biotechnology
AND THE LAW

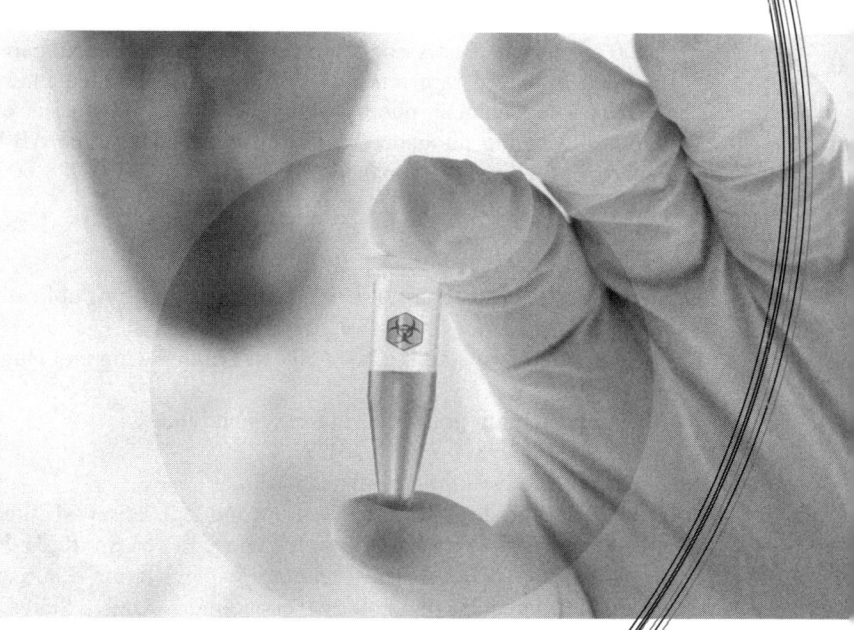

HUGH B. WELLONS, EILEEN SMITH EWING
ROBERT COPPLE, WILLIAM WOFFORD, ERIKA LEITZAN

ABA
Defending Liberty
Pursuing Justice

Cover design by ABA Publishing

The materials contained herein represent the opinions and views of the authors and/or the editors, and should not be construed to be the views or opinions of the law firms or companies with whom such persons are in partnership with, associated with, or employed by, nor of the American Bar Association unless adopted pursuant to the bylaws of the Association.

Nothing contained in this book is to be considered as the rendering of legal advice for specific cases, and readers are responsible for obtaining such advice from their own legal counsel. This book and any forms and agreements herein are intended for educational and informational purposes only.

© 2007 American Bar Association. All rights reserved. No part of this publication may be reproduced, stored in a retrieval system, or transmitted in any form or by any means, electronic, mechanical, photocopying, recording, or otherwise, without the prior written permission of the publisher. For permission contact the ABA Copyrights & Contracts Department, copyright@abanet.org or via fax at (312) 988-6030.

11 09 08 07   5 4 3 2 1

Library of Congress Cataloging-in-Publication Data

Biotechnology and the law / Eileen Smith Ewing and Hugh B. Wellons, editors.
 p. cm.
 Includes bibliographical references and index.
 ISBN-13: 978-1-59031-761-7
 ISBN-10: 1-59031-761-0
  1. Biotechnology industries—Law and legislation—United States.
2. Biotechnology—United States. I. Ewing, Eileen Smith. II. Wellons, Hugh B.
   [[DNLM: 1. Biomedical Technology—legislation & jurisprudence—United States. 2. Biomedical Technology—economics—United States. 3. Biomedical Research—legislation & jurisprudence—United States. 4. Health Care Sector—legislation & jurisprudence—United States. W 32.5 AA1 B616 2006]
 KF3133.B56B563 2006
 343.73'0786606—dc22   2006033073

Discounts are available for books ordered in bulk. Special consideration is given to state bars, CLE programs, and other bar-related organizations. Inquire at Book Publishing, ABA Publishing, American Bar Association, 321 North Clark Street, Chicago, Illinois 60610.

www.ababooks.org

Contents

Preface xxxi
About the Editors xxxv
About the Contributors xxxix

Chapter I
Introduction to Biotechnology and the Law 1
Robert F. Copple
A. The Biotech Primer 4
B. Biotech Defined 4
    1. Three-Branch Approach 5
C. The Biotech Company Life Cycle 5
    1. Phase I: Start-up 6
        a. Intellectual Property 6
        b. Company Formation 7
        c. Investment Capital 7
    2. Phase II: Early Development 8
        a. Additional Investment 8
        b. The Regulatory Track 9
        c. Business Growth and Complexity 9
    3. Phase III: Later-Stage Development and Product Approval 10
    4. Phase IV: Challenges Facing the Now Mature Company 10
        a. Commercialization 11
        b. Regulatory Oversight 11
        c. Litigation 11
D. Conclusion 12
Glossary 13

Chapter II
Managing Innovation: Patent Basics for Biotechnology Counsel 25
Dr. Michael H. Brodowski, Thomas A. Turano, and Dr. Christine C. Vito
A. Introduction 25
B. U.S. Patent Portfolios 26
    1. Patent Rights—The Claims 26
    2. Types of Patents 28
        a. Provisional Patent Applications 29
        b. Continuing Patent Application Practice 30

3. Requirements for Patentability 31
　　　4. Preparation of a Patent Application 34
　　　5. Patent Application Formalities 35
　　　6. Publication of Patent Applications 38
　　　7. Patent Prosecution 39
　　　　　a. Appeal of Patent Office Final Rejections 41
　　　　　b. Notice of Allowance 42
　　　8. Post-Issue Patent Considerations 43
　C. Foreign Patent Portfolios 45
　　　1. Protection Strategy 46
　　　2. Patentability Differences 49
　　　3. Other Considerations 51
　　　4. Prerequisites to Filing 52
　　　5. Options for Filing in Other Jurisdictions 53
　　　　　a. Additional Considerations 57
　D. Managing the Company's Patent Estate 58
　　　1. A Family Portrait 58
　　　2. Keeping It in the Family 60
　　　3. Skeletons in the Closet 62
　　　　　a. Rights of Ownership 63
　　　　　b. Correspondence to Products or Business Strategies 64
　　　　　c. Freedom to Operate 66

Chapter III
Company Formation 69
Andrew T. Hoyne, Steven E. Pozaric, and Mark L. Stoneman
　A. Introduction 69
　　　1. "But will it help us get money?" 69
　　　2. The Importance of the Board of Directors 70
　　　3. Speed 72
　　　4. Simplicity 73
　　　5. The Role of the Company's Attorneys 73
　B. Biotechnology Company Models 73
　　　1. Company Formed Before In-Licensing While R&D Continues at University 74
　　　2. Technology Flip 75
　　　3. Revenue-Funded Company 75
　　　4. Corporate Deal-Funded Company 75
　　　5. Venture Fund–Launched Company 76
　　　6. Angel Investor–Funded Company 76
　　　7. Significant Self-Funded Company 77
　　　8. Shoestring Self-Funded Company 77
　　　9. Charitable Corporation or Foundation 78
　　　10. Debt-Funded Company 79

Contents

- C. Entity Selection and Formation 79
  1. No Perfect Choice 79
  2. Sole Proprietorships and Partnerships 80
  3. C-corporations 81
     a. Limited Liability 82
     b. Centralized Management 82
     c. Owners 82
     d. Transferability of Ownership 82
     e. Classes of Ownership 83
     f. Incentive Compensation 83
     g. Taxation 83
  4. S-corporations 84
  5. Limited Liability Companies 88
     a. Problems Using an LLC 88
     b. LLC Organization 91
  6. Exotic Entity Types 95
  7. State of Organization 95
  8. Name Selection 97
- D. Capital Structure and Stock Grants 99
  1. Introduction 99
  2. Securities Law Compliance 99
  3. Founders Stock, Restricted Stock, and Stock Options 100
  4. Common and Preferred Stock 105
- E. Relationships with Early Participants 107
  1. Founders 108
  2. Board of Directors 109
  3. Scientific Advisory Board (SAB) 110
  4. Management 111
     a. Chief Executive Officer 111
     b. Chief Financial Officer 112
     c. Chief Scientific Officer 112
     d. Clinical/Regulatory 113
  5. Employees 113
- F. Incubators 114
- G. University Relationships 115
- H. Early-Stage Company Agreements 117
  1. Brief Review of Intellectual Property for the Non-IP Attorney 117
     a. Patents 118
     b. Trade Secrets 118
     c. Trademarks 119
     d. Copyrights 121
  2. Confidentiality Agreements 122

	3. Material Transfer Agreements	124
	4. Research Collaboration Agreements	126
I.	Positioning for an Exit	127
	Appendix A: Mutual Confidentiality Agreement	132

Chapter IV
Acquisition of Biotechnology— Technology Transfer 139
Hugh B. Wellons

A.	Technology Creation	140
	1. Protecting Propriety of the Invention in the Early Stages	140
	a. Confidentiality Agreements	140
	b. Who Was First?	141
	c. Company Records	142
	2. Keeping Necessary Records	143
	3. Who Owns What? (Employer v. Employee and JV Issues)	143
	a. Work Made for Hire	143
	b. Employee Rights	145
	c. State Laws	145
	d. Canadian and European Union Laws	146
	e. Trade Secrets	147
	f. Joint Venture Ownership	148
	4. Patent Filing: Protecting an Invention and Limiting Others' Use	149
	a. Why File a Patent?	149
	b. Patent Requirements	149
	c. Patent Claims and Rights	150
	d. Types and Stages of Patents	150
	e. Patent Prosecution	151
	f. Post-Issue Considerations	151
	g. Foreign Patent Filing	152
	5. Possible Effects of Outside Funding	152
	a. Ownership	152
	b. Public Domain	154
	c. Manufacturing or Sales Restrictions	154
B.	Forms of Technology Transfer	155
	1. Acquisition of Owner	155
	a. Acquiring the Owner	155
	b. Employing the Owner	155
	2. Assignment	156
	3. License and Sublicense	156
	a. Common Form of Transfer	156
	b. Alternative to Assignment	156
	c. Sublicense	158
	4. Fair Use Agreement	158

		a. Fair Use and Experimental Use	158
		b. Fair Use Agreements	160
		c. Doctrine and Agreements' Effect on Intellectual Property Ownership and Due Diligence	160
	5.	Public Domain	161
C.	Transfer from Academia		162
	1.	University Considerations	162
	2.	Material Transfer Agreements	168
	3.	Principal Investigator Considerations	169
		a. Conflict of Interest and Conflict of Commitment	169
		b. Conflict of Interest	169
		c. Conflict of Commitment	170
		d. Special Knowledge	171
	4.	Licensee Considerations	171
		a. Policies and Procedures	172
		b. It's a Long Way to Market, So Wrap Up the People You Need	172
		c. Public Disclosure?	173
		d. Stakeholders	173
	5.	Interests of Other Stakeholders	174
		a. Other Underwriters	174
		b. Government Agencies	174
		c. Special Government Considerations	174
		d. Nonprofits	175
	6.	Common Restrictions	175
		a. License Only, Not an Assignment	175
		b. Time Limitations	176
		c. Restrictions on Participation by the Inventors	176
		d. Audit	176
		e. Scope of License	176
		f. Indemnification	176
		g. Sublicense Approval	176
		h. Sublicensee Subject to License Terms	176
		i. Original Licensee Always Liable	177
		j. Cannot Use the Name of the University	177
		k. Government Has a License	177
		l. Other General Restrictions You Would Find in Most Other Licensing Agreements	177
	7.	Common Guidelines for Price and Provisions of the License	177
		a. Standstill Fee	177
		b. Up-front License Fee	177
		c. Minimum Annual Payment	178
		d. Periodic Licensing Fees (Such as Quarterly or Annual)	178
		e. Participation in Third-Party Payments	178

		f.	Lump-Sum Royalties 178
		g.	Milestone Payments 178
		h.	Sales-Based Royalties 178
		i.	Equity in the Licensee 179
		j.	Equity Protections 179
		k.	Put of Shares 179
		l.	A Time for Sale 179

      8. When Equity Is the Primary Consideration for the License 179
      9. Applicability of Bayh-Dole Act 180
    10. Application of "CREATE" Act of 2004 183
    11. Conflict between Publication and Protection of IP 183

D. Transfer from Other Nonprofit Entities 184
      1. Implications of Nonprofit Status 184
      2. Unrelated Business Income Tax 185
      3. Priorities of Nonprofit Technology Owner 185
      4. Joint Venturing (especially qualification for STTR grants) 186
          a. SBIR Grants 186
          b. STTR Grants 187
          c. Problems with STTR and SBIR Grants 187
      5. Common Misconceptions 187
      6. Case Study—Howard Hughes Medical Institute 188
          a. Assignment of Rights 188
          b. Sharing Patent Costs and Royalties 189
          c. Equity Ownership 189
          d. Collaborations 189
          e. Time Limitations 189
          f. Start-up Companies 189
          g. Summary 190

E. Transfer from Individuals 190
      1. Consideration of Terms 190
          a. Parties 190
          b. Recitals 190
          c. Definitions 190
          d. Property Licensed 190
          e. Scope of the Assignment or License 191
          f. Territory 191
          g. Right to Sublicense 192
          h. Follow-on and Later-Developed Technology 192
          i. Term and Renewal of License 192
          j. Termination 193
          k. Deliveries 193
          l. Retention of Rights 193

		m.	Payments, Including Fees, Royalties, Stock (Options, Warrants), Milestone, etc. 193
		n.	Audit Rights 194
		o.	Reporting and Marketing Responsibility 194
		p.	Representations and Warranties of the Inventor 194
		q.	Indemnification 194
		r.	IP Protection 194
		s.	Insurance 194
		t.	Assignability 195
		u.	Amendments 195
		v.	Alternative Dispute Resolution (ADR) 195
		w.	"Boilerplate" Language 195
	2.	Common Negotiation Points 196
		a.	Price Paid/Consideration 196
		b.	Fees and Royalties Are Both Negotiable Points 196
		c.	Records and Reporting 197
		d.	Warranty 197
		e.	Indemnification 197
		f.	IP Matters 197
		g.	Confirmation of Ownership 198
	3.	Patent Filing 199
F.	Summary 199

Chapter V
Financing a Biotech Company 203
William N. Wofford

A.	Overview 204
	1. Drug Development Costs 204
	2. Product Development Time Lines 206
B.	Basic Securities Law Considerations 209
	1. Registration or Exemption Under the Securities Act 209
	2. Section 4(2) Exempt Transaction 210
	3. Regulation D Exempt Transaction 210
	4. Rule 701—Compensation Plans 212
	5. State "Blue Sky" Laws 213
C.	Pre-seed and Seed Capital 214
	1. Founders' Stock 214
	a. Restrictions on Transfer 215
	b. Vesting 215
	c. Lock-up 216
	d. Drag-along 217
	2. Employee Stock 218
	a. Plan Basics 218
	b. Securities 219

		c.	Tax 219
		d.	Corporate 220
		e.	Commercial 221
	3.	Stock to Service or Technology Providers 221
		a.	Securities 222
		b.	Tax 222
		c.	Conflicts of Interest 223
	4.	Friends and Family 223
		a.	Securities 223
		b.	Corporate 224
	5.	Loans 224
	6.	Generating Revenues to Reduce or Defer Need for Investment 225
		a.	Intellectual Property 225
		b.	Commercial 226
	7.	Government Funding 226
		a.	SBIR Grants 226
		b.	STTR Grants 227
		c.	Advantages to Receiving Federal Grant Funding 228
		d.	Disadvantages to Receiving Federal Grant Funding 228
		e.	Eligibility/51 Percent Rule 228
		f.	State Resources 230
D.	Venture Capital 230
	1.	Financial Rights 231
		a.	Valuation 231
		b.	Liquidation Preference 231
		c.	Participating Preferred 231
		d.	Accruing Dividends 232
		e.	Protection of Ownership Percentage 232
	2.	Governance Rights 233
		a.	Board Representation 233
		b.	Protective Provisions/Class Voting 233
	3.	Exit Rights 233
		a.	Registration Rights 234
		b.	Redemption Rights 234
		c.	Co-sale Rights 235
	4.	Series B—Time to Start All Over 235
E.	Corporate Investment 236
F.	Initial Public Offering 237
G.	Post-IPO Financing 239
	1.	PIPES 239
	2.	Convertible Debt 240
	3.	Project Finance 241

H. Conclusion	241
Glossary of Frequently Used Terms	253

Chapter VI
Employment Issues for Biotechnology Companies 265
Jeffrey A. Van Doren

A.	Employment At Will		265
B.	Employee or Independent Contractor		266
	1.	The Common-Law Control Test	267
	2.	The IRS Control Test	268
	3.	The Economic Reality Test	270
	4.	Potential Liability	271
C.	Employer Coverage Under Federal Civil Rights Laws		272
	1.	Title VII of the Civil Rights Act of 1964 (42 U.S.C. § 2000e et seq.)	272
		a. Basic Coverage	272
		b. Sexual Harassment	273
	2.	Age Discrimination in Employment Act (ADEA) (29 U.S.C. § 621 et seq.)	273
		a. Basic Coverage	273
		b. Older Workers' Benefit Protection Act	273
	3.	Americans with Disabilities Act (42 U.S.C. § 12,101 et seq.)	274
		a. Basic Coverage	274
		b. Reasonable Accommodation	274
	4.	Equal Pay Act (29 U.S.C. § 206(d))	275
D.	Employer Coverage Under State and Local Civil Rights Laws		275
	1.	State Civil Rights Law	275
	2.	Local Laws and Ordinances	275
E.	Equal Opportunity and Affirmative Action Obligations of Government Contractors and Subcontractors		276
F.	Other Federal Employment Laws		277
	1.	Fair Labor Standards Act (FLSA) (29 U.S.C. § 201 et seq.)	277
		a. Basic Coverage	277
		b. Basic Requirements	277
	2.	Family and Medical Leave Act (29 U.S.C. § 2601 et seq.)	281
	3.	National Labor Relations Act (29 U.S.C. § 151 et seq.)	281
		a. Coverage of the NLRA	281
		b. Employee Rights under the NLRA	282
		c. "Protected Concerted Activity"	282
		d. Union Organizing	282
		e. NLRA Applicability to Non-union Employers	283
	4.	Employee Retirement Income Security Act (ERISA) (29 U.S.C. § 1001 et seq.)	285

5. Occupational Safety and Health Act (OSHA) (29 U.S.C. § 651 et seq.) 285
6. Immigration Reform and Control Act 1986 (IRCA) (18 U.S.C. § 274A-274C) 286
7. Uniformed Services Employment and Reemployment Rights Act of 1994 (USERRA) (38 U.S.C. § 4301 et seq.) 287
8. Fair Credit Reporting Act (FCRA) (15 U.S.C. § 1681 et seq.) 287
    a. Written Notice and Authorization 287
    b. Adverse Actions Procedures 288
9. Employee Polygraph Protection Act (29 U.S.C. § 2001 et seq.) 288
G. Use of Employment Contracts 288
    1. When Is an Employment Agreement Useful? 289
        a. Security 289
        b. Recruitment Incentive 289
        c. Defined Performance Expectations 289
        d. Defined Compensation Expectations 289
        e. Confidentiality and IP Ownership 290
    2. Items to Be Covered 290
        a. Duration 290
        b. Position and Title 291
        c. Compensation 291
H. Employee Handbooks 299
    1. Pros and Cons of Using 299
        a. Reasons for Using 299
        b. Reasons for Not Using 300
    2. Items to Be Covered 301
        a. Disclaimers and At-Will Statements 301
        b. EEO Policies 301
        c. Harassment Policy 302
        d. Family and Medical Leave Policy 302
        e. E-mail and Computer Usage Policy 303
        f. Description of Benefits 303
        g. Discipline Policy 303
I. Immigration Options for Biotech Employees 304
    1. Obtaining a Visa and U.S. Entry 304
    2. Non-immigrant Visas 305
        a. H-1B "Specialty Worker" Visa 305
        b. TN "NAFTA Professional" Visa 307
        c. L-1 "Intracompany Transfer" Visa 308
        d. E-1 "Treaty Trader" and E-2 "Treaty Investor" Visas 309
        e. O-1 "Extraordinary Ability Alien" Visa 310
    3. Immigrant Visas and Permanent Residence Status 312

		a.	Employment-Based Preferences	312
		b.	Visa Backlogs and Priority Dates	314
		c.	Labor Certification	314
		d.	Immigrant Visa and Adjustment of Status	315

Appendix A: Coverage of State Equal Rights Statutes 318

Chapter VII
Federal Regulation of Research Through Funding 325
G. Melissa Ince and Jenny Kim

- A. Grants and Contracts 326
  - 1. Federal Research Grants 326
    - a. Subgrants 327
    - b. Terms and Conditions 328
    - c. Grantor Agencies 330
      - i. Small Business Innovation Research (SBIR) and Small Business Technology Transfer (STTR) Program Grants 330
      - ii. SBIR 331
      - iii. STTR 331
  - 2. Contracts 332
    - a. Sale of Commercial Items and Services 332
    - b. Procurement Integrity: Off-Limits Information 337
    - c. Allowable and Unallowable Costs 340
    - d. Product Substitution 342
- B. SBIR and STTR Grants 344
  - 1. SBIR Grants 344
  - 2. STTR Grants 345
  - 3. Basic Characteristics 346
  - 4. NIH Guidance 347
    - a. Significance 347
    - b. Approach 348
    - c. Innovation 348
    - d. Environment 349
  - 5. Protection of Human Subjects 349
  - 6. Vertebrate Animals 350
  - 7. Criteria 351
  - 8. Phase II Application Review Criteria 351
  - 9. Amended Applications 352
  - 10. Phase I/Phase II Fast-Track Application Review Criteria 352
  - 11. Phase II—Competing Continuation Application Review Criteria 352
- C. Ethics, Outside Activities, and Employment 353
  - 1. Grants 353
    - a. Standards of Conduct 353
    - b. Financial Conflict of Interest 353

c. Misconduct in Science and Engineering 354
2. Contracts 354
   a. Organizational Conflicts of Interest 354
   b. Employment Discussions With and Hiring of U.S. Government Personnel 356
   c. The National Institutes of Health (NIH) Government Employee Supplemental Regulations on Permitted Outside Activities 358

Chapter VIII
Regulation of Preclinical Research 407
Daniel T. Pancamo
A. Animal Use in Biomedical Research and Testing 408
   1. The Basic Regulatory Scheme—the Animal Welfare Act (7 U.S.C. §§ 2131-2159) and Regulations (9 C.F.R. Parts 1-4). 408
      a. Overview of the AWA 408
      b. Overview of the AWA Regulations 411
         i. General Overview 411
         ii. Registration 412
         iii. The IACUC 412
         iv. Personnel Qualifications, Veterinary Care, Record Keeping 415
      c. Implementation and Enforcement of the AWA and the AWA Regulations by the USDA Animal and Plant Health Inspection Service (APHIS) 417
   2. U.S. Government Principles for the Utilization and Care of Vertebrate Animals Used in Testing, Research and Training (50 Fed. Reg. 20,864-02 (1985)) 418
   3. Memorandum of Understanding Among APHIS/USDA, the FDA and the NIH 419
   4. NIH Considerations 420
      a. Health Research Extension Act; NIH 420
      b. NIH Extramural Research 421
      c. Guide for the Care and Use of Laboratory Animals; Institutional Animal Care and Use Committee Guidebook 422
   5. FDA Considerations 423
   6. CDC Considerations 424
   7. State Law 424
   8. Conclusion 424
B. Other Regulatory Schemes Applicable to Preclinical Research— Protection of the Environment and Public Heath 425
   1. Introduction 425
   2. EPA Jurisdiction and RCRA 425

    3. Issues in Applying Environmental Law to Research Facilities 433
    4. IACUC Responsibility 434
    5. The Public Health Security and Bioterrorism Preparedness and
       Response Act of 2002; Select Agents and Toxins 434
C. Other Regulatory Schemes Applicable to Preclinical Research—
   Occupational Safety and Health Considerations and the Protection of
   Individuals Conducting Preclinical Research 438
    1. Introduction 438
    2. Occupational Safety and Health Administration (OSHA) Regulation;
       Standards; Resources 439
    3. Selected Resource Tools—Chemicals and Biohazards 441
    4. Radioactive Materials in the Research Setting 442
D. Conclusion 442

Chapter IX
Research and Development Collaborations 445
Eileen Smith Ewing
A. Introduction: The Collaborator as Biotechnology's White Knight 445
B. Finding a Strategic Partner: Beating the Mathematical Odds 446
C. Negotiating a Term Sheet 449
    1. The Importance of the Term Sheet to the Transaction 449
    2. Issues Crucial to Address at the Term Sheet Stage 450
    3. Issues to Avoid Negotiating at the Term Sheet Stage 451
D. Key Issues in a Research Collaboration Agreement 452
    1. Governance of the Research Collaboration 452
       a. Composition of the Joint Steering Committee 452
       b. Duties of the Joint Steering Committee 453
       c. Meetings of the Joint Steering Committee 453
       d. Decisionmaking by the Joint Steering Committee 453
    2. The Scope of the Collaboration 454
       a. Field 455
       b. Scope Limitations Based on Patent Family 456
       c. Scope Limitations Based on Timing 456
       d. Scope Limitations Based on Project Funding 456
    3. Intellectual Property 456
       a. Core Intellectual Property of the Smaller Partner, Developed
          Prior to the Collaboration but Highly Relevant 457
       b. Core Intellectual Property of the Larger Funding Partner,
          Developed Prior to the Collaboration but Highly Relevant 457
       c. Background Intellectual Property of the Smaller Partner,
          Developed Prior to the Collaboration but of Possible Utility 457
       d. Background Intellectual Property of the Larger Funding
          Partner, Developed Prior to the Collaboration but of Possible
          Utility 458

        e. Intellectual Property Developed by One or Both Parties Arising out of the Collaboration 458
        f. Intellectual Property Developed by the Smaller Partner During, but Outside of, the Collaboration 458
        g. Novel Intellectual Property Developed by One or Both Parties During the Collaboration That Does Not Arise out of the Existing Intellectual Property of Either Party 459
    4. License Grants 459
        a. Research Licenses 460
        b. Development and Commercialization License 460
        c. Cross-Licenses; Freedom to Operate 460
        d. Enabling License 461
        e. License as Protection Against Infringement Claims 461
    5. Financial Terms 462
        a. Signature Payments 462
        b. Research Funding 463
        c. Equity Investments 463
            i. Pricing the Equity 463
            ii. Multiple Tranches 464
            iii. Advantages of Equity Investment by a Collaborator 464
            iv. Disadvantages of Equity Investment by a Collaborator 465
        d. Milestone Payments 465
    6. Option to Develop and Commercialize 469
        a. Notice of Exercise 469
        b. Right of First Refusal 469
        c. Right of First Negotiation 470
        d. Rights in Unoptioned Intellectual Property 470
    7. Term and Termination 471
        a. Term 471
        b. Early Termination 471
E. Post-Closing Pitfalls That Can Derail a Research and Development Collaboration 472
    1. Change in Strategic Fit or Commitment to the Project 472
    2. Communication and Control Issues 475
    3. Unrealistic Expectations 475
F. Alliances with Third Parties— Keeping Other Options Open 475
    1. Right of First Refusal May Preclude Other Transactions 476
    2. Right of First Negotiation May Also Have a Chilling Effect 476
    3. The Deal May Be Worth It; Rely on Contractual Protections 476
G. Conclusion: Where Do the Parties Go From Here? 477

Chapter X
FDA Regulation of Biomedical Research 479
Robert B. Nicholas
- A. Introduction 479
  1. Introductory Note on Biotechnology and Clinical Trials 480
- B. Part One—Overview of the Regulatory Framework 481
  1. The History, Goals, and Purpose of Regulation 481
  2. Government Regulation of Clinical Research 481
  3. The Roles and Obligations of the Parties 483
     a. Sponsor 484
     b. Contract Research Organization (CRO) 484
     c. Institutional Review Board (IRB) 485
     d. Principal Investigator (PI) 486
     e. The Legal Relationships Between the Parties: Contractual Agreements 487
        i. The Sponsor and Principal Investigator 487
        ii. The Sponsor and the CRO 488
        iii. The Principal Investigator and the Study Subject 489
- C. Part Two—Anatomy of a Clinical Trial 490
  1. Before the Trial Can Begin 490
     a. Drugs: Investigational New Drug Applications (IND) 490
     b. Devices: Investigational Device Exemption (IDE) 490
     c. IRB Approval of the Protocol, ICF, and Study Advertisement 491
  2. Beginning and Conducting the Trial 491
     a. Subject Enrollment and Test Article Administration 491
     b. Control of the Trial: Record Keeping and Reporting 493
  3. After the Trial 494
     a. Submission and Audit 494
     b. FDA Inspection 495
     c. Administrative Actions—Civil and Criminal Penalties 497
  4. Preparing for FDA Inspections and Responding to FDA Allegations of Misconduct 497
  5. FDA Criminal Actions and Other Potential Consequences: Qui Tam Suits and Adverse Publicity 498
- D. Part Three—Conduct and Use of Non-U.S. Studies 499
  1. IND/IDE or Not 499
  2. FDA Acceptance and Use of Non-U.S. Clinical Data 500
  3. Export of Test Article 500
  4. EU Clinical Trial Directive 500
- E. Conclusion 501

Chapter XI
Privacy Issues for Biotechnology Companies 509
Steve A. Schwarm and Anne Stohr O'Brien
A. Introduction 509
B. The National Approach to Health-Care Privacy 512
   1. Health Insurance Portability and Accountability Act of 1996 512
   2. HIPAA Privacy Regulations 518
      a. Individual Rights 518
          i. Notice of Privacy Practices 519
          ii. Restriction of PHI by Individual Patient 521
          iii. Access of Individuals to PHI 521
          iv. Amendment or Change of PHI 523
          v. Accounting of Disclosures 524
      b. Use and Disclosure for Treatment, Payment, and Health-Care Operations 525
      c. Disclosure of PHI with Authorization or by Agreement 526
          i. Authorizations 526
          ii. Defective Authorization 528
          iii. Combined Authorizations 528
          iv. Conditioning of Authorizations 528
          v. Revocation of Authorizations 529
          vi. Authorizations for Marketing 529
          vii. Use or Disclosure Requiring Patient Opportunity to Agree or Object 529
      d. Disclosure Pursuant to a Public Policy Exception 530
          i. As "Required by Law"—45 C.F.R. § 164.512(a) 530
          ii. Uses and Disclosures for Public Health Activities— 45 C.F.R. § 164.512(b) (Includes child abuse reporting) 531
          iii. Disclosures About Victims of Abuse, Neglect or Domestic Violence—45 C.F.R. § 164.512(c) 532
          iv. Uses and Disclosures for Health Oversight Activities— 45 C.F.R. § 164.512(d) 534
          v. Disclosures for Judicial and Administrative Proceedings— 45 C.F.R. § 164.512(e) 534
          vi. Disclosure for Law Enforcement Purposes—45 C.F.R. § 164.512(f)* 536
          vii. Uses and Disclosures about Decedents—45 C.F.R. § 164.512(g) 536
          viii. Uses and Disclosures for Cadaveric Organ, Eye or Tissue Donation Purposes—45 C.F.R. § 164.512(h) 536
          ix. Uses and Disclosures for Research Purposes—45 C.F.R. § 164.512(i) 537

		x.	Uses and Disclosures to Avert a Serious Threat to Health or Safety—45 C.F.R. § 164.512(j) 539
		xi.	Specialized Government Function—45 C.F.R. § 164.512(k) 539
		xii.	Disclosures for Workers' Compensation—45 C.F.R. § 164.512 (l) 539
	e.	Disclosure Pursuant to a Business Associate Agreement—(45 C.F.R. § 164.502(e) and § 164.504(e)) 539
	f.	Disclosure Pursuant to a Data Use Agreement 542
3.	Preemption Issues 543
C.	Recognition of State Approach to Health-Care Privacy 544
D.	HIPAA Interplay with Federal Common Rule and Federal Certificates of Confidentiality 545
1.	Introduction 545
2.	Research and HIPAA 545
	a.	When Research Is Subject to HIPAA 545
	b.	Permission to Use or Disclose Research Information 546
		i.	Use or Disclosure Without Authorization 546
		ii.	Research Use/Disclosure with Individual Authorization 547
3.	The Common Rule and HIPAA 547
4.	Research and Business Associate Status Under HIPAA 549
5.	Federal Certificates of Confidentiality 549
	a.	Certificates of Confidentiality Explained 549
	b.	National Institutes of Health Statement on Certificates of Confidentiality 550
E.	Research Issues and Academic Medical Centers 551
F.	Canadian Privacy Legislation 551
1.	Accountability 552
2.	Identifying Purpose 553
3.	Consent 553
4.	Limiting Collection 554
5.	Limit Use, Disclosure, and Retention 554
6.	Accuracy 554
7.	Safeguards 554
8.	Openness 554
9.	Individual Access 555
10.	Challenging Compliance 555

Chapter XII
Medical Reimbursement 563
Paul W. Radensky
A. Reimbursement Basics 563
   1. Key Terms and Concepts 563
   2. Coverage 564

		a.	Determining the Scope of Benefits 564
		b.	Checking for Specific Exclusions from Coverage 565
		c.	The Reasonable and Necessary Test 565
		d.	Medical Necessity for the Particular Patient 566
		e.	Implications of Coverage/Non-coverage 567
		f.	Coverage Process 567
	3.	Payment Law and Policy 568
	4.	Coding 569
	5.	Appeals 571
	6.	Who Are the Payers? 574
B.	Applying the Basics 574
	1.	Coverage, Payment, and Coding for Drugs and Biologicals 574
	2.	Coverage, Payment, and Coding for Procedures Involving the Use of Medical Devices 576
	3.	Coverage, Payment, and Coding for Durable Medical Equipment, Prosthetics, Orthotics, and Supplies 578
	4.	Coverage, Payment, and Coding for In Vitro Diagnostics 579
C.	Special Payment Rules for New Technologies 579
	1.	Inpatient Prospective Payment System 579
	2.	Outpatient Prospective Payment System 580
	3.	Ambulatory Surgical Centers—Payment for New Technology Intraocular Lenses 580
	4.	Private Payer Carve-outs 581
D.	Reimbursement for Investigational Products 581
	1.	National Coverage Determination on Routine Costs of Qualifying Clinical Trials 581
	2.	Investigational Device Exemptions 582
E.	Compliance Considerations 583
	1.	Requirements for Proper Billing 583
	2.	Reimbursement Support Services 586
	3.	Discounts and Related Fraud and Abuse Considerations 586
F.	Conclusions 587
Table of Acronyms 588

Chapter XIII
Approval of Products for Human Use 591
Areta L. Kupchyk

A.	Standard Pathways to Market 591
	1.	Drugs 591
		a.	Preclinical 591
		b.	Investigational New Drug Applications 592
			i. Exemption from Law 592
			ii. Institutional Review Boards 593
			iii. Clinical Hold 593

	iv. Types of INDs 595
	v. Phases of Clinical Trials 595
	c. New Drug Applications 596
	i. New Drug Application Content and Format Requirements 597
	ii. Facility Inspection 600
	iii. Labeling Review 600
	iv. Advisory Committees 602
	v. Completion of Review and Decision 602
	d. Generic Drugs 603
	i. Abbreviated New Drug Applications 603
	e. 505(b)(2) Applications 605
2.	Biological Products 605
3.	Human Cells, Tissues, and Cellular and Tissue-Based Products 607
4.	Medical Devices 608
	a. Device Classifications 609
	i. Class I Medical Devices 609
	ii. Class II Medical Devices 609
	iii. Class III Medical Devices 609
	b. The 510(k) Notification Process 609
	c. The Premarket Application Process 610
	d. Investigational Device Exemption 610
5.	Combination Products 610

B. Special Pathways to Market 612
   1. Fast-Track Programs 612
   2. Orphan Drug Designation 614
C. Future Pathways to Market 615

Chapter XIV
The Regulation of Biomedical Products for Animal Use 623
Robert B. Nicholas and Kent D. McClure

A. Regulation of Animal Health Products 623
B. The Animal Health Industry 625
   1. Development Incentives 625
   2. Size Matters 625
   3. Complexity 627
C. Biotechnology-Derived Products 628
D. Overview of FDA Regulation of Animal Drugs 629
   1. FDA Regulates Animal Drugs: Defined 629
   2. Critical Elements in the Regulatory Regime 630
      a. Approval of New Animal Drugs 631
      b. Denial and Withdrawal of Approval of New Animal Drugs 632
      c. Post-approval Requirements 632
      d. Inspection, Enforcement, and Compliance 632

E. Distinguishing Factors Between FDA Regulation of Animal and Human Drugs 633
   1. Drugs for Food Animals: Human Food Safety 633
   2. Drugs Administered in Animal Feed 635
   3. Import of Use of an Approved Drug in Different Species; Minor Species and Uses; Use in Pets; Animal Drug Availability 636
   4. Practical Considerations for Interacting with the Center for Veterinary Medicine (CVM) 637
F. CVM Regulation of Biotechnology Products 639
G. Overview of USDA Regulation of Animal Biological Products 641
   1. USDA Regulates Veterinary Biologics 641
   2. Overview: Virus-Serum-Toxin Act 642
   3. Critical Elements in the APHIS Regulatory Requirements 642
      a. Veterinary Biologics Defined 642
      b. Licensing 643
      c. Permits 644
      d. Standard Requirements 644
      e. Record Keeping 644
      f. Adverse Event Reports 645
      g. Enforcement Procedures 645
      h. Exemptions to the Regulations 645
   4. The Agricultural Bioterrorism Protection Act of 2002 646
   5. Animal Health Protection Act 646
   6. Special Consideration for Biotech Biologics 647
H. Conclusion 648

Chapter XV
Approval Process for Biotechnology Products in Agricultural Use 661
Dr. J. Winston Porter
A. Coordinated Federal Framework 662
B. Role of the Environmental Protection Agency 664
C. Role of the U.S. Department of Agriculture 666
D. Role of the Food and Drug Administration 668
E. Role of the States in Regulation of Biotech Crops 670
   1. EPA and the States 670
   2. USDA and the States 670
   3. FDA and the States 671
F. Biotech Crop Regulation in Other Countries 671
   1. Argentina 672
   2. Brazil 672
   3. Canada 673
   4. China 674
   5. European Union 674

Chapter XVI
Legal Requirements After Approval 677
Areta L. Kupchyk
- A. The Food and Drug Administration 677
- B. Office of Inspector General, Department of Health and Human Services 679
- C. The *Neurontin* Case 679
- D. Import and Export Requirements 680
- E. Current Good Manufacturing Practice Requirements 682
- F. Reporting Requirements to FDA 683
  1. Drug and Biological Products 683
  2. Medical Devices 684
  3. Promotional Materials: Form FDA-2253 686
- G. Sales and Marketing Regulations 686
  1. Prescription Drug Marketing Act 686
  2. FDA Regulation of Advertising 687
  3. Three Basic Types of Advertisements 691
     a. Product-Claim Advertisements 691
     b. Reminder Advertisements 691
     c. Help-Seeking Advertisements 691
  4. Requirements for Product Claim Advertisements 691
  5. Print Advertisements: the Brief Summary 692
  6. Broadcast Advertisements: the Major Statement 692
  7. Prior Approval and Post-Marketing Notification 693
  8. FDA Notification 694
  9. Promotion of Off-Label Use 694
  10. Exchange of Scientific Information 695
  11. The First Amendment 696
  12. Other Cases of Interest—Product Liability 699
  13. The Federal Trade Commission 699
- H. Withdrawal of FDA Approval 700
  I. False Claims Act 701
  J. Anti-kickback Statute and Other Illegal Remuneration 701

Chapter XVII
Development and Commercialization Alliances 707
Eileen Smith Ewing
- A. Introduction: Why Choose to Partner? 707
- B. Considerations in Choosing a Partner 708
- C. The Stage of the Drug Candidate Will Define the Alliance 708
  1. Early-Stage Deals 709
     a. Target Identification and Validation 709
     b. Hits 710
     c. Leads 710

		d.	Optimized Leads 710
	2.	Preclinical-Stage Licensing 710
		a.	ADME/Tox Studies 710
		b.	Investigational New Drug Application 711
	3.	Clinical-Stage Licensing 711
		a.	Phase I 711
		b.	Phase II 711
		c.	Clinical Trials (Phase III) 711
	4.	Pre-launch Licensing 711
D.	The Development and Commercialization License Agreement 712
	1.	Nature and Scope of License Grant 712
		a.	Identifying the Subject Technology 712
		b.	The Rights Granted 713
		c.	Scope of Rights 714
		d.	Retained Rights of the Licensor 715
	2.	Consideration for the License Grant 716
		a.	Milestone Payments 716
		b.	Royalty Payments, Generally 718
		c.	Term of Royalty Payments 721
		d.	Punitive Reduction in Royalty Rates 722
		e.	Reduction in Royalty Rates for Third-Party Licenses 723
	3.	Other Intellectual Property Issues 723
		a.	Responsibility for Patent Prosecution and Maintenance 723
		b.	Abandoned Jurisdictions 723
		c.	Ongoing Cooperation 724
		d.	Trademarks, etc. 724
		e.	Prosecution of Infringers 724
	4.	Cooperation of the Parties During the Regulatory Approval Process 725
	5.	Participation in the Upside 726
		a.	"Co-rights" 726
		b.	Bulk Supply Rights 728
E.	Anticipating Changes of Control of Either Party 728
		a.	Licensor Issues 729
		b.	Licensee Issues 729
		c.	Tailoring a Solution 730
F.	Terminating the Agreement if the Alliance Fails 730
	1.	Material Breach by the Licensee 731
		a.	The Licensor's Perspective 731
		b.	The Licensee's Perspective 731
	2.	Material Breach by the Licensor 732
		a.	The Licensor's Perspective 732

		b. The Licensee's Perspective 732
	3.	Termination Without Cause 732
G.	Conclusion: The Importance of Getting It Right 733

Chapter XVIII
Expansion: European and International Considerations for Biotechnology Companies 735
Daniel Pavin

A.	An Overview of Relevant European Institutions, Regulatory Bodies, and Legislative Framework 737
	1. The European Commission 737
	2. The European Medicines Agency 737
	3. National Regulatory Bodies (Competent Authorities) 739
	4. European Legislation and Other Instruments 739
B.	The Definition of "Medicinal Products" Under European Law 740
C.	Standards for Non-clinical Tests: Good Laboratory Practice and Laboratory Animal Welfare 741
	1. Introduction 741
	2. Guidance from the ICH and the EMEA 742
	3. Laboratory Animal Welfare 742
	4. Non-clinical Studies and Animal Testing: Other Countries 742
	a. GLP 742
	b. Animal Testing 743
D.	Clinical Trials in the EEA 743
	1. Introduction: The Regulatory Framework 743
	2. Provisions of the Clinical Trials Directive 744
	3. Scope of the Clinical Trials Directive: What Is a "Clinical Trial"? 745
	4. What Is an "Investigational Medicinal Product"? 745
	5. Who Is the "Sponsor" under the Clinical Trials Directive? 746
	6. Sponsors Who Are Not Established in the EEA 747
	7. Applying for Clinical Trial Authorization 747
	8. Manufacture and Importation of Investigational Medicinal Products (IMPs) 748
	9. GMP and GCP Inspections 749
	10. Notification of Adverse Events and Suspected Unexpected Serious Adverse Reactions 750
	11. Suspension of Trials 750
	12. Effect of Noncompliance 751
	13. Liability and Insurance 751
	14. Clinical Trials and Data Protection (Privacy) Law 751
	15. GCP and the GCP Directive 753
E.	Obtaining a Marketing Authorization in Europe 753
	1. Introduction 753

- 2. What Information Must Be Contained in a Marketing Authorization Application? 755
- 3. What Is the Format of a Marketing Authorization Application? 756
- 4. Summary of the Centralized Procedure 756
- 5. Duration of a Marketing Authorization 757
- 6. Responsibilities of the Holder of the Marketing Authorization 757
- 7. Can Patented Inventions Be Used for Uses Relating to Applying for a Marketing Authorization? 758
  - a. The Historical Position in Europe 758
  - b. The New Bolar Exemption 758
- F. Clinical Trials and Marketing Authorizations: International Strategies and Issues 759
  - 1. Product Development Strategies 759
  - 2. Where to Conduct a Clinical Trial 761
  - 3. Use of U.S. Non-clinical and Clinical Trials Data to Support a Marketing Authorization Application 762
  - 4. International Coordination 763
    - a. Introduction: The ICH 763
    - b. The Common Technical Document 763
- G. Post-marketing Issues in the EEA 764
  - 1. Pharmacovigilance 764
    - a. Introduction 764
    - b. Roles and Responsibilities of an MAH 764
    - c. Supervision and Enforcement 765
  - 2. Advertising, Promotion, and Labeling 766
  - 3. Manufacture, Importation, Classification, and Inspections 767
    - a. Manufacturing and Importing 767
    - b. Classification 767
    - c. Inspections 767
  - 4. Abridged Applications 768
    - a. Introduction 768
    - b. Abridged Applications for "Generic Medicinal Products" 768
    - c. Abridged Applications for Similar Biological Medicinal Products 769
  - 5. Bibliographic or "Well-Established Use" Applications 769
  - 6. Regulatory Data and Marketing Exclusivity 769
  - 7. Price Controls and Government Purchasing 771
  - 8. Parallel Importation and Parallel Distribution 771
    - a. Parallel Importation 771
    - b. Trademark Issues: Repackaging and Relabeling 772
    - c. Medicines Legislation 773
    - d. Parallel Distribution 773

		9.	Confidentiality and Freedom of Information	774
H.	Other Areas of Regulation			775
	1.	Regulation of Human Embryonic Stem Cell Research		775
		a.	Introduction	775
		b.	The Council of Europe's Convention on Human Rights and Biomedicine	775
		c.	European Harmonizing Legislation—The Current Position	776
		d.	National Regulation within the EEA	776
		e.	Other Countries	777
	2.	Human Tissue and Cells		777
		a.	Introduction	777
		b.	The Human Tissues and Cells Directive	777
	3.	Advanced Therapies		779
		a.	Europe	779
		b.	International	780
	4.	Blood and Blood Components		780
	5.	Medical Devices		781
I.	Regulation of GMOs			781
	1.	Regulation of GMOs: Legislation and Practice in the EEA		781
	2.	The EEA Legislative Framework with Respect to GMOs		782
		a.	Experimental Release of GMOs into the Environment	782
		b.	Placing on the Market of GMOs for Cultivation, Import, or Processing into Industrial Products	782
		c.	Placing on the Market of GMOs for Food or Feed/Food or Feed Containing GMOs	783
		d.	Safeguard Clause	783
		e.	Labeling and Traceability	783
		f.	Sanctions	784
		g.	Practical Implications for Industry	785
		h.	Developing and Marketing Authorizations for Medicinal Products Consisting of or Containing GMOs	786
	3.	International GMO Regulation		787
J.	Intellectual Property			788
	1.	Introduction		788
	2.	Patents		788
		a.	Legislative Background	788
		b.	Obtaining Patents in Europe	789
		c.	Substantive Patentability Criteria; Differences to the U.S. Position	790
		d.	Excluded Subject Matter	791
		e.	Microbiological Processes and Products	791
		f.	Human Material	792
		g.	Morality: Stem Cells	792

		h.	Morality: Transgenic Animals 793

        h. Morality: Transgenic Animals 793
        i. Transgenic Plants 793
    3. Trademarks 793
    4. Copyright and Database Right 794
    5. Plant Breeders' Rights 795
    6. The Interplay Between Intellectual Property Rights and European Community Law 795
    7. Enforcement of Intellectual Property Rights 796
K. EC Competition Law 796
    1. Introduction 796
    2. EC Competition Procedures 796
    3. Article 81 797
        a. Introduction 797
        b. Block Exemptions 798
    4. Article 82 798

Chapter XIX
Biotechnology Patent Litigation for the Non-Patent Attorney 813
Julie Fleming Brown

A. Judicial and Extrajudicial Proceedings 815
    1. Reexamination 816
        a. Ex Parte Reexamination 816
        b. Inter Partes Reexamination 817
        c. Director-Initiated Reexamination 818
    2. Reissue 819
B. General Overview of Patent Litigation Issues (Substantive) 819
    1. Claim Interpretation 821
    2. Definition of Infringement 822
        a. Types of infringement 824
    3. Proof of Infringement 825
        a. Possible Defenses and Counterclaims 825
        b. Non-infringement 826
        c. Patent Invalidity (§§ 102, 103, 112) 828
            i. Anticipation 829
            ii. Obviousness 830
            iii. Section 112 defenses 831
        d. Patent Unenforceability 833
        e. Antitrust 834
            i. Patent Misuse 834
            ii. Walker Process Counterclaim 835
            iii. Handgards Counterclaim 836
        f. Other Defenses Not Special to Patent Cases 836
    4. Damages Issues 837

	a. "No Less than a Reasonable Royalty"	838
	b. Lost Profits	840
	c. Enhanced Damages	841
	i. Willfulness	842
	ii. Attorneys' Fees	843
	d. Equitable Relief	843
C.	Phases of a Patent Case (Procedural/Strategic)	843

Chapter XX
Litigation Issues 857
Robert F. Copple

A. Intellectual Property and Confidential Business Information 858
   1. Trademark Issues 859
      a. Registration and Protection 859
      b. Litigation Claims—Infringement and Dilution 859
   2. Trade Secrets 863
      a. Trade Secrets Defined 863
      b. Establishing the Foundation for Trade Secret Protection 864
      c. Misappropriation 865
      d. Inevitable Disclosure Doctrine 866
B. Products Liability 867
   1. Defects and Causation 868
   2. Establish a Record of Compliance and Responsibility 868
C. Business Liability 869
   1. Corporate Disclosures and Insider Trading 870
      a. Misstatements and Omissions 870
      b. Insider Trading 871
   2. Corporate Governance 871
   3. False Claims and Whistleblowers 872
   4. Average Wholesale Price Drug Litigation 873
D. Document and Information Retention 873
   1. Regulatory Record-Keeping Requirements 874
   2. Litigation Discovery Issues 874
   3. Data Management Policy 875
E. Alternative Dispute Resolution 880
   1. ADR Defined 880
      a. Arbitration 880
      b. Mediation 881
   2. ADR Myths and Misconceptions 881
      a. A Sign of Weakness 881
      b. Free Discovery 882
   3. An Integrated Strategy for ADR 882
      a. Before the Dispute Arises 882

		b.	In the Early Stages of the Dispute 883
		c.	Parallel Strategies 884
		d.	Private Forums and Confidentiality 884
	4.	A Special Case for Patent Litigation 885
		a.	Participation by Senior Management.. 886
		b.	Advantages of ADR Confidentiality 886
		c.	ADR as an Alternative to Foreign Litigation 887
	5.	ADR Guidelines 888

Chapter XXI
Biotechnology Resources 893
Jennifer Korpacz
Treatises 893
National Academies Press 894
Major Federal Acts 896
Selected *Federal Register* Documents 900
Federal Agency Resources 900
Key Federal Cases 912
State Laws 918
Additional Resources 918
Europe 923
Foreign Countries 933

Index **935**

Preface

Biotechnology is frequently identified as one of the fastest-growing industries in the world. To speak of a single "biotechnology industry," however, is quite misleading. Biotechnology applies the myriad branches of the life sciences (for example, the various medical and surgical specialties, biology, biochemistry, pharmacology, biomedical engineering, genomics, proteomics, regenerative medicine, nanotechnology) to the development of products and technologies useful in a broad range of industry sectors (for example, human health care, veterinary care, food and agriculture, textiles, chemicals, alternative energy sources, biodefense). Some of biotechnology's applications, such as stem cell research, may challenge our preconceived notions—and, indeed, our comfort level—about the very nature of life. Other applications of biotechnology are more mundane—the enzymes that improve our laundry detergents or enhance the flavors of our foods. There are nascent products of biotechnology under development that pose potential solutions to some of the world's greatest problems: disease, famine, environmental pollution, nonrenewable energy sources.

The twentieth century looked to physics and chemistry to better the human condition. The twenty-first century looks to the life sciences with the same hope. This is not a North American or European or Asian phenomenon; it truly is global. These days, intellectual property developed in collaboration across a variety of technological specialties and industry sectors, in a number of countries on several continents, typically underlies any major medical breakthrough. Winston Churchill once said, "The empires of the future will be empires of the mind." He could have been talking about the so-called biotechnology industry when he spoke those words.

Not surprisingly, companies developing biotechnology products have very broad legal needs. Seminal technology often originates in universities and nonprofit research organizations. Government and private grant money plays a crucial role in fostering this fledgling technology. Once the academic institution licenses the technology to a company (frequently a start-up organized for this very purpose), the company takes on the task of raising enough capital to advance the technology toward commercialization. Financing, always difficult for a start-up business, is further complicated by the tremendous risks and long lead time involved in bringing a product from concept to market. In the case of pharmaceuticals and biologics, it often takes more than 10 years to navigate the U.S. Food and Drug Administration approval process—and most products never achieve marketing approval. In addition, many products also must contend with the regulations of the U.S. Department of Agriculture, the U.S. Environmental Protection Agency, and their foreign counterparts. Although the European Union rules are similar in some respects, they are not the same. These great risks, long lead time, and regulatory complexities encourage collaborations by smaller players with more established, deep-pocketed companies. The expenses involved almost mandate a worldwide marketing strategy involving one or more strategic partners. Even after achieving marketing approval, these products can expose their companies to substantial risks of patent infringement claims, product liability claims, government reimbursement and pricing claims, regulatory compliance actions, and a host of other legal nightmares.

Successful leaders of biotechnology companies will view these issues as related. Rather than pieces of a puzzle, they will see them more as strands of a rope, separate but intertwined. Their lawyers need to view them the same way. The legal adviser to a biotechnology company, whether in-house or outside, needs to take a holistic approach in order to serve that company's strategic needs. This is difficult to do: these legal problems cover numerous disciplines, any one of which requires years of experience to practice well. No one person can be master of all these specialties. As a result, lawyers (and the biotechnology clients they serve) need a resource that will enable them to spot legal issues critical to companies in this industry—a tool that will, at very least, tell them the right questions to ask in order to avert difficulties.

Two years ago, the Biotechnology Committee of the American Bar Association acknowledged the pressing need for such a resource. Committee members, and especially the then chair and chair-elect, Julie Fleming Brown and Erika Lietzan, respectively, recognized that lawyers practicing in this area (and the clients they serve) needed a comprehensive reference book. Books then available were typically so technical that a non-lawyer, or a lawyer outside a given legal discipline, would find them daunting. The Committee proposed a primer providing sufficient information to introduce the issues in each legal discipline that are critical to a biotechnology company.

Before a word of the book was written, a year and a half was invested in developing the book's format and scope. Hugh Wellons, the subsequent Committee chair, assembled a dedicated editorial team to carry the task forward: he and Eileen Smith Ewing as co-editors-in-chief; Robert F. Copple as stylistic editor; and Erika Lietzan and Bill Wofford as topic editors. Benefiting from the input of other legal experts, this editorial team shaped the book's content and recruited as chapter authors national experts in a range of fields. The topic editors assumed editorial responsibility based on their individual areas of expertise: Erika oversaw the scientific and regulatory chapters, and Bill shepherded the business law chapters. Subsequent chapter drafts, polished by their authors under Erika's and Bill's guidance, were further edited by the editors-in-chief and by Bob, who was in charge of style and consistency of content. In short, each chapter was edited multiple times in a grueling process that took well over a year from first drafts to last.

This, however, gives too much credit to the editors. The authors are the true stars of this book. They worked hard to meet demanding deadlines; they accepted our suggestions graciously; and they embraced the difficult task of distilling their complex professional expertise into simple explanations. We editors found it an education to work with these experts; we hope you will feel similarly enlightened by their work.

And now, the disclaimer: this book is meant to be a primer. No chapter will educate you sufficiently to practice in that area. The information in the book should not be taken as legal advice; given space and scope limitations, it does not seek to address all legal and regulatory concerns that companies or lawyers might have to consider in a specific situation. Each chapter could have been expanded into a book, but that was not our mission. We hope this primer will provide enough information for counsel and management to plan strategically, and enough guidance to know when you need an expert's advice.

This book was clearly a team effort, and many thanks are due. The ABA, especially its Biotechnology Committee and Division of Science and Technology, have provided a great deal of support. The ABA's book publishing division has been generous with its help and guidance. The American Association for the Advancement of Science provided general advice, and the

University of California–Berkeley Division of Agricultural and Natural Resources was kind enough to allow us to use its fine glossary of materials. Authors relied on various sources, which are identified in the individual chapters. We sincerely thank all the authors and the editorial staff—they have created a book in which they can take great pride. Special thanks go to our firms and our families, who put up with longer hours, fewer billings, and increased stress. We hope they, too, will take pride in the results.

Hugh B. Wellons and Eileen Smith Ewing
June 2006

About the Editors

Robert F. Copple (stylistic editor; chapter author) consults with major corporations on complex litigation, intellectual property, crisis management, government relations, and regulatory matters. He is also a trained mediator specializing in technology and environmental disputes. He practiced as a litigator with major law firms in Denver and Phoenix, and was senior litigation counsel for Motorola. While at Motorola, he was the lead attorney for all environmental litigation, all litigation for the Semiconductor Sector, and the majority of the company's intellectual property litigation. In addition, he reorganized and managed the company's Superfund liability, developed risk-management systems for the Iridium Satellite Launch Program, led the eCommerce law team, coordinated all alternative dispute resolution, and developed decision science methods for litigation evaluation and strategy analysis.

Mr. Copple has written and spoken extensively on litigation practice, communications law, economics, environmental, intellectual property, and alternative dispute resolution topics. In addition, he has lectured and taught graduate and law school courses at the University of North Carolina at Chapel Hill, Arizona State University, the University of Nebraska, and the University of Houston Law Center. He has provided training seminars for the CPR International Institute for Conflict Prevention and Resolution and the American Arbitration Association.

Mr. Copple received his undergraduate, masters, and law degrees from the University of Nebraska, where he was the executive editor of the *Nebraska Law Review*, and his Ph.D. in mass communications from the University of North Carolina at Chapel Hill. He also clerked for a state supreme court chief justice and for a federal district judge. Prior to his legal career, Mr. Copple was a working journalist on several newspapers and a legislative aid in the U.S. Congress and the Nebraska Unicameral Legislature.

Mr. Copple may be contacted at 9274 East Desert Trail, Scottsdale, AZ 85260; (480) 614-1561 (telephone); (480) 694-3403 (cell); rfcopple@cox.net (e-mail).

Eileen Smith Ewing (co-editor-in-chief; chapter author) is a partner in the Corporate, Licensing, and Life Sciences Practice Groups of K&L Gates. She co-coordinates both the firm's Licensing Practice Group and its interdisciplinary Life Sciences Practice Group across its 21 offices. Ms. Ewing represents private and public life sciences companies in strategic alliances, ranging from traditional mergers, acquisitions, joint ventures, and securities offerings to complex, cutting-edge drug discovery, development, and commercialization collaborations. Ms. Ewing's transactional practice is informed by a strong background in intellectual property licensing and technology transfer. Ms. Ewing speaks Japanese and has particular experience in Pacific Rim biopharmaceutical transactions. Her clients range from tiny biomedical start-ups to major multinational pharmaceutical companies.

Ms. Ewing has published more than 50 articles on corporate and intellectual property legal issues with respect to the life sciences industries. She is an executive editor of the *Journal of BioLaw and Business* and a regular speaker at BIO and other industry conferences. Ms. Ewing received a bachelor's degree *summa cum laude* from Harvard in 1984, M.A. and M.Phil. degrees in Japanese from Columbia University, and a J.D. from Columbia Law School in 1989.

Ms. Ewing may be contacted at K&L Gates, State Street Financial Center, One Lincoln Street, Boston, MA 02111; (617) 951-9227 (telephone); (617) 261-3175 (facsimile); eileen.ewing@klgates.com (e-mail); www.klgates.com (Web site).

Erika King Lietzan (science/regulatory section editor) is chair of the Biotechnology Committee in the American Bar Association's Section of Science and Technology Law and on the Section's governing council. She is special counsel in the food and drug practice group at Covington & Burling in Washington, D.C., where she specializes in pharmaceutical, biological drug, and medical device law. She has published on a wide range of topics, including clinical trial regulation, the Hatch-Waxman amendments to the FDCA, FDA's enforcement authority in GMP cases, prescription drug importation, FDA regulation of health claims for dietary supplements, FDA's litigation history, and privacy law. She has spoken on topics in drug, biologic, and device law, including direct-to-consumer advertising, bioterrorism, counterfeiting, and First Amendment issues. She is also on the Editorial Advisory Board of the *Food and Drug Law Journal* (published by the Food and Drug Law Institute). Ms. Lietzan graduated from the University of North Carolina in 1990, with honors. She earned an M.A. in intellectual history from UCLA and earned her J.D. from Duke Law School in 1995, with high honors. She clerked on the 11th Circuit Court of Appeals before coming to Covington in 1996. From 2002 to 2005, Ms. Lietzan was assistant general counsel of the Pharmaceutical Research and Manufacturers of America.

Ms. Lietzan may be contacted at Covington & Burling, 1201 Pennsylvania Ave. N.W., Washington, D.C. 20004; (202) 662-5165 (telephone); (202) 778-5165 (facsimile); elietzan@cov.com (e-mail).

Hugh B. Wellons (co-editor-in-chief; chapter author) is a partner at LeClair Ryan, where he focuses on biotechnology law, including aspects of corporate law, securities law, intellectual property, and mergers and acquisitions. He counsels biotech businesses, including public companies and emerging growth companies, and assists clients with intellectual property transfer involving universities, nonprofits, and larger corporations. Mr. Wellons is the immediate past chair of the American Bar Association Committee on Biotechnology and is a member of the Virginia Bar.

Mr. Wellons is a requested lecturer on biotech and nanotechnology matters for the ABA and for a number of Virginia and Washington, D.C., organizations. He also has lectured on securities law, strategic transactions, business formation, exit strategies, venture capital, and other funding concerns. Mr. Wellons has represented a variety of biotechnology companies, including companies specializing in transgenics, bioinfomatics, new drug development, and telemedicine.

Mr. Wellons has an undergraduate degree and masters in business administration from Duke University and a law degree from Washington & Lee University. Prior to practicing law, he worked at IBM in the Research Triangle Park. He was a partner at two other law firms before joining LeClair Ryan. Mr. Wellons has served as lead counsel on approximately 10 initial public offerings, seven secondary public offerings, 20 acquisitions of larger companies, and many private offerings. In addition, he has helped numerous companies in licensing transactions.

Mr. Wellons may be contacted at LeClair Ryan, 1800 Wachovia Tower, Drawer 1200, Roanoke, Virginia 24006; (540) 510-3057 (telephone); (540) 510-3050 (facsimile); www.leclairryan.com (Web site).

William N. Wofford (business/litigation section editor; chapter author) is a partner with Hutchison Law Group a law firm focused on serving life sciences and information technology companies based in the Southeast. Mr. Wofford's practice focuses on corporate and transactional matters for life sciences and technology companies. Many of Mr. Wofford's clients are bringing new and improved medical products and services to the clinic and the marketplace. Others are active in providing healthcare services, software, and media. Mr. Wofford helps growing and established companies raise capital, acquire and out-license technology, collaborate with strategic partners, and engage in mergers and acquisitions. A graduate of the University of Virginia (B.A. in 1989 and J.D. in 1994), Mr. Wofford began his legal career with White & Case in New York City. In 1997, Mr. Wofford moved to the Research Triangle, where he practiced with Womble Carlyle Sandridge & Rice prior to joining Hutchison+Mason in 2001. Mr. Wofford is active in numerous business organizations, including the Licensing Executives Society, the American Bar Association's Business Section and Biotechnology Committee, the Council for Entrepreneurial Development, the North Carolina Bioscience Industry Organization, and Southeast BIO. His charitable endeavors include a founding role with the Carrboro Parks Project and service on the board of directors of the American Lung Association of North Carolina and the Kramden Institute.

Mr. Wofford may be contacted at Hutchison Law Group, 5410 Trinity Road, Suite 400, Raleigh, NC 27607; (919) 829-4292 (telephone); (866) 479-7550 (facsimile); bwofford@hutchlaw.com (e-mail); www.hutchlaw.com (Web site).

About the Contributors

Michael H. Brodowski, Ph.D. (chapter author) is a partner in the Intellectual Property Practice Group of K&L Gates. Dr. Brodowski counsels individuals, start-up and established companies, research and educational institutions, investors, and underwriters in all aspects of the law relating to the protection, enforcement, and transfer of intellectual property rights. He concentrates on the establishment, maintenance, and exploitation of patent rights in the United States and abroad to support clients' business objectives. Dr. Brodowski has experience in creative and strategic patent prosecution, including patent reexamination, reissue, and foreign opposition proceedings. He renders patent infringement and invalidity opinions, conducts freedom-to-operate studies and due-diligence investigations, and advises trial counsel in patent infringement litigation. He counsels clients regarding the transfer and license of technology, including patent licenses and technology development agreements. He is experienced in trademark, copyright, and trade secret matters. Dr. Brodowski advises clients in the fields of chemistry, including complex multi-step organic synthesis, pharmaceuticals and small molecules, rational drug design, drug delivery, plastics and polymers, and chemical manufacturing; materials science, including metal composite materials, specialty papers, fuel cells, and separations media; biotechnology, including protein and nucleic acid compositions, synthesis and sequencing, and bioinformatics; health care, including diagnostic assays, medical and dental devices, and personal care products; and analytical instrumentation, including mass spectrometry, chromatography, and electrophoresis. Before entering the legal profession, Dr. Brodowski was a project chemist in the Product Development Group of the Toiletries Technology Laboratory at the Gillette Company. He is the first-named inventor on a number of issued U.S. and foreign patents.

Dr. Brodowski may be contacted at K&L Gates, State Street Financial Center, One Lincoln Street, Boston, MA 02111; (617) 261-3113 (telephone);

(617) 261-3175 (facsimile); michael.brodowski@klgates.com (e-mail); www.klgates.com (Web site).

Julie Fleming Brown (chapter author) is a registered patent attorney with a practice focused on patent litigation, though she also has substantial experience in trademark, trade secret, and complex commercial litigation. She has represented clients in a wide range of technologies, including medical devices, electrostatics, and telecommunications. Ms. Brown is active with the American Bar Association's Section of Science and Technology Law. She is currently a member of the Board of Editors of *The SciTech Lawyer* and serves as the Section's liaison to the Special Committee on Bioethics and the Law. Her previous appointments in the Section include chair, Biotechnology Committee (1997-2002); chair, Life Sciences and Physical Sciences Division (2001-2004); and council member (1999-2004). Before entering private practice, Ms. Brown clerked for the Hon. J. Owen Forrester of the U.S. District Court for the Northern District of Georgia.

Ms. Brown may be contacted at (404) 374-7500 (telephone) or jflemingbrown@aol.com (e-mail).

Andrew T. Hoyne (chapter author) is a partner in the St. Louis–based law firm of Armstrong Teasdale LLP, where he chairs the firm's Biotechnology and Life Sciences Practice. His practice includes life science company licensing, manufacturing, research, collaboration, financing, and venture capital agreements and relationships. He is chair of the St. Louis Capital Alliance, listed in *The Best Lawyers in America*, a former member of the Executive Committee of St. Louis Technology Gateway, and a former vice-chair of the Biotechnology Committee of the American Bar Association Science and Technology Section. He received J.D. and LL.M. degrees from Washington University School of Law and a B.A. from Knox College. From 1987 through 1990, he was associate general counsel of Invitron Corporation, a publicly held biotechnology spin-off of Monsanto Company.

Mr. Hoyne may be contacted at Armstrong Teasdale LLP, One Metropolitan Square, Suite 2600, St. Louis, MO 63102; (314) 342-8066 (telephone); ahoyne@armstrongteasdale.com (e-mail).

G. Melissa Ince (chapter author) is an associate with the Kansas City law firm of Polsinelli Shalton Welte Suelthaus, PC, practicing in the regulatory and compliance aspects of life sciences and environmental law. Ms. Ince serves as co-chair of the American Bar Association's Genetic and Medical Research Committee, deputy editor-in-chief of the *Sci-Tech Lawyer*, and is past chair of the Life Sciences Grants Compliance Subcommittee. She was graduated from the University of Missouri-Rolla with a B.S. in geological engineering, *cum laude*, in 1994, and from Washington University School of Law in 2000.

Ms. Ince may be contacted at Polsinelli Shalton Welte Suelthaus, PC, 700 W. 47th Street, Suite 1000, Kansas City, MO 64112; (816) 360-4229 (telephone); mince@pswslaw.com (e-mail).

Jenny Kim (chapter author) is an associate in the Government Contracts Group of Miller & Chevalier Chartered, where she has a broad-based practice focusing on government contracts, government ethics, compliance, and election/lobbying laws. Her expertise includes evaluating and developing public contracting compliance programs, resolving suspension and debarment matters, federal criminal conflicts-of-interest laws counseling, particularly on the revolving-door restrictions, U.S. Postal Service discount mail compliance counseling, and advising senior corporate executives on formation of and the parameters of political action committee fund-raising, contribution, and communications. Prior to joining Miller & Chevalier, Ms. Kim served as a U.S. Presidential Management Fellow and worked in the White House and the Missile Defense Agency. As an ethics adviser in the Office of Counsel to the President at the White House, she served as a de facto special assistant to an Associate Counsel to the President. She counseled senior White House officials and employees regarding criminal conflict of interest statutes, Executive Branch Standards of Ethical Conduct regulations, financial disclosure requirements, travel-related issues, and other matters that required a legal and public relations strategy. At the Missile Defense Agency, she participated in the development of internal guidance memoranda and a study to recommend export control changes to facilitate international missile defense cooperation. In 2005, the American Bar Association Young Lawyers Division (YLD) appointed Ms. Kim to the position of YLD Liaison to the

Standing Committee on Election Law. She was also a 2005 delegate to the YLD Assembly at the 2005 American Bar Association Annual Meeting.

Ms. Kim may be contacted at Miller & Chevalier Chartered, 655 15th St., NW, Washington, D.C. 20005, (202) 626-1571 (telephone); (202) 626-5801 (facsimile); jkim@milchev.com (e-mail).

Jennifer Korpacz, J.D., M.S.L.S (chapter author) is the assistant librarian–research for the Washington, D.C., office of Covington & Burling. She leads a team of seven research librarians, and she specializes in food and drug and legislative research. A graduate of the University of Colorado at Boulder, she earned her law degree from St. John's University and is admitted to practice in New York. She obtained her library science masters degree from The Catholic University of America, and she just finished a two-year term as the president of the Private Law Libraries Special Interest Section of the Law Librarians' Society of Washington, D.C. Prior to joining Covington & Burling, she was a case administrator with the American Arbitration Association.

Ms. Korpacz may be contacted at Covington & Burling, 1201 Pennsylvania Ave., N.W., Washington, D.C. 20004-2401; (202) 662-6000 (telephone).

Areta L. Kupchyk (chapter author) is a partner in Reed Smith's healthcare practice group in Washington, D.C., and counsels on FDA-related drug, device, biologic, and biotechnology matters. Ms. Kupchyk joined Reed Smith in 2003 after spending nearly 10 years at the Food and Drug Administration as Associate Chief Counsel for Biologics and for Drugs, as well as Assistant General Counsel for Litigation. During her tenure, Ms. Kupchyk contributed significantly to the development of some of the FDA's most dynamic issues, including new human cell and tissue regulations, the policy on bioengineered plants grown to produce medical products, BSE-related enforcement, xenotransplantation, and fast-track approvals. Ms. Kupchyk also provided technical assistance to Congress and regulatory counsel to FDA officials on enforcement strategies, including the FDA's Application Integrity Policy and debarments under the Generic Drug Enforcement Act. Ms. Kupchyk has received numerous awards, including the prestigious Department of Health and Human Services (HHS) Distinguished Service Award, the FDA Commissioner's Special Recognition Award, and the HHS General Counsel's Leadership Award. Ms. Kupchyk's FDA practice is augmented by prior federal and state litigation experience at the Federal Trade Commission and at the Office of the Attorney General of Maryland. In 1990, Ms. Kupchyk earned her J.D., with honors, from the University of Maryland School of Law and was awarded the Order of the Coif. Ms. Kupchyk is admitted to practice in Maryland, the District of Columbia, the Maryland Court of Appeals, and the U.S. District Court for the District of Maryland.

Ms. Kupchyk may be contacted at Reed Smith LLP, 1301 K Street N.W., Suite 1100 - East Tower, Washington, D.C. 20005; (202) 414-9362 (telephone); (202) 414-9299 (facsimile); akupchyk@reedsmith.com (e-mail).

Kent D. McClure, D.V.M., J.D. (chapter author) is general counsel to the Animal Health Institute (AHI), the U.S. national trade association for research-based manufacturers of animal health products—the biologics, pharmaceuticals, and pesticides that are used in modern food production and that keep livestock, poultry, and pets healthy. He received his doctor of veterinary medicine degree from Texas A & M and his legal degree from the University of Texas. He provides general legal counsel for the association as well as guidance on scientific and policy issues. Prior to joining AHI, Dr. McClure practiced in Dallas, Texas, representing a variety of manufacturers of pharmaceuticals and medical devices as well as health-care providers.

Dr. McClure may be contacted at Animal Health Institute, 1325 G Street N.W., Suite 700, Washington, D.C. 20005; (202) 637-2440 (telephone); (202) 393-1667 (facsimile).

Robert B. Nicholas (chapter author) is a partner in the law firm of McDermott Will & Emery LLP based in the Washington, D.C., office. He is head of the firm's FDA practice and co-chairs the firm's Life Sciences/Biotechnology Practice Group. He focuses his practice on representing clients at all stages of development and marketing of human and animal drugs, biologics, medical devices, and foods. Mr. Nicholas works with clients developing and implementing strategic and regulatory plans for product approvals; compliance counseling; enforcement defense; litigation; and government relations. In addition to representing clients before the FDA, the courts, and Congress, Mr. Nicholas has experience on NIH funding and research compliance, and USDA/APHIS biotechnology permit approval and research matters. His clients include multinational companies, research institutions, development-stage companies, and individual investigators and scientists. Prior to joining McDermott, Mr. Nicholas served on the senior staff of the Oversight Subcommittee, U.S. House Committee on Science and Technology, and in the Executive Office of the President. Other past positions include service as a deputy attorney general for Pennsylvania, as vice chairman of the Special Committee on Biotechnology of the ABA, and as an editor of the *Biotechnology Law Journal*. He has been a consultant to the National Academy of Sciences and the Congressional Office of Technology Assessments. Mr. Nicholas is admitted to practice in the District of Columbia, Massachusetts, and before the Supreme Court of the United States.

Mr. Nicholas may be contacted at McDermott Will & Emery LLP, 600 13th St., N.W., Washington, D.C. 20005; (202) 756-8170 (telephone); rnicholas@mwe.com (e-mail).

Anne Stohr O'Brien (chapter author) is of counsel in the Health Care Law Group of Polsinelli Shalton Welte Suelthaus PC, where she concentrates her practice on health-care regulatory, licensing, compliance, and risk management matters. Since entering private practice in 1986, she has had experience in business litigation, managed-care litigation, and national mass tort liability litigation with emphasis on medical witness development. She has represented physicians, allied health professionals, hospitals, and other health-care institutions with risk management, regulatory, licensure and medical staff issues, preparation and review of health-care-related contracts, HIPAA compliance and violations and clinical research trials. Ms. O'Brien received her BS, *cum laude*, in nursing from St. Louis University in 1983 and worked as a registered nurse on a medical/surgical unit at a large metropolitan hospital in St. Louis before law school. She has given presentations on nursing liability and licensure issues at medical service corporation seminars.

Ms. O'Brien may be contacted at Polsinelli Shalton Welte Suelthaus PC, 700 West 47th Street, Suite 1000, Kansas City, MO 64112; (816) 753-1000 (telephone); (816) 753-1536 (facsimile); aobrien@pswslaw.com (e-mail).

Daniel T. Pancamo (chapter author) is counsel in the New Orleans regional law firm Phelps Dunbar, L.L.P. He practices in business, commercial, and regulatory law. He is a 1989 graduate of Tulane Law School. He is also a member of the board of directors of the National Tay-Sachs & Allied Diseases Association, one of the nation's oldest genetic disease support organizations.

Mr. Pancamo may be contacted at Phelps Dunbar, L.L.P., 365 Canal Street, Suite 2000, New Orleans, LA 70130; (504) 584-9265 (telephone); pancamod@phelps.com (e-mail).

Daniel Pavin (chapter author) is a partner in the London office of European law firm Taylor Wessing. He works mainly in the life sciences, technology, and IT sectors and acts for a wide range of clients, from university spin-outs and entrepreneurs to multinational life sciences and medical device companies. Mr. Pavin's practice covers both non-contentious and contentious intellectual property and information technology matters and includes:

- Transactional and commercial work, including alliance agreements, patent and software licensing, research and development agreements, clinical trials agreements, and distribution and agency agreements.
- Intellectual property and regulatory advice in the context of mergers, acquisitions, investments, and joint ventures.
- Life sciences, technology, and IT contract disputes.
- Data protection, freedom of information and privacy.

Mr. Pavin has a degree from Cambridge University in computer science and physics and a diploma in intellectual property law and practice from Bristol University. Mr. Pavin is one of the authors of the UK Law Society's *Data Protection Handbook*.

Mr. Pavin may be contacted at Taylor Wessing, Carmelite, 50 Victoria Embankment, Blackfriars, London EC4Y 0DX, United Kingdom; +44 (0)20 7300 7000 (telephone); +44 (0)20 7300 7100 (facsimile); d.pavin@taylorwessing.com (e-mail); www.taylorwessing.com (web site).

Dr. J. Winston Porter (chapter author) is a leading environmental and management consultant whose experience includes solid and hazardous waste management, urban rivers restoration, and agricultural biotechnology. He is president of the Waste Policy Center (WPC) in Leesburg, Virginia. The WPC is a private research and consulting organization that deals with environmental management and policy issues. Dr. Porter is also a frequent communicator on environmental matters through speeches and media appearances. From 1985 to 1989, Dr. Porter was the Assistant Administrator for Solid Waste and Emergency Response at the U.S. Environmental Protection Agency. In this position, he was the national program manager for the Superfund and other solid and hazardous waste programs. Earlier, Dr. Porter was with the Bechtel engineering and construction organization, where he managed the environmental department and later directed the master plan for the $30 billion Jubail Industrial City in Saudi Arabia. He received his B.S. in chemical engineering from the University of Texas at Austin and his Ph.D. in the same field from the University of California at Berkeley. He is a registered professional engineer in California, Texas, and Virginia. In 1999 he was named a Distinguished Engineering Graduate of the University of Texas at Austin.

Dr. Porter may be contacted at 104 Dry Mill Road, Suite 103, Leesburg, VA 20175; (703) 777-9800 (telephone); jwp@winporter.com (e-mail); www.winporter.com (Web site).

Steven E. Pozaric (chapter author) is an associate of the St. Louis–based law firm of Armstrong Teasdale LLP. He is a member of the firm's Business Services Department and helps leads the firm's efforts involving biotechnology and life sciences companies, particularly in the area of formation, financing, and collaborative efforts. Mr. Pozaric also focuses on mergers and acquisitions and regularly counsels clients with respect to corporate formation matters, financing strategies and plans, securities issues, and general business matters. Mr. Pozaric received his B.B.A. from Texas Christian University, his M.B.A. from the John M. Olin School of Business at Washington University and his J.D. from St. Louis University. Prior to his career in law, he worked in corporate finance for a division of Emerson Electric and for Lockheed Martin (formerly General Dynamics).

Mr. Pozaric may be contacted at Armstrong Teasdale LLP, One Metropolitan Square, Suite 2600, St. Louis, MO 63102; (314) 552-6643 (telephone); spozaric@armstrongteasdale.com (e-mail).

Paul W. Radensky, M.D. (chapter author) is a partner at McDermott Will & Emery LLP based in the firm's Miami office and concentrates in the Life Sciences practice. He works on Medicare, Medicaid, and third-party payer reimbursement matters relating to pharmaceuticals, biologics, medical devices, *in vitro* diagnostics, and clinical laboratory services. He also works on clinical development, promotional compliance, and outcomes research matters for FDA-regulated products. Dr. Radensky did his undergraduate work in biochemical sciences at Princeton University (A.B., 1975), received his M.D. degree from the University of Pennsylvania (1979), completed an internal medicine residency and fellowship in liver diseases at Mount Sinai in New York, and received his J.D. degree from Harvard Law School (1988).

Dr. Radensky may be contacted at McDermott Will & Emery LLP, 201 S. Biscayne Blvd., Suite 2200, Miami, FL 33131; (305) 347-6557 (telephone); (305) 347-6500 (facsimile); pradensky@mwe.com (e-mail).

Steve A. Schwarm (chapter author) is a shareholder in the Health Care Law Group of Polsinelli Shalton Welte Suelthaus PC, where he concentrates his practice on health-care regulatory, licensing, and compliance matters. Since entering private practice in 1992, he has represented physicians, hospitals, drug distributors, and other health-care providers and entities in investigations and trial-type administrative hearings before state and federal agencies throughout the country. He has clients throughout the United States, and he serves as regulatory compliance counsel to a multi-state independent clinical laboratory and to an academic medical center hospital's HIPAA Privacy and Security Committees, in addition to serving on numerous hospital committees relating to regulatory issues. Mr. Schwarm is a former assistant attorney general for Kansas and litigation counsel/general counsel for a multi-health care provider state regulatory agency. He has completed the Federal Associations Regulatory Board's attorney certification course in professional regulatory law. Mr. Schwarm litigates, teaches, and writes extensively in the area of health-care administrative law. He is the author of numerous health care/administrative books and articles and is recognized as a leading authority in the area of the Health Insurance Portability and Accountability Act of 1996 (HIPAA). He is the co-author of *HIPAA Privacy Clear View—Digital Desk Reference* and a contributor to DRI's *MedLaw Update*; American Health Lawyers' Association publications; *Report on Patient Privacy*; *Report on Medicare Compliance*; HIPAA Privacy Compliance Guide; and the *KADC Legal Letter*.

Mr. Schwarm may be contacted at Polsinelli Shalton Welte Suelthaus PC, 555 South Kansas Ave., Topeka, KS 66603-3443; (785) 233-1446 (telephone); sschwarm@pswslaw.com (e-mail).

Mark L. Stoneman (chapter author) is a partner in the St. Louis–based law firm of Armstrong Teasdale LLP, where he practices business and corporate law. Mr. Stoneman has represented both new and established life science companies. His practice focuses on areas involving formation, capitalization, acquisitions, divestitures, and joint ventures. In many instances, Mr. Stoneman has acted as outside general counsel to companies of various sizes. Mr. Stoneman serves on The St. Louis Capital Alliance and related subcommittees. Mr. Stoneman is involved in various charitable activities, including the United Way and Junior Achievement. Mr. Stoneman received his B.S. in business administration, *cum laude*, in 1993, his J.D. in 1996, and his Master of Accountancy in 2002—each from the University of Missouri.

Mr. Stoneman may be contacted at Armstrong Teasdale LLP, One Metropolitan Square, Suite 2600, St. Louis, MO 63102; (314) 552-6629 (telephone); mstoneman@armstrongteasdale.com (e-mail).

Thomas A. Turano (chapter author) is a partner in the Intellectual Property Practice Group at K&L Gates. Mr. Turano focuses on intellectual property counseling, patent and trademark prosecution, licensing, opinions, transactional due diligence, and litigation. He counsels both international and U.S. clients on creating a patent portfolio that will maximize the business value of a company's intellectual property in the individual jurisdictions of interest. Mr. Turano practices in both the health science–related and the high tech–related technologies. Prior to joining K&L Gates, Mr. Turano was a partner in the Patent and Intellectual Property Practice Group of Testa, Hurwitz & Thibeault, LLP. He is also a former adjunct professor at Suffolk University School of Law, having taught a course on patent prosecution. Mr. Turano has presented a number of seminars and talks in the United States, Canada, and Europe on patent strategy and portfolio development, and he has published numerous scientific, engineering, and legal articles and is the author of a book on patent prosecution. Mr. Turano earned a J.D. from Suffolk University Law School (1988), M.S. degrees from Worcester Polytechnic Institute, Brown University, and the University of Rhode Island, and a B.S. from the University of Rhode Island.

Mr. Turano may be contacted at K&L Gates, State Street Financial Center, One Lincoln Street, Boston, MA 02111; (617) 261-3148 (telephone); (617) 261-3175 (facsimile); thomas.turano@klgates.com (e-mail); www.klgates.com (Web site).

Jeffrey Van Doren (chapter author) is a partner in the Employment and Labor practice group at LeClair Ryan, where he specializes in immigration and labor law matters. Listed in *The Best Lawyers in America* for immigration law, Mr. Van Doren focuses on assisting U.S.-based and foreign companies with their business immigration needs. He represents both public and private employers in securing non-immigrant (temporary) and immigrant (permanent) visas on behalf of employers and employees. Jeff has broad experience representing clients in immigration-related proceedings before federal administrative agencies including the Department of Homeland Security's immigration bureaus (U.S. Citizenship & Immigration Services and the Bureau of Customs Enforcement), the Department of Labor, and the Department of State and its U.S. consulates abroad. He also advises U.S. employers on compliance with the I-9 "employer sanctions" provisions of federal law. Mr. Van Doren also has extensive experience representing management on traditional labor matters, including union avoidance and decertification, developing strike plans, collective bargaining, contract compliance, and arbitration. He regularly appears before the NLRB in such matters. He has frequently been called upon to assist clients in defense of discrimination, wrongful discharge, wage and hour, breach of contract, and other employment claims before federal and state courts. He has been named by *Virginia Business* magazine as one of "Virginia's Legal Elite" in the field of labor/employment law.

Mr. Van Doren may be contacted at LeClair Ryan, 1800 Wachovia Tower, Drawer 1200, Roanoke, VA 24006; (540) 510-3054 (telephone); (540) 510-3050 (facsimile); www.leclairryan.com (Web site).

Christine C. Vito, Ph.D. (chapter author) is a partner in the Intellectual Property Practice Group at K&L Gates. Dr. Vito advises clients in all matters relating to patent procurement and strategic portfolio development, technology licensing and asset management; and general intellectual property counseling regarding patent infringement, validity and enforcement. Dr. Vito's practice concentrates on the life/medical sciences and biotechnology, and her clients include venture-backed companies, multinational corporations, venture firms, nonprofit organizations, and universities. Prior to joining K&L Gates in 2005, Dr. Vito was a partner in the Patent and Intellectual Property Practice Group of Testa, Hurwitz & Thibeault, LLP. She was previously a research scientist in both the academic and industry sectors. While at Children's Hospital and Harvard Medical School in Boston, Dr. Vito studied developmental neuroendocrinology and collaborated with many of the field's leading behavioral biologists. After leaving academia, Dr. Vito joined Ventrex Laboratory of Portland, Maine, where she served as manager of scientific affairs and coordinator of technology-related legal matters, including patent and licensing matters. From 1989 to 1993, Dr. Vito was a member of the Maine State Commission on Biotechnology and Genetic Engineering.

Dr. Vito may be contacted at K&L Gates, State Street Financial Center, One Lincoln Street, Boston, MA 02111; (617) 261-3150 (telephone); (617) 261-3175 (facsimile); christine.vito@klgates.com (e-mail); www.klgates.com (Web site).

Chapter I

Introduction to Biotechnology and the Law

Robert F. Copple
Scottsdale, Arizona

Technology, or "tech," is a driving force in our culture and economy. Beginning in the late 1950s with the development of television, the invention of the transistor, and the launch of Russian satellite Sputnik, Americans evolved into a culture of technophiles. We drank Tang instant breakfast drink (supposedly a mainstay of the astronauts' space diet) while watching Walter Cronkite count down the minutes to the next nail-biting space launch. We listened to major news and sporting events, such as the Cassius Clay/Sonny Liston title fight, on our miniature transistor radios. Even our automobiles took on design elements of jet airplanes and rocket ships.

During this same time frame, advances in health care also leaped into our lives. The mass production of vaccines and the inoculation of millions of schoolchildren put to an end many devastating diseases that ravaged the previous generations. We witnessed the first heart transplant. And, increased medical sophistication gave women a new level of reproductive and economic freedom. It's no wonder that we began to believe in better living through chemistry.

These technological advances were, at least in part, driven by two foundational scientific events that foretold the future of the tech culture and the tech economy. The first was Bell Labs' invention of the transistor, which resulted in a Nobel Prize for the research team in 1956. That simple, almost inert, replacement for the vacuum tube was the initial and necessary step that made possible powerful microprocessors, each containing millions of circuits. Increasingly smaller chunks of silicon and copper, in turn, led to the development of the modern computer, the creation of the Internet, the invention of previously impossible scientific instruments and processes, and the mass production of electronic consumer devices that pervade virtually every aspect of our lives and have created a global tech economy.

The second, but equally breathtaking, scientific development was the discovery of the DNA double helix by two Cambridge University researchers, which earned them the Nobel Prize in 1962. This first glimpse at the source code of life fueled a research explosion in the biological and medical sciences. Biotech joined semiconductor technology as a potential driver of the new economy and culture.

While the semiconductor revolution (consistent with the tech "law" that microprocessor power doubles every 18 months) blazed along at geometric speed, biotech seemed to linger as the great unfulfilled promise. Even though biotech discoveries and developments continued to progress incrementally, at least from the consumer point of view, biotech did not seem to have the same raging momentum. There are many reasons for this perceived disparity in developmental speeds. Chief among these is that even the most sophisticated microprocessor does not approach the mysterious complexities of living systems. And, because biotech often involves direct or indirect application to human life, there is little room for error. It is one thing for an office computer to crash and quite another for an inadequately tested medical application to impair life and physical well-being. In other words, "Intel Inside" is much different from "Got DNA?"

While the benefits of biotech are too numerous to list, it has also been a source of great controversy. Most recently, developments regarding stem cell research (a biotech poster child), cloning, and athletic performance-enhancement drugs have created public debate that goes far beyond pure science into the realms of ethics, religion, and to the basic definition of what it is to be human. At the concrete level, more serious are the examples of biotech innovation gone wrong, resulting in death and disabling conditions, such as the Thalidomide babies of the 1960s.

But while biotech research and development moves along at a more deliberate path, recent scientific and economic events have altered the potential, if not the pace, of biotech application. First, the mapping of the human genome, perhaps the greatest biological achievement since the identification of the double helix, has provided medical researchers with enhanced ability to study and treat disease. Second, the investment community, hungry for the addictive excitement and extraordinary profits of the 1990s electronic tech boom, now busted, is looking for a new fix, and biotech may be just the ticket. Third, individual, university, and corporate researchers, seeing what invention, innovation, and intellectual property licensing did for the Microsofts, Apples, and Sonys of the world, are working to build their biotech portfolios in anticipation of greater value, leverage, and profit.

If it isn't already obvious, the biotech boom is largely about money and the race for that money. True, the actual applications may be altruistic, such as creating vaccines to avoid pandemic outbreaks of deadly diseases. Even so, with an aging population of Baby Boomers who are determined to live forever, there is a great deal of money to be made by the successful competitors in the consumer market. As is true of most new technologies, such as the Internet, the initial commercialization that provides the necessary capital to go forward often does not come from the most sophisticated and erudite uses of the technology, but, instead, from consumer applications catering to more superficial wants and desires.

It is this potential for great riches that is causing biotech investors and inventors to seek each other out. One of the best examples of this trend is the relatively recent rise of the university technology transfer office mandated to increase university funding through the commercialization of academic research. Accordingly, investors are willing to take a risk with biotech development despite the high failure rate of new biotech ventures, and the great costs and exceedingly long time frames required to get a biotech product to market.

A. The Biotech Primer

What does this all have to do with a primer on biotechnology law? The answer is this. Biotech has expanded from the largely exclusive realm of a few major corporations and research organizations to include a multitude of biotech start-ups and other entities looking for a stake in this next boom. As a result, legal practitioners who previously were unlikely to be faced with biotech issues are now finding themselves representing these new players. Biotech legal practice involves specialized subject matter and regulatory schemes that, generally, are not part of the business lawyer's repertoire and that can present many hazards for the uninitiated. Because of this expansion of the biotech practice beyond the traditional organizations and their representatives, the American Bar Association's Biotechnology Committee determined that the time was right for a biotech book to help lawyers find their way through the biotech maze.

This primer was never meant to be the last word on biotech law. Instead, it is intended to serve as a starting place for lawyers faced with the challenge of identifying the legal issues and processes that must be faced by their clients in building, marketing, and protecting a biotech business. The authors of the individual chapters, each of whom are experts in their respective fields, have endeavored to provide thorough, yet accessible, overviews of biotech subspecialties with an eye to practical application. We hope you will find this volume a useful and often consulted resource in your biotech practice.

B. Biotech Defined

Before going any further, it is necessary to attempt to come up with a working definition of "biotechnology." In its narrowest and most traditional sense, "biotech" is a term of art that encompasses the alteration and application of living matter—for example, the genetic manipulation of microbes—for a human use. With growth of the industry and the integration of many different technologies, however, a working definition becomes more elusive. As the field has grown, the term has evolved to include research, development, and application of medicines, devices, analytical aids, and therapies intended to contribute to the health and physical well-being of humans. The working definition must also include fields, activities, and subject matter that indirectly impact or contribute to wellness or lifestyle. For example, the broader definition of biotech includes activities such the development of pesticides, altered or improved agricultural plants and animals intended for food or other uses, microbes engineered to perform specific tasks such as the breakdown of wastes and hazardous substances or the creation of chemical compounds, and even veterinary science aimed at the well-being of the family pet. It is this definition of biotech that is exemplified by the broad-based membership of many biotech industry groups. This is also the definition applied in this primer.

1. Three-Branch Approach

Because of the vastness of biotech development and application, it might be better to define biotech to encompass all things medicinal and/or biological, and then break the area down into three functional branches. The first branch is pharmacological, referred to in the industry as "pharma," which includes medicines, vaccines, and some diagnostic tools. The second branch is medical devices, used for research, diagnostics, and the application of medicines and therapies. The third branch might be described as the genetics, biologics or "Jurassic Park" branch and includes DNA technologies to create medical therapies, as well as agricultural plants and animals.

While this three-branch approach is a good starting point, the demarcation gets very fuzzy at the edges. So, for example, how do you characterize a therapeutic system involving a device that is implanted in a patient to dispense particular medications to specific cells or parts of the body? Or, what about a semiconductor designed to analyze a drop of a patient's blood (the "lab on a chip") to determine the genetic source of a disease? In the end, for the lack of a better taxonomy method, these examples all fall into the general category of "biotech."

C. The Biotech Company Life Cycle

To focus on the application of specific areas of biotech law, it is first necessary to understand the overall biotech company life cycle. Beginning with idea conception and corporate formation through product development and marketing, next-level business development, and post-product sale, the life cycle is intended to provide the reader with a frame of reference for the issues that arise at various points in the biotech business process. Accordingly, we have attempted to organize this primer in a manner consistent with the biotech life cycle. From a practical standpoint, the biotech company life cycle can be divided into four general phases.

1. Phase I: Start-up

The Start-up Phase is characterized by two distinct elements: idea inception and company formation, which are discussed in Chapters II-V. Biotech is an idea-driven industry dependent upon creative minds to come up with scientific discoveries that can be converted into new products. To be economically successful, however, those ideas and inventions must be backed by substantial financial investment within the context of a company structure. Therefore, representation of the start-up company requires expertise in both intellectual property protection and corporate formation and financing.

a. Intellectual Property

On the intellectual property side of the start-up equation, fortunes can be lost for failure to take the proper legal steps to protect discoveries and applications. This step in the legal process is the realm of the intellectual property lawyer with expertise in legal specialties including patent, trade secret, trademark, and copyright. Recognition of this representational need can go a long way toward building a foundation that will contribute greatly to acquiring adequate business development funding and achieving maximum profitability at the next major stage of biotech business development.

For the business lawyer representing the biotech client, and particularly the start-up client, it is very important to get intellectual property counsel involved early in the process. Patent lawyers, who by definition are required to have technical training in addition to a law degree, generally have backgrounds that mirror their clients' scientific disciplines. For example, semiconductor patent attorneys also tend to be electrical engineers ("Double E's") or chemical engineers ("Chem E's"), like their clients or their clients' inventors. Similarly, in the world of biotech, patent lawyers tend to come from the life sciences disciplines and often hold Ph.D.'s in relevant areas such as biochemistry and molecular biology. Such team efforts help avoid the pitfalls inherent in the intellectual property protection process and also set the stage for a successful business strategy.

b. Company Formation

While company formation is important for any start-up business, it is particularly crucial for the biotech start-up. In contrast to the Internet start-ups, which seemed to move from inception to an individual public offering about as soon as the domain name was registered, the biotech company may take up to 10 years from idea inception before a product has been approved for sale. Because of this long lead time, strategic company formation is critical to keeping the company, its key executives, and its brain power together for the duration of the life cycle. Therefore, the business lawyer involved in biotech company formation must be able to think well into the future and to anticipate the types of corporate issues that might be triggered, including long-term corporate governance, key executive longevity, and the allocation of corporate equity.

c. Investment Capital

These business formation issues are further complicated by the fact that getting a biotech product to market is a costly enterprise that will not show a profit for years after idea inception. Therefore, the biotech start-up needs great amounts of outside investment capital from venture capitalists, sophisticated "angels," or the large biotech company seeking to purchase or partner with the start-up. Once money is at issue, the financial relationships between the start-up principals and the outside investors can become very complex as the start-up's equity begins to migrate away from the principals to those investors. Therefore, the start-up's lawyer has the challenge of helping her client form a company that protects the principals' interests while also being financially attractive to the essential outside investors.

Even though all of the players are focused, more or less, on the money, as with any tech speculation, there is a natural tension between investors and inventors. Typically, the outside money people are looking for speedy returns on investment. Inventors, on the other hand, and particularly academic inventors, are often driven by an obligation to complete fully the necessary research without shortcuts that could cause professional embarrassment. It is at this early intersection where biotech lawyers can work with their clients by creating business entities specifically tailored to address the need for speed while avoiding unnecessary research and development risks that could lead to exorbitant liability and business failure. By helping the client select a strong board of directors and the assignment of watchdogs, such as a science advisory board, the company can create a sort of business détente between investors and inventors that may allow them to survive the tumultuous early years of the relationship and see them through to business success.

2. Phase II: Early Development

Once the basic foundation of the start-up is in place, the new company is now on the long road to development, regulatory approval, and product sale. The early development phase is marked by continued financing issues, the search for development partners, the beginnings of the regulatory trials process, and the business issues faced by any tech company as it grows beyond a few principals to become a more complex organization. Chapters VI-IX address many of these early development issues.

a. Additional Investment

If there is one reoccurring theme throughout the biotech business lifecycle, it is financing and the virtually constant need for new capital. Financing issues are not as critical for the larger, established biotech companies with a diversified portfolio of products at different stages of maturity. For the start-up, however, finding capital and the right partners often means the difference between a successful business and early demise. These relationships can take different forms, both public funding and private investment, each of which presents strategic issues for the new company and challenges the biotech business lawyer in helping to shepherd his client to success.

b. The Regulatory Track

The early development phase is also marked by the all-important relationships between the company and the relevant governmental agencies, as well as the beginning of the years of scientific testing and trials necessary to ultimately achieve regulatory approval. Because biotech company development is based on an inherent tension between time and money, missteps in terms of damage to agency relationships or failure to comply with the required regulatory protocols can result in serious delays that strain the time/money critical path and endanger the company's chances for success. Here, the biotech lawyer, who will likely be better versed in regulatory compliance and relationship building than his science-driven client, can provide great value by helping the company to avoid the small missteps that often lead to business disaster.

c. Business Growth and Complexity

Once the fledging biotech company grows beyond the initial principals, it will become a more complex business organization, complete with employees and consultants who may have personal agendas different from those of the founders. As the principals move from the role of researchers to business managers, counsel can be invaluable in helping to set up these relationships in a manner that protects the company's assets and mitigates the inevitable tensions. For example, tech companies are typically havens for bright young scientists and engineers anxious to apply their training and make a name for themselves in their respective disciplines. It is also a well-recognized phenomenon that a disproportional degree of the actual idea advancement that occurs in tech companies is done by these young innovators fresh from academia and exposure to the most recent theoretical developments. When their ambitions motivate them to make their own ways and, perhaps, to start their own companies, there are often disputes about who owns the research and inventions. By anticipating these issues, the legal counsel can help his clients create employer/employee relations that may not stop the departure of brain power, but could prevent them from leaving with the family jewels.

3. Phase III: Later-Stage Development and Product Approval

In reality, the early stages of the biotech regulatory process are only a warm-up for the real race, which is clinical trials and final agency product approval. Only after this stage is completed is the biotech company positioned to reap the rewards from years of investment and hard work. But, successful navigation of this phase requires a high level of legal proficiency in the respective regulatory disciplines. As a result, this is another point in the process where the lead biotech lawyer will likely want to partner with other lawyers with specialized expertise—this time, experienced biotech regulatory lawyers.

The unknown wonders of biological systems are yet to be revealed, in addition to the potential for great harm associated with human tampering. It is no wonder that biotech is subject to an exceedingly complex set of federal and state laws and regulations. These regulatory schemes dictate virtually every aspect of biotech development from research protocols to product testing, clinical trials, record keeping, marketing, labeling and packaging. Given the number and levels of agencies regulating some aspect of biotech, it is no wonder that the field is a virtual sea of acronyms comparable only to the rise of environmental regulation in the 1980s. Any given biotech regulatory analysis might include references to the FDA, USDA, EPA, and so on, as well as to the procedures prescribed by each, also referred to in their acronym form. The biotech business lawyer or general counsel charting an efficient and effective course through the agency morass needs at least a conversational familiarity with the language and an understanding of the scope and reach of the respective agencies. Chapters 10-15 will provide the business lawyer with a strong and accessible first-reference source.

4. Phase IV: Challenges Facing the Now Mature Company

While successful completion of clinical trials is the last major step to getting a product to market, the biotech company's business and legal challenges continue as the company shepherds its products, builds its capital, and looks for the next innovation, application, or market. As with any mature company, these related issues involve future business development, additional regulatory strictures, and potential liability.

a. Commercialization

On the business development side, the ownership of an approved product can result in a biotech company becoming much more attractive to outside investors and other large established biotech companies. Therefore, if the biotech company has not already entered into such partnerships, it is now in a position to seek additional investment and commercialization relationships aggressively, thus creating a new role for legal counsel. In addition, the biotech company will likely want to seek other markets for its product beyond the United States. Entry into the international marketplace will require the company and its legal counsel to engage in and comply with the separate regulatory schemes in each new jurisdiction. Finally, while the biotech company may possess an exclusive right to produce and market its product, that right is limited to a term of years. Consistent with the business adage of "stand still and die," the biotech company will want to explore ways to extend that limited monopoly through additional product applications and new "follow on" products that may not require the same level of, and time for, regulatory scrutiny.

b. Regulatory Oversight

Regulatory requirements do not end with product approval. The biotech company is required to monitor the performance of its product, report any side effects or dangers that are discovered in the course of its use, and take the actions necessary to avoid or mitigate those dangers, including issuing warnings, recalling product, and, possibly, termination of sales. In addition, there are strict regulations governing how a product may be marketed and for what purposes. Marketing a product for purposes beyond the scope of the agency approval can subject the biotech company to severe financial penalties and additional regulatory limitations.

c. Litigation

Success, however, often attracts opportunists, competitors, accusers, and thieves, against whom the biotech lawyer must be ready to defend her client. In addition to the typical civil litigation experienced by other businesses, the types of disputes most often faced by biotech companies are those relating to intellectual property rights and the safety of their products. The lure of a commercially successful product often entices infringers, both domestic and international, to take advantage of the biotech company's years of research, investment, and marketing to achieve quick and ill-gotten profits. A strong intellectual property enforcement program, although often expensive to fund, can send a strong message to potential infringers while, at the same time, providing investors and public shareholders with a sense of security that can result in increased company value. Likewise, continuous monitoring of product performance coupled with a willingness to take responsible action can go a long way toward deflecting potentially crippling product liability suits and protecting the brand.

D. Conclusion

This introduction merely provides an overview of the world of biotech law. The real value of this primer is in the pages that follow, which provide the expert analysis and recommendations of the biotech practitioners who have graciously contributed to this effort. We are all greatly indebted to these legal experts. We would also like to thank the American Bar Association for its vision and continued support of this project. Biotech law is a dynamic subject matter, and this primer provides a snapshot in time of this rapidly growing and evolving area. What is particularly noteworthy about this effort is that it represents what we believe to be the most comprehensive resource on this highly diverse and increasingly pervasive area of law, for which our authors must be thanked.

Glossary

University of California – Berkeley*
Division of Agricultural and Natural Resources
Statewide Biotechnology Workgroup
www.ucbiotech.org

Agrobacterium Microorganism (bacterium) that produces crown gall disease in the wild; it does so by introducing a part of its genetic material into the plant to direct it to make compounds it needs to live.

Agro-ecosystem A complex mixture of pastures, farm fields, businesses, home sites, natural habitats, and cities and towns.

Agronomy The science and economics of crop production; management of farm land.

Antibiotic Chemical sometimes synthesized by other organisms, sometimes manufactured, that is a deterrent to other organisms.

Antibiotic resistance Resistance mechanisms to antibiotics exist that render cells "immune" to the antibiotic; the genes for these characteristics are found in certain organisms. The genes are used in some genetic-engineering experiments as tools to identify cells that have received new DNA.

Antibody Protein produced by humans and higher animals in response to the presence of another protein, termed an antigen. The interaction of the antigen and the antibody can cause certain human health problems, like allergies or autoimmune diseases.

Antigen Substance, usually a protein, that when introduced into the body causes the body to make an antibody, usually specific to the antigen.

Autoradiography Technique used to visualize DNA that is labeled with radioactivity. It can be used to determine the presence or absence of certain DNA fragments and the length or number of DNA molecules.

Bacillus thuringiensis See Bt.

Bacteriophage Virus that infects bacteria, sometimes causing the death of the host organism.

---

* Special Thanks to the University of California – Berkeley Division of Agricultural and Natural Resources for its permission to use this glossary. See www.ucbiotech.org for updates of this site.

Bacterium/pl. bacteria Simplest form of life that exists as a single cell without a distinct structure called a nucleus that contains the genetic information of the cell. Also known as a prokaryote.

Base pair One unit of DNA composed of two complementary nucleic acid molecules (nucleotides) on opposing strands of DNA. The base adenosine always pairs with thymidine; the base guanidine pairs with cytidine.

Biodegradable Capable of being broken down by microorganisms. Breakdown products can often be re-used by other organisms as food and energy sources.

Bioinformatics Assembly of data from genomic analysis into accessible and usable forms.

Biomass Total weight of all organisms in a sample after drying.

Biomining Use of living organisms (e.g., bacteria, plants) to accumulate in their cells precious metals, like gold, silver, platinum, from mine tailings. Organisms can be collected and the metal recovered.

Bioreactor Vessel or container in which a biological reaction occurs. Often used in manufacturing efforts to produce pharmaceuticals.

Bioremediation Use of organisms (e.g., bacteria, plants) to remove environmental contaminants from soils and water. The contaminants can include organic molecules, like PCPs, or metals, like mercury, selenium and lead.

Biotechnology See "Know GMOs" Basics section. Historically means use of an organism to perform a function, like making cheese or wine. Contemporary meaning includes the use of the new genetic tools of recombinant DNA to make a new genetically modified organism.

BST/BGH Bovine somatotropin or bovine growth hormone. This is a hormone produced by cattle naturally. The genetic information for this hormone was cloned and can now be made in microorganisms for injection into cattle to increase milk production.

Bt Bacillus thuringiensis. A naturally occurring microorganism that produces a toxin that only kills organisms with alkaling stomachs, namely insect larvae. As a whole killed organism, this toxin has been used for biological control for decades. The genetic information that encodes the toxin was identified and moved into plants to make them insect tolerant.

"Bug" Colloquial or slang term for bacterium.

Callus Undifferentiated plant cells resulting from cell division of differentiated organs, such as leaves, roots, seeds. The undifferentiated callus can be triggered by hormones to develop into a whole plant.

cDNA DNA that is synthesized to be complementary to an mRNA molecule. By definition a cDNA represents a portion of the DNA that specifies a protein (is translated). If the sequence of the cDNA is known, by complementarity, the sequence of the DNA is known.

Cell Basic unit of life, the smallest living structure that is able to function independently. The human body is composed of trillions of cells; bacteria are a single cell.

Centimorgan Unit of measurement for studying genetics. One centimorgan is equivalent to a 0.01 chance that a particular genetic location (locus) will be separate from a particular marker in a single generation. In humans a centimorgan is about 1 million base pairs.

Chromosome Spring-like structures of tightly coiled DNA that contains the genetic information (genes) that instructs the cell on its function. Genes are present on chromosomes. Organisms contain differing but characteristic numbers of chromosomes; humans contain 2 strands of 23.

Clone Exact genetic replica of a single unit of the genetic information in the form of DNA (e.g., gene) or of an entire cell or organism.

Cloning Means of isolating particular parts of the genome in small fragments of DNA and making copies of and studying the sequence in another organism. Can also mean the process of producing by nonsexual means an identical copy of an organism.

Codon Unit of three nucleotide bases contained in the DNA and mRNA that specifies the information for one of the 20 amino acids; the entire array of codons is known as the genetic code. Strings of codons form genes and strings of genes form chromosomes.

Contigs Group of DNA sequences that are overlapping or contiguous on the genome. Such sequences are necessary to obtain the entire, uninterrupted sequence of the genome.

Cosmids Vehicles that are used to separate out discrete sections of the DNA for cloning purposes. These vehicles contain bacterial phage lambda DNA to allow them to make copies of themselves in their bacterial host and also DNA fragments of about 40,000 base pairs from the source being studied.

Cross-infection The simultaneous infection with different types of viruses.

Culture A particular type or subset of organisms growing under controlled conditions in the laboratory; a cell culture.

Cytoplasm Liquid portion inside of a cell in which other parts of the cell reside, e.g., ribosomes, mitochondria.

Dietary supplement Food product ingested to correct a perceived deficit in the overall diet; typically not a whole food.

DNA Deoxyribonucleic acid. The chemical building block of the genetic information in the cell, genes; it specifies the characteristics of most living organisms. The DNA is usually in the form of two complementary strands.

DNA probe Short piece of DNA that is complementary to a specific piece of DNA in the cell. By marking the probe, it is possible to visualize whether the DNA is present in the genetic material. This forms the basis for DNA diagnostics.

E. coli/Escherichia coli Specific single-celled organism or bacterium that lives in the intestinal tract of most vertebrates; some strains of this bacteria are harmful to humans, e.g., E. coli 0157. This organism has been used to do much of the genetic manipulation with recombinant DNA methods because it is well-characterized genetically.

Ecology Study of interaction of organisms with the physical environment and with one another.

Ecosystem Living system that includes all organisms in a "natural community" that live and interact with their environment.

Electrophoresis Method using an electrical field which leads to the separation of proteins or DNA fragments based on their size. Smaller proteins or DNA fragments move faster; larger ones slower. Samples are normally placed in the electrical field loaded in a gel-like substance, called agar or agarose.

Endophyte Organism living inside another organism. In some cases the endophyte cannot live outside its host, an "obligate endophyte"; in other cases the endophyte can live outside its host, "facultative endophyte."

Enzyme Protein that facilitates or speeds up certain chemical reactions. Enzymes are used inside of cells to aid in cell growth and reproduction. Enzymes have also been isolated from organisms and used in products like cheese and laundry detergents.

Eucaryote/eukaryote Organism that contains a defined nucleus; includes all organisms except viruses, bacteria, and blue-green algae, which are known as prokaryotes.

Exons Portion of the DNA sequence that codes for the protein parts of the gene.

Explant Portion of living tissue that is removed from the organism (e.g., plant) and cultured independently in the laboratory.

Fermentation Conversion of one substance into a more desirable substance through the actions of microorganisms under controlled growth conditions.

Functional food Food that provides health benefits beyond energy and essential nutrients (e.g., yogurt, which promotes beneficial microflora in the gut).

Fungicide Some agent, like a chemical, that kills fungi.

Fungus/ pl. fungi Type of microorganism that lacks chlorophyll used for photosynthesis, for example, yeasts and molds.

Gene Segment of DNA specifying a unit of genetic information; an ordered sequence of nucleotide base pairs that produce a certain product that has a specific function.

Gene flow The incorporation of genes from one organism into the complement of genes in another population of organisms.

Gene mapping Determination of the relative locations of genetic information (genes) on chromosomes.

Gene pool The combination of all genes and gene variations of a specified group, e.g., species.

Genetics Study of the patterns of inheritance of genetic information in organisms.

Genome Entire genetic material in an organism, comprising all chromosomes.

Genomic library Collection of DNA clones that represent the entire genome.

Genomics Molecular characterization of all the genes and gene products of a species.

Genotype Collection of genetic material in an organism that gives rise to its characteristics.

Germplasm

GMO Genetically modified organism, term used to refer to organisms modified by the new methods of genetic engineering.

Herbal supplement The subset of botanical supplements derived from herbaceous plants.

Hybridization 1. Joining of two complementary strands of DNA, or of DNA and RNA, to form a double-stranded molecule. 2. Process of sexual exchange between two plants to produce hybrid plants.

Intellectual property Intellectual property rights include patent rights, plant variety protection certificates, unpublished patent applications, and inventions that may or may not be legally protectable.

Intron DNA sequences that interrupt the protein-coding sequence of a gene; introns are transcribed into mRNA but the sequences are eliminated from the RNA before it is used to make protein.

Immunoassay Diagnostic assay that uses antibodies to confirm the presence/absence of certain compounds.

In vitro Direct translation is "in glass." Describes biological reactions that take place in laboratory containers, such as test tubes. Although they attempt to achieve conditions in living organisms, such reactions only simulate real-life situations.

In vivo Direct translation is "in life." Describes biological reactions taking place inside living organisms.

Library Collection of fragments of the genome in an unordered array. Relationships of fragments can be determined by physical (sequencing, RFLP maps, ESTs) or genetic means.

Linkage Physical relationship between markers on a chromosome; the linkage number gives an estimate of the probability that two markers will be inherited together. The closer together the markers, the lower the probability that they will be separated during chromosome pairing after fertilization.

Locus Location of a gene on a chromosome.

Marker Identifiable physical location on a chromosome, the inheritance of which can be monitored.

Marker gene Gene used during genetic engineering attempts that helps to identify cells that have received new DNA. Genes usually include either a selection advantage, e.g., antibiotic or herbicide resistance, or visualization advantage, e.g., beta glucuronidase (GUS) or green fluorescent protein (GFP) expression.

Metabolites Substances that are used by or produced by enzyme reactions or other metabolic processes.

Microbe Any small, microscopic organism.

Micrometer Unit used for measurement, equivalent to 10^{-6} meters or one-millionth of a meter; abbreviation um.

Molecular breeding Identification and evaluation of useful traits in breeding programs using marker-assisted selection.

Monoclonal antibody Highly specific, purified antibody derived from only one subset of cells and which recognizes only one antigen or epitope.

Morphology Form and structure of organisms, like plants and animals; their structural appearance.

Mutagen Agent or process that causes mutation, like chemicals, radiation or transposable elements.

Mutant Variant organism that differs from its parent because of mutation.

Mutation Genetic change caused by natural phenomena or by use of mutagens. Stable mutations in genes are passed on to offspring; unstable mutations are not. From latin word for "change."

Mycorrhiza/pl. mycorrhizae Fungal microorganisms that form close, symbiotic relationships with the roots of higher plants. Such relationships often provide the plant with micronutrients.

Nanometer Unit used for measurement, equivalent to 10^{-9} meters or one-billionth of a meter; abbreviation nm.

Nitrogen fixation Change of atmospheric nitrogen into nitrogen compounds by certain microorganisms, usually living in close relationship with plant roots. Nitrogen compounds can be used by plants as food. See **rhizobia**.

Nodule Swelling or enlargement of roots of plants, predominantly legumes, due to the presence of nitrogen-fixing microorganisms.

Nutraceutical Food or food product that decreases the risk of disease establishment or progression.

Nucleic acids Long chains of molecules known as nucleotides, that perform important functions in the cell; two kinds of nucleic acids function in the cell, i.e., DNA and RNA.

Nucleotide Building blocks of DNA and RNA. Nucleotides are composed of phosphate, sugar, and one of four bases, adenine, guanine, cytosine and uracil (RNA) or thymine (DNA). Three bases form a codon, which specifies a particular amino acid; amino acids are strung together to form proteins. Strings of thousands of nucleotides form a DNA or RNA molecule.

Nucleus Central compartment in cells of higher organisms (eukaryotes); it houses most of the heritable genetic information in a cell in higher organisms.

Oligonucleotide probe Short piece of DNA that is complementary to a specific piece of DNA in the cell. By marking the probe, it is possible to visualize whether the DNA is present in the genetic material. This forms the basis for DNA diagnostics.

Pathogen Any organism capable of producing disease.

Peptide Two or more amino acids, building blocks of proteins, that are chemically linked to each other.

Phage Virus that infects bacteria, sometimes causing the death of the host organism.

Phenotype Visible characteristics or traits of an organism, like a plant or an animal.

Phytochemical Substances found in plants and plant-derived products.

Plasmid Independent, free-floating circular piece of DNA in a bacterium, capable of making copies of itself in the host cell. Plasmids can be used in recombinant DNA experiments to clone genes from other organisms and make large quantities of their DNA.

Polymerase chain reaction Commonly used technique that leads to the selective amplification of a nucleotide sequence of interest. The amplified DNA becomes the predominant sequence in the mixture upon PCR amplification. Often used to make nucleotide probes for diagnostics.

Polymeorphysm A visible or molecular difference between two contrasting individuals.

Prion A small protein found in the brain cell membrane. The distorted form of this protein is responsible for mad cow disease and causes new Creutzfeld-Jakob disease in humans.

Prokaryote/procaryote Microbial or bacterial cell lacking a true nucleus. Its genetic information is usually in the form of a single long strand of DNA; plasmids exist separate from the primary DNA strand. Contrast with eukaryote.

Promoter A control region of a gene that determines in which tissue and at what time points a gene product is produced.

Proteomics The study of proteins.

Protoplast Cellular material, cytoplasm, mitochondria, nucleus, etc., remaining after the cell wall has been removed.

PST Porcine somatotropin. Version of growth hormone or somatotropin produced by swine.

Recombinant DNA (Abbr. rDNA) As a process: broad range of techniques that involve the manipulation of the genetic material of organisms, also known as genetic engineering or biotechnology. As a product: fragments of DNA from two sources or organisms joined together.

Regeneration Process of triggering the formation of whole plants from cells removed from the plant and grown in the laboratory under controlled growth conditions. One of the steps involved in the process of demonstrating **totipotency**.

Restriction enzymes Class of enzymes that cut DNA at specific locations identified by the sequence of the nucleotides. At the site of the cut, other pieces of DNA, sometimes sharing the same recognition sequence, can be inserted.

Rhizobia Microorganisms or bacteria belonging to the genus Rhizobium, which are commonly involved in fixing nitrogen; normally reside in close relationship (symbiotic) with roots of leguminous plants.

Rhizosphere Area of soil near the plant roots, normally the location of large populations of microorganisms.

Ribonucleic acid (Abbr. RNA) Chemical chains made up on the sugar ribose attached to nucleic acid molecules. Different types of RNA exist in cells, some of which serve as the immediate code for proteins, some of which are involved in the physical process of protein synthesis. RNA can also serve instead of DNA as the only genetic information in certain viruses.

Sexual reproduction Process in which two cells, termed gametes, come together to form one fertilized cell that contains genetic information from both parental cells.

Somaclonal variation Genetic changes that occur within non-reproductive cells, often during the process of culturing the cells in the laboratory. Some of these changes are heritable and result from actual changes in the genetic code.

Species Term used to describe the group of like individuals. Classically, species were defined as organisms that share certain characteristics.

Somatotropin Protein hormone secreted by a special organ in mammals, the pituitary gland, and each animal produces its own specific version of the hormone that is active in its own species and in species of lower order but not higher. The hormone directs milk production.

Spore Particular form of certain microbes that allows the organisms to survive in a dormant stage until conditions improve, at which time the spores can germinate and the life cycle resumes.

Sterile Free of living organisms; the term usually refers to lack of microorganisms or bacteria. Process of sterilization refers to killing all life forms by heating, chemical treatment or other means.

Strain Different organism within same species.

Substrate Material or substance acted upon by an enzyme.

Symbiosis Two or more dissimilar organisms living together in close association with one another. Includes parasitism, where one of the organisms harms the other(s), mutualism, where association is advantageous to all, and commensalism, where association is advantageous to one organism but doesn't affect other organism(s).

Tissue culture Process of introducing living tissue into culture in the laboratory where tissues or cells can be grown for extended periods of time.

Totipotency Capability of certain cells to be cultured in the laboratory and undergo sustained cell divisions. Application of hormonal and other signals triggers the tissue to undergo a programmed, developmental pathway that leads to the re-formation of the entire organism.

Transformation Process of introducing into an organism new genetic information that can be stably maintained.

Transgenic Organism that contains genetic materials introduced through recombinant DNA techniques. Usually implies that organism contains DNA from another organism.

Transposon Naturally occurring DNA sequence that is capable of moving its location within the genome; movement is due to the presence of an enzyme that can mediate the movement and which is encoded within the transposon itself. Transposable elements are responsible

Vaccine Utilization of a killed or debilitated organism or a part of its contents that is capable of inducing protection against the disease caused by that organism.

Value-added Trait introduced into an organism/plant that gives that organism added value, like the addition of a valued trait or the capability to produce a new, valued substance, like a pharmaceutical or a biomaterial.

Vector Agent, such as an insect, virus or plasmid, that is able to mechanically or biologically transfer itself or its contents from one organism to another. In genetic engineering this refers to any virus or plasmid into which a gene is introduced and which is capable of carrying DNA to other cells.

Virulence Degree or severity of disease-causing potential of an organism.

Virus Small genetic element composed of either DNA or RNA that is protected by a protein coat. Virus is capable of existing either inside a cell (intracellular) or outside a cell (extracellular). Viruses cannot make copies of themselves without invading another cell and using some of its machinery.

Wild-type Organism as discovered in nature.

Yeast Kind of fungi or microbe. Yeasts are used in bread-, wine-, and beer-making to produce fermentation.

Chapter II

Managing Innovation: Patent Basics for Biotechnology Counsel

Dr. Michael H. Brodowski, Esq.
Thomas A. Turano, Esq.
Dr. Christine C. Vito, Esq.
K&L Gates
Boston, Massachusetts

A. Introduction

Among the various intellectual property rights available for a life sciences business, patents usually are the most common and important rights, often forming the foundation of a company. Unlike computer-related businesses, biotechnology and small molecule therapeutics companies often require many years to bring a product to the marketplace and achieve profitability. However, even late-stage and Fortune 500 companies in the life science space rely heavily on their patent portfolios to have a competitive advantage in the marketplace and exclusivity for their products to assist in recouping the research and development expenses. Accordingly, a successful entrepreneur or manager of a life sciences business needs to understand the fundamentals of patents and their use in creating and growing a business.

Important considerations to keep in mind while building a patent estate include developing a patent portfolio that protects the business, both domestically and in foreign markets of interest, and maintaining the patent portfolio so that it adapts to the changing business. The following discussion provides a high-level overview of the principles and issues of patent law, as many specific nuances and details are too voluminous to mention.

B. U.S. Patent Portfolios

Patents are obtained for a variety of reasons. Because of their ability to exclude others from a particular technological space, patents can provide an avenue for entry into a marketplace while keeping competitors at a distance. Patents also attract money. Investors frequently look for early-stage companies or raw ideas that have commercial potential provided that adequate patent rights have been or can be secured to protect the underlying business. Patents can facilitate discussions and entry into licensing arrangements and technology partnerships such as joint ventures.

Patents can provide counterclaims and cross-licensing possibilities if faced with defending a litigation. Not only can a more favorable settlement be reached, but if the patent estate is large enough, it may prevent the litigation in the first instance. Finally, patents can be used offensively to threaten or actually file a lawsuit against an alleged infringer as part of an overall business strategy. The bottom line is that a well-developed patent estate is a valuable business asset that can help a company achieve its business objectives.

1. Patent Rights—The Claims

The rights granted by the government for a patent include the right for a limited period of time to exclude others from making, using, selling and offering to sell in, and importing into the United States the patented invention (the so-called "patent monopoly"). In exchange for these rights, an inventor needs to describe fully the invention as dictated by the patent laws as codified in Title 35 of the United States Code. The policy behind the patent system is to encourage creativity and the advancement of the sciences through the public disclosure of the invention in exchange for the exclusive rights of a patent.

The life of a patent generally expires 20 years from the filing date of the earliest filed patent application in the chain of priority. For applications filed prior to June 8, 1995, which matured into patents, the patents have a term that is the longer of 20 years from the filing date of the earliest filed application and 17 years from the issue date of the patent. There are various provisions to extend the term of a patent, usually for delays that limit the enjoyment of the full benefit of the patent rights.

Patent rights often are described in terms similar to a land deed. The territory circumscribed and covered by the deed represents the scope of coverage provided by a patent. But how does a company know when another is trespassing on its turf? The patent claims, similar to the metes and bounds of a deed, define the scope of protection. Claims frequently are referred to as being broad, that is, covering a large area often using generic terminology, or as being narrow, that is, covering a smaller, more well-defined area usually using more specific terminology.

Keep in mind that patents provide the right to exclude others from practicing that which is claimed. Consequently, a patent doesn't necessarily mean that a company can practice what it's protected. For example, company A has a patent to a four-legged chair having four legs, a seat, and a back. Company B obtains a patent on a four-legged rocking chair having four legs, a seat, a back, and two rockers each connecting two legs. Because the rocking chair has four legs, a seat and a back, company A's patent would be infringed by making and selling the rocking chair. Company A's patent is called a "dominating" patent. However, company A is unable to make a rocking chair without infringing the patent rights of company B. Thus, for either company to be in the rocking chair business, each company needs the other. In such a scenario, a cross-license agreement

> **Practice Points**
>
> Types of patents commonly include:
>
> - Utility (protects apparatus, compositions of matter, or methods of making or using the same)
> - Design (protects ornamental design of manufactured item)
> - Plant (protects asexually reproduced plants)

usually is negotiated between the companies so each is able to reap some financial benefit in the rocking chair marketplace.

Regardless of the scope of the claims, it is paramount to craft them to include the important commercial embodiments. Although a patent application may be well written and include use of the technology, if the claims are not carefully drafted to coordinate with the business plan, the resulting patent is less valuable. That is, the claims of the patent application should be drafted not only to be patentable, but also to cover aspects of the technology that are commercially significant. For example, an application that is directed to a new diagnostic assay typically would include claims to the test method itself. However, if the diagnostic assay will be sold as a test kit, then claims directed to the test kit should be included too.

Consequently, a company needs to devise a patent portfolio strategy that integrates its business plan with its patents. Although the underlying technology may be sophisticated, it is insufficient to understand merely the science. Rather, it is critical to understand the use of the technology in a business context so as to maximize the value of the patent rights. For example, a patent that fully describes the technology, including its commercial applications, will support protection of the significant commercial embodiments. However, the content of the patent should not be limited solely to the commercial uses but should describe and claim the full scope of protection available in view of the prior art.

2. Types of Patents

Different types of patents exist depending on the subject matter and protection sought. A utility patent is the most common and provides protection for apparatus, compositions of matter, methods or processes of making apparatus and compositions of matter, and methods or processes of using apparatus and compositions of matter. Methods of doing business can be patented—for example, an accounting method. Although mainly thought of in a financial context, business method patents have issued in other areas, including life sciences.

Other types of patents include design patents, which protect the ornamental design of an article of manufacture, and plant patents, which protect asexually reproduced plants. Applications for each of these patents have specific requirements and forms in which they are filed with the United States Patent and Trademark Office ("Patent Office" or "PTO") as well as providing rights particular to each.

What type of patent application should be filed? It depends on the subject matter for which patent protection is sought. The type of patent application is usually clear when a design or plant patent application is appropriate. However, when seeking a utility patent, should a provisional patent application be filed first?

a. Provisional Patent Applications

Provisional patent applications ("provisionals"), when used properly, can be valuable tools in the development of a patent estate. For example, the filing date of a provisional typically is not taken into account when calculating patent term. This advantage can be significant, for example, in the case of patents covering drug products, where it is desirable to have the patent expire at the latest possible date when profitability and market share of the products covered by a patent is usually highest.

> **Practice Points**
>
> Types of patent applications include:
>
> - Provisional ("placeholder" that preserves rights but is not examined by PTO)
> - Continuation (may claim subject matter that was just described but not actually claimed in earlier application)
> - Divisional (parallel application covering inventions split off by PTO from another application)
> - Continuation-in-Part (introduces new subject matter to an earlier application)

Because a provisional is not examined, its filing fee is much lower than a utility application. During its one-year life and prior to filing a utility application that is examined and published, an applicant can seek licensees to develop the technology and possibly to pay or share the patent prosecution expenses. The applicant also can analyze the marketplace and develop its products in that year to determine whether it is worthwhile to pursue patent protection.

Another advantage is that a provisional does not need to be as formal as a non-provisional patent application and thus can be easier and less expensive to prepare. When confronted with an impending disclosure of an invention outside the company, a quickly filed provisional can preserve valuable rights.

However, to the extent that time and resources permit, an applicant should attempt to identify the invention and its commercial significance, formulate patent claims that cover the invention and its commercial applications, and then craft an adequate application to support the claims. Without such analysis and preparation, there is greater risk that the claims that issue from a patent application claiming the benefit of a provisional will not be adequately supported by the disclosure in the provisional. Consequently, the benefit of the filing date of the provisional is lost, possibly rendering the resulting patent claims invalid due to intervening prior art that the provisional filing date shielded.

b. Continuing Patent Application Practice

A continuing patent application is an application that claims the benefit of the filing date of an earlier-filed patent application or applications. The earlier filing date defines what information is prior art. A continuing application must be filed prior to the issue or abandonment of the earlier-filed application(s), have at least one common inventor with each of the earlier-filed application(s), and refer to the earlier-filed application(s) in its specification or inventor declaration. Continuing patent applications include continuation applications, divisional applications, and continuation-in-part applications.

A continuation patent application ("continuation") is substantially identical in content to the application(s) to which it claims priority. Continuations can be filed to continue prosecution of an application that is under a final Patent Office action. Continuations also can be used to claim subject matter described in the application but not claimed in an earlier application and to pursue claims of varying scope and different terminology. In addition, a continuation application frequently is filed on core technology simply to maintain a pending application to which a later-filed application can claim priority.

A divisional patent application ("divisional") is substantially identical in content to the application(s) to which it claims priority, but results from a restriction requirement imposed by the Patent Office. If the Patent Office believes that more than one invention is described by the claims submitted in the patent application, the Patent Office restricts the prosecution of the application to the claims directed to one of the inventions. The non-elected claims then can be pursued in a divisional application either in parallel with or serially to the restricted application.

In both continuations and divisionals, no new matter can be added to the later-filed application. If new matter is introduced into a continuing application prior to its filing, the resulting application is a continuation-in-part patent application. Continuations-in-part were commonplace when the term of a patent was determined based on its issue date. Today, because the term of a patent is 20 years from the earliest claimed priority date, the reason for filing a continuation-in-part patent application should be carefully considered.

First, the new matter in the continuation-in-part is entitled only to the benefit of the date on which the new matter is filed, not the filing date of the earlier application. Thus, it may not be effective to overcome recently discovered prior art. Second, the new matter, if supporting patentability of the original claims, often may be effectively introduced via a declaration. Finally, the new matter may actually constitute a new invention that is deserving of an original application filing and a full 20-year patent term.

3. Requirements for Patentability

An invention needs to be new and unobvious in view of the state-of-the-art at the time the application was filed, that is, in view of the "prior art." This legal phrase is statutorily defined. An understanding of what constitutes prior art is necessary to know what the claims are compared when determining their patentability. Prior art includes printed publications and patents throughout the world that were available prior to the filing date of the patent application. Knowledge of or use by others of the claimed invention in the United States prior to the filing date of the application also is prior art. In addition, prior art includes commercial public use, offers to sell, and sales of the claimed invention. For example, trade show exhibits, scientific meeting posters, test marketing, and beta site use can be prior art. The United States provides a one-year grace period for certain public disclosures of the invention.

For prior art to render a claim unnovel, each and every element of the claim needs to be present in a single piece of prior art, that is, the prior art anticipates the claim. If not identically described or found in the prior art, a claim can be considered obvious based on a combination of prior art publications and patents reciting each of the elements of the claim. Keep in mind that the unobviousness of a claim in view of the prior art is a separate and distinct requirement from novelty.

The determination of obviousness is made from the perspective of one having ordinary skill in the art at the time the invention was made (a "skilled artisan"). A finding of obviousness is not merely locating each element or step in the prior art. Rather, at least one of the publications must include some teaching or suggestion to motivate a skilled artisan to make the claimed combination and provide an expectation that the combination would successfully produce the claimed invention.

A claimed invention also needs to be useful, that is, demonstrate a minimal beneficial use or utility. The use should be related to the intended purpose of the invention. The invention doesn't need to be an improvement over the state-of-the-art, but must possess at least some utility.

In addition to the claimed subject matter being new, useful, and unobvious, an application needs to satisfy the "written description" and "enablement" requirements and disclose the "best mode."

To enable an invention, the application needs to describe the claimed invention in such a way that a skilled artisan can understand how to make and use the invention without undue experimentation. In other words, a skilled artisan should be able to read a patent and, coupled with his knowledge of the technical field, reproduce the invention without undue experimentation.

Different information can enable a different scope of invention. For example, disclosure of a nucleotide sequence can support a claim to the amino acid sequence it encodes because a skilled artisan can, without undue experimentation, determine the amino acid sequence from the nucleotide sequence. That is, knowing the nucleotide sequence permits a skilled artisan to know and make the amino acid sequence. However, the reverse is not true. The disclosure of an amino acid sequence does not provide the requisite information to make, without due experimentation, the nucleotide sequence from which it is produced.

To satisfy the written description requirement, the application should expressly use the claim language or describe the claim language with specificity so it is clear that the inventor(s) had possession of the claimed invention at the time the application was filed. This requirement is distinct from enablement. Although an application can teach how to make and use an invention, the application may not necessarily include the precise terminology now being used in the claims to describe the invention. Thus, the application can enable the invention but might fall short on the written description requirement.

For claims directed to biological materials, the deposition of the biological material in a publicly accessible depository can satisfy the written description. Making such a deposit is recommended, as typographical errors in long sequences in the application can occur, but the deposit can be sequenced to provide the correct sequence.

To satisfy the best mode requirement, the inventor(s) need to disclose the best way known at the time of filing the application of how to carry out or practice the invention. An inventor can't conceal the most viable or commercially significant embodiments of the claimed invention. To do so would not further enrich the art and advance development of the technology. Although at times it's seemingly difficult to do, disclosure of the best mode is part of the bargain struck for the grant of exclusive patent rights, and non-disclosure of the best mode can render claims of the patent invalid.

Another of the technical requirements of a patent application is that the claims be "definite." That is, a skilled artisan should understand the meaning of a claim to be able to ascertain when he's trespassing on the patent rights of another, or infringing the patent. The use of relative terms, such as *substantially* and *high* or *low*, should be avoided, as the coverage of the claim tends to be too uncertain. Likewise, generic terminology can suffer from being poorly defined and understood. When coining terms or phrases, the application often contains a section that provides a definition of those terms to provide the metes and bounds of the claim. A definition, along with examples, also can provide support for future claim amendments to satisfy this requirement as well as to distinguish the prior art from the claims if the claims are initially too broad.

Each of the above-described requirements for a patent is applied to the claims in view of the rest of the application. That is, the analysis begins with an understanding of the claimed invention, which may be assisted by reference to the specification or drawings.

4. Preparation of a Patent Application

In light of the above discussion regarding the importance of the patent claims, it is common practice in drafting a patent application to begin with those claims. Prior to preparing the whole application, a draft claim set should provide an outline to review efficiently with the inventors the understanding of the invention. Answers to the following questions should be confirmed about the invention. What does it do? How does it work? What are its required components/steps? What is the best way to practice the invention? How is it different from similar products and the state-of-the-art in the field?

Reviewing the draft claims provides a check that the distinctions from the known prior art and the commercial applications of the invention are embodied in the claims. Furthermore, the claims define the legal rights of the patent. The remainder of the application is merely support for those claims. Accordingly, beginning with the claims provides guidance as to what description of the invention must be included in the application.

To avoid unexpected difficulties in procuring patent protection and strengthen a patent in view of the prior art, it is advisable to conduct a patentability search prior to preparing and filing an application. Such a search seeks to identify prior art—state-of-the-art patents, printed publications and other publicly available information—that may impact the ability of the company to secure patent protection for its own ideas. Knowledge of the prior art provides an opportunity to present claims that are distinguishable, thereby increasing the likelihood of successfully issuing a patent. In addition, consideration of the relevant prior art will strengthen the resulting patent against an invalidity attack.

Moreover, the claims initially submitted for examination can be drafted to avoid the known prior art and possibly limit the introduction of claim amendments to issue the patent. If the claims are unamended, a full range of equivalents will be available when asserting the patent claims against an alleged infringer. Further, if the patent application publishes, the possibility of provisional rights exist, such as a reasonable royalty (discussed more below).

After the claims are acceptable, the remainder of the application is drafted. Many different styles of applications exist, some dependent upon the subject matter of the invention. Drawings are prepared that may help to illustrate various aspects and embodiments of the invention. Working examples are particularly beneficial for inventions in the unpredictable chemical and biological arts.

Prophetic examples can be included in an application. A prophetic example describes an experiment or process that was not actually performed, but is helpful to understand and practice the invention. Prophetic examples should be written in the present tense to make clear the experiment was not performed. To suggest otherwise could render the patent invalid or unenforceable.

If the description or claims contain amino acid or nucleotide sequences, a hard copy and an electronic copy on disk of the sequence is submitted with the application. If not submitted with the application, the disk copy can be submitted later in response to a notice to comply with sequence listing requirements.

5. Patent Application Formalities

To perfect a filing date for a provisional application, the appropriate fees and required identifying information of the applicant(s) must be provided. If such fees and information are not provided at the time of filing the application, a Notice to File Missing Parts of Provisional Application will issue, requesting the missing fee and information along with a surcharge fee. If a response to complete these requirements is not filed in the allotted time, the application will be deemed abandoned. Consequently, the filing date of the application will be lost.

After its filing date, a provisional application cannot be amended. The application is checked for formalities by the Patent Office, accorded a filing date, then sits on a shelf until it expires one year after its filing date. If changes need to be made or additional information added to the application, another provisional application must be filed. A provisional cannot claim priority to any earlier-filed patent application. However, in the case of multiple related provisionals, the filing date of the earliest-filed provisional is not lost if, within one year of its filing, a utility patent application is filed that claims priority to each of the earlier-filed provisionals.

To that end, before the one-year anniversary of the filing date of a provisional, at least one of a U.S. utility application, an international application under the Patent Cooperation Treaty (PCT), and a non-U.S. national or regional patent application needs to be filed and claim priority to the provisional application. If such an application is not later-filed, the priority date of the provisional is irrevocably lost. Consequently, prior art coming into existence between the provisional's filing date and the later application's filing date could prevent an otherwise valid patent from issuing because the invention no longer is considered new or unobvious in view of the intervening prior art, all because the priority date had not been maintained.

A priority claim is applicable not only to provisionals, but also to initially foreign-filed applications and continuing applications. Because maintaining a priority date is so important, it's critical to ensure the formal requirements are met to perfect the date. Both timing and proper notice of the priority claim must be satisfied. If the earlier-filed applications are in a foreign language, certified copies of English language translations must be timely submitted to perfect priority rights to foreign language–filed applications. Further, the subject matter of the prior application should be incorporated by reference into the later-filed patent application in the event that a portion of the application inadvertently is left out.

To perfect a patent application filing date for a utility patent application, a proper application containing at least one claim must be filed along with the formal transmittal papers, including identifying indicia and other applicant information. Filing fees and an oath or declaration of the inventors also is required, but they can be subsequently filed with a surcharge fee in response to a Notice to File Missing Parts of Nonprovisional Application. The Patent Office also can object to certain informalities of the filed papers and require correction within a specified time or lose the filing date.

Who is an inventor? An oath or declaration for a patent application must be executed by each of the inventors of the claimed subject matter. An inventor is a person who thought of the idea of the invention and had a definite plan as to how to carry it out. An inventor is not simply a technician who implements the instructions of another. For example, an inventor is not necessarily a co-author of a scientific publication. Co-authors often are those individuals who made significant contributions to the work done and described in the paper. However, such contribution may not be an inventive contribution, but rather the the carrying out of another's idea (often referred to as "a pair of hands").

Defining an inventive entity for a set of claims can be one of the more grey areas in the patent process. If done wrong, claims of the patent can be invalid or the patent held unenforceable. However, if an error in the inventive entity is discovered—for example, if the claims change such that an originally named inventor is no longer an inventor or another person should be added as an inventor—correction is possible provided the error in naming the inventive entity was without deceptive intent.

For example, consider the scenario that involves a disgruntled party that allegedly was involved in making the invention, but was not named as an inventor on the patent. The patented product or service becomes a huge commercial success and the disgruntled party wants a piece of the action. The disgruntled party files a declaratory judgment claim to be added to the inventive entity. If successful, the disgruntled party can end up being a co-owner of the patent, thereby able to exploit the patent for his own benefit and to the detriment of the company. Thus, when multiple parties are involved in developing a technology where patent rights may be created, such as in a joint venture or collaborative research arrangement, a preexisting agreement to distribute the patent rights between the parties is recommended.

An assignment of the invention from each of the inventors to the company needs to be secured, preferably when the inventors sign the declaration. A more complete discussion of the importance of the complete assignment of the patents rights of the inventors to the company is provided below.

Government funding is common in life sciences research. If an invention was made or developed using money from the federal government, the government gets certain rights in the invention, for example, a non-exclusive, irrevocable, royalty-free license to the patent. The assistance of the particular government agency needs to be expressly acknowledged in the patent along with the rights of the government. Failure to properly recognize the funding and to elect title from the government could result in the government taking ownership of the patent. Although the government has not yet taken such action, the patent law gives it the right to do so.

Another consideration at the time of filing a provisional or utility patent application is whether the application qualifies for payment of reduced PTO fees. If the patent owner qualifies as a "small entity," it is possible to pay one-half of certain fees. Misrepresentation of small-entity status can render a patent unenforceable. Accordingly, payment of large-entity fees avoids any subsequent patent enforceability issues based on payment of small-entity fees.

U.S. patent law imposes on individuals associated with the filing and prosecution of a patent application an absolute duty of candor and good faith in dealing with the Patent Office. This includes a duty to disclose information known to persons substantially involved with the application, including the applicant or its attorneys, that may be pertinent to examination of each pending claim. Failure to meet this duty may result in an otherwise valid patent being declared unenforceable. Conversely, information properly brought to the attention of the Patent Office creates a presumption that the information has been considered by the examiner.

To comply with the duty of disclosure, an Information Disclosure Statement ("IDS") is submitted to the Patent Office. Any publications or prior art that relate to the field of the invention, even if the publication was of limited distribution, such as a copy of a thesis in a library or a handout at a conference, should be submitted. Careful thought should be given to include any publications by the inventors relating to the invention. Further, any commercial activity occurring before the filing of the application and involving the invention, including any trade show exhibits, scientific meeting posters, test marketing, beta site use, sales, offers for sale, or acts or communications that might be viewed as offers for sale, also should be considered as being included in an IDS. In bringing such information to the attention of the Patent Office, it's better to err on the side of thoroughness and disclose.

6. Publication of Patent Applications

About 18 months after the earliest claimed priority date, a patent application should publish. In the case of applications with a priority chain greater than 18 months, the application typically publishes within months after the application formalities are completed. The application is published electronically by the Patent Office and can be accessed via the PTO's Web site, currently at http://www.uspto.gov/patft/. Additionally, after a patent application publishes, a copy of the application and all related papers in its file at the Patent Office may be accessed by the public on the PTO's Patent Application Information Retrieval (PAIR) Web site—currently available at http://www.uspto.gov/ebc/—or by a written request to the Patent Office.

The publication of a patent application may entitle the patent owner to provisional rights in the form of a reasonable royalty from the date of publication to the date the patent issues. To benefit from provisional rights, the infringer must have had actual notice of the published patent application, and the invention as claimed in the issued patent must be substantially identical to the invention as claimed in the published application.

7. Patent Prosecution

After the patent application filing formalities are complete, the prosecution stage of the patent process begins. The Patent Office assigns the application to an examiner, who will object to, reject or allow each pending claim. However, before doing so, the examiner may issue a restriction requirement on the claims. If the examiner believes that more than one invention is present in the claims, the patent applicant(s) must elect for further prosecution one of the groups of claims that represent one invention. The non-elected invention(s) are withdrawn from prosecution but not lost, as they can be pursued in a divisional patent application.

A common example of a claim set facing restriction is one that contains both composition of matter and method claims. The patent applicant often elects the composition of matter claims to pursue in the pending application, as these claims typically provide more valuable, enforceable rights. To pursue the non-elected method claims, the patent applicant files a divisional patent application, which claims the benefit of the filing date of the earlier-filed pending application. The divisional application is substantially identical to the pending application, except the claims will be limited to the methods of the invention. A divisional application can be filed immediately after receiving a restriction requirement and any time prior to the abandonment of the earlier-filed application or issue of a patent.

After electing an invention, the patent applicant(s) may also need to elect a species within that group of claims, such as IL-12 in a listing of interleukins. The election of a species does not withdraw the non-elected species from prosecution, but is to direct the examiner's prior art searching efforts.

The real negotiating with the Patent Office begins upon the receipt of a first Office action that objects to or rejects at least one claim. Although a first action Notice of Allowance is possible, it tends to be rare, as claims are usually drafted to test the limits of the known prior art. Consequently, a first Office action will issue most likely rejecting all the claims.

The first Office action typically is a non-final action. A response usually is due within three months from the mailing date of the Office action without any extension fee. One-month extensions of time can be obtained retroactively upon payment of the appropriate fee. A maximum of three months can be purchased, for a total of six months to reply, including the initial extension-free period. Six months is the maximum statutory response period. If some action is not taken within the six-month period, the application will be deemed abandoned. Unlike loss of a priority claim, an abandoned patent application can be revived if the abandonment of the application was unintentional, but only under specific circumstances. Consequently, unintentional abandonment of an application should be avoided.

A rejection of a claim typically is based on one of the statutory requirements for patentability. Accordingly, a claim can be found to lack utility (a § 101 rejection) or novelty (a § 102 rejection), and/or be obvious (a § 103 rejection). A claim also can be rejected based on the "technical" requirements of the statute, such as written description, enablement, best mode, and claim definiteness (§ 112 rejections). A claim also can be objected to for a variety of reasons or be rejected based on the judicially created doctrine of double-patenting.

A response to a non-final Office action most frequently involves not only rebuttal remarks to the examiner's rejections, but also claim amendments to distinguish the claims from the prior art. Amendments to the claims or potentially to the specification also can address § 112 rejections.

It is critical that the claims of the application be distinguished from the prior art. All too often an argument is made as to why an invention is different from the prior art, yet the distinguishing feature is found in the specification of the application, not the claims. Such a feature needs to be included in the claims to overcome such prior art effectively. Describing or illustrating the distinguishing feature elsewhere in the application is not sufficient.

Declarations from skilled artisans, experts, and the inventors can be submitted to support particular arguments and to assist in convincing the examiner that the claims are patentable. Declarations also provide an avenue for submitting experimental results relevant to the invention. While declarations can be helpful in getting an application allowed, they should be carefully thought out and prepared, as the declarant and declaration will undergo heavy scrutiny in any evaluation of the validity of the patent.

If an application is not placed in condition for allowance in response to a non-final Office action, the Patent Office typically issues a final Office action. Subsequent actions in response to a final Office action are somewhat limited. The claims can be amended, but the examiner usually will only enter the amendments if they either place the claims in condition for allowance or reduce the number of issues that would need to be addressed if the rejections were appealed. Accordingly, if substantial claim amendments are to be made, a Request for Continued Examination (RCE) should be filed along with the claim amendments. An RCE will remove the finality of the Office action and provide at least one additional non-final Office action if the claim amendments are unsuccessful in placing the application in condition for allowance. Alternatively, if a response to the final Office action is filed without an RCE, it should be filed within 2 months of the mailing date of the Office action to ensure that the examiner reviews the response and provides an Advisory Action prior to the final deadline for taking action in the application.

When faced with a final Office action, another option is to file a continuing application as discussed above.

a. Appeal of Patent Office Final Rejections

If an impasse is reached with an examiner, the final rejection(s) of the claims can be appealed to the Board of Patent Appeals and Interferences (BPAI or the Board). A Notice of Appeal is filed, followed by a formal Appeal Brief. The Appeal Brief contains, among other required information, argument as to why the examiner is incorrect and a patent should be granted. No claim amendments or declarations can be submitted to support the appeal. Any such changes or supporting evidence must be entered during the prosecution stage.

After receiving the Appeal Brief, the Patent Office can reply with an Examiner's Answer. The patent applicant(s) can file a rebuttal to the Examiner's Answer, having the last word before the Board renders a decision. The Board, composed of three Senior Administrative Judges, reviews the submissions by each party and rules on the patentability of the claims at issue. An oral hearing can be requested. If claims are found to be patentable or if unresolved matters exist, the patent application is returned to the Patent Office for further processing. If the Board affirms the rejections, the patent applicant(s) can appeal to the Court of Appeals for the Federal Circuit (CAFC), which is the federal court of appeals for patents.

> **Practice Points**
>
> Possible responses to a final PTO rejection include:
> - Amend claims through a Request for Continued Examination
> - File a continuation application
> - Appeal to the Board of Patent Appeals and Interferences

b. Notice of Allowance

After receiving a Notice of Allowance, which indicates the Patent Office's intent to grant a patent, careful review of the correspondence with and actions before the Patent Office should be undertaken. For example, was all known relevant prior art, including publications, cited in foreign patent prosecution submitted to and considered by the examiner as evidenced by initialed IDS's? Do the claims have any typographical errors or other changes that should be made before they issue? Did the examiner provide reasons for allowance and are the reasons accurate or do they require clarification? Is the Patent Term Adjustment (discussed below) correct or should more days be added to the end of the patent term due to Patent Office delay in prosecuting the application? If corrections or other submissions are needed, they should be filed prior to payment of the issue fee, due three months from the mailing of the Notice of Allowance. No extensions to this payment deadline are permitted. After the issue fee is paid, any remedial action is much more difficult and costly to accomplish.

Also upon receipt of a Notice of Allowance, thought should be given as to whether a continuing application should be filed (see previous discussion on continuing applications). If so, the continuing application needs to be filed prior to the issue date of the patent. The later-filed continuing patent application will claim priority, that is, the benefit of the filing date of the earlier-filed application that matured into the patent.

8. Post-Issue Patent Considerations

When a patent issues, enforceable rights come into existence. These rights need to be maintained by the payment of renewal fees. In the United States, these fees are called maintenance fees and are due 3.5, 7.5, and 10.5 years from the issue date of the patent. The Patent Office allows these fees to be paid up to six months late upon payment of a surcharge fee.

Delays in advancing the prosecution of an application that are caused by the Patent Office can add time to the term of a patent. Such additional term for administrative delays is referred to as Patent Term Adjustment (PTA). Other delays encountered by a patent applicant resulting from suspension of prosecution due to a secrecy order or interference, or idle time during a successful appeal to the Board, also can add term to the life of a patent. Moreover, if a drug product covered by a patent undergoes Food and Drug Administration (FDA) marketing approval, certain time that the product underwent the regulatory review process may be added to the end of the patent term. Each of these patent life-extending events should be considered and appropriate action taken to extend the term of the

> **Practice Points**
>
> The following events may add valuable time to a patent's life:
> - Filing a provisional application
> - Obtaining a Patent Term Adjustment for PTO delays
> - Extension of term due to suspension of prosecution (secrecy order or interference)
> - Extension of term to cover delay during successful appeal of a rejection
>
> Certain FDA regulatory review periods also extend term.

patent. Such extensions may be especially desirable in the life sciences area, as the end of the patent term often is when a product covered by the patent is most profitable.

For example, a patent covering a drug usually issues well before the drug is approved for commercial use by the FDA. After a drug is available, it often takes years for the market share of the drug to increase. In addition, after a drug has been produced for some time, the manufacturing and distribution costs may decrease. Consequently, the profitability of the drug tends to be highest toward the end of the patent term, possibly reaching millions of dollars a day. Accordingly, to take advantage of the increased profitability and prevent competitors (e.g., generic pharmaceutical companies) from entering the marketplace any earlier than necessary, the term for such patents should be extended whenever possible. Moreover, as discussed previously, the initial filing of a provisional patent application can shift the patent term up to one year into the future, thereby further extending the expiration date of the patent.

Errors discovered in an issued patent have a specific path for correction. If the error is a typographical or other non-substantive error, a Certificate of Correction can be requested. If granted, the Certificate issues with an official seal, and the amendments listed on the Certificate are present as if they were in the patent as originally granted.

If the errors are more serious, a reexamination proceeding or a reissue application may be necessary. A reexamination proceeding reevaluates the allowed claims in view of prior art patents and printed publications, typically ones that were not considered by the Patent Office in allowing the patent. Reexaminations can be requested by the patent owner or by third parties. In an *ex parte* proceeding, the patent owner or third party files a request for examination along with arguments as to why the patent claims are unpatentable in view of the published prior art. Subsequently, the remaining proceeding is limited to the patent owner and the Patent Office.

For applications filed after November 29, 1999, that matured into patents, *inter partes* reexamination is available. This proceeding attempts to reduce court disputes where the validity of the patent claims is challenged based on published prior art by permitting a third-party requestor to reply to the patent owner's claim amendments and arguments as if the third-party requestor was an examiner throughout the proceeding. Both parties have a right to appeal.

If the error involves a defect in the specification or drawings, or in claiming too little or too much, a reissue patent application may be appropriately filed. Unlike reexaminations, reissue proceedings are not limited to the consideration of prior art patents and printed publications in determining patentability of the claims. A reissue application is frequently used to broaden the scope of the claims that originally issued. However, such a reissue application must be filed within two years of the date the patent issued.

C. Foreign Patent Portfolios

A U.S. company having gotten its U.S. patent portfolio in order may be inclined to breathe easier believing that it has sufficiently protected its patentable intellectual property. This might, in fact, be the case if that company never does any business outside of the United States.

But the truth of the matter is that although the United States has a dynamic economy, most business today is really global in character. For example, even very small companies provide parts and services to large multinational conglomerates or overseas corporations. Further, it should be apparent that manufacturing and service facilities move with relative ease around the planet seeking the cheapest labor or the best regulatory environment. Thus, items that were once fabricated locally or services that were once provided locally now may be produced in any one of hundreds of locations worldwide.

Add to this flexibility in manufacturing and service provisioning the fact that buying power is now global in scope and you can easily see why companies look outward in defining markets. For example, Europe has a potential market as large as the United States, and China and India have potential markets exceeding that of the United States. With these kinds of statistics floating around the media daily, one can understand why non-domestic sales play such an important role in many companies' balance sheets. So to protect themselves, companies operating globally must have a global patent strategy. Further, because the patent laws in various jurisdictions vary significantly, this strategy must be present from the very beginning. A U.S. patent portfolio development strategy alone is generally insufficient.

A patent is only enforceable in the jurisdiction in which it is issued. Therefore, although a U.S. patent can be enforced against anyone making, using, and selling the patented product in the United States, it will not stop someone from making, using or selling the patented invention anywhere else in the world. To do so, a patent application must be filed in each jurisdiction of interest. So what prevents companies from simply filing patent applications in each country of interest? The costs to file, prosecute, issue, and maintain the multiple patent applications and resulting patents deter this strategy.

The filing, prosecution, issuance, and maintenance of a single patent family over the 20-year life of the patents can easily exceed $100,000. (A patent family is generally the U.S. and foreign patents that all derive from a single patent filing. Thus, the patents that arose from a U.S. patent application that became the basis of a European patent application which then issued in Germany and France as a patent would be a single family.) As a result, a portfolio of even a modest number of U.S. patents can result in foreign filing costs that are truly exciting. There are a number of things to consider in order to keep from breaking the bank in developing a global patent portfolio.

1. Protection Strategy

The first issue that arises is: "Where should I file?" The answer to this question depends heavily on the business plan of the company. Companies generally consider filing in jurisdictions in which they sell or manufacture their products. Companies also consider filing in jurisdictions in which they have a large potential base of customers.

For example, Europe has a large, affluent potential customer base and a source of skilled labor for manufacturing purposes. The fact that the European Union is also a free trade zone and includes a large number of countries makes filing in this jurisdiction especially attractive. However, as will be discussed below, there is to date no single European patent, so patents for countries in Europe must be obtained individually. So how do companies make filing in Europe economically feasible?

One way is to file for patent protection only in countries with the biggest economies and populations and rely on the fact that if patents are obtained in these countries, sellers will be discouraged from making infringing products that cannot be sold everywhere in the European Union (EU) free trade zone. That is, if the product cannot be sold in the United Kingdom, France, and Germany because of patents in those countries, it is less likely that a seller will try to manufacture and sell the product in Belgium, the Netherlands, and the remaining smaller countries in Europe.

Another consideration is to file in countries that have a reputation for enforcing patent rights and in which that enforcement is the easiest to accomplish. For example, companies might consider filing for patent protection in countries in which issues of validity and infringement can be decided in a single court, or in jurisdictions that permit some form of discovery.

Once the decision is made where to file the applications in general, the next question is which of the patents in the portfolio should be filed where. Some companies categorize their inventions into levels of importance. The hierarchy can be simply three-tiered: very important or core technology, significant technology, and other.

Thus core technology—technology that is essential to the operation of the business and upon which the remaining technology depends—would be given the broadest protection. This technology would be filed "worldwide," which typically includes the United States, Europe, and Japan, and potentially includes Russia, China, and India as well as other countries that are important to the specific business of

> **Practice Points**
>
> In deciding on foreign jurisdictions in which to file patent applications, consider:
>
> - Size and strategic importance of marketplace
> - Likelihood and ease of enforceability
> - Whether this invention is actually patentable in certain jurisdictions
> - Whether public disclosure precludes patentability in certain jurisdictions
> - Secrecy orders and national security issues of U.S. government
> - Cost of filing and maintaining patents in each jurisdiction

the company. For example, if the company is involved in stem cell research, Singapore and South Korea might be included in the list.

Important technology, which is not core technology but which still provides a significant economic advantage, is filed in a fewer number of countries. Typically these countries would include the major markets for the company's products. As such, companies frequently file for protection of these inventions in the United States, Europe and Japan.

"Other technology" is technology that would not provide that great of an economic advantage but is being filed for other reasons. These reasons include political reasons (for example, to keep an important scientist or engineer happy) or to make the patent portfolio larger (to keep the investors happy). This technology is frequently filed only within the jurisdiction in which it was developed or in which the company's main office is located.

The next question that arises is whether filing in some of the above-mentioned countries is of any value because their intellectual property protection policies are so poor. Again, this becomes a question of business strategy. Take for example China.

With a potential consumer market of over one billion people, most companies find the Chinese market difficult to ignore. China, however, does not have a good reputation for enforcing intellectual property rights. So what should a company do? The company should be realistic in its ability to break into the Chinese market. The company should ask: Is the product made by the company one that will sell well in China? Will the company be able to find and maintain a Chinese partner company to help it understand the market? Is the company's product easily copied and manufactured?

If the answer to these questions is yes, then potentially the company should consider filing for patent protection in China. Why? Because the business proposition indicates that the company eventually may sell into China. An additional consideration is that patent filing and prosecution in China is not that expensive. Finally, and perhaps most important, even if the chances of enforcing the patent are low, they are greater than zero. And zero is the chance of protecting the intellectual property if there is no patent protection. Together these considerations mean that filing for patent protection in China in this situation should not be disregarded.

So, after the countries and the importance of the technologies have been determined, you have all that is needed to decide what to file where. Correct? No! Next, the individual invention must be considered in view of its patentability under the patent laws of the various jurisdictions in which filing is contemplated.

2. Patentability Differences

Before an application is filed in other jurisdictions, it is important to consider patentability issues according to the laws of the jurisdiction in which the patent application is intended to be filed. Although the patent laws are remarkably similar in the various jurisdictions in the world, they are not identical, and these differences appear in many places in the statutory scheme. So, after the company decides in which jurisdictions a patent application might be filed, it should consider the chances of a patent actually issuing in those jurisdictions. The company should also consider whether a potentially losing fight with a patent office over an invention of questionable patentability in a given jurisdiction is worth the time, money, and effort such a fight will take.

The first issue to be considered is what is patentable under the statutes of the various jurisdictions. The United States has arguably the most liberal statutory provisions of any of the jurisdictions. As was said in the *Chakrabarty* case almost 30 years ago, substantially anything made by the hand of man is patentable.[1]

Four areas in which patentability differences appear between the United States and most of the rest of the world include: methods of treating disease in a human or an animal; software per se; methods of doing business; and plant or animal species.

Methods of treatment are generally patentable in the United States but are not generally patentable elsewhere. What is meant by the words "generally patentable" is that a U.S. inventor can invent a method for performing a medical or surgical procedure that is patentable in the United States but cannot typically charge a medical practitioner with infringement for performing the patented method without a license.[2] In the majority of other jurisdictions, treatments of humans or animals, whether by surgical or medical means, are simply not patentable.

What would be patentable in the jurisdictions are the specific drugs and devices used for treating the human or animal. Also, what are known as "second medical use"–type claims are patentable in many jurisdictions. These claims are often directed to using known compounds in producing drugs for treating specific diseases. These claims are patentable even if the compounds were known previously to have other medical uses.

In the United States, software is patentable simply as an algorithm. That is, the steps themselves as defined in the algorithm and executed by the computer are patentable. In most other jurisdictions, software per se is not patentable, and it is necessary to claim the algorithm in conjunction with hardware. So for an algorithm to be patentable, in many jurisdictions it is necessary to claim the algorithm as a system for accomplishing the function performed by the algorithm.

Further, in most jurisdictions methods of doing business are not patentable unless the method is closely tied to computer hardware. As such, business methods in these jurisdictions are treated substantially as software patents. In the United States no such connection is required.[3]

Finally, in many jurisdictions claims are not granted with respect to plant or animal varieties or essentially biological processes for the production of plants or animals.[4] However, animals and plants are "not excluded from patentability if the technical feasibility of the invention is not confined to a particular plant or animal variety."[5] This is in contrast to the United States, where any novel plant or non-human animal variety is patentable.

So whether the company is located within or outside the United States, the claims being made in the first patent application should be vetted to determine if the claims as written would be allowable in other jurisdictions and whether, for companies located outside the United States, broader claims can be obtained in the United States than are available in their home jurisdictions. If so, then the applicant must make sure support for those broader U.S. claims is included in the specification of the patent application as filed in the home jurisdiction. Failure to do so will result in the patent being rejected for lack of enablement, and any attempt to introduce support after the application has been filed in the home jurisdiction will be rejected as new matter.

3. Other Considerations

In addition to statutory patentability differences, there are differences with the way various jurisdictions treat the issue of novelty. For example, in the United States, if information about the invention is published prior to the filing of a patent application on the invention, an application can still be filed as long as it is filed within a year of the first public disclosure. In many other jurisdictions, publication of information about the invention is a novelty-destroying event. Such jurisdictions are referred to as absolute or strict novelty jurisdictions. In an absolute or strict novelty jurisdiction, once information about the invention is published, no patent application can be filed which requires that information for novelty. Therefore, to maintain patentability outside the United States, a patent application should be filed prior to any public disclosure.

As stated previously, in the United States an offer for sale of the claimed invention starts a statutory clock running. If a patent application is not filed within one year of the first offer for sale of a product incorporating the invention, no application can be filed in the United States. Most other jurisdictions do not have this limitation.

Also, in most jurisdictions, the inventor's own prior patents act as prior art to new inventions. However, in the United States, as described previously, continuing applications may be filed.

Although additional (equivalent to divisional) applications are available in some jurisdictions, only the United States permits such continuing applications to be filed consecutively for 20 years from the date of filing of the first application. In addition, in the United States, continuation-in-part applications are possible in some circumstances that allow new matter to be incorporated into a new application that claims priority to an already filed application, thereby possibly preventing the already filed but unpublished application of the same inventor from being used as prior art to the inventor's new application. In most other jurisdictions, for any such new invention to be patentable, it must be novel and unobvious in view of previously filed patents by the same inventor.

By carefully considering the laws in the various jurisdictions in which patent protection is desired and doing so prior to filing the first patent application, the laws of the other jurisdictions can be kept in mind to obtain the maximum amount of protection. Such protection may in fact be greater than that permitted by your home jurisdiction.

4. Prerequisites to Filing

But before filing a patent application outside your resident jurisdiction, certain steps may be required by your resident jurisdiction. For example, many jurisdictions require that its citizens either file an application for a patent in their jurisdiction first or that they obtain a foreign filing license before filing the application in other jurisdictions. In the United States, a foreign filing license is automatically granted if the government has not placed a secrecy order on the invention within six months of the application filing date. A secrecy order is issued by one of the U.S. security organizations. The security agencies responsible for reviewing patent applications and determining if the application poses a security threat include the Atomic Energy Commission and the Department of Defense. For example, a security reviewer might place cryptographic techniques and military-grade weapons under a secrecy order.

If a secrecy order is placed on the application, the applicant generally cannot file another patent application outside of his or her home jurisdiction. In the United States, the secrecy orders may take on one of several levels of secrecy, and these levels determine in which, if any, other jurisdictions patent applications may be filed. These secrecy levels are fairly complex and are beyond the scope of this chapter. Suffice it to say there are many ways to deal with secrecy orders, and the imposition of an order is not necessarily the end of your foreign filing options.

In any event, failure to abide by a security order in the United States can make the patent unenforceable and can result in a fine. Other jurisdictions may incarcerate as well as fine anyone who fails to obtain a license prior to filing in another country. On the other hand, many countries do not require a security determination at all.

After the prefiling requirements are met, it is then necessary to determine how you will file the application in other jurisdictions.

5. Options for Filing in Other Jurisdictions

As yet, and for the foreseeable future, there is no worldwide patent. So, generally, there are three ways of obtaining patent protection outside of the country in which the application was originally filed. The patent applicant can refile the application in each of the countries in which he or she desires patent protection. This is called a national filing. For example, an owner of a U.S. patent application could directly file that application in Japan, the United Kingdom, Germany, etc., individually.

Alternatively, the application owner could file the application in one of the Regional Patent Offices. A Regional Patent Office is a patent office that is typically formed by treaty among several countries in a region. At the moment there are four regional offices: the European Patent Office (EPO), which has 30 countries of Europe as members (Austria, Belgium, Bulgaria, Cyprus, Czech Republic, Denmark, Estonia, Finland, France, Germany, Greece, Hungary, Iceland, Ireland, Italy, Liechtenstein, Lithuania, Luxembourg, Monaco, Netherlands, Poland, Portugal, Romania, Slovakia, Slovenia, Spain, Sweden, Switzerland, Turkey, and United Kingdom); the Eurasian Patent Office (EAPO), which has nine of the former republics of the Soviet Union as members (Armenia, Azerbaijan, Belarus, Kazakhstan, Kyrgyzstan, Republic of Moldova, Russian Federation, Tajikistan, and Turkmenistan); the African Regional Intellectual Property Organization (ARIPO), which has 15 English-speaking African states (Botswana, The Gambia, Ghana, Kenya, Lesotho, Malawi, Mozambique, Namibia, Sierra Leone, Sudan, Swaziland, Tanzania, Uganda, Zambia, and Zimbabwe) as members; and Organisation Africaine de la Propriete Intellectuelle (OAPI), which has 16 French-speaking African states as members (Benin, Burkina Faso, Cameroon, Central African Republic, Chad, Congo, Côte d'Ivoire, Equatorial Guinea, Gabon, Guinea, Guinea-Bissau, Mali, Mauritania, Niger, Senegal, and Togo). A regional filing allows a patent applicant to file a single application and designate in which countries belonging to the regional office the applicant wishes ultimately to obtain a patent.

A third alternative is to file an "international patent application" under the Patent Cooperation Treaty (PCT), termed a PCT filing. Although there is no single global patent, a majority of countries have signed the Patent Cooperation Treaty. This treaty, which is administered by the World Intellectual Property Organization (WIPO), a United Nations organization, does several things. First, it guarantees that in any jurisdiction there are reciprocal patent rights for non-residents of the jurisdiction (non-citizens will be treated no differently than citizens of the jurisdiction). Thus, if, say, the United States grants its citizens a grace period in which to file a patent application after an inventor has published an article about the invention, the United States must provide that same grace period to non-U.S. applicants applying for patent protection in the United States.

Second, the treaty provides that anyone filing a patent application under the treaty can do so within one year of its earliest priority filing, that is, the earliest patent application that was first filed describing the invention, and obtain a date of filing as if the PCT application had been on the same date as the original filing. Thus, if a U.S. provisional application were filed on January 2, 2005, and the applicant wanted to make use of the PCT filing procedure, he or she must do so by January 2, 2006. If the application is filed within the year, then for certain prior art purposes, the applicant filing date is equivalent to January 2, 2005.

Third, by using a PCT filing, the applicant equivalently files in each of the countries and regions that are signatories to the treaty. So an applicant can apply not only to all the countries that are signatories but also to all the regional offices.

The filing of an application under the PCT is referred to as Chapter I. The applicant files the PCT application through a Receiving Office (typically the patent office of the applicant's resident jurisdiction). The use of the Receiving Office guarantees that a foreign filing license will be requested even if the first application to be filed is the PCT application.

If an earlier-filed application is to be used for priority, a Chapter I filing must occur within one year of the original application filing. Eighteen months after the original filing date, several things happen. First the International Search Authority (ISA) issues a search report called an International Search Report (ISR) that reports all the prior art the search agency finds that may have an impact on the patentability of the invention. Presently the following patent offices are permitted to act as an International Searching Authority (ISA) and an International Preliminary Examination Authority (IPEA) (as described below): Austria, Australia, Canada, European Patent Office, Finland, Japan, Korea, Peoples Republic of China,

Russian Federation, Spain, Sweden, and the United States. Near or at the same time as the ISR is issued, the ISA issues a Written Opinion which includes a brief patentability analysis of the claims in view of the ISR references.

Response to this Written Opinion is voluntary. Informal comments can be filed by the applicant, and these will be placed in the file and be accessible by the later national and regional examiners but will not be considered by the ISA examiner. Also, the applicant can simply do nothing and not respond to the Written Opinion. In both of these cases the Written Opinion will issue as an International Preliminary Examination Report (IPER).

If the applicant wishes to file a more formal reply potentially including claim amendments in order to influence the IPER, the application must enter Chapter II. To enter Chapter II, the applicant pays a fee and submits a Chapter II Demand along with remarks on the Written Opinion and any claim amendments. The International Preliminary Examination Authority (IPEA) will issue an IPER taking into account any arguments and amendments to the claims made by the applicant. If the applicant decides not to enter Chapter II, the applicant need do nothing for 30 months, when the application first enters the National Phase as described below.

In either case, the IPER is based on the most restrictive common denominator of patentability. Accordingly, many applicants choose not to amend the claims at this time. For example, if the claims are rejected as being obvious in view of some prior art, an applicant potentially could lose rights by amending the claims because in some jurisdictions the cited art might not be considered prior art. Instead, many applicants wait to amend the claims when the application has entered the National Phase.

At 30 months from the original filing date, the application enters the National Phase. By entering the National Phase, the applicant chooses countries or regions in which he or she wishes a patent to issue. At this point prosecution takes place before the patent offices in the jurisdictions selected.

When the application enters the National Phase, the application must then comply with all the local rules of the jurisdiction in which the patent is being prosecuted. For example, translations become due and examination fees need to be paid. The prosecution then proceeds just as it does in the United States. It should also be noted that although U.S. companies can use their U.S. patent attorneys to file applications with the PCT, when the National Phase is entered, attorneys in the jurisdiction of interest must be retained, and this is usually done by the U.S. patent attorneys.

If an application entering the National Phase enters through a Regional Office such as the European Patent Office (EPO) and not simply one or more country patent offices, the process becomes a bit more extended. First, the application is examined in the EPO by a European Patent Examiner. The prosecution is again similar to that in the United States. If the searching authority (ISA) during Chapter I of the PCT was the EPO, the application will be examined directly. If the ISA was not the EPO, then a second search may take place.

After the search is conducted, the application will be examined for patentability. If an examination report (IPER) was issued in Chapter II by the EPO as the examining authority (IPEA), the first office action issued by the EPO will be substantially the same as the IPER. As in U.S. prosecution, the applicant has the ability to amend the claims at this time.

It is important to note that the flexibility to amend the claims in the United States does not generally extend to other jurisdictions. In the United States, for example, if a claim claims a range of "100-200 mg," the claim can generally be amended, if necessary to overcome prior art, to claim "150-200 mg." Support for this claim is in the fact that the range 150-200 mg is inherently contained in the range 100-200 mg. However, in the EPO, if the sub-range 150-200 mg is not specifically mentioned in the specification, then potentially the claim may not be so amended and any attempt to do so will result in a new matter rejection.

After the claims are allowed and the EPO "grants" a patent, the application must then be validated in each country in which the applicant wishes to have a patent issue. Validation requires paying of fees and having the claims of the patent translated into the three official languages of the EPO: English, French, and German. At this point a patent will issue in each country selected in Europe for validation.

In Europe and in many other jurisdictions, but not in the United States, the allowed patent is next published for opposition. During the opposition period, any third party can oppose the issuance of the patent by citing prior art. If an opposition is filed, the patent applicant and the opposer ultimately meet in an opposition proceeding. During the opposition, the opposer raises its objection to the issuance of the patent (based typically upon prior art grounds) and the applicant gets to rebut the opposer's assertions. If the applicant is successful, the patent then issues.

To understand the interplay of the various offices, consider the following example in which a U.S. applicant files for a provisional application in the United States on May 1, 2005. By May 1, 2006, the applicant must convert the application to a utility application in the United States and file in any other jurisdiction in which he or she wishes to claim priority to the U.S. provisional application. In this example, the applicant also files a PCT application through the Receiving Office of the U.S. Patent Office.

Six months after the PCT and U.S. applications are filed (18 months from the filing date of the provisional application), the PCT and U.S. applications publish. In this example, the patent applicant does not wish to enter Chapter II of the PCT and so nothing substantive happens until 30 months from the filing date of the provisional application. At 30 months, the PCT application enters the National Phase, and in this example the applicant wishes to file in Japan and Europe. The applicant requests examination in Japan and prosecution in Japan then begins.

In Europe, the applicant also requests examination and the prosecution at the regional level also begins. Once the European examination is complete and the patent application is allowed, the applicant validates the European patent application in the United Kingdom, Germany, and France, the European countries of interest to the applicant in this example.

a. *Additional Considerations*

As in the United States, in most jurisdictions, once the patent issues it must be maintained by paying periodic renewal fees. Many jurisdictions also require annual fees to maintain the applications during prosecution. Typically these payments are made yearly and are called annuities.

Because of these maintenance payments, the cost of maintaining a portfolio is significant. As a result, as part of its patent strategy, a company should periodically review its portfolio to allow no-longer-useful patents to lapse and thereby reduce their maintenance costs.

Thus, the obtaining of a patent portfolio in multiple jurisdictions is costly and complex. However, by planning a global strategy early on and executing on the strategy, the greatest protection can be obtained for the least amount of money.

D. Managing the Company's Patent Estate

Now that the company has committed time, resources, and money to develop a patent estate, it must now become a good steward of that estate. Just as a land steward strives to maintain precious resources, the company as patent steward must implement good business practices to manage its patent estate, not only to preserve its integrity in the near term but also to extract maximal value from it over the long term. Toward this end, the following discussion attempts to outline some general do's and don'ts of estate stewardship and housekeeping while providing some practical recommendations for success.

1. A Family Portrait

A company should think broadly when asking the question, "What are the patent and patent-related assets that reside in our estate?" The assets properly included in any estate survey are: issued and granted patents worldwide; pending and allowed or accepted patent applications worldwide; patent applications currently in preparation; invention disclosures submitted to the company currently under consideration; invention disclosures submitted to the company but not acted upon; and patent assets to which the company has rights by virtue of an agreement(s) with a third party(ies).

At minimum, a company should maintain a current status report itemizing each of the foregoing assets together with a summary of certain basic facts, such as: title; filing date; issue date; inventor names; identity of assignee or licensor; reel and frame data for ownership documents recorded with the U.S. Patent Office; current procedural status; type of filing (e.g., U.S. provisional application, utility application or design application; original, continuation or divisional); identity of priority and/or parent application; jurisdiction; and identity of a product or other commercial embodiment corresponding to each asset.

Objectively speaking, this recommendation may appear trivial and obvious but it is not. Many companies do not follow this practice, and an equally large number of those that do fall short of the objective. This is not simply an administrative exercise. As will be discussed below, the value of a patent estate to the company's business can often rise or fall on such a disciplined approach. While there is expense associated with preparation and maintenance of a status report, its value to the company cannot be understated. This report can serve as an inventory for budget discussions, as a basis for talking points when appropriate marketing or collaborative discussions arise, and, most important, as a road map for keeping the patent estate objectives aligned with the business development objectives. More on these points later.

In the case of the invention disclosure assets identified above, a status report will likely assume a different form and purpose. Invention disclosures memorialize an idea or discovery. As such, a completed disclosure form should describe in detail the idea or discovery, including materials and references to company notebooks; identify the inventive contributors; state the first date of discovery or conception; disclose the identity of any individuals to whom the idea or discovery was communicated (internally and externally); and be signed and dated by inventive contributors and witnesses.

At bottom, the recommendations for innovation management are simple: first, the company should have a process for collecting and archiving invention disclosures; and second, the company should regularly review and consider whether such disclosures warrant a patent filing or perhaps serve to embellish an already-existing filing. In certain instances, these invention disclosures can belie a research or development direction that has strayed from the business objectives or a discovery that can foreshadow a second generation core technology. Again, a disciplined approach can bring value in this regard. The company's estate should be, at least, a reflection of its current business and marketing plan, but the estate should also foreshadow how the business is evolving. Do not mortgage the future for want of simple asset management practices.

As suggested above, third-party patent rights contributed by agreement to the company should also be catalogued. In practice, this goes beyond merely keeping a copy of the license in the corporate files. Typically, the schedule of patent rights that accompanies the agreement is only current as of the date of execution of the agreement. Thus the company should regularly obtain updates from the third party. The company may, however, also wish to monitor independently the third party's patent activities to ensure full disclosure by the third party and resolve any dispute as to the actual rights that should flow to the company. Such a proactive approach can save face later during a due diligence and avoid a potential deficiency in the estate and/or remove a potential cloud on the company's ability to do business. More on these points later.

In practice, the company whose management appoints a patent/intellectual property coordinator and institutes a patent committee populated by management will most likely achieve these objectives. The most effective patent committee will have members from business development, product development, marketing and sales, legal, and operations as well as research and development. Similarly, the most effective patent/intellectual property coordinator is not necessarily a scientist or other individual strictly devoted to technical innovation at the company. Patent counsel should certainly attend but need not direct meetings or control agendas. In essence, the patent committee is a committee making business decisions and should be conducted accordingly.

2. Keeping It in the Family

Innovation and product enhancements are the hallmark of a healthy company. Naturally, a company expects undiluted or uncompromised opportunities to exploit these to their fullest measure, so loss management practices are a must, especially regarding patent assets. Toward that end, a company must engage in loss prevention measures.

Untimely disclosure of an innovation or incremental improvement can certainly compromise future patent rights. While it is generally appreciated that an inventor's scientific articles can be problematic, other forms of disclosure can result in a loss of rights. For example, transfer of a material such as a protein or cell line to a party outside the company is a disclosure. Even if the transfer is to a party with whom the company has a preexisting confidential relationship, the transfer will still be a damaging disclosure unless the material is specifically and directly covered by the preexisting confidential relationship. In short, if a transfer is not accompanied by a specific materials transfer agreement, not only is there a likely loss of rights to the existing invention, but certain downstream invention rights are likely lost as well.

Another example of a potentially damaging disclosure involves grant applications, particularly applications submitted to federal funding agencies. While the fact of the grant and its contents may remain non-public for some period of time, it is subject to publication under an FOIA (Freedom of Information Act) request; subsequently submitted technical reports to the funding agency can also be subject to such requests. Thus another possible loss of rights to valuable intellectual property can occur unless the company has taken appropriate measures.

Similar concerns may arise when collaborators are involved but not monitored adequately by the company. While the company should expect to benefit from a collaborator's discoveries, a collaborator's unmonitored practices may jeopardize the company's ability to do so.

Once again, the company should rely on good asset management practices to mitigate risks such as those described above. In each of the foregoing situations, a company should review every form of external communication and determine whether the subject matter of the communication is already protected by a patent application, and if not, whether it should be so protected. Good business practices dictate that the company should designate an individual to monitor the activities of scientists in-house as well as at a collaborator's facility, and to monitor submissions or technical publications of any type. Often, the IP/patent coordinator can fulfill this role.

An equally important and complimentary role for this individual is that of in-house educator. An informed employee is another safeguard to loss of potentially valuable patent assets. On a regular basis, the company should conduct in-house seminars to educate the work force on patent and intellectual property concepts and to describe the company's policies and practices. This brings immediate and real benefit to the company.

Similarly, incomplete or improper documentation can potentially compromise future rights. Perhaps the best-known example is a company's laboratory notebooks. There are very specific administrative formalities that should be recited in a notebook so it can serve as a proper legal document. More often than not, a company professes to have this under control but, upon inspection, does not. Notebooks and technical records can be critical in resolving any future disputes as to inventorship, entitlement to a patent, or misappropriation of confidential information and/or trade secrets, to name but a few. Again, best practices in this regard would involve the watchful eye of a designated individual who has been trained appropriately and a work force that is informed.

Another example of incomplete or improper documentation is a poorly drafted nondisclosure agreement (NDA). Unfortunately, NDAs do not generally command the attention of company management, yet they are routinely employed as the company's first line of defense against misappropriation of intellectual property rights.

One version of NDA does not fit all. A company should carefully define and limit the scope of an NDA for two reasons: first, it serves to keep the company's eventual disclosure focused (hopefully, on current ideas already subject to patent protection of some form) rather than open-ended (e.g., on amorphous future ideas not already subject to patent protection); and second, it serves to document accurately what exactly has been disclosed and to whom, often a concern of investors. In fact, just the exercise of discussing internally the scope of an NDA can make clear to the company that it has not yet taken measures to protect the subject matter of the NDA. In this situation, no NDA should be executed prior to filing a patent application or, at least, preparing a complete (signed, executed, dated, witnessed) invention disclosure to memorialize the origins of the ideas and discoveries. This is discussed further in Chapter VI.

At bottom, the company should remember that NDAs are a weak form of defense. While everyone who participates in a confidential exchange will remember that the exchange was in fact confidential, do not expect everyone to recall accurately or agree on who contributed "Idea X" to the group discussion. Thus, it is always prudent to file a patent application in advance of the exchange if only to serve as objective documentation of the fact that "Idea X" originated at the company, and create a written summary of exactly what was discussed by whom for the company's files.

3. Skeletons in the Closet

Even the best of families have skeletons in the closet. The key is knowing about them, particularly before your investors, collaborators or competitors do. The following discussion focuses on three basic business considerations: First, does the company own the patent rights in the estate? Second, does the patent estate correspond to the company's products, services and/or business plan? And, third, does the company require any third-party rights to conduct its business—that is, is the company free to operate in the marketplace?

a. Rights of Ownership

As a threshold matter, a company should take affirmative steps to perfect ownership rights in patent assets. In brief, this begins with the company's employment agreement, which should have an explicit and broad assignment of invention obligation recited as a condition of employment. This is the safety net. On a case-by-case basis, however, the company still must conduct a thorough investigation of who is an inventor of the particular invention claimed in any patent or application. Once the true inventors are identified, the company should prepare an assignment form for signature by each inventor at the time a patent application is filed. Ideally, the assignment form identifies specifically the patent or application being assigned, and further recites language that anticipates all subsequent patents and applications world-wide derived from this particular parent. This prophetic language operates to capture future ownership rights for the company. Such prophetic language is a safeguard for the possibility that future related applications or patents are themselves not actually assigned by operation of a separate assignment. It is also a safeguard for the possibility that an inventor leaves the company and/or becomes uncooperative. Even when this prophetic language is used, it is prudent to have an inventor sign an assignment form for each application filed by the company at the time of filing, even if it is a provisional patent application. As discussed in more detail below, an inventor who does not affirmatively assign the entirety of his/her patent rights remains an owner of the patent under the law of the United States.

Why is ownership important? The most obvious answer is: Ownership is essential for securing exclusivity for the company. Exclusivity is synonymous with value and translates into intellectual capital. For example, exclusivity impacts the magnitude of an investment and gives the company leverage—for example, bargaining power during settlement of litigation.

If a company does not wholly own its patent assets, the question then becomes "Who else does?" In the United States this is particularly critical, since co-owners can each commercially exploit the entirety of the patent rights without the obligation of accounting to the others. There is no recourse available to the company. So, if a company does not wholly own its rights, a co-owner can compete directly or grant a license to a competing party, including the company's nemesis. When multiple parties have rights to the same patent, then the maximum commercial value of the patent to any one of them has been diminished.

Unfortunately, an inventor will often own rights, in whole or in part, in a company patent because of a company failure to act timely. While the company may be able to rely on a well-crafted employment agreement as evidence of an obligation to assign, the absence of an actual assignment document creates a cloud on the company's title. In the course of an investment or merger, for example, the importance of the particular patent asset and the extent to which the patent estate per se is affected (i.e., the extent to which a chain of related patents is affected) may weigh heavily on valuation or, in certain circumstances, delay or break the deal.

Of equal importance is the negative impression left upon the parties to the transaction. Poor housekeeping at this level raises questions about company management's diligence and attention to detail. When something as fundamental as asset ownership is not well managed or documented by the company, investors or collaborators may begin to lose confidence in the company's management.

b. *Correspondence to Products or Business Strategies*

As stated earlier, sole ownership of a patent is essential for securing exclusivity for a legally protected term of years. Exclusivity is, in turn, critical to commercial success because, during this legally protected term of years, the patent owner is empowered to prevent others from making, having made, using, selling, offering to sell, and importing the patented invention. So, when a company is maximally exploiting its patent estate, it is making, having made, using, selling, offering to sell and/or importing a product or service that corresponds exactly to one or more claims of the patent. If a company's product or service does not correspond exactly to one or more claims of a patent in the company estate, the company will be unable to rely on its patent estate to prevent a third party from copying the company's product or service. It is as if the company has no patent estate at all.

Imagine the following scenario: Company A's patent applications were filed approximately five years ago at the time its first-generation product configuration was finalized. Patents have since issued with claims that correspond exactly to this product configuration. Company B is a competitor that has studied Company A's patents and has designed a comparably performing product that does not correspond to any of Company A's patent claims. Company A then evaluates Company B's product and determines that it is identical to Company A's current product. But Company A cannot assert its patent estate against Company B, and more important, Company A has lost the opportunity to secure exclusivity for its current product. Even more unfortunate is the fact that Company B has already filed a patent application on this improved product configuration, thereby being able ultimately to exclude Company A!

This is an example of a fundamental disconnect between products and patents. Company A's product evolved but its patent estate did not, with serious consequences—loss of market exclusivity and no immediate recovery plan. If this deficiency in the patent estate was uncovered during a financing-related due diligence, the investors would withdraw. If uncovered during a negotiation pursuant to a merger, acquisition, strategic alliance or dispute resolution, the company's leverage would evaporate.

This would be far less likely to happen to a company that follows basic loss prevention practices. First, a company should regularly audit its patent estate to confirm at least that it is staying abreast of and corresponds to product developments and improvements. This includes patents and applications directed to embodiments that may not correspond exactly to the company's preferred product configuration but may have commercial value nevertheless. Competitors should not be permitted to benefit from the company's basic discoveries merely by selling a variant or incremental improvement.

Second, monitor competitors for possible design-around technologies and products. It is possible in most instances to glimpse a competitor's future product strategies by reviewing its patent publications. Third, designate an individual or team of individuals to carry out these tasks in consultation with company patent counsel. The success and value of such an audit will depend directly upon the depth of legal scrutiny. Do not delegate these tasks only to scientists at the company; these tasks require a blend of technical sophistication and patent law expertise.

c. Freedom to Operate

As stated earlier, a patent owner can exclude others from making, having made, using, selling, offering to sell, and importing the patented invention. A patent does not confer any affirmative right on the owner. So, even if the company wholly owns a patent that corresponds to its key product, it may not be enough—the company can still be enjoined or sued for selling its product.

Potential dominating or blocking patents can issue at any time. A dominating patent can broadly extend to the company's business per se; a blocking patent can cover a specific product or service. The bottom-line test is whether the patent's claims describe—literally or by virtue of equivalent teachings—each element or feature of the company's business, products, and/or services. If the answer is "yes," the company's freedom to operate is in possible jeopardy. The company must act diligently. More details later on this point.

For these reasons, a company should monitor newly issued patents on a regular basis, no less than semi-annually and preferably quarterly. A company can develop appropriate search terms/search strings and deploy them regularly to interrogate appropriate patent databases; searches need only refresh those conducted previously. Several free databases are available, such as the U.S. Patent Office database; the European Patent Office database; and the Patent Cooperation Treaty database. One note of caution: a company should review its search terms/search strings regularly to confirm their continued relevance, particularly when using competitors' company names or inventors as search terms. A company can contract with a variety of service providers who can assume these monitoring tasks and provide search results to the company for its review.

Issuance of dominating or blocking patents in the United States should not be difficult to predict, particularly since U.S. patent applications are now published no more than 18 months after filing. Also, a publicly accessible online database hosted by the U.S. Patent & Trademark Office houses all prosecution-related documents so that a company can track the progress of a published U.S. patent application. Similar accessibility to prosecution-related documents is available outside the United States, for example, via a database hosted by the European Patent Office or the World Intellectual Property Organization. Thus patent surprises should be at a minimum.

Again, the company's basic objective should be to learn of the existence of third-party patents as early as possible and have a plan to manage the risks posed, if any. Once a potential dominating or blocking patent is identified, company patent counsel should be asked as soon as possible to confirm whether the patent is enforceable. Threshold determinations of enforceability include whether the patent has naturally expired, lapsed (e.g., for failure to pay requisite maintenance fees), been disclaimed, withdrawn or challenged in whole or in part post-issuance (e.g., subject to reexamination or reissue). Next, confirmation of the identity of the patent owner is a useful determination at an early stage. For example, perhaps on its face the patent is assigned to a nonprofit entity, yet the true current owner is a *Fortune* 100 company. A company is likely to assess risk differently when the owner is a *Fortune* 100 company. Another important step at an early stage is identifying all relevant members in the patent's family, if any. An analysis of actual risk cannot be accurate unless the scope and extent of the potential risk is recognized at the outset.

Having completed the steps outlined above, the company should now instruct its patent counsel to prepare an opinion of non-infringement. To do so, counsel must be provided with an accurate and detailed description of the company's business activities and/or its on-sale products and services. Counsel should also have access to technical as well as business personnel; again, a designated individual such as the IP/patent coordinator should oversee the patent opinion process.

Depending on the extent of infringement risk identified by patent counsel in consultation with company management, the company may wish to proceed to obtain an invalidity opinion from patent counsel. Obviously, if the company has decided to seek a license from the patent owner, patent counsel should be advised accordingly, and any work related to an opinion should be suspended. Again, designating a specific individual to manage this process minimizes failed communications and exposure to new, unintended risks.

A disciplined approach to issues raised by third-party patents permits the company to act proactively in the face of potential risks. The company can thoughtfully consider various alternatives, such as risk abatement—redesigning its products or services; risk mitigation—licensing third-party patents; or risk allocation—continuing business as usual, having obtained an opinion of patent counsel.

Notes

1. *See* Diamond v. Chakrabarty, 447 U.S. 303 (1980). "The Committee Reports accompanying the 1952 Act inform us that Congress intended statutory subject matter to 'include anything under the sun that is made by man.' S. REP. No. 1979, 82d Cong., 2d Sess., 5 (1952); H. R. REP. No. 1923, 82d Cong., 2d Sess., 6 (1952)."
2. 35 U.S.C. 287(c).
3. *See Ex parte* Carl A. Lundgren, BPAI Appeal No. 2003-2088.
4. Article 53(b) European Patent Convention.
5. EPO Enlarged Board of Appeal decision G 01/98.

Chapter III

Company Formation[1]

Andrew T. Hoyne
Steven E. Pozaric
Mark L. Stoneman
Armstrong Teasdale LLP
St. Louis, Missouri

A. Introduction

1. "But will it help us get money?"

One of this chapter's authors was attending a biotechnology company board meeting almost 20 years ago. The question on the table was whether a particular university faculty member should be engaged as a consultant/scientific advisor to the company. The faculty member had great credentials, and management thought attracting him would be a coup. Then the veteran venture capitalist brought the conversation in focus with the simple question: "But will it help us get money?"

Biotechnology companies seem to be always either raising money or getting ready to raise money. And not just a small amount of money, but

> **Practice Point**
>
> Biotechnology companies are almost always either raising money or getting ready to raise money.
>
> The company's attorney is encouraged to view legal issues through the additional filter of "will it help us raise money?"

substantial amounts. This factor separates an attorney's representation of a biotechnology company from many other businesses: essentially every substantive (and sometimes minor) business and legal decision needs to be filtered through the question of "will it help us get money?" In this chapter, we will discuss many of the elements that need to be considered when forming a biotechnology company. But, when considering these points, the reader is encouraged to remember an overriding consideration of whether a particular action will help or hurt the company when it seeks to raise money.

As a starting point in this discussion, some of the early considerations relating to biotechnology company formation that can have an impact upon the company's ability to raise funds include the following:

- Selection of a protectable company name so that name recognition can be built up over time, an Internet domain name can be secured, and management is shown to pay attention to details.
- A state of organization or incorporation familiar to investors in other locations (very often, Delaware).
- A board of directors with contacts and credentials, and a willingness to assist in attracting funding.
- A capital structure that is as simple and straightforward as possible.
- Avoiding a high valuation of the company by early-round investors that presents a roadblock later to attracting financing from investors more experienced in market valuations.
- A set of legal documents (including those related to corporate governance, securities laws, confidentiality arrangements, employment terms, etc.) that both reasonably protects the company's interests and conveys the impression that the company is well-run and pays attention to details.

2. The Importance of the Board of Directors

The board of directors plays several important roles in an early-stage biotechnology company (whether as a corporation or limited liability company). While experience shows that a company with a strong board will not always be successful, the converse is often true: a company without a strong board will have a very difficult time achieving success.

Company Formation

Very early in the company formation stage, the identification and recruitment of as strong a board as possible should be undertaken. And, further, this process should not stop, as a key role of the board and management going forward should be the identification and recruitment of additional board members to expand the board, to replace members who leave, and/or to upgrade the board to add key skill sets, credentials, and contacts. Some of the reasons why a strong board is important are as follows:

> **Practice Point**
>
> **Board of Directors**
>
> The board plays key roles in a company's development.
>
> Directors are needed who:
> 1. Provide credibility, either as scientists or business leaders
> 2. Provide industry and funding contacts
> 3. Are experienced and provide good business judgment, especially for strategic decisions and in times of crisis
> 4. Are willing to put in the time to be actively involved in the company's development and fund-raising

- Strong board members provide important credibility to the company, its technology, and its management, and as such they can, simply by being members of the board, enhance the ability of the company to raise money.
- Board members with financing and industry contacts can open doors that the company's management may not be able to open.
- A board that meets regularly and exercises overall control of the company's business affairs can cause the company to focus beyond the day-to-day and instead look at longer-term strategic options and alternatives.

Having a strong board on paper is not enough. It is important that the board be actively engaged in the company's affairs. In many cases, this can be achieved through regular meetings (e.g., every two months) where the company's affairs are reviewed in detail, as well as through periodic updates between meetings.

3. Speed

Biotechnology companies and their founders (as opposed, for example, to start-up information technology companies), especially those with a strong academic orientation, sometimes act as if time is not a primary factor for the company's success. Science takes time, of course. But, it seems that there can sometimes be a tendency for other elements of the company's growth to be allowed to drag on while the company does just one more experiment, holds out for a better deal or pursues an interesting diversion, or while the founder finishes a paper or an academic grant application. Nevertheless, it is generally in the best interests of the company to push forward rapidly. Several reasons for this stand out. First, investors get impatient. They are much more likely to invest in the next round if they see significant rapid progress being made. Second, even initial investors have exit expectations; the general rule of thumb has been that investors tend to look for an exit in about five years from the date of the investment (although current trends in venture capital investing suggest that this period may be getting longer in some circumstances). The faster the company moves during that period and the more progress that is made, the more likely that it will have good alternatives as that period comes to an end. Third, the company's competitors are moving fast. Therefore, the company must continue to develop its technology to stay ahead of its competitors and maintain its vitality. The United States patent system is based upon a "first-to-invent" system, which makes continued development important to maintain a U.S. patent position. Likewise, many non-U.S. patent systems provide patent rights on a "first-to-file" basis, which provides a further incentive to companies to not only invent, but also to promptly make their patent filings. Fourth, patent fees can become quite expensive, especially when a patent moves to the international phase. The more progress a company can make before funds are needed to pay the sizable patent costs that are coming, the more likely that it will be able to attract funding to pay those costs. And fifth, many of a company's costs are time-based—rent, wages, etc. The more progress that can be made in any particular period of time, the more progress that can be made before the funding is gone and the company is raising more money.

Company Formation

4. Simplicity

Many early-stage biotechnology companies are nothing more than a collection of legal contractual rights—licenses, leases, consulting agreements, collaboration agreements, investment agreements, and so on. While there are always exceptions to the general rule, a goal of keeping these arrangements and agreements as simple and consistent as possible can be beneficial to the company's long-term growth. First, simpler is usually easier to document and implement, thereby facilitating transactions and reducing transaction time. And second, the more complicated, the greater the potential for the complication to come back and interfere with a plan down the road. Certainly, some complexity goes with the territory and provides protection to the company. But all too often it seems that what appears to be an innocuous term turns out to be a troublesome roadblock to another desired action down the road.

5. The Role of the Company's Attorneys

When biotechnology companies are formed, they often lack many of the elements of a traditional business. They may operate in leased space, perhaps with equipment provided as part of the lease. They often will have in-licensed technology from a university. Instead of inventory, they have a patent portfolio and trade secrets. Some of the company's key personnel will be employed by others, including universities and collaborators. Investors will provide funds with numerous strings attached. And research, testing, product development, and other technology advancements are often done by third parties. It is the role of the company's attorney to keep these various relationships in order—both reasonable and protective of the company's interest—so that investors (and prospective investors) can have confidence in the company's legal affairs and are willing to provide funding for further growth.

B. Biotechnology Company Models

When forming a biotechnology company, there can often be an assumption that there is a "standard" model that must be used—the company receives some initial funding followed by multiple rounds of venture funding. This model is not uncommon. But many companies are formed using other models.

The funding plan of the biotechnology company—the anticipated funding sources, together with the goals, expectations, and abilities of the founders and other company principals—is the primary determinant in the selection of a formation model. Once the funding plan is established, the implementation steps can flow from the practical and other requirements to achieve that funding. Often business models can be combined to address the funding opportunities present in a particular situation.

Discussed below are several business models that have been used to form biotechnology companies.

1. Company Formed Before In-Licensing While R&D Continues at University

In this model, the company forms as a legal entity and obtains the agreement of the university that technology will be licensed to the company at some point in the future. The company then begins to build out its team, apply for grants, have discussions with funding sources, and generally organize so that it is in a position to launch when it has funding in place, while continuing research and development at the university.

The primary potential advantages of this model are that cash outflow is limited prior to the company's launch and research continues within the university, potentially adding to the intellectual property to be out-licensed to the company. When the company launches, it has a team, resources, and arrangements in place for a potentially faster ramp-up. And, with the licensing delayed until the funded launch, the funding sources may bring another perspective to the final licensing negotiations, resulting in a potentially better arrangement. This approach may be especially appropriate if a funding source is anticipated but is not yet in a position to invest.

There are several potential disadvantages to this model. The launch of the company is delayed, which may result in loss of competitive advantage or intellectual property leadership. Delay may also result in a shorter period of time for the company to get to a point where it can fund major patent costs. In addition, without the definitive in-license of technology, funding may be harder to attract. And, there could be a risk of the company not being able to obtain the technology license due to a change in some aspect of the arrangement. Finally, it can be difficult to coordinate all the activities in order to bring the pieces together at one time.

Company Formation

2. Technology Flip

In this model, after limited development, the company's technology is packaged and sold to another company. This approach may provide a rapid up-side to founders, while at the same time requiring a limited initial capital investment. However, this approach has limited applicability (the technology generally must be at a stage where it is marketable); it requires skill and contacts to work a corporate deal; it can involve significant patent, legal, and travel costs; and licensing and technology rights may not permit a technology flip or may require a significant portion of any funds received for the licensed technology to be paid to the licensor.

3. Revenue-Funded Company

The company's operations in this model are funded by revenues from out-licensing non-essential technology, services provided to customers, SBIR and other grant revenue, and other revenue sources.

This model presents several potential advantages: The time and effort of attracting investors and ownership dilution can be reduced or eliminated. Operating revenues may be easier to obtain than investment. And ongoing operations allow the company to build a team and infrastructure over time to support future growth of the company's proprietary technology.

However, this model has several potential risks or disadvantages: Revenues may not be adequate or near-term enough for the company to grow its proprietary technology at a competitive speed or to cover expensive patent protection costs. The SBIR grant process can take a long period of time before the more significant Phase II grants are obtained and funded. Out-licensing may cause concerns regarding the mix of technology rights retained versus the rights out-licensed. And it can be difficult for the company management and personnel to mix time, skills, vision, and operations of an R&D-based company with a revenue-based company.

4. Corporate Deal-Funded Company

In this model, the company's operations are funded by a deal with a more established company. This approach can be attractive for several reasons. The company's scientific founder may be much better positioned to deal with corporate scientists with whom the founder can discuss the technology as technology, rather than with prospective investors whose focus is on the investment deal. And this approach may provide significant funding to the company, without the need to attract numerous investors while valuation of future rights may be higher in such a strategic investment. Further, the corporate investment provides the company with credibility. On the other hand, these types of investments are very hard to find, take a long time to put together, come with numerous strings attached, and the company usually lacks negotiating leverage.

5. Venture Fund–Launched Company

A venture capital fund participates in the formation and organization of the company and is the initial investor in the company in this model.

In this approach, the company initially deals with only one investor, rather than many. It brings in a professional investor and future funding source at the start. It also allows the scientific founders to focus on the science while the fund brings in management to run the company.

At the same time, this model has limited applicability, as it generally requires a broad platform technology; a venture fund that has the interest, time, and resources to devote to the project; and a company located in or willing to relocate to a location acceptable to the venture fund. Further, valuation will often be low, with the founder's upside adversely impacted by requirements of the venture fund investor of a low valuation, a liquidation preference, and possibly a cumulative dividend. Also, with the five-year or so window in which venture capital funds have historically planned to exit from their investments, the involvement of the venture capital fund at formation starts the clock ticking earlier than some of the other models. Finally, the venture fund will control the company and the company's options will be limited if the fund decides not to participate in a necessary funding round or to participate at terms that are not attractive to the founders. This model has become rarer as venture funds have concentrated on later-stage investments.

6. Angel Investor–Funded Company

In an angel investor–funded company, the company attracts one, two, or more rounds of angel investor funds to launch and grow the company.

This approach requires the formation of the company and establishment of at least part of the management team before funds are raised, as angel investors tend to invest on the basis of the quality of the team, not the underlying science, which they may not fully understand. Raising funds from angels can take a lot of time and generally requires a solid and active board of directors with contacts and credibility who are able and willing to make connections and be involved in the fund-raising process. Finally, the angels may not have the ability to fund subsequent rounds.

However, this approach may result in much better investment terms than a venture fund investment, as the investment terms are often set by the company and either accepted by an investor or the investor passes. (But, of course, the terms will need to be attractive enough to secure investment.)

7. Significant Self-Funded Company

The founders use significant personal funds (e.g., $500,000 to $1,000,000) to launch the company with the expectation that future funding will come from angel investors, venture funds or revenues. Unfortunately, few academic founders have the necessary funds to risk investment in a start-up biotechnology company; and if they have such funds, then they are often hesitant to put so much personal wealth at risk, since their life's work (the technology) is already at risk in the venture. And a large initial investment by the founder may be difficult to integrate with subsequent investment rounds in terms of valuation, control, and other issues. However, this approach allows the company to professionally launch and ramp-up without needing to spend time raising funds for that purpose.

8. Shoestring Self-Funded Company

In this model, the founders launch the company with limited personal funds in order to move the technology forward until other funding options are available. The advantages of this model are that there is no initial need to spend time raising funds and there is no initial dilution of ownership. However, the lack of capital to rapidly move forward with technology advances may result in the company falling behind competitors, and, due to a lack of funds, the company may not be able to pay for patent costs, adequately compensate team members, access appropriate laboratory space, and cover other costs. Further, use of this approach may cause unprofessional results or reputation. In addition, the local start-up industry personnel (incubators, etc.) may shy away from the company as one with extremely limited likelihood of success. In most cases, this model is not practical for a start-up biotechnology company.

9. Charitable Corporation or Foundation

The company is formed and conducts research and development efforts as a nonprofit charitable corporation or foundation focused upon specific diseases or conditions. Funds are raised from donors and grants, rather than investors and venture capitalists.

There are difficulties with this approach. First, when the company is actually formed as a foundation or charity (as opposed to those instances in which funding is merely provided by such an entity), there is no financial upside potential (whether or not such potential is realistic) to founders and employees other than compensation and bonuses. Second, the large blocks of funding from venture capital investments are not available. And third, the charitable company's activities are subject to the legal and tax standards that apply to nonprofits.

But this approach does have several potential advantages. When a company is formed as a nonprofit, it is more likely to be able to obtain funding from government agencies and private foundations that either limit funds available to for-profit companies or are restricted from making grants to for-profit companies. Further, if the charitable company is focused upon a particular disease or condition, donations from persons afflicted with such disease or condition, their family members, and various organizations involved in the field are possible. And stock-related issues including valuation, preferential venture capital rights, and so on can be ignored. Finally, some persons may want to avoid the "stigma" of commercialism and instead be involved with a charitable entity. It is also conceivable that in the right set of circumstances, technology (e.g., commercial development of a piece of the technology outside of the nonprofit's area of research) could be licensed later to an indirectly related for-profit company, thereby allowing for some potential upside.

10. Debt-Funded Company

Some founders will consider funding their companies using debt. Nonconvertible debt does not dilute ownership, and it may be easier to obtain than an equity investment. And the founder may believe that the debt can be used as a bridge until revenues or another investment round. There are several significant difficulties with debt in a biotechnology company. First, the debt must be repaid when due. Biotechnology companies by their nature often do not have sufficient funds for operations, let alone for repaying debt. If the company goes into default, then its existence can be at risk. Second, in most cases, the debt is used to fund ongoing research and operations, which may not result in the creation of an identifiable asset on the company's balance sheet (e.g., inventory is not created). Third, agreements to which the company is subject (including most university licenses) may have termination rights that are triggered upon insolvency and similar conditions. Failure to pay debt as it comes due or having the debt liability on the company's balance sheet without a corresponding asset can put a cloud on the company's solvency and, as a result, upon such agreements. If a company enters the "zone of insolvency," then the responsibility of the board can shift to a duty to protect the assets of the company for the benefit of its creditors. And fourth, investors in subsequent rounds usually will not want the funds that they are investing used to repay an existing note holder unless the amount is modest. Other than a company projecting immediate revenues, a determination to use debt to provide financing should be very carefully made, and the assumptions upon which debt is to be taken on should be considered very carefully, as the risks of the use of debt can be significant.

C. Entity Selection and Formation

1. No Perfect Choice

Just as there are a number of means by which a company may be funded, there are several types of legal entities that can be used for the conduct of the company's business. There is no ideal solution to the choice of entity question when forming a biotechnology company. Each of the types of entities available has its advantages and its disadvantages. The choice should be driven by what type of entity makes obtaining funding, both immediate and longer-term, easier. In starting a venture, founders are presented with the following choices:

- sole proprietorship;
- partnership;
- C-corporation;
- S-corporation;
- limited liability company; and
- exotic entity types

2. Sole Proprietorships and Partnerships

Biotechnology companies are not typically formed as sole proprietorships or partnerships. A sole proprietorship is essentially what results when an individual decides to enter into business and starts working, developing ideas, and entering into agreements in his or her own name. A sole proprietorship is not a separate legal entity. As a result, the individual is personally liable for all of the sole proprietorship's liabilities.

A partnership is very similar to a sole proprietorship except that more than one person is involved. Depending on the sophistication of the parties involved and the subject matter of the partnership, the partners might enter into a partnership agreement that outlines each partner's responsibilities and respective share of profits and losses. Like a sole proprietorship, a partnership is not recognized as a separate legal entity for liability purposes, and each partner is personally liable for the obligations of the partnership. In addition, individual partners are able to bind the partnership (and the other partners) to decisions; therefore, each partner will be obligated for liabilities created by the other partner.

> **Practice Point**
>
> **Form of Entity**
>
> Most biotech companies need to be either a(n):
>
> 1. C-corporation,
> 2. S-corporation, or
> 3. Limited liability company

Some biotechnology companies might, at their very early stages, start as de facto sole proprietorships or partnerships. Due to the lack of a shield from liability and other requirements of prospective investors (such as readily definable and transferable ownership interests), any venture that is growing should quickly take the form of either a corporation (be it a C-corporation or an S-corporation) or a limited liability company (LLC). Further, a biotechnology company in formation is generally well advised to establish the entity as early as possible so that licenses, confidentiality, employment, and other agreements can be in the name of the entity, initial intellectual property rights (e.g., Internet domain names and intent-to-use federal trademark applications) can be held by the company, key advisors can be issued or purchase restricted stock rather than delaying until later when the company's valuation is increased and less attractive stock options must be used, and the enterprise can be taken more seriously by investors and others.

3. C-corporations

Many biotechnology companies are formed as C-corporations. There are several reasons for this. First, the C-corporation is generally well understood, simple, and straightforward—there is neither the complexity nor the need to consider the details of a limited liability operating agreement and partnership taxation. Second, the C-corporation has room to grow—it is the typical entity in which venture funds invest. A C-corporation can be sold in a tax-free reorganization under Internal Revenue Code Section 368, and a C-corporation is typically the entity that would be used if the company were

> **Practice Point**
>
> **C-corporation Pluses and Minuses**
>
> + Form known and understood by investors
> + Initial organization is simple and straightforward
> + Multiple classes of ownership facilitate VC investment
> + Exits available through IPO and tax-free exchanges
> + Tax advantages of stock options and restricted stock
> + Tax advantages of long-term capital gains and small-business stock upon sale
> + Limited liability
> + Centralized management
> + Unlimited number of owners
>
> − No immediate pass-through of losses to investors
> − Double taxation of profits

to go public. And there will be no need down the road to convert the entity from one form of organization (e.g., an LLC) to a C-corporation, with attendant issues, time, and expense (see Section C.5.a.(v)). Third, the various forms of incentive compensation (options and restricted stock) are available and understood. Fourth, ownership is on the easily understood basis of stock rather than the complexities inherent in capital accounts of an LLC. Fifth, investors in a C-corporation may be eligible for tax relief upon the sale, exchange or worthlessness of their stock as discussed in Section C.3.g.

A corporation is organized under the laws of its state of incorporation and is created when articles (or a certificate) of incorporation (i.e., charter) are filed with the applicable state filing office. Each state has its particular laws regarding corporations; however, all corporations have the traits summarized below.

a. Limited Liability

Shareholders of a corporation are not generally personally liable for the debts or other liabilities of the corporation. A shareholder normally risks only the amount of the investment made in acquiring the stock.

b. Centralized Management

Management of a corporation is vested in its board of directors. The board of directors delegates this authority to the officers for day-to-day operational decisions. Shareholders have a voice in the governance of a corporation due to their power to elect directors and to vote on amendments to the articles of incorporation, mergers or other fundamental transactions as provided for in the relevant state statutes, the corporation's charter, or a shareholders' agreement (if in effect).

c. Owners

Stock in a C-corporation may be owned by any number and any type of investor, be it an individual, corporation, LLC, trust or otherwise. Further, there is no restriction on the residency of stockholders of a C-corporation.

d. Transferability of Ownership

A shareholder may, subject to restrictions imposed by federal and state securities laws, freely transfer its shares of stock. The founders and early investors may enter into a shareholder's agreement that imposes restrictions on the transfer of shares. These restrictions might include the grant of a right of first refusal to the corporation or other shareholders upon a proposed transfer of shares (although intra-family and estate planning transfers often are excepted). However, some investors tend to be troubled by such restrictions, and the administration of these agreements can be time-consuming as the number of shareholders grows. Consequently, although shareholder's agreements (or transfer restrictions in other governing documents) are common for many small businesses, the long-term benefit of such an agreement for a biotechnology company should be carefully considered.

e. Classes of Ownership

A C-corporation's charter may provide for different classes of ownership (i.e., both common stock and one or more different classes of preferred stock). These classes typically possess different rights and powers with regard to approval of transactions, issuance of additional shares of stock, election of directors, rights to dividends, and rights to proceeds upon the sale or dissolution of the corporation.

f. Incentive Compensation

In order to incentivize its management and employees, corporations are able to grant incentive stock options (options that do not give rise to tax liability when exercised), non-qualified stock options (options that, when exercised, do have immediate tax effects), and restricted stock (stock that may be forfeited if certain events do not occur or if the recipient leaves the employ of the corporation prior to the time that such events occur). For a more thorough discussion of incentive compensation, see Section D.3 and Chapter VII.E.3.

g. Taxation

A biotechnology company conducting business as a C-corporation can provide its investors with potential long-term tax-sheltered growth that is ultimately realized by the sale or exchange of the investors' stock. Investors may be eligible to receive tax relief through the lower tax rates that generally apply to long-term capital gains upon sale, as well as the exclusion of capital gains upon the sale of small business stock under Internal Revenue Code Section 1202 and the rollover of capital gains from small business stock under Internal Revenue Code Section 1045. In addition, holders of stock in a C-corporation may be able to exit through a tax-free exchange of their stock in the company for the stock of a public acquiring company pursuant to Internal Revenue Code Section 368. Further, investors may be eligible for the ordinary loss deduction for the sale, exchange or worthlessness of small business stock pursuant to Internal Revenue Code Section 1244. Each of these tax provisions has limitations and special rules, and consultation with the Company's tax advisor is recommended.

A potentially significant drawback for some investors to a C-corporation (in contrast with an S-corporation or an LLC, both of which are discussed below) is that it is subject to what is referred to as "double-taxation." A corporation must pay income taxes on its earnings. And when it distributes those earnings to its shareholders by means of dividends, redemptions or liquidation, the shareholders then must pay taxes on the distributed income. While most biotechnology companies will not be remitting dividends or repurchasing shares, some companies might, as part of the company's exit strategy, sell all or a portion of the company's assets and then make a liquidating distribution to the company's shareholders. The sale of assets by the corporation would give rise to a taxable event for the corporation, and the receipt of funds by the shareholder would give rise to an additional tax being imposed.

4. S-corporations

An S-corporation is a C-corporation that has filed a tax election on IRS Form 2553. This election allows the corporation to have pass-through tax status similar to an LLC electing partnership tax status, thereby passing through losses to its investors subject to the passive loss limitation and at-risk rules and avoiding the double taxation of a C-corporation's income, discussed above.

> **Practice Point**
>
> **IRS Forms**
>
> IRS forms are available from the IRS Web site: www.irs.gov

While S-corporation status can be attractive to some investors, there are significant restrictions on S-corporations contained in the Internal Revenue Code[2] and related regulations, as summarized below.

> **Practice Point**
>
> **S-corporation Pluses and Minuses**
>
> + Benefits of corporate form
> + Profits and losses passed through to shareholders, but subject to limitations
> + Conversion to C-corporation does not involve change of entity
> - Limited to 100 owners
> - Owners must be U.S. resident individuals
> - Only one class of stock allowed
> - Generally must convert to C-corporation for VCs to invest
> - Company must timely and accurately distribute tax information to shareholders for filing each year
> - Profitable companies typically must distribute cash to allow shareholders to pay taxes

a) Most important, shareholders must be individuals and not corporations, certain trusts, limited liability companies or partnerships. This restriction also means that individual investors may not invest in the S-corporation through a corporation, limited liability company or certain trusts. While some prospective investors may have the flexibility to invest as individuals, others may not. As a result, this requirement can, in practice, significantly increase the difficulty of fund-raising. (Venture capital funds are typically limited partnerships, limited liability companies or corporations, and so could not invest in an S-corporation. Venture capital funds typically desire to invest in a C-corporation in any event.)

b) The number of shareholders is limited to 100. This restriction will probably not have a significant effect on most biotechnology companies early in their respective lives. But as a company grows, this could become a problem if funding comes from an increasing number of angel investors, if the existing investors transfer shares to additional parties, or if many employees and others become stockholders upon the exercise of stock options.

c) Shareholders are essentially limited to United States residents.

d) An S-corporation may only have one class of stock. A corporation is deemed to have different classes of stock if the classes have different rights to distribution and liquidation proceeds. Different shares may have different voting rights without violating the prohibition on multiple classes of stock. This restriction means that an S-corporation could not issue preferred stock or other second class of stock which may be necessary to attract investments from investors who require preferred stock.

The restrictions outlined above mean that an S-corporation is not a suitable type of entity if the company will be seeking funding from multiple angel investors, some of whom may desire to invest through an LLC or other investment vehicle, or from venture capital funds. However, an S-corporation could be a good interim entity choice prior to the entry of such investors while the company has only a limited number of individual angel investors, those investors desire the tax treatment of an S-corporation, *and* those investors understand that the company will likely need to terminate its election upon future funding in order to attract investments from investors other than individuals or from investors requiring preferred stock. This circumstance could exist either where the entity has a business model under which it is likely that the entity would generate profits, in which case profits could be distributed to investors, or if the entity is expected to generate losses, and the investors have the ability to utilize such losses as offsets against other income-generating investments.

Many early-stage biotechnology companies focus upon research and development of their science and lack a strong administrative infrastructure. If organized as an S-corporation, the company will need to ensure that it provides the necessary tax information to its shareholders following year-end so that the shareholders are able to file their tax returns in a timely manner. The providing of this information by an early-stage biotechnology company can sometimes be difficult. In many cases, the S-corporation will need to engage outside tax support to ensure that the information is provided in a timely and professional manner. Because the company's information flows through to the investors' tax returns, the company will need to be especially careful to ensure that the information provided is correct, as any adjustment at a later date would trigger not just an amendment of the company's tax return, but the amendment of each investor's tax return.

S-corporation status may be voluntarily terminated with the consent of shareholders holding more than 50 percent of the company's stock. In addition, S-corporation status is automatically lost if any of the above restrictions are violated. For example, if an S-corporation were to sell shares of preferred stock to a venture capital fund that was a limited partnership, it would automatically forfeit the S-corporation status. In addition, termination causes the corporation to have two tax returns for the year in which termination occurs—one for the period in which it was an S-corporation and a second for the remaining portion of the year. One risk of S-corporation status is that a shareholder might take an action that results in the termination of that status prior to the time that the corporation would otherwise deem the change desirable.

Since conversion from being an S-corporation to a C-corporation is one of a change of tax status and not a change of legal entity, the conversion does not otherwise impact the company, its assets, contracts, agreements or relationships. This compares to the potentially significant impact that is triggered by the legal entity change of converting an LLC into a corporation or converting a corporation organized under the laws of one state into a corporation organized under the laws of another state. (See Section C.5.a.(v).)

Note that losses of an S-corporation are allocated among shareholders, including the company founders, based upon the number of shares held. This has two impacts. First, cash investors do not receive all the losses. And the founders, who typically have a very low tax basis in their stock, have losses that they cannot currently utilize, since the loss can only offset the basis of the stock held. As noted above, the current use by the investor of losses that have been passed through is subject to the passive loss limitation and at-risk rules.

Finally, since profits of an S-corporation are passed through to the shareholders, where they are subject to taxes, it is common that a shareholder's agreement include a provision that an amount of cash will also be distributed to the shareholders so that they have cash with which to pay resulting income taxes. This pulls funds out of the company when the company is profitable even though the company may need the funds for its growth and ongoing business development. This compares to a C-corporation, which may have losses carried forward from its early years to offset the current income and thereby avoid paying tax. For example, if a company enters into a licensing agreement and receives an up-front license fee, it may have positive net income for the year. A C-corporation might have prior-year losses that it can use to offset the income, thereby using the full amount of the license fee for company operations. The S-corporation, having previously passed the losses out to its shareholders, might need also to pass out a portion of the license fee to its shareholders so that they can pay their taxes on their proportionate share of the company's income.

5. Limited Liability Companies

An LLC can be an attractive form of entity in those cases where the founders and early investors desire the pass-through tax treatment available when the LLC elects partnership tax status. There are no limitations on who may invest in an LLC, and consequently, the burdensome permitted investor limitations of an S-corporation do not apply here. Further, losses can be allocated to the cash investors rather than prorated among shares held, which results in potentially more losses flowing back to the cash investors rather than being allocated to founders.

a. Problems Using an LLC

At the same time, there can be problems associated with LLCs as the choice of entity for biotechnology companies, which problems are summarized below.

(i) Standard LLC operating agreements are often not appropriate for biotechnology companies. Care needs to be taken to ensure that the operating agreement provides a governance structure that allows for control to be held by a board of directors and day-to-day activities to be conducted by the company's officers, and that the operating agreement does not include provisions that unnecessarily add to the company's administrative burdens (such as requiring that each existing investor must approve each new investor).

Company Formation

(ii) Partnership tax rules are complex. In the event of a sale or wind-up of the LLC (including a conversion of the LLC to a corporation), these rules generally provide for an allocation of the LLC's assets on the basis of capital accounts. In such an event, these rules can make it difficult to ensure treatment of all LLC owners (including founders, employees, option holders, and multiple-investment round investors) in a manner that replicates the conventional economic model of a C-corporation. The complicating nature of the arrangement alone may be enough to scare off some potential investors. In any event, consultation with the company's tax advisor is essential.

(iii) Although an LLC that has elected to be taxed as a partnership may pass through losses to its investors, those losses are subject to the at-risk loss limitation rules of Internal Revenue Code Section 465 and the passive loss limitation rules of Internal Revenue Code Section 469,

---

Practice Point

Limited Liability Companies Pluses and Minuses

+ Limited liability
+ Centralized or decentralized management
+ Profits and losses can be passed through to investors, but subject to limitations
+ Unlimited number of owners
+ No limit on kinds of owners

- Initial organization often involves complex operating agreement
- Capital account rules add complexity upon sale or wind-up
- Likely will be converted to another form for VC to invest
- Generally impractical for an IPO
- Company cannot be sold in a tax-free reorganization
- No tax advantages for stock options
- Company must timely and accurately distribute tax information to shareholders for filing each year
- Company typically must distribute cash to allow shareholders to pay taxes
- Conversion to a C-corporation is not a simple process

which limit the extent to which losses from passive investments may be deducted from non-passive income.

(iv) An LLC faces the same administrative problems as an S-corporation with respect to timely and accurate preparation and distribution of individual tax information to investors. See Section C.4.

(v) Although an LLC can be converted into a corporation, for example, in preparation for a venture capital financing, the process can be time-consuming and expensive. The process involves a number of steps, including the following: First, a corporation must be established. That requires that the desired corporate name must be available. (One alternative is to form the corporation when the LLC is formed and then carry that corporation forward as an inactive shell in order to ensure that the name is available.) Second, company agreements should be reviewed to ensure that the effects of the conversion upon such agreements can be properly addressed. Third, the required level of investor approval must be received, which often requires the preparation of a disclosure statement outlining the change and the impact upon the investors, including allocation of assets pursuant to capital accounts as set out in Section C.5.a.(ii). Any concerns of individual investors may also need to be addressed. Fourth, if the company's operating agreement includes contractual provisions between the company and its investors (e.g., confidentiality terms), then new contracts with the investors may need to be entered into replacing the operating agreement terms. (The alternative is to keep all such agreements out of the operating agreement and in separate investment agreements that are structured to continue in the event of a conversion.) Fifth, share certificates typically need to be exchanged. Sixth, employees and others holding options must be informed of the conversion and the impact of such conversion upon their options. Seventh, any necessary filings must be made. For example, notice of the conversion must be filed with respect to all intellectual property filings. Eighth, third parties must be notified of the change as necessary (e.g., insurance companies). And ninth, final LLC tax returns must be prepared and appropriate information provided to the investors for the filing of their individual returns.

Company Formation

(vi) Company personnel holding ownership interests in the LLC are treated as partners rather than employers, with the resulting need to pay their own employment taxes, estimated tax payments, and so on. In some cases, this status as "partners" can impact the manner in which the personnel can participate in the company's employee benefit plans.

(vii) An LLC is typically subject to the same arrangement among investors as an S-corporation to distribute funds so that investors can pay taxes attributable to their share of the LLC's income, even when the company may need those funds for its ongoing operations. See Section C.4.

(viii) Venture capital funds typically do not invest in LLCs (although some funds will now do so) without first converting to a C-corporation.

(ix) LLCs typically cannot make an initial public offering or enter into an Internal Revenue Code Section 368 tax-free reorganization without first converting to a C-corporation.

(x) The tax laws of the LLC's state must be reviewed to determine if an out-of-state investor's holding of an interest in the LLC subjects such out-of-state investor to income taxation by such state, and appropriate disclosures made to prospective out-of-state investors.

b. LLC Organization

An LLC is organized by filing a certificate or articles of organization with the applicable state office (the choice of domicile, or where an entity will be organized, is discussed in Section C.6). An LLC generally has the following characteristics:

(i) *Flexibility.* For corporations, state statutes provide the framework for the management of the entity. However, for LLCs, the statutes generally contain default provisions that can be varied by the operating agreement of the LLC. The operating agreement is the governing document of the LLC, and in that respect is similar to the bylaws of a corporation. However, since the operating agreement modifies the default provisions in the state statutes, the operating agreement goes beyond what is normally found in a corporation's bylaws and contains essential information about the operations of the LLC and the relationship among the members and the company. Thus, in many ways an LLC operating agreement is like a combination of articles of incorporation, bylaws, and a shareholders agreement for a corporation, plus relevant portions of state corporate law.

Since each operating agreement can modify the default provisions in the statutes, each LLC may be different from the next. This factor gives an LLC flexibility that corporations do not have. However, this flexibility also means that formation of an LLC can be more expensive, since "standard"-form corporate governance documents often used for corporations will not be appropriate and each operating agreement may need to be more carefully tailored to the specific situation faced by the entity. As a result, investors need to carefully consider and evaluate the operating agreement.

One of the more interesting aspects of the flexibility of an LLC is that percentage ownership interests can be completely separated from capital contributions or participation in various revenue streams. The operating agreement can specify that certain members are the only ones to benefit from certain revenue streams or that certain members are entitled to an interest in profits of the LLC prior to the profits being divided among the members as a group. The ability to give a "profits interest" enables a company to grant a meaningful stake in the successful outcome of the business to a person who arrives late in the life of the entity without the necessity of incurring substantial out-of-pocket costs. Those types of unusual allocations will need to be considered in light of applicable laws and regulations concerning partnership taxation.

(ii) *Limited Liability.* The LLC is a separate legal entity, and, by virtue of the state statutes, provides its members (i.e., the owners of the company) with limited liability. As a result, generally the members will not be personally liable for the debts or obligations of the LLC and can only lose the amount of their investment.

(iii) *Management.* An LLC can be managed by either the members or managers. This governance choice is typically one that must be made when making the initial filing with the state filing office. As noted in the introduction to this chapter, the board of directors plays a crucial role in a biotechnology company. If an LLC form of entity is to be used, careful consideration should be given to a management structure that mirrors that of a corporation—a solid board of directors and solid team of officers.

(iv) *Ownership.* When an investor invests in an LLC, the investor becomes a member of the LLC and, under the terms of a typical operating agreement, acquires a percentage ownership based on the amount of the investment relative to the total amount invested by all investors. This ownership sometimes is denominated in "membership units" or "shares" (in some states, which can be thought of as similar to shares of stock of a corporation) if a company's operating agreement so provides. An LLC may have multiple classes of owners with different rights (similar to common stock and different classes of preferred stock for a corporation). As mentioned above under "*Flexibility,*" the characteristics of the ownership interests as to decision-making matters and rights to profits, losses, and distributions can be varied by the operating agreement.

(v) *Transferability of Ownership.* In addition to applicable federal and state securities laws restrictions, many state statutes provide that approval of either a majority of or all the existing members is required for a new party to become a member, unless otherwise provided by the operating agreement. In practice, company operating agreements often provide that new members may be admitted upon the approval of managers. However, operating agreements commonly will have restrictions on to whom ownership may be transferred and the process by which such a transfer must follow. The process will often provide for rights of first refusal that may be exercised by the company and/or the other members. Care needs to be taken when drafting any such provisions, if they are to be included at all, as the mechanics can create administrative complexities for a biotechnology company.

(vi) *Voting.* In general, voting on matters by members is based on the percentage ownership. However, the operating agreement can modify this general rule, allowing greater control over company actions to be vested in certain types or classes of members.

(vii) *Limited History.* Limited liability companies are a type of entity that is relatively new in the legal area. Of course, "new" is somewhat relative, as limited liability companies were first created in 1977 with the passage by Wyoming of its LLC act.[3] While that was nearly 30 years ago, it is significantly less than the time over which corporations have been in existence. Moreover, the use of LLCs as an entity choice did not become widespread until 1996, when the "check the box" rules were adopted. Therefore, the body of law surrounding limited liability companies is not as well developed as for corporations.

(viii) *Incentive Compensation.* Another drawback to an LLC is that incentive stock options are not available to limited liability companies, because the Internal Revenue Code limits those types of options to corporations.[4] That being said, an LLC can still have incentive-based compensation for its directors, officers, employees, and consultants. However, such programs are potentially more complicated and costly to implement relative to a conventional corporate stock option, and they will not have the favorable tax features of an incentive stock option.

(ix) *Taxation.* An LLC may elect to be taxed either as a corporation or a partnership. An LLC with more than one member will be treated as a partnership for federal income tax purposes, unless an affirmative election to the contrary is made. Such a contrary election can be made on IRS Form 8832. Usually, an LLC will elect to be taxed as a partnership in order to avoid the double taxation discussed above, in which case income and losses pass through to owners rather than being taxed at the entity level. This is one of the most significant benefits of choosing an LLC as the type of entity. A potentially significant aspect of the pass-through is the pass-through of losses from the early stages of a biotechnology company, rather than the pass-through of income. The pass-through can provide significant appeal to investors who have taxable income that can be offset by the losses that are passed through from the company. The pass-through of losses is subject to the passive loss limitations of Internal Revenue Code Section 469 and the at-risk rules of Internal Revenue Code Section 465. The allocation of losses must have a substantial economic effect, as set out under the partnership tax rules.

Please see Section C.5.a for a discussion of other tax considerations with respect to LLCs.

6. Exotic Entity Types

There are other types of entities available from which the organizers of a new biotechnology venture may theoretically choose. They include limited partnerships, limited liability partnerships (LLP), and limited liability limited partnerships (LLLP). These entities possess certain of the attributes of partnerships and limited liability companies. A limited partnership is a partnership form created under state law that affords a class of partners limited liability, but also restricts their involvement in the operation of the business. A limited partnership still requires a general partner to have unlimited liability for the debts of the entity. An LLP is a general partnership that has been registered with the state. Generally, the partners of an LLP remain personally liable for their own wrongful acts and the acts of those whom they directly supervise. Otherwise, the partners' liability is typically limited to the amount of their collective investment in the LLP.

An LLLP is a limited partnership that registers under state law that enables a general partner to have limited liability as well. The process of a limited partnership transforming into an LLLP is similar to a general partnership registering as an LLP. The characteristics of limited partnerships, LLPs and LLLPs can vary from state to state. This variability, together with their genesis as partnerships, make them unlikely choices for a new biotechnology company. This is due to the often widespread nature of biotechnology company fund-raising—investors can often be sought from throughout the United States and, in some cases, from foreign countries. Generally, the more standard the investment opportunity, the greater the chance exists of receiving funding, all other things being equal.

7. State of Organization

In most cases, the state of organization should be narrowed to two choices: Delaware or the state in which the entity is to be located, if it is a state in which investors throughout the United States are familiar and reasonably comfortable (e.g., California). If the entity is to be located in another state, then incorporation or organization under the laws of that state has the benefit of only local lawyers and investors being familiar with the laws that govern business entities in the state.

Delaware, on the other hand, is widely viewed as being an appropriate venue in which biotechnology companies are organized. Delaware has a well-developed body of law dealing with corporations, and most lawyers that practice corporate law (including those that represent venture capital funds) are familiar with Delaware law requirements. Due to this familiarity, it is common for a venture capital investor to require that a company reincorporate as an entity formed under the laws of Delaware. Further, sophisticated angel investors may be more comfortable with an investment in a Delaware-based entity. A further practical benefit to incorporating under Delaware law is that shareholder approval may be obtained by majority (or other applicable standard) written consent, rather than the unanimous or super-majority written consent required in some states. If a start-up biotechnology company anticipates that financing from venture funds or sophisticated investors will be sought, it is often simpler to start life as a Delaware entity. But note that the choice of the state of organization may be further affected by the applicable laws of a state where the company has significant operations and shareholders if such state attempts to impose provisions of its corporate law upon the foreign corporation to the exclusion of the corporate law of the state of incorporation (e.g., California[5]).

> **Practice Point**
>
> **State of Organization**
>
> If the company does not expect to need VC or sophisticated investor funding, the state where the company is founded may suffice. If VC funding is expected, forming the company as a Delaware C-corporation should be considered.

The organizers of the start-up company should consider, however, the extra costs incurred as a Delaware corporation or LLC rather than a local-state corporation or LLC, namely Delaware filing fees, agent fees, and franchise taxes, in addition to qualifying to do business in the state where the business is located. But such expenses often are relatively modest compared to the cost of later converting an entity to one chartered under Delaware law. (See Section C.5.a.(v) with respect to the conversion of an LLC into a corporation. The change of a corporation's state of incorporation would trigger similar steps.)

The state of organization of an LLC may be more flexible, although Delaware remains a good choice for the same reasons that many select it as the state of incorpoation. However, in many cases, the LLC is only an interim entity for early-stage investment rounds. Consequently, the issues associated with use of the local state of organization may not be significant. And many LLC statutes are based upon Model Acts, making differences among state laws less significant.

8. Name Selection

Trademark law is the umbrella body of law that governs brand names and other indicators of the source of a product or service, including company names. Many biotechnology companies are formed with an intention of conducting business nationally and internationally rather than being active in a purely local market. For these reasons, it is important to consider trademark law at the time the name of the biotechnology company is selected. Here are some general suggestions regarding name selection:

> **Practice Point**
>
> The PTO's trademark database may be searched for confusingly similar names at www.uspto.gov.

a) Trademark law is based upon first use of mark. As a result, when a proposed name is being considered, a review should be conducted to confirm that the name, or a confusingly similar name, is not already being used by others for a similar product or service. This search can be done in stages—first by a search of the proposed name using an Internet search engine (e.g., Google), then by a search of the U.S. Patent and Trademark Office database for confusingly similar marks, and finally by what is referred to as a "full" trademark search. Failure to search fully for the mark risks a claim for infringement or a need to change the name of the company after the company has built up recognition of the name. Many or most of the "good" names have already been taken. Consequently, it is important to allow sufficient time to select a name that is both available and protectable.

b) Trademark law places a premium on unique and clever names (e.g., Genentech, Amgen), rather than names that are descriptive of the product or service being offered.

c) A unique and clever name also may provide a better opportunity to obtain an Internet domain name consistent with the company's name. Many prospective investors, employees, collaborators, and so on will go first to the company's Web site to find out information about the company. If the Internet dot-com domain is not available for a particular name, then the Web site may prove difficult for others to find. Further, in order to protect the name, many companies will register similar domain names.

d) Federal trademark registration strengthens and adds to the trademark rights derived from use. For a trademark to be registered in the U.S. Trademark Office, there must first be "use" in a trademark sense. There is a procedure under U.S. trademark law that allows an applicant to file an application based upon a good-faith intent to use the mark. In most cases, use of this procedure is recommended as part of the company formation process in order to take advantage of the priority date achieved by filing (which will become effective if the registration process is completed) and to put others on notice of the company's intentions to use the name.

e) Trademark laws are territorial. Trademark rights in the United States generally do not provide trademark rights in other countries. Companies planning an international business should consider registration of their trademark in additional countries. The European Union provides a centralized trademark registration in 25 European countries.

f) Even though a particular company name is available from the relevant secretary of state, it may not be clear for trademark purposes. That is because trademark law will supersede state corporate law. So, for example, assuming the corporate name "Amgen" were available in a state other than California for a corporate name, the use of such name by a biotechnology company would infringe the trademark rights of the California corporation.

D. Capital Structure and Stock Grants

1. Introduction

In contrast to many small businesses that are owned entirely by the proprietors and the founders, the ownership structure for the typical biotechnology company is likely to be significantly more complicated. There are two primary reasons for this. First, biotechnology companies almost uniformly require cash and other support for product and corporate development; the sale or grant of company stock or stock rights can provide a means to generate that cash; and many biotechnology companies have no other way to obtain the significant funding they need other than selling their stock. Second, there can be more constituencies in a biotechnology company that want to have ownership in the company. Importantly, the converse also can be true. In other words, the company itself can benefit when various constituencies see themselves as having an ownership interest in the company. In short, ownership in the biotechnology company can create powerful incentives for founders, universities or other licensors of key intellectual property to the company, investors, employees, directors, and consultants. While there is an infinite degree of variation available to any particular biotechnology company, most of the companies seem to use the same set of tools in reaching an optimum capital structure. These tools are generally discussed below.

> **Practice Point**
>
> A "percentage interest of the company" can be subject to confusion—is that pre or post the issuance? Is it dilutable? On the other hand, a specific number of shares is clear.
>
> A capital structure with more shares each with a lesser value (e.g., a founder's round of 1 million shares) can facilitate the grant to employees and others of a significant number of shares of stock.

2. Securities Law Compliance

The offer, sale, and grant of stock and stock-based rights (including options, warrants, LLC membership interests, and convertible debt) are subject to both federal and state securities laws. All such offers, sales, and grants must comply with the requirements of full disclosure, and there must be an applicable exemption from the registration requirements of federal and state law. Failure to fully comply and to document compliance will create serious problems for the company, both in terms of potential claims from existing investors and from prospective new investors, who will often avoid investments where the company has not been in compliance with the securities laws because of the risks associated with potential claims. In addition, securities law governs the payment of commissions to raise funds for the company. The use of "finders" or unregistered brokers for this purpose can be a trap for the unwary. See Chapter V for a detailed discussion of this important topic.

3. Founders Stock, Restricted Stock, and Stock Options

Before outside funding is received, the company founders and other persons involved with the company will typically be granted an ownership interest in the company in the form of common stock. Sometimes other interested parties are provided with ownership in order to obtain needed technology or development skills.

The value of the company must be considered carefully when the founders and other early investors receive stock or are granted their shares (or other equity). If the company is truly a new start-up with no assets other than the initial capital contributions by persons granted equity in the founder's round, then the founder and others may be able to reasonably assert that shares acquired at par value or other modest valuation were acquired at their fair market value at that time.

> **Practice Point**
>
> All offers, sales, and grants of stock and stock-based rights are subject to state and federal securities laws.
>
> The use of "finders" or unregistered brokers to raise funds from investors can be a trap for the unwary.
>
> See Chapter V.

The founders and other persons receiving stock at the founder's round may purchase their stock for cash at the value established or contribute property to the company in exchange for the stock. If stock is awarded in exchange for services, then the award of such stock would constitute taxable compensation income to the person performing the services.

At the founder's round, consideration should be given to granting stock subject to vesting so that if a person acquiring the stock (e.g., founders, officers, directors, employees, consultants, etc.) leaves the company within a reasonable period of time (often three to four years) or prior to attaining agreed-upon milestones, then the company will have the right to buy back the portion of the stock that has not vested at the initial investment price. This can send a positive message to future investors and stakeholders that the founder and others are committed to staying involved with the company going forward, and to preserve shares for persons who are actively involved with the company.

This is done best through the use of restricted stock. Restricted stock provides significant advantages to the holder compared to option grants at the founding round. This is because the shareholder receiving the restricted stock owns the

> **Practice Point**
>
> Arrangements where founders or others are granted non-dilutive stock may create a problem in attracting sophisticated funding.

stock, and will own it free of restrictions as the stock vests. If the company is ultimately sold, then the holder has capital gains. On the other hand, if the company increases in value, an option holder must first exercise the option, which requires payment of the strike price as well as applicable taxes for non-qualified options. As a result, many persons holding options seek to defer exercise until a liquidation event. However, this can be problematic if the option holder must exercise an option that is scheduled to expire, if the holder leaves the company and the option provides that it must be exercised within a limited period after termination of employment, or if there is a sale, in which case the option holder will have ordinary compensation income.

The restricted stockholder and the company will typically enter into a restricted share agreement that memorializes the conditional nature of the grant of shares. Taxable compensation income is calculated on the difference between the fair market value of the stock received and the amount paid for such stock. The person receiving the restricted shares has the option of being taxed at the time the shares are received or at the time the restrictions lapse and the stock vests. If the recipient elects to be taxed at the time of grant of the shares, then he or she must file an election under Internal Revenue Code Section 83(b) with the Internal Revenue Service within 30 days of grant. If the recipient does not file a Section 83(b) election, then the recipient is taxed as the stock vests on the basis of the fair market value on such date. The 30-day period cannot be extended. The use of restricted stock must be examined carefully if the company is an S-corporation to ensure that a second class of stock is not created.

At later stages in the company's life cycle, restricted stock arrangements become less viable as the amount of cash that must be paid or the income imputed becomes prohibitive. In this context, stock options or warrants are more useful. Warrants are rights to purchase stock in the future, usually at a set price, which are not issued in compensation of employment or management. Options compensate an employee, advisor or director by giving the employee the right to acquire shares of the company's stock at a future date for a fixed price (i.e., the exercise price). There are two types of options: incentive stock options and non-qualified stock options.

Companies desiring to grant options typically first establish a stock plan that allocates a portion of the company's outstanding stock for use in granting stock options and restricted stock. Although the number of shares in a plan will vary from company to company, in many cases a typical range is between 10 percent and 20 percent of outstanding shares. Specific stock options are then approved by a company's board or compensation committee for grant to employees, directors, and advisors. Each option grant is reflected in a stock option agreement.

Companies granting options will need to ensure that the option grant is in compliance with the applicable blue-sky laws and regulations of the state where the company is located and the residence of the option recipient. (Many states exempt options granted under plans. Some states require filings and payments of fees.) SEC Rule 701 sets forth the requirements and limitations of an exemption from the federal registration requirement of options.

A requirement of incentive stock options is that they are made at no less than fair market value on the date of grant.[6] Pursuant to Internal Revenue Code Section 409A, non-qualified options are treated as deferred compensation, and if the option grants are not made at fair market value, then the provisions of that section apply to the option. Proposed regulations under Section 409A outline requirements for determining fair market value. With the new Section 409A rules, many early-stage, non-public companies are beginning to move toward granting options only a limited number of times (perhaps once or twice) per year so that the fair market value determinations (e.g., by third-party appraisal, self-valuation using Section 409A methodology, or other reasonable method) can be made with more care.

Incentive stock options are provided favorable tax treatment under the Internal Revenue Code. In connection with an incentive stock option, there is no income taxation to the employee on either the grant or exercise of the option.[7] Conversely, the employer does not take a compensation deduction upon the grant or exercise of an incentive stock option (although such a deduction would be available in those instances in which the employee makes a disqualifying disposition). When the incentive stock option is exercised, the holding period for capital gains taxes begins, and the employee may be entitled to receive capital gains treatment, as long as the stock is not sold during the two-year period following the grant of the stock option.[8] To obtain this favorable treatment and qualify as an incentive stock option, certain requirements must be met:[9]

> **Practice Point**
>
> **Restricted Stock**
>
> 1. Typically, common stock granted or sold is subject to repurchase right of the company if shareholder leaves.
> 2. Repurchase right is eliminated over time in reverse vesting or reaching of milestones.
> 3. Time period is often three or four years.
> 4. If stock is granted as compensation for services, shareholder can elect to be taxed at time of grant or as restrictions lapse.
> 5. If taxed at grant, shareholder must file 83(b) election within 30 days.

   a) Incentive stock options may only be granted to employees. (Non-employee directors and advisors may not be granted incentive stock options and may only be granted non-qualified options. Employees may also be granted non-qualified options.)

b) The options must be granted pursuant to a written plan specifying the number of shares to be issued and the class of employees eligible to receive options;
c) The shareholders must approve the plan within 12 months before or after the adoption of the plan;
d) Options must be granted within 10 years from the date such plan is adopted or the date such plan is approved by the stockholders, whichever is earlier;
e) Options must be exercised within 10 years of the grant (or five years in the case of a greater than 10 percent shareholder);
f) Option price must be at least equal to the fair market value of the stock on the date of the grant (or 110 percent of the fair market value in the case of a greater than 10 percent shareholder);
g) The option must not be exercised by or transferred to any person other than the employee during the employee's lifetime; and
h) The option holder must be an employee during the entire period between the date of the option grant and the date three months before the option exercise.

> **Practice Point**
>
> **Incentive Stock Options**
> 1. May only be granted to employees.
> 2. Strike price must be fair market value or greater at time of grant.
> 3. Limited by Internal Revenue Code requirements.
> 4. Option grant is not a tax event.
> 5. Option vesting is not a tax event.
> 6. Option exercise is not a tax event (employee must pay option price).
> 7. Stock held for one year receives long-term capital gains (if stock not sold within two years of option grant).

Employees and non-employees may be granted non-qualified stock options. There can be more flexibility with the non-qualified options, and these are subject to different tax consequences. For most early-stage biotechnology companies, the grant of a non-qualified option at fair market value and its vesting are not taxable events for either the option recipient or the company. However, ordinary compensation income is recognized by the option holder (and a corresponding deduction available to the company) when the option is exercised, based on the spread between the option price and the fair market value at the time of exercise. Upon sale of the stock issued upon exercise of the option, the difference between fair market value at the time of exercise (which becomes the basis of the stock) and the proceeds from the sale are taxed as long- or short-term capital gain income, and there is no corresponding deduction for the employer.

4. Common and Preferred Stock

In the context of a biotechnology company, it is typical to have a different series of preferred stock issued in connection with each successive financing round, although delay in issuing preferred until later rounds when the investors demand it will help keep a company's capital structure simpler and keeps all investors in an equal position. The founders, employees, consultants, "friends and family," and other early investors generally receive common stock. Subsequent investors receive Series A preferred shares, Series B preferred shares, etc., with each successive series being issued later in the company's life cycle. Venture capital funds and corporate investors will almost universally require preferred stock.

> **Practice Point**
>
> **Non-qualified Stock Options**
> 1. May be granted to employees and non-employees
> 2. Must be granted at fair market value to avoid tax on vesting
> 3. Grant of option is not a tax event
> 4. Vesting of option is not a tax event (if option granted at fair market value)
> 5. Exercise of option is a tax event—spread between option price and fair market value at exercise is taxable compensation income

A preferred class of stock is any class of stock which has rights that are not identical to the "common" class of stock. In general, common stock holders have the right to one vote per share, share in dividends as they are declared for the benefit of common stock holders on the basis of their relative ownership percentages, and share in any proceeds upon liquidation (after satisfaction of all prior obligations) based on relative ownership percentage of common stock. A preferred class of stock, in contrast, can have different voting powers, different liquidation preference amounts or priority, or other rights as authorized by the corporation's charter.[10] Within a separate class of stock, there may be one or more series of stock. Stockholders holding shares of the same class but different series may vote together with respect to matters affecting the class as a whole.[11] For further information regarding preferred stock, see Chapter V.

> **Practice Point**
>
> **Typical VC Preferred Stock Rights may include:**
>
> 1. Liquidation preference
> 2. Cumulative dividends
> 3. Anti-dilution rights
> 4. "Put" rights to force redemption (repurchase) of the stock

A brief summary of certain key terms pertaining to preferred stock is set out below.

a) Perhaps the most important right that preferred holders typically have in a biotechnology company is a liquidation preference. Preferred shareholders are typically entitled to receive payments in advance of the common stockholders upon any "liquidation" of the corporation. "Liquidation" usually includes not just a dissolution and wind-up of the company, but also its sale or a sale or exclusive license of substantially all the assets. While corporate law generally provides the company with the flexibility to establish the nature of this payment,[12] it is not unusual to require payment to the preferred shares in an amount equal to the initial preferred investment prior to distribution of the balance to common stockholders. (The preference on liquidation is sometimes set at multiples of the amount of the preferred shareholder's original investment.) In the event that dividends are cumulative and have accrued but are unpaid as of liquidation, it is typical that this unpaid dividend amount would be satisfied prior to any distribution to the common shareholders. Preferred shareholders will often then still share in the distribution to common shareholders on the same basis as if converted to common stock.

b) Preferred shareholders may be entitled to receive a specified dividend, which must be paid in full before any dividend can be distributed to common shareholders. This is typically a cumulative dividend that accrues but is not paid until there is a liquidation event. As a practical matter, the general expectation is not that the dividend will be paid in the ongoing conduct of the company's business, but that at the time of the sale of the company, the preferred holders will be paid the cumulative dividend as part of their liquidation preferences before any payment is made to the holders of common stock.

c) Another feature often found in preferred stock is anti-dilution rights included within the conversion rights of the preferred. Basically, anti-dilution rights are a mechanism that revalues the preferred holder's investment if there is a subsequent investment in the company at a lower price. There are two general methods used to calculate anti-dilution—full ratchet and weighted average (with full ratchet being more onerous to the company's early investors and founders). And there are usually exceptions to the application of these rights, such as stock options awarded pursuant to a specified incentive stock plan. The important practical points are that once anti-dilution rights are granted to one round of investors, all subsequent rounds will require them. And, if there is a subsequent funding round at a lower valuation triggering these rights, the effect on ownership allocation can be significant.

d) Finally, preferred shares can be subject to a right of redemption. For example, venture capital funds may require that, at the fund's option, the company buy back its shares at the greater of the investment price or fair market value a specified number of years (five is common) after the investment. The purpose of such clauses is often not to force a redemption but to provide the venture fund leverage to push the company to an exit, that is, a sale of the company.

E. Relationships with Early Participants

Other than intellectual property and access to capital, one of the most crucial aspects in ensuring the success of the biotechnology company can often be creating a strong nucleus of people involved in the company, including the founders, the board of directors, scientific advisory board, consultants, collaborators, and management. As noted in the introduction to this chapter, the company business attorney and patent attorney play a key role in the company as well.

1. Founders

The founders are the individuals with the vision of the company and the technical and/or business expertise to move it forward. (The title of a "founder" is an honorific title and has no formal legal significance, compared to a director or officer, which are discussed below.) While founders might have strong science credentials and expertise and a basic understanding of how to transform these ideas into business opportunities, they may lack the necessary business skills to staff, organize, and run a company. As a result, it is usually necessary to enlist the aid of a board of directors, officers, and employees to develop the vision and core technology to a point where significant value is created.

> **Practice Point**
>
> Arrangements where the founder licenses (rather than assigns) technology into the company either with or without a royalty may cause investors to lose interest because of the naiveté of the founder and are typically not tolerated by venture funds.

It is important to consider carefully the role and involvement of the founders in the company's activities. This role can vary based upon the status of the company, the founders' other activities, the founders' strengths and expertise, and the message that is desired to be sent as part of the company's fund-raising efforts. At one end of the spectrum, the founders might continue in university positions while chairing or serving on the company's scientific advisory board, while industry veterans are brought in to manage the company's day-to-day business. On the other end of the spectrum, the founders might join the company full-time in roles appropriate for the founders' abilities, such as chief scientific officer. It can be important for fund-raising purposes that the founders, at least in the early years of a company's existence, be actively involved in the company in some significant capacity, while at the same time not occupying positions more appropriately filled by others. If the company is in an early-stage or start-up mode and the founders are holding several positions that will be passed on to others as the company matures, it can often be helpful to note that roles being held by the founders are on a temporary or interim basis to make it clear that an expanded management team is planned when conditions warrant it and, importantly, that the founder recognizes the need to add capable management.

Care needs to be taken with respect to founders who are involved with academic research related to the company while also having a role with the company. Both founder and company must ensure that such relationship complies with applicable university conflicts of interest and conflict of commitment policies. These policies can apply at all stages of research, not just research involving human clinical subjects. In addition, careful consideration needs to be given to the university's intellectual property policy, as discussed below. See Chapter IV.

2. Board of Directors

The board is the nucleus of people who will guide the company and assist in decision making. While the board will delegate operational decisions to the company's officers, it will retain decision-making responsibility for the more significant decisions faced by a company (selling stock, entering into material agreements and developing the company's strategic plan). The rights and responsibilities of directors are set in statutes and case law as well as the corporation's charter and bylaws. To the extent possible, it is advisable from the beginning to enlist as strong a board as possible rather than simply relying upon the founders' family and friends.

In searching for board candidates, the founders should look for individuals whose skill-sets complement the founders' skill-sets. For example, the founders will likely have a scientific background, but perhaps have no experience running a business or raising money. Therefore, ideal candidates for the board of directors might include current or retired executives of companies in the same industry. Further, someone who has previously had success in raising money (perhaps a successful entrepreneur or a veteran of other start-ups) might also be a good candidate.

Operationally, an experienced board can help the founders avoid mistakes that have plagued other companies. It can aid in key decisions regarding personnel, developing strategic plans, staffing the scientific advisory board, selecting the appropriate management, and selecting candidates for other key positions. When the company is faced with decisions that involve a wide array of important aspects, such as strategic partnering, decisions among different product candidates and others, the board can draw on its collective knowledge and experience in making key decisions. Further, if the members of the board are experienced business people, they can temper some of the more unrealistic and overly aggressive ideas that a founder who is unschooled in running a company may have.

Equally important as assisting in operational aspects, the contacts of the individual board members can be helpful when attempting to access funding sources. A board with solid experience and credentials provides additional credibility when the company is discussing its prospects with prospective investors. Directors familiar with the local investment climate can also provide introductions to angel investors. If the company is lucky enough to attract a person who has successfully run a start-up company or has other experience in dealing with venture capital funds, then the company may be able to use those contacts to tap into potential funding sources.

3. Scientific Advisory Board (SAB)

For many biotechnology companies, the SAB plays key roles in focusing the concepts at the core of the company's science while lending credibility to the company. For these reasons, the recruitment of a strong SAB is often one of the early steps that biotechnology company founders take in building the company.

Ideally, the company will be able to populate its SAB with individuals who are recognized as the experts in their field. In many cases, the founders and other members of the company will have previously worked with potential SAB candidates through research collaborations or other academic and professional ventures. Other times, potential SAB members are identified through their publications and presentations. And in some cases, an individual is considered for the SAB for defensive reasons—because he or she is one of the most likely candidates for developing a competing technology or to preclude a competitor from engaging the individual as a consultant or SAB member.

SAB members are often compensated with a relatively modest annual cash retainer and stock options issued pursuant to the company's option plan. The number of SAB members often ranges from about four to seven. Meetings are often held twice yearly for a day or two per meeting. Experience has shown that including a fixed term in SAB appointments (e.g., three years) can provide an opportunity to evaluate the current and anticipated involvement of the SAB member and, accordingly, put into place a system to rotate off the SAB members as the company's science evolves.

4. Management

While the board and SAB can provide some of the expertise that the founders lack, by the nature of these groups, their role is not to conduct the day-to-day operations of the company. Many founders of biotechnology companies have scientific backgrounds. While the founders may have the vision, a solid management team will be needed to ensure that the vision is accomplished. Furthermore, adding management personnel allows the founders to concentrate more on the things they are the best at doing. A strong and experienced management team is often cited by sophisticated investors as the primary or a key factor in their investment decision.

a. Chief Executive Officer

One of the key hires by a company is a chief executive officer. This position might carry with it the title of president, but, no matter what the title, the role is the same—to take care of the business operations of the company. The CEO will need to lead, manage, and motivate the company. A good candidate for the position of a CEO will have experience in the field. This will provide understanding of the competitive landscape facing the company and insights into product development, sales and distribution issues, as well as contacts that can prove helpful in developing strategic alliances.

Depending on the size and development stage of the company, the CEO may have various roles. The CEO will take on responsibilities for implementing the strategies decided upon by the board. The CEO will work with the founders to ensure that the company's research and product development efforts stay on track and continue to progress. This person could also take the lead in negotiations with strategic partners, suppliers, consultants, and customers. In a smaller organization, the CEO might take on the functions that in a larger organization would be handled by a chief financial officer, human resources department, and others.

In any size organization, the CEO will be one of the company's primary "public faces" as the company deals with investors. This person will, together with the founders, identify likely investors, including venture capital funds, introduce the company to these investors, and (hopefully) negotiate terms pursuant to which investments will be made in the company. After investments are made, the CEO will need to keep in contact with the investors and make sure that they are kept aware of the company's progress and remain happy with their investment.

b. Chief Financial Officer

The chief financial officer plays a key role in the company. Besides the "standard" CFO job requirements, in an early-stage biotechnology company, the CFO must translate the vision of the founder, the board, and management into a supportable financial plan. Further, the CFO is responsible for clearly demonstrating to investors and funding sources that the company understands that it is spending their funds and will exercise appropriate controls to ensure the funds are wisely spent. The CFO also will work with company scientific personnel to ensure that grant applications for which the company may be eligible are timely filed and the company is in compliance with reporting and monitoring obligations under any resulting grants.

In smaller companies, the role of the CFO might be taken on by the CEO or another person, possibly a contractor on a part-time basis. In any event, the person performing this role will need to focus on top-level issues ranging from ensuring that the company remains in compliance with the financial covenants contained in investment documents to the more mundane functions, such as writing checks (at least in smaller organizations). In any size start-up organization, the person in charge of this function will need to monitor the rate at which the company is using cash (its "burn rate"), so the company is able to know well in advance when it needs to start the money-raising process.

c. Chief Scientific Officer

The founders often fill the role of the chief scientific officer of the company and head the company's research and product development activities. However, depending on the founders' skills, it can be prudent to retain an internal research and development expert to help move the company's technology along the product development pathway. This process will involve

Company Formation

coordination with the board of directors, the SAB, and the company's other researchers and scientists. In addition to coordinating research activities, a key duty of the CSO is the coordination of patent and intellectual property matters. As the company grows, this responsibility is often delegated to another senior scientist.

d. Clinical/Regulatory

Biotechnology companies operate in a heavily regulated environment and, depending upon their products, are subject to regulation by various government entities, including the Food and Drug Administration and the United States Department of Agriculture. Early in the company's existence, it will need to retain a specialist in the area of the company's product development to ensure the company follows the necessary steps in product development. Animal and human trials can be expensive and take months to complete. Adopting a well-thought-out plan and strategy with the assistance of qualified and experienced consultants and advisors can, in the long run, result in savings of cost and time. Usually, this is not a field the company can effectively handle without competent and experienced internal and/or external expertise.

5. Employees

While relationships between the company and its employees will be discussed in Chapter VI, a brief comment regarding one aspect of employment may be helpful. As biotechnology companies grow and evolve, their employee needs change. If the company is successful, it may need persons of increasing skill levels. If the company has trouble raising funds, then it may need to scale back. Consequently, it is important for a company to maintain flexibility. Long-term employment contracts and severance plans are typically luxuries that early-stage biotechnology companies are not in a position to commit to provide. Instead, in order to ensure necessary flexibility, many companies hire employees on an at-will basis so that the employees can be terminated at any time, subject to applicable state law. This result can be assisted by carefully crafted letters that offer employment, discuss the terms, and explicitly state that the relationship has no definite term. Then, if unpleasant employment decisions must be made, the company can do so in a way that balances its needs for survival and success with fairness for the departing employees.

It is standard practice that all employees are expected to enter into confidentiality agreements and invention rights agreements that protect the company's intellectual property and trade secrets. While non-competition agreements are desirable from an employer's perspective, the laws of many states limit their enforceability, and potential employees can often be reluctant to enter into non-compete agreements that could adversely affect their ability to obtain employment should they leave the company. Key points to include in an employee confidentiality and inventions rights agreement include the following:

- An obligation to protect the company's confidential information.
- An obligation to protect third-party confidential information received by the company.
- If there is an expiration of the obligations of confidentiality, then it should be at least 10 years to ensure that third-party information received with a 10-year term does not trigger a need to revise the employee agreements (among other reasons).
- Assignment to the company of all intellectual property created by the employee during the term of employment (and a reasonable period thereafter if based upon the company's technology or business). This may be limited by applicable state statute, for example, to work done during working hours, involving company assets, or related to the company's business.
- A process regarding patent assignments, review of patent applications, and other patent procedures.

F. Incubators

One of the many challenges faced by a newly created entity is deciding where to locate its facilities. The nature of a biotechnology company's product candidates might necessitate that a facility possess certain specialized characteristics to be suitable, including, for example, laboratory space, sophisticated data infrastructure, areas to grow cultures, hazardous waste removal services, clean-room manufacturing space, and a well-designed security system. A typical office building will not be able to provide what these companies need. Building out laboratory space or controlled manufacturing space can be very expensive, and generally is not a prudent use of the funds that the company worked so hard to raise.

Research facilities such as technology incubators have come to fill this need. In addition to the physical facilities incubators possess, they often offer services to their tenants to help the ventures succeed. These services may include assistance in developing a business plan, coaching provided by experienced business leaders, identification of and access to angel and venture capital investors, various types of seminars, and other services. A company seeking to locate in an incubator will be required to enter into a lease agreement that will have many of the customary provisions found in a normal office lease but often with more flexibility than a standard commercial lease. A landlord that is an incubator may require equity in its biotechnology company tenant (either outright or in the form of a warrant or option) or some royalties over a certain level of sales to compensate for the intangible values provided by the services it offers.

G. University Relationships

A biotechnology company will typically have relationships with one or more universities or other research institutions. When preparing to enter into discussions with a university, a good place to begin can often be the university's intellectual property policy, usually available on its Web site. Other research institutions will have policies and concerns similar to those of universities as set out in this section.

1. Faculty members, staff, and students at many universities are often subject to policies that generally provide as follows, subject to exceptions at various institutions:

   - All inventions made using university facilities, staff, property, biological materials or other assets, or made pursuant to a federal or other grant made to the university are owned by the university.
   - The result of any sponsored research is owned by the university. The sponsor may typically obtain a royalty-bearing license to any intellectual property resulting from the sponsored research. When research is sponsored, a significant administrative overhead fee is added on by the university.

- The out-licensing of the university's inventions is through the university technology transfer office.
- Faculty members can spend a portion of their time (often 20 percent—one business day of each week) consulting for companies at non-university locations. Intellectual property created while consulting and not using university facilities can be owned by the company for which the consulting is performed. Time spent at night and on weekends might not count toward the 20 percent.
- There are typically approvals required by the dean, department chair, and others.
- Universities have conflict of interest committees. Often, the emphasis is on reporting and transparency of arrangements involving the university's faculty and staff, although the committee may have the authority to limit any deemed conflict of interest. Faculty and staff members will periodically need to report their involvement with the company.
- The intellectual property policy will often specify the percentage allocation among the university, the department, and the faculty and staff of royalty and other license income attributable to university-licensed inventions.

2. Arrangements with universities are generally assembled with the general guidelines set out immediately above, subject to modification for each individual institution's requirements. For example:

   - If the company founder desires to retain a university position, then (unless the founder takes a leave of absence from the university) the founder must limit participation in the company so that it falls within the consulting exception. The founder's ability to use the consulting exception will depend upon the extent of other consulting arrangements that count toward the 20 percent.
   - If the company desires to out-license a body of technology developed by the founder at the university, the company will need to enter into a license agreement with the university. These licenses can be royalty-bearing, may include an up-front license fee, and so on. The university may negotiate for a portion of the company's equity. If the researcher conducting the research has an owner-

ship position in the company, then it is not uncommon for the researcher to be expected to waive his or her share of the resulting royalty income, and there will be a corresponding reduction in the royalty rate payable by the company.
- If the company desires to have the faculty member continue to conduct research at the university, it will need to enter into a sponsored research agreement with the university. The company will provide funding (including administrative overhead). The university will own the results. The company will need to out-license the results from the university either in a separate license or in the license referenced immediately above.
- If the company desires to develop its own proprietary technology, it must typically do so at its own labs or use commercial contract researchers, as opposed to use of university equipment and facilities.
- SAB members and other university consultants must be engaged through the consulting exception.
- All arrangements require the appropriate level of university approval.

See Chapter IV for more details relating to university technology transfer.

H. Early-Stage Company Agreements

1. Brief Review of Intellectual Property for the Non-IP Attorney

The creation, protection, exploitation, and enforcement of intellectual property rights is the key value-driver of a biotechnology company. For that reason, it is necessary for all attorneys engaged in the representation of the company to have, at the least, a general understanding of intellectual property law and the company's plans and strategies to develop, protect, exploit, and defend its intellectual property. In this regard, it is important to understand that the general "default" rule is that an item of intangible property, as opposed to tangible property, may freely be used by anyone. A protectable interest in intellectual property is established only if an item of intangible property falls into a protectable category, it is then protected pursuant to the specific requirements of that category, and any resulting rights are enforced.

The four primary types of intellectual property are: patents, trade secrets, trademarks, and copyrights. Each of these will be briefly addressed in turn. It is important to note that this summary is not only extremely abbreviated, but relates only to the laws relevant to intellectual property in the United States. In many contexts, emerging biotechnology companies will also want to seek international protection for intellectual property rights as well.

a. Patents

Much of the value of a biotechnology company is achieved through the aggressive patenting of the company's inventions and discoveries. Please refer to Chapter II for a discussion of this very important topic.

b. Trade Secrets

Many of the states in the United States have adopted the Uniform Trade Secrets Act or variations thereof. Under the Uniform Act, a trade secret is any information or process that derives value as a result of its secrecy and is subject to reasonable efforts to maintain its secrecy. The comments to the Uniform Act indicate that the definition was purposefully drafted in a broad fashion and is intended to include the concept of "know-how," which is occasionally used as a synonym for a trade secret.

In a biotechnology company, common trade secrets include inventions that have not yet been filed as patent applications, pending patent applications prior to publication, proprietary technical methods and processes, research results and data, and proprietary business and financial data. As noted above, a company desiring to protect information as a trade secret must use reasonable efforts to maintain it as a secret. Common techniques include, at minimum, (i) the requirement that all company employees, collaborators and third parties having access to the information first enter into a confidentiality agreement with the company covering the information, (ii) taking physical steps to limit internal company access to confidential information only to those persons who need access to such information, and (iii) logging and marking as "confidential" trade secrets made available to third parties.

A party that owns and protects a trade secret has the right under the Uniform Act to file suit with respect to any misappropriation of the trade secret. This suit can be for either an injunction or damages. Misappropriation of a

Company Formation

trade secret is essentially acquisition by improper means (e.g., industrial espionage) or improper disclosure or use without consent.

There are a number of means by which another party can come to use a trade secret without engaging in misappropriation. These include, for instance, independent discovery of the trade secret, reverse engineering (e.g., purchase of a product on the open market and then deriving the trade secret through an analysis of the product), a license from the owner of the trade secret, or obtaining knowledge of the trade secret through appropriate public means (e.g., observation and public use, review of published literature, etc.).

c. Trademarks

While trade secrets and patents relate to various types of information and/or inventions, a trademark is a means by which a trademark owner can distinguish its goods and services from those provided by others. A trademark can be a word, name, symbol or other device to distinguish goods and services from those offered by a competitor. Logos, sounds, images, colors, and various other devices can be used as trademarks. A "service mark" is a trademark for services. Service marks are generally subject to the same rules as trademarks. (A discussion of trademark rights relating to a company's name is set out at Section C.8.)

There are different types of trademarks based upon their relationship with the good or service provided. These types run on a continuum and are generally described as follows:

1. Arbitrary or fanciful marks that have no apparent relationship to the good or service that is being provided;
2. Marks that are suggestive of the good or service that is being provided;
3. Marks that are descriptive of some feature of the goods or services to be provided; and
4. Marks that are purely generic (generally not protectable as trademarks).

Owners of trademarks have three different means by which they can seek protection of their rights. By taking no action at all, the owner of a trademark can obtain common-law rights with respect to its trademark for which there is trademark "use." With respect to arbitrary and suggestive marks, the owner obtains rights immediately upon use of the mark. For descriptive marks, no rights are obtained until users have associated a trademark and the goods and services with which it is associated. In any instance, the common-law rights extend only to the geographic area in which the trademark holder is engaged in the business. Because the scope of common-law rights can be subject to significant debate, they are not often seen as a viable means of protecting significant intellectual property rights in a trademark. Further trademark "use" generally includes only commercial sales of products or services bearing a trademark. So, unless a biotechnology company is performing services for others or selling products bearing the trademark, the company will not have trademark "use" and will not be building common-law trademark rights. Simply raising funds and conducting research does not typically constitute trademark use.

Another means by which trademark rights may be obtained is registration of the trademark with a particular state. While the rights vary based upon applicable state law, such a registration has limited value in that it is tied only to the state in which the registration is found. Again, there generally must be trademark use to acquire rights under state trademark law.

Federal registration of the trademark with the United States Patent and Trademark Office (PTO) is the most advisable means to protect significant trademarks. An application for a federal trademark registration can be based on actual use or a bona fide "intent to use" a mark. The federal intent to use procedure is an especially effective tool for a biotechnology company with a long product development cycle. When a product candidate is identified, a product name can be selected (subject to appropriate clearance with the FDA) and an "intent to use" application filed with the PTO. While the application works through the PTO (a process that can take years), the priority of the company in the mark is established if there is ultimate trademark use leading to registration and the company can be more confident that its use of the mark, even on a product candidate, is clear of third-party rights. Ultimately, the mark must be used within the applicable time periods or the application is cancelled; but the process does allow the company to hold onto rights with respect to the mark for an extended period of time.

After a federal trademark registration has been granted, the ® symbol should be used. Prior to such a grant, the ™ should be used for trademarks, with ˢᴹ being used in connection with service marks. These designations serve to identify the trademark or service mark as such and are intended to place others on notice of the holder's intent to avail itself of trademark protections.

Finally, it is important for any trademark holder to enforce its rights. Once a federal trademark registration is obtained, the trademark holder can sue in federal court to protect its rights and seek various remedies, including injunctive relief, treble damages (in appropriate circumstances), and attorneys' fees.

d. Copyrights

Federal law establishes copyright protections to works of authorship (each a "Work") in categories including the following: (1) literary Works; (2) musical Works; (3) dramatic Works; (4) pantomimes and choreographic Works; (5) pictorial, graphic, and sculptural Works; (6) motion pictures and other audiovisual Works; (7) sound recordings; and (8) architectural Works.[13] Generally, copyright protection provides the owner with the exclusive right (a) to reproduce the Work; (b) to prepare derivative Works (i.e., modify original Work); (c) to distribute copies of the Work; (d) to perform the Work publicly; and (e) to display the Work.[14] There are various exceptions to these exclusive rights, and federal law makes it clear that copyright protection does not "extend to any idea, procedure, process, system, method of operation, concept, principle, or discovery, regardless of the form in which it is described, explained, illustrated, or embodied[.]"[15]

Copyright protection begins upon creation of a Work. The protections offered by federal law last for 70 years following the death of the author (for Works created after January 1, 1978). In the case of anonymous works or those created for hire, the copyright endures for a term of 95 years from the year of its first publication, or a term of 120 years from the year of its creation, whichever expires first.[16]

While copyright protection is automatic, providing copyright notice and registration with respect to the Work can strengthen the rights of the owner. Depending upon the form of the Work, the notice of copyright protection can be affected by various means. For instance, in a written work, the notice could simply consist of the "©" symbol or the word "Copyright," the year of first publication of the Work, and the name of the owner of copyright in the

Work.[17] Like the notice, registration of a copyright is not required for protection, but registration increases the rights of the copyright owner and is generally a prerequisite for filing suit.[18] Timely registration can permit the owner to sue for statutory damages and attorneys' fees.[19]

In the case of a biotechnology company, copyright often comes into play with respect to computer software and printed, promotional, and graphic works. When these materials are authored by third parties (e.g., other companies, moonlighters, or independent contractors), it is important for the company to ensure that it acquires the copyright to the work, not simply the physical manifestation of the work itself. The copyright can be acquired from the author pursuant to a copyright assignment. Simply paying for the work does not acquire the underlying copyright. Although some agreements provide that works done by third parties are "works for hire" and any resulting copyrights are owned by the company, the specifics for "works for hire" generally do not apply to such situation. Instead, it is necessary that there be a specific assignment of the copyright.

2. Confidentiality Agreements

Negotiation of confidentiality agreements, to some degree, tracks the discussion of trade secrets. While the subjects included in confidentiality agreements have become somewhat standardized, these agreements can have varying specific terms and can be crafted to either favor or disfavor disclosure and more strongly protect the disclosing party or the recipient. In general, there are a few key terms to consider in reviewing or preparing a confidentiality agreement.

First, it is important to consider the scope of the coverage. From the perspective of the information recipient (i.e., the one who is bound by confidentiality), the more narrow the scope the better. The most narrow scope is probably a description that tracks the scope of the applicable trade secret law. To some extent, trade secrets are already protected by applicable trade secret law and the agreement has little additional impact (other than to support claims under the trade secret laws that the purported trade secret has been subject to reasonable protections) if it only covers the same scope. The scope, however, may be broadened and the parties may include information that, while not technically within the definition of a trade secret, may be restricted as to use or disclosure by the recipient. This information may include certain customer lists, data formulations, processes, or other information that (for some reason or another) is not accorded full protection under the trade secret laws.

Second, there are typical exceptions to the coverage of the agreement. Usually there is a list of exceptions, which (to a lesser or greater degree) track the exceptions contemplated by the comments to the Uniform Trade Secrets Act. These exceptions often exclude the following types of confidential information from coverage of the agreement: confidential information that (a) is or becomes part of the public domain, through no unauthorized act or omission of the recipient; (b) is lawfully in the recipient's possession prior to disclosure by the disclosing party; (c) is disclosed to the recipient independently by a third party not subject to a confidentiality obligation; (d) is independently developed by the recipient without access to the disclosed confidential information; and (e) is disclosed by the disclosing party to a third party free of any confidentiality obligation or restriction upon use. These exceptions can be coupled with standards of proof, which may limit their use (for the benefit of the disclosing party). For example, the disclosing party might only allow an exception for independent development when such independent development can be proved by "clear and convincing" evidence.

Third, it is important to express the recipient's obligations with respect to the information received. Typically, this includes a restriction on the recipient's ability to use the information in a manner outside of the limited use permitted by the disclosing party. Also, the recipient may be obligated to return all documentation containing or derived from disclosed confidential information to the disclosing party upon such party's request. Of course, there should be an express prohibition on the recipient's disclosure of the confidential information.

Finally, it is important to consider the term of the agreement. Really, the agreement can have two terms: the period during which confidential information may be disclosed, and the period during which the obligation to maintain confidentiality survives. On the first point, a shorter term can appropriately narrow the scope to fit the anticipated duration of the transaction. Of course, a narrow term may also create a trap for the unwary, who assume that any information can be safely disclosed at any time, as long as there once existed a confidentiality agreement on the subject matter. On the second point, the nature of the information disclosed should be considered in determining the length of the obligation. With respect to trade secrets that may maintain value far into the future, it may be appropriate to have no limitation on this term.

A disclosure of confidential information under a confidentiality agreement carries with it several risks. One such risk is that once disclosed, the information can be diffused either purposely or unintentionally among the recipient's personnel and those with whom they are in contact. A second risk is that the recipient will know the disclosing party's plans, technologies, and intellectual property position and can modify its own plans to reflect that information. Third, the terms of the confidentiality agreement will typically provide a permitted basis for the recipient to use the disclosed information for its own purposes (e.g., after the expiration of any duration of obligations). And fourth, there is a risk that the recipient will use the information in violation of the agreement, either inadvertently or intentionally. Possible ways to balance these risks with the need to engage in substantive discussions and relationships that require such disclosure can include being careful to whom information is disclosed and then to disclosing only the minimum amount of information necessary for the particular project at that specific time.

While most attention is given to the protection of a company's trade secrets, it is also important to note that a company needs to be selective with respect to the trade secrets that it accepts from others under an explicit or implicit obligation of confidentiality. At the least, acceptance of such information obligates the company to protect the information's confidentiality. But further, acceptance may "taint" the company personnel who have access to the third-party information, thereby precluding them from taking steps which they might have taken if they had not had access to that information. Some companies, when dealing with third-party information that closely overlaps their internal information, may have the information reviewed by an independent consultant or limit employees who have access to the third-party information to those who will not likely be engaged in overlapping research.

A sample mutual confidentiality agreement appears in Appendix A at the end of this chapter.

3. Material Transfer Agreements

Material transfer agreements are typically entered into when one party delivers materials and information related to those materials to another party, which will use or evaluate the materials for the purposes provided in the agreement. These agreements can be executed frequently by biotechnology companies, and companies may establish forms that they prefer (much like a confidentiality agreement). These forms assume that a confidentiality agreement already exists between the parties, as the parties are likely to have exchanged some information or had confidential discussions in order to determine if the further step of transferring materials is an appropriate next step.

While there are various forms for these documents, they tend to cover the same general subjects. The agreement will identify the type and quantity of material that is to be provided. The recipient may request representations concerning the transferor's rights in the material and lawful authority to deliver the material. Similarly, the recipient may also make representations or covenants with respect to its authority to fulfill its obligations, its use of the materials (that is, the scope and nature of any evaluation and obligation to report with respect to any such evaluation), and limitations on further transfer of the materials. Often representations by both parties will be accompanied by disclaimers with respect to matters not intended to be covered by such representations. One such disclaimer that is typically included is that the transferor does not make a representation or warranty that the use of the materials by the transferee will not infringe the intellectual property rights of any third party. Also, the transferor may disclaim any warranties with respect to merchantability or fitness of the materials for any particular purpose. Similarly, the recipient may desire to include similar disclaimers with respect to its deliveries under the agreements. These representations and covenants may be supported by indemnification obligations. These indemnification provisions are much as would be found in other commercial agreements and can be subject to similar limitations. For instance, the parties may impose limits on the scope of damages and exclude claims for matters such as punitive damages or lost profits.

The agreement will also cover issues related to property ownership. Even though the transferor usually retains ownership of the materials and licenses the transferee to use the materials, this is not universal.

There is even more variance with respect to any improvements, inventions, and data with respect to the materials. Transferors may be concerned that the use of the materials by the transferee will result in a patentable invention that could limit the rights of the transferor to grow and expand its intellectual property position. To address such concerns, the transferor can refrain from providing materials to the transferee until the transferor has filed for patent protection over the transferee's intended use or unless the transferee has agreed to assign to the transferor rights to any such inventions. Access to data developed by the recipient is also a point of negotiation. The transferee will often desire to withhold such information from the transferor, while the transferor may seek such data for its internal purposes and to provide to investors, prospective investors, and others. These positions are negotiable, and the parties may settle upon a situation where one party retains ownership while the other is given a license with respect to the improvements, inventions, and data. In a similar vein, the transferor normally wants to impose restrictions upon the use of any information derived from the evaluation of the transferred materials.

4. Research Collaboration Agreements

Although Chapter IX discusses research arrangements in more detail, it is appropriate to provide a brief summary of these agreements here, as they are likely to be encountered relatively early in the life cycle of the typical biotechnology company. Generally, these agreements are executed to protect the intellectual property of both parties when they are engaged in a collaborative research project. For instance, these types of agreements could be entered into between two biotechnology companies; a biotechnology company and a pharmaceutical or medical device company; or a biotechnology company and the government or a university.

Even though some of these agreements can be mutual, it is easier to think of these documents in terms of having two parties each with distinct roles: a sponsor who provides materials or intellectual property for the research, and the researcher who conducts the research that is subject to the agreement. Typically, these agreements will either supplement or contain provisions similar to confidentiality agreements and material transfer agreements. There are a few additional elements that are found in most agreements of this nature.

First, the agreement will establish the purpose of the arrangement. That is, it will describe the parties, the scope and purpose of the research (this will likely include a detailed protocol for the research), who will conduct the research (including the individuals responsible, or investigators), and the anticipated results in terms of milestones, deliveries, or term. Because of the degree of uncertainty involved in endeavors concerning scientific research, it is not uncommon for these agreements to establish a committee populated by representatives of each party to deal with unforeseen circumstances during the term of the agreement. For instance, the agreement may form a committee or designated individuals to monitor progress toward milestones and to make adjustments to the protocol as necessary.

One of the critical reasons to execute such an agreement is to delineate clearly the ownership of intellectual property related to the research project. This includes both the property that exists before the collaboration and property that is developed (independently or jointly) during the course of the collaboration. In addition to allocating the ownership rights of the parties in these various types of properties, the agreement typically will regulate the process for protecting these rights. For instance, the agreement may establish procedures for dealing with infringers, procuring patent protection, and publishing results of any research.

Finally, these agreements contain many of the same provisions that are included in agreements of a commercial nature. For instance, these agreements typically contain indemnification provisions and procedural mechanisms concerning default and termination. In addition to these provisions, these documents will contain "boilerplate" provisions relating to choice of law, severability, and similar matters. Although it is typically included within the boilerplate provisions, it may make sense to ensure that a clause is included establishing an independent contractor relationship. Given the nature of these arrangements, there is a risk that the parties would be viewed as partners jointly pursuing the same end. While a provision in the agreement may not alleviate this risk as it involves third parties, it can establish a clear understanding between the parties themselves.

I. Positioning for an Exit

As described in this chapter, a biotechnology company will likely have many key constituencies, each of which may have differing ideas as to whether or when an "exit strategy" should be discussed. Given the capital-intensive nature of these companies, however, the discussion of possible exit will likely come fairly early with the addition of venture capital or other professional investors. While founders, employees, and friends and family may be willing to delay these discussions, professional investors will require that this discussion take place in advance of making any investment. The term "exit strategy" generally refers to a strategy to plan a means by which investors can achieve a return on and of their investment. Given the low likelihood that a biotechnology company will pay a dividend adequate to provide sufficient return on capital (or any dividend at all), most exit strategies focus on one of two primary avenues: initial public offering (IPO) of the capital securities of the biotechnology company, or sale of the equity interests in the biotechnology company to an acquiring entity.

It is always best to plan for the end at the beginning. Even though return of capital can come through liquidation of the company, redemption by the company, or sale of equity interests to other investors, these are not generally the exit strategies that biotechnology companies and their investors strive to achieve. For this reason, we focus on strategies related to a sale of the company and public offerings.

> **Practice Point**
>
> Begin with the end in mind. In order to organize and develop the company properly, it is vital to have an exit strategy in mind at the beginning. That strategy can affect many decisions in the development of the company.

Given that these are two exit strategies commonly considered by biotechnology investors, founders and managers should keep these strategies in mind even at the earliest stages of the biotechnology company's formation and operation. Anyone who purchases the biotechnology company's securities (whether through an IPO or acquisition) will expect that the company has properly documented transactions related to both capital transactions and its operations. For instance, it is routine to require that an opinion of counsel be delivered in connection with either of these exit events. Such an opinion would need to cover matters such as those related to the legal organization of the company, the authorization of the company and officers to execute transactional documents, and the fact that all prior security issuances complied with applicable corporate law and securities laws. This means that activities that appear fairly mundane at the time (e.g., maintaining of corporate record books, holding annual meetings, completing Form D and related state law filings, etc.) can take on increased significance in the face of an acquisition or IPO. It is critical that the significance of this information be conveyed at the earliest stages to ensure these important activities are not ignored in favor of activities that are (justifiably) seen as more directly important to the business (e.g., licensing arrangements, research and development, etc.).

While some biotechnology managers who are new to the process may be surprised to find that problems with "paperwork" such as corporate records and Form D filings could impact their company's ability to engage in an IPO or sale transaction, most would not be surprised that documentation surrounding operational details could have the same impact. It should be anticipated that an underwriter, in the context of an IPO, or buyer, in the context of a sale, will conduct thorough due diligence of the biotechnology company. While a portion of this due diligence will rely upon interviews of the company's personnel, it will be expected that the company's documentation supports the assertions made by these individuals. For example, in either of these instances, there will be high expectations that the ownership of all intellectual property has been documented properly. These same types of concerns relate to various operational aspects of the company, and the company should be prepared to present written documentation with respect to all significant aspects of its operations, including areas such as intellectual property ownership, licensing terms, confidentiality agreements, and employee confidentiality and inventions rights obligations; compliance with environmental, immigration, employment and tax laws; internal controls for accounting systems; and contractual relationships with suppliers, vendors, collaborators, and investors.

The point, of course, is that the biotechnology company must prepare itself constantly for these events. It is critical to establish appropriate procedures and controls to ensure that the company will be able to respond quickly and credibly to due diligence requests about its business.

While these preparations are common to both an IPO and an acquisition, an IPO imposes some additional obligations on the company (many of which may exist in the context of an acquisition by a public company). These additional obligations include matters such as meeting the requirements of the applicable listing entity, meeting requirements for compliance with securities laws, and operating in a manner that will not result in adverse accounting treatment.

The two major listing entities (the New York Stock Exchange and the Nasdaq Stock Market) have requirements that are similar to each other and some of the applicable securities laws and regulations, but they are not uniform. In addition to establishing financial requirements, both major listing entities regulate matters such as the degree of director independence required for the issuer's board of directors, as well as the existence and composition of the board's audit committee.

In addition to the traditional disclosure and reporting requirements imposed upon public companies, the Sarbanes-Oxley Act, passed in 2002, imposes a number of additional rules regarding public companies. This Act covers items such as limitations on loans to insiders, reporting with respect to the issuer's internal controls, and financial statement certification by certain of the issuer's officers.

Finally, any public reporting company must prepare its financial statements in compliance with generally accepted accounting principals (GAAP). Although most larger private companies already report the majority of their activities in compliance with GAAP, complete compliance with GAAP can require significant changes in some areas. For start-up companies, GAAP issues can arise in connection with the way that employee stock options and revenues are reported. The debate over employee stock options has been public for a number of years and is ongoing. Issues of revenue reporting can be more subtle, but can arise in those situations, among others, where the biotechnology company receives payments based upon the satisfaction of certain milestones. These and other atypical contracts may result in unique accounting issues that need to be addressed in a fashion consistent with GAAP for those companies that intend to take advantage of the public markets in the medium-term future.

The above summary is intended to highlight issues for biotechnology companies that intend to either conduct an IPO or be acquired by a public company. Frequently, biotechnology companies can plan best for these events by preparing for them well in advance with the advice of counsel and accountants skilled in the representation of companies intending to follow these exit strategies.

Notes

1. Comments with respect to matters of taxation in this chapter are given with respect to general matters only and should not be relied upon with respect to any specific situation. All taxation comments in this chapter are subject to conditions, limitations, and restrictions. Further, tax authorities are subject to change, retroactively and/or proactively, and any such changes could affect the validity of comments set out in this chapter. Any tax advice contained in this chapter is not intended or written to be used, and may not be used, for the purposes of avoiding penalties that may be imposed on any taxpayer by the Internal Revenue Service or for promoting, marketing or recommending to any other party any tax matters addressed in this chapter. Each reader should obtain tax advice with respect to all matters of taxation discussed in this chapter.
2. *See* 26 C.F.R. § 1.1361-1.
3. *See* LARRY E. RIBSTEIN & ROBERT R. KEATINGE, RIBSTEIN & KEATINGE ON LIMITED LIABILITY COMPANY, § 1.2 (2d ed. 1995).
4. 26 U.S.CA. § 422(b).
5. Section 2115 of the California Corporations Code; *see also* VantagePoint Venture Partners 1996 v. Examen, Inc., 2005 WL 1047285 (Del. Supr. May 5, 2005).
6. 26 U.S.C. § 422(b)(4).
7. 26 U.S.C. § 421(a).
8. 26 U.S.C. § 421(b).
9. 26 U.S.C. § 422.
10. *See, e.g.*, § 151(a) of the Delaware General Corporation Law.
11. *See, e.g.*, § 242(b)(2) of the Delaware General Corporation Law.
12. *See, e.g.*, § 151(d) of the Delaware General Corporation Law.
13. 17 U.S.C. § 102.
14. 17 U.S.C. § 106.
15. 17 U.S.C. § 102(b).
16. 17 U.S.C. § 302.
17. 17 U.S.C. § 401.
18. 17 U.S.C. § 411.
19. 17 U.S.C. § 412.

Appendix A
Mutual Confidentiality Agreement

This Mutual Confidentiality Agreement (this "Agreement"), is entered this [DAY] day of [MONTH], 20[XX] ("Effective Date"), between ABC, Inc., a _____ corporation ("ABC") and XYZ, Inc., a _____ corporation ("XYZ"). XYZ and ABC are collectively referred to herein as "Parties", in singular or plural usage, as required by context.

1. **Purpose of This Agreement.** The intent of this Agreement is for the Parties to discuss the possibility of [DESCRIBE PROPOSED TRANSACTION] (the "Transaction") and to protect the confidential nature of such discussions.[1] In order to facilitate discussions contemplated hereunder, the Parties may receive from, and provide to each other, certain Confidential Information, as defined below. Each Party's information is proprietary, secret, and confidential, and will be disclosed by one Party (the "Disclosing Party") to the other Party (the "Receiving Party") only on the following terms and conditions.

2. **Definition of Confidential Information.** The term "Confidential Information" shall mean all trade secrets that are disclosed by the Disclosing Party to the Receiving Party to the extent that, (a) when disclosed in writing, the disclosure is marked as "confidential"; or (b) when disclosed orally, the disclosure is accompanied contemporaneously by a writing describing the nature of the information disclosed and its confidential nature.[2]

3. **Exceptions.** Confidential Information shall not include that which: (a) is or becomes part of the public domain, through no unauthorized act or omission on the part of the Receiving Party[(provided, however, that no Confidential Information shall be deemed to be a part of the public domain merely because it may be derived from one or more items of information that are a part of the public domain)]; (b) is lawfully in the Receiving Party's possession prior to disclosure by the Disclosing Party[, to the extent that such prior possession is confirmed by clear and convincing evidence]; (c) is disclosed at any time to the Receiving Party by an independent third party not subject to a confidentiality obligation to the Disclosing Party; (d) is independently developed by one or more employees of the Receiving

Party with no access to the disclosed Confidential Information[, to the extent that such independent development is confirmed by clear and convincing evidence]; or (e) is disclosed by the Disclosing Party to a third party free of any confidentiality obligation or restriction upon use.

4. **Obligations of Protection.** The Receiving Party shall take and maintain proper and appropriate steps to protect the Confidential Information received. Dissemination of Confidential Information shall be limited to directors, officers, employees, contractors or agents (collectively, "Agents") that are directly involved with discussions contemplated by this Agreement, and even then only to such extent as is necessary and essential in connection with the Transaction. The Parties shall inform their Agents of the confidential nature of the information disclosed hereunder and cause all such Agents to[(a) execute agreements similar to this Agreement in favor of the Disclosing Party and the Receiving Party and (b)] abide by the terms of this Agreement. [The Receiving Party shall be responsible for any breach of this Agreement by any of its Agents and shall, at its sole expense, take all reasonable measures (including legal proceedings) to restrain such Agents from prohibited or unauthorized use or disclosure of Confidential Information.][3]

5. **Obligations of Non-disclosure.** The Receiving Party shall not disclose the Disclosing Party's Confidential Information to any unauthorized person or entity without prior express written consent of the Disclosing Party or unless required by law or court order. If the Receiving Party is required by law or court order to disclose Confidential Information of the Disclosing Party, then the Receiving Party shall give the Disclosing Party prompt notice of such requirement so that an appropriate protective order or other relief may be sought.

6. **Authorized Use and Ownership of Confidential Information.** Confidential Information will be used by the Receiving Party only in connection with evaluation of the Transaction; no other use will be made of it by the Receiving Party, it being recognized that both Parties have reserved all rights to their respective Confidential Information not expressly granted herein. Except as expressly provided herein, no license or right is granted hereby to the Receiving Party, by implication or otherwise, with respect to or under any patent application, patent, claims of patent or proprietary rights of the Disclosing Party. [The Parties agree that no warranties are made

expressly or implicitly regarding accuracy or completeness of Confidential Information provided under this Agreement.]

All documents that contain Confidential Information shall remain the property of the Disclosing Party, and all such documents, and copies thereof (no matter the media of storage), shall be returned or destroyed upon the request of the Disclosing Party. Documents prepared by the Receiving Party using Confidential Information of the Disclosing Party, or derived therefrom, shall be destroyed upon request of the Disclosing Party, confirmation of which shall be provided in writing.[Even if a document is requested to be returned or destroyed, the Receiving Party may keep one copy of any document in the files of its legal department or outside counsel for record purposes only.]

7. **Term of Disclosure and Duration of Confidentiality.** The period for disclosure of Confidential Information between the Parties under this Agreement shall be [two] year[s] from the Effective Date (the "Disclosure Term"). With respect to Confidential Information disclosed during the Disclosure Term, the obligations imposed by this Agreement shall endure during and after the Disclosure Term, subject to the provisions in Section 3.[4]

8. **Injunctive Relief and Additional Remedy.** The Disclosing Party acknowledges that the injury that would be suffered by the Receiving Party as a result of a breach of the provisions of this Agreement would be irreparable and that an award of monetary damages to the Receiving Party for such a breach would be an inadequate remedy. Consequently, the Receiving Party will have the right, in addition to any other rights it may have, to obtain injunctive relief to restrain any breach or threatened breach or otherwise to specifically enforce any provision of this Agreement, and the Receiving Party will not be obligated to post bond or other security in seeking such relief.

9. **No Business Obligation.** It is expressly understood and agreed that neither Party shall have any legal duty or obligation to the other Party with respect to either entering into any future business transaction, including any arrangement involving the Transaction, except as may be set forth in a mutually acceptable written agreement which has been fully executed and delivered between the parties with respect to the Transaction. Neither Party shall be under any obligation to provide the other Party with Confidential Information.

Company Formation 135

10. **General Provisions.**

(a) Entire Agreement. This Agreement constitutes the entire agreement between the Parties and supersedes any prior understandings, agreements, or representations by or between the Parties, written or oral, to the extent they related in any way to the subject matter hereof.

(b) Succession and Assignment. This Agreement shall be binding upon and inure to the benefit of the Parties named herein and their respective successors and permitted assigns. No Party may assign either this Agreement or any of its rights, interests, or obligations hereunder without the prior written approval of the other Party.

(c) Counterparts. This Agreement may be executed in one or more counterparts, each of which shall be deemed an original but all of which together will constitute one and the same instrument.

(d) Headings. The section headings contained in this Agreement are inserted for convenience only and shall not affect in any way the meaning or interpretation of this Agreement.

(e) Notices. All notices, requests, demands, claims, and other communications hereunder will be in writing. Any notice, request, demand, claim, or other communication hereunder shall be deemed duly given if (and then two business days after) it is sent by registered or certified mail, return receipt requested, postage prepaid, and addressed to the intended recipient as set forth below:

If to _____   If to _____

XYZ: _____   ABC: _____
    Attn: Attn:

Any Party may send any notice, request, demand, claim, or other communication hereunder to the intended recipient at the address set forth above using any other means (including personal delivery, expedited courier, messenger service, telecopy, telex, ordinary mail, or electronic mail), but no such notice, request, demand, claim, or other communication shall be deemed to have been duly given unless and until it actually is received by the intended recipient. Any Party may change the address to which notices, requests, demands, claims, and other communications hereunder are to be delivered by giving the other Party notice in the manner herein set forth.

(f)   Governing Law. This Agreement shall be governed by and construed in accordance with the domestic laws of the State of _____ without giving effect to any choice or conflict of law provision or rule that would cause the application of the laws of any jurisdiction other than the State of _____. In the event of any dispute under this Agreement, the prevailing Party shall be entitled to recover its attorneys' fees and court costs from the other Party.

(g)   Amendments and Waivers. No amendment of any provision of this Agreement shall be valid unless the same shall be in writing and signed by the Parties. No waiver by any Party of any default, misrepresentation, or breach of covenant hereunder, whether intentional or not, shall be deemed to extend to any prior or subsequent default, misrepresentation, or breach of covenant hereunder or affect in any way any rights arising by virtue of any prior or subsequent such occurrence.

(h)   Severability. Any term or provision of this Agreement that is invalid or unenforceable in any situation in any jurisdiction shall not affect the validity or enforceability of the remaining terms and provisions hereof or the validity or enforceability of the offending term or provision in any other situation or in any other jurisdiction.

(i)   Construction. The Parties have participated jointly in the negotiation and drafting of this Agreement. In the event an ambiguity or question of intent or interpretation arises, this Agreement shall be construed as if drafted jointly by the Parties and no presumption or burden of proof shall arise favoring or disfavoring any Party by virtue of the authorship of any of the provisions of this Agreement. The word "including" shall mean including without limitation.

IN WITNESS WHEREOF, the undersigned have entered into this Agreement as of the Effective Date.

XYZ

XYZ, Inc.

By: _____
Printed Name:_____
Title:_____

ABC

ABC, Inc.

By: _____
Printed Name:_____
Title:_____

Notes

1. The scope of this purpose clause will impact the "use" restrictions found below. A narrow purpose clause, however, could create the suggestion that information not delivered in connection with such narrow purpose was not intended to be protected by the agreement.

2. This definition is fairly narrow, as it is limited to "trade secrets" and must be accompanied by written notice of confidentiality. This language can be made much broader to cover items that, while not technically trade secrets, are also deserving of protection. This definition could be broadened to include specific items such as patent applications, inventions, research plans, financial reports, business plans, customer data or other similar information.

3. These exceptions are fairly typical, except for the last one, which is not uncommon. The last exemption may be appropriate when the agreement only applies to trade secrets. The bracketed language has the effect of narrowing these exemptions. Finally, it is notable that disclosures required by law are not excluded from the coverage of this agreement (as the other exclusions are) and are dealt with under Section 5.

4. It is more common to have a term imposed upon the duration of the obligations of the parties. This might make sense for disclosures of financial information, which becomes stale after a few years, but does not make sense for trade secrets, which may maintain value for many years into the future. From the perspective of the disclosing party, it is better to make the obligations indefinite, subject only to the exceptions already contemplated above.

Chapter IV

Acquisition of Biotechnology—Technology Transfer[1]

Hugh B. Wellons
LeClair Ryan, a Professional Corporation
Roanoke and Blacksburg, Virginia

With Special Thanks to Michael J. Martin, TechTransfer Associates

One of the first critical steps in the creation of any technology company is acquisition of the core technology. This is especially critical for a biotech company. Biotech products are often very complex, involving many building blocks from various sources. Very few successful biotech products are invented "in whole cloth" by one person. Commonly, critical components are invented at and owned or controlled by universities and nonprofit companies. Specific federal and state laws and institutional rules often govern who owns this technology and how this technology can be used or transferred outside of the institution where it was created. We cannot provide comprehensive information, because the laws and rules differ between location and institution and are in flux constantly. We can provide current best practices, highlight the theories behind these rules, and provide issue-spotting and research tips for the practitioner attempting to discover what factors influence the negotiation to acquire technology by his or her client.

This issue of transfer of technology is further complicated by ownership questions. Individuals and companies do not always own what they think they own. We will provide a very brief overview of ownership issues, with reference to a more detailed explanation of this in Chapter II, dealing with patent prosecution. This chapter is written primarily from the point of view of the licensee, although we try to provide insight into the perspective of the licensor as well.

A. Technology Creation

Creating technology is not transfer of technology, although it is at its heart a form of "acquisition" of technology. Approaching this in the right manner is especially critical in biotechnology, both because the stakes are so high and because the process of creating that technology often takes a very long period of time. It is not unusual, for example, for isolation of a single protein and determination of its best use to take many years. Opportunities for errors in recordkeeping and protecting technology are magnified. Also, there often is a "race to the finish line" in developing treatments or cures for various illnesses and medical conditions. We will list below some primary steps that any inventor should take in this process. Please refer to the more detailed commentary in Chapter II.

1. Protecting Propriety of the Invention in the Early Stages

a. Confidentiality Agreements

Protecting propriety of an early-stage invention is critical. Confidentiality agreements are almost always necessary. These not only protect against someone stealing an idea, but they often are necessary for an invention to qualify for patent protection. In general, a disclosure of an invention to a third party may disqualify that invention from U.S. patent protection if the application is filed more than one year after that disclosure. Perhaps more damaging, disclosure of an invention to a third party prior to patent filing may disqualify the invention from international patent protection immediately. This is not a hard and fast rule, and it depends on the level of disclosure and possible relations between the parties. This problem can be cured, however, by executing a confidentiality and nondisclosure agreement prior to the disclosure. Typically, this is a separate agreement between unrelated parties, but in an employment relationship it sometimes is a clause in the employment agreement.

b. Who Was First?

(i) *Workbooks or laboratory notebooks*—The question of who first invented a new product, process or component comes up all the time. In those cases, evidence is submitted of workbooks detailing the steps in the invention process. Since it is common for life science inventions to take many years and to have many steps in the process, this review can be very cumbersome. Often, the best protection an inventor has is her workbook or laboratory notebook, written in ink, filling every consecutively numbered page, which details by date experiments attempted and results. This is discussed in more detail in Chapter II.

(ii) *When and what resources?*—Another record that is important for an individual inventor is a detailed record of where and when she developed the invention and what equipment she used. Inventions by an employee at her place of employment on matters relating to her employer are generally owned by the employer under the "works made for hire" doctrine. We will discuss that in more detail below and in Chapter VI. Often, however, an individual has an idea that is unrelated to her specific employment. These inventions sometimes are owned by the individual, if she is careful in how she develops and records the invention. For example, many universities specify that anything done on behalf of the university or using any university facilities is owned by the university. A graduate student

> **Practice Points**
>
> 1. Keep accurate and detailed workbooks of the development, in ink, dating work, leaving no blanks, showing all mistakes and "blind alleys," and have it signed by another knowledgeable in the field.
> 2. Never disclose seminal parts of what you are doing without a written NDA in place.
> 3. Check employment agreements, outside funding, and policies to determine who really owns the IP.

or professor working on a product that is outside the scope of university activities and a biotech company working with a university employee should be careful to develop that invention offsite and keep detailed records of how that invention was developed, or they may find that the university has a claim to her invention. This may not help in a commercial setting, however, because many employment contracts provide that any invention in a broad spectrum by an employee during the term of employment belong solely to the employer. Moreover, the university may have a claim to the invention nonetheless: many academic institutions have conflict of interest policies that prohibit a faculty member from directly accepting remuneration for industry-sponsored research; the institution may deem the remuneration part of the professor's salary, and it may claim intellectual property rights in any resulting invention. Again, please see Chapters II and VI.

c. Company Records

Companies have a similar interest in detailed records of the invention. Companies should have specific procedures that employees must follow in order to ensure that employees' inventions are owned by the employer and remain protectable. Employers should audit these procedures on a regular basis. Employers also should interview employees on a regular basis (at least annually) to ask what projects each is working on and to ensure that records are being filed and kept, so that the employer can enforce its rights in that invention. It is important to keep IP strategy in mind when considering new direction or a new invention. As early in the inventing process as practical, an employer should perform a patent and/or copyright search to ensure that the proposed invention is not infringing on another product. It is never too early to plan a strategy or defense relating to continued development of a possibly infringing invention. The earlier that a company can check this, the earlier it can plan its strategy. Finding a possible infringement early allows the company to make a decision of whether to continue to invest money in the product, look at licensing alternatives, or try to design around the potential infringement. Any company's IP development strategy should include examination of both internal and external IP with an emphasis on how to design around that IP (for defensive purposes regarding the internal IP) and identifying likely new areas of development in hopes of defining them first and filing a patent. See Chapter II.

2. Keeping Necessary Records

Workbooks and laboratory notebooks always should be bound volumes with preprinted, consecutively numbered pages. Avoid spiral or any other types of notebooks from which pages can be removed easily. Entries should be written in ink; pages should be filled from top to bottom. When completed, workbooks and laboratory notebooks should be signed by another who is knowledgeable in the field and kept under lock, with access to keys limited, in order to support testimony that the records have not been changed. All work should be dated and described carefully. In addition, it is as important to keep records of mistakes and "dead ends" as the successes, in order to demonstrate the process used to create the invention.

3. Who Owns What? (Employer v. Employee and JV Issues)

a. Work Made for Hire

(i) *Copyright law*—Work made for hire is fundamentally a copyright issue. Generally, a work prepared by an employee within the scope of his or her employment or a work specially ordered or commissioned for use as a contribution to a collective work is a work made for hire. If an invention is a work made for hire, the employer or person for whom the work was prepared is the initial owner of the copyright, unless there is a written agreement to the contrary signed by both parties. As we indicated, however, this applies specifically to copyright law, and most intellectual property developed in biotechnology is protected by patents or trade secrets.

(ii) *Shopright rule ≠ work made for hire*—Under patent law, an employee's invention may not belong to the employer except in certain circumstances. Unlike copyright law, the employee-employer relationship does not necessarily create an ownership right in an employee invention. However, if an employee was hired for the purpose of inventing a product or the employee is acting under specific instructions to invent a product, the employer probably owns that product. Most universities now have contracts giving the university sole ownership of any inventions using university resources. This often trips up faculty who leave one university for another, only to find out that the invention she intended to continue developing or perfect at the new place actually belongs to the university she just left.[2] Even if the employee owns the product, however, the "Shopright Rule" of patents provides the employer who funded the work with a non-exclusive license to use, manufacture, and sell the invention without additional compensation to the employee. Of course, in many biotechnology settings, this non-exclusive right is of marginal benefit to the employer because it erodes the exclusivity that is often central to a biopharmaceutical business model. Put simply, many biotechnology products require large capital investments and bear considerable risk of failure; as a result, high margins associated with market exclusivity are needed to justify the risks. If an employee can simply sell rights to others, the value of the invention will be drastically reduced. In addition, employees generally own inventions made on their own time and at their own expense, even if they relate to the employer's business. The employer generally has no rights to such an invention. All of this helps explain why most biotech companies, particularly those with venture capital investors, require that employees enter into an employment agreement that makes it clear what belongs to the employer and also includes a prior assignment of any such inventions to the employer. See Chapter VI.

(iii) *Employee v. contractor*—An important question frequently raised in connection with intellectual property ownership is whether an inventor actually was an employee or a mere independent contractor. In making this determination, the IRS looks primarily at three factors:

1. *Behavioral Control:* To what extent does/did the company control the person's behavior, looking at both detail of work instructions and training? The rules affecting independent contractors are different.
2. *Financial Control:* How does the company control the business aspects of the person's job, looking primarily at who decides how and when the person is paid?

3. *Type of Relationship:* How is the relationship documented, how "permanent" is it, and what benefits are provided?[3]

The rules affecting independent contractors are different. The "work made for hire" doctrine applies differently to third-party contractors. A product made by an independent contractor does not belong to the person who contracted its creation unless the contract specifically says so. Without the benefit of contract terms, an invention developed by an independent contractor belongs to the contractor, although the party who paid for it may retain a license to use and manufacture it. Similar to the rights retained by the employee in the case of a patentable invention, this right to use is of limited benefit to the party who paid for it, because the independent contractor can sell the invention to the competition. Although slightly different, the same general analysis applies to patentable inventions. Once again, a contract spelling out the ownership rights of the parties is critical.

b. Employee Rights

As indicated above, employees have broad rights under copyright and patent law. If a patentable invention is not within the employee's scope of employment, and there is no contract providing ownership or rights to the employer, the employee may own that invention outright. Similarly, an employee generally retains ownership of an invention, subject to a non-exclusive license in favor of the employer, even when the invention was made in the course of employment. Also, filing for patent protection requires the signatures of the individual inventors. In most cases, the company itself cannot sign the patent application; it must have the employee's signature in order to complete the application. Accordingly, this may create negotiating leverage for a difficult employee/inventor. Again, the ready answer is an employment agreement that specifies the rights of both employee and employer. Any well-advised biotechnology company has all of its employees and contractors under an agreement that covers this issue. See Chapter VI.

c. State Laws

Many states have their own rules regarding intellectual property ownership in the employment context. You should look for these laws under statutes relating to intellectual property, a specific statute related to trade secrets, or sometimes under the labor code provisions. An example of this is California law, which provides that everything that an employee acquires or creates by virtue of her employment, except compensation due her, belongs to the employer.[4] However, California law also provides that any employment agreement that requires an employee to assign or offer to assign her rights to an invention to the employer shall not apply to an invention that the employee developed entirely on her own time without using employer equipment, supplies, trade secrets, etc., except where the invention results from work performed on behalf of the employer by the employee or reduces to practice or anticipates research or development of the employer.[5] California, like many states, also provides that an employment agreement that goes further than the state law is considered against public policy and unenforceable.[6] This makes it very important that a practitioner understands the state laws where the company operates and is careful in selecting the law that applies to the employment contract. See Chapters II and VI.

d. Canadian and European Union Laws

(i) *Canada*—In Canada, as a general rule, an employee owns her invention even if it was made during the course of employment, unless the employee was hired expressly for the purpose of inventing.[7] Similarly, as a general rule, faculty in Canada own their own inventions, not their university employers. This general rule can be avoided by an employment agreement that deals with the issue specifically and assigns ownership rights to any invention to the employer. The agreement also must require that the employee cooperate in the prosecution of the patent or litigation relating to it. A similar rule and a similar solution would apply to industrial designs. Copyright ownership is similar to the United States law. The question is whether the work was done by the employee in the normal course of employment and also who controlled the work in question—whether the ultimate responsibility fell on the employer or the employee. Courts also may use an economic reality test to determine whether there was in fact an employment relationship and also whether the employer treated the inventor as an employee. Canada also considers "moral rights," which involve the right of an author to remain associated with his/her work even after an assignment of rights has occurred.[8] Employers operating in Canada should include a waiver of these rights and any assignment as a part of the agreement. Canada also may allow a reversionary interest in the inventor in some cases.

(ii) *European Union*—Employee ownership of an invention is not completely consistent across the European Union, and laws governing employee rights differ from country to country. One important point to note is that the EU, in general, is a "first to file" jurisdiction, so when there are two inventors, the first to file for patent generally is considered to own it. That provides employers a mechanism for protecting rights to employee inventions, although it may not help in the case of an invention that an employee has not disclosed to the employer. For more details, please see the discussion in Chapter XIX.J.

e. Trade Secrets

(i) *What are they?*—Trade secrets generally are state law rights recognizing that some inventions are not suitable for patent or copyright protection, either because of the nature of the invention or because the inventor may wish to avoid public disclosure of the details so that it might extend the secrecy of the invention. The typical example of a trade secret is the formula for Coca-Cola, which has been kept secret for many decades. If the formula were ever copyrighted (or patented, if that were possible), then it would have to be disclosed in the filing. This would leave the specific formula open to infringement in countries that do not recognize international copyright or patent laws. After the patent or copyright expired, it also would allow anyone to make a product identical to Coca-Cola and to compete with Coca-Cola with that product. We see that now with generic drug makers competing with the pharmaceutical companies that developed the innovative product. The issue is somewhat more complicated in the biotechnology industry. The Food and Drug Administration until now has taken the position that it usually cannot adequately ensure that a biologic produced by a generic manufacturer is truly identical to its patent-protected counterpart. Nonetheless, many consider it inevitable that regulatory changes will permit the first follow-on biologics to enter the marketplace soon. In fact, both the EU and the FDA have approved follow-on biologics under limited circumstances. Please see the discussion of generic drugs and follow-on biologics in Chapter XII.A.1.d.

(ii) *Not as helpful in biotechnology*—Trade secrets generally are not as applicable to biotechnology companies, because most products developed by biotechnology companies for therapeutic use must go through an extensive disclosure process, testing, and trials in order to be approved for manufacture and commercial sale. However, some parts of a complex product or manufacturing process may be suitable for trade secret protection. Particularly if follow-on biologics win regulatory approval, the value of trade secrets to the manufacturer of the original product will increase.

(iii) *Uniform Act*—The Uniform Trade Secrets Act has been adopted by many states and may be seen as the standard.[9] This Act defines as a trade secret any information, including formulas, patterns, compilations, techniques, etc., that derive an actual or potential economic value from not being generally known or ascertainable in the marketplace, and that is subject to reasonable efforts to maintain secrecy. The Act allows the owner of such a trade secret to enjoin actual or threatened misappropriations. The Act also provides for actual damages in the case of misappropriation and exemplary damages if the misappropriation is willful or malicious. However, the owner must demonstrate reasonable steps to protect the secret. Trade secrets generally are considered to be less helpful than federal intellectual property rights, such as patent or copyright, but they may be useful, especially in a case in which a theft of data has occurred before a patent or copyright could be filed or in the case of a method or component that will not have to go through the regulatory approval process.

f. Joint Venture Ownership

It is common practice in the biotechnology industries for parties to collaborate in developing a final product or, in some cases, a common component or discovery tool needed by both parties in their different products. This is often done through joint ventures. Collaboration allows parties to combine strengths and build shared knowledge, lines of communication, and trust, potentially setting the stage for a more extensive later collaboration or combination. Every joint venture agreement is different, because the resources of the parties and the technical, legal, and commercial challenges facing them are unique. The contract controls any joint venture. This applies to ownership as well as other provisions of the joint venture. If the contract does not clearly spell out who owns the result and how, then the resulting technology sometimes is considered to be owned by both parties. Accordingly, if party A and party B jointly develop protein Y, and their agreement does not specify ownership and license terms, then once protein Y is fully developed, A and B might be in a race to the marketplace, competing against each other. Joint venturing often is a useful way of developing or perfecting a particular product. It is usually only the first step in that process, however, and much thought needs to be given to the contract and who controls the resulting product (or who controls which part of the resulting product[s]) very early in the process. This subject is dealt with in much more detail in Chapter IX.

4. Patent Filing: Protecting an Invention and Limiting Others' Use[10]

a. Why File a Patent?

Patents provide the most robust of any of the federal IP protections. Patents exclude others from a technological space and often are a prerequisite for attracting money. The filing procedure is complicated and arcane, not a practice for the unexperienced, but the result, absolute exclusion of competition in a specific commercial space, often is worth the trouble and expense.

b. Patent Requirements

In general, in order to qualify for a patent, an invention must be useful, new, and non-obvious. It also is critical that the patent application meet the technical requirements of patentability, including a description of the invention specifically, so someone expert in the field could re-create it. In a biological invention, deposition of the new material in a publicly accessible depository can assist in satisfying certain of these requirements.

c. Patent Claims and Rights

A patent does not provide a right to make and sell something, but it permits exclusion of others from making and selling what the patent claims cover. It is not freedom to operate. A patent may be granted on a product that, because it includes other restricted (especially patented) material, cannot be made without third-party approval. For example, a compound produced in part with a patented genetic process (belonging to another party) may receive a patent. However, before the inventor can legally make and sell that compound made by the patented process, she must obtain a license or other right from the owner of the protected genetic process.

Patent rights generally expire 20 years after the earliest patent filing date. This sometimes can be extended if there was a delay in the granting process.

d. Types and Stages of Patents

(i) Types of patents include the following:

1. Utility patents are the most common type, and they protect compositions of matter, apparatuses, and methods for making compositions of matter or apparatuses.
2. "Business methods" are a form of utility patent covering a way of doing something, often including mathematical formulas. This is found most often in the financial industries, but it also might apply in bioinformatics or other biotech-related fields.
3. Design patents cover ornamental design.
4. Plant patents cover asexually reproduced plants.

(ii) Stages of patent filing include:

1. *Provisional Patent Application.* This application is not examined. The filing fee is lower. It establishes a priority date for the invention, but its filing date typically does not affect the patent term. However, a utility patent application claiming the benefit of the filing date of the provisional application must be filed within one year of filing the provisional patent.

2. *Utility Patent Application.* This is an application that is examined and can mature into a granted patent. A utility application can claim the benefit of the filing date of a provisional application.
3. *Continuing Patent Application.* This is a patent application that claims the benefit of an earlier-filed application, but it must have much in common with that earlier filing.
4. *Divisional Patent Application.* Sometimes the Patent Office places restrictions on a patent filing, limiting the claims. The claims that were excluded can be pursued in the divisional patent application.

e. Patent Prosecution

Patent "prosecution" begins after the application is filed. This is the process for pushing the application through to patent issuance. There are basically four possible steps in this process.

(i) Patent Office review and rejection of the claims of the patent application. Although a few applications are accepted as filed, the majority are rejected for technical reasons, questions about the claims, or both.
(ii) The inventor (and her attorney) must draft a response to that rejection and in some cases negotiate directly with the examiner. The response generally amends the claims and rebuts the examiner's position on the material points. Turnaround time for answering an objection is three months, although up to three additional months' time is available for a fee.
(iii) The Patent Office then makes a final determination of whether to allow or reject each claim in the patent.
(iv) If the inventor does not want to accept the final decision of the Patent Office, she may appeal that decision to the Board of Patent Appeals and Interferences, which requires a formal briefing process or filing a continuing application.

Please see Chapter II for more detail on this subject.

f. Post-Issue Considerations

In order to maintain any rights you have in a patent, you must pay the required renewal fees. Maintenance fees are due in the United States 3.5, 7.5, and 10.5 years after the U.S. issue date of the patent. Virtually every other country in which the patent is filed will have renewal fees due, on different schedules. There are companies that specialize in performing this administrative task. In some cases in which a drug goes through a lengthy FDA approval process, the inventor may petition the Patent Office to extend the life of the patent.

g. Foreign Patent Filing

A U.S. patent is good only in the United States. In order to pursue patent rights in other countries, the inventor should file directly in those countries or file an international patent application under the PCT (the Patent Cooperation Treaty, a treaty between most developed countries) within one year of the initial patent application filing. This, in effect, sets your priority date in the non-U.S. countries. However, that alone merely stays the tolling of the time to prosecute the application. After the PCT filing, the inventor has 30 months to elect in which countries she wishes to file, paying fees for prosecution in each country. In the EU, the inventor can elect to pay a separate fee for each country or an EU fee, with a reduced country fee. The key point here is to plan well in advance which countries are good potential markets and will provide reasonable protection, so that the patent filing makes business sense.

5. Possible Effects of Outside Funding

a. Ownership

Development of a human therapeutic biotech product takes a long time and is expensive, so a combination of grants, outside investments, and revenue-generating deals are usually necessary to fund it. Licensing or outright acquisition of technology is a faster route, but that, too, may require capital. Money always comes at a price, and that is certainly true with outside funding of IP. Funding by commercial entities usually requires either (i) ownership or rights to future ownership in the company developing the product, or (ii) ownership, license or other rights in the technology being developed. The sources, cost, and dilutive effect of outside capital must be factored into the inventor's business plan to ensure that the full effect is well understood.

Research funding from a nonprofit institution also may come at a price: many nonprofit corporations limit the extent to which researchers they sponsor may own an interest in companies that license the resulting technology. An example of this is the Howard Hughes Medical Institute, which generally limits the percentage of equity a sponsored researcher can hold in a company benefiting from that research. (See Section IV.D.4.d. below.)

In general, the most financially favorable approach to acquiring rights in IP, at least in the short run, is to license the IP from an academic or research institution in return for a royalty stream back to the licensing entity. This avoids dilution of company stock and creates no payment obligation unless the product sells. This approach is most commonly acceptable to a university or other nonprofit research institution, although our experience is that the licensor generally also requires a small amount of equity, milestone payments, or other "kicker." However painless it seems at the outset, in the long run, it may be financially detrimental to burden a product (particularly a composite product comprising IP from multiple licensors) with significant royalty obligations. In the worst-case scenario, a product may carry a chain of royalty-bearing licenses leading from the ultimate developer back to the original inventor through multiple sublicensees. This is the so-called "royalty-stacking" problem. A company that has been overly profligate in incurring royalty obligations may find, when the time comes to enter into a commercialization collaboration with, for example, a major pharmaceutical partner, that the royalty rate offered by the commercial developer will barely cover other existing royalty obligations—leaving little or no revenue for the biotech company.

Another possibility is to transfer the technology to a new company owned jointly by the party controlling the technology and the party investing the capital. This limits the intellectual property and revenue-sharing rights to the technology being developed. It does little good, however, for a small start-up company to develop technology in which a larger, more able company has

> **Practice Points**
>
> 1. If acquiring an IP owner, look carefully at typical license reps and warranties. You want similar IP protection in the stock or asset purchase agreement.
> 2. If IP is the primary motivation, the buyer should push for asset purchase to avoid or mitigate a future claim of past infringement resulting from use of the key IP. The seller will want a stock purchase to shed that same risk.

co-exclusive rights. The smaller company will lose that game, although in some cases the larger company loses also, because the smaller company, having the same "freedom to operate" with respect to the technology, can either undercut prices or license the IP to a more able competitor.

b. Public Domain

Some nonprofit companies still have in their charters that any inventions they fund go into the public domain. In addition, some nonprofits still push inventions in this direction, due in part to a mission to spread knowledge, but possibly also in fear that a successful invention will create revenue that might disqualify the company from nonprofit status. This must be discussed early in the process, if the funding entity is pushing for all or part of the invention to go into the public domain. A possibly persuasive argument against that inclination is that technology in the public domain generally will not receive the massive additional funding needed to obtain regulatory approval, because the parties that would go to the trouble and expense of doing that have no economic incentive to do so. This is particularly true for novel human therapeutics, a mainstay of biotechnology, where the FDA approval process alone requires years and millions of dollars.

c. Manufacturing or Sales Restrictions

Many entities place manufacturing or sales "strings" on sponsored technology. Many universities have rules governing the manufacture or sales of technologies that they sponsored. Federal law (see discussion of Bayh-Dole Act below under IV.B.9) places a manufacturing limitation on products developed using federal funds. It generally requires that a product developed with federal funding and sold in the United States must have some substantial portion of that product manufactured in the United States, to the extent practicable.[11] The funding agreement may provide other restrictions, so that must be reviewed carefully.

B. Forms of Technology Transfer

1. Acquisition of Owner

a. *Acquiring the Owner*

Perhaps the simplest way to acquire technology, besides creating it, is acquiring the owner of the technology. Acquisition of any business generally takes two forms, stock purchase or asset purchase. Stock purchase (often accomplished by way of merger) refers to acquiring all of the equity interest in that company, and therefore owning the company as the sole shareholder. Asset purchase involves acquiring specified assets—sometimes substantially all of the assets—of a business and assuming identified liabilities and obligations. Excellent standard forms for these agreements are provided by the ABA in its "Model Stock Purchase Agreement and Commentary" and "Model Asset Purchase Agreement and Commentary." If the owner of the technology has already created a market or has developed certain goodwill in the company itself, it sometimes makes sense to acquire the whole company. In most cases, it is more advantageous to the buyer to acquire the assets of the company, especially if you can acquire only the assets you want. This can limit the buyer's potential exposure for contingent liability, provided the agreement is drafted carefully. There are many factors that need to be considered in choosing a stock or asset form for the deal, and that detailed consideration is beyond the scope of this book. In the case of transfers of patents, it may require that assignments are filed with the Patent and Trademark Office in order to confirm that transfer.

b. *Employing the Owner*

Another common method of acquiring technology, which will be described in more detail below, involves receiving an assignment or license of the technology from the individual(s) who developed it. Often, the inventor(s) will also be hired as a consultant or employee to continue developing the technology and to prevent competitors from gaining access to the expertise. Sometimes the inventors require equity interest in the acquirer or other accommodations, depending on the value of the technology acquired and the negotiating leverage of the parties.

2. Assignment

Another relatively simple method of acquiring technology is to have it assigned.[12] Assignment differs from license and sublicense, as described below, because it is a transfer of all rights to that technology. The assignee is the new effective owner of the technology. Acquirors generally prefer to "own" technology so they do not have to manage any reservation of rights or comply with ongoing financial and performance obligations. Some academic institutions and nonprofit companies, however, have a policy against assignment and only license or sublicense, creating some tension in dealing with potential buyers. The Bayh-Dole Act, described in more detail in IV.C.8 below, discourages assignment of IP generated in government-sponsored research. The terms for an assignment vary widely and, as referred to above, often require a way for the assignor to share in the profits and opportunities of the technology through equity interests, employment, wages and benefits, or even a form of royalty stream. Most assignment documents, however, are straightforward. Assignment is the means usually used with employees or independent contractors to document that the owner of the copyright or patent filed is the company that paid for its development.[13]

3. License and Sublicense

a. *Common form of transfer*

A common form of technology transfer is a license or a sublicense. Most of the operating systems and computer programs that we use on a daily basis are made available under a license or sublicense agreement. Even open source programs are distributed under a limited license that places certain responsibilities on the user. Similarly, much of biotechnology acquisition is done by license or sublicense.

b. *Alternative to assignment*

Many academic institutions and nonprofit companies have policies against assigning technology they own. In those cases, the needed technology is licensed. In many cases, all the user needs is a license, often a nonexclusive license. If your client has a product that is complete except for a single process, for example, then it probably does not care if other people can use that

Acquisition of Biotechnology—Technology Transfer

process as long as it can, too. In those cases, a very limited license will suffice. In other cases, your client may need an exclusive worldwide license, which effectively prohibits anyone else in jurisdictions where patent protection is maintained from using the product. The amount an acquirer will pay for a license will be dependent upon a number of factors, including the strength of the patent claims, the level of development of the patents and related products, the degree of exclusivity, geographic scope, whether others are competing for rights to the technology, and other matters.

Typical license terms include:

- Parties
- Recitals
- Definitions
- Property licensed
- Scope of the license
- Exclusivity
- Uses
- Territory
- Right to sublicense
- Follow-on and later-developed technology
- Term and renewal of license
- Termination
- Deliveries
- Retention of rights
- Payments, including fees, royalties, stock (options, warrants), milestone, etc.
- Audit rights
- Reporting and marketing responsibility
- Reps and warranties of the inventor
- Indemnification
- IP protection
- Insurance
- Assignability
- Amendments
- Alternative dispute resolution (ADR)
- "Boilerplate" language

c. Sublicense

A sublicense is a derivative of the original license. A sublicensee, in most cases, cannot hold more than the license grants, no matter what the sublicense says. It is important to scrutinize the license to ensure that the licensor can provide the rights needed, and that the sublicensee will have adequate protections against losing its rights due to the fault of the sublicensor/original licensee. In this regard, it is useful if the original license contains "springing license" terms: namely, if the original license terminates through the fault of the licensee, any sublicenses that had been granted by the defaulting sublicensor are automatically converted to direct licenses on identical terms between licensor and sublicensee. In other words, the sublicensor steps into the licensor's shoes with respect to any sublicensees.

> **Practice Point**
>
> Practically, experimental use as an exception to patent exclusion does little good in a commercial setting, except for possibly allowing "Beta-testing" to see if the IP works in that setting and using patent rights of other parties during clinical development.

4. Fair Use Agreement

a. Fair Use and Experimental Use

(i) *Fair Use Doctrine*—The Fair Use Doctrine under the Copyright Act provides that it is not infringement under certain circumstances to use a copyrighted work.[14] The definition of fair use is very vague. The factors considered are the purpose and character of use (especially whether it is for a commercial purpose), the nature of the copyrighted work, the amount or portion of the copyrighted work used in comparison to the whole produced, and the effect of the use on the market for the copyrighted work. Key considerations, in addition to those listed in the Act, seem to be the financial benefit to the user and the detriment, if any, to the owner. Most commercial uses of copyrighted property will not qualify for the fair use exception.

(ii) *Experimental Use Exception Under Patent Law*—A corollary to the Fair Use Doctrine under copyright law has been developed by the courts under patent law. It is the experimental use exception. Generally, a purely scientific research use of a patented technology, especially for educational purposes, is considered to be an exception to infringement under patent law. This dates back to a famous decision by Joseph Story, a later Supreme Court Justice. In *Whittemore v. Cutter,* 29 F.Cas. 1120, 1121 (no. 17, 600, c.c.d. Mass. 1813) (Story, J.), Story identified an exemption from patent infringement for "philosophical" experimental use. He felt that an exemption for philosophical (scientific) uses was at the very core of the constitutional mandate to create a patent system that promoted the progress of "the useful art." As courts over the years have interpreted this exemption from infringement, academic and non-profit institutions were generally the winners of these cases. However, the exception has been limited, especially in the case of *Madey v. Duke University.*[15] Under recent rulings, it is not clear that academic institutions or nonprofit companies have a special standing with regard to the exception for infringement. It appears that courts will continue to look at whether the use of the patented technology was really for the sole purpose of gratifying curiosity, scientific inquiry, or mere amusement. There also is a statutory exemption for use or import of specific types of biotech inventions for the purpose or preparing for or carrying out clinical trials or otherwise preparing for a federal filing.[16] Outside of those exceptions, the experimental use exception may not exist. This is limited in comparison to other treatments of this doctrine around the world.

(iii) *Experimental Use Doctrine in Europe and Japan*—Experimental use is a broader and more recognized exception from patent infringement in most of Europe. Some European courts even have hinted that only a commercial use under disguise is prohibited. Patented products sometimes are even allowed as a test or base against which clinical trials can be conducted, although that is a minority position in Europe. The point is that the experimental use exception is much broader in Europe than in the United States.

Similarly, Japan provides a statutory exception to experimental use, although there is no definition of what constitutes an "experiment." In practice, experimental use also is broader in Japan than in the United States. For more details on other countries' treatment of experimental use and fair use, please see discussion at Chapters II and XIX.

b. Fair Use Agreements

Since fair use and experimental use are not crystal clear in the United States, it is relatively common for companies and institutions to enter into what are often called fair use agreements with owners of technology prior to using that technology for further experimentation or development. For example, a university performing research on blood-clotting factors may wish to use constructs owned by a pharmaceutical company. Historically, university researchers would do nothing, relying on the experimental use doctrine. Recently, in the wake of the *Madey* case, researchers appear to have become more cautious, and sophisticated institutions are increasingly likely to contact the pharmaceutical company to obtain an agreement that the limited experimentation and development they will perform constitutes fair use or experimental use, and therefore is not infringement. Sometimes these agreements provide a limited license of any results back to the pharmaceutical company. They seldom if ever provide any rights to the university beyond the rights to use the patented or copyrighted material for limited research purposes.

c. Doctrine and Agreements' Effect on Intellectual Property Ownership and Due Diligence

Anyone contemplating an acquisition of rights to technology should perform substantial due diligence into the components of that technology and any rights reserved by third parties. Since fair use and experimental use provide no commercial rights to the property, it is possible that the resulting technology, because it includes a component patented by a third party, may require a license from that third party to be "free and clear" with respect to the technology needed. Negotiating this at the "back end" can be difficult. Due diligence should determine all component parts of the technology to be acquired and consider also all possible fair use agreements that may have been executed relating to the developed technology. Some fair use agreements are so broadly written that they provide a license to all technology developed in a project, including related technologies, whether or not the recipient actually uses the patented fair use technology covered by that agreement. In other words, a university could obtain a fair use agreement for a particular construct patented by a pharmaceutical company, decide that that construct is not the best approach to take, and yet still find that the resulting product that it develops is licensed in part to the pharmaceutical company. These agreements must be reviewed carefully.

5. Public Domain

Some technology is already in the public domain. It is not unusual to find that a component of a larger piece of technology, or a possible replacement component for unavailable technology, is already in the public domain, because it was developed at an academic institution or nonprofit company and put in the public domain intentionally or accidentally. It is not unusual to find, for example, that needed technology, while "protected" by a patent, actually was fully disclosed in an academic treatise long before the patent was filed, nullifying the patent rights. Accordingly, a search of academic papers and other records may help to "free up" needed technology that is otherwise unavailable.

Similarly, it is important that an acquirer determine whether all or part of the technology she desires to acquire is already in the public domain, as that can have a significant impact on the outcome, or even the need for negotiations with the ostensible owners of the technology. As we indicated above, public disclosure of the critical parts of intellectual property may disqualify that property for patent protection. A more detailed discussion of what constitutes property in the public domain can be found in Chapter II.

Open source codes are becoming more and more common. They are used often by companies involved in bioinformatics, but they also are used in analytical programs and for other purposes by more standard biotech companies. This is a terrific boon to computer programmers of all types, but there is a potential landmine in their use. Under the GNU General Public License, which governs a large number of open-source products, open source code can be integrated only into other open-source products.[17] Any modification of the code generally must be published. It is critical that companies that use open source documents pay close attention to the governing license and act accordingly. Insurance products are beginning to spring up to reduce this risk, but care in reviewing the underlying license is the best protection.

C. Transfer from Academia

1. University Considerations

Many universities in the past considered themselves to be morally superior to, and removed from, much of the commercial world.[18] Universities focused primarily on developing and expanding knowledge, whether scientific, literary, or philosophical. Commercialization generally was considered inconsistent with that mission. Many professors and researchers, even in highly technical fields, were more interested in publishing papers in prestigious journals explaining the work they were doing and informing their colleagues of developments than in keeping developments secret until they could file patents on them. In fact, in the tenure process, publication was rewarded and patents were not. This orientation came into question in 1925, when the University of Wisconsin (Madison) developed a method for producing vitamin D in milk by ultraviolet radiation, which could help to eliminate the childhood disease rickets. The University of Wisconsin created a foundation to bring in revenues from this invention.[19] The prevailing attitude began to change after World War II. The combination of military development growing out of the World War and the Korean War and the vastly growing space program resulted in a host of federal agencies providing funding to many universities.[20] Because of the academic mind-set, which encouraged open publication without the retention of exclusive rights, many of the developments of those universities either never were commercialized or were commercialized by other parties, often based in other countries, as new technical developments were made public. The process for trying to license the technology granted was incredibly cumbersome, discouraging commercialization of many inventions.

The United States in the early 1970s began to see a host of competitors from Europe and Asia threatening its two-decade run as the manufacturing leader of the world. It was even stated in Congress that "[f]ederal agencies are not as successful in delivering new products and inventions to the marketplace as the private sector. . . .The public is not receiving the full benefits of the research and development efforts that it is supporting. It is in the public interest that new discoveries are commercialized as quickly as possible without artificial restraints. . . ."[21] Congress decided to enact the University and Small Business Patent Procedure Act, commonly known as the Bayh-

Dole Act, in 1980 to foster development and patenting of federally sponsored research.[22] The provisions of the Bayh-Dole Act, as explained under the section "Applicability of Bayh-Dole Act" on page 191, had an extraordinary effect on technology transfer in universities.

In order for a university to qualify for federal research funds, it has to meet the requirements of Bayh-Dole, which includes written employment agreements clarifying the employee relationship with the university and obligating the employee to disclose and cooperate in patenting inventions, a requirement that universities share royalties with inventors, and several reporting requirements.[23] Universities scrambled to create policies that were consistent with the Bayh-Dole Act and debated among themselves the best way both to maximize federal research funding and to encourage development of university inventions. The Association of University Technology Managers (AUTM) was founded to create a forum for discussing the best way to encourage commercial development of federally sponsored research, support the university's mission of spreading knowledge, and also meet the specific requirements of the Bayh-Dole Act. AUTM now is a national group of over 300 colleges and universities and helps to define the standards for university technology transfer.[24]

Technology transfer practices and priorities continue to evolve at universities. Initially, universities attempted to concentrate their technology transfer programs on maximizing the revenues produced for the university. In many cases this focus proved to be counterproductive: universities were often no better than the investing world at predicting future success; internal university politics, rather than commercialization potential, often governed which faculty members' inventions received expensive patent protection; and cumbersome licensing terms and protracted negotiations reduced the incentive for businesses to seek licenses to university-owned technology. Later, at least for public universities, other priorities became recognized, including the commercial development in the home state of the university, growth in jobs, increase in prestige, and the level of jobs created. Many universities began to take a broader view of what constitutes "best practices" in university transfer. Universities still differ in terms of the specific techniques and requirements they have. Some are easier to negotiate with than others in licensing technology. Some have fully staffed offices of specialists to make these decisions, while others use a committee of faculty or a mix. Universities also use different metrics to gauge the success of their technology transfer system. The following are some of the priorities that universities consider in both their policies and in the deals they do.[25]

(i) Considerations of universities include the following:

1. *Legal requirements*. Technology transfer availability is required by Bayh-Dole, but the specific process is mostly up to the university, within legal constraints.
2. *No assignment*. Universities will generally require that they retain legal title to inventions, but scope and terms of licenses can be flexible.
3. *Incentives for innovation*. Providing for a meaningful stream of potential royalties or other license income to inventors helps encourage disclosures of new inventions.
4. *Faculty preferences*. Technology transfer offices will also seriously consider the preferences of faculty inventors in determining the best recipient for a technology license.
5. *Recover sunk costs*. Universities, especially with biotech IP, tend to have out-of-pocket patent costs that they hope to recover immediately. This enables these funds to be recycled to cover the costs of the next generation of patentable inventions.
6. *Running royalties*. Receiving a share of future revenues is a way for the university and the licensee to share in commercial success if and when it occurs.
7. *Appreciation in stock value*. Universities, as discussed below, are becoming more willing to take an equity stake in the business of the licensee. As with royalties, this enables a licensee to preserve cash early while giving the university the ability to participate financially in the success of a licensee.
8. *Level of say-so in the process*. Most universities do not want any management responsibility (such as a board seat), as that would impose ongoing responsibility. They often do want the ability to revoke the license if milestones are not achieved. Furthermore, a nonprofit academic institution may fear that excessive involve-

Acquisition of Biotechnology—Technology Transfer 165

ment in the board or management of a for-profit spin-off company may threaten the institution's tax-exempt standing.

9. *Confidence in licensee.* A university is more likely to accept a back-end-loaded license from an entity they believe will still exist on the back end. However, some universities' technology transfer offices are generally forgiving to start-ups, especially when one of the company principals was an inventor of the IP.
10. *Future grants or research investments.* Companies that have a record or a real prospect of supporting work at the university through grants or sponsored research may get a more sympathetic ear.
11. *Attracting other faculty to the university.* Universities are competing for faculty, and a reputation for being "inventor-friendly" and "entrepreneurial" can help attract other inventors.
12. *Reimbursement of patent costs.* As mentioned above, universities like to pay off out-of-pocket costs. Some universities consider reimbursement of patent costs, sometimes the largest out-of-pocket expense, a high priority.
13. *Consultation/say-so in approving sublicensees.* Especially in biotechnology, this is important. Biotechnology tends to get more attention and press coverage. In addition to wanting an assurance of payment when due, a university may care about the reputation of the party handling the IP.
14. *Requirement that sublicensees are subject to license terms.*
15. *Who is on the hook?* Original licensee often remains ultimately (additionally) liable to the university. Sublicensing is not a way to get "off the hook."
16. *Indemnification.* There often is very broad indemnification for the university and related parties. This is required by most state laws for public institutions. In many states, universities have statutory or common-law immunity for many actions. They want to ensure that they are not put at risk of liability if their IP results in a product that harms a patient, or if their IP infringes the rights of a third party.
17. *Minimal representations and warranties.* For the reasons discussed in the immediately preceding subsection, universities are more likely to favor licensees who do not expect burdensome

representations and warranties. For example, most universities refuse to represent that their IP is non-infringing, even though they, as licensors, are in the best position to know.

18. *Sufficiency of insurance.* See above. Again, universities want to be sure that they are protected.
19. *Trademark protection.* Usually there are restrictions on use of university or related parties' names. The university does not want publicity related to their IP unless they can be sure it is good.
20. *Original missions.* Some universities include language appealing to the three basic missions of education, research, and public service. These are the critical missions of any university.
21. *Due diligence milestones and fair return targets* to satisfy Bayh-Dole Act.
22. *Reporting.* Specific reporting obligations, as required to enable the institution to meet its reporting obligations under Bayh-Dole, NIH or other rules, usually are required.
23. *Sponsored research opportunities.* Some universities favor licensors who will agree to sponsor additional related research outside the bounds of the license agreement, and may grant a right of first refusal to license the fruits of the additional research to the sponsor.
24. *Compliance with IRS Rev. Proc. 97-14* requiring that any license from a university receiving federal funds be granted for fair market value. This concept can cause a problem in licensing future developments.

(ii) Considerations of employee/researcher:

1. *Chance for invention to find use.*
2. *Research grants or joint ventures.* These can help fund future projects and aid in obtaining tenure.
3. *Royalties to employee.* Again, money is good.
4. *Equity to employee.* Beware of conflicts of interest and commitment, as described below. Since biotech IP is often slow to develop and take to market, equity often is the best long-term option for both parties, unless cumulative royalty obligations end up overburdening the technology and chilling further development deals.

5. *Employee participation in management v. conflicts of interest and commitment.* See more detail below.
6. *Points toward tenure (only in some universities).* As mentioned above, added research grants may actually help this more than the IP itself. Some universities are starting to reward patents and inventions, but most still favor publication and grant dollars.
7. *Political.* Does it help with departmental hierarchy?
8. *Limiting personal risk.* Many academics want to limit personal risk to zero. Don't we all? The type of person who teaches or researches in a university often is more risk-averse than the average inventor, so this may be more important.
9. *Unrealistic expectations of cost to get to marketplace.* What Thomas Edison said is true: "genius," like successful businesses, is 2 percent inspiration and 98 percent perspiration, but the inventor often cannot recognize that. University inventors often take a "but for" approach. "But for my invention, there would not even be a project and product." Yes, but when someone has put millions of dollars, personnel, and/or months of time into a project solely on the inventor's prediction of what it will do, they expect to be fully rewarded for their risk. This is always a battle. At the heart of it is ego.
10. *Failure to appreciate the limitations on an academic inventor's rights.* The university inventor often loses sight of the fact that he may be the inventor, but he is not the owner. Ownership resides in his employer, the academic institution—and if the project was federally funded in whole or part, certain rights tantamount to ownership also rest in the federal government, on behalf of the taxpayers. Because of ego or personal greed, a faculty inventor may create obstacles to a technology transfer opportunity that is in the best interests of the university, independent investors, and the public. In this case, the inventor may need to be reeducated about his role in the process.

(iii) Considerations of community and society (and also, sometimes, the university):

1. *Reduces waste of ideas/inventions.* This was important to Congress in passing Bayh-Dole.

2. *More rapid dissemination of the benefits of medical research* to the ultimate consumers of health care, the public.
3. *New jobs developed.*
4. *Possibility of attracting like-kind investments.*
5. *Publicity and prestige* to the university and the community.
6. *Royalty payments* to the university, to the benefit of future research efforts.
7. If structured properly from the university's perspective, *licensing deals* need not place undue restrictions on faculty's freedom to publish and disseminate knowledge.
8. *Atmosphere of encouraging inventors can attract other inventors.* This can be a chicken/egg issue, but if an area has successful inventors, it attracts venture capital, and that attracts more inventors.
9. *Can stretch the local investor market*—a few successes can encourage the local equity market for private equity transactions. Profit attracts profit.
10. *Attraction of proven faculty from other universities.*
11. *Revenues/tax dollars generated.* Many states are realizing that biotech has more multiplier impact than most other industries. Job skills and salaries tend to be high. Educational needs tend to be high. Components often require labs or GMC manufacturing. All of this requires support functions. That is why many states are encouraging biotech start-ups now.

Common restrictions, guidelines, and practice tips are provided below under "Common Restrictions" and "Common Guidelines for Price and Provisions."

2. Material Transfer Agreements

Sometimes when the IP is early-stage, the company first must conduct further research to determine if the IP warrants commercial development. Universities often start by offering a material transfer agreement. These are appropriate when no collaboration is immediately anticipated with a third party, and the use of the material will be for research only at that stage.[26] Universities not certain of the company's prospects sometimes offer this first to allow the company to establish the commercial viability of both the IP and the company itself. Companies going down this road need to be careful to protect whatever IP they develop. Attaching a clause or separate document providing a means of negotiating future freedom to operate should be considered.

3. Principal Investigator Considerations

a. Conflict of Interest and Conflict of Commitment

(i) Inventors of technology at universities must be very careful in how they handle their inventions. In most cases, the inventions do not belong to them. Under Bayh-Dole and under most employment contracts with both for-profit and not-for-profit entities, the institution—not the inventor—owns the invention. Under the Bayh-Dole Act, a university must share any royalties it receives with the employee/inventor. Many nonprofits do not have a similar rule. Some nonprofits allow an inventor funded by the institute to have an equity interest in the company commercializing the product. However, many that allow equity interests restrict the percentage that the inventor might have.

(ii) Universities have a number of considerations in developing technology. Chief among them is maintaining the tax-free status of the institution. This requires that the institution does not become a commercial venture that makes a profit. Universities are primarily research and teaching institutions, where the objectivity and integrity of their researchers are considered paramount. Two related concerns in this regard are conflict of interest and conflict of commitment.

b. Conflict of Interest

A conflict of interest is when a party is motivated to take an action that is not in the best interests of his employer or fiduciary beneficiary. Universities and nonprofits worry that too high an equity stake in an entity or too much possible future payment can motivate the employee to act in ways that are not in the best interest of the university. In other words, many believe that a small equity interest or future royalty stream that may provide the employee with reasonable rewards from an invention may be okay, but a larger interest can skew the employee's orientation away from the university. It is too much of a good thing. If Tom is earning X from the university and 2X from the company pushing his invention, it's easy to see where loyalties might lie. Also, especially with complicated biotech products, some developments may involve companies or acts that are in opposition to the university's interest.

The general concern is that financial incentives can undermine the objectivity, or perceived objectivity, of research results.

The author had a client who developed several patents providing for a possible new method of testing pharmaceuticals against a specific pathogen. The university, his primary employer, became concerned that his possible profits from his invention would interfere with his ability to teach electrical engineering, which was largely unrelated to his invention. Accordingly, most universities have specific policies that must be considered relating to conflict of interest. Most universities now also have independent review processes that protect against a conflict of interest becoming a problem, thus freeing the employee to hold a more substantial portion of the vehicle for developing the technology. Consistent with that approach and concern about conflicts of interest, the NIH has addressed this issue in its rules.[27]

Practice Points

1. Review university guidelines for IP transfer, including rules relating to conflict of interest and commitment.
2. Ensure that the license includes later, related inventions by the listed inventors.
3. Engage the inventors to ensure effective technology transfer and continued access to relevant expertise.
4. Due diligence: Find out if there are other stakeholders, including someone funding the lab or the inventor's salary.
5. Especially with universities, research extensively to ensure no disclosure of the IP prior to patent filing.
6. Try to negotiate back-end payment—keep up-front payments to a minimum.

c. Conflict of Commitment

Similarly, many universities and nonprofits have rules relating to conflict of commitment. The theory is basically the same, but the concern here is that the inventor will be motivated to spend so much time on the invention that she will ignore duties to the employer. Many universities have specific rules limiting the number of hours a week that can be worked, on average, by a professor on matters outside of the university. Some nonprofits have similar restrictions. In putting together a deal with a university employee, an attorney should ask for copies of the conflict of interest and conflict of commitment policies to ensure that the deal offered will meet the required standards. Many a deal has been reworked to accommodate these standards.

d. Special Knowledge

Even though an inventor may have no ownership interest in her invention and be restricted in how much equity or revenue she can receive by conflict of interest or conflict of commitment, she may have substantial bargaining power. There is always a perception, and usually a fact, that the inventor did not put everything in her head into the invention. Any company licensing that invention wants to know what else is there. It is often that additional piece of the puzzle that allows an inventor to negotiate additional cash or equity compensation, a contingent royalty payment, or a significant sponsored research grant earmarked for the inventor's own laboratory or program at the university. Companies developing new technology often will pay a consulting fee to ensure that they have the inventor's input into matters related to the technology.

4. Licensee Considerations

Companies licensing IP from universities or nonprofits in most cases cannot own the invention because the Bayh-Dole Act restricts the assignment of inventions. Accordingly, the licensee must give a lot of thought to what restrictions it is willing to accept in a license of technology. Some companies try to take the position that only an assignment is acceptable. In practice, an exclusive, worldwide, unrestricted license, including any later developments, generally is virtually the same as an assignment, but it is permitted under Bayh-Dole, with minor reservations. In fact, an exclusive, worldwide, unrestricted license may be more intrusive than a simple assignment, because it usually includes follow-on technology.

a. Policies and Procedures

The licensee must be very careful to understand the policies and procedures of the university, including conflict of interest and commitment, as described above. In particular, licenses sometimes contain references to state statutes that further restrict the transfer of the IP or retain some right of further development to the university. You must review these references carefully to ensure that they do not place unworkable restrictions on the deal.

b. It's a Long Way to Market, So Wrap Up the People You Need

Most biotech inventions at the university level are not close to being ready to commercialize. Sometimes only one or a few people, including the inventor, truly understand how the invention works and how it can be improved or modified. There often is a steep learning curve for in-house engineers or scientists to understand the technology. Accordingly, it is often critical that the licensee obtain some degree of promised cooperation from the inventor in the purchase. Often, it also is critical to obtain rights, options, or a right of first refusal for any later, related inventions by the inventor and his/her team. Universities are understandably reluctant to pledge the results of future work. Some universities will provide rights to any later, related inventions at the university, but beware: these are often unenforceable against the inventor, because they are too broad. In most cases, the university cannot commit inventions by parties not under the contract. For example, a blanket license of later, related inventions at the university may not apply to an inventor (new faculty member?) who was not on the earlier license. Similarly, the license to later inventions most certainly will be unenforceable if the faculty member leaves that university and joins another. The best that a licensee might get is some level of license for related inventions later developed by the inventor of the principal product licensed. An example of this conflict was demonstrated in 1992 when the Scripps Research Institute, which received substantial federal funding, entered into a contract with Swiss pharmaceutical company Sandoz (now Novartis), providing Sandoz a license to all future Scripps discoveries. The NIH investigated, resulting in new NIH rules and a modified agreement for Scripps and Sandoz. In particular, the NIH now requires that universities receiving NIH funding, before entering sponsored research agreements with commercial interests, take into consideration whether the sponsor has the commitment and means to develop the research, require a written commitment to develop the invention, and limit the sponsor to six months to "pull the trigger" on its commitment to develop the invention.[28]

c. Public Disclosure?

A primary concern for the licensee is whether the invention was publicly disclosed prior to protection. There are numerous inventions that have received a great deal of investment for development and commercialization only to find out that the inventor presented the invention at a small gathering of scientific fellows more than a year before the patent was filed. Similarly, many academicians, not understanding that international patent filing rules are different from those in the United States, freely disclose their ideas when they know that the patent is in the process of being prepared. This may not spoil the U.S. patent, which allows disclosure within a year before filing, but it almost certainly spoils any chance for patenting internationally. This can considerably reduce the value of the intellectual property.

d. Stakeholders

Understand who the other stakeholders in the project are. The university and the inventor are clear stakeholders, but sometimes the work or the inventors' salary is partially underwritten by a government agency, a nonprofit, or a commercial entity. It is important to discover whether there are other parties funding the professors' salary. Also ask whether anyone is funding this particular research or the lab itself. If other parties are funding these, find out what restrictions they may place on the transactions or what rights they may take in the inventions. It is very common for a commercial enterprise to fund a project with no specific rights to the project, but with a contract or an unwritten understanding that it will have a right of first refusal on any attempt to commercialize the resulting invention. Sometimes this hidden promise does not come up until the last stages of negotiating the license.

5. Interests of Other Stakeholders

a. Other Underwriters

We referred above to the fact that many other parties may have an interest in a transfer of technology. The university and the inventor have been explored. Often an academic salary is partially underwritten by a nonprofit entity, a government agency, or a commercial enterprise. Similarly, a specific lab and its equipment often are underwritten by another institution. In some cases, these underwritings come with strings attached. Government agencies providing funding usually pose no additional restrictions other than the Bayh-Dole Act, but many, like the NIH, do have specific rules for disclosure and other actions.

b. Government Agencies

The NIH, for example requires that any institution receiving NIH funds, in order to acquire title to a sponsored invention, must have an administrative process in place that that accomplishes the following:

(i) Provide notification to the NIH Technology Office (in writing or by email to www.edison.gov).
(ii) Provide notification to any sponsoring agency.
(iii) Specifically elect in writing to retain title within two years of initial disclosure.
(iv) Provide to the NIH copies of all U.S. patent applications and all granted patents, including patent serial numbers, related to the invention.
(v) Note on the face of any patent application that the research was sponsored by a federal agency, listing the agencies that sponsored it.
(vi) Grant in writing a nonexclusive license to the U.S. government to use the invention for government purposes.[29]

c. Special Government Considerations

Some federal agencies have additional restraints and procedures, including the Department of Defense and the Department of Homeland Security. These agencies often place very precise restrictions on what can be done with inventions they fund, for obvious national security reasons. A university usually will not permit a commercial enterprise to place large restrictions on projects, professors, or even laboratories that it funds. However, the university sometimes will provide the commercial enterprise a right of first refusal or other contract rights or license-sharing rights for any invention that it funds. Sometimes these are verbal promises, history of operations or understandings that have no paper trail. Although usually not enforceable, these understandings can place the university in a difficult position when faced with the choice between an uncertain development venture versus an almost certain alienation of a large contributor. It is important to perform due diligence and discover what other stakeholders there are and what rights they have.

d. Nonprofits

Nonprofit organizations commonly place restrictions on deals that can be done with technology they helped to underwrite. These restrictions can vary quite a bit. One of the largest nonprofit underwriters of biotechnology inventions is the Howard Hughes Medical Institute. It places a host of rules and restrictions on the professors and the projects it funds. These generally are well-thought-out and very clearly stated, but it is vital to consider what these are. An example is that any scientist funded by HHMI cannot take more than a 5 percent equity interest in a commercial venture licensing that scientist's technology, in most cases. There are exceptions for start-up ventures. Similarly, there are restrictions on royalties, work, and other matters placed on funded scientists. It is critical that an attorney perform due diligence and receive, if possible, written verification from the university listing any other stakeholders in the deal.

6. Common Restrictions

The following are common restrictions in university technology transfer agreements. Some of these are explained in more detail above.

a. License Only, Not an Assignment

As we explain above, a license is not an assignment. In general, universities license IP, they do not assign it. Depending on the terms, a license may be substantially the same as an assignment or very much less.

b. Time Limitations

University technology transfer licenses often have milestones to reach in order for the license to continue. These may or may not be renegotiable at a later date depending on likelihood of success and other interests in the technology.

c. Restrictions on Participation by the Inventors

These can be both restrictions on the amount of equity held, restrictions on the amount of royalties offered, and, more commonly, restrictions on the number of hours that can be devoted to a project by inventors unless the inventors' salary is partially funded by the licensee.

d. Audit

Broad right of audit to confirm sales figures for purposes of verifying royalties due. This, of course, is common in most well-written licenses.

e. Scope of License

The licensee will want as broad a scope of license as possible. The university may offer a limited scope with a chance to reach certain benchmarks to expand the scope of the license, or it may offer a very broad scope that will be pulled back if certain benchmarks are not met.

f. Indemnification

Broad indemnification language protecting the university and all related parties, as well as making the university a named insured under the policy.

g. Sublicense Approval

Requirement that the licensee obtain university permission before sublicensing, although some practitioners have experienced universities softening on this.

h. Sublicensee Subject to License Terms

Requirement that all sublicensees abide by the original license terms.

i. Original Licensee Always Liable

With respect to the university, the original licensee remains primarily liable for any violations of the license or any sublicense, although some practitioners have experienced universities softening on this.

j. Cannot Use the Name of the University

Prohibition against the use of names or symbols identifying the university, especially in any marketing material.

k. Government Has a License

Statement that the U.S. government, pursuant to Bayh-Dole, has a restricted license to use the technology for its own purposes.

l. Other General Restrictions You Would Find in Most Other Licensing Agreements

7. Common Guidelines for Price and Provisions of the License

The following are common payment schemes that are often incorporated in standard university licenses. It is standard to see a combination of the following, but not all.

a. Standstill Fee

The university may wish to see a good-faith effort on the part of the licensee to raise capital before it will agree to a license. In this case, the university may agree in the meantime to a simple Standstill Agreement, pursuant to which the university agrees, in return for a modest payment, that it will not license the technology to a third party for a fixed period of time.

b. Up-front License Fee

This commonly is due upon signing the license and is often crafted to reimburse the university for its out-of-pocket patent costs. Sometimes this is the only up-front payment.

c. Minimum Annual Payment

These often commence after a grace period of a few years and can serve as a substitute for onerous performance milestones.

d. Periodic Licensing Fees (Such as Quarterly or Annual)

This is virtually the same as the minimum annual payment, except that this sometimes is structured as a separate fee, not a minimum payment that can be eliminated by payment of royalties.

e. Participation In Third-Party Payments

During the early years of product development, a biotech's most significant revenues are likely to come from third-party payments—signature or milestone payments or research funding—made by a larger partner who has agreed to collaborate on product development. Savvy universities explicitly insist on receiving a percentage of these payments.

f. Lump-Sum Royalties

This is usually due prior to commercialization or sales. This is often based on a present value of expected royalty, so the licensee needs to be careful about its projections on future sales. That number may come back to haunt him.

g. Milestone Payments

Payments are often due on specific events, such as filings of an IND or NDA/BLA with the FDA or the completion of a phase of clinical trials.

h. Sales-Based Royalties

This is either on a per-unit or per-dollar basis. There often is some give and take on whether this is based on revenues, net sales, or net profits. Net sales is most common, with the major battle revolving around what is included in that calculation. Keep in mind that although the percentage based on revenues will be lower, it is much easier to verify revenues than it is to verify profit. If the client wants to base it on profits, ensure that the license provides a broad right of audit and a detailed description of what can and cannot go into the profit calculation. Creative accounting is always a risk.

i. Equity In the Licensee

This is becoming more common, especially for early-stage technology or other IP that the university does not believe is easily marketed.

j. Equity Protections

These provisions sometimes provide the university the ability to increase its equity percentage, or maintain that percentage, in the event of an unexpected dilution of the university's interest.

k. Put of Shares

A put allowing the university to sell its stock to the licensee at a minimum amount, pending a certain event. A common example is a put allowing the university to sell a majority of its equity interest upon an IPO of the licensee, and a right to require the licensee to register the university's shares for sale when the licensee registers its own shares.

l. A Time for Sale

This allows the university to force a sale of the licensee or technology in certain events, usually in the case of the licensee not meeting expectations. The author has seen this language but believes that in most cases the company can negotiate to have this paragraph removed.

8. When Equity Is the Primary Consideration for the License

Many universities today license unproven, cutting-edge technology to fledgling companies associated with members of the faculty or other interested parties. Often, the business plan of the licensee relies completely on the technology coming from the university. In these cases, the university often demands an equity interest, sometimes a sizable one. Universities in general do not want to exert control over the companies licensing their inventions. They recognize that they have neither the expertise nor the time to devote to running a business or managing its affairs. Also, "operating" a for-profit company might endanger a university's tax status and its statutory immunity from certain types of liability (depending on the state law). However, universities sometimes demand a "seat at the table," a seat on the board of directors or, more often, a veto right over senior officers and certain activities, such as debt or equity financing, and the right to step in if certain milestones are not met. This can present conflict between the company, the inventor, and the university. In addition, company management must keep in mind that it has a fiduciary duty to all of its shareholders, including the university, to act in the company's long-term best interest. In some cases, the university and company management have different "best interests" in mind. An example of this is when the company is developing a product that has the potential for negative publicity, such as transgenic medicines.

Counsel for the licensee should negotiate to limit the university's activity in the management of the company. Try to limit the amount of equity the university holds or limit the voting rights of the equity granted. Many universities will accept a lack of voting rights in exchange for stronger powers in the event that the company does not meet its projected goals. This can provide management more flexibility at the outset of the project. Many universities will accept or even request that their equity interests be in the form of warrants that give the university equity up-side participation but no stockholder rights or even a non-voting class of stock. Counsel for the licensee should seek to have universities accept post-IPO lockups, obligations to vote in favor of a board approved sale of the company, and other restrictions that apply to shares held by founders (though universities are unlikely to accept vesting provisions, since the stock represents part of the purchase price for the technology).

9. Applicability of Bayh-Dole Act

The Bayh-Dole Act (1980) and the Trademark Clarification Act of 1984 both help to support government funding of nongovernmental research. The Trademark Clarification Act provides broader technology transfer authority in government-owned, contractor-operated laboratories and permits those laboratories to enter into cooperative research and development agreements with non-federal entities and to require federal employees to receive a fraction of resulting royalties.

a) The Bayh-Dole Act (35 U.S.C. § 200, et seq.) was written specifically to improve the protection of federally funded university developments and encourage their commercialization. Specifically, the Bayh-Dole Act requires the following:

(i) *Written employee agreements*—Universities must have written employee agreements that protect the technology developed, require prompt disclosure to the university, and require cooperation in the filing of patent applications.

(ii) *Royalty sharing*—Universities must share royalties with the inventors.

(iii) *Reporting*—Universities must report to the federal agencies that have provided funding regarding the inventions developed with its funds, commercial sales, and royalties earned.

(iv) *U.S. manufacturing*—Universities must give preference to U.S. manufacturers, and especially small businesses. In fact, to the extent possible, products licensed pursuant to Bayh-Dole must be "substantially manufactured in the United States." 37 C.F.R. § 401.14(i). The government may revoke title to an invention if it determines that commercialization has been inadequate.

(v) *U.S. retains license*—The federal government generally retains a non-exclusive, non-transferable, irrevocable, paid-up license to use the invention on behalf of the United States.[30] Generally, licenses from a university to a business contain a sentence confirming that the United States retains such a license.

(vi) *License only, no assignment*—Bayh-Dole does not allow the assignment of technology, but merely the license of the technology. As discussed above, this does not present a major barrier except that it runs afoul of some company's internal rules. An exclusive (except for U.S. government use), worldwide license provides virtually the same use of the technology and protection that ownership would provide.

(vii) *Termination of license if commercialization is inadequate*—If the government determines that efforts to commercialize a product were inadequate, the title to the IP may revert back to the government.

b) The "license only," U.S. manufacturing preference, and title reversion right may seem to be barriers to use, but they are not in most cases. The "license only" standard may conflict with the preferences of some technology acquirers, but it need not present a practical problem in the marketplace. The U.S. manufacturing preference would present a problem if it were strictly enforced. In the worldwide marketplace we live in today, this can provide a substantial challenge for companies that are developing products in which price will be a major consideration. Manufacturing often is cheaper elsewhere. The United States, however, has more than inertia on its side. The need to keep IP, especially trade secrets, under wraps, strong legal protection for IP, the need to approve both product and manufacturing for sale in the United States, high profit margins, and a greater number of GMP-compliant and specialty manufacturing sites (as well as people trained to work in them) all help to keep much of this manufacturing in the United States. After polling the other authors of this book, none of us could find one example that we were aware of in which the federal government enforced this right. The supposition is that the government takes the view that if it is commercially reasonable to produce here, generally a company will do so. Many companies using such technology go to great lengths to manufacture in the United States, but it sometimes is just not feasible economically. However, if the government ever decided to enforce this provision, it could impose additional costs on the manufacture of products whose initial inventions were funded in part by federal dollars. Finally, Bayh-Dole does allow the federal government to revoke university title if commercialization has been inadequate. Again, we are aware of no case in which that has happened. We are aware of only one case in which a third party attempted to force the government to exercise "march in" rights, and it was refused.[31] If a product is being commercialized and is being sold or prepared for sale, that alone should be a substantial defense against a claim that commercialization was inadequate.

c) Despite the lack of enforcement of some restrictions under Bayh-Dole, it is still important to recognize the possible restrictions and address them in drafting the license agreement and any sublicense agreements. Bayh-Dole does not specifically restrict sublicensing, but it does require that any sublicenses carry forward the restrictions imposed by Bayh-Dole on the university and the initial license.

10. Application of "CREATE" Act of 2004

The "CREATE" Act of 2004 was signed into law in December of that year. It was passed in response to the problem that joint development relationships between companies and universities, because of the sharing of information, often disqualified the IP for patent protection. This act was written to solve that problem and encourage collaborative research efforts. It revises the treatment of "prior art" under the patent laws so that it does not include (and therefore does not disqualify for patent protection) an invention when:

- The invention was made by or on behalf of parties to a joint research agreement in effect before the invention was made;
- The invention was the result of activities within the scope of that agreement; and
- The patent application for the invention discloses the names of the parties to the joint research agreement.[32]

This is not as simple as it seems. Some believe that the rules promulgating this act are not completely helpful. One of the seemingly clearest exemptions under this act is when both parties have confidential disclosure agreements. You should review any existing joint research agreements to ensure that they are in compliance with this act. You should consider recording that agreement with the PTO, which recent regulations permit. In order to do that without extensive amendment or redaction of portions of the agreement, the scope of the joint research should be set forth separately, in an exhibit or appendix. For more details, please see Chapter II.

11. Conflict between Publication and Protection of IP

We included this as a separate heading precisely because it is so often overlooked. Publication under patent laws is a very broad term. Any disclosure to a party that is not employed by the university or nonprofit, or under an NDA (nondisclosure agreement) may disqualify the invention for patent protection.

a) Academicians want to publish. Academicians want to speak at conferences and announce their developments. This helps them obtain tenure, maintain tenure, and increase their status in their professional community. Perhaps more important for most, it fulfills their desire to spread knowledge as broadly as possible so that the bounds of human knowledge can expand more quickly. This mind-set dates back centuries, but we might call this today the "open source mentality." These are wonderful goals, but they run afoul of patent requirements. And if the biotechnology is available to everyone, what business will spend the great resources required to perfect the technology and take it through the regulatory approval process?

b) It is absolutely critical before executing a license with the university that the licensee perform due diligence to ensure that no disclosure has been made of the licensed invention. If possible, it is recommended for purposes of documenting due diligence that the practitioner obtain from the inventor written and signed confirmation that she has not disclosed any part of the invention to anyone else except as specifically indicated. If any disclosures were made, it is imperative to ensure that an NNDA was effective prior to the disclosure, or that the disclosure was within the time frame allowed for patent filing (one year in the United States).

D. Transfer from Other Nonprofit Entities

It is becoming more and more common for technology to be developed in nonprofit entities and then transferred to or shared with commercial entities. Nonprofits are beginning to accept, as the federal government did, that in order to have innovation funded and commercialized, thereby spreading it broadly, for-profit companies need to be involved and motivated. With a few exceptions related to nonprofit development of products to treat diseases prevalent only in less developed countries, only for-profit companies have the infrastructure, skills, connections, and financial resources to shepherd a new biological development through the FDA and other regulatory processes.

1. Implications of Nonprofit Status

Any nonprofit, in order to maintain its tax-free status, must not make and keep more money than its spends, in general. Accordingly, nonprofits have to be very careful to draft policies that will ensure that a "home run" product does not result in them becoming a profit-making entity. Some, like Howard

Hughes Medical Institute, eschew most forms of payment or royalties resulting from the technology, or monitor them closely. Others allow some royalties to come their way in hopes of funding future developments.

2. Unrelated Business Income Tax

Unrelated business income tax (UBIT) is tax that applies to certain activities that are not related to the nonprofit's primary nonprofit activity.[33] Basically there are three tests of whether net income from the activity are taxable: (i) the activity must be a trade or business; (ii) the trade or business must be carried on regularly; and (iii) it must not be substantially related to exempt purposes.[34] Fortunately, there are a number of exceptions. Some primary exceptions are dividends, royalties, and dispositions of property, including sales of stock in a for-profit business.[35] Accordingly, it is common for nonprofits to negotiate any license favoring a payout through one of these methods. However, these exceptions are not absolute, so anyone negotiating with or representing a nonprofit should consult a tax expert to ensure that UBIT does not apply in that case.

3. Priorities of Nonprofit Technology Owner

a) The nonprofit selling technology generally will be most concerned with the following:

- Maintaining nonprofit status.
- Minimizing institutional risk.
- Maximizing development potential of the invention.
- Providing support and motivation for development by employees of the nonprofit entity.
- Expanding potential for sharing of ideas and joint venturing with both nonprofit and for profit partners.
- Provide funding for the nonprofit entity.

b) Nonprofit entities typically are very risk-averse. Accordingly, two priorities sometimes become paramount in negotiations. They are (i) reimbursement immediately for any patent or other out-of-pocket costs, and (ii) liberal indemnification and insurance provisions to ensure that the nonprofit is fully protected against product liability claims in the event of a death or injury due to the invention.

c) Different nonprofits organize these priorities differently. Some nonprofits, such as Howard Hughes Medical Institute, have little interest in or need for substantial funding supplements. Others hope for additional funding to offset expenses. In order to negotiate effectively with the nonprofit, you must understand its policies and procedures and also understand the priorities behind those policies and procedures.

4. Joint Venturing (especially qualification for STTR grants)

It has become much more common for nonprofits to "joint venture" with for-profit entities in developing inventions. Biotechnology in particular is so multi-layered, often requiring a combination of several different inventions to create a commercially viable product, that joint venturing has become very common. It is particularly common for a nonprofit entity to develop and possibly even patent a technique that is vital to the completion of another product. In these cases, the commercial interest can license the product directly from the nonprofit or enter into a joint development project to complete the product. The benefits to the nonprofit are often many, including the possibility of a royalty stream, advancement of its scientific base, possible development of techniques or products that are vital either to other projects or its stated mission, encouragement of researchers and sharing of knowledge, and development of a relationship that may bear further fruit on future projects.

a. SBIR Grants

Government agencies provide grants to small businesses for technology development. At least five federal government departments provide such grant funding, including the Department of Defense, Department of Energy, Department of Health and Human Services, NASA, and the National Science Foundation. The most well known of these is the Small Business Innovation Research Program (SBIR), which provides grants in two phases to small businesses. SBIR grants require that the grantee is a U.S.-owned, for-profit company with 500 or fewer employees, and that the primary researcher (inventor) is employed by the company. This is not a fit with a joint-venturing arrangement between a for-profit and a nonprofit entity.

b. STTR Grants

Recognizing this, the federal government instituted the Small Business Technology Transfer Program (STTR) to facilitate joint ventures between commercial entities and nonprofits. Like SBIR grants, grants are provided in two stages, and the requirements to qualify are a little looser. The commercial entity must be a U.S.-owned, for-profit small business with 500 or fewer employees, but the principal researcher need not be an employee. The nonprofit merely must be located in the United States and either a nonprofit university, a nonprofit research organization, or a federally funded research and development center. Proposals are accepted annually on development of projects. For more details regarding these federal funding programs, please see Chapter 7 (Federal Regulation of Research Through Funding).

c. Problems with STTR and SBIR Grants

The major problem in using these grants, besides the fact that the application process is very competitive, is that they are not available in general to companies owned or controlled in majority by another entity that does not qualify. For example, if the applying company is owned more than 50 percent by a large corporation, or if it receives funding from a venture fund with assets over the allowed limit, this funding is not available. Both the granting agencies and Congress have been petitioned to change this position, but that is the current situation. This must be addressed by the developing company in its capital-planning process.

5. Common Misconceptions

Many companies often assume that technology held by a nonprofit is not available for use. Usually, that is not correct. Many nonprofits encourage their researchers to find commercial outlets for their developments. Many nonprofits, especially in biotechnology, recognize that any new drug or device must go through a long, rigorous, and very expensive FDA and EU process before it ever reaches the market. This process, of course, follows an equally rigorous development schedule, including computer models and animal testing. A good idea may never get to a market if some company is not sufficiently motivated to spend the money to get it there.

6. Case Study—Howard Hughes Medical Institute

Howard Hughes Medical Institute (HHMI) is a large, nonprofit research institute that funds thousands of researchers employed in its own facilities and also faculty and researchers in universities across the United States. HHMI has very specific and well-traveled rules and procedures dealing with technology transfer. We use it as an example because it is a large player in biotechnology, funding many of the leading researchers in the nation, and it has had to deal internally with the issues that nonprofits face in seeking ways to encourage collaboration while maintaining their nonprofit status, consistent with their own policy statement. In short, it is an intelligent leader in this field. Please see www.hhmi.org/pdf/investigator-guide.pdf. The example below is as of the most recent experience of this author. HHMI may have adjusted the procedure since.

> **Practice Points**
>
> What nonprofits care about most:
> 1. Preserving tax-exempt status.
> 2. Minimizing institutional risk of liability.
> 3. Preventing damaging publicity.
> 3. Motivating institution's researchers.
> 4. Developing projects—making inventions available.
> 5. Protecting academic independence and ability to disseminate knowledge freely.

Nonprofits have different priorities, but they share an aversion to any risk. Be prepared to provide extensive indemnification and more expensive insurance coverage. The trade-off can be IP that would cost more coming from a commercial entity or individual.

a. Assignment of Rights

Every employee agrees to assign to HHMI all rights to any invention or other IP. If the employee is also an employee at the university, then in our experience IP generally is assigned by the researcher to HHMI and then by HHMI to the university.

b. Sharing Patent Costs and Royalties

HHMI and the host institution share the costs of patenting any resulting invention and the royalties that may accrue. The inventor's royalty share is determined by the formula set at the host institution.

c. Equity Ownership

When equity is at issue, HHMI has many rules regarding the ownership of equity. In general, an HHMI researcher may not own more than 5 percent of any class of equity in a for-profit company licensing HHMI-funded IP. There are temporary exceptions for start-up entities.

d. Collaborations

Collaborations between HHMI researchers and for-profit companies are encouraged, provided they are driven by scientific considerations. There are specific forms to fill out regarding collaboration. However, researchers are restricted in their ability to consult with (i.e., earn regular income from) a company that is licensing the researchers' invention. An exception is provided in the context of human subject research, but there are limitations on what the researcher can do.

e. Time Limitations

An HHMI investigator is required to spend at least 75 percent of his or her time on research, with the remainder spent on academic duties. Consulting activities are limited to no more than 36 days per year, in general. Consulting is also limited to an exchange of ideas; it may not involve research or directing research.

f. Start-up Companies

Start-up companies are treated a bit differently. An HHMI researcher may own up to 20 percent of any class of equity security of a start-up, but no group of researchers may own more than 40 percent of that equity. In addition, by the end of one year, the ownership must be reduced to not more than 5 percent of any class of equity.

g. Summary

Policies and procedures such as these are not uncommon with well-established nonprofits. It is important to understand these and to take them into account when developing the strategy to negotiate with the inventor and with both the nonprofit or related university.

E. Transfer from Individuals

1. Consideration of Terms

The basic terms of a technology transfer from an individual are not materially different from a technology transfer from a university, nonprofit or business. The nature of transferring directly from an individual, however, raises certain issues. Let us look at the standard terms of a license agreement and discuss how those issues might affect those terms.

a. Parties

Make sure all the inventors are listed by their correct, legal names.

b. Recitals

Explain what the parties are trying to accomplish. Some courts use these "whereas" clauses to interpret definitions or intent of the parties.

c. Definitions

Little needs to be said here. Definitions, although usually the first part of any agreement, are often the last section finished.

d. Property Licensed

Carefully describe the subject of the license. Include related and later-developed inventions, if relevant and possible. Use patent numbers, heading names on disclosure materials, etc., to define the property specifically. Depending on how sophisticated the individual, this may need to be rather broad.

e. Scope of the Assignment or License

Scope must include:

(i) *Assignment*—Unlike universities and nonprofits, individuals usually can assign the IP if they are willing. This provides more freedom and autonomy to the assignee, and it makes many other issues moot. In some cases, there may be an assignment back to the inventor in the event of uncured material breach by the assignee. However, you must be careful not to create a license when you intend to create an assignment by providing too many rights back to the inventor, or you will defeat part of your purpose.

(ii) *Exclusivity*—If the transaction is structured as a license, will the license be exclusive, non-exclusive, co-exclusive, or exclusive except for some reservation?

(iii) *Uses/Field*—Any company wants its uses to be as broad as possible, including any possible use of the technology. Individuals are less likely to object to this, because in most cases they do not need to retain uses for their own purposes. An exception is that the individual may want the ability to continue research and development. Generally speaking, the more broad the transfer of rights, the more likely the transfer should be structured as an assignment rather than a license. This also may provide more protection in a bankruptcy scenario. Although the circuits currently split on the issue, bankruptcy courts have a great deal of leeway in amending or forcing assignment of licenses, even if the terms of the license deny that right. However, even an assignment, if within six months of the bankruptcy filing (12 months for a related party in some instances), might be overturned by a bankruptcy court.

f. Territory

Will this be worldwide, limited to certain countries, etc.? Again, unless an individual has the ability to market the product in a specific territory or believes that he or she can find another company to purchase rights in other countries, generally the individual has less concern about granting a worldwide license than a corporation or even a nonprofit or university might have.

g. Right to Sublicense

The licensee will need the right to sublicense the invention, in case later development or its own determinations lead it to believe that another company or even a subsidiary of the licensee would be a better vehicle for developing or marketing the product. Individuals should have little objection to the licensee sublicensing the product, provided that royalty streams would apply to any sublicensee or other mechanisms are in place to provide the individual with rights to participate financially in sublicensing (e.g., sharing a specified portion of sublicense revenues rather than having royalty apply to sales by sublicensees).

h. Follow-on and Later-Developed Technology

This is often a contested issue, except in patent estates that are mature and not the subject of current work at the institution. The licensee will want to ensure that it is obtaining the best technology available both today and tomorrow. Individuals, because they often have an emotional attachment to their inventions, often resist a right to later developments related to that product. A compromise sometimes is to ensure that any later-developed technology that is in the same line as or makes use of the licensed technology will belong to the licensee. Nonetheless, courts have been reluctant to enforce "mortgage-on-brain" provisions, which purport to grant rights in all of an individual's future inventions and effectively render the inventor an indentured servant to the investor for the rest of his useful life. These clauses are usually found void as against public policy.

i. Term and Renewal of License

The initial term must be long enough to provide for development, regulatory process, and marketing. The term is most often for the life of the patents and sometimes longer (with a step down in royalty rate after patent expiration) when there is meaningful know-how (and sometimes even when there is not). Individuals sometimes require milestones, but it is less likely than for universities, nonprofits, or other companies. Automatic extension rights, sometimes depending on milestones, are important.

j. Termination

Provide causes for termination, when the license may be terminated without cause, automatic expiration, and notice provisions. Typical effects of termination are damages (sometimes liquidated), reversion of ownership of the IP (and sometimes any improvements) back to the inventor, return of materials and confidential data, and certain terms surviving (confidentiality, noncompetes, choice of law and venue, etc.).

k. Deliveries

Typically these are workpapers and lab notebooks, patent filings, biological or chemical materials, training, and anything else the licensee may need. In some cases, training in the practice of complex methods is also conducted to ensure effective technology transfer.

l. Retention of Rights

Individuals are less likely than a university or a nonprofit to want to retain certain rights for later development, although sometimes the inventor wants to continue tinkering with an invention. It is key that the licensee confirms that it is obtaining all marketing rights to the product.

m. Payments, Including Fees, Royalties, Stock (Options, Warrants), Milestone, etc.

Possible payment obligations include:

- Up-front or periodic payments
- Set fees over time or at milestone events
- Royalties based on sales
- Royalties based on sublicense revenue
- Collateral or guarantee of royalties (or not)
- Minimum royalties
- Possible reductions or credits against other royalties (for example, additional patent costs)
- Stock rights—either earned stock, stock options, warrants, or ability to convert debt (royalties owed?) into stock
- Employment or independent contractor fees

n. Audit Rights

This runs the gamut, but individuals sometimes are less sophisticated in demanding the right to audit the books and records of the licensee. Of course, this should be equally critical to any licensor, no matter the form.

o. Reporting and Marketing Responsibility

Individuals generally are less involved in reporting on progress or contributing to marketing efforts than other licensors. It is sometimes critical, especially in the case of a major technological development, to have the inventor available to aid in marketing and fund-raising efforts. It also is critical that the licensee be notified of any further developments in the technology.

p. Representations and Warranties of the Inventor

These should always include ownership, non-infringement of other patents, no pending or threatened litigation or claims against patents or licensor, patentability of IP, and compliance with specific laws, including export/import laws and laws governing handling, treatment, labeling, environmental treatment, etc., of possible biohazards. There is no need for "authorization," although a representation about the individual having capacity may help.

q. Indemnification

The inventor should agree to indemnify the licensee for all breaches in the agreement, especially related to ownership and infringement. Individuals tend to be more leery of this than entities because of personal liability.

r. IP Protection

Clarify who has the continuing duty to perfect or maintain patent rights, trade secret rights, manage infringement claims, etc., and how that will be paid. Also state that all products will be marked appropriately (i.e., patent pending, ™, ®, ©, etc.).

s. Insurance

Sometimes individuals do not ask for this, especially in an assignment, but generally a licensee is required to demonstrate or provide some or all of the following:

Acquisition of Biotechnology—Technology Transfer

- Comprehensive general liability
- Products liability coverage
- D&O coverage
- Employer liability
- Coverage against environmental and pollution problems
- Infringement coverage
- Waiver of subrogation
- Prior notice of change or cancellation
- Name of licensor as additional insured
- Copies of all related policies

t. Assignability

Licensees will want this to be assignable. Inventors may not care, as long as the assignee has the ability to pay and is bound by all terms and conditions. Original licensee may remain bound.

u. Amendments

Who can amend the agreement and how? Usually in these cases it is by mutual consent, only in writing.

v. Alternative Dispute Resolution (ADR)

Much more common in these contracts, ADR provisions usually require mediation before a suit is brought and often require that suits be subjected to arbitration. Licensees will want to name or limit the possible arbitrators, if possible.

w. "Boilerplate" Language

- Notice information
- Force majeure (if a party cannot deliver through no fault of its own, it is not in breach)
- Entire agreement/integration clause (but beware of inadvertently superseding other related agreements, such as an NDA)
- Choice of law and forum (licensee want its home state in most cases)
- Confidentiality

- Non-competition and non-solicitation. It is advisable to deal with these as separate primary sections and tailor them to the transaction, but some put them in the "boilerplate" section.
- Attorney's fees and court costs
- Counterparts
- No agents or brokers
- No beneficiaries not in privity to the contract
- Headings are not for construction of the contract
- Survivability
- Severability of provisions declared void or unenforceable if the rest of the agreement is still valid

2. Common Negotiation Points

a. Price Paid/Consideration

Individuals, depending on the level of sophistication, often want royalties, fees, and an equity stake. The size of the company and the potential of the technology may dictate whether equity compensation is appropriate. In the case of a company with little cash reserves, this may be the best solution. The licensee must weigh the company's stock, which is "cash-free," vs. its obligations to limit dilution of other shareholders. The individual inventor may want to ensure that the language in the license applies any percentage royalty payment, whether from sales or profits, against any later sublicensee. Compromise alternatives include negotiating sublicense sharing in lieu of reach through royalties or even a combination approach, where the patent owner receives a specified portion of the sublicense revenues attributable to the licensed IP.

b. Fees and Royalties Are Both Negotiable Points

The company usually will want minimal up-front fees and possibly base fees on milestone events such as Phase I, Phase II and Phase III, filing or approval of an NDA filing with the FDA, or the first commercial sale of product. The licensee should want any royalty to be based on net profits as it calculates profits on the matter, including all applicable overhead and other charges. The individual should want royalties to be based on revenues or sales. A possible middle ground is to base revenues on net sales, which are revenues minus specific, defined expenses. That is the most common basis for royalties, although what is included in net sales can vary from deal to deal.

c. Records and Reporting

The company may resist providing detailed records to the individual. The individual may not ask for them. However, in order to ensure development of the product and to check results against royalty payments, individuals may demand access to records and that specific records be kept in a certain way. In some cases the individual will request the right to have a CPA inspect the financial records of the sales.

d. Warranty

The company will want any warranty that it can get. It must have a warranty that the individual transferring the technology owns the technology, did not disclose the technology prior to patent application, and that the technology, to the best of the inventor's knowledge, does what it has claimed to do. The licensee may want additional warranties confirming its safety and efficacy, although the licensor should resist. A compromise may be to warrant the accuracy of the information provided, perhaps with a knowledge qualifier.

e. Indemnification

Indemnification from an individual usually is not worth much. The company will clearly want to be indemnified against any ownership issues or other violations of the warranty term, and against the IP infringing the IP rights of a third party. The company should state in the indemnification language that it can withhold fees and royalty payments and sue for return of previously paid fees in order to protect its right to indemnification.

f. IP Matters

(i) *Patent handling*—The company needs to confirm in the license (as well as in due diligence) that the invention was not publicly disclosed prior to patent application and that the patent application fairly and fully describes the invention. The license may state how costs will be covered for future patent filing matters. Sometimes costs are shared, but more often the licensee incurs the future patent costs. This, however, depends on the degree of exclusivity; the more exclusivity you have, the more likely you are to be responsible for patent costs. In some cases, a licensee negotiates to deduct some portion of the future patent costs from the royalty payments. The inventors must assign their rights to any future patent filings on the technology and agree in advance to cooperate with any such filings.

(ii) *Name and trademark usage*—If the individual has already developed a name for the product, and especially if the invention is already known in the trade press under that name, the licensee may want the rights to the use of that name. In most cases, for practical and liability purposes, it is more sensible for the company to create its own name.

(iii) *Secrecy and confidentiality*—The licensee will want to ensure that the individual inventor maintains all secrets and confidences in her possession relating to the licensee. Often in negotiations, the licensee must disclose its projections for the product and, in some cases, in order to prove its ability to fund and pay royalties, its own financial situation. If the company is not public, it will want to ensure that the individual keeps these matters confidential.

Similarly, in investigating the individual's invention, the licensee may discover other inventions in process or other matters that the individual wishes to keep confidential.

g. Confirmation of Ownership

Confirmation of ownership, always critical, is especially important in acquiring technology from individuals. It is vital that the licensee perform adequate due diligence to ensure that the individuals transferring the technology are the only inventors of the technology. It is critical that the technology is investigated thoroughly to ensure that no parts of it are owned by anyone else, especially with a patent on file. Due diligence both in the inventors' records (especially lab workbooks) and in the U.S. PTO database and other sources is essential. This is especially important, because breach of contract claims and indemnification are less likely to be of value in these cases.

3. Patent Filing

Has a patent been filed on the invention? Is the patent adequate? Are there possible defenses against the validity of the patent? Were there any prior disclosures of the technology? If there were disclosures, did they include elements critical to the patent itself? If a patent has not been filed, who will file it? Are the inventors assigning their rights to the patent and agreeing to cooperate in filing the patent in the license? Is there anyone else who has an arguable claim that they were an inventor of some portion of the technology?

All of these questions must be asked to verify that an adequate patent has been filed or can be filed by the company at a later date.

F. Summary

Biotechnology is a broad industry. Products often are built upon other products or other technology. Most new biotech products begin in a university or nonprofit institution. Getting the IP out of those settings is not simple. Since the IP deals with life sciences, which are complex by nature, it is rare that any commercial product is the result of a single development in a single laboratory. Sharing and transferring technology is the rule. Accordingly, any practitioner should allow ample time to understand who owns all necessary technology and plan a strategy to ensure that the company has freedom to operate with regard to the final product.

Critical to this process are three lessons we all learned in kindergarten. The first lesson is to look both ways before crossing the street. In this case, look at all the IP and determine what the various components are. When you have done that, you can determine whether IP belongs to others and how best to negotiate with them for rights to use that IP. The second lesson is to put yourself in the other's shoes. Understand what they need and why. This is important whether you are the licensee or the licensor. Only then can you begin to understand what is important to the other side and foresee negotiation points before they become problems. Failure to understand the indemnification needs of a university, for example, will delay a deal for no real purpose. The third lesson is to play well with others. Cooperative agreements, joint ventures and the like are common in this industry. You may have to give up some equity (and control) or provide certain rights to the resulting invention in order to gain access to the needed IP or to avoid substantial early cash penalties. You are more likely to get the deals done and continue developing the product for future deals if you take a reasonable approach. There are a lot of competing products out there, especially products in the development stage, and not many products that cannot be replaced or substituted with something else. In southwest Virginia, where I grew up, we say that pigs get fat and hogs get slaughtered. This is an important concept, especially when dealing with larger companies and nonprofit entities that often have greater resources and a different set of priorities. These concepts are developed more fully in Chapters IX and XVII.

Notes

1. This is merely an overview of this practice area. This chapter does not seek to address all legal and regulatory issues that companies or lawyers would have to consider in this practice. Some specific omissions are local laws, regulation with respect to the use and transportation of hazardous or restricted materials (if applicable), environmental law, product liability law, and "generic" issues such as local contract, labor, real estate, corporate, taxation, and anti-trust law.

2. *See* Madey v. Duke Univ., 307 F.3d 1351 (Fed. Cir. 2002).

3. *See* a brief discussion of these factors in the IRS's publication *at* http://www.irs.gov/govt/fslg/article/0,,id=110344,00.html.

4. *See* CAL. LAB. CODE § 2860.

5. *See* CAL. LAB. CODE § 2870.

6. *See* CAL. LAB. CODE § 2870; *see also* Amendariz v. Foundation Health Psychcare Svcs., Inc., 24 Cal. 4th 83, 100, 6 P.3d 669, 680 (Cal. Sup. Ct. 2000).

7. *See* Spiroll Corp. Ltd. v. Putti, et al. (1975), 22 C.P.R. 2d 261, 1975 C.P.R. Lexis 306 (finding in favor of employee where employee was not hired to invent for employer and invention did not derive from job duties). *Compare* W. J. Gage Ltd. v. Sugden (1967), 51 C.P.R. 259, [1967] 2 O.R. 151, 62 D.L.R. (2d) 671 (discussing theory that employee holds inventions made during course of employment as trustee for employer where invention derives from job duties).

8. Copyright Act § 14.1.

9. *See, e.g.,* VA. CODE ANN. §§ 59.1-335 et seq.

10. See Chapter II for a detailed discussion of this topic. We borrowed liberally from Chapter II in drafting this summary.

11. 35 U.S.C. § 204.

12. Copyrights, patents, and trade secrets generally are "assigned" rather than "sold," because they are intangible assets.

13. The U.S. Patent and Trademark Office now accepts patent assignments in an online format. Online forms may be viewed *at* http://epas.uspto.gov.

14. 17 U.S.C. § 107.

15. *See* Roche Products v. Bolar Pharm. Co., 733 F.2d 858, 862-63 (Fed. Cir. 1984) and the recent circuit court ruling in Madey v. Duke Univ., 307 F.3d 1351 (Fed. Cir. 2002).

16. *See* 35 U.S.C. § 271(e)(1) and (2):

> (1) It shall not be an act of infringement to make, use, offer to sell, or sell within the United States or import into the United States a patented invention (other than a new animal drug or veterinary biological product (as those terms are used in the Federal Food, Drug, and Cosmetic Act and the Act of March 4, 1913) which is primarily manufactured using recombinant DNA, recombinant RNA, hybridoma technology, or other processes involving site specific genetic manipulation techniques) solely for uses reasonably related to the development and submission of information under a Federal law which regulates the manufacture, use, or sale of drugs or veterinary biological products.
>
> (2) It shall be an act of infringement to submit—
>
> (A) an application under section 505(j) of the Federal Food, Drug, and Cosmetic Act or described in section 505(b)(2) of such Act for a drug claimed in a patent or the use of which is claimed in a patent, or
>
> (B) an application under section 512 of such Act or under the Act of March 4, 1913 (21 U.S.C. 151–158) for a drug or veterinary biological product which is not primarily manufactured using recombinant DNA, recombinant RNA, hybridoma technology, or other processes involving site specific genetic manipulation techniques and which is claimed in a patent or the use of which is claimed in a patent,
>
> if the purpose of such submission is to obtain approval under such Act to engage in the commercial manufacture, use, or sale of a drug or veterinary biological product claimed in a patent or the use of which is claimed in a patent before the expiration of such patent.

17. *See* http://www.gnu.org.

18. Michael J. Martin, one of the authorities in this area, who has worked for both commercial interests and universities, says in jest, "Universities are morally superior to those money-grubbing, blood-sucking capitalists." Actually he points out that businesses and universities have different missions and measure success differently. The mission of a university is to create and disseminate knowledge, and technology transfer affords another method to package knowledge for use by society. That is why it may appear to commercial interests that universities are not driven solely by monetary rewards.

19. Kenneth S. Dueker, *Biobusiness on Campus; Commercialization of University-Developed Biomedical Technologies*, 52 FOOD & DRUG LAW J. 453 (1997).

20. *Id.*

21. S. Rep. No. 480, 96th Cong., First Sess., at 19 (1979); Dueker, *supra* note 19, at 460.

22. 35 U.S.C. §§ 200 *et seq.*

23. *Id.*

24. http://www.autm.net/aboutTT/aboutTT_faqs.cfm

25. For an excellent summary of the history of technology transfer in the United States, see Kenneth S. Dueker, *supra* note 19. Much of what I know of this history I learned from Mr. Dueker's writings, and that may be reflected here unitentionally. For an excellent overview of the current considerations of university technology transfer officials, please see the AUTM Web site at www.autm.net or consult a member of AUTM. This chapter author's knowledge on this subject was increased substantially over the years by referring to those sources.

26. *See* http://www.fda.gov/oc/ofacs/partnership/techtransfer/purpose.htm.

27. http://ethics.od.nih.gov/LawReg/FR-New-5501-5502.pdf and 5 C.F.R. §§ 5501 and 5502.

28. *See* Association of University Technology Managers, Inc., AUTM Technology Transfer Practice Manual, Vol. III (1994) and NIH guidelines.

29. 35 U.S.C. § 202(c)(1) et seq.; and 37 C.F.R. § 401.

30. 34 U.S.C. § 202(c)(4) and 37 C.F.R. § 401.14(a).

31. Dr. Harold Varmus, Director, National Institutes of Health, Office of the Director, Determination in the Case of Petition of Cellpro, Inc. (August 1997).

32. *Also see* 35 U.S.C. §§ 102(e), (f), and (g) and 103(c)(2)–(3), and an assortment of articles on the Web.

33. *See primarily* Internal Rev. Reg. § 1.51301(a) and United States v. American Bar Endowment, 477 U.S. 105, 111 n.1 (1986).

34. *Id.*

35. I.R.C. §§ 512(b)(1), 512(b)(2), and 512(b)(5).

Chapter V

Financing a Biotech Company

William N. Wofford
Hutchison Law Group, PLLC
Raleigh, North Carolina

With Special Thanks to Don Novajowsky and J. Robert Tyler
of Hutchison Law Group, PLLC

A fledgling biotech company has numerous hurdles to overcome in its path toward achieving the long-term goals of commercialization of its products and technology and, ultimately, profitability. Other chapters address many of these challenges. Few of these challenges, however, are more daunting than finding the capital to fund the huge investments in intellectual property, clinical trials, operations, and personnel necessary to discover, develop, and commercialize safe, effective, novel therapeutic products.[1]

This chapter will discuss challenges associated with funding a biotech company. Particular attention will be given to funding issues from the time of formation until an initial public offering (IPO), because most biotech companies will be acquired or go out of business before reaching a point where an IPO is a viable option. Many of those that remain independent will eventually need access to the large pools of capital available in the public markets and will, accordingly, need to avoid missteps that could jeopardize an IPO.

A. Overview

If a company can develop a proprietary idea into a safe and effective new therapy, chances are good that the investors in the company will realize exceptional returns because of the strong margins typically earned on novel biopharmaceutical products in the United States and, to a lesser extent, other developed countries. However, the biotechnology and pharmaceutical industries are characterized by: 1) high costs of labor, materials, and intellectual property rights; 2) intense government regulation; 3) low success rates; and 4) complex manufacturing and distribution processes. To be successful, most biotech companies will require outside capital over six, eight, ten or more years. And the large amount of capital needed at more advanced stages will compel them to tap venture capital and the public equity markets to meet their capital needs. As a result, those companies that achieve promising results with initial funding are rewarded with the task of having to raise additional capital.

1. Drug Development Costs

Before considering the particulars of various kinds of funding, it is essential to understand the scale of the funding challenge. One of the most widely reported studies of the costs getting a drug to market is published periodically by the Tufts Center for the Study of Drug Development.[2] In May 2003, the Tufts Center estimated that the total cost to develop a new prescription drug was $897 million, including the costs of post-approval studies. Earlier studies included estimates of $54 million in 1979, $231 million in 1991, and $802 million in 2001. These studies are controversial, in part, because they account for the cost of failures in the development process, including research on potential products abandoned during development, as well as the opportunity costs of incurring research and development expenditures before generating revenues from sales. From the perspective of a biotech company, the studies might overstate the costs involved because they are based on a survey of major pharmaceutical companies, many of which may have higher overhead and personnel costs compared to smaller biotech companies. Nevertheless, few would argue that the cost to bring a new human therapeutic product from conception to the marketplace is enormous and growing.

Financing a Biotech Company 205

A large part of new-product development costs are funded with profits earned by established companies from the sale of existing drugs and biotech products. As shown in Figure 5-1,[3] much of the rest is funded with proceeds from the sale of securities by public companies.

Exhibit 5-1
Total Financing, 1998-2004 (in billions of U.S. dollars)

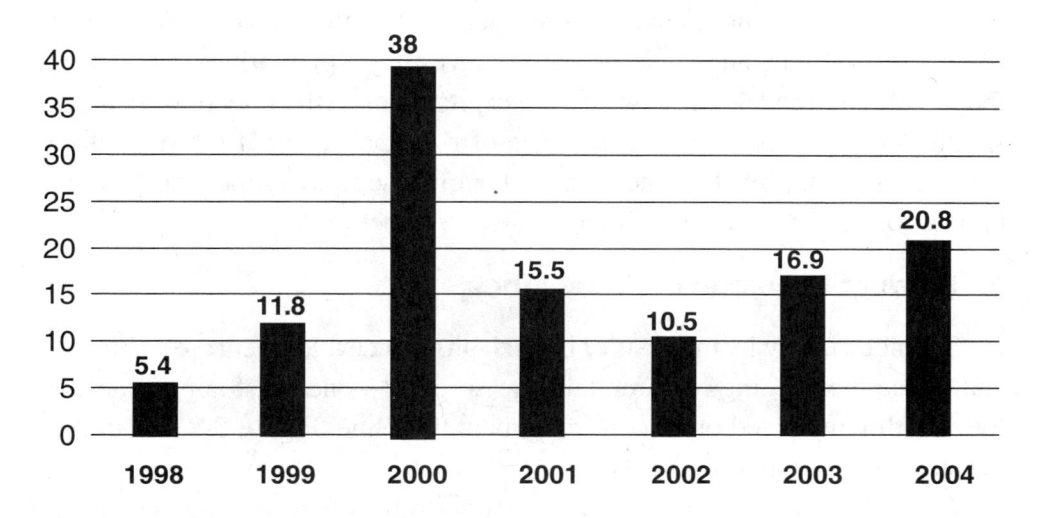

Year	Amount
1998	5.4
1999	11.8
2000	38
2001	15.5
2002	10.5
2003	16.9
2004	20.8

Figure 5-2
Biotech Industry Financing, 2004

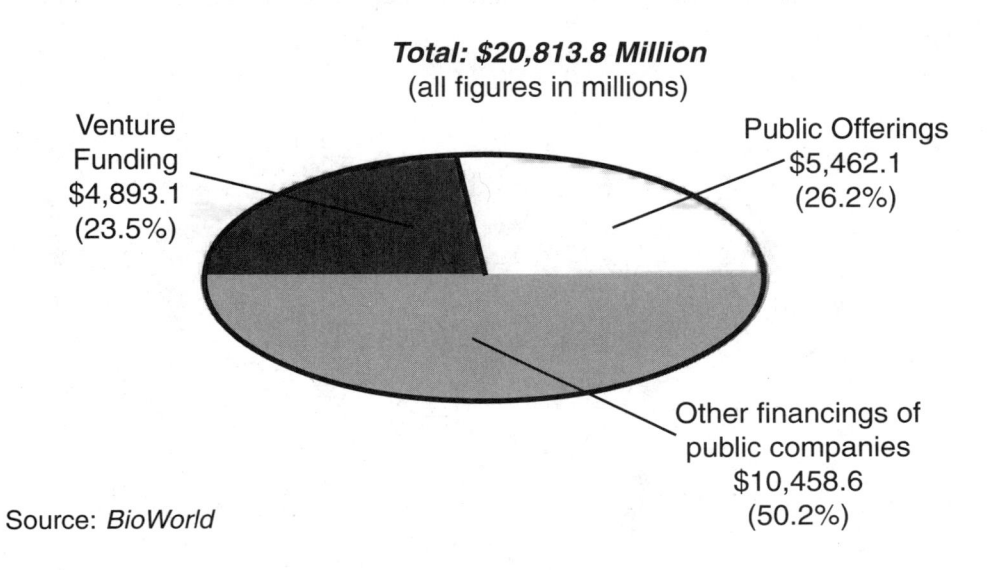

Total: $20,813.8 Million
(all figures in millions)

- Venture Funding $4,893.1 (23.5%)
- Public Offerings $5,462.1 (26.2%)
- Other financings of public companies $10,458.6 (50.2%)

Source: *BioWorld*

Clearly, tremendous amounts of capital are invested in private companies by venture capital firms and in public companies. The amount invested in public companies far exceeds the amount of venture investment. Reasons for this include: (a) the supply of capital in the public securities markets dwarfs the amount of funding in venture capital funds; (b) public capital markets are more willing to finance late-stage clinical trials than early-stage clinical trials because the chance of failure is lower and, if the trials are successful, the amount of time to get a product to market is shorter; and (c) the high costs and lower risk associated with later-stage trials make investing in these trials a poor fit for the investment models of most venture capital firms, which tend to focus on smaller investments with greater levels of risk and potential return. Before companies are eligible for funding by either of these sources, they must clear a number of hurdles, some of which are discussed below.

2. Product Development Time Lines

To understand why the costs of biotech product development are so high—and hence the funding requirements are so great—one must appreciate the long, highly regulated product development time line. Figure 5-3[4] illustrates the steps involved in this process.

In order to fully appreciate why the time from inception of an idea for a novel therapeutic to receipt of regulatory approval is so extensive, it is important to have a basic understanding of the regulatory process governing clinical trials. That process is discussed in detail in Chapter X, but a brief summary is provided here.

Figure 5-3
Biotech Drug Discovery Process

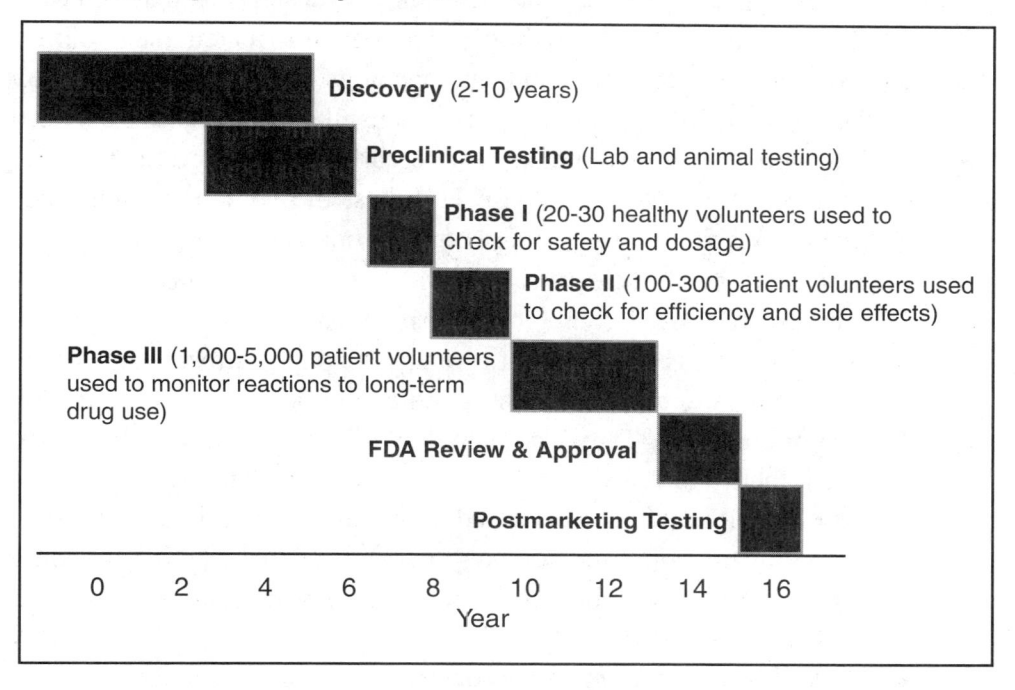

- **Discovery** (2-10 years)
- **Preclinical Testing** (Lab and animal testing)
- **Phase I** (20-30 healthy volunteers used to check for safety and dosage)
- **Phase II** (100-300 patient volunteers used to check for efficiency and side effects)
- **Phase III** (1,000-5,000 patient volunteers used to monitor reactions to long-term drug use)
- **FDA Review & Approval**
- **Postmarketing Testing**

Year: 0 2 4 6 8 10 12 14 16

As shown in Figure 5-3 above, it often takes years for researchers to identify compounds, proteins or other biologic material that may serve as the basis for a drug development program. This discovery phase may involve screening a vast number of potentially useful compounds or isolating and characterizing numerous complex biologic materials. Once a suitable candidate is found, the potential product enters pre-clinical development (i.e., testing in animals) and clinical development (i.e., clinical trials in humans). The U. S. Food and Drug Administration (the FDA) summarizes the process as follows:

> Once a candidate drug is identified, the sponsor notifies the FDA of its intent to conduct clinical studies on human subjects. This is called filing an initial new drug application, also referred to as an IND. The IND involves a detailed review process, which, if successful, paves the way to clinical studies. Clinical development typically involves three phases of study, as follows.

- Phase I studies may be conducted in patients, but typically involve healthy volunteer subjects. These studies are designed to determine the pharmacokinetic (how the drug is absorbed, distributed, metabolized, and excreted by the body) and pharmacologic (the effect of the drug on the body) actions of the drug in humans, the side effects associated with increasing doses, and, if possible, early evidence on effectiveness.

   Upon conclusion of Phase I studies, the company determines whether results are promising enough to pursue a Phase II study to help determine the scientific validity of the drug. If the answer is negative, research on the compound is terminated.
- Phase II studies are designed to obtain data on the effectiveness of the drug for a particular indication or indications in patients with the disease or condition. They also help determine the common short-term side effects and risks associated with the drug. Phase II studies are closely monitored and conducted in a relatively small number of patients. At this point, the company again evaluates whether it should pursue further research on the molecule. A positive decision will lead to Phase III studies.
- Phase III studies are expanded controlled and uncontrolled trials. They are done to gain additional data about effectiveness and safety needed to evaluate the benefits and risks of the drug. Results from Phase III studies also yield data that will provide the information that eventually will go on physician labeling.[5]

Each stage of clinical development is considerably more expensive than the previous step. This is largely a function of the increasing number of physicians and patients involved in larger studies. As a result, when favorable results are achieved in pre-clinical studies or a Phase I or Phase II clinical trial, the sponsoring company (assuming it does not already have a product on the market or other sources of funding) will generally need to raise capital to fund the next costly phase of clinical development. As discussed in Chapters VII, IX, and XVIII, government funding and commercial partnerships may serve as an attractive alternative to raising capital from investors to fund clinical trials. Where those options are unavailable, unattractive, or inadequate, a company will generally need to sell stock to investors to raise the necessary funds.

Financing a Biotech Company

The rest of this chapter will address how a developing biotech company can find the resources to fund its development while avoiding legal mis-steps that could jeopardize future access to capital.

B. Basic Securities Law Considerations

Counsel to a biotech company will serve his client well by helping prepare the company for the rigors of due diligence that future funding sources will conduct. He will earn client loyalty by helping to avoid unpleasant tax traps. But nothing will please a client's management and directors more than keeping them out of jail. For that, compliance with the securities laws is a must.

1. Registration or Exemption Under the Securities Act

The Federal Securities Act of 1933, as amended (the Securities Act), and related regulations and interpretations are the main body of law regulating the sale of securities. The Securities Act, enforced by the Securities and Exchange Commission (the SEC), is very broad in scope. As stated in the Securities Act: "Unless a registration statement is in effect as to a security, it shall be unlawful for any person, directly or indirectly . . . to sell such security through the use or medium of any prospectus or otherwise."[6] The definition of a "security" under the Securities Act is very expansive and encompasses many types of financial instruments that a company may issue, including shares of stock and options to purchase stock. The Securities Act provides for exceptions and states that a company cannot sell its securities without either (a) first registering its securities with the SEC, or (b) issuing a security that is exempt from registration (i.e., issuing an "exempt security"), or (c) consummating the transaction in accordance with an exemption from registration (i.e., issuing a security in an "exempt transaction").

Registering securities with the SEC requires extensive and ongoing disclosure. For more developed companies, registering securities, completing an IPO, and enjoying the visibility and access to public capital markets associated with having listed shares of stock is an essential element of its financing strategy. For an early-stage company, the high costs of compliance alone are probably enough to make registering its securities prohibitive. These costs, coupled with a lack of interest in the public markets for early-stage technologies and the enormous potential liability associated with securities, make registration a distant dream of early-stage companies. The Securities Act provides that certain types of securities are automatically exempt. However, exempt securities include securities such as government securities, railroad equipment trusts, and certificates issued by a trustee in bankruptcy, which are generally not relevant to a biotech company. As a practical matter, early-stage companies will not be able to register their securities or issue "exempt securities," so they must issue securities in "exempt transactions."

The Securities Act provides exemptions for a number of types of transactions, but only a few of these are generally relevant to an early-stage biotech company. The most commonly used exemptions are provided for in Section 4(2) of the Securities Act and the related Rules 501-506 (also known as Regulation D - Limited Offerings) and Rule 701 (Rule 701 - Compensatory Benefit Plans).

2. Section 4(2) Exempt Transaction

Section 4(2) provides an exemption for "transactions by an issuer not involving any public offering." The plain text suggests that so long as a company does not advertise its shares or indiscriminately offer them to unsuspecting widows and orphans, a company could rely on the exemption provided by 4(2). However, case law and regulatory guidance tend to narrowly interpret the exemption. As a result, there is considerable uncertainty regarding the scope of 4(2), making reliance on 4(2) a risky affair. Companies that do not anticipate facing intense scrutiny of their history of securities transactions from the SEC and investors' attorneys may be inclined to rely on 4(2) for many transactions. For a biotech company that expects to need venture capital and eventual access to the public markets, however, greater certainty is a priority. In addition, non-compliance can result in substantial fines, sanctions and even, potentially, criminal charges, so counsel should avoid reliance on 4(2) when other exemptions are available.

3. Regulation D Exempt Transaction

To provide issuers with greater certainty, the SEC adopted a number of "safe harbors." Transactions that comply with the specific provisions of these safe harbors are deemed to be covered by 4(2). A transaction that does not comply with the safe harbor requirements may still be exempt under 4(2), but there is risk that it will not. Biotechnology companies seeking the assurance of a safe harbor exemption will often look to Regulation D (often called "Reg. D").

Reg. D comprises Rules 501 through 506 promulgated under the Securities Act. The basic policy of Reg. D is to provide issuers with a safe harbor while maintaining standards for disclosure and other matters to provide protection of investors, particularly less wealthy or sophisticated investors who are believed to need greater protection under the law. Rules 501 through 503 provide definitions and general conditions and procedural requirements. Each of Rules 504, 505, and 506 provides a specific exemption, with variations regarding specific thresholds and disclosure requirements. For instance, 504 is limited to offerings of up to $1 million, 505 covers offerings up to $5 million, and 506 has no limit on the amount of money raised.

Perhaps the most important aspect of Reg. D is the concept of the "accredited investor." The regulation makes it relatively simple to comply if the securities will be offered and sold only to "accredited investors." Rule 501 defines an "accredited investor" as a person who meets one or more of the following qualifications:

- a director, executive officer or general partner of the issuer or any general partner of the issuer, or
- a person with a net worth, together with his or her spouse, of more than $1 million, or
- a person who has had income in excess of $200,000 in each of the two most recent years or joint income with his or her spouse in excess of $300,000 in each of those years and has a reasonable expectation of reaching the same income level in the current year.[7]

Reg. D does not prohibit the sale of securities to unaccredited investors. However, enhanced disclosure requirements, limitations on the number of unaccredited investors, and other provisions make compliance with Reg. D more difficult and less certain if unaccredited investors are permitted to invest. As a result, in many cases, companies seeking to rely on the safe harbor provided for in Reg. D will offer and sell securities only to accredited investors.

To qualify for the Reg. D safe harbor, a company must make a filing with the SEC. The company must complete a short form (called a Form D) and submit it to the SEC together with a filing fee no later than 10 days after the first sale of securities in the offering. The form includes disclosures regarding the identity of the company's officers, directors, and principal stockholders, the amount of the investment, and the state(s) where securities have been sold, among other disclosures.

4. Rule 701—Compensation Plans

Rule 701 promulgated under the Securities Act provides another exemption commonly used by biotech companies. Unlike Reg. D, which is used in connection with fund-raising, Rule 701 applies to companies issuing securities that are compensatory in nature. The purpose of this rule is to provide a clear and relatively simple exemption to enable companies to make equity-based compensation available to employees and others serving the company. The rule is based on the premise that securities offered to these persons are often means of providing incentive-based compensation to the individuals, not ways to finance a company. The basic requirements of Rule 701 are as follows:

> **Practice Points**
>
> Form Ds are publicly available documents. For a company that wishes to keep the status of its fund-raising activities or the identity of its investors confidential, the company should consider filing the Form D before the first sale is made. If the filing is made after the investment, it must disclose the identity of parties that have become directors and major stockholders as part of the transaction. If the filing is made prior to the investment, it serves as notice of the company's intent to sell up to a specified amount of a particular security, but details about expected future investors need not be disclosed.

- The plan must be a bona fide compensation plan, not a scheme to obtain financing.
- Sales under the plan in any 12-month period must not exceed the greatest of $1 million, 15 percent of the total assets of the company, or 15 percent of the outstanding amount of the relevant class of securities.
- If more than $5 million of securities will be sold under this exemption in any 12-month period, certain financial and other information must be disclosed.

Unlike Reg. D, Rule 701 is a self-executing exemption, meaning that no filing with the SEC or other federal agency is required.

5. State "Blue Sky" Laws

In addition to the federal rules, each state has specific rules and regulations governing the sale, distribution, and issuance of securities to residents within its borders. These "Blue Sky" laws once imposed duplicate and even inconsistent regulations on the sale of securities. Much of the regulatory burden of compliance with federal and state securities laws was reduced with the adoption of the National Securities Markets Improvement Act of 1996 ("NSMIA"). This act provided for federal law to preempt many, but not all, elements of state regulation of securities. Although NSMIA streamlined compliance, it did not entirely preempt state regulation of securities, so practitioners still need to review the securities laws of the states where the clients and other purchasers of securities (including employees and others who receive options under a Rule 701 plan) are based.

> **Practice Points**
>
> 1. Don't act like the U.S. government—be frugal with cash.
> 2. Remember that a modest share of something big is better than 100 percent of nothing—use stock to reward and motivate key contributors.
> 3. But pay attention to securities laws when issuing stock.

In summary, counsel representing biotech companies must be particularly mindful of securities laws, because biotech companies will likely need to raise capital multiple times from sophisticated sources and will be subject to thorough due diligence review. Noncompliance can cause considerable expense and other difficulties. For example, in some cases the only practicable way to cure prior noncompliance with securities laws is to conduct a rescission offer. This is a transaction where the company offers to rescind the offending sale of securities by offering to repurchase them. Rescission offers are time-consuming and expensive exercises that can be avoided with compliance. Fortunately, compliance is feasible for companies that carefully consider the securities law issues associated with each issuance of securities.

C. Pre-seed and Seed Capital

Prudent cash management is important to any business. For a biotech company that will face large cash outlays for operating costs, intellectual property, and clinical trials well in advance of generating significant revenues, the importance of making efficient use of capital cannot be overstated. The challenge is to make as much progress as possible with as little funding as possible, so that when selling stock to investors, the company can command the highest price per share practicable, enabling the current stockholders to retain the largest practicable stake in the company.

Before venture capital firms and the public markets get interested, the main sources of funding at early stages include equity investments or loans from founders, initial officers, and "angel" investors (i.e., individuals who qualify as accredited investors). Other sources include "sweat equity," where founders, employees or providers of services forgo cash compensation in exchange for shares of the company. In some cases, bank loans may be available. In addition, many early-stage companies will look for ways to generate revenue to offset some of the costs of research, development, and overhead. Finally, grants from government or nonprofit organizations may be available for companies engaged in innovative research or pursuing treatments for "orphan" indications (rare diseases or conditions that are generally not viewed as attractive market opportunities for businesses). Although some of these activities are not financing activities in the conventional sense of the sale of debt or equity securities, each can play an important role in ensuring that a biotech company will have adequate financial resources to execute its business plan.

1. Founders' Stock

When a biotech company issues stock to its founders, the founders rarely make a large cash investment in the company. Nevertheless, founders' stock plays an important role in financing a biotech company at its earliest stages. Instead of cash, a biotech company obtains the benefit of the founder's hard work, reputation, experience and, sometimes, intellectual property in exchange for the founders' stock. These contributions help launch the venture and position it to be eligible to raise capital from other sources at subsequent stages. This is generally one of the few situations where a biotech company will issue stock in reliance on the exemption of 4(2) of the Securities Act.

Even though a founder's cash stake in the company's stock may be nominal, the legal implications of this investment are sizable. A founder will generally control a substantial ownership interest in the company. Although this interest will likely get diluted (i.e., the number of shares will stay the same but it will represent a smaller percentage) over time as investors and other stakeholders obtain shares of the company, founders' stock can represent a large portion of the company's capital stock for many years. Therefore, it is essential that the founder's stock be subject to appropriate restrictions that align the economic interests of each founder with those of the company and its other stakeholders. Because biotech companies are scrutinized very closely by lawyers representing potential investors, counsel to the company should make every effort to ensure that the expectations of potential investors will be met during due diligence.

To that end, company counsel should consider having the following restrictions apply to shares issued to founders at the time the company is first organized and capitalized.

a. Restrictions on Transfer

Federal securities laws impose significant restrictions on the transferability of unregistered stock, but investors will generally expect founders to hold all or most of their shares until a sale of the company or following an IPO, so restrictions that are more stringent than those required by law will often be required. With limited exceptions (e.g., transfers to family members, charitable organizations or estate-planning entities), founders should not be able to transfer their shares without the approval of the company. Many early-stage companies will include restrictions of this kind in the company's bylaws.

b. Vesting

It is common for co-founders to agree that shares should vest. With vesting, a founder receives stock up front, but agrees that all or a portion of the shares will be forfeited if he or she does not meet certain commitments, typically consisting of continuing to be an active contributor to the company for a specified period of time. The concept of vesting effectively ties the economic interests of the founder with that of the company's other stockholders. For example, if a founder receives 100,000 shares of stock that contain provisions calling for "four-year vesting with a one-year cliff," the shares will all be issued to the founder at about the time the company is formed. If the founder remains involved for the full four-year period, she will keep all 100,000 shares. However, if she leaves during the four-year period, a pro rata portion of the shares will be cancelled. The "one-year cliff" means that if she leaves during the first year, she will forfeit all of her shares. Although vesting based on time appears to be the most common form of vesting, it is also possible to provide for vesting based on performance of the founder, the company, or other factors as may be determined by the company's board of directors.

c. Lock-up

If the company ever aspires to sell shares in an IPO, founders and other significant stockholders will likely be required to sign a "lock-up" or "market stand-off." This is an agreement prohibiting them from selling their shares for a determined period (often 180 days) following the IPO. Although many founders remain active and supportive of companies at the time of an IPO and generally have an economic incentive to help facilitate such a transaction even if they are no longer actively involved, it is not unheard of for an estranged founder to be inaccessible or even uncooperative. If the lock-up agreement is obtained in advance, the company can avoid additional logistics and negotiations that might be required to obtain a lock-up agreement later.

Practice Points

Beware "phantom income." In any situation involving vesting, the parties should consider filing an election under Section 83(b) of the Internal Revenue Code. If stock is subject to vesting and no 83(b) election is made, the stockholder will be required to recognize as taxable ordinary income the difference between the value of the stock at the time of vesting and the amount paid for the stock. Because the stockholder incurs a tax liability without receiving any cash, the income is sometimes referred to as "phantom income." If an 83(b) election is made, the difference (if any) between the value and the price paid is treated as income at the time the shares are purchased (when the shares may have virtually no value), but later vesting will not result in phantom income.

d. Drag-along

In order to protect the company's liquidation options in the future, a founder's stock may be subject to drag-along rights. A drag-along right is a right that enables majority stockholders to require another stockholder to vote in favor of and otherwise help facilitate a future sale of a company. Drag-along rights are designed primarily to protect majority stockholders from one or more minority stockholders that might seek to disrupt a sale or other transaction or to demand additional benefits as a condition to cooperation. The potentially adverse effects of drag-along rights are often ameliorated by providing assurances that the minority stockholder will be subject to the same terms and conditions as other similarly situated stockholders. In some cases, a stockholder subject to a drag-along obligation will also receive a "tag-along" right that gives him the ability to sell his shares if other holders are selling theirs.

> **Practice Points**
>
> Equity compensation arrangements can have a considerable impact on the company's financial statements because the value of the equity interest can be treated as a compensation expense, increasing the expenses of a company for financial reporting purposes, even when cash is not changing hands. While many believe that basic valuation metrics such as earnings have limited practical significance to a development-stage biotech company, qualified accountants should be consulted to confirm that a company is aware of and prepared for the accounting consequences associated with its stock-based compensation arrangements.

These kinds of obligations do more than just help prepare the company for some of the rigors of legal due diligence for future financing activities. They can also serve to help founders understand that a biotech venture will require sustained effort and contributions from numerous participants before parties can "cash out." Nevertheless, in many cases, companies and founders will defer imposing many of these restrictions unless and until it becomes a requirement of a venture capital financing. Deferral can reasonably be justified by the KISS (keep it simple, stupid) principle. Nevertheless, counsel should consider advising companies to adopt appropriate restrictions early, when the stakes are low and the sense of shared purpose among founders may be at its zenith.

2. Employee Stock

Many early-stage companies wish to provide incentives to employees by granting them shares of the company's stock or options to purchase shares of the company's stock. These arrangements will rarely result in a meaningful cash infusion to the company. However, as with founders, employees may accept lower cash compensation in exchange for stock or stock options. The resulting savings in compensation from utilizing equity as a component of compensation may be part of the company's overall financing strategy.

The cornerstone of most employment-related stock programs for early-stage companies is a stock option plan. A properly designed and implemented stock option plan will provide a fairly simple way for companies to ensure compliance with applicable corporate and securities laws and to avoid unpleasant surprises when preparing audited financial statements. The plan will also enable the company to meet the commercial expectations of future investors while providing employees and other optionees tax-advantaged ways to enjoy some of the benefits of ownership of a high-growth company.

a. Plan Basics

An option plan is a written arrangement that provides for the grant of stock options to employees and other persons. A stock option is the right to purchase a share of stock on specific terms and conditions. If a stock option meets requirements specified under the Internal Revenue Code (the "IRC"), the option can qualify as an "incentive stock option" ("ISO") and be eligible for favorable treatment under the IRC. Options that do not qualify as ISOs are called "non-qualified stock options" ("NQSOs"). To qualify as an ISO, the options must satisfy certain criteria, such as:

- The option must be in writing.
- The company's stockholders must approve the option plan within 12 months before or after the plan is approved by the company's board of directors.
- ISOs cannot have a term greater than 10 years (five years if the options are granted to persons holding 10 percent or more of the company's stock) and cannot be granted later than 10 years following stockholder approval of the plan.

- ISOs can only be granted to employees of the company (not directors or consultants).
- An ISO must be exercised during employment or within 90 days after the end of employment, though a longer period may be available if employment is terminated due to death or disability.
- The exercise price of options cannot be less than the fair market value of the underlying stock on the date of grant (or 110 percent of the fair market value if the option holder is a 10 percent stockholder).
- The company must limit the value of stock underlying options granted to any recipient that may vest in any particular calendar year to $100,000, based on the value of the stock on the date of grant.
- The options are subject to restrictions on transfer.

b. Securities

As discussed above, any issuance of stock or other securities must be registered or exempt. Rule 701 provides an exemption under federal law for securities issued under a plan that meets certain requirements. Because compliance with Rule 701 is pretty straightforward (as discussed above), many companies will operate all of their compensatory stock arrangements under this rule. Practitioners still need to be mindful of state Blue Sky laws. Some states take the view that regulation under Rule 701 and other federal standards (e.g., ERISA) provide adequate oversight of employment-related stock or option plans. Others consider employment-related equity programs as an appropriate area for state regulation. For example, California securities law imposes both procedural requirements (filings with the state) and substantive requirements (certain terms and conditions must be included in the option plan or agreement). Because so many biotech companies have employees or consultants in California, many companies will incorporate the California standards into their option plans either on a general basis or at least for employees based in California.

c. Tax

NQSOs are generally less favorable to the optionee from a tax perspective than ISOs because the optionee will recognize taxable income when he or she exercises the option, even if the optionee does not sell the underlying stock. Moreover, the income will generally be taxed at ordinary income tax rates rather than lower capital gains tax rates. An ISO permits an optionee to defer income recognition from the time the optionee exercises the option until the time the employee sells the shares. In addition, the holding period for the stock starts at the time of exercise, so if the optionee holds the shares for at least one year after exercise (and more than two years from the date the option was first granted), the entire difference between the exercise price and the market value at sale will be taxed at the lower capital gains rate. In other words, an ISO can enable the optionee to defer tax and pay tax at a lower rate as compared to an NQSO. Following the adoption of Section 409A of the Internal Revenue Code in 2004, companies should be very cautious about granting stock options with an exercise price that is less than fair market value, or else the option grant will not only fail to qualify as an ISO, but it could also subject the recipient to phantom income (see practice point above) and cause the company additional tax withholding and reporting obligations. A detailed discussion of corporate and personal income tax issues associated with equity compensation is outside the scope of this chapter. However, any practitioner should recognize that if a company adopts and properly implements a stock option plan, the company can provide its employees and others with potentially valuable long-term benefits while minimizing or at least deferring unfavorable tax consequences.

d. Corporate

The most basic corporate law considerations associated with granting stock or options to employees are ensuring that the shares to be issued are duly authorized and that the company receives adequate consideration for shares that it issues. A properly designed and implemented stock option plan will help ensure compliance with these requirements in a few ways. First, an option plan will be adopted by the company's board of directors and, in most cases, will also be approved by the stockholders (as noted above, stockholder approval of an option plan is a requirement for an option granted under the plan to be an ISO). At the time the plan is approved, the board will typically reserve the requisite number of shares of the company's capital stock for issuance upon exercise of options granted under the plan. As a result, the company should be confident that shares issued under the option plan have been duly authorized. In addition, each time an option is granted under the plan, the board of directors (or a committee or person that the board has delegated authority to) will need to determine the terms and conditions of the option, including the exercise price. This process will help the board meets its obligation to ensure that the company receives adequate consideration for shares that it issues.

e. *Commercial*

Stock option plans provide a number of commercial benefits to a company. As noted above, the potential value of stock options enables companies to conserve cash by paying lower salaries than would otherwise be required. In addition, vesting provisions and the requirement that ISOs must be exercised during employment, or within a short period after termination of employment, provide employees with an incentive to stay with the company, because if they leave they may lose the value of the stock options. Finally, stock option plans may be used to meet investor expectations regarding restrictions on transfer, vesting, lock-ups and drag-along rights.

There are other arrangements that companies may use to provide stock-based compensation to employees, which may be suitable in particular circumstances. However, for the reasons discussed above, many early-stage biotech companies will use stock option plans as the primary or exclusive tool to provide stock-based compensation. Companies using other approaches will need to carefully consider the securities, tax, accounting, corporate, and commercial issues associated with different vehicles. These issues were further complicated with the effectiveness in 2005 of Section 409A of the Internal Revenue Code, which imposes excise taxes on a broad range of arrangements that involve deferred compensation.

3. Stock to Service or Technology Providers

Professional advisors and others accustomed to working with early-stage biotech companies understand the financial challenges faced by these companies. They also recognize that a successful biotech company may be a valuable client for many years and a potentially lucrative investment. Consequently, some will be prepared to accept stock or options in exchange for deferring or forgoing some or all of the cash compensation they might otherwise charge. Similarly, as discussed in Chapter IV, many universities and other research institutions will generally expect full reimbursement of out-of-pocket patent expenses as part of the compensation for the grant of an exclusive license to intellectual property rights. Knowledgeable technology transfer professionals recognize that requiring an early-stage company to pay all of these costs immediately may put undue burden on the company, particularly where an extensive or mature international patent portfolio is being licensed on an exclusive basis. Consequently, it is often possible for an early-stage biotech company to negotiate a deferred payment schedule based on time or the achievement of commercial or funding milestones and to provide the institution with some stock as part of the license agreement.

As with other grants of stock, it is necessary to consider securities, tax, and other legal issues in connection with issuing stock or options to service or technology providers.

a. Securities

Institutional technology providers will typically meet the financial requirements to qualify as an "accredited investor." In addition, because a transfer of technology from one or a very small number of institutions for stock of a closely held private company as part of a negotiated license agreement is a unique transaction, the transaction should readily qualify under the 4(2) exemption. Transactions with service providers may qualify under 4(2), Regulation D or even Rule 701, but counsel should consider carefully the relative merits of these exemptions.

b. Tax

A transaction involving the exchange of services or technology for stock will typically be a taxable transaction. As a result, the party that receives the stock will generally have taxable income equal to the value of the stock. Of course, the value of the stock of a privately held company may be difficult to determine because there is no market trading in the shares of stock. In the absence of a market, it is appropriate to consider comparable, contemporaneous transactions. If the transaction with the service or technology partner is not properly structured, it could complicate other stock-based arrangements. For example, if a service provider agrees to accept 1,000 shares of common stock in lieu of fees of $1,000, it would seem clear that the company and the service provider have agreed that the common stock has a value of $1.00 per share. If the company then granted an option to an employee with an exercise price of less than $1.00 per share, the option might not qualify as an ISO because the exercise price was less than the fair market value of the stock (i.e., $1.00 per share) at the time of grant. In addition, Section 409A could require that the recipient recognize taxable income and that the company withhold tax on the phantom income. To avoid creating this kind of problem, it may be advisable to engage in separate and distinct transactions. For instance, a service provider might purchase stock at the same time and the same price as the founders or might receive an NQSO under the stock option plan. Separately, the service provider and the company could agree on a discount or fee deferral arrangement.

c. Conflicts of Interest

Owning stock in a client company may raise conflict of interest concerns for legal counsel or other service providers. Ethics rules, malpractice insurance requirements, and other guidance vary considerably from state to state, and consideration of those issues is outside the scope of this chapter. Universities and other research institutions also maintain policies governing conflicts of interest. While these also vary considerably, companies should, at a minimum, not expect to conduct human clinical trials at an institution that has an equity or royalty interest in the company or technology that is the subject of the trial.[8]

4. Friends and Family

Many entrepreneurs looking to raise early-stage capital will approach their friends and family for seed capital. This type of investor is likely to be less sophisticated and demanding than venture capitalists, so the transaction will rarely be subject to the type of negotiation that is part of a venture capital financing (discussed below). Instead, the company will typically decide the terms of the offering. As a result, it is possible that the company will have the opportunity to complete a financing on terms (such as price per share) that are more favorable to the company than a well-informed investor would accept.

a. Securities

Companies seeking to raise investment capital from individuals—including friends and family—are well advised to deal only with accredited investors and to comply with the procedural and filing requirements of Reg. D.

b. Corporate

Individual investors may be willing to overpay for shares. This presents something of a dilemma to the company. On the one hand, the company's board has a responsibility to current shareholders to obtain adequate value for the shares. This would suggest that obtaining the highest price that the market will bear for the company's stock is appropriate, because it would minimize dilution to current shareholders by raising the greatest amount of money while issuing the fewest possible shares. It could also be argued that it sets a precedent for valuation, so any later financing activity would have to occur at a higher price. Experience, however, suggests a more cautious approach that would balance the desire of the company and its founders to minimize dilution with a realistic understanding of what subsequent investors will expect regarding valuation. A "down round" (i.e., a later financing at a lower price per share) can be fraught with legal risk for many of the parties involved. There are legal strategies to ameliorate the risks associated with a down round, but counsel would be well advised to recommend that clients establish a realistic valuation when raising capital from individuals.

5. Loans

Another alternative, at least in theory, for a company to satisfy its capital requirements is to borrow money. Debt has a number of attractive features, including that it does not dilute the ownership interests of the stockholders. On the other hand, for the early stage biotech company, debt has very serious limitations. With revenues a distant possibility and with limited assets to serve as collateral, early-stage biotech companies are generally viewed as poor credit risks, so loans are generally unavailable. If a founder, officer or other person has substantial assets and is willing to guaranty a loan, lenders may be more willing to advance funds, but will typically still expect to see a business model that indicates that the loan will be repaid with interest on a timely basis. Although exceptions exist, loans are rarely a realistic financing tool for early-stage biotech companies. An exception to this general rule is the convertible "bridge loan." A convertible bridge loan is temporary financing that is meant to bridge the gap to a larger, more permanent round of financing. For example, an investor might lend a company money. The loan would be evidenced by a note and the note would be convertible (on either an optional or a mandatory basis) into shares of stock issued by the company in its next financing that

Financing a Biotech Company

meets specified criteria. The investor that makes the loan would typically get some benefit from investing at an earlier, riskier stage. The benefit would customarily be in the form of a reduced conversion rate (where, for example, $1.00 of loan principal would convert into $1.25 worth of stock issued in the financing) or warrant "coverage" (where the loan principal would convert into shares at the standard price, but the investor would also receive warrants to purchase additional shares of stock in the future at the current (presumably low) price).

6. Generating Revenues to Reduce or Defer Need for Investment

To reduce its need for investment capital, a company can generate revenue to offset some of its operating expenditures. For example, an early-stage biotech company may provide research services for a fee on a contract basis to a larger, more established company. Or it may license or sublicense some of its intellectual property rights to raise funds to support development of the retained rights. Although the company might be able to command a greater price later for the same intellectual property rights after generating additional pre-clinical or clinical data, the need for capital may make it reasonable to give up the rights to potential future benefits in exchange for funding up front. Generating revenues of this kind can create some risks.

a. *Intellectual Property*

Care must be taken in contracts of this kind, or the company may find that it has assigned improvements to its core technology to a third party. As discussed in considerable detail in Chapters IX and XVIII, biotech licensing is a complex, high-stakes game in which many factors need to be taken into account to ensure that the value of a company's technology is not reduced by the activities of hostile or irresponsible licensees. A biotech company will want to make sure that its early, revenue-generating activities do not create impairments on its intellectual property portfolio that will make it harder to complete an important strategic alliance later. This can usually be handled by making sure that service contracts confirm that while the client obtains ownership to data and inventions related to its own drug, the biotech company retains ownership to its core technology and any improvements created during the project.

b. Commercial

In many cases, engaging in revenue-producing work is disfavored by companies and potential investors because it can interfere with the primary objective of developing a product. Nevertheless, some companies that can successfully devote resources to generating revenue will conclude that the benefits, including reduced dependence on investment capital, outweigh the costs. Some companies are successful in achieving the best of both worlds, where they get paid to develop their core technology and retain substantially all of the rights.

7. Government Funding

Various federal and state programs offer grants and contracts that may present an attractive alternative or complement to other sources of capital. Federal support of research is covered in great detail in Chapter VII, so this section will only touch on key characteristics of a few of the most popular programs for early-stage biotech companies: the Small Business Innovation Research ("SBIR") Program and the Small Business Technology Transfer ("STTR") Program.

a. SBIR Grants[9]

The SBIR program funds early-stage research and development at small technology companies and is designed to: (a) stimulate technological innovation; (b) increase private-sector commercialization of federal R&D; (c) increase small-business participation in federally funded R&D; and (d) foster participation by minority and disadvantaged firms in technological innovation. To participate in the SBIR program:

- a firm must be a U.S. for-profit small business of 500 or fewer employees;
- work must be performed in the United States;
- during Phase I, a minimum of two-thirds of the effort must be performed by the proposing firm; a minimum of one-half of the effort in Phase II; and
- the principal investigator must spend more than one-half of the time employed by the proposing firm.

SBIR funding is conducted in two distinct stages, and applications must be submitted to the appropriate federal entity at predetermined dates. First, companies apply for a Phase I (note, these phases are unrelated to the phases of clinical trials discussed above and elsewhere in this book) award, which may be in amounts of up to $100,000. Phase I awards are meant to test the scientific, technical, and commercial merit and feasibility of a particular concept. Upon successful completion of a Phase I award, the company may then be invited to apply for a two-year Phase II award of up to $750,000 to further develop the concept, usually to the prototype stage. Proposals are judged competitively on the basis of scientific, technical, and commercial merit. Following completion of Phase II, small companies are expected to obtain funding from the private sector and/or non-SBIR government sources (in "Phase III") to develop the concept into a product for sale in private sector and/or governmental markets.

b. STTR Grants[10]

In 1992, Congress established the STTR pilot program. STTR is similar in structure to SBIR but funds *cooperative* R&D projects involving a small business and a research institution (i.e., university, federally funded R&D center, or nonprofit research institution). The purpose of STTR is to create an effective vehicle for moving ideas from our nation's research institutions to the market, where they can benefit both private-sector and governmental customers.

To participate in the STTR program:

- a firm must be a U.S. for-profit small business of 500 or fewer employees (there is no size limit on the research institution);
- the research institution must be a U.S. college or university, FFRDC or nonprofit research institution;
- work must be performed in the United States;
- the small business must perform a minimum of 40 percent of the work and the research institution a minimum of 30 percent of the work in both Phase I and Phase II;
- the small business must manage and control the STTR funding agreement; and
- the principal investigator may be employed at the small business or research institution.

Like SBIRs, STTR grants are awarded in a two-stage process.

c. Advantages to Receiving Federal Grant Funding

There are a number of benefits to obtaining government grant funding. Grant funds are cash awards, have no impact on the ownership of the company and, unlike loans, do not need to be repaid. Further, the SBIR and STTR funds are potentially recurring. Not only can a company progress through the process by receiving successive Phase I and Phase II funding, but a single company can obtain additional SBIR/STTR funds for various projects it may be exploring and developing. Other benefits include the fact that success in winning grant awards provides external validation that the company's science is valid and potentially valuable. Some companies find success in using grant funds to help bridge the gap from the formation stage to a point where venture capital may be available.

d. Disadvantages to Receiving Federal Grant Funding

Conversely, there are certain drawbacks to these programs. The funds must be used for specific purposes, so the company does not have much flexibility in how it uses the funding. Grant expenditures are subject to strict accounting rules and auditing by governmental agencies. Further, the funding process can be slow. Finally, the funds are generally unavailable for commercialization activities, so while they can complement other sources of capital, grant funds cannot provide all of the funding to move a product development effort toward commercialization.

e. Eligibility/51 Percent Rule

One hot topic in recent years has been the question of eligibility for SBIR and similar grants. As the name suggests, and as the requirements noted above state, only certain small businesses are eligible to receive these awards. In particular, eligibility requires compliance with the 51 Percent Rule—the requirement that an SBIR recipient must be a for-profit business concern that is at least 51 percent owned and controlled by one or more individuals who are citizens of, or permanent resident aliens in, the United States; or it must be a for-profit business concern that is at least 51 percent owned and controlled by another for-profit business concern that is at least 51 percent owned and controlled by one or more individuals who are citizens of, or permanent resident aliens in, the United States.[11]

Part of the rationale behind the 51 Percent Rule is to prevent large companies from creating subsidiaries that would artificially qualify as "small." However, until January 2001, many companies took the position that domestic venture capital firms should be treated as U.S. "individuals." In January 2001, an Administrative Law Judge ruled that "individuals" must mean "natural persons." As a result, companies that are majority-owned by venture capital firms (as is common in biotech) were no longer eligible to receive SBIR funding.

Some companies that consider continued eligibility for SBIR funding a priority may adopt corporate structures designed to ensure ongoing compliance with the applicable requirements. Potential structures might include:

- *Convertible Debt*—Debt securities are not equity ownership interests in a company, and even convertible debt, which can be converted into shares of a company stock, is not considered an equity security. Therefore, a company may be eligible for continued SBIR funding even though one or more venture capital firms hold convertible debt that represents a majority of the economic value of the company.
- *Voting Trusts*—The 51 Percent Rule regulates ownership in the context of voting control over the company. Therefore, if voting control of the company is transferred to a trust controlled by qualified individuals, the requirements of the 51 Percent Rule may be met even if venture capital firms or other disqualified persons own a majority of the beneficial interests of the company.
- *Separate Research and Development Companies*—It may be possible to establish a subsidiary or other special purpose company having an ownership structure that meets the requirements of the 51 Percent Rule and to then have this company contract with the other company for a portion of the research and development activities for which the grant is made.

As the law in this area is not very well developed, the risks and benefits of approaches that might be viewed as circumventing the intent of regulations should be carefully considered.

f. State Resources

Many states provide incentives to recruit and support biotechnology companies. Practitioners will generally be aware of the programs available in their own states, but a good survey of state programs is maintained by the Bioscience Industry Organization (www.bio.org).

D. Venture Capital[12]

Venture capital is a professionally managed pool of capital that is raised from public and private pension funds, endowments, foundations, banks, insurance companies, corporations, and wealthy families and individuals. Venture capitalists (VCs) generally invest in companies with high growth potential that have a realistic exit scenario within five to seven years. As noted in Figure 5-1 above, VCs invested nearly $5 billion in biotech companies in 2004. Other published figures show that these funds may be invested in 300-400 companies, making for an average investment in the range of $10 million.[13]

Each of these transactions involves substantial due diligence, negotiation and documentation, and requires that numerous legal issues be addressed. Before discussing particular legal issues, however, it is important to understand the principal elements of a venture capital financing. From the perspective of the company, of course, venture capital financing is important because it provides substantial infusions of capital to fund research and development activities. In addition, many VCs have valuable connections with relevant industry experts and investment bankers, so investments by VCs can be leveraged into other important business and finance activities. For the VCs, investments in biotech companies represent potentially lucrative, albeit long-term, investments.

Following is a discussion of key provisions of a venture capital transaction. Exhibit A following this chapter provides a glossary of terms associated with a venture capital investment and a sample venture capital term sheet for a first round of funding. In the first round of funding, the company will generally issue Series A Convertible Preferred Stock. Subsequent rounds of investment will generally involve the sale of Series B Convertible Preferred Stock, Series C Convertible Preferred Stock and so on, until an initial public offering (when the preferred stock will generally convert to common stock), a sale of the company (in which the stockholders will all exchange their shares for cash and/or other securities) or a recapitalization. A recapitalization generally involves a situation where a struggling company raises money and some or all of the rights and preferences of existing stockholders are eliminated or substantially reduced. Issues associated with recapitalizations are outside the scope of this chapter.

1. Financial Rights

a. Valuation

A key factor in any venture capital investment is the value of the company. In particular, VCs and other stakeholders will need to determine what percentage of the company the VCs will receive in exchange for a particular investment amount. This is frequently discussed in terms of "pre-money" valuation and "post-money" valuation. For example, if a VC invests $4 million in a company for 40 percent of the company's shares, the company would have a pre-money valuation of $6 million and a post-money valuation of $10 million. The price per share paid by the investor would generally be set at whatever price is necessary to ensure that the $4 million investment would result in the investor owning 40 percent of the shares. In these calculations, the total number of shares generally includes a significant number of shares reserved for employee stock options (often referred to as the "option pool").

b. Liquidation Preference

Most venture capital investments are structured as convertible preferred stock. A fundamental feature of preferred stock is that it has a liquidation preference. A liquidation preference is a feature of the stock that provides that the holder of that stock is entitled to receive a specified dollar amount per share before holders of common stock or other "junior" securities receive value for their stock.[14] The amount of the liquidation preference will generally be at least equal to the original purchase price of the stock. In some cases, the liquidation preference will be a multiple of the amount invested.[15] If the company is sold or liquidated, the VCs get their liquidation preference before the holders of the common stock (typically founders, management, and employees) receive any value for their shares.

c. Participating Preferred

Many VCs insist that the preferred stock be "participating" preferred stock. This means that *after they receive the liquidation preference,* they share on a pro rata basis with the holders of the common stock in any proceeds that remain. These participation rights allow the VCs to share in a greater portion of the proceeds if the company is sold on favorable terms. If convertible preferred stock is non-participating, then the VCs will have the right to choose between the liquidation preference or converting the preferred stock into common stock and receiving a pro rata share of the proceeds of the sale.

d. Accruing Dividends

Preferred stock might bear a fixed-rate dividend that, due to the cash-constraints of early-stage companies, is not currently payable, but is cumulative and becomes part of the liquidation preference upon a sale or liquidation of the company. The payment of dividends on the preferred stock will have priority over common stock dividends. These cumulative dividend rights provide a priority minimum rate of return to the VCs.

e. Protection of Ownership Percentage

After VCs obtain a specified percentage interest in a company, they will want to ensure that the interest cannot be diminished against their will. VCs protect their ownership percentages through preemptive rights, anti-dilution protection, and price protection. Preemptive rights give investors the right to purchase a portion of the shares of stock sold in future financing rounds, enabling them to maintain their percentage ownership in the company. Anti-dilution protection adjusts the investors' ownership percentages if the company effects a stock split, stock dividend or similar transaction. Price protection protects the VCs from the risk that they overpaid for their stock if the pre-money valuation turns out, in retrospect, to have been too high. There are two common types of price protection: full ratchet and weighted average ratchet. A full ratchet retroactively reduces the price per share paid by the VC to the lowest price at which the company subsequently sells its common stock regardless of the number of shares of stock the company issues at the lower price. A weighted average ratchet adjusts the price according to a formula that takes into account the lower issue price and the number of shares that the company issues at that price. Nearly all VC investments will have either a full ratchet or a weighted average ratchet, but these terms, like many others, fluctuate over time in response to and as part of overall market conditions for capital (see, e.g., survey cited in prior footnote).

2. Governance Rights

a. Board Representation

Most venture capital investments provide VCs with considerable ability to control a company. Even where VCs obtain a minority interest in a company, they will insist that the company's governance structure ensure that they have considerable protections and control. For example, investment structures generally provide that some or all of the VCs have the right to elect a member of the board of directors. This ensures that their representatives have regular opportunities to confer with management and to review and vote upon executive employment matters, budgets, material transactions, and other strategic matters. In some cases, investment documents will require that certain actions must have specific approval of the investor-designated members of the board, even where general corporate law principles would provide that the matter could be approved by a simple majority.

b. Protective Provisions/Class Voting

In addition, preferred shares will often have "protective provisions." These provide that a company may not engage in certain activities or complete certain transactions without first having received the affirmative vote of a designated group of stockholders. For example, terms of an investment may require that the company obtain the consent of holders of a majority of the company's Series A Convertible Preferred Stock in order to amend the company's certificate of incorporation, to issue additional shares of stock, to deviate from an approved budget, to incur debt, to enter into a strategic license or partnership or to merge with, acquire, or be acquired by another company. These rights may be included in the company's certificate of incorporation or may be specified in an "Investor Rights Agreement" or other contract entered into as part of the financing transaction.

3. Exit Rights

VCs must achieve liquidity in order to provide the requisite rate of return to their investors. In other words, they must convert their shares of portfolio companies into cash or marketable securities so they can distribute these proceeds to their owners. Most VC funds have a limited life of 10 years, and most investments from a fund are made in the first four years. Therefore, investments are structured to provide liquidity within five to seven years so that investments made in a fund's third and fourth years are liquidated as the fund winds up and its assets are distributed to the fund's investors. The primary liquidity events for VCs are the sale of the company for cash or marketable securities or the sale of company stock following an IPO by the company.

Generally, VCs do not have a contractual right to require the company to be sold but have enough influence that they have the practical ability to force a sale. For example, if VCs believe that a sale of the company will provide a more favorable return on investment than continuing to invest in development efforts, the VCs have the ability to prevent the company from selling additional stock to raise capital, leaving the company with no alternative to pursuing a sale of the business.

a. Registration Rights

VCs typically obtain registration rights. "Demand" registration rights give the VCs the right to require the company to register its shares with the SEC, so that the VCs can sell their shares in the public capital markets. Also, VCs will generally have "piggyback" registration rights that give them the right to include their stock in future registered offerings that the company may wish to complete. Although it is very uncommon for VCs to exercise registration rights to compel a company to go public, the existence of the rights enables VCs to put pressure on a company to sell or go public.

b. Redemption Rights

VCs also insist on redemption rights to give them a way to achieve liquidity if it is not available through a sale or public offering. This gives the investors the right to require the company to repurchase their stock after a specified period, typically four to seven years. The purchase price for the stock may be based upon the liquidation preference discussed above or the fair market value of the stock as determined by an appraisal or a formula. A private company that is struggling may not be able to finance the buyout of an investor, meaning that the redemption right may not be a practical way to achieve liquidity. However, this right gives the VCs tremendous leverage to force management to deal with their need for an exit and can result in a forced sale of the company. Also, if the VCs trigger their redemption right and the company does not meet its payment obligations, the VCs might have the right to take over control of the board of directors, putting them in a position to direct any future activities of the company.

c. Co-sale Rights

Other exit rights that VCs typical require are "co-sale" rights. Co-sale rights give the investors the right to include their stock in any proposed sale of stock by management or founders.

4. Series B—Time to Start All Over

It is not uncommon for the financial, governance, and exit rights of VCs to get revised during the life of a biotech company. The typical biotech company seeking to develop a novel therapeutic may require three or more rounds of venture capital before it reaches the stage of development where it is suitable to attempt to access public capital markets through an IPO. Each new round of financing may include new and current investors.

Nearly all of the rights associated with a VC investment may be renegotiated. As a general rule, new investors will seek to have preferences and priorities over existing investors. In the case of financial rights, for example, later investors will normally want their liquidation preference to have priority over (or be "senior" to) the liquidation preference of earlier investors. Existing investors, however, can be expected to prefer a *pari passu* arrangement, where all preferred investors share equally in proceeds of a sale or liquidation. With respect to governance rights, holders of Series A Convertible Preferred Stock may wish to retain a class vote over important company transactions, whereas new investors—who may be making a larger investment—may believe that class voting privileges should be exercised only by the Series B Convertible Preferred Stock holders. A compromise might involve the holders of Series A and Series B voting together as a single class on some or all of the protective provisions. Series B investors may wish to have one or more of their representatives replace an existing member of the board of directors. Regarding exit rights, later-stage investors will require assurance that earlier investors cannot exercise redemption rights or registration rights in a way that adversely affects the interests of the later-stage investors. Initial investors may have difficulty accepting these adjustments if the effect is that their ability to force a liquidity event is deferred until after the 10-year life of their investment funds. Market conditions, notably the perceived attractiveness of the company relative to other investment opportunities, will significantly affect the negotiations regarding these relative rights. While the company and investors may renegotiate many terms as part of successive rounds of financing, the effect of precedent should not be ignored: if a company grants its Series A investors a favorable provision, it will be very difficult to avoid granting the same or a similar benefit to subsequent investors.

E. Corporate Investment

Venture capital firms are not the only outside parties to invest in the stock of developing biotech companies. Often, larger biotech or pharmaceutical companies will also invest in the stock of a privately held or publicly traded biotech company. These investments are generally completed as part of a broader strategic alliance, including a license or a collaboration for research, development, and/or commercialization. Alliance issues are discussed in Chapters IX and XVIII, but there are certain aspects of equity investment by a strategic partner that merit particular attention.

For a biotech company, selling shares of its stock to a strategic partner is generally considered a welcome, positive development for several reasons. The most obvious is that the investment provides additional capital to fund operations. The next major reason is that corporate investors (also referred to as "strategic" investors) will often have lower financial return requirements on these investments than venture capital firms or other "financial" investors. For the biotech company, this can translate into less demanding financial rights (often in the form of a higher share price) and less onerous governance and exit rights than would be available from a financial investor. Finally, the strategic relationship with the larger company is often viewed as important validation of the technology and commercial prospects of the biotech company.

In many ways, the terms of investment for a strategic investor will be similar to those of a financial investor. However, counsel representing a biotech company must be careful not to simply mirror the terms of the latest VC investment round.

As noted above, one of the advantages of receiving investment capital from a strategic investor is that other strategic considerations may make the investor more accommodating on price and other terms than a financial investor. These strategic considerations most frequently involve the expectation that successful development of the technology of the biotech company will provide significant commercial value to the strategic investor. For example, the strategic investor may have rights to commercialize one or more products resulting from a collaboration between the parties, and the investor expects that these commercialization rights, rather than its investment in the stock of the biotech company, will provide the most valuable return to the strategic investor.

On the other hand, strategic considerations of the corporate investor may result in conflicts or difficulties for the biotech company and its other stockholders. For example, governance rights granted to VCs often include the ability to veto a merger or other major transaction. This veto right is considered reasonable and customary in VC transactions, because VCs, as financial investors, can be expected to act in a way that is intended to maximize the value of their stock holdings in the biotech company. Normally, a VC can be expected to support a merger or other transaction that results in the greatest financial benefit (on a risk-adjusted basis) to the stockholders of the company, since the VC, as a major stockholder, will directly benefit. On the other hand, a strategic investor may view a merger very differently. For instance, if the other party in a proposed merger is a competitor of the strategic investor, the strategic investor may wish to prevent the competitor from acquiring control over the biotech company's technology. If the governance rights granted to the strategic investor in connection with its investment include a veto over the transaction, the strategic investor could prevent a transaction even if the transaction would result in an excellent return to all of the biotech company's stockholders. Because the grant to a strategic investor of a right of this kind could prevent the biotech company from getting acquired, future potential investors in the company might be unwilling to invest in the company, leaving the company unduly reliant on the good will of—or at the mercy of—the strategic investor.

F. Initial Public Offering

Many biotech companies and their investors consider an IPO to be a crowning achievement. An IPO is a transaction in which a company registers its securities and sells them to the public through a syndicate of investment banks. Typically, an IPO will involve only the sale of new shares, meaning that the company keeps all of the proceeds after transaction expenses.

There are good reasons for a biotech company to relish the opportunity to complete an IPO. Among the benefits are:

- Raising a large sum of money (perhaps $30-$100M) in a single transaction.
- Reducing the cost of capital for future transactions.
- Being relieved of the sometime onerous provisions of venture capital investments (because the preferred stock will generally convert into common stock and many of the other special rights of venture capital investments will end upon the completion of an IPO).
- Becoming more visible to potential investors and collaborators.
- Attracting talented personnel.
- Providing investors the opportunity to liquidate their investments and realize a return on their investment.

On the other hand, pursuing an IPO can be a painful process for the biotech company for a variety of reasons, including:

- Long days and nights with investment bankers and lawyers.
- Comprehensive scrutiny of business activities and historical transactions by regulators and teams of attorneys.
- High costs to complete the transaction, in both professional fees and lost management time.
- Chance that uncontrollable factors (e.g., unfavorable clinical trial developments by the company, favorable or unfavorable clinical trial results for competitors or general market conditions) will stop the deal before it can be completed.
- High ongoing compliance costs, in terms of both out-of-pocket expenses and potentially cumbersome business processes.

Often, stockholders think of an IPO as a liquidity event. While it is certainly a momentous event in the life of a biotech company, it may not be accurate to consider it a liquidity event. That is because "lockup" agreements and other factors will impose significant restrictions on the ability of insiders to sell their shares. While it is possible for current stockholders to sell some of their shares as part of an initial sale of shares to the public, stockholders will generally need to wait at least six months after the IPO to begin selling their shares. In addition, sustained sales by insiders or other large stockholders can cause the share price to decline significantly.

G. Post-IPO Financing

As demonstrated in Figure 5-1, most of the capital invested in biotech companies is invested during IPOs and other transactions involving public companies. For the most part, these transactions involve conventional stock offerings, in which a company, working with a syndicate of investment banks, will offer new shares of its stock to institutional investors (such as mutual funds) and individuals. It is not uncommon, however, for biotech companies to utilize more exotic securities and transaction structures to raise capital. While there is not room for a detailed discussion of legal and commercial considerations associated with these types of transactions, it is worth identifying a few structures and some of their salient features.

1. PIPES

As noted above, an IPO is not only a way of raising a sizable amount of capital in a single financing transaction. It is also a step that ensures that the company will, in general, have greater future access to capital than a similarly situated private company. Once public, a company may raise additional funds with the help of its bankers, or underwriters, by selling additional shares of stock which it has registered with the SEC in subsequent underwritten public offerings. A public company can also engage in privately negotiated transactions with investors. In fact, these happen on a regular basis, and they are often structured as a "PIPE" (private investment in public equity). In a typical PIPE deal, a company will sell shares of its stock to a small group of hedge funds or other institutional investors. At the time of the transaction, the shares will be unregistered shares, meaning that the company has not registered the shares with the SEC, and without an intervening registration of the shares, investors would typically need to hold their shares for at least one year before they could sell them into the market under a securities laws exemption known as Rule 144. However, the company will normally agree to register the shares within a specified period of time (with the initial registration filing typically to be made with the SEC within 30 to 60 days after the sale of the stock). The SEC does not review all registrations of stock. If the SEC notifies the company that it will not review a particular registration, the registration is deemed to be immediately effective and the purchasers can begin trading immediately after notification, but if the SEC does decide to review a company's registration, it may take an additional two or three months after the initial filing for the SEC to approve the registration of shares (at which time the investors can begin trading). To compensate the investors for taking the risk that the shares will decline in value between the time of their investment and the time that they can sell the shares, the company will typically accept a price that is a discount to the public trading price at the time of the sale (perhaps 10-20 percent of the trailing trading price average over a period of days). In some cases, investors may be able to ameliorate the risk of a stock price decline by engaging in hedging transactions related to the stock of the issuer (e.g., the investor could sell the stock short, so a decline in the price of the stock would generate a benefit to the investor). Investors may also receive warrants to purchase additional shares at a stated price for a specified period of time, giving them additional ability to share in potential success of the company.

2. Convertible Debt

During the biotech financing boom of 2004, many companies chose to raise capital by selling convertible notes. Convertible notes are a hybrid security, meaning that they have some features of both debt and equity. Typically, a convertible note will be a promise to pay a stated amount, plus interest (which may be fixed or variable and may be payable in regular installments or in a "balloon" payment at maturity), at a particular time (the maturity date). As with other debts or liabilities, the obligation to repay a convertible note is senior to the rights of stockholders to receive proceeds from the sale or liquidation of the company. Unlike other creditors, however, the holder of a convertible note will have the right to convert the note into stock of the company.

Many biotech companies have found that by structuring a financial instrument that gives investors the enhanced security of being a creditor of the company while having some opportunity to participate in appreciation in value of the stock if the company is successful, the company can obtain capital at the lowest overall cost. If the company simply borrowed money, lenders would generally require a higher interest rate and perhaps other concessions. And if the company simply sold additional stock, it might receive an undesirable price per share, resulting in excessive dilution to current stockholders.

3. Project Finance

At the time this book was going to press, a new type of financing—project finance—had emerged to fund biotech development.[16] Project finance involves a transaction or series of related transactions in which financing is provided to support a particular project (e.g., one or two phases of clinical trials for a drug candidate). The funding can be used only for the particular project and the capital providers can look only to the project for payment. This can be structured by forming a special-purpose entity that is owned in whole or in part by the investors. The biotech company would have an agreement in place to purchase the stock of the special-purpose entity on certain terms and conditions. In essence, if the project was successful, the biotech company would have an incentive to reacquire the assets that had been transferred to the special-purpose entity. If the clinical development program were unsuccessful, the biotech company would not exercise its right, leaving the investors to bear the burden of the unsuccessful trial. At the time of publication, there is no way of knowing whether project finance will become a prevalent and enduring piece of the biotech financing puzzle.

There are also international variations on the project finance concept. For instance, it may be feasible for a biotech company to license rights to certain of its technology to a separate entity in a country that offers grants, tax credits or other governmental incentives for biotech research and development activities. The company and the investors in the new entity could share in the benefits of the governmental incentives and the benefits of successful R&D efforts. Of course, these would need to be balanced against additional overhead costs of a separate entity and political, legal, regulatory, and other risks associated with operating in the particular country.

The permutations are nearly endless, limited only by the creativity of capital market participants and the laws and regulations that doggedly seek to keep pace with their innovations.

H. Conclusion

Biotech companies present founders, management, and investors with financing challenges. The potential that a medical breakthrough will create tremendous value for stakeholders is balanced by the long and uncertain product development time line and costly regulatory and intellectual property environment. Compounding matters is the fact that preliminary success with modest initial investments generally translates into a need to raise larger sums to fund later-stage development activities. But simply locating the capital is only part of the solution. Companies must take care to navigate various legal regimes—most notably, the federal and state securities laws—to ensure that each stage of capital-raising paves the way for future commercial and fund-raising success.

Notes

1. The authors acknowledge that the field of biotechnology is broad, encompassing many companies that are not focused on developing novel human therapeutics. Those companies—such as research service providers and companies marketing "tools" to enhance discovery or development—will generally face different financing challenges. Nevertheless, the focus of this chapter will be on addressing legal issues and presenting practical tips for counsel advising a venture that seeks to develop new medical treatments.

2. The Tufts Center Web site is http://csdd.tufts.edu/ and a copy of the Tufts Center Study can be found at http://www.cptech.org/ip/health/econ/dimasi2003.pdf.

3. http://www.bio.org/speeches/pubs/er/statistics.asp.

4. *Id.*

5. http://www.fda.gov.

6. Section 5(a), Securities Act of 1933, as amended.

7. 1933 Act Rules.

8. Most major research universities and other medical centers publish their conflict of interest policies on their Web sites. The issues were summarized by former FDA Commissioner Jane E. Henney, Ph.D, in remarks made in 2000, including:

> Relationships between industry and academia are also becoming more complex. Academic researchers now serve not only as clinical investigators, but also in the roles of sponsors of IND investigations, inventors named on patents, and product manufacturers. Industry's mechanisms for paying clinical investigators to conduct research vary widely from one organization to the next and can be quite complicated. Often they're murky at best. Patients become increasingly vulnerable as individuals assume the multiple roles of physician, investigator and sometimes sponsor, and when research institutions stand to benefit financially as well. Legitimate questions arise about an investigator's objectivity, and concern for patients, versus his or her concern about the bottom line.
>
> Let's be realistic. Profits do drive this business. Financial incentives have long been an important, and necessary, motivating force behind medical advancements. As a result, financial conflicts of interest—whether real or perceived—are now an inherent part of the process and we must

deal with them. It's never been more important to ensure that adequate controls are in place to guard against improper behavior or bias—conscious or not—caused by conflicting loyalties on the part of clinical researchers.

Human Subject Protection and Financial Conflicts of Interest, NIH Campus, Bethesda, Md., Aug. 15, 2000, http://www.fda.gov/oc/speeches/2000/humansubject.html.

9. http://www.acq.osd.mil/sadbu/sbir/overview/index.htm.

10. *Id.*

11. http://www.nvca.org/pdf/SBA%20published%20rule%20change.pdf#search='sbir%2051%25%20rule.

12. Material in the section on Venture Capital is based on an article previously published by J. Robert Tyler in the TRIANGLE TECHJOURNAL.

13. http://www.pwcmoneytree.com.

14. Exhibit A includes a glossary of terms associated with venture capital.

15. According to the Fenwick & West survey (http://www.fenwick.com/vctrends), 12-33% of the venture capital deals in a given quarter include liquidation preferences that are a multiple of the original investment amount.

16. *See, e.g.,* Roger Longman, *Symphony & Guilford Try Out Project Financing*, IN VIVO: BUSINESS & MEDICINE REP. (July 1, 2004).

Exhibit A
Summary of Terms for Series A Convertible Preferred Stock of [Name of Company]

This summary of terms (the "Term Sheet") outlines the terms and conditions of a proposed investment by [Name of Lead Investor] ("Lead Investor") [and other investors listed below (collectively, the "Investors")] in _____, a Delaware corporation (the "Company").

Founders:	_____, _____ and _____.
Type of Security:	Series A Convertible Preferred Stock of the Company (the "Series A Preferred").
Pre-Money Valuation:	$_____.
Number of Shares/ Purchase Price:	Up to _____ shares of Series A Preferred at $_____ per share (the "Purchase Price").
Aggregate Purchase Price:	The aggregate purchase price will be $_____ (representing ___ percent of the Company on a fully diluted basis post-financing including an available option pool of ___ percent).
Investors:	[Lead Investor] $_____ Investor #2] $_____ [Investor #3] $_____
Post-Financing Ownership: **(Fully-Diluted Basis)**	A Pro-Forma Capitalization chart that shows the ownership of the Company immediately after the investment described in this Term Sheet is attached as an Exhibit.
Rights, Preferences, Privileges and Restrictions of Series A Preferred:	(1) *Dividend Provisions.* The Holders of the Series A Preferred will be entitled to receive, prior to the payment of any dividend on the Common Stock of the Company (the "Common Stock"), a [cumulative dividend of __ percent per share, which will accrue whether or not declared by the Board of Directors] [non-cumulative dividend of __ percent per share, as and when declared by the Board of Directors].

(2) *Liquidation Preference*. In the event of any liquidation or winding up of the Company, the holders of the Series A Preferred will be entitled to receive, in preference to the holders of the Common Stock, an amount equal to the Purchase Price per share plus all accrued but unpaid dividends. ["Participating" Preferred would include a provision such as: After the payment of such liquidation preference, the holders of the Series A Preferred and the holders of the Common Stock will be entitled to receive, pro rata on an as-converted basis, the remaining assets of the Company available for distribution to its stockholders.] ["Non-participating" Preferred would include a provision such as: After the payment of such liquidation preference, the Common Stock will be entitled to receive, pro rata, the remaining assets of the Company available for distribution to its stockholders.] A merger, consolidation (other than one in which the holders of the capital stock of the Company prior to such merger or consolidation continue to hold at least 51 percent by voting power of the capital stock of the surviving entity), sale, or exclusive license of all, substantially all or a significant portion of the assets or intellectual property of the Company will be deemed to be a liquidation event

(3) *Optional Conversion*. The holders of the Series A Preferred will have the right to convert the Series A Preferred, at the option of the holder, at any time, into shares of Common Stock. One share of Series A Preferred will initially be convertible into one share of Common Stock.

(4) *Automatic Conversion*. The Series A Preferred will automatically be converted into Common Stock at the then applicable conversion rate in the event of either: (i) the closing of an underwritten initial public offering with aggregate gross offering proceeds to the Company of at least $_____ and a per share price to the public of at least _____ times the Purchase Price (a "Qualified Public Offering") or (ii) the election of the holders of at least a majority of the outstanding shares of Series A Preferred.

(5) *Price Protection and Antidilution Protection.* The conversion price of the Series A Preferred (the "Series A Conversion Price") will be adjusted to prevent dilution if the Company issues additional shares of Common Stock or any right or option to purchase Common Stock or any other security convertible into Common Stock (other than shares issued to employees, consultants or directors in accordance with plans approved by the Board of Directors and the Series A Directors (as defined herein) at a purchase price less than the then applicable Series A Conversion Price. In such an event, the Series A Conversion Price will be reduced, concurrently with such issuance, to the consideration per share received by the Company for the additional shares of Common Stock. In addition, the Series A Conversion Price will be proportionately adjusted for stock splits, stock dividends, recapitalizations, and the like.

(6) *Redemption Provisions.* The shares of Series A Preferred will be redeemed by the Company in three equal annual installments (as legally permissible) at any time after the fifth anniversary of the Closing (as defined herein), commencing 60 days after receipt by the Company, from the holders of a majority of the then-outstanding shares of Series A Preferred, of written notice requesting redemption of all shares of Series A Preferred. The redemption price will be the Purchase Price plus all accrued but unpaid dividends.

(7) *Voting Rights.* Each share of Series A Preferred will be entitled to that number of votes equal to the number of shares of Common Stock issuable upon the conversion of a share of Series A Preferred. The Series A Preferred and Common Stock will vote together as a class except: (i) the Series A Preferred as a class will be entitled to elect _____ members of the Board of Directors (the "Series A Directors"), (ii) as required by law, and (iii) as set forth in Section 8 below.

(8) *Protective Provisions.* The consent of the holders of a majority of the Series A Preferred will be required for, among other things: (i) an amendment or repeal of any provision of the Company's Certificate of Incorporation

or Bylaws if such action would change the rights, preference or privileges of the Series A Preferred; (ii) the authorization or issuance of any class of stock having any right, preference, or priority superior to or on a parity with the Series A Preferred; (iii) the payment of dividends; (iv) a merger, sale of all, substantially all or a significant portion of the assets, recapitalization, reorganization, liquidation or dissolution of the Company; (v) the redemption, retirement, purchase or acquisition, directly or indirectly, through subsidiaries or otherwise, of any shares of the capital stock of the Company (other than repurchases of Common Stock at cost upon termination of employment or service); (vi) the entering into any lines of business that are not primarily related to the business of the Company as conducted as of the Closing; (vii) the grant of an exclusive license to any of the Company's material intellectual property rights; (viii) the acquisition of all or substantially all of the properties, assets, or stock of any other company or entity; (ix) the incurrence of indebtedness in excess of $_____ in the aggregate; (x) any capital expenditures (including expenditures for capitalized leases and expenditures by subsidiaries) in excess of the budget duly adopted by the Board of Directors for any fiscal year, without the approval of the Board of Directors and the Series A Directors; (xi) the issuance of any equity securities (other than options or restricted stock issued to employees, consultants, or directors in accordance with plans approved by the Board of Directors and the Series A Directors); (xii) the issuance by any subsidiary of any equity securities other than issuances to the Company and issuances approved by the Board of Directors and the Series A Directors; (xiii) the making of any loan or advance to, or acquisition of any stock or other securities of, any entity unless it is wholly owned by the Company; (xiv) the making of any loan or advance to any person, including, without limitation, any employee or director of the Company or any subsidiary, except advances and similar expenditures in the ordinary course of business or under the terms of an employee stock or option plan approved

	by the Board of Directors and the Series A Directors; (xv) the guarantee, directly or indirectly, of any indebtedness or obligations except for trade accounts of any subsidiary arising in the ordinary course of business; or (xvi) without the approval of the Board of Directors and the Series A Directors, the amendment, modification or adoption of any stock option plan or any transfer, vesting or repurchase provisions with respect to any restricted stock or option with any employee, or any new equity-based agreements that contain more favorable provisions with respect to vesting, repurchase or transfer.
Information Rights:	The Company will furnish each holder of Series A Preferred with an annual budget, annual financial statements audited by an accounting firm of national reputation, and quarterly and monthly unaudited financial statements. These obligations will terminate upon a Qualified Public Offering.
Registration Rights:	(1) *Demand Registration*. At any time after the earlier of: (i) [five] years following the Closing or (ii) six months following the Company's initial public offering, the holders of at least [20] percent of the Common Stock issuable upon the conversion of the Series A Preferred may require that the Company file a registration statement with regard to such shares. The Company will not be obligated to effect more than [two] registrations under this demand provision. (2) *Company Registration*. The holders of the Series A Preferred will be entitled to "piggyback" registration rights on registrations by the Company, subject to the right of the Company and its underwriters to reduce the number of shares proposed to be registered in view of market conditions. (3) *S-3 Rights*. If the Company is eligible as a registrant to use Form S-3 and the holders of the Series A Preferred request that the Company effect a registration on Form S-3 for shares having an aggregate sale price to the public of at least [$1,000,000], the Company will cause such shares to be registered.

	(4) *Market "Stand-off" Agreements.* Each holder of Series A Preferred, if requested by the Company and the managing underwriter of an underwritten public offering by the Company of Common Stock, will not sell or otherwise transfer or dispose of any shares (excluding shares acquired in or following the Company's initial public offering) for such period of time as required by the underwriters (not to exceed 180 days) following the effective date of the registration statement for such offering; provided, that: (a) such agreement will only apply to the Company's initial public offering; (b) all directors, officers, and 1 percent stockholders of the Company enter into similar agreements; and (c) the Company will agree to use its best efforts to ensure that such agreement: (i) provides for periodic early releases of portions of the securities subject thereto upon the occurrence of certain specified events and (ii) provides that in the event of any early release, all Investors will be released on a pro rata basis from such market stand-off agreements. (5) *Expenses.* All registration expenses (exclusive of underwriting discounts and commissions) including the fees of one special counsel of the Investors will be borne by the Company.
Rights to Purchase Additional Shares:	The holders of the Series A Preferred will have the right to purchase their pro rata share based on their ownership of the outstanding shares of Series A Preferred of any future equity offering by the Company, subject to customary exclusions (such as issuances pursuant to an employee stock plan approved by the Board of Directors and the Series A Directors). Such rights will terminate upon a Qualified Public Offering.
The Purchase Agreement:	The investment will be made pursuant to a Stock Purchase Agreement reasonably acceptable to the Company and the Investors, which Agreement will contain, among other things, appropriate and customary representations and warranties of the Company and conditions to Closing which will include, among other things, qualification of the shares under applicable Blue Sky laws, receipt of a

	customary opinion of counsel to the Company (in a form satisfactory to the Investors), and the filing of an Amended and Restated Certificate of Incorporation establishing the rights and preferences of the Series A Preferred.
Board Composition:	The Board of Directors will consist of ___ persons, comprised of: (i) ___ representative(s) designated by the Investors; (ii) ___ representative(s) designated by the Founders; (iii) the Chief Executive Officer of the Company; (iv) and ___ director(s) who are not employed by the Company. The Board of Directors will meet no less frequently than once every ___ months.
Key Man Insurance:	After the Closing, the Company will procure and maintain key man life insurance policies on the lives of [Founder 1], [Founder 2] and [Founder 3] in the amount of $_____ each, with proceeds payable to the Company.
Founders' Stock:	Each of the Founders will execute a Stock Restriction Agreement covering the shares of Common Stock held by such Founder as of Closing (the "Founders' Stock"), which provides that: (i) any unvested Founders' Stock may be repurchased by the Company for their original issue price if the employment of such Founder is terminated for "cause" by the Company or by such Founder other than for "good reason" and (ii) ___ percent of each such Founder's unvested Founders' Stock will become vested if the employment of such Founder is terminated by the Company without "cause" or by such Founder for "good reason" or as a result of the death or permanent disability of such Founder. "Good reason" will mean a material adverse change in employment responsibilities or compensation or a relocation beyond a ___-mile radius from the Company's headquarters. The Founders' Stock will be subject to four-year vesting, with 25 percent of the Founders' Stock vesting on the first anniversary of the Closing and the remainder vesting monthly over the three years following such anniversary. In the event of an acquisition of the Company, 100 percent of each Founder's unvested Founders' Stock will become vested.

Right of First Refusal and Co-sale on Founders' Stock:	If a Founder proposes to sell any shares of Founders' Stock (the "Offered Shares"), the Company will be entitled to a right of first refusal to purchase such Offered Shares. If the Company does not elect to purchase all of the Offered Shares, then each of the Investors will be entitled to a right of first refusal to purchase their pro rata portion (based on their ownership of the outstanding shares of Series A Preferred) of the remaining shares, with rights to purchase Offered Shares not subscribed for by the other Investors. If this right of refusal is not exercised, the Investors will have co-sale rights with respect to such Offered Shares. Such rights will terminate upon a Qualified Public Offering.
Vesting Requirements:	All options to purchase Common Stock of the Company, will be subject to four-year vesting, with 25 percent of the shares vesting on the first anniversary of the date of grant and the remainder vesting monthly over the three years following such anniversary.
Proprietary Agreements:	All Founders and employees will execute confidentiality agreements in a form acceptable to the Investors. All Founders and key employees will execute non-competition and non-solicitation agreements with the Company in a form acceptable to the Investors and covering a one-year period following termination of employment.
Expenses:	The Company will pay legal fees of the Lead Investor's counsel of up to $___ and disbursements incurred by such counsel in connection with this financing.
Closing:	The closing of the transaction is expected to occur on or before _____, 20__ (the "Closing"). The Closing is subject to completion of a satisfactory due diligence review of the Company by the Investors and the execution of satisfactory legal agreements, which will be drafted by the Lead Investor's counsel, incorporating the terms hereof.
Confidentiality:	The Company will not disclose the terms of this Term Sheet with any person other than officers, members of the Board of Directors, and the Company's accountants and attor-

	neys without the written consent of the Investors.
Exclusivity:	In consideration of the time and expense devoted and to be devoted by the Investors in consideration of this investment, the Company and the Founders agree that, for a period of 30 days after the execution of this Term Sheet, they will not solicit any offers, engage in any discussions, or enter into any agreements or commitments with respect to an equity investment in the Company or another entity organized by the Founders.
Nature of Document:	Except as provided above under "Confidentiality," "Expenses," and "Exclusivity," this Term Sheet does not constitute a legally binding obligation of the Investors, the Company or the Founders, and the Investors may terminate discussions with the Company and the Founders at any time.

Glossary of Frequently Used Terms

Basic Equity Terms

Authorized Shares: The total number of shares of capital stock that a company is authorized to issue in its certificate of incorporation.

Capitalization Chart: A spreadsheet or table that shows the ownership, on a particular date, of a company's issued and outstanding shares of capital stock and other securities that are convertible into or exercisable for shares of capital stock.

Common Stock: Common Stock is the basic ownership interest in a company. Common stockholders have voting rights, dividend rights, and liquidation rights that are proportionate to the number of shares that they own. The liquidation rights of the holders of Common Stock are subordinate to those of the company's creditors and the holders of the company's Preferred Stock. The dividend rights of the company's Common Stock may be subject to the Dividend Preference of the company's Preferred Stock.

Convertible Stock: Convertible Stock is stock (generally Preferred Stock) that is convertible into another type of stock (generally Common Stock) at a predetermined Conversion Price or Conversion Ratio.

Founders' Stock: Founders' Stock refers to the shares of the Common Stock that are issued to the founders of a company upon its establishment. The Founders' Stock may be subject to a Stock Restriction Agreement that provides for vesting of the Founders' Stock over time.

Fully Diluted Shares: A company's Fully Diluted Shares refers to the total number of shares of Common Stock that the company has issued, plus all shares of Common Stock that would be issued if all outstanding options, warrants, convertible Preferred Stock, and convertible debt were exercised or converted and all shares of Common Stock that are reserved under the Option Pool.

Incentive Stock Options (ISOs): Incentive Stock Options are options that satisfy certain criteria under the Internal Revenue Code. Principal among these is that ISOs may be granted to employees only and the exercise price must be equal to or greater than the fair market value of the underlying stock on the grant date. The advantage of ISOs is that there is generally no tax to the option holder until the underlying stock is sold, provided that the option holder satisfies certain holding periods that are imposed by the Internal Revenue Code. (However, the option holder may be subject to alternative minimum tax when the option is exercised.)

Issued and Outstanding Shares: A company's issued and outstanding shares refers to the total number of shares of stock that the company has actually issued to stockholders on a particular date.

Non-Qualified Stock Options (NQSOs): Non-Qualified Stock Options are options that do not satisfy one or more of the criteria to be ISOs. A company can issue NQSOs to non-employees and the exercise price may be less than the fair market value of the underlying stock on the grant date. Unlike ISOs, when NQSOs are exercised, the option holder is subject to ordinary income tax on the difference between the exercise price and the fair market value of the underlying stock on the date of exercise. When the stock is sold, the option holder is subject to capital gains tax on the difference between the sales price and the fair market value of the underlying stock on the date of exercise.

Option Pool: The Option Pool refers to the total number of shares of stock (generally Common Stock) that a company has reserved for issuance to employees, directors, and advisors under its stock option plan. The size of the Option Pool will depend upon the number of shares that the company and the investors determine to be necessary to hire the employees that the company will need to execute its business plan.

Options: Options are securities that permit the holder to purchase a specified number of shares of the company's stock (generally Common Stock) at a predetermined price (the exercise price) and for a certain period of time. Generally, the right to purchase the shares vests and the option becomes exercisable over a period of time.

Preferred Stock: Preferred Stock is a class of stock that has rights and preferences that are superior to those of the company's Common Stock. Generally, these rights and preferences include Affirmative Covenants, Anti-dilution Protection, Conversion Rights, Co-sale Rights, Dividend Preference, Drag-Along Rights, Liquidation Preference, Preemptive Rights, Price Protection, Protective Provisions or Negative Covenants, Redemption Rights or Put Rights, Registration Rights, and Rights of First Refusal. Preferred Stock is designated by series, such as Series A, Series B, and so forth.

Stock Restriction Agreement: A Stock Restriction Agreement gives the company the right to purchase a decreasing number of the shares of Common Stock owned by a founder over of period of generally three to four years if the founder's employment with the company is terminated. Generally, the repurchase price of the shares is the same price that the founder paid for the shares. Under a Stock Restriction Agreement, a founder's shares will vest as the company's repurchase rights lapse over the term of the agreement. Even though the unvested shares are subject to the company's repurchase rights, the founder has full voting and other rights with respect to all of the shares.

Warrants: Warrants are securities that permit the holder to purchase a specific number of shares of the company's capital stock at a predetermined price (the exercise price) and for a certain period of time. Generally, a company will issue warrants to investors, lenders, or strategic partners as an "equity sweetener" to enhance the underlying investment, credit facility, or other business arrangement.

Venture Capital Terms

Affirmative Covenants: Affirmative Covenants require a company to provide certain information to its investors on a regular basis or to take or maintain certain corporate actions. Typical Affirmative Covenants give the investors the right to receive monthly, quarterly, and annual financial statements and annual budgets or require the company to maintain certain insurance (including key man life insurance on the founders) or to maintain the size and composition of the company's board of directors.

Anti-dilution Protection: Anti-dilution Protection adjusts the investors' ownership percentages if the company effects a stock split, stock dividend, or recapitalization.

Board Observation Rights or Board Visitation Rights: Major investors in a company will require the right to one or more seats on the company's board of directors. Other investors in the company may require the right to have a representative attend meetings of a company's board of directors as a non-voting observer.

Conversion Price or Conversion Ratio: The Conversion Price or the Conversion Ratio determines the number of shares of Common Stock into which each share of Preferred Stock is convertible and is adjusted based on the investors' Anti-dilution Protection and Price Protection.

Conversion Rights: Investors generally have the right to convert their shares of Preferred Stock into shares of Common Stock at any time at the applicable Conversion Price or Conversion Ratio.

Co-sale Rights: Co-sale Rights give the investors the right to sell all or a portion of their shares as a condition to the founders of the company selling any of their shares. This protects the investors from being locked into an investment if the founders have sold their shares.

Cram Down Round: Generally, a Cram Down Round is a Down Round in which the new investors require the previous round investors to waive all or a portion of their Price Protection. A Cram Down Round may also be effected by the new investors requiring the previous round investors to convert their shares of Preferred Stock into shares of Common Stock or by recapitalizing the previous round investors' shares of Preferred Stock into a lesser number of shares. In a Cram

Down Round, the equity interests of the previous round investors are diluted, and the new investors own a greater equity interest in the company.

Cumulative Dividends: Cumulative Dividends means that if the dividend is not declared during the applicable time period, it accrues and is payable at a later time.

Dilution: Dilution refers to a decrease in the percentage ownership of a stockholder as a result of the issuance by the company of additional equity securities.

Dividend Preference: The payment of dividends on the Preferred Stock that a company issues to its investors will have priority over Common Stock dividends. Generally, the investment documents will provide that the company cannot pay any dividends on the Common Stock unless the company pays equivalent dividends on the Preferred Stock. Often, the Preferred Stock will bear a fixed dividend rate, and, due to the cash constraints of early-stage companies, the dividends will not be payable currently but will accrue and become part of the Liquidation Preference that is payable upon the liquidation of the company.

Down Round: A Down Round is a financing in which the Pre-money Valuation of the company is less than the Post-money Valuation of the company in the company's previous round of financing. A Down Round will trigger the Price Protection of the investors in the previous rounds of financing.

Drag-Along Rights: Drag-Along Rights give the investors the right to require the founders of the company (and possibly other key stockholders) to sell their shares if the investors decide to sell their shares. Generally, the buyer of the company wants to ensure that it will be able to purchase all of the stock of the company. Drag-Along Rights protect the investors by preventing the founders (and possibly other key stockholders) from blocking a sale of the company that the investors desire.

Due Diligence Review: The Due Diligence Review refers to the analysis by a potential investor of a possible investment in a company. Among other things, the potential investor will evaluate the company's technology, products, business strategy, potential markets, management, corporate and legal documents and affairs, and accounting and financial matters.

Exit Strategy: A company's Exit Strategy is the method by which it intends to achieve a return for its investors, founders, and employee option holders. The most common exit strategies are the sale of the company or an Initial Public Offering.

Full Ratchet: A Full Ratchet is a form of Price Protection that adjusts the Conversion Price to the lowest price at which the company subsequently sells shares of its Common Stock regardless of the number of shares that the company sells at that price.

Liquidation: Liquidation typically means the sale of the company, whether through a sale of the voting control of its stock, a merger, or sale of all or substantially all of its assets. A liquidation also includes the voluntary or involuntary dissolution of the company as a result of the company not succeeding and going out of business.

Liquidation Preference: Upon the liquidation of a company, the holders of the company's Preferred Stock have the right to receive distributions of money or assets prior to any class of subordinate stock. The Liquidation Preference is generally equal to the purchase price of the Preferred Stock, plus accrued but unpaid dividends. The Liquidation Preference ensures that the investors get their investment back, plus a fixed return, before the founders, management, and employees receive any proceeds of the liquidation.

Mandatory Conversion: Upon the closing of a Qualified Initial Public Offering, the investors are required to convert their shares of Preferred Stock into shares of Common Stock at the applicable Conversion Price or Conversion Ratio.

Pari Passu: Upon a liquidation, the Liquidation Preferences are generally paid to the investors in the reverse order of that in which their investments were made. That is, the last investors get paid their Liquidation Preferences first. However, some investors require that the Liquidation Preferences are paid to the investors Pari Passu, meaning at the same time or at the same level and without regard to the order in which the investments were made. If the proceeds of the liquidation are insufficient to pay all of the Liquidation Preferences, then the investors divide the proceeds on a pro-rata basis.

Participating Preferred Stock or Participation Rights: Participation Rights mean that the investors share on a pro-rata basis with the holders of Common Stock in any proceeds of the liquidation that remain after the payment of their Liquidation Preference. If the investors do not have Participation Rights, they must choose either to receive their Liquidation Preference or convert their shares of Preferred Stock into Common Stock and participate on a pro rata basis with the holders of Common Stock in the liquidation proceeds.

Pay-to-Play Provisions: Pay-to-Play Provisions provide that if an investor does not participate in a company's subsequent financing rounds, then the non-participating investor will lose its Anti-dilution Protection, Price Protection, or Preemptive Rights. These provisions are intended to keep the investment syndicate in place to continue to fund the company by being punitive to non-participating investors.

Post-money Valuation: The Post-money Valuation is the value of the company immediately after the investment. It is determined by adding the amount that is invested in the financing to the Pre-money Valuation of the company. For example, if the Pre-money Valuation of the company is $8 million and the investors invest $4 million in the financing, then the Post-money Valuation of the company is $12 million.

Pre-money Valuation: The Pre-money Valuation is the value of the company immediately prior to the investment that is agreed upon by the company and the investors. It is generally expressed as a total dollar amount, such as $8 million. However, it may also be expressed as a price per share, such as $2 per share. If the Pre-money Valuation of the company is $8 million, and the company has 4 million Fully Diluted Shares prior to the investment, then the price that the investors will pay in the financing is $2 per share. If the investors invest $4 million, the company will issue 2 million shares to the investors, and the investors will own 33 percent of the company (2 million shares/6 million shares).

Preemptive Rights: Preemptive Rights give the previous round investors the right to purchase stock in future financings by the company on the same terms and conditions as the investors in future financing rounds. Preemptive Rights enable the previous round investors to purchase a pro-rata portion of the shares of stock sold by the company in future financing rounds.

Price Protection: Price Protection adjusts the Conversion Price if a company issues Common Stock or other securities that are convertible into or exercisable for Common Stock at a price per share below the current Conversion Price. The result is that the investors will be issued more shares of Common Stock upon the conversion of their Preferred Stock. This protects the investors from the risk that they overpaid for their stock if the Pre-money Valuation turns out to be too high.

Protective Provisions or Negative Covenants: Protective Provisions or Negative Covenants give the investors the right to approve certain corporate actions. Typical Protective Provisions give the investors the right to approve amendments to the company's certificate of incorporation and bylaws, future issuances of stock, the declaration and payment of dividends, increases in the company's Option Pool, expenditures in excess of approved budgets, the incurrence of debt, the sale of the company, and changes in the company's line of business.

Redemption Rights or Put Rights: Redemption Rights or Put Rights give the investors the right to require the company to repurchase the investors' stock after a period of generally four to seven years. The repurchase price for the stock may be based upon the amount of the Liquidation Preference, the fair market value of the stock as determined by an appraiser, or the value of the stock based upon a multiple of the company's earnings.

Rights of First Refusal: The investors generally require the founders of the company to agree that if they ever desire to sell all or a portion of their stock, the founders must first offer to sell the stock back to the company and then to the investors. Rights of First Refusal protect the investors and the non-selling founders from the stock being sold to an unfriendly party.

Financing a Biotech Company

Term Sheet: A non-binding summary of the major terms and conditions of a proposed investment in a company by the investors. A Term Sheet may have a binding exclusivity or no-shop provision whereby the company and the founders agree that they will not initiate or hold discussions with other potential investors for some period of time after the Term Sheet is signed. Also, some investors require the company to pay their legal fees and due diligence expenses even if the investment set forth in the Term Sheet does not close for any reason.

Weighted Average Ratchet: A Weighted Average Ratchet is a form of Price Protection that adjusts the Conversion Price according to a formula that takes into account the lower issue price and the number of shares that the company issues at that price. In other words, the larger the number of dilutive shares that the company issues, the greater the adjustment to the Conversion Price.

Securities Law Terms

Accredited Investor: Under Rule 501 of Regulation D of the Securities Act, an individual is deemed to be an Accredited Investor if his or her net worth or joint net worth with a spouse exceeds $1 million or if the individual had income in excess of $200,000 in each of the two most recent years or joint income with a spouse in excess of $300,000 in each of those years and has a reasonable expectation of reaching the same level of income in the current year. Directors and executive officers of the company and entities with assets in excess of $5 million are also considered Accredited Investors.

Best Efforts Underwriting: In a Best Efforts Underwriting, the Underwriter is obligated only to use its reasonable best efforts to sell the stock that is being offered by the company in a public offering. The Underwriter has the right to return any unsold shares to the company.

Blue Sky Laws: Blue Sky Laws are state laws that regulate the issuance of securities. All issuances and transfers of securities must comply with both the federal securities laws and the Blue Sky Laws of the state in which the securities are being offered and sold.

Cutback Rights: Cutback Rights apply in situations where investors have exercised their Registration Rights and desire that some of their shares be sold under the company's Registration Statement. The Underwriter may determine that there is not a market for all of the shares that are proposed to be sold in the offering. Cutback Rights give the Underwriter the right to reduce the number of the investors' shares that are being sold in the offering.

Demand Registration Rights: Demand Registration Rights are a type of Registration Rights that allow the investors to require the company to file a Registration Statement with respect to their shares. Typically, the investors cannot exercise their

Demand Registration Rights until after the company is public. However, absent this restriction, the investors could exercise their Demand Registration Rights and require the company to conduct an Initial Public Offering.

Exchange Act: The Exchange Act refers to the Securities Exchange Act of 1934. The Exchange Act provides for the filing of various periodic reports with the SEC by public companies, the regulation of proxy solicitations, and limitations on insider trading. Also, the Exchange Act governs the operations of stock exchanges and over-the-counter trading.

Federal Exemptions from Registration; Section 4(2); and Regulation D: When a company makes an offer to sell its securities (including shares of stock, options, warrants, and convertible debt), the company must either register the stock with the SEC pursuant to a Registration Statement filed under the Securities Act, or issue the stock pursuant to an exemption from the registration requirements of the Securities Act. The most common exemption from registration is Section 4(2) of the Securities Act, which exempts from the registration requirements of the Securities Act "transactions by an issuer not involving any public offering" (i.e., private placements). The shares that are issued in a private placement are referred to as "restricted shares," and they cannot be resold unless they are registered under the Securities Act or pursuant to an exemption from registration. Regulation D, promulgated by the SEC, provides several "safe harbors" under Section 4(2) of the Securities Act if the offering meets certain criteria specified in Regulation D.

Firm Commitment Underwriting: In a Firm Commitment Underwriting, the Underwriter agrees to buy all of the shares that are offered by the company in a public offering at a fixed price and then resells those shares to the public at the higher offering price. Before signing the underwriting agreement for a Firm Commitment Underwriting, the Underwriter contacts investors and solicits "indications of interest," which are non-binding obligations of the investors to purchase the shares from the Underwriter. The Underwriter will not sign the underwriting agreement until it has accumulated "indications of interest" for at least the number of shares of stock that are being offered by the company. The Underwriter cannot return any unsold shares to the company.

Follow-on Offering or Secondary Offering: A Follow-on or Secondary Offering refers to the sale by a company of shares of its Common Stock in a public offering after it has completed its Initial Public Offering.

Form 8-K: Form 8-K is a report that a company must file with the SEC to report certain material events that might affect its business or financial condition.

Form 10-K: Form 10-K is a comprehensive overview of a company's business and financial condition that the company must file with the SEC within 90 days after the end of each fiscal year.

Form 10-Q: Form 10-Q is an overview of a company's business and financial condition that the company must file with the SEC within 45 days after the end of each of the first three quarters of each fiscal year. The company will file a Form 10-K at the end of each fiscal year.

Form S-1: Form S-1 is the Registration Statement that is filed with the SEC in connection with a company's Initial Public Offering.

Form S-3: Form S-3 is a short-form Registration Statement that permits a company to incorporate by reference information that is contained in its previous periodic filings that it made with the SEC under the Exchange Act (Form 8K's, Form 10-K's, Form 10-Q's, etc.). To be eligible to use Form S-3, a company must have been public for more than 12 months and be current in its Exchange Act filings.

Form S-4: Form S-4 is the Registration Statement that a company uses to register shares of its stock that it is issuing in an acquisition to the stockholders of the target company.

Form S-8: Form S-8 is the Registration Statement that a company uses to register shares of its stock that are issuable to employees pursuant to the company's stock option plans or stock award plans.

Initial Public Offering (IPO): An Initial Public Offering is a company's first sale of shares of its Common Stock to the public. The company accomplishes an Initial Public Offering by filing a Registration Statement (generally on Form S-1) with the SEC. Most Initial Public Offerings are Firm Commitment Underwritings.

Market Stand-off Agreement and Lock-up Period: In connection with a public offering of stock, the Underwriters typically insist that certain stockholders of the company agree not to sell their shares for some period of time (usually 180 days, which is referred to as the Lock-up Period) after the company's public offering. A Market Stand-off Agreement is the agreement that those stockholders sign agreeing to this restriction.

NASD: The abbreviation for the National Association of Securities Dealers, which is a self-regulating organization that is responsible for regulating stock brokers and dealers.

NASDAQ: The abbreviation for the National Association of Securities Dealers Automated Quotations system that facilitates stock trading on the Nasdaq Stock Market.

NYSE: The abbreviation for the New York Stock Exchange, which is the world's oldest (it was founded in 1792) and largest stock exchange.

Piggyback Registration Rights: Piggyback Registration Rights give the investors the right to have shares that are owned by them included in a Registration

Statement that the company files for itself or for a selling stockholder. Generally, Piggyback Registration Rights are not applicable to the company's Initial Public Offering.

Prospectus: A Prospectus is a document that summarizes an issuer's Registration Statement. The issuer must give a Prospectus to all potential purchasers of the company's securities in the offering. An issuer's preliminary Prospectus is called a "red herring" because it contains red legends on the front cover.

Qualified Initial Public Offering: A Qualified Initial Public Offering is an Initial Public Offering that raises gross proceeds for the company of a size and at a price per share that are agreed upon by the company and the investors. A Qualified Initial Public Offering will trigger the mandatory conversion of the Preferred Stock into Common Stock. An Initial Public Offering that raises gross proceeds for the company of at least $20 million to $30 million and at a price per share of at least three to five times the price per share that the investors paid are typical requirements for a Qualified Initial Public Offering.

Registration Rights: Registration Rights give the investors the right to require that the company include shares of Common Stock that are owned by the investors in the company's Registration Statements that are filed with the SEC.

Registration Statement: A Registration Statement is a disclosure document that a company (known as the issuer) files with the SEC pursuant to Section 5 of the Securities Act in order to register its shares of stock so that they can be sold to the public and become freely tradable. It contains a description of the issuer's business and financial condition and of how the proceeds of the offering will be used. It also includes background information on the issuer's executive officers and directors, information on the issuer's capitalization, and audited financial statements.

Rule 144 Exemption: Rule 144 under the Securities Act is the principal exemption that is relied upon after a company goes public for resales of shares that were issued privately pursuant to exemptions from registration either before or after the company is public. It provides an exemption from registration under the Securities Act for resales by stockholders of restricted shares if certain requirements are met. Generally, these requirements include: (a) a one-year holding period; (b) a limit on the volume of securities that may be sold by any person in any three-month period (1 percent of the outstanding shares or the average trading volume in the company's shares during the four calendar weeks prior to the notice filing described below, whichever is greater); (c) a requirement that the sales be made through a broker; and (c) a requirement that the seller file a notice of sale on Form 144 with the SEC prior to the first sale covered by the notice.

SEC: The SEC is the United States Securities and Exchange Commission, which is an independent, quasi-judicial, federal agency that administers the federal securities laws, including the Securities Act and the Exchange Act.

Securities Act: The Securities Act refers to the Securities Act of 1933 that was intended to protect investors by ensuring that persons offering to sell stock provided accurate and complete information about the stock being sold. The Securities Act requires the registration of securities or the sale of securities pursuant to an exemption from registration and the disclosure of all material information regarding the issuer and the securities being sold so that investors may make informed investment decisions.

Underwriter: An Underwriter is an investment banker that facilitates the sale of shares that are offered in a public offering. An Underwriter buys the stock from the company and resells it to investors. The Underwriter makes a profit on the spread between the price at which it buys the stock from the company and the price at which it resells the stock to investors.

Chapter VI

Employment Issues for Biotechnology Companies

Jeffrey A. Van Doren
LeClair Ryan, a Professional Corporation
Roanoke, Virginia

One of the first things most biotechnology companies will do—after raising funds and setting up the company—is hire employees. Hiring, training, rewarding, motivating, protecting, and firing employees probably trips up more companies than financing or technology concerns. You can do the right thing only slightly the wrong way and suffer tremendous penalties. This is especially true in biotechnology, because the training, rewarding, and protecting issues are often more complicated than most realize. Problems are often magnified. In addition, employees are, on average, better educated than in other industries and better able to discover if some obscure legal right has been violated.

A. Employment At Will

Traditionally, in the absence of a contract for a specific duration, both employers and employees were free to terminate the employment relationship at any time. This concept, known as "employment at will," means that employers did not need a reason to terminate employees, *and* employees did not need cause to quit. Courts for many years considered this an equivalent relationship, since both parties had the same right. More recently, however, legislatures and courts have questioned the equality of the parties' respective bargaining positions and developed numerous exceptions to the employment-at-will doctrine. Employment at will is still the basic rule in most states, but the exceptions must be heeded. Especially in biotechnology, where employees are generally better educated and less easy to replace, and where employment contracts are common, employment and labor laws must be understood.

A basic knowledge of federal, state, and local employment laws will help biotechnology employers avoid common pitfalls and structure the employment relationship properly from the start. With this in mind, we will first look briefly at the most significant laws affecting the employment relationship. Second, we will look in greater detail at the use of employment contracts and employee handbooks. Third, we will explore the laws regarding hiring of foreign nationals to work for U.S. biotechnology companies.

B. Employee or Independent Contractor

Many biotechnology companies, especially when they are in a start-up phase, may be reluctant to hire employees and instead hire persons as "independent contractors." Companies do not have to withhold federal, state, and Social Security (FICA) taxes, or pay unemployment or workers' compensation insurance for independent contractors. They also do not need to offer benefits like paid sick leave, vacation, health insurance, and stock options, as they do to attract and retain employees. The cost savings both in actual dollars terms and in not having to do all the paperwork necessary to hire an actual employee can be significant.

Despite the obvious temptation to avoid the costs associated with employing someone, employers must be careful about misclassifying workers as independent contractors when they really are employees. Employee status triggers employer obligations under the various federal and state statutes discussed below that do not apply to independent contractors.

Employment Issues for Biotechnology Companies

While misclassification of employees can be expensive, there is no simple test for determining whether a particular worker qualifies as an employee. Rather, there are multiple tests used for deciding whether an employment relationship exists, depending on which statute is at issue. These tests focus on different criteria. Thus, a worker may be considered an employee for purposes of one statute and an independent contractor under another. The confusion is further exacerbated by court decisions that reach different results often from similar facts. Since the inquiry in any particular case is necessarily fact-specific, courts can (and often do) reach conflicting results. Nonetheless, the responsibility for making the correct decision falls squarely on the employer, and making an erroneous decision can result in liability.

1. The Common-Law Control Test

The traditional common-law approach to determining employee status is the common-law control test. This test was initially applied to determine whether an employer should be held responsible for the actions of its workers when they cause some injury to a third party. As new employment-related statutes were enacted, most courts continued to apply the common-law approach, modified by the IRS 20-factor test, which is discussed below. Courts have weighed and applied the factors of the common-law control test in the following manner:

- The greater the *skill required to do the job*, the more likely the individual is an independent contractor;
- The fact that the individual *supplies his or her own tools and materials* suggests independent contractor status;
- *The longer the relationship*, the more likely that there is an employer/employee relationship;
- The fact that the person who pays for the work has the *right to assign additional projects* to the worker without additional compensation and without altering the terms of a contract indicates employee status — an independent contractor relationship is generally contractual;
- The fact that the *employer determines the work schedule* suggests an employment relationship;

- An *individual who is paid by the hour or other time period* is more likely to be considered an employee, while payment by the job or project suggests independent contractor status;
- Where the *employer hires, fires, and pays the worker's assistants* (rather than the worker himself or herself), the worker will more likely be deemed an employee;
- An individual who works in a field that is *not the company's ordinary line of business* will be more likely to be found an independent contractor;
- The fact that a worker is *in business for himself or herself* and has all the appropriate licenses suggests independent contractor status;
- The fact that a worker receives *employee benefits* from the person who pays for the work suggests an employment relationship; and
- The fact that a worker is *treated as an employee for tax purposes* indicates an employment relationship.

The common-law control test continues to be used in determining whether an employer should be held vicariously liable for the acts of its employees. Although application has expanded, it is not generally used to determine employee status under anti-discrimination statutes.

2. The IRS Control Test

The Internal Revenue Service (IRS), building on the common-law test, has set forth a more detailed test for determining whether an individual is an independent contractor for purposes of paying employment tax and withholding. These factors and their application are as follows:

- An individual who is *required to follow instructions* is more likely to be considered an employee;
- The greater the *amount of training* needed for the individual to complete an assigned task, the greater the likelihood that the individual will be considered an employee;
- Where an individual is *integrated into the employer's business* to a great extent, the individual is more likely to be considered an employee;

- The fact that an individual *personally renders services* will weigh in favor of employee status;
- The fact that the *individual hires, fires, and pays assistants*, and the employer has no right to do so, indicates independent contractor status;
- The existence of a *continuing relationship* is indicative of employee status;
- The establishment of a *set amount of work hours* suggests employee status;
- An individual whose *time is substantially devoted* to the job is more likely to be considered an employee;
- The fact that an individual *works on the employer's premises* suggests employee status;
- An individual who works according to a *sequence set by the employer* will more likely be deemed an employee;
- The fact that an individual *submits regular or written reports* to the employer will weigh in favor of employee status;
- An individual who is *paid by the project, rather than by the hour* or other period of time, will more likely be considered an independent contractor;
- An individual who is *reimbursed for expenses* is more likely an employee;
- An individual who *furnishes the necessary tools and materials* for the job is more likely an independent contractor;
- That an individual *makes an investment in the facilities* in which he or she works weighs in favor of independent contractor status;
- The fact that an individual's work results in *the possible realization of a profit or the risk of a loss* suggests independent contractor status;
- An individual who *works for more than one firm* at a time is more likely to be an independent contractor;
- An individual who *makes his or her services available to the general public* is more likely to be considered an independent contractor;
- The fact that the employer has the *right to discharge* the individual suggests an employment relationship (independent contractor relationships are more likely to be contractual); and

- The fact that the *individual has the right to terminate the relationship* also suggests an employment relationship because independent contractors are usually bound by a contract.

This test is applied by the IRS and by some state tax agencies to determine liability for contributions for Social Security and Medicare benefits, unemployment taxes, penalties, and interest. Courts have also used this test to determine employee status under the National Labor Relations Act (NLRA), the Employee Retirement Income Security Act (ERISA), and the Americans with Disabilities Act (ADA).

3. The Economic Reality Test

The test that construes employee status most broadly is the "economic reality" test. This test first gained ascendancy in the context of federal wage and hour law, but has been generally used to determine employee status under a variety of federal and state statutes designed to provide employee protections. The economic reality test considers the circumstances of the whole activity, focusing on the degree to which the worker is dependent on the relationship. Among the factors weighed in the economic reality test are the following:

- The *right to control* the manner in which the individual performs his or her services suggests an employment relationship;
- The *opportunity for financial profit or risk of financial loss* on the part of the individual indicates an independent contractor relationship;
- The fact that an individual has made an *investment in the equipment to run the operation and employs workers* indicates an independent contractor status;
- The fact that a worker uses *special skills* suggests independent contractor status;
- The more *permanent and exclusive the relationship*, the more likely that the worker will be considered an employee; and
- Where the relationship between the worker and the company is *integral to the company's operations*, the likelihood is greater that the worker will be deemed an employee.

The economic reality test has been used in determining employee status for purposes of Title VII of the Civil Rights Act of 1964, the Age Discrimination in Employment Act (ADEA), and the Family and Medical Leave Act (FMLA). Some courts construing anti-discrimination statutes have combined the control factors of common-law/IRS tests, along with the "whole activities" focus of the economic realities test to determine employee status.

4. Potential Liability

The danger of misclassifying workers was highlighted in a class-action lawsuit, *Vizcaino v. Microsoft Corp.*, 97 F.3d 1187 (9th Cir. 1996), *aff'd on reh'g,* 120 F.3d 1006 (1997), *cert. denied,* 522 U.S. 1098 (1998), where the court found that Microsoft had mischaracterized certain workers it called "freelancers" as independent contractors. Although the workers were hired for specific projects, some had been kept on, working on successive projects for a number of years. They were fully integrated into Microsoft's work force, worked on site and on work teams along with Microsoft's regular employees, performed identical functions, shared the same supervisors, and worked the same core hours as regular employees. Microsoft provided the freelancers with admittance card keys, office equipment, and supplies. However, as independent contractors, these workers were not eligible for the same employee benefits as Microsoft's regular employees.

Microsoft's troubles started when the Internal Revenue Service (IRS) performed an audit to determine whether Microsoft was in compliance with federal tax laws. Applying the 20-factor test for employee status, the IRS ruled that the freelancers and other temporary employees were not independent contractors, but rather were regular employees. Microsoft was required to pay overdue taxes and issue retroactive W-2 forms.

Armed with the IRS decision, the newly designated employees then filed a class-action suit demanding the same employee benefits as other employees at Microsoft had received. Finding that the test for employee status is the same under federal tax laws and under the Employee Retirement Income and Security Act (ERISA), the court held that these workers were also eligible to participate in the same employee benefit plans as Microsoft's regular employees. For Microsoft, this meant that the mischaracterized workers were entitled to retroactive medical benefits, pension and retirement benefits, and, most significantly, stock options.

This widely reported case is a prime illustration of the danger of mischaracterizing the status of a worker. It can be expensive not only in terms of overdue taxes but could also subject employers to unexpected employee benefits costs, sometimes determined years after the fact. Biotechnology employers should carefully review their arrangements with any "independent contractors" to ensure that those workers are properly classified.

C. Employer Coverage Under Federal Civil Rights Laws

Most of the federal civil rights laws have employee thresholds (e.g., 15 employees for Title VII) that may not apply to small biotechnology companies. This is important to note, since many companies may be "immune" from coverage for a few years but then gradually slide into coverage as they grow. Moreover, as reflected in Appendix A, many states have much lower thresholds for their civil rights law coverage. Employers and counsel must be sure that their policies and practices comply with both federal and, where applicable, state laws.

1. Title VII of the Civil Rights Act of 1964 (42 U.S.C. § 2000e et seq.)

a. Basic Coverage

Prohibits discrimination on the basis of race, color, religion, sex (including pregnancy) or national origin. Applies to employers with *15 or more employees* and any agent of such employer.

Most claims under Title VII are brought under two major theories. The first theory, known as "disparate treatment," makes it unlawful for employers to treat certain individuals differently from others based on their protected status or traits. For example, a policy that expressly excludes women from participating in an employee fitness program is discriminatory in treatment. Second, a policy that is neutral on its face but is not applied equally to all employees is discriminatory in enforcement. For example, when minority employees are terminated for a first offense rule infraction while whites receive only a warning for the same offense, the employment practice is considered discriminatory in enforcement.

The second theory, known as "disparate impact," applies when employment practices that appear neutral on their face operate more harshly on one protected group than another and cannot be justified by business necessity. Disparate impact cases often are used to challenge education requirements and other neutral hiring criteria. For example, the use of arrest records (as opposed to convictions) to determine an applicant's suitability for employment has been found to have a discriminatory impact on minority applicants.

b. Sexual Harassment

Sexual harassment is a form of sex discrimination prohibited by Title VII. The courts have recognized two basic types of sexual harassment: (1) harassment that creates an offensive or hostile working environment, and (2) harassment in which a supervisor demands sexual favors as a condition of employment or in return for certain benefits. Employers must have a policy prohibiting sexual harassment and a procedure so that complaints of harassment can be raised and investigated.[1] Title VII requires employers to take prompt and effective action to end sexual harassment when it is found to have occurred.

2. Age Discrimination in Employment Act (ADEA) (29 U.S.C. § 621 et seq.)

a. Basic Coverage

Prohibits discrimination on the basis of age against persons age 40 and over. It is unlawful "to fail or refuse to hire or to discharge any individual or otherwise discriminate against any individual with respect to his/her compensation, terms, conditions, or privileges of employment, because of such individual's 'age.'" Applies to employers with *20 or more employees* and any agent of such employer.

b. Older Workers' Benefit Protection Act

The Older Workers' Benefit Protection Act (OWBPA) in part restricts an employer's ability to settle actual or threatened age discrimination claims or to secure releases under the ADEA. Most significantly, if an employee has not filed a charge of discrimination or a lawsuit under the ADEA, a waiver of ADEA rights or claims will not be effective unless the employee is given at least 21 days to consider it and the ability to revoke the agreement for seven days after execution. When exit incentive programs are offered to a group or class of employees, this consideration period is extended to 45 days, and other requirements apply. All waivers of ADEA claims must be in writing, specifically refer to the ADEA, and be supported by consideration. Employees must also be advised in writing to consult with an attorney before signing any release agreement.

3. Americans with Disabilities Act (42 U.S.C. § 12,101 et seq.)

a. Basic Coverage

Prohibits discrimination against qualified individuals with disabilities. Applies to employers with *15 or more employees* and any agent of such employer. Under the ADA, a disabled person is anyone who:
- has a physical or mental impairment which substantially limits one or more major life activities,
- has a record of such an impairment, or
- is regarded as having such an impairment.

The ADA prohibits discrimination based on disability. An employer cannot refuse to hire or take negative employment action against an otherwise qualified disabled applicant or employee on the basis of the disability alone. A "qualified" individual with a disability is an individual with a disability who, with or without "reasonable accommodation," can perform the essential functions of a particular job.

b. Reasonable Accommodation

Reasonable accommodation may include:

- modification of employee facilities to provide ready accessibility and usability to such a person;
- job restructuring (reassigning nonessential duties and/or using part-time or modified work schedules);
- acquisition or modification of equipment or devices;

- provision of readers or interpreters; and/or
- other similar actions.

Adjustments must be made for the known limitation of otherwise qualified disabled applicants and employees, unless a particular adjustment or alteration is demonstrated to impose undue hardship.

4. Equal Pay Act (29 U.S.C. § 206(d))

Prohibits employers from wage-based discrimination on the basis of gender for jobs with equal skill, effort, and responsibility that are performed under similar working conditions

D. Employer Coverage Under State and Local Civil Rights Laws

1. State Civil Rights Law

As noted above, most of the federal civil rights laws have a threshold for coverage. That doesn't mean that small employers are completely off the hook!

Most states have fair employment practices or civil rights laws that parallel Title VII, but many have lower thresholds for coverage. In fact, quite a few state laws provide coverage for employers with only one employee in the state. The chart in Appendix A reflects the basic coverage requirements of the various state fair employment practices laws. Counsel should carefully review the state statute and any applicable case law to determine state-specific requirements.

2. Local Laws and Ordinances

In addition to federal and state laws, many cities, counties or other local government entities have employment practices ordinances that apply to employers located within their jurisdiction. Local ordinances often protect individuals from discrimination on additional bases, such as marital status, sexual orientation, political beliefs or personal appearance.

The specific coverage of such local laws and ordinances are beyond the scope of this book. Company management or human resources personnel

E. Equal Opportunity and Affirmative Action Obligations of Government Contractors and Subcontractors

Executive Order 11,246, Section 503 of the Rehabilitation Act of 1973, and the Vietnam Veterans' Readjustment Assistance Act require federal contractors to take affirmative action when hiring minorities, women, the disabled, and veterans. In general, these affirmative action obligations apply to federal contractors who do over $10,000 in business with the federal government. Since many biotechnology companies receive federal government funding for research, they may be required to comply with these federal affirmative action requirements. Companies covered under Executive Order 11,246 and related laws must maintain three different types of affirmative action plans: (1) minorities and women; (2) disabled individuals; and (3) Vietnam era, special disabled, and other protected veterans.

> **Practice Point**
>
> Because of the complexity of government regulations, many biotechnology companies have determined that it is more cost-effective to outsource their affirmative action plans. The detailed statistical analysis needed is better left to professionals who have the expertise, software tools, and dedicated time to spend on their plans, and outsourcing assures clients of compliance with the regulations.

The Office of Federal Contract Compliance Programs (OFCCP), the Department of Labor division charged with enforcing affirmative action requirements, has developed detailed regulations affecting the required contents of a company's narrative affirmative action plans and also regarding how the annual statistical analysis and reporting requirements are met.

F. Other Federal Employment Laws

1. Fair Labor Standards Act (FLSA) (29 U.S.C. § 201 et seq.)

The Fair Labor Standards Act (FLSA) establishes minimum wage, overtime pay, recordkeeping, and child labor standards affecting full-time and part-time workers in the private sector and in federal, state, and local governments.

a. Basic Coverage

An employee can be covered under the FLSA either because his or her employer is a covered enterprise or because the employer is engaged in interstate commerce.

  (i) An "enterprise" is covered if it directly or indirectly employs workers and has gross sales of at least $500,000.
  (ii) The FLSA contains an expansive definition of interstate commerce. Any business that "has employees engaged in commerce or in the production of goods for commerce or that has employees handling, selling, or otherwise working on goods that have been moved in or produced for commerce by any person" is covered by the FLSA.

This definition is so broad that nearly every employer in the United States is covered by FLSA.

> **Practice Point**
>
> Many states provide for a minimum wage higher than $5.15 per hour. For example, California and Massachusetts, two states with a large number of biotechnology companies, have minimum wage rates of $6.75 per hour. While most biotechnology positions will likely pay far higher than the minimum rate, employers should be sure that wages of any support personnel meet both federal and state minimum wage rates.

b. Basic Requirements

  (i) *Minimum Wage*—Employees who are covered by the FLSA must be paid a minimum wage of not less than $5.15 per hour.
  (ii) *Overtime Pay*—Overtime pay at a rate of not less than one and one-half times their regular rate of pay is required after 40 hours of

work in a workweek. There are a number of exemptions to the overtime pay requirements. For biotechnology companies, the most likely exemptions that may apply are the so-called "white collar" exemptions, which exempt executive, administrative or professional employees from the time and one-half requirement. Also exempt are computer professionals.

The white-collar exemptions are often difficult to apply to real-life situations. For example, many researchers with advanced degrees in a scientific field would be covered by the "professional" exception, but only if the employee is paid on a salary basis. A technical employee with no degree but many years of research experience, however, likely would not qualify, since he or she does not possess an actual degree. Counsel should refer to the detailed DOL regulations contained at 29 C.F.R. § 541.

A brief summary of the most likely exemptions that may be used by biotechnology employers follows:

1. To qualify for the **executive employee exemption**, all of the following tests must be met:

    - The employee must be compensated on a salary basis at a rate not less than $455 per week[2];
    - The employee's primary duty must be managing the enterprise, or managing a customarily recognized department or subdivision of the enterprise;
    - The employee must customarily and regularly direct the work of at least two or more other full-time employees or their equivalent; and
    - The employee must have the authority to hire or fire other employees, or the employee's suggestions and recommendations as to the hiring, firing, advancement, promotion or any other change of status of other employees must be given particular weight.

2. To qualify for the **administrative employee exemption**, all of the following tests must be met:

- The employee must be compensated on a salary or fee basis at a rate not less than $455 per week;
- The employee's primary duty must be the performance of office or non-manual work directly related to the management or general business operations of the employer or the employer's customers; and
- The employee's primary duty includes the exercise of discretion and independent judgment with respect to matters of significance.

3. To qualify for the **professional employee exemption**, all of the following tests must be met:

    - The employee must be compensated on a salary or fee basis at a rate not less than $455 per week;
    - The employee's primary duty must be the performance of work requiring advanced knowledge, defined as work that is predominantly intellectual in character and that includes work requiring the consistent exercise of discretion and judgment;
    - The advanced knowledge must be in a field of science or learning; and
    - The advanced knowledge must be customarily acquired by a prolonged course of specialized intellectual instruction.

4. To qualify for the **computer employee exemption**, all of the following tests must be met:

    - The employee must be compensated either on a salary or fee basis at a rate not less than $455 per week or, if compensated on an hourly basis, at a rate not less than $27.63 an hour;
    - The employee must be employed as a computer systems analyst, computer programmer, software engineer or other similarly skilled worker in the computer field performing the duties described below;
    - The employee's primary duty must consist of:

- the application of systems analysis techniques and procedures, including consulting with users, to determine hardware, software or system functional specifications;
- the design, development, documentation, analysis, creation, testing or modification of computer systems or programs, including prototypes, based on and related to user or system design specifications;
- the design, documentation, testing, creation or modification of computer programs related to machine operating systems; or
- a combination of the aforementioned duties, the performance of which requires the same level of skills.

(iii) *Child Labor*—For nonagricultural operations, the FLSA restricts the hours that children under age 16 can work and forbids the employment of children under age 18 in certain jobs deemed too dangerous.

(iv) *Record Keeping*—Every employer covered by the FLSA must keep records for each covered, nonexempt worker. There is no required form for the records, but the records must include accurate information about the employee and data about the hours worked and the wages earned. The following is a listing of the basic records that an employer must maintain.

- Employee's full name and Social Security number;
- Address, including Zip code;
- Birth date, if younger than 19;
- Sex and occupation;
- Time and day of week when employee's workweek begins, hours worked each day, and total hours worked each workweek;
- Basis on which employee's wages are paid;
- Regular hourly pay rate;
- Total daily or weekly straight-time earnings;
- Total overtime earnings for the workweek;
- All additions to or deductions from the employee's wages;
- Total wages paid each pay period;
- Date of payment and the pay period covered by the payment.

2. Family and Medical Leave Act (29 U.S.C. § 2601 et seq.)

This statute requires covered employers to provide up to 12 weeks of unpaid, job-protected leave to eligible employees for certain medical and family reasons. Employees are eligible for FMLA leave if they have worked for a covered employer for at least 12 months and have worked for the employer at least 1,250 hours in the 12 months immediately preceding the leave. To be covered, the employees must be located at a U.S. work site which, when combined with all of the employer's other work sites within 75 miles, has 50 or more employees. Some state and local governments have their own family and medical leave requirements.

3. National Labor Relations Act (29 U.S.C. § 151 et seq.)

The National Labor Relations Act (NLRA) is the primary federal statute protecting the rights of employees to organize a union or to refrain from organizing a union. Employees have collective rights as well as individual rights under the statute. Employers also have certain rights protected by the statute, including the right to a fair secret ballot election. The NLRA is enforced by the National Labor Relations Board (NLRB), an independent federal agency.

Many employers mistakenly believe that the NLRA applies only to unionized companies. The NLRA, however, protects an employee's right to engage in "concerted activity," which the NLRB has held applies to both union and non-union companies. As discussed below, there are several common employment policies or practices that have been held to violate the NLRA.

a. Coverage of the NLRA

The NLRA applies to all employers engaged in interstate commerce, with a few specifically defined exceptions. The following employees are not covered by the NLRA: persons primarily engaged in agricultural work; domestic workers; workers employed by a parent or spouse; independent contractors; supervisors; employees whose employer is covered by the Railway Labor Act; or employees of the United States government, state governments, Federal Reserve banks, political subdivisions of a state or local government or of a governmental corporation.

b. Employee Rights under the NLRA

(i) *Section 7 Rights*—The basic provision of the NLRA guaranteeing employee rights is Section 7, which provides:

"Employees shall have the right to self-organization, to form, join, or assist labor organizations, to bargain collectively through representatives of their own choosing, and to engage in other concerted activities for the purpose of collective bargaining or other mutual aid or protection, and shall also have the right to refrain from any or all of such activities."

c. "Protected Concerted Activity"

This is a key concept under the NLRA. It is defined as activity by one person or employee, relating to wages, hours, and working conditions, that affects other employees of the same employer. Significantly, the NLRB has held that an employee can act *alone* but still be engaging in "concerted activity" as long as his or her activities relate to issues that affect other employees.

d. Union Organizing

The NLRB regulations and procedures along with the many rules developed through NLRB case decisions make this a particularly challenging area. It is imperative that any biotechnology company facing a threat of union organizing retain experienced labor relations counsel.

(i) *NLRB Procedures*—The NLRB has very detailed regulations for determining whether a labor organization is entitled to represent a particular group of employees. The standard procedure is for a labor organization to obtain "union authorization cards" from at least 30 percent of the proposed employee unit. Once the union has achieved this "showing of interest" it will file a petition with the NLRB seeking to represent the identified group of employees.

(ii) *Secret Ballot Election*—Within a few weeks after the election petition is filed, the NLRB will conduct a secret ballot election among the employees to determine whether they wish to be represented by the union for purposes of collective bargaining with the employer regarding wages, hours, and other working condition. A simple majority of employees actually voting will determine the outcome of the election.

(iii) *Campaign*—During the period between the election petition being filed and the election, it is normal for both the union and the company to engage in a campaign to urge the employees in the unit to vote for or against the union in the secret ballot election. In general, the NLRB treats the campaign like a political campaign and will not evaluate the truthfulness of the campaign statements of either party.

(iv) *Unlawful Employer Conduct*—In its quest to convince employees not to vote for union representation, there are certain *TIPS* employers must follow: An employer may *not*:

- *T*— Threaten employees with discharge, demotion, transfer, or any other reprisal from the company if they do not support the company or if they engage in any conduct supporting the union.
- *I*— Interrogate employees about whether or why they support the union or the company.
- *P*— Promise employees a benefit if they do not support the union or do support the company.
- *S*— Spy on union meetings or union organizers or give the impression of keeping these employees under surveillance.

e. NLRA Applicability to Non-union Employers

As noted above, while the NLRA is generally thought to cover only unionized workplaces, the NLRB has held that many common personnel polices violate the NLRA. Thus, biotechnology employers and their counsel should familiarize themselves with these issues.

(i) *Policy Barring Discussion of Compensation*—The right to engage in "concerted activity" includes the right of employees to communicate with one another regarding self-organization at the job site. Since compensation is a key objective of organizational activity, the NLRB has held that *any* rule (even an oral rule) that restrains an employee's ability to discuss wages may interfere with the employee's right to engage in protected concerted activity. Accordingly, any formal or informal rules prohibiting discussions of compensation should be discontinued.

(ii) *Employee Committees*—The NLRA contains provisions outlawing employer domination of labor unions. While designed to protect against "company unions" created in the auto and steel industries in the 1930s, the NLRB takes an expansive view of what constitutes a "labor organization" and has applied this view to many commonly found employee committees.

1. The NLRB evaluates the legality of employee committees using a two-part analysis. First, it considers whether the committee constitutes a "labor organization" under the NLRA. A committee is a labor organization if its employee-members participate and "deal with" the employer regarding issues such as wages, hours, or other terms and conditions of employment.
2. The NLRB next considers whether the employer has dominated or interfered with the formation or administration of the committee. This second point is satisfied if management created the committee and determines the committee's structure, function, and continued existence.

(iii) *Inconsistent E-mail Policies*—Another area that can be challenging for non-union employers is e-mail. Many employers allow employees to use e-mail to disseminate and exchange a wide variety of information, including personal materials. Some, however, try to prevent employee use of e-mail to discuss union and other nonbusiness activities and so restrict their e-mail and other communication systems to business use only. The NLRB generally upholds policies limiting the use of communication equipment and systems as long as the rules do not discriminate against unions while allowing other employee personal activities. In short, if a company allows employees to use e-mail for nonbusiness purposes, such as selling Girl Scout cookies or the like, the company may not lawfully prohibit employees from using the company's e-mail system to solicit union support. See the discussion *infra* at Section G.2.e regarding e-mail policies.

(iv) *Individual Representation of Group Concerns*—Keep in mind that an employee acting alone may be found to be engaging in "concerted activity" protected by Section 7 even in the absence of any union or union-organizing activity. For an individual's complaints to constitute concerted action, the complaints may not be made solely on behalf of an individual employee, but must be made on behalf of other employees or at least with the object of inducing or preparing for group action. Significantly, it is not necessary that an employee be appointed by his or her fellow employees in order to represent their interests. The question is whether the employee acted with the purpose of furthering group goals. Thus, protests by an employee on behalf of other employees concerning wages, hours, and working conditions, as well as the presentation of job-related grievances, are activities protected by the NLRA. Employers considering discipline against employees who have engaged in such action on behalf of other co-workers must carefully consider whether the employee or the NLRB will link the discipline to the concerted activity.

4. Employee Retirement Income Security Act (ERISA) (29 U.S.C. § 1001 et seq.)

ERISA prohibits adverse action against any person who exercises any right to which he is entitled under an employee benefit plan or interference with the attainment of any right to which such participant may become entitled under the plan.

5. Occupational Safety and Health Act (OSHA) (29 U.S.C. § 651 et seq.)

OSHA requires employers to furnish a place of employment that is free from recognized hazards that are causing or likely to cause death or serious physical harm to employees. Among the major provisions of OSHA are the following:

- Provide a workplace free from serious recognized hazards and comply with standards, rules, and regulations issued under the OSHA Act.
- Examine workplace conditions to make sure they conform to applicable OSHA standards.
- Make sure employees have and use safe tools and equipment and properly maintain this equipment.

- Use color codes, posters, labels or signs to warn employees of potential hazards.
- Establish or update operating procedures and communicate them so that employees follow safety and health requirements.
- Provide medical examinations and training when required by OSHA standards.
- Post, at a prominent location within the workplace, the OSHA poster (informing employees of their rights and responsibilities).
- Report to the nearest OSHA office within 8 hours any fatal accident or one that results in the hospitalization of three or more employees.
- Keep records of work-related injuries and illnesses. (Note: Employers with 10 or fewer employees and employers in certain low-hazard industries are exempt from this requirement.)
- Provide employees, former employees, and their representatives access to the Log of Work-Related Injuries and Illnesses (OSHA Form 300).

Twenty-three states operate state OSHA programs covering private-sector workers as well as state and local government employees. Counsel should check their state laws to see if there is a state OSHA program. For additional information relating to OSHA standards, particularly as they apply to biotech companies, please see Chapter VIII.F.

6. Immigration Reform and Control Act 1986 (IRCA) (18 U.S.C. § 274A-274C)

IRCA requires employers to complete a Form I-9 verifying the employment eligibility of persons working in the United States who are citizens of the United States, nationals of the United States, or aliens authorized to work in the United States.

IRCA requires employers to hire only U.S. citizens, nationals of the United States, or aliens who are authorized to work in the United States. The law requires every employer to verify the employment eligibility of every employee hired after November 6, 1986. Employers are not to discriminate against individuals on the basis of national origin or citizenship.

This means that an employer should have an I-9 form on file for all employees, regardless of citizenship status, hired after November 6, 1986.

7. Uniformed Services Employment and Reemployment Rights Act of 1994 (USERRA) (38 U.S.C. § 4301 et seq.)

USERRA protects service members' reemployment rights when returning from a period of service in the uniformed services, including those called up from the Reserves or National Guard, and prohibits employer discrimination based on military service or obligation. USERRA covers nearly all employees, including part-time and probationary employees, and applies to virtually all U.S. employers, regardless of size. USERRA also provides health insurance protections for the employee and his/her dependents for up to 24 months while on active duty.

8. Fair Credit Reporting Act (FCRA) (15 U.S.C. § 1681 et seq.)

FCRA provides restrictions on employer use of consumer reports to obtain background information about employees or prospective employees. A consumer report contains information about a person's personal and credit characteristics, character, general reputation, and lifestyle. To be covered by the FCRA, a report must be prepared by a consumer reporting agency (CRA)—a business that assembles such reports for other businesses.

Employers often do background checks on applicants and get consumer reports during their employment. Some employers only want an applicant's or employee's credit payment records; others want driving records and criminal histories. For sensitive positions, it's not unusual for employers to order investigative consumer reports—reports that include interviews with an applicant's or employee's friends, neighbors, and associates. All of these types of reports are consumer reports if they are obtained from a CRA.

a. Written Notice and Authorization

Before an employer obtains a consumer report for employment purposes, it must notify the individual in writing, in a separate document consisting solely of the notice, that a report may be used. The employer must also must get the person's written authorization, in the proper form, before procuring the report. There are stiff penalties for noncompliance.

b. Adverse Actions Procedures

If an employer relies on a consumer report for an "adverse action," such as refusing to hire an applicant, reassigning or terminating an employee, or denying a promotion, it must take the following steps:

(i) **Before** taking the adverse action, the employer must give the individual a *pre-adverse action disclosure* that includes a copy of the individual's consumer report and a copy of "A Summary of Your Rights Under the Fair Credit Reporting Act"—a document prescribed by the Federal Trade Commission. The CRA that furnishes the individual's report should provide the employer with the summary of consumer rights.

(ii) **After** the employer has taken an adverse action, it must give the individual notice (orally, in writing, or electronically) that the action has been taken in an adverse action notice. It must include:

- the name, address, and phone number of the CRA that supplied the report;
- a statement that the CRA that supplied the report did not make the decision to take the adverse action and cannot give specific reasons for it; and
- a notice of the individual's right to dispute the accuracy or completeness of any information the agency furnished, and his or her right to an additional free consumer report from the agency upon request within 60 days.

9. Employee Polygraph Protection Act (29 U.S.C. § 2001 et seq.)

This act prohibits the use of lie detector tests for almost all private employers.

G. Use of Employment Contracts[3]

The vast majority of employer-employee relationships are not derived from any formal employment agreement but arise instead in the traditional employment-at-will context mentioned in the chapter introduction. In some instances, however, either one or both of the parties to an employment relationship may want to formalize the relationship in a written employment agreement. Generally, such employment agreements involve executives or key technical employees rather than lower-level employees. Most employment agreements are entered into at the beginning of what both parties typically hope will be an enduring relationship. Counsel, in advising on the drafting of employment agreements, should assist clients in anticipating the impact of the agreement if the employment relationship falters.

1. When Is an Employment Agreement Useful?

A variety of reasons motivate both employers and employees to seek a formal employment agreement. Although both parties often give up certain rights in entering into such an agreement, the agreement can be mutually beneficial in a way that offsets the loss of those rights. Either the employer or the employee may derive the following benefits from the existence of a written employment agreement:

a. Security

An employment agreement provides job security to the employee by setting forth the expected duration of the employee's employment, or the grounds under which the employee's employment may be terminated by the employer.

b. Recruitment Incentive

Written employment agreements are beneficial to the employer because, by providing the additional job security to the employee, the employer may be able to attract talented employees who would not enter into an employment relationship without such security.

c. Defined Performance Expectations

The written employment agreement articulates the expectations of the employer with respect to many aspects of the employee's performance.

d. Defined Compensation Expectations

The written employment agreement articulates the expectations of the employee with respect to compensation during the course of employment, and any severance payment that might be due to the employee following the termination of the employment relationship.

e. Confidentiality and IP ownership

On the employer's side, a well-written biotech employment agreement imposes strict confidentiality on the employee's work for the employer and makes it clear that any intellectual property developed by the employee (within legal limitations) belongs to the employer. It also contains assignment language, legally assigning any related IP developed to the employer and contractually obligating the employee to cooperate in patent filing.

2. Items to Be Covered

a. Duration

An employment agreement should define the expected duration of the employment relationship between the employer and the employee. This duration may be set forth in terms of the number of years for which the employer and the employee agree to be bound by the agreement. Typically, an employment agreement also contains provisions that allow the relationship to be terminated in accordance with its terms. In drafting such agreements, counsel should inquire whether the agreement is intended to last for a definite period of time or only until one of the parties is able to exercise one of the grounds under the agreement for terminating the employment relationship.

(i) *Agreements With a Finite Term*—Placing a finite term in the agreement gives the employee the security of knowing the duration of the relationship. It benefits the employer by allowing the relationship to end without having to terminate the employee's employment prematurely. Agreements with specific terms should state whether, at the end of the term, the relationship will end, convert to an at-will relationship, or renew for a successive period. The typical term may be anywhere from one to five years, although it is only rarely more than three years.

(ii) *"Evergreen" Clauses*—Some agreements contain "evergreen" clauses under which the contract, while set to expire on a finite date, is automatically renewed for a successive period if neither party gives notice of intent to terminate. This extra period may be of the same duration as the original period or for a shorter time. A typical evergreen clause might read as follows: "Following the expiration of the initial term, this Agreement shall be renewed for successive one-year terms unless either party gives notice of intent to terminate the Agreement at least 30 days prior to the expiration date" OR "Following the expiration of the first year of each term, this Agreement shall be renewed for successive term equaling the original term unless either party gives notice of intent to terminate the Agreement at least 30 days prior to the end of the term."

> **Practice Point**
>
> Counsel should be aware that an evergreen clause may become a trap for the client. If the employer consents to the inclusion of an evergreen clause, it must ensure a mechanism by which it calendars the notice date, or the employer may unwittingly find itself subject to a renewed employment period under the agreement. In addition, broad evergreen clauses, like the second one mentioned in the main text, have been attacked in shareholder actions as a breach of the board of directors' fiduciary duty.

b. Position and Title

Employment agreements are most typically put in place for key employees. Thus, the employment agreement generally should set forth the title and position that will be filled by the employee so there is no misunderstanding with respect to the job that the employee is accepting. However, the employer will generally seek to retain the unilateral right to change the employee's title, duties, and reporting relationship at any time, whereas a well-advised executive may seek to have changes in responsibility treated as "constructive dismissal" without cause, with all the ensuing penalties that may impose.

c. Compensation

One of the most critical aspects of any employment agreement is the compensation structure that is being provided to the employee in the agreement. If the employee is merely receiving a certain base salary, that is not particularly complicated. Even if the agreement addresses only base salary, however, counsel should be certain how the parties intend for the base salary to be reviewed and adjusted with any regular frequency, such as at the time of an annual performance review.

(i) *Base Salary*—Employers have long stated salary figures in monthly or weekly terms rather than annual terms for fear that a court might view the statement of the salary in annual terms as an implied contract to pay salary for a year. While courts in many states have discounted this theory, it is still good practice to state base salary in monthly or weekly as well as annual terms when drafting documents such as letters offering employment. In employment contracts, however, it is probably not as much a concern, since the terms of the relationship and the rights of the parties upon termination are likely to be delineated specifically in the agreement.

In an express employment contract, it is particularly helpful to define "base salary" as a term in the agreement because it is likely that other provisions of the agreement (such as severance pay or bonus) will make reference to base salary.

(ii) *Bonuses and Profit-Sharing Incentive Compensation*—In many agreements a bonus may be a component of the employee's compensation. There are numerous ways to design an employee bonus provision, but generally the earning potential is defined in one of the following ways:

- A set amount that is guaranteed to the employee regardless of results;
- A set amount that is contingent upon the achievement of individual employee objectives and/or company achievement of broader corporate objectives;[4]
- An amount equal to a percentage of revenues, profits, EBITDA,[5] development arrangements, or some other measure; or
- An amount left solely to the discretion of the CEO or Board.

(iii) *Commissions*—If the employee is engaged in a sales-related activity, often his or her compensation will include commissions based upon revenue generated by the employee or by other employees for whom he or she has responsibility. Where commissions are involved, particularly commissions based on the work of other employees (often called override commissions), the parties should carefully define in the employment agreement the basis upon which the override commissions will be calculated. For example, if the executive will be entitled to an override on the gross margin of the employer's sales, the term "gross margin" should be defined carefully so that both parties understand how the gross margin will be calculated.

Moreover, it is critical that the agreement state explicitly when the commissions are earned. For example, the agreement should state whether the commission is due (i) upon the execution of the contract with the customer, (ii) when the goods or services are delivered, (iii) when the goods or services are invoiced, or (iv) when the revenue is finally collected from the customer. These terms are common for employees involved in wholesale sales, but relatively rare for biotech companies. However, compensation based primarily on sales or some other measure of new business is common in pharmaceutical sales.

(iv) *Stock Options*—Stock options have become common for executives or other high-level employees in biotechnology companies. This may be true especially where the company is in a start-up mode and the employee may forgo a higher base salary in exchange for a promise of a future equity position within the company. These provisions should be written carefully to comply with federal securities laws, if the employer is or expects to be a publicly traded corporation, and with the requirements of the Internal Revenue Code applicable to stock options. Since securities and tax implications are beyond the scope of this chapter, counsel unfamiliar with such issues should consult corporate or tax counsel for guidance in drafting these provisions.

Apart from the corporate formalities of the stock option plan generally, there are several aspects of stock options that should be considered in a specific employment agreement if they are not addressed in the stock option plan.

1. *Vesting*—Many stock option plans do not spell out vesting schedules but allow each grant to be tied to a specific vesting schedule. There are a myriad of different events that could trigger vesting, such as a specific length of employment, termination of the employment relationship, a change in control of the employer, or completion of FDA trial phases. Counsel should carefully examine the vesting of options in light of the company's overall business plans and remind the company to ensure that it has a full understanding of the accounting implications of a stock option

program. Although vesting regimes vary from across companies and industries, a common vesting regime for biotech companies involves 25 percent of options vesting after one year of employment, with the remaining 75 percent vesting in equal monthly installments over the next 36 months. In addition, it is common for some or all unvested options to vest following an acquisition or change of control of the company, based either upon the occurrence of the transaction (sometimes referred to as a "single trigger") or upon the termination of employment within a specified period after the change of control (a "double trigger").

2. *Right to Exercise Options*—Separate from the issue of vesting is the question of how long the employee retains the right to exercise the options once the relationship has ended. Some stock option plans state that all options terminate when the employment ceases. Again, counsel should advise a client which options are best in light of the company's overall business plans.

3. *Buy-back Provisions*—Where the corporation is privately held, counsel should consider the means by which the company will buy or may back the employee's stock if the employee's relationship with the company is terminated. The company may not want a former employee to be in possession of company stock. Similarly, counsel for the employee should consider a provision that will allow the executive to compel a sale of the stock back to the company in the event of a termination. Otherwise, the employee may be left a minority shareholder with an illiquid stake in a company over which he or she has no control.

See Chapter V for further discussion of stock options.

(v) *Duties and Responsibilities*—Many employment agreements are deficient in describing the duties and responsibilities that are expected of the employee. Some agreements go no further than identifying the employee's title and position and including a general reference to the employee's duties. As a result, if the employee's performance is considered unsatisfactory, it is difficult for the employer to refer back to the employment agreement as the grounds for its dissatisfaction. Therefore, counsel should consider including a section on the employee's general duties (remaining loyal to the company, not undertaking acts that might injure the company, and similar obligations) and also encourage the employer to specify particular expectations of the employee. If the agreement makes reference to a job description, the job description should be attached as an exhibit to the agreement.

(vi) *Termination*—One aspect of the employment agreement that is valuable to both parties is a provision establishing the grounds upon which the employment relationship may come to an end. However, a termination clause in an employment agreement does not have to provide for termination only for cause. Rather, the termination section might provide for termination without cause, termination with cause (including a definition of what would constitute cause under the agreement), termination by the employee for "good reason" or constructive termination (a provision favored by executives), or termination based on other grounds, such as permanent disability of the employee.

1. *Termination for Cause*—The employer should define those actions or failures to act that would rise to the level of "cause" to terminate the employment agreement before the end of its term. Although "cause" may be defined however the parties may agree, the following infractions are the types that are typically included:

   - Failure to perform duties in a satisfactory manner. [Note that this is much easier to prove if the employee's duties are described with some detail, as discussed above.]
   - Fraud, misappropriation, embezzlement or acts of similar dishonesty.
   - Conviction of a felony.
   - Illegal use of drugs or excessive use of alcohol in the workplace.
   - Intentional or willful misconduct by the employee that may subject the company to criminal or legal liability.
   - Insubordination or deliberate refusal to follow the instructions of the employee's supervisor.
   - Breach by employee of any material terms of the agreement.

- Breach of loyalty by the employee, including diversion or usurpation of corporate opportunities.
- Willful or persistent violation of the company's policies and procedures.
- Violation of confidentiality or noncompete clauses.

2. *Termination Without Cause*—Employees may decline to sign employment agreements that do not provide them with some level of security beyond simple employment-at-will status. Nonetheless, employers should, whenever possible, retain their right to terminate an employee without cause, even if it means providing that such termination will entitle the employee to some measure of severance pay. When an agreement restricts termination to termination for cause, the employer may find itself having to live with an employee who, while not engaging in conduct that arises to "cause," is nonetheless no longer useful to the company.

    - *Severance Pay*—In designing an appropriate severance package for the employee, the parties should consider the nature of the employee's position, the degree of difficulty likely to be faced by the employee in obtaining new employment, and the extent of the employee's compensation package. In some instances, one or two months' severance pay may be appropriate for a termination without cause. In other circumstances, the employee might require a more significant severance package, such as one extending six months or a year.
    - *Obtaining a Release*—In drafting a severance provision, counsel for employers should consider tying receipt of severance pay to the execution of a release of claims. In other words, the employee will only receive the severance after executing an agreement that releases any and all claims against the employer. This will prevent the employee from using the severance payment as a means of financing litigation against the employer.

3. *Termination by the Employee for Good Reason*—Employees may also seek to include a provision that permits the employee to ter-

minate the relationship for "good reason" and specifies that the termination be treated by the company as a termination without cause. "Good reason" to terminate may include such employer actions as relocating the employee's place of work to a location more than 50 miles away, substantially reducing the employee's work responsibilities, reducing the employee's base salary, requiring the employee to engage in unlawful conduct or withholding bonus amounts that are due. Such a clause would typically include a requirement for written notice to provide the employer an opportunity to cure the objectionable condition.

    4. *Termination for Death or Disability*—If the employee should become disabled and, after a reasonable period, can no longer perform the duties required of the position, or dies, the agreement should terminate. The agreement should address the effect of termination by death or disability on the employee's compensation.

(vii) *Fringe Benefits*—To the extent the employee's fringe benefits—for example, vacation, sick leave, health benefits, and retirement benefits—are different from those offered to the company's other employees, they should be set forth in the agreement. In addition, if the employer will pay for an employee's membership at a local country club or provide a company car, such perquisites should be spelled out in the agreement.

(viii) *Confidentiality and Trade Secret Protection*—An employer providing an employee access to proprietary information may seek to restrict the employee's use and dissemination of that information both during and after the period of employment. This is critical for biotech companies. Every employee must sign a confidentiality agreement or have a clause in the employment agreement dealing with this. It is preferable to do this with a separate agreement in most cases, so if the employment agreement is voided by court, the confidentiality requirements still stand.

(ix) *Noncompetition and Nonsolicitation Clauses*—In exchange for the security that the employer is providing to an employee in an employment agreement, the employer may seek to restrict the employee from competing against the employer in some manner should the relationship terminate. Noncompetition provisions may be drafted to provide protection in a variety of ways. The employer may wish to prohibit the employee from engaging in a competing business within a certain mileage radius of the employer's place of business or may simply seek to prevent the employee from contacting the employer's customers or clients for a certain period of time. Unfortunately for biotech companies, a noncompetition obligation based on geographic proximity is unlikely to be particularly helpful, as competition is national and international in scope. This consideration, coupled with the fact that some states with strong biotechnology industries, such as California, take a particularly dim view of noncompetes, reinforces the view that biotech companies will need to look to patents and other intellectual property and regulatory regimes to protect them against competition from former employees.

> **Practice Point**
>
> **Noncompetition clauses**
> The broader the clause, the less likely it will be enforceable. For example, a noncompetition clause that restricts an employee from competing with the employer on a worldwide basis for five years will likely be found unenforceable, unless the employer can show that both the scope and length of the restriction is actually necessary to protect its legitimate business interests. A two-year restriction limited only to the geographic area of the employer's business would stand a much better chance of enforcement.

In general, such non-competition clauses are disfavored by the courts, since they restrict an employee's right to earn a living. How such agreements are interpreted and when they may be entered into are determined by state law. Counsel should carefully review the law in the state of intended employment to ensure that any noncompetition or nonsolicitation clause will be valid and enforceable.

(x) *Duty of Loyalty/Disclosure of Other Pursuits*—Increasingly, employees are not limiting themselves to serving only their employer. Rather, many employees seek to maintain other business ventures "on the side." Employers should require employees, particularly high-level employees, to disclose any business or ownership interests that they hold in business ventures other than the ownership of stock in a public corporation. The employee should also be reminded of his or her duty of loyalty to the employer and should be required to affirm his or her obligation to bring all corporate opportunities to the attention of the corporation. Violation of this clause should be noted as grounds for possible termination for cause.

(xi) *Boilerplate Provisions*—Most employment agreements, like other contracts, contain a series of "boilerplate" provisions that cover a number of miscellaneous issues. Among the provisions typically included are the following:

- Notice;
- Severability;
- Waiver;
- Governing law;
- Forum selection clause; and
- Integration/prior agreements.

H. Employee Handbooks

Employers often wish to publish their employment policies in an Employee Handbook that is given to new employees during orientation. While Employee Handbooks can be a useful tool for communicating the employer's polices, because of potential legal and employee-relations problems, employers must take care in drafting and administering Employee Handbooks. If an employer cannot ensure that it will have a well-drafted Employee Handbook *and* administer it consistently and fairly for all employees, then it should not have one.

Written personnel policies and handbooks can alert employees to an organization's rules and procedures but also can be a source of misunderstanding and potential liability if not properly prepared.

1. Pros and Cons of Using

a. Reasons for Using

There are many reasons why employers should consider creating and distributing information in an employee handbook.

- Employee handbooks can inform employees of policies, work rules, and expected standards of behavior.
- Employee handbooks can also create a positive image of the employer within the workplace and community and be an effective tool to promote favorable benefits and working conditions. These can be a substantial advantage in recruiting and keeping morale high among current employees.
- Employee handbooks reduce misunderstandings about employer expectations. If an employee is disciplined for violating a policy, the employee cannot plead ignorance or surprise.
- The employer can reinforce its EEO commitment and its position on sexual harassment by publishing its EEO and sexual harassment policies in a handbook.
- Handbooks provide supervisors, as well as employees, with a clear set of rules and policies, thereby increasing the likelihood of uniform treatment throughout the company.

b. Reasons for Not Using

Having an employee handbook is not without risks. Many employees have sought to use employee handbooks as evidence to overcome the presumption of at-will employment.

- Employees often try to avoid the at-will presumption by claiming that they were employed pursuant to an expressed or implied contract of employment that required the employer to have "just cause" before they were discharged or required that certain disciplinary procedures be followed before termination. In some cases, former employees make both claims. Poorly drafted employee handbooks are frequently used as the basis of such claims. This risk can generally be eliminated through a carefully worded disclaimer tailored to the specific jurisdiction.
- Employers also must ensure that handbooks are administered consistently and fairly for all employees because even a well-written employee handbook can lead to serious legal problems if not properly administered. For example, the handbook may become evidence

of discriminatory treatment where the employer failed to apply it consistently to all employees. In addition, employers who do not follow their own written policies or change policies without justification can provoke employee morale and productivity problems, since employees experience discontent when policies are changed in a seemingly arbitrary fashion.

2. Items to Be Covered

Assuming your company decides to develop an employee handbook, there are certain basic items that should be included.

a. Disclaimers and At-Will Statements

All employee handbooks and company policies should state that they are not contracts or conditions of employment and that the policy or handbook can be modified, interpreted or eliminated at the company's sole discretion. Handbooks should state that the employee's relationship with the company will be at will and that either the company or the employee can terminate it at any time, with or without notice. This "disclaimer" statement should also provide that the employee's at-will status can be changed only by a written document signed by both the employee and a designated officer of the company.

b. EEO Policies

There is no legal requirement that a company promulgate an equal opportunity/nondiscrimination policy. However, one of the first items that will be requested by the Equal Employment Opportunity Commission in an investigation of a discrimination charge is the company's nondiscrimination policy. The handbook should contain a short and simple statement that the company will not discriminate on the basis of race, color, sex, religion, national origin, age or disability with respect to any personnel decision. In jurisdictions where state or local laws provide additional protections (i.e., for sexual orientation), those bases should be included in the policy statement.

c. Harassment Policy

In a pair of cases decided in 1998,[6] the U.S. Supreme Court set forth the standard for an employer's liability for sexually harassing conduct. The court held that to establish an affirmative defense to a claim of hostile work environment harassment, an employer must be able to present evidence that it had taken reasonable preventive measures, such as distribution of a sexual harassment policy.

In light of the Supreme Court decisions, all employers—even those who elect not to publish employee handbooks—should adopt a harassment policy that includes the following elements:

- A definition of what conduct is considered harassing.
- A statement that such conduct is inappropriate and will not be tolerated by the company.
- An explanation of the steps that an employee should take to register a complaint of sexual or other harassment.
- A brief description of the steps that the employer will take to investigate any complaint of harassment.
- A statement that an employee who files a complaint under the policy will not be subject to any form of retaliation for having made a complaint.
- A statement that the company will make every reasonable effort to maintain confidentiality in its investigation. However, a blanket policy of confidentiality should not be given, since the employer may need to confront the alleged harasser in order to conduct an effective investigation.

d. Family and Medical Leave Policy

The Department of Labor has adopted regulations implementing the Family and Medical Leave Act (FMLA). Among the regulations is a requirement that if an employer provides written guidance to employees covering employee benefits or rights, such as an employee handbook, information concerning the FMLA *must* be included in the handbook.

The regulations further provide that even in the absence of a written policy, a covered employer must provide written guidance about FMLA rights when employees seek to invoke such rights. This can be in the form of a Department of Labor fact sheet, which is available on the Internet (http://www.dol.gov/esa/regs/compliance/whd/whdfs28.htm).

e. E-mail and Computer Usage Policy

With the advent of e-mail, voice mail, and office Internet access, legal issues have arisen out of employees' use (or misuse) of employer computer systems. Employers should make known to employees that voice mail, e-mail, and office computers are the employer's property and therefore subject to monitoring by the employer at any time, with or without prior notice to the employee. An employer's policy should also prohibit the display or transmission of any material that could be construed as creating a hostile work environment, such as sexually explicit or obscene images, messages, jokes or cartoons.

f. Description of Benefits

The handbook is an excellent place to briefly describe the benefits available to employees, such as insurance benefits (health, life), retirement benefits, tuition reimbursement, leave policies, etc. If the handbook contains a summary of benefits, it should also contain a disclaimer that the official insurance policy or summary plan description will prevail if there is a conflict in terms. The handbook should also note that benefits may be changed or terminated at any time at the company's sole discretion.

g. Discipline Policy

There are three approaches to addressing discipline and termination matters in an employee handbook: (1) say nothing to avoid any implication that employees may be terminated only for specific reasons; (2) remind employees of their at-will status; or (3) describe the types of conduct and levels of performance and other circumstances that may lead to termination.

If the third approach is taken, employers must be careful to preserve the at-will status of employees and to avoid inadvertently failing to list legitimate grounds for termination. Since no policy can address every situation that may arise or every type of conduct that is prohibited, employers should retain the discretion to terminate employees for other conduct it deems inappropriate.

I. Immigration Options for Biotech Employees

Because biotechnology companies are often on the cutting edge of research and new product development, they may discover that the candidate needed to fill a key position is not a U.S. citizen or permanent resident. The candidate may be graduating from a university in the United States, be employed by another company, or perhaps be living abroad and working in a field of interest. In such circumstances, the employer likely will need to obtain the appropriate work visa to authorize the foreign national's employment in the United States.

The government agency that grants most immigration benefits is U.S. Citizenship & Immigration Services (USCIS). This agency is one of three agencies created in March 2003 by the breakup of the Immigration and Naturalization Service (INS) and the placement of both immigration adjudication and enforcement functions into the newly created Department of Homeland Security. The reorganization, unfortunately, has not resulted in increased efficiency, and lengthy processing delays for immigration benefits should be expected and anticipated. Moreover, if the foreign national is overseas, he or she should prepare to encounter substantial delays in visa processing due to increased security concerns.

Since biotechnology is an international industry, the United States will continue to need significant foreign talent and expertise in almost all fields of research. Thus, biotechnology employers must understand the different ways a foreign national can legally work in the United States on a temporary basis (pursuant to a non-immigrant visa) or on a long-term basis (as an immigrant or permanent resident).

1. Obtaining a Visa and U.S. Entry

Foreign nationals who intend to come to the United States can seek to do so under one of two basic categories: non-immigrants and immigrants. Non-immigrants are aliens coming to the United States only for a temporary, limited period. Immigrants are those coming to the United States to remain and reside permanently. Whether the foreign worker comes to the United States as a non-immigrant or immigrant will depend upon the particular business objectives and whether the alien meets the specific eligibility requirements of a particular immigration category, or "classification."

In general, aliens must be in possession of a visa in order to come to the United States. The actual visa is issued only at U.S. consular posts (embassies and consulates general) abroad. In the case of non-immigrants, the visa consists of a "machine-readable," laminated paper that is permanently affixed to a righthand page of the alien's passport. The visa can be thought of as an entry permit, specifying one of the many non-immigrant categories for which the alien is found eligible and qualified.

Upon presentation of the visa to an immigration inspector at arrival in the United States (either at an international airport or border or seaport), the inspector typically will question the alien in order to reassess his or her eligibility to enter the country and then will issue the alien a Form I-94 card, or "Arrival/Departure Record." The I-94 card can be thought of as a stay permit, which shows what non-immigrant status has been granted to the alien and shows how long he can stay in this country—that is, when the specified status expires. Employers and aliens should be cautioned that the expiration dates on the visa and I-94 card frequently are not the same. The visa must be valid only at the time the alien seeks to enter the United States, whereas the I-94 card controls how long the alien is authorized to stay in the country.

In summary, it should be remembered that aliens generally need both an entry permit (visa) and stay permit (I-94 card) in order to travel to and be admitted for entry into the United States.

2. Non-immigrant Visas

Although there are a large number of non-immigrant visa categories available to foreign nationals who desire to come temporarily to the United States, those most frequently used by biotechnology companies are the Temporary Worker (H-1B); NAFTA Professional (TN); Intracompany Transferee (L1); Treaty Trader or Investor (E1 or E2); and Extraordinary Ability Alien (O-1) The following discussion will examine in further detail these various non-immigrant "working visa" categories so as to familiarize counsel and human resources professionals with each category's basic eligibility requirements.

a. H-1B "Specialty Worker" Visa

(i) *Basic Requirements*—The classification of H-1B Temporary Worker in a "Specialty Occupation" is available to any employer in the United

States to hire foreign professionals for a temporary assignment. Aliens are eligible for H-1B classification if they qualify as members of a professional occupation. This includes scientists, engineers, computer systems analysts, and any other occupation for which attainment of at least a bachelor's degree in a specific course of study is the usual minimum requirement for an entry-level position in the occupation. To qualify, individuals must show that they have the requisite four-year U.S. college degree or its equivalent. In addition, aliens must have satisfied any U.S. state licensure requirements of their particular profession before being eligible for H-1B classification.

H-1B aliens not only must satisfy the foregoing criteria, but the positions in which they intend to work in the United States must require the employment of persons having such professional qualifications. In addition, an employer's intent must be to hire the alien for only a temporary period.

These visas are employer-specific, so if the prospective hire is currently working for another U.S. company pursuant to H-1B authorization, the new employer must file an H-1B application for the employee before he or she can start working for the new company. Those foreign nationals who are currently in valid H-1B status are allowed to "port" to a new employer, which allows the H-1B worker to commence employment for the new employer at the time USCIS receives the new employer's H-1B application—the new employer does not have to wait for visa approval before the H-1B worker can begin working.

(ii) *Labor Condition Application*—Any employer wishing to sponsor an H-1B non-immigrant must file a labor condition application (LCA) with the U.S. Department of Labor for the H-1B position certifying that the wage to be paid is the greater of the actual wage for the occupation at the place of employment or the "prevailing wage." Employees can obtain a prevailing wage determination from their state employment services office, which will be a "safe harbor" for the employer in terms of an acceptable prevailing wage calculation. The company must also post notice at its place of business that it is filing for an H-1B visa. The representations of the company can be challenged by any interested party, and if it is found to have willfully misrepresented any factual aspect of the filing, the company faces civil fines, liability for back wages, and other penalties, including prohibitions against hiring new H-1B workers for up to one year.

(iii) *Length of Stay*—The H-1B non-immigrant can be admitted typically for an initial period of three years, with extensions available up to a maximum consecutive stay of six years. Certain H-1B non-immigrants on whose behalf a labor certification application (discussed in a later section) has been pending for more than one year prior to the end of their six years in H-1B status, i.e., before the end of year 5, may seek an extension beyond six years in one-year increments.

(iv) *H-1B Visa Cap*—U.S. immigration law limits to 65,000 the number of new H-1B visas that can be approved each year. Because of the popularity of the H-1B visa classification, the cap has been reached *before the start of the federal government's fiscal year* for each of the past three years. Congress granted some relief in late 2004, creating an exemption from the cap for up to 20,000 aliens who possess master's degrees from U.S. colleges or universities. Nonetheless, unless the cap is raised by future legislation, it can be expected that the annual allotment of new H-1B visas will continue to be used quickly. As of publication of this book, the H-1B cap for fiscal year 2007 (starting October 1, 2006) was reached on May 26, 2006, more than four months before the start of the fiscal year. Employers interested in an H-1B visa for a particular candidate should consult with experienced immigration counsel to ensure proper planning to obtain one of the limited number of visas.

b. TN "NAFTA Professional" Visa

(i) *Basic Requirements*—Certain Canadian and Mexican nationals can enter the United States to work on a year-by-year basis under immigration provisions in the North American Free Trade Agreement (NAFTA). The TN visa category can be used only for specific positions identified in a schedule found in Appendix 1603.D.1 of NAFTA. Of specific interest to the biotech industry are the following professional areas: scientist (including biochemist, biologist, chemist, geneticist, pharmacologist), medical laboratory technologist, scientific technician, pharmacist, and physician (research). A complete list of the professions listed under NAFTA and the minimum education requirements for each can be found at: http://travel.state.gov/visa/temp/types/types_1274.html#16.

Similar to the H-1B visa category, this category is employer-specific, in that the Canadian or Mexican national may work only for the sponsoring employer and must obtain new TN authorization before transferring to a new employer.

(ii) *Application Procedure*—For Canadians, the process is much simpler than using the H-1B category, as the application is presented to the USCIS at a port of entry and is adjudicated the same day. Mexican nationals must file and obtain the appropriate TN visa at a consulate in Mexico and then seek admission at the border.

The application for TN status typically includes documents proving the necessary degree background, a written offer of employment from the U.S. employer, documentation of Canadian or Mexican citizenship, and a filing fee.

(iii) *Length of Stay*—TN status can be renewed indefinitely on a year-by-year basis by submitting new petitions at the border (for Canadians) or consulate (for Mexicans) or through a USCIS service center. Nonetheless, since the applicant must have "non-immigrant intent" to qualify under this category, it is often difficult to renew TN authorization for longer than four or five years, and USCIS service centers have started to deny TN extensions filed in the United States if an immigrant visa petition has also been filed on behalf of the applicant.

c. L-1 "Intracompany Transfer" Visa

(i) *Basic Requirements*—For those biotech companies that have parent or subsidiary operations in other countries, the L-1 visa category allows certain personnel (executives/managers and employees with specialized knowledge) to be transferred temporarily to work for the U.S. parent, branch, subsidiary or affiliate of the foreign organization. To qualify, the employee must have worked for the foreign company for at least one of the immediately preceding three years in an executive, managerial or "specialized knowledge" capacity.

(ii) *Length of Stay*—Basic scientific staff can typically be transferred for up to five years as L-1B employees with specialized knowledge, although the USCIS is becoming extremely strict in its interpretation of this category. Managerial and executive employees can remain in L-1A status for up to seven years. Finally, spouses (but not children) of L-1 visa holders may now apply for working authorization in the United States, which is a significant benefit to working couples.

d. E-1 "Treaty Trader" and E-2 "Treaty Investor" Visas

(i) *Basic Requirements*—E visas are available only to nationals of countries that have either a Treaty of Friendship, Commerce and Navigation or a Bilateral Investment Treaty with the United States.[7] The "E-1 treaty trader" is an alien coming solely to carry on substantial trade principally between the United States and his home country. The "E-2 treaty investor" is an alien coming solely to develop and direct the operations of an enterprise in which he has made, or is in the process of making, a substantial investment.

In practice, the E category is used not so much by individual traders or investors as by U.S. companies owned by one or more persons who are nationals of a country having the required treaty with the United States ("treaty nationals") in order to bring aliens of that same nationality to work in managerial or other key positions for such a foreign-owned company.

Biotech companies that are U.S. subsidiaries of a foreign parent company owned by treaty nationals or a completely independent U.S. business established by treaty national owners may qualify for E visa status.

(ii) *Application Procedure*—Qualified E-1 and E-2 non-immigrants must obtain such visas directly from a U.S. embassy or consulate abroad. (This visa requirement also applies to Canadian nationals who otherwise are generally exempt from passport and visa requirements to enter the United States.) The applicant for an E visa must submit the standard non-immigrant visa application and present his passport and passport-type photograph. The E visa applicant also should present a letter from the prospective U.S. employer (or himself if an independent businessperson) that describes the nature of the business, provides all information necessary to show that the business satisfies the various E-1 or E-2 requirements, and shows that the individual applicant is coming to perform the requisite E non-immigrant duties.

The Department of State's Visa Office has created a special E Supplement form that also must be completed in applying for the E visa. Each U.S. consular officer has discretion to require submission of various corporate and financial documents to verify that the U.S. business qualifies under the E-1 or E-2 requirements. The spouse and minor dependent children of the principal E-1 or E-2 alien also may qualify for the same visa (that is, unlike most other visa types, there is no separate E category for dependents). Unlike most visa categories, spouses of E-1 or E-2 visa holders may apply for work authorization in the United States. Dependent children of E-1 or E-2 visa holders are not allowed to work.

e. O-1 "Extraordinary Ability Alien" Visa

A little-used visa category that may be of particular use in the biotechnology category is the O-1 Visa for Aliens of "Extraordinary Ability." As discussed below, the requirements for this category are quite high, but in the light of the H-1B visa cap, many biotech employers may wish to consider an O-1 visa for highly qualified researchers or scientists.

(i) *Basic Requirements*—To qualify as an alien of extraordinary ability in the sciences, arts, education, business, or athletics, the alien must be recognized as being prominent in his or her field of endeavor, as demonstrated by the following:

1. Evidence that the alien has been nominated for, or has been the recipient of, significant national or international awards or prizes in the particular field such as a Nobel Prize. [Obviously, this is a very, very high standard that only a few people will meet. Thus, the law allows an alternative standard that is far easier to meet.]
2. At least three of the following forms of documentation:
    - Documentation of the alien's receipt of nationally or internationally recognized prizes or awards for excellence in the field of endeavor;

- Documentation of the alien's membership in associations in the field for which classification is sought, which require outstanding achievements of their members, as judged by recognized national or international experts in their disciplines or fields;
- Published material in professional or major trade publications or major media relating to the alien's work in the field for which classification is sought, which shall include the title, date, and author of such published material;
- Evidence of the alien's participation on a panel, or individually, as a judge of the work of others in the same or in an allied field of specialization to that for which classification is sought;
- Evidence of the alien's original scientific, scholarly, or business-related contributions of major significance in the field;
- Evidence of the alien's authorship of scholarly articles in the field, in professional journals or other major media;
- Evidence that the alien has been employed in a critical or essential capacity for organizations and establishments that have a distinguished reputation;
- Evidence that the alien has either commanded a high salary or will command a high salary or other remuneration for services, evidenced by contracts or other reliable evidence.

(ii) *Peer Group Consultation*—As part of the petition package for an O-1 visa, the employer must solicit an advisory opinion from an appropriate U.S. "peer group" (normally a labor union) regarding the nature of the work to be done and the alien's qualifications.

The consultation requirement was designed for the entertainment and athletics industries in which labor unions may wish to argue against importation of competing aliens on an individualized basis. In the biotech field, there may not be a labor union "peer group" whose opinion can be solicited. In that case, the employer should be prepared to submit affidavits or other evidence from non-related entities establishing that no peer group exists.

3. Immigrant Visas and Permanent Residence Status

As an alternative to the above non-immigrant, or temporary, classifications, foreign nationals may seek to come to the United States to remain and reside permanently as immigrants based primarily either upon sponsorship by a close family relative or upon permanent offer of employment. With the exception of those aliens who are spouses, unmarried minor children, and parents of United States citizens, all prospective immigrants are subject to an annual quota which limits the number of persons who can immigrate to the United States.

Approximately 675,000 total visas are allocated to the family and employment-based categories annually, of which only 140,000 are set aside for employment-based immigration. Each county is allocated a maximum of approximately 26,000 permanent visas annually.

a. *Employment-Based Preferences*

The employment-based (EB) preference categories allocate the 140,000 annually available visas as follows:

(i) *EB First Preference* (40,000 visas annually)
1. *Priority Workers*—These workers consist of: (i) aliens with extraordinary ability in the arts and sciences, business, education, and athletics; (ii) outstanding professors and researchers; and (iii) multinational managers and executives.
2. These first preference aliens are exempt from obtaining an approved labor certification application (described below). However, the eligibility standards are very high. For example, extraordinary ability aliens are those who have attained "a level of expertise indicating that the individual is one of those few who have risen to the top of the field of endeavor." Outstanding professors and researchers must demonstrate "international recognition" in their particular academic area, three years of actual teaching or research experience, and be coming to fill a tenured or tenure-track position.
3. Of these three EB first preference subcategories, the last one regarding multinational managers and executives is potentially

the most useful one for companies and international businesspeople. This applies to aliens who have been or could be admitted to the United States as L-1A non-immigrants to perform managerial or executive duties, working within the same or related international organization. Again, a key benefit of this and the other categories of the first preference classification is that no labor certification is required (see later discussion of labor certifications).

(ii) *EB Second Preference* (40,000 visas annually)

Members of the professions holding advanced degrees or persons of "exceptional ability." This category is for professionals holding advanced (beyond baccalaureate) degrees and aliens of "exceptional ability" in the sciences, arts or business. This category is for those with substantially more than entry-level professional qualifications and generally requires the individual to be the recipient of a job offer by a U.S. employer, and thus be subjected to the rigors of the labor certification process. In relatively rare instances, the requirement of obtaining individual labor certification in this second preference category can be waived where it is demonstrated that the alien's work would be in the "national interest."

(iii) *EB Third Preference* (40,000 visas annually)

Skilled workers, professional and other workers. This category is for aliens who hold baccalaureate degrees (or an equivalent degree) and who are members of the professions, skilled workers with at least two years of training or experience, and unskilled workers. Unskilled workers means workers in jobs requiring less than two years of training or experience. Forty thousand total visas are available in this category, but unskilled workers are restricted to receiving only 10,000 of these visas. Additionally, all EB third preference aliens must first obtain approval of an individual labor certification application.

(iv) *EB Fourth Preference* (10,000 visas annually)

Ministers of religion and certain workers in religious organizations.

(v) *EB Fifth Preference* (10,000 visas annually)

Employment creation immigrants. This category is for aliens who invest generally a minimum of $1 million in a new commercial enterprise that will provide full-time employment for at least 10 U.S. workers. Of the 10,000 allotted annual visas in this fifth preference category, 3,000 are designated for investment enterprises located in special "targeted areas" of high unemployment, which permits a minimum qualifying investment of only $500,000.

b. Visa Backlogs and Priority Dates

Because permanent immigration to the United States is limited by the annual quota system, and because the demand by aliens for these permanent visas frequently exceeds the available supply in both the family-based and employment-based categories, some of these categories can become over-subscribed—that is, prospective immigrants are placed on a waiting list based on their "priority date," which is the time when they first applied for labor certification (as described below) or filed the immigrant visa petition for their particular preference classification. This backlog, or waiting list, is revised each month by the Department of State and, depending upon whether the demand has increased or decreased for the particular preference category, the waiting period can become longer or shorter. Since the demand and number of visas allocated for each preference category is different, waiting periods will vary.

c. Labor Certification

Persons seeking to immigrate in the second and third preference (EB 2 or EB 3) must first obtain a permanent labor certification, which is issued only if the U.S. Department of Labor can verify there is an insufficient number of available, willing, and qualified U.S. workers for the particular job. Labor certifications often can be difficult or even impossible to obtain and are always a somewhat troublesome, lengthy, and costly procedure.

(i) *Filing Requirements*—Under recently adopted regulations known by the acronym "PERM" (Program Electronic Review Management), the labor certification application must be filed online through a DOL-maintained Web portal. Before filing, the employer must register and create an account at the DOL Web site: http://www.plc.doleta.gov/.

(ii) *Prefiling Recruitment*—Before filing the application, the employer must undertake a number of specific recruitment steps to prove that there are no "qualified, interested and willing" U.S. workers, including:

- Internal posting for at least 10 consecutive business days between 180 and 30 days prior to filing.
- Use of any and all in-house media, whether electronic or printed, utilized in an employer's normal recruitment process.
- Posting of a job order with the local employment office for a period of 30 days.
- Two print advertisements on two different Sundays in the newspaper of general circulation in the area of intended employment. Both ads must be placed more than 30, but not more than 180, days prior to filing and can be placed on consecutive Sundays. If the job requires experience as well as an advanced degree, the employer may (but need not) use a professional journal in lieu of one of the Sunday ads.
- If the position is for a "professional" job, i.e., one that requires at least a bachelor's or higher degree (and is included in a list of such occupations published by the Department of Labor), an employer is required to undertake additional recruitment in the form of three (3) of the following: (i) job fairs; (ii) employer's Web site; (iii) job search Web site other than employer; (iv) on-campus recruiting; (v) trade or professional organization; (vi) private employment firms; (vii) employment referral program; (viii) notice of the job opening at a campus placement office; (ix) local and ethnic newspapers; or (x) radio and television advertisements.

(iii) *Recruitment Summary*—At the end of the above-described recruitment campaign, the employer is required to prepare a recruitment report describing the recruitment undertaken and results. This report is not submitted to the DOL as part of the application process. However, the DOL may request the recruitment summary as part of an audit prior to approving the application. The recruitment report must establish that there were no U.S. workers who were qualified for and interested in the position.

d. Immigrant Visa and Adjustment of Status

Following approval of the labor certification, the prospective employer must file a Form I-140 Immigrant Visa Petition in which the USCIS examines whether the alien is qualified under the terms of the labor certification and is eligible for either second or third preference employment-based preference classification.

Once an alien's immigrant visa petition has been approved by the USCIS, he or she must await the time when his priority date becomes "current" on the visa numbers quota list.[8] The alien will then apply for his or her immigrant visa from the United States consular post abroad, or make application for status as a permanent resident from the appropriate local office of the USCIS without leaving the United States. This latter process is known as "adjustment of status," and generally is available only to aliens who at all times have maintained a valid non-immigrant status (e.g., have not worked without authorization or overstayed).

As of the publication of this book, the U.S. Congress was debating a number of measures to reform U.S. immigration law. These changes, if passed and signed into law, could have a significant impact on immigration options for biotech employees.

Notes

1. *See* Section H.2.c. *infra* for a discussion of effective harassment policies.

2. The dollar figures are not updated regularly or tied to other laws such as in increase in the minimum wage. Regulations updating the white-collar exemptions took effect in August 2004. Prior to then, the minimum salary figures had not been updated since 1975.

3. By definition, this is a brief overview of employment contracts. There are many wonderful treatises on employment contracts, including the ABA's *Employment Termination: Rights and Remedies*, 2d ed., W. Holloway & M. Leech eds. (Product Code 5250208P9184) and *The American Bar Association Guide to Workplace Law* (Product Code 2350038). Every company's employment needs are a little different, so any form or model should be read carefully and adjusted as needed.

4. In biotech companies this may be tied to benchmarks, such as FDA Phase I, II, or III completion, or completion of a license or joint venture.

5. EBITDA means earnings before income taxes, depreciation and amortization. It is often used in early-stage businesses as the basis for calculating valuation and sometimes (less often) for rewarding compensation. It is less applicable to most biotech companies, because their value is based more on potential and less on current status.

6. Burlington Indus. v. Ellerth, 524 U.S. 742 (1998); Faragher v. City of Boca Raton, 524 U.S. 775 (1998).

7. A current list of countries with eligible treaties is published in the U.S. State Department's Foreign Affairs Manual and can be found online at http://foia.state.gov/masterdocs/09fam/0941051X1.pdf. Note that some treaties allow both E-1 and E-2 status, while others allow only one type of visa.

8. As of the publication date of this book, there were significant backlogs in the EB-2 and EB-3 categories, especially for citizens of India, China, and Mexico. The most recent State Department Visa Bulletin, with current priority dates, may be obtained at http://travel.state.gov/visa/frvi/bulletin/bulletin_1360.html.

Appendix A
Coverage of State Equal Rights Statutes

State	Coverage*	Threshold for Coverage
Alabama *Ala. Code § 25-1-20*	Covers only age discrimination (over 40)	20 or more employees
Alaska *Alaska Stat. § 18.80.220 951 et seq.*	Prohibits discrimination based on parenthood or marital status	Any person with one or more employee in the state
Arizona *Ariz. Rev. Stat. § 41-1401 et seq.*	Same as federal law except that state law provides only equitable remedies and does not permit compensatory or punitive damages	15 or more employees except for sexual harassment claims, the employer need only have one employee
Arkansas *Ark. Code Ann. § 16-123-101 et seq.*	Same basic coverage as federal law	9 or more employees
California *Cal. Gov't Code § 12940*	Prohibits discrimination based upon marital status, sexual orientation, Native American tribal affiliation or any "arbitrary criterion"	5 or more employees
Colorado *Colo. Rev. Stat. § 24-34-301 et seq.*	Prohibits discrimination based upon marital status and discharge for engaging in any lawful activity off the employer's premises during nonwork hours	All employers
Connecticut *Conn. Gen. Stat. § 46(a)-60(a)(1)*	Prohibits discrimination based upon marital status, sexual orientation, or learning disability. Must grant reasonable leave for disability resulting from pregnancy	Same as federal statues except for pregnancy discrimination, which applies to 3 or more employees

* Unless otherwise noted, the state employment practices laws all cover the same protected categories as federal law, i.e., race, color, religion, sex, pregnancy, national origin, disability or age (over 40).

Delaware *19 Del. Code § 711*	Prohibits discrimination based upon marital status or genetic information	4 or more employees for race, marital status, genetic information, color, age, religion, sex or national origin. 20 or more for disability
District of Columbia *D.C. Code § 2-1401.01 et seq.*	Prohibits discrimination based upon marital status; sexual orientation; personal appearance; outward appearance of any person, irrespective of sex, with regard to bodily condition or characteristics, manner or style of dress, and manner of personal grooming, including but not limited to hairstyle and beards; matriculation, family responsibilities; political affiliation; familial status; and place of residence or business	All employers regardless of size except for religious accommodation, which applies to employers with 5 or more employees
Florida *Fla. Stat. Ann. § 760.01 et seq.*	Same as federal law except that pregnancy is not expressly covered	15 or more employees
Georgia *Ga. Code Ann. § 45-19-20 (public employers)* *Ga. Code Ann. § 34-1-2 and 34-6A-1 (private employers)*	Protections against race, color, religion, sex, pregnancy, national origin cover **public employers** only. Prohibits discrimination on account of age or disability by private employers	All employers
Hawaii *Haw. Rev. Stat. Chapter 378*	Prohibits discrimination based upon marital status or sexual orientation	All employers
Idaho *Idaho Code Ann. § 18-7301 et seq.*	Same basic coverage as federal law	All employers
Illinois *775 Ill. Comp. Stat. 5/1-101 et seq.*	Prohibits discrimination based upon marital status; sexual orientation; citizenship status; arrest record; military status; and unfavorable military discharge	15 or more employees

Indiana *Ind. Code § 22-9-1-1*	Same as federal law except disability provisions don't require reasonable accommodation	6 or more employees
Iowa *Iowa Code § 216.6 et seq.*	Same basic coverage as federal law	More than 4 employees
Kansas *Kan. Stat. Ann. § 44-1001 et seq.*	Same basic coverage as federal law	4 or more employees
Kentucky *Ky. Rev. Stat. Ann. Ch. 344*	Prohibits discrimination based upon status as a smoker or nonsmoker	8 or more employees except for disability, where threshold is 15 employees
Louisiana *La. Rev. Stat. Ann. § 23:301 et seq.*	Same as federal law except disability provisions don't require reasonable accommodation; prohibits discrimination because of sickle cell trait or genetic information	20 or more employees
Maine *Me. Rev. Stat. Ann. tit.5, § 4551 et seq.*	Prohibits discrimination based upon sexual orientation or genetic information	All employers
Maryland *Md. Code Ann., art. 49B, § 1 et seq.*	Prohibits discrimination based upon marital status, sexual orientation or genetic information	15 or more employees
Massachusetts *Mass. Gen. Laws Ch. 151B, § 4(1)*	Prohibits discrimination based upon sexual orientation or genetic information	6 or more employees
Michigan *Mich. Comp. Laws § 37.2202 & § 37.1202*	Prohibits discrimination based upon height; weight; familial or marital status; genetic information	All employers

Minnesota *Minn. Stat. Ann. § 363A.01 et seq.*	Prohibits discrimination based upon sexual orientation; marital status; status with regard to public assistance	All employers
Mississippi *Miss. Code Ann. § 79-1-9*	Applies only to **public employers**	
Missouri *Mo. Rev. Stat. Ch. 213*	Same basic coverage as federal law	6 or more employees
Montana *Mont. Code Ann. tit. 49, Ch. 2*	Prohibits discrimination based upon marital status	All employers
Nebraska *Neb. Rev. Stat. § 48-1101 et seq.*	Prohibits discrimination based upon marital status	15 or more employees
Nevada *Nev. Rev. Stat. § 613.300*	Prohibits discrimination based upon sexual orientation	15 or more employees
New Hampshire *N.H. Rev. Stat. Ann. § 354-A:7*	Prohibits discrimination based upon marital status or sexual orientation	More than 6 employees
New Jersey *N.J. Stat. Ann § 10:5.1 et seq.*	Prohibits discrimination based upon marital status; sexual orientation; source of lawful income used for rent or mortgage payment; atypical hereditary cellular or blood trait; genetics; refusal to submit to genetic testing or refusal to provide genetic information	All employers
New Mexico *N.M. Stat. Ann. 1978, § 28-1-7(A)*	Prohibits discrimination based upon spousal affiliation, sexual orientation or gender identity	4 or more employees except for spousal affiliation (50 employees); sexual orientation (15 employees)
New York *N.Y. Exec. Law § 296(1)(a)*	Prohibits discrimination based upon marital status; sexual orientation; genetic predisposition or carrier status	4 or more employees

North Carolina *N.C. Gen. Stat. § 143-422.2*	Prohibits discrimination based upon sickle cell trait or hemoglobin C trait; genetic testing or information	15 or more employees
North Dakota *N.D. Cent. Code § 14-02.4-01 et seq.*	Prohibits discrimination based upon marital status; having received public assistance; for engaging in any lawful activity off the employer's premises during nonwork hours	All employers
Ohio *Ohio Rev. Code Ann. § 4112.01 et seq.*	Same basic coverage as federal law	4 or more employees
Oklahoma *Okla. Stat. tit. 25, § 1302*	Same basic coverage as federal law	15 or more employees
Oregon *Or. Rev. Stat. § 659A.030*	Prohibits discrimination based upon marital status or genetic information	All employers
Pennsylvania *Pa. Stat. Ann. tit. 43, § 951 et seq.*	Prohibits discrimination based upon familial status	4 or more employees
Rhode Island *R.I. Gen. Laws § 28-5-1 et seq.*	Prohibits discrimination based upon sexual orientation or genetic information	4 or more employees
South Carolina *S.C. Code Ann. § 1-13-10 et seq.*	Same basic coverage as federal law	15 or more employees
South Dakota *S.D. Codified Laws § 20-13-1 et seq.*	Same basic coverage as federal law	All employers
Tennessee *Tenn. Code Ann. § 4-21-101 et seq.*	Same basic coverage as federal law	8 or more employees

Texas *Tex. Lab. Code Ann. § 21.001 et seq.*	Prohibits discrimination based upon genetic information or refusal to submit to genetic testing	15 or more employees
Utah *Utah Code Ann. § 34A-5-101 et seq.*	Same basic coverage as federal law	15 or more employees
Vermont *Vt. Stat. Ann. tit. 21, § 494 et seq.*	Prohibits discrimination based upon genetic information or refusal to submit to genetic testing	All employers
Virginia *Va. Code Ann. § 2.2-2639B*	Prohibits discrimination based upon genetic information	6 to 15 employees. Law is narrower than Title VII in that it only outlaws termination. Prohibition against genetic testing applies to all employers.
Washington *Wash. Rev. Code § 49.60.010 et seq.*	Prohibits discrimination based upon marital status or genetic information	8 or more employees
West Virginia *W. Va. Code Ann. § 5-11-1 et seq.*	Same basic coverage as federal law	12 or more employees
Wisconsin *Wis. Stat. § 111.31 et seq.*	Prohibits discrimination based upon marital status; sexual orientation; genetic information; arrest or conviction record; use or nonuse of lawful products off the employer's premises during nonwork hours	All employers
Wyoming *Wyo. Stat. Ann. § 27-9-105 et seq.*	Prohibits discrimination because of use of tobacco	2 or more employees

Chapter VII

Federal Regulation of Research Through Funding

G. Melissa Ince
Polsinelli Shalton Welte Suelthaus PC
Kansas City, Missouri
and
Jenny Kim
Miller & Chevalier Chartered
Washington, D.C.

Recognizing the need to encourage scientific development and the impracticality and inefficiency of attempting to conduct all of the associated research itself, the government funds a great deal of research by private, non-and for-profit entities. There are two main instruments the government uses to fund research: grants and contracts. The instrument selected depends on the purpose of the research.

Grants are used when executive agencies, such as the National Institutes of Health (NIH), wish to support a research project because it will benefit the public through the expansion of scientific knowledge. Contracts are the mechanism the government uses when it wishes to purchase a product or service, whether that product is a computer program or an antigen.

The legal obligations that are imposed on a recipient of grant or contract funds are very different, as is the mechanism by which the obligations are made part of the agreement. In practical terms, the difference between grants and contracts is this: the bulk of the government's requirements for accepting grant funds are obliquely incorporated by reference into the award instrument and attach on withdrawal of funds. Contract conditions, on the other hand, are explicitly—if at times confusingly—set out in the document the client executes.

If a client accepts a subgrant (called a "subaward") or a subcontract, particularly if it is its first, it is very important to explain what the client is agreeing to, because the consequences of noncompliance can have lasting and costly effects. The failure to comply with the terms and conditions of funding can result in more stringent monitoring of your client's activities, the loss of funding, debarment (which results in a bar to receiving *any* federal funds), and even criminal charges.

The first part of this chapter deals with grants and contracts. It is intended to provide an explanation of how the regulatory scheme is imposed. It is not intended to provide a comprehensive analysis of the compliance requirements. To learn more about the specific compliance requirements for grants or contracts, consult the associated tables at the back of this chapter. The tables provide interpretation of most of the conditions that cause problems or confusion and provide reference sources for more information.

The second part of the chapter addresses ethical issues that arise for governmental employees. While these regulations are not strictly part of the regulation of extramural funding, they affect how and when one may hire a governmental employee, which is useful for a biotechnology company to know.

A. Grants and Contracts

1. Federal Research Grants

The purpose of grants is the advancement of the public good. There is an altruistic ideal in grant-making that is reflected in the compliance scheme. Violations of the vast majority of the obligations that attach under a grant are self-discovered, self-reported, and self-corrected. This concept is particularly apparent in the structure of the human subjects protection and animal welfare programs.

This altruistic, self-regulating ideal is also reflected in the format in which the grant obligations are presented. Not for scientists are the tedious and imposing Federal Acquisition Regulation (FAR) clauses governing the interactions of private contractors with the government! No, they prefer their regulations presented in an easy-to-read, nicely indexed, friendly little "Manual" or

"Guidebook." But don't be fooled: every one of the conditions in that friendly guidebook is as binding and enforceable as those hard-to-read FAR clauses.

"But wait!" you say, "The grant isn't a contract! There are no 'whereas' clauses or warranties and representations! It doesn't even require execution!" The truth is that the federal research grant is just a contract with a friendly face. It is a contract in which acceptance is indicated by action. The action in this case is withdrawal of the grant funds. Thus, when your client withdraws the funds, it has just agreed to adhere to all the terms and conditions, even entire manuals, that are incorporated by reference.

There is no "generic" set of terms and conditions that apply to research grants, even those made by a single agency. Grants can be made pursuant to special legislative directives that impose unique terms on the use of funds. Grants are also subject, from year to year, to any quirky obligations attached to the funds by means of a rider in the appropriations bill that provides the funding to the agency or for that particular program. An amusing example is the "Prohibition of Student Unrest" provision that one of us saw in a boilerplate subaward agreement. A lengthy search turned up a rider in a 1968 Appropriations Bill that was intended to clamp down on student anti-war protests. That institution had clearly been including that provision in all of its subaward agreements since 1968. What a waste of ink! Appropriations riders, in fact, are only effective for a specific funding year.

> **Practice Points**
>
> **Government Grants**
> — Have as their purpose advancement of the public good;
> — Are legally enforceable;
> — Constitute a contract once funds are withdrawn by grantee;
> — Incorporate binding terms from policy manuals and guidelines; and
> — Can impose requirements on an entire institution.

a. *Subgrants*

The above example raises the tricky issue of ensuring subawardee compliance. The main grant recipient (called the "awardee" or sometimes the "grantee") will often enter into an agreement with another entity to help with some aspect of the research. This is known as a "subaward," and the assisting entity is the "subawardee." Awardees often try to develop a single subaward form contract that contains, cumulatively, every possible provision of every agency from which they have ever received funding. This can lead to your client, as a subawardee, agreeing to obligations that are not required by the awarding agency.

Negotiating a subaward is tricky. The awardee will never want to let the subawardee see the award document, justifying it on confidentiality or intellectual property bases, so the subawardee cannot verify for itself whether any of the provisions really need to be included. There is no point, however, in agreeing to and complying with conditions that are not required by the funding agency.

For this reason, when your client asks you to help negotiate a subaward, you will need to actually read the terms and conditions in the subaward instrument and compare them to the standard terms and conditions for that agency for that funding year. Anything nonstandard should be questioned. You should also check to see whether the listed terms and conditions actually "flow down" to subawardees, or require a certification. You will need to check the funding agency's manual—or the handy chart attached to this chapter—to make sure.

Depending on the leverage your client has, you may be able to get unnecessary provisions deleted if you can show they are not normally required by the relevant government agency. It is a good idea to seek a representation and warranty that the terms and conditions set out in the subaward instrument do not exceed those imposed under the original award, but don't hold your breath. Subawardees don't usually have much negotiating power when it comes to the terms of subawards.

b. Terms and Conditions

What are these terms and conditions, and how do they apply to your client? On the one hand, there will be explicit requirements in the award instrument, such as "you must contact your grants management officer within 30 days of receipt." Those are easy enough to understand. Then there are the ones that the casual reader might pass over entirely, like "Awardee must adhere to OMB Circular A110 and the NIH Grants Policy Manual." Many attorneys will slide right over these clauses, because they do not sound like regulations, statutes, or anything else with the force of law. It is a big mistake, however, to ignore these provisions.

The NIH Grants Policy Manual, for instance, contains obligations like "Nondelinquency on Federal Debt," which means that if the Awardee or Subawardee has a judgment lien against it for a federal debt, it cannot receive funds.[1] Another example is the Drug-Free Workplace requirement, which mandates that the awardee establish a policy prohibiting drug use in the workplace and report to NIH within 10 days if any employee is convicted of a drug-related crime.[2] These requirements are codified—the Nondelinquency on Federal Debt is at 28 U.S.C. § 3201(e), and the Drug-Free Workplace policy at 42 U.S.C. § 702—as are most of the requirements. The funding agency's grants policy manual is just a convenient collection of the requirements and generally can be relied upon as an accurate representation of the obligations applicable to your client.

General terms and conditions may include organizational ethics, nondiscrimination, funding-related administrative requirements, and ethical and safety standards for conducting the research.

- Ethics provisions include the Byrd Anti-Lobbying Act, which generally prohibits the use of federal funds for lobbying activities; financial conflict-of-interest prohibitions; Organization Standards of Conduct; and social objectives such as increasing seat belt use.
- Nondiscrimination provisions include the Age Discrimination Act; Rehabilitation Act; Title IX of the Educational Amendments of 1972 (sex discrimination); and Title VI of the Civil Rights Act of 1964.
- Funding-related provisions are not comprehensively addressed in this chapter; those requirements are voluminous and generally dealt with by specialized administrative personnel. But the significant provisions that affect a client's operations include incorporation of the Office of Management and Budget Circulars on procurement, usually Circular A-110, audits, and allocation of program income.
- Ethical and safety standards for conducting research include compliance with the Animal Welfare Act, obtaining a Federal Wide Assurance for human subjects research (which obligates the institution to utilize Institutional Review Boards for human subjects research), various provisions limiting and prohibiting certain types of stem cell research, and compliance with the NIH's "Guidelines for Research Involving Recombinant DNA," which sets the standard for safely working with rDNA, toxins, and many other biological materials.

Some of the requirements apply to the whole institution, once funding is accepted for the first grant. While this may sound overreaching, it has worked well in practice. For instance, the rDNA Guidelines referenced above are one of the institution-wide conditions. The little-known alternative regulatory scheme to the rDNA Guidelines is Section 700 of the Toxic Substances Control Act (TSCA). TSCA mandates a lengthy federal review and approval process for the creation of any "intergeneric" (genes from one species put into another species) organisms. The rDNA Guidelines allow most research to proceed after brief review by an internal institutional biosafety committee (IBC), a comparatively quick and easy process.

c. Grantor Agencies

There are many federal agencies that make research grants, and each agency may have its own policy manual and implementing regulations. The Health and Human Services Department contains many agencies that make grants, including the National Institutes of Health, the National Science Foundation, and the National Cancer Institute. The NIH has the most developed (some would say too developed) grants management program. The NSF has a well-developed program, but it is not as detailed as that of the NIH. But the agencies have many similar requirements, which makes sense because they are both overseen by HHS. The attached table compares the requirements of the NIH and NSF grants manuals, and notes the many differences.

Other federal agencies that make grants include NASA and the Department of Defense ("DoD"), although these agencies tend to prefer contracts as their award instruments. The attached table also sets out certain DoD requirements for the sake of comparison. Generally, the DoD grants tend to be more "contract-like" than NIH and NSF grants, in that the provisions are more onerous and less flexible.

i. Small Business Innovation Research (SBIR) and Small Business Technology Transfer (STTR) Program Grants

SBIR and STTR are programs that provide grant funds to increase the participation of domestic small businesses in research and development. They are neither entirely contracts nor entirely grants, although for the purposes of compliance, the theory is more akin to the traditional federal research grant than a contract. The programs have certain participation and eligibility requirements, discussed below, and to the extent any generalizations can be made about the programs, the compliance scheme is largely self-imposed by the awardees.

ii. SBIR

The Small Business Innovation Research (SBIR)[3] program is a set-aside program (2.5 percent of an agency's extramural budget) for domestic small business concerns to engage in Research/Research and Development (R/R&D) that has the potential for commercialization and public benefit. Participation in the program is mandatory for federal agencies whose external funding budgets exceed $100 million per year. Currently, 11 federal agencies participate in the SBIR program: the Departments of Health and Human Services (DHHS), Agriculture (USDA), Commerce (DOC), Defense (DOD), Education (DoED), Energy (DOE), Homeland Security, and Transportation (DOT); the Environmental Protection Agency (EPA), the National Aeronautics and Space Administration (NASA), and the National Science Foundation (NSF). To date, over $12 billion has been awarded by the SBIR program to various small businesses. To participate in the program, businesses must be for-profit, have 500 or fewer employees, and the funded work must be performed in the United States. In addition, there are certain effort levels required by the principal individuals involved in the project. Depending on the agency, there can be requirements that the principal investigator be employed primarily by the proposing firm, or that the proposing firm not subcontract/subaward more than a certain percentage of the work.

iii. STTR

Similarly, federal agencies with extramural R&D budgets over $1 billion are required to administer STTR[4] programs using an annual set-aside of 0.30 percent. Currently, five federal agencies participate in the STTR program: DOD, DOE, DHHS (NIH), NASA, and NSF. In fiscal year 2003 (October 1, 2002–September 30, 2003), the NIH made SBIR grant and contract awards totaling over $525 million and STTR grant awards totaling over $31 million. To participate in the STTR program, the business must either be for-profit with 500 or fewer employees or a research institution; the funded work must be performed in the United States; and certain effort levels and project control thresholds are required of the entities involved in the project.

Compliance-wise, the programs are much less subject to generalization than the traditional federal research grants. SBIR and STTR grant funds are usually subject to a traditional contract, the terms of which vary according to the funding agency and type of research to be performed. The compliance scheme is much less concrete, though; many of the same elements as in a regular research grant are reviewed by the agency in the course of the grant award process, but there are few hard-and-fast rules that apply to all such grants. Typically, the business seeking the grant may be required to develop and submit a work plan or cooperative agreement that will govern how the work will be carried out, and will be incorporated into the terms of the contract. Ideally, you as the applicant's counsel should review the work plan or cooperative agreement before it is submitted to the agency. Additional detail regarding SBIR and STTR grants is provided below in Section C.

2. Contracts

The Federal Acquisition Regulations (FAR) and relevant federal statutes outlined briefly below apply both when a private contractor does business directly with the federal government as a prime contractor and when it does business indirectly with the federal government as a subcontractor. In addition, separate rules also apply to a private contractor's relationships with third parties, such as teaming partners, vendors, and suppliers, who are working with the private contractor to meet the federal government's needs. The attached appendix of FAR Federal Procurement Requirements and Policy clauses presents additional obligations of which a potential contractor must be aware.

a. *Sale of Commercial Items and Services*

The federal government has a policy preference for acquisition of commercial items and services. FAR Parts 10, 11, and 12 prescribe policies for acquisition of commercial items and encourage government agencies to procure commercial items. For example, a biotech company would need to be aware of these obligations when entering into an arrangement with the government regarding the sale or supply of, for example, vaccines, standard drugs, or biomedical equipment.

Under FAR § 12.207, agencies may only use firm fixed-price contracts[5] or fixed-price contracts with economic price adjustment[6] for acquisition of commercial items. Indefinite-delivery contracts also may be used, which base prices on a firm fixed price or fixed price with economic price adjustment.

Commercial products must meet the "commercial item" definition of FAR § 2.101. Generally, a product will qualify as a commercial item when it is provided to the general public for non-governmental purposes. Under the FAR definition, a commercial item is any item, other than real property, that is of a type customarily used for non-governmental purposes. It is generally an item that has been sold, leased or licensed to the general public or that has been offered for sale, lease or license to the general public.

FAR Parts 10, 11, and 12 implement the government's preference for acquisition of commercial items and components and non-developmental items, rather than items developed and produced to government-unique requirements. Under these FAR requirements, procuring agencies must:

> **Practice Points**
>
> **Government Contracts:**
> — Have as their purpose acquisition of commercial goods/services;
> — Are legally enforceable;
> — Constitute a contract once executed by the parties;
> — Are governed by the Federal Acquisition Regulations; and
> — Must obligate subcontractors' compliance on certain key terms.

(i) Conduct market research to determine whether commercial items or non-developmental items are available to meet agency requirements.

(ii) To the maximum extent practicable, specify agency needs in functional, performance or physical terms that encourage offerors to supply either commercial items or, if such items are not available, non-developmental items.

(iii) Acquire commercial items or non-developmental items when available to meet agency needs.

(iv) Require prime contractors and subcontractors at all tiers to incorporate, to the maximum extent practicable, commercial items and non-developmental items as components of items supplied to the agency.

An agency may use sealed bid, negotiation or simplified acquisition procedures when acquiring commercial items. Standard Form 1449, Solicitation/Contract/Order for Commercial Items, is the form that must be used for all solicitations, contract awards, and orders for commercial items.

An agency may combine the required synopsis and the terms of a written solicitation in a single Federal Business Opportunities ("FedBizOpps") (www.fedbizopps.gov) notice. In such instances, the private contractor will be allowed a minimum of 15 days to respond to the solicitation.

An agency may use streamlined evaluation procedures to evaluate offers for commercial items. These include:

- "Best Value" evaluations based solely on technical, price, and past performance factors.
- Evaluations without specification of technical subfactors.
- Technical evaluations based on existing product literature, product samples and warranty provisions.
- Submission of alternate proposals.
- Proposal response times of less than 30 days.

The FAR has been revised to reduce the complexity of contracting for commercial items. Agencies may only use, to the maximum extent practicable, contract clauses that are required by law or determined to be consistent with customary commercial practices. While some tailoring is permitted, agencies generally must use one set of solicitation provisions, one list of representations and certifications, one set of standard terms and conditions, and one set of additional terms and conditions to implement laws applicable to commercial item acquisitions.

FAR § 12.503 lists the laws that are no longer applicable to commercial item prime contracts: the Walsh-Healey Act,[7] Contingent Fees,[8] Drug-Free Workplace, Contract Work Hours and Safety Standards Act,[9] Clean Air Act, and modified clauses relating to the Truth in Negotiations Act (TINA)[10] and Cost Accounting Standards (CAS).[11] For a complete list of those laws and clauses no longer applicable to subcontracts for commercial items, see FAR § 12.504. The Department of Defense also includes in the DFARS, Subpart 212.5, a list of defense-related laws and regulations that are not applicable to commercial-item contracts and subcontracts.

FAR § 15.4031 prohibits the government from obtaining cost or pricing data for acquisitions at or below the simplified acquisition threshold,[12] although the contracting officer may request information other than cost or pricing data.[13] Auditable information includes books, documents, accounting procedures and practices, and other data, including computer data. A private contractor's failure to provide accurate information to the government may expose the private contractor and its individual employees to possible violations of false statement laws. Also, private contractor employees should cooperate with audits conducted for these purposes, since obstructive conduct may be viewed as a criminal violation of the Obstruction of a Federal Audit statute.[14]

The government will evaluate a private contractor's past-performance data "from a variety of sources both inside and outside the Federal government."[15] Past performance will be considered in accordance with FAR Subpart 9.1 for all solicitations of commercial items.

The following representation and certification clauses are frequently included in solicitations and contracts for commercial items and services:

- Certificate of Independent Price Determination[16]
- False Statements in Bids[17]
- Utilization of Small Business Concerns, Small Disadvantaged Business Concerns, and Woman-Owned Small Business Concerns[18]
- Equal Opportunity[19]
- Certification of Non-Segregated Facilities[20]
- Previous Contracts and Compliance Reports[21]
- Affirmative Action Compliance[22]
- Gratuities[23]
- Certification and Disclosure Regarding Payments to Influence Certain Federal Transactions[24]

A private contractor's purchasing and subcontracting relationships are governed by FAR Part 44, applicable laws, and the terms of applicable government contracts. Among other things, government requirements can affect the type of contract used, the amount and type of competition employed, and the terms and conditions that are required to be flowed down to subcontractors in written agreements. In addition to the FAR, government contractors should also look to the agency-specific FAR supplement for additional information. For example, in a Department of Health and Human Services contract, clause HHSAR 352.22370 (Safety and Health) must flow down to the subcontract between the prime and sub where the subcontract involves the use of toxic substances, hazardous materials, or hazardous operations.

A contractor's purchasing and subcontracting program must operate in a reasonable and fair manner with suppliers and vendors. In this regard, the contractor must avoid any actual or potential conflicts of interest (including a financial stake in the outcome) in awarding or administering subcontracts and purchase orders and must not receive personal benefits from suppliers in exchange for favorable treatment (that is, "kickbacks"). To ensure that the interests of the government and a contractor are protected, purchasing and subcontracting should be accomplished at arm's length, preserving market competition.

Many government decision-makers believe that vigorous competition produces pricing more favorable to the government and tends to keep subcontractors "honest." Additionally, competition at the vendor and subcontractor level is viewed as a means of reducing the risk of kickbacks and fraudulent practices.

> **Practice Points**
>
> **Evaluation of Vendor Proposals:**
> — Document process carefully in writing;
> — Apply consistently across vendors;
> — Evaluate on objective, demonstrable factors such as performance history, experience, pricing, timeliness, personnel, and management;
> — Ensure subcontractor eligibility.

The process of evaluating vendors' proposals should be well documented and consistently applied to avoid any allegations of improprieties or preferential treatment. Bids and proposals should be evaluated and rated on the basis of the best value to the contractor, which can include, where applicable: (1) past performance on prior similar jobs; (2) past experience on prior similar jobs; (3) price reasonableness; (4) record of timely performance; (5) key personnel; and (6) management or technical approach of the vendor. Ratings of bids and proposals and a recommendation for award, including the underlying rationale, should be made in writing and retained in the private contractor's files.

Prior to awarding a purchase order or subcontract, it is necessary to ensure that the selected supplier or subcontractor has not been debarred or suspended from doing business with the government and, therefore, is ineligible to perform services for the private contractor.

A contractor's purchasing department must review the General Services Administration's "List of Parties Excluded from Federal Procurement and Nonprocurement Programs" (http://epls.arnet.gov) in order to ensure that proposed vendors and suppliers have not been debarred or suspended from doing business with the federal government.

Once a vendor is selected for performance of a government subcontract, the private contractor will need to determine which contract clauses must be included in the purchase order or subcontract. Government contractors are required to obligate subcontractors under certain prime contract clauses and requirements as well as certain standard FAR clauses. Additionally, there are several contract clauses that, while not legally required, are necessary to protect the private contractor's interests under federal government contracts. These clauses include the authority of the contractor to *terminate* a subcontract if the underlying government contract or program is terminated and the authority of the contractor to *change* the subcontract when the government makes unilateral changes in the contractor's federal contract. Mandatory flow-down clauses are listed in FAR § 52.2446, and a contractor should inform its subcontractors that they are required to include the FAR § 52.2446 clauses in all lower-tier subcontracts.

b. Procurement Integrity: Off-Limits Information

Federal law known as the "procurement integrity provisions" addresses restrictions on the exchange of protected information, including contractor bid and proposal information and government source selection information. These provisions make it illegal for a private contractor to have in its possession or use certain types of information. During the competitive procurement process, certain information generally may not be requested or obtained by the private contractor, unless the information is released to all competitors. Therefore, it is important for private contractor personnel to be alert when offered information that is marked in any of the following ways:

(i) "Source Selection or Procurement Integrity Sensitive" is information that is prepared for use by a federal agency for the purpose of evaluating a bid or proposal to enter into a federal agency procurement contract, if that information has not been previously made available to the public or disclosed publicly. This includes:

- Bid prices submitted in response to a federal agency invitation for bids or lists of those bid prices before bid opening;
- Proposed costs or prices submitted in response to a federal agency solicitation or lists of those proposed costs or prices;
- Source selection plans;
- Technical evaluation plans;
- Technical evaluations of proposals;
- Cost or price evaluations of proposals;
- Competitive range determinations that identify proposals that have a reasonable chance of being selected for award of a contract;
- Rankings of bids, proposals or competitors;
- Reports and evaluations of source selection panels, boards or advisory councils; and
- Other information marked as "SOURCE SELECTION INFORMATION—SEE FAR 3.104," based on a case-by-case determination by the head of the government agency or designee or the contracting officer that its disclosure would jeopardize the integrity or successful completion of the federal agency procurement to which the information relates.

(ii) "Contractor Bid or Proposal Information" is information submitted to a federal agency as part of or in connection with a bid or proposal to enter into a federal agency procurement contract, if that information previously has not been made available to the public or disclosed publicly. This includes:

- Cost or pricing data;[25]
- Indirect costs and direct labor rates;
- Proprietary information about manufacturing processes, operations or techniques marked by the contractor in accordance with applicable law or regulation;
- Information marked by the contractor as "contractor bid or proposal information" in accordance with law or regulation; and

- Information marked in accordance with FAR 52.21512, "Restriction on Disclosure and Use of Data," which contains instructions to offerors on how to mark information they wish to protect. Offerors can protect information with one or more of the following markings:

    (iii) Private Contractor Proprietary or Trade Secrets
    (iv) For Official Use Only (FOUO)
    (v) Not Releasable Under the Freedom of Information Act
    (vi) Draft—Not for Release Outside of the Government

In addition, certain other information about the private contractor's competitors is *off-limits irrespective of any legends or other markings*. This includes cost or pricing data and proprietary information and trade secrets. Information available publicly, such as on a competitor's Web site, does not fall into these protected categories. Private contractors should always exercise due diligence to ensure that they are authorized to receive information provided by government employees or third parties, including consultants. Private contractor personnel should not assume such authorization.

After the procurement process is complete, some otherwise protected information may be releasable by the federal government under the Freedom of Information Act (FOIA) or during debriefings held by the government. Debriefings are meetings between the government and unsuccessful offerors and occur after the government has announced the award of a contract.

It is essential that private contractor personnel understand what conduct is prohibited under the procurement integrity provisions and that information concerning a possible violation by the government or its competitors be brought to its immediate attention, so that an early assessment can be made regarding the 14-day reporting requirement. The procurement integrity provisions prohibit the filing of a bid protest with the Government Accountability Office (GAO) against the award or proposed award of a contract alleging a violation of any one of the procurement integrity provisions, unless the protester first reports to the federal agency responsible for the procurement no later than 14 days after the person becomes aware of the possible violation.

Keep in mind that if a private contractor does not wish for *its confidential and proprietary materials* to be released to a competitor pursuant to a FOIA request under FOIA exemption four, it needs to clearly identify its materials as proprietary and confidential to demonstrate that its information does not belong in the public realm. However, even if confidential and proprietary materials have been properly marked, an agency may still release such materials based on a recent Department of Justice "FOIA Post" memorandum (September 8, 2005), which advises agencies to look to certain Fourth and Ninth Circuit decisions[26] that supported the disclosure of unit prices and discusses various ways that agencies can interpret those decisions in favor of disclosure of unit-price information (http://www.usdoj.gov/oip/foiapost/2005foiapost17.htm).

c. Allowable and Unallowable Costs

(i) *Regulatory Requirements*—FAR Part 31, Cost Principles, identify unallowable costs applicable to the following types of contracts or contract-related transactions:

1) Pricing of fixed-price contracts and modifications whenever a cost analysis is required under FAR Part 15.
2) Determination of negotiation of costs under a fixed-price contract clause.
3) Determining reimbursable cost under a cost-reimbursable contract.
4) Negotiating indirect cost rates, including those for interim and progress payments.
5) Proposing, negotiating or determining cost where the contract has been terminated.
6) Redetermining the price under a price-redetermination contract.
7) Revising the price of a fixed-price incentive contract.
8) Pricing changes and contract modifications.

(ii) *Exceptions to Applicability*—The FAR Cost Principles do not apply to firm fixed-price contracts awarded under sealed-bid procedures or procedures involving adequate price competition. These principles, however, may apply to modifications to such contracts.

(iii) *Basic Allowability Requirements*—Under the FAR Cost Principles, for a cost to be allowable, there are five basic requirements:

1) The cost must be reasonable.
2) The cost must be allocable to the contract. Costs are allocable if:
   a. incurred specifically for a contract;
   b. they benefit more than one contract or cost objective; or
   c. they are necessary to the overall operation of a business.
3) Allocation methods should equitably assign costs to contracts and reflect the degree of causal or beneficial relationship of a cost to a contract.
4) When in doubt as to whether a cost is allowable, questions should be directed to the business unit.
5) The cost must be allocated to the contract in accordance with Cost Accounting Standards, if applicable, otherwise, generally accepted accounting principles and practices.
6) The cost must be in accordance with the terms of the contract.
7) The cost must not be made unallowable by FAR § 31.205.

(iv) Regulations require business units to identify expressly unallowable cost, including any directly associated cost, and to exclude these costs from any billing, claim or proposal to which the FAR Cost Principles apply.
1) FAR 31.001 defines "unallowable cost" as follows: Any cost which, under the provisions of any pertinent law, regulation or contract cannot be included in prices, cost reimbursements or settlements under a government contract to which it is allocable.
2) "Directly associated cost" means any cost that is generated solely as a result of the incurrence of another cost and that would not have been incurred had the other cost not been incurred.
3) In some circumstances, more than one cost principle covering allowability under FAR 31.205 will apply to a specific cost. In such instances, guidance should be obtained from the business unit to determine how such cost should be treated. Classification of a cost should be made prior to the time the cost is incurred in order to ensure that the essential nature of the cost is identified and the cost is charged to the correct cost account.

(v) *Certification*—When required by the government, the controller is required to certify that, to the best of his or her knowledge and belief, all indirect costs included in the interim and final rate proposals are allowable under applicable FAR Cost Principles and do not include any costs that are unallowable.

1) Failure to submit a signed certificate may result in payment of rates unilaterally established by the Contracting Officer.

2) FAR 42.7093 provides for the assessment of a penalty when a submitted cost is expressly unallowable under a FAR Cost Principle or an executive agency supplement that defines allowability. The amount of this penalty is equal to the amount of unallowable cost plus interest. Further, for a cost that was determined to be unallowable prior to proposal submission, the penalty is two times the amount of the unallowable cost. These penalties are in addition to other administrative, civil, and criminal penalties provided by law.

(vi) *Government Audits*—The Defense Contract Audit Agency (DCAA) or GAO generally will conduct government audits.[27]

d. Product Substitution

FAR Part 46 and requisite contractual requirements require the implementation of a Quality Assurance Program. Only supplies and services that strictly conform to contract and subcontract ("contract") requirement shall be tendered to customers.

Product substitution is a form of fraud against the government that can be instigated in a number of ways. The U.S. Justice Department has succeeded in prosecutions in instances where contractors falsified test and inspection reports for products delivered or delivered lower-priced but "acceptable" parts that were not in accordance with the terms of the contract.

The government requires strict compliance with contract requirements because often the substituted product is not as good as the item or service specified. Introduction of substitute goods into the government supply channels undermines the reliability of the entire supply system.

The DoD Office of the Inspector General and the GAO define "product substitution" as any attempt by a contractor to deliver goods or services that do not conform in every respect to contract requirements while seeking reimbursement based on delivery of allegedly conforming products or services.

Supplies or services provided by contractors must "strictly comply" with contract specifications. As a result, contractors can be charged with product substitution even if deviations are (a) minor in nature, (b) in accordance with best commercial practice or (c) in fact, benefit the government in that the nonconforming item tendered is as good as, or better than, the item called for by the contract.

Even if the substitute item is "as good as" that specified in contract documents, acceptance introduces harm to the integrity of the competitive procurement system, which is based on all competitors offering to furnish only the item identified in procurement specifications. Permitting each offeror to substitute his or her own judgment as to the quality of the item proposed defeats this fundamental idea of bidding or proposing on an equal basis. This especially may become an issue for a biotech company that is in the business of providing reagents, kits or equipment.

> **Practice Points**
>
> **Nonconforming Goods**
> — Substitution of goods is deemed fraud on the government.
> — Strict conformity to contract specifications is required.
> — Offering "better" goods than required is no defense.
> — Failure to test products as required by contract is deemed impermissible product substitution.
> — Evaluate on objective, demonstrable factors, such as performance history, experience, pricing, timeliness, personnel, and management.
> — Ensure subcontractor eligibility.

Failure to perform tests on products to the extent contractually required constitutes a prohibited product substitution, regardless of whether the untested products are actually deficient. For example, a contractor who manufactures vaccines delivers the products to the government. Because the contractor was running behind in production, however, it omitted the required test of the vaccines to ensure absence of contamination. Nevertheless, the contractor certified that the test had been conducted and that the test results conformed to the contract specifications. Even if subsequent testing of the product confirms that there were no defects, the contractor is still liable for product substitution when the contract required that the product be pretested.

The DoD Inspector General has noted that product substitution encompasses not only the substitution of goods but also "worker substitutions." For example, the government issues a solicitation for the provision of clinical trial services that requires offerors to submit with their proposal the resumés of individuals who are to be assigned to work on the contract, as well as describe the commitment levels of certain key employees. After the contractor is awarded the contract, no attempt is made to contract or hire many of the individuals whose resumés were included in the proposal. Instead, the contractor hires individuals who may or may not be as qualified as those proposed. This substitution of workers constitutes an improper "worker substitution" when the contract requires that the contractor provide the workers named in the proposal.

B. SBIR and STTR Grants

Small Business Innovation Research (SBIR) and Small Business Technology Transfer (STTR) Program Grants are two of the most common forms of grants received by small businesses developing a biotechnology product. However, in terms of what they are, these grant types really are "neither fish nor fowl." Grants by definition, their terms also resemble contracts in some ways. While SBIRs and STTRs are awarded by a number of federal agencies—each of which operates by its own rules—most SBIR and STTR grants to biotech companies come from the NIH, so the NIH rules are discussed below. Because the rules change frequently, the following discussion is meant simply to provide a general overview, and is no substitute for careful review of the rules of the agency offering the grant.

1. SBIR Grants

a) The Small Business Innovation Research (SBIR)[28] program is a set-aside program (2.5 percent of an agency's extramural budget) for domestic small business concerns to engage in Research/Research and Development (R/R&D) that has the potential for commercialization. Federal agencies with extramural research and development budgets over $100 million are required to administer SBIR programs using an annual set-aside of 2.5 percent for small companies to conduct innovative research or R/R&D that has potential for commercialization and public benefit. Currently, 11 federal agencies participate in the SBIR program: the Departments of Health and Human Services (DHHS), Agriculture (USDA), Commerce (DOC), Defense (DOD), Education (DoED), Energy (DOE), Homeland Security, and Transportation (DOT); the Environmental Protection Agency (EPA), the National Aeronautics and Space Administration (NASA), and the National Science Foundation (NSF). Through 2005, over $12 billion had been awarded by the SBIR program to various small businesses.

b) The SBIR Program includes the following objectives: using small businesses to stimulate technological innovation, strengthening the role of small business in meeting federal R/R&D needs, increasing private-sector commercialization of innovations developed through federal SBIR R&D, increasing small-business participation in federal R/R&D, and fostering and encouraging participation by socially and economically disadvantaged small-business concerns and women-owned business concerns in the SBIR program.

c) To participate in the SBIR program:

- a firm must be a U.S. for-profit small business of 500 or fewer employees;
- work must be performed in the United States;
- during Phase I, a minimum of two-thirds of the effort must be performed by the proposing firm; in a Phase II grant, the recipient must perform at least one-half of the effort (the rest may be subcontracted); and
- the principal investigator must be primarily employed by the grant recipient.

2. STTR Grants

a) Similarly, federal agencies with extramural R&D budgets over $1 billion are required to administer STTR[29] programs using an annual set-aside of 0.30 percent. Currently, five federal agencies participate in the STTR program: DOD, DOE, DHHS (NIH), NASA, and NSF. In fiscal year (FY) 2003 (October 1, 2002–September 30, 2003), the NIH made SBIR grant and contract awards totaling over $525 million and STTR grant awards totaling over $31 million. Proposals are accepted annually for collaborative projects between research institutions and small businesses. Because many biotech companies are formed to commercialize technology developed at universities or other research institutions and it is common for key scientists to retain their positions with the institution while helping the biotech company, the STTR can provide an excellent source of funding for joint work between the SBIR and the scientists' institution.

    b) To participate in the STTR program:

- a firm must be a U.S. for-profit small business of 500 or fewer employees;
- the research institution must be a U.S. college or university, federally Funded Research and Development Center (FFRDC) or nonprofit research institution;
- work must be performed in the United States;
- the small business must perform a minimum of 40 percent of the work and the research institution a minimum of 30 percent of the work in both Phase I and Phase II;
- the small business must manage and control the STTR funding agreement; and
- the principal investigator may be employed at the small business or research institution.

3. Basic Characteristics

The STTR and SBIR programs are similar in that both programs seek to increase the participation of small businesses in federal R&D and to increase private-sector commercialization of technology developed through federal R&D. The unique feature of the STTR program is the requirement for the small-business concern applicant organization to formally collaborate with a research institution in Phase I and Phase II.

However, the SBIR and STTR programs differ in two major ways:

(i) First, under the SBIR Program, the principal investigator must have his/her primary employment with the small-business concern at the time of award and for the duration of the project period; under the STTR Program, primary employment is not stipulated.

(ii) Second, the STTR Program requires research partners at universities and other nonprofit research institutions to have a formal collaborative relationship with the small-business concern. At least 40 percent of the STTR research project is to be conducted by the small-business concern and at least 30 percent by the single, "partnering" research institution.

The SBIR/STTR Programs are structured in three phases:

1) *Phase I*—The objective of Phase I is to establish the technical merit and feasibility of the proposed R/R&D efforts and to determine the quality of performance of the small-business awardee organization prior to providing further federal support in Phase II. Support under Phase I is normally provided for six months/$100,000 for SBIR and one year/$100,000 for STTR.
2) *Phase II*—The objective of Phase II is to continue the R/R&D efforts initiated in Phase I. Only Phase I awardees are eligible for a Phase II award. SBIR and STTR Phase II awards normally may not exceed $750,000 total. However, applicants may propose longer periods of time and greater amounts of funds necessary for completion of the project.
3) *Phase III*—The objective of Phase III, where appropriate, is for the small-business concern to pursue with non-SBIR/STTR funds the commercialization objectives resulting from the Phase I/II R/R&D activities. In some federal agencies, Phase III may involve follow-on non-SBIR/STTR funded R&D or production contracts for products, processes or services intended for use by the U.S. government.

4. NIH Guidance

The NIH provides the following guidance for potential SBIR/STTR applicants on the type of criteria that will be used in considering the scientific and technical merit of each SBIR/STTR application:

a. *Significance*

(i) Does the proposed project have commercial potential to lead to a marketable product, process or service? Does this study address an important problem?
(ii) What are the anticipated commercial and societal benefits that may be derived from the proposed research?

(iii) If the aims of the application are achieved, how will scientific knowledge or clinical practice be advanced? What will be the effect of these studies on the concepts, methods, technologies, treatments, services, or preventive interventions that drive this field?
(iv) Does the application lead to enabling technologies (e.g., instrumentation, software) for further discoveries?
(v) Will the technology have a competitive advantage over existing/alternate technologies that can meet the market needs?

b. Approach

(i) Are the conceptual or clinical framework, design, methods, and analyses adequately developed, well-integrated, and appropriate to the aims of the project?
(ii) Is the proposed plan a sound approach for establishing technical and commercial feasibility?
(iii) Does the applicant acknowledge potential problem areas and consider alternative strategies?
(iv) Are the milestones and evaluation procedures appropriate?

c. Innovation

(i) Are the aims original and innovative?
(ii) Does the project challenge existing paradigms or clinical practice or address an innovative hypothesis or critical barrier to progress in the field?
(iii) Does the project develop or employ novel concepts, approaches, methodologies, tools, or technologies for this area?
(iv) Investigators
(v) Is the principal investigator appropriately trained and capable of coordinating and managing the proposed SBIR/STTR?
(vi) Are the investigators well suited to carry out this work? Does the investigative team bring complementary and integrated expertise to the project (if applicable)?
(vii) Is the work proposed appropriate to the experience level of the principal investigator and other researchers, including consultants and subcontractors (if any)?
(viii) Are the relationships of the key personnel to the small business and to other institutions appropriate for the work proposed?

d. Environment

(i) Is there sufficient access to resources (e.g., equipment, facilities)?
(ii) Does the scientific and technological environment in which the work will be done contribute to the probability of success?
(iii) Do the proposed studies benefit from unique features of the scientific environment or subject populations, or employ useful collaborative arrangements? Is there evidence of institutional support?

5. Protection of Human Subjects

In conducting peer review for scientific and technical merit, Scientific Review Groups (SRGs) will also evaluate the involvement of human subjects and proposed protections from research risk relating to their participation in the proposed research according to the following review criteria: (1) risk to subjects, (2) adequacy of protection against risks, (3) potential benefits of the proposed research to the subjects and others, (4) importance of the knowledge to be gained, and (5) data and safety monitoring for clinical trials.

a) When human subjects are involved in the proposed clinical research, the SRG will also evaluate the proposed plans for inclusion of minorities and members of both sexes, as well as the inclusion of children in clinical research, as part of the assessment. The evaluation will be factored into the overall score for scientific and technical merit of the application.

b) Under NIH policy, the following criteria will be applied to *all* applications:

(i) *Protection of Human Subjects*—For all studies involving human subjects, see instructions and Decision Table for Human Subjects Research, Protection and the Inclusion of Women, Minorities, and Children.[30]

- If an exemption is claimed, is it appropriate for the work proposed? If no exemption is claimed, are the applicant's responses to the six required points appropriate?
- Are human subjects placed at risk by the proposed study? If so, are the risks reasonable in relation to the anticipated benefits to the subjects and others? Are the risks reasonable in

relation to the importance of the knowledge that reasonably may be expected to be gained?
- Are the plans proposed for the protection of human subjects adequate?

(ii) *Inclusion of Women Plan—for clinical research only*
- Does the applicant propose a plan for the inclusion of both genders that will provide their appropriate representation
- Does the applicant provide appropriate justification when representation is limited or absent?
- Does the applicant propose appropriate and acceptable plans for recruitment/outreach and retention of study participants?

(iii) *Inclusion of Minorities Plan—for clinical research only*
- Does the applicant propose a plan for the inclusion of minorities that will provide their appropriate representation? Does the applicant provide appropriate justification when representation is limited or absent?
- Does the applicant propose appropriate and acceptable plans for recruitment/outreach and retention of study participants?

(iv) *Inclusion of Children Plan—for all studies involving human subjects*
- Does the applicant describe an acceptable plan in which the representation of children of all ages (under the age of 21) is scientifically appropriate and recruitment/retention is addressed realistically?
- If not, does the applicant provide an appropriate justification for their exclusion?

(v) *Data and Safety Monitoring Plan—for clinical trials only*
- Does the applicant describe a Data and Safety Monitoring Plan that defines the general structure of the monitoring entity and mechanisms for reporting Adverse Events to the NIH and the IRB?

6. Vertebrate Animals

The proposed involvement of vertebrate animals will be evaluated by SRGs as part of the scientific assessment according to the following five points: (1) detailed description of the proposed use of the animals; (2) justification for the use of animals and for the appropriateness of the species and numbers proposed; (3) adequacy of proposed veterinary care; (4) procedures for limiting pain and distress to that which is unavoidable; and (5) methods of euthanasia.

7. Criteria

In accordance with NIH policy, the following criteria will be applied to *all* applications:

a) *If vertebrate animals are involved, are adequate plans proposed for their care and use?*
b) *Are the applicant's responses to the five required points complete and appropriate?*
c) *Will the procedures be limited to those that are unavoidable in the conduct of scientifically sound research?*
d) *Budget*:
   - For all applications, is the percent of effort listed for the principal investigator appropriate for the work proposed?
   - On applications, is the overall budget realistic and justified in terms of the aims and methods proposed?
e) *Biohazards:*
   - Is the use of materials or procedures that are potentially hazardous to research personnel and/or the environment proposed?
   - Is the proposed protection adequate?

8. Phase II Application Review Criteria

Following a successful Phase I grant, a company may seek to move to Phase II. In that event, the company will be evaluated on the following criteria:

a) How well did the applicant demonstrate progress toward meeting the Phase I objectives, demonstrating feasibility, and providing a solid foundation for the proposed Phase II activity?
b) Did the applicant submit a concise Commercialization Plan that adequately addresses the specific areas described in Item K of the Phase II Research Plan?
c) Does the project carry a high degree of commercial potential, as described in the Commercialization Plan?

9. Amended Applications

In addition to the above criteria, the following criteria will be applied to revised applications:

a) Are the responses to comments from the previous SRG review adequate?
b) Are the improvements in the revised application appropriate?

10. Phase I/Phase II Fast-Track Application Review Criteria

For Phase I/Phase II Fast-Track applications, the following criteria also will be applied:

a) Does the Phase I application specify clear, appropriate, measurable goals (milestones) that should be achieved prior to initiating Phase II?
b) Did the applicant submit a concise Commercialization Plan that adequately addresses the specific areas described in Item K of the Phase II Research Plan?
c) To what extent was the applicant able to obtain letters of interest, additional funding commitments, and/or resources from the private sector or non-SBIR/STTR funding sources that would enhance the likelihood for commercialization?
d) Does the project carry a high degree of commercial potential, as described in the Commercialization Plan?

Phase I and Phase II Fast-Track applications that satisfy all of the review criteria will receive a single rating. Failure to provide clear, measurable goals may be sufficient reason for the scientific review group to exclude the Phase II application from Fast-Track review.

11. Phase II—Competing Continuation Application Review Criteria

In addition to the review criteria stated above for "All SBIR/STTR applications," the following items will be applied to ALL Competing Continuation Phase II applications in the determination of scientific merit and the priority score.

- Does the activity as proposed address issues related to federal regulatory approval processes?
- Did the applicant submit a concise Commercialization Plan that adequately addresses the specific areas described in Item K of the Phase II Research Plan?
- Does the project carry a high degree of commercial potential, as described in the Commercialization Plan?

C. Ethics, Outside Activities, and Employment

1. Grants

Most federal grantor agencies require awardees to develop general standards of conduct, including a financial conflict of interest policy for researchers carrying out grant-funded research, and to establish policies for addressing research misconduct. Each of these requirements is addressed in Section C.2.c, but briefly, they are as follows:

a. Standards of Conduct

The company must require everyone involved in grant-supported activities, including employees, consultants, and administrative personnel, to adhere to written standards regarding basic ethics. The policies may be pre-existing, but they must set standards for accepting gifts, giving gratuities and favors, nepotism, financial conflict of interest (discussed below), political participation (lobbying, generally), and bribery. The policies must set out specific penalties and a review process for violations of the standards.

b. Financial Conflict of Interest

The financial conflict of interest policy must minimize the opportunity for improper financial gain, as well as limit the potential for research results to be tainted by personal financial impact. The policy must apply to every employee and consultant working on grant-supported projects or activities, as well as to the officers and members of the awardee's governing board. It must also contain an administrative process to identify, manage, reduce, or eliminate conflicting financial interests for projects proposed for federal grant funding. If an adverse action is taken against a principal investigator on a federal research grant because of financial conflict of interest, notification of the grants management officer is usually mandatory.

c. Misconduct in Science and Engineering

"Misconduct in science and engineering" refers to improper or unethical conduct of the research itself. Plagiarism and falsification of research results are the two most common issues. The various federal agencies have different positions as to whether an awardee may carry out its own investigation. Awardees typically do wish to investigate such allegations on their own where allowed, so it is a good idea to have a policy in place to address how such an investigation will be carried out. Although there are various suggested policies available for adaptation through federal agencies, they are all quite complex, and debating alterations to the process may consume much time and energy on the part of the scientists who will be subject to it. There is no easy way to address this issue.

2. Contracts

a. Organizational Conflicts of Interest

FAR Subpart 9.5 limits the ability of the private contractor to perform a federal government contract under certain circumstances where the government believes an organizational conflict of interest exists, as defined in the regulations. Under FAR § 9.501 an "organizational conflict of interest" occurs when, because of other activities or relationships, a contractor is unable or potentially unable to render impartial assistance or advice to the government, the contractor's objectivity in performing the contract work is or might be otherwise impaired, or the contractor has an unfair competitive advantage. Under certain circumstances, the contractor may be permitted to mitigate the conflict of interest, as long as the government approves the mitigation plan.

    (i) *Types of Conflicts of Interest*—The FAR prescribes the following four categories of conflicts that may, depending on the circumstances, prevent the private contractor from obtaining the award of a government contract: (1) providing systems engineering and technical direction to the government, (2) preparing specifications or work statements for inclusion in a competitive procurement, (3) providing technical evaluation of advisory and assistance services relating to evaluation of the private contractor's or a competitor's products or services, or (4) obtaining access to proprietary information of a competitor.

First, in providing systems engineering or technical direction for a government project, FAR 9.5051 precludes the private contractor from being selected as a contractor, subcontractor, or consultant for a subsequent system or major component follow-on procurement.

Second, when the private contractor prepares or assists in preparing a work statement to be used in competitively acquiring services for the government, the private contractor is precluded by FAR 9.5052 from supplying those services unless (1) it is the sole source or (2) more than one contractor has been involved in preparing the work statement.

Third, as a general rule, if the private contractor provides technical evaluations, advice, or assistance to the government, the private contractor will not be permitted under FAR 9.5053 to receive the award of a contract that includes the evaluation of private contractor products or competitor products.

Fourth, when, by the terms of a contract, the government provides the private contractor under contract or otherwise with proprietary information of a competitor, FAR § 9.5054 requires the private contractor to protect the information from unauthorized use or disclosure. The private contractor cannot use non-public information for any purpose other than that for which it was provided. Receiving solicitation information, such as a draft statement of work, also can place a contractor at an unfair advantage in a government procurement and may preclude a contractor from participating in the procurement.

(ii) *Consequence of Organizational Conflicts of Interest*—A government procurement that requires the private contractor to perform one of the above activities should contain a provision stating the nature of conflicts that may arise in performing a subsequent contract. These government contract provisions that will limit the private contractor's ability to pursue follow-on contracts in the future may be subject to negotiation. In some instances, the government may make arrangements to preserve the private contractor's ability to bid follow-on procurements when the private contractor's obligations under a predecessor contract involve one or more of the above-described activities. This may provide an opportunity to develop a mitigation plan acceptable to the government.

Organizational conflicts of interest rules also apply to any consultants working on behalf of the private contractor. The use of consultants who have had access to the proprietary information of competitors, source selection information, or any other information creating an unfair advantage to the private contractor over competitors may preclude the private contractor from pursuing government contracts relating to that information or advantage.

b. Employment Discussions With and Hiring of U.S. Government Personnel

The laws and regulations regarding this subject can be divided into two categories:

(i) Restrictions on contractors holding employment discussions with current government personnel; and
(ii) Restrictions on tasks and work assignments that government personnel (both current and former) can perform for private-sector employers.

Because of their government duties, some government personnel cannot hold employment discussions with contractors unless they obtain advance agency approval.[31] In most cases, government personnel must notify their supervisor and their agency ethics official when contacted by or prior to contacting contractors to discuss employment, even if the official rejects the possibility of non-government employment at the outset.[32]

What constitutes "employment discussions" is interpreted broadly. Even e-mail correspondence, exchanging a resumé, or a conversation over lunch or at a conference can be considered employment discussions. References to salary or other terms of employment are not necessary to trigger employment discussions.

At other times, because of their government duties, certain former government employees are prohibited from working for and receiving compensation from certain government contractors for one year after they leave government service.[33] Others have a one- or two-year ban that precludes them from contacting their former agencies and/or any senior officials in the executive branch.³⁴ The restrictions are imposed based upon the individual's responsibilities and, in some cases, grade level while with the government. The determination of which restrictions apply to each current and former government employee is complex and usually requires a legal analysis. This legal analysis has become more difficult with the issuance of U.S. Office of Government Ethics (OGE) Advisory Opinion 02 x 5, where OGE fails to draw a distinction between policy and "particular matter." The legal analysis has also become more complex due to the fact that non-federal employee workers who have been brought into the federal workplace through other personnel vehicles, such as the Intergovernmental Personnel Act,³⁵ the detailee system, and the Information Technology Exchange Program,³⁶ are subject to the federal conflict of interest laws as if they were federal employees.

If a biotech company is looking to hire a current or recent NIH/NSF/NCI employee, it should carefully:

- ascertain who made the first contact—the company or the government employee;
- keep note of dates when contact first began, and any documentation;
- determine the scope of the employee's official duties and particular projects involving the company; and
- require that the employee produce a written disqualification statement, signed by authorized agency counsel.

In addition to other potential restrictions, current government personnel are prohibited from "representing" any non-government entity while they are employed by the government, even if such government personnel are on annual or transition leave.³⁷ Further, there are restrictions on the form of compensation that may be paid by the private contractor to a current government employee.³⁸

This is a complex area of government law, requiring analysis on two levels: first, a determination as to whether the private contractor is permitted by law to discuss job or consultant opportunities with the particular government employee; and second, even if the private contractor may talk to the individual about future business opportunities, whether there are restrictions applicable to the person's activities as an employee or consultant of the private contractor—for example, whether certain matters, contracts, or government agencies will be "off-limits" to the former government employee, and the length of any such restrictions.

Sanctions available to the government for violations in this area include criminal and civil penalties, exclusion from the procurement competition, cancellation of the contract, and suspension and debarment from doing business with the government. These sanctions may be applied by the government to the private contractor, the government employee, or the private contractor employee involved, as appropriate.

c. The National Institutes of Health (NIH) Government Employee Supplemental Regulations on Permitted Outside Activities

If a biotech company and/or association is interested in asking a government employee to serve on a private scientific advisory board, it should carefully consider that:

- The new FDA and NIH regulations generally require that an FDA/NIH employee must obtain prior approval from an ethics counsel on outside activities, including consultative or professional services; teaching, writing, or editing related to the government employee's official duties; or providing services to a non-federal entity as an officer, director, or board member, or as a member of a group that provides advice, counsel or consultation;
- All NIH employees are prohibited from engaging in employment (which includes serving as an officer, director, or other fiduciary board member, serving on a scientific advisory board or committee, and consulting or providing professional services) and compensated teaching, speaking, writing, or editing with a substantially affected organization (SAO), a supported research institution (SRI), a health-care provider or insurer (HCPI), or a related trade, professional, or similar association (RTPSA); and
- All NIH employees are also prohibited from engaging in any self-employed business activity that involves the sale or promotion of products or services of an SAO or HCPI.[39]

Despite the description of the above requirements, each grant or contract warrants an individual factual analysis—the descriptions above present just a few of the minefields of which a potential federal grantee or contractor must be aware. Unfortunately, easy template policies to ensure compliance with these obligations are not available. When conducting business with the government, a contractor must be aware of its obligations and be ready to "negotiate" with the government over any discrepancies.

Notes

1. Nat'l Institutes of Health, Grants Policy Manual 52-53.
2. *Id.* at 47.
3. The SBIR program was established under the Small Business Innovation Development Act of 1982 (P.L. 97-219), reauthorized until Sept. 30, 2000 by the Small Business Research and Development Enhancement Act (P.L. 102-564), and reauthorized again until Sept. 30, 2008, by the Small Business Reauthorization Act of 2000 (P.L. 106-554).
4. The STTR program was established by the Small Business Technology Transfer Act of 1992 (Public Law 102-564, Title II), reauthorized until the year 2001 by the Small Business Reauthorization Act of 1997 (P.L. 105-135), and reauthorized again until Sept. 30, 2009, by the Small Business Technology Transfer Program Reauthorization Act of 2001 (P.L. 107-50).
5. "Fixed-price types of contracts provide for a firm price or, in appropriate cases, an adjustable price. Fixed-price contracts providing for an adjustable price may include a ceiling price, a target price (including target cost), or both. Unless otherwise specified in the contract, the ceiling price or target price is subject to adjustment only by operation of contract clauses providing for equitable adjustment or other revision of the contract price under stated circumstances. The contracting officer shall use firm-fixed-price or fixed-price with economic price adjustment contracts when acquiring commercial items." Fed. Acquisition Regs. (FAR) § 16.201.
6. Pursuant to FAR § 16.203-1 (a), a fixed-price contract with economic price adjustment "provides for upward and downward revision of the stated contract price upon the occurrence of specified contingencies." "Economic price adjustments are of three general types:

> (1) *Adjustments based on established prices.* These price adjustments are based on increases or decreases from an agreed-upon level in published or otherwise established prices of specific items or the contract end items.
> (2) *Adjustments based on actual costs of labor or material.* These price adjustments are based on increases or decreases in specified costs of labor or material that the contractor actually experiences during contract performance.
> (3) *Adjustments based on cost indexes of labor or material.* These price adjustments are based on increases or decreases in labor or material cost standards or indexes that are specifically identified in the contract."

7. Walsh-Healy Act is a public law designed to prevent the practice of "bid brokering," i.e., the practice of buying items and then reselling them to the government without the adding of any value to the item by the reseller. The act provides that contracts subject to its provisions (generally contracts over $10,000) may be awarded only to "manufacturers" or "regular dealers," as defined.

8. FAR subpart 3.4, Contingent Fees, prescribes policies and procedures that restrict contingent fee arrangements for soliciting or obtaining government contracts to those permitted by 10 U.S.C. § 2306(b) and 41 U.S.C. § 254(a).

9. The Contract Work Hours and Safety Standards Act (CWHSSA) applies to federal service contracts and federal and federally assisted construction contracts over $100,000. It requires contractors and subcontractors on covered contracts to pay laborers and mechanics employed in the performance of the contracts one and one-half times their basic rate of pay for all hours worked over 40 in a workweek.

10. Congress enacted TINA for the purpose of providing for full and fair disclosure by contractors in the conduct of negotiations with the government. The most significant provision in TINA is the requirement that contractors submit certified cost and pricing data for negotiated procurements above a defined threshold.

11. The Cost Accounting Standards are a result of concern for the pricing and accounting practices of defense contractors. There was no consistency within and between contractors' cost accounting practices, making it difficult to conduct standard audits.

12. Pursuant to FAR § 2.101(b), "Simplified acquisition threshold" means $100,000, except for acquisitions of supplies or services that, as determined by the head of the agency, are to be used to support a contingency operation or to facilitate defense against or recovery from nuclear, biological, chemical, or radiological attack (41 U.S.C. 428a), the term means—

> (1) $250,000 for any contract to be awarded and performed, or purchase to be made, inside the United States; and
> (2) $_ million for any contract to be awarded and performed, or purchase to be made, outside the United States.

13. FAR § 15.4033; FAR § 52.21520 (Requirements for Cost or Pricing Data or Information Other than Cost or Pricing Data).

14. 18 U.S.C. § 1516.

15. FAR § 12.206.

16. FAR § 52.2032.

17. FAR § 52.2144..

18. FAR § 52.2191; § 52.2198; § 52.2199; § 52.21910.

19. FAR § 52.22226.

20. FAR § 52.22221.

21. FAR § 52.22222.

22. FAR § 52.22225.
23. FAR § 52.2033.
24. FAR § 52.20311.
25. As defined by 10 U.S.C. § 2306a(h), with respect to procurements subject to that section and section 304A(h) of the Federal Property and Administrative Services Act of 1949 (41 U.S.C. § 254b(h)), with respect to procurements subject to that section.
26. Acumenics Research & Tech., Inc. v. United States Dep't of Justice, 843 F.2d 800, 808 (4th Cir. 1988); Pacific Architects & Engineers v. United States Department of State, 906 F.2d 1345, 1347-48 (9th Cir. 1990).
27. *See* DEFENSE CONTRACT AUDIT MANUAL, DCAAM 7640.1.
28. The SBIR program was established under the Small Business Innovation Development Act of 1982 (P.L. 97-219), reauthorized until Sept. 30, 2000, by the Small Business Research and Development Enhancement Act (P.L. 102-564), and reauthorized again until Sept. 30, 2008, by the Small Business Reauthorization Act of 2000 (P.L. 106-554).
29. The STTR program was established by the Small Business Technology Transfer Act of 1992 (P. L. 102-564, Title II), reauthorized until the year 2001 by the Small Business Reauthorization Act of 1997 (P.L. 105-135), and reauthorized again until Sept. 30, 2009, by the Small Business Technology Transfer Program Reauthorization Act of 2001 (P.L. 107-50).
30. http://www.hhs.gov/ohrp/humansubjects/guidance/decisioncharts.htm.
31. 41 U.S.C. § 423; FAR § 3.104.
32. *Id.*; 18 U.S.C. § 208.
33. 41 U.S.C. § 423.
34. 18 U.S.C. § 207.
35. 5 U.S.C. §§ 3371 *et seq.*
36. 5 U.S.C. §§ 3701 *et seq.*
37. 18 U.S.C. §§ 203, 205.
38. *Id.*
39. 5 C.F.R. §§ 5501.106-.109 (Aug. 31, 2005, 70 Fed. Reg. 51,559).

Obligations Arising From Federal Research Grant Funds
LAWS AND REGULATIONS

Title and Summary	Agency Requirements	Sources of Obligation
Age Discrimination Act The Age Discrimination Act prohibits the use of age as a criteria for excluding, discriminating against, or limiting the opportunity to participate in an activity (such as a study or research program) supported by Federal funds. The Awardee must maintain records, provide information, and allow access to its records to an agency for the purposes of determining compliance with the Act. The Awardee must maintain a policy stating institutional commitment to non-discrimination on basis of age, but no affirmative action program is required.	**NIH** Sub-recipients of NIH awards must be "notified" of Awardee's policies under this Act. 45 CFR §90.43(a) Awardee certifies compliance by executing HHS form 690 **NSF** An implementing clause will be included in the award instrument to the Awardee. A provision identical to NSF GPM §617.4 must be included in each subagreement or subcontract. Unlike NIH, NSF does not have the authority to require self-evaluation as part of a compliance review.	42 USC §§ 6101 et seq **NIH**: • 45 CFR 91 • GPS p. 68 **NSF**: • 45 CFR 617 • GC-1, Article 26 • GPM 705
Animal Welfare Act ("AWA") The Animal Welfare Act ensure humane treatment of live or dead, warm-blooded, vertebrate animals used in research. Rats, mice, and most birds are excluded. An Assurance of Compliance ("Assurance") must be filed with the Office of Laboratory Animal Welfare ("OLAW"). Must register with APHIS. Funded institutions must also establish policies for the humane treatment of all vertebrate animals (including mice, rats, birds, and reptiles). Interestingly, the DOD however, requires that the AWA Standards be extended to mice and rats (any vertebrate animal) used in DOD-funded research. The standards include:	**NIH** All subawardees must comply with the Animal Welfare Act, including suppliers of goods and services and consortium participants. **NSF** NSF expects Awardees to comply with the "Guide for Care and Use of Laboratory Animals" and the "Public Health Service Policy and Government Principles Regarding the Care and Use of Animals.""IACVC approval or an OLAW multi-project assurance or NSF's single project assurance must cover the project before the grant is awarded. Compliance must be "appropriately addressed" in subawards.	7 USC §§2131-21599 CFR 1.1-4.11 **NIH** GPS pp. 65-66 **NSF** • GC-1, Article 28 • GPM 713

Federal Regulation of Research Through Funding

Title and Summary	Agency Requirements	Sources of Obligation
<ul><li>adequate veterinary care, food, water, and shelter;</li><li>consideration of alternatives to procedures likely to cause pain or distress;</li><li>use of anesthesia, analgesics, and tranquilizers to reduce and eliminate pain;</li><li>pre- and post-surgical care and limitations on the number of surgical procedures for animals;</li><li>a committee must review animal research, and conduct semi-annual reviews;</li><li>persons performing research must be adequately trained; and</li><li>animals may generally only be purchased from a licensed dealer.</li></ul>	**DOD** The DOD rules are more expansive than mere AWA compliance. The rules govern <u>all</u> live, non-human vertebrate animals used in research. This includes mice, fish, and rats. Other requirements for protocol review include a written description of the literature search for unnecessary duplication of research and consultation with a statistician to document the minimum number of animals has been used. Another requirement is licensing and inspection by the USDA as well as a site visit by a DOD-trained veterinarian within six months of delivery of animals under the grant. The Awardee must also immediately report to DOD any change in AALAC accreditation status or investigation by USDA.	**DOD** DOD Directive 3216.1, April 17, 1995. Guidance document "Research Involving Animals," located at http://mrm-www.army.mil/docs/rcq/FY02AnimalAppendix.doc **NIH** GPS p. 39
Standards of Conduct Written standards of conduct must be established by the Awardee for its employees, consultants, and others involved in grant-supported activities. Pre-existing standards can be used, but they must cover at least the following issues:<ul><li>financial interests</li><li>gifts</li><li>gratuities and favors</li><li>nepotism</li><li>political participation</li><li>briberyand must specify penalties, a review process for violations of the standards, and provide advance notification of outside activities, relationships, or financial conflicts of interest to a responsible individual in the organization.</li></ul>		**NIH** GPS p. 44 **NSF** GPM 510

Title and Summary	Agency Requirements	Sources of Obligation
Bayh-Dole Act The Bayh-Dole Act preserves invention rights for Awardees (and sometimes employee inventors) provided that the grant's reporting, filing, and acknowledgement requirements are met. The Government retains a royalty-free license.[1] To comply with Bayh-Dole, the Awardee must establish and implement an employee invention reporting policy. The invention date starts a chain of timed events the Awardee must complete to retain title, including filing the patent, notifying OPERA, and submitting various types of reports. 1. Fellowships, scholarships, and training grants are not subject to invention reporting requirements, and the Federal Government has no rights to inventions developed during the course of such activities.	**NIH** Standard clause (37 CFR 401.14) must be included in all awards and subawards for experimental, research or development activities. Detailed information for NIH grantees may be found at www.iedison.gov. **NSF** Specified clause (NSF GPM 731.3; 45 CFR 50.4(a)) must be included in all awards and subawards for experimental, research, or developmental activities. NSF requires that invention reports and notices be sent to it instead of OPERA. NSF also reserves the right to transfer title to a foreign government if required by treaty.	35 USC §§200-212 **NIH** • 37 CFR 401 *et seq* • GPS pp. 113-114 **NSF** • 45 CFR 650 • GC-1, Article 21 • GPM 730, 731
Byrd Anti-Lobbying Act The Awardee and each tier that receives a subaward or subcontract for more than $100,000, must file a certification with the tier above that it has not and will not use Federal funds to do the following: pay any person or organization to influence or attempt to influence any officer or employee of an agency, a member of Congress, officer or employee or Congress, or an employee of a member of Congress, in connection with obtaining any Federal contract, grant, or any other award covered by 31 USC §1352. The Awardee must also disclose any lobbying with non-federal funds that takes place in connection with obtaining any federal award in an annual report.	**NIH** "Legislative liaison" activities, and professional and technical services, are not subject to this prohibition, as set out in HHS regulation 45 CFR Part 93. The required certification for NIH grant recipients includes a statement that the recipient has not and will not make a prohibited payment; that it will report the use of non-federal funds used for lobbying purposes; and that the recipient will include this certification requirement in consortium agreements and contracts under grants that will exceed $100,000, and obtain the certifications from others where required.	31 USC §§1352 **NIH** • 45 CFR 93 • GPS pp. 49-50

Title and Summary	Agency Requirements	Sources of Obligation
	Specific prohibitions include using NIH-appropriated funds to pay the salary or expenses of an employee of a grantee, consortium participant, or contractor or agent related to any activity designed to influence legislation or appropriations pending before Congress or any State Legislature. This prohibition includes the use of funds for any kit, pamphlet, booklet, publication, radio, television or video presentation for that purpose. **NSF** The NSF has no separate requirements other than those listed in the summary above.	**NSF**: • 45 CFR 604 • OMB A-110, Appx. A
Acknowledgement of Federal Funding Awardee-issued documents describing Federally-Funded projects or programs must acknowledge the percent and dollar amount of funds, and percentage and dollar amount of total costs financed by non-government sources. Bid invitations, requests for proposals, press releases and statements are all included.		**NIH** GPS p. 69 **NSF** GPM 744
Freedom of Information Act ("FOIA") and Research Data Data produced with Federal support, that is cited publicly and officially by a federal agency in support of an action that has the force and effect of law, are subject to public access under FOIA. These agency actions include regulations and administrative orders. This provision only applies to the data <u>first</u> produced in a project supported with Federal funds, under a <u>competing</u> award <u>after</u> April 17, 2002.	**NIH** Will generally release records in its possession under FOIA, such as funded applications, continuations, grant progress reports, and final reports that have been transmitted to Awardee. Other information will generally be withheld. NIH can release "research data" produced by Awardees that are consortium participants or providers of routine goods and services.	45 CFR 612, 613, 614 5 USC § 522 45 CFR Part 5 **NIH** • GPS p. 69-71 • NIH Guidance: "Notice of Amendment to A110," December, 1999

Title and Summary	Agency Requirements	Sources of Obligation
"Research data" does not include drafts, plans for future research, physical objects, trade secrets, confidential information, intellectual property, medical files, or information that could identify a particular person in a medical study. Data may still be discarded after NIH retention times pass, and it is then not subject to FOIA.	**NSF** All NSF formats and correspondence received from Awardees are subject to public release, with limited exceptions.	**NSF** • http://www.NIH.gov/icd/od/form • 45 CFR 74.36 • http://grants.NIH.gov/grants/policy/data-sharing/index.htm **NSF** • GPM 812.3 • 45 CFR 612, 613, 614
Human Pluripotent Stem Cell ("HPSC") Research Human pluripotent stem cells are cells that are self-replicating, derived from human embryos or human fetal tissue, and known to develop into cells and tissues of the three primary germ layers. Although HPSCs may be derived from embryos or fetal tissue, such stem cells are not in themselves embryos. NIH funded research that incorporates the NIH GPS into the grant, which will involve human pluripotent stem cells derived: (1) from human fetal tissue, or (2) from human embryos that are the result of *in vitro* fertilization, can only be conducted using lines created before August 9, 2001. A more detailed explanation of the criteria that the cell lines must meet is found in the documents in the "Sources" column to the right. The approved lines can be located through NIH's Human Embryonic Stem Cell Registry y at http://escr.nih.gov.	**NIH** In addition to the traditional peer review process HPSC research must undergo a review of documentation of compliance with the Guidelines, conducted by the Human Pluripotent Stem Cell Review Group (HPSCRG), which is a working group of the Center for Scientific Review Advisory Council (CSRAC). The review focuses on the source of the cells, ethical issues, and involves public meetings.	*NIH Guidelines for Research Using Human Pluripotent Stem Cells* (Guidelines), effective August 25, 2000, http://stemcells.NIH.gov/policy/guidelines.asp. This document still contains useful information, although some sections have been withdrawn. The President's criteria can be found at: http://grants.NIH.gov/grants/guide/notice-files/NOT-OD-02-005.html **NIH** GPS pp. 53-54.

Federal Regulation of Research Through Funding 367

Title and Summary	Agency Requirements	Sources of Obligation
Metric Conversion Act of 1975 All reports, measurement values in applications, publications, and data must be kept in metric units. This requirement applies to consortium participants and suppliers of goods and services as well as Awardees.		15 USC §205 a-k E.O. 12770 15 CFR 1170 **NIH** GPS p. 72 **NSF** GPM 863
Nondelinquency on Federal Debt (Federal Debt Collection Procedure Act) Federal Debt Collection Procedure Act, 28 U.S.C. § 3201(e) prohibits receipt of grant funds for any entity with a judgment lien against it for a Federal debt. It is the Awardee's duty to determine whether subawardees are eligible to receive funds.	No agency-specific requirements.	28 USC § 2301(e) **NIH** GPS p. 52-53
OMB Circular A110, "Awardee Responsibilities and Federal Requirements" The circular sets out grant administration standards, such as procurement, conduct, equipment standards, and notes which conditions must pass through to subawardees.	The CFR sections noted simply re-state OMB Circular A-110's terms. **NIH** Some subawardee provisions contained in Appendix A of OMB A-110 do not apply to NIH grants/contracts. Always check the GPS for the most complete information, or see specific topics in this table.	**NIH** 45 CFR 74 **NSF** • 45 CFR 689 • GC-1 • GPM 500

Title and Summary	Agency Requirements	Sources of Obligation
Protection of Human Subjects All Federally-funded research involving human subjects must be carried out in accordance with the conditions in the institution's Assurance of Compliance (where applicable) and the applicable portions of the Federal Common Rule, 45 CFR 46. If an institution conducts research that does not fall into the "exempt" category (mostly use of pre-existing materials), it <u>must</u> obtain a Federal-Wide Assurance of Compliance, the primary requirement of which is that the research must be reviewed and approved by an Institutional Review Board ("IRB").	**NSF** Most terms are also mentioned in the NSF's "GC-1." **NIH** NIH simply restates the common rule requirements, and requires that key personnel engaged in human subjects research be educated on the protection of human subjects. **NSF** The NSF does have its own slightly abbreviated/condensed rules for human subjects research, but these do not apply when an institution has a Federal-Wide Assurance. NSF does require that any human subjects research be IRB-approved <u>before</u> the grant is issued, or that the IRB or Awardee (not PI) certify that the research is exempt. **DOD** The DOD definition of human materials includes established human cells lines. This means that an IRB determination of "exemption" is required for virtually every protocol. The DOD also requires for each protocol that an IRB provide a letter with documentation of the risk level to any human subjects, as well as an original consent form that documents the type of research being conducted. Any protocol modifications and continuing review reports must be submitted to the DOD's human subjects review board.	45 CFR 46 <u>NIH</u> • 45 CFR 46 • GPS pp. 58-61 <u>NSF</u> • 45 CFR 690 • GC-1, Article 32 • GPM 711 <u>DOD</u> Guidance document "Research Involving Human Subjects and/or Anatomical Substances," located at http://mrmc-www.army.mil/docs/rcq/HSAppendix19Feb02.pdf.

Federal Regulation of Research Through Funding

Title and Summary	Agency Requirements	Sources of Obligation
Rehabilitation Act of 1973 Awardees may not exclude handicapped persons from participation in, deny benefits to, or subject to discrimination under, any program or activity (while would include conducting or participating in research) receiving federal funds, solely by reason of the handicap. Awardees may not discriminate in employment of the handicapped, and must make reasonable accommodations for handicap. The Awardee must designate a person to coordinate its efforts to comply with the Act, adopt grievance procedures that provide for prompt resolution of any violations, and take continuing action to notify participants, beneficiaries, applicants, employees and entities holding collective bargaining agreements with it that it does not discriminate on the basis of handicap.	**NIH** Awardee certifies compliance through executing Form HHS-690. All subawardees (including those who supply goods and services via contract) and consortium participants must certify compliance to NIH. **NSF** Awardee certifies compliance by means of an Assurance. Compliance must be "appropriately addressed" in subawards. This is done through a certification certificate for research, science, or technical experimentation. A certificate does not have to be obtained from providers of routine goods and services. The NSF provides guidance for the Awardee to determine what constitutes "reasonable physical qualifications" for participation in science, research, and technical experimentation under §504 of the Rehabilitation Act. The guidance should be provided to the Awardee's human resources to evaluate candidates for science-related positions.	29 USC 794 **NIH/HHS**: • 45 CFR 84 • GPS p. 68 **NSF**: • 45 CFR 605 • GPM 703 • GC-1, Article 27

Title and Summary	Agency Requirements	Sources of Obligation
The Privacy Act of 1974 This provision does not normally apply to records maintained by Awardees. The Privacy Act establishes certain safeguards for the privacy of information about individuals maintained in a system of records, as identified by the Act (i.e., information may be retrieved by the individual's name or other identifying information). These safeguards include the rights of individuals to determine what information about them is maintained in Federal agencies' files (hard copy or electronic) and how it is used, to have access to such records, and to correct, amend, or request deletion of information in their records that is inaccurate, irrelevant, or outdated.	**NIH** Records maintained by NIH with respect to grant applications, grant awards, and the administration of grants are subject to the provisions of the Privacy Act. NIH has two Privacy Act systems, which provide guidance on requirements for the management of grant records in the possession of NIH and include appropriate routine uses of such information. They also include requirements for safeguarding the records and for record retention and disposal.	5 USC §552a 45 CFR Part 5b **NIH** GPS p. 72
Title IX of the Education Amendments of 1972 No person in the United States shall, on the basis of sex, be excluded from participation in, be denied the benefits of, or be subjected to discrimination under any education program or activity receiving federal financial assistance. This means that participating in the conduct of research, and participating in studies carried out as part of the research are covered. The recipient must "commit itself to take whatever remedial action is necessary . . . to eliminate existing discrimination on the basis of sex, or to eliminate the effects of past discrimination whether occurring prior or subsequent to the submission to the Director of such assurance." A compliance coordinator must be designated, grievance procedures adopted, and applicants notified of the Awardee's commitment to non-discrimination on the basis of sex. No affirmative action program is required.	**NIH** Must submit Certificate of Assurance HHS Form 690. Certification from consortium participants and providers of routine goods and services is required. **NSF** An implementing article is usually contained in the award instrument.	20 USC §1681-1686 **NIH** • 45 CFR 86 • GPS p. 68 **NSF** • 45 CFR 618 • GC-26 • GPM 704

Title and Summary	Agency Requirements	Sources of Obligation
Title VI of the Civil Rights Act of 1964 No person in the U.S. shall exclude persons from participation in, deny persons the benefits of, or subject persons to discrimination, on the basis of race, color or national origin, for any program or activity receiving Federal financial assistance. Grant-funded programs or research are included in programs or activities receiving federal financial assistance. The regulations contain a general recordkeeping requirement, but HHS has not adopted any specific form to use when compiling and maintaining this information or any regulation that requires a recipient to make definite, scheduled reports to it that track its efforts to comply with the act. HHS has the authority to review a grant recipient's practices from "time to time" to determine whether they are in compliance with the Act.	**NIH** All grant recipients and subawardees must file the required Assurance, form HHS-690. **NSF** An Assurance is required by Awardee. For subawardees, contractors and subcontractors the Awardee must include a compliance provision in the subaward instrument.	42 USC §§2000d et seq. **NIH** • 45 CFR 80 • GPS p. 68 **NSF** • 45 CFR 611 • GC-1, Article 27 • GPM 702

POLICY ISSUES

Title and Summary	Agency Requirements	Sources of Obligation
Ban on Human Embryo Research and Cloning Federal agency funds may not be used to support human embryo research under any extramural (award made to entities outside the agency) award or instrument. This means the Federal agency funds may not be used for the creation of a human embryo(s) for research purposes or for research in which a human embryo(s) is destroyed, discarded, or knowingly subjected to risk of injury or death greater than that allowed for research on fetuses *in utero* under 45 CFR 46.208(a)(2) and subsection 498(a) and (b) of the PHS Act. The term "human embryo(s)" includes any organism not protected as a human subject under 45 CFR 46, as of the date of enactment of the governing appropriations act, that is derived by fertilization, parthenogenesis, cloning, or any other means from one or more human gametes or human diploid cells.	**NIH** In addition to the statutory restrictions on human fetal research under subsections 498(a) and (b) of the PHS Act, by Presidential memorandum of March 4, 1997, NIH is prohibited from using Federal funds for cloning of human beings.	**NIH** GPS p. 54-55
Confidentiality/Identifying Information Certificates of Confidentiality can be obtained, by application, that allow researchers to engage in research activities with protection from being required to provide patient identity information in any civil, criminal, administrative, or other proceeding. This provision is primarily used for researchers that "de-identify" data—the Certificate prevents any outside entity from requiring the researcher to divulge the source of the materials. It is a necessary protection to ensure the privacy that is the basis of such human subjects research.		PHS Act §301(d) 42 USC § 241(d) http://grants.nih.gov/grants/policy/coc/index.htm. **NIH** GPS p. 57

Federal Regulation of Research Through Funding

Title and Summary	Agency Requirements	Sources of Obligation
Confidentiality of Substance Abuse Patient Records The records of substance abuse patients must be kept confidential except under conditions specified in the Act.		PHS Act §543 42 USC § 290dd-2 **NIH** • 42 CFR Part 2 • GPS p. 57
Data and Safety Monitoring for Human Subjects When appropriate, research plans must make adequate provisions for monitoring data to ensure the safety of the subjects.	**NIH** NIH has requirements for oversight and monitoring of data and safety of human subjects in clinical trials that are much more detailed than the regulatory standard. For instance, the NIH mandates that a detailed plan be prepared and approved by the IRB and NIH before any human subjects are recruited.	45 CFR 46.111(a)(6) **NIH** • GPS pp. 62-63
Debarment and Suspension Awardees, and some subawardees, must certify that principals have not been debarred or suspended, proposed for debarment, declared ineligible, or voluntarily excluded from covered transactions. Grounds for suspension or debarment include: • a civil judgment or criminal conviction, or indictment for same, within the past three years for commission of fraud or a criminal offense in connection with obtaining, attempting to obtain, or performing a public transaction or contract; • Violation of a state or Federal antitrust statute; • commission of embezzlement, theft, forgery, bribery, falsification or destruction of records; or • for making false statements or receiving stolen property. • within the past 3 years had any public transaction determined by default.	**NIH** Certification must be submitted by prime awardee, subawardees receiving more than $100,000 for goods or services, and all Consortium participants. Regardless of whether a certification is made, entities that are currently debarred or suspended cannot be paid with Federal grant funds. **NSF** A certification must be submitted by the grantee institution and by each subawardee receiving NSF funds.	Executive Orders 12549 and 12689 OMB A-110 **NIH/HHS** • 45 CFR 76 • GPS p. 52, 53 **NSF** • 45 CFR 620 • GPM 912, 930 • GC-1, Articles 24, 25

Title and Summary	Agency Requirements	Sources of Obligation
Drug-Free Workplace The Awardee must establish a drug-free awareness program, prohibit drug use in the workplace, report any employee's drug-related conviction to the funding agency within ten days of the time it receives notice of the conviction, and either sanction employees convicted of drug offenses or require completion of a rehabilitation program.	**NIH** Must establish a drug-free awareness program, and must notify NIH within 10 days of learning of an employee's drug conviction. **NSF** Must certify to NSF that the policy is in place.	**NIH** • 42 USC § 702 • 45 CFR § 76 • GPS p. 47 **NSF** • 45 CFR 630 • 48 CFR 9.2, 23.5, 52.2
Facility Safety Program An adequate safety program is required. A summary of the programs must be submitted for approval, which is granted on a five-year basis. Annual updates are also required. Any significant impact on the environment or violation of any applicable environmental law or regulation must be reported to the Management Grants Officer ("MGO") for the Awardee's grant.	**DOD** If the research is part of the "Biological Defense Research Program", many additional requirements exist. *See* 32 CFR 626.5.	NIH and NSF have no comparable requirement. **DOD** Appendix "L", Safety Program located at http://mrmc-www.army.mil/docs/RCQ/F702FSPAppendix.doc.

Federal Regulation of Research Through Funding 375

Title and Summary	Agency Requirements	Sources of Obligation
Financial Conflict of Interest Awardee must establish and enforce policies that minimize the opportunity for improper financial gain on the part of the Awardee and associated persons, and that limit the potential for research results to be tainted by possible personal financial or other gain. Standards of conduct must address financial conflict of interest, gifts, gratuities, favors, nepotism, political participation and bribery. Specific penalties (in addition to those that might be imposed by the government for violation of grant conditions) must be set out, as well as a notification and review process for potential or actual violations, and a way to provide advance notice of outside activities, relationships, and financial interests to the Awardee.	<u>NIH</u> • A copy of the standards of conduct must be made available to each officer and member of the Awardee's governing board, and to each employee and consultant working on the grant-supported project or activity. • If a suspension or separation action is taken against a PI or other key personnel under an NIH grant, the designated GMO must <u>be notified</u>. • The Awardee's signature on the grant application certifies that there is an administrative process (written and enforced) to identify, manage, reduce or eliminate conflicting financial interests with respect to research projects for which NIH funding is sought. • If a financial conflict of interest occurs on an NIH grant, it must be reported to the NIH GMO. • Consortium participants must be subject to one of the Awardee's conflict of interest policies. <u>NSF</u> • Policy only required for institutions employing more than 50 persons. • Refers to guidance issued by universities and scientific societies. • Provides detailed examples of what "significant" financial interests are, and enumerates exemptions. • Initial disclosure must be made at time proposal is submitted to NSF. • Requires updates yearly or when new financial interests are acquired.	NIH • 42 CFR 50 Subpart F • GPS pp. 44-46 <u>NSF</u> • 45 CFR 689 • GC-1, Article 33 • GPM 510

Title and Summary	Agency Requirements	Sources of Obligation
Inclusiveness in Research Design Women and members of minority groups must be included in any NIH-supported research project involving human subjects, unless a clear and compelling rationale and justification establishes that inclusion is inappropriate. Cost is not an acceptable reason for exclusion. Women of childbearing potential should not be routinely excluded from participation in clinical research (i.e., any biomedical or behavioral research involving human subjects). All new applications involving human subjects research must include children (i.e., individuals under the age of 21) in the research design unless there are scientific or ethical reasons not to include them.[2] If children will be excluded from the research, the application must present an acceptable justification for the exclusion. This policy applies to both exempt and nonexempt research activities (see "Human Subjects" in this section). The inclusion of children as subjects in research must comply with all applicable provisions of 45 CFR Part 46 and other pertinent Federal laws and regulations. Information on race must also be collected. 2. This policy has been in effect since October 1, 1998 for new applications submitted for a receipt date after that date. It is not mandatory for applications submitted for receipt dates prior to that date, competing awards made prior to that date, or non-competing awards resulting from competing awards made prior to that date.		OMB Directive No. 15 **NIH** GPS pp. 66-67 http://grants. NIH.gov/grants/funding/ women_min/ guidelines_amended_ 10_2001.htm. http://grants. NIH.gov/grants/guide/ notice-files/NOT-OD-01- 053.html http://grants. NIH.gov/grants/funding/ children/children.htm
Increasing Seat Belt Use in the United States A policy encouraging seat belt use in personal vehicles and institutional vehicles must be established.	**NIH** Only Awardee must comply (does not flowdown). **NSF** Compliance must be "appropriately addressed" in all subawards.	E.O. 1304 **NIH** GPS p. 54 **NSF** GC-1, Article 41

Federal Regulation of Research Through Funding 377

Title and Summary	Agency Requirements	Sources of Obligation
Investigational Drug Exceptions Note that where clinical research involving investigational new drugs ("INDs") occurs, it must meet FDA's IND regulations and human subjects protection regulations, in addition to HHS's human subjects requirements.		FDA regulations: 21 CFR Parts 50 and 312 **NIH** GPS pp. 63-64
Misconduct in Science and Engineering Administrative policies for investigating and promptly resolving all instances of alleged or apparent research misconduct must be established and communicated to all persons involved in grant-funded research or administration.	**NIH** Any instance of research misconduct that is investigated must be reported to the Federal Office of Research Integrity. An annual report must also be submitted. Where the validity or reliability of data has been affected by research misconduct, the Awardee and its employee/collaborator authors are responsible for submitting a correction or republishing of the data to a journal (as appropriate) and/or publishing the corrected data, if required. **NSF** NSF's position is that it has the primary authority to investigate scientific misconduct and that if an Awardee wishes to conduct its own investigation in lieu of NSF, it must keep NSF informed, complete its inquiry in 90 days, and, if an investigation is warranted, the Awardee must complete the investigation and come to a conclusion within 180 days.	**NIH** • 42 CFR 93 • GPS pp. 50-51 **NSF** • 45 CFR 689 • GPM 900-909, 930, 932

Title and Summary	Agency Requirements	Sources of Obligation
National Security If an Awardee generates information it believes should be classified, there are specific steps to follow. There are also steps that must be taken to guard against transnational terrorism.		E.O. 12356 E.O. 12958 **NSF** • GPM 850 • GC1 Article 28
Patriot Act Background checks are necessary to ensure that "Restricted Persons" do not possess, ship, transport, or receive any listed select agent.		18 U.S.C. 10 42 CFR 73.7 **NIH** • GPS 48
Public Health Security and Bioterrorism Preparedness and Response Act The Act requires registration of facilities that use more than threshold quantities of select agents. The registration program is run by the CDC. Note that there are DOT regulations that appear to apply (they are in force on the books), but that have, for all practical purposes, been superseded by the CDC program.	There are no specific agency requirements.	42 CFR 73 **NIH** • GPS 48
Publications, Exhibits, Copyright, and Funding Acknowledgement The Awardee may own or permit others to own copyright in all subject writings, subject to a royalty-free license for the government, and unless otherwise specified in the award documents. An acknowledgement of funding must appear in all publications of work produced by grant-related activities; there is boilerplate language in the NIH GPS. Note that grants not primarily for research (travel, conferences) do not contain copyright provisions.	**NIH** Agreements with contractors or consortium participants may not diminish NIH's rights to copyrighted material. **NSF** Special provisions may be negotiated to further the objectives of the NSF. All subawardees must comply.	**NIH** • 45 CFR 74.36 • GPS pp. 114-115 **NSF** • GPM 732, 733 • GC-1 Article 18-20

Federal Regulation of Research Through Funding

Title and Summary	Agency Requirements	Sources of Obligation
Research Involving Recombinant DNA & Human Gene Transfer The document (see "Sources" column) sets out the necessity for and duties of an Institutional Biosafety Committee, registration requirements, adverse event reporting, risk assessment, and other reporting obligations. If any grant-funded activity occurs at an Awardee's facility, ALL research at the facility must comply with the requirements of the document.	**NIH** The Awardee, consortium participants, and suppliers of routine goods and services must all comply. **NSF** Compliance must be appropriately addressed in all subawards.	*Guidelines for Research Involving Recombinant DNA* http://www4.od.NIH.gov/oba/rac/guidelines/guidelines-html **NIH** GPS p. 51-52 **NSF** • GPM 712 • GC-1, Article 30
Research on Human Fetal Tissue & Human Fetal Tissue Transplant Human fetal tissue is defined as tissue or cells obtained from a dead human embryo or fetus after a spontaneous or induced abortion or stillbirth, and does not include established human fetal cell lines. Federal statute specifically prohibits any person from knowingly acquiring, receiving, or transferring any human fetal tissue for valuable consideration. "Valuable consideration" is a concept similar to profit, and does not include reasonable payment for costs associated with the collection, processing, preservation, storage, quality control or transportation of these tissues.	**NIH** There are additional legal requirements for research on the transplantation of human fetal tissue for therapeutic purposes that is conducted or supported by the NIH, most of which relate to the content of the informed consent document, and certifications by the attending physician and PI that the material was obtained ethically. The authorized organizational official that signs the application must certify that, if research on the transplantation of human fetal tissue is conducted under the grant-supported project, the organization will make the physician statements and informed consent required by subsections 498A(b)(2) and (2) of the PHS Act available to HHS.	42 USC § 289g-1 and 289g-2 Sections 498A and 498B(b) of the Public Health Service Act.FDA – http://www.Fda.gov/cber/ltr/fetal/113000.htm. Guidance available at http://grants. http://grants.nih.gov.grants.gov/grants/guide/notice-files/not93-235.html. FDA also claims jurisdiction under its "Part 1271" regulations. **NIH** GPS pp. 55-56.

Title and Summary	Agency Requirements	Sources of Obligation
Restriction on Distribution of Sterile Needles NIH appropriated funds may not be used to carry out any program involving distribution of sterile needles or syringes for the hypodermic injection of any illegal drug.		**NIH** • GPS p. 54
Sharing of Unique Research Resources Unique research resources—such as cell lives, DNA sequences, and synthetic organisms, as well as computer programs, transgenic animals and intellectual property—should be shared to enhance the value of funded research. An Awardee's policies on sharing these resources should comport with this principle, but it is not mandatory.	**NIH** NIH published a document, "Principles and Guidelines for Recipients of NIH Research Grants and Contracts on Obtaining and Disseminating Biomedical Research Resources," 64 FR 72090, which sets out guidelines for an Awardee's terms and conditions to disseminate and acquire research tools in a manner consistent with the Bayh-Dole Act and the terms and conditions of NIH awards. Biological information should be submitted to appropriate databases. Streamlined procedures should be adopted for disseminating research tools, including to for-profit organizations for internal use (not sale or commercial development). **NSF** Software samples, data, physical collections, and research.	**NIH** • 64 FR 72090 • GPS pp. 115-116 • http://ott.od.NIH.gov/neropages/rtguide-final.html **NSF** • GPM 734 • GC-1, Article 38

Federal Regulation of Research Through Funding 381

GRANT ADMINISTRATION

Title and Summary	Agency Requirements	Sources of Obligation
Audits and Record Retention An annual audit by a public, federal, state, or local government audit organization is required where an Awardee spends more than $500,000 in grant funds in one year. The auditing entity must use the Generally Accepted Government Auditing Standard ("GAGAS"). Records must be maintained for 3 years after the final financial report is submitted for a funded project. Access to records must be granted to agency officials for auditing, if requested. Records such as audits, appeals, litigation or settlement of claims must be retained until the issue has been resolved.	**NIH** Only subawardees receiving amounts greater than $100,000 need comply. **NSF** All subawards must address appropriately.	31 USC §§7501-7507 OMB Circular A-133 **NIH** • 45 CFR 74.26, 74.48 • GPS pp. 134-136 **NSF** • GPM 350 • GC-1, Article 23
Equipment "Equipment Management," also called "Property Standards" in the regulations, governs the management and ultimate disposition of property purchased with federal grant funds. The Awardee is permitted to use its own property management standards, provided they meet the standards of OMB A-110.33 to 110.37. Notably, the Awardee must: • provide the same/equivalent insurance coverage for federally-purchased property as grantee's own property. • provide an annual report of federally-owned property in its possession, unless the property is declared "exempt" by the awarding agency.	NIH and NSF are not permitted to have their own rules governing NSF property management. Materials in the agency manuals simply restate the OMB rules, although they provide agency-specific contact information and give examples that relate to that agency's work.	**NIH** GPS p. 124-125 **NSF** • 45 CFR 74.34 • OMB Circular A-110, .31-.37 • GC-1, Article 6 • GPM 530, 540, 541-544, 546

Title and Summary	Agency Requirements	Sources of Obligation
• May not use equipment in which the Federal government owns an interest, supplies, or expendable property, to provide services to non-federal outside organizations for a fee less than private companies' charges, unless specifically authorized by federal statute. • Must use the equipment in the project/program for which it was acquired for as long as needed, whether or not the project/program continues to be supported by federal funds. • Extensive records must be kept on the equipment: title vests, federal percentage of ownership in the equipment, and disposition data. • A physical inventory must be taken at least once every 2 years, and a control system must be in place to safeguard against loss, damage, or theft. Any loss, damages or theft must be investigated and reported to the Federal government. Title to supplies and expendable property vests in the Awardee upon purchase. Note: Intangible property rights and management discussed separately.		
Procurement Standards	NIH and are required to use the procurement standards of OMB Circular A-110 and can not alter them. **NIH** All agreements with third parties for goods or services must comply. **NSF** Only contracts or awards over $100,000 must include these standards.	OMB Circular A-110.40-110.48 **NIH** • 45 CFR 74.40-74.48 • GPS pp. 138-139 **NSF** GC-1, Article 9

Title and Summary	Agency Requirements	Sources of Obligation
Program Income There are administrative rules governing how income generated by a sponsored program may be spent. Program income includes income from fees for services performed, the use or rental of real or personal property acquired under the grant, the sale of commodities or items fabricated under the grant, license fees for and royalties on and copyrights and interest on loans made with grant funds. Program income is defined as gross income earned.	**NIH** Program income may be used as set out in Table II-3 p. 132 of NIH GPS, unless otherwise specified in the grant documents. The NIH generally only requires the alternative uses if the grantee has a history of large unobligated grant balances or has requested multiple time or budget extensions. **NSF** The funds should be used to further the objectives of the sponsored project unless otherwise provided for in the grant documents. If the funds generated are in excess of the grant amount, and the grant agreement so requires, the NSF may recover the income which is in excess of the grant amount.	**NIH** GPS p. 120, Table II-3 **NSF** • GPM 444, 752 • GC-1, Article 18

Legend:

NIH	=	National Institutes of Health	NSF	=	National Science Foundation
EPA	=	Environmental Protection Agency	HHS	=	Department of Health and Human Services
E.O.	=	Executive Order	GPS	=	The NIH's "Grants Policy Statement"
USC	=	United States Code	GPM	=	The NSF's "Grants Policy Manual"
CFR	=	Code of Federal Regulations	GC1	=	The NSF's "Grant Conditions1" Document
DOD	=	Department of Defense			

*Note – Health service provider requirements (Child Protection Act (no smoking)), United English Proficiency (health and social services providers); Construction-related provisions, Military Recruiting and Reserve Officer Training Corps access to Institutions of Higher Education (grant can be pulled if access not granted) and HIPAA (no different or special requirements) are not included in the table. Also excluded are requirements only applicable to Consortium Participants.

FEDERAL PROCUREMENT REQUIREMENTS AND POLICY

Provision or Clause	Source	Summary	Additional Agency Requirements
FAR 52.202-1 Definitions	FAR 2.201	Definitions for federal procurement transactions.	
FAR 52.203-2 Certificate of Independent Price Determination	FAR 3.103-1	A contractor must certify that prices were not disclosed to or discussed with other offerors or competitors.	
FAR 52.203-3 Gratuities	FAR 3.202	Generally, this provision prohibits the contractor, its agents or representatives from offering or giving a gratuity to a government official, officer or employee with the intent to obtain a contract or favorable treatment under a contract. The government may terminate the contract in addition to civil, criminal and other administrative penalties, including suspension and/or debarment from government contracting and government-approved subcontracting.	**DFARS 203.7000** Contractor Standards of Conduct Policy: Government contractors must conduct themselves with the highest degree of integrity and honesty. Contractors should have standards of conduct and internal control systems that— (1) Are suitable to the size of the company and the extent of their involvement in Government contracting, (2) Promote such standards, (3) Facilitate timely discovery and disclosure of improper conduct in connection with Government contracts, and (4) Ensure corrective measures are promptly instituted and carried out. **HHSARS 303.203** (Reporting suspected violations of the Gratuities clause)

FEDERAL PROCUREMENT REQUIREMENTS AND POLICY

Provision or Clause	Source	Summary	Additional Agency Requirements
FAR 52.203-5 Covenant Against Contingent Fees	FAR 3.404	A contractor must certify that no contingent fees exist except between contractor and its "bona fide" employees or agents.	**HHSARS 303.405** (Misrepresentations or violations of Covenant Against Contingent Fees)
FAR 52.203-6 Restrictions on Subcontractor Sales to Government	FAR 3.503-2	A contractor must agree not to enter into any agreement with either actual or prospective subcontractors that would restrict the subcontractor in making direct sales to the government by the prime contractor pursuant to the prime's contract with the government or pursuant to any follow-on contract.	
FAR 52.203-7 Anti-Kickback Procedures	FAR 3.502-3	This provision prohibits any person from providing or attempting to provide or offering to provide any money, fee, commission, credit, gift, gratuity, thing of value, or compensation of any kind which is provided, directly or indirectly, to any prime contractor, prime contractor employee, subcontractor, or subcontractor employee for the purpose of improperly obtaining or rewarding favorable treatment in connection with a prime contract or in connection with a subcontract relating to a prime contract, or soliciting, accepting, or attempting to accept any kickback; or including, directly or indirectly, the amount of any kickback in the contract price charged by a prime contractor to the United States or in the contract price charged by a subcontractor to a prime Contractor or higher tier subcontractor. The contractor shall have in place and follow reasonable procedures designed to prevent and detect possible violations. The contractor shall promptly report in writing any possible violation. The contractor shall cooperate fully with any Federal agency investigating a possible violation.	**DFARS 203.502-2** (Subcontractor kickbacks) **HHSARS 303.502** (Subcontractor kickbacks)

FEDERAL PROCUREMENT REQUIREMENTS AND POLICY

Provision or Clause	Source	Summary	Additional Agency Requirements
FAR 52.203-11 Certification and Disclosure Regarding Payments to Influence Certain Federal Transactions (Byrd Amendment)	FAR 3.808(a)	Any contractor who requests or receives a Federal contract exceeding $100,000 shall submit the certification and disclosures required by the provision at 52.203-11, Certification and Disclosure Regarding Payments to Influence Certain Federal Transactions, with its offer. Disclosures under this section shall be submitted to the contracting officer using OMB standard form LLL, Disclosure of Lobbying Activities. The contractor shall file a disclosure form at the end of each calendar quarter. All subcontractor disclosure forms (but not certifications), shall be forwarded from tier to tier until received by the prime contractor. The prime contractor shall submit all disclosure forms to the contracting officer at the end of the calendar quarter in which the disclosure form is submitted by the subcontractor. Each subcontractor certification shall be retained in the subcontract file of the awarding contractor. The certification for contractors includes a statement that the contractor has not and will not make a prohibited payment, that it will report the use of non-federal funds used for lobbying purposes, and that they will include this certification requirement in consortium agreements and contracts that will exceed $100,000, and obtain certifications where required.	Under DFARS 231.205-22, legislative lobbying costs and any costs associated with preparing any material, report, list, or analysis on the actual or projected economic or employment impact in a particular State or congressional district of an acquisition program for which all research, development, testing, and evaluation has not been completed also are unallowable.

FEDERAL PROCUREMENT REQUIREMENTS AND POLICY

Provision or Clause	Source	Summary	Additional Agency Requirements
FAR 52.203-12 Limitation on Payments to Influence Certain Federal Transactions	FAR 3.808(b)	Any contractor who requests or receives a Federal contract exceeding $100,000 shall submit the certification and disclosures required by the provision at 52.203-11, Certification and Disclosure Regarding Payments to Influence Certain Federal Transactions, with its offer. Disclosures under this section shall be submitted to the contracting officer using OMB standard form LLL, Disclosure of Lobbying Activities. The contractor shall file a disclosure form at the end of each calendar quarter. All subcontractor disclosure forms (but not certifications), shall be forwarded from tier to tier until received by the prime contractor. The prime contractor shall submit all disclosure forms to the contracting officer at the end of the calendar quarter in which the disclosure form is submitted by the subcontractor. Each subcontractor certification shall be retained in the subcontract file of the awarding contractor. The certification for contractors includes a statement that the contractor has not and will not make a prohibited payment, that it will report the use of non-federal funds used for lobbying purposes, and that they will include this certification requirement in consortium agreements and contracts that will exceed $100,000, and obtain certifications where required.	

FEDERAL PROCUREMENT REQUIREMENTS AND POLICY

Provision or Clause	Source	Summary	Additional Agency Requirements
FAR 52.204-2 Security Requirements	FAR 4.404(a)	The contractor shall comply with— (1) the Security Agreement (DD Form 441), including the National Industrial Security Program Operating Manual (DoD 5220.22-M); and (2) any revisions to that manual, notice of which has been furnished to the contractor.	
FAR 52.209-5 Certification Regarding Debarment, Suspension, Proposed Debarment, and Other Responsibility Matters	FAR 9.409(a)	A contractor must certify that you have or have not been suspended or debarred, indicted, convicted, or found liable for certain enumerated civil and criminal violations in the last three years, or had a contract terminated for default in the last three years.	DFARS 252.203-7001, 203.570-3 (Prohibition on persons convicted of fraud or other defense-contract-related felonies)
FAR 52.209-6 Protecting the Government's Interest When Subcontracting with Contractors Debarred, Suspended, or Proposed for Debarment	FAR 9.409(b)	A contractor must certify that you have or have not been suspended or debarred, indicted, convicted, or found liable for certain enumerated civil and criminal violations in the last three years, or had a contract terminated for default in the last three years.	DFARS 252.203-7001, 203.570-3 (Prohibition on persons convicted of fraud or other defense-contract-related felonies)
FAR 52.214-4 False Statements in Bids	FAR 14.201-6(b)(2)	This clause is included in all invitations for bids. This provision provides that bidders must provide full, accurate and complete information, as required by the government Invitation for Bid ("IFB"). This provision ensures that the government has all necessary information needed to evaluate competitive bids and fairness to competing bidders and the government in the award. Violation of this provision invokes such actions as the annulment of the contract, suspension and/or debarment from government contracting and subcontracting. The criminal penalty for making false statements is prescribed in 18 U.S.C. § 1001.	

FEDERAL PROCUREMENT REQUIREMENTS AND POLICY

Provision or Clause	Source	Summary	Additional Agency Requirements
FAR 15.406-2 Certificate of Current Cost or Pricing Data		For negotiated contracts expected to exceed $550,000 or modification to any sealed bid or negotiated contract involving a price adjustment over $500,000, a contractor must supply the government with all cost or pricing data that a prudent seller would reasonably expect to affect price negotiations. The contractor must certify that the data is current, accurate and complete to the best of its knowledge.	
FAR 52.214-26 Audit and Records – Sealed Bidding	14.201-7(a)	If the contractor has been required to submit cost or pricing data in connection with the pricing of any modification to this contract, the contracting officer, or an authorized representative of the contracting officer, in order to evaluate the accuracy, completeness, and currency of the cost or pricing data, shall have the right to examine and audit all of the Contractor's records, including computations and projections. The Contractor shall make available at its office at all reasonable times the materials described above for examination, audit, or reproduction, until 3 years after final payment under this contract, or for any other period specified in FAR Subpart 4.7. Subpart 4.7 (Contractor Records Retention) is incorporated by reference in its entirety and made a part of a contract.	DFARS 252.237-7001 Compliance with audit standards: The Contractor, in performance of all audit services under this contract, shall comply with "Government Auditing Standards" issued by the Comptroller General of the United States.

FEDERAL PROCUREMENT REQUIREMENTS AND POLICY

Provision or Clause	Source	Summary	Additional Agency Requirements
FAR 52.215-2 Audit and Records – Negotiation	15.209(b)(1)	If the contractor is required to furnish cost, funding, or performance reports, the contracting officer or an authorized representative of the contracting officer shall have the right to examine and audit the supporting records and materials, to evaluate: (1) The effectiveness of the Contractor's policies and procedures to produce data compatible with the objectives of these reports; and (2) The data reported. The Contractor shall make available at its office at all reasonable times the records, materials, and other evidence described above for examination, audit, or reproduction, until 3 years after final payment under this contract or for any shorter period specified in Subpart 4.7, Contractor Records Retention, of the FAR, or for any longer period required by statute or by other clauses of this contract.	
FAR 52.215-12 Subcontractor Cost or Pricing Data	15.408(d)	The contractor shall require the subcontractor to certify in substantially the form prescribed in FAR 15.406-2 that, to the best of its knowledge and belief, the data submitted under this clause were accurate, complete, and current as of the date of agreement on the negotiated price of the subcontract or subcontract modification.	

FEDERAL PROCUREMENT REQUIREMENTS AND POLICY

Provision or Clause	Source	Summary	Additional Agency Requirements
FAR 52.219.1 Small Business Program Representation	19.308(a)(1)	This clause is included in solicitations when the contract will be performed in the United States. It is Government policy to promote the utilization of small business concerns, small disadvantaged business concerns, and woman-owned business concerns. Prime contractors must represent that they will carry out this policy in awarding of subcontracts and may be required to cooperate with any study conducted by the Small Business Administration to determine such compliance. Making a false or incorrect representation and thereby violating these provisions may result in the imposition of liquidated damages and may result in a breach of contract claim, common law fraud and may be considered a violation of the False Statements Act.	
FAR 52.219-8 Utilization of Small Business Concerns; FAR 52.219-9 Small Business Subcontracting	FAR 19.708(a); FAR 19.708(b)	This clause is included in solicitations when the contract will be performed in the United States. It is Government policy to promote the utilization of small business concerns, small disadvantaged business concerns, and woman-owned business concerns. Prime contractors must represent that they will carry out this policy in awarding of subcontracts and may be required to cooperate with any study conducted by the Small Business Administration to determine such compliance. Making a false or incorrect representation and thereby violating these provisions may result in the imposition of liquidated damages and may result in a breach of contract claim, common law fraud and may be considered a violation of the False Statements Act.	
FAR 52.222-4 Contract Work Hours and Safety Standards Act – Overtime Compensation	FAR 22.305	No Contractor or subcontractor employing laborers or mechanics shall require or permit them to work over 40 hours in any workweek unless they are paid at least 1 and 1/2 times the basic rate of pay for each hour worked over 40 hours.	

FEDERAL PROCUREMENT REQUIREMENTS AND POLICY

Provision or Clause	Source	Summary	Additional Agency Requirements
FAR 52.222-5 Davis-Bacon Act	FAR 22.407(a)	For solicitations and contracts in excess of $2,000 for construction within the United States, all laborers and mechanics employed or working upon the site of the work will be paid unconditionally and not less often than once a week, and without subsequent deduction or rebate on any account (except such payroll deductions as are permitted by regulations issued by the Secretary of Labor under the Copeland Act (29 CFR part 3), the full amount of wages and bona fide fringe benefits (or cash equivalents thereof) due at time of payment computed at rates not less than those contained in the wage determination of the Secretary of Labor which is attached hereto and made a part hereof, or as may be incorporated for a secondary site of the work, regardless of any contractual relationship which may be alleged to exist between the contractor and such laborers and mechanics. Any wage determination incorporated for a secondary site of the work shall be effective from the first day on which work under the contract was performed at that site and shall be incorporated without any adjustment in contract price or estimated cost. Laborers employed by the construction contractor or construction subcontractor that are transporting portions of the building or work between the secondary site of the work and the primary site of the work shall be paid in accordance with the wage determination applicable to the primary site of the work.	

FEDERAL PROCUREMENT REQUIREMENTS AND POLICY

Provision or Clause	Source	Summary	Additional Agency Requirements
FAR 52.222-20 Walsh-Healey Public Contracts Act	FAR 22.610	If the contract is for the manufacture or furnishing of materials, supplies, articles or equipment in an amount that exceeds or may exceed $10,000, the following terms and conditions may apply: (a) All stipulations required by the Act and regulations issued by the Secretary of Labor (41 CFR Chapter 50) are incorporated by reference. (b) All employees whose work relates to this contract shall be paid not less than the minimum wage prescribed by regulations issued by the Secretary of Labor (41 CFR 50-202.2). Learners, student learners, apprentices, and handicapped workers may be employed at less than the prescribed minimum wage (see 41 CFR 50-202.3) to the same extent that such employment is permitted under Section 14 of the Fair Labor Standards Act (41 U.S.C. 40).	
FAR 52.222-21 Prohibition of Segregated Facilities	FAR 22.810(a)(1)	This clause is included in all solicitations when the Equal Opportunity clause (52.222-26) is included in the solicitation and contract. Certification as to the nonsegregation of facilities ensures that neither the offeror, nor any of its proposed subcontractors, operates segregated facilities. This implements Government policy not to award contracts to contractors who maintain segregated facilities. The Private contractor certifies that it does not and will not maintain segregated facilities for its employees and, further, that the Private contractor agrees to obtain identical certifications from any proposed subcontractors.	

FEDERAL PROCUREMENT REQUIREMENTS AND POLICY

Provision or Clause	Source	Summary	Additional Agency Requirements
FAR 52.222-22 Previous Contracts and Compliance Reports	FAR 22.810(a)(2)	This clause is included in all solicitations when the Equal Opportunity clause (52.222-26) is included in the solicitation and contract. This representation addresses the existence of equal opportunity compliance reports by the offeror on file with the Government and enables review of those reports before contract award. The Private contractor represents that it has or has not participated in previous contracts or subcontracts which are subject to an Equal Opportunity clause. Violation of this provision may result in the rejection of the bid if no representation is made. Suspension and/or debarment from Government contracting or Government approved subcontracting may be imposed if the certification is false, and criminal penalties may be imposed under the False Statements Act.	
FAR 52.222-25 Affirmative Action Compliance	FAR 22.810(d)	This clause is included in all solicitations where the Equal Opportunity clause (FAR 52.222-26) is included in the solicitation and contract. This representation regarding the filing of an offeror's affirmative action program reports with the Government enables review of those reports before contract award. Also, the representation states that the private contractor has or has not participated in previous contracts or subcontracts that are subject to the written affirmative action program requirements. Violation of this provision may result in the rejection of the bid or proposal if no certification is made. Suspension and/or debarment from Government contracting and Government-approved subcontracting also may be imposed if the Certification is false, and in criminal penalties under the False Statements Act.	**NOTE:** Recently, the Office of Federal Contract Compliance Programs ("OFCCP") issued a final rule clarifying the definition of an "applicant" in the context of internet recruitment and amending recordkeeping requirements regarding internet applications. 70 Fed. Reg. 58946 (Oct. 7, 2005). This clarification narrows the applicant definition previously utilized by the OFCCP, but will require many contractors to

FEDERAL PROCUREMENT REQUIREMENTS AND POLICY

Provision or Clause	Source	Summary	Additional Agency Requirements
			modify existing data collection and recordkeeping practices by February 6, 2006, so contractors should initiate a comprehensive review of their selection, applicant tracking, and record retention processes promptly to ensure compliance with this new rule.
FAR 52.222-26 Equal Opportunity	FAR 22.810(e)	This clause is included in all solicitations and contracts unless the contract is exempt from all of the requirements of Executive Order 11246. The provision requires an offeror to comply with equal opportunity requirements promoting Government policy against discrimination and prohibiting the award of Government contracts to those who discriminate. The provision requires the offeror to agree that, during performance of the contract, it will not discriminate as to race, sex, color, religion or national origin. Further, the offeror agrees to take affirmative steps to ensure nondiscrimination, including the posting of notices to inform employees of whom to contact in cases of discrimination and that it will comply with the equal opportunity clause, as well as Executive Order 11246, as amended. Violation of this provision may result in annulment of the contract, suspension or debarment from Government contracting and subcontracting, civil monetary penalties under Executive Order 11246, publication of names of the noncomplying contractor, and criminal actions instituted by the Department of Justice and the Equal Employment Opportunity Commission (EEOC).	**NOTE:** Recently, the Office of Federal Contract Compliance Programs ("OFCCP") issued a final rule clarifying the definition of an "applicant" in the context of internet recruitment and amending recordkeeping requirements regarding internet applications. 70 Fed. Reg. 58946 (Oct. 7, 2005). This clarification narrows the applicant definition previously utilized by the OFCCP, but will require many contractors to modify existing data collection and recordkeeping practices by February 6, 2006, so contractors should initiate a comprehensive review of their selection, applicant tracking, and record retention processes promptly to ensure compliance with this new rule.

FEDERAL PROCUREMENT REQUIREMENTS AND POLICY

Provision or Clause	Source	Summary	Additional Agency Requirements
FAR 52.223-4 Recovered Material Certification	FAR 23.406(a)	A contractor must certify that it will use recovered materials (as defined in FAR 23.402) as required by applicable specifications.	
FAR 52.223-5 Pollution Prevention and Right-to-Know Information	FAR 23.1005	Executive Order 13148 requires Federal facilities to comply with the provisions of the Emergency Planning and Community Right-to-Know Act of 1986 (EPCRA) (42 U.S.C. 11001-11050) and the Pollution Prevention Act of 1990 (PPA) (42 U.S.C. 13101-13109). The contractor shall provide all information needed by the federal facility to comply with the following: (1) The emergency planning reporting requirements of Section 302 of EPCRA. (2) The emergency notice requirements of Section 304 of EPCRA. (3) The list of Material Safety Data Sheets, required by Section 311 of EPCRA. (4) The emergency and hazardous chemical inventory forms of Section 312 of EPCRA. (5) The toxic chemical release inventory of Section 313 of EPCRA, which includes the reduction and recycling information required by Section 6607 of PPA. (6) The toxic chemical, priority chemical, and hazardous substance release and use reduction goals of Sections 502 and 503 of Executive Order 13148.	Under DFARS § 209.405(b), the Procurement Cause and Treatment Code "H" annotation in the GSA List of Parties Excluded from Federal Procurement and Nonprocurement Programs identifies contractors that are declared ineligible for award of a contract or subcontract because of a violation of the Clean Air Act (42 U.S.C. 7606) or the Clean Water Act (33 U.S.C. 1368). Under 40 C.F.R. § 32.215(b), the agency head may grant an exception permitting award to a Code "H" ineligible contractor if it is in the paramount interest of the United States. Such agency head with this exception authority may be ranked no lower than a general or flag officer or a member of the Senior Executive Service. Furthermore, the official granting the exception must provide written notice to the Environmental Protection Agency debarring official.

Federal Regulation of Research Through Funding

FEDERAL PROCUREMENT REQUIREMENTS AND POLICY

Provision or Clause	Source	Summary	Additional Agency Requirements
FAR 52.223-6 Drug-Free Workplace	FAR 23.505	The contractor must establish a drug-free awareness program, prohibit drug use in the workplace, report any employee's drug-related conviction to the granting agency within ten days of the time it receives notice of the conviction, and sanction employees convicted of drug offenses, or require completion of a rehabilitation program.	DFARS 252.223-7004 (Drug-Free Work Force) NASA-ARS 1852.223-74 (Drug – and Alcohol- Free Workforce)
FAR 55.224-1 Privacy Act Notification	FAR 24.104(a)	The Contractor will be required to design, develop, or operate a system of records on individuals, to accomplish an agency function subject to the Privacy Act of 1974, Public Law 93-579, December 31, 1974 (5 U.S.C. 552a) and applicable agency regulations.	
FAR 55.224-2 Privacy Act Notification	FAR 24.104(b)	See above.	
FAR 55.225-2 Buy America Certificate	FAR 25.1101(a)(2)	The contractor certifies that offeror certifies that each end product of this provision (except those specifically listed), is a domestic end product and that the offeror has considered components of unknown origin to have been mined, produced, or manufactured outside the United States.	DFARS 252.225-7000 (Buy American Act – Balance of Payments Program Certificate); DFARS 225-7001 (Buy American Act - Balance of Payments Program)

FEDERAL PROCUREMENT REQUIREMENTS AND POLICY

Provision or Clause	Source	Summary	Additional Agency Requirements
FAR 55.227-1 Authorization and Consent	FAR 27.201-2(a)	The government authorizes and consents to all use and manufacture, in performing this contract or any subcontract at any tier, of any invention described in and covered by a United States patent (1) embodied in the structure or composition of any article the delivery of which is accepted by the government under this contract or (2) used in machinery, tools, or methods whose use necessarily results from compliance by the contractor or a subcontractor with (i) specifications or written provisions forming a part of this contract or (ii) specific written instructions given by the Contracting Officer directing the manner of performance. The entire liability to the Government for infringement of a patent of the United States shall be determined solely by the provisions of the indemnity clause, if any, included in this contract or any subcontract hereunder (including any lower-tier subcontract), and the Government assumes liability for all other infringement to the extent of the authorization and consent hereinabove granted. The contractor agrees to include, and require inclusion of, this clause, suitably modified to identify the parties, in all subcontracts at any tier for supplies or services (including construction, architect-engineer services, and materials, supplies, models, samples, and design or testing services expected to exceed the simplified acquisition threshold); however, omission of this clause from any subcontract, including those at or below the simplified acquisition threshold, does not affect this authorization and consent.	

FEDERAL PROCUREMENT REQUIREMENTS AND POLICY

Provision or Clause	Source	Summary	Additional Agency Requirements
FAR 55.227-2 Notice and Assistance Regarding Patent and Copyright Infringement	FAR 55.202-2	The Contractor shall report to the Contracting Officer, promptly and in reasonable written detail, each notice or claim of patent or copyright infringement based on the performance of this contract of which the Contractor has knowledge. The Contractor agrees to include, and require inclusion of, this clause in all subcontracts at any tier for supplies or services (including construction and architect-engineer subcontracts and those for material, supplies, models, samples, or design or testing services) expected to exceed the simplified acquisition threshold at FAR 2.101.	NASA-ARS 1852.227-84 (Patent Rights Clauses)
FAR 52.227-3 Patent Indemnity	FAR 27.203-1(b); FAR 27.203-2(a); FAR 27.203-4(a)(2)	The contractor shall indemnify the government and its officers, agents, and employees against liability, including costs, for infringement of any United States patent (except a patent issued upon an application that is now or may hereafter be withheld from issue pursuant to a Secrecy Order under 35 U.S.C. 181) arising out of the manufacture or delivery of supplies, the performance of services, or the construction, alteration, modification, or repair of real property (hereinafter referred to as "construction work") under this contract, or out of the use or disposal by or for the account of the Government of such supplies or construction work.	
FAR 55.227-5 Waiver of Indemnity	FAR 27.203-6	The government hereby authorizes and consents to the use and manufacture, solely in performing this contract, of any invention covered by the United States patents identified below and waives indemnification by the contractor that are specifically identified by the contracting officer.	

FEDERAL PROCUREMENT REQUIREMENTS AND POLICY

Provision or Clause	Source	Summary	Additional Agency Requirements
FAR 52.227-6 Royalty Information	FAR 27.204-2	When the response to a solicitation contains costs or charges for royalties totaling more than $250, specific information shall be included in the response relating to each separate item of royalty or license fee.	
FAR 55.227-7 Patents – Notice of Government Licensee	FAR 27.204-3(c)	The government is obligated to pay a royalty applicable to the proposed acquisition because of a license agreement between the Government and the patent owner.	
FAR 55.227-9 Refund of Royalties	FAR 27.206-2	The contractor shall furnish to the contracting officer, before final payment under this contract, a statement of royalties paid or required to be paid in connection with performing this contract and subcontracts hereunder together with the reasons. Such contractor will be compensated for royalties only to the extent that such royalties were included in the contract price and are determined by the contracting officer to be properly chargeable to the government and allocable to the contract. To the extent that any royalties that are included in the contract price are not in fact paid by the contractor or are determined by the contracting officer not to be properly chargeable to the government and allocable to the contract, the contract price shall be reduced.	
FAR 52.227-11 Patent Rights – Retention by the Contractor; FAR 52.227-12 Patent Rights – Retention by the Contractor (Long Form)	FAR 27.303(a); FAR 27.303(b)	Generally, these provisions preserve invention rights for contractors, and sometimes, employee inventors, provided that reporting, filing, and acknowledgement requirements are met. The Government retains a royalty-free license.	

FEDERAL PROCUREMENT REQUIREMENTS AND POLICY

Provision or Clause	Source	Summary	Additional Agency Requirements
FAR 52.227-13 Patent Rights – Acquisition by the Government	FAR 27.303(c)	The Contractor agrees to assign to the Government the entire right, title, and interest throughout the world in and to each subject invention, except to the extent that rights are retained by the Contractor under the following: With respect to each subject invention to which the Contractor retains principal or exclusive rights, the Contractor agrees as follows: (i) The Contractor hereby grants to the Government a nonexclusive, nontransferable, irrevocable, paid-up license to practice or have practiced each subject invention throughout the world by or on behalf of the Government of the United States (including any Government agency). (A) The contractor agrees that with respect to any subject invention in which it has acquired title, the federal agency has the right in accordance with the procedures in FAR 27.304-1(g) to require the contractor, an assignee, or exclusive licensee of a subject invention to grant a nonexclusive, partially exclusive, or exclusive license in any field of use to a responsible applicant or applicants, upon terms that are reasonable under the circumstances, and if the Contractor, assignee, or exclusive licensee refuses such a request, the Federal agency has the right to grant such a license itself; OR (B)Under the "greater rights determination," the contractor, or an employee-inventor after consultation with the contractor, may retain greater rights than the nonexclusive license, in accordance with the procedures of paragraph 27.304-1(a) of the FAR. A	

FEDERAL PROCUREMENT REQUIREMENTS AND POLICY

Provision or Clause	Source	Summary	Additional Agency Requirements
		request for a determination of whether the contractor or the employee-inventor is entitled to retain such greater rights must be submitted to the Head of the contracting agency or designee at the time of the first disclosure of the invention not later than 8 months thereafter, unless a longer period is authorized in writing by the contracting officer for good cause shown in writing by the contractor.	
FAR 52.229-3 Federal, State, and Local Taxes	FAR 29.401-3	Unless otherwise provided in this contract, the contract price includes all applicable Federal, State, and local taxes and duties. The government shall, without liability, furnish evidence appropriate to establish exemption from any Federal, State, or local tax when the contractor requests such evidence and a reasonable basis exists to sustain the exemption.	
FAR 52.229-4 Federal, State and Local Taxes (State and Local Adjustments)	FAR 29.401-3	Unless otherwise provided in this contract, the contract price includes all applicable Federal, State, and local taxes and duties. The contract price shall be increased by the amount of any after-imposed tax, or of any tax or duty specifically excluded from the contract price by a term or condition of this contract that the Contractor is required to pay or bear, including any interest or penalty, if the Contractor states in writing that the contract price does not include any contingency for such tax and if liability for such tax, interest, or penalty was not incurred through the Contractor's fault, negligence, or failure to follow instructions of the Contracting Officer. No adjustment shall be made in the contract price under this clause unless the amount of the adjustment exceeds $250.	

FEDERAL PROCUREMENT REQUIREMENTS AND POLICY

Provision or Clause	Source	Summary	Additional Agency Requirements
		The government shall furnish evidence appropriate to establish exemption from any Federal, State, or local tax when— (1) The Contractor requests such exemption and states in writing that it applies to a tax excluded from the contract price; and (2) A reasonable basis exists to sustain the exemption.	
FAR 52.230-1 Cost Accounting Standards Notices and Certification	FAR 30.201-3	The contractor must certify that it has submitted a written Disclosure Statement describing its cost accounting practices and that its practices are consistent with what is described in the Disclosure Statement. Any contract in excess of $500,000 is subject to the Cost Accounting Standards.	
FAR 52.230-2 Cost Accounting Standards	FAR 30.201-4(a)	Section IV.	
FAR 52.230-6 Administration of Cost Accounting Standards	FAR 30.201-4(d)	Section IV.	
FAR 52.232-2 Payments Under Fixed-Price Research and Development Contracts	FAR 32.111(a)(2)	Section IV.	
FAR § 47.402		Federal employees and their dependents, consultants, contractors, grantees, and others must use U.S.-flag air carriers for U.S. Government-financed international air travel and transportation of their personal effects or property, if available.	Guidelines for Implementation of the Fly America Act (B-138942), issued by the Comptroller General of the United States (March 31, 1981).

FEDERAL PROCUREMENT REQUIREMENTS AND POLICY

Provision or Clause	Source	Summary	Additional Agency Requirements
DFARS 252.235-7002	DFARS 235.071(a)	The contractor shall register its research facility with the Secretary of Agriculture in accordance with 7 U.S.C. 2316 and 9 CFR subpart C, and § 2.30, and furnish evidence of such registration to the contracting officer before beginning work under this contract. The contractor shall acquire animals only from dealers licensed by the Secretary of Agriculture under 7 U.S.C. 2133 and 9 CFR subpart A, § 2.1 through 2.11, or from sources that are exempt from licensing under those sections. The contractor agrees that the care and use of animals will conform with the pertinent laws of the United States and regulations of the Department of Agriculture (see 7 U.S.C. 2131 et. seq. and 9 CFR subchapter A, parts 1 through 4).	
HHSARS 352.270-8 Protection of Human Subjects	HHSARS 370.304	Notice to Offerors of Requirements of 45 CFR Part 46, Protection of Human Subjects (Jan. 2001) In accordance with 45 CFR Part 46, prospective contractors being considered for award shall be required to file with OPRR an acceptable Assurance of Compliance with the regulations, specifying review procedures and assigning responsibilities for the protection of human subjects. The initial and continuing review of a research project by an institutional review board shall assure that the rights and welfare of the human subjects involved are adequately protected, that the risks to the subjects are reasonable in relation to the potential benefits, if any, to the subjects and the importance of the knowledge to be gained, and	

FEDERAL PROCUREMENT REQUIREMENTS AND POLICY

Provision or Clause	Source	Summary	Additional Agency Requirements
		that informed consent will be obtained by methods that are adequate and appropriate. The contracting officer will direct the offeror/contractor to the OHRP IRB Registration and Assurance Filing website.	
HHSARS 352.270-9 Care of laboratory animals	HHSARS 370.404	Notice to Offerors of Requirement for Compliance with the Public Health Service Policy on Humane Care and Use of Laboratory Animals (Revised 1986, Reprinted 2000).	

Chapter VIII

Regulation of Preclinical Research

Daniel T. Pancamo
Counsel, Phelps Dunbar, L.L.P.
New Orleans, Louisiana

Preclinical research is one of the intermediate steps in the drug development process. It occupies the position between the discovery phase, which identifies a potential drug for therapy or cure of a disease, and Phase I clinical trials, which are trials on human subjects to test safety of an experimental drug. Preclinical research involves both in vitro testing (testing in the petri dish) and in vivo testing (testing in animal models) for the purpose of evaluating a potential drug's:

- toxicity (looking at a range of dosage levels and evaluating the effect of the drug's metabolic breakdown);
- specificity (the potential drug's ability to affect specific cells or tissues without affecting other cells and tissues); and
- blood absorption rates.

In very limited circumstances, preclinical research is also conducted as a precursor to the therapeutic use of a drug by humans when it would not be feasible or ethical to do clinical trials of that drug on humans. One of the benefits of preclinical research in animal models is that, given that the lifespan of experimental animals is generally shorter than that of humans, it enables investigators to evaluate a potential drug's effect over multiple generations within a relatively compressed time frame.

This chapter will address the major regulatory framework applicable to preclinical research, primarily as a matter of federal law, including the requirements for compliance and the penalties for noncompliance. It is conceptually useful to think of regulation of preclinical research in terms of three categories of regulatory protections: (1) protection of the animals used in biomedical research; (2) protection of the environment and public health; and (3) protection of the individuals actually conducting preclinical research and ancillary personnel. The chapter is organized along these categories. The order is completely arbitrary and one category should not be assumed to have priority over another (although a scientist once remarked to the author that his laboratory mice cost more than his postdoctoral fellows).

A. Animal Use in Biomedical Research and Testing

1. The Basic Regulatory Scheme—the Animal Welfare Act (7 U.S.C. §§ 2131-2159) and Regulations (9 C.F.R. Parts 1-4).

The use of animals in biomedical research and testing is highly regulated. Companies engaged in biomedical research and testing are required to comply with the Animal Welfare Act (AWA) and its accompanying regulations (the AWA Regulations). The AWA expresses congressional policy that the use of animals in research is critical for advancing the knowledge of cures and treatments for disease, and that measures that address the public's concern that laboratory animals are humanely treated are important in ensuring that such research will continue.

a. Overview of the AWA

The AWA is broad in its reach. It applies to any "research facility," which is defined as any school, institution, organization or person (which is further defined to include any legal entity) that uses live animals in research, testing or experiments, and that either purchases or transports live animals in commerce or receives funds under a grant, award, loan, or contract from an agency of the United States for the purpose of carrying out research, tests or experiments. The definition of "research facility" is sufficiently broad to apply to any private company using animals in biomedical research. The AWA protections extend to any warm-blooded animal, dead or alive (although it excludes rats and mice bred for use in research).

AWA administration falls within the jurisdiction of the Secretary of the U.S. Department of Agriculture (USDA). Under the AWA, the Secretary is directed to develop standards for the humane handling, care, and treatment of animals used in biomedical research. This includes basic requirements for handling, shelter, and feeding. With respect to research facilities, there are further requirements, which include:

- Ensuring that during experimental procedures, animal distress and pain are minimized, including providing adequate veterinary care and the appropriate use of anesthesia, pain relief, and, when appropriate, euthanasia.
- Consideration by the principal investigator of alternatives to any procedure likely to cause pain to an animal involved in an experiment.
- Consultation with a veterinarian regarding any procedure likely to cause pain, including the consideration of anesthesia, pain relief, and presurgical and postsurgical care in accordance with established veterinary medical practices.

While the AWA establishes minimum standards for all covered research or experimental procedures, the act expressly provides that it does not preempt or prohibit any state or political subdivision from developing and implementing additional or more stringent standards. Thus, research facilities will also need to ensure compliance at the state and local levels.

The AWA also contains express limitations on the USDA's authority. The Secretary is not authorized to promulgate rules and regulations concerning the focus or goals of actual research or experimentation by a research facility. Thus, the Secretary cannot prescribe the content of research, or the parameters of an experiment. Additionally, the USDA is not authorized, during the performance of an inspection, to interrupt the conduct of actual research or experimentation.

The AWA empowers the USDA to make such inspections as the USDA deems necessary to determine whether a research facility is in compliance with the AWA. USDA officials are granted access at all reasonable times to the research facility, its animals, and the research facility's records to ensure compliance. Further, the USDA is required to inspect each research facility at least annually. If violations are noted, the USDA may conduct follow-up investigations. USDA officials may confiscate any animal found to be suffering due to a research facility's failure to comply with the AWA.

The AWA requires that each research facility register with the USDA. The specific registration requirements are discussed more fully below in the overview of key regulations. In addition, each research facility is required to establish an institutional animal care and use committee (IACUC). In a nutshell, the IACUC is charged with ensuring the research facility's compliance with the AWA and its accompanying regulations. The composition and specific obligations of the IACUC, and the critical role it serves, are described more fully below.

Penalties for violation of the AWA can be severe. Any research facility that violates the AWA or the AWA Regulations may be assessed a civil penalty of up to $2,500 for each violation, and the Secretary may issue a cease and desist order in connection with the violation. Each violation and each day during which a violation continues are considered a separate offense. In establishing a penalty, the Secretary may consider the size of the business of the person involved, the gravity of the violation, the person's good faith, and its history of previous violations. Prior to assessing any penalty or issuing a cease and desist order, the violator must be given notice and an opportunity for a hearing. The Secretary's order is final and conclusive unless the violator files an appeal with the applicable U.S. Courts of Appeals, which have exclusive jurisdiction to determine the validity of any such order. The appeal must be brought within 60 days after entry of the Secretary's order. In addition to the foregoing civil penalties, if a violator knowingly fails to obey a cease and desist order, the violator shall be subject to a civil penalty of $1,500 for each offense, and for each day the failure continues. Finally, any person who assaults, resists, intimidates or interferes with an inspecting USDA official may be fined up to $5,000, or imprisoned up to three years, or both; if a deadly or dangerous weapon is used in the commission of such acts, the person can be fined up to $10,000 or imprisoned up to 10 years, or both.

The AWA recognizes that animal research can generate proprietary information and data deserving of intellectual property protection. Accordingly, the AWA makes it unlawful for any member of the IACUC to release any confidential information of the research facility, including:

- Trade secrets, processes, operations, styles of work, or apparatus.
- The identity, confidential statistical data, and amount or source of any income, profits, losses or expenditures of the research facility.

Additionally, it is unlawful for any IACUC member to use such information to his or her advantage, or to reveal such information to another person. An IACUC member who violates the foregoing is subject to removal from the IACUC, a fine of up to $1,000, and imprisonment of up to one year; if the violation is willful, the fine may be up to $10,000 with potential imprisonment of up to three years. A research facility injured by reason of a violation may recover all actual and consequential damages it sustains, as well as reasonable attorneys' fees. This remedy is not exclusive, and is in addition to any other remedies available to the research facility. Given the potentially serious consequences—both to the research facility and to the IACUC member—resulting from a disclosure of confidential information (whether inadvertent or willful), each IACUC member, as a condition to joining the IACUC, should be required to sign a written acknowledgment of his or her responsibilities with respect to confidential information, which expressly sets forth the possible consequences of a violation.

b. *Overview of the AWA Regulations*

i. General Overview

The rules, regulations, and standards promulgated by the Secretary in connection with the AWA are found in Title 9 of the *Code of Federal Regulations*, Chapter I, Subchapter A, Parts 1-4. Part 1 includes the definition of terms used in the AWA Regulations. Part 3 sets forth the standards, which are specific requirements with respect to housing, handling, care, and treatment that research facilities must comply with. Each Subpart of Part 3 sets forth specifications for the handling, care, treatment, and transportation of different species of animals (for example, Subpart A sets forth specifications for dogs and cats; Subpart D sets forth specifications for nonhuman primates). Part 4 sets forth the rules of practice governing proceedings under the AWA as applied by the Animal and Plant Health Inspection Service of the U.S. Department of Agriculture (APHIS), the division within the USDA charged with enforcing the AWA. Part 2 contains the heart of the AWA Regulations, and for purposes of this chapter the key regulations are found in Subpart C, which are the regulations applicable to research facilities.

ii. Registration

The first key set of regulations applicable to a research facility are those pertaining to registration. Each research facility is required to register with the Secretary by completing a prescribed registration form. The form is provided by the AC Regional Director, who is the person in charge of the official work of APHIS in the particular state in which the research facility has its principal place of business. The registration form, when completed, is filed with the AC Regional Director. The registration form must be signed by an official with the legal authority to bind the research facility (under the AWA Regulations, this person is designated as the "institutional official"). As a general proposition, a subsidiary of a business corporation, rather than the parent corporation, is registered as a research facility. At the time the registration form is filed, the research facility must acknowledge its receipt from APHIS of a set of the AWA Regulations and must sign a form agreeing to comply with them; the form is filed with the AC Regional Director. It should be noted that there is an Eastern and Western region in APHIS; the research facility needs to check the APHIS Web site to determine which region its particular state of operation falls under.

iii. The IACUC

The second key set of regulations applicable to a research facility are those applicable to its IACUC. The IACUC is the cornerstone of a research facility's compliance with the AWA, and an effective compliance program will depend directly upon an effective IACUC. The purpose of the IACUC in general is to assess and monitor the research facility's animal programs, facilities, and procedures. Comparable to the limitations placed on the Secretary of the USDA, the IACUC may not prescribe methods or set standards for the design, conduct or performance of research or experimentation.

Under the AWA Regulations, the IACUC must have at least three members, who are appointed by the chief executive officer of the research facility. The minimum membership consists of a chairman and at least two additional members. At least one member of the IACUC must be a doctor of veterinary medicine, trained or experienced in laboratory animal science and medicine, who has program responsibility for the animals involved in research and experimentation at the research facility. Another committee member must be a person completely unaffiliated with the research facility (it is the intention that this person represent the interest of the general community). If the IACUC has more than three members, no more than three members may be from the same administrative unit of the research facility.

The IACUC is charged with very specific obligations under the AWA Regulations, including:

- A review, at least once every six months, of the research facility's program for the care and use of its animals.
- An inspection, at least once every six months, of the research facility's animal facilities.
- Preparation of semiannual reports documenting its evaluations of the research facility's programs and animal facilities. Reports must be signed by a majority of the IACUC members and must document any deficiencies, with a plan and schedule to correct deficiencies. A deficiency that remains uncorrected for 15 business days must be reported to APHIS and any federal agency, such as the National Institutes of Health (NIH), that may be funding the particular research activity in which the deficiency is noted.
- Review and investigate complaints from the public and from laboratory personnel concerning noncompliance.
- Make recommendations to the institutional official concerning the research facility's animal program, facilities or personnel training.
- Under appropriate circumstances, suspend research activities.

With respect to procedures involving animals, the IACUC must determine that:

- The procedures are designed to avoid or minimize pain. A procedure is deemed "painful" if it is reasonably expected to cause more than slight or momentary pain in humans.
- The principal investigator has considered alternatives to procedures that may cause more than slight or momentary pain to the animals, and that the principal investigator has provided written assurance that the research activities are not unnecessarily duplicative of previous experiments.
- If a procedure may result in more than slight or momentary pain, it must be performed with appropriate anesthetics and analgesics, and in consultation with the attending veterinarian.
- Medical care for the animals will be available by a qualified veterinarian.
- Personnel conducting procedures will be appropriately trained.
- Research involving surgery must provide for pre-operative and post-operative care in accordance with established veterinary medical practice. Major operative procedures must be performed in dedicated facilities with the use of sterile instruments, surgical gloves and masks, and aseptic procedures. However, procedures involving rodents, a mainstay of preclinical research, do not require dedicated facilities, but must be performed under aseptic conditions.

The foregoing review must be done in advance of any such research activity taking place, and written descriptions of all such activities must be made available to all IACUC members. Any IACUC member can request full IACUC review of a proposed research activity. If full IACUC review is not requested, the chairman of the IACUC must designate at least one qualified member of the IACUC to conduct the review. If full IACUC review is requested, the proposed research activity may be approved only upon the majority vote of a quorum of the IACUC, at a meeting convened to specifically review such activity. IACUC members having a potentially conflicting interest in the activity are prohibited from reviewing or approving that activity. The IACUC must notify the principal investigator in writing of its decision to approve or disapprove a proposed research activity involving animals, and if the IACUC disapproves a proposed research activity, it must give the principal investigator written reasons for disapproval together with

Regulation of Preclinical Research

an opportunity for the principal investigator to respond in person or in writing. The IACUC must conduct continuing reviews of such activities at appropriate intervals and at least annually, and may suspend any activity it previously approved if it determines that the activity is not being conducted pursuant to the approved parameters. Any suspension of a research activity must be reported to APHIS and any federal agency that may be funding the particular research activity.

As described above, the IACUC has substantial responsibilities. Those responsibilities, together with the significant penalties that may be imposed for violation of the AWA and the AWA Regulations, should be clearly understood by each prospective member of the IACUC before he or she is appointed to the IACUC.

In addition to the IACUC requirements and obligations imposed by the AWA and the AWA Regulations, federal agencies such as NIH that award grants involving animal research have specific requirements relating to the IACUC. This is discussed more fully below. Lawyers advising entities that are conducting animal research need to be conversant with both sets of requirements.

iv. Personnel Qualifications, Veterinary Care, Record Keeping

In addition to the registration and IACUC requirements, the AWA Regulations impose specific rules regarding personnel qualifications, veterinary care, record keeping and reporting, and access by APHIS officials. These requirements are summarized briefly below.

With respect to personnel qualification, the research facility is obligated to ensure that all of its personnel involved in animal care and use (including both scientists and research technicians) are qualified to perform their duties. The research facility must provide training and instruction to its personnel, including guidance in:

- Humane methods of animal experimentation.
- Pre-procedural and post-procedural care of animals, and aseptic surgical methods.
- The use of research methods that limit animal use or minimize pain.
- Proper use of anesthetics and analgesics.
- Methods for reporting deficiencies.

The AWA Regulations expressly prohibit discrimination and reprisals against research facility employees, lab personnel and IACUC members who report violations of the AWA and the AWA Regulations.

The research facility is obligated to have an attending veterinarian to provide veterinary care for the laboratory animals. The veterinarian must be employed by the research facility under a "formal arrangement"; if the veterinarian is part-time, the formal arrangement must include regularly scheduled visits. The attending veterinarian must be a voting member of the IACUC.

The AWA Regulations establish fairly extensive record keeping and reporting requirements applicable to research facilities. Each research facility is required to maintain the following IACUC records:

- Minutes of IACUC meetings.
- Records of proposed research activities involving animals and any proposed significant changes.
- Records of semiannual IACUC reports and recommendations.

All records must be maintained for at least three years. Records relating to a proposed research activity must be retained for the duration of the activity, and for an additional three years thereafter. All records must be available for inspection and copying by APHIS officials and the representative of any federal agency providing funding for a particular research activity. APHIS officials are obligated to respect the confidentiality of such records and may not remove them from the research facility's premises, unless the records relate to an alleged violation and are needed in connection with an enforcement action. The release of records containing privileged or confidential trade secrets or commercial or financial information is governed by the Freedom of Information Act and the Federal Trade Secrets Act.

The research facility is further obligated to provide an annual report of its activities to the AC Regional Director of the state in which the research facility is located. The report must be submitted by December 1 of each calendar year, and must be signed and certified by the research facility's chief executive officer or institutional official. Among other things, the report must:

- Assure that the research facility followed professionally accepted standards governing care, treatment and use of animals.
- Assure that each principal investigator has considered alternatives to painful procedures.
- Assure that the research facility is complying with the AWA and the AWA Regulations.
- State the location of all facilities where animals were housed or used in research or experimentation.

Finally, each research facility is obligated to provide APHIS officials with access to both its physical facilities and its records to ensure compliance with the AWA and the AWA Regulations. Among other things, APHIS officials may enter a research facility's premises during business hours and examine and make copies of records, inspect facilities in animals, and document noncompliance. APHIS officials are empowered to correct instances of noncompliance on the inspection site, including requiring that a suffering animal's pain be alleviated or that an animal be euthanized; additionally, an APHIS official may confiscate animals if a research facility fails to comply with a request to correct a violation.

c. Implementation and Enforcement of the AWA and the AWA Regulations by the USDA Animal and Plant Health Inspection Service (APHIS)

As discussed above, APHIS has the responsibility to implement and enforce the AWA and the AWA Regulations. In this regard, there are a few items that research facilities should take note of that will aid them in their efforts to effect compliance. APHIS has an *Animal Care Policy Manual*[1] that outlines its policies on a number of topics. Policy Number 15, dated April 14, 1997, addresses IACUC membership. Additionally, APHIS has prepared a set of *Institutional Animal Care and Use Committee (IACUC) Guidelines*,[2] in a check-the-box format, that provides a helpful checklist for IACUC members; the checklist is cross-referenced against the applicable AWA Regulation (see APHIS § 41-35-036). Policy Number 17, dated March 17, 1999, addresses the annual report that research facilities are obligated to submit to the applicable AC Regional Office responsible for the state in which the research facility is located. Among other things, it describes the APHIS forms that must be used and includes instructions on completing the forms. Finally, the APHIS Animal Care section has prepared a *Research Manual*[3] which includes a "Research Facility Inspection Guide"; the purpose of this document is to establish a reference guide for APHIS officials for the inspection of USDA-registered research facilities. Sections include registration; conducting the inspection (along with pre- and post-inspection procedures); physical facilities and husbandry; veterinary care; and IACUC membership and functions. Research facilities and their IACUCs would be well advised to be familiar with the Inspection Guide and to be proactive in addressing areas of potential noncompliance.

2. U.S. Government Principles for the Utilization and Care of Vertebrate Animals Used in Testing, Research and Training (50 Fed. Reg. 20, 864-02 (1985))

Under the U.S. Government Principles for the Utilization and Care of Vertebrate Animals Used in Testing, Research and Training (the U.S. Government Principles), federal agencies that develop requirements for research involving animals must consider nine principles, and when any such agency sponsors research, the responsible official of the agency must ensure compliance with those principles. For example, the NIH has promulgated policies both for extramural and intramural research involving animals; the policies concerning extramural research are discussed more fully below. Any researcher conducting federally funded animal research should be aware of the U.S. Government Principles, including:

- The care and use of animals should be in accordance with the AWA.
- Prior to their performance, researchers conducting procedures involving animals should consider their relevance to human or animal health, the advancement of knowledge or the good of society.
- The minimum number of animals required to obtain valid results should be used.
- The avoidance or minimization of pain is imperative.
- Procedures that may cause more than momentary or slight pain should be performed with appropriate sedation, analgesics or anesthetics.
- Euthanasia must be considered if an animal is likely to suffer chronic or severe pain subsequent to a procedure.

- There should be species-specific appropriate housing and veterinary care.
- The principal investigator and other personnel engaged in the research must be appropriately qualified.
- Exceptions to the U.S. Government Principles must be considered by an IACUC, not the investigators involved in the research.

3. Memorandum of Understanding Among APHIS/USDA, the FDA and the NIH

Effective January 1, 2001, APHIS, the Food and Drug Administration (FDA) and the NIH entered into a *Memorandum of Understanding*[4] concerning laboratory animal welfare. The memo was extended for an additional five years, effective February 14, 2006. While acknowledging that each agency has necessary operational differences, the three agencies nonetheless recognized that each share a common concern for the care and use of laboratory animals. Further, while the AWA and the AWA Regulations assign primary responsibility to APHIS for enforcement, there is recognition by the three agencies that a shared perspective on standards of laboratory animal care and use presents a consistent federal approach, and should help entities engaged in animal research comply with applicable requirements. Given that the AWA and the AWA Regulations are largely predicated on voluntary compliance (albeit with APHIS enforcement and a fairly stringent set of penalties for violations), a uniform federal approach by key agencies can give companies engaged in animal research a road map for compliance and a degree of predictability in dealing with these agencies on issues relating to animal research. Under the Memorandum of Understanding, the three agencies agree to do the following:

- Share information contained in their respective registries and listing the organizations under their purview.
- Provide one another with information concerning adverse findings regarding animal care and use at organizations that have been investigated or inspected, and any agency action that may have been taken.

- Provide one another with information regarding evidence of serious noncompliance with required standards for laboratory animal care.
- Avoid redundant evaluations of the same organization.
- Consult and coordinate with one another on regulatory or policy proposals and significant policy interpretations involving laboratory animal care.
- Provide each other with resource persons for scientific and educational information related to laboratory animal welfare.

This interagency cooperation is no small matter. Companies would be well advised to consider that an instance of serious noncompliance reported by one agency (for example, the NIH) could have material adverse consequences for the company in its subsequent dealings with another agency (for example, the FDA).

4. NIH Considerations

a. Health Research Extension Act; NIH

Having examined the AWA and the AWA Regulations, the U.S. Government Principles, and the Memorandum of Understanding among APHIS, the NIH, and the FDA, it is beneficial to look briefly at the individual policies and requirements of the NIH, the FDA, and the Centers for Disease Control and Prevention (CDC) concerning laboratory animals. An understanding of the requirements applicable from the NIH's perspective begins with the Health Research Extension Act of 1985 (Pub. L. 99-158, Section 402(b)(6)). Under the Health Research Extension Act of 1985, the Secretary of the U.S. Department of Health and Human Services, acting through the Director of the NIH, is required to establish guidelines for the care and use of animals in biomedical research and for the organization of IACUCs. The Director of the NIH is obligated to require each applicant for a grant, contract or cooperative agreement involving research on animals that is administered by the NIH to include in its application or proposal: (i) assurances that the applicant will meet the standards governing the care of animals and biomedical research, that the investigators will be appropriately trained, and that an IACUC will be in place; and (ii) a statement of the reasons for the use of animals in the research to be funded by the NIH. The Director can revoke a grant or contract if applicable standards are not being met or if any required corrective action is not undertaken. Comparable to what is provided in the AWA, the guidelines cannot be construed to prescribe methods of research, nor may they be used to require a research entity to disclose trade secrets or commercial or financial information that is privileged or confidential. It should be noted that the Health Research Extension Act of 1985 constitutes a second law obligating entities engaged in preclinical research involving animals to establish an IACUC (in addition to the requirements of the AWA).

b. NIH Extramural Research

NIH extramural research is subject to the Public Health Service Policy on the Humane Care and Use of Laboratory Animals (the "PHS Policy"), which was created by the Public Health Service of the U.S. Department of Health and Human Services to implement and supplement the U.S. Government Principles (the Public Health Service exists under the U.S. Department of Health and Human Services and includes, among other agencies, the NIH, the FDA, and the CDC). By its terms, the PHS Policy applies to all PHS-conducted or -supported research involving animals (see 42 C.F.R. § 52.8). The PHS Policy does not supplant the AWA, nor does it preempt applicable state or local law, which may be more stringent. It is administered by the Office of Laboratory Animal Welfare (OLAW) at the NIH.

Under the PHS Policy, no research activity involving animals may be supported by the NIH until the "institution" (defined as any public or private organization, business or agency) has provided the requisite "assurance" (defined as the documentation from an institution assuring compliance with the PHS Policy) to the OLAW. The assurance must be signed by an individual with the legal authority to commit on behalf of the institution that the PHS Policy requirements shall be met. The assurance can be thought of as the functional equivalent of the USDA registration requirement under the AWA. Among other things, the assurance must:

- Describe the institution's program for the care and use of laboratory animals.

- State whether the institution's program and facilities either are accredited by the Association for Assessment and Accreditation of Laboratory Animals Care International, or are evaluated by the institution's IACUC.
- State the names, titles, and credentials of the IACUC chairperson and members.

An IACUC's obligations under the PHS Policy generally parallel those set forth in the AWA and the AWA Regulations, including the record-keeping and reporting requirements (with the OLAW having basically the same rights to review records and reports as APHIS). However, there are some differences with respect to the IACUC's composition. Under the PHS Policy, there must be at least five rather than three members, which must include: (i) a doctor of veterinary medicine; (ii) one practicing scientist experienced in research involving animals; (iii) a member whose primary concerns are nonscientific (the examples given include ethicist, lawyer, and clergyman); and (iv) an individual completely unaffiliated with the institution. Finally, under the PHS Policy, the OLAW has essentially the same rights to investigate allegations of noncompliance and to conduct inspections of an institution's facilities as does ASPHIS under the AWA and the AWA regulations.

It should be further noted that, as set forth in the NIH Grants Policy Statement (December 1, 2003), the NIH will not make an award for research unless the applicant organization has filed the required assurance with the OLAW and has provided verification that its IACUC has reviewed and approved those portions of its applications pertaining to the use of live vertebrate animals.

c. Guide for the Care and Use of Laboratory Animals; Institutional Animal Care and Use Committee Guidebook

Another important feature of the PHS Policy is that the IACUC is required to develop and implement its program for laboratory animals in accordance with the *Guide for the Care and Use of Laboratory Animals,*[5] prepared by the National Research Counsel and published by the National Academy Press. The stated purpose of the Guide is "to assist institutions in caring for and using animals in ways judged to be scientifically, technically, and humanely appropriate." While the Guide must be adhered to in connection with all PHS-conducted or -supported research, it is intended for a wider audience; that is, any institution or setting in which animals are used for research, teaching and testing. As such, it is intended to be a primary reference, and would be an essential tool for any IACUC. It is divided into four major chapters, covering: (i) institutional policies and responsibilities; (ii) animal environment, housing and management; (iii) veterinary medical care; and (iv) physical plant. Each chapter provides an extensive set of references, and the Guide also contains an extremely comprehensive bibliography. The Guide expressly points out in a number of places that to the extent it makes recommendations different from the requirements of the AWA or the PHS Policy, any entity covered by the AWA or the PHS Policy requirements, as applicable, must adhere to them.

One excellent resource is the *Institutional Animal Care and Use Committee Guidebook*[6] (2d Edition 2002), prepared by OLAW and the Applied Research Ethics National Association. It is both reader-friendly and extremely comprehensive, covering a broad range of topics that are essential to an IACUC member's understanding of his or her responsibilities and obligations.

5. FDA Considerations

For the most part, FDA jurisdiction arises at the Phase I clinical trial stage in the drug development process. However, the FDA, in a position paper dated October 1992, acknowledges that animal testing is often necessary to ensure product safety and, accordingly, that it adheres to and supports all applicable laws relating to animal testing, including the AWA. Additionally, as a Public Health Service agency, any animal research done in connection with an application for a research permit or a permit for marketing a regulated product must be conducted in accordance with the PHS Policy (and, by virtue of its incorporation into the PHS Policy, the *Guide for the Care and Use of Laboratory Animals*).

Given that preclinical research is a necessary condition precedent to Phase I clinical trials, the FDA has prescribed good laboratory practices for conducting "nonclinical laboratory studies." The FDA defines these as in vivo or in vitro experiments (in which test articles are studied prospectively in test systems under laboratory conditions to determine their safety) to support applications for research or marketing permits for FDA-regulated products. Entities conducting preclinical research that intend to qualify their research for clinical trials must comply with these regulations.

6. CDC Considerations

The CDC, as a Public Health Service agency, requires that any research involving animals that it funds must comply with all federal law applicable to animal care and use (including the AWA and the Health Research Extension Act of 1985) and must conform to the PHS Policy.

7. State Law

A review of applicable state law on animal care and use in biomedical research is beyond the scope of this chapter. The reader is referred to *State Laws Concerning the Use of Animals in Research*,[7] published by the National Association for Biomedical Research, as a reference source for individual state law.

8. Conclusion

As noted at the outset of this chapter, biomedical research using laboratory animals is highly regulated. The failure to comply with applicable rules and standards can have severe consequences, including enforcement actions resulting in fines and prison terms and the loss of research funding. The good news is that there are substantial resources available for entities involved in biomedical research using laboratory animals, much of it available over the Internet. Both APHIS and the OLAW have exceptionally detailed Web sites with an abundance of resources concerning laboratory animal care and use. Additionally, IACUC members should be aware of the Web site maintained by the American Association for Laboratory Animal Science (www.IACUC.org), which is another excellent and comprehensive resource.

B. Other Regulatory Schemes Applicable to Preclinical Research—Protection of the Environment and Public Heath

1. Introduction

One of the most daunting challenges facing entities engaged in the conduct of preclinical research is compliance with the welter of federal and state regulations concerning protection of the environment and protection of public health. An entity conducting preclinical research may generate materials and waste that are potentially hazardous, including toxic, corrosive, flammable and mutagenic chemicals, radioactive materials, infectious agents including viruses and bacteria, and recombinant DNA. There is an enormous number of potentially applicable federal, state and local laws that may govern. Further, there are multiple agencies at the federal, state and local level to which the research entity may need to report its activities and that may have enforcement authority over the research entity. At the federal level, these agencies might include the Environmental Protection Agency (EPA), the Nuclear Regulatory Commission (NRC), the Department of Transportation (DOT), the Department of Health and Human Services (DHHS), the USDA, and the CDC. These agencies may have overlapping jurisdiction, and at the same time may have inconsistent policy interpretations and enforcement practices. In sum, it creates a potential regulatory minefield for entities conducting preclinical research.

This section of the chapter will focus on environmental protection and enforcement by the EPA, along with some of the potential problems in applying environmental law in a research setting. Additionally, this section of the chapter will focus on public health considerations implicated by preclinical research, and specifically the constraints imposed by the Public Health Security and Bioterrorism Preparedness and Response Act of 2002 (Pub. L. 107-188) and the implementing regulations published by the CDC.

2. EPA Jurisdiction and RCRA

This discussion will begin with a brief overview of the EPA's jurisdiction and some of the basic concepts set forth in the Resource Conservation and Recovery Act of 1976 (42 U.S.C. §§ 6901, *et seq.*) and its accompanying regulations (RCRA), as applicable to preclinical research.[8] RCRA and its regulations are voluminous and it is not possible to summarize them here. Thus, the focus of this section will be limited to those provisions of RCRA that may affect preclinical research.

RCRA was passed to address the increase in the amount of solid waste produced by the American population requiring disposal in landfills and dumping sites, and to create a regulatory scheme for the handling and disposal of hazardous wastes that pose a substantial threat to human health and the environment. RCRA gives the EPA the authority to regulate and control hazardous waste from "the cradle to the grave," including the generation, transportation, treatment, storage, and disposal of hazardous waste. In general, our concern is with the status of entities conducting preclinical research as "generators" of hazardous waste.

Under RCRA, a person generating hazardous waste is obligated to report to the EPA the activity giving rise to the generation of such waste. To determine whether or not an entity conducting preclinical research falls under the EPA's RCRA jurisdiction, that entity, as the "person" generating the waste, must first determine whether the waste it is generating is hazardous waste. The following RCRA definitions specify what waste constitutes "hazardous waste":

> "Hazardous Waste" means a solid waste, or combination of solid wastes, which because of its quantity, concentration, or physical, chemical, or infectious characteristics may—
> (A) cause, or significantly contribute to an increase in mortality or an increase in serious irreversible, or incapacitating reversible, illness; or
> (B) pose a substantial present or potential hazard to human health or the environment when improperly treated, stored, transported, or disposed of, or otherwise managed.

> "Solid waste" means any garbage, refuse, sludge from a waste treatment plant, water supply treatment plant, or air pollution control facility and other discarded material, including solid, liquid, semisolid, or contained gaseous material resulting from industrial, commercial, mining, and agricultural operations.

In a nutshell, the person charged with making the determination of whether a waste is hazardous must first determine whether the waste is excluded from regulation. If it is not excluded, that person must then determine whether the waste is listed as a hazardous waste in the RCRA regulations, and if it is not listed, whether it nonetheless meets the requirements of being considered as a hazardous waste. The reader should note that, in the Appendix to Part 260 (Hazardous Waste Management System: General) of C.F.R. Title 40, there are a series of helpful flowcharts that aid in the determination of whether a particular waste is hazardous and in the identification of the particular regulations applicable to an entity's activities in connection with hazardous waste. The definition of "person" includes an individual, firm, corporation, partnership and association, and accordingly is not limited to a specific individual. Thus, even though an individual researcher conducting preclinical research may actually generate hazardous waste, under the regulations it is permissible for another individual (for example, an entity's environmental compliance officer) to make the determination as to whether a particular waste is a hazardous waste, provided that both individuals are part of the same "person" (that is, the entity conducting the preclinical research). Indeed, the EPA recommends that in laboratory settings, hazardous waste determination ideally is a collaborative effort between the individual researcher and the environmental compliance officer.

To help parties determine whether or not wastes that they are generating are hazardous, the EPA has established and/or designated:

- Criteria for identifying the characteristics of hazardous waste and for listing particular hazardous wastes (e.g., it contains a toxic constituent listed in Appendix VIII of 40 C.F.R. Part 261).
- The characteristics of hazardous waste (e.g., ignitability, corrosiveness, reactivity, and toxicity).
- Lists of particular solid wastes that qualify as hazardous wastes, with certain exclusions referenced in Appendix IX to 40 C.F.R. Part 261.

Title 40, Part 261 of the Code contains extensive regulations concerning the identification and listing of hazardous waste. The EPA has further established particular testing procedures for evaluating the extent to which waste materials exhibit the characteristics of, or otherwise qualify as, hazardous wastes. These procedures appear in certain Appendices to Part 261 of Title 40. The regulations, however, also allow for parties to petition to use "equivalent" testing or analytical methods to determine whether a waste is hazardous.

Assuming that an entity conducting preclinical research is generating hazardous waste, it must also determine its particular generator status. Among other things, this status will determine certain reporting requirements and the length of time it is permitted to accumulate hazardous waste on-site. There are three categories of generator; which category an entity conducting preclinical research will fall into depends upon the amount of hazardous waste the entity generates *each month*. The categories are (1) large quantity generators (LQG), (2) small quantity generators (SQG), and (3) conditionally exempt small quantity generators (CESQG), each of which is discussed briefly below.

LQGs are generators that generate 1,000 kilograms or more of hazardous waste per month, or more than 1 kilogram of acutely hazardous waste per month (an acutely hazardous waste is one found to be fatal to humans in low doses or capable of causing or significantly contributing to an increase in serious irreversible or incapacitating reversible illness). LQGs are permitted to accumulate hazardous waste on-site for up to 90 days. Waste must be accumulated in closed containers that are labeled and marked with the date that accumulation began. LQGs are required to have an employee available to respond to emergencies who can coordinate all emergency responses. Additionally, they are required to have a formal, written emergency response contingency plan and a formal training program for the proper handling of hazardous wastes. Finally, they are required to provide a biennial hazardous waste report.

SQGs are generators that generate more than 100 kilograms but less than 1,000 kilograms of hazardous waste per month. SQGs are permitted to accumulate hazardous waste on-site for up to 180 days, or up to 270 days if they will be transporting hazardous wastes off-site a distance greater than 200 miles. SQGs may not accumulate more than 6,000 kilograms of hazardous wastes at any time. They must have an employee serve as emergency response coordinator; however, they are not required to have formal written contingency plans or a formal training program. Additionally, SQGs are exempt from the biennial hazardous waste report requirement.

CESQGs are generators that generate 100 kilograms or less of hazardous waste per month or 1 kilogram or less of acutely hazardous waste per month. CESQGs are permitted to accumulate waste on-site for up to 90 days; they may not accumulate more than 1,000 kilograms of hazardous waste at any time. Significantly, CESQGs are exempt from the regulations under Part 262 (Standards Applicable to Generators of Hazardous Waste) of C.F.R. Title 40, but are nonetheless required to identify their hazardous waste, to comply with the storage limit requirements, and to ensure that the hazardous waste they generate is delivered to an approved facility for treatment or disposal.

To the extent the applicable accumulation limits imposed on CESQGs or SQGs are exceeded, or to the extent the applicable time limits imposed on SQGs or LQGs are exceeded, the sites are then deemed to be storage facilities. A storage permit will be required, and additional regulatory burdens relating to standards applicable to owners and operators of hazardous waste treatment, storage, and disposal facilities will be imposed under 42 U.S.C. §§ 6924 and 6925 and 40 C.F.R. Parts 264, 265 and 270.

It should further be noted that a research facility may accumulate up to 55 gallons of hazardous waste or up to one quart of certain specifically identified acutely hazardous waste at the point of generation, provided the hazardous waste is accumulated in containers marked "hazardous waste." If the "satellite accumulation" provisions of RCRA apply, the containment and record-keeping requirements are somewhat reduced. However, if the maximum quantities of hazardous waste or acutely hazardous waste are exceeded, the research facility then has three days within which to comply with the full-blown requirements.

Finally, it should be noted that the determination of whether a facility is a LQG, SQG, or CESQG is made on a *monthly* basis. Accordingly, the facility's category, and its corresponding regulatory obligations, can change from month to month. As discussed below, in the context of a research facility or laboratory engaged in preclinical research, this can become highly problematic.

Having briefly reviewed the determination of what constitutes a hazardous waste that subjects a research facility's preclinical research activities to the EPA's RCRA jurisdiction, and the particular categories of "generator" that may be applicable to a research facility, it is beneficial to review in summary form the standards applicable to hazardous waste generators. The standards are set forth in Part 262 of C.F.R. Title 40. The reader should bear in mind that, as the name suggests, conditionally exempt small quantity generators are exempt from compliance with Part 262. The reader should further bear in mind, however, that the requirements to obtain CESQG status are not straightforward in their application, and CESQG status can change at any time the quantity limits are exceeded.

There are essentially four sets of standards that generators must comply with, although the level of compliance depends in part on the generator's status as either a SQG or LQG. They are: (i) general requirements, including the requirements for EPA identification numbers; (ii) manifest requirements for off-site transportation of hazardous materials; (iii) pre-transport requirements, which govern, among other things, labeling and accumulation of hazardous materials on-site; and (iv) record-keeping and reporting requirements.

Under the general requirements, a generator is prohibited from treating, storing, disposing of or transporting hazardous waste unless it has received an EPA identification number from the EPA. Further, a generator is prohibited from offering its hazardous waste to a transporter or to a treatment, storage or disposal facility that has not received an EPA identification number. This enables the EPA to monitor generators and the quantities of hazardous waste they are generating.

Under the manifest requirements, a generator who transports hazardous waste for off-site treatment, storage or disposal must prepare a detailed manifest on the EPA's prescribed form. Among other things, the manifest must: (i) designate the facility permitted to handle the waste described on the manifest, and designate an alternate facility if the primary facility is not available due to an emergency; (ii) be certified in writing by the generator; and (iii) identify the particular hazardous waste being transported and the specific quantities of waste. The manifest must be done in multiple originals; the generator must receive a signed copy back from the initial transporter of the waste, as well as the owner of the designated receiving facility. The purpose of the manifest system is to ensure that hazardous waste designated for treatment, storage or disposal is documented properly for shipment and to ensure that such hazardous waste is delivered to an authorized facility (that is, a facility that has obtained a permit from the EPA to conduct storage, treatment, and disposal services).

The pre-transport requirements are very broad. Among other things, they address: (i) packaging, marking, and placarding of hazardous waste prior to transportation off-site in accordance with DOT requirements; (ii) accumulation of hazardous waste on-site in approved containers, tanks, and containment facilities, all clearly marked to indicate that they contain hazardous waste (note that the permitted accumulation times applicable to SQGs and LQGs are described in this subpart); and (iii) emergency response measures in the event of a spill, fire, explosion or other event that threatens human health.

Under the record-keeping and reporting requirements, each generator must maintain a copy of each signed manifest for a period of three years from the date the hazardous waste was accepted by the initial transporter. Further, each generator must keep records of any hazardous waste determinations for at least three years from the date that the waste was sent for off-site treatment, storage or disposal. The foregoing retention periods are automatically extended during any enforcement action, or as otherwise requested or required by the EPA (the EPA has broad authority to require generators to furnish additional reports concerning the quantities and dispositions of hazardous wastes). Generators further must file exception reports with the EPA if they do not receive confirmation (in the form of a signed manifest) of delivery of the hazardous waste by the owner of the designated receiving facility. Finally, LQGs must file a comprehensive biennial report to the EPA by March 1 of each even-numbered year.

RCRA and the corresponding EPA regulations also regulate the transportation, storage, treatment, and disposal of hazardous wastes. To the extent research facilities engage in these activities, the transportation of hazardous waste is governed generally by 42 U.S.C. § 6923 and 40 C.F.R. Part 263, and the storage, treatment, and disposal of hazardous waste is governed by 42 U.S.C. §§ 6924 and 6925 and 40 C.F.R. Parts 264 and 270 (regarding permits).

RCRA allows the states to apply to the EPA to assume responsibility for hazardous waste management within their own states. See 42 U.S.C. § 6926. If a state's program is authorized, a state's enforcement action under its own program will have the same force and effect as action by the EPA under RCRA. A state can have a program that is more stringent than RCRA, and those individuals counseling entities conducting preclinical research will need to review applicable state law to determine whether their individual states have enacted their own authorized hazardous waste management programs and counsel their clients on compliance and enforcement issues accordingly.

Generators of hazardous waste must provide information related to such hazardous waste to duly designated officers, employees, or representatives of the EPA (or a state having an authorized hazardous waste program), and must allow such duly designated parties to access and copy all records related to such hazardous waste. Additionally, the duly designated officers are authorized to inspect any establishment or premises where hazardous wastes are handled, and they may inspect and obtain samples of hazardous wastes from such establishment or premises.

Information obtained by the EPA (or by a state with an authorized hazardous waste program) through the inspections described above or otherwise in accordance with the EPA's authority under RCRA is considered information available to the public. However, a person may assert a claim of business confidentiality covering all or part of such information. Information covered by such a claim will remain confidential, except in limited circumstances.

There are severe penalties for violation of RCRA. Noncompliance can result in the EPA's imposition of a civil penalty of $25,000 per day of noncompliance for each violation (the same penalty applies with respect to violation of a noncompliance order issued by the EPA). Violations that are done knowingly (for example, dumping hazardous material or making false material statements) are criminal violations punishable by fines of up to $50,000 per day of violation or two years' imprisonment (the fines and prison terms can be doubled for subsequent convictions). Finally, there is the "knowing endangerment" penalty; if any person knowingly transports, treats, stores or disposes of any hazardous waste in violation of the statute and knows at the time that he thereby places another person in imminent danger of death or serious bodily injury, then the violator, upon conviction, can be subject to a fine of up to $250,000, or imprisonment for up to 15 years, or both. If the violator is an organization (any legal entity other than a government), it can be subject to a fine of up to $1 million.

3. Issues in Applying Environmental Law to Research Facilities

The EPA has undertaken a review of the application of the RCRA regulations to academic research facilities, and some of the problems inherent in applying those regulations. The EPA's review arose out of the *Report on Consensus Best Practices for Managing Hazardous Wastes in Academic Research Institutions*,[9] prepared by the Howard Hughes Medical Institute in October 2001. Similarly, the NIH in a *Workgroup Report*[10] has identified its concerns relating to the regulatory burden imposed upon academic research institutions in complying with RCRA. The fundamental issue is that while RCRA functions well in regulating industrial settings, it can be difficult and burdensome to apply in the research setting. Though the EPA and the NIH focused on academic research institutions, many of the same concerns should be shared by private commercial research facilities.

Among the issues to consider (as identified by the EPA and the NIH), and where the current RCRA regulatory framework can be problematic, are the following:

- In a research setting, relatively small quantities of a large number of chemicals are in use on a non-production basis.
- The chemicals in use in a research setting often vary depending on the frequently changing direction of a research endeavor.
- The potential environmental risks are of a different magnitude than those posed by industrial facilities.
- The overall potential for harm to human health or the environment can often be less than in an industrial setting because of the smaller quantity of chemicals in use.
- Lab staff generally has a high level of awareness of health, safety, and environmental hazards associated with working with chemicals.

- The time limits to dispose of hazardous wastes are fairly inflexible and not cost-effective for research facilities.
- Typically, the amount of hazardous waste generated fluctuates significantly from month to month, based on the nature of the experimentation taking place. Correspondingly, the research facility's status as a SQG, a LQG or a CESQG can vary from month to month, which entails compliance with different sets of requirements.

Both the NIH Workgroup Report and the Howard Hughes Medical Institute Report advocate giving academic research facilities greater flexibility in complying with the RCRA regulations by moving to a performance-based model for managing hazardous waste in research settings. It is arguable, and a case can be made, that private commercial research laboratories should have the benefit of the same flexibility.

4. IACUC Responsibility

With respect to in vivo preclinical research, the proper handling and disposal of hazardous waste generated from research is yet another area over which the IACUC has oversight responsibility (although, as noted above, the organization's environmental compliance officer would be the appropriate person to actually ensure compliance).

5. The Public Health Security and Bioterrorism Preparedness and Response Act of 2002; Select Agents and Toxins

In 2002, Congress enacted the Public Health Security and Bioterrorism Preparedness and Response Act (Pub. L. 107-188). Its purpose is to regulate the possession and use of certain select agents and toxins in order to protect the public against their misuse, whether inadvertent or as the result of acts of terrorism against the United States. The act is implemented by the Select Agents and Toxins regulations (42 C.F.R. Part 73), which are administered by the CDC under its Select Agent Program.

The regulated entities include any academic institution, corporation, partnership, and any other legal entity. In particular, the regulations are targeted at biomedical centers, commercial pharmaceutical manufacturing facilities, clinical and diagnostic laboratories, and research facilities.

"Select agents and toxins" in general are defined to include "biological agents" and "toxins." "Biological agents" means any microorganism or infectious substance or any naturally occurring, bioengineered, or synthesized component of any such microorganism or infectious substance capable of causing death or disease in humans, plants, or animals, or degradation of food or water supplies, or degradation of the environment. A "toxin" is defined as the toxic material or product of plants, animals, microorganisms or infectious substances, or a recombinant or synthesized molecule (which may include bioengineered poisons and products). There are two categories of select agents and toxins. "HHS' select agents and toxins" are regulated by the Department of Health and Human Services (DHHS) to protect public health and safety. They include designated viruses (such as Ebola, Marburg, and smallpox), bacteria, fungi, toxins such as ricin, and certain genetic elements, recombinant nucleic acids, and recombinant organisms that can encode any of the select agent viruses or listed toxins or that genetically modify any of the designated viruses, bacteria, fungi, and toxins. "Overlap select agents and toxins" are subject to joint regulation by both the DHHS and the U.S. Department of Agriculture (USDA) (the act gives the USDA authority to regulate select agents and toxins in order to protect animal and plant health and animal and plant products).

In general, an entity may not possess or use in the United States, receive from outside the United States, or transfer within the United States any select agent or toxin unless it has complied with the requirements of the regulations. An overview of the regulations follows:

a. The entity must have applied for and been granted a certificate of registration by either the DHHS or the USDA. The certificate of registration will only cover the specific select agents and toxins described in the entity's application, and will be valid only as to the activities and facility locations described in the application. The certificate of registration is valid for up to three years.
b. The entity, its owner(s), and any individual(s) handling select agents or toxins (including the entity's "responsible official," described below) must be approved by the DHHS or the USDA based on a security risk assessment conducted by the Attorney General. The

approval of an entity or individual is valid for up to five years. Certain categories of persons (such as those affiliated with terrorist organizations) are, of course, automatically excluded.

c. Each entity must designate a responsible official who is familiar with the select agent and toxin regulations and has the authority and responsibility to ensure the entity's compliance. The responsible official must have been approved under the security risk assessment procedures. The responsible official may designate alternate officials to act in his or her absence, provided they meet all the requirements to be a responsible official (including satisfying the security risk assessment). Among other things, the responsible official is charged with implementing the entity's safety, security, and emergency response plans, allowing only approved individuals access to select agents and toxins, implementing training, providing notices of any theft, loss or release of a select agent or toxin, and maintaining the required records.

d. The entity must implement a biosafety program. It should be noted that entities are expressly prohibited, without prior DHHS approval, from conducting experiments using recombinant DNA to bioengineer a drug resistance trait in an agent that would otherwise not acquire the resistance trait naturally (like antibiotic resistance in bacteria) if the acquisition of the trait could compromise the drug's ability to control the agent in humans, plants or animals. Thus, for example, prior DHHS approval would be required to conduct experiments involving the transfer of a gene into a virus such as smallpox for the purpose of making the virus resistant to vaccines. This is a serious concern. Several years ago a team of Australian scientists announced that they had genetically engineered a mousepox virus that killed mice specifically vaccinated against mousepox. It involved the introduction of a single gene into the mousepox genome. The findings evoked considerable debate over the concern that bioterrorists would have a road map for developing bioweapons—such as smallpox bioengineered to have resistance to existing smallpox vaccine—that would have devastating consequences if used.

e. The entity must implement a security plan to ensure the security of areas containing select agents and toxins. The plan must provide, among other things, for inventory control and other physical security measures, reporting procedures, and security plan review by the responsible official at least annually and after any "incident."
f. The entity must implement an emergency response plan that meets OSHA requirements and is coordinated with the entity's other plans for emergencies.
g. The entity must provide safety and security training for those individuals who will be handling select agents and toxins. The training must be provided prior to the individual's initial work assignment, and prior to any new assignments that may involve exposure. The training must be documented.
h. The entity through its responsible official is obligated to maintain complete records documenting its compliance with the select agents and toxins regulations, including: (i) current lists of individuals approved for access to select agents and toxins; (ii) a detailed inventory of select agents and toxins on-site; (iii) records documenting an individual's specific access to select agents and toxins and storage and use areas, including specific dates and times; (iv) inspection records; (v) sets of the required safety, emergency response and security plans, and training records; (vi) permits for approved transfer of select agents and toxins from one entity to another; and (vii) incident reports. All records must be maintained for three years.
i. There are limited exemptions from the requirement to comply with the select agents and toxins regulations. For example, the DHHS may exempt an entity from compliance in whole or in part if the DHHS determines that the exemption is necessary for the entity's timely participation in response to a public health emergency. Additionally, a laboratory conducting diagnosis or verification involving select agents or toxins may be exempt, provided it notifies the DHHS immediately if particular agents or toxins are identified (such as smallpox, any of the hemorrhagic fevers, or botulinum neurotoxins) and the agents or toxins are thereafter destroyed, unless law enforcement directs otherwise after consulting with the DHHS.

j. The DHHS, without prior notice and without cause, may inspect any site where select agents or toxins are used or stored and may inspect and copy any records it requires.
k. If an entity discovers the theft or loss of a select agent or toxin, or if there has been a release causing an occupational exposure or outside of the facility's primary containment barriers, the entity must immediately (by phone, fax or e-mail) notify the DHHS and state and local enforcement (if there's been theft or loss) or state and local public health agencies (if there's been a release).
l. Finally, in addition to potential criminal penalties that may apply, under the act violators may be liable for civil penalties; penalties against individuals may be up to $250,000, and penalties against entities may be up to $500,000.

C. Other Regulatory Schemes Applicable to Preclinical Research—Occupational Safety and Health Considerations and the Protection of Individuals Conducting Preclinical Research

1. Introduction

The preclinical research setting can be extremely hazardous to human health and safety. The entity conducting research is obligated to provide a safe workplace for all of the individuals engaged in the research, including the scientists, lab technicians, animal handlers, and maintenance staff. These individuals can be exposed to a broad array of hazards, including (i) physical hazards from interactions with animals and from laboratory equipment and machinery (such as syringes and scalpels and radiation sources); (ii) hazards from exposure to chemicals that may be toxic, corrosive, carcinogenic or mutagenic; and (iii) hazards from exposure to infectious diseases resulting from viruses, bacteria, and parasites.

To the extent the entity is conducting in vivo preclinical research, occupational health and safety is a matter that should be considered jointly by the entity's IACUC as well as its environmental compliance personnel and occupational safety and health personnel.

2. Occupational Safety and Health Administration (OSHA) Regulation; Standards; Resources

Similar to the EPA's regulation of hazardous wastes under RCRA, the Occupational Safety and Health Administration (OSHA), a subdivision of the Department of Labor, regulates the management of hazardous wastes. Unlike the EPA, however, OSHA does not focus on public welfare, but rather on the protection of workers exposed to or handling hazardous wastes. In laboratory settings, OSHA has established performance-based standards for the use and handling of hazardous chemicals (as opposed to the substance-specific health standards established by OSHA for the use and handling of hazardous chemicals in non-laboratory settings).

In the research laboratory setting, a key OSHA regulation is the standard governing "Occupational Exposure to Hazardous Chemicals in Laboratories" (29 C.F.R. § 1910.1450). "Hazardous chemicals" have a very specific definition under the standard:

> "Hazardous chemical" means a chemical for which there is statistically significant evidence based on at least one study conducted in accordance with established scientific principles that acute or chronic health effects may occur in exposed employees. The term "health hazard" includes chemicals which are carcinogens, toxic or highly toxic agents, reproductive toxins, irritants, corrosives, sensitizers, hepatotoxins, nephrotoxins, agents which act on the hematopoietic system, and agents which damage the lungs, skin, eyes, or mucous membranes.

There are four key compliance requirements under the hazardous chemicals standard. The first is the requirement that an employer develop and implement a chemical hygiene plan that sets forth procedures, equipment, personal protective equipment, and work practices that are capable of protecting employees from the health hazards presented by hazardous chemicals in the workplace. The chemical hygiene plan must be written, and it must include each of the following elements:

- Standard operating procedures when laboratory work involves hazardous chemicals.

- Criteria that the employer will use to determine and implement control measures to reduce employee exposure to hazardous chemicals.
- A requirement that all protective equipment is operating properly.
- Provisions for employee training.
- The circumstances under which a particular laboratory activity will require the employer's prior approval.
- Provisions for medical consultation and examinations.
- Designation of personnel responsible for implementing the chemical hygiene plan.
- Provisions for additional employee protections for work with particularly hazardous substances.

The second key compliance requirement is that the employer provide its employees with information and training to ensure that they are aware of chemical hazards. The information must be provided at the time of an employee's initial assignment to a workplace where hazardous chemicals are present. The employee's training must include methods that may be used to detect the presence of hazardous chemicals, the physical and health hazards presented by hazardous chemicals in the workplace, and the measures employees can take to protect themselves from such hazards.

The third key compliance requirement is that the employer provide all employees who work with hazardous chemicals the opportunity to receive medical attention whenever an employee develop signs or symptoms associated with hazardous chemical exposure, or when exposure monitoring reveals an exposure level in excess of OSHA-prescribed limits, or whenever an event such as a spill, leak or explosion occurs in the workplace. The medical examination must be performed under the direct supervision of a licensed physician, at no cost to the employee, and without any loss of pay. The employer is obligated to provide the physician with information identifying the particular hazardous chemicals involved and the circumstances under which the exposure occurred, and the employer must obtain a written opinion from the examining physician that, among other things, sets forth the results of the examination and identifies any recommendations for follow-up examinations or treatment.

The fourth key compliance requirement is that the employer maintain for each employee an accurate record of any measurements taken to monitor employee exposures and any medical examinations.

It should be noted that the OSHA hazardous chemicals standard includes an appendix containing recommendations for laboratory chemical hygiene prepared by the National Research Council. The recommendations are intended to provide a quick reference during laboratory operations and during development of the chemical hygiene plan. Among many other items, the recommendations address animal work with chemicals of high chronic toxicity.

In addition to the OSHA standard regulating hazardous chemicals in laboratories, OSHA has a standard regulating bloodborne pathogens (which are defined as pathogenic microorganisms present in human blood, including hepatitis B virus (HBV) and human immunodeficiency virus (HIV)) and other potentially infectious materials (which may include blood, organs, or other tissues from experimental animals infected with HIV or HBV) (29 C.F.R. § 1910.1030). Similar to the requirement for a chemical hygiene plan under the hazardous chemicals standard, the bloodborne pathogens standard requires employers, where there is potential for occupational exposure to blood and other potentially infectious materials, to develop and implement an exposure control plan. Its purpose is to develop procedures and facilities designed to minimize or eliminate such occupational exposure. Like the hazardous chemicals standard, the bloodborne pathogens standard has employer requirements for medical consultation and examinations for employees who may have sustained an occupational exposure, for employee training, and for individualized employee record keeping. There are also specific requirements related to a "research laboratory," which is defined as a laboratory producing or using research laboratory scale amounts of HIV or HBV. Among other things, there are requirements pertaining to animal rooms and the handling of infected animals, the permissible use of syringes, and disposal requirements.

3. Selected Resource Tools—Chemicals and Biohazards

In addition to the OSHA standards (which of course are mandatory), there are a number of resource tools that entities conducting preclinical research should be aware of. The following in particular merit careful review:

- *Occupational Health and Safety in the Care and Use of Research Animals*[11] (1997), National Academy Press. (Among other things, this publication identifies the various hazards present in the research setting and identifies the principal elements of an occupational health and safety plan).
- *Prudent Practices in the Laboratory: Handling and Disposal of Chemicals*[12] (1995), National Research Council, National Academy Press.
- *Biosafety in Microbiological and Biomedical Laboratories,*[13] CDC and NIH, DHHS. DHHS Publication No. (CDC) 93-8395.
- *Biosafety in the Laboratory: Prudent Practices for Handling and Disposal of Infectious Materials*[14] (1989), National Research Council, National Academy Press.
- *NIH Guidelines for Research Involving Recombinant DNA Molecules,*[15] NIH, DHHS.

4. Radioactive Materials in the Research Setting

In addition to hazardous chemicals and biohazardous materials, personnel conducting preclinical research may have occupational exposure to radioactive materials. Reference is made to the Energy Reorganization Act of 1974 (42 U.S.C. §§ 5801 *et seq.*) and the regulations set forth in Title 10 of the *Code of Federal Regulations* for statutes and regulations that may be applicable in the research setting.

D. Conclusion

As should be evident from this chapter, preclinical research is subject to a significant regulatory burden. The compliance costs are high, and similarly the costs for noncompliance can be high as well. If in vivo preclinical research is being conducted, the IACUC has substantial responsibilities as a matter of federal law. Additionally, state and local authorities may impose regulatory burdens that are actually more stringent than those imposed under federal law. Unfortunately, budgetary constraints mean that more money spent on compliance means less money available for actual research. The challenge for entities conducting preclinical research is to ensure that its compliance is at the same time both cost-effective and responsive to applicable legal requirements.

Notes

1. www.aphis.usda.gov/ac/polmanpdf.html.
2. www.aphis.usda.gov/ac/iacuc.pdf.
3. www.aphis.usda.gov/ac/researchguide.html.
4. www.grants.nih.gov/grants/olaw/references/finalmou.htm.
5. www.nap.edu/readingroom/books/labrats/.
6. www.grants.nih.gov/grants/olaw/Guidebook.pdf.
7. www.nabr.org/Animallaw.
8. The author does not specialize in environmental law. Consultation with an environmental practitioner (whether an attorney or other consultant) is highly recommended when evaluating compliance.
9. www.hhmi.org/research/labsafe/projects/report_congress.pdf.
10. www.grants2.nih.gov/grants/policy/regulatoryburden/hazardouswastes.htm.
11. www.books.nap.edu/books/0309052998/html/index.html.
12. www.nap.edu/books/0309052297/html/R1.html.
13. www.cdc.gov/od/ohs/biosfty/bmbl3toc.htm/
14. www.nap.edu/books/0309039754/html/index.html.
15. www.4.od.nih.gov/oba/rac/guidelines/guidelines.html.

Chapter IX

Research and Development Collaborations

Eileen Smith Ewing
K&L Gates
Boston, Massachusetts

A. Introduction: The Collaborator as Biotechnology's White Knight

Major pharmaceutical companies need smaller, emerging biotechnology companies. The internal research and development efforts of these behemoths simply cannot sustain their required growth rate.[1] They must collaborate with nimble, creative biotechnology companies to feed their huge appetites for novel science.

On the other hand, a biotechnology company that seeks to discover and develop a marketable drug product is facing a Sisyphean struggle. The average cost to develop a new drug is about $900 million, requiring an average development period of 10 to 12 years.[2] Only one in 5,000 compounds that enter preclinical testing ever becomes an approved drug product.[3] Similar challenges face devices and other biotechnology products, although their path toward regulatory approval may not be as long as that for biopharmaceuticals. How can a small biotechnology start-up company with a few million dollars in angel financing and venture capital ever hope to push the rock up this hill? Even a more mature biotechnology company is likely to find the high cost of clinical trials a burden too heavy to be borne alone.

Enter Big Pharma[4]—to the cheers not only of the struggling biotech company, but also of its weary individual and institutional investors, its patient academic licensors, its visionary management, even its venerable scientific advisory board. The huge in-licensing machinery of major pharmaceutical companies is biotechnology's life-support system, and it also supports all the stakeholders on the sidelines. A global pharmaceutical company may spend between 10 and 50 percent of its annual research and development budget on in-licensing.[5]

Twelve out of the 25 largest revenue-producing drugs currently on the market were developed and commercialized by companies other than the companies that discovered or designed them—in other words, through biopharmaceutical alliances.[6] Typically, the parties do not enter directly into a development and commercialization license. They are more likely first to explore their scientific compatibility by means of a research collaboration. The stakes are high. A failed research collaboration can kill a start-up company. A successful one lays the groundwork for a prestigious drug development alliance. And more than 50 percent of research collaborations end in failure.[7]

B. Finding a Strategic Partner: Beating the Mathematical Odds

The problem facing the biotechnology industry is that, despite Big Pharma's huge appetite for innovation and its driving need to maintain profit margins, only a small percentage of biotechnology companies that seek a research collaboration opportunity are chosen. The business development and licensing group of a large pharmaceutical company may review several thousand proposals a year. A few hundred of these will enter negotiations; a few tens actually will close. How does a biotechnology company become one of the fortunate few?

Research and Development Collaborations

Exhibit 9-1
Stakeholders in the Research Collaboration

Party	End Goals
Pharmaceutical Company	—Become biotechnology companies' "partner of choice" over competitors
	—Build strong drug development pipeline
	—Develop and market blockbuster drugs
	—Seize worldwide market share with respect to treating a particular disease state
Biotechnology Company	—Develop profitable drugs that will generate substantial royalty revenues
	—Utilize pharmaceutical companies' development and marketing expertise
	—Utilize pharmaceutical companies' worldwide distribution channels
	—Use royalty revenues from early drug product successes to develop other drug candidates independently
	—Build strong drug development pipeline
	—Achieve exit strategy for investors (acquisition or IPO)
	—Become Big Pharma?
Biotechnology Company's Institutional Investors	—Return on investment through timely exit strategy (acquisition or IPO)
Academic Licensor	—Royalty stream on IP licensed to biotechnology company
	—Advancement of science
U.S. Government (e.g., National Institutes of Health)	—Federally funded academic research developed, commercialized, and made available for the public's benefit, as envisioned by the Bayh-Dole Act

1) *Don't Expect Big Pharma to Find You.* A key business development executive at Astra-Zeneca noted that of the licensing opportunities reviewed by his company, 95 percent were based an introduction made at the smaller company's initiative, and only 5 percent resulted from Astra-Zeneca's identifying and approaching a company on its own initiative.[8] "If you build it, they will come" appears not to apply to pharmaceutical collaborations.

2) *It's About the Science.* Scientist-to-scientist interaction (as opposed to business development connections) seems to have the best chance at succeeding. Even if the initial communication is between business development executives, it is important to get the scientists talking to each other as soon as possible. It is the scientists who will have to carry the deal through the pharmaceutical company's typically byzantine approval process; they need to believe strongly in the scientific opportunity.

> **Practice Points**
>
> 1. Draft a one- to two-page summary of your key scientific points, but not at a level that would require an NDA.
> 2. Find a scientific "godfather" at the larger company, even if you need to use a third party to make the connection—a cold call will rarely work.
> 3. At the first meeting, let your scientists make the case to theirs; use that to leverage a subsequent meeting with business development team.

3) *Approaching Big Pharma with an Opportunity to Collaborate.* Both scientists and business development officers within pharmaceutical companies tend to dislike cold calls. A one- or two-page summary of the scientific opportunity should be sent by e-mail to the appropriate science chief within the larger company. The smaller company should send enough information to whet the recipients' interest, but the amount of the material should not overwhelm them, and the nature of the material should not require a confidential disclosure agreement; the larger corporation will not sign one at this stage. Focus on the science, not on the projected market opportunity—remember, this is not a business plan for presentation to venture capitalists.

4) *Use of Third Parties as Valuable Contacts.* The company may benefit from any contacts its officers, board members, or venture capital investors have within the pharmaceutical community. Similarly, if their lawyers or accountants deal with the industry regularly, they may prove a valuable resource. These contacts can help identify:

- Which pharmaceutical companies have a "sweet spot" in the relevant area of science, and which are not worth targeting
- Who are the right people to approach initially within the targeted pharmaceutical companies
- How the approval process at a particular pharmaceutical company works

These contacts should not be expected to obtain a research collaboration for the company—they can only expedite the process by providing the biotech company with better access to potential collaborators. In the final analysis, the science either will sell itself or not. If it does, the pharmaceutical company will offer to summarize the proposed collaboration in a term sheet.

C. Negotiating a Term Sheet

1. The Importance of the Term Sheet to the Transaction

One would think collaboration term sheets were enforceable, from the attention the parties typically pay to negotiating them. While it is true that most term sheets explicitly state that they are non-binding on the parties, one should not underestimate the moral imperative they wield. Some of the most crucial aspects of the deal will be hammered out at this stage: for example, the intellectual property to be licensed, the scope of the license grant, and the financial compensation.

Unenforceability notwithstanding, the parties will turn again and again to the term sheet as they negotiate the definitive agreement. It is an intrepid lawyer who will try, in the course of later negotiations, to change his client's position from what was clearly agreed in the term sheet. Cries of "That's not what was in the term sheet!" will echo around the negotiating table. The danger, of course, is that the other side will respond by threatening to renege on some of its own earlier commitments. If the ensuing lack of trust between the parties does not derail the deal entirely, it may set the deal back weeks or even months. Craft the term sheet with care, and then respect it in subsequent negotiations.

The foregoing is particularly true with respect to a research collaboration with a larger pharmaceutical partner. Generally speaking, the finalized term sheet in almost any corporate transaction likely will serve to summarize the deal terms for the parties' boards of directors; it will be the tool by which the boards give management the green light to proceed. A research collaboration may not be sufficiently material to a large pharmaceutical partner to require board approval. However, the pharmaceutical business development team is likely to have to present these terms to a number of internal committees for approval. Typically, this is a cumbersome and time-consuming process that requires input and support from many groups and departments within the pharmaceutical company. Once the business development team gains the tentative approval of these internal committees to the terms of the deal, they understandably will be extremely reluctant to start the process over again to obtain approval of a changed term.

2. Issues Crucial to Address at the Term Sheet Stage

Certain terms are so essential to the deal that the parties cannot afford to proceed beyond the term sheet stage with different notions of what these terms will look like. The smaller party will be vulnerable to the costs (in lost dollars, lost opportunities, and diminished reputation among other suitors) of a deal that fails several months into negotiations. Although perhaps less vulnerable to financial costs of a failed deal, the larger partner likely will have invested resources in building internal interdepartmental support for the collaboration as part of a larger disease program. A late-stage deal breakup slows the momentum of the larger research program and saps the morale of the scientists and business development executives associated with it. Both parties to a collaboration should avoid post-term sheet surprises by addressing the following issues in the term sheet with appropriate specificity:[9]

- *Scope of collaboration.*[10] In other words, whose intellectual property will be rolled into the effort: yours, theirs, that of a third party? For what specific purposes?

- *Term of collaboration.*[11] For how long will both parties commit to work together?
- *Joint steering committee.*[12] Address composition, the identity of key representatives from each side, selection of a chair, and voting mechanisms. (The specific issues over which the joint steering committee will have control may be left to the definitive agreement.)
- *Financial terms regarding the collaboration itself.*[13] Signature payments, research funding, equity investments, early milestone payments.
- *Rights in intellectual property, old and new.*[14] The parties need to establish what rights each will have in any technology arising from the collaboration, as well as their respective rights, if any, in each other's background intellectual property.
- *Development and commercialization rights.*[15] While it may not be necessary, and from the perspective of the smaller party not even advisable, to pin down the financial terms of a commercialization license this early in the process, it is crucial that the parties at least agree on structure. Will the funding partner have development and commercialization rights automatically, or must it exercise an option to license? Will a form of license or "heads of agreement" be negotiated contemporaneously with the collaboration agreement, or will the parties wait until later to negotiate terms?
- *Development and commercialization financial terms.*[16] If the parties are indeed going to commit to a form of license agreement or "heads of agreement" that will include financial terms (milestone and royalty payments), address the numbers at the term sheet stage to avoid deal-breaking surprises during contract negotiation.

3. Issues to Avoid Negotiating at the Term Sheet Stage

Precisely because the parties recognize the value to later negotiations of precisely pinning issues down at the term sheet stage, they often become hopelessly bogged down in details. Some issues can, and perhaps should, be left for negotiation in the definitive agreement:

- *Authority of the joint steering committee.* Postpone detailed discussion of what matters it will control with respect to the collaboration,

and which party, if any, will have the tie-breaking vote. This discussion, although largely symbolic, can elicit considerable negativity around the negotiating table.
- *Defined terms.* Particularly with respect to thorny issues involving intellectual property rights, it is usually a mistake at this stage to engage in a duel over the precise language of defined terms. Accept agreement as to what is generally meant, but not as to specific wording. Negotiation of the definitive agreement will provide much more scope for precise wordsmithing.
- *Termination rights.* This is a debate to have much later in the negotiating process, because it speaks to each side's insecurities about the relationship.
- *Change of control provisions.* Again, this is an issue that awakens each side's concerns about industry consolidation and predatory behavior by competitors. This discussion should be postponed not merely to the collaboration agreement stage, but until the development and commercialization agreement is under negotiation.

D. Key Issues in a Research Collaboration Agreement

1. Governance of the Research Collaboration

a. Composition of the Joint Steering Committee

A research collaboration is typically governed by a joint steering committee composed of an equal number of members from each party to the alliance. The chair may be the senior representative of the funding partner, or the chair may rotate between the parties, perhaps on an annual basis. The joint steering committee is critical to the success of the alliance, both from business and scientific perspectives. Thus it is useful to include among a party's representatives on the committee:

- the principal investigator or chief scientist for the project, preferably the one who has already invested time to build a consensus within his company supporting the project; and
- a business development executive empowered by her company with sufficient authority to make ongoing decisions relevant to the collaboration.

b. Duties of the Joint Steering Committee

The joint steering committee has general oversight over the collaboration. More particularly, its express duties may include the following:

- Agreeing on a research plan outlining the scientific objectives of the collaboration;
- Periodically reviewing the goals and strategy of the collaboration;
- Facilitating technology transfer, if one of the parties is an academic or research institution;
- Facilitating exchange of information between the parties;
- Receiving and reviewing deliverables under the research plan;
- Reviewing publications related to the results of the research;
- Reviewing and allocating financial and personnel resources, as well as determining the number of full-time-equivalent (FTE) scientists that may be needed for the collaboration;
- Resolving disputes between the parties;
- Serving as a liaison between the team and their respective organizations;
- Determining when certain milestones in the collaborative process have been met (for example, when scientific proof of concept has been achieved); and
- Deciding on behalf of both parties to terminate the collaboration early, based on failure of the science or otherwise.

c. Meetings of the Joint Steering Committee

The interests of the parties will be served best if the collaboration agreement requires a certain number of meetings per year, whether in person or telephonically. If the meetings are in person, the parties may bear their own expenses, or the partner funding the collaboration may do so for both parties.

d. Decisionmaking by the Joint Steering Committee

The collaboration agreement will identify how decisions are to be made by the joint steering committee: unanimously, by majority vote, or by collective voting. The agreement should also provide a mechanism for breaking deadlocks. These may include:

- A requirement that the joint steering committee reach a decision on the issue within a set time period;
- Chair has the tie-breaking vote;
- Funding partner has the tie-breaking vote; or
- The joint steering committee refers the matter to certain identified senior executives in each company for resolution within a set time period.

Often, when the funding partner is a major pharmaceutical company, it will insist that it have the tie-breaking vote on any deadlocked issues before the joint steering committee. After all, the argument goes, it *is* their money at stake. Furthermore, in multinational pharmaceutical companies, it may not be practical or efficient to bring a minor dispute in one of hundreds of research collaborations to an overburdened senior executive. A possible compromise is to offer the tie-breaking committee vote to the larger partner on all but a small handful of "bet-the-company" issues, which would need to be referred to senior management for resolution or compromise with the smaller partner. These might include:

- Proposed early termination of the collaboration;
- Proposed change of direction that would require the smaller partner to invest significantly greater resources than originally contemplated; or
- Proposed change of direction that would require the smaller partner to focus on areas of science outside its core competencies.

2. The Scope of the Collaboration

From the outset, the parties to a research collaboration need clarity as to the scope of the collaboration. Inevitably, there are good practical reasons for defining scope: it may determine which scientists will be assigned to the project, which representatives will sit on the joint steering committee that oversees the project, and how much research funding may be necessary from the collaborating party.

More important, however, the scope of the collaboration is likely to affect the parties' future intellectual property rights. Although this is a matter for negotiation, it is likely that the funding partner will have limited, if any, rights to intellectual property developed by the other party after the research agreement execution date and outside the collaboration.

Sometimes the funding partner seeks rights to the platform technology that the other party brings to the collaboration, although the latter was developed outside and prior to the research alliance. This may be a reasonable position. Interest in the platform technology may have motivated the strategic alliance in the first place. In this case, the licensing party would be wise to restrict scope by field. If intellectual property created as a result of the collaboration has applications beyond the project's scope, the funding partner may or may not have rights outside the field. This is a matter for negotiation.

There are a number of reasons why scope limitations may be advisable or necessary:

- *Licensee's interest.* Licensee has determined that a specific disease program of its own is likely to benefit from this collaboration;
- *Third-party licenses.* Licensor has already granted, or hopes to grant, licenses to third parties with respect to other fields; or
- *Independent development.* Licensor wishes to retain rights to develop and commercialize in certain fields independently.

Typically, one may limit the scope of a collaboration in several ways:

a. Field

In a biotechnology research collaboration, "field" is frequently limited to a particular disease or group of related diseases. It may also be limited as to use of the ultimate product—for example, diagnostic, therapeutic, prophylactic, or palliative—or by the expected method of drug delivery—for example, oral, buccal, topical, or by intravenous or intramuscular injection.

If the goal of the collaboration is to identify compounds that act on a particular target (e.g., a virus, an enzyme or a receptor on the surface of a cell), the target itself may limit the field—or there may be further limitations by disease state, if the parties expect that a particular target may be implicated in a number of diseases. Or the goal may be to identify targets implicated in a disease, in which case the particular disease, again, may define the field.

b. Scope Limitations Based on Patent Family

The parties may be able to circumscribe the collaboration by identifying particular patents (and their progeny of related patents) of interest to the licensee. This is a relatively clean and precise way to limit deal scope, particularly if the licensee resists field limitations. The larger party typically will insist on rights to prosecute the patent for all the related technologies to ensure proper and timely patent filing and to guard against leaving holes in the patent protection, either in terms of subject or geography.

c. Scope Limitations Based on Timing

It is not uncommon for a research collaboration to grant a license under all patents of the licensor applied for or granted as of the commencement date of the alliance. Alternatively, the scope of certain research alliances may be limited to intellectual property developed during the term of the agreement. In the latter case, it is often a good idea to add a "tail" period of 6 to 12 months to give the parties the benefit of late-arriving research results. In either case, time is the determining factor in limiting the intellectual property made available to the collaboration.

d. Scope Limitations Based on Project Funding

For a company or research institution that receives research funding from multiple sources, determining scope of collaboration based on who funded the project is a possibility. This is a less precise and, for the licensee, much riskier approach than the others discussed. Particularly when the same scientists work on multiple scientifically related but independently funded projects, it is crucial to combine this approach with other methods of limiting scope, such as field of use. Otherwise, later attempts to grant exclusive development and commercialization rights to a particular licensee may be challenged by other research sponsors.

3. Intellectual Property

As mentioned above, the collaboration's scope will relate closely to the scope of each party's intellectual property rights, both during the alliance and in the future. Thus the parties must have a clear understanding of what intellectual property the collaboration does, and does not, cover. Consider, for example, the following strategic categories of intellectual property that may be made available to a collaborator.

a. Core Intellectual Property of the Smaller Partner, Developed Prior to the Collaboration but Highly Relevant

Inclusion of this intellectual property is crucial; it is probably the motivation behind the transaction. The smaller partner needs to consider whether a field restriction will enable it to enter into other research collaborations—or whether the healthy consideration offered, possibly with back-end compensation, by a motivated licensee is sufficient to justify tying up the company's crown jewels with one partner.

b. Core Intellectual Property of the Larger Funding Partner, Developed Prior to the Collaboration but Highly Relevant

The larger partner may feel motivated to bring its own intellectual property—for example, a library of many thousands of compounds to be tested against the collaborator's targets—into the collaboration if the smaller partner's technology is likely to narrow or validate its own drug discovery efforts. Otherwise, the larger partner may well continue with multiple other research projects addressing the same disease or target. The smaller partner may wish to consider whether this backing of multiple horses may at some point give rise to a competitor product that will keep its own product on the shelf. This situation may be aggravated by a "not invented here" prejudice at the larger entity.

c. Background Intellectual Property of the Smaller Partner, Developed Prior to the Collaboration but of Possible Utility

The core intellectual property sought by the larger partner may not be all the smaller partner has to offer. For this reason, the larger partner will often seek a wrap-up clause in which all other intellectual property of the licensor not specifically covered by the collaboration agreement but identified post-execution as useful to the collaboration will be deemed licensed non-exclusively along with the core intellectual property. This is often called a "reach-in." In general, the smaller partner will find this clause acceptable, as long as there is a carve-out for intellectual property that the smaller partner may not license, because it is encumbered by licenses to or from third parties. Even in this case, some sort of "best efforts" may be required to resolve that encumbered license.

d. Background Intellectual Property of the Larger Funding Partner, Developed Prior to the Collaboration but of Possible Utility

As a general rule, the larger partner is not going to make its own background intellectual property available to the collaboration, except in instances where such intellectual property is directly relevant to the matter under study. This usually is not an issue, because the larger partner, who expects to market the result, will be motivated to offer this background IP if they determine that the resulting product warrants development and testing. It won't be available, however, to the smaller partner for other uses.

e. Intellectual Property Developed by One or Both Parties Arising out of the Collaboration

This is the work product of the collaboration. It may derive from the intellectual property of one party or the other. It may be created by employees for either or both parties. The collaboration agreement is likely to state that ownership of this intellectual property will be determined pursuant to United States patent law (that is, ownership follows inventorship). In other words, each party owns what its own employees invent, regardless of who files the patent, and what is jointly invented is jointly owned. However, control over this intellectual property is not necessarily an issue of ownership, but one of license. Thus the licensing section of the collaboration agreement will address rights to collaboration intellectual property.

f. Intellectual Property Developed by the Smaller Partner During, but Outside of, the Collaboration

The larger partner may understandably fear that the scientific advances of its smaller partner outside the collaboration may outstrip what is accomplished within the collaboration. Despite a significant financial investment, the funding partner might find itself pursuing technology or concepts rendered obsolete by discoveries made independently or in a third-party collaboration by its smaller partner. Funding partners often will argue vociferously for a wrap-up license that provides them rights to anything the collaborator discovers in the field during the term of the collaboration. Smaller partners will want to resist this vociferously, because of its potential chilling effect on other collaboration opportunities. A compromise position is to offer the funding partner a right of first negotiation on new intellectual property in the field developed during the term but outside the collaboration, as long as that intellectual property is not encumbered by a third-party license. The smaller partner should resist, however, a right of first refusal, which also would have a chilling effect on any potential collaboration with other parties.

g. Novel Intellectual Property Developed by One or Both Parties During the Collaboration That Does Not Arise out of the Existing Intellectual Property of Either Party

Although research collaboration is typically limited by field, one can never predict what unrelated scientific advances may arise from the parties' collaborative efforts. For example, a new tool may be developed that has potential utility beyond the specific research under way. In such a case, the collaboration agreement will usually provide for ownership based on United States patent laws. However, access to the new invention by license is a matter of negotiation. The collaboration agreement may contemplate cross-licenses of each party to the other's rights, if any, in the new invention, affording both parties freedom to operate.

4. License Grants

At the heart of the collaboration agreement are the licenses granted by the parties to intellectual property used or developed in the alliance. Some collaboration agreements also automatically grant a development and commercialization license with respect to any potential products. More typically, the collaboration agreement covers only the exploratory courtship period between the parties. In that case, the collaboration agreement may grant a license option to the funding partner, exercisable during the term of the collaboration and perhaps for a tail period thereafter. The parties may negotiate in advance the terms that will govern any development and commercialization license, or they may postpone negotiation until a license agreement is actually needed. License terms negotiated in advance may be memorialized by simple "heads of agreement" attached as an appendix to the collaboration agreement. Alternatively, a full-scale form of license agreement may be hammered out at the commencement of the collaboration, to be attached as an exhibit to the collaboration agreement.

a. Research Licenses

At a minimum, the collaboration agreement must render the parties capable of conducting research using certain intellectual property they might not otherwise have the right to use. Thus, the parties will identify as crucial to the alliance certain of the categories of intellectual property listed above; they will grant each other a non-transferable, royalty-free license for the term of the collaboration to use that intellectual property for non-commercial, internal research purposes only. This license may be co-exclusive as to the field, or it may be non-exclusive.

b. Development and Commercialization License

As discussed above, the collaboration agreement may contemplate that the funding party will obtain a license to develop, manufacture, market, and sell products based on intellectual property used in or arising out of the collaboration. For example, the research license may have involved pharmaceutical compounds with potential efficacy against a particular target. Once certain pharmaceutical compounds show promise in the collaboration, a development and commercialization license will be necessary for the pharmaceutical company to take these compounds into development as drug candidates. Typically this license is exclusive as to field and territory; the field may be as narrow as a single disease or as broad as all human and/or veterinary health care; the territory may be a single country or worldwide. This license will rarely be non-exclusive in nature—it is the ability to keep other players out of the marketplace that gives the license value.

c. Cross-Licenses; Freedom to Operate

Certain jointly owned intellectual property that emerges from the collaboration may not be the appropriate subject of an exclusive development and commercialization license but may have future utility to the parties nonetheless. While the funding partner may not require an exclusive license in these cases, it will, at least, want "freedom to operate"—reassurance that its use of the technology will not infringe the collaborator's rights. It is quite reasonable for the smaller partner to seek similar protection. The result is usually a symmetrical pair of cross-licenses, giving the parties equal co-exclusive or non-exclusive access to the jointly owned technology. If the cross-licenses are co-exclusive, both parties need to ensure that rights to sublicense are discussed.

d. Enabling License

Particularly in those cases in which not all of the smaller partner's intellectual property is being licensed—where, for example, the scope of the collaboration is limited to certain, but not all, patent families under the control of the licensor—the funding partner may feel justifiably concerned that it may have overlooked a crucial piece of the puzzle. There may not be time to do sufficient due diligence on all of the licensor's patents or to analyze their possible usefulness within the collaboration. Even if there is sufficient due diligence, no one can predict all the twists and turns that future development may take. For this reason, the funding partner will often bargain for an enabling license, a catch-all grant that gives the licensee the right to use whatever other unidentified intellectual property of the licensor is necessary to enable the use of the licensed intellectual property. The breadth of this grant is open to discussion. Some licensees will accept "necessary" as the limiting word; others will argue for "necessary or desirable"; a few will push for "necessary or desirable, in the sole judgment of the licensee." The problem with the latter two approaches, of course, is that desirability is highly subjective. Arguably, access to all the licensee's intellectual property may be a desirable thing. However, if the smaller company's strategy is to limit the scope of the collaboration, perhaps to permit other parallel collaborations, such a broad enabling license may undercut that strategy.

e. License as Protection Against Infringement Claims

Another legitimate concern of the funding partner is that the smaller partner may develop intellectual property independent of the collaboration that will block the rights granted by the collaboration agreement. Hence we often see a clause protecting the licensee from a claim of infringement by the collaborator: it grants the licensee a license under any unidentified blocking intellectual property sufficient for the licensee at least to be able to exercise the rights granted under the collaboration agreement. It is reasonable for the funding partner to seek this protection.

5. Financial Terms

Parties to a research collaboration spend a lot of time fighting over milestone payments and royalty rates. The smaller company may want to announce the deal in terms of its potential value, in order to excite the industry. The larger company may resist this, because it may set a false financial precedent for future deals. Given the long and perilous process of drug development and approval, however, the odds are great that a biotech company will never see the late-stage milestone payments, much less the royalties on net sales of products, that were so fiercely debated at the start of the journey. (This is particularly true in early-stage deals.) Or the milestones may be achieved and the product approved for sale, but by then the company may have been acquired, its investors having found their desired exit strategy after providing multiple infusions of capital, its smaller stockholders diluted, and its management replaced. The early payments under a research collaboration are the ones that count. Those payments will have a real and immediate impact on the company.

> **Practice Points**
>
> The smaller company should press for more money up front and less on the back end. Smaller companies generally need money now, and the odds of actually receiving even a portion of the back-end payments are remote in most deals.
>
> The financial consideration typically offered in a research collaboration may include a combination of signature payments, research funding, equity investment, and milestone payments.

a. Signature Payments

These are dollars offered just for closing the deal, regardless of whether scientific results are achieved. This is trophy money—nominal for early-stage collaborations and increasingly substantial along the development time line. The only catch is that the receiving company may be encumbered by in-licensing arrangements with research institutions that require it to share a percentage of non-royalty income in respect of the licensed intellectual property. If the latter is the case, it may be beneficial to structure the transaction so some of this consideration falls in categories not typically reachable by in-licensors, such as equity investments or reimbursement of research costs.

b. Research Funding

A typical approach to research funding is for the parties to determine how many full-time equivalent (FTE) scientists will be needed to staff the collaboration annually throughout the term of the agreement. That number is then multiplied by an FTE rate, which varies depending on the funding partner's own practices and the geographical region in which the research will be done. The FTE rate takes into account salary and benefits payable to the scientist as well as a certain percentage of company overhead attributable to the scientist. Alternatively, the funding partner may allocate a lump sum annually to the project, but may empower the joint steering committee to determine if additional FTEs are necessary beyond what the initial funding permits.

c. Equity Investments

The purchase of equity by a collaborator is truly a sweetener to the deal. Unlike signature payments, milestones, and royalties, equity infusions are usually not reachable by third parties who have in-licensed underlying intellectual property to the smaller partner. More important, perhaps, is the signal the equity purchase sends to the marketplace: the collaborator is betting not just on this research project, but on the company as a whole. For a private company, this validation from a major player can (and frequently does) set the stage for an initial public offering or an acquisition play. For a company already public, this message to the capital markets is likely to be a boon to the stock price. Dilution of existing investors is usually a trivial concern alongside these other considerations.

i. Pricing the Equity

Private companies may peg the price of stock sold in connection with a research collaboration to the most recent capital round. The purchaser may want to establish to its satisfaction that the most recent round was predominantly composed of new investors, not insiders setting an artificially high price. This is even more of an issue if the equity is to be sold in multiple tranches, with the price per share tied to intervening future institutional capital rounds.

In the case of public companies, purchasers will insist that their per-share price reflect the market price *before* the market absorbed the good news of a major research collaboration. One favored approach is to calculate an average of closing prices over a period of several days. The relevant period is usually between 10 and 30 days before the closing date.

ii. Multiple Tranches

Allies in a research collaboration will rarely make their investment in a single tranche. More typically, there will be several tranches, timed to coincide with achievement of research milestones. The first tranche is a given; subsequent tranches may depend on whether deliverables are received, whether scientific proof of concept is achieved, or whether the larger partner decides to exercise an option to enter into a development and commercialization license.

iii. Advantages of Equity Investment by a Collaborator

In addition to the positive signals sent to the market when a major industry player makes a significant investment in a smaller research partner, there are other advantages to this method of raising capital:

- The funding partner is not likely to be an overly controlling, activist investor, particularly if it is a multinational pharmaceutical company with other focuses for its corporate energies;
- The funding partner is likely to accept stock on terms similar to those offered in the most recent institutional capital round, rather than seeking more draconian terms;
- Existing institutional investors, such as venture capitalists, are likely to welcome the validation of the company signaled by this investment, rather than expressing concern about dilution;
- The funding partner is not likely to challenge board control or in other ways antagonize existing institutional investors;

- Willingness of the collaboration partner to invest in future tranches is likely to depend specifically on scientific achievements related to this collaboration, not on meeting broader company goals;
- If the collaborator takes a large stake in its partner, it arguably may be less motivated to pull out of the collaboration early and take a loss on the stock price if the initial collaboration results fall short.

iv. Disadvantages of Equity Investment by a Collaborator

- Most collaborators will equire a board seat or board information rights in return for a significant equity investment. This could give a specific collaborator access to more information than is strategically appropriate about prospective collaborations with its competitors.
- Similarly, a board seat or board information rights could inform this collaborator about a potential merger or acquisition opportunity faced by the company, giving the larger partner an opportunity to block a competitor's interest in the smaller company. The biotech company should seek the ability to restrict information related to potential transactions with competitors of the pharma company. Unfortunately, it may be hard to control the flow of information between directors off-line.

See Chapter V for additional discussion regarding equity investments by corporate partners and other outside investors.

d. Milestone Payments

While payments on later milestones are more appropriately considered in the context of a commercialization license[17] (as are royalty payments[18]), payments on achievement of early milestones are a standard part of a research collaboration agreement. Early milestones, achievement of which may trigger payment, may include:

- Achievement of scientific proof of concept[19]
- Successful completion of ADME/toxicity studies;[20]
- Filing of an Investigational New Drug application;
- "First dosing in man"; or
- Successful completion of Phase IIa studies.[21]

Typically, it will be the joint steering committee that will determine whether a milestone has been achieved, although this may be an issue on which the funding partner insists that its sole judgment should prevail, given the money it is investing. Where possible, to avoid controversy, the smaller partner should have negotiated in advance clear, objective standards for achievement of each of these milestones.

One area of controversy often involves the number of times a particular milestone must be paid. In the case of drug compounds, for example, it is usual to provide that the same milestone will only be paid once for compounds having the same active moiety;[22] in other words, if, during development, a closely related compound with better "druggability" is substituted for a lead compound, the pharmaceutical company will typically expect not to pay again for milestones already achieved by the initial, closely related compound. Some deals will allow for multiple payments for achievement of the same milestone in limited circumstances or reduced payments for milestones achieved more than once: for example, if a compound is retested for its efficacy against a different medical indication, new milestone obligations may be triggered.

In general, biotechs can expect that early milestone payments will be considerably lower than those paid down the development path; in other words, milestone payments will be "backloaded." This is a standard industry practice, particularly for very early-stage deals, and it merely reflects the perceived risks of the collaboration to the larger partner. Where there is room to argue for greater front-loading of the transaction, however, the smaller partner will want to do so as strenuously as the relationship will allow, remembering the very different impact on the company of early versus later payments in deals of this nature.

Exhibit 9-2
Pros and Cons of Various Approaches to Structuring Development Rights

	Commercialization License within Collaboration Agreement	*Option within Collaboration Agreement; Heads of Agreement Annexed*	*Option within Collaboration Agreement; Form of License Annexed*
PROS (Big Pharma Perspective)	—Pharma, as licensee, gets development and commercialization rights automatically —No need for corporate decisionmaking as to whether to exercise option —Early milestone payments linked to scientific progress, not option exercise	—Relative ease of subsequent option exercise, depending on the extent to which substantive terms are addressed in advance	—Greatest ease of subsequent option exercise —All substantive terms, including financial, are determined in advance —Financial terms offered now may be less generous when dealing with theoretical milestones and products than might later be offered
CONS (Big Pharma Perspective)	—Knowledge that pharma has no deadline on choosing among compounds may lead to internal complacency and missed patent filing/development opportunities	—Biotech partner may use this structure to avoid pinning down financial terms until more information about the science is available	—Financial terms offered now may be more generous when dealing with theoretical milestones and products than might later be offered

Exhibit 9-2
Pros and Cons of Various Approaches to Structuring Development Rights *(continued)*

	Commercialization License within Collaboration Agreement	*Option within Collaboration Agreement; Heads of Agreement Annexed*	*Option within Collaboration Agreement; Form of License Annexed*
PROS **(Biotech Perspective)**	—Predictability —Cachet of early announcement that Big Pharma has taken a license to develop and commercialize results of collaboration	—Biotech partner may use this structure to avoid pinning down financial terms until more information about the science is available	—Predictability —Ease of entering into license—no further negotiations
CONS **(Biotech Perspective)**	—May preclude 3rd-party development deals —Terms fixed	—Predictability of other terms —Pharma may insist on financial terms —Option exercise not guaranteed	—Terms fixed —Option exercise not guaranteed

6. Option to Develop and Commercialize

Although some research collaborations build in an automatic right to commercialize the fruits of the alliance in return for the funding partner's investment, an option grant is the more typical approach. The funding partner is given the option to enter into one or more development and commercialization licenses. (Sometimes one license covers commercialization of all the fruits of the alliance; sometimes the licensee may pick and choose what it wishes to license under individual agreements, leaving the unpicked fruit for the smaller partner to develop independently or with a third party.) The option can take the form of a mere notice of exercise, a right of first refusal, or a right of first negotiation. The terms of the resulting license may be established contemporaneous with negotiation of the research collaboration agreement (either as a full-blown form of license agreement or as simple "heads of agreement"), or negotiation of terms may be left to the future.

a. Notice of Exercise

Under this scenario, the funding partner has a fixed period of time to give notice that it intends to enter into a development and commercialization license with respect to the relevant collaboration intellectual property. Sometimes, this time period commences with some identifiable event (such as notice from the joint steering committee that proof of concept has been achieved). Alternatively, it may extend throughout the research term and into a fixed tail period of 6 to 12 months thereafter. License terms have previously been negotiated; once notice of exercise is given, the parties merely must act in a timely manner to execute the form of license agreement already agreed upon.

b. Right of First Refusal

Even if license terms have not yet been finalized, this scenario puts the licensee in a relatively strong position. The funding partner gets the first opportunity to enter into a commercialization deal with its collaborator. If the funding partner declines the opportunity to enter into a transaction on terms acceptable to the biotech, then the smaller partner may take the intellectual property to a third party for development. The general terms set out as "heads of agreement" and attached to the research collaboration agreement may govern the resulting transaction. Alternatively, the parties may negotiate license terms in good faith, with the smaller partner required to accept any reasonable terms the larger partner may propose. In any case, the funding partner will have a limited time period during which to exercise its right of first refusal. This time period is typically calculated in the same manner as is the option period referred to in the preceding section. If the time lapses without consummation of a transaction, the smaller partner may usually shop the intellectual property elsewhere. Since this often is a matching right—the right to match another offer received by the smaller partner—the smaller partner should resist this term strongly. Few companies will be interested in spending time negotiating a possible deal if they know the funding partner can step in and take that deal away.

c. Right of First Negotiation

This is a gentler approach, more favorable to the licensor. For a stated time period during and after the term of the collaboration, the funding partner must be approached first with an opportunity to enter into a development and commercialization license, even if the smaller partner is considering another commercialization partner. The parties again have a fixed period during which they will attempt to negotiate a license. In this case, unlike a right of first refusal, the licensor is not compelled to accept terms proposed by the licensee. On the contrary, the licensor may run out the clock if it does not feel the terms offered are favorable. Because of the stronger position in which this scenario places the licensor, licensees usually ask for a "most favored nation" clause to accompany a right of first negotiation: for a fixed period of time after negotiations fail, the licensor may not enter into a transaction with a third party on terms more favorable to that party than those offered under the right of first negotiation.

d. Rights in Unoptioned Intellectual Property

When the funding partner seeks an option to pick and choose among the intellectual property it will develop—compounds, for example—this may create a strategic business opportunity for the smaller partner with respect to the leftovers. If at all possible, the smaller partner should retain its rights (including development and commercialization rights) with respect to unoptioned leftovers from the research collaboration. The smaller partner should also seek a license under the funding partner's intellectual property rights, if any, in the unoptioned leftovers. Sophisticated collaborators will understandably want to block development by a former collaborator of anything too close to what they themselves are developing. They know they could be establishing a future competitor to their own product. However, the funding partner may be more flexible about granting rights to unoptioned leftovers that are clearly distinguishable, whether in chemical structure, method of action, or otherwise, from what has been optioned.

7. Term and Termination

a. Term

A research collaboration may extend for several years. On the other hand, if the funding partner's purpose is merely to kick the tires in preparation for a more substantial transaction between the parties, the collaboration may last as little as six months.

b. Early Termination

There are a number of reasons why either party may want the ability to end the collaboration early, acting either unilaterally or by mutual agreement. The parties are likely to want a unilateral right to terminate in the event of material breach or bankruptcy. They are likely to favor termination by mutual agreement (usually upon the vote of the joint steering committee) in the event the science fails.

The funding party also may want a unilateral right to end the collaboration without cause, at its own discretion—a proposal the smaller company should resist strongly. The funding partner may lose interest in the project, either because the science seems less promising over time or because the funding partner itself would rather focus its resources on other collaborators, other diseases. Some large companies also are prone to the syndrome of "the newest marble in the drawer," showing little patience and reassigning resources to newer projects. This is another reason to resist a unilateral right to terminate.

There is an immediate financial loss to the smaller partner if its collaborator withdraws: it may be left, for example, with an obligation to pay its FTEs for the remainder of the collaboration term. Much more important, though, is the reputational damage to a smaller partner when its collaborator withdraws early from the alliance: inevitably, doubt is cast on the science, regardless of the spin the parties may use in the press release. If the smaller company is publicly traded, its stock price may fall drastically; if the company is privately held, its next round of financing, if any, may be a "down" round, with much harsher terms.

A compromise position might be to accept the funding partner's right to terminate unilaterally without cause, but to stipulate that this can only happen during the final year (or other appropriate time period) of the collaboration. It is fair to ask that, in the event of its early termination without cause, the funding partner will continue to carry all or a portion of the smaller partner's FTE costs, if the smaller partner is contractually committed to keep those scientists on the payroll for the full collaboration term. Large pharmaceutical companies are likely to see the public relations value of "doing the right thing" by a collaborator's employees in the event of a failed collaboration.

E. Post-Closing Pitfalls That Can Derail a Research and Development Collaboration

Parties enter a research collaboration with high hopes. No one expects the science to fail; no one expects the term of the collaboration to expire without either party producing results worth licensing. But that is the biotechnology business—it is not for the risk-averse. Pharmaceutical companies know that they are taking a gamble with each collaboration.

Beyond the risks inherent in scientific research, there are other pitfalls the parties need to watch for if their research collaboration is to be successful. The most common include:

1. Change in Strategic Fit or Commitment to the Project

For the pharmaceutical partner, any one external research collaboration is but a single piece in a large jigsaw puzzle. The pattern of the overall puzzle may change, and as a result, the importance of a single piece to the puzzle may be diminished. For example, the pharmaceutical partner may acquire another major company, and it may be distracted for the next year or two trying to digest and restructure that company's research alliances. Or the pharmaceutical company itself may be acquired, with a similar result. Even if the company remains independent, it may reevaluate its strategies and decide that the focus of this collaboration no longer fits a "sweet spot."

Research and Development Collaborations

Exhibit 9-3
In Case the Collaboration Terminates Early

Financial Issues:	—Collaboration Agreement may provide for continuing support of scientists specifically assigned to the collaboration for the remainder of the term, or at least for several months after early termination.
	—Collaboration Agreement may provide for post-termination reimbursement for capital costs incurred at the funding partner's request solely to aid the collaboration, e.g., special retrofitting of laboratories.
Public Relations Issues:	—Collaboration Agreement may require joint press release.
	—If the collaboration is being terminated for reasons other than problems with the science (e.g., pharmaceutical partner is restructuring its own research focus), the Collaboration Agreement may require the larger partner to provide negative reassurance to the market: "Our decision is not related to the merit of the science."
Confidentiality Issues:	—Ensure mutual return of all proprietary biological and other materials.
	—Ensure mutual return of all proprietary written and electronic data and records.
	—Document communications to collaboration scientists and relevant company executives that the confidentiality obligations of the Collaboration Agreement survive termination.

Exhibit 9-3
In Case the Collaboration Terminates Early *(continued)*

Post-Termination Intellectual Property Issues:	—Consider that valuable intellectual property may have been created, even in a failed collaboration.
	—Where cross-licenses give each party non-exclusive rights to collaboration intellectual property, consider whether these rights are for research purposes only or permit development and commercialization—the rights are probably not symmetrical between the parties.
	—Even where Collaboration Agreement grants each party freedom to operate with respect to collaboration IP, larger party may want (and smaller party should resist) post-termination notice requirements with respect to further development of that and derivative IP.
Public Company Issues:	—Early termination of a key research collaboration may, for the smaller partner, be a material event requiring disclosure to the markets.
	—Avoid selective disclosure liability under Regulation FD: ensure that the bad news does not reach some investors earlier than others.
	—Until this bad news is disclosed to the markets, it constitutes "insider information"; anyone in the know should not buy or sell company stock.

2. Communication and Control Issues

The role of the joint steering committee is vital, not only in terms of project oversight, but also as a channel of communication between the management of the respective companies. If this channel fails in its role, or if management on either side disdains it, the collaboration is in trouble. In particular, the joint steering committee must take care not to let scientific and business issues be cast in terms of which party is in control.

3. Unrealistic Expectations

A biotechnology company in the heady days of its early successes—a thriving research collaboration with Big Pharma; perhaps a registration statement filed for an initial public offering, or lucrative offers to acquire the company before its Board of Directors—may overestimate its strength in the relationship. At the key stage where the parties are considering moving from a short-term research collaboration to a much longer-term development and commercialization relationship, unrealistic expectations about financial and other licensing terms can sink an alliance.

F. Alliances with Third Parties— Keeping Other Options Open

When negotiating the research collaboration agreement and any option grant or pre-agreed license terms, it is very important to consider how this deal may affect opportunities for other alliances. From the biotech company's perspective, it does not want to be a captive to a single pharmaceutical ally. Its investors want opportunities to expand the company beyond this specific collaboration—otherwise, the biotechnology company becomes a mere extension of its pharmaceutical partner. And depending on the medical indication, another pharmaceutical company might make a better partner for a different therapeutic. Nonetheless, the pharmaceutical company, for its part, does not want to invest hundreds of millions of dollars in bringing to market a product that its competitor controls for other indications. A few particularly problematic areas:

1. Right of First Refusal May Preclude Other Transactions

Frequently, the parties may agree to a right of first refusal in the pharmaceutical partner with respect to intellectual property developed outside the agreed-upon field, or even outside the collaboration. The consideration offered may be attractive, but consider also the chilling effect this may have on third-party interest. This chilling effect may last until such time as the original pharmaceutical partner exercises its right of refusal—but then that refusal itself may have a negative impact on third-party interest. As mentioned above, few third parties will spend the time in due diligence and negotiating a deal that the funding partner can choose to take away.

2. Right of First Negotiation May Also Have a Chilling Effect

Even a right of first negotiation with respect to intellectual property developed outside the agreed-upon field, or outside the collaboration, depending on how it is written, may have a chilling effect on third-party interest. If all third-party proposals must be temporarily shelved while the pharmaceutical collaborator considers matching or bettering the offer, third-party offers will be less forthcoming.

3. The Deal May Be Worth It; Rely on Contractual Protections

For the struggling biotechnology company, the opportunity to have a major pharmaceutical company make such a broad commitment may outweigh these theoretical concerns—indeed, the breadth of the commitment may be quite validating in the marketplace. Just keep a close eye on the wording of these rights, however. In particular, insist on absolute clarity with regard to the following:

- Notice requirements and deadlines
- Trigger events (should be objective and verifiable, not subjective)
- Expiration of rights of first refusal or negotiation
- Expiration of any time period during which no more favorable deal can be entered into with a third party than was proposed by the pharmaceutical partner

Clarity on these points will go a long way toward allaying third-party concerns about the pharmaceutical partner's overarching rights to attractive intellectual property.

G. Conclusion: Where Do the Parties Go From Here?

Lawyers try their hardest to craft research collaboration terms that will benefit their pharmaceutical or biotechnology clients. Ultimately, however, there is only one measure of success in a biopharmaceutical research collaboration: did the parties uncover or validate something that may, given sufficient time and resources, lead to a marketable drug that will benefit human health? If the answer is positive, then the parties are ready to move from a short-term research alliance to a long-term licensing commitment. If the answer is negative, the company must look for new research collaboration opportunities with other partners. Either way, the lawyers will be along for the ride.

Notes

1. *Growth Strategies for Large Biopharma Companies: Sustaining Future Growth Through Expanded Capabilities and Targeted Innovation*, Deloitte Research, 2004.

2. *Collaborations and Licensing in Global Pharmaceuticals and Biotech*, Visiongain Management Reports, 2005.

3. *Id.*

4. References in this chapter to "Big Pharma" or to major pharmaceutical companies should be read to include "Big Biotech." Similarly, references to smaller biotechnology start-ups or emerging companies are meant to include early-stage pharmaceutical companies also. The industries are converging, and old distinctions are becoming less meaningful.

5. *Collaborations and Licensing in Global Pharmaceuticals and Biotech*, *supra* note 2.

6. *The McKinsey Quarterly*, 2004 Number 1.

7. *Learning the BioPartnering Game: How to Achieve More from Your Alliance*, IBM Business Consulting Services, 2004.

8. Presentation by Dr. Campbell Wilson, Discovery Alliances, AstraZeneca, March 2003.

9. Each of these issues will be discussed in greater detail later in Section D of this chapter, "Key Provisions of the Research Collaboration Agreement."

10. *See* Section D.2 of this chapter, "Scope of the Collaboration."

11. *See* Section D.7 of this chapter, "Term and Termination."

12. *See* Section D.1 of this chapter, "The Joint Steering Committee."

13. *See* Section D.5 of this chapter, "Financial Terms."

14. *See* Section D.3 of this chapter, "Intellectual Property."

15. *See* Section D.6 of this chapter, "Option to Develop and Commercialize."
16. *Id.*
17. *Id.* at Section D.2.a.
18. *Id.* at Section D.2.b.
19. "Scientific proof of concept" with respect to drug discovery and development refers to the scientific study of the mechanism of action in humans of, for example, a particular compound. A positive result from this study will support a decision to proceed with development of the compound as a drug candidate.
20. These are studies that screen and eliminate potential drug candidates that manifest toxic properties *in vivo*. The term "ADME/Tox" (absorption, distribution, metabolism, excretion, and toxicity) is generally applied to the group of tests that are used to characterize a compound's properties with respect to absorption by the intestine, distribution to the organism, metabolism by the liver, excretion by the kidneys, and toxicity profiles.
21. "Phase IIa" refers to clinical studies of a drug candidate in human patients to determine initial dose-ranging tolerability and safety in single-dose, single ascending-dose, multiple-dose, and/or multiple ascending-dose regimens. Please see more detail in Chapters X and XIII.
22. "Active moiety" is defined under 21 C.F.R. § 314.108(a) as "the molecule or ion excluding those appended portions of the molecule that cause the drug to be an ester, salt (including a salt with hydrogen or coordination bonds), or other noncovalent derivative (such as a complex, a chelate or cathrate) of the molecule, responsible for the physiological or pharmacological action of the drug substance." More simply put, the active moiety of a drug molecule is the part that does the therapeutic work, regardless of what changes or deletions are made to other parts of the molecule.

Chapter X

FDA Regulation of Biomedical Research

Robert B. Nicholas
McDermott Will & Emery LLP
Washington, D.C.

A. Introduction

In the United States, most new prescription drugs and many medical devices must first be approved by the U.S. Food and Drug Administration (FDA) before they can be legally marketed. Clinical research is frequently a prerequisite to FDA approval of new therapeutics and diagnostics.[1] Clinical research is defined as a research study or investigational trial that uses human volunteers to test the safety and efficacy of new drugs or medical treatments.[2] Data resulting from clinical research trials are reviewed by the FDA as part of its application approval process. The FDA's clinical trial regulations, including those for devices and drugs (including biologics), provide a comprehensive set of rules designed to protect the welfare of human subjects and ensure the quality and integrity of clinical data.[3] Failure to comply with the clinical trial regulations may result in injury to study subjects; the FDA's refusal to consider the study data; administrative, civil, and criminal penalties; and civil liability.

This chapter discusses the FDA's rules governing clinical research trials of investigational drugs, biologics, and medical devices, three categories identified in the Federal Food, Drug, and Cosmetics Act (FFDCA).[4] The chapter is organized to provide a general understanding of those clinical trial regulations.

- Part One describes the history and purpose of the FDA's clinical trial regulations, briefly describes the role of other regulators, and identifies the roles and obligations of the parties subject to FDA regulation.
- Part Two provides an anatomy of a clinical trial and describes the basic regulatory framework governing a clinical investigation.
- Part Three discusses the rules for clinical studies conducted outside the United States when the sponsor intends to submit the resulting data to FDA.

This chapter does not thoroughly explore the differences between biotechnology drugs and traditional, chemically synthesized drugs. However, biotech drugs may present some unique issues for clinical studies because of the protein manufacturing process, and some trials, such as those for gene therapy, may also raise additional ethical and policy issues.

1. Introductory Note on Biotechnology and Clinical Trials

As biomedical knowledge has rapidly expanded during the past two decades, and new techniques have been developed to produce novel therapies and diagnostics, biotech products have constituted an ever-increasing percentage of clinical trials. Biotechnology-based therapeutics offer cutting-edge clinical research opportunities because they provide the potential for creating new medical treatments for a variety of conditions and illnesses that presently lack fully effective treatment options, such as AIDS, cancer, anemia, hemophilia, arthritis, diabetes, and Parkinson's disease.[5]

Under the existing regulatory structure, biotechnology is largely viewed as another technique for producing new drugs rather than a process producing therapeutic agents different from standard chemically synthesized drugs.[6] Thus, clinical trials that test the safety and efficacy of biotechnology-based products are subject to the same regulations as more traditionally produced drugs, biologics, and medical devices.[7] The FDA may, however, more closely scrutinize and impose additional requirements on biotech products. In terms of clinical trials and also, ultimately, product approval, one of the principal areas of additional attention can be the source and the development of the biological material used to produce the therapeutic or diagnostic product and the resulting manufacturing process.[8] These areas may be more heavily scrutinized because biotechnology may introduce new contaminants or create small differences in protein structures from those that are naturally occurring. Even small structural differences may have the potential to impact the safety and efficacy of a product.[9]

B. Part One—Overview of the Regulatory Framework

1. The History, Goals, and Purpose of Regulation

Modern-day regulation of investigational trials has its foundation in the reaction to testing of unwilling subjects during World War II, which was condemned by "The Nuremberg Code."[10] It is not surprising, therefore, that the primary focus of governmental and non-governmental regulations and guidelines for conducting clinical research is to protect the rights and welfare of human subjects. In addition, the FDA's regulations establish a system of checks and balances intended to ensure the integrity and scientific comparability of research data generated at multiple sites and submitted to the FDA as part of the product application approval process.

2. Government Regulation of Clinical Research

There are three governmental authorities that regulate clinical trials involving investigational drugs (including biological products) and medical devices: 1) the FDA; 2) the Department of Health and Human Services' (HHS) Office for Protection of Research Subjects (OHRP); and 3) the individual states. The FDA regulates clinical research involving drugs, medical devices, and food products within its jurisdiction (sometimes referred to as an FDA-regulated article or "test article").[11] The FDA defines a "clinical investigation" of a drug as any experiment in which a drug is used on one or more human subjects.[12] An experiment means "any use of a drug except for the use of a marketed drug in the practice of medicine."[13] Device investigations are defined as "an investigation or research involving one or more subjects to determine the safety or effectiveness of a device."[14]

OHRP oversees human subjects "research"[15] funded by HHS (e.g., National Institutes of Health (NIH), Center for Medicare and Medicaid (CMS)) and research conducted at institutions that have signed a research "assurance" of compliance with OHRP.[16] OHRP is responsible for the implementation of HHS requirements. HHS regulations, frequently referred to as the "Common Rule," primarily focus on institutional review boards (IRBs) and informed consent (IC) requirements. OHRP and FDA share similar requirements but differ in several significant ways, such as when research is subject to regulation and record-keeping requirements.[17] Most if not all academic medical centers and hospitals have signed assurances, as have some companies that are conducting federally funded human subjects research.[18] Compliance with both FDA's and OHRP's regulations is necessary when such institutions conduct clinical studies involving the use of a FDA-regulated drug or device.

> **Practice Points**
>
> — The FDA regulates clinical research involving use of an FDA-regulated product in humans ("test article"). Prior approval is required before research can begin.
> — OHRP regulates "human subjects research" generally at institutions receiving funding from federal government agencies, regardless of whether a test article is used. Prior OHRP approval is not required before research begins. Compliance with FDA regulations is also required when a test article is involved.
> — States generally do not require prior state approval to conduct clinical research, but specific state requirements may apply.

Nearly all states impose additional requirements for the conduct of clinical trials.[19] State laws regulating clinical trial research are generally not preempted by federal law.[20] For example, federal law defers to respective state jurisdictions regarding the age of consent to participate a clinical trial.[21] While many states set the requisite age at 18, certain states, such as Nebraska (legal consent at 19) and Alabama (legal consent at 14) diverge from the majority.[22] Confidentiality of medical records provides further example of the role of state law in the regulation of clinical trials. The Health Insurance Portability and Accountability Act (HIPAA)[23] preempts state privacy laws *except* where state law is more stringent than HIPAA regulations.[24] Because individual states may regulate medical research differently, practitioners need also to be aware of relevant state-based considerations.

Noncompliance with clinical trial regulations can result in adverse consequences, including increased risk to human subjects, delay in approval of applications of important new drugs and devices, and the compromise of business investments. At the administrative level, consequences may include the rejection of data by the sponsor or by the FDA and, accordingly, the delay of the sponsor's approval application. Since a principal investigator (PI) is charged with knowledge of the FDA's requirements, even innocent failures to comply with the regulations can result in publicly available notices of compliance deficiencies, such as the issuance of an FDA Form 483 or warning letter. In cases of deliberate misconduct, including conduct putting subjects at risk, the FDA may seek to impose criminal and/or administrative sanctions. When a study subject is injured, the failure to comply with the FDA's requirements may constitute evidence of negligence in a lawsuit.

3. The Roles and Obligations of the Parties

FDA regulations establish a system of checks and balances to achieve the dual goals of research subject protections and data integrity. Clinical research requirements target three specific parties: the "sponsor," PI, and IRB. Under current regulation, each party has specific obligations. The FDA acts as the gatekeeper to commencement of a clinical investigation, requiring approval (active or passive) of the "investigational new drug" application IND (drugs) or an "investigational new device" application IDE (devices). The IND/IDE must contain detailed information on the drug or device, including manufacturing information, preclinical safety testing, and a detailed investigational plan sufficient to justify the proposed clinical investigation. After a study is completed (and sometimes during the conduct

> **Practice Points**
>
> FDA regulations govern the activities of three parties:
> — Sponsor and/or CRO, the party who initiates the study and holds the IND/IDE;
> — PI, the party conducting the test using the test article;
> — IRB, the organization responsible for oversight of the study.

of the study), the FDA acts as the "policeman" seeking to ensure compliance with its regulations by inspections and audits of the studies and regulated parties. Failure to comply with FDA requirements can lead to administrative, civil, and criminal compliance and enforcement actions.

a. *Sponsor*[25]

The sponsor initiates and takes responsibility for the clinical trial. A sponsor does not conduct the study unless it is also the PI (sponsor-investigator) and thereby required to comply with the obligations of both the sponsor and the PI.[26] In the case of a drug, the sponsor holds and maintains the IND or, if a device is involved, the IDE. The sponsor's responsibilities include: 1) selecting qualified investigators; 2) providing the investigator with information needed to conduct a proper investigation; 3) monitoring and ensuring that the investigation conforms to the research plan and established IND/IDE protocols; 4) maintaining an effective IND/IDE; and 5) keeping the FDA and investigators informed of any significant adverse effects or risks associated with the drug. The sponsor is also responsible for developing and obtaining, when required, FDA approval of amendments to the clinical research protocol.

The FDA encourages sponsors of clinical trials, including sponsors of investigational products testing the efficacy of biotech-based therapeutics and diagnostics, to interact with the agency early in the drug development process.[27] Such early consultation is particularly recommended for novel proteins and similar products, including those qualifying for orphan drug designation, and fast-track or accelerated approval.[28]

b. *Contract Research Organization (CRO)*

The sponsor of an IND may legally transfer some or all of its responsibilities to a "contract research organization" (CRO).[29] To be legally effective, the delegation must be in writing. Sponsors frequently rely on CROs to monitor the investigation and may rely on CROs to perform additional functions, such as selecting and training the PI in the study protocol and requirements. In some instances, the CRO may take on the full responsibilities of the sponsor. The "monitor" is required to regularly visit a site and review the conduct of the study, help spot and correct difficulties in protocol compliance, compare forms for data discrepancies between the source documentation (patient charts and records) and case report form (CRF) (the sponsor's designated form for submission to the sponsor of required study data), and otherwise oversee and facilitate a site's conduct of the study. The FDA's oversight of a CRO is bounded by the sponsor's responsibilities assumed in writing by the CRO.

c. Institutional Review Board (IRB)

The primary purpose of the institutional review board is to protect the rights and welfare of human research subjects.[30] In this regard, the IRB is acting on behalf of the FDA in overseeing the day-to-day conduct of the clinical study. The IRB consists of an independent review group, responsible for review, modification, and approval or rejection of the study protocol and related documents. Enrolling study subjects and administration of the test article cannot begin unless and until the IRB approves, with or without required modification, the research protocol, the written informed consent form (ICF) required to be signed by the study subject, as well as any advertising used to recruit test subjects. The FDA requires that IRBs be composed of a qualified and diverse membership and possess the authority and competency to review (initially and on an ongoing basis), require modifications to, and approve, reject, and suspend clinical research.

The IRB is required to maintain detailed records of its operations and

> **Practice Points**
>
> — IRBs need written procedures clearly defining their policies and procedures, including when submissions are required, confidentiality and conflict of interest provisions, and FDA reporting obligations.
> — IRBs need to keep accurate and timely records of all activities. IRBs should develop forms and systems to be able to readily monitor studies and support regulatory compliance.
> — Institutions housing IRBs need to have clear policies on how to handle research misconduct and conflicts of interest.
> — IRBs should conduct periodic audits of their activities to ensure that the board is following procedures and in compliance with legal requirements.

to operate under written procedures. These procedures include requiring IRB review of research, initially and on an ongoing basis (at least once per year, unless more frequent review is necessary), review of changes to the investigational plan, and modification to the ICF.[31] IRB procedures also require notification to the IRB, and in some circumstances to the FDA, of changes in research activity, adverse event reporting, protocol deviations, and the suspension and/or termination of a study. IRBs frequently are part of the institution where the research is being conducted but also may be free-standing.

d. Principal Investigator (PI)

The principal investigator is the party conducting the scientific study[32] and the experimental article is administered by the investigator or someone acting under his/her direction. As the leader of the team, the investigator is frequently referred to as the PI, with other team members designated as "sub-investigators." The investigator is generally responsible for: 1) ensuring that the clinical study is conducted in accordance with the signed investigator statement (Form FDA-1572)[33] when drugs make up the test article, or an "investigator agreement" with devices, the investigational plan, and applicable regulations; 2) protecting the rights, safety, and welfare of the subjects; 3) control of the drugs or devices under investigation; 4) obtaining appropriate subject informed consent; and 5) obtaining IRB review and approval of the protocol, ICF, and advertisements used to recruit subjects.

The PI is required to follow the study protocol, which is the standard by which compliance is mea-

> **Practice Points**
>
> — PIs are responsible for the activities of staff assisting the PI on the study. PIs need to ensure that tasks are clearly delegated to qualified and trained staff, who are familiar with the protocol and regulations, and sufficient in number to conduct the study.
> — The PI is responsible for accurate and timely documentation of study activities. PIs cannot depend on study monitors or sponsor to perform their responsibilities.
> — The PI is responsible for keeping the IRB and sponsor informed of all significant study related activities.

sured. The PI is also responsible for reporting adverse events, protocol deviations, and other relevant matters to the IRB and the sponsor. It is important to understand that while the sponsor may prepare the protocol, informed consent form and advertising, the obligations to the IRB are largely those of the PI and not the sponsor. While the study is monitored by the sponsor, the PI has an independent obligation to follow the approved protocol and to otherwise perform the study according to the FDA's regulations, and cannot rely on the monitor for this purpose.

The PI is also required to maintain accurate and necessary records regarding the conduct of the study. The signed investigator agreement (devices) or Form 1572 (drugs) certifies to the FDA that the PI understands the FDA's requirements, has expertise in the subject of the trial, and will take personal responsibility for the conduct of the trial. In some circumstances the PI may initiate as well as conduct the study. In such circumstance the PI is considered a "sponsor-investigator" and is responsible for compliance with both the sponsor and investigator regulations. PIs at academic institutions may serve in this dual capacity when investigating new uses of approved drugs and biologics, when investigating drugs or devices developed by the PI, or when obtaining an IND to treat a patient with an unapproved drug or device.

e. *The Legal Relationships Between the Parties: Contractual Agreements*

In addition to the various governmental regulations governing the conduct of clinical trials of investigational products, the roles and rights of the various non-governmental parties are frequently governed by contract.

i. The Sponsor and Principal Investigator

The legal relationship between the sponsor and the PI is largely defined by the "Clinical Trial Agreement," or CTA. The CTA establishes the sponsor's and PI's responsibilities, including payment for the trial, and commits the parties to compliance with FDA and related requirements. Frequently the CTA contains the PI's representations and warranties concerning expertise, and certifies that the PI has not been disbarred or disqualified by the FDA from conducting the investigation and that the PI does not have a conflict of interest. The CTA usually obligates the PI to notify and cooperate with the sponsor in any FDA audit or investigation of the trial and also contains other provisions pertaining to confidentiality, rights in data and patents, and control over publication of study results. Importantly, the CTA contains the provisions for medical expense coverage in case of injury to the subject and potential liability arising out of the study. Liability is almost always retained by the sponsor and is subject to a standard indemnification agreement whereby the sponsor indemnifies the PI and the PI's institution for all potential liability relating to the clinical investigation. Ordinarily, when a PI is affiliated with a medical institution where the research is to be conducted, the institution also needs to be a party to the CTA. In these circumstances the sponsor also commits to compliance with the institution's rules and regulations, including the institution's IRB.

ii. The Sponsor and the CRO

As previously noted, the sponsor may transfer legal responsibility for compliance with FDA requirements to a CRO *provided* the transfer is in writing. Given the wide range of duties that a CRO may assume in an investigation, from merely monitoring the study to actually conducting the study, it is difficult to set out particularly what should be included in the agreement. However, the contract between the CRO and the sponsor needs to be carefully drafted so that there is no ambiguity about what obligations are being transferred and assumed. Standard clauses in-

> **Practice Points**
> — The CTA should clearly specify the respective rights and obligations of the parties, including the obligation of all parties to comply with FDA regulations, and state and federal law.
> — Critical elements of a CTA include liability and indemnification and rights to intellectual property, publication, and confidentiality. PIs need to ensure funding adequate to staff and properly conduct the study. Sponsors need to provide for notification by PIs of FDA audits and certification regarding conflicts of interest and debarment.
> — Institutions where research is being conducted ordinarily require that CTAs be between the institution and the sponsor; the PI's role is acknowledged.

clude confidentiality, intellectual property rights, liability and indemnification, cooperation and notification, and regulatory compliance.

iii. The Principal Investigator and the Study Subject

The principal agreement between the PI and the study subject is the ICF. Unless exemptions apply, a PI may only use a human research subject in a clinical investigation after obtaining legally effective informed consent from the subject or the subject's legally authorized representative.[34] The FDA requires that a person may only freely consent to being a research subject after being provided accurate and understandable information about the risks and benefits of the study. Unless exceptional circumstances exist, the subject must sign the IRB-approved ICF. Modification to the ICF, including those necessary to add newly discovered risks, require IRB review and approval before being used, and may require seeking new consent from the study subject. The PI has to make certain that, whenever legally possible, the study participants fully understand the potential risks and benefits of the experiment before the experiment begins. The information provided must be in a language understandable to the subject and, by regulation, cannot require the subject to waive any legal rights or release those conducting the study from liability for negligence.[35]

> **Practice Points**
>
> — The study protocol, ICF, and recruitment advertisement are ordinarily drafted by the study sponsor, though submitted by the PI for approval to the IRB.
> — IC is a process and not merely a written document. Special considerations apply when dealing with minors and other persons not able to legally give consent.
> — FDA inspections frequently find missing witness signatures, dates, and other problems with subject ICFs.
> — Newly discovered risks may require IRB approval of a new ICF and study subjects may need to be consented on the new ICF. Be sure to discard unused copies of obsolete ICFs so that the old form is not inadvertently used.

The FDA recognizes three exceptions to the IC requirement.[36] Exceptions exist (i) for a physician to preserve the life of an individual patient; (ii) for the conduct of a narrow class of research in emergency settings where IC is ordinarily not possible; and (iii) for use by the Department of Defense for specific investigational products in combat exigencies.

C. Part Two—Anatomy of a Clinical Trial

1. Before the Trial Can Begin

a. Drugs: Investigational New Drug Applications (IND)

A clinical study of a new drug ordinarily cannot begin until a sponsor has submitted, and FDA has approved, an IND. The IND contains information about the drug product and the investigational plan, including the research protocol. Prior approval[37] of an IND is required for all clinical investigations of drug products subject to FDA jurisdiction under § 505 of FFDCA,[38] or for biological products subject to the licensing provisions of the Public Health Service Act (PHSA).[39] Certain investigations, principally some investigations of legally marketed products, are exempt from the IND requirement.[40] However, such investigations are, nevertheless, ordinarily still required to be conducted in compliance with the IRB and informed consent regulations.[41]

b. Devices: Investigational Device Exemption (IDE)

FDA approval of an IDE is required before a device investigation can begin. For investigations of non-significant risk devices (NSR), IDE approval is assumed and the IDE does not actually need to be submitted to the FDA. The sponsor is, nevertheless, still required to comply with other IDE regulatory requirements, including IRB approval and informed subject written consent.[42] The IRB must also confirm that the investigation involves an NSR device. FDA approval of an IDE is required for all significant risk (SR) devices before an investigation can begin. An SR device is defined essentially as one that presents a potential for serious risk to the safety, health or welfare of a subject and is (i) intended as an implant, (ii) is purported for use in supporting or sustaining human life, (iii) is for use of substantial importance in diagnosing, curing, mitigating or treating, or otherwise preventing impairment of human health, or (iv) otherwise presents such a risk.[43] The research protocol, ICF, and recruitment ads for SR device study must also be approved by the IRB before the study can commence.

c. IRB Approval of the Protocol, ICF, and Study Advertisement

Before the study can begin, the IRB must approve the protocol, the ICF, and the advertisements to be used to recruit study subjects. The IRB has ongoing responsibility as the trial proceeds to review and approve any changes to the protocol, ICF, and study advertisements. The IRB is also responsible for "continuing review" at least yearly and more frequently if necessary to ensure the protection of the research subjects.

2. Beginning and Conducting the Trial

a. Subject Enrollment and Test Article Administration

Eligible subjects may be selected and the test article administered after the FDA and the IRB conduct their respective reviews and approvals. Drugs are ordinarily tested in "controlled" clinical investigations. In order to determine whether the drug has its intended effect, it is usually necessary to compare the effects on those who receive it (treatment group) and a "control group." A control group is comprised of subjects who

> **Practice Points**
>
> **Anatomy of a Clinical Study**
> — Before the trial begins
>   - Obtaining the IND/IDE
>   - Obtaining IRB approval
> — Beginning and conducting the study
>   - Subject recruitment and screening
>   - Administration of the test article
>   - Record keeping and reporting
> — After the study
>   - Completion of the study report and submission of the NDA/BLA/PMA
>   - FDA inspection/audit and review
> — Post-inspection compliance and enforcement actions
>   - 483s and warning letters
>   - debarment and disqualification
>   - administrative, civil, and criminal sanctions

meet the same study inclusion criteria as the treatment group but may receive no treatment, an inactive substance that looks identical to the investigational drug (placebo), a drug known to be effective for the condition being studied, or a different dose of the study drug. In prospective studies, the control group is studied at the same time as the treatment group. Historical controls, subjects from historical records who fit the study-specific criteria, may be appropriate depending on the study protocol.

Studies are frequently "blinded" and "randomized" to reduce the possibility of bias and control the placebo effect that occurs when subjects being treated with an identified experimental drug consciously believe their condition is improving. In blinded studies, neither the subject nor the PI knows which subjects will receive the study treatment and which are in the control group. In a randomized study, all subjects who meet the same inclusion criteria are randomly separated into groups that either receive the treatment drug or serve as the control. Such studies are called double-blinded, randomized, or placebo controlled trials.

Clinical trials involving drugs generally have four research stages, sometimes with sub-phases:[44]

- Phase I studies involve the administration of the test article (drug) ordinarily to a small number of healthy individuals (20-100), primarily to gather safety data, such as safe dosage for future tests.
- Phase II studies are designed to gather additional short-term safety data and dose range findings, but also effectiveness data. The drug is administered to a small number of subjects (up to several hundred) with the target disease.
- Phase III studies are similar to Phase II studies but operate on a larger scale (several hundred to several thousand), are statistically designed to determine whether the drug is safe and effective for the target indication, and to more precisely identify any drug-related adverse effects.
- Phase IV studies are conducted to continue evaluation of the safety and efficacy of drugs or therapies already approved by the FDA.

Products subject to CDER's accelerated procedure are approved on Phase II data, using surrogate endpoints, and Phase III studies are conducted post-approval.[45]

b. Control of the Trial: Record Keeping and Reporting

Record keeping is a crucial aspect of biotech regulatory compliance. The FDA takes the position that if there is no written record, the task was not performed. In the event of significant discrepancies between the source documentation (subject medical records) and the "case report form" (CRF; study data record), a PI faces the possibility of the data being discarded, resulting in delay or failure to obtain product approval. Egregious cases may also lead to a civil liability to sponsors and possibly study subjects and to FDA compliance or enforcement actions.

The PI has the principal responsibility to maintain timely and accurate records, including source documentation, CRFs, study article control records, and regulatory correspondence.[46] Specific reporting requirements include reports to the IRB (e.g., adverse event reporting, protocol deviations, changes in the study protocol), to the study sponsor, and to the FDA.

One of the PI's most significant responsibilities is to report adverse events. For drugs and biologics, a PI is required to "promptly" report to the sponsor any adverse effect that may reasonably be regarded as caused by, or probably caused by, the drug. If the adverse effect is alarming, the investigator should report it immediately.[47] For devices, a PI must submit to the IRB and the sponsor " a report of any unanticipated adverse device effect[48] occurring during the investigations as soon as possible, but no later than 10 working days after the investigator first learns of the effect."[49]

Practice Points

— FDA takes the position that if something was not documented, it was not done.
— Discrepancies between CRFs and source documents may indicate sloppiness or fraud. Periodic audits help detect missing data and discrepancies.
— Written procedures and systems are necessary to ensure timely reporting and accurate study documentation.
— Systematic failure in documentation or reporting can lead to termination of an IRB's right to approve FDA-regulated research or a PI being barred from future participation in FDA-regulated studies.

The device regulations, specifically, and the drug regulations, by implication, require the PI to report to the sponsor and IRB any deviations from the investigational plan to protect the life and well-being of a study subject. Other PI protocol deviation constituting serious or continuing noncompliance with FDA, sponsor, or IRB requirements, or otherwise results in an IRB termination or suspension of a study, the rules of the reviewing IRB should require the PI to report to the IRB (and the IRB's affiliated institution, if any), and perhaps the FDA, and the sponsor.

Generally, the FDA requires the PI to maintain study-related documents for two years after approval of the investigational product. The PI may physically maintain the study documents or transfer the responsibility to a third party.[50]

The sponsor must also comply with FDA record-keeping and reporting requirements. For example, a sponsor is required to report to the PI new information as the trial proceeds, and report to the FDA certain exceptions to IC involving emergency research[51] and the termination of any PI for noncompliance with the FDA requirements. If the drug presents an "unreasonable and significant risk" to subjects, the sponsor is required to stop the study and report to the FDA.[52] In order to identify any potential bias by the PI in the conduct of the study, the sponsor is required to submit to the FDA at the time of filing an approval application a list of clinical investigators who conducted covered clinical studies and certify certain financial arrangements, including: 1) that no financial arrangements with an investigator have been made where study outcome could affect compensation; 2) that the investigator has no proprietary interest in the tested product; 3) that the investigator does not have a significant equity interest in the sponsor of the covered study; and 4) that the investigator has not received significant payments of other sorts. If financial arrangement does exist between the sponsor and investigator, the nature of that relationship must be disclosed and any steps taken to minimize bias explained.[53]

3. After the Trial

a. *Submission and Audit*[54]

Once the necessary data has been developed, the sponsor submits a new drug or biological product application (respectively, NDA or BLA), or in the case of a medical device, a PMA or sometimes a 510(k). The FDA will approve the product if, in addition to meeting other requirements, the clinical data demonstrates the device, drug, or biological product is safe and effective for the labeled use, or in the case of a 510(k), if the device is shown to be "substantially equivalent" to another legally marketed device. As part of the NDA, BLA, and PMA approval process, FDA will conduct an audit/inspection of pivotal clinical studies relied on for approval.

b. *FDA Inspection*[55]

FDA has explicit statutory authority to conduct certain inspections, including inspection of clinical investigations subject to regulation by FDA.[56] Bioresearch monitoring inspections are conducted of PIs, sponsors, and IRBs and may be conducted: 1) routinely (randomly); 2) for cause (where there are allegations of fraud, subject safety concerns, or extensive allegations of noncompliance or other serious misconduct); and 3) on a pre-approval basis (pivotal studies relied on for approval of FDA-regulated products). Most inspections of IRBs and PIs are prearranged.

An inspection generally begins when an FDA inspector arrives at the site, presents his/her credentials, and issues a "Notice of Inspection" (Form FDA 482). If the inspection is for cause, a PI may receive prior notification, although the FDA will sometimes conduct a preliminary "routine" inspection to be followed by a for cause inspection. Generally, the FDA inspector is from the local district office and acts under the direction of the relevant center: the Center for Drug Evaluation and Research (CDER) for drugs; the Center for Biologics Evaluation

> **Practice Points**
>
> — Preparation for an FDA inspection begins long before the FDA arrives. Knowledge about the regulatory requirements and familiarity with the study protocol are essential for compliance. Standard Operating Procedures are useful, but only if adherence is monitored by periodic audits.
> — FDA inspections follow an established protocol. The FDA expects a study to be "controlled," e.g., conducted in accordance with the study protocol, as demonstrated by the study documentation.
>
> *(continued on page 451)*

and Research (CBER) for biologics; and the Center for Devices and Radiological Health (CDRH) for medical devices. Criminal investigations are conducted by FDA's Office of Criminal Investigation (OCI), sometime in association with the local Office of the U.S. Attorney.

The FDA's inspection authority for drug-related clinical studies is very broad. An authorized FDA representative may, at a reasonable time and upon request, have access to, copy, and verify "any records and reports" required to be kept, such as drug disposition records and case histories (including primarily subject-specific records and sponsor data reporting forms).[57] The FDA's authority for device studies is similarly broad and also allows inspection of "all records relating to the investigation."[58] However, records identifying individual subjects by name need be made available to the FDA only if the agency "has reason to suspect" that adequate IC was not obtained or if required reports were not submitted, incomplete, inaccurate, false, or misleading.

> **Practice Points**
>
> *(continued from page 450)*
> — Study documentation should be well organized, readily accessible, and complete and accurate. CRFs should be kept by subject identification number, and there should be separate binders for regulatory correspondence.
> — One person should be designated to interact with the FDA inspector(s). The person should be knowledgeable about FDA requirements and the specific study. Accurate records should be kept of the FDA's questions and documents copied by FDA.
> — Interactions with the FDA should be respectful and truthful. It is a criminal offense to lie to the FDA or to refuse an FDA inspection. However, you are free to disagree with the FDA.

The inspection can last anywhere from several days to months, depending on the size and complexity of the study and the focus of the inspection. At the conclusion of the inspection, the inspectors will conduct an "exit interview" during which the inspector(s) will inform the PI (or IRB administrator or chairperson, in the case of an IRB inspection, or sponsor) of any compliance issues noted. If the inspector has found deficiencies, he or she may issue a Form FDA 483 or "Notice of Inspectional Observation," commonly called a "483," which highlights the main findings. The most common observations from FDA inspections of PIs are: 1) failure to obtain proper informed consent; 2) failure to conduct the study in accordance with the investigational plan; 3) failure to maintain accurate, complete, and current study records; 4) failure to use IRB-approved informed consent forms: 5) failure to report unanticipated adverse events in a timely manner to the sponsor and the IRB; and 6) failure to maintain accurate, complete and current drug/device accountability records.

c. Administrative Actions—Civil and Criminal Penalties

Inspection may result in the recommendation of regulatory or administrative actions, including investigator disqualification[59] and fines, imprisonment, and other penalties under the FFDCA[60] or the United States criminal statutes. Potential FDA actions include: 1) warning and untitled letters; 2) re-inspection; 3) termination of an exemption (IND, IDE); 4) refusal to approve, license or clear the product (NDA, BLA, PMA, 510(k)); 5) withdrawal of approval or clearance (PMA, BLA, NDA, 510(k)); 6) implementation of the Application Integrity Policy;[61] 7) initiation of stock recovery or recall;[62] 8) seizure of test articles; 9) injunction; and, 10) prosecution under the FFDCA and other federal statutes.[63]

4. Preparing for FDA Inspections and Responding to FDA Allegations of Misconduct

FDA inspections of pivotal clinical studies are routine, particularly study sites with large enrollment or with results significantly different from other sites. For a party subject to regulation, compliance starts long before the inspection and requires a thorough understanding of FDA requirements and familiarity with the study protocol, as well as proper implementation of those regulations. Practitioners who seek to counsel and represent parties subject to FDA inspection need to be familiar with the FDA's inspectional protocol,[64] understand the limits of the FDA's inspectional authority, and know how to interact with FDA representatives. For example, it is important for the FDA to conclude that the investigation has been "controlled." This means demonstrating that the records are readily available and accurate, and that the PI is familiar with the protocol.

At the conclusion of the inspection, the FDA may issue a Form 483 or a warning letter for more serious infractions.

- *Reply to 483.* Reply to a 483 is optional, though a written reply is generally useful in communicating the party's position, demonstrating to the FDA a party's intent to cooperate, and creating a record for the future. If a party is going to reply, it should be delivered before the FDA makes any further decisions, ordinarily within 10 days to three weeks of receiving the 483. The reply should discuss in detail how the PI/IRB/Sponsor intends to address the cited deficiencies. Often, adoption of new procedures and/or staff training will address the specific problem and lessen the possibility of a reoccurrence. If appropriate, the party should make any necessary document corrections that can be made after the fact. Replies to a 483 and warning letters are public documents, after being redacted for confidential information. The former is available by request under the Freedom of Information Act (FOIA), whereas the latter is ordinarily posted on the FDA's Web site.[65]
- *Reply to warning letter.* The warning letter requires a reply, ordinarily within 15 or 30 days. The reply to the warning letter follows the same guidelines as that for a 483 reply.

5. FDA Criminal Actions and Other Potential Consequences: Qui Tam Suits and Adverse Publicity

In cases of extensive or deliberate noncompliance with the clinical trial regulations,[66] particularly if the FDA concludes that a PI or IRB is unwilling or incapable of compliance and in cases of fraud or other similar misconduct, the FDA may seek to disqualify a PI or IRB from conducting further FDA-regulated clinical research. If the PI or IRB is unable to convince the FDA not to pursue disqualification, the FDA offers an opportunity for the PI to voluntarily agree to disqualification in an informal conference, and will post the disqualification on the FDA Web site. If the voluntary method fails, the PI will receive an opportunity for a formal evidentiary hearing before the FDA's administrative law judge (ALJ), followed by appeals to the FDA's commissioner, and thereafter to federal court. The offer of an opportunity for hearing and related actions are matters of public record. Other options for FDA action include civil and criminal proceedings, the latter conducted in conjunction and under the direction of the local U.S. Attorney.

The PI may also face civil liability from sponsor-initiated legal actions. Additionally, if the clinical study was funded by NIH or another agency, or if medical costs were reimbursed by CMS, the PI faces the possibility of a qui tam suit brought by a private individual in a private attorney general capacity. In these circumstances, violations of FDA regulations and other federal and state laws may provide a basis for liability. In qui tam actions, the federal or state governments may intervene and become a party to the suit in order to increase the likelihood of success and participate in any negotiations and conduct of the case.

D. Part Three—Conduct and Use of Non-U.S. Studies

Historically, most clinical research submitted to the FDA was undertaken in the United States, initially in academic medical centers and more recently in private specialty medical practices. Increasingly, however, clinical research studies submitted to the FDA are being conducted outside the United States, including studies conducted under the European Union's clinical trial directive.[67] The FDA's regulations address: 1) the conduct of research performed abroad that is intended for submittal to FDA in support of a marketing application; 2) use in the approval process of clinical data from studies conducted outside the United States; and 3) the export of investigational products from the United States to other countries where the clinical investigation is taking place.

1. IND/IDE or Not

Studies conducted outside the United States may be conducted under an IND/IDE. Those studies must meet same the requirements as domestic studies conducted under an IND or IDE.[68] However, it is not necessary for foreign clinical studies to be conducted under an IND/IDE in order to be considered by the FDA.

2. FDA Acceptance and Use of Non-U.S. Clinical Data

When data from a clinical study that has been conducted outside the United States without an IND/IDE are submitted to the FDA, two questions arise. The first inquiry involves an evaluation of the adequacy of the protection afforded the study subjects. Generally, the FDA will accept clinical data for consideration obtained from clinical investigations performed outside the United States when the study conforms to the ethical principles established in the Declaration of Helsinki, or the laws of the respective country in which the research is conducted, depending on which provides greater protection to human subjects.[69] Additionally, the sponsor must provide assurances concerning the validity and integrity of the data submitted to the FDA. Among the factors considered, the study must be well designed, well conducted, and performed by qualified investigators.[70]

Foreign clinical data meeting the above standards may also form the *sole* clinical evidence for approval of a PMA or NDA, provided the data meet additional requirements. Those requirements are that the data be relevant to U.S. medical practice and determined to be valid without an FDA inspection, or, if an inspection is necessary, it is possible to conduct such an inspection.[71]

3. Export of Test Article

For studies to be conducted outside of the United States, the FDA permits export of the investigational products for use in clinical investigations in limited circumstances. An investigational drug generally may be exported without any special consideration under an IND, but only to a PI listed on the Form 1572 (drug).[72] In the absence of an IND, an investigational product may be exported for use in a clinical trial only with FDA approval.[73] Export of unapproved medical devices for use in a clinical study generally requires FDA approval.[74]

4. EU Clinical Trial Directive

The 2001 European Union Clinical Trial Directive, effective in EU member states in May 2004, increased clinical trial standards community-wide by adopting regulations comparable to the United States regarding the design, conduct, recording, and reporting aspects of clinical trials. The "ethics committee," defined as an independent body responsible for approving protocol, informed consent, and PI credentials, is the counterpart of the IRB. "Sponsors" and "investigators" are also provided for within the Directive.[75] The Directive: 1) provides specific time scales for ethics review; 2) requires submission to the Licensing Authority of an application for authorization[76] of clinical studies and approval by the respective authority in the Member State; 3) regulates manufacturing of the investigational medical product; and 4) establishes routine inspections. The Directive includes certain exceptions for drug development of particular biotechnology-based products. Specifically, time limits for approval by the Ethics Committee and Licensing Authority authorization are extended for clinical trials of "gene therapy, somatic cell therapy, and medicinal products containing genetically modified organisms."

E. Conclusion

Compliance with the FDA's clinical trial regulations is necessary for the protection of research subjects and the use of data from clinical studies to support marketing applications made to the FDA. Given the importance of clinical data for FDA submissions, practitioners can provide useful counsel and representation to parties involved in biomedical research, from the initiation of the research plan through acceptance of the data.

Notes

1. Certain drugs and devices do not require clinical research to support marketing of the product. Clinical research is not required, and in fact cannot be submitted when seeking approval of "generic" drugs, for example, copies of approved drugs, once patent protection has ended. 21 C.F.R. pt. 314 (2005). Due to potential safety and legal issues, FDA has not yet approved any generic biotech drug (called "follow-on biologics"). Clinical data also are not required to market non-prescription drugs subject to "monographs" for over-the-counter or "OTC" drugs. 21 C.F.R. pt. 330 (2005). At present no biotech drugs are subject to an OTC monograph. Most medical devices do not required clinical data to be legally marketed. For example, most low-risk devices do not require premarket review by the FDA. Many other devices are allowed to be marketed because they are "substantially equivalent" to grandfathered devices, for example, devices legally in commerce before May 28, 1976, the effective date of the medical device amend-

ments to the FFDCA. To gain market entry, manufacturers of devices claiming to be substantially equivalent must have FDA "clear" a premarket notification or 510(k). 21 C.F.R. pt. 807 (2005). Only infrequently will a demonstration of substantial equivalence require clinical data. Some devices however, including principally high-risk devices and some new devices, cannot be marketed without an approved premarket approval application (PMA). Clinical data are ordinarily required in PMAs to demonstrate a reasonable assurance of safety and effectiveness of the device for the labeled indication. 21 C.F.R. pt. 814 (2005).

2. Before a pharmaceutical, biotechnology or medical device company, or other sponsor can conduct clinical research, the sponsor must conduct preclinical research, which involves nonhuman testing methods, such as analytical testing and tests using cells, animals, and other biological systems. Preclinical research is intended to demonstrate to FDA that there is sufficient information concerning the safety of the investigational article to justify further evaluation in humans.

3. FDA's regulation of clinical trials of drugs, biologicals, and medical devices share a common set of regulations pertaining to informed consent (21 C.F.R. pt. 50 (2005)) and institutional review boards (21 C.F.R. pt. 56 (2005)). However, the process of commencing and conducting clinical studies of devices is subject to regulations different from but similar (21 C.F.R. pt. 812 (2005)) to those for drugs and biologics (21 U.S.C. pt. 312 (2005)).

4. 21 U.S.C. § 321 (2004). "The term 'drug' means articles intended for use in the diagnosis, cure, mitigation, treatment, or prevention of disease in man or other animals; and articles (other than food) intended to affect the structure or any function of the body of man or other animals." 21 U.S.C. § 321(g) (2000 & Supp. III 2003). "The term 'device' means an instrument, apparatus, implement, machine, contrivance, implant, in vitro reagent, or similar or related article, including any component, part, or accessory, which is . . . intended for use in the diagnoses of disease or other conditions or in the cure, mitigation, treatment, or prevention of disease, in man or other animals, or intended to affect the structure or any function of the body of man or other animals. . . ." 21 U.S.C. § 321(h) (2000 & Supp. III 2003). "Biological product" is defined as 'a virus, therapeutic serum, toxin, antitoxin, vaccine, blood, blood component or derivative, allergenic product, or analogous product, or arsphenamine or derivative of arsphenamine (or any other trivalent organic arsenic compound), applicable to the prevention, treatment, or cure of a disease or condition of human beings.'" Public Health Service Act, Pub. L. No. 85-881, 72 Stat. 1704, 42 U.S.C. 262(i) § 262 (2000 & Supp. III 2003).

5. *See* Center for Biologics Evaluation and Research, Food & Drug Admin., Commemorating 100 Years of Biologics Regulation 26-30 (September 2002), www.fda.gov/cber/inside/centennial.html.

6. Coordinated Framework for the Regulation of Biotechnology, 51 Fed. Reg. 23,301 (Exec. Off. of the Pres./Off. of Sci. and Tech. Policy, June 26, 1986). The Coordinated Framework examined the regulatory authorities of FDA, USDA, EPA and NIH over various biotechnology products and set out an overall approach intended to fill gaps in and coordinate potentially overlapping agency regulation. The document is based on the premise that biotech products are not different from, and should not be regulated differently than, their traditionally produced counterparts.

7. For example, most biological products, including products produced by newer biotech techniques, meet the definition of "drugs" under the FFDCA, yet are regulated as biologics. Center for Biologics Evaluation and Research, Food & Drug Admin., Frequently Asked Questions, http://www.fda.gov/cber/faq.html.

8. 21 U.S.C. §§ 372-374 (2000 & Supp. III 2003); 21 U.S.C. § 331(e), (f) (2000 & Supp. III 2003). *See also* Michelle Meadows, *The FDA's Drug Review Process*, FDA CONSUMER MAGAZINE (July-Aug. 2002), http://www.fda.gov/fdac/features/2002/402_drug.html.

9. Robert L. Zeid, *Regulatory and Development Issues in the Demonstration of Therapeutic Equivalence for Multisource Biotech-Derived Pharmaceuticals*, 34 DRUG INFO. J. 919, 921 (2000); *also* Robert L. Zeid, *Multi-Source Biotech–Derived Pharmaceuticals: Regulatory, Legal, and Scientific Issues in Development*, http://biotech.about.com/od/regulation/; Center for Drug Evaluation and Research, Food & Drug Admin., *Guidance for Industry: Content and Format of Investigative New Drug Applications (IND), For Phase 1 Studies of Drugs* (November 1995), http://www.fda.gov/cder/guidance/phase1.pdf (discussing manufacturing differences in biotechnology-derived products); Center for Drug Evaluation & Research, Food & Drug Admin., *Guidance for Industry: S6 Preclinical Safety Evaluation of Biotechnology-Derived Pharmaceuticals* (July 1997), http://www.fda.gov/cder/guidance/1859fnl.pdf (discussing the safety concerns arising from the presence of impurities or contaminants in biotechnology-derived pharmaceuticals).

10. *See, e.g.*, THE NUREMBERG CODE, TRIALS OF WAR CRIMINALS BEFORE THE NUREMBERG MILITARY TRIBUNALS UNDER CONTROL COUNCIL LAW No. 10, Vol. 2, pp. 181-82. Washington, D.C.: U.S. Gov't Print. Off., 1949 (http://www.hhs.gov/ohrp/references/nurcode.html). *See also* HORST H. FREYHOFER, THE NUREMBERG MEDICAL TRIAL: THE HOLOCAUST AND THE ORIGIN OF THE NUREMBERG MEDICAL CODE (Peter Lang Publishing, 2005).

11. Protection of Human Subjects, 21 C.F.R. pt. 50 (2005); Institutional Review Boards, 21 C.F.R. pt. 56 (2005); Investigational New Drug Application, 21 C.F.R. pt. 312 (2005); Investigational Device Exemptions, 21 C.F.R. pt. 812 (2005), http://www.fda.gov/oc/gcp/regulations.html; Good Clinical

Practice in FDA-Regulated Clinical Trials, Regulations (http://www.fda.gov/oc/gcp/default.html); International Conference of Harmonization-Good Clinical Practices (ICH-GCP); guidelines for the conduct of clinical research which have been accepted by the EU, U.S. and Japan. *See* http://www.fda.gov/oc/gcp/guidance.html.

12. 21 C.F.R. § 312.3 (2005).

13. *Id.* (emphasis added). The "practice of medicine" exemption permits a physician to use an approved drug for any purpose, including uses not contained in the FDA-approved label (*e.g.*, off-label uses) subject only to state laws governing the practice of medicine. However, the exemption does not apply to the use by a physician of an unapproved product.

14. 21 C.F.R. § 812.3 (2005).

15. "Research" refers to a systematic investigation, including research development, testing, and evaluation, designed to develop or contribute to generalizable knowledge. Activities that meet this definition constitute research for purposes of this policy, whether or not they are conducted or supported under a program that is considered research for other purposes. OHRP jurisdiction is invoked by this definition of research rather than by whether the study involves an investigational article, or the off-label use of an approved drug or device. 45 C.F.R. § 46.102 (2005). *See* Office for Human Research Protections (OHRP), http://www.hhs.gov/ohrp/.

16. As a condition of receipt of federal funds for human subjects research, an institution is required to sign an "assurance" to the effect that *all* research at the institution will be conducted in compliance with the Common Rule, not merely federally funded research.

17. A comparison of the principal differences between FDA regulations and the Common Rule is contained at *Comparison of FDA and HHS Human Subject Protection Regulations*, http://www.fda.gov/oc/gcp/comparison.html.

18. Federal Policy for the Protection of Human Subjects, Final Rule, 56 Fed. Reg. 28,003 (HHS, NSF, June 18, 1991).

19. Sandra P. Kaltman & John M. Isidor, *State Laws Affecting Institutional Review Boards*, 4 MED. RESEARCH LAW & POLICY 417 (2005). For example, states may regulate such issues as age and capacity of consent, genetic research, confidentiality of medical records, protection of vulnerable patients, clinical research, IRBs, investigational drugs, delegation of authority to perform medical practice, or referral fees and recruitment methods of clinical trials.

20. *Id.*

21. 45 C.F.R. § 46.402(a) (2005).

22. Kaltman, *supra* note 20, at 417.

23. Health Insurance Portability and Accountability Act of 1996, Pub. L. No. 104-191, 110 Stat. 1936 (codified at 42 U.S.C. § 201). HIPAA estab-

lishes minimum federal standards for the privacy/confidentiality and security of certain individually identifiable health-related information developed or maintained in electronic format.

24. Kaltman, *supra* note 20, at 417.

25. Responsibilities of Sponsors and Investigators, 21 C.F.R. §§ 312.50–312.70 (2005), drugs; Investigational Device Exemptions, 21 C.F.R. §§ 812.1–812.47 (2005), devices.

26. A sponsor does not conduct the study unless the sponsor is also the PI ("sponsor-investigator") and thereby is required to comply with the obligations of both the sponsor and the PI, 21 C.F.R. § 312.3 (2005).

27. Specifically, eligible sponsors must be engaged in clinical study to support a claim of efficacy, and the product at issue must have "the potential to represent a significant advance in the treatment, diagnosis, or prevention of a disease or condition, or to address an unmet medical need." *See* Center for Biologics Evaluation and Research, Food and Drug Administration, Guidance for Industry: Independent Consultants for Biotechnology Clinical Trial Protocols 2 (August 2004), http://www.fda.gov/ohrms/dockets/98fr/03d-0112.gdl00001.pdf. This program is available for a subset of products covered by the Prescription Drug User Fee Amendments of 2002 (PDUFA III), Pub. L. No. 107-188, 116 Stat. 594 (codified at 21 U.S.C. § 356b (2000 & Supp. III 2003)).

28. 21 C.F.R. pt. 314 (2005).

29. 21 C.F.R. § 312.52 (2005).

30. *See* General Requirements for Informed Consent, 21 C.F.R. § 50.20 (2005); IRB Functions and Operations, 21 C.F.R. § 56.108 (2005); Assurance of IRB Review, 21 C.F.R. § 312.66 (2005), drugs; and IRB Review and Approval, 21 C.F.R. §§ 812.60–812.66 (2005), devices.

31. 21 C.F.R. § 56.108 (2005).

32. 21 C.F.R. §§ 50, 54, 56, 312(D), 812(E) (2005).

33. *See* Information for Sponsor-Investigators Submitting Investigational New Drug Applications (INDs), Instructions for FDA Form 1572. Form 1572 is required to be signed by the PI. Form 1572 specifically acknowledges the PI's understanding of FDA's regulations and the study protocol and his/her agreement to conduct the study in accordance with the regulations and the protocol. *See* http://www.fda.gov/cder/forms/1571-1572-help.html.

34. 21 C.F.R. § 50 (2005); 21 C.F.R. § 312.60 (2005) (IND); 21 C.F.R. § 812.100 (2005) (IDE).

35. 21 C.F.R. § 50.20 (2005).

36. 21 C.F.R. §§ 50.23, 50.24 (2005).

37. An IND becomes effective 30 days after FDA receives it unless the sponsor is notified by FDA that a clinical hold has been placed on the investigation. 21 C.F.R. § 312.40 (2005).

38. 21 U.S.C. § 355 (2000 & Supp. III 2003).
39. 42 U.S.C. § 262 (2000 & Supp. III 2003).
40. 21 C.F.R. § 312.2 (2005).
41. *Id.*
42. 21 C.F.R. § 812.2 (2005).
43. 21 C.F.R. § 812.3 (2005).
44. *See generally* Center for Drug Evaluation and Research, Food & Drug Admin., Guidance for Industry: General Guidelines for the Clinical Evaluation of Drugs, http://www.fda.gov/cder/guidance/old034fn.pdf.
45. 21 C.F.R. subpt. H (2005).
46. 21 C.F.R. § 312.62 (2005), drugs; 21 C.F.R. § 812.140 (2005), devices.
47. 21 C.F.R. § 312.62 (2005).
48. An "unanticipated adverse device effect" is any serious adverse effect on health or safety; any life-threatening problem or death caused by or associated with a device if that effect, problem, or death was not previously identified in nature, severity, or degree of incidence in the application; or any other unanticipated serious problem associated with a device that relates to the rights, safety, or welfare of subjects. Investigator Recordkeeping and Record Retention, 21 C.F.R. § 312.62 (2005).
49. 21 C.F.R. § 812.150 (2005).
50. 21 C.F.R. §312.62 (2005), drugs; 21 C.F.R. § 812.140 (2005), devices.
51. 21 C.F.R. § 50.24 (2005).
52. 21 C.F.R. §§ 312.53–312.57 (2005).
53. 21 C.F.R. pt. 54 (2005).
54. Applications for FDA Approval to Market a New Drug, 21 C.F.R. pt. 314 (2005), Premarket Approval of Medical Devices, 21 C.F.R. pt. 814 (2005), Establishment Registration and Device Listing for Manufacturers and Initial Importers of Devices, 21 C.F.R. pt. 807 (2005).
55. Investigational New Drug Application, 21 C.F.R. pt. 312 (2005); Premarket Approval of Medical Devices, 21 C.F.R. pt. 814 (2005).
56. Investigational New Drug Application, 21 C.F.R. pt. 312 (2005); Premarket Approval of Medical Devices, Investigational Device Exemptions, 21 C.F.R. pt. 814 (2005).
57. The names of study subjects are not required to be divulged unless the records of particular individuals require a more detailed study or if fraud is suspected.
58. 21 C.F.R. pt. 814 (2005).
59. 21 C.F.R. § 312.70 (investigator disqualification/drugs), § 812.119 (investigator disqualification/devices) (2005).

60. 21 U.S.C. § 333 (2000 & Supp. III, 2003).

61. HHS/FDA, Fraud, Untrue Statements of Material Facts, Bribery, and Illegal Gratuities, Final Policy, 56 Fed. Reg. 46,191 (Nov. 10, 1991). A company found to have submitted false data to FDA, or otherwise to have engaged in fraudulent actions, may be subject to the AIP. Data in support of approval or other application submitted by a company subject to an AIP receive additional scrutiny before acceptance by FDA.

62. FDA withdrawal of a product approval results in the product being considered adulterated, misbranded, and otherwise violative of the FFDCA. In lieu of FDA seizure of products in commerce, the manufacturer may have the option of removing the product from the market via a recall or market recovery, or stock recovery of product still subject to the firm's direct control. Recalls are generally voluntary because, except for medical devices, FDA does not have the authority to order the mandatory recall of a product. 21 C.F.R. pts. 7 (Enforcement Policy), 810 (Medical Device Recall Authority).

63. *Id.*; *see also* 18 U.S.C. § 371 (conspiracy), § 1001 (fraud and false statements), §§ 1341, 1343 (mail and wire fraud), and § 1505 (obstruction of justice) (2000 & Supp. III, 2003).

64. *See* FDA's INVESTIGATIONS OPERATIONS MANUAL 2005, http://www.fda.gov/ora/inspect_ref/iom/default.html.

65. Availability for public disclosure of data and information in an IND, 21 C.F.R. § 312.130 (2005). Confidentiality of data and information in a premarket approved application (PMA) file, 21 C.F.R. § 814.9 (2005).

66. 21 C.F.R. pts. 50, 56, 312, and/or 812 (2005).

67. Council Directive 2001/20/EC, art. 2, 2001 O.J. (L121/34).

68. 21 C.F.R. pts. 312, 812 (2005).

69. A clinical study involving a medical device must adhere to the ethical principles of the 1983 version of the Declaration, Research Conducted Outside the United States, 21 C.F.R. § 814.15(a) (2005), devices; whereas a clinical study involving drugs must conform to the 1989 version of the Declaration, Foreign Clinical Studies Not Conducted Under an IND, 21 C.F.R. § 312.120 (2005), drugs. *See also FDA Guidance for Industry, Acceptance of Foreign Clinical Studies* (March 2001), http://www.fda.gov/cder/guidance/fstud.html.

70. *Id.* 21 C.F.R. § 312.120 and 314.106 (drugs), § 814.15 (devices) (2005).

71. *Id. See* International Conference on Harmonisation; Guidance on Ethnic Factors in the Acceptability of Foreign Clinical Data; Availability, 63 Fed. Reg. 31,790 (HHS, FDA, June 10, 1998). *See also Guidance for Industry, E5 Ethnic Factors in the Acceptability of Foreign Clinical Data Questions and Answers,* http://www.fda.gov/cber/gdlns/iche5ethnic.pdf.

72. 21 C.F.R. § 312.110 (2005).

73. *Id.*

74. 21 C.F.R. § 812.18 (2005). There is an extensive discussion of various FDA export requirements for unapproved drugs and devices in FDA, *Guidance for Industry on: Exports and Imports Under the FDA Export Reform and Enhancement Act of 1996* (Draft, March 1998), http://www.fda.gov/oc/guidance/frexport.html.

75. Council Directive 2001/20/EC, art. 2, 2001 O.J. (L121/34).

76. For example, the Medicines and Health-care Products Regulatory Agency (MHRA) is the regulatory and licensing authority of the U.K.

Chapter XI

Privacy Issues for Biotechnology Companies

Steve A. Schwarm
Polsinelli Shalton Welte Suelthaus PC
Topeka, Kansas

Anne Stohr O'Brien
Polsinelli Shalton Welte Suelthaus PC
Kansas City, Missouri

A. Introduction

In 1996 Congress passed a national privacy law, the Health Insurance Portability and Accountability Act of 1996 (HIPAA), Public Law 104-191 (August 21, 1996). Under authority granted by HIPAA, the Department of Health and Human Services (HHS) promulgated Privacy Regulations that control the use and disclosure of health information. HIPAA and the Privacy Regulations apply to "Covered Entities," consisting of health-care providers, health insurance companies, health-care clearinghouses, and prescription drug card sponsors.[1] Biotechnology companies are generally not considered to be Covered Entities, and thus it is not immediately obvious how HIPAA may affect such companies. There are, however, instances in which biotech organizations may fall within HIPAA and the Privacy Regulations. Additionally, a biotech company may interact with a Covered Entity and will have to know the HIPAA requirements.

First, a biotech company should not automatically assume that it falls outside the definition of a Covered Entity. Counsel for the company should carefully examine the functions and services provided by the company, and the billing of those functions/services, in the context of the definition of a Covered Entity in the Privacy Regulations. The Centers for Medicare and Medicaid Services provides a decision tool for determining covered entity status at http://www.cms.hhs.gov/hipaa/hipaa2/support/tools/decisionsupport/default.asp.

In addition, a researcher for a biotech company may be a Covered Entity if he or she furnishes health-care services to individuals, including the subjects of research, and transmits any health-care information in a HIPAA standard transaction. For example, a researcher who conducts a clinical trial that involves the delivery of routine health care to the research subjects and transmits health information in electronic form to a third-party payer for payment would be a Covered Entity under the HIPAA Privacy Regulations.

Second, biotech companies need health data from Covered Entities in order to conduct research. Biotech company researchers will need to have an understanding of the HIPAA Privacy Regulations so they can effectively work with the Covered Entities to obtain the needed information. For example, a Covered Entity may request HIPAA-compliant authorizations, signed by the subjects of the information, from a biotech company requesting health-care information. As an alternative to an authorization, a Covered Entity may want to obtain a waiver of authorization from an Institutional Review Board or Privacy Board pursuant to the procedure for such outlined in the Privacy Regulations. If the requested review of health information is preparatory to research, the Covered Entity might request that the researcher provide the necessary HIPAA representations before disclosing health information to the researcher. If the requested information constitutes a "limited data set" under the Privacy Regulations, the researcher and the Covered Entity might want to enter into a HIPAA-compliant Data Use Agreement for the use and disclosure of health information.

Third, although HIPAA does not require a business associate agreement for disclosures from a Covered Entity to a researcher for research purposes, the Covered Entity may request that the researcher enter into such an agreement. The business associate agreement will control how the biotech company can further use and disclose the health information, including how it

Privacy Issues for Biotechnology Companies

can respond to subpoenas, discovery requests, and other legal process, and impose upon the biotech company certain obligations to assist the Covered Entity with access to and amendment of personal health information (PHI) and accounting of disclosures of PHI. For the above reasons, it is very important for a biotech company to have a general understanding of HIPAA and the Privacy Regulations.

In addition to HIPAA, there are other federal laws, such as the federal common-law rule relating to human research and federal certificates of confidentiality, which may affect biotech companies. In this chapter, we will provide a general overview of HIPAA, with particular attention to the Privacy Regulations related to research, as well as other federal laws relevant to the privacy of health-care information that may be pertinent to biotech companies. Further, because of the large number of biotech companies in Canada, this chapter will also briefly explore Canadian privacy laws that may impact biotech companies.

Although state privacy laws will not be discussed in this chapter due to the sheer volume of material, it is important to note that some state privacy laws may cover the same subject matter as the HIPAA Privacy

Practice Points

Useful Terms for Understanding HIPAA

— "Covered Entity": typically includes health-care providers, health insurance companies, health-care clearinghouses, and Prescription Drug Card Sponsors, who transmit healthcare information in an electronic form in connection with a transaction covered by HIPAA.

— "Individually Identifiable Health Information" or "IIHI": a subset of health information collected from an individual that could reasonably be used to identify that person.

— "Protected Health Information": IIHI that is maintained or transmitted via written or electronic records or orally.

— "Notice of Privacy Practices" or "NPP": Adequate notice provided to an individual of the possible uses and disclosures of their PHI and the individual's rights under HIPAA.

— "Business Associate": an entity that uses or discloses PHI to perform services or functions on behalf of a Covered Entity under the terms of a Business Associate Agreement with a Covered Entity.

Regulations. If that is the case and if the HIPAA Privacy Regulations are contrary to state privacy law, the general rule is that the HIPAA Privacy Regulations will preempt the state law. There are, however, exceptions to this general rule; for example, where the state law is "more stringent" than the HIPAA Privacy Regulations, the state law controls. Before using or disclosing protected health information, biotech company counsel should be familiar with the state privacy laws in the states in which the biotech company is located and/or does business.

If a biotech company conducts clinical research trials in a foreign country or otherwise conducts business internationally, counsel for that company needs to be aware of foreign privacy requirements, particularly if the biotech company moves health-care data from one country to another. Some foreign countries may prohibit the transfer of data within their borders if the data has not been collected in compliance with that country's privacy law. For an in-depth discussion of international privacy laws, see Chapter XIX, "Expansion: European and International Considerations for Biotechnology Companies."

B. The National Approach to Health-Care Privacy

1. Health Insurance Portability and Accountability Act of 1996

The Health Insurance Portability and Accountability Act of 1996 (HIPAA) was enacted by Congress with the intent of improving the efficiency and effectiveness of the country's health-care system. One area of improvement was in the protection of individual health-care information from unauthorized use or disclosure. The Secretary of the Department of Health and Human Services promulgated standards for the privacy and security of this type of information. The final security standards (Security Regulations) (45 C.F.R. Parts 160, 162, and 164) became effective April 21, 2003. Covered Entities, with the exception of small health plans, had to comply with the security standards by April 21, 2005. Small health plans had to comply with the security standards by April 21, 2006. The Privacy Regulations (45 C.F.R. Parts 160 and 164) became effective April 14, 2001. The deadline for compliance with the Privacy Regulations for most Covered Entities was April 14, 2003. Small health plans had until April 14, 2004 to comply.

HIPAA establishes a "federal floor" for protection of "individually identifiable health information."[2,3,4] Individually identifiable health information (IIHI) is defined in 45 C.F.R. § 160.103 as a "subset" of health information collected from an individual and includes demographic information that:

a) Is created or received by a health-care provider, health plan, employer or health-care clearinghouse;
b) Relates to the past, present, or future physical or mental health or condition of an individual, the provision of health care to an individual, or the past, present or future payment for the provision of health care to an individual; and
   (i) that identifies the individual; or
   (ii) with respect to which there is a reasonable basis to believe the information can be used to identify the individual.

Individually identifiable health information includes:

- Name;
- Address (all data smaller than a state);
- Phone numbers;
- Fax numbers;
- E-mail address;
- Social Security number;
- Medical Record number;
- Health Plan Beneficiary number;
- Dates (except year) directly related to the individual, such as date of birth, date of death, admission date, discharge date, etc.;
- Account numbers;
- Finger and voice prints;
- Account numbers;
- Certificate/license numbers;
- Vehicle identifiers, serial numbers, including license plate;
- Device identifiers and serial numbers;
- Web Universal Resource Locators (URLs);
- Internet Protocol (IP) address numbers;
- Full-face photographic images and any comparable images; and
- Any other unique identifying number, characteristic, or code, except as permitted by the Privacy Regulations.[5]

Health information that does not contain the above identifiers and with respect to which there is no reasonable basis to believe that the information can be used to identify an individual is *not* individually identifiable health information. Such information is considered "de-identified" information, and the constraints of the HIPAA Privacy Regulations do not apply.

IIHI is also referred to as Protected Health Information (PHI). PHI means individually identifiable health information that is:

(i) Transmitted by electronic media;
(ii) Maintained in any medium described in the definition of electronic media at 45 C.F.R. § 162.103; or
(iii) Transmitted or maintained in any other form or medium. Protected health information excludes individually identifiable health information in: (i) education records covered by the Family Educational Rights and Privacy Act, as amended, 20 U.S.C. § 1232g; (ii) records described at 20 U.S.C. § 1232g(a)(4)(B)(iv); and (iii) employment records held by a Covered Entity in its role as employer. If IIHI is not maintained or transmitted in the manner described in this definition, it is not considered PHI and thus is not covered by the HIPAA Privacy Regulations.
(iv) In summary form, PHI is personal health information that includes written records, electronic health records, and "oral" information.

Compliance with the Privacy Regulations requires observance of complex privacy and access requirements for PHI as defined by HIPAA. Under the Privacy Regulations, the persons/entities to which HIPAA applies are called "Covered Entities" (45 C.F.R. § 160.103). The general rule is that: "[a] Covered Entity may not use or disclose an individual's protected health information, except as otherwise permitted or required by this subpart." 45 C.F.R. § 164.502(a). The Privacy Regulations also create a new set of rights for patients with respect to PHI, requiring the Covered Entities to provide patients with benefits such as notice of privacy practices, access to health information in certain circumstances, the right to amend their PHI, and an accounting of health information disclosures in certain circumstances.

"Covered Entity" means (i) a health plan, (ii) a health-care clearinghouse, or (iii) a health-care provider that transmits any health information in

Privacy Issues for Biotechnology Companies 515

electronic form in connection with a transaction covered by HIPAA. It also includes a prescription drug card sponsor under the Medicare Prescription Drug, Improvement, and Modernization Act of 2003 (MMA). Health-care provider means a provider of services (as defined in Section 1861(u) of the Social Security Act (the Act), 42 U.S.C. § 1395x(u)), a provider of medical or health services (as defined in Section 1861(s) of the Act, 42 U.S.C. § 1395x(s)), and any other person or organization who furnishes, bills, or is paid for health care in the normal course of business.

When using or disclosing PHI or when requesting PHI from another Covered Entity, a Covered Entity must make reasonable efforts to limit PHI to the *minimum necessary* to accomplish the intended purpose of the use, disclosure or request (45 C.F.R. § 164.502(b)). This minimum standard does not, however, apply to the following situations:

Practice Points

Covered Entities Must Designate:
— A "privacy official"
— A complaint contact (person or office)
— In access denial cases, a "reviewing official" who is also a licensed health-care provider
— Persons responding to requests for access to information
— Persons responding to requests for amendments to information
— Persons responding to requests for accounting of disclosures

- Disclosure to or request by a health-care provider for treatment;
- Uses or disclosures made to an individual or required under HIPAA;
- Uses or disclosures made pursuant to a HIPAA compliant authorization signed by the individual;
- Disclosures made to the Secretary of Health and Human Services;
- Uses and disclosures that are required by law; and
- Uses or disclosures that are required for HIPAA compliance.

45 C.F.R. § 164.502(b)(2)

The HIPAA Privacy Regulations contain several special regulations that relate specifically to research, which will be discussed at length in this article. Under HIPAA, "research" is the "systematic investigation, including research development, testing, and evaluation, designed to develop or contribute to generalizable knowledge" (45 C.F.R. § 164.501).

HIPAA requires Covered Entities to do very specific acts, designate certain individuals, and have certain mandated policies and procedures in place. These are as follows:

- Designate a privacy official;
- Designate a contact person or office who is responsible for receiving complaints;
- Be prepared to designate a "reviewing official" who is a licensed health-care professional who will be designated by the Covered Entity to review any denial of access of an individual to PHI;
- Document the titles of the persons or offices responsible for receiving and processing requests for access by individuals under 45 C.F.R. § 524, document the titles of the persons or offices responsible for receiving and processing requests for amendments under 45 C.F.R. § 526, and document the titles of the persons or offices responsible for receiving and processing requests for accounting under 45 C.F.R. § 528.
- Train all members of its "work force" on the policies and procedures with respect to PHI;
- Have in place appropriate "administrative, technical and physical safeguards to protect the privacy of PHI";
- Provide a process for individuals to make complaints concerning the Covered Entity's policies and procedures or its compliance/noncompliance with such policies and procedures;
- Have and apply appropriate "sanctions" against members of its work force who fail to comply;
- Mitigate, to the extent practicable, any harmful effect that is known to the Covered Entity of a use or disclosure of PHI in violation of its policies and procedures;
- A Covered Entity may not intimidate, threaten, coerce, discriminate against, or take other retaliatory action against individuals for the exercise by the individual of any right under or for participation by the individual in any process established by HIPAA or for filing a complaint with the Secretary of Health and Human Services, or for

testifying, assisting or participating in any investigation, compliance review, proceeding or hearing under HIPAA or opposing any act or practice made unlawful by HIPAA (provided the individual or person has a good-faith belief that the practice opposed is unlawful and the manner of the opposition is reasonable and does not involve a disclosure of PHI in violation of this HIPAA subpart);
- The Covered Entity may not require individuals to waive their rights under 45 C.F.R. § 160.306 (complaint made to Secretary of Health and Human Services);
- Implement policies and procedures to meet all the requirements of HIPAA (taking into account the size of and type of activities that relate to PHI undertaken by the specific Covered Entity); and
- Maintain its policies and procedures for a minimum of six years from the date of creation or the date when such policies and procedures were last in effect, whichever is later, in written or electronic form.

The federal privacy "floor" set by the Privacy Regulations is subject to more stringent state laws. Counsel for a biotech company should be familiar with the privacy of health-care information laws in the state(s) in which the biotech company is located and does business so that a determination can be made whether a HIPAA Privacy Regulation is contrary to state law and, if so, whether the state law is more or less stringent than the HIPAA regulation. If such state law is more stringent than the HIPAA regulation, it "preempts" the HIPAA regulation and controls (45 C.F.R. § 160.203).

The following publications pertaining to Privacy Regulations related to research may be helpful:

- The U.S. Department of Health and Human Services, Food and Drug Administration, Office of the Commissioner, "Guidance for Industry-IRB Review of Stand-Alone HIPAA Authorizations Under FDA Regulations."
http://a257.g.akamaitech.net/7/257/2422/14mar20010800/edocketaccess. gpo.gov/2003/03-28044.htm
  - United States Department of Health and Human Services, "Protecting Personal Health Information and Research: Understanding the HIPAA Privacy Rule."

http://privacyruleandresearch.nih.gov http://privacyruleandresearch.nih.gov/pr_02.asp

Additional U.S. Department of Health and Human Services resources include:

- Institution of Review Boards and HIPAA Privacy Rule.
  http://privacyruleandresearch.nih.gov/irb_default.asp
- Privacy Boards and the HIPAA Privacy Rule.
  http://privacyruleandresearch.nih.gov/privacy_boards_hipaa_privacy_rule.asp
- Research Repositories, Databases, and the HIPAA Privacy Rule.
  http://privacyruleandresearch.nih.gov/research_repositories.asp
- Clinical Research and the HIPAA Privacy Rule.
  http://privacyruleandresearch.nih.gov/clin_research.asp
- HIPAA Authorization for Research.
  http://privacyruleandresearch.nih.gov/authorization.asp

2. HIPAA Privacy Regulations

a. *Individual Rights*

The individual rights given to patients under HIPAA are as follows:

(i) To receive written notice of a Covered Entity's information practice and individual rights.
(ii) To obtain access to a copy of the individual's own health information.
(iii) To obtain an accounting of how the individual's health information has been disclosed.
(iv) To request a correction and/or amendment to the individual's health information.
(v) To request the Covered Entity to further restrict use and disclosure of their PHI or request the covered entity use alternative means or locations to communicate confidential information.
(vi) The right to file a complaint if the individual believes his or her rights have been violated (complaint to be filed within the Covered Entity's organization).

i. Notice of Privacy Practices

Under 45 C.F.R. § 164.520, an individual has the right to adequate notice of the uses and disclosures of PHI that may be made by the Covered Entity and of the individual's rights and the Covered Entity's legal duties with respect to PHI. A Covered Entity can fulfill its notice obligation by providing each of its patients with a written Notice of Privacy Practice (NPP) that is in plain language and contains certain required elements.

The required elements of an NPP, as outlined in 45 C.F.R. § 164.520(b), include:

- Header of NPP: "THIS NOTICE DESCRIBES HOW MEDICAL INFORMATION ABOUT YOU MAY BE USED AND DISCLOSED AND HOW YOU CAN GET ACCESS TO THIS INFORMATION. PLEASE REVIEW IT CAREFULLY."
- A description, including at least one example, of the types of uses and disclosures that the Covered Entity is permitted to make for treatment, payment, and health-care operations.
- A description of each of the other purposes for which the Covered Entity is permitted or required by HIPAA to use or disclose PHI without the individual's written consent or authorization. For example, if the Covered Entity is going to provide PHI to a researcher, the NPP should contain such a notice.
- If use or disclosure is prohibited or materially limited by any other applicable law, the description of such use or disclosure must reflect the more stringent law (state law).
- Each required description must include sufficient detail to place the individual on notice of the uses and disclosures that are permitted or required by HIPAA and any other applicable law.
- A statement that other uses and disclosures will be made only with the individual's written authorization.
- A statement that the individual may revoke such authorization as provided by 45 C.F.R. § 164.508(b)(5).

The NPP must also contain a statement of the individual's rights with respect to PHI and a brief description of how the individual may exercise those rights. Those rights are as follows:

- The right to request restrictions as provided by 45 C.F.R. § 164.522(a) on certain uses and disclosures of PHI, including a statement to put the individual on notice that the Covered Entity is not required to agree to a requested restriction.
- The right to receive confidential communications of PHI as provided by 45 C.F.R. § 164.522(b) as applicable [a covered health-care provider must permit individuals to request and must accommodate reasonable requests by individuals to receive communications of PHI from the covered health-care provider by alternative means or alternative locations].
- The right to inspect and copy PHI as provided by 45 C.F.R. § 164.524 [right of access to inspect and obtain a copy of PHI *except for* psychotherapy notes, information compiled in reasonable anticipation of or for use in civil, criminal or administrative action or proceeding and PHI maintained by a Covered Entity that is subject to CLIA to the extent the provision of access to the individual would be prohibited by law or exempt from CLIA pursuant to 42 C.F.R. § 493.3(a)(2)].
- The right to amend protected health information as provided by 45 C.F.R. § 164.526.
- The right to receive an accounting of disclosures of protected health information as provided by 45 C.F.R. § 164.528.
- The right of an individual, including an individual who has agreed to receive notice electronically, to obtain a paper copy of the notice from the Covered Entity upon request.

Optional elements: A separate statement is required in the NPP if the Covered Entity plans to do any of the following:

- Contact the individual to provide appointment reminders for information about treatment alternatives or other health-related benefits or services that may be of interest to the individual;
- Contact the individual to raise funds for the Covered Entity; or
- Disclose protected information to the sponsor of a group health plan.

A CE may use what HHS calls a "layered" notice as long as all of the NPP requirements are included in the document that is actually provided to the individual. A layered notice is one that provides a summary of the individual's rights and other NPP provisions. The layered notice provision was first addressed in the August 14, 2002 *Federal Register* preamble. It is important to note that nothing in the final August 2002 modifications to the HIPAA Privacy Rule relieve a CE of its duty to provide the entire notice in plain language so the average reader can understand it. Thus, if a layered notice is used, it will be in addition to the regular NPP. It is not a substitute for the regular NPP.

ii. Restriction of PHI by Individual Patient

Pursuant to 45 C.F.R. § 164.522, a Covered Entity must permit an individual to request that the Covered Entity restrict uses or disclosures of PHI about the individual to carry out treatment, payment, or health-care operations and disclosures permitted under 45 C.F.R. § 164.510(b). A Covered Entity is not required to agree to a restriction; however, a Covered Entity that agrees to a restriction is bound by the restriction except in cases of emergency treatment. Restrictions, even if agreed to, are not effective to prevent uses and disclosures required by § 164.502(a)(2)(ii) pertaining to an HHS privacy rule investigation under § 164.510(a) regarding facility directories or any subparagraph under § 164.512.

A Covered Entity/provider may terminate an agreement for a restriction if:

- The individual requests the termination in writing;
- The individual orally agrees to the termination and the oral agreement is documented in writing;
- The Covered Entity/provider informs the individual that it is terminating its agreement to a restriction except that such termination is effective only with respect to PHI created or received after it has so informed the individual.

iii. Access of Individuals to PHI

Under 45 C.F.R. § 164.524 an individual has a right of access to inspect and copy his or her PHI in a "designated record set" for as long as the PHI is maintained in the designated record set, with the exception of the following:

- Psychotherapy notes;[6]
- Information compiled in reasonable anticipation of, or for use in, a civil, criminal, or administrative action or proceeding; or
- PHI maintained by a Covered Entity that is:
  - subject to the Clinical Laboratory Improvement Amendments of 1988 (CLIA) (45 U.S.C. 263a) to the extent the provision of access to the individual would be prohibited by law; or
  - exempt from CLIA pursuant to 42 C.F.R. § 493.3(a)(2).

The Covered Entity may require individuals to make requests for access in writing (provided it informs the individuals of such requirement). A Covered Entity's deadline to respond to such request is 30 days after receipt of request.

A Covered Entity must provide the individual with access to the PHI in the form or format requested by the individual if it is readily producible in such form or format (if not, in a readable hard-copy form or other form or format as agreed to by the Covered Entity and the individual). A summary may be provided if the individual agrees in advance to such summary. To the extent possible, the Covered Entity must give the individual access to any other PHI requested after excluding the PHI for which the Covered Entity has a ground to deny access.

A Covered Entity can deny an individual access to his/her PHI without an opportunity for review in certain circumstances. Any de-

> **Practice Points**
>
> **Tips for Dealing with Personal Health Information Access Requests**
> — Make certain PHI is not in an exempt category (e.g., psychotherapy notes, records in preparation for litigation).
> — Require requests in writing.
> — Respond to requests within 30 days.
> — Provide information in summary form, if the individual agrees in advance.
> — Provide information in the format requested by the individual, if possible; otherwise, provide readable hard copy.
> — Charge only reasonable copying and postal costs.

nial of access must be written in plain language and contain the basis for the denial, a statement of an individual's review right, and a description of how the individual may complain to the Covered Entity (which includes the name or title and telephone number of the contact person or office to receive such complaint).

A covered entity may charge an individual only a reasonable cost-based fee that is limited to the actual copying costs, any postage costs when the individual has requested the copy be mailed, and costs of preparing a summary if agreed to by the individual.

iv. Amendment or Change of PHI

Under 45 C.F.R. § 164.526, an individual has a right to have a Covered Entity amend his/her PHI. The Covered Entity may require that a request for amendments be in writing and that the individual provide a reason to support a requested amendment, provided the Covered Entity informs individuals in advance of such requirements.

The time deadline for a Covered Entity to respond to a request for an amendment is 60 days after receipt of the request. If PHI is amended, the Covered Entity must identify the records in the designated record set that is affected by the amendment and append or otherwise provide a link to the location of the amendment. The Covered Entity must also inform the individual that an amendment is accepted and obtain the individual's identification of and agreement to have the Covered Entity notify the relevant persons with whom the amendment needs to be shared.

A Covered Entity that is informed by another Covered Entity of an amendment to an individual's PHI must amend the PHI in the designated record set using the same procedure and in the same format as required by the sending Covered Entity.

A Covered Entity may deny an individual's request for amendment under certain circumstances. The denial must be in writing, use plain language, and contain certain required information, such as the basis for the denial and the individual's right to submit a written statement disagreeing with the denial (the Covered Entity may reasonably limit the length of a statement of disagreement that an individual may file).

The individual may submit a statement of disagreement with the denial. The Covered Entity may then prepare a written rebuttal to the individual's statement of disagreement and provide a copy to the individual who submitted the statement of disagreement. The Covered Entity must append or otherwise link all of the above documents (individual's request for an amendment, Covered Entity's denial of the request, the individual's statement of disagreement, and the Covered Entity's rebuttal) to the individual's designated record set. All these documents must be appended to any subsequent disclosure of the PHI to which the disagreement relates.

v. Accounting of Disclosures

Pursuant to 45 C.F.R. § 164.528, an individual has a right to receive an accounting of disclosures of PHI made by a Covered Entity in the six years prior to the date on which the accounting is requested. Exceptions to the rule are as follows:

- The Covered Entity does not have to provide accounting relating to PHI to carry out treatment, payment or health-care operations relative to release of PHI to an individual;
- Pursuant to a consent that complies with 45 C.F.R. § 164.506(b);
- Disclosures without consent subject to 45 C.F.R. § 164.502(a)(1)(iii) for facility directory or to persons involved in the individual's care with other notifications as allowed by 45 C.F.R. § 164.510;
- For national security or intelligence purposes;
- To correctional institutions or law enforcement officers as provided in § 164.512(k)(5) [inmate matter]; or
- Disclosures that occurred prior to the compliance date for the Covered Entity.
- "Suspension" requests properly made under § 164.528(a)(2).

Special considerations apply to accounting of disclosures for research. Pursuant to 45 C.F.R. § 164.528(b)(4)(i), if the Covered Entity has made disclosures of PHI for a particular research purpose in accordance with 45 C.F.R. § 164.512(i) for 50 or more individuals during the period covered by the requested accounting, then the accounting may, with respect to such disclosures for which the protected health information about the individual may have been included, provide the following:

- The name of the protocol or the research activities;
- A description, in plain language, with a research protocol or other research activity, including the purpose of the research and the criteria for selecting particular records;
- A brief description of the type of PHI that was disclosed;
- The date or period of time during which disclosures occurred, or may have occurred, including the date of such disclosure during the accounting period;
- The name, address, and telephone number of the entity that sponsored the research and the researcher to whom the information was disclosed; and
- A statement that the PHI of the individual may or may not have been disclosed for a particular protocol or other research activity.

If it is reasonably likely that the PHI of the individual requesting the accounting was disclosed for such research protocol or activity, the Covered Entity must, at the request of the individual, assist that individual in contacting the entity that sponsored the research and the researcher (45 C.F.R. § 164.528(b)(4)(ii)).

b. Use and Disclosure for Treatment, Payment, and Health-Care Operations

A health-care provider is free to disclose an individual's PHI without an authorization signed by the individual for its own treatment, payment, and health-care operations (TPO); for treatment activities and payment activities of another health-care provider; and for limited health-care operations of a Covered Entity (45 C.F.R. § 164.506(c)).

The term "healthcare operations" is broadly defined in the Privacy Regulations (45 C.F.R. § 164.501) to include a multitude of business-related activities, including *but not limited to* business planning and development, business management and general administrative activities, legal services, financial auditing services, review of the competence and qualifications of health-care professionals, quality assessment and improvement activities, and activities relating to the renewal or replacement of a contract for health insurance.

c. Disclosure of PHI with Authorization or by Agreement

i. Authorizations

In the past, written permission to release medical records was done with a form such as a Medical Records Release Form. HIPAA has given us a new term for this: "authorization."

If the Covered Entity wants to use or disclose an individual's PHI for any reason *other than* TPO, the Covered Entity must obtain that individual's written authorization (unless otherwise specifically allowed under another HIPAA provision, e.g., court order).

A special category of PHI, psychotherapy notes, are generally subject to the authorization regulation, even with respect to treatment, payment or health-care operations.

A valid authorization must be written in plain language, signed, and dated. Any authorization must contain certain "core elements" and "required statements." The authorization must contain:

- A description of the PHI to be used or disclosed;
- Names of the persons or classes of persons to whom the PHI will be disclosed or from whom such PHI will be requested;
- Name of the persons or classes of persons authorized to make the requested use or disclosure;
- The purpose of the requested use or disclosure. The statement "at the request of the individual" is a sufficient description of the purpose when an individual initiates the authorization and does not, or elects not to, provide a statement of the purpose;
- An expiration date or an expiration of event that relates to the individual or the purpose of the use or disclosure. The statement "end of research study," "none," or similar language is sufficient if the authorization is for a use or disclosure of PHI for research purposes, including the creation and maintenance of a research database or research repository;
- Signature of the individual and date (if the authorization is signed by a personal representative of the individual, a description of such representative's authority to act for the individual must be recorded on the form);

- Statement to place the individual on notice of the individual's right to revoke the authorization in writing, how the individual may revoke the authorization, and any exceptions to the right to revoke;
- Statement adequate to place the individual on notice of the ability or inability of the Covered Entity to condition treatment, payment, enrollment in a health plan or eligibility for benefits on the individual's signing the authorization; and
- Statement adequate to place the individual on notice of the potential for information disclosed pursuant to the authorization to be redisclosed by the recipient and no longer protected by HIPAA.

Covered Entities are required to obtain an authorization for uses and disclosures of PHI unless the use or disclosure is required or otherwise permitted by the HIPAA Privacy Regulations. Covered Entities may only use authorizations that meet the requirements of 45 C.F.R. § 164.508(b), and any such use or disclosure of PHI will be lawful only to the extent it is consistent with the terms of such authorization. A voluntary consent document will not constitute a valid permission to use or disclose health information for a purpose that requires an authorization under the rule.[7]

As noted above, a Covered Entity may use or disclose PHI, including psychotherapy notes, without an authorization for its own treatment, payment, and health-care operation; however, a Covered Entity may *not* use or disclose psychotherapy notes for purposes of *another* Covered Entity's treatment, payment, or health-care operations without obtaining the individual's authorization.[8]

Covered Entities may include additional, non-required elements in an authorization as long as they are not inconsistent with the elements and statements required under 45 C.F.R. § 164.508.

If an individual is signing the authorization as a personal representative, the HIPAA Privacy Regulations require that Covered Entities verify and document an individual's authority to sign an authorization on a patient's behalf. Covered Entities are required to document and retain all authorizations under 45 C.F.R. § 164.508

ii. Defective Authorization

Under 45 C.F.R. § 164.508(b)(2), an authorization is considered to be defective if any of the following occur:

- The expiration date has passed or the expiration event has occurred, and the Covered Entity is aware of the fact;
- Any of the required core elements or notification statements are omitted or incomplete;
- The authorization violates the specifications regarding compounding or conditioning authorizations [according to HHS this means that authorizations for the use or disclosure of psychotherapy notes may be combined only with another authorization for the use or disclosure of psychotherapy notes]; or
- The Covered Entity knows that material information in the authorization is false.

iii. Combined Authorizations

Except for psychotherapy note authorizations, generally authorizations may be combined. An authorization for the use or disclosure of PHI for a research study may be combined with any other type of written permission for the same research study, including another authorization for the use or disclosure of PHI for such research or a consent to participate in such research (45 C.F.R. § 164.508(b)(3)(i)). A Covered Entity generally may not combine an authorization with any other type of document, such as the Notice of Privacy Practices or a written voluntary consent.[9]

iv. Conditioning of Authorizations

A Covered Entity may not condition treatment, payment or enrollment in a health plan or eligibility for benefits on the individual's signing of an authorization. There are exceptions to this general rule. For example, a Covered Entity may condition the provision of research-related treatment on provision of an authorization for the use or disclosure of PHI for such research (45 C.F.R. § 164.508(b)(4)(i)). In addition, a health plan may condition enrollment in the health plan or eligibility for benefits on the provision of an authorization requested by the health plan prior to an individual's enrollment if certain conditions are met (45 C.F.R. § 164.508(b)(4)(ii)).

v. Revocation of Authorizations

45 C.F.R. § 164.508(b)(5) provides individuals the right to revoke an authorization any time in writing; however, an individual may not revoke an authorization if a Covered Entity has acted in reliance on the authorization or if the authorization was obtained as a condition of obtaining insurance coverage and other law gives the insurer the right to contest the claim or policy itself.

vi. Authorizations for Marketing

Except as provided for at 45 C.F.R. § 164.508(a)(3), a Covered Entity must have the individual's prior written authorization to use or disclose PHI for marketing[10] communications. A marketing authorization must include a statement of remuneration, if any.

The exceptions to the requirement of an authorization for use or disclosure of PHI for marketing communication are: (1) when the communication occurs in a face-to-face encounter between the Covered Entity and the individual; or (2) the communication involves a promotional gift of nominal value. It is important to keep in mind that the marketing authorization exclusion is narrowly crafted to permit only face-to-face encounters between the Covered Entity and the individual. HHS has rejected expansion of the face-to-face authorization exception to include telephone, mail, and other common carriers, fax machines or the Internet, if any.

It is important to note that the HIPAA privacy marketing provisions do not modify or change any other federal or state law relating to anti-kickback statutes, Stark regulations or self-referral prohibitions.

vii. Use or Disclosure Requiring Patient Opportunity to Agree or Object

Under 45 C.F.R. § 164.510, there are generally three situations where a Covered Entity may use or disclose PHI without patient consent or authorization *if* the patient is given prior notice and a "meaningful" opportunity to agree or object. In an emergency, that meaningful opportunity to object or restrict can be afforded the individual after the emergency has passed.

- Covered Entity may use or disclose limited general information about patients for creation or maintenance of a facility directory.[11] The requirements relating to a facility directory are very specific. This has been defined as an "opt out" provision in which an individual patient can "opt out" of having his/her information in a hospital facility directory. If the patient consents and information is placed in the facility directory, then only certain types of identifiable information can be released. For the most part, the information can only be released if the patient is asked for by name. Information from a hospital facility directory can be released to a member of the clergy even if the clergy does not ask for the patient by name.

- The Covered Entity may disclose PHI to certain relatives, close friends, or other designees of a patient when it is relevant to that person's involvement in the care or payment for care of that patient.
- A Covered Entity may use or disclose PHI to notify family members or representatives of a patient of the patient's location, general condition, or death. The required notice and subsequent agreement or objection may be oral.

The individual's agreement or objection to the use or disclosure of PHI may be oral.

d. Disclosure Pursuant to a Public Policy Exception

Covered Entities are permitted to disclose PHI without a written authorization or giving the individual an opportunity to agree or object for what has been described as "public policy" purposes (45 C.F.R. § 164.512). Disclosure under these exceptions depends heavily on the factual circumstances and may be very limited depending on the circumstances.

i. As "Required by Law"—45 C.F.R. § 164.512(a).[12]

In 45 C.F.R. § 164.512(a), a Covered Entity is permitted to release PHI to comply with laws requiring the use or disclosure of PHI provided the use or disclosure meets and is limited to the relevant requirements of such other laws.[13] Section 164.512 also contains specific paragraphs that have *additional requirements* with which Covered Entities must comply. These additional requirements and grounds relate to disclosures about victims of abuse, neglect or domestic violence (45 C.F.R. § 164.512(c)), for judicial and administrative proceedings (45 C.F.R. § 164.512(e)), and for law enforcement purposes (45 C.F.R. § 164.512(f)). Be aware that the "verification" requirement under 45 C.F.R. § 164.514(h) applies to all disclosures under 45 C.F.R. § 164.512(a).[14]

ii. Uses and Disclosures for Public Health Activities—45 C.F.R. § 164.512(b) (Includes child abuse reporting)

Under 45 C.F.R. § 164.512(b), a Covered Entity is permitted, but is not required, to disclose PHI without individual authorization to: (1) a public health authority authorized by law to collect or receive such information for the purpose of preventing or controlling disease, injury, or disability, including, but not limited to, the reporting of disease, injury, vital events such as birth or death, and the conduct of public health surveillance, public health investigations, public health intervention; (2) a public health authority or other appropriate authority authorized by law to receive reports of child abuse or neglect; (3) a person or entity other than a governmental authority that can demonstrate that it was acting to comply with the requirements or direction of a public health authority (e.g., FDA matters); or (4) a person

> **Practice Points**
>
> **A Covered Entity may release Protected Health Information without individual authorization if the disclosure:**
>
> — Is to a public health agency for purposes of preventing or controlling illness, recording vital events, investigating reports of child abuse, or preventing serious threats to health or safety;
> — Is to law enforcement authorities in connection with domestic violence, other adult abuse or neglect, location of missing persons, or reports of crime;
> — Is to a "health oversight agency" of the government for that agency's legally mandated activities, or otherwise is for use in connection with certain specialized government functions;
> — Is required in a judicial or administrative proceeding;
> — Is in connection with organ, eye, or tissue donation;
> — Is for research purposes (if a waiver has been obtained);
> — Is for workers' compensation claims; or
> — Is otherwise required by law.
> — Charges only reasonable copying and postal costs
>
> (Nonexclusive list)

who may have been exposed to a communicable disease or may otherwise be at risk of contracting or spreading a disease or condition and was authorized by law to be notified as necessary in the conduct of a public health intervention or investigation.[15, 16]

The provisions of this section relating to reporting child abuse or neglect will be interpreted and applied under an "other law" approach. This means that HIPAA permits a Covered Entity to make reports relating to child abuse and neglect, but such reports must be made to a public health authority or other appropriate authority authorized by law to receive such reports. This means that the Covered Entity for the most part will follow state laws relating to any type of report, to include a mandatory report, to be made to a public agency that is "authorized by law" to receive such reports. In those cases, the "other law" must be followed. Even though in many cases child abuse would be a crime and the child would be deemed to be a crime victim, this paragraph of § 512 controls over the general crime victim provision found in § 512(f).

To make a disclosure that is not one of those listed in 45 C.F.R. § 164.512(b), Covered Entities must obtain individual authorization or must meet the requirements of another provision of this rule that would permit disclosure of information.

iii. Disclosures About Victims of Abuse, Neglect or Domestic Violence—45 C.F.R. § 164.512(c)[17]

45 C.F.R. § 164.512(c) allows Covered Entities to report PHI to specified authorities regarding certain abuse, neglect and domestic violence *other than* child abuse and neglect.[18] Child abuse and neglect is addressed in 45 C.F.R. § 164.512(b).

It is important to note that the provisions of 45 C.F.R. § 164.512(c) [abuse (non-child abuse), neglect and domestic violence] supersede the provisions of 45 C.F.R. § 512(a) ["required by law"] and 45 C.F.R. § 164.512(f)(1)(i) ["required by law to include" wound reporting] to the extent that those provisions address the subject matter contained within 45 C.F.R. § 164.512(c).[19]

The regulation specifies three circumstances in which disclosures of PHI are allowed in order to report abuse, neglect or domestic violence. First, this regulation allows disclosure of PHI related to abuse if required by law and the disclosure complies with and is limited to the relevant requirements of such law. Covered Entities are required to make such disclosures pursuant to a state's mandatory reporting law and inform the individual of the report.

Second, this regulation allows Covered Entities to disclose PHI related to abuse if the individual has agreed to such disclosure. When considering the possibility of disclosing PHI in an abuse situation pursuant to this section, HHS encourages Covered Entities to seek the individual's agreement whenever possible.

Third, this same regulation allows Covered Entities to disclose PHI about an individual without the individual's agreement if the disclosure is expressly authorized by statute or regulation and either:

- The Covered Entity, in the exercise of its professional judgment, believes that the disclosure is necessary to prevent serious harm to the individual or to other potential victims; or
- If the individual is unable to agree due to incapacity, a law enforcement or other public official authorized to receive the report represents that the protected health information for which disclosure is sought is not intended to be used against the individual, and that an immediate enforcement activity that depends on the disclosure would be materially and adversely affected by waiting until the individual is able to agree to the disclosure.[20] HHS emphasizes that disclosure under this third part of the paragraph may be made only if it is expressly authorized by statute or regulation.[21]

Covered Entities are required to inform the individual in all of the situations described above that the Covered Entity has disclosed PHI to report abuse, neglect or domestic violence except when:

- The Covered Entity, in the exercise of professional judgment, believes that informing the individual would place the individual at risk of serious harm; or
- The Covered Entity actually would be informing a personal representative (such as a parent of a minor) and the Covered Entity reasonably believes that such person is responsible for the abuse, neglect, or other injury that has already occurred and that giving information to the person would not be in the individual's best interest.[22]

iv. Uses and Disclosures for Health Oversight Activities—45 C.F.R. § 164.512(d)

Pursuant to 45 C.F.R. § 164.512(d), a Covered Entity may disclose PHI to a "health oversight agency" for oversight activities authorized by law. Such activities include audits; civil, administrative or criminal investigations; inspections; licensure or disciplinary actions; civil, administrative or criminal proceedings/actions; or other activities necessary for appropriate oversight of:

- The health-care system;
- Government benefit programs for which health information is relevant to beneficiary eligibility;
- An entity subject to government regulatory programs for which health information is necessary for determining compliance with program standards; or
- An entity subject to civil rights laws for which health information is necessary for determining compliance.

A health oversight activity does not include an investigation or other activity in which the individual is the subject, and such investigation or other activity does not arise out of and is not directly related to:

- The receipt of health care;
- A claim for public benefits related to health; or
- Qualification for, or receipt of, public benefits or services when a patient's health is integral to the claim for public benefits or services.

Even if a biotech company is not a Covered Entity, the company must be aware of the access a "health oversight agency" may have to its records.

v. Disclosures for Judicial and Administrative Proceedings—45 C.F.R. § 164.512(e)

1. *Special Requirements for Subpoenas and Discovery Requests*: HIPAA Privacy Regulations specifically authorize the disclosure of PHI for some judicial and administrative proceedings absent authorization. Under 45 C.F.R. § 164.512(e), a Covered Entity may disclose PHI if the health-care provider receives a properly issued order

from a court or administrative tribunal, which for the most part requires no further HIPAA analysis. (Privilege analysis and special law analysis will be necessary.) A court order is an actual order signed by a judge, not a subpoena signed by an attorney for a party. A Covered Entity may also disclose PHI in response to a subpoena, discovery request or other lawful process when the health-care provider receives "satisfactory assurance" as prescribed under the regulations.

2. *Satisfactory Assurances Are Required in Certain Circumstances*: A health-care provider that receives a subpoena, discovery request, or "other lawful process," not accompanied by a court or administrative tribunal order, receives "satisfactory assurances" from the party seeking PHI in the following two circumstances: (1) the health-care provider receives from the requesting party a written statement and accompanying documentation demonstrating that (a) the requesting party has made a good-faith attempt to provide written notice to the individual; (b) the notice included sufficient information about the litigation or proceeding for which the PHI is requested to permit the individual to raise an objection to the court or administrative tribunal; (c) the time for the individual to raise objections to the court or administrative tribunal has elapsed; and (d) no objections were filed, or all objections filed by the individual have been resolved by the court or the administrative tribunal (and the disclosure now sought is consistent with the resolution of any objections); and (2) the "satisfactory assurance" requirement can also be met if (a) the requesting party has made "reasonable efforts" to secure a qualified protective order, and (b) the requesting party's written statement and accompanying documentation demonstrate that the parties have agreed to a protective order; (c) the requesting party has presented the protective order to the involved court or administrative tribunal, or (d) the party seeking the PHI has requested a qualified protective order from the court or administrative tribunal. A qualified protective order prohibits the parties from using or disclosing PHI for any purpose other than the litigation or proceeding for which the information was requested and requires that the PHI be returned to the Covered Entity

or destroyed (including destruction of all copies) at the conclusion of the litigation or proceeding (45 C.F.R. § 164.512(e)(1)).

These requirements apply to any discovery request, even one under Federal Rule of Civil Procedure 45.[23]

vi. **Disclosure for Law Enforcement Purposes—45 C.F.R. § 164.512(f).**[24]

A Covered Entity may disclose protected health information for a law enforcement purpose to a law enforcement official if the conditions in 45 C.F.R § 164.512(f)(1) through (f)(6) are met, as applicable.

- Pursuant to Process and as Otherwise Required by Law (45 C.F.R. § 164.512(f)(1)).
- Disclosures for Identification and Location Purposes: Suspects, Fugitives, Material Witnesses, and Missing Persons—45 C.F.R. § 164.512(f)(2).[25]
- Victim of a Crime—45 C.F.R. § 164.512(f)(3).[26]
- Disclosures About Decedents—45 C.F.R. § 164.512(f)(4).
- Reporting Crime on Premises—45 C.F.R. § 164.512(f)(5).
- Reporting Crime in Emergencies—45 C.F.R. § 164.512(f)(6).

vii. **Uses and Disclosures about Decedents—45 C.F.R. § 164.512(g)**

A Covered Entity may disclose PHI to a coroner/medical examiner for the purpose of identifying a deceased person, determining a cause of death, or other duties as authorized by law.

viii. **Uses and Disclosures for Cadaveric Organ, Eye or Tissue Donation Purposes—45 C.F.R. § 164.512(h)**

A Covered Entity may use or disclose all PHI to organ procurement organizations or other entities engaged in the procurement, banking or transplantation of cadaveric organs, eyes, or tissues for the purpose of facilitating organ, eye or tissue donation and transplantation.

ix. Uses and Disclosures for Research Purposes—45 C.F.R. § 164.512(i)

A Covered Entity may use or disclose PHI for research, regardless of the source of funding for the research, if it obtains a waiver (in whole or in part) of the individual authorization required by 45 C.F.R. § 164.508 (for use or disclosure of all PHI) that has been approved by either an Institutional Review Board[27] (IRB) or a privacy board[28] (composed as set out in § 512(i)(1)(i)(B)).

The waiver documentation must include:

- A statement identifying the IRB or privacy board and the date on which the waiver was approved;
- A statement that the IRB or privacy board has determined that the waiver satisfies the following criteria:
  — The use or disclosure of PHI involves no more than minimal risk to the subjects;
  — That there is an adequate plan to protect the identifiers from improper use and disclosure;
  — That there is an adequate plan to destroy the identifiers at the earliest opportunity consistent with conduct of the research unless there is a health or research justification for retaining the identifiers or such retention is otherwise required by law;
  — Adequate written assurances that the PHI will not be reused or disclosed to any other person or entity, except as required by law, for authorized oversight of the research study, or for other research for which the use or disclosure of PHI would be permitted by the subpart;
  — That the research could not practically be conducted without the waiver; and
  — The research could not practically be conducted without access to and use of the PHI.
- A brief description of the PHI for which use or access has been determined by the IRB or privacy board to be necessary;
- A statement that the waiver has been reviewed and approved under either normal or expedited review procedures as outlined in § 164.512 (i)(2)(iv)(A), (B) & (C); and

- The signature of either the IRB or privacy board Chair, as applicable, or the Chair's designee.

(45 C.F.R. § 164.512(i)(1)(i))

In addition to the waiver procedure, access to PHI by a researcher for use in the development of a research hypothesis and formal research protocol is allowed under § 164.512(i) (reviews preparatory to research). This exception gives a researcher the ability to develop a clinical research study and to recruit patients into the study. A Covered Entity must obtain from a researcher certain representations prior to the use or disclosure of PHI. These representations must include a statement that:

- Use or disclosure of PHI is sought solely as necessary to prepare a research protocol or for singular purposes preparatory to research;
- No PHI will be removed from the Covered Entity by the researcher in the course of the review; and
- The PHI for which use or access is sought is necessary for the research purposes.

(45 C.F.R. § 164.512(i)(1)(ii))

If the researcher seeks a decedent's PHI, the researcher must provide the Covered Entity with the following:

- Representation that the use or disclosure sought is solely for research on the PHI of decedent;
- Documentation, at the request of the Covered Entity, of the death of such individual; and
- Representation that the PHI for which use or disclosure is sought is necessary for the research purposes.

(45 C.F.R. § 164.512(i)(1)(iii))

If, prior to the effective date of the Privacy Regulations (April 14, 2003), a Covered Entity obtained the informed consent or authorization (presumably non-HIPAA compliant) of an individual to participate in research or a waiver of informed consent by an IRB, the Covered Entity may, to the extent allowed by the consent or authorization, use or disclose PHI for research notwithstanding the authorization requirement in § 164.508 or the waiver provisions in § 164.512(i) (45 C.F.R. § 164.532(a) & (c)).

x. Uses and Disclosures to Avert a Serious Threat to Health or Safety—45 C.F.R. § 164.512(j)

A Covered Entity may disclose PHI, if the Covered Entity, in good faith, believes the use or disclosure is necessary for law enforcement authorities to identify or apprehend an individual because of a statement of a patient admitting participation in a violent crime that the Covered Entity reasonably believes may have caused serious physical harm to the victim or where it appears from all the circumstances that the individual has escaped from a correctional institution or from lawful custody. There are certain limitations on the disclosure of this information. This HIPAA Privacy Regulation does not permit disclosure if the information was learned in the course of treatment to affect the propensity to commit the criminal conduct that is the basis for the disclosure.

xi. Specialized Government Function—45 C.F.R. § 164.512(k)

Under 45 C.F.R. § 164.512(k), a Covered Entity may use and/or disclose PHI for certain specialized government functions, including military and veterans' activities, national security and intelligence activities, protective services for the President and other authorized persons, medical suitability determinations if the Covered Entity is a component of the Department of State, correctional institutions and other law enforcement custodial situations, and under certain circumstances when a health plan is a government program providing public benefits or is a government agency administering a government program providing public benefits.

xii. Disclosures for Workers' Compensation—45 C.F.R. § 164.512 (l)

A Covered Entity may disclose PHI as authorized by and to the extent necessary to comply with laws relating to workers' compensation or similar programs, established by law, that provide benefits for work-related injuries or illnesses without regard to fault.

e. **Disclosure Pursuant to a Business Associate Agreement—(45 C.F.R. § 164.502(e) and § 164.504(e))**

Covered Entities may need to disclose PHI to persons who or business entities that provide services or perform functions *on behalf of* the Covered

Entities without an authorization from the individual. Such persons and/or business entities who perform functions or services *on behalf of* a Covered Entity, and to whom the Covered Entity must disclose PHI in order for that function/activity to be performed, are called "business associates" under the HIPAA Privacy Regulations (45 C.F.R. § 160.103). Business associates are *not* members of the Covered Entity's work force, but rather persons and entities outside the Covered Entity's organization. The functions and activities performed by the business associate which involve the use or disclosure of PHI include, but are not limited to, claims, processing or administration data analysis, processing or administration, utilization review, quality assurance, billing, benefit management, practice management, repricing, and services such as legal, actuarial, accounting, consulting, data aggregation, management, administrative, accreditation, or financial (45 C.F.R. § 160.103).

A Covered Entity may disclose PHI to a business associate and may allow the business associate to receive or create PHI on its behalf only if the Covered Entity obtains "satisfactory assurances" that the business associate will appropriately safeguard the PHI (45 C.F.R. § 164.502(e)(1)(i)). Such "satisfactory assurances" must be provided by the business associate to the Covered Entity in a written contract and must establish the permitted and required uses and disclosures of such PHI by the business associate. In addition, the contract must provide that the business associate will:

- Not use or further disclose the information other than as permitted and required by the contract as required by law;
- Use appropriate safeguards to prevent use or disclosure of the information other than as provided for by its contract;
- Report to the Covered Entity any use or disclosure of the information not provided for by its contract of which it becomes aware;
- Ensure that any agents, including a subcontractor, to whom it provides PHI received from, or created or received by the business associate on behalf of, the Covered Entity agrees to the same restrictions and conditions that apply to the business associate with respect to such information;
- Make PHI available so that the Covered Entity may give the individual right of access to his/her PHI as required under 45 C.F.R. § 164.524;

- Make PHI available for amendment and incorporate any amendments in accordance with the requirements of 45 C.F.R. § 164.526;
- Make available the information for the Covered Entity to provide an accounting of disclosures to an individual in accordance with 45 C.F.R. § 164.528;
- Make its internal practices, book, and records relating to the use and disclosure of PHI received from, or created or received by the business associate on behalf of, the Covered Entity available to the Secretary of Health and Human Services for purposes of determining the Covered Entity's compliance with HIPAA; and
- At termination of the contract, if feasible, return or destroy all PHI received from, or created or received by the business associate on behalf of, the Covered Entity that the business associate still maintains in any form and retains no copy of such information. If such return or destruction is not feasible, the agreement must extend the protections of the contract to the information and limit further uses and disclosures to those purposes that make the return or destruction of the information infeasible.

The business associate agreement must also authorize termination of the agreement by the Covered Entity if the Covered Entity determines that the business associate has violated a material term of the agreement. The agreement may not authorize the business associate to use or disclose the PHI in any manner that would violate the requirements of HIPAA if done by the Covered Entity. The business associate agreement may include a number of permissive paragraphs, including permission for the business associate to use and disclose PHI for the proper management and administration of the business associate and may provide data aggregation services relating to the health-care operations of the Covered Entity.

A Covered Entity may be the "business associate" of another Covered Entity if that Covered Entity performs a function or service *on behalf of* another Covered Entity. If, however, a Covered Entity is receiving an individual's PHI in its capacity as a health-care provider and is treating the individual, that Covered Entity is *not* considered a business associate of the Covered Entity disclosing the PHI and no written contract is needed before disclosure can be made (45 C.F.R. § 164.502(e)(1)(ii)).

f. Disclosure Pursuant to a Data Use Agreement

A Covered Entity may use or disclose PHI that constitutes a "limited data set" only for purposes of research, public health or health-care operations provided that the Covered Entity enters into a "data use agreement" with the limited data set recipient (45 C.F.R. § 164.514(e)(1) & (3)). A limited data set is PHI that excludes 16 direct identifiers of the individual or relatives, employers or household members of the individual as listed in 45 C.F.R. § 164.514(e)(2). A data use agreement regarding the limited data set must:

- Establish the permitted uses and disclosures of such information by the limited set recipient for either the purposes of research, public health, or health-care operations. The data use agreement may not authorize the limited data set recipient to use or further disclose the information in a manner that would violate the requirements of § 164.514 if done by the Covered Entity;
- Establish who is permitted to use or receive the limited data set; and
- Provide that the limited data set recipient will:

  — Not use or further disclose the information other than as permitted by the data use agreement or as otherwise required by law;
  — Use appropriate safeguards to prevent use or disclosure of the information other than as provided for by the data use agreement;
  — Report to the Covered Entity any use or disclosure of the information not provided for by its data use agreement of which it becomes aware;
  — Ensure that any agents, including a subcontractor, to whom it provides the limited data set agrees to the same restrictions and conditions that apply to the limited data set recipient with respect to such information; and
  — Not identify the information or contact the individuals.
  (45 C.F.R. § 164.514(e)(4)).

A Covered Entity that becomes aware that a limited data set recipient has violated a provision of the data use agreement must take steps to cure the breach of the agreement and, if steps to cure are not successful, must discontinue disclosure of PHI to the recipient and report the problem to the Secretary of HHS (45 C.F.R. § 164.514(e)(4)(iii)(A)).

3. Preemption Issues

If a HIPAA Privacy Regulation is contrary to a provision of state law, the HIPAA Privacy Regulation prevails[29] (45 C.F.R. § 160.203). There are four exceptions to this general rule outlined in § 160.203. The most talked about exception is the one which holds that if the state law "relates to privacy of individually identifiable health information"[30] and is "more stringent" than the HIPAA Privacy Regulation, then the state law controls and HIPAA does *not* preempt (45 C.F.R. § 160.203(b)). To be "more stringent" than a HIPAA Privacy Regulation, a state law must meet one or more of the following criteria:

- Prohibits or restricts a use or disclosure of PHI in circumstances under which such use or disclosure otherwise would be permitted under HIPAA, except if the disclosure is:
  — required by the Secretary of HHS in connection with determining whether a Covered Entity is in compliance with this subchapter; or
  — to the individual who is the subject of the individually identifiable health information.
- With respect to the rights of an individual who is the subject of the PHI, permits greater rights of access or amendment, as applicable;
- With respect to information to be provided to an individual who is the subject of the PHI about a use, a disclosure, rights and remedies, provides the greater amount of information;
- With respect to the form, substance or need for express legal permission from an individual who is the subject of the PHI for use or disclosure of PHI provides requirements that narrow the scope or duration, increase the privacy protections afforded (such as by expanding the criteria for), or reduce the coercive effect of the circumstances surrounding the express legal permission, as applicable;
- With respect to record-keeping or requirements relating to accounting of disclosures, provides for the retention or reporting of more

detailed information or for a longer duration; or
- With respect to any other matter, provides greater privacy protection for the individual who is a subject of the PHI.

(45 C.F.R. § 160.202)

The issue of whether a state law is "contrary to" and "more stringent" than a HIPAA Privacy Regulation has been debated by several federal courts. (See *Northwestern Memorial Hospital v. Ashcroft*, 362 F.3d 923 (7th Cir. 2004); *United States* ex rel. *Pogue v. Diabetes Treatment Centers of America*, No. 993298 (D.D.C., May 17, 2004); *United States* ex rel. *Stewart v. Louisiana Clinic*, No. 99-1761 (E.D. La. June 4, 2003).

In addition to the "more stringent" exception, § 160.203 also excepts from HIPAA preemption state procedures for the reporting of disease or injury, child abuse, birth, or death, or for the conduct of public health surveillance, investigation, or intervention (45 C.F.R. § 160.203(c)).

Other exceptions to the general preemption rule include certain determinations made by the Secretary of HHS[31] and state laws, which require health plans to report[32] or provide access to certain information.

C. Recognition of State Approach to Health-Care Privacy

State-specific regulations pertaining to privacy of protected health information, research, and/or biotech matters are too voluminous in number to be addressed in this resource publication. The Health Privacy Project in Washington, D.C. maintains a Web site that provides a summary of state laws pertaining to privacy. The Health Privacy Project also staffs the Consumer Coalition for Health Privacy. For further information on state health privacy laws and related health privacy matters, check out the Health Privacy Web site at www.healthprivacy.org.

D. HIPAA Interplay with Federal Common Rule and Federal Certificates of Confidentiality

1. Introduction

The HIPAA Privacy Regulations establish the conditions under which protected health information may be used or disclosed by Covered Entities for research purposes. The Privacy Regulations also define the means by which individuals will be informed of uses and disclosures of their medical information for research purposes, and their rights to access information about them held by Covered Entities. The Privacy Regulations build upon the existing federal protections for research involving human subjects called the "Common Rule." [See the Common Rule (45 C.F.R. Part 467, Subpart A) and/or the Food and Drug Administration's (FDA) human subject protection regulations (21 C.F.R. Parts 50 and 56).] Where both the Privacy Regulations and the Common Rule apply, both regulations must be followed. More important, the Privacy Regulations create equal standards of privacy protection for research governed by the existing federal human subject regulations and research that is not. In the course of conducting research, researchers may obtain, create, use and/or disclose individually identifiable health information. Under the Privacy Regulations, Covered Entities are permitted to use and disclose protected health information for research with individual authorization, or without individual authorization under limited circumstances.

2. Research and HIPAA

a. When Research Is Subject to HIPAA

A researcher is a covered health-care provider if he or she furnishes health care services to individuals, including the subjects of research, and transmits any health information in electronic form in connection with a transaction covered by the Transactions Rule.[33] (See 45 C.F.R. § 160.102 § 160.103.) For example, a researcher who conducts a clinical trial that involves the delivery of routine health care, such as an MRI or liver function test, and transmits health information in electronic form to a third-party payer for payment, would be a covered health-care provider under the Privacy Regulations. Researchers who provide health care to the subjects of research or other individuals would be covered health-care providers even if they do not themselves electronically transmit information in connection with a HIPAA transaction, but have other entities, such as a hospital or billing service, conduct such electronic transactions on their behalf. For further assistance in determining Covered Entity status, see the "decision tool" at the Office of Civil Rights HIPAA Web site.[34]

b. *Permission to Use or Disclose Research Information*

i. Use or Disclosure Without Authorization

An often confusing issue is when a researcher needs a participant's permission to use PHI for research. As discussed *infra* in sections B.2.d.(ix) and B.2.f., to use or disclose PHI information without authorization by the research participant, a Covered Entity must obtain one of the following:

- Documented Institutional Review Board (IRB) or Privacy Board Approval. This provision of the Privacy Regulations might be used, for example, to conduct records research when researchers are unable to use de-identified information, and the research could not practicably be conducted if research participants' authorization were required.
- Representations from the researcher, either in writing or orally, that the use or disclosure of the PHI is solely to prepare a research protocol or for similar purposes preparatory to research; that the researcher will not remove any PHI from the Covered Entity; and that the PHI for which access is sought is necessary for the research purpose. This provision might be used, for example, to design a research study or to assess the feasibility of conducting a study.
- Representations from the researcher, either in writing or orally, that the use or disclosure being sought is solely for research on the protected health information of decedents, that the PHI being sought is necessary for the research, and, at the request of the Covered Entity, documentation of the death of the individuals about whom information is being sought.
- A data use agreement entered into by both the Covered Entity and the researcher, pursuant to which the Covered Entity may disclose a limited data set to the researcher for research, public health, or health

Privacy Issues for Biotechnology Companies

care operations. A limited data set excludes specified direct identifiers of the individual or of relatives, employers, or household members of the individual. The elements of the data use agreement were discussed *infra* in section B.2.f.

ii. Research Use/Disclosure with Individual Authorization

To use or disclose PHI with authorization by the research participant, the Covered Entity must obtain an authorization that satisfies the requirements of 45 C.F.R. § 164.508. The Privacy Regulations have a general set of authorization requirements that apply to all uses and disclosures, including those for research purposes. However, several special provisions apply to research authorizations:

- Unlike other authorizations, an authorization for a research purpose may state that the authorization does not expire, that there is no expiration date or event, or that the authorization continues until the "end of the research study"; and
- An authorization for the use or disclosure of PHI for research may be combined with a consent to participate in the research or with any other legal permission related to the research study.

3. The Common Rule and HIPAA

An interesting issue is the interplay between the HIPAA Privacy Regulations and the "Common Rule," the federal policy for the protection of human research subjects. Under the Privacy Regulations, a patient's authorization is for the use and disclosure of protected health information for research purposes. In contrast, an individual's informed consent, as required by the Common Rule and the Food and Drug Administration's (FDA) human subjects regulations, is a consent to participate in the research study as a whole, not simply a consent for the research use or disclosure of PHI. For this reason, there are important differences between the Privacy Regulations' requirements for individual authorization and the Common Rule's and FDA's requirements for informed consent. However, the authorization elements in the Privacy Regulations are compatible with the Common Rule's informed consent elements. Thus, both sets of requirements can be met by use of a single, combined form, which is permitted by the Privacy Regulations. For example, the Privacy Regulations allow the research authorization to state that the authorization will be valid until the conclusion of the research study, or to state that the authorization will not have an expiration date or event. This is compatible with the Common Rule's requirement for an explanation of the expected duration of the research subject's participation in the study. It should be noted that where the Privacy Regulations, the Common Rule, and/or FDA's human subjects regulations are applicable, each of the applicable regulations must be followed.

The Common Rule is codified throughout the federal regulations depending upon the federal department involved. The following is a list of the federal regulations codifying the Common Rule:

- U.S. Department of Agriculture, 7 C.F.R. Part 1c
- U.S. Department of Energy, 10 C.F.R. Part 745
- National Aeronautics and Space Administration, 14 C.F.R. Part 1230
- U.S. Department of Commerce, 15 C.F.R. Part 27
- Consumer Product Safety Commission, 16 C.F.R. Part 1028
- International Development Cooperation Agency, Agency for International Development, 22 C.F.R. Part 225
- U.S. Department of Health and Human Services, 45 C.F.R. Part 46, Subpart A
- U.S. Department of Housing and Urban Development, 24 C.F.R. Part 60
- U.S. Department of Justice, 28 C.F.R. Part 46
- U.S. Department of Defense, 32 C.F.R. Part 219
- U.S. Department of Education, 34 C.F.R. Part 97
- Affairs, 38 C.F.R. Part 16
- Environmental Protection Agency, 40 C.F.R. Part 26
- National Science Foundation, 45 C.F.R. Part 690

If informed consent or reconsent (i.e., asked to sign a revised consent or nother informed consent) is obtained from research subjects after the HIPAA compliance date, the Covered Entity must obtain individual authorization as required at 45 C.F.R. § 164.508 for the use or disclosure of protected health information once the original consent expires. The revised informed consent document may be combined with the authorization elements required by 45 C.F.R. § 164.508.

4. Research and Business Associate Status Under HIPAA

In the August 14, 2002 Preamble to publication of the Final Privacy Regulations, HHS provided some guidance as it relates to research, HIPAA, and business associate requirements. HHS opined that disclosures from a Covered Entity to a researcher for research purposes as permitted by the Privacy Regulations do not require a business associate contract. HHS explained that this is true even in those instances where the Covered Entity has hired the researcher to perform research on the Covered Entity's own behalf because research is not a covered function or activity. HHS did note, however, that the Privacy Regulations do not prohibit a Covered Entity from entering into a business associate contract with a researcher if the Covered Entity wishes to do so. In addition, if the Covered Entity desires to give the researcher a limited data set for research purposes, then the Covered Entity must enter into a data use agreement as required by 45 C.F.R. § 164.514(e).[35]

5. Federal Certificates of Confidentiality

a. Certificates of Confidentiality Explained

A special type of protection afforded to research information is identification of research participants when the research is coupled with a Certificate of Confidentiality. Certificates of Confidentiality are issued by the National Institutes of Health and other HHS agencies to protect identifiable research information from forced or compelled disclosure. Certificates of Confidentiality are addressed under 42 C.F.R. Part 2a, Protection of Identity—Research Subjects. This federal regulation states, in part, that the Secretary of HHS may authorize persons engaged in the research of mental health, including research on the use and effect of alcohol and other psychoactive drugs, to protect the privacy of individuals who are the subjects of such research by withholding from all persons not connected with the conduct of such research the names or other identifying characteristics of the research subjects. The person authorized to protect the privacy of such individuals may not be compelled in any federal, state, or local civil, criminal, administrative, legislative or other proceeding to identify such individuals.

The regulations that accompany 42 C.F.R. § 2a.1 identify to whom a Certificate of Confidentiality application may be made, the effect of a Confidentiality Certificate if issued, and the impact of the determination of such a certificate.

Like the certificate of confidentiality provisions in 42 C.F.R. Part 2a, the Public Health Service Act § 301(d), 42 U.S.C. § 241(d) affords the protection of the identity of research subjects in biomedical, behavioral, clinical, or other research.

b. National Institutes of Health Statement on Certificates of Confidentiality

In March 2002, the National Institutes of Health (NIH) announced its statement on certificates of confidentiality. The statement indicates that certificates of confidentiality allow the investigator and others who have access to research records to refuse to disclose identifying information of research participants in any civil, criminal, administrative, legislative, or other proceedings, whether at the federal, state, or local level. NIH indicated in its statement that certificates of confidentiality may be granted for studies collecting information that, if disclosed, could have adverse consequences for subjects or damage their financial standing, employability, insurability, or reputation. The NIH provides a special Web page relating to certificates of confidentiality that can be accessed at http://grants.nih.gov/grants/policy/coc/index.htm.

Background information relating to certificates of confidentiality, as issued by the NIH–Office of Extramural Research, indicate that, in general, certificates of confidentiality are issued for "single, well-defined research projects rather than groups or classes of projects." If the certificate of confidentiality is issued, it will be very specific and state the date upon which it becomes effective and the date upon which it expires. A certificate of confidentiality protects all information identifiable to any individual who participates as a research subject during the time the certificate is in effect. Additional background information on NIH certificates of confidentiality may be obtained from its Web site.[36]

Additionally, the NIH maintains a Web site of frequently asked questions (FAQs) on certificates of confidentiality. One such FAQ dated July 21, 2003, discusses the interplay between the HIPAA Privacy Rule and certificates of confidentiality. This FAQ indicates that certificates of confidentiality offer an important protection for the privacy of research subject participants by protecting identifiable health information from forced disclosure (e.g., by court order). While the Privacy Regulations establish protection for the use and disclosure of PHI by Covered Entities, the Regulations do permit use or disclosure of PHI in response to certain judicial or administrative orders. Therefore, researchers/contractors may obtain certificates of confidentiality to protect them from being forced to disclose information that would have to be disclosed under the Privacy Regulations.[37]

E. Research Issues and Academic Medical Centers

Research at academic medical centers may present its own special set of issues. As an additional resource pertaining to academic medical center research, the reader is referred to the Association of American Medical Colleges *Guidelines for Academic Medical Centers on Security and Privacy*. In May 2001, the AAMC published *Practical Strategies for Addressing the Health Insurance Portability and Accountability Act*. This excellent publication not only identifies the HIPAA requirement, but also addresses a section under each regulation titled "AMC Explanation of HIPAA Regulation," "Key Issues," and "Guidelines." The guideline can be accessed at www.aamc.org/members/gir/gasp/start.htm.

F. Canadian Privacy Legislation

Canada has legislation very similar in intent and nature to the United States Gramm-Leach-Bliley Act (GLBA) and HIPAA. The Canadian legislation is commonly referred to as "Bill C-6" and/or Personal Information Protection and Electronic Documents Act (PIPED Act).

One of the main purposes of the PIPED Act is to provide privacy protection for "personal information"[38] collected, used or disclosed by the private sector. While the PIPED Act does have specific provisions, the "Privacy Commissioner of Canada" has represented that he plans to rely on the courts to provide an interpretation of the Act. Therefore, it is somewhat challenging to provide legislative intent as it pertains to the PIPED Act. The PIPED Act generally requires organizations to obtain an individual's consent for the collection, use or disclosure of the individual's personal information, including personal information collected before the PIPED Act was passed. Organizations[39] are required to protect personal information with safeguards appropriate to the "sensitivity" of the information.

In addition to addressing how personal information can be collected and used, the PIPED Act also addresses how transactions are electronically stored. This is similar to the HIPAA Security Rule, 45 C.F.R. § 164.300 *et seq.*

The PIPED Act applies to organizations differently based on the phase of the PIPED Act. On January 1, 2001, the PIPED Act applied to federally regulated organizations including banks, telephone companies, shipping and air carriers; information about the employees of these organizations; and the transmission of personal information across provincial and national borders. On January 1, 2002, the PIPED Act became applicable to personal health information used by the organizations (that were affected July 1, 2001). Health information includes both mental and physical health information. As of January 1, 2004, the PIPED Act applies to personal information used by all organizations in Canada unless the organization operates within a province that has similar legislation.

The essential principles of the PIPED Act are similar to those found in the European Union (E.U.) Directive.

In Part 1 of the PIPED Act, certain individual rights are identified relating to the protection of personal information. This part outlines 10 essential principles of privacy. The Model Code for the Protection of Personal Information form is an essential part of the PIPED Act. The Model Code was developed by the Canadian Standards Association and contains ten principles. A summary of these 10 principles follows:

1. Accountability

Organizations are responsible for all personal information under their control and remain responsible when personal information is processed by third parties on their behalf. Organizations must designate at least one individual who is accountable for the organization's compliance with the act. Organizations must implement security to protect personal information and establish procedures to receive and respond to complaints, train staff, and otherwise develop policies and practices relating to the protection of personal information.

Privacy Issues for Biotechnology Companies 553

2. Identifying Purpose

Organizations are required to document the purpose of the collection and use of personal information before the organization can collect or use it. The organization must have permission to use the information if the documented purpose changes.

3. Consent

The knowledge and consent of the individual who is the subject of the personal information is required to collect, use or disclose personal information. Consent may also be withdrawn. As with the HIPAA requirement that the Notice of Privacy Practice be in plain language, notice under the PIPED Act must be written in an understandable manner and contain the following information:

- The name, or title, and address of the person accountable for the organization's compliance and to whom complaints or inquiries can be sent;
- The purposes for which personal information is collected;
- The means by which data subjects can gain access to personal information;
- The types of personal information held by the organization;
- A copy of any informational material that explains the organization's policies; and
- The type of personal information that is shared with affiliates or agents of the organization.

The PIPED Act provides that an organization should generally seek "express consent" when the information is likely to be considered sensitive and "implied consent" when the information is considered less sensitive. For the most part, medical record information will always be considered sensitive.

Much like § 164.512 of the HIPAA Privacy Regulations, the PIPED Act recognizes that in certain circumstances personal information can be collected, used or disclosed without the knowledge and consent of the individual. Examples include:

- Certain legal, medical or security situations;
- Fraud detection and prevention;
- Collection by law enforcement where seeking consent might defeat the purpose of collection;
- When consent is impossible or inappropriate; and
- When an organization does not have a direct relationship with the individual.[40]

4. Limiting Collection

The amount and type of information is limited to what is necessary for the identified purpose. The identified purpose is that which relates to the "identifying purpose" under principle #2 above.

5. Limit Use, Disclosure, and Retention

Information can only be disclosed or used for the purpose for which it was collected. Personal information should be kept only as long as necessary to fulfill the specific purpose.

6. Accuracy

Personal information has to be accurate, complete, and as up-to-date as necessary for the purpose for which it is to be used.

7. Safeguards

Organizations must ensure the confidentiality and integrity of personal information whether it is stored on paper or electronically. Additionally, organizations must take appropriate steps to protect personal information from theft and loss as well as unauthorized access, disclosure or improper use.

8. Openness

Organizations must provide the public with general information on their personal information protection policies and practices. Accordingly, a copy of the material that explains the organization's practices must be made available.

9. Individual Access

Individuals must have access to their personal information and details on how it has been used. Upon request, individuals must be informed of the existence, use, and disclosure of all their personal information and also be given access to that information. An individual has the right to challenge the accuracy and completeness of the information and have it amended when appropriate.

10. Challenging Compliance

The organization must provide a method to address complaints or challenges to its compliance, must investigate and document all complaints, and, if necessary, update its practices.

The Privacy Commissioner of Canada has published a document titled *Your Privacy Responsibilities: A Guide for Businesses and Organizations to Canada's Personal Information Protection and Electronic Documents Act*. This guide includes an introduction section and a section regarding an organization's responsibilities and how to fulfill those responsibilities, as well as a "tips" section. This guide is part of the "E-Kit" put together by the Privacy Commissioner of Canada. The Privacy Commissioner of Canada's Web site is www.privcom.gc.ca/ekit/ekit_e.asp. One of the more helpful sections of this Web site is the section containing questions and answers regarding the application of the PIPED Act and the Alberta and British Columbia Personal Information Protection Acts.

In addition, the section of the Web site titled "Commissioner's Findings" contains summaries of the Commissioner's cases from 2001 through 2005. These case summaries are helpful in interpreting the PIPED Act and applying it to a given factual scenario.

Notes

1. This fourth category was added as part of the Medicare Prescription Drug, Improvement, and Modernization Act of 2003 (MMA) signed into law on December 8, 2003. *See also* 42 C.F.R. § 403.812. An endorsed sponsor is a HIPAA covered entity and must comply with the standards, implementation specifications, and requirements in 45 C.F.R. Parts 160, 162, and 164 as identified in 42 C.F.R. § 403.812. As to the Privacy Regulations, the endorsed sponsor must comply with Part 160 and 164, Subparts A and E

that relate to "health plans." For Security Regulation compliance, the endorsed sponsor must comply with Parts 160 and 164, Subparts A and C as other covered entities.

2. This "general rule" is explained by the U.S. Department of Health and Human Services (HHS) in both the December 28, 2000 (65 Fed. Reg. 82,462) and the August 14, 2002 (67 Fed. Reg. 53,182) Preamble to those *Federal Register*s as follows:

> This final rule establishes, for the first time, a set of basic national privacy standards and fair information practices that provide all Americans with a basic level of protection and peace of mind that is essential to their full participation in their [health] care. This rule sets a floor of ground rules for health care providers, health plans, and health care clearinghouses to follow, in order to protect patients and to encourage them to seek needed care (65 Fed. Reg. 82,464) and ". . . the Privacy Rule creates, for the first time, a floor of national protections for the privacy of their [consumer] most sensitive information—health information. . . . Under the Privacy Rule, health plans, health care clearinghouses, and certain health care providers must guard against misuse of individuals' identifiable health information and limit the sharing of such information, and consumers are afforded significant new rights to enable them to understand and control how their health information is used and disclosed." (67 Fed. Reg. 53182).

3. *See* Duckett & Burns, *Responding to Subpoenas for Medical Records: In Compliance with HIPAA,* 39 Tenn. B.J. 18 (May 2003) ("HIPAA is a serious set of regulations for hospitals and physicians. The regulations impose substantial duties on physicians and hospitals to safeguard the privacy of the patients they treat. Failure to comply with the regulations may result in significant civil fines and serious criminal penalties.")

4. *See* Averill, *Lawyers Helping Lawyers—HIPAA Privacy Rules,* 51 L.A. Bar J. 280 (December 2003-January 2004).

5. 45 C.F.R. § 164.514(b)(2).

6. Psychotherapy Notes means notes recorded (in any medium) by a health-care provider who is a mental health professional documenting or analyzing the contents of conversion during a private counseling session or a group, joint, or family counseling session and that are separated from the rest of the individual's medical record (45 C.F.R § 164.501).

7. 67 Fed. Reg. 53,220.

8. 67 Fed. Reg. 53,220.

9. 45 C.F.R. § 164.508. *See* 67 Fed. Reg. 53,221.

10. Marketing is defined expressly to include "an arrangement between a Covered Entity and any other entity whereby the Covered Entity discloses protected health information to the other entity, in exchange for direct or indirect remuneration, for the other entity or its affiliate to make a communication about its own product or service that encourages recipients of the communication to purchase or use that product or service." These communications are marketing and can only occur if the Covered Entity obtains the individual's authorization pursuant to 45 C.F.R. § 164.508. There are three categories of communications that are *excluded* from the definition of "marketing." A Covered Entity is not engaged in marketing when it communicates to individuals about: (1) the participating providers in health plans' network, the services offered by a provider, or the benefits covered by a health plan; (2) the individual's treatment; or (3) case management or care coordination for that individual, or directions or recommendations for alternative treatments, therapies, health-care providers, or settings of care to that individual. A communication that merely promotes health in a general manner and does not promote a specific product or service from a particular provider does not meet the general definition of "marketing." Therefore, communications such as mailings reminding women to get an annual mammogram, and mailings providing information on how to lower cholesterol, about new developments in health care, about health or "wellness" classes, about support groups, and about health fairs are permitted, and are not considered marketing. This means that Covered Entities may make communications in newsletter format without authorization as long as the content of such communication is not "marketing," as defined by the rule.

11. A common example is the hospital patient directory maintained at many hospital information desks.

12. In December 2000, HHS indicated that the Final Rule "does not create any new duty or obligation to disclose protected health information." Rather, according to HHS, the Final Rule permits Covered Entities to use or disclose PHI when they are "required by law to do so." 65 Fed. Reg. 82,666. In December 2000, HHS expanded the definition of "law" to include "binding legal authority" such as constitutions, statutes, rules, regulations, common law, or other government actions as having the effect of law. 65 Fed. Reg. 82,668. In the December 2000 Preamble, HHS explained how the "required by law" provision relates to the rest of the privacy rule. "We note that this rule does not affect what is required by other law, nor does it compel a Covered Entity to make a use or disclosure of protected health information required by the legal demands or reporting requirements listed in the definition of 'required by law.' Covered Entities will not be sanctioned under this rule for responding in good faith to such legal process and reporting requirements. However, nothing in this rule affects, either by expanding or

contracting, a Covered Entity's right to challenge such process or reporting requirements under other laws. The only disclosures of protected health information compelled by this rule are disclosures to an individual (or the personal representative of an individual) or to the Secretary for the purpose of enforcing this rule." 65 Fed. Reg. 82,525. This concept is again repeated in the December 2000 Preamble at 65 Fed. Reg. 82,668, in which HHS stated as follows:

> We do not agree that the Final Rule should require Covered Entities to comply with uses or disclosures of protected health information mandated by law. The purpose of this rule is to protect privacy, and to allow those disclosures consistent with sound public policy. Consistent with this purpose, we mandate disclosures only to the individual who is the subject of the information, and for purposes of enforcing the rule. Where a law imposes a legal duty on the Covered Entity to use or disclose protected health information, it is sufficient that the privacy rule permit the Covered Entity to comply with such law. The enforcement of that legal duty, however, is a matter for that other law." Uses and disclosure permitted under paragraph 512(a) must be limited to the PHI necessary to "meet the requirements of the law that compels the use or disclosure." 65 Fed. Reg. 82,525.

13. 65 Fed. Reg. 82,525.

14. *Id.*

15. In the December 2000 Preamble, HHS indicated that the Final Rule continues to permit Covered Entities to disclose PHI without individual authorization directly to public health authorities and listed examples such as the Food and Drug Administration, the Occupational Safety and Health Administration, the Centers for Disease Control and Prevention, as well as state and local public health departments as long as it is for a public health purpose. 65 Fed. Reg. 82,526.

16. HHS was very specific in the December 2000 Preamble that state laws continue to apply with respect to child abuse and that the Final Rule does not in any way interfere with a Covered Entity's ability to comply with those laws. 65 Fed. Reg. 82,527.

17. The December 28, 2000 Preamble indicated that HHS recognized that most, if not all, states had laws that mandated reporting of child abuse or neglect to the appropriate authorities. Additionally, HHS recognized that many states have laws mandating the reporting of abuse, neglect or exploitation of the elderly or other vulnerable adults. HHS indicated that it "did not intend to impede reporting in compliance with these laws." 65 Fed. Reg. 82,527.

18. HHS indicates that this paragraph "addresses reports to law enforcement as well as to other authorized public officials." 65 Fed. Reg. 82,527.
19. 65 Fed. Reg. 82,527.
20. *Id.*
21. 65 Fed. Reg. 82,528.
22. In the December 2000 Preamble, HHS explained its rationale as follows:

> We believe that in abuse situations—to a greater extent than in situations involving crime victims in general—there is a clear potential for abusers to cause further serious harm to the victim or to others, such as other family members in a household or other resident of a nursing home. The provisions allowing reporting of abuse when authorized by state law, as described above, are consistent with principles articulated by the AMA's Council on Ethical and Judicial Affairs, which state that when reporting abuse as voluntary under state law, it is justified when necessary to prevent serious harm to a patient.

65 Fed. Reg. 82,528.

23. Fed. R. Civ. P. 45 is specifically referenced in the Preamble to the December 28, 2002 final HIPAA privacy regulations, 65 Fed. Reg. 82,529. In *United States of America v. Franklin Sutherland*, 143 F. Supp. 2d 609 (W. Dist.Va. May 1, 2002) the court addressed this specific provision of the HIPAA privacy regulations relative to a subpoena obtained by the U.S. Attorney pursuant to Fed. R. Crim. P. 17. The court held that "although issued by the clerk of the court, the subpoena did not constitute an order of the court because the rules provide that the clerk may issue a blank subpoena to be completed later by the party seeking documentary evidence." The court specifically cited 45 C.F.R. § 164.512(e) and 65 Fed. Reg. 82,814-15 in its analysis.

24. In addressing the disclosure of PHI to law enforcement, HHS "balanced" the law enforcement need against an individual's right to privacy. This is reflected in HHS's statements contained in the December 2000 publication of the Final Rule:

> Disclosure of protected health information by law enforcement is not at issue in this regulation. Law enforcement access to protected health information in the first instance, absent any re-disclosure by law enforcement, impinges on individuals' privacy interests and must therefore be justified by a public purpose that outweighs individuals' privacy interests. We do not agree that sufficient safeguards already exist in this area.

65 Fed. Reg. 82,678-79.

25. The purpose of this provision was explained by HHS as follows:

> The purpose of this provision is to permit law enforcement to obtain limited time-sensitive information without the process requirements applicable to disclosures for other purposes. Only limited information may be disclosed under this provision, and disclosure is permitted only in limited circumstances. We believe that these safeguards are sufficient, and that creating additional restrictions would undermine the purpose of the provision and that it would hinder law enforcement's ability to obtain essential, time-sensitive information.

65 Fed. Reg. 82,684-85.

26. A person may be both a suspect and a victim. In that situation HHS states that only the more limited information under § 164.512(f)(2) may be disclosed and not all of the PHI that may be disclosed under § 164.512(f)(3).

27. The Institutional Review Board must be established in accordance with 7 C.F.R. 1c.107, 10 C.F.R. 745.107, 14 C.F.R. 1230.107, 15 C.F.R. 27.107, 16 C.F.R. 1028.107, 21 C.F.R. 56.107, 22 C.F.R. 225.107, 24 C.F.R. 60.107, 28 C.F.R. 46.107, 32 C.F.R. 219.107, 34 C.F.R. 97.107, 38 C.F.R. 16.107, 40 C.F.R. 26.107, 45 C.F.R. 46.107, 45 C.F.R. 690.107, or 49 C.F.R. 11.107 (45 C.F.R. § 164.512(i)(1)(i)(A)).

28. The Privacy Board must meet the following criteria: 1) Have members with varying backgrounds and appropriate professional competency as necessary to review effect of the research protocol on the individual's privacy rights and related interests; 2) Include at least one member who is not affiliated with the Covered Entity, not affiliated with any entity conducting or sponsoring the research, and not related to any person who is affiliated with any of such entities, and 3) Does not have any member participating in a review of any project in which the member has a conflict of interest (45 C.F.R. § 164.512(i)(1)(i)(B)).

29. "State law" means a constitution, statute, regulation, rule, common law, or other state action having the force and effect of law (45 C.F.R. § 160.202).

30. The phrase "relates to the privacy of individually identifiable health information" means, with respect to a state law, that the state law has the specific purpose of protecting the privacy of health information or affects the privacy of health information in a direct, clear, and substantial way (45 C.F.R. § 160.202).

31. A HIPAA exception to the Privacy Regulations general preemption provision is if a determination is made by the Secretary of HHS that a provision of state law 1) is necessary i) to prevent fraud and abuse related to the provision of or payment for health care; ii) to ensure appropriate state regulation of insurance and health plans to the extent expressly authorized by

statute or regulation; iii) for state reporting on health-care delivery or costs; or iv) for purposes of serving a compelling need related to public health, safety, or welfare, and, if a standard, requirement or implementation specification of the HIPAA Privacy Regulations is at issue, if the Secretary determines that the intrusion into privacy is warranty when balanced against the need to be served; or 2) has as its principal purpose the regulation of the manufacturer, registration, distribution, dispensing, or other control of any controlled substances (as defined in 21 U.S.C. § 802), or that deemed a controlled substance by state law. (45 C.F.R. § 160.203(a)).

32. 45 C.F.R. § 160.203(d) excepts from the general HIPAA preemption provision state law that requires a health plan to report, or to provide access to, information for the purpose of management audits, financial audits, program monitoring and evaluation, or the licensure or certification of facilities or individuals.

33. See the Question and Answer section of the CMS Web site at www.cms.hhs.gov. Click on the HIPAA link for further information.

34. http://www.hhs.gov/ocr/hipaa.

35. *See* 67 Fed. Reg. 53,252.

36. http://grants1.nih.gov/grants/policy/coc/background.htm.

37. http://grants1.nih.gov/grants/policy/coc/faqs.htm.

38. "Personal information" means information about an identifiable individual, but does not include the name, title, business address or telephone number of any employee of an organization. Recorded speech of Jennifer Stoddart, Privacy Commissioner of Canada; "An overview of Canada's new private law – The *Personal Information Protection and Electronic Documents Act.*" *See* http://www.privcom.gc.ca/speech/2004/vs/vs_sp-d_040331_e.asp ("It is important to understand some of the main concepts behind *PIPEDA*. *PIPEDA* applies to organizations engaged in commercial activities that collect, use or disclose personal information. *PIPEDA* describes personal information as 'information about an identifiable individual,' but this does not include the name, title or business address or telephone number of an employee of an organization. The Act describes 'commercial activity' as 'any particular transaction, act or conduct or any regular course of conduct that is of a commercial character, including the selling, bartering or leasing of donor, membership or other fundraising lists.'" See also Section 3 of the Act.

39. An organization is an association, a partnership, a person or a trade union.

40. *Privacy Law Advisor*, Pike & Fischer, Inc., 2001. Pike & Fischer, Inc. is a subsidiary of the Bureau of National Affairs, Inc., page 14.

Chapter XII

Medical Reimbursement

Paul W. Radensky, M.D., J.D.
McDermott Will & Emery
Miami, Florida

Reimbursement is one of the most important keys to successful commercialization of a new drug or biological or medical device. Obtaining approval from the Food and Drug Administration provides a license to market the product. However, unless providers will be compensated adequately for using or ordering the item, they will have no incentive to do so. Reimbursement planning can be a complex and time-consuming process, in some cases requiring several years to reach a desired goal. Accordingly, reimbursement planning should be as much a part of product development as planning for FDA clearance. The sections below provide a basic framework for considering reimbursement plans for new technologies. Reimbursement practice is heavy on acronyms. These are defined throughout the text, and a Table of Reimbursement Acronyms is included at the end of this chapter.

A. Reimbursement Basics

1. Key Terms and Concepts

When talking about reimbursement for biotechnology items or services—or any other medical items or services—three key terms or concepts must be understood: (1) *coverage*, (2) *payment rate*, and (3) *coding*.

All three must be addressed to have successful reimbursement for a biotechnology product.

2. Coverage

"Coverage" refers to whether or not an item or service is eligible for reimbursement under the terms of a health-care benefit plan. For private payers, coverage is determined by contract: the benefit plan documents subject to applicable federal laws (e.g., ERISA) or state laws (e.g., state insurance laws). Under public benefit programs, such as Medicare and Medicaid, the scope of covered benefits is determined by law—statutes and regulations. Coverage is a threshold matter—if there is no coverage, there can be no payment whatsoever for an item or service.

Determining whether coverage is available is a four-step process: (1) determine whether the item or service fits within the scope of the benefits of the plan; (2) determine if any specific exclusions would deny coverage; (3) determine whether the item or service is reasonable and necessary and not experimental or investigational as a general matter; and (4) determine whether the item or service is medically necessary for the particular patient and provided in an appropriate setting.

> **Practice Points**
>
> **For a treatment to be covered, it must:**
> 1. Fit within the scope of the plan benefits;
> 2. Not be excluded by the Plan;
> 3. Be reasonable and necessary (not experimental); and
> 4. Be medically necessary for the patient and administered appropriately.

a. Determining the Scope of Benefits

The Medicare statute provides several distinct benefits. Under Medicare Part A, Medicare provides coverage for hospital inpatient, skilled nursing facility, hospice, and some home health services.[1] Under Medicare Part B, Medicare provides coverage for physicians' services, hospital outpatient services, diagnostic tests, clinical laboratory tests, durable medical equipment, some home health services, and many other services.[2] Medicare Part C provides the scope of benefits for beneficiaries who elect to receive benefits outside the traditional fee-for-service benefit, including Medicare managed care plans.[3] Medicare Part D provides the prescription drug benefit approved in 2004 under the Medicare Prescription Drug, Improvement and Modernization Act of 2003 (the MMA—Pub. L. 108-173).[4]

Biotechnology products would not be covered as a discrete class of products, but rather would fit under many established benefit categories. For example, if a novel biotechnology drug is given to patients with septic shock who are admitted as inpatients at a hospital, the drug would be covered as an inpatient item/service. If a biotechnology device comprises a diagnostic laboratory test, the service would be covered as a diagnostic laboratory test. Coverage for biotechnology items and services fall under established rules and may differ depending upon the type of product and the setting in which it is provided.

b. Checking for Specific Exclusions from Coverage

Being included in the scope of benefits is just the first step in determining coverage. The next step is to ensure that the item or service is not otherwise excluded as a non-covered item or service. Certain items and services may be specifically excluded from coverage. For example, when oncologists began to treat metastatic breast cancer patients with high-dose chemotherapy combined with bone marrow transplantation, numerous payers adopted specific terms in their benefit plans to exclude coverage for these services even though they otherwise could have been covered as hospital services and/or physician services.

c. The Reasonable and Necessary Test

An important coverage determination is whether an item or service is considered "reasonable and necessary" and not experimental or investigational. Under this determination, items and services are excluded from coverage if they are considered not medically necessary for the diagnosis or treatment of patients (Social Security Act § 1862(a)(1)(A)). There are no regulations that specify the criteria for meeting the reasonable and necessary test, but the Centers for Medicare and Medicaid Services (CMS) is developing guidance documents in this area.[5] Despite the lack of firm criteria, certain principles are clear: (1) effectiveness and safety evidenced in published clinical studies is important for determining coverage; and (2) the more rigorous the evidence (e.g., randomized, controlled trials are preferred to non-randomized studies), the larger the study, and the longer the duration of follow-up will more likely cause payers to find the evidence sufficient to determine that the item or service is reasonable and necessary.

Also important in this determination is the relevance of the clinical endpoints in the studies presented to the payers. Payers are generally interested in "health outcomes," which are endpoints that patients can understand and appreciate without interpretation by a health-care professional. For example, a product that opens narrowed coronary arteries can be a major breakthrough. If the clinical study simply shows that the coronary channel is opened but does not show that this results in reduction in chest pain, avoidance of heart attacks or increased survival, payers may determine that the evidence is insufficient to warrant coverage.

In addition to evidence from published clinical studies, to support a determination for coverage, payers also may consider clinical practice guidelines, policies or assessments prepared by authoritative sources. If sponsors of a new biotechnology drug or device approach payers for coverage, the payers will often look to see whether or not the relevant medical specialty society has issued any practice policies about the technology. If the medical provider community is not asking for the item or service to be covered, the payers are unlikely to grant coverage.

d. Medical Necessity for the Particular Patient

Beyond a threshold determination that a new product or service can be reasonable and necessary for some patients, payers will consider whether the item or service is medically necessary for a specific patient at a particular time. An item or service will be considered reasonable and necessary only for patients with certain diagnoses. In addition, payers may determine that an item or service is medically necessary only among patients who have failed or have had side effects on other therapies that are more effective, safer or less costly. For example, a blockbuster therapy that opens coronary arteries may be considered medically necessary only in patients with 70-percent narrowing of the coronary arteries, as shown by cardiac catheterization.

e. Implications of Coverage/Non-coverage

As explained above, coverage is a threshold issue, and without coverage there can be no payment. Nevertheless, a service may be covered and yet there may be no separate payment for it. For example, under the Medicare inpatient Prospective Payment System that determines payment for most acute-care hospitalizations, hospitals are paid an all-inclusive fee that covers all services provided during the admission other than physician services. The payment is determined by the Diagnosis Related Group (DRG) assigned to the admission. The DRG, in turn, is based on the reason the patient was hospitalized (the principal diagnosis) as well as any major operating room procedures that may have been performed. If during the admission the patient develops an infection and requires a novel biotechnology antimicrobial, there may not be any incremental payment for the agent.

f. Coverage Process

Under Medicare, most coverage decisions are made by local Medicare contractors, which are private entities that process Medicare claims; however, some coverage determinations are made nationally by CMS. These coverage determinations are called National Coverage Determinations (NCDs) and are binding on all local contractors and beneficiaries (although Medicare managed-care organizations can provide coverage greater than what is otherwise required). In 2005, CMS released draft guidance on: (1) when CMS will initiate the NCD process on its own; (2) when CMS will refer an NCD under consideration for an external technology assessment (managed by the Agency for Healthcare Research and Quality); (3) when CMS will refer an NCD to its Medicare Coverage Advisory Committee; and (4) linking coverage to collection of evidence ("Coverage with Evidence Development"). Medicare announced plans to release draft guidance on the agency's considerations when reviewing evidence in making an NCD, but this guidance was not available at the time of publication. (For current information on coverage guidance and coverage policies, see http://www.cms.hhs.gov/coverage/guidance.asp.)

Local Medicare contractors may adopt local coverage policies to define the indications and limitations of coverage, covered diagnosis codes, non-covered diagnosis codes, and documentation requirements for coverage for services provided in their regions. Local coverage policies may provide for coverage or non-coverage of an item that is not subject to an NCD. When an NCD applies, the local coverage policies cannot be inconsistent with the national policy, but may provide additional information to implement the national policy.

Local coverage policies were called Local Medical Review Policies (LMRPs) until December 2003 and included identification of the benefit category, reference to any statutory exclusions, and coding guidelines, as well as indications and limitations of coverage under the reasonable and necessary requirements. Beginning in December 2003, local coverage policies are now called Local Coverage Determinations (LCDs), and include only those sections of the LMRP that address the reasonable and necessary requirements. Coding guidelines are still prepared, but these are released as separate documents. All LMRPs must have been converted to LCDs by December 2005.[6]

Most Medicare claims for items and services do not fall under either national or local coverage determinations. The services are either paid on an automated basis without going through any specific review or are reported under an unlisted or non-specific code and set aside for manual review. NCDs and LCDs are developed only when Medicare intends to put in place specific requirements for coverage that apply nationally (NCD) or locally/regionally (LCD).

Private payers have similar procedures and policies that determine when items and services will be covered by the plans. In addition to the Medicare NCD process, several payers look at technology assessments prepared by the national Blue Cross and Blue Shield Association's (BCBSA) Technology Evaluation Center (TEC, a joint program of the BCBSA and Kaiser-Permanente) or assessments published by Aetna for its plans, or the payers may purchase assessments from private technology assessment organizations, such as ECRI or Hayes, Inc.

3. Payment Law and Policy

Medicare and private payers have different methods for determining payment depending upon the site of service and the benefit category. For example, in a hospital inpatient setting under Medicare, all items and services—including any biotechnology products—are paid under an inclusive fee according to the DRG assigned for the admission.[7] In a skilled nursing facility (SNF) setting, most items and services are included in a per-diem payment amount determined by Resource Utilization Groups (RUGs).[8] Per-diem payments are also common among private insurance contracts with hospitals, although there may be different per-diem amounts for medical versus surgical admissions or for intensive care beds versus regular care beds. In the hospital outpatient setting, services are paid under the Outpatient Prospective Payment System comprising Ambulatory Payment Classification (APC) groups.[9] Generally, discrete services are assigned to separate APCs, but some bundling of items and services does occur. For example, through 2006 drugs and biologicals that cost less than $50 per day are bundled into the APC payment. Payment for most medical devices is bundled into the payment for the associated procedure in which the device is used. Physicians' services in the office setting are paid under the Medicare Physician Fee Schedule. Drugs and biologicals administered by the physician are paid separately. Since January 2005, payment has been based upon manufacturer-reported average sales price (generally set at 106 percent average selling price).[10]

4. Coding

Codes are the languages of the payers and indicate what items and services were provided, and why and where they were provided. There are several coding systems, each of which is used for a different purpose.

The major coding systems are shown in Exhibit 12-1.

Exhibit 12-1
Major Coding Systems

ICD-9-CM Diagnosis Codes	The International Classification of Diseases, 9th Revision, Clinical Modification tabular list of diseases is used to identify diagnosis or nature of illness or injury on the claim forms. Diagnosis codes answer the question, "why was the service performed?" Diagnosis codes are key to determining whether an item or service will be covered. ICD-9-CM diagnosis codes may be three, four or five characters (e.g. xxx.xx) and are either numeric or alpha-numeric. Payers generally require codes to be selected at the highest level of specificity that describes a patient's condition. ICD-9-CM diagnosis codes are coordinated and maintained by the National Center for Health Statistics within the Centers for Disease Control and Prevention. ICD-9-CM are updated twice yearly, with the main update occurring every October.
ICD-9-CM Procedure Codes	These comprise a limited set of codes describing significant procedures that are reported on claims forms for inpatient admissions. ICD-9-CM codes consist of four characters (e.g. xx.xx) in numeric format. ICD-9-CM procedure codes are coordinated and maintained by the Centers for Medicare and Medicaid Services.
CPT©	Current Procedural Terminology codes describe nearly all physician and outpatient services. CPT® codes answer the question—what was performed? Most CPT® codes are five characters and are numeric (Category I CPT® codes). New categories of CPT® codes have been created for use as performance measures (Category II CPT® codes) or to describe emerging technologies (Category III CPT® codes); these new code categories are alpha-numeric in format. CPT® codes are coordinated and maintained by the American Medical Association (which holds the copyright to the CPT® coding system as well as the registered trademark for CPT®). Determinations on new and revised codes are made by an independent CPT® Editorial Panel comprising representatives from major specialty organizations and payers. CPT® is updated on an annual basis effective January 1.

Medical Reimbursement

Exhibit 12-1
Major Coding Systems

HCPCS	Healthcare Common Procedure Coding System (HCPCS) codes describe items and services not included in CPT®, such as durable medical equipment, injectable drugs and certain codes used solely by Medicare, Medicaid or private payers. HCPCS codes answer the question, "what was provided or performed?" HCPCS codes are alpha-numeric in format. HCPCS is coordinated and maintained by the Centers for Medicare and Medicaid Services and is updated on an annual basis effective January 1.
Revenue Codes	These describe departments within institutions to which charges for items and services are applied. Revenue codes comprise four characters and are numeric; most start with a leading zero (e.g., 0xxx). Revenue codes are coordinated and maintained by the National Uniform Billing Committee. Revenue codes are reported on the institutional billing form—CMS-1450/UB-92 form.
Place of Service Codes	These codes describe the setting and provider type that performed the service. Place of Service codes are reported on the CMS-1500 non-institutional billing form.

5. Appeals

When a request for payment for Medicare benefits is submitted, the Medicare contractor will make an initial determination on coverage. If a beneficiary (or a physician or provider that has taken the claim on assignment) is dissatisfied with the initial determination, that person may appeal the decision. The steps for appeal include:

1. Redetermination;
2. Reconsideration;
3. Administrative Law Judge Hearing;
4. Departmental Appeals Board; and
5. Judicial Review in Federal Court.

Major changes in the appeal procedures were enacted under the Benefits Improvement and Protection Act of 2000 (BIPA) and the Medicare Modernization Act. Many of these changes were intended to make the basis for determinations clearer to providers and beneficiaries and to make the procedures more streamlined and fair. Interim final regulations implementing the new appeals procedures were published in the *Federal Register* on March 8, 2005. A summary of the new appeals procedures, including time lines for making appeals, time lines for decision making on the appeals, and amount in controversy requirements, are shown in Exhibit 12-2. Also shown for comparison purposes are the former appeal procedures for Part A and Part B. Although the new regulations became effective May 1, 2005, implementation of most of the new procedures will be phased in. In general, implementation of the new appeals procedures for Medicare contractors handling institutional claims began May 1, 2005. Implementation of most new appeals procedures for Medicare contractors handling non-institutional claims became effective as of January 1, 2006. Medicare health maintenance organizations and private insurers may have similar appeal processes, but specific procedures may vary.

Medical Reimbursement

Exhibit 12-2
Comparison of Former and Current 1869 Fee-For-Service Appeals

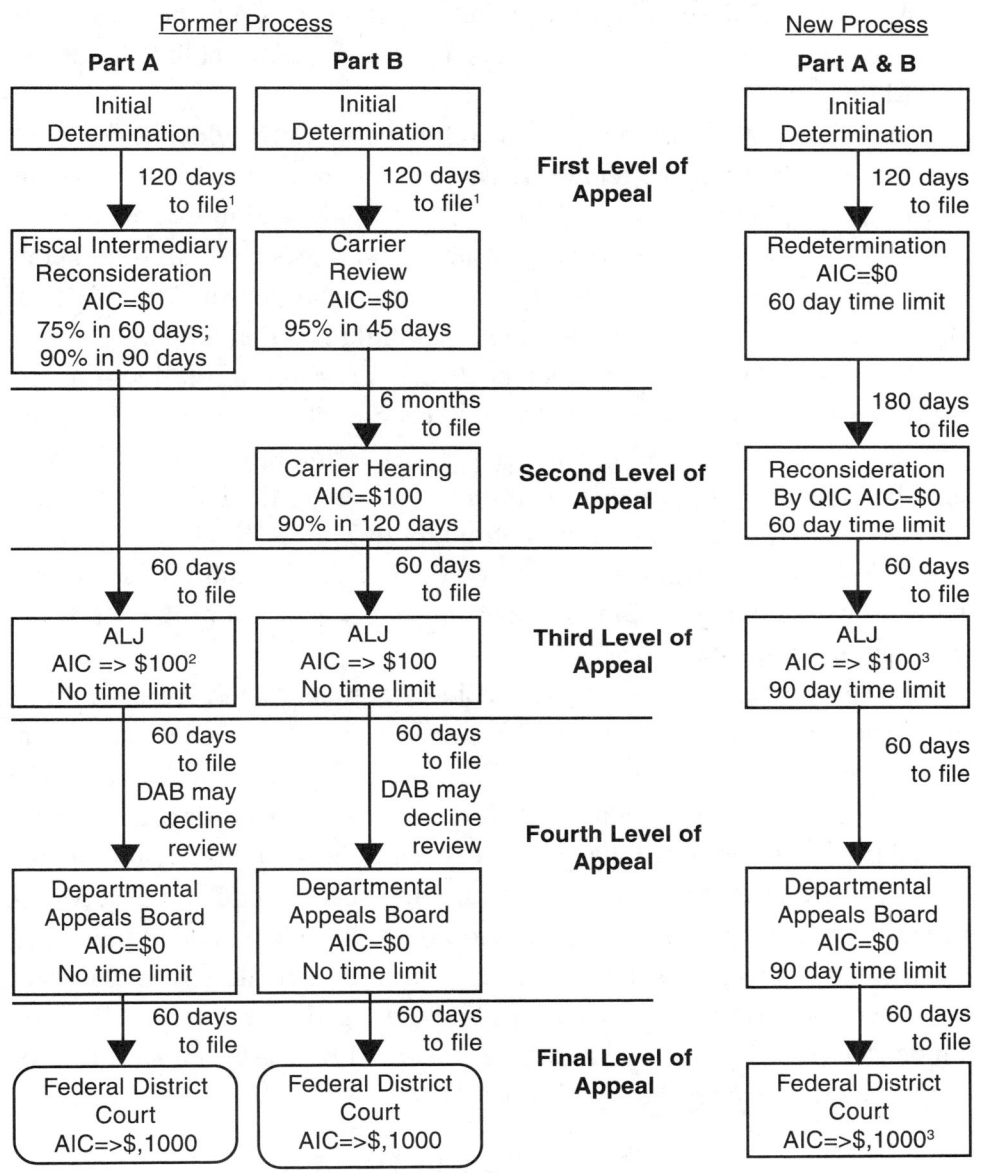

Former Process			New Process
Part A	**Part B**		**Part A & B**

Former Part A	Former Part B	Level	New Part A & B
Initial Determination	Initial Determination		Initial Determination
↓ 120 days to file[1]	↓ 120 days to file[1]	**First Level of Appeal**	↓ 120 days to file
Fiscal Intermediary Reconsideration AIC=$0 75% in 60 days; 90% in 90 days	Carrier Review AIC=$0 95% in 45 days		Redetermination AIC=$0 60 day time limit
	↓ 6 months to file		↓ 180 days to file
	Carrier Hearing AIC=$100 90% in 120 days	**Second Level of Appeal**	Reconsideration By QIC AIC=$0 60 day time limit
↓ 60 days to file	↓ 60 days to file		↓ 60 days to file
ALJ AIC => $100[2] No time limit	ALJ AIC => $100 No time limit	**Third Level of Appeal**	ALJ AIC => $100[3] 90 day time limit
↓ 60 days to file DAB may decline review	↓ 60 days to file DAB may decline review	**Fourth Level of Appeal**	↓ 60 days to file
Departmental Appeals Board AIC=$0 No time limit	Departmental Appeals Board AIC=$0 No time limit		Departmental Appeals Board AIC=$0 90 day time limit
↓ 60 days to file	↓ 60 days to file	**Final Level of Appeal**	↓ 60 days to file
Federal District Court AIC=>$,1000	Federal District Court AIC=>$,1000		Federal District Court AIC=>$,1000[3]

[1] For initial determinations prior to 10/1/02, the time frame to file was 6 months for a review and 60 days for a reconsideration.

[2] For initial determinations prior to 10/1/02, the AIC required for an ALJ hearing was $500 for all services other than home health.

[3] Starting in 2005, the AIC requirement for an ALJ hearing and Federal District Court will be adjusted in accordance with the medical care component of the Consumer Price Index.

6. Who Are the Payers?

As explained in section 2 above, items and services may be paid for by public or private health benefits payers. Public programs include Medicare and Medicaid.

Medicare. Medicare provides health benefits to the elderly, disabled, and those with end-stage renal disease (patients requiring kidney dialysis or transplant). Medicare is a federal program, but it is administered regionally or locally by administrative contractors who process claims and conduct medical reviews. The Medicare program is set out in Title XVIII of the Social Security Act and regulations promulgated thereunder.

Medicaid. Medicaid provides health benefits to eligible low-income individuals. Medicaid is a jointly funded program between the federal and state governments. Broad federal guidelines define eligibility and coverage, but specific program criteria are maintained by the individual states. The Medicaid program is set out nationally in Title XIX of the Social Security Act and regulations promulgated thereunder. In addition, each state has its own statutory and regulatory framework governing the Medicaid program it administers.

Private payers. Private payers include large national insurers as well as smaller regional or local plans. The largest national payers include Aetna, Blue Cross and Blue Shield plans, CIGNA, and United Healthcare. These payers offer a range of products, such as managed care organizations, preferred provider organizations, point of service plans, and indemnity plans. Some private payers also offer Medicare managed care plans (e.g., Medicare Advantage). In addition, many employers have self-funded plans and contract with payers for administrative services. Private payer plans are governed by various state insurance and managed care laws, while self-funded employer plans are generally governed by the Employee Retirement Income Security Act (ERISA).

B. Applying the Basics

1. Coverage, Payment, and Coding for Drugs and Biologicals

Many biotechnology drugs and biologicals require administration by a physician or other health-care professional and are, therefore, covered under Part B of the Medicare program. As of January 1, 2006, oral drugs are covered, in general, under the new Part D program. Some drugs may be covered under Part B and Part D depending upon use. For example, an immunosuppressive drug used to prevent rejection of a kidney transplant graft in a patient who had a Medicare-covered transplant is covered under Part B. The same drug used for other purposes would be eligible for coverage under Part D. Under Medicaid and private payer plans, injectable drugs and biologicals may be covered as medical benefits or as outpatient prescription drugs. Oral drugs and biologicals are generally covered under prescription drug benefits.

Labeled uses of these drugs and biologicals are almost always covered. Off-label uses may be covered if the uses are listed as accepted in reference drug compendia, such as the USP-DI (formerly maintained by the *U.S. Pharmacopoeia* and now maintained by Thomson Micromedex), American Hospital Formulary Service or DRUGDEX (recognized by Medicaid), supported by clinical evidence in published, peer-reviewed publications, or if such uses are considered generally accepted by the medical community. Medicare does not have a formulary for coverage of Part B drugs and biologicals, nor does it employ any prior authorization/determination to approve coverage before the drug is ordered or used. By contrast, some Medicaid programs have formularies or preferred drug listings, and many private payers have formularies. Medicaid and private payers also frequently require prior authorization/determination approval.

Medicare payment for drugs and biologicals under Part B is generally set at 106 percent of the manufacturer-reported average sales price. Manufacturers report sales prices quarterly, 30 days after the end of each quarter. These prices are then used to set payments for the quarter following the report. In other words, there is a four- to six-month delay between pricing changes and the date when these are reflected in payment rates.

Beginning in July 2006, physicians will have an option to continue to purchase and bill Medicare for Part B drugs and biologicals or to select a vendor who will purchase, deliver the drugs, and bill Medicare instead of the physician.[11] Under this new Competitive Acquisition Program, mandated under the MMA, Medicare has initially selected one vendor to offer Part B drugs and biologicals that are included under this program.

Under Medicare Part D, Medicare does not pay directly for drugs and biologicals. Part D Prescription Drug Plans (PDPs) are at risk (subject to certain limits) for the costs of the drugs. Payments to participating network pharmacies are negotiated between PDPs and the pharmacies. Prices paid for covered drugs and biologicals are negotiated between PDPs and manufacturers and suppliers.

Medicaid payment for drugs and biologicals varies from state to state. Some states pay at a discount off national average wholesale price (AWP or the price paid to wholesalers by retailers) as reported in published pricing compendia. Other states pay based upon wholesale acquisition cost (WAC or the price paid by wholesalers to manufacturers). Payments for drugs paid as medical benefits may be the same as or different from those paid under prescription drug benefits. In addition, there are dispensing fees paid to pharmacies for filling prescriptions. At the time of publication, Congress recently made some changes to payment rates for drugs and biologicals provided under Medicaid.

Private payers frequently provide prescription drug coverage through Pharmacy Benefit Managers (PBMs). The PBMs may negotiate pricing with manufacturers or suppliers. Plans may negotiate payments with participating pharmacies as well. Plan enrollees typically pay variable (tiered) copayment rates for generic drugs, preferred branded drugs, and non-preferred branded drugs. Higher-cost biotechnology drugs and biologicals may be assigned to a fourth, higher-cost tier that is higher than other non-preferred drugs.

2. Coverage, Payment, and Coding for Procedures Involving the Use of Medical Devices

Most medical devices are not provided directly to patients, but instead are used to perform diagnostic or therapeutic procedures. Coverage, coding, and payment for these devices are determined by the policies that apply to the associated procedures. Coverage for these services generally requires that the underlying device be approved or cleared by the Food and Drug Administration. Unlike with most drugs or biologicals, however, many payers require more than just FDA approval/clearance to approve coverage. Clinical evidence comprising peer-reviewed publication reports of well-designed clinical trials may be required to obtain coverage.

Payments for medical procedures involving devices depends upon the type of service and the setting. Services provided in physician offices or free-standing settings are generally paid by Medicare under the Physicians' Fee Schedule, with payments assigned to each CPT® and HCPCS code payable under the PFS. The PFS determines payments by multiplying relative value units (RVUs) by a nationally uniform conversion factor and locally varying geographic practice cost indices (GPCIs). The conversion factor is updated annually and is set at $37.8975 for 2006.

The conversion factor update is based upon changes in input costs for providing medical care services, but is also constrained by comparing the growth in expenditures with target rates of growth. Over the past several years, actual growth exceeded targeted rates of growth. This would have triggered a reduction in the conversion factor for each year in 2003, 2004 and 2005, but Congress intervened and mandated 1.5 percent increases for each of those years. A reduction in the conversion factor for 2006 was also proposed, but Congress mandated a one-year freeze in the conversion factor.

For the purpose of determining RVUs, there are three types of relative values: work, practice expense and malpractice expense. Work addresses the time, mental effort and judgment, technical skill, physical effort, and psychological stress involved in performing a procedure. Work is determined through physician surveys conducted and submitted by interested medical specialty groups. The surveys do not capture work through scientific time-and-motion studies, but rather seek physician estimates of the apparent intensity of one service compared to reference service with known valuations.

Practice expense comprises non-physician labor, supplies, and medical equipment. Non-physician labor is priced on a per-minute basis depending upon the type of practitioner (e.g., RN). Equipment is also priced on a per-minute basis using a standardized formula that incorporates the list price and useful life of the device. In general, equipment costs do not drive practice expense inputs unless the procedures are lengthy.

Malpractice expenses contribute only a small portion to the relative values and are intended to reflect malpractice insurance costs for the specialties that perform the procedure.

There are distinct geographic practice cost indices for each RVU component (work, practice expense, and malpractice expense). These are multiplied by the component RVUs, and the geographically adjusted RVUs are then summed to compute the total RVUs, to which the conversion factor (CF) is applied to determine the payment rate:

$$\text{Payment} = ((\text{RVU-work} \times \text{GPCI-work}) + (\text{RVU-practice expense} \times \text{GPCI-practice expense}) + (\text{RVU-malpractice} \times \text{GPCI-malpractice})) \times \text{CF}$$

3. Coverage, Payment, and Coding for Durable Medical Equipment, Prosthetics, Orthotics, and Supplies

Some medical devices are covered directly by payers, including items of durable medical equipment (DME) and prosthetics, orthotics, and supplies. To be eligible for coverage as DME, an item must be capable of withstanding repeated use, principally be used for a medical purpose and not generally useful in the absence of illness or injury, and be used by patients in their homes.[12] Prosthetics are devices that replace a non-functioning body part. In general, if an item of DME or a prosthetic device is covered, associated supplies are covered.

DME and prosthetics are paid under a complex payment system. Relatively low-cost items are paid on a lump-sum basis, and items that are more costly and used over a period of time are paid on a rental basis subject to an overall cap. Other policies apply to payments for oxygen and prosthetics.

Payment rates for DME are determined by imputing a reference, historical charge amount for the device from 1987. For devices that were not marketed at that time, current charges are deflated to 1987 levels and then re-inflated to current levels. The deflators are substantially greater than the inflators.

When a new item is approved or cleared by the FDA, a manufacturer may seek a determination from the Medicare contractor called the Statistical Analysis Durable Medical Equipment Regional Carrier (SADMERC) as to the appropriate coding assignment for the device. If assigned to an established code, the payment rate for the established code will apply. When a new code is assigned to a DME item, the four regional DME contractors, who process DME claims for Medicare, determine local fee amounts (using the deflators and inflators described above). The local fees are reported back to CMS, which sets national limits for the fees going forward.

4. Coverage, Payment, and Coding for In Vitro Diagnostics

In vitro diagnostic products are generally paid under the Clinical Laboratory Fee Schedule. Unlike most other outpatient items and services, laboratory tests paid under the CLFS do not require a co-payment. When a new laboratory test is adopted and new codes are approved, CMS seeks comments from stakeholders as to whether payment for the new procedure should be set by cross-walk to payment for an established service or by a de novo rate-setting process of gap-filling. Because gap-filling is time-consuming for all parties and has a lot of uncertainty, most stakeholders recommend cross-walks, and CMS generally agrees to some cross-walk to set payment rates for new procedures.

C. Special Payment Rules for New Technologies

1. Inpatient Prospective Payment System

Under the Medicare inpatient prospective payment system (IPPS), payments for most new items and services are determined by assignment to a specific DRG. If the charges for the procedure increase due to higher costs for the new item or service, then the payments for the DRG to which the procedure is assigned will increase over time. This process takes years, however, and will result in increased payments for all procedures under the DRG, not merely those involving the new technology. For this reason, Congress enacted a provision to allow for separate payment for certain new technologies where specific cost, clinical superiority, and novelty criteria are met. CMS has applied these criteria very restrictively, however, and very few technologies have been granted new technology add-on payments under the inpatient IPPS. Even when new technology add-on payments are allowed, CMS only pays a portion of the incremental cost for the new technology rather than the full incremental cost.

2. Outpatient Prospective Payment System

Under the Medicare OPPS, new technologies may be assigned to established APCs or may be assigned to so-called New Technology APCs. The latter are not grouped clinically, but rather by the estimated cost for performing the procedure. The intent in assigning procedures to these APCs is to gather data over a period of time so that the procedure ultimately can be assigned to standard APCs. Distinct from the New Technology APCs, for drugs, biologicals or medical devices inserted into the body, separate pass-through payments may be made if the drug, biological or medical device category is new, if the new technology is determined to provide substantial clinical benefits, and if the cost is considered not insignificant considering the costs otherwise accounted for under the APC to which the procedure involving the technology is assigned. Pass-through items are paid separately at 106 percent of manufacturer-reported average sales price (ASP) for drugs or at estimated costs for devices for a period of two to three years. After the pass-through period is finished, payments for the drugs or biologicals are switched to the rules that otherwise apply for these items, and payments for devices are generally folded into the payment for the procedure in which the device is used.

3. Ambulatory Surgical Centers—Payment for New Technology Intraocular Lenses

Most intraocular lens (IOL) implantations are made in ambulatory surgical centers (ASC). Payment for the IOL is included in the payment for the associated ASC procedure and is fixed at $150 regardless of the actual cost of the lens. Recognizing that the fixed payment would disincentivize advances in IOL technology, Congress provided for incremental payments for approved categories of new technology IOLs. The criteria for approval of new technology IOLs are that an IOL comprises a new technology material or predominant characteristic and that this new technology results in clinical superiority compared to established lenses. FDA labeling must include the claim of superiority. Given the highly restrictive criteria, very few categories of lenses have been approved for new technology payments.

4. Private Payer Carve-outs

In addition to the new technology payment provisions set by statute under Medicare, private payer contracts may include carve-outs for new technology items or services. In general, new technology carve-outs are intended to account for items and services that were not in commercial use when the contract between the payer and provider was negotiated. Like Medicare, these carve-outs may include novelty, clinical superiority, and cost thresholds to allow for incremental payments for new technologies.

D. Reimbursement for Investigational Products

1. National Coverage Determination on Routine Costs of Qualifying Clinical Trials

Medicare coverage denials for items and services provided to patients in clinical trials was considered to be a barrier to enrolling Medicare beneficiaries into clinical trials. To address this concern, CMS issued a National Coverage Determination allowing Medicare coverage of routine clinical costs provided to patients in qualifying clinical trials.[13] Qualifying clinical trials include: (1) trials funded by the National Institutes of Health (NIH), the Centers for Disease Control and Prevention (CDC), the Agency for Healthcare Research and Quality (AHRQ), CMS, the Department of Defense (DoD), and the Department of Veterans Affairs (VA); (2) trials supported by centers or cooperative groups that are funded by NIH, CDC, AHRQ, CMS, DoD or VA; (3) Investigational New Drug (IND) application trials and drug trials exempt from IND; and (4) trials meeting multi-agency panel-developed criteria following principal investigator certification and enrollment of the trial in a registry (not developed as of mid-2006).

The following requirements also must be met for coverage to be provided: (1) the purpose of the trial must be evaluation of an item or service that falls within a Medicare benefit category; (2) the trial must have therapeutic intent and not merely be designed exclusively to test toxicity or pathophysiology; (3) the trial must enroll patients with diagnosed diseases or conditions rather than healthy volunteers (except trials of diagnostic interventions, which may enroll healthy patients for controls).

Routine clinical costs include: (1) items and services typically provided absent a clinical trial; (2) items or services required solely for the provision of the investigational item or service; (3) items or services required for the clinically appropriate monitoring of the effects of the item or service; (4) items or services required for the prevention of complications; (5) items or services needed for reasonable and necessary care arising from provision of the investigational item or service.

Excluded from coverage are the investigational items themselves, items and services provided solely to satisfy data collection and analysis needs and that are not used in the direct clinical management of the patient, and items and services customarily provided by the research sponsors free of charge for any enrollee in the trial.

In addition, Medicare will pay for reasonable and necessary items and services to treat complications from any clinical trial (i.e., not solely qualifying clinical trials).

2. Investigational Device Exemptions

Separate from the NCD on coverage of routine costs for qualifying clinical trials, Medicare also may pay for certain investigational devices and related services. When an investigational device exemption application is approved by the Food and Drug Administration, FDA will assign the device to one of two reimbursement categories: Category A (experimental/investigational) or Category B (non-experimental/investigational).[14]

Category A is assigned to Class III devices for which absolute risk is not established. These include devices of a type for which no marketing application has been approved through the premarket approval (PMA) process for any indication for use, and devices that have undergone significant modification for a new indication for use. For more detail regarding the FDA approval process, please see Chapter XIII.

Category B is assigned to Class I or II devices or Class III devices about which incremental risk is the question. These include Class III devices whose technological characteristics and indications are comparable to a PMA-approved device; devices with technological changes that represent advances to a device that has already received PMA approval (i.e., generational changes); devices comparable to a PMA-approved device but which are under investigation for a new indication for use and where no significant modifications to the device were required; devices that become the subject of an IDE after the FDA requires premarket approval; and investigations of devices determined by Institutional Review Boards to be "nonsignificant risk" but for which the FDA required the submission of an IDE.

Specific billing requirements must be followed to obtain payment for Category B devices and related services. Payments may not exceed the amount that otherwise would have been paid for a currently used device serving the same medical purpose.

E. Compliance Considerations

1. Requirements for Proper Billing

The following general requirements must be met for essentially all items and services billed to any payer:

1. The item or service must be necessary and ordered and performed by an appropriately licensed practitioner.
2. The item or service must have been performed as billed.
3. The medical record must document meeting the requirements.

Failure to submit properly completed claims is a common reason for claims denials. Hospitals, skilled nursing facilities, and other institutional providers submit claims on the form CMS-1450, which is also referred to as the Uniform Bill or UB-92. Although most hospitals bill electronically, sample claim forms and instructions often refer to the paper version of the form. Instructions for completing this form are developed by the National Uniform Billing Committee and are published in the *Medicare Claims Processing Manual* (Chapter 25, Section 60).

The Field Locators (FL) shown in Exhibit 12-3 are key elements of the CMS-1450/UB-92.

Exhibit 12-3
Field Locators

FL42 Revenue Code	Identifies the department to which the charges for the service are assigned.
FL43 Revenue Description	Provides a narrative or standard description for each line item corresponding to the revenue code.
FL44 HCPCS (Healthcare Common Procedure Coding System)	Describes the item or service provided and is used for outpatient claims.
FL67 Principal Diagnosis	For inpatient admissions, this is the condition determined after study to be chiefly responsible for the admission. For outpatient encounters, this is the diagnosis shown to be chiefly responsible for the outpatient services.
FL68-75 Other Diagnoses	For inpatients, list of up to eight additional conditions that co-existed at the time of admission or developed during the stay and which had an effect upon treatment or length of stay. For outpatients, up to eight additional diagnoses that co-existed with the principal diagnosis.
FL76 Admitting Diagnosis/ Reason for Visit	For inpatients, this is the condition identified by the physician at the time of the admission requiring hospitalization. For outpatients, it is the patient's reason for visiting the hospital.
FL80 Principal Procedure	Required only for inpatients, this is the procedure performed for definitive treatment or to take care of a complication and which is most closely related to the principal diagnosis.
FL81 Other Procedures	Required only for inpatient admissions, these include up to five significant procedures in addition to the principal procedure.

Medical Reimbursement

A new version of the CMS-1450 (the UB-04) is under development and may be released for use in the near future.

Physician offices and freestanding facilities bill using the CMS-1500 form, which is also referred to as the Health Insurance Claim Form. The CMS-1500 is developed by the National Uniform Claim Committee and instructions are published in the *Medicare Claims Processing Manual* (Chapter 26, Section 10).

Key elements of the CMS-1500 are shown in Exhibit 12-4.

Exhibit 12-4
Key Elements of the CMS-1500

Item 21—Diagnosis or Nature of Illness or Injury	Up to four codes are listed in priority order.
Item 24B—Place of Service	A code is entered to identify the place of service. Relevant places of service include 11—office, 20—urgent care facility, 21—inpatient hospital, 22—outpatient hospital, 23—emergency department—hospital, 24—ambulatory surgical center, 31—skilled nursing facility, 49—independent clinic, 81—independent laboratory.
Item 24D—Procedures, Services or Supplies	These are listed using HCPCS/CPT® codes. If an unlisted or not otherwise classified code is used, a narrative explanation of the procedure must be included in item 19 or attached to the claim.
Item 24E—Diagnosis Code Reference	These refer to the diagnosis codes listed in item 21 to relate the procedure and date of service to the relevant primary diagnosis.

Providers are held to know about national and local coverage determinations that impact coverage for items and services they order or perform. National coverage determinations are posted to the CMS Web site and may be accessed at http://www.cms.hhs.gov/coverage/default.asp. This site also provides a search engine to research LCDs for specific local contractors or among all local contractors. In addition to NCDs and LCDs, all Medicare contractors issue regular bulletins that supplement the NCDs and LCDs with information about coverage and payment policies. Providers who have questions about billing should consult these resources before contacting their local contractors.

2. Reimbursement Support Services

Many manufacturers have programs to assist providers or patients with reimbursement. These programs may include reimbursement support newsletters, Web sites, and telephone hotline services. The programs may provide general information about coverage, coding or payment for the manufacturer's drug, biological or device or may provide more specific information related to particular payers or patient claims. In addition to these services, many manufacturers run or support patient assistance programs to provide financial support or free goods to patients meeting medical and financial need criteria.

3. Discounts and Related Fraud and Abuse Considerations

Discounts provided on drugs, biologicals, and medical devices that are included under claims submitted to Medicare, Medicaid or other federal or state health-care programs may implicate the federal fraud and abuse laws, including the Anti-Kickback Statute,[15] the Stark Self-Referral Prohibition Law[16] or the Federal False Claims Act.[17] Similar provisions under state law may apply regardless of payer status. A full description of these laws and considerations for compliance is beyond the scope of this chapter; however, some important points may be summarized. Discounts generally should be reported on invoices along with information advising provider customers of their obligations to inform payers about these discounts. Mark-ups of charges above provider acquisition costs may be permissible depending upon the type or item or service, but specific facts and circumstances should be analyzed before any mark-ups are billed to payers.

F. Conclusions

Successful commercialization of novel biotechnology drugs, biologicals. and medical devices requires careful reimbursement planning. In addition to obtaining FDA approval or clearance to market, coverage and adequate payment must be obtained. One should consider the benefit category under which the item will be paid. Will there be separate payment for the item or will be it be bundled or packaged into payment for a related procedure? Are there established codes to report the use of the item or service? If not, plans for obtaining such codes should be developed and implemented, and may require one to two years or more to complete. Once new codes are established, additional planning is needed to ensure that the payment rate reflects the resources required to provide the item or perform the procedure. Reimbursement planning often requires a significant commitment of time and resources and should not be left to last-minute planning just prior to commercialization. Successful reimbursement planning can make the difference between a failed product and one that achieves or exceeds expectations.

Table of Acronyms

APC: Ambulatory Payment Classification (group)

ASC: Ambulatory Surgical Center

ASP: Average Sales Price

AWP: Average Wholesale Price

BCBSA: Blue Cross and Blue Shield Association

BIPA: Benefits Improvement and Protection Act of 2000

CF: Conversion Factor

CMS: Centers for Medicare and Medicaid Services

CPT®: Current Procedural Terminology (copyright American Medical Association)

DME: Durable Medical Equipment

DMERC: Durable Medical Equipment Regional Carrier

DRG: Diagnosis Related Group

ERISA: Employee Retirement Income Security Act of 1974

GPCI: Geographic Practice Cost Index

HCPCS: Healthcare Common Procedure Coding System

IDE: Investigational Device Exemption

IND: Investigational New Drug (Application)

IPPS: Inpatient Prospective Payment System (or PPS)

LCD: Local Coverage Determination

LMRP: Local Medical Review Policy

MMA: Medicare Prescription Drug, Improvement and Modernization Act of 2003

NCD: National Coverage Determination

OPPS: (Hospital) Outpatient Prospective Payment System (or HOPPS)

PBM: Pharmacy Benefit Manager

PDP: Prescription Drug Plan (under Medicare Part D)

PMA: Premarket Approval

RUG: Resource Utilization Group

RVU: Relative Value Unit

SADMERC: Statistical Analysis Durable Medical Equipment Regional Carrier

SNF: Skilled Nursing Facility

TEC: Technology Evaluation Center (of the Blue Cross and Blue Shield Association)

UB: Uniform Bill (i.e., UB-92; UB-04)

WAC: Wholesale Acquisition Cost

Notes

1. Soc. Sec. Act § 1812 (42 U.S.C. § 1395d).
2. Soc. Sec. Act § 1832 (42 U.S.C. § 1395k).
3. Soc. Sec. Act § 1852 (42 U.S.C. § 1395w-22).
4. Soc. Sec. Act § 1860D-2 (42 U.S.C. § 1395w-102).
5. *See* http://www.cms.hhs.gov/coverage/guidance.asp.
6. MEDICARE PROGRAM INTEGRITY MANUAL (Pub. 100-08), Transmittal 63 (Jan. 23, 2004).
7. 42 C.F.R. §§ 412.2, 412.60.
8. 42 C.F.R. §§ 413.335, 413.343, 413.345.
9. 42 C.F.R. §§ 419.2, 419.31.
10. Soc. Sec. Act §§ 1842(o), 1847A (42 U.S.C. §§ 1395u(o), 1395w-3a).
11. Soc. Sec. Act §§ 1842(o), 1847B (42. U.S.C. §§ 1395u(o), 1395w-3b).
12. 42 C.F.R. § 414.202.
13. MEDICARE NATIONAL COVERAGE DETERMINATIONS MANUAL (CMS Pub. 100-03), ch. 1, § 310.1.
14. 42 C.F.R. §§ 405.201 et seq.
15. Soc. Sec. Act § 1128B(b) (42 U.S.C. § 1320a-7b(b)).
16. Soc. Sec. Act § 1877 (42 U.S.C. § 1395nn).
17. 31 U.S.C. § 3729 et seq.

Chapter XIII

Approval of Products for Human Use

Areta L. Kupchyk, Esq.
Reed & Smith, LLP
Washington, D.C.

Developing a new medical product and taking it through the regulatory review process to obtain marketing approval is challenging, costly, and yet enormously rewarding. The process of moving a product successfully and efficiently from "bench to bedside" requires a strategic plan to navigate extensive federal regulations and the bureaucratic policies and procedures of the U.S. Food and Drug Administration. This chapter outlines the standard and special FDA pathways to market that are available for drugs, biological products, devices, and human cellular and tissue products.

A. Standard Pathways to Market

1. Drugs

a. Preclinical

Marketing approval for human drugs depends on the submission of clinical data that demonstrate the safety and efficacy of a drug product for its intended use. Before beginning clinical trials to support a marketing application, a sponsor must submit data showing that the drug is reasonably safe for use in initial, small-scale human studies. The submission to

FDA should include nonclinical data from past *in vitro* laboratory or animal studies, if available; data from previous clinical testing or marketing of the drug in the United States or another country whose population is relevant to the U.S. population, if available; and, if not available, new preclinical studies designed to provide the evidence necessary to support the safety of administering the compound to humans.

Preclinical studies should identify a drug's toxic and pharmacologic effects through *in vitro* and *in vivo* laboratory animal testing. The FDA will generally ask sponsors to: (1) develop a pharmacological profile of the drug; (2) determine the acute toxicity of the drug in at least two species of animals; and (3) conduct short-term toxicity studies ranging from two weeks to three months, depending on the planned duration of use of the substance in the proposed clinical studies. Results from animal studies, both short-term and long-term, are submitted to FDA when a sponsor submits an application to begin human clinical trials. The FDA reviews the preclinical research data and then makes a decision as to whether to allow the clinical trials to proceed. Some animal testing continues after clinical trials begin to learn whether long-term use of a drug may cause cancer or birth defects.

b. Investigational New Drug Applications

i. Exemption from Law

To begin human clinical trials, a sponsor must first submit to FDA an investigational new drug application (IND). The IND is not an application for marketing approval. Rather, it is a request for an exemption from the federal law that prohibits an unapproved drug from being shipped in interstate commerce.[1] This exemption is necessary because a sponsor typically ships the yet unapproved investigational drug to clinical investigators across one or more state lines.[2] To obtain the exemption, a sponsor must submit to FDA an IND containing sufficient information and data to document that the drug is reasonably safe to begin human testing.

An IND includes data and information in three broad areas: 1) animal pharmacology and toxicology studies to permit an assessment as to whether the product is reasonably safe for initial testing in humans; 2) information detailing the composition, manufacture, stability, and controls used for manufacturing the drug substance and the drug product to ensure that the company can adequately produce and supply consistent batches of the drug; and 3) clinical protocol and investigator information to assess the potential risks to which subjects will be exposed and to assess whether the investigators are qualified to conduct the trials.

ii. Institutional Review Boards

Institutional Review Boards (IRBs) are charged with protecting the rights and welfare of human subjects participating in clinical trials. IRBs are established typically at hospitals and research institutions throughout the country and are responsible for ensuring that volunteers in clinical trials are fully informed and have given their written consent before studies begin.

IRBs are subject to FDA regulations and FDA inspections.[3] FDA regulations require that an IRB be composed of no less than five experts and lay people with varying backgrounds to ensure a complete and adequate review of research activities. In addition to professional competence, an IRB and its members must have the experience and expertise to ascertain the acceptability of applications and proposals with respect to institutional commitments, applicable laws and regulations, and standards of professional conduct and practice, as well as community attitudes.[4]

iii. Clinical Hold

FDA has 30 calendar days after an IND submission to decide whether a clinical trial may begin or should be delayed because of concerns that patients would be exposed to an unacceptable risk. Generally, if there are no concerns about the safety of the drug in the proposed trial, FDA is not obligated to contact the sponsor or formally issue any type of approval. If the sponsor hears nothing from FDA, then on day 31 after submission of the IND, the study legally may proceed as submitted. More typically, however, a conscientious sponsor will contact the FDA division responsible for reviewing the IND and obtain verbal affirmation that FDA has no safety concerns that would impede the initiation of a trial. If an unacceptable risk exists or if there is insufficient data to make such a risk determination, FDA will notify the sponsor to obtain more information or, if necessary, issue a "clinical hold" to prohibit the trial from going forward.

A "clinical hold" is the mechanism that FDA uses when it believes the study cannot be conducted without unreasonable risk to the participants in the trial. A clinical hold is an administrative order issued by FDA to the sponsor to delay a proposed clinical investigation or suspend an ongoing investigation. It may be applied to one or more of the investigations covered by an IND. When an ongoing study is placed on clinical hold, subjects may not be given the investigational drug and new subjects may not be recruited. As applied to a proposed study, a hold prohibits the recruitment of subjects. In addition, FDA will require patients already in the study to be taken off the investigational drug unless FDA specifically allows continuation in the interest of patient safety.[5]

> **Practice Points**
>
> In issuing a "clinical hold," the FDA postpones a trial phase or test. The best way to avoid this is to try to increase dialogue with the FDA, listen carefully, and try to anticipate and develop responses to possible concerns.

If a clinical hold order issues, FDA will contact the sponsor within the 30-day initial review period to stop the clinical trial from beginning. FDA may either delay the start of an early-phase trial on the basis of information submitted in the IND or stop an ongoing study based on a review of newly submitted clinical protocols, safety reports, protocol amendments, or other information. The hold will be lifted only after a sponsor adequately addresses or resolves the pertinent issues. The sponsor must submit to the FDA a response addressing the hold. FDA will review the sponsor's response and notify the sponsor within 30 days whether the hold will be lifted.[6]

If other deficiencies are found in an IND that the review division determines are not serious enough to justify delaying clinical studies, FDA will inform the sponsor that it may proceed with the planned clinical trials, but that additional information is necessary to complete or correct the IND file, or that there are issues that need to be addressed prior to the submission of a new drug application (NDA).[7]

iv. Types of INDs

INDs are applications typically submitted by companies whose ultimate goal is to obtain marketing approval for a new product. However, many INDs are filed for reasons other than to obtain marketing approval. These INDs include "Investigator INDs," "Emergency Use INDs," and "Treatment INDs," which are subject to specific regulatory requirements.[8] Treatment INDs are intended to make promising new drugs available to desperately ill patients as early in the drug development process as possible. FDA will permit an investigational drug to be used under a treatment IND if there is preliminary evidence of drug efficacy and the drug is intended to treat a serious or life-threatening disease, or if there is no comparable alternative drug or therapy available to treat that stage of the disease in the intended patient population.[9]

v. Phases of Clinical Trials

There are three basic phases for clinical research conducted under an IND. The phases start with small studies to establish initial safety data and then proceed to involve more and more patients to establish efficacy data. The ultimate goal is to gather sufficient clinical data of efficacy to meet the legal requirement for marketing approval.

1) Phase 1 is when an investigational new drug is first introduced into humans. These studies, conducted in healthy or patient volunteers, are designed to determine the metabolic and pharmacologic actions of the drug in humans, the side effects associated with increasing doses, and, if possible, to gain early evidence on effectiveness. During Phase 1, sufficient information about the drug's pharmacokinetics and pharmacological effects should be obtained to permit the design of well-controlled, scientifically valid, Phase 2 studies. In addition, Phase 1 studies evaluate drug metabolism, structure-activity relationships, and the mechanism of action in humans. The total number of subjects included in Phase 1 studies varies with the drug, but is generally in the range of 20 to 80.[10]

2) Phase 2 clinical studies are conducted to obtain preliminary data on the effectiveness of the drug for an intended use. This phase helps

identify common short-term side effects and risks associated with the drug. Phase 2 studies are typically well controlled, closely monitored, and conducted in a relatively small number of patients, usually involving several hundred people.[11]

3) Phase 3 studies are intended to gather the additional information about effectiveness and safety needed to evaluate the overall risk/benefit of the drug. This evaluation will determine whether there is sufficient evidence of efficacy needed for approval. Phase 3 studies also are intended to provide sufficient information for extrapolating the results to the general population and determining what information is necessary for physician labeling. Phase 3 studies usually include several hundred to several thousand people.[12]

> **Practice Points**
>
> **Phase I**—First introduction of a drug to humans designed to determine initial safety, side effects, and evidence of effectiveness.
> **Phase II**—Obtain preliminary data regarding effectiveness.
> **Phase III**—Usually a larger, double-blind study, aimed at determining effectiveness over something resembling a more general population.

c. New Drug Applications

To obtain marketing approval for a drug, a sponsor must submit all the data gathered during the animal studies and human clinical trials in a new drug application (NDA) to the FDA. The applicant must demonstrate that its new drug is both safe and effective for its intended use. FDA charges fees to facilitate speedier reviews each time a company submits a marketing application for review.[13] The fees are intended to support the costs of the review process. In exchange for this user funding, FDA has agreed to meet drug-review performance goals to help ensure the timeliness of reviews and provide a measure of accountability.[14]

Before submitting an NDA, generally at the end of phase 2 (EDP2) and again at the end of phase 3, an applicant is entitled to meet with FDA to discuss what data the agency needs in an application to demonstrate the specific drug product's safety and effectiveness. The meetings are intended to identify any major unresolved problems or issues, help the reviewers become acquainted with the general information to be submitted, and discuss the presentation of the data in the NDA. Another meeting may also be scheduled 90 days after the initial NDA submission to discuss additional issues uncovered in the initial review.[15]

i. New Drug Application Content and Format Requirements

The content and format of an NDA are dictated by regulation and generally should include the following 15 separate sections:[16]

- Index;
- Summary;
- Chemistry, Manufacturing, and Control;
- Samples, Methods Validation Package, and Labeling;
- Nonclinical Pharmacology and Toxicology;
- Human Pharmacokinetics and Bioavailability;
- Microbiology (for anti-microbial drugs only);
- Clinical Data;
- Safety Update Report (typically submitted 120 days after the NDA's submission);
- Statistical;
- Case Report Tabulations;
- Case Report Forms;
- Patent Information;
- Patent Certification; and
- Other Information.

Although the exact requirements and the quantity of information and data required to be submitted in a NDA depend on the nature of the specific drug, the NDA must include *all* relevant data and information available to a sponsor up through the time of submission. To assist applicants, FDA has published numerous guidance documents related to NDA content and format issues.[17,18]

FDA classifies new drug applications with a code number (1 through 7) that reflects both the type of drug being submitted and its intended uses.

1. New Molecular Entity
2. New Salt of Previously Approved Drug (not a new molecular entity)
3. New Formulation of Previously Approved Drug (not a new salt OR a new molecular entity)
4. New Combination of Two or More Drugs
5. Already Marketed Drug Product—Duplication (i.e., new manufacturer)
6. New Indication (claim) for Already Marketed Drug (includes switch in marketing status from prescription to OTC)
7. Already Marketed Drug Product—No Previously Approved NDA

Upon receiving an NDA submission, FDA screens the submission for completeness. This evaluation, which generally is completed within 60 days of submission, is intended to ensure that all required elements of an NDA are included and that sufficient data and information have been submitted to justify "filing" the application. Only when an NDA is "filed" does FDA's official review begin. If an NDA is deemed incomplete, FDA issues a "refuse-to-file" (RTF) letter in which FDA describes the NDA deficiencies.[19] In such a case, the NDA is not "filed" and the review does not begin. The applicant must resubmit the NDA with the deficiencies corrected (in some cases with additional data), which usually requires payment of additional user fees before FDA will consider the application for filing and thus begin the review clock.

FDA's medical and clinical reviewers, often called medical officers, are almost exclusively physicians. Medical reviewers are responsible for evaluating the clinical sections of submissions, such as the safety of the clinical protocols in an IND and the test results. Within most divisions, reviewers take the lead role in analyzing the results of the animal toxicology, human pharmacology, and clinical tests to formulate the overall basis for FDA's ultimate action on the application.

FDA's review team will include pharmacologists and toxicologists who are responsible for evaluating the results of animal testing and determining the relationship between animal drug effects and potential effects in humans. The pharmacology/toxicology section of the application typically will contain, if known: 1) a description of the pharmacologic effects and mechanism(s) of action of the drug in animals; and 2) information on the absorption, distribution, metabolism, and excretion of the drug. FDA regulations do not further describe the appropriate presentation of these data, in contrast to the more detailed description of how to submit toxicologic data. However, FDA will accept a summary report without individual animal records or individual study results. The NDA must also include an integrated summary of the toxicologic effects of the drug in animals and *in vitro*. The particular studies needed depend on the nature of the drug and the phase of human investigation.[20]

Each review division employs a team of chemists responsible for reviewing the chemistry and manufacturing control sections of drug applications. In general, chemistry reviewers evaluate data related to drug identity, manufacturing control, and analysis. The reviewing chemist is responsible for looking at the manufacturing and processing procedures for a drug to ensure that the compound is adequately reproducible and stable. Pharmacokineticists evaluate the rate and extent to which the drug's active ingredient is made available to the human body and the way it is distributed in, metabolized by, and eliminated from the body. Statisticians evaluate the statistical relevance of the data in the NDA primarily to evaluate the methods used to conduct studies and to analyze the data. The purpose of these evaluations is to give the medical officers a better idea of the power of the findings to be extrapolated to the larger U.S. patient population.

Under current regulations, FDA may allow evidence of effectiveness in adults to be extrapolated to form the basis for concluding that a drug is effective in the pediatric population if the course of the disease and effects of the drug are sufficiently similar between the child and adult populations. Additional information supporting pediatric use, such as pharmacokinetics data, safety data, and pharmacodynamics data, may also be required to determine the appropriate pediatric dose.[21]

Microbiology information is required only in NDAs for anti-infective drugs. Since these drugs affect microbial rather than human physiology, reports on the drug's *in vivo* and *in vitro* effects on the target microorganisms are critical for establishing product effectiveness. A microbiology section usually includes data describing:

- The biochemical basis of the drug's action on microbial physiology;

- The drug's antimicrobial spectra, including results of *in vitro* preclinical studies demonstrating concentrations of the drug required for effective use;
- Any known mechanisms of resistance to the drug, including results of any known epidemiologic studies demonstrating prevalence of resistance factors; and
- Clinical microbiology laboratory methods needed to evaluate the effective use of the drug.[22]

ii. Facility Inspection

When an NDA is filed and the review process begins, FDA may also schedule a preapproval inspection (PAI) of the manufacturing facilities and clinical trial sites. During such inspections, FDA investigators audit manufacturing-related statements and commitments made in the NDA against the sponsor's actual manufacturing practices. Such inspections may involve:

- Verification of the accuracy and completeness of manufacturing information described in the NDA;
- Evaluation of the manufacturing controls;
- Evaluation of current Good Manufacturing Practice (cGMP) compliance; and
- Collection of drug samples for analysis, *e.g.*, methods validation, methods verification, and forensic screening for substitution.

PAIs generally are conducted for drug products that: 1) are new chemical or molecular entities; 2) have narrow therapeutic ranges; 3) represent the first approval for the applicant; or 4) are sponsored by a company with a history of cGMP problems.[23] The results of the PAI may affect the final approval decision for an NDA. If FDA documents significant cGMP problems during a PAI, FDA may withhold approval of the NDA until these issues are corrected.

iii. Labeling Review

Each statement proposed for drug labeling must be justified by data and results submitted in the NDA.[24] The labeling requirements are organized into the sections shown in Exhibit 13-1.

**Exhibit 13-1
Labeling Requirements**

Description	Proprietary and established name of drug; dosage form; ingredients; chemical name; and structural formula.
Clinical Pharmacology	Summary of the actions of the drug in humans; *in vitro* and *in vivo* actions in animals if pertinent to human therapeutics; pharmacokinetics.
Indications and Usage	Description of use of drug in the treatment, prevention or diagnosis of a recognized disease or condition.
Contraindications	Description of situations in which the drug should not be used because the risk of use clearly outweighs any possible benefit.
Warnings	Description of serious adverse reactions and potential safety hazards, subsequent limitation in use, and steps that should be taken if they occur.
Precautions	Information regarding any special care to be exercised for the safe and effective use of the drug. Includes general precautions and information for patients on drug interactions, carcinogenesis/mutagenesis, pregnancy rating, labor and delivery, nursing mothers, and pediatric use.
Adverse Reactions	Description of undesirable effect(s) reasonably associated with the proper use of the drug.
Drug Abuse/ Dependence	Description of types of abuse that can occur with the drug and the adverse reactions pertinent to them.
Overdosage	Description of the signs, symptoms, and laboratory findings of acute overdosage and the general principles of treatment.
Dosage/Administration	Recommendation for usage dose, usual dosage range, and, if appropriate, upper limit beyond which safety and effectiveness have not been established.
How Supplied	Information on the available dosage forms to which the labeling applies.

FDA evaluates draft labeling for accuracy and consistency against the data and information provided in the NDA. All claims, instructions, and precautions must accurately reflect data submitted in support of the NDA. If FDA has concerns about statements in the draft labeling, FDA will contact the applicant and may require revisions. Although FDA is the final arbiter of labeling content, convention permits a negotiation process between the applicant and FDA. Through this labeling negotiation process, a drug's final approved labeling is determined.

iv. Advisory Committees

FDA uses advisory committees to obtain independent professional opinions from expert advisors outside the agency.[25] In this way, final agency decisions will have the benefit of wider national expert input. FDA typically asks an advisory committee to respond to specific questions. For example, FDA may ask an advisory committee to make recommendations about the adequacy of data to support the safety and effectiveness of a new drug indication, the appropriateness of an expanded or additional indication for an already approved drug, or the need for a special regulatory requirement, such as a boxed warning in a drug's labeling. Advisory Committees may also advise FDA on appropriate labeling information, or help with guidelines for developing particular kinds of drugs. However, recommendations by an Advisory Committee are just that, advisory, and are not binding on FDA.[26]

Advisory meetings are usually public, but may be closed if requested by the sponsor and if the need for such protection is justified—for example, if confidential and proprietary information will be discussed. Whether the subject of an advisory committee meeting will be considered confidential and the extent to which an advisory committee's deliberations must be made public is governed by the Federal Advisory Committee Act (FACA).[27]

v. Completion of Review and Decision

When the technical reviews are completed and the division reviewing the NDA decides on the appropriate action, the result is communicated to the applicant via an action letter. There are three possible action letters that can be sent to the applicant:

- *Not Approvable Letter:* Lists the deficiencies in the application and explains why the application cannot be approved.
- *Approvable Letter:* Signals that, ultimately, the drug can be approved. Lists minor deficiencies that FDA believes can be corrected; may involve conducting one or more studies; often involves labeling changes; and possibly requests commitment to do post-approval studies.
- *Approval Letter:* States that the drug is approved. May follow an approvable letter, but can also be issued directly.

If the action taken is either an approvable or a not approvable action (as opposed to an approval), FDA provides applicants with an opportunity to meet and discuss the deficiencies. The purpose of this "end of review conference" is to identify what further steps are necessary before the NDA can be approved.

d. Generic Drugs

i. Abbreviated New Drug Applications

New drugs are typically developed under patent protection, which gives the patent holder the sole right to sell the drug while the patent is in effect. The Hatch-Waxman Amendments, passed in 1984, authorized an abbreviated pathway to market for generic copies of new drugs.[28] Under the Hatch-Waxman Amendments, when new drug patents expire, manufacturers can apply to the FDA to market generic versions of those drugs by submitting an abbreviated new drug application (ANDA). The ANDA applicant is not required to conduct independent and costly clinical research to establish safety and effectiveness. Instead, the generic applicant may rely on the innovator's safety and effectiveness data submitted in the NDA.[29]

> **Practice Points**
>
> Generic drugs sometimes qualify for an abbreviated new drug application, allowing the generic to rely on some parts of the innovator's clinical study. However, the generic must demonstrate that it is bioequivalent to the innovator's product, which is difficult in the case of a biological product.

A generic drug product is one that is comparable to an innovator drug product[30] in dosage form, strength, route of administration, quality, performance characteristics, and intended use. Although an ANDA applicant may rely on the innovator's original scientific data to establish the safety and effectiveness of the generic drug product, the applicant must demonstrate that the generic is comparable, or bioequivalent, to the innovator.[31] Bioequivalence to the reference listed drug (RLD) is based upon a demonstration that both the rate and extent of absorption of the active ingredient of the generic drug fall within established parameters when compared to that of the RLD.[32] Applicants may request a waiver from performing *in vivo* bioequivalence studies for certain drug products where bio-availability may be demonstrated by submitting data such as 1) a formulation comparison for products whose bioavailability is self-evident—for example, oral solutions, injectables, or ophthalmic solutions where the formulations are identical; or 2) comparative dissolution.[33]

An ANDA must include a patent certification in which the applicant must make one of the following statements: (1) such patent information has not been filed; (2) such patent has expired; (3) the date on which such patent expires; or (4) such patent is invalid or will not be infringed by the manufacture, use, or sale of the drug product for which the ANDA is submitted.[34] The fourth certification is known as a "paragraph IV certification." The ANDA applicant who makes a paragraph IV certification must provide appropriate notice to each owner of the patent identified in the certification and to the holder of the relevant NDA.[35] Generic manufacturers who are first to file paragraph IV certifications and successfully challenge listed patents as invalid, or not infringed, are rewarded with a 180-day period of marketing exclusivity.[36] In other words, an applicant who submits an ANDA with the first paragraph IV certification to a patent will be given exclusive right to market its generic version over other generic versions of the same drug product for 180 days.[37] This 180-day period begins after the earliest of either the initial marketing of the first applicant's drug or a court decision that holds that the patent that is the subject of the paragraph IV certification is invalid or not infringed. This marketing protection is commonly known as "180-day exclusivity."

After FDA determines that an ANDA is acceptable, an approval or tentative approval letter is issued to the applicant. If the approval occurs prior to the expiration of any patents or exclusivities applicable to the RLD, a *tentative* approval letter is issued to the applicant that delays final approval until all applicable patents and exclusivities have expired.[38]

e. 505(b)(2) Applications

The FDCA also contains an alternative mechanism through which a sponsor can obtain approval of a drug product. Known as "the 505(b)(2) application," this mechanism applies to drug products that differ from an approved innovator product (and therefore don't qualify as generics) or drug products (and some biological drug products) that require additional human studies for approval.[39] The 505(b)(2) mechanism permits a sponsor to rely on published, peer-reviewed scientific literature, or on the FDA's previous finding of safety and effectiveness for an approved product, to determine whether such a drug product is safe and effective for its intended uses and thereby meets the statutory requirements for marketing approval.[40] It is not clear, however, whether FDA can go so far as to rely on proprietary data in another applicant's approved NDA to determine the safety and effectiveness of a 505(b)(2) drug. FDA has taken the position that it may do so; however, its interpretation has drawn criticism, and whether it can do so ultimately may be resolved by the courts. Despite this apparent encroachment on the proprietary rights of the NDA holder, the 505(b)(2) approval process, similar to the ANDA process, acknowledges the innovator's intellectual property rights. For example, the patents listed with FDA by an NDA holder at the time of NDA approval must be recognized by the 505(b)(2) applicant, if applicable, and approval will be delayed until patent protections and statutory marketing exclusivity have expired.

2. Biological Products

Biological products include a diverse range of substances,[41] such as vaccines, blood and blood components, allergenics, gene therapy, cellular and tissue-based products, recombinant therapeutic proteins, and xenotransplantation products.[42] Most biologics are complex mixtures that are not easily identified, characterized, or manufactured. For example, they tend to be heat-sensitive and susceptible to microbial contamination, and, therefore, require aseptic manufacturing processes. By contrast, most conventional drugs are chemically synthesized and well characterized, and have manufacturing processes that are easier to control. Despite these differences and challenges, biological products often represent cutting-edge breakthroughs that one day may provide needed treatments for many serious and life-threatening illnesses.

Biological products are usually licensed for marketing under the Public Health Service Act (PHSA) based on the submission to FDA of a biological license application (BLA).[43] However, biological products may also meet the definition of a drug or a device and, thus, may be subject to approval through the NDA, 505(b)(2), or device approval processes. The BLA approval process for biologic products is very similar to the NDA approval process for human drugs. Following laboratory and animal research, a biological product is studied in human clinical trials. Data from research and clinical trials are submitted in a BLA to demonstrate that the biological product meets requirements for safety, purity, and potency.[44] Because most biological products meet the definition of "drugs" under the FDCA, they are also subject to many drug regulations and requirements.[45] For example, a clinical trial involving an investigational biological product must be subject to a valid and effective IND and must be manufactured in accordance with CGMP regulations for drugs as well as additional biological product manufacturing regulations.[46]

After FDA approves a BLA, the biological product may also be subject to official lot release to ensure consistency in manufacturing.[47] This is a uniquely distinct aspect of biological product marketing approval. As part of the manufacturing process, the manufacturer is required to perform certain tests on each lot of the product before it is released for distribution.[48] If the product is subject to official lot release, the manufacturer submits samples of each lot of product to FDA together with a release protocol showing a summary of the history of manufacture of the lot and the results of all of the manufacturer's tests performed on the lot. FDA may also perform certain confirmatory tests on lots of some products, such as viral vaccines, before releasing the lots for distribution by the manufacturer.[49]

Unlike the pathway to market for drugs under the FDCA, the pathway for biological products has no formal abbreviated process. The PHSA makes no explicit accommodation for biological ANDAs, that is, for an abbreviated application that would permit approval of a "generic" or "follow-on" biologic based on FDA's prior approval of another manufacturer's application. Although FDA has suggested that a generic version of a biological product that was originally approved under section 505 of the FDCA might be approved as a "follow-on" through the 505(b)(2) mechanism, nothing has been settled. Indeed, whether a generic or follow-on biological product is possible has been subject to scientific, legal, and policy debate within the FDA as well as the industry for several years. To date, FDA has been reluctant to issue any formal guidance or opinion on the topic. However, FDA approved a "follow-on protein product" on May 30, 2006, despite intense opposition by the manufacturer of the innovator product. In approving the follow-on, FDA issued a 53-page response to the opposition that sets out its reasons for approval.[50] In approving a 505(b)(2) application for Omnitrope, a recombinant human growth hormone (rhGH), FDA acknowledged that advances in manufacturing technology, process control, and protein characterization helped establish an appropriate scientific basis for a finding of safety and effectiveness. At the same time, FDA reiterated that the use of the 505(b)(2) pathway would not be available for approving follow-on versions of biological products that were licensed under section 351 of the PHSA or that pose scientific challenges by more complex and not as well understood licensed biological products.

3. Human Cells, Tissues, and Cellular and Tissue-Based Products

On May 25, 2005, FDA finalized the implementation of a comprehensive new system for regulating human cells, tissues, and cellular and tissue-based products (HCT/Ps). This new system creates a tiered, risk-based approach to the regulation of different types of HCT/Ps. The new regulatory scheme includes establishment registration and product listing, donor screening, testing, eligibility requirements, good tissue practice regulations, and other requirements.[51] In addition, the applicable rules permit regulation of certain HCT/Ps solely to prevent the introduction, transmission, and spread of communicable disease under the authority of § 361 of the Public Health Service (PHS) Act.[52] Other HCT/Ps would be regulated under the FDCA as drugs, devices, and/or biological drugs.[53]

To be regulated solely under § 361 of the PHS Act ("a 361 product"), and thus avoid premarket approval requirements, the HCT/P must meet the all of the following criteria:

a) The HCT/P is minimally manipulated;
b) The HCT/P is intended for homologous use only, as reflected by the labeling, advertising, or other indications of the manufacturer's objective intent;
c) The manufacture of the HCT/P does not involve the combination of the cell or tissue component with a drug or a device, except for a sterilizing, preserving, or storage agent, if the addition of the agent does not raise new clinical safety concerns with respect to the HCT/P; and
d) Either:
   (i) The HCT/P does not have a systemic effect and is not dependent upon the metabolic activity of living cells for its primary function; or
   (ii) The HCT/P has a systemic effect or is dependent upon the metabolic activity of living cells for its primary function, and:
   - Is for autologous use;
   - Is for allogeneic use in a first-degree or second-degree blood relative; or
   - Is for reproductive use.[54]

Put another way, an HCT/P will be regulated as a drug, biological product, or device and may be subject to preapproval requirements, if it is more-than-minimally manipulated,[55] used for a non-homologous purpose,[56] combined with some other article,[57] or used for an unrelated allogeneic purpose.[58]

4. Medical Devices

The regulatory pathway to market for a medical device depends on the device classification. Medical devices are classified into Class I, II, and III, with regulatory requirements and oversight increasing from Class I to Class III. Most Class I devices are exempt from Premarket Notification requirements; most Class II devices require Premarket Notification; and most Class III devices require Premarket Approval, because they present the greatest risk to public health and safety.

a. Device Classifications[59]

i. Class I Medical Devices

Class I medical devices present minimal risks of harm to the user and are often simpler in design than Class II or Class III devices. Examples include enema kits and elastic bandages. According to the FDA, approximately 47 percent of medical devices fall under this category, and the majority of these are exempt from the regulatory process because they present high assurances of safety and little risk to the public health. If a device falls into an exempted Class I device category, no premarket notification application is required before marketing the device in the United States. However, the manufacturer of an exempt Class I device is required to comply with "general controls" and register its establishment and list its product(s) with FDA.[60] Examples of exempt Class I devices are manual stethoscopes, mercury thermometers, and bedpans.

ii. Class II Medical Devices

Most medical devices are considered Class II devices. Examples of Class II devices include powered wheelchairs and some pregnancy test kits. Approximately 43 percent of medical devices fall under this category. To ensure ongoing safety of Class II devices, FDA generally imposes "special controls," in addition to general controls, on various categories of Class II devices.

iii. Class III Medical Devices

Class III medical devices usually sustain or support life, are implanted, or present potential high or unreasonable risk of illness or injury. Examples of Class III devices include implantable pacemakers and breast implants. Approximately 10 percent of medical devices fall under this category.

b. The 510(k) Notification Process

Medical devices that are "substantially equivalent" to a medical device that is being legally marketed do not require premarket review and approval. Instead, the manufacturer is required to first notify FDA and demonstrate that its device is substantially equivalent (SE) to a predicate device. This is referred to as premarket notification (PMN) or "510(k) notification" because it is § 510(k) of the FDCA that authorizes this streamlined pathway to market.[61] A device is SE if, in comparison to a predicate device it: 1) has the same intended use as the predicate device, and 2) has the same technological characteristics as the predicate device, or 3) has different technological characteristics that do not raise new questions of safety and effectiveness, and the sponsor demonstrates that the device is as safe and effective as the legally marketed device.[62] Clinical trials to demonstrate safety and effectiveness are not required. Instead, the manufacturer must show that its device is comparable to the predicate device. If FDA finds that the device is SE, the manufacturer can market the device. Most Class I and Class II devices require no more than the submission of a 510(k) notification to get to market.[63]

c. The Premarket Application Process

Due to the greater level of risk associated with Class III devices, FDA has determined that general and special controls alone are insufficient to ensure their safety and effectiveness. Therefore, Class III devices, the highest-risk devices, require the submission and approval of a premarket application (PMA) before they can be marketed or distributed in the United States.[64] FDA will approve a PMA if it contains sufficient valid scientific evidence to ensure that the device is safe and effective for its intended use.

d. Investigational Device Exemption

Similar to the drug IND, an investigational device exemption (IDE) allows the investigational device to be used prior to approval as long as it is used in an approved clinical study intended to collect safety and effectiveness data for a PMA submission and, in some situations, a 510(k) submission.[65] As with drug clinical trials, clinical studies of devices are also monitored by IRBs located at the hospitals or other facilities where the clinical studies are conducted.[66]

5. Combination Products

A combination product is composed of any combination of a drug and a device; a biological product and a device; a drug and a biological product; or a drug, device, and a biological product.[67] Combination products do not have a separate pathway to market, so they raise a variety of regulatory

Approval of Products for Human Use

and review challenges both for manufacturers and for FDA. Although the pathway to market for drugs, biological products, and medical devices is similar, each of these medical products has unique characteristics. These unique characteristics are addressed through the separate review process and marketing applications for drugs, devices, and biological products, that is, NDA, BLA, PMA, and 510(k) submissions. When drugs and devices, drugs and biologics, or devices and biologics are combined to create a new product, how the combination product as a whole will be regulated depends on the "primary mode of action" (PMOA) of the overall product.

Based on a determination of the PMOA, FDA assigns a component of the agency to have primary jurisdiction for the regulation of a combination product.[68] For example, if the primary mode of action of a combination product is that of a biological product, the product will be assigned to the FDA component responsible for biological product premarket review.[69] Depending upon the type of combination product, marketing approval, clearance, or licensure may be obtained through the submission of a single marketing application, or through separate marketing applications for the individual constituent parts of the combination product. Formal procedures to request that FDA determine the PMOA and designate the appropriate regulatory oversight for a combination product are referred to as "Request for Designation" (RFD) and are set forth at 21 C.F.R. Part 3.[70]

Primary mode of action is defined as "the single mode of action of a combination product that provides the most important therapeutic action of the combination product. The most important therapeutic action is the mode of action that is expected to make the greatest contribution to the overall intended therapeutic effects of the combination product." For purposes of PMOA, "therapeutic" effect or action includes any effect or action of the combination product intended to diagnose, cure, mitigate, treat, or prevent disease, or affect the structure or any function of the body.[71]

Examples of combination products with *biological product* PMOA include:

- Interferon and injector for treatment of hepatitis C
- Injectable protein with delivery device for orthopedic use
- Radiolabeled antibody with detector device
- Autologous cells and scaffold for orthopedic use

- Blood-derived protein and delivery device/dressing for wound treatment
- Device and biologic to separate stem cells for reinfusion after chemotherapy

Examples of combination products with *drug* PMOA include:

- Cytotoxic agent and biological product for targeted cancer treatment
- Gynecologic drug and delivery device
- Photosensitizing drug and light source for cancer treatment
- Drug and transdermal iontophoretic delivery system
- Fluoride-containing dental device for anticaries treatment
- Fluoride varnish for anticaries treatment

Examples of combination products with *device* PMOA include:

- Breath collection/analysis devices and drug for *H. pylori* diagnosis
- Laser and photosensitizing agent for antimicrobial use
- Dialysate with drug component
- Heparin-coated cardiovascular stent
- Drug-eluting cardiovascular stent[72]
- Vascular graft with antibiotic
- Dental floss with fluoride

B. Special Pathways to Market

1. Fast-Track Programs

In 1997, Congress directed FDA to take actions appropriate to facilitate the development and expedite the review of an application for any new drug that is intended to treat serious or life-threatening conditions *and* that demonstrates the potential to address *unmet medical needs* (fast-track products).[73] As a result, Congress codified FDA's long-standing programs that facilitate development and review of products for serious and life-threatening conditions. Such programs included (a) the procedures for drugs intended to treat life-threatening illnesses,[74] and (b) the priority review procedures of the Center for Biologics Evaluation and Research and the Center for Drug Evaluation and Research (CDER).[75] Collectively, these programs provide "fast-track" review of many important drug and biological products.

Under the Fast-Track Program, FDA is permitted to approve an NDA or BLA if the product "has an effect on a clinical endpoint or on a surrogate endpoint that is reasonably likely to predict clinical benefit." Where an accelerated approval is based upon a surrogate endpoint or on an effect on a clinical endpoint other than survival or irreversible morbidity, FDA will ordinarily require postmarketing studies "to verify and describe the drug's clinical benefit and to resolve remaining uncertainty as to the relation of the surrogate endpoint upon which approval was based to clinical benefit, or the observed clinical benefit to ultimate outcome."[76] In addition, FDA is permitted to accept and review portions of a marketing application prior to receipt of the complete application, thus procedurally expediting the review process.[77]

> **Practice Point**
>
> If a new drug qualifies for Fast Track, the sponsor must identify the serious condition or unmet need, explain why the drug should address that need, and demonstrate how the trials will evaluate this potential.

Fast-track programs are different from "expanded access" programs, which are applicable to investigational drugs.[78] Fast-Track is intended to facilitate development and expedite review of drugs to treat serious and life-threatening conditions so that an approved product can reach the market quickly. Expanded access programs, such as the treatment IND, are intended to facilitate access to investigational drugs *before* approval specifically for patients with serious and life-threatening conditions who are without therapeutic alternatives.

A sponsor may submit a request for fast-track designation at the time of original submission of its IND, or at any time thereafter prior to receiving marketing approval of its BLA or NDA. A request for fast-track designation should be submitted as an amendment to the sponsor's IND with Form FDA 1571 attached or, if the request is simultaneous with submission of the original IND, should accompany the IND. The sponsor should identify the serious condition and the unmet medical needs, provide a plausible basis for the assertion that the drug has the potential to address such unmet medical needs, and include in the development plan (at a level of detail appropriate to the stage of development) trials designed to evaluate this potential. FDA is required to respond to a request for fast-track designation within 60 calendar days of receipt of the request.

It is important to note that FDA may withdraw fast-track designation if the drug development does not continue to meet the criteria for fast-track designation. A product in a fast-track development program may lose its designation if the drug: 1) no longer demonstrates a potential to address unmet medical needs, or 2) is being studied in a manner that would show the product is able to treat a serious or life-threatening condition and fulfills unmet medical needs. For example, designation could be withdrawn if a new product were approved under a conventional approval that addressed the same needs, or if emerging clinical data failed to show that the product in a fast-track development program had the anticipated advantage over existing therapy.[79]

2. Orphan Drug Designation

An "orphan drug" is a drug product that treats a rare disease affecting fewer than 200,000 Americans. The Orphan Drug Act

> **Practice Point**
>
> An orphan drug is one designed to treat a rare disease affecting fewer than 200,000 Americans. It is not necessarily a drug treating a deadly illness.

was intended to stimulate the research, development, and approval of products that treat rare diseases,[80] and since its enactment, over 100 orphan drugs and biological products have been brought to market. Under the Orphan Drug Act, sponsors are rewarded with seven years of marketing exclusivity after approval of an orphan drug product. Sponsors also are granted tax incentives for clinical research involving orphan drugs. FDA provides research study design assistance through its Office of Orphan Products Development.[81] In addition, FDA offers grant funding to defray costs of qualified clinical testing expenses related to the development of orphan products.[82]

C. Future Pathways to Market

In addition to follow-on biological products and other abbreviated pathways to market, advances in technology and medicine will be the single most significant contributor to developing future pathways to market. Perhaps the most promising advancement in the immediate future may be pharmacogenomics.

Voluntary Genomic Data Submissions (VGDSs) are a novel way to share information with the FDA. At the current time, most pharmacogenomic data are of an exploratory or research nature and FDA regulations do not require that these data be submitted to an IND, or that complete reports be submitted to an NDA or BLA. However, voluntary submissions can benefit both the industry and the FDA in a general way by providing a means for sponsors to ensure that regulatory scientists are familiar with and prepared to appropriately evaluate future genomic submissions. The FDA has requested that sponsors conducting such programs consider providing pharmacogenomic data to the agency voluntarily, when such data are not otherwise required under the regulations.[83]

Notes

1. The Federal Food, Drug, and Cosmetic Act (FDCA), 21 U.S.C. § 301 et seq., requires that a drug be the subject of an approved marketing application before it is transported or distributed across state lines.

2. Even if a clinical trial is conducted in one state and the investigational drug is not shipped across state lines, virtually every drug is made up of one or more components that have crossed state lines. Therefore, FDA considers any use of such drug, even if only in one state, to require approval before it can be used. Use of such a drug in an investigational trial may proceed without approval *only if* the sponsor submits an IND to obtain an exemption from the requirement.

3. 21 C.F.R. Part 56.
4. 21 C.F.R. § 56.107.
5. 21 C.F.R. § 312.42(a).
6. 21 C.F.R. § 312.42(d) and (e).
7. *See* FDA, Center for Drug Evaluation and Research (CDER), MANUAL OF POLICY AND PROCEDURES (MAPP) 6030.1, *IND Process and Review Procedures.*
8. *See* 21 C.F.R. §§ 312.34, 312.35, and 312.36.
9. 21 C.F.R. § 312.34.
10. 21 C.F.R. § 312.21(a).

11. 21 C.F.R. § 312.21(b).

12. 21 C.F.R. § 312.21(c).

13. In 1992, Congress passed the Prescription Drug User Fee Act (PDUFA), which was reauthorized in 1997 through the Food and Drug Modernization Act (FDAMA) (PDUFA II), and again in 2002 by the Public Health Security and Bioterrorism Preparedness and Response Act (PDUFA III), which extended the PDUFA authority through 2007.

14. For example, under the PDUFA III performance goals, FDA is expected to review and act on 90 percent of standard original filed NDA and BLA submissions within 10 months of receipt, and 90 percent of priority original filed NDA and BLA submissions within 6 months of receipt. For a complete list of current PDUFA performance goals, *see* http://www.fda.gov/oc/pdufa/PDUFAIIIGoals.html.

15. *See* FDA, CDER, *Formal Meetings Between CDER and CDER's External Constituents,* MAPP 4512.1.

16. 21 C.F.R. § 314.50; *also see* Form FDA-356h, Application to Market a New Drug for Human Use.

17. *See* CDER's Drug Information Branch (DIB) Guidance Documents for a complete list of available guidelines online and instructions on how to obtain them.

18. FDA is an active participant in the International Conference on Harmonisation of Technical Requirements for Registration of Pharmaceuticals for Human Use (ICH). This is a cooperative effort between the drug regulatory authorities and the innovative pharmaceutical company professional organizations in the European Union, Japan, and the United States to reduce the need to duplicate the testing conducted during the research and development of new medicines. Information on ICH developments is available through the official ICH Internet Home Page.

19. For the NDA "Refuse to File (RTF) Policy," *see* http://www.fda.gov/cder/guidance/rtf.pdf; for NDA filing procedures, *see* http://www.fda.gov/cder/mapp/6010.5.pdf; for the BLA RTF Policy, *see* http://www.fda.gov/cber/regsopp/8404.htm.

20. 21 C.F.R. § 312.23(a)(8)(i).

21. *See* FDA guidance, *The Content and Format for Pediatric Use Supplements* (March 1996).

22. *See* FDA's *Guideline for the Format and Content of the Microbiology Section of an Application* (February 1987).

23. *See* FDA *Compliance Program Guide 7346.832.*

24. 21 C.F.R. Part 201.

25. Regulations that establish the general procedures for FDA's use of advisory committees are set forth at 21 C.F.R. Part 14.

26. *See* overview of FDA Advisory Committees at http://www.fda.gov/oc/advisory/default.htm.

27. 5 U.S.C. App. § 2. *Also see* FDA's Disclosure Guidance, *Disclosure of Information Provided to Advisory Committees in Connection with Open Advisory Committee Meetings Convened by the Center for Drug Evaluation and Research Beginning on January 1, 2000* (the disclosure policy guidance), http://www.fda.gov/cder/guidance/3479dft.htm.

28. The Drug Price Competition and Patent Term Restoration Act of 1984 (Pub. L. No. 98-417) (the Hatch-Waxman Amendments) created § 505(j) of the FDCA (21 U.S.C. 355(j)). Section 505(j) established the ANDA approval process.

29. 21 U.S.C. § 355(j).

30. An "innovator drug" is also known as the "reference listed drug" or "RLD" product and is listed in FDA's publication called *Approved Drug Products with Therapeutic Equivalence Evaluations* (more commonly referred to as the "Orange Book" because of its orange cover). FDA, however, is gradually phasing out the Orange Book as electronic record keeping and publication become more acceptable and accessible.

31. 21 U.S.C. § 355(j).

32. 21 C.F.R. Part 320.

33. 21 C.F.R. § 320.22.

34. 21 U.S.C. § 355(j)(2)(A)(vii).

35. 21 U.S.C. § 355(j)(2)(B)(i); 21 C.F.R. § 314.95.

36. 21 U.S.C. § 355(j)(5)(B)(iv).

37. FDA's policy regarding multiple first filers is that it intends to treat all ANDAs containing a paragraph IV certification to a listed patent that are submitted on the same day as being submitted at the same time for purposes of 180-day exclusivity when no ANDA for the same drug product containing a paragraph IV certification to the same patent has been submitted on a previous day. *See* FDA Guidance, *180-Day Exclusivity When Multiple ANDAs Are Submitted on the Same Day*, July 2003, http://www.fda.gov/cder/guidance/5710fnl.pdf.

38. 21 C.F.R. § 314.105(d).

39. The "505(b)(2) application" refers to applications filed under section 505(b)(2) of the FDCA; 21 U.S.C. § 355(b)(2).

40. 21 U.S.C. § 355(b)(2).

41. The term "biological product" is defined in the Public Health Service Act (PHSA) to mean "a virus, therapeutic serum, toxin, antitoxin, vaccine, blood, blood component or derivative, allergenic product, or analogous product, or arsphenamine or derivative of arsphenamine (or any other trivalent organic arsenic compound), applicable to the prevention, treatment, or cure of a disease or condition of human beings." 42 U.S.C. § 262(i). No further description or definition is provided. As a result, the meaning or scope of the term "analogous product,"

for example, is unclear. FDA has already relied on this vague term to extend its regulatory authority over biologicals to include human cellular and tissue-based products, which are not specifically enumerated in the definition of a biological product.

42. Xenotransplantation is any procedure that involves the transplantation, implantation, or infusion into a human recipient of a xenotransplantation product, which is either (a) live cells, tissues, or organs from a nonhuman animal source or (b) human body fluids, cells, tissues or organs that have had *ex vivo* contact with live nonhuman animal cells, tissues, or organs.

43. Section 351 of the PHSA; 42 U.S.C. § 262.

44. 21 C.F.R. § 601.2.

45. The FDCA defines drugs by their intended use, for example, as "articles *intended for use* in the diagnosis, cure, mitigation, treatment, or prevention of disease," and "articles (other than food) *intended* to affect the structure or any function of the body of man or other animals." 21 U.S.C. § 321(g)(1). A biological product is defined, in relevant part, under the PHSA as "a virus, therapeutic serum, toxin, antitoxin, vaccine, blood, or blood component or derivative, allergenic product, or analogous product . . . *applicable* to the prevention, treatment or cure of a disease or condition of human beings." 42 U.S.C. § 262(i).

46. *See e.g.*, 21 C.F.R. Parts 210, 211, 600, 601, and 610.

47. 21 C.F.R. § 610.2.

48. 21 C.F.R. § 610.1.

49. 21 C.F.R. § 610.2(a).

50. *See* FDA Citizen Petition Response, Docket Nos. 2004P-0231/CP1 and SUP1, 2003 P-0176/CP1 and EMC1, 2004 P-0171/CP1, and 2004N-0355 (May 30, 2005).

51. The new regulatory scheme is composed of three HCT/P rules that were published separately: Establishment Registration and Listing rule, 66 Fed. Reg. 13 (January 19, 2001); Donor Eligibility rule, 69 Fed. Reg. 101 (May 25, 2004), and the Good Tissue Practice (GTP) rule, 69 Fed. Reg. 226 (November 24, 2004). The Donor Eligibility and GTP rules became effective May 25, 2005. The entire HCT/P regulatory scheme is codified at 21 C.F.R. Part 1271.

52. 42 U.S.C. § 264.

53. For HCT/Ps recovered on or after May 25, 2005, *see* 21 C.F.R. Part 1271. For HCT/Ps recovered before May 25, 2005, *see* 21 C.F.R. part 1270.

54. 21 C.F.R. § 1271.10.

55. 21 C.F.R. § 1271.10(a)(1). "*Minimal manipulation* means: (1) For structural tissue, processing that does not alter the original relevant characteristics of the tissue relating to the tissue's utility for reconstruction, repair, or replacement; and (2) For cells or nonstructural tissues, processing that does not alter the relevant biological characteristics of cells or tissues." 21 C.F.R. § 1271.3(f).

56. 21 C.F.R. § 1271.10(a)(2). *"Homologous use* means the replacement or supplementation of a recipient's cells or tissues with an HCT/P that performs the same basic function or functions in the recipient as in the donor." 21 C.F.R. § 1271.3(c).

57. 21 C.F.R. § 1271.10(a)(3) states in relevant part: "The manufacture of the HCT/P does not involve the combination of the cells or tissues with another article, except for water, crystalloids, or a sterilizing, preserving, or storage agent, provided that the addition of water, crystalloids, or the sterilizing, preserving, or storage agent does not raise new clinical safety concerns with respect to the HCT/P."

58. 21 C.F.R. § 1271.10(a)(4), which states in relevant part: "Either (i) The HCT/P does not have a systemic effect and is not dependent upon the metabolic activity of living cells for its primary function; or (ii) The HCT/P has a systemic effect or is dependent upon the metabolic activity of living cells for its primary function, and: (*a*) Is for autologous use; (*b*) Is for allogeneic use in a first-degree or second-degree blood relative; or (*c*) Is for reproductive use.

59. 21 U.S.C. § 360c(a)(1).

60. General controls are baseline requirements that apply to all medical devices necessary for marketing, proper labeling, and monitoring the performance of any device on the market. *See* 21 C.F.R Parts 800 et seq.

61. 21 U.S.C. § 360(k).

62. 21 C.F.R. Part 807.

63. *See* http://www.fda.gov/cdrh/databases.html.

64. 21 U.S.C. § 360e.

65. 21 C.F.R. Part 812.

66. *See* 21 C.F.R. Parts 50 and 56. The same human subject protection regulations and IRB regulations applicable to drugs also apply to medical devices.

67. 21 C.F.R. § 3.2(e), which states in relevant part that "a combination product is defined to include: (1) A product comprised of two or more regulated components (*i.e.,* drug/device, biologic/device, drug/biologic, or drug/device/biologic) that are physically, chemically, or otherwise combined or mixed and produced as a single entity; (2) Two or more separate products packaged together in a single package or as a unit and comprised of drug and device products, device and biological products, or biological and drug products; (3) A drug, device, or biological product packaged separately that according to its investigational plan or proposed labeling is intended for use only with an approved individually specified drug, device, or biological product where both are required to achieve the intended use, indication, or effect and where, upon approval of the proposed product, the labeling of the approved product would need to be changed (*e.g.*, to reflect a change in intended use, dosage form, strength, route of administration, or significant change in dose); or (4) Any investigational drug, device, or biological product packaged separately that according to its proposed label-

ing is for use only with another individually specified investigational drug, device, or biological product where both are required to achieve the intended use, indication, or effect."

68. 21 U.S.C. § 353(g).

69. Currently, most biological product applications are reviewed by FDA's Center for Biologics Evaluation and Research (CBER); however, certain biological product applications, such as therapeutic biologics, are now being reviewed by FDA's CDER.

70. *See* general information about combination products at http://www.fda.gov/oc/combination/default.htm.

71. 70 Fed. Reg. 49,848 (August 25, 2005), amending 21 C.F.R. § 3.2(m).

72. *See* http://www.fda.gov/oc/combination/stents.html.

73. Section 112 of the Food and Drug Administration Modernization Act of 1997 (FDAMA) (P.L. 105-115) amended the FDCA by adding new § 506; 21 U.S.C. § 356.

74. *See* 21 C.F.R. §§ 312.80–312.88 (Subpart E). Under the Subpart E regulations for investigational new drugs, drug development is considered a continuum from early preclinical and clinical studies through submission of a marketing application. The regulations emphasize the critical nature of close early communication between the FDA and a sponsor, outline procedures such as pre-IND and end of phase 1 meetings as methods to improve the efficiency of preclinical and clinical development, and focus on efforts by the FDA and the sponsor to reach early agreement on the design of the major clinical efficacy studies that will be needed to support approval.

75. Products regulated by CBER are eligible for priority review if they provide a significant improvement in the safety or effectiveness of the treatment, diagnosis, or prevention of a serious or life-threatening disease. *See* CBER Manual of Standard Operating Procedures and Policies, SOPP 8405, *Complete Review and Issuance of Action Letters*, June 11, 1998. Products regulated by CDER are eligible for priority review if they provide a significant improvement compared to marketed products in the treatment, diagnosis, or prevention of a disease; eligibility is not limited to drugs for a serious or life-threatening disease. *See Priority Review Policy*, April 22, 1996, CDER, MAPP 6020.3.

76. 21 C.F.R. §§ 314.500–314.560 and Preamble at 57 Fed. Reg. 58,942 (December 11, 1992).

77. 21 U.S.C. § 356.

78. *See, e.g.*, treatment IND regulations set forth at 21 C.F.R. § 312.34.

79. *See* FDA Guidance for Industry, *Fast Track Drug Development Programs—Designation, Development, and Application Review,* July 2004, at http://www.fda.gov/cder/guidance/5645fnl.htm.

80. 21 U.S.C. § 360aa. The Orphan Drug Act was signed into law on January 4, 1983.

81. For more information on the Office of Orphan Products Development, go to http://www.fda.gov/orphan/grants/info.htm.

82. For grant information, go to http://www.fda.gov/orphan/grants/info.htm.

83. The process for voluntarily submitting genomic data to the FDA is detailed at http://www.fda.gov/cder/mapp/4180.3.pdf.

Chapter XIV

The Regulation of Biomedical Products for Animal Use

Robert B. Nicholas
McDermott Will & Emery LLP
Washington, D.C.
and
Kent D. McClure
Animal Health Institute
Washington, D.C.

A. Regulation of Animal Health Products

Jurisdiction over medical products for use in animals is divided among three agencies, each with differing primary statutory authorities: the Food and Drug Administration (FDA), under authority of the Federal Food, Drug and Cosmetic Act (FFDCA);[1] the U.S. Department of Agriculture's (USDA) Animal and Plant Health Inspection Service (APHIS), under the Virus-Serum-Toxin Act (VSTA);[2] and the Environmental Protection Agency (EPA), under the Federal Insecticide, Fungicide and Rodenticide Act (FIFRA).[3] Determining the appropriate regulatory pathway for any animal health product is critical to understanding the legal and regulatory environment, creating product development strategies, and predicting key business parameters, such as time to market and research and development costs.

This chapter discusses the regime for regulation of medicinal products for animal use, including products produced by the newer molecular biology techniques. This includes animal drugs, regulated by FDA's Center for Veterinary Medicine (CVM), comprising animal drugs used to treat diseases in companion animals (e.g., dogs and cats); animal drugs used to prevent or treat diseases or to enhance feed efficiency (growth promotion) in livestock, poultry, and fish ("food animals"); and animal drugs administered in feed. Also discussed is the regulation of therapeutic, diagnostic, and other biological products used in animals. These products are not regulated by FDA[4] but fall within the exclusive jurisdiction of APHIS. However, the regulation of insecticides by EPA is generally beyond the scope of this book and therefore is not discussed.[5]

FDA's regulatory regime for drug products used in veterinary medicine generally parallels that used to regulate drugs for use in humans, and historically, the regulation of drugs for humans and animals have largely followed the same path. However, because many veterinary drugs are used in animals consumed as food by humans, the regulation of these drugs in most respects also has followed the pathway used by FDA for the regulation of food for human use.

Significant differences in FDA's regulation of human use and animal use products generally reflect the agricultural setting in which many animal drugs are used. Some of these factors accounting for the differences in regulatory treatment include: animal use products are often intended for use in multiple species; different species often have significant pharmacokinetic differences; and many intended uses are in species that are also used for human food and can be sources of potentially harmful animal drug residues or vectors for bacterial, viral, or protozoan food-borne diseases in humans.[6]

To the extent there is overlap between FDA regulation of human drugs and veterinary drugs, this chapter focuses on the unique aspects of regulation of veterinary products.[7] Additionally, this chapter does not specifically discuss veterinary medical devices regulated by FDA. Generally, medical devices used to detect disease in animals (veterinary medical devices) fall within the definition of "device" in the FFDCA.[8] However, veterinary medical devices are largely unregulated by FDA, except for the general statutory prohibition on misbranding and adulteration.[9] This chapter also does not discuss the regulation of animal feed and non-drug feed ingredients by the Center for Veterinary Medicine, which largely parallels FDA regulation of food consumed by humans. This latter topic is included in Chapter 14.

B. The Animal Health Industry

1. Development Incentives

An important consideration when representing animal health companies is that the animal health industry is very different from the human health sector of the economy. The economic incentives supporting the development of drugs for human use, such as third-party insurance and the value placed on human life and health, support the necessary development costs and attendant higher prices for drugs for human use. These incentives are largely absent in the veterinary drug market. For example, in the food animal sector, all treatment decisions are largely economically driven. A producer of food animals has little reason to pay for a drug to treat an animal unless there is an economic return. There is, however, somewhat more pricing flexibility and ability to recover development costs in drugs for companion animals, but not on the scale of products for human use. Ironically, however, because companion animals are not consumed by humans as food, the regulatory requirements for marketing of drugs for pets are significantly less than those for food animals.

2. Size Matters

The animal health industry is also very much smaller in terms of gross revenue than the human pharmaceutical and medical device industry.[10] Sales of even blockbuster animal drugs are a mere fraction of even the most modestly successful human drugs. However, the regulatory requirements for animal drugs are nevertheless significant, and particularly in case of drugs for food animals, even more extensive and complex than those involving drugs, devices, and food for humans. Failure to comply with regulatory requirements for products for veterinary use can lead to the full panoply of administrative, criminal, and civil liability.

Another difference between the animal health industry and the human health industry is that the major companies producing animal drugs, biologics, and insecticides are often relatively small divisions or companies within the major pharmaceutical companies. While these large companies have devoted significant resources to animal drug development and have very sophisticated regulatory departments, the animal drug companies frequently must take a back seat to their sister human health companies when competing internally and externally for funding and political support. For start-up companies and other small companies, obtaining financing for animal drug development can be very problematic. Generally, the independent companies producing animal health products tend to be relatively small. The challenge for the practitioner in the animal health arena is, therefore, to understand and address in a cost-effective manner the regulatory concerns of animal drug, biologic, and feed companies and their customers and clients.

> **Practice Points**
>
> **Federal and State Government Agencies Relevant to Animal Health Products**
> — USDA: the Department of Agriculture
> — APHIS: the Animal and Plant Health Inspection Service of the USDA
> — CVB: APHIS's Center for Veterinary Biologics
> — EPA: the Environmental Protection Agency
> — OPP: EPA's Office of Pesticide Programs
> — FDA: the Food and Drug Administration
> — CVM: the FDA's Center for Veterinary Medicine
> — CBER: the FDA's Center for Biologics Evaluation and Research
> — CDER: the FDA's Center for Drug Evaluation and Research
> — CDRH: the FDA's Center for Devices and Radiological Health
> — CFSAN: the FDA's Center for Food Safety and Applied Nutrition
> — AAFCO: the Association of American Feed Control Officials

What may be said about the relative significance of the animal health companies as part of larger pharmaceutical companies may also be said about CVM in contrast to the FDA centers regulating products for human use. CVM has a much smaller budget and staff than CBER (biologics), CDER (drugs), CDRH (medical devices), and CFSAN (food).[11] From a practitioner's viewpoint, the practical implications of CVM's position in the FDA hierarchy is that it may take longer for CVM to make decisions on product approvals[12] as well as on cutting-edge issues. Additionally, it may be more difficult to find support at higher levels in the agency when such support is useful to resolving policy issues. Also, frequently CVM will be guided by precedents set by CBER or CDER.

3. Complexity

As is the case with human drugs, the regulation of individual drugs can occasionally become the focus of debate about societal issues. For human drugs, the hot-button issues have been stem cell research and reproductive drugs,[13] whereas in the veterinary arena, hot-button issues include environmental questions, animal welfare, large-scale agricultural production, and loss of family farms. Finding common understanding in this wider debate involving animal drugs is made more difficult because of limited public understanding of modern livestock and food production. The lack of exposure to production agriculture also can affect the medical profession's views on animal drug regulatory matters. This can include physicians (MDs), who ordinarily are not exposed to veterinary medicine in medical school, as well as many veterinarians (DVMs) who are typically affiliated with small animal practices and not familiar with production agriculture—including, ironically, veterinarians who work at CVM.

Significant state involvement in the regulation of agriculture, particularly in the farm states and largely focusing on animal feed, also may create overlapping compliance obligations. For example, while animal drugs are largely regulated by FDA, pet food and food animal feed are significantly regulated under standards set by the Association of American Feed Control Officials (AAFCO), the formal association of state feed officials, and enforced by the states and FDA.

C. Biotechnology-Derived Products[14]

For many years, traditional agricultural production, including production of food animals, has been grounded in biology and chemistry, such as the use of selective breeding techniques, prophylactic immunization with biologics, and the use of chemically synthesized animal drugs. The ability of the new biotechnology-derived products (r-DNA technologies used for production of drugs and animals, such as cloning, transgenics, and the use of genetically modified organisms to produce animal drugs) to navigate the regulatory pathways and obtain market acceptance varies by the agency with jurisdiction. In APHIS and in the user community there is widespread use and acceptance of biologics such as gene-deleted vaccine strains, subunit vaccines, or live recombinant-vectored vaccines. In contrast, despite the fact that many of the techniques of biotechnology were first developed in animal models, the commercialization of the technology has been slow to develop in the areas regulated by CVM. Questions have been raised about whether, and the extent to which, FDA has jurisdiction over the new technologies; what data are required to approve various applications; how to assess the potential risks of new products; and whether the products of biotechnology present new and additional risks to human health and the environment.[15] The difference between CVM's and APHIS's experience relative to biotechnology may be related to the historic division of responsibility. The USDA has regulated biologic products since 1913 and has vast experience addressing regulatory and scientific issues presented by the use of modified living organisms. In contrast, CVM matured as an organization focused on chemically synthesized compounds that much more readily lend themselves to precise chemical definition and analysis.

Questions faced by CVM, and to a lesser extent by APHIS, have sometimes resulted in uncertainty in the regulatory landscape, including controversy and delays in product submissions and decisions, notwithstanding government-wide efforts to address such questions over the past 20 years or more.[16]

The Coordinated Framework for the Regulation of Biotechnology (Coordinated Framework), published in 1986, remains today the primary, comprehensive federal statement outlining the basis of federal agency jurisdiction over various biotechnology products.[17] The Coordinated Framework is grounded in the principle that the products of biotechnology should be regulated under the same authorities and in a similar manner as similar products produced using conventional technologies. While many biotech products have been approved for human health and consumption, and numerous field trials of transgenic plants have taken place, in the intervening years since publication of the Coordinated Framework, CVM's approval of recombinant bST in 1993[18] is perhaps the only recombinant protein approved as an animal drug by FDA. In contrast, APHIS's Center for Veterinary Biologics (CVB) has approved numerous biologics that are the product of biotechnology, including more than a dozen live recombinant-vectored vaccines, and has licensed the world's first DNA vaccine. Indeed, since 1990, the USDA program to vaccinate wildlife against rabies has distributed more than 48 million doses of a live recombinant-vectored subunit rabies vaccine in the form of oral baits.[19] The ongoing discussion about how to assess and regulate market entry of transgenic animals and cloned animals approved for food production, begun many years ago,[20] confirms that aspects of the regulatory regime are still works in progress, though perhaps a resolution is now closer.[21]

D. Overview of FDA Regulation of Animal Drugs[22]

1. FDA Regulates Animal Drugs: Defined

The history of FDA's regulation of animal drugs parallels the history of FDA's regulation of human drugs, principally because the statute defines "drug" to mean articles used in "man or other animals."[23] Prior to the 1968 animal drug amendments to the FFDCA[24] (1968 Amendments), persons intending to introduce an animal drug into interstate commerce were regulated under the same statutory authority as those applicable to human drugs. Various pre-1968 amendments to what is now the FFDCA imposed on human and animal drug manufacturers alike new requirements for safety (1938) and effectiveness (1962), and, for animal drugs intended for use in food animals as well as animal feed producers, requirements similar to those imposed on producers of food and feed ingredients (1958) for human use.[25]

Prior to the 1968 Amendments, manufacturers of animal drugs for food animals were required to obtain a drug approval from the Bureau of Veterinary Drugs and also file a food additive petition with the Bureau of Foods to set a residue tolerance for any residue of the drug in the edible tissue of the animal.[26] The 1968 Amendments created a more streamlined scheme for the regulation of new animal drugs and animal feed. The 1968 Amendments, among other things, combined parts of the existing food additive provisions (§ 348) and the drug approval provisions (§ 355) into a new section of the FFDCA (§ 360b), created a new category of drugs called "new animal drugs," excluded new animal drugs from the existing definition of "new drug" and "food additive," and made new animal drugs subject to the new section of the FFDCA.[27] "New Animal Drug" (as subsequently amended) is broadly defined and includes any unapproved drug, or drug not generally recognized as safe by experts, intended for use in animals other than man, including drugs for use in animal feed.[28] Under the 1968 Amendments, introduction into interstate commerce of an unapproved new animal or food containing a residue of an unapproved new animal drug constituted a violation of the FFDCA.[29] The 1968 amendments put in place the basic regulatory regime still in effect.

> **Practice Points**
>
> **Milestones in Regulatory Approval and Marketing of an Animal Drug:**
> — Preclinical investigations subject to good laboratory practices (cGLP)
> — Field studies pursuant to a Notice of Claimed Investigational Exemption for a New Animal Drug (INAD)
> — Submission of New Animal Drug Application (NADA)
> — Pre-approval inspection of manufacturing facilities
> — Pre-approval audit of field studies
> — Approval of NADA published in *Federal Register*
> — Post-approval manufacturing (current good manufacturing practices or cGMP), record-keeping and reporting requirements

2. Critical Elements in the Regulatory Regime

Not surprisingly, CVM's regulation of new animal drugs follows the basic FDA regulatory regime for human medical and food products: (i) applicable regulatory requirements determined by the intended use of the product, as described in the product labeling, (ii) pre-market evaluation of scientific data derived from scientific studies and tests, (iii) approval required to the extent applicant meets statutory safety, effectiveness, and other applicable requirements for labeled indication(s), including manufacturing requirements, (iv) approval for specific labeled indications, (v) post-approval reporting, record-keeping, manufacturing, and promotional requirements, and (vi) FDA enforcement based on inspections and residue monitoring.

a. Approval of New Animal Drugs

The route to approval to market a new animal drug parallels that for marketing a new drug for human use, namely, an approved application (a "new animal drug application" or "NADA") is required.[30] The NADA must contain adequate information on the drug substance and formulation (including manufacturing, chemistry, and controls), proposed labeling, "full reports of adequate tests by all methods reasonably applicable to show whether or not the new animal drug is safe and effective" for its intended use, including "substantial evidence" of effectiveness.[31] "Field study(s)," used to generate data for approval, require CVM approval of a "Notice of Claimed Investigational Exemption for a New Animal Drug," or INAD. Laboratory studies ordinarily must be conducted in accordance with "good laboratory practices," or GLPs.[32]

CVM has the authority to approve important new animal drugs on an expedited basis.[33] Also, as with human use drugs, generic new animal drugs may be approved on abbreviated applications (called an abbreviated new animal drug application, or ANADA).[34] Sponsors are also required to register manufacturing establishments, list products in distribution, and pay certain user fees.[35] Animal drug approvals are subject to the National Environmental Policy Act, 21 U.S.C. § 4321 (2000 & Supp. 2003), requiring procedural consideration (but not substantive decision) of potential environmental impacts, unless exempt.[36] As part of the NADA review process, CVM or the field staff will conduct a pre-approval inspection of the manufacturing establishment and audit of the pivotal filed study(s). In contrast to human drug approvals, approval of an NADA is published as a regulation in the *Federal Register* (codified at 21 C.F.R. pts. 520-529, 558), together with any associated residue tolerance (codified in 21 C.F.R. pt. 556).

b. Denial and Withdrawal of Approval of New Animal Drugs

Denial of approval of an NADA entitles the sponsor to the same procedural remedies as the denial of a New Drug Application for human use, including an opportunity to request a hearing before FDA. Various hearing fora may be available, including a hearing before a neutral fact-finder (e.g., an administrative law judge or ALJ), assuming one can establish that there is a material factual dispute. The ALJ's "initial decision" is appealable to the FDA Commissioner. The Commissioner's "final decision" is considered final agency action and is appealable to the Circuit Court.[37]

c. Post-approval Requirements

Subsequent to approval, sponsors are required to timely report adverse events, file annual reports, keep certain records, and manufacture in compliance with current good manufacturing practices (cGMPs).[38] NADA supplements are required for significant post-approval changes to labeling, manufacturing, and additional species and use indications.[39] Advertising of prescription animal drugs as well as labeling is subject to regulation by FDA, similar to the regime and standards established for human drugs.[40] However, in comparison to drugs for human use, animal drugs are generally more readily available as over-the-counter drugs than by prescription, based in large measure on the fact that users of animal drugs in food-producing animals frequently are ranchers, growers, and producers with extensive knowledge about the drugs being used and experience in drug use generally. In contrast, human patients do not generally have the training and experience to use many drugs safely.

d. Inspection, Enforcement, and Compliance

Holders of approved NADAs are subject to inspection and the same panoply of FDA enforcement and compliance actions as NDA holders. In the event an animal drug presents an "imminent hazard" to human health, the Secretary of the Department of Health and Human Services can immediately suspend the approval of an NADA and a hearing must be provided to the sponsor within 90 days thereof.[41] Alternatively, the FDA can withdraw an NADA after an opportunity for hearing based on various grounds related to safety matters, fraud, or failure to comply with specific requirements.[42]

As discussed in detail in the section following, drugs administered to food animals also are subject to a food safety assessment and, unless exempt, the food from the animal cannot be offered for consumption unless a residue tolerance and/or withdrawal time have been established in the final approval for the drug. A tolerance and withdrawal time can also be set for an investigational new animal drug.[43] Additionally, CVM has authority to establish "import tolerances" for residues of drugs in imported animal products, where the drug is not approved or intended for use in the United States.[44] Import tolerances are based, generally, on the same food safety standards used to establish tolerances for drugs used domestically, but since the drug is not intended for use in the United States, target animal safety and effectiveness as well as other data ordinarily required in an NADA need not be submitted.

E. Distinguishing Factors Between FDA Regulation of Animal and Human Drugs

Significant issues in the regulation of animal drugs, in contrast to human drugs, include: (i) human food safety, (ii) use of drugs in animal feed, including drugs for growth promotion, and (iii) multiple species, minor species, and companion animals. This section also discusses some practical considerations for understanding and interacting with CVM.

1. Drugs for Food Animals: Human Food Safety

Of the factors distinguishing the regulation of animal drugs from their human counterparts, the most significant is human food safety issues involving drugs intended to be used in food-producing animals. Such drugs must not only be shown to be safe in the target animal,[45] but any food product of that animal that may be consumed by humans must also be "safe."[46] CVM has interpreted "safe" in the context of target animal safety to mean that the "risks outweigh the benefits" to the animal, and for the food safety decision, that any residue of the animal drug, including any metabolites formed in or on the food, must be at or below a level that, when consumed, results in " a reasonable certainty of no harm."[47]

CVM's regulation of residues of animal drugs in edible tissue follows closely the substantive and legal standards utilized for indirect food additives by FDA's Center for Food Safety and Applied Nutrition (CFSAN). An essential step in the approval of a new animal drug in a food animal involves submission by the sponsor of data adequate to establish a residue tolerance. Based on acute and/or chronic testing, the FDA will establish (i) a residue tolerance, expressed as the maximum amount of the allowable drug residue (kg/mg or ppm) remaining in the target tissue after slaughter, that results in a "reasonable certainty of no harm" from consumption of the food product, and (ii) a withdrawal time, the time that the drug can no longer be administered to the animal before slaughter, based on the time necessary for the drug residue to become depleted to or below the established tolerance. For compliance purposes, the NADA sponsor must provide a reliable (validated, sensitive) methodology for detecting the drug residue (or metabolite) in the "target" tissue.

The safety determination for animal drug residues in food for humans ("human food safety") is not dictated by the drug claims but by the chemical nature and biological activity of the drug entity.[48] The human food safety concern for animal drug residues focuses on the assessment of chronic low-level exposure effects of drug residues in edible tissues. Generally, the concentration of drug residues in edible tissues is not high enough to produce acute toxicity.

The human food safety evaluation ordinarily involves the completion of the standard battery of toxicology tests and residue and metabolism studies. These toxicology tests are designed to determine the dose at which the compound produces an adverse effect in test animals and a dose at which the drug produces no adverse effect—that is, the no observed effect level (NOEL). The observed effect does not always represent a toxic effect. Pharmacological, hormonal, and microbiological effects are all considered adverse biological effects in the human food safety evaluation. For certain drug classes, additional specialized tests are required to establish a NOEL for these physiological effects.

In addition to the general food safety provisions of the FFDCA, the Delaney Clause[49] prohibits the use of carcinogenic compounds as animal drugs when they leave residues in food. Therefore, if the animal drug or its metabolites are structurally related to a demonstrated carcinogen or if the compound tests positive in the genetic toxicology studies, additional carcinogenicity studies may be required.[50]

Following completion of all the toxicology studies, the NOEL of the most sensitive effect from the most appropriate toxicology study is divided by a safety factor to determine an acceptable daily intake (ADI). The ADI represents the highest amount of total residue of the compound that is allowed in edible tissues of the target animal. This total residue consists of parent compound, free metabolites, and metabolites that are covalently bound to endogenous molecules, and is very difficult to measure on a routine basis. Rather than measuring the total residues in all the edible tissues, CVM establishes one value, a tolerance, in one tissue, the target tissue for monitoring drug residues. The tolerance is established so that when residues are below the tolerance in the target tissue, the whole carcass is safe. To establish the tolerance for the drug, the drug sponsor conducts a residue depletion study to determine when the concentration of total drug residues is below the ADI.[51]

2. Drugs Administered in Animal Feed

Another difference between the regulation of animal and human use drugs is that some animal drugs are mixed with feed before being sold to end users. In some instances the feed is the most effective, and in some cases the only, practical way to deliver a therapeutic dose of the medication to the animal.[52] In other instances, the medication is primarily administered to enhance the animal's growth (growth promotion drugs). In addition to regulating the drug manufacturer (NADA holder), FDA also regulates feed mills producing medicated feed.[53] A feed mill is required to obtain annually a license from FDA to manufacture medicated feed. Medicated feed must be manufactured in accordance with cGMPs and must be labeled in accordance with currently approved feed labeling for the drug;[54] feed mill operations (and manufacturers) are required to keep certain records and submit specified reports. Feed mills also are subject to FDA inspection. A drug manufacturer cannot sell a drug for use in manufacturing a medicated feed except to a licensed feed mill. The manufacturer or other seller of a drug for use in a medicated feed is required to obtain from the purchaser a statement to the effect that the purchaser is a licensed feed mill (or is providing the drug to a licensed feed mill).

The Animal Drug Availability Act (ADAA) created a new category of veterinary drugs called "veterinary feed directive drugs" or "VFD" drugs.[55] Prior to 1996, an animal drug could be regulated as either an OTC drug or a prescription drug. However, CVM determined that certain new animal drugs, considered vital to animal health, should be able to be approved for use in animal feed, but only if these medicated feeds were administered under a veterinarian's order and professional supervision. For example, according to CVM, control over the use of certain non-prescription antimicrobials is critical to reducing unnecessary use of such drugs in animals, and to slow or prevent potential for the development of bacterial resistance to antimicrobial drugs. Safety concerns relating to difficulty of diagnosis of disease conditions, high toxicity, or other reasons may also dictate that the use of a medicated feed is limited to use by order and under the supervision of a licensed veterinarian.

When a new animal drug application is submitted to the CVM for approval, the appropriate CVM division determines whether a drug will be an OTC, prescription, or VFD drug. A practicing veterinarian may not write a VFD order for an OTC drug, nor may he/she write a VFD order to be used contrary to the FDA regulation for that drug. A veterinarian may only write a VFD order for drugs approved for that category and only in the context of a valid client-patient relationship (VCPR), as defined in 21 C.F.R. § 530.3(i) (2005).[56]

3. Import of Use of an Approved Drug in Different Species; Minor Species and Uses; Use in Pets; Animal Drug Availability

An additional difference between the regulation of animal use and human use drugs is that a drug may be used in several different animal species. Each labeled indication, including a label to treat the same disease in another species, ordinarily can be approved only if species-specific data are submitted in a NADA, ANDA or supplement to an NADA.[57] Given the generally high costs of developing and obtaining approval of animal drugs, CVM has several mechanisms available to make animal drugs potentially more readily available.

Similar to human use drugs, a manufacturer of an animal drug cannot promote an approved drug for an off-label use, but a veterinary practitioner can use an approved animal drug (and human drugs) for non-labeled indications, provided certain conditions are met.[58] As one would expect, there is considerably more flexibility for the use of a drug in a non-food animal than in a food animal. FDA has the authority by regulation to prohibit extra-label use of individual animal drugs and has done so where safety or other concerns would justify such action.[59]

As has the human health community, the animal health community has struggled over the years with having approved drugs available for uses that may not ordinarily justify the high costs of drug development. FDA provides assistance in the development of "orphan" drugs for humans, defined generally as drugs used to treat limited populations.[60] The parallel for animal drugs are drugs for "minor" uses and drugs for "minor" species (MUMS drugs).[61] The Minor Use and Minor Species Animal Health Act (MUMSAHA) was passed in 2004 and generally provides for restricted animal drug approval based on reduced data requirements.[62] Incentives for development of MUMS drugs include "conditional approval," "indexing," and "designation."[63] "Conditional approval" permits FDA approval and marketing of a MUMS drug for up to five years (one-year renewals required) before all effectiveness data is collected, but only after safety is proven.[64] "Indexing" that permits CVM to establish a list of new MUMS drugs that may be legally marketed, notwithstanding the absence of an NADA. Indexed drugs are restricted to drugs where the market potential is so limited (e.g., zoo animals) that conditional approval is not a realistic alternative. Indexed drugs may be used in non-food-producing animals and in food-producing animals only in the early life stages—the non-food-use stages.[65] Conditional approval and indexing may not be granted for a new animal drug that is contained in, or is a product of, a transgenic animal.[66] "Designation" is similar to an orphan drug designation for human drugs. Designated drugs are eligible for marketing exclusivity, grants, and other economic incentives and assistance.[67]

4. Practical Considerations for Interacting with the Center for Veterinary Medicine (CVM)

In terms of advocating for a client on animal health matters, it is important to understand how CVM is organized to regulate animal drugs and how CVM makes decisions about animal drugs.

Similar to FDA's other centers, CVM has a "director" and operates with functional divisions, the principal ones being the Office of New Drug Approval (ONDA), the Office of Surveillance and Compliance (OSC), and the Office of Research. ONDA has primary responsibility for new drug approvals, including investigational drugs and food/feed tolerances, while OSC has responsibility generally for post-approval matters.

From a political perspective, as with FDA's other centers, CVM is subject to the authority of the FDA Commissioner, a political appointee confirmed by the Senate. In turn, the Commissioner reports to the Secretary of the Department of Health and Human Resources. The distinction of importance is that FDA is not an independent regulatory agency but it is part of the executive branch, headed by political appointee, and subject to the control and influence of both the executive branch, consistent with the law, and Congress. Given, however, the relatively narrow import of many animal drug regulatory issues (particularly in contrast to competing human health issues), it may be difficult to gain the attention of those who have oversight over CVM. For example, congressional oversight of FDA is largely not within the animal health industry's natural constituency on the agriculture committees but rather within the province of committees dealing with human health matters—for example, the Senate Committee on Health, Education, Labor, and Pensions (HELP), or the House Committee on Energy and Commerce. However, this may be ameliorated to some extent by the fact that FDA and USDA, and indeed all appropriations, are handled in the House and the Senate by one committee. The health-focused committees have very large constituencies, with many health-care issues beyond FDA regulatory matters, and animal health plays a very small part in the committees' agendas. Notwithstanding the relatively junior position of CVM, there has been significant new legislation affecting animal drug regulation during the past 10 years.[68]

In terms of decision making, CVM is similar to the rest of FDA; in the first instance, FDA is a science-based regulatory agency. The best route to being an effective client advocate is develop high-quality scientific data, organize it well, and present it in an effective manner. As with the other FDA centers, informal and formal dispute resolution mechanisms exist to resolve scientific disagreements with CVM, including access to CVM's Ombudsperson.[69] On policy matters (including CVM), FDA is not impervious to outside influences, and frequently solicits input from constituent groups, including public interest groups and industry, that are seeking to influence FDA policy and decisions. However, the ability of parties to informally influence CVM actions may be limited in some circumstances, depending on the statutory requirements applicable to particular agency action. For example, administrative hearings are largely conducted on the record, and activities under an INAD and NADA are confidential and restricted to the sponsor and FDA.[70]

F. CVM Regulation of Biotechnology Products

FDA/CVM has claimed jurisdiction over a wide variety of products, which generally can be grouped under the heading "biotechnology." Such products include but are not limited to genetically modified animals, including transgenic[71] and cloned animals; meat, milk, eggs, and other edible food products derived from genetically modified animals used for human and animal use; animal drugs produced in genetically engineered animals; and genetically engineered plants and microorganisms used for feed, or as feed ingredients.[72] However, while there has been significant public debate over the past dozen or more years, CVM has issued no new regulations or formal guidance addressing whether and how it would regulate differently transgenic or cloned animals and food products from such animals.[73] To date, it does not appear that any of these products have been approved by CVM, although research in these area is taking place. For example, CVM investigated the disposal of transgenic pigs under an INAD by the University of Illinois and concluded that the pigs were improperly allowed to enter the human food chain.[74]

FDA's assertion of jurisdiction over animal drugs manufactured using the new biotech techniques and injected or fed to animals for drug-related purposes has largely been accepted, regardless of whether the drug is produced in a genetically modified macro- or microorganism. Approval of such drugs generally raises no new considerations, such as safety and effectiveness, although the method of manufacture can raise additional or novel safety and perhaps environmental issues. However, as the pathway to approval and use of r-bST demonstrates, political, social, ethical, and environmental factors can have an impact on the timing and data required for approval, even when no one would seriously question the animal drug status of r-bST when administered to dairy cows to enhance milk production.[75]

FDA also has asserted jurisdiction over cloned animals, transgenic animals, and similar "products." The asserted rationale is that these products are "animal drugs" because the genetic constructs and techniques used are intended to treat, mitigate, cure, diagnose or prevent disease in animals and/or affect the structure or function of the animal.[76] In the case of transgenic fish (and presumably other transgenic animals), FDA has used this rationale to assert jurisdiction over the genetic construct and the expression product of the construct. Furthermore, because the construct is integrated into the genome and is to be stably inherited by the progeny, subsequent generations as well are considered "animal drugs."[77] Even those who would readily accept CVM authority wonder how CVM will address certain scientific and legal questions raised by the critics of biotechnology generally, as well as by others.

Because of uncertainty, FDA and product developers are going slowly while the public debate takes place. For example, for some years there has been a voluntary moratorium on the introduction of food from cloned and transgenic animals into the human food chain.[78] Numerous conferences and discussions over the past decade have addressed various questions involved in regulation and commercialization of such products. Much of the discussion has focused on factors traditionally considered by FDA, such as how to assess target animal safety and human food safety. The latter includes the inadvertent introduction in transgenic animals of new toxins and proteins (allergens) into the food chain. However, and not surprisingly, a substantial part of the public debate has centered on issues not traditionally considered by FDA in regulating veterinary drugs and issues that FDA may not have statutory authority to consider.[79] These issues include ethical questions in producing genetically modified and cloned animals; the impact of potential monoculture on genetic diversity; animal welfare; environmental impacts; religious concerns; and the impact on small-scale/family farming.[80] While occasionally some similar questions have arisen with biotech products in the human health arena—for example, cloning and stem cell research—the march of many biotechnology products through CDER, CBER, and CDRH has generally engendered much less controversy. This is perhaps not surprising, as human health products ordinarily focus on treating or preventing important human health diseases or illnesses in individual people with which most people can readily identify. By contrast, food and agricultural inputs are infrequently seen as having such urgent and positive public health impacts and have, therefore, more readily become the focus of debate of the larger societal issues, notwithstanding their potential to more efficiently produce safer and more beneficial foods with environmental benefits.

The full extent and/or limit on FDA's jurisdiction over these biotech "products" has not been tested in the courts. Generally researchers and sponsors have not challenged FDA, preferring to have an FDA "seal" of safety as a counterpoint to public opinion and concern.

G. Overview of USDA Regulation of Animal Biological Products[81]

1. USDA Regulates Veterinary Biologics

The regulation of veterinary biological products lies with the USDA. In 1913, Congress enacted provisions dealing with viruses, serums, toxins, antitoxins, and analogous products for use in domestic animals,[82] commonly known as the Virus-Serum-Toxin Act, or VSTA. VSTA was initially enacted in response to substantial losses from the unregulated manufacture and distribution of anti-hog cholera serum.[83] It prohibited the interstate shipment of any "worthless, contaminated, dangerous, or harmful virus, serum, toxin, or analogous product intended for use in the treatment of domestic animals."[84] In 1985, VSTA was amended (1985 Amendments) to provide, among other things, sole regulatory jurisdiction over veterinary biological products to USDA.[85]

Within USDA, CVB is tasked with oversight of the implementing regulatory scheme. Structurally, CVB is part of Veterinary Services, which in turn is part of APHIS. CVB is headed by a director and has two main functional units, one dealing with policy and the evaluation of license applications and one dealing with inspection and regulatory compliance issues. The established regulatory regime is similar to FDA's regulation of human use biological products. Applicants must demonstrate the purity, safety, potency, and efficacy of products and the capability to manufacture consistently within the parameters of an approved outline of production. The spectrum of data required ranges from characterization of seed materials and ingredients, laboratory and target animal safety, and efficacy studies to stability testing and post-marketing surveillance. Because many traditional biological products have been developed and manufactured using live attenuated organisms, rather than synthesized chemical molecules, the regulatory pathway for biotechnology-derived vaccines and other biological products for animal use is relatively well established

2. Overview: Virus-Serum-Toxin Act

VSTA prohibits the preparation, sale, barter, and exchange of "worthless, contaminated, dangerous, or harmful virus, serum, toxin, or analogous products intended for use in the treatment of domestic animals."[86] With some minor exceptions, VSTA also requires that all entities that prepare, sell, barter, exchange or ship such products have a license and comply with the regulations enacted by the Secretary of Agriculture.[87] Under VSTA, the federal government has the authority to inspect all biological products coming into the country[88] and to regulate the preparation and sale of such products within the United States.[89] CVB has broad inspection powers, permitting inspection of any facility that produces biologics at any hour, both day and night.[90]

A violation of VSTA is punishable as a misdemeanor and can result in up to a $1,000 fine or one year in jail.[91] The 1985 Amendments expanded the Secretary of Agriculture's rulemaking authority by authorizing the promulgation of rules and regulations necessary to carry out the act.[92] Additionally, the 1985 Amendments expanded USDA's inspection power by permitting inspection of any establishment that produces or sells biologics, rather than just licensed establishments.[93] USDA has enacted regulations to carry out VSTA and its goal of ensuring the safety and effectiveness of veterinary biologics.[94] Generally, states may not create additional restrictions, except in the case that such additional regulations are necessary to control local disease.[95]

3. Critical Elements in the APHIS Regulatory Requirements

a. Veterinary Biologics Defined

The mechanism of action is the primary distinguishing feature that determines whether a potential product is a biologic regulated by CVB, a new animal drug regulated by CVM, or an insecticide regulated by EPA. Biological products are defined by APHIS as those that act primarily through the direct stimulation, supplementation, enhancement, or modulation of the immune system or immune response and are intended for the treatment of animals.[96]

b. *Licensing*[97]

Manufacturers of veterinary biologicals must hold a U.S. Veterinary Biologics Establishment License for each manufacturing site and a U.S. Veterinary Biologic Product License for each biological product that the establishment intends to prepare.[98] APHIS will not issue one type of license without the manufacturer satisfying requirements for both establishment and at least one product license.[99] Before issuing an Establishment License, the Administrator must inspect the facility and equipment of the establishment and ensure that it is in compliance with all applicable regulations.[100] In order to obtain a Product License, the establishment must demonstrate the "purity, safety, potency, and efficacy of each product."[101] For each biological product, the establishment must prepare an Outline of Production and place it on file with APHIS,[102] as well as create a label that must be submitted to APHIS for its approval.[103]

> **Practice Points**
>
> **Licenses and Permits Commonly Issued by APHIS for Veterinary Biologic Products:**
>
> — Biologics Establishment License (for each manufacturing site)
> — Biologics Product License (for each product)
> — Conditional License (under emergency conditions, with proof of efficacy/safety)
> — Research and Evaluation Permit
> — Distribution and Sale Permit
> — Transit Shipment Only Permit

Conditional licensure is available in order to meet an emergency condition, limited market, local situation, or other special circumstance.[104] Under conditional licensure, a manufacturer is allowed to develop efficacy data while marketing a product, having demonstrated purity, safety, and a reasonable expectation of efficacy. CVB generally requires those holding conditional licensure to conduct additional efficacy studies and/or to develop additional data to support the validity of a proposed potency test. An important use of conditional licenses has been in allowing rapid access to the market for products designed to counter emerging diseases and unmet needs. For example, the first West Nile Virus vaccine was originally marketed under a conditional license before a regular product license was issued.

c. Permits

In order for a facility to import biologics, it must first obtain a permit.[105] Permits are divided into three categories: (1) Research and Evaluation; (2) Distribution and Sale; and (3) Transit Shipment Only.[106] The regulations restrict the importation of biologics from certain countries, such as those countries known to have exotic diseases.[107] Additionally, although the Department of Homeland Security is in charge of physically inspecting the imported biologics, the USDA is still given the authority to develop the governing regulations.

d. Standard Requirements

The regulations provide detailed standard requirements for biological products. They specify standard procedures for various kinds of tests as well as specific requirements for many different types of biologics.[108] Additionally, the regulations provide for production requirements and require the establishment to create an Outline of Production for each biological product that it produces.[109]

e. Record Keeping

The regulations also require record keeping. The establishments must create and maintain records of "successive steps in the development and preparation of biological products."[110] Records of the quantity and location of each biological product and a record of all labels currently in use must also be kept.[111] Additionally, the facility must record information pertaining to all animals maintained in the facility, as well as the disposition of every animal used in the preparation of biologics.[112]

f. Adverse Event Reports

CVB maintains a passive adverse event reporting system. End users of veterinary biologics products are not required to report adverse events. However, manufacturers of veterinary biologics are obligated to inform CVB immediately when they are aware of problems with the purity, potency, safety, efficacy, preparation, testing or distribution of a product.[113] Manufacturers must also contemporaneously record and maintain information that will allow the creation of such reports.[114] In practice, information that would lead to stoppage of sale and distribution is immediately reported to CVB, with manufacturers maintaining records of all adverse events reported to them, which are then made available to CVB as requested during inspection. Currently, these reports are not periodically transmitted to CVB. However, this is an area of regulatory interest.[115]

g. Enforcement Procedures

The Secretary may revoke or suspend both licenses and permits, after an opportunity for a hearing, if he determines that that the license or permit is being used to facilitate the production or movement of any worthless, contaminated, dangerous, or harmful biological product contrary to the VSTA.[116] Additionally, under the VSTA, the USDA has the power to detain, seize, or condemn any biological product that is in violation of the Act.[117]

h. Exemptions to the Regulations

There are several statutory and regulatory exemptions to the VSTA and its implementing regulations. The USDA itself may be exempted from one or more of the requirements for biological products used in federal disease eradication programs or an emergency.[118] Additionally, veterinarians and animal owners can be exempted from the establishment and product licensure requirements under certain circumstances. USDA continues to have the authority to enforce the statutory provision prohibiting the sale, barter or exchange of a worthless, contaminated, dangerous or harmful virus, serum, toxin or analogous product. Veterinarians can prepare and use biologic products in the course of their professional practice outside of the licensure and regulatory requirements.[119] Animal owners also can prepare and use biological products for their own animals outside of the licensure and regulatory requirements.[120] (This has interesting implications in today's climate of large corporations controlling the production of millions or billions of food animals.) Finally, the Administrator can exempt those people who prepare and distribute biologics within the same state pursuant to a state license if he or she has determined that the state program effectively reviews products for purity, potency, safety and efficacy.[121] The only state that has such authority is California.[122]

4. The Agricultural Bioterrorism Protection Act of 2002[123]

In March 2005, the USDA issued final rules implementing the Agricultural Bioterrorism Protection Act of 2002: Possession, Use, and Transfer of Biological Agents and Toxins.[124] The regulations govern the "possession, use, and transfer of biological agents or toxins that have been determined to have the potential to pose a severe threat to both human and animal health, to animal health, or to animal products."[125] Under these regulations, those persons who possess, use, or transfer a listed agent or toxin[126] must register with APHIS and agree to comply with all safety procedures. Such regulations are intended to ensure safety and protect against terrorism.

5. Animal Health Protection Act

Another overlapping authority is the Animal Health Protection Act (AHPA).[127] The AHPA was intended to consolidate animal quarantine and related laws, some dating from the late 1800s, and provide new authority in one flexible statutory framework in order to allow APHIS to best protect the health and safety of all aspects of U.S. animal agriculture. At its essence, the AHPA allows APHIS to seize, destroy or prohibit entry into the United States of any "article" necessary to prevent the introduction into or dissemination within the United States of any pest or disease of livestock seize.[128] In turn, "article" is defined very broadly and includes "any material or tangible object that could harbor a pest or disease."[129] The relevance to veterinary biologic products is twofold. Due to the manufacturing methods and ingredients utilized in many products, they have the potential to be contaminated with extraneous organisms or materials. In such cases, APHIS could use the broad authority of the AHPA in considering the product an "article." Additionally, APHIS has a strong incentive to bring enforcement actions under the AHPA rather than the VSTA due to the substantial penalties available under the AHPA, which makes criminal penalties and civil fines of up to $500,000.[130]

6. Special Consideration for Biotech Biologics

The regulation of veterinary biologics is geared toward ensuring that the end product is pure, safe, potent, and effective, regardless of whether it is derived from modern biotechnology techniques. Whether a particular biotechnology-derived product will present novel regulatory issues is a fact-driven analysis. However, APHIS has previously addressed many of the issues presented by biotechnology-derived veterinary biologics. CVB uses risk analysis procedures to evaluate license applications for biotechnology-derived products. To facilitate their preparation of scientifically valid and credible risk analyses, CVB has developed a set of guidance documents called "Summary Information Formats" or "SIFs."[131] SIFs coherently identify the relevant information needed for CVB's risk analysis and guide potential applicants in evaluating data needs for potential products. There are several SIFs, with three addressing different categories of biotechnology products, one focused on environmental releases, and one addressing importation into the United States. CVB also provides examples of the completed forms to assist applicants in understanding the data requests.

The Category I SIF identifies the information and data an applicant must provide in order to allow for the characterization of recombinant microorganisms for inactivated (not living) biotechnology-derived veterinary biologics.[132] This category of SIF is appropriate for bacterins, killed viruses, subunit vaccines, monoclonal antibodies for therapeutic or prophylactic use, monoclonal antibodies, and expressed proteins for use in diagnostic test kits. The example provided by CVB is a complete Category I SIF for an inactivated, subunit feline immunodeficiency virus vaccine.[133] The Category II SIF identifies the information and data an applicant must provide in order to allow for the characterization of live biotechnology-derived vaccine microorganisms containing gene deletions and/or heterologous marker genes.[134] The example provided by CVB is for a live gene deleted (thymidine kinase negative) swine poxvirus vaccine.[135] The Category III SIF identifies the information and data an applicant must provide in order to allow for the characterization of biotechnology-derived live vector vaccines containing heterologous genes encoding immunizing antigens and/or other immune stimulants.[136] The example provided by CVB is a live swine pox-vectored vaccine expressing the envelop gene of the feline immunodeficiency virus.[137]

Additionally, the FDA and USDA have drafted a joint document on bioengineered plants in order to provide additional guidance.[138] The draft guidance document addresses considerations for filing for a Veterinary Biologics Product License as well as for filing for an NADA when bioengineered plants are used. For example, the guidance document notes that the manufacturer should provide detailed information about the source plant, the host plant biology, and the recombinant DNA constructs or viral vectors used.[139] There are also certain processes that must be described in the product's Outline of Production, such as steps of the purification process.[140]

The guidance document seems particularly concerned with ensuring that the manufacturer address environmental concerns, such as confinement measures.[141] The document discusses measures that the manufacturer should take in transporting and storing bioengineered plants so that they do not adversely affect the environment.[142]

Depending upon the technology utilized, there may be other regulatory factors involved as well. For example, certain bioengineered products are prohibited altogether in the absence of notice to the Administrator of APHIS or a permit.[143] CVB will take the lead and typically interact with other governmental offices that have regulatory input into the product. Therefore, it is in an applicant's best interest to initiate discussions with the agency during the early stages of product development.

H. Conclusion

CVM and APHIS have well-established and comprehensive programs to regulate animal drugs and biological products, respectively. The clarity of the pathway for the newer biotechnology-derived products, however, depends largely on the nature of the technology used. At least for the moment, those pathways seem clear at APHIS, while those at CVM appear to be more of a work in progress.

Notes

1. Federal Food, Drug, and Cosmetic Act, 21 U.S.C. § 301 (2000 & Supp. III 2003).
2. Virus-Serum-Toxin Act, 21 U.S.C. §§ 151-159 (2002 & Supp. III 2003).
3. Federal Insecticide Fungicide and Rodenticide Act, 7 U.S.C. §§ 136–136y (2000 & Supp. III 2003).
4. 21 U.S.C. § 391(c) (2000 & Supp. III 2003); 21 C.F.R. § 510.4 (2005).
5. Products intended to kill fleas, ticks, and other pests are potentially subject to regulation as both animal drugs under the FFDCA and pesticides under the FIFRA. A 1973 Memorandum of Understanding (MOU) between EPA and FDA seeks to coordinate the actions of the agencies and eliminate overlaps. 38 Fed. Reg. 24,233 (Sept. 6, 1973), republished as FDA Compliance Policy Guide (CPG) No. 7155b.03 (Oct. 1, 1980). The CPG was partially superseded by an FDA/EPA MOU. 48 Fed. Reg. 22,799 (May 20, 1983), stayed (48 Fed. Reg. 37,077) (August 16, 1983). Generally speaking, products falling within the definitions of a pesticide and an animal drug are regulated as a "drug" by FDA if the product operates systemically, whereas EPA will regulate as "pesticide" products that act externally.
6. FDA has regulatory authority over veterinary drugs, including setting limits on animal drug residues in poultry, fish, and livestock food products. However, USDA's Food Safety and Inspection Service (FSIS) is largely responsible for the anti-mortem, slaughter, and post-slaughter wholesomeness of meat, poultry, and eggs entering interstate commerce. Federal Meat Inspection Act, 21 U.S.C. § 601 (2000 & Supp. III 2003); Poultry Products Inspection Act, 21 U.S.C. § 451 (2000 & Supp. III 2003); Egg Products Inspection Act, 21 U.S.C. § 1031 (2000 & Supp. III 2003). For example, control of microbial contamination of food of animal origin is generally within FSIS's jurisdiction. However, FDA has jurisdiction to prohibit the use of an antimicrobial in a food animal when use of the antimicrobial is "not shown to be safe" because the antimicrobial, by selection pressure, gene mutation, or otherwise, contributes to development and spread of antibiotic-resistant microorganisms, and to human infections of antibiotic resistant microorganisms when people consume food. Final Decision of the Commissioner, Withdrawal of Approval of the New Animal Drug Application for Enrofloxacin in Poultry, Docket No. 2000N-1571 (U.S. Health & Human Services, July 27, 2005) [hereinafter Enrofloxacin Decision].
7. FDA's primary drug-related authority for the regulation of both human and animal drugs is contained in Chapter V of the FFDCA, and many of the act's

other provisions (*e.g.,* adulteration, misbranding, establishment registration, drug listing, inspectional authority) do not distinguish between animal and human use drugs. To the extent FDA imposes identical or similar requirements on the manufacturers of human and animal drugs, FDA's veterinary requirements are summarized and the reader is generally referred to the chapters discussing FDA regulation of human drugs.

8. "The term 'device'... means an instrument... which is (2) intended for use in diagnosis of disease ... in man or *other animal* . . . or (3) intended to affect the structure or function of the body of man *or other animal.* . . ." 21 U.S.C. §§ 321(h)(2), (3) (2000 & Supp. III 2003) (emphasis supplied). Additionally, many diagnostic devices used for detection of diseases in animals are regulated by APHIS rather than FDA if they work via an immunologic mechanism of action.

9. Unlike manufacturers of devices for human use, manufacturers of devices for veterinary use are not required to register their establishments or list devices in commerce, nor is there a premarket submission requirement. How FDA Regulates Veterinary Devices, http://www.fda.gov/cvm/regofdevices.htm.

10. For example, according to the Animal Health Institute (AHI), the animal health products industry trade association, 2004 net U.S. sales for all animal health products (drugs, biologicals, feed additives, and insecticides) was about $5 billion. An animal drug with annual sales of $100 million, of which there are not many, would be considered a "blockbuster." *Id.* By contrast, many individual human drugs have annual sales in the billions, and Pfizer's cholesterol-lowering drug Lipitor, the world's largest-selling drug, had worldwide sales in 2003 of over $9 billion. Pfizer, Performance Report: Letter to Shareholders, http://www.pfizer.com/pfizer/are/investors_reports/annual_2003/review/p2003ar01_02_03.jsp.

11. 2004 appropriations and Full Time Equivalents (FTE) by center: CVM ($88,897/FTE 631), CDER ($476,220/FTE 3,205), CFSAN ($410,674/FTE 2,987), CDRH ($ 224,664/FTE 1,644), and CBER ($168,700/FTE 1,064), Food and Drug Administration, All Purpose Table – Total Program Level (Dollars in Thousands), http://www.fda.gov/oc/oms/ofm/budget/2005/BIB/apt-totalproglev.html.

12. Passage of the Animal Drug User Fee Act of 2003 (ADUFA), Pub. L. No. 108-130, 117 Stat. 1361 (codified at 21 U.S.C. § 379j-12 (2000 & Supp. III 2003)), may help advance the timeliness of product approvals at CVM as it did at CDER with implementation of user fees for human use pharmaceuticals. *See* http://www.fda.gov/cvm/adufa.html. *See also* Guidance for Industry, Animal Drug User Fees and Fee Waivers and Reductions, CVM Guidance 170 (March 15, 2004), http://www.fda.gov/cvm/Guidance/published.html [hereinafter CVM Guidance Page, all CVM's guidance will be cited by title and number, http://www.fda.gov/cvm/Guidance/published.html].

13. For example, approval of "Plan B," a morning-after pill for over-the-counter (OTC) use, has been delayed several times, notwithstanding positive advisory committee recommendations. It has been widely speculated that FDA's slowness in approving the product is based on conservative opposition that the product's OTC availability could promote promiscuity among teenagers. *See* Marc Kaufman, *FDA Commissioner Steps Down after Rocky Two-Month Tenure*, WASH. POST, Sept. 24, 2005, at A-7; *see also* Marc Kaufman, *Decision on Plan B Called Very Unusual*, WASH. POST, Oct. 13, 2005, at A-9.

14. CVM's Web page has links to many of CVM's activities, policies, and regulations for biotechnology, including those pertaining to animal drugs and genetically engineered animals, cloning, animal feeds, and genetically engineered plants, http://www.fda.gov/cvm/bioengineered.html.

15. Pew, Initiative on Food and Biotechnology, *Biotech in the Barnyard: Implications of Genetically Engineered Animals*, http://www.pewagbiotech.org, (2002); Pew, Initiative on Food and Biotechnology, *Future Fish: Issues in Science and Regulation of Transgenic Fish* (2003), http://www.pewagbiotec.org; Pew, Initiative on Food and Biotechnology, *Bugs in the System: Issues in the Science and Regulation of Genetically Modified Insects* (2004), http://www.pewagbiotech.org; NATIONAL RESEARCH COUNCIL, ANIMAL BIOTECHNOLOGY: SCIENCE BASED CONCERNS (Natl. Academies Press, 2002); Executive Office of the President, Council on Environmental Quality and Office of Science and Technology Policy, 2001, Case Studies of Environmental Regulation of Biotechnology (Washington, D.C.; OSTP), http://www.ostp.gov/html/012201.html (CEQ-OSTP 2001). The Council on Environmental Quality case studies consist of an introduction and six case studies: (1) salmon, (2) Bt-Maize, (3) soybean, (4) pharmaceutical producing animal, (5) bioremediation using trees, and (6) bioremediation using bacteria.

16. Between 1980 and 1987 the U.S. House of Representatives House Science and Technology Committee held numerous hearings to examine the laws potentially applicable to the regulation of the new biotech products. *See, e.g.*, Staff of Subcomm. on Investigations and Oversight, Comm. on Sci. and Tech., The Environmental Implications of Genetic Engineering, 98th Cong. (1984).

17. Coordinated Framework for the Regulation of Biotechnology, 51 Fed. Reg. 23,301 (Exec. Off. of the Pres./Off. of Sci. and Tech. Policy, June 26, 1986). The Coordinated Framework examined the regulatory authorities of FDA, USDA, EPA, and NIH over various biotechnology products and set out an overall approach intended to fill gaps in and coordinate potentially overlapping agency regulation.

18. 21 C.F.R. § 552.2120 (2005). Bovine growth hormone occurs naturally in cows. Recombinant bovine growth hormone (r-bST) was approved by FDA to enhance milk production in dairy cows. While CVM examined in great detail the safety and effectiveness of the drug and the potential environmental impacts,

public concerns about biotechnology and other issues resulted in a protracted approval process spanning many years. *See* Mandala Project, TED Case Studies Number 399, Bovine Growth Hormone (rbST) and Dairy Trade, (TED/BST), http://www.american.edu/TED/bst.htm [hereinafter TED/BST].

19. http://www.aphis.usda.gov/ws/rabies/vaccine.html.

20. FDA/CVM, Update on Livestock Cloning, July 13, 2000, http://www.fda.gov/cvm/CVM_Updates/clones.htm; FDA/CVM, Animal Cloning: A Risk Assessment (Draft, Oct. 21, 2003), http://www.fda.gov/cvm/Documents/CLRAES.pdf; L. Bren, *Cloning: Revolution or Evolution in Animal Production?*, FDA Veterinarian Newsletter, V. XVIII, No. V (September/October 2003), http://www.fda.gov/cvm/Sep-Oct03.htm; Pew, 2002; Pew, 2003; Pew, 2004; NAS, 2002, op cit at n.17.

21. L. Crawford, 28th Annual National Food Policy Conference Speech (Washington, D.C., 2005, http://www.fda.gov/oc/speeches/2005/nfpc0919.html. Commissioner Crawford's oral presentation outlines FDA's plans for continuing development of FDA's position on cloned and transgenic animals, although his resignation shortly after the speech may delay the finalization of an FDA policy.

22. CVM's basic authority over animal drugs is found at 21 U.S.C. § 360b (2000 & Supp. III 2003), with regulations in 21 C.F.R. pt. 500 (2005). CVM's Web site (http://www.fda/cvm.gov) contains many guidance documents and procedures of value to the practitioner. In addition, the CVM's Web site contains CVM's *Policies and Procedures Manual.* The FDA Web site (http://www.fda.gov) also has links to various FDA compliance and enforcement materials, such as the *Inspection Operation Manual,* the *Compliance Policy Guide Manual,* established dockets for rules and petitions, and warning letters. Familiarity with these documents is critical to an understanding of how CVM operates.

23. Even today the FFDCA does not contain a separate and distinct definition of "animal" or "veterinary" drugs; "drug" encompasses "articles" intended for use in or affecting the structure or function of "man *or other animals.*" 21 U.S.C. § 321(g) (2000 & Supp. III 2003) (emphasis supplied).

24. Animal Drug Amendments Act of 1968, Pub. L. No. 90-399, 82 Stat. 342 (codified at 21 U.S.C. § 301) (2000 & Supp. 2005) added section 512 to the FFDCA.

25. The regulation of animal drugs as well as human drugs can be traced back to the Pure Food and Drugs Act of 1906, 59 Pub. L. No. 384, 59th Cong. ch. 3915, § 67; 34 Stat. 768 (1906) (codified at 21 U.S.C. § 301) (2000 & Supp. 2005). The Federal Food, Drug, and Cosmetic Act of 1938 greatly expanded the regulatory requirements and FDA's authority of human and veterinary drugs, adding essentially the requirement to prove a drug is "safe" before approval, Fed. Food, Drug & Comestics Act, Pub. L. No. 75-717, 75 Stat. 1040 (1938) (codified at 21 U.S.C. § 355) (2000 & Supp. III 2003). The FFDCA has been amended many times since 1938. The Food Additive Amendments of 1958, Pub.

L. No. 85-929, 72 Stat. 1784, 21 U.S.C. § 301 (2000 & Supp. III 2003), addressed largely the regulation of food additives, including residues of animal drugs, while the Drug Amendments Act of 1962, Pub. L. No. 87-781, 76 Stat. 780 (codified at 21 U.S.C. § 301 ((2000 & Supp. III 2003) mandated the efficacy requirements for drugs, including animal drugs.

26. However, it was not until 1983 that what is now CVM was given responsibility for regulating the human food safety aspect of animal drug approval and use, Food & Drug Admin., Statements of Organization, Functions and Delegations of Authority, 48 Fed. Reg. 337 (Food & Drug Admin., Jan. 4, 1983). Until that time the Bureau of Foods had the responsibility for establishing safe drug residues in food.

27. Enrofloxacin Decision, *supra* note 8, at 94.

28. 21 U.S.C. § 321(v), (w) (2000 & Supp. III 2003). Conceptually, products regulated by APHIS operate in a "safe harbor" with respect to the FFDCA. They are subject to VSTA and APHIS's implementing regulations and policies, but not to the FFDCA or to FDA's implementing regulations or policies. *See* 21 U.S.C. § 352(c) (2000 & Supp. III 2003); 21 C.F.R. § 510.4 (2005). However, the definition of a "new animal drug" or "drug" under the FFDCA is sufficiently broad to encompass virtually any animal health product, and if APHIS does not assert jurisdiction over a biological product, the product will likely be regulated by FDA.

29. 21 U.S.C. §§ 331, 360b (2000 & Supp. III 2003). The reader is referred to Chapter X, *supra*, containing a detailed discussion of the definition of "drug" under the FFDCA.

30. 21 U.S.C. § 360b(a)(1) (2000 & Supp. III 2003). CMC Guidance, *supra* note 14: *Guidance for Industry #83: Chemistry, Manufacturing and Controls Changes to an Approved NADA or ANADA* (Draft Guidance #83), June 1999; *Guidance for Industry #169: Drug Substance: Chemistry, Manufacturing, and Controls Information* (January 2004).

31. 21 U.S.C. § 360b(b) (2000 & Supp. III 2003); 21 C.F.R. pt. 514 (2005). One or more "adequate and well-controlled" studies are necessary to establish by substantial evidence that a new animal drug is safe. 21 C.F.R. § 514.117 (2005).

32. 21 C.F.R. pt. 514 (2005).

33. CVM Guidance Page, *supra* note 14, Guidance to Industry # 28, Animal Drug Applications Expedited Review Guideline (June 1990); CVM Guidance to Industry # 121, Expedited Review for New Animal Drug Applications for Pathogen Reduction Claims (March 6, 2001).

34. 21 U.S.C. § 360b(c)(2) (2000 & Supp. III 2003). While many of the FDA requirements for ANADAs parallel those for human drugs, there are significant differences, largely based on the differences in veterinary and human medicine and the use of drugs in food-producing animals and in humans. For example, while an ANDA sponsor can only be required to demonstrate that its

product is bioavailable and bioequivalent, CVM is not so limited and can request, in addition to bioequivalence data in each species for which the drug is approved and tissue residue studies in each such species, "such other data or studies as [CVM] considers appropriate based on scientific principles," 21 U.S.C. § 369b(c)(H)(2) (2000 & Supp. III 2003). Another example involves drugs produced by biotechnology. Biotechnology-produced animal drugs are excluded from the abbreviated approval process and patent term restoration provisions. The situation involving human biological drugs is more complex and is currently subject to debate. *See* Chapter __ on human drug approval and follow-on biologics. *See also* CVM Guidance Page, *supra* note 14, *CVM Guidance to Industry # 35, Bioequivalence Guideline*, October 9, 2002.

35. 21 C.F.R. pt. 207 (2000 & Supp. III 2003); 21 U.S.C. § 379j-12 (2000 & Supp. III 2003). The Animal Drug User Fee Act (2003) establishes four different kinds of user fees: (1) fees for certain types of animal drug applications and supplements, (2) annual fees for certain animal drug products, (3) annual fees for certain establishments where such products are made, and (4) annual fees for certain sponsors of animal drug applications and/or investigational animal drug submissions. S*upra* note 14.

36. 21 C.F.R. § 514.1 (2005); 21 C.F.R. pt. 25 (2005).

37. 21 U.S.C. § 360b(c) (2000 & Supp. III 2003); 21 C.F.R. pt. 514, subpt. B (2005).

38. 21 C.F.R. pts. 210, 225, 226, 202, 510, subpt. D, § 514.80 (2005).

39. 21 C.F.R. pt. 514 (2005).

40. For example, sponsors are required to submit advertising within 30 days of use, and pre-launch advertising is subject to pre-approval review. As with human-use drugs, FDA does not have jurisdiction to regulate advertising (as opposed to "labeling") of animal drugs available over-the-counter (OTC). Advertising of OTC animal drugs is subject to jurisdiction of the Federal Trade Commission.

41. 21 U.S.C. § 360b(d) (2000 & Supp. III 2003).

42. 21 C.F.R. pt. 514, subpt. B (2005).

43. 21 C.F.R. pt. 511 (2005). The "withdrawal period" is the period before slaughter during which the drug cannot be administered to the animal. It is intended to allow depletion of the drug and drug metabolites (residue) to a safe level. The tolerance is the safe level established based on residue depletion studies, toxicology data, and safety factors, as explained below.

44. 21 U.S.C. § 360b(a)(6) (2000 & Supp. III 2003).

45. CVM Guidance Page, *supra* note 14, Guidance to Industry # 33, Target Animal Safety Guidelines for New Animal Drug, June 1989 (Guidance # 33).

46. 21 U.S.C. § 360b (2000 & Supp. III 2003). Drugs for use in companion animals follow a pathway largely similar to drugs for human use, since such

drugs do not ordinarily implicate food safety issues and, therefore, do not require a residue tolerance.

47. CVM has no regulations defining "safe." The D.C. Circuit court has interpreted section 360b as requiring a risk/benefit analysis. Hess & Clark, Inc. v. FDA, 497 F.2d 975 (D.C. Cir. 1974); Rhone-Poulenc Inc. v. FDA, (D.C. Cir. 1979). However, FDA has concluded that, with respect to the human food safety evaluation of animal drug residues in food, the two cases have been implicitly overruled, FDA is not permitted to consider risks and benefits, and the standard for approval is "a reasonable certainty of no harm." Enrofloxacin Decision, *supra* note 8, at 84-107. *See also* CVM Guidance Page, *supra* note 14, CVM Guidance to Industry # 3, General Principles for Evaluating the Safety of Compounds Used in Food-Producing Animals (June 2005).

48. *Id. See also* Miller et al., *Food Safety Evaluation of Transgenic Animals,* FDA VETERINARIAN NEWSLETTER (March/April 1996), *available at* http://www.fda-gov/cum/4404.htm#TRFTOC19.

49. The Delaney Clause, added as part of the 1958 Food Safety Amendments, prohibits generally the use of a food additive if it is found to induce cancer when ingested by man or animal. The so-called "DES Proviso" was added in 1962. The Drug Amendments Act of 1962, Pub. L. No. 87-781, § 104(x)(1), 76 Stat. 780, 785 (codified at 21 U.S.C. §§ 348(c)(3)(A), 379e(b)(5)(B), 360(b)(d)(1)(I)). Generally the DES Proviso allows the use of a carcinogenic animal feed additive, provided the animal is not adversely affected and there is "no residue" remaining in the edible part of the tissue. The 1968 Animal Drug Amendments extended the DES Proviso to all residues of animal drugs, including those directly administered to the animal. Animal Drug Amendments Act of 1968, Pub. L. No. 90-399, § 10, 82 Stat. 342, 343 (codified at 21 U.S.C. § 360b).

50. 21 C.F.R. pt. 500, subpt. E (2005).

51. *Id.*

52. Some animal drugs may be administered in drinking water, primarily because water delivery may be the most, and in some cases the only, effective way to medicate the animal. Water medications are not generally mixed in feed and, therefore, are not ordinarily subject to the feed medication rules.

53. 21 C.F.R. pts. 515, 558 (2005). The Animal Drug Availability Act (1996) amended Section 512(m) of the FFDCA to revise and simplify FDA regulation of drugs used in animal feed, 21 C.F.R. pts. 514, 515, 558 (2005).

54. 21 C.F.R. § 514.80 and pts. 515, 558 (2005), and 21 C.F.R. §§ 510.301, 510.305 (2005). The NADA holder obtains feed mill labeling for the drug at the time of approval of the NADA and the label is available to the feed mill operator.

55. Animal Drug Availability Act of 1996, Pub. L. No. 104-250, 110 Stat. 3151 (codified at 21 U.S.C. § 301).

56. *See generally* CVM Guidance Page, *supra* note 14, *CVM Guidance for Industry* # 120, Veterinary Feed Directive Regulation (March 1, 2000).

57. 21 C.F.R. §§ 514.1, 514.4 (2005).

58. The Animal Medicinal Drug Use Clarification Act of 1994, Pub. L. No. 103-396, 52 Stat. 1040 (codified at 21 U.S.C. § 301). *See also* 21 C.F.R. pt. 530 (2005). As a matter of enforcement discretion, absent a significant safety concern, FDA ordinarily leaves enforcement of off-label animal drug use in companion animals to the states.

59. *Id.*

60. Orphan Drug Act of 1983, Pub. L. No. 97-414, 96 Stat. 2049 (codified at 21 U.S.C. §§ 360aa-360dd).

61. "Minor species" are defined as "animals other than humans that are not major species." "Major species" are cattle, horses, swine, chickens, turkeys, dogs, cats, and other species added by regulations. "Minor use" is defined as a drug use in a major species for an "indication that occurs infrequently and only in a small number of animals or in limited geographical areas and only in a small number of animals annually." Minor Use and Minor Species Animal Health Act of 2004, Pub. L. No. 108-282, 118 Stat. 891 (to be codified at 21 U.S.C. § 301).

62. *Id.*

63. CVM has established a MUMS office. Links to various MUMS-related documents are *available at* http://www.fda.gov/cvm/minortoc.htm.

64. 21 U.S.C. § 360 ccc (2000 & Supp. III 2003).

65. 21 U.S.C. § 360 ccc-1 (2000 & Supp. III 2003).

66. 21 U.S.C. § 360 ccc(a)(3)(A), 360 ccc(a)(2) (2000 & Supp. III 2003).

67. 21 U.S.C. § 360 ccc-2 (2000 & Supp. III 2003); HHS/FDA, Designation of New Animal Drugs for Minor Use or Minor Species, Proposed Rule, 70 Fed. Reg. 56,394 (Sept. 27, 2005).

68. Significant animal health-related amendments to the FFDCA since 1980 include Generic Animal Drug and Patent Term Restoration Act of 1988, Pub. L. No. 100-670, 102 Stat. 3971 (codified at 21 U.S.C. § 301); Animal Medicinal Drug Use Clarification Act of 1994, Pub. L. No. 103-396, 108 Stat. 4153 (codified at 21 U.S.C. § 301); Animal Drug Availability Act of 1996, Pub. L. No. 104-250, 110 Stat. 3151 (codified at 21 U.S.C. § 301); Food and Drug Administration Modernization Act of 1997, Pub. L. No. 105-115, 111 Stat. 2296 (codified at 21 U.S.C. § 301); Animal Drug User Fee Act of 2003, Pub. L. No. 108-130, 117 Stat. 1361 (codified at 21 U.S.C. § 301); Minor Use and Minor Species Animal Health Act of 2004, Pub. L. No. 108-282, 118 Stat. 891 (codified at 21 U.S.C. § 301), http://www.fda.gov/opacom/laws/.

69. CVM Guidance, *supra* note 14, CVM, Guidance for Industry # 79: Dispute Resolution Procedures for Science-Based Decisions on Products Regulated by the Center for Veterinary Medicine (July 2005).

70. Separation of Functions; *ex parte* communications, 21 C.F.R. § 10.55 (2005); 21 C.F.R. pts. 512, 514 (2005) (confidentiality of INAD and NADA).

71. *See* http://www.fda.gov/cvm/bio_drugs.html.

72. HHS/FDA, *Guidance for Industry: Drugs, Biologics, and Medical Devices Derived from Bioengineered Plants for Use in Humans and Animals* (Draft Guidance, September 2002), http://www.fda.gov/cvm/bio_feeds.html.

73. CVM Guidance, *supra* note. 14, CVM *Guidance for Industry (#177), Specifications: Test Procedures and Acceptance Criteria for New Biotechnological/Biological Veterinary Medicinal Products*, VICH GL-40, Draft Guidance (May 24, 2005).

74. CVM letter to the University of Illinois, September 29, 2003, http://www.fda.gov/cvm/bio_drugs.html.

75. TED/BST, *supra* note 18.

76. 21 U.S.C. § 321(g)) (2000 and Supp. 2003).

77. Pew, 2001, *supra* note 15, at 41; FDA/CVM, Questions and Answers and Answers About Transgenic Fish, http://www.fda.gov/cvm/transgen.htm; FDA/CVM, Letter to Land Grant University Presidents, May 13, 2003, http://www.fda.gov/cvm/bio-drugs.html; FDA/CVM, FDA Statement Regarding Glofish, December 9, 2003, http://www.fda.gov/cvm/bio_drugs.html.

78. Crawford Speech, *supra* note 21.

79. Enrofloxacin Decision, *supra* note 6, at 120.

80. *Supra* notes 17, 18, 20.

81. CVB's basic authority over the regulation is found at 21 U.S.C. § 151 (2000 & Supp. III 2003), with regulations in 9 C.F.R. pts. 101-123 (2005). CVB's Web site (http://www.aphis.usda.gov/vs/cvb/) contains many guidance materials of value to the practitioner.

82. Now codified at 21 U.S.C. §§ 151-159 (2000 & Supp. III 2003).

83. Congressional Research Service, The Virus-Serum-Toxin Act: A Brief History and Analysis (Code RS22014), Jan. 3, 2005.

84. 21 U.S.C. § 151 (2000 & Supp. III 2003).

85. Prior to the 1985 amendments to VSTA, USDA's jurisdiction was construed to cover only *interstate* shipment of finished veterinary biological products, with FDA jurisdiction over all other such products, such as those made and sold within a single state. Grand Laboratories, Inc. v. Harris, 66 F.2d 1288 (8th Cir. 1981) (*en banc*). The Homeland Security Act of 2002, which among other things consolidated many different agency border inspection functions, transferred certain functions pertaining to VSTA from USDA to the Department of Homeland Security, including principally the physical inspection of imports. 6 U.S.C. § 231 (2000 & Supp. III 2003). However, USDA still maintains responsibility for VSTA regulations and policies. *See also* Viruses, Serums, Toxins, and Analogous Products; Experimental Products and Exempted Products, 42 Fed. Reg. 30,128 (Aug. 13, 1987).

86. 21 U.S.C. § 151 (2000 & Supp. III 2003).

87. *Id.*

88. 21 U.S.C. § 153 (2000 & Supp. III 2003).
89. 21 U.S.C. § 154 (2000 & Supp. III 2003).
90. 21 U.S.C. § 157 (2000 & Supp. III 2003).
91. 21 U.S.C. § 158 (2000 & Supp. III 2003).
92. *Id.*
93. *Id.*
94. VSTA implementing regulations promulgated by APHIS are found in 9 C.F.R. pts. 101-123 (2005).
95. *See* Viruses, Serums and Toxins and Analogous Products: Restrictions on Distribution and Use, 57 Fed. Reg. 38,758 (U.S. Dep't of Agric., Aug. 27, 1992) (to be codified at 9 C.F.R. pt. 102 (2005)).
96. 9 C.F.R. § 101.2 (2005).
97. *See* V.S. Memorandum 800.50: Basic License Requirements and Guidelines for Submission of Materials in Support of Licensure (http://www.aphis.usda.gov/vs/cvb/memos/2002/800_50.pdf). This guidance document provides detailed information relative to specific information and data requirements.
98. Formerly, manufacturers of human biologics were also required to obtain both a product and establishment license. However, currently FDA requires only a single license. FDA regulation of biological products is discussed in detail in Chapter I, *supra*. 9 C.F.R. § 102.2 (2005).
99. *Id.*
100. 9 C.F.R. § 102.4 (2005).
101. 9 C.F.R. § 102.3 (2005).
102. 9 C.F.R. § 114.8 (2005).
103. 9 C.F.R. § 102.3(b)(2)(iv) (2005).
104. 9 C.F.R. § 102.6 (2005).
105. 9 C.F.R. § 104.1 (2005).
106. 9 C.F.R. § 104.2 (2005).
107. *Id.*
108. *See* 9 C.F.R. pt. 113 (2005).
109. 9 C.F.R. § 114.8-9 (2005).
110. 9 C.F.R. § 116.1 (2005).
111. 9 C.F.R. § 116.2-3 (2005).
112. 9 C.F.R. § 116.6 (2005).
113. 9 C.F.R. § 116.5(b) (2005).
114. 9 C.F.R. § 116.1(b) (2005).
115. APHIS has published a proposed rule that would require periodic submission of summary adverse event information to CVB. 70 Fed. Reg. 48,325 (Aug. 17, 2005) (to be codified at 9 C.F.R. § 116.9).
116. 9 C.F.R. § 105.1 (2005).
117. 9 C.F.R. pt. 118 (2005).
118. 9 C.F.R. § 106.1 (2005).

119. 21 U.S.C. § 154a(2) (2000 & Supp. III 2003); 9 C.F.R. § 107.1 (2005).
120. 21 U.S.C. § 154a(1) (2000 & 2003).
121. 21 U.S.C. § 154a(3) (2000 & Supp. III 2003); 9 C.F.R. § 107.2 (2005).
122. Cal. Food & Agric. Code § 14288 (2005).
123. Public Health Security and Bioterrorism Preparedness and Response Act of 2002, Pub. L. No. 107-188, Title II, Subtitle B (§ 211-213) (2002) (codified at 7 U.S.C. § 8401) (2000 & Supp. III 2003).
124. 70 Fed. Reg. 13,242 (USDA, March 18, 2005) (to be codified at 9 C.F.R. pt. 121).
125. 9 C.F.R. § 121.2 (2005).
126. Veterinary Services Select Agents are those listed in 9 C.F.R. § 121.3 (2005). Those intending to work with these agents must register and have a certificate from the APHIS Administrator. Overlap select agents subject to both APHIS and CDC are listed in 9 C.F.R. § 121.4 (2005). Those intending to work with overlap select agents, those of both agricultural and public health interest, can register with either APHIS or CDC. The agencies will coordinate, and both will be involved in the process of providing a certificate from both the APHIS Administrator and the HHS Secretary. 9 C.F.R. § 121.7 (2005).
127. Congress worked on varying versions of the Animal Health Protection Act for more than 18 years before the AHPA became a part of the Farm Security and Rural Investment Act of 2002, better known as the 2002 Farm Bill. The relevant provisions are primarily codified at 7 U.S.C. § 8301.
128. 7 U.S.C. § 8303 (2000 & Supp. III 2003).
129. 7 U.S.C. § 8302(2) (2000 & Supp. III 2003).
130. 7 U.S.C. § 8313 (2000 & Supp. III 2003).
131. *Available at* http://www.aphis.usda.gov/vs/cvb/lpd/sifs.htm.
132. http://www.aphis.usda.gov/vs/cvb/lpd/sifs/sif_cat_I.htm.
133. http://www.aphis.usda.gov/vs/cvb/lpd/sifs/sif_cat_I_example.htm.
134. http://www.aphis.usda.gov/vs/cvb/lpd/sifs/sif_cat_II.htm.
135. http://www.aphis.usda.gov/vs/cvb/lpd/sifs/sif_cat_II_example.htm.
136. http://www.aphis.usda.gov/vs/cvb/lpd/sifs/sif_cat_III.htm.
137. http://www.aphis.usda.gov/vs/cvb/lpd/sifs/sif_cat_III_example.htm.
138. *See* Draft, *Guidance for Industry: Drugs, Biologics, and Medical Devices Derived from Bioengineered Plants for Use in Humans and Animals; Availability*, 67 Fed. Reg. 57,828 (USDA, Sept. 12, 2002). Although the comment period has closed, neither FDA nor USDA have announced any new or modified guidance on the subject.
139. *Id.*
140. *Id.*
141. *Id.*
142. *Id.*

143. 7 C.F.R. § 340 (2005). The regulations list those organisms that they consider to be plant pests at 7 C.F.R. § 340.2 (2005). There are certain exemptions, however, for "genetic material from any plant pest contained in *Escherichia coli* genotype K-12, sterile strains of *Saccharomyces cerevisiae*, or asporogenic strains of *Bacillus subtilis*." 340.2(b).

Chapter XV

Approval Process for Biotechnology Products in Agricultural Use

*Dr. J. Winston Porter**
Waste Policy Center
Leesburg, Virginia

This chapter deals with the approval process for biotechnology products used in agriculture. We will demonstrate this process by example, discussing the regulation of agricultural crops that have been genetically modified to impart a useful trait, such as pest resistance or herbicide tolerance. These are the primary products in this category. Such crops have grown rapidly in the United States, with about 90 percent of soybeans, 70 percent of cotton, and 40 percent of corn being of the biotech variety. (Biotech crops are also referred to by some as genetically engineered or genetically modified crops.)

Our primary focus is the Coordinated Framework for Regulation of Biotechnology, a policy document regulating biotechnology products that

---

* The author wishes to acknowledge the very helpful assistance provided by various experts in the United States Environmental Protection Agency, Department of Agriculture, and Food and Drug Administration. Particular thanks are also expressed for the overall editorial support provided by Dr. Janet Andersen, Director of the Biopesticides and Pollution Prevention Division of the EPA.

was published by the U.S. Office of Science and Technology Policy in 1986. The Framework involves key roles for the U S. Environmental Protection Agency (EPA), the U.S. Department of Agriculture (USDA), and the U.S. Food and Drug Administration (FDA).

The Framework is summarized below, followed by more detailed discussions of the responsibilities of the three federal agencies. Following this information, we will briefly discuss the roles of states and of selected foreign countries in biotech crop regulation.

A. Coordinated Federal Framework

Biotech crops undergo a food safety and environmental review process conducted by the EPA, USDA, and FDA. Each agency operates under its own laws and regulations, and some of the mandates are somewhat overlapping. The three agencies often interact during their regulatory processes. Briefly, each agency's role is as follows:

- The USDA ensures that biotech products are not a pest to agriculture.
- The EPA protects human health and the environment.
- FDA's role is to protect the safety of the food supply and ensure proper labeling.

> **Practice Point**
>
> EPA, USDA and FDA all regulate genetically modified plants in some way. The USDA regulates agriculture. The EPA is concerned with human health and the environment. The FDA is concerned with a safe food supply and proper labeling.

All agricultural biotech plants are first reviewed by USDA to assess their potential to become a plant pest in the environment. A plant pest is an organism that can cause damage or disease in a plant or plant product. This definition is broader than most would think, and might encompass a crop that could damage another crop, in addition to the typical insect or mold "pest." The USDA's Animal and Plant Health Inspection Service (APHIS) regulates the safe testing of biotech plant varieties. APHIS issues field-testing permits annually based on facts about the new genes and gene products, the origin of the genes (bacteria, plant virus, plant, etc.), purpose of the test, manner in which the test will be conducted, and specific precautions to prevent escape of pollen, plants, or plant parts from the test site. Before commercialization, APHIS typically makes a determination of "nonregulated status" for the product. Some products, such as those that produce pharmaceutical compounds, require permits for production.

The EPA reviews a biotech product if the plant product is to produce a pesticide (i.e., an insecticide, fungicide, or herbicide). The agency regulates only the pesticidal substance within the plant, not the entire plant.

First, the EPA must grant an Experimental Use Permit (EUP) if field testing is 10 acres or more, even if there is a USDA permit. Additional approvals are needed if the experimental plants will end up in the food or animal feed supply, or the pollen from the plants can drift and pollinate food or feed crops.

An EPA registration or license to sell and distribute the product is required prior to commercial sales. Applicants must submit data showing that the pesticide does not pose an unreasonable risk to human health and the environment when used appropriately. EPA considers both human toxicity and ecotoxicity as well as allergenicity related to the pesticidal compound produced by the plant. EPA may prohibit the sale and distribution of a pesticide if it poses unacceptable risks, or restrict where and/or how the crop is grown to ensure that the product can be used without unacceptable risks.

FDA's process generally involves voluntary consultation aimed at ensuring that any new biotech foods are as safe as comparable foods that are already being consumed. Thus, new biotech foods are tested to determine if they are essentially the same as their non-biotech counterparts in terms of stability, allergenicity, and direct protein toxicity. FDA does not consider the pesticidal substances reviewed by EPA, but does focus on the rest of the food. FDA also has authority to remove from the market, or take action against, any food it believes to be unsafe. Some key questions FDA uses to determine if the biotech food is as safe as other food on the market are as follows:

- Is the substance produced from the inserted material safe?
- Does the inserted gene cause unexpected changes in the plant compared with the conventional variety of a given crop?

- Do nutrients, vitamins, and minerals in the new plant occur at the same level as in the conventionally bred plant?

More detail on the roles of the three federal agencies is provided below, followed by general discussions of the regulatory activities of the states and selected foreign countries.

B. Role of the Environmental Protection Agency

The EPA regulates products that contain pesticides and are regulated under the Federal Insecticide, Fungicide and Rodenticide Act (FIFRA). This act requires that all pesticides sold or distributed in the United States must be registered with the EPA unless they are specifically exempted. It is not the nature of the substance but its intended use that determines if a product is a pesticide. Thus, when a plant is genetically modified—for example, to ward off an insect pest—it serves the function of a traditional pesticide and is thereby subject to FIFRA regulations. EPA has exempted from regulation the natural pesticidal substances that occur in plants and traditional plant-breeding techniques to add or enhance desired traits.

> **Practice Point**
>
> The EPA is concerned primarily with pesticides, and it defines that broadly to include pesticides incorporated in the plant itself, if not occurring naturally.

The EPA also regulates the amount of pesticide residues that can be in the food or feed supply under the Federal Food, Drug and Cosmetic Act (FFDCA). Most of this law is the purview of FDA, but the authority to establish pesticide tolerances or exemptions from tolerance resides in the EPA.

In 1994, the Biopesticides and Pollution Prevention Division was established within EPA's Office of Pollution Prevention (OPP) to facilitate the registration of "biopesticides" or "biological pesticides."

There are several categories of biopesticides, but the category of interest here is called "plant-incorporated protectants" (PIPs). These are pesticidal substances that plants produce from added genetic material.

Examples of PIPs are crops that are genetically modified to produce traits such as insect resistance or plant virus tolerance. Herbicide-tolerant plants are not considered PIPs because the regulated pesticide is the conventional chemical herbicide. In such cases, EPA regulates the chemical herbicide and USDA and FDA regulate the herbicide-tolerant plant.

As with conventional pesticides, EPA can register PIPs only if they do not pose an unreasonable risk to human health and the environment and a tolerance or tolerance exemption meets the FFDCA standard of "reasonable certainty of no harm." All of the registered products to date have been granted tolerance exemptions because the substances produced did not show toxicity when tested at very high levels.

Any applicant for registration must have an EPA establishment number, which is provided by EPA's appropriate regional office. Next, the applicant is strongly encouraged to visit with EPA to explain its product and development plans. EPA will provide guidance on the testing required and, when needed, the regulatory process.

EPA's regulations do not require an Experimental Use Permit (EUP) when field trials will be less than 10 acres (cumulative) across the United States. However, if the PIP could be in the food or feed supply or be fed to animals that would enter the food supply, then a tolerance or tolerance exemption must be obtained before field trials are conducted, regardless of whether an EUP is required or not. An applicant may choose to test several closely related "genetic constructs" under one EUP, but a commercial registration would be for only a single genetic construct.

Based on field trials, laboratory studies, and other information, EPA scientists assess a wide variety of potential effects associated with the PIP.

These include acute reactions such as toxicity, allergenicity, and skin and eye irritations, as well as potential long-term effects such as cancer, birth defects, and reproductive and neurological system disorders. Such long-term testing has not been required for the products approved to date, which have all been proteins. However, other compounds that might be used as PIPs in the future may require such testing.

In addition, extensive ecological testing is done to assess potential risks to birds, fish, bees, aquatic invertebrates, and representative species of both predatory and parasitic insects important in controlling insect pests. Also, earthworms and springtails, which are part of the decomposition process, are tested for potential adverse effects from the PIP. The length of time it takes the PIP to be degraded in the environment is also determined. All of these data are used for a risk assessment that includes special consideration for children and workers, as well as endangered species.

EPA considers public comments for every new PIP and often holds Scientific Advisory Panel meetings to have outside experts peer-review its risk assessments. Before approving the registration of the PIP, EPA may also impose conditions on the registration in order to minimize the possibility of risks, such as the genes moving into a wild plant relative or the target insect developing resistance to the PIP.

Insect resistance is a concern for certain of the registered PIPs because similar, non-genetically engineered pesticides are also used by organic and conventional farmers and gardeners. EPA may also require post-registration monitoring of field insect populations to ensure that resistance is not developing. In addition, an annual report is required that indicates the amount and location of the PIP.

Time frames for EPA decisions vary by type of application, with a non-food use EUP usually taking about six months. A food-use EUP can take up to approximately 15 months if a Scientific Advisory Panel meeting is required. Time frames for a new PIP registration decision vary from approximately 12 to 24 months. EPA also has a fee system associated with its pesticide registration under the Pesticide Registration Improvement Act of 2004.

C. Role of the U.S. Department of Agriculture

The U.S. Department of Agriculture (USDA) has two major roles in dealing with genetically engineered organisms (GEOs), both of which are based on USDA's role in preventing plant pests in the environment. (As noted earlier, a plant pest is an organism that can cause damage or disease in a plant or plant product.) USDA's authorities over GEOs are derived from the Plant Protection Act (PPA) of 2000. The USDA activities regarding GEOs are conducted by the Animal and Plant Health Inspection Service (APHIS).

The first role is reviewing field-test permits for new plants that have the potential to become a plant pest in the environment. Developers of

Approval Process for Biotechnology Products in Agricultural Use

biotech products must obtain APHIS approval before releasing genetically engineered plants into the environment. Permits are not needed for laboratory or contained-greenhouse situations.

However, a permit is needed for a GEO that is a "regulated article" before it can be imported or moved through interstate transport. A regulated article is defined as "any organism that has been altered or produced through genetic engineering, if the donor organism, recipient organism or vector or vector agent belongs to any genera or taxa in the relevant regulations," and meets the definition of a plant pest.

> **Practice Point**
>
> The USDA reviews biotech products to be used in agriculture in order to ensure that they will not cause harm to agriculture and the natural ecosystem.

To obtain a permit, a researcher or plant breeder must provide detailed information on the regulated article, including the scientific details relating to its development and identity, the purposes for introduction, and the procedures, processes, and safeguards that will be employed to prevent escape and dissemination. A permit will be granted if APHIS determines that the conduct of the trial, under confinement conditions specified by the applicant or required by the agency, will not pose a plant pest risk.

Permits for environmental releases are generally processed within 120 days of receipt of a complete application. That period may be extended if an Environmental Impact Statement (EIS) is required in addition to an Environmental Assessment (EA). APHIS provides the state in which the release is planned with a copy of the application and the risk assessment prepared by the APHIS staff.

Before commercial use of a biotech plant that is not producing pharmaceuticals or industrial compounds, the applicant can petition APHIS for "nonregulated status." To support such a petition, the applicant must supply information on the biology of the crop, description of the transformation that has been done, identification of the donor genes and regulatory sequences, genetic analysis, and results from the field trials, including agronomic performance and any potential environmental effects.

APHIS then evaluates potential plant pest risks, the products produced by the new genes (new enzymes or changes in the plant's metabolism), increase in weediness, potential impacts on other plants, animals, and insects, changes in agricultural practices, and the potential for transfer of the new genetic material to other plants. A notice announcing the petition request for deregulation is published in the *Federal Register* and public comments are considered before APHIS makes its determination. If the petition is granted, the biotech crop is no longer considered a "regulated article" and will not be subject to oversight by APHIS.

D. Role of the Food and Drug Administration

The Food and Drug Administration (FDA) uses the food safety and food additive authorities in the Federal Food, Drug and Cosmetic Act of 1938 (FFDCA), as amended, to regulate the safety of biotech foods.

Under these laws, FDA operates a voluntary premarket notification and consultation system that provides biotech companies an opportunity to demonstrate that foods produced from their biotech crop are as safe as their traditional counterparts.

If a biotech food contains a protein or other new substance that is not "generally recognized as safe" (GRAS), the food must go through a formal FDA premarket approval process in which the sponsor must prove scientifically that the new substance in the food is safe. FDA's presumption has been that transferred genetic material is GRAS.

FDA's oversight of biotech foods is managed through the Division of Biotechnology and GRAS Notice Review, Office of Food Additive Safety, in FDA's Center for Food Safety and Applied Nutrition, which coordinates reviews with FDA's Center for Veterinary Medicine.

In 1992, FDA issued a policy statement regarding how the agency intended to regulate human foods and animal feeds derived from new plant varieties, including varieties developed using DNA technology, which were referred to as "bioengineered foods." In general, FDA announced that bioengineered foods would be regulated no differently than foods developed through traditional plant breeding. FDA would look to the objective characteristics of the food and its intended use, not the method by which the food was developed.

FDA also acknowledged the food industry's long-standing practice of consulting with FDA in the early stages of developing food through new technologies. This practice, although not required, allowed the agency to identify and address issues regarding foods and food ingredients before they were marketed. FDA expressed its expectation that such consultation would continue with regard to bioengineered foods.

A company that intends to commercialize a biotech food meets with FDA at an "initial consultation" to identify and discuss possible issues regarding safety, nutritional, or other regulatory issues. A "final consultation" is held once the company believes it has developed the data and information necessary to address issues or concerns raised by FDA.

> **Practice Point**
>
> The FDA permits voluntary pre-market notification and consultation. It is critical that you consult an expert professional before taking advantage of this process.

Another aspect of FDA's involvement has to do with labeling.

In January 2001, the agency issued draft guidance regarding the labeling of biotech foods. In this draft FDA reaffirmed that special labeling is not required because there is "no basis for concluding that bioengineered foods differ from other foods in any meaningful or uniform way, or that, as a class, foods developed by the new techniques present any different or greater safety concern than foods developed by traditional plant breeding."

Nonetheless, the draft guidance sets out several scenarios in which a bioengineered food might require information on the label to indicate what in the bioengineered food is different from its conventional counterpart food. (The fact that it was developed through bioengineering would give no information as to the difference, so that fact would not be required on the label.) The scenarios are:

- If there is an issue regarding how a food is used or the consequences of its use;
- If the bioengineered food has a significantly different nutritional property; or

- If the bioengineered food contains an allergen that consumers would not expect to be in the food.

E. Role of the States in Regulation of Biotech Crops

The states' regulatory activities are, or could be, parallel with the EPA, USDA, and FDA programs described earlier. Thus, in this brief overview, the states' roles are outlined in conjunction with these three federal agencies.

1. EPA and the States

At the federal level, the EPA regulates pesticidal substances using the Federal Insecticide, Fungicide, and Rodenticide Act (FIFRA), as well as the pesticide tolerance provisions of the Federal Food, Drug and Cosmetic Act (FFDCA). FIFRA authorizes states to regulate pesticides and to enter into cooperative agreements with the EPA to support state pesticide programs. It also provides that states have the primary enforcement authority for pesticide use violations. However, despite the clarity of the states' role for conventional pesticides, their role is much less clear for plant-incorporated protectants (PIPs).

EPA's position has been that the PIP itself is a pesticide. The seeds and plants that contain the PIP do not have to be regulated as pesticides. In other words, at the point in the system where states normally have a key role, overseeing pesticide use in the field, there is no FIFRA-regulated pesticide use. States and EPA's Regional Offices have been involved in overseeing testing of PIPs under Experimental Use Permits.

Currently, no states have laws governing pesticide tolerances for biotech crops or the general safety of such crops.

2. USDA and the States

At the federal level, the USDA regulates biotech crops through the Plant Protection Act of 2000 (PPA). As noted earlier, the PPA gives the USDA broad authority to regulate plant pests and noxious weeds to protect agriculture, public health, and the environment. Among other things, this involves the regulation of field or greenhouse testing of biotech crops.

Most states have some type of statutory authority to control plant pests and protect plant health through such measures as quarantines. However, the PPA has a provision that preempts state regulation of plant pests or noxious weeds if the USDA has acted to regulate the plant in question, unless the state regulations are "consistent with and do not exceed" the USDA requirement.

Thus, once the federal government has acted to regulate a biotech crop, there is some uncertainty about a state's authority to regulate the same crop. Part of the uncertainty has to do with the fact that few states have adopted laws or regulations governing biotech crops. Despite these uncertainties, the USDA has established a cooperative relationship with the states in the oversight of biotech field trials.

3. FDA and the States

At the federal level, FDA utilizes the food safety and additive authorities in the Federal Food, Drug and Cosmetic Act (FFDCA) to ensure the safety of biotech foods. FDA operates a voluntary permanent notification and consultation approach to allow applicants to show that their proposed biotech food is as safe as the traditional counterparts. If the applicant cannot show that the biotech product is GRAS, a formal FDA premarket approval process is triggered.

Most states have food and drug laws that are similar to the FFDCA. These laws usually provide for the removal of unsafe foods, but do not generally get into premarket reviews, leaving this to FDA. However, in the commercial phase, FDA usually coordinates any response to biotech food contamination with the states.

F. Biotech Crop Regulation in Other Countries

A number of other countries are also active in the area of biotech agriculture. Some, such as Argentina, are large growers of biotech crops, while many others import foods made from biotech crops. For illustration purposes, the approval processes are outlined for five key biotech countries or regions.

1. Argentina

Argentina has approved for commercialization 10 genetically engineered crops, including soybeans, cotton, and corn. Acceptance of genetically engineered crops in Argentina has been almost universal, with more than 90 percent of the country's soybean crop planted with genetically engineered seeds in 2004.

The Argentine review and approval system utilizes an intragovernmental commission called CONABIO, the National Advisory Commission on Biotechnology. CONABIO is the body of consultation and technical support that advises the Secretary of Agriculture, Livestock, Fisheries and Food on the technical and biosafety support requirements to be met in the release into the environment of genetically engineered crops and material for veterinary use. CONABIO's review includes scientific analysis and sometimes incorporates an economic component (i.e., third-country market approval); until recently, a genetically engineered crop was approved for cultivation only after confirmation that it had been approved for consumption in important export markets.

In 2004, the Secretary of Agriculture, Livestock, Fisheries and Food created the Office of Biotechnology, whose responsibility will be to provide advice and assistance in the development of all the activities related to biotechnology and biosafety, especially those related to the environmental release and trade of genetically engineered plants and/or animals. It also provides assistance in defining policy, designing specific regulations, and promoting activities of the Secretariat.

2. Brazil

Brazil enacted a Biosafety Bill in March 2005, which replaced the previous legal framework for agricultural biotechnology, in use since 1995. Enactment of this law follows three consecutive years in which the Brazilian government legalized the marketing of genetically engineered soybeans despite the lack of governmental review and approval for their planting and commercialization. Under this new law, a technology provider must apply to the National Technical Commission of Biosafety (CTNBio) for approval to commercialize agricultural biotechnology products. CTNBio conducts a scientific review, which includes a review of environmental impact. Once approved by CTNBio, the application goes before the Ministries of Agriculture, Livestock, and Food Supply (for products used in agriculture, livestock, and agribusiness (processing); Health (for products having human uses or pharmaceutical application); and/or Environment (for products requiring registration and inspection for release into the environment).

CTNBio must approve all field trials prior to their being carried out. In 2004, CTNBio approved 21 field trials: 11 for corn, 3 each for soybeans and eucalyptus, 2 for cotton, and 1 each for rice and dry edible beans.

To date, Brazil has approved three genetically engineered items: an insect-resistant cotton, a herbicide-tolerant soybean, and corn with both insect resistance and herbicide tolerance traits. The corn application is approved for feed use only at this time.

3. Canada

Canada was the third largest worldwide producer of biotechnology crops in 2004. Approximately 77 percent of Canada's canola crop was herbicide-tolerant.

Although market acceptance is a concern for many Canadian agricultural exporters, the government of Canada to date relies exclusively on science in determining whether to allow the commercialization of a genetically engineered crop. Canada's regulatory system has approved approximately 63 genetically engineered crops for commercialization.

Agricultural biotechnology products seeking approval for commercialization must go through a six-step regulatory process. The Canadian Food Inspection Agency (CFIA), Health Canada, and Environment Canada are the primary agencies responsible for monitoring and regulating the approval of a new product. The CFIA is responsible for granting approval for commercial release and use of a new product in livestock feed. Prior to approval for commercial release, CFIA also approves and monitors field trials to comply with guidelines for environmental safety and to ensure confinement. Health Canada is responsible for approving the consumption of a new product in the human food market. Environment Canada addresses any potential impact on the environment posed by a new product.

4. China

China first released the details of its biotechnology regulations in January 2002, using an interim system of regulation until the government instituted the permanent regulatory system in April 2004. All biotech products entering China require a safety certificate as well as labeling approval, both of which are issued by China's Ministry of Agriculture (MOA).

Before issuance of a safety certificate, a product must have been approved in the country of origin and have completed the food and environmental safety assessment process in China. This includes feeding studies as well as in-country field tests. Once these assessments are complete, the data packages and technical reports are submitted to an MOA-convened National Biosafety Committee (NBC) for review. MOA considers the NBC recommendation and makes the official announcement of safety, issuing safety certificates on a time-limited basis, usually with a three-year expiration date.

Prior to import, biotech products must also have been issued a "labeling approval" by the MOA. Currently, China requires labeling for the following biotech products:

- Soybeans seed, soybeans, soybean flour, soybean oil, soybean meal;
- Corn seed, corn, corn oil, and corn flour;
- Rape (canola) seed, rapeseed, rapeseed oil, rapeseed meal;
- Cotton seed for planting; and
- Tomato seed, fresh tomato, tomato sauce.

With the exception of biotech cotton, China has not completed the assessment process or issued safety certificates for domestic propagation of any biotech crops.

5. European Union

The debate concerning biotechnology in the EU is highly politicized. Many of the contentious biotech issues now confronting the EU are not related to human health and environmental safety. However, over the last six years the EU has implemented a comprehensive regulatory system to ensure that biotech products are fully evaluated to ensure their safety. The

European Food Safety Authority (EFSA) and the member state authorities have the final say before a product is authorized for release.

The EU and member states are currently debating a number of issues that are based on economic consideration, and not safety: 1) the ongoing search for seed-labeling legislation for biotech products approved by EFSA, and 2) the development of coexistence measures for biotech, conventional, and organic agriculture that equally protect the interests of all farmers. Similarly, the EU Commission has stated that the marketing bans in six member states are not based on legitimate safety concerns.

Under the EU regulatory framework, technology providers can file an application for the authorization of agricultural biotech products under two EU regulations. Under Regulation (EC) No. 1829/2003, a company can file a single application for the biotech product and all its uses. The company submits the application to the authorities of the member state where the product will first be marketed. Within 14 days, the member state must forward the application to the European Food Safety Authority (EFSA) for review.

EFSA conducts a single risk assessment, and a single authorization can be granted for a biotech product and all its uses (cultivation, importation, processing into food/feed or industrial products). While EFSA attempts to issue an opinion within six months, it may request additional information from the applicant, which may lengthen the process. If EFSA issues a positive risk assessment, the application is forwarded to the European Commission, which has responsibility for risk management.

The Commission has three months to draft a proposal recommending that the member states authorize the product. In the proposal the Commission may impose certain product conditions (e.g., harvesting, transport, and monitoring). The member states then review and vote on the proposal in a regulatory committee.

If the proposal fails to obtain a "qualified majority" (QM), the proposal then goes to the Council of Ministers for review. The Council has three months to make a decision. If the Council fails to reach a decision, the Commission may then authorize the marketing of the product.

A company can also file an application under Directive 2001/18/EC for the purpose of marketing a biotech event for cultivation, importation, and processing into different products. While the procedure under this directive resembles that of Regulation (EC) No. 1829/2003, there are some differences. When the application is submitted in the member state, that county's authoritie's perform an assessment. Should they issue a negative assessment, the applicant's only option is to submit the file in another member state. However, if the member state does issue a favorable assessment, then the results are shared with the Commission, and all other member states may approve the event for marketing within the EU or raise objections. Should objections be raised, then the Commission will ask EFSA to conduct a study. From this point the approval procedure resembles that of Regulation (EC) No. 1829/2003.

The Commission's Directorate General for Health and Consumer Protection—known by the French acronym SANCO—handles applications that are submitted under Regulation (EC) No. 1829/2003. Typically, the Agriculture Council of Ministers reviews Commission proposals under this legislative authority when the member states are deadlocked. The Directorate General for the Environment handles applications submitted under Directive 2001/18/EC with the Environment Council of Ministers reviewing Commission proposals when the member states fail to reach a QM.

Chapter XVI

Legal Requirements After Approval

Areta L. Kupchyk, Esq.
Reed & Smith, LLP
Washington, D.C.

After approval, a biotechnology product continues to be subject to regulation in that it must be manufactured, distributed, and marketed in accordance with various federal and state laws and regulations. Accordingly, companies must implement an intricate web of post-approval procedures and carefully monitor compliance. Missteps are easy and can be costly. Government seizures, injunctions, civil money penalties, consumer restitution, profit disgorgement, and even criminal prosecution are among the potential consequences facing companies, and in some cases individuals, who are found noncompliant. This chapter provides an overview of notable federal laws and regulations that affect product manufacture, distribution, and marketing strategies.

A. The Food and Drug Administration

The Food and Drug Administration (FDA) regulates the manufacture, sale, distribution, and marketing of drugs, biological products, and medical devices in the United States.[1] FDA publishes regulations to implement the statutory mandate of Congress as set forth in the Federal Food, Drug and Cosmetic Act (FDCA). FDA's regulations are published in the *Code of Federal Regulations* (CFR). Title 21 of the CFR contains all regulations pertaining to FDA-regulated products.

FDA also publishes "guidance documents" that provide recommendations about how to comply with a law or regulation. A recommendation in a guidance document represents one way, but not necessarily the only way, to ensure compliance. An alternative approach may be used if that approach satisfies the requirements of the applicable statute and regulations. Ultimately, however, FDA determines whether an alternative approach satisfies regulatory and statutory requirements. Generally, a guidance document has been published after careful consideration of various approaches and after an opportunity for public comment. Therefore, any deviation from FDA's recommendation in a guidance document should be done only after careful review and, when appropriate, discussion with the agency. As FDA states in each guidance document, its recommendations "represent the Agency's current thinking" on a particular subject. Determining whether to develop an alternative approach should include consideration of the age of the guidance document (the older the document, the less current it may be), current industry practice, and scientific support for an alternative. FDA also publishes procedures for its own staff to follow. These procedures are intended to standardize the review process and are available on FDA's Web page.[2]

Post-approval product surveillance is an important part of the FDA regulatory scheme and includes monitoring, investigating, and reporting to FDA adverse events. FDA also regulates the labeling of all drugs, biological products, and devices, and advertising for the riskiest medical products, such as prescription (Rx) drugs and restricted devices (i.e., some Class III devices).[3] The Federal Trade Commission (FTC) regulates advertising only for the less-risky products, such as non-prescription, over-the-counter (OTC) drugs and non-restricted medical devices.[4] The FDA and the FTC cooperate with each other's investigations and share technical and regulatory support whenever appropriate.[5]

The FDA also works with the Securities and Exchange Commission (SEC), whose primary mission is to protect the investing public and to maintain the integrity of the securities market. FDA assists SEC staff by assessing the accuracy of statements in SEC filings relating to FDA issues. And FDA officials routinely provide technical and scientific information and expert advice to the SEC to assist in its investigations of possible violations of federal securities laws. The cooperation between FDA and the SEC continues after approval, particularly with respect to evaluating the accuracy of statements related to adverse events and compliance with good manufacturing practice. FDA and the SEC now have a centralized procedure to enable FDA personnel to refer information directly to the SEC about statements that may be false or misleading. In addition, FDA has given certain of its employees a "blanket" authorization to share non-public information with the SEC without obtaining individualized authorizations.[6]

B. Office of Inspector General, Department of Health and Human Services

The FDA is one of many agencies within the Department of Health and Human Services (HHS). Another unit of the HHS is the Office of Inspector General (OIG), which provides independent oversight of HHS and all of its agencies. The OIG's stated mission is to promote economy, efficiency, and effectiveness through the elimination of waste, abuse, and fraud. The OIG enforces other laws that affect the biotechnology industry, including the False Claims Act and the anti-kickback statute.

On May 5, 2003, the OIG published the "Office of Inspector General's Compliance Program Guidance for Pharmaceutical Manufacturers" to promote voluntary compliance programs for the health-care industry. This compliance guidance encourages pharmaceutical companies to implement internal controls and procedures that promote compliance with applicable statutes, regulations, and requirements of the federal health-care programs. The OIG's Compliance Program guidance identifies fundamental elements and principles for an effective compliance program that every biotechnology manufacturer should consider when developing and implementing a compliance program or evaluating an existing one.

C. The *Neurontin* Case

The potential consequences of not having an effective compliance program are best illustrated by the *Neurontin* case. On May 13, 2004, Warner-Lambert Company and its parent, Pfizer, settled criminal and civil claims related to the promotion and marketing of Neurontin (gabapentin) by its

Parke-Davis Division. The case was brought by the government in a qui tam action filed under the False Claims Act.[7] The government's case was based on information from a whistleblower, Dr. David Franklin, who had been employed as a medical science liaison by Parke-Davis. Dr. Franklin claimed that the company had promoted Neurontin for uses not approved by FDA, which resulted in ineligible Medicaid reimbursement payments for Neurontin prescriptions.

The settlement included two felony violations of the FDCA (misbranding based on promotion of off-label use).[8] Warner-Lambert agreed to pay more than $430 million, including a $240 million criminal fine, the second-largest criminal fine ever imposed in a health-care fraud prosecution. This settlement also represents one of the largest fines ever paid for violations relating to off-label promotion of pharmaceuticals. In addition, Pfizer entered a Corporate Integrity Agreement (CIA) with the OIG.[9] The CIA mandated widespread and strict efforts to institute and maintain compliance with the FDA's promotional policies. The CIA also required unprecedented oversight of non-promotional activities.

D. Import and Export Requirements

In addition to marketing and promotional restrictions, manufacturers of biotechnology products must comply with U.S. and foreign laws regarding import and export of medical products and components. All imported finished products intended for distribution in the United States must meet the same standards as products produced in the United States.

Exported products are often required to meet similar requirements by the importing country. Firms exporting products from the United States are routinely asked by foreign customers or foreign governments to supply a "certificate" for products regulated by FDA. To facilitate this need, FDA issues export certificates containing information about a product's regulatory or marketing status. Typically, foreign governments want official statements that products exported to their countries can be marketed in the United States or meet specific FDA requirements, such as cGMP regulations. Examples of the various types of Export Certificates include:

- The Certificate of a Pharmaceutical Product, which conforms to the format established by the World Health Organization (WHO) and is often used by the importing country when considering whether to license the product for sale in that country.
- The Non-Clinical Research Use Only Certificate, which is for the export of a product, material, or component intended for non-clinical research use only, and which may be marketed in, and legally exported from, the United States.[10]
- The Certificate to Foreign Government, which is for the export of human drugs and biologics, animal drugs, and devices that can be legally marketed in the United States.
- The Certificate of Exportability, which is for the export of human drugs and biologics, animal drugs, and devices that cannot be legally marketed in the United States, but meet specific export requirements.[11]

> **Practice Point**
>
> Be careful in both import and export. Imported products must meet U.S. standards. Exported products must meet the standards of the receiving country, but in some cases also must contain a "certificate" that the products meet U.S. standards.

FDA includes an attestation of cGMP compliance when issuing an export certificate for a U.S.-approved drug, biological product, or medical device. FDA bases its attestation of compliance with cGMP regulations on the manufacturer's most recent FDA inspection and other available information. FDA will not issue a Certificate to Foreign Government or a Certificate of a Pharmaceutical Product if:

1. FDA has initiated an enforcement action such as a seizure or an injunction;
2. The manufacturing facility failed to operate in compliance with cGMP regulations (unless the particular exported product is not affected by the specific cGMP deficiencies);

3. The manufacturing facility is not registered or listed with FDA; and
4. The product is not exported from the United States.

E. Current Good Manufacturing Practice Requirements

After FDA approval, a manufacturer of a drug, biological product, or device must maintain compliance with current Good Manufacturing Practice (cGMP) requirements to ensure: 1) that the product adheres to the terms and conditions of approval established in the approved marketing application; and 2) that the product is manufactured in a consistent and controlled manner.

CGMP requirements for drugs and biological products describe the methods to be used in, and the facilities or controls to be used for, the manufacture, processing, packing, or holding of the product. These requirements are intended to ensure that it meets the legal requirements for safety, and has the identity and strength and meets the quality and purity characteristics that it purports or is represented to possess.[12] The cGMP requirements for devices are similar and are set forth in the quality system regulation.[13] CGMP regulations include specific requirements for a quality control unit, facilities, equipment, production controls, storage, distribution, labeling, and record keeping.

FDA monitors compliance with cGMP regulations by sending trained field inspectors to conduct periodic, unannounced inspections of manufacturing facilities and by conducting general surveillance activities. These activities are intended to ensure that medical products are not adulterated during production and distribution.[14]

FDA describes its inspectional and compliance strategies in its Compliance Program Guides (CPGs).[15] Specific strategies for ensuring cGMP compliance include:

1. Factory inspections, including the collection and analysis of associated samples, through which FDA evaluates the conditions and practices under which drugs and drug products are manufactured, packed, tested, and held. Products from production and distribution

facilities are consistently of acceptable quality if the firm is operating in a "state of control." (CPG 7356.002).
2. Surveillance activities, such as sampling and analyzing products in distribution, through which FDA monitors the product quality. (CPG 7356.008).

F. Reporting Requirements to FDA

Information about actual and suspected adverse events related to marketed products is essential to ensure a current safety profile of a product. Preapproval studies provided to FDA and relied upon to demonstrate a product's safety and efficacy typically involve only several hundred to several thousand patients. Because all possible side effects of a drug or medical device cannot be identified or anticipated based on such limited data, FDA relies on post-marketing surveillance and risk assessment programs to monitor for any additional adverse events. Such post-marketing data are used to keep product labeling current, and, if the adverse events are serious, may be used to reconsider the marketing approval of the product.[16]

> **Practice Point**
>
> The FDA continues to monitor the safety and efficiency of a product after approval, and companies selling approved products continue to have an obligation to report problems they discover.

1. Drug and Biological Products

Holders of approved marketing applications, including new drug applications (NDA), abbreviated new drug applications (ANDA), biological license applications (BLAs), and manufacturers of prescription drugs for human use marketed without approved NDAs or ANDAs, are required to report adverse experiences to FDA.[17]

Every adverse experience report must contain four basic elements: (1) an identifiable patient; (2) an identifiable reporter; (3) a suspect drug or biological product; and (4) an adverse event or fatal outcome.[18] This information must be proactively set out in the initial report. However, if any of these basic elements remains unknown after a thorough investigation, a report is not required to be filed, and should not be filed, with the FDA. FDA considers reports without such information difficult, if not impossible, to interpret. If a report is lacking any of the four basic elements, FDA typically will return it marked "insufficient data for a report." Nevertheless, detailed records of such efforts should be maintained in product safety files, which are routinely reviewed by FDA during a facility inspection to determine whether the incident was appropriately investigated. Adverse experiences may also be reported to FDA by physicians, patients, and any other interested person through a voluntary system called MedWatch.[19]

2. Medical Devices

Device manufacturers are required to notify FDA if they receive complaints of device malfunctions, serious injuries, or deaths associated with their medical devices. The requirements for making such a report are set forth in the medical device reporting (MDR) regulations.[20] In addition, FDA can require that a device manufacturer: (1) conduct specific post-market surveillance, and (2) track certain high-risk devices to enable traceability to the user level.

Medical device manufacturers are required (1) to review all reports of adverse events associated with their products, and (2) to report to FDA certain events associated with their products. In addition, user facilities, such as hospitals and nursing homes, are legally required to report suspected medical device-related deaths to both FDA and the manufacturer, if known, and serious injuries to the manufacturer or to FDA, if the manufacturer is unknown.[21]

An FDA summary of the reporting requirements for manufacturers is provided in Exhibit 16-1. An FDA summary of reporting requirements for user facilities and distributors is provided in Exhibit 16-2.

Legal Requirements After Approval

Exhibit 16-1
Summary of Reporting Requirements for Manufacturers

Who Must Report	What to Report	Report Form #	To Whom	When
Manufacturer	30-day reports of deaths, serious injuries and malfunctions	Form FDA 3500A	FDA	Within 30 calendar days after becoming aware of an event
Manufacturer	5-day reports on events that require remedial action to prevent an unreasonable risk of substantial harm to the public health	Form FDA 3500A	FDA	Within 5 work days after becoming aware of an event
Manufacturer	Baseline reports to identify and provide basic data on each device that is subject of an MDR report	Form FDA 3417	FDA	30 calendar and 5 work day reports when device is reported for the first time. Interim and annual updates if any baseline information changes after initial submission.
Manufacturer	Annual Certification	Form FDA 3381	FDA	Coincide with firm's annual registration dates.

Exhibit 16-2
Summary of Reporting Requirements for User Facilities and Distributors[22]

Reporter	What to Report	Report Form #	To Whom	When
User Facility	Death	Form FDA 3500A	FDA & Manufacturer	Within 10 work days
User Facility	Serious injury	Form FDA 3500A	Manufacturer. (To FDA only if manufacturer is unknown.)	Within 10 work days
User Facility	Annual reports of death and serious injury	Form FDA 3419	FDA	January 1

3. Promotional Materials: Form FDA-2253

FDA requires that the holder of an approved NDA submit all prescription drug advertising and promotional labeling (including mailing pieces and labeling designed to contain samples) to FDA at the time such materials are initially disseminated or published.[23] The NDA holder must submit two copies of each marketing material with a "Transmittal of Advertisements and Promotional Labeling for Drugs for Human Use," also referred to as Form FDA-2253 as well as the product's current professional labeling. These submissions are made at the time of launch, as well as each time a new promotional material is introduced or an existing material is modified. This is discussed in more detail below under "Prior Approval and Post-Marketing Notification" and "FDA Notification."

G. Sales and Marketing Regulations

1. Prescription Drug Marketing Act

The Prescription Drug Marketing Act (PDMA) was enacted in 1987 to curb the distribution of counterfeit, adulterated, misbranded, subpotent, and expired drugs, which fed the secondary diversion market for prescription drugs in the United States. FDA implemented the PDMA through regulations that:

a. Prohibited re-importation, except by a manufacturer or for emergency medical care;
b. Prohibited the sale, purchase, or trade of Rx drugs if: purchased by hospital or health care entity, or donated or discounted to charitable organization;
c. Established requirements for the distribution of Rx drug samples by manufacturers and their sales representatives; and
d. Established requirements for drug wholesalers, other than distributors who are authorized by the manufacturer, to document each transaction with a "pedigree," which generally involves maintaining documentation of the chain of custody through which a product travels.

Under the "pedigree" provision, authorized distributors are exempt from the requirement of maintaining a pedigree or passing one along when they resell prescription drugs to another wholesaler or retail outlet. As written, this provision has raised concerns among many distributors as well as FDA. For example, an unscrupulous wholesale distributor seeking to introduce a counterfeit or diverted drug into commerce could do so by selling it to an unknowing authorized distributor, who is not required to maintain or pass on a pedigree when the drugs are resold. As a result of this gap, FDA has stayed enforcement of this provision and asked Congress to consider statutory changes to address these issues, which it believes are not within its authority to correct.[24]

2. FDA Regulation of Advertising

FDA regulates promotional labeling for all drugs and devices and advertising for prescription drugs and restricted devices. The FTC is responsible for regulating the advertising of non-prescription (or "over-the-counter") drugs and medical devices that are not restricted devices.[25]

Specific words and phrases are used repeatedly in FDA's regulation of drug marketing. Three words are essential to an understanding of FDA regulation: label, labeling, and advertising.

a. *Label.* A "label" is defined as "a display of written, printed or graphic matter upon the immediate container of any article."[26]

b. *Labeling.* "Labeling" is defined as "all labels and other written, printed or graphic matter (1) upon any article or any of its containers or wrappers, or (2) accompanying such article."[27] (The Supreme Court has held that "accompanying" does not mean that the material must be physically connected to the product. The connection can be textual. The test is whether the material "supplements or explains" the drug.)[28]

In regulations, FDA has deemed labeling to mean:

Brochures, booklets, mailing pieces, detailing pieces, file cards, bulletins, calendars, price lists, catalogs, house organs, letters, motion pictures, film strips, lantern slides, sound recordings, exhibits, literature, and reprints and similar pieces of printed, audio, or visual matter descriptive of a drug and references published [*e.g.*, PDR] for use by medical practitioners, pharmacists, or nurses containing drug information supplied by the manufacturer, packer, or distributor of the drug and which are disseminated by or on behalf of the manufacturer, packer, or distributor. . . .[29]

There are two general categories of labeling:

(i) "FDA-approved patient labeling" is also called "Information for the Patient," "Patient Information," "Medication Guide," or "patient package insert." This labeling is written for patients and focuses on the product's more serious risks, as well as less serious but more frequently occurring risks, rather than detailing each specific risk. Some patient labeling describes risks more fully than other patient labeling does. For example, some patient labeling focuses only on giving instructions for use or provides only a single warning.

(ii) "FDA-approved product labeling" is also called the "package insert," "professional labeling," "physician labeling," "prescribing information," or "direction circular." This labeling is written for health professionals using medical terminology. Each risk is specified. However, the language used for health professionals may be difficult for some consumers to understand.

c. *Advertising.* The FDCA gives FDA limited authority to regulate the advertising of prescription drugs, but does not define the term "advertising."[30] FDA also does not define "advertising" in regulation, but instead gives only examples, which include: "advertisements published in journals, magazines, other periodicals and newspapers, as well as broadcast advertisements in media such as radio, television, and telephone communications."[31] FDA's only guidepost to the definition of "advertising" (besides the dictionary) has been the Supreme Court, which rather broadly defines it as that which disseminates information about "who is producing and selling what product, for what reason, and at what price."[32]

d. *Promotional materials.* Although the term "promotional materials" is often used by FDA, it is defined neither in the statute nor in FDA regulation. In various FDA guidance documents, however, FDA uses the term "promotional materials" to refer to both labeling and advertising collectively.[33]

In regulating drug and device promotional materials, FDA relies primarily on two provisions of the FDCA: the intended use provision of the new drug application requirements and the misbranding provision. An NDA can only be approved if, among other things, there is "substantial evidence" to demonstrate that the drug is safe and effective "under the conditions of use prescribed, recommended, or suggested in the proposed labeling," and such labeling, "based on a fair evaluation of all material facts," is not "false or misleading in any particular."[34] The FDCA makes it illegal to introduce or deliver for introduction into interstate commerce any drug product that does not have an approved application for the uses prescribed, recommended, or suggested in the labeling.[35]

The FDCA also makes it illegal to receive, introduce, or deliver for introduction into interstate commerce any drug that is "misbranded."[36] A drug is misbranded if any one of several circumstances exists, such as:

(i) *False or Misleading.* A drug is misbranded if its labeling is "false or misleading in any particular."[37]

(ii) *Prominence.* A drug is misbranded if required information is not prominently placed with such conspicuousness and in such terms as to make it likely to be read and understood by an ordinary individual.[38]

(iii) *Adequate Directions for Use.* A drug is misbranded if its labeling fails to bear adequate directions for use, including adequate warnings.[39]

> **Practice Point**
>
> It is illegal for a drug label to be either:
> 1. False or misleading, or
> 2. Misbranded—having required information provided in an inconspicuous or confusing manner.

(iv) *Truth in Advertising.* A prescription drug is misbranded if its advertising does not provide a "true statement" with respect to side effects, contraindications, or effectiveness.[40] Advertising cannot be "false, lacking in fair balance, or otherwise misleading,"[41] and it will be so deemed if, for example, it:

- Contains a representation or suggestion, not approved for use in the labeling, that the drug is better, safer, more effective, or effective in a broader range of conditions than demonstrated by substantial evidence;[42]
- Contains an unsupported comparative claim or superiority claim;[43]
- Contains unsupported favorable information or opinions;[44]
- Selectively presents favorable information on safety or side effects;[45]
- Suggests that study information has more general application;[46]
- Uses literature references that do not support the claim in question;[47]
- Uses data that have no clinical significance;[48]
- Uses statements from authorities out of context, or ignoring negative or inconsistent views;[49]

- Uses literature, quotations, or references to recommend or suggest an unapproved indication or to inaccurately support an approved indication;[50] or
- Cites scientific studies that are defective in construction or contain criteria making them inapplicable to the sponsor's purpose.[51]

3. Three Basic Types of Advertisements

FDA recognizes three basic types of advertising, regardless of whether the advertisement is in print or broadcast.

a. *Product-Claim Advertisements*

A "product-claim advertisement" is an advertisement that includes both a product's name and its use, or that makes any claims or representations about a prescription drug.

b. *Reminder Advertisements*

Reminder advertisements typically include: (1) the product name and (2) sponsor name, but not (3) the indication or dosage recommendation.[52]

c. *Help-Seeking Advertisements*

Help-seeking advertisements do not mention a drug or product, but only discuss a disease or condition and advise the audience to "see your doctor" for possible treatments. Help-seeking advertisements are not regulated by FDA because they do not mention a product.[53]

4. Requirements for Product Claim Advertisements

A "product claim advertisement" cannot be false or misleading and must present a "fair balance" between the risks and benefits of the drug.[54] Every advertisement must meet FDA's fair balance requirements. The risks of the product must be clearly identified and set off against its benefits.[55] Fair balance applies equally to both the content and format of promotional materials.[56] To ensure compliance with these requirements, FDA regulations require the inclusion of a "Brief Summary" or "Major Statement" with every advertisement. A "Brief Summary" is required on all print advertisements. A "Major Statement" is required for all broadcast advertisements.

5. Print Advertisements: the Brief Summary

All print advertisements require a "Brief Summary." The Brief Summary, contrary to its name, is neither brief nor a summary,[57] and must include all risks listed in the approved product labeling, including side effects, contraindications, warnings, and precautions.[58] In January 2004, FDA proposed a draft guidance document on "Brief Summary: Disclosing Risk Information in Consumer-Directed Print Advertisements" that makes recommendations on the disclosure of risk information in prescription drug product advertisements directed toward consumers in print media. This draft guidance supersedes the draft guidance titled, "Using FDA-Approved Patient Labeling in Consumer-Directed Print Advertisements," which was issued in April 2001. In the current draft guidance, FDA proposes that a manufacturer be able to choose how it will present risk information from at least three recommended options: (1) present all risk information from the FDA-approved professional labeling; (2) reproduce FDA-approved patient labeling, either in its entirety or as modified to omit less important risk information; or (3) provide the risk information that would be appropriate for the proposed FDA-approved Highlights Section in prescription drug labeling. The agency has not yet finalized the guidance.

The Brief Summary is not required for all print advertisements. In reminder advertisements, FDA has permitted omission of a Brief Summary if the product name and indications for use are not included in the advertisement. FDA has also permitted "coming soon" advertisements without a Brief Summary, where the only information in the advertisement was the company name and the indication.[59] However, FDA does not permit reminder advertisements for any drug product that carries a "Black Box warning."[60,61] Advertisements for bulk sale drugs may not contain any claims for therapeutic safety or effectiveness.[62] Advertisements for Rx compounding drugs may not contain any claims for therapeutic safety or effectiveness.[63]

6. Broadcast Advertisements: the Major Statement

A "Major Statement" is required for all broadcast (radio, TV, or telephone communication) advertisements. This statement must include the product's major risks and make "adequate provision" for the dissemination to viewers of the product labeling, which includes all of the risks associated with the product. Instead of listing each risk as provided in a drug product's label, an Rx drug broadcast advertisement must include, at least, information about the major risks of the drug in either the audio or the audio and visual part of the presentation.[64] Instead of the Brief Summary, the sponsor may make "adequate provision" for the dissemination of approved package labeling in connection with the broadcast presentation.[65] FDA has recommended that compliance with the adequate provision requirements includes all of the following components:

a. An operating toll-free telephone number through which a consumer can hear the labeling read or have the labeling mailed to him or her in a timely manner (mailed within two business days; received within four to six days);
b. A statement directing consumers to pharmacists and/or physicians, who may provide additional product information;
c. An Internet Web page (URL) address that provides full access to the product labeling; and
d. Reference to an alternative mechanism for obtaining package labeling information for consumers who do not have access to technology such as the Internet.[66]

7. Prior Approval and Post-Marketing Notification

The FDCA expressly prohibits FDA from requiring prior approval of the content of any advertisement, except in "extraordinary circumstances."[67] An "extraordinary circumstance" includes a situation when a sponsor or FDA receives information, not widely publicized in medical literature, that a drug may cause fatalities or serious injuries, and despite notification from FDA, the sponsor fails to adequately publicize such information.[68] For example, FDA implicitly considers NDA reviews and approval under its "Accelerated Approval" program to be an extraordinary circumstance and requires pre-clearance submissions.[69]

8. FDA Notification

FDA requires that all prescription drug advertising and all drug promotional labeling (including mailing pieces and labeling designed to contain samples) be submitted to FDA at the time they are initially disseminated or published.[70] Two copies of each submission along with Form FDA-2253 (Transmittal of Advertisements and Promotional Labeling for Drugs for Human Use) are to be submitted along with the product's current professional labeling.

> **Practice Point**
>
> In some cases, even if it is not required, it is wise to consider asking the FDA to review advertising material before it is disseminated.

Although FDA is prohibited from preapproving any advertising, it is not prohibited from reviewing such materials if voluntarily submitted. Whether to seek FDA's review of advertising materials before dissemination or publication may depend on several factors. FDA review before dissemination may be appropriate if: (1) time allows; (2) the cost of revising or revoking a marketing campaign in response to an FDA enforcement action would be excessive; or (3) a split exists between a company's marketing and regulatory affairs personnel.

9. Promotion of Off-Label Use

Off-label use refers to an unapproved use for an FDA-approved product. In other words, the "use" is not described, prescribed, recommended, or suggested on the FDA-approved label.

FDA generally refrains from regulating the "practice of medicine." When a drug is prescribed for an off-label use by a health-care provider licensed to prescribe such drug, such activity is considered to be within the practice of medicine. FDA generally considers the "practice of medicine" primarily to be the interaction between a doctor and his or her patient.

If an activity falls within the "practice of medicine," FDA has not considered it to be "promotion" of the product. FDA regulates promotion but not the practice of medicine. FDA prohibits the promotion of a drug product for unapproved uses. Marketing an approved new drug product for an unapproved use will render the product unapproved and, therefore, misbranded.[71] According to FDA, no one—neither physician nor manufacturer—is permitted to "promote" a prescription drug product for off-label uses outside of the doctor-patient relationship. Violations of FDA's restrictions on promotion may lead to one or more FDA enforcement actions. FDA may request that a manufacturer issue a Dear Doctor letter, or it may take more assertive actions, such as moving to seize or recall the product, enjoining its distribution or production, or withdrawing marketing approval.

10. Exchange of Scientific Information

Although FDA restricts promotional materials, it does not restrict the exchange of scientific information.[72] The scientific exchange of information about unapproved or "off-label" uses has historically occurred through the sponsorship of Continuing Medical Education (CME) forums and the distribution of published, peer-reviewed medical journal articles. Speakers at CME seminars often present research and discuss off-label applications. Manufacturers may sponsor these seminars and not have the statements attributed to them by FDA, as long as the program is not under the manufacturer's control—for example, as long as it is run by an independent educational provider.

After much debate, FDA issued a guidance permitting manufacturers to circulate reprints of peer-reviewed articles discussing off-label uses, in response to physician requests, under limited conditions. A linchpin in FDA's flexibility with respect to dissemination of information about off-label use was "independence." The guidance set forth criteria for determining independence, including restrictions on manufacturers' input regarding selection of speakers and topics. Subsequently, in the FDA Modernization Act (FDAMA), Congress attempted to codify this guidance and permitted broader dissemination if a manufacturer committed to filing a supplemental NDA for the off-label use. The FDA guidance document and the subsequent regulations pursuant to FDAMA were the subject of the three cases against FDA known as the *Washington Legal Foundation* cases (WLF cases), which challenged FDA's right to regulate commercial speech under the First Amendment of the United States Constitution.

11. The First Amendment

On July 30, 1998, the U.S. District Court for the District of Columbia voided three guidance documents issued by FDA as violating the First Amendment commercial free speech right of manufacturers.[73] Those guidance documents addressed manufacturer dissemination of peer-reviewed journal articles, medical texts, and continuing medical education material that included off-label or unapproved uses of drugs, biologics or medical devices. In a second decision a year later, the district court struck down Section 401 of FDAMA and FDA's implementing regulations, which had taken the place of the FDA guidance documents struck down in the prior decisions and which again limited the dissemination of reprints.[74] Taken together, the two decisions permitted manufacturers to:

- Disseminate to health-care professionals reprints of articles in peer-reviewed scientific journals or chapters from bona fide scientific reference texts that discuss off-label uses; and
- Sponsor independent CME programs that feature discussions of off-label uses, and take part in recommending speakers or topics for discussion. The criteria for independence discussed in FDA's guidance are still of value.

FDA appealed the decision of the district court. On February 11, 2000, the Court of Appeals for the D.C. Circuit vacated the lower court's decisions, based on FDA's representation that it did not have power to enforce section 401 of FDAMA in and of itself. This procedural decision did not address the legal merits of the district court's decisions and has left the legality of restrictions on commercial speech unsettled. However, FDA took the position that even though it may not charge a violation of section 401 of FDAMA for promotion of an off-label use, it may use the dissemination of a reprint on off-label uses as evidence of a misbranding violation under the FDCA. A misbranding violation would be based on a manufacturer's to promote the product for a new "intended use." Whether it has the authority to act on the basis of dissemination of a reprint alone is an open question, which will likely be settled in subsequent litigation.

Nevertheless, FDA may still bring an action against a person for marketing an *un*approved drug or device under the FDCA misbranding provisions. Indeed, the promotion of an unapproved drug or device is prohibited under 21 C.F.R. §§ 312.7 and 812.7. FDA's guidance as to what "independence" means is helpful in distinguishing between promotion and the exchange of scientific information, a distinction FDA will still use to determine whether an advertisement has rendered a drug or device misbranded. FDA will consider the following factors in evaluating programs and activities and determining independence:[75]

(a) Control of Content and Selection of Presenters and Moderators
  (i) Has the provider maintained full control over the content of the program, planning of the program's content, and selection of speakers and moderators?
  (ii) Has the supporting company engaged in scripting, targeting points for emphasis, or other actions designed to influence the program's content?
  (iii) Has the company suggested speakers who are or were actively involved in promoting the company's products or who have been the subject of complaints or objections with regard to presentations that were viewed as misleading or biased in favor of the company's products?

(b) Meaningful Disclosures at the time of the program to the audience regarding:
  (i) The company's funding of the program;
  (ii) Any significant relationship between the provider, presenters or moderators, and the supporting company (e.g., employee, grant recipient, or owner of significant interest or stock); and
  (iii) Whether any unapproved uses of products will be discussed.

(c) The Focus of the Program
  (i) Is the intent of the company and the provider to produce an independent and non-promotional activity that is focused on educational content and free from commercial influence or bias?
  (ii) Does the title of the activity fairly and accurately represent the scope of the presentation?

(iii) Is the central theme based on a single product marketed by the company or a competing product, except when existing treatment options are so limited as to preclude any meaningful discussion of alternative therapies? (Each treatment option need not be discussed with precisely equal emphasis; however, emphasis on a newer or, in the view of the presenter, more beneficial treatment modality should be provided in the context of a discussion of all reasonable and relevant options.)

(d) **Relationship Between Provider and Supporting Company**—whereby the company may exert influence over the content (e.g., a provider that is owned by, or is not viable without the support of, the company supporting the activity).

(e) **Provider Involvement in Sales or Marketing**—Are individuals employed by the provider and involved in designing or conducting scientific or educational activities also involved in advising or otherwise assisting the company with respect to sales or marketing of the company's product?

(f) **Provider's Demonstrated Failure to Meet Standards**—i.e., programs that repeatedly fail to meet standards of independence, balance, objectivity, or scientific rigor.

(g) **Multiple Presentations**—(but FDA recognizes that some repeat programs can serve public health interests, and it sometimes actively encourages multiple presentations on selected urgent topics).

(h) **Audience Selection**—by the sales or marketing departments of the supporting company, or are intended to reflect sales or marketing goals (e.g., to reward high prescribers of the company's products, or to influence "opinion leaders").

(i) **Opportunities for Meaningful Discussion During Program**

(j) **Further Dissemination** after the initial program by or at the behest of the company, other than in response to an unsolicited request or through an independent provider

(k) **Ancillary Promotional Activities** (e.g., presentations by sales representatives or promotional exhibits) taking place in the meeting room.

(l) **Complaints** by the provider, presenters, or attendees regarding attempts by the supporting company to influence content.

(m) **Additional Considerations.** While not required, a written agreement, coupled with the factors described above, can provide persuasive evidence of independence. Is there any documentation of the measures taken to ensure independence of an activity? Is there a written agreement between the provider and the supporting company that reflects that the provider will be solely responsible for designing and conducting the activity, and that the activity will be educational, non-promotional, and free from commercial bias?

12. Other Cases of Interest—Product Liability

In *Perez v. Wyeth Laboratories*,[76] the Supreme Court of New Jersey held that: (1) manufacturers are not shielded from liability by the "learned intermediary" rule for injuries to consumers when they engage in direct-to-consumer advertising; and (2) there is a rebuttable presumption that a manufacturer's duty to consumers is met when the manufacturer is in compliance with FDA regulations concerning advertising, labeling, and warning.

13. The Federal Trade Commission

In general, under a FTC-FDA Liaison Agreement issued on September 9, 1971, FDA regulates advertising of Rx drugs, biologics, "restricted" medical devices, and all promotional labeling. FTC regulates advertising of OTC drugs, dietary supplements, and all other medical devices. The FDA standard to support content and claims is much more rigorous than the FTC's standard. "Substantial evidence" must exist to support a claim. Under FDAMA, this standard requires generally two adequate and well-controlled clinical trials.

The FTC Bureau of Consumer Protection Division of Advertising Practices generally evaluates ads for "unfair or deceptive acts or practices."[77] Advertisers must have a reasonable basis for objective claims before the claims are disseminated.[78] For health and safety claims, FTC has typically required "competent and reliable scientific evidence." Competent and reliable scientific evidence has been defined as tests, analysis, research, studies, or other evidence based on the expertise of professionals in the relevant area, that has been conducted and evaluated in an objective manner by persons qualified to do so using procedures generally accepted in the profession to yield accurate and reliable results.[79] The primary difference between FDA and the FTC is that FDA must approve new products for marketing and then reviews promotional materials for conformance with the approved labeling. The FTC, on the other hand, does not have a role prior to market entry. If the FTC challenges a claim after market entry, the company merely has to have scientific evidence that would provide a reasonable basis for the claims made.

H. Withdrawal of FDA Approval

FDA can withdraw approval to market a drug, biological product, or medical device for various reasons, generally but not exclusively related to information about a product's safety or efficacy. Specifically, FDA can withdraw marketing approval if it finds that:

1. Clinical or other experience, tests, or other scientific data show that the product is unsafe for use under the conditions of use upon which basis the application was approved;
2. New evidence of clinical experience not contained in the application or not available to FDA until after the application or abbreviated application was approved, or tests by new methods, or tests by methods not deemed reasonably applicable when the application was approved, evaluated together with the evidence available when the application was approved, reveal that the product is not shown to be safe for use under the approved conditions of use;
3. Upon the basis of new information before FDA with respect to the drug, evaluated together with the evidence available when the application or abbreviated application was approved, there is a lack of substantial evidence from adequate and well-controlled investigations that the drug will have the effect it is purported or represented to have under the conditions of use prescribed, recommended, or suggested in its labeling;
4. The application contains any untrue statement of a material fact; or
5. Required patent information was not submitted.[80]

I. False Claims Act

The False Claims Act provides a civil money penalty against anyone who defrauds the federal government by submitting a false claim "knowingly."[81] Section 3729(b) explains that "knowingly" includes actual knowledge, deliberate indifference, and reckless disregard. There is no need to prove that the defendant specifically intended to defraud the government. The act covers schemes by contractors to obtain government funds in violation of contractual requirements, as well as schemes to avoid paying for benefits and services received from the government and to obtain payment for services not provided to the government. The False Claims Act authorizes claims for treble damages—three times the actual damages—plus $5,000 to $10,000 for each false claim for payment.

The False Claims Act also allows individuals (also called "whistleblowers") who discover such schemes to bring suit on behalf of the government.[82] These suits—called "qui tam" suits—have been a powerful and successful enforcement tool. Although whistleblowers may be eligible to receive 15 percent to 30 percent of the government's recovery, the act includes substantial procedural and jurisdictional hurdles that must be cleared before any judgment is obtained.[83]

J. Anti-kickback Statute and Other Illegal Remuneration

The federal anti-kickback statute prohibits anyone from knowingly or willfully offering, paying, soliciting, or receiving remuneration in order to induce or reward business reimbursable under federal or state health-care programs.[84] The statute establishes criminal penalties for its violations and permits the OIG to bring an administrative proceeding to exclude a provider from Medicare or Medicaid participation, or to collect civil money penalties without first obtaining a criminal conviction.[85] There are six exceptions to the anti-kickback statute: (1) properly disclosed discounts or other reductions in price; (2) payments to bona fide employees; (3) payments to group purchasing organizations; (4) waiver of coinsurance for Medicare Part B services for certain individuals who qualify for PHS programs; (5) risk-sharing arrangements; and (6) payment practices that meet the "safe harbor" elements set forth in regulations defining conduct that will not be subject to enforcement.[86] The "safe harbor" regulations exempt arrangements that do not represent remuneration intended to prohibit referrals or recommendations for a product or services. Several established safe harbors are easily applicable to drug and device manufacturers, and involve payment practices related to equipment rental, personal services contracts, warranties, discounts, and certain payments to group purchasing organizations.

State anti-kickback laws generally contain similar prohibitions to the federal statute. Typically, state laws will apply only to goods and services furnished under the state's Medicaid program, but occasionally, a state statue will apply to all health-care services.[87]

Notes

1. Individual states may also impose additional requirements on biotechnology products that are manufactured or distributed within their borders. State requirements are beyond the scope of this chapter but should be researched before distribution or manufacturing begins in any state.

2. The Center for Drug Evaluation and Research (CDER) procedures are published as a *Manual of Policies and Procedures* (MaPPs); *see* http://www.fda.gov/cder/mapp.htm. The Center for Biologics Evaluation and Research (CBER) procedures are published as a *Manual of Standard Operating Procedures and Policies* (SOPPs); *see* http://www.fda.gov/cber/regsopp/regsopp.htm.

3. Labeling includes "all labels and other written, printed or graphic matter (1) upon any article or any of its containers or wrappers, or (2) accompanying such article," such as pamphlets, sales aids, instructions, abstracts, journal articles, or any other material distributed to supplement or explain the product. 21 U.S.C. § 321(m).

4. 21 U.S.C. §§ 352(a), (n), (q), and (r); 15 U.S.C. § 52. *See also* 36 Fed. Reg. 18,539 (Sept. 16, 1971).

5. To provide for more efficient use of FDA and other agency manpower and resources and to prevent duplication of effort, FDA and various agencies often enter into formal or informal agreements and/or understandings called "Memorandums of Understanding" (MOUs). MOUs specify areas in which each agency will assume primary responsibility.

6. *See* http://www.fda.gov/bbs/topics/NEWS/2004/NEW01019.html.

7. 31 U.S.C. §§ 3729 *et seq.*

8. Franklin v. Parke-Davis, 147 F. Supp. 2d 39 (D. Mass. 2001).

9. *See* http://oig.hhs.gov/fraud/cia/index.html.

Legal Requirements After Approval

10. Non-clinical research-use-only materials must be specifically labeled to indicate research use only. *See* 21 C.F.R. § 809.10(c)(2) and 21 C.F.R. § 312.160.

11. There are numerous legal requirements for exporting unapproved products and other products that do not comply with FDCA requirements for marketing in the United States. *See* 21 U.S.C. § 381(e) or § 382; http://www.fda.gov/opacom/laws/fdcact/fdcact8.htm. For example, a drug or device may be exported even if it does not fully comply with all applicable requirements under the FDCA if it:

  (A) accords to the specifications of the foreign purchaser,
  (B) is not in conflict with the laws of the country to which it is intended for export,
  (C) is labeled on the outside of the shipping package that it is intended for export, and
  (D) is not sold or offered for sale in domestic commerce.

21 U.S.C. § 381(e)(1).

12. Drug cGMP regulations are set forth at 21 C.F.R. Parts 210 and 211; additional cGMP regulations applicable to biological products are set forth at 21 C.F.R. pts. 600-10.

13. 21 C.F.R. pt. 820. Device cGMP regulations describe "the methods used in, or the facilities or controls used for, its manufacture, packing, storage, or installation . . . are not in conformity with applicable requirements under section 360j(f)(1) of this title or an applicable condition prescribed by an order under section 360j(f)(2) of this title." 21 U.S.C. § 351(h).

14. FDA will consider a drug or device to be adulterated if it was not manufactured according to cGMP requirements. 21 U.S.C. § 351(a)(2)(B).

15. Compliance Policy Guides (CPGs) explain FDA policy on regulatory issues related to laws and regulations that FDA enforces. These include cGMP regulations and application commitments. The CPG Manual is the repository for all agency compliance policy, including statements or correspondence by headquarters offices or centers reflecting new policy or changes in compliance policy, agency correspondence with trade groups and regulated industries, and advisory opinions; precedent court decisions; multicenter agreements regarding jurisdiction over FDA-regulated products; applicable preambles to proposed or final regulations or other *Federal Register* documents; and individual regulatory actions. The CPG Manual is *available at* http://www.fda.gov/ora/compliance_ref/cpg/default.htm.

16. *See* FDA's recommended premarketing/post-marketing risk assessment processes and post-marketing surveillance programs, *Managing the Risks from Medical Products Use: Creating a Risk Management Framework*, at www.fda.gov/oc/cder/tfrm/riskmanagement.pdf, May 1999.

17. 21 C.F.R. §§ 310.305 (records and reports concerning adverse drug experiences on marketed prescription drugs for human use without approved new

drug applications), 314.80 (post-marketing reporting of adverse drug experiences), 314.98, and 600.80 (post-marketing reporting of biological product adverse experiences).

18. The four basic elements are consistent with international harmonization initiatives. *See* § III.B.3, International Conference on Harmonization (ICH); *Guideline on Clinical Safety Data Management: Definitions and Standards for Expedited Reporting* (ICH E2A document; 60 Fed. Reg. 11,284 (March 1, 1995)).

19. More information on MedWatch is *available at* www.medwatch.gov.

20. 21 C.F.R. pt. 803.

21. These reports must be made on the MedWatch 3500A Mandatory Reporting Form.

22. MDRs may also be voluntarily reported to FDA by physicians, patients, and any other interested person through MedWatch.

23. 21 C.F.R. § 314.81(b)(3)(i).

24. *See* FDA's Report to Congress, *The Prescription Drug Marketing Act,* June 2001.

25. *See* 21 U.S.C. §§ 352(a), (n), (q), and (r). 15 U.S.C. § 52. *See also* 36 Fed. Reg. 18,539 (Sept. 16, 1971).

26. 21 U.S.C. § 321(k).

27. 21 U.S.C. § 321(m).

28. Kordel v. United States, 335 U.S. 345 (1948).

29. 21 C.F.R. § 202.1(l)(2) (2004).

30. 21 U.S.C. § 352(n).

31. 21 C.F.R. § 202.1(l)(1).

32. Virginia State Board v. Virginia Citizens Council, 425 U.S. 748, 765 (1976).

33. *See e.g.*, Draft Guidance, Accelerated Approval Products—Submission of Promotional Materials (March 1999).

34. 21 U.S.C. § 355(d).

35. 21 U.S.C. § 331(d).

36. 21 U.S.C. § 331(a)-(c).

37. 21 U.S.C. § 352(a).

38. 21 U.S.C. § 352(c).

39. 21 U.S.C. § 352(f).

40. 21 U.S.C. § 352(n).

41. 21 C.F.R. § 202.1(e).

42. 21 C.F.R. § 202.1(e)(6)(i).

43. 21 C.F.R. § 202.1(e)(6)(i) and (ii).

44. 21 C.F.R. § 202.1(e)(6)(iii).

45. 21 C.F.R. § 202.1(e)(6)(iv).

46. 21 C.F.R. § 202.1(e)(6)(v).

47. 21 C.F.R. § 202.1(e)(6)(vi).

48. 21 C.F.R. § 202.1(e)(6)(vii).

49. 21 C.F.R. § 202.1(e)(6)(viii)-(ix).

50. 21 C.F.R. § 202.1(e)(6)(x)-(xi).

51. 21 C.F.R. § 202.1(e)(6)(xiii)-(xx).

52. 21 C.F.R. § 202.1(e)(2)(i).

53. Technically, "help-seeking" advertisements are not regulated because they do not contain any product claims. When done correctly, such an advertisement (1) does not identify a drug by name, (2) generally discusses a disease or condition, and (3) advises the audience to consult a physician. In January 2004, FDA proposed new draft guidance specifically to address the use of "'Help-Seeking' and Other Disease Awareness Communications By or On Behalf of Drug and Device Firms."

54. 21 C.F.R. § 202.1(e)(6).

55. 21 C.F.R. § 202.1(e)(5)(ii). FDA's criteria to establish "fair balance" are provided in the negative in the advertising regulation, 21 C.F.R. § 202.1(e)(6)-(7), where examples of information that are not fairly balanced are presented.

56. FDA guidance document, "Current Issues and Procedures, in DDMAC" (April 1994; rescinded in 1997, but FDA plans to revise and reissue).

57. As former FDA Commissioner Dr. Mark McClellan has said, the disclosure of all risk information renders the Brief Summary "neither brief nor much of summary, so not very helpful." Speech to National Association of Health Underwriters Legislative Conference in Washington, D.C., March 25, 2003.

58. 21 U.S.C. § 352(n); 21 C.F.R. § 202.1(e)(1) and (e)(3)(iii).

59. FDA has also challenged running a "reminder ad" that lists only the company name and the name of an investigational drug where the ad is placed in a journal issue in which is also published the results of a study testing the drug for a stated indication, thus bringing together all three elements (drug, company, and indication). *See* Warning Letter from DDMAC, FDA to Steven Quay, President, Sonus Pharmaceuticals, Inc. (March 26, 1998), *available at* http://www.fda.gov/cder/warn/mar98/6003.pdf.

60. 21 C.F.R. § 202.1(e)(2)(i).

61. A "Black Box warning" is a term used to describe any special warning that FDA requires to be displayed prominently in a box on the labeling. Boxed warnings typically include serious problems associated with the use of the product, such as those that may lead to death or serious injury. FDA will specify the location of a boxed warning if one is required. 21 C.F.R. § 201.57(e).

62. 21 C.F.R. § 202.1(e)(2)(ii).

63. 21 C.F.R. § 202.1(e)(2)(iii).

64. *See* "Consumer Directed Broadcast Advertisement, FDA Guidance for Industry," 64 Fed. Reg. 43,197 (Aug. 8, 1999).

65. 21 C.F.R. § 202.1(e)(1).

66. *Id.*

67. 21 U.S.C. § 352(n).
68. 21 C.F.R. § 202.1(j)(1).
69. 61 Fed. Reg. 24,314, 24,315 (May 14, 1996). For drugs and biological products under accelerated approval reviews, FDA requires pre-approval submission of all promotional materials, including advertisements, that the sponsor intends to disseminate in the first 120 days after approval. 21 C.F.R. §§ 314.550 and 601.45.
70. 21 C.F.R. § 314.81(b)(3)(i).
71. 21 U.S.C. §§ 355(a), 331(d). "No person shall introduce or deliver into interstate commerce any new drug, unless an approval of an application filed pursuant to [21 U.S.C. § 355(b) or (j)] is effective with respect to such drug." An application approved under 21 U.S.C. § 355 must identify the particular uses to which the new drug will be put, and an approval of such an application for interstate distribution can become effective only with respect to such uses. *See* 21 U.S.C. § 355(b), (d), and (j).
72. 21 C.F.R. § 312.7(a).
73. Washington Legal Found. v. Friedman, 13 F. Supp. 2d 51 (D.D.C. 1998), *amended by* 36 F. Supp. 2d 16 (D.D.C. 1999), *amended by* 36 F.S upp. 2d 418 (D.D.C. 1999), *motion denied, summ. judgment granted*, 56 F. Supp. 2d 81 (D.D.C. 1999), *vacated in part sub nom.* Washington Legal Found. v. Henney, 202 F. 3d 331 (D.C. Cir. 2000), *motion denied*, 128 F. Supp. 2d 11 (D.D.C. 2000).
74. *See also* Thompson v. Western States Med. Center, 535 U.S. 357 (2002) (the Supreme Court held that FDAMA's prohibitions on soliciting prescriptions for and advertising compounded drugs amount to unconstitutional restrictions on commercial speech).
75. FDA Guidance, *Industry-Supported Scientific and Educational Activities* (November 1997).
76. Perez v. Wyeth Labs., 734 A.2d 1245 (1999).
77. 15 U.S.C. § 45.
78. *In re* Pfizer, Inc., 81 F.T.C. 23 (1972).
79. *See e.g.,* Global World Media Corp. Consent Order, No. 962-3210 (July 1997).
80. 21 C.F.R. § 314.150.
81. 31 U.S.C. § 3729.
82. 31 U.S.C. § 3730(b).
83. 31 U.S.C. § 3730(d).
84. 42 U.S.C. § 256b.
85. *Id.*
86. 42 U.S.C. § 1320a-7b(b)(3); 42 C.F.R. § 1001.952.
87. *See, e.g.,* Mass. Gen. Laws ch. 175H, § 3.

Chapter XVII

Development and Commercialization Alliances

Eileen Smith Ewing
K&L Gates
Boston, Massachusetts

A. Introduction: Why Choose to Partner?

Given the acceleration of scientific breakthroughs across the biopharmaceutical, device, and genetic engineering sectors, it is nearly impossible for one company—particularly a small, highly focused biotech—to avail itself of the myriad technologies and resources that could expedite its own product development. The tremendous cost of discovering and developing a biotechnology product (development of a drug, for example, averages approximately $900 million over 10-12 years[1]) further handicaps the odds against an emerging biotechnology company.

Development alliances would appear to be the answer: they bring the enormous financial resources of the pharmaceutical sector, along with that industry's time-honored drug commercialization capabilities, to bear on the fertile scientific creativity of the biotechnology community. It should come as no surprise that in a study by researchers from Wharton Business School of more than 500 biopharmaceutical alliances, drugs developed in partnership were significantly more likely to win approval from the U.S. Food and Drug Administration than were drugs developed by a single company.[2]

B. Considerations in Choosing a Partner

While it is true that pharmaceutical-biotechnology collaborations have produced some of the most successful drugs on the market—12 out of the 25 largest revenue-producing drugs currently on the market were developed and commercialized through biopharmaceutical alliances[3]—a marriage of incompatible partners can sink the best science. Consider the following case:

> A recent oncology alliance between a large pharma and a biotech suffered a setback as a result of the imbalance of power between the two companies. The biotech had pioneered a promising technology in cancer treatment, and initial studies demonstrated its superior clinical profile. . . . The pharma, certain that it would get its way, attempted to strong-arm the biotech into accepting [a trial in combination with existing drugs]. The biotech's leadership resisted—having staked the company on a new technology, they did not want to endorse a competitor. Alienated by the one-sided strategies of their partner, the small company exercised its contractual right to veto the trial. As a result, the drug's uptake failed to meet expectations, and after a year of lackluster growth and mounting competition, the pharma shifted its focus to a similar pipeline drug.[4]

Despite this disheartening example, increasing competition among Big Pharma[5] for the best licensing opportunities has spearheaded in recent years a race to become biotech's "partner of choice." In general, this paradigm shift has bettered the opportunities of the small biotech licensor to negotiate fair, favorable alliance terms on a more balanced playing field. What terms are deemed fair depends largely on the stage of the technology brought to the table.

C. The Stage of the Drug Candidate Will Define the Alliance

Pharmaceutical companies prefer later-stage development alliances: the closer the drug candidate is to approval, the lower the risk. Lower risk justifies higher cost. But it is increasingly hard to find high-quality, late-stage drug candidates, so pharmaceutical companies have been pushed toward earlier-stage development alliances. This trend has been a boon to emerging biotechnology companies. Those companies can share the financial and logistical burdens of drug development earlier. They are also less reliant on venture capital funding.

A drug candidate's stage at the start of an alliance will define many aspects of the deal: financial terms, parties' rights and responsibilities, and how rapidly the pharmaceutical partner will assume control over the development process. Noted below are the stages of drug discovery and development, along with their relative attractiveness as entry points into a development and commercialization alliance.

> **Practice Point**
>
> Typical entry points for licensing deals:
> — Validated targets (typically nonexclusive licenses)
> — Leads, particularly if optimized
> — Post-ADME/Tox screening
> — Post-IND filing
> — During Phase II or III clinical trials

1. Early-Stage Deals

a. Target Identification and Validation

(i) *Unvalidated Targets*—An example would be a full-length gene sequence that is without functional assignment or disease association. Unvalidated targets are unattractive licensing candidates; there is no shortage of validated targets under study, so the risk is not worth the effort.

(ii) *Validated Targets*—A validated target is a gene with an association to a particular disease that can be demonstrated *in vivo*. This gene's function, when modulated by chemical or biological means, results in a phenotypic change in a relevant cell line. Validated targets are of interest as licensing candidates, but only if the licensor has a valid, enforceable patent or license—freedom to operate is the main concern here. Typically, pharmaceutical companies would rather take a non-exclusive license to a validated target at low cost than an exclusive license at higher cost.

b. Hits

These are molecules that show an effect on validated targets when put through high-throughput screening. Hits are not good licensing candidates. High-throughput screening identifies many false positives. Additionally, many genuine hits prove difficult, if not impossible, to design into "druggable" molecules.[6]

c. Leads

These are chemically modified high-throughput screening hits or rationally designed molecules that show, for example:

- Dose-related *in vitro*[7] potency
- Appropriate *in vitro* selectivity
- Activity and selectivity in cells
- Suitable physico-chemical properties suggesting "druggability"

Leads may be early-stage licensing candidates if the licensor has a patent claiming composition of the compound.

d. Optimized Leads

After a lead has been identified, parties will synthesize a number of similar related compounds to generate one with a more favorable profile of "druggable" characteristics—an optimized lead. Optimized leads will meet tighter specifications and present *in vivo* and disease model data. Optimized leads are certainly candidates for early-stage licensing deals.

2. Preclinical-Stage Licensing

a. ADME/Tox Studies

An optimized lead will typically undergo *in vitro* and animal testing to determine if it is likely to manifest toxic properties in living organisms. The term "ADME/Tox" (absorption, distribution, metabolism, excretion, and toxicity) is generally applied to the group of tests that are used to characterize a compound's properties with respect to absorption by the intestine, distribution to the organism, metabolism by the liver, excretion by the kidneys, and toxicity profiles. An optimized lead for which complete preclinical toxicology and ADME studies are available is definitely of licensing interest to pharmaceutical companies.

b. Investigational New Drug Application

Prior to initiating clinical trials, an Investigational New Drug (IND) application must be submitted to the FDA. Filing an IND is an important milestone in the drug development process that markedly increases the attractiveness of a drug candidate to potential licensees.

3. Clinical-Stage Licensing

a. Phase I

Phase I studies involve the initial introduction of an investigational new drug into humans, usually healthy volunteer subjects. These studies are designed to determine the metabolic and pharmacological actions of the drug in humans, the side effects associated with increasing doses, and, if possible, to gain early evidence on effectiveness. Phase I studies also evaluate drug metabolism, structure-activity relationships, and the mechanism of action in humans. The total number of subjects included in Phase I studies is generally in the range of 20 to 80.

b. Phase II

During this phase of development, clinical studies are conducted in human patients to determine dosage tolerability, safety, and efficacy.

c. Clinical Trials (Phase III)

During this phase, much broader human clinical trials of the drug candidate are conducted, generally at multiple sites.

4. Pre-launch Licensing

A drug candidate near completion of Phase III clinical trials is a low-risk licensing proposition for a pharmaceutical company. After all, little remains to accomplish but the things Big Pharma does best: sales and marketing. Major pharmaceutical companies have the machinery in place to guide a late-stage drug candidate through the final stages of regulatory approval and into the marketplace, often on a worldwide level. The company that waited this long to license its successful drug candidate can expect high royalties in exchange for having borne almost all the development risk and expense, as well as having forgone milestone payments from a partner along the way.

D. The Development and Commercialization License Agreement

The Development and Commercialization License Agreement is an important document. It may govern the relationship of the parties for decades—typically for as long as royalties are due to the licensor on the sale of any drug developed by the licensee. Yet, too often it is the Research Collaboration Agreement, with a lifespan of just a few years, that is the subject of intense negotiation. The License Agreement (or the "Heads of Agreement" summarizing license terms) gets short shrift as a mere exhibit. It is true that some 50 percent of research collaborations end in failure,[8] rendering long-term development and commercialization terms moot. For those parties who expect success in bringing a drug to market, however, the following terms deserve particular attention.

1. Nature and Scope of License Grant

The license grant is the critical core of the License Agreement. It establishes the parameters of what the licensee may do with the licensor's technology. It also identifies the outer limits of the technology in which rights will be granted.

a. Identifying the Subject Technology

Let us say, for example, that their collaborative research suggests to the parties that a certain family of compounds shows promising activity against a validated target. In that case, the pharmaceutical partner will seek a license under all patents with claims covering:

- the compounds themselves;
- any related formulation or prodrug;[9]
- any method of making or using the compounds; and
- any improvements to the foregoing.

Development and Commercialization Alliances

The pharmaceutical partner is likely also to seek a license under any know-how relating to the above.

In some cases, the license grant will relate to patents and know-how covering a particular compound—actually, a specific compound and any other compounds sharing the same active moiety. In other instances, the license may refer to a broad family of compounds, or perhaps any compounds identified by means of the licensor's drug discovery platform within a specified field.

b. The Rights Granted

Typically, a License Agreement will include several different license grants with respect to the subject technology:

- A license under the relevant patents and know-how to carry out its obligations under the License Agreement and to "develop, manufacture, have manufactured, market, use, sell, and import for sale" bulk drug substance and drug products containing the compound(s).
- A right to sublicense and, in particular, to subcontract manufacturing of the drug product. This right may (if the licensor is in a strong bargaining position) require licensor's notice of, and consent to, any sublicensing arrangements.
- There may also be a non-exclusive license to such other technology of the licensor as is necessary (with a strong licensee, this may read, "necessary or desirable") to carry out the intent of the License Agreement.[10]

> **Practice Point**
>
> Be careful to distinguish between the License Agreement term and the royalty term. They may not be identical.
>
> The royalty term will determine for how long the licensor will receive royalty payments.
>
> The License Agreement term will govern other contractual obligations, such as indemnification responsibilities in the event of a product liability or intellectual property infringement claim.
>
> In the event the License Agreement and royalty terms are identical, pay particular attention to those clauses identified as surviving termination of the agreement.

- Alternatively, many agreements contain an "enabling" license with respect to blocking intellectual property: in the event the licensee's exercise of its rights under the License Agreement infringes other intellectual property rights of the licensor, the licensee is granted a non-exclusive license sufficient to exercise its rights.
- The scope of the license should not include rights of the licensor's affiliates, since that could serve as a "poison pill" blocking a potential merger or acquisition with respect to the affiliate.

c. Scope of Rights

(i) *Exclusivity*—In consideration of the significant investment the pharmaceutical partner may be making, and because a non-exclusive license would leave the pharmaceutical partner open to competition, it is to be expected that the development and commercialization license will be exclusive, at least as to products arising out of the licensed technology in the field.[11]

(ii) *Territory*—This is commonly worldwide, unless the parties have agreed that the licensor or a third party will have certain rights in specific countries. For example, in the event of a co-marketing provision, the parties' rights to market may be defined geographically; this will affect the territory under relevant terms of the license grant. As noted in Section D.5.a.ii below, retention of this kind of right can enable a biotech to accelerate the development of its own sales and marketing capabilities.

(iii) *Duration*—In the case of patent licenses, the term of the agreement is typically the life of all relevant patents (including "all divisionals, continuations, continuations-in-part, re-examinations, reissues, extensions, registrations, and supplementary or complementary certificates"). Some agreements less favorable to the licensor have a shorter term—for example, 10 years from first commercial sale—which results in licensee royalty obligations of shorter duration. The know-how license grant is usually perpetual; a licensor-friendly agreement may provide that some small portion of royalties attributable to know-how will continue to be payable to the licensor on net sales of the licensed product, even after patent protection is no longer available in a particular jurisdiction.

(iv) *Field*—This may be as broad as "all therapeutic, diagnostic, palliative, or preventive uses in respect of human and animal health care." Where the subject of the License Agreement is a single compound (including all compounds having the same active moiety), pharmaceutical companies are likely to seek the broadest possible definition of field. Where the subject of the License Agreement includes a wider family of compounds, the pharmaceutical development partner may be more amenable to a narrower field. For example, the field may be as narrow as a particular disease. Alternatively, the expected method of drug delivery—for example, orally, buccally, topically, or by injection—may be used to limit the field. This is a particularly sensitive issue for the pharmaceutical partner: the more restrictions on field, the more likely that the biotechnology partner will be able to license the compound to a third party for other indications. This aggravates the risk the pharmaceutical company faces of subsequent competition from off-label use.

d. Retained Rights of the Licensor

If all or part of the license grant is "exclusive even as to licensor," the licensor may no longer exercise those rights under the licensed patents and know-how. However, in some instances, the licensor may be able to negotiate retention of certain rights.

(i) *Internal Research Only*—In this case, the licensor may continue to use the subject technology internally for research purposes. This may be valuable if the subject technology might lead to innovations that do not infringe the licensee's rights.

(ii) *Rights in Other Fields*—If the license to the pharmaceutical partner is limited by field, then the licensor retains rights to the technology in other fields. It may develop the technology in other fields independently or with third parties.

(iii) *Rights in Abandoned Compounds*—When the License Agreement relates to a family of compounds, it is likely the pharmaceutical partner will not use them all. One compound with the most favorable characteristics will be advanced as the "lead compound." If the lead compound fails, the pharmaceutical company will often turn to a related compound as a substitute. Ultimately, if all goes well, one compound advances into Phase III clinical trials, and the other licensed compounds lie unused. Occasionally, a licensee in a very strong negotiating position will be able to retain rights (or receive a license back) to abandoned compounds.

> **Practice Point**
>
> A savvy licensor realizes that one alliance is rarely a strong foundation for its continued growth as a company. To keep future product development options open, a licensor should attempt, when possible, to bargain for:
>
> — Retained internal research rights;
> — Rights in other fields/indications;
> — Rights to all compounds that the pharmaceutical partner declines to pursue and market.

This approach tends to worry a pharmaceutical partner. If it gives up rights to abandoned compounds, that compound might be developed years later into a competing product. Licensees can expect strenuous pushback on this issue. Nonetheless, it is sometimes possible to prevail, particularly if the retained right (or license back) is drafted with great care, building in protections against the scenarios of most concern to the pharmaceutical company.

2. Consideration for the License Grant

Revenues to be received by the licensee in consideration of a development and commercialization license fall into two temporal categories: pre-commercialization and commercialization. Pre-commercialization considerations may include signature payments,[12] research funding,[13] equity investments,[14] and milestone payments. Chapter IX addressed in detail the first three of these. Thus this chapter will focus on milestone payments and on royalties (consideration received on product sales once the drug is commercialized).

a. Milestone Payments

The principle of milestone payments is that key events on the path to commercialization should generate financial rewards for the licensor. Typically, the developing partner will want to "backload" the milestone payments: in other words, early payments are low; payments get larger the closer the drug candidate is to approval and commercialization. This is a risk-sharing device.

(i) *Early milestone events*—Examples of these may include scientific proof of concept;[15] execution of the development and commercialization agreement; successful completion of ADME/Tox studies;[16] successful initiation of, first patient enrollment in, or completion of Phase I or Phase IIa[17] trials.

(ii) *Clinical stage milestone events*—Examples of these may include initiation of or first patient enrollment in Phase IIb[18] or Phase III[19] clinical trials and/or filing of an Investigational New Drug (IND) application (or, for biologic materials, a Biologics License Application (BLA)) with the U.S. Food and Drug Administration (or an analogous filing with the equivalent agency of a major foreign government or regional regulatory authority).

(iii) *Pre-launch milestone events*—These may include successful completion of Phase III clinical trials, filing of a New Drug Application (NDA) with the U.S. Food and Drug Administration (or an analogous filing with the equivalent agency of a major foreign government or regional regulatory authority), and/or first regulatory approval of the drug product in the United States (or a major foreign country).

(iv) *Post-launch milestone events*—A typical post-launch milestone event is the first approved sale of the drug product in the United States (or certain specified foreign countries). Milestone payments might also be generated when worldwide annual sales of the drug product pass certain threshold amounts.

(v) *Milestone payments on compounds in the same class*—Typically, development and commercialization licenses will provide that a specific milestone will only be paid once for any compound in the same class. In other words, if certain milestones are paid with respect to a lead compound, and then another closely related compound is substituted as the lead, the developing partner will receive credit for previous milestones paid on the earlier compound.

(vi) *Milestone payments on subsequent indications*—Some development and commercialization agreements provide that once milestones have been paid on a compound, no additional milestones will be generated as a result of the approval of the drug for additional medical indications. Other agreements allow repeat milestone payments on the second indication; this is a matter of negotiation.

b. Royalty Payments, Generally

Royalty rates vary depending on a number of factors, including the extent of patent protection in place, the type of product, the stage at which the pharmaceutical partner took responsibility for development, and the third-party royalty obligations already incurred by the licensor. Licensees generally expect to calculate royalties based on their "net sales" of the product, although, admittedly, basing royalties on a lower percentage of total sales would be a simpler approach. The specific deductions resulting in "net sales" may differ from deal to deal.

(i) *Net Sales*—The net sales amount is calculated by subtracting from sales receipts a variety of expenses the pharmaceutical partner may have to cover. These deductions may include any or all of the following:

- Trade discounts, credits, or allowances;
- Credits or allowances granted upon returns, rejections, or recalls;
- Reserve for bad debts;
- Freight, shipping, and insurance charges;
- Taxes, duties, or other governmental tariffs; and
- Government-mandated rebates.

> **Practice Point**
>
> In negotiating the net sales definition, the licensee wants as many deductions as possible. The licensor wants as few. From the licensor's standpoint, the closer it can get to gross sales revenue, the better—not only monetarily, but in practical terms. A complex net sales definition requires continuing due diligence on the licensor's part to ensure that the net sales obligations are calculated fairly. Periodic accounting audits may be necessary.

Development and Commercialization Alliances

Some pharmaceutical companies will also include a blank check deduction of 2 to 5 percent of net sales to cover overhead or to allow for any expenses that the company is unable to track. It is possible to negotiate the finer points of the "net sales" definition—in particular, the size of the blank check deduction—but at the end of the day, when one is dealing with a huge, multinational conglomerate, one realizes that much of this is simply a reflection of the company's standard internal accounting practices—for better or worse, the net sales definition is what it is.

(ii) *Typical Royalty Rates*—Each deal is individual; it is hard to predict royalty rates with great accuracy. Exhibit 17-1 offers a rough guide to royalty rates, based on developmental stage of the technology at the time the License Agreement was executed. Bear in mind, however, that these royalty rates will be adjusted downward if:

- The underlying patent protection is not watertight;
- The licensee is assuming any existing obligations to pay royalties to third parties, such as academic institutions;

Exhibit 17-1
Rough Guide to Royalty Rates, Based on Developmental Stage

Developmental Stage	Rate	Comments
Validated Targets (Nonexclusive)	$\geq 1\%$	Lower if patent is insecure or if third-party royalties are payable
Validated Targets (Exclusive)	1-2%	
Leads	4-5%	Subject to royalty stacking; multi-tier royalties may be staged by annual net sales achieved
Optimized Leads	6-7%	
Development Candidates	7-8%	
Clinical Stage (Phase I)	~10%	Better benchmarking data available; can be reduced to Net Present Value
Clinical Stage (Phase II)	~15%	
Clinical Stage (Phase III)	~20%	

- There is an expectation that this therapy will be bundled with other products (whether other therapeutics or drug delivery devices) for sale.

(iii) *Multi-tiered Royalties*—Some agreements will provide for staggered royalty rates that increase as certain annual net sales thresholds are reached. Thus, for example, a licensor might receive 4 percent on annual net sales of less than $100 million, 5 percent on annual net sales of at least $100 million but less than $500 million, and 6 percent on annual net sales of at least $500 million.

The licensee should propose minimum royalty obligations to protect itself from these scenarios.

(iv) *Royalties on Combination Products*—When the parties expect that the licensee will sell the licensed technology as one component of a product, the License Agreement typically provides for royalties payable only on that portion of the product's net sales price attributable to the licensed technology. Where each component of the product could be sold as a stand-alone product, this is an easy calculation: one multiplies total net sales by a fraction, $A / (A + B)$, where A would be the price of the licensed component if it were sold alone, and $(A + B)$ is the total sales price. Where the components could not be sold alone, the method of calculation is a matter for negotiation. Some agreements look to the relative cost to manufacture each component of

> **Practice Point**
>
> Frequently, the licensor does not have title to the intellectual property being licensed to a larger partner for development and commercialization. The IP will have been in-licensed from an academic institution or another company. In this case, it is important that:
>
> — any discrepancies in the net sales definitions be identified and reconciled, and
> — the licensee's obligation to report net sales be timed to mesh with the licensor's own reporting obligations under the original in-license.

the product. Where the licensed technology improves a product previously sold by the licensee, some agreements provide for royalties on the difference in annual net sales of the new, improved product over the old. There are drawbacks to each of these approaches from the licensor's perspective: for example, neither takes into account the value the licensed technology may add in terms of retaining market share versus a competitor, even though revenues on the improved product may not outstrip those generated by the old.

c. Term of Royalty Payments

(i) *Royalties on Patents*—Where the parties acknowledge that the royalty obligation is primarily tied to patent protection, then the royalty payment term will typically survive with respect to sales in a particular jurisdiction only for as long as there is patent protection in that jurisdiction. However, from the perspective of the licensor, there are flaws to this approach, which should be considered in negotiating the term of patent royalties:

> **Practice Point**
>
> In determining royalties for combination products or next-generation products, bear in mind that calculations based on increases in net sales price of the combination product over the licensee's stand-alone product, or of annual sales revenue of the next-generation product over its unimproved predecessor, may result in little or no royalty income for the licensor if the licensee:
>
> — chooses to sell the new product at the same price as the old; or
> — fails to increase sales revenues of the new product over the old.

- The pharmaceutical partner may derive significant revenue on the licensed drug product from countries where, at least until recently, patents received little respect. The licensor may want to argue that it deserves a percentage of that revenue, regardless of the existence of patent protection in those jurisdictions.

- Even after a patent expires in a particular jurisdiction, the protection that had been afforded by the expiring patent allowed the pharmaceutical partner to build up protection in terms of market share. The licensor may assert that until such time as the licensee's market share in that jurisdiction drops below a specified percentage, full or partial royalty payments should continue.
- Another approach to the same argument is to propose that full or partial royalties will continue until generic competition in a certain jurisdiction (in the absence of patent protection) drives the pharmaceutical partner's market share below a specified percentage.

(ii) *Know-How Royalties*—Where significant know-how has been transferred from licensor to licensee, there is another argument for continuing partial royalty payments (perpetually or for a period of several years—such as 10 years from the first commercial sale) with respect to net sales in jurisdictions that no longer provide patent protection to the product. The licensor may bargain for royalty payments on the know-how once the patent royalties are no longer payable. The argument is that proprietary know-how with respect to the drug product still gives the pharmaceutical company a marketing edge over its generic competitors, and thus the licensor of the know-how deserves some compensation. This argument will be supported by including in the License Agreement definition of "know-how" the various documents filed and correspondence exchanged with the U.S. Food and Drug Administration or the analogous agency in the country or region for which know-how royalties are sought.

If obtained, know-how royalties will be significantly lower than patent royalties.

d. Punitive Reduction in Royalty Rates

In the event of the licensor's material breach of the License Agreement, the pharmaceutical partner will want a cudgel with which to enforce its rights. When the pharmaceutical company has invested tens or even hundreds of millions of dollars in bringing the product to market, however, termination is not a reasonable solution. Termination would only result in the pharmaceutical partner's loss of its own license to market the product.

A drastic reduction in royalty obligations (by 50 percent or more) is a more reasonable punitive strategy. Less draconian is a mechanism under which a certain percentage of royalties is paid into escrow, rather than to the licensor, after a breach has been alleged. In the event that a judge or arbitrator finds there was no breach, then the licensor receives all withheld royalty amounts.

e. Reduction in Royalty Rates for Third-Party Licenses

Many agreements provide that in the event the licensed intellectual property infringes that of a third party, necessitating negotiation of a license from that third party, then royalty payments will be reduced to offset any license fees payable to the third party. As protection, the licensor may negotiate that its royalties may, in any case, never be reduced by more than a certain percentage, such as 50 percent.

3. Other Intellectual Property Issues

a. Responsibility for Patent Prosecution and Maintenance

Licensor and licensee will typically remain responsible for filing and maintaining patents on their own respective background intellectual property. As for the key patents addressed by the License Agreement, prosecution and maintenance rights and obligations depend on several factors:

- If the licenses granted the pharmaceutical partner under the patents are restricted to a narrow field, such as one or more related diseases, then the licensor is likely to retain rights to file and maintain patents, given the expectation that the licensor may enter multiple alliances across fields. It is a matter of negotiation who will bear the expense of this patent protection.
- If the field of the license grant is broad in scope, it is more likely that the pharmaceutical partner will wish to take over prosecuting and maintaining the relevant patents at its own expense.

b. Abandoned Jurisdictions

Most agreements provide that if the party first charged with prosecuting and maintaining the relevant patents fails or chooses not to do so, the other party may take over the obligation at its own expense rather than see its patent protection lapse. This may be true generally or jurisdiction by jurisdiction.

The parties may agree on a list of jurisdictions in which patent protection must be maintained. Electing additional patent protection usually will be at the discretion of the party principally charged with patent prosecution and maintenance under the agreement, although the other party may have the right to do so in neglected jurisdictions.

c. Ongoing Cooperation

Every License Agreement will provide that, regardless of which party is charged with prosecuting and maintaining patents, the other party must cooperate with its efforts. Such cooperation typically will include:

- Executing such certificates and instruments as will establish ownership rights and enable the other party to apply for and prosecute patents; and
- Promptly informing the other party of information that may affect the preparation, filing, or prosecution of patents.

d. Trademarks, etc.

The licensee, as marketer of the drug product, will almost always insist on ownership of and control over product trademarks, trade dress, and packaging.

e. Prosecution of Infringers

The right to pursue infringers is often heavily negotiated, but common sense would dictate that, with respect to late-stage drug candidates, at least, the pharmaceutical partner has the stronger economic motivation to pursue infringers zealously and the greater financial resources to do so effectively. The licensor may wish to retain the right to prosecute infringers until development reaches a late enough stage—Phase III clinical trials, perhaps. Another reason for the licensor to retain the first right to pursue infringers might be that there are multiple licensees across fields, all of whom may be affected by the alleged infringement. Who has the rights to prosecute and enforce the patent, however, may depend a great deal on the scope of the license. A broad license often will provide the licensee the right to prosecute or enforce, or assume prosecution or enforcement, of a patent in some cases. A mere "freedom to operate," non-exclusive license is less likely to contain such language, although it still may include rights to step in if patent prosecution or enforcement does not meet certain time lines or standards.

Giving the pharmaceutical partner the first right to pursue infringers throughout the development process presents little risk to the licensor. Most agreements provide that if the party first entitled to pursue infringers fails or is uninterested in doing so, the other party may step in at its own expense. Alternatively, a licensor with sufficient resources may wish to join the pharmaceutical partner's prosecution of the infringer, on the licensor's own behalf and at its own expense.

Another frequently debated issue involves division of any damages. In fairness, the party that pursued the infringer will, quite reasonably, expect its legal expenses to be paid out of the settlement. It is a matter of negotiation, then, how the remainder of the spoils will be treated:

- Entire amount of damages payable to party who pursued the infringer?
- Damages (net of legal expenses) split evenly between the parties?
- Entire amount of damages (net of legal expenses) payable to pharmaceutical partner, in lieu of lost sales?
- Entire amount of damages (net of legal expenses) payable to pharmaceutical partner, in lieu of lost sales—but subject to a royalty payment at the otherwise agreed rate to the licensor, as in the case of any other net sales revenues?
- Or, if sublicense revenues are shared at a different rate, treat damages as revenues from sublicensing?

4. Cooperation of the Parties During the Regulatory Approval Process

Although it may appear that the pharmaceutical partner has assumed all essential obligations with respect to bringing the drug candidate to market—and, indeed, most licensees controlling development and commercialization will insist that regulatory submissions be in the licensee's name—

still, the licensor will remain obligated under the License Agreement to provide cooperation and assistance throughout the approval process in dealing with regulatory agencies.

5. Participation in the Upside

a. "Co-rights"

In the classic development and commercialization alliance, Big Pharma takes on virtually all the risks of developing a smaller company's drug candidate—and then reaps nearly all the rewards if the risks pan out. Increasingly, however, biotechnology companies with confidence in their own future ability to develop and market drugs (not to mention an eye on Wall Street, which favors companies with revenue potential beyond mere royalty streams) have been pressing for an option to participate more fully in the upside of the drug development process. As a result, one sees in some (though by no means the majority of) alliances over the past several years what are colloquially referred to as "co-rights." Most commonly, these involve co-development and co-promotion rights, each of which involves the optional sharing of certain responsibilities and financial rewards between the pharmaceutical partner and its smaller licensor.

> (i) *Co-development Rights*—This is a scenario seen more frequently in early-stage than in later-stage deals, but only where the licensor is perceived as extremely sound financially and otherwise possessed of the resources to carry its own weight in a drug development program. Under this scenario, the licensee initially assumes full responsibility for developing the drug candidate. However, the parties agree to revisit this issue upon the occurrence of a specific event—perhaps the initiation of Phase IIb or Phase III clinical trials. At that time, the licensor may opt into the development process, assuming a previously agreed percentage of development expenses and obligations. However, this opt-in right usually involves certain conditions:
>
> - The pharmaceutical partner typically retains a veto right at its sole discretion. From the perspective of the pharma partner, it

does not want a promising drug development program burdened by a partner that cannot carry its weight financially, scientifically, or in terms of the critical mass necessary to get the job done. And with the clock ticking on patent life for a product that might generate peak sales of millions of dollars per day, the pharma partner can not tolerate unnecessary delays in decision-making.

- There is usually a prohibition on sublicensing a co-development right. Otherwise, the pharmaceutical company might find itself dealing with a range of other parties—from contract research organizations to major pharmaceutical competitors—in place of its biotechnology partner.

- Opting into co-development may translate to a reduction in milestone payments. This makes sense, if one considers milestone payments the "rent" paid by the developing partner during the course of the drug approval process. There is less justification to pay rent to a co-developer (although some obligation does remain, given the licensor's overarching intellectual property rights).

- Opting into co-development should translate into a significantly increased royalty share; alternatively, the parties may agree on another method of increasing the licensor's share of the profits on net sales of the drug product.

(ii) *Co-promotion Rights*—In this scenario, the licensor may give notice to its pharmaceutical partner, within a specified period of time prior to the first commercial sale of the drug product, that it wishes to participate in promotion of the drug product. This option may be limited to certain geographical territories, such as the licensor's home country, where it is determined the licensor has the best opportunity as a co-promoter. Co-promotion rights may have some or all of the following features:

- The pharmaceutical partner almost always retains a veto right, at its sole discretion, in the event it determines that the licensor does not have the resources to be an effective co-promoter. These

resources may include not only financial wherewithal, but also pharmaceutical sales and marketing experience (and the accompanying regulatory understanding), market reputation, and the like.
- There is usually a prohibition on sublicensing the co-promotion right. As in the case of a co-development sublicense, the pharmaceutical partner fears loss of control over who its co-promotion partner actually would be.
- Typically, the parties will enter into a co-promotion agreement at the time of option exercise, allocating respective responsibilities.
- If the parties are co-promoting in a shared territory (as opposed to dividing the promotion opportunities geographically), then there will often be a limit placed on what percentage of the overall sales detail force and product-specific marketing expenses shall be borne by each party.
- When the parties agree to co-promote in a given territory, the licensor's share of net sales for that territory will no longer be calculated as a royalty on net sales, but rather a percentage of the profits, usually commensurate with the percentage of marketing expenses borne by the licensor.

b. Bulk Supply Rights

Another way licensors may participate in the upside is to enter into a Supply Agreement to manufacture and supply to the licensee the bulk drug substance from which the drug product will be produced. Along with its royalty stream from the licensee, this arrangement gives the licensor another source of revenue with respect to the licensed product.

E. Anticipating Changes of Control of Either Party

It is not unreasonable to expect that at some point during the term of the License Agreement—which may, as previously noted, continue for decades—one or both parties will undergo a change of control.

a. Licensor Issues

In recent years, the trend for larger pharmaceutical companies has been to consolidate. Consider the Sanofi acquisition of Aventis or Pfizer's takeover of Pharmacia. It is understandable, then, that a small biotechnology company entering into a long-term development and commercialization alliance with one major pharmaceutical company may wonder, quite understandably, with which other industry player it may end up partnering. The concerns of the small licensor include:

- What if the acquiror has no use for this particular drug candidate, either because it is not interested in that area of science or because it has a competing product of its own under development? Will this drug candidate end up ignored on the acquiror's shelf?
- What if the acquiror lacks comparable marketing capabilities and distribution channels in certain key territories around the world? Will we lose substantial royalties as a result?
- We have confidence in meeting our co-development and/or co-promotion obligations with our current licensee—but if we have a weaker relationship with an acquiror, will we still be able to maximize those rights?

b. Licensee Issues

Many biotechnology companies, for their part, dream of acquisition opportunities. For their institutional investors, an eventual sale of the company would be a welcome liquidity event—particularly given an unpredictable, indeed chilly, market for initial public offerings. Yet a pharmaceutical partner to a drug development initiative may wonder, quite understandably, whether it will ultimately be doing business with this licensor or some unknown future acquiror. Pharmaceutical companies may have the following anxieties about a licensor change of control:

- What if the licensor is acquired by another major pharmaceutical company? Will our know-how with respect to this initiative, such as marketing strategies, end up in the hands of our biggest competitor?

- What if the licensor is acquired by a less reliable or less competent company—will we have an argument on our hands to prevent the exercise of co-development or co-promotion rights?
- What about any bulk drug substance manufacturing for which we were planning to rely on our licensor—can we still count on reliable supply?

c. Tailoring a Solution

In order to allay concerns, each party may agree to provide notice or even to obtain consent before a change of control. Most companies would find this far too burdensome, however: the need to bring each development partner to the table before effecting a change of control would have a chilling effect on most mergers or acquisitions.

Alternatively, the smaller partner may agree that it will need consent from the larger partner prior to any merger with or acquisition by another pharmaceutical company with a similar market capitalization to the larger partner. This, along with standard veto powers over exercise of "co-rights" by any successor in interest to the smaller partner, should allay the concerns of the larger partner. Another possibility is providing the larger partner with advance notice of the potential transaction so it will have the opportunity to make a competing offer. The smaller partner—in particular its Board of Directors—will need to consider carefully whether the potential chilling effect of such a provision is outweighed by the validation and financial benefits of inking a major development partnership.

A small biotechnology licensor is unlikely to obtain a commitment from a major pharmaceutical partner to notify, much less seek consent from, that licensor prior to a change of control. However, there are other contractual protections, binding on any successor to the pharmaceutical partner, which may provide the smaller party with some comfort. Most useful of these is the right to terminate if the larger partner is failing to exercise diligence in developing the drug candidate.

F. Terminating the Agreement If the Alliance Fails

The odds are dauntingly against maintaining a successful development alliance all the way through commercialization. More than one-third of alliances get canceled or renegotiated prior to the end of their intended term, while fewer than two out of five meet their stated objectives.[20] Even while maintaining a strong commitment to the relationship, it is in each party's interest to negotiate termination rights and other material breach penalties carefully.

In structuring the rights of the parties in the event of, for example, a material breach, one must bear in mind that the same penalty can affect each party quite differently. Termination rights by and large favor the licensor: with its intellectual property rights returned to it, the licensor can presumably start again with another collaborator. The licensee, on the other hand, is in a different position. The pharmaceutical partner may have hundreds of millions of dollars invested in a drug candidate on the verge of product launch; it may have a large sales force lined up and waiting to market the product worldwide; it may have third-party manufacturing and distribution contracts outstanding. How can termination of the License Agreement serve its interests, even in the event of the licensor's breach?

1. Material Breach by the Licensee

a. *The Licensor's Perspective*

In the event of an uncured material breach—for example, failure to pay royalties, to maintain confidentiality, or to develop the drug candidate diligently—the licensor will want the right to terminate. It is likely to obtain a much better deal from another collaborator now that it has a drug candidate closer to commercialization.

b. *The Licensee's Perspective*

The larger pharmaceutical partner to the development alliance will resist inclusion of this remedy in the License Agreement. Given its investment in the drug candidate, it will argue for some intermediate remedy, even in the event of its own material breach: monetary damages, a higher royalty rate, or even loss of exclusivity is preferable to termination of the license.

2. Material Breach by the Licensor

a. *The Licensor's Perspective*

The smaller biotech partner may attempt to argue that termination is an appropriate remedy against it in the event it materially breaches the License Agreement. But for the reasons stated above, the later the development stage, the more likely that a termination event will hurt the pharmaceutical partner—while potentially creating new business opportunities for the breaching licensor.

b. *The Licensee's Perspective*

One remedy that the pharmaceutical partner may propose in the event of the licensor's uncured material breach is a significant reduction in royalty rates. This serves the appropriate punitive function in respect of the licensor's breach, but it does no harm to the licensee. If the licensor resists this remedy, a compromise position might be for the licensee to pay a significant portion of its royalties into escrow, while awaiting arbitration or adjudication of the dispute. If the licensee is found not to have breached the agreement materially, it will receive the withheld royalties at that time.

3. Termination Without Cause

The parties may wish to consider scenarios under which they might no longer wish to work together, even if there has been no material breach or other termination event. Perhaps one party is acquired by a party unacceptable to the other. Perhaps one party desires to be acquired, but this particular development alliance is one of the obligations the acquiror would prefer not to assume. Perhaps the science has failed, or regulatory approval has been denied. In such cases, the License Agreement should provide a mechanism by which the parties may mutually agree to part ways. For the reasons discussed above, however, a unilateral right of termination by the licensor—particularly late in the development process—generally should be avoided.

G. Conclusion: The Importance of Getting It Right

Development alliances are crucial to the viability of both the pharmaceutical and biotechnology industries. Spurred by weak pipelines and expiring patents, pharmaceutical companies pumped more than $11 billion into biotech development alliances in 2004—the highest level in history.[21] Yet, as noted above, a significant percentage of these deals fail. As lawyers representing pharmaceutical or biotechnology clients, we can do nothing when science itself poses the obstacles. But most other obstacles to these deals are, at bottom, business issues. Through careful drafting and insightful counsel, we can assist our clients over many of the hurdles that might otherwise result in a failed alliance.

Notes

1. *Collaborations and Licensing in Global Pharmaceuticals and Biotech*, Visiongain Management Reports, 2005.

2. S. Nicholson, P. Danzon, and J. McCullough, "Biotech-Pharmaceutical Alliances as a Signal of Asset and Firm Quality," *NBER Working Paper*, June 2002, No. 9007.

3. THE MCKINSEY QUARTERLY, 2004, No. 1.

4. *Pharma Alliances: Bridging the Gap,* The Kerdan Group, 2005.

5. When used in this chapter, the terms "Big Pharma," "major pharmaceutical companies," and the like are meant to include the biggest of the biotechnology companies also. Convergence of the two industries has led to great similarities between the large players, and indeed, between the smaller players, of both groups.

6. An "undruggable" molecule is one that, for example, may be too large, too chemically unstable, or otherwise impractical or unsuitable for delivery into the human body as a drug.

7. *In vitro* techniques include utilizing cell or tissue cultures, isolated cells, tissue slices, subcellular fractions, transgenic cell cultures, and cells from transgenic organisms, as well as *in silico* modeling.

8. *Learning the Biopartnering Game: How to Achieve More from Your Alliance*, IBM Business Consulting Services, 2004.

9. A prodrug is a drug that is administered in an inactive (or significantly less active) form. Once administered, the prodrug is metabolized in the body into the active compound. The rationale behind the use of a prodrug is generally for ADME optimization. Prodrugs are usually designed to improve oral bioavailability—poor absorption from the gastrointestinal tract is usually the limiting factor, and it is often due to the chemical properties of the drug.

10. *But see* Chapter IX, Section D.3.C, for concerns raised by a grant of this right.

11. *See* Section D.1.c.iv of this chapter.

12. *See* Chapter IX, Section D.5.a.

13. *See* Chapter IX, Section D.5.b.

14. *See* Chapter IX, Section D.5.c.

15. "Scientific proof of concept" with respect to drug development refers to the scientific study of the mechanism of action of the subject compound in humans. A positive result from this study will support a decision to proceed with development of the compound as a drug candidate.

16. *See* note 2, above.

17. "Phase IIa" refers to clinical studies of a drug candidate in human patients to determine initial dose-ranging tolerability and safety in single-dose, single ascending-dose, multiple dose, and/or multiple ascending-dose regimens.

18. "Phase IIb" refers to continued clinical trials of a drug candidate on sufficient numbers of human patients to establish efficacy and dose for the desired indications.

19. "Phase III" refers to continued clinical trials of a drug candidate on sufficient numbers of human patients to establish safety and efficacy for the desired indications. These trials are typically much larger than those in Phase IIb and are likely to be conducted at multiple sites.

20. *Critical Factors for Alliance Formation: Insights from the Deloitte Research Biotech Alliance Survey,* Deloitte Research, 2005.

21. *Id.*

Chapter XVIII

Expansion: European and International Considerations for Biotechnology Companies*

Daniel Pavin, Esq.
Taylor Wessing
London, England

This chapter examines legal and regulatory issues of relevance to a company expanding its business beyond the United States.

The geographic focus of this chapter is on Europe, though commentary is included as to certain legal and regulatory matters of note in various other non-U.S. jurisdictions.

---

* This chapter does not seek to address all legal and regulatory issues that companies or lawyers would have to consider in this practice, such as local health and safety laws, regulation with respect to the use and transportation of hazardous or restricted materials (if applicable), environmental law (outside of the context of the discussion in the GMO section of this chapter), product liability law, and "generic" issues such as local contract, labor, real estate, corporate, taxation, and antitrust law.

The author would like to thank his colleagues in the Taylor Wessing Life Sciences and Healthcare Group, and in particular Yvonne Roberton, Director of Roberton Limited Regulatory Consultancy, for their assistance in the preparation, writing, and review of this chapter. Any errors or omissions are, however, the author's alone.

In 2004, the European Union expanded from 15 Member States to 25 Member States,[1] and it now has a population of approximately 500 million. This presents great opportunities to an expanding U.S. company. At the same time, access to, and operating within, the European market presents a significant number of legal and regulatory challenges. Whatever form expansion takes—for example, setting up a research facility in a country outside the United States or entering into a collaboration agreement with a non-U.S. partner—it is essential to have an understanding of the local legal and regulatory framework in order to conduct research, development, and marketing effectively and efficiently.

This chapter provides an overview of:

- relevant European institutions, regulatory agencies and the European legislative framework (section A);
- what is a "medicinal product" under European law (section B);
- the regulation of product development: non-clinical trials (section C) and clinical trials (section D);
- the regulation of marketing authorizations (section E);
- strategies and issues associated with international clinical trials and marketing authorizations (section F);
- post-marketing activities, including pharmacovigilance, manufacturing and supply controls, abridged marketing authorization applications, and regulatory data exclusivity (section G);
- other areas of regulation of particular relevance to the biotechnology sector, such as that governing stem cell research, the use of human tissue and cells, and medical devices (section H);
- the regulation in Europe and internationally of genetically modified organisms or "GMOs" (section I);
- key aspects of European intellectual property law (section J); and
- European competition (antitrust) law (section K).

A. An Overview of Relevant European Institutions, Regulatory Bodies, and Legislative Framework

1. The European Commission

The European Commission's four main roles are to propose legislation to the European Parliament and the European Council, to administer and implement Community policies, to enforce Community law (jointly with the Court of Justice) and to negotiate international agreements, mainly those relating to trade and cooperation. The European Commission is divided into different administrative departments (Directorates-General or DGs), each of which has responsibility for a different area or areas of European policy.[2] Key relevant DGs (with their responsibilities in brackets) include:

a) the Enterprise and Industry DG (pharmaceuticals,[3] including advanced therapies such as human tissue engineering, gene therapy, and cell therapy;[4] biotechnology[5] and cosmetics;[6] and medical devices[7]);
b) the Health and Consumer Protection DG (approvals and labeling of genetically modified food and feed[8]);
c) the Environment DG (the release of genetically modified organisms into the environment and for contained use[9] and protection and welfare of laboratory animals[10]);
d) the Internal Market DG (intellectual property matters[11]); and
e) the Research, Development, Technology and Innovation DG (promoting and facilitating research into biotechnology, including funding of transnational projects under the "Framework" initiative[12]).

In addition to providing further information about the work of the various DGs, their respective Web sites are very useful sources of information, containing links to relevant legislation and guidance, consultation papers, press releases, and speeches.

2. The European Medicines Agency

The European Medicines Agency (EMEA) is a decentralized body of the European Union, with headquarters in London. The EMEA's main responsibility is the protection and promotion of public and animal health through the evaluation and supervision of medicines for human and veterinary use, which it coordinates throughout the European Union.[13]

Specific activities of the EMEA include assessing marketing authorization applications made using the Centralized Procedure (see below at section E.1.a) and processing variations to them; providing scientific advice, protocol assistance, regulatory and procedural guidance to companies; receiving safety reports concerning medicinal products and coordinating action relating to their safety and quality; and coordinating Member States' inspections activity.

The EMEA is organized into a Management Board, the Committee for Medicinal Products for Human Use (CHMP), the Committee for Medicinal Products for Veterinary Use (CVMP), the Committee for Orphan Medicinal Products (COMP), and the Committee for Herbal Medicinal Products (HMPC).

The Inspections Sector of the EMEA is, among other things, responsible for coordinating any good manufacturing practice (GMP), good clinical practice (GCP), or good laboratory practice (GLP) inspections requested by the CHMP or CVMP in connection with the assessment of marketing authorization and clinical trial applications and/or the assessment of matters referred to those committees in accordance with European legislation.[14]

There are a number of key "Working Parties" within the EMEA, covering topics such as Blood Products, Biotechnology (see below), Efficacy, ICH, Pharmacovigilance, Quality, Safety, and Vaccines. The EMEA's Biotechnology Working Party (BWP) undertakes various activities in relation to biotechnological products, such as supporting marketing authorization assessment and providing scientific advice. There is also a Blood Products Working Group, set up to address efficacy and safety aspects of blood products (including recombinant-DNA medicinal products). Quality aspects of blood products are covered by the BWP. A Working Party on Similar Biological Medicinal Products (BMWP) has also been established to provide recommendations to the CHMP on biosimilars.[15] These Working Parties have issued Concept Papers, and Draft and Adopted Guidelines applicable to their fields.[16] The EMEA's Gene Therapy Expert Group and Human Cell Therapy Expert Working Group has issued guidance documents in the fields of gene transfer, lentiviral vectors, gene therapy, human somatic cell therapy, xenogenetic cell therapy medicinal products, biobanks and pharmacogenetics, and medicinal products containing active substances produced by stable transgene expression in higher plants.[17]

3. National Regulatory Bodies (Competent Authorities)

Each Member State has its own national regulatory body, or "competent authority." They play an extremely important role in European regulation of medicinal products. Functions of the competent authorities include:

a) authorization and supervision of medicinal products via the national route and clinical trial authorizations;
b) acting as rapporteur/co-rapporteur in the Centralized Procedure (see section E.4 below);
c) inspections; and
d) participation in the work of the *European Pharmacopoeia* (see section A.4 below).

A list of European competent authorities, which includes links to their Web sites, is set out on the following Web page of the EMEA Web site: http://www.emea.eu.int/Inspections/Links.html.[18]

4. European Legislation and Other Instruments

This chapter makes reference to European "Regulations" and "Directives." When brought into force, a "Regulation" takes effect in all Member States and is directly enforceable in those states. Unlike a Regulation, a Directive needs to be implemented into Member States' national legislation. Differences can arise between Member States' implementations, through (for example) different interpretations of the language of the Directive, where the Directive simply sets a minimum standard (and does not prevent a stricter position being taken), or where the Directive allows for discretion on the part of the Member State as to how to implement a particular provision. However, national courts must interpret the resulting national laws in light of the parent Directive, with disputes ultimately being resolved by the European Court of Justice, further smoothing out national differences in interpretation.

When looking at the legal position in Europe with respect to various matters (such as clinical trials), this chapter generally only considers legislation at the Regulation and Directive level. In practice, one must also consider the applicable national law that implements the Directives, and in effect read the two together.

In addition, and of relevance specifically to the pharmaceutical and biotechnology sectors, are the *European Pharmacopoeia* monographs. The *European Pharmacopoeia* is the authoritative collection of standards for medicines in Europe. Its texts (termed "monographs") are the primary standards for medicines and are legally binding, through an international treaty. Applicants for marketing authorizations for medicinal products must use terminology identical to that in the *European Pharmacopoeia* and observe the quality standards (for example, with respect to raw materials, dosage forms, and tests) set out in it.

Guidelines issued by the European Commission, the EMEA Committees, ICH, and guidelines of national competent authorities, to which subsequent sections of this chapter make reference, are not legally binding as such, but regulatory agencies expect applicants to comply with them where applicable. If an applicant deviates from the guideline or considers that it is not applicable, then a robust justification for noncompliance must be given.

B. The Definition of "Medicinal Products" Under European Law

Whether something is or is not a medicinal product[19] determines which laws apply to it. The definition of "medicinal product" is:

a) any substance or combination of substances presented as having properties for treating or preventing disease in human beings; or
b) any substance or combination of substances which may be used in or administered to human beings either with a view to restoring, correcting or modifying physiological functions by exerting a pharmacological, immunological or metabolic action, or to making a medical diagnosis.[20]

In the definition above, a "substance" is defined to be any matter irrespective of origin, whether human, animal, vegetable or chemical. Therefore, the definition of "medicinal product" is very broad in scope and includes new therapies such as gene therapy. It is important to note that a substance is a "medicinal product" if claims are made that it is capable of treating or preventing disease in humans, or it is presented or marketed as such, even if it is subsequently found not to do so.

Products whose classification is unclear (for example, where it is not clear whether a product is a medicine or a food supplement) are commonly termed "borderline products." If a product falls within the definition of "medicinal product" and within the definition of a product covered by other European legislation, then pharmaceutical legislation applies.[21] If the product is clearly, for example, a food supplement, biocidal or a cosmetic, rather than a medicinal product, then pharmaceutical legislation will not apply. Medicinal product/medical device combinations are discussed below at section H.5.

C. Standards for Non-clinical Tests: Good Laboratory Practice and Laboratory Animal Welfare

1. Introduction

Applications for authorizations to conduct clinical trials (see section D) and for marketing authorizations (see section E) must be supported by certain prescribed non-clinical data. The studies to derive those data must be planned, performed, recorded and reported in accordance with Good Laboratory Practice (GLP).

GLP in the European Economic Area (EEA)[22] is governed by two Directives.[23] The first, Directive 2004/9/EC,[24] lays down the obligation of the Member States to designate the authorities responsible for GLP inspections in their territory. Additionally, it sets out reporting requirements and requirements in respect of mutual acceptance of data within the EEA, and requires that the Organisation for Economic Co-operation and Development (OECD) Revised Guides for Compliance Monitoring Procedures for GLP and the OECD Guidance for the Conduct of Test Facility Inspections and Study Audits be followed during laboratory inspections and study audits. The second, Directive 2004/10/EC,[25] requires Member States to take all measures necessary to ensure that laboratories carrying out safety studies on chemical products comply with the OECD Principles of Good Laboratory Practice.

Depending on the nature of the materials being used in the tests, other Directives may be applicable—for example, Directive 2004/33/EC, concerning technical requirements for blood and blood components (see further at section H.3 below).

2. Guidance from the ICH and the EMEA

The ICH has issued guidelines as to quality and safety standards to be applied in non-clinical studies. An example of relevance to the biotechnology sector is the note for "Guidance on Preclinical Safety Evaluation of Biotechnology-Derived Pharmaceuticals."[26] The EMEA has also issued its own guidelines with respect to non-clinical testing.

3. Laboratory Animal Welfare

Directive 86/609/EEC governs the protection of animals used for experimental and other scientific purposes.[27] This Directive sets out certain standards with respect to carrying out experiments on animals; for example, experiments on animals must be performed by authorized persons only (or under the authority of such a person),[28] experiments on animals must not be performed if there is another scientifically satisfactory method of obtaining the result sought,[29] and user establishments[30] and breeding and supplying establishments[31] must be registered.

The European Commission has set up a Technical Expert Working Group (TEWG) to assist in the revision and review of Directive 86/609. The final reports of all the subgroups of TEWG have been submitted and the Commission is currently analyzing the reports.[32]

A number of multinational and national organizations within the EEA have issued guidelines with respect to aspects of animal testing. Examples include those set out by the Federation of European Laboratory Animal Science Associations (FELASA).[33]

4. Non-clinical Studies and Animal Testing: Other Countries

a. GLP

The principles of GLP have been developed in the framework of the Organization for Economic Cooperation and Development (OECD) and were first published in 1981. Subsequently, a series of further documents on related issues, notably compliance, monitoring, and inspections, have been published.³⁴ OECD member countries have adopted the GLP principles developed by the OECD, and a number of non-member countries have agreed to adhere to the principles as part of a mutual recognition scheme.

b Animal Testing

Most countries in which non-clinical studies are likely to be conducted have in place laws governing the use of animals. There are also various national and international initiatives aimed at promoting the so-called "3Rs" (replacement, refinement, and reduction of the use of animals in research).³⁵

D. Clinical Trials in the EEA

1 Introduction: The Regulatory Framework

The European regulatory framework for clinical trials that are conducted in the EEA is provided by the so-called "Clinical Trials Directive,"³⁶ (discussed in more detail below), together with:

a) other Directives applicable to aspects of clinical trials, such as the GCP Directive³⁷ (when implemented), the GMP Directive,³⁸ and the Data Protection Directive;³⁹
b) other Directives that may be applicable depending on the nature of the trial, such as Directives regulating the use of GMOs (see further at section I below);
c) guidance⁴⁰ issued by the European Commission;⁴¹ and
d) guidelines issued by the European Medicines Agency.⁴²

A U.S. company conducting clinical trials in Europe (whether to support a marketing authorization application in Europe, the United States or elsewhere) must comply with this framework.

The Clinical Trials Directive was adopted by the European Parliament and Council on April 4, 2001. Prior to its adoption, there was no harmonized European legislation with respect to the conduct of clinical trials.

The Directive should have been implemented by all Member States by May 1, 2004, but a number of Member States missed that deadline.⁴³ The

Clinical Trials Directive has not been implemented uniformly throughout the remaining Member States, and each Member State has its own detailed administrative procedures to be followed with respect to the application for, and running of, a clinical trial. Therefore, those who conduct pan-European clinical trials will have to continue to be aware of differences in the application process for, approval of, and reporting requirements for clinical trials between Member States, taking steps to comply with local variations in the implementation and interpretation of the Clinical Trials Directive.[44]

2. Provisions of the Clinical Trials Directive

Broadly speaking, the main aims of the Directive are to:

- reinforce ethical principles and protect the rights of subjects in clinical trials;
- simplify and harmonize regulatory and approval procedures with respect to the conduct of clinical trials of medicinal products in Europe, including in particular making adherence to GCP a legal requirement; and
- improve the quality of clinical research in Europe.

To these ends, the Directive sets out provisions with respect to:

a) conduct (including compliance with GCP) and suspension of clinical trials;
b) clinical trials on minors;[45]
c) subject consent and the consent of incapacitated subjects;
d) establishment and operation of Ethics Committees, approvals from Ethics Committees, and the authorization process for clinical trials by competent authorities;
e) establishment of a European clinical trials database (known as "Redact"[46]);
f) adverse event and serious adverse reaction reporting;
g) establishment of a European database of suspected unexpected serious adverse reactions;
h) manufacture and importation of investigational medicinal products, the labeling of them, and certification of relevant activities by a Qualified Person; and
i) insurance/indemnity requirements.

3 Scope of the Clinical Trials Directive: What Is a "Clinical Trial"?

The Clinical Trials Directive defines a clinical trial as:

> any investigation in human subjects intended to discover or verify the clinical, pharmacological and/or other pharmacodynamic effects of one or more investigational medicinal product(s), and/or to identify any adverse reactions to one or more investigational medicinal product(s) and/or to study absorption, distribution, metabolism and excretion of one or more investigational medicinal product(s) with the object of ascertaining its (their) safety and/or efficacy.[47]

Accordingly, the Clinical Trials Directive covers Phase I-IV clinical trials. No distinction is made between commercial studies and non-commercial studies (academic research or investigator-led studies). In all cases, non-interventional trials (i.e., those where a medicinal product is prescribed in the usual manner strictly in accordance with the terms of its marketing authorization) are excluded from the ambit of the Clinical Trials Directive.[48]

4 What Is an "Investigational Medicinal Product"?

An "investigational medicinal product" (IMP) is defined to be a:

> pharmaceutical form of an active substance or placebo being tested or used as a reference in a clinical trial, including products already with a marketing authorization but used or assembled (formulated or packaged) in a way different from the authorized form, or when used for an unauthorized indication, or when used to gain further information about the authorized form.

The term "investigational medicinal product" includes biological and biotechnology products, cell therapy products, gene therapy products, plasma-derived products, and products containing GMOs.

5. Who Is the "Sponsor" under the Clinical Trials Directive?

The Directive defines a sponsor as "an individual, company, institution or organization which takes responsibility for the initiation, management and/or financing of a clinical trial." The sponsor can be a single organization or a group of individuals/organizations. A group of sponsors can either be co-sponsors (agreeing on allocation of liability between them) or joint sponsors (each taking full liability for the trial).

Legal responsibilities of the sponsor include:

> **Practice Points**
>
> The duties of a sponsor under the Clinical Trials Directive include:
>
> 1. Obtaining official authorizations and approvals.
> 2. Amending non-accepted applications.
> 3. Notifying authorities about significant protocol changes.
> 4. Reporting on safety, including adverse events reports.
> 5. Responding in the event authorities wish to stop a trial.
> 6. Insuring or indemnifying against risks.

a) Obtaining authorization from the competent authorities, approval from the Ethics Committees, and additional approvals for certain types of trial, such as gene therapy trials.
b) Amendment of the application in the event of non-acceptance by the competent authority.[49]
c) Notification to competent authorities in the event of significant changes to the trial protocol.[50]
d) Recording and reporting details of adverse events[51] and suspected serious unexpected adverse reactions,[52] and providing annual safety reports to competent authorities and Ethics Committees.[53]
e) Having in place insurance or indemnity arrangements.[54]

6. Sponsors Who Are Not Established in the EEA

Article 19 of the Clinical Trials Directive requires sponsors, or their legal representatives, to be established within the EEA. Accordingly, it is not possible for a U.S.-based sponsor with no establishment or representative in the EEA to conduct a clinical trial within the EEA.

Options available to a non-EEA sponsor, which should be evaluated on a case-by-case basis, include:

a) appoint an EEA-based group company (if one exists) to be the legal representative;
b) set up a subsidiary in the EEA to act as the legal representative; or
c) enter into a contract with a contract research organization (CRO) under which the CRO agrees to act as legal representative (and take on liability for some or all of the sponsor's obligations).

7. Applying for Clinical Trial Authorization

While specifics vary from Member State to Member State,[55] the basic rule is that before commencing a trial, the sponsor must first obtain a favorable opinion from an Ethics Committee (or Ethics Committees) and authorization from the relevant competent authority (or authorities). Each opinion issued by an Ethics Committee covers the proposed trial in a single Member State. Multi-centre trials running in several Member States will therefore require an Ethics Committee approval from an Ethics Committee in each of those Member States.[56]

Ethics Committees are required to provide reasoned opinions within 60 days of receipt of a valid application,[57] except where the application relates to a trial in-

Practice Points

The Clinical Trials Directive requires sponsors, or their legal representatives, to be established within the EEA. Options for a non-EEA sponsor include:

1. appoint an EEA-based group company to be the legal representative;
2. set up a subsidiary in the EEA to act as the legal representative.
3. enter into a contract with a contract research organization under which the CRO agrees to act as legal representative.

volving investigational medicinal products for gene therapy or somatic cell therapy or containing GMOs. In those cases, extensions are permitted, up to a total of 180 days. In the case of xenogenic cell therapy, there is no time limit on the authorization period.[58]

The sponsor must submit a clinical trial application to the competent authority in each Member State in which the trial is to be conducted. Applications are made on prescribed forms, with supporting data being provided in the Common Technical Document (CTD) format.

Authorizations are granted at a national level; they are not granted centrally.[59] Each competent authority must review and approve or reject the application submitted to it within 60 days, except again in the case of gene therapy medicinal products, somatic cell therapy medicinal products (including xenogenic cell therapy medicinal products), and GMOs. As with Ethics Committee approvals, in those cases, extensions are permitted, up to a total of 180 days. In the case of xenogenic cell therapy, there is no time limit on the authorization period.[60]

Written authorization from each relevant competent authority is required in the case of gene therapy medicinal products,[61] somatic cell therapy medicinal products (including xenogenic cell therapy medicinal products), and GMOs.[62] No gene therapy trials may be carried out that result in modifications to the subject's germ line genetic identity.[63]

The European Commission has issued detailed guidance on requesting authorization for, notifying substantial amendments in respect of, and declaring the end of, clinical trials under the Clinical Trials Directive.[64]

8. Manufacture and Importation of Investigational Medicinal Products (IMPs)

Manufacturers of IMPs must hold a manufacturing authorization from the relevant competent authority.[65] If an IMP is imported from a country outside the EEA, then the importer must have an IMP manufacturer's authorization. Authorizations for marketed medicinal products do not cover IMPs.

Before an IMP is used in a clinical trial, a Qualified Person (QP) must ensure that, where the IMP has been manufactured in the relevant Member

State, each batch of IMPs has been manufactured in accordance with GMP and that each batch is appropriately certified. The Qualified Person must be "permanently and continuously" at the disposal of the manufacturer or importer.[66] Where the IMP has been manufactured in a third country, the QP must ensure that each production batch has been manufactured and checked in accordance with GMP. Once an IMP has been imported and released by a QP, it can move freely within the EEA.

Under the terms of mutual recognition agreements (MRAs) entered into between the EU and various non-EEA countries,[67] inspectors in countries party to MRAs can perform inspections locally on behalf of other party countries. There is no current GMP MRA between the European Union and the United States, and therefore GMP audits must be conducted on U.S. manufacturing sites of IMPs for use in European clinical trials and certified by the QP.[68]

The Qualified Person must hold certain minimum qualifications (for example, in the United Kingdom, the Qualified Person must be a member of the Institute of Biology, the Royal Society of Chemistry, or the Royal Pharmaceutical Society of Great Britain).

9. GMP and GCP Inspections

Trial sites, manufacturing (or importing) sites of IMPs, any laboratory used for the analysis of clinical trial data, and the sponsor's premises may be subject to inspections by inspectors appointed by the relevant competent authority.[69]

> **Practice Points**
>
> The duties of the "Qualified Person" under the Clinical Trials Directive include:
>
> 1. Ensuring GMP for each batch of investigational medical product.
> 2. Releasing investigational medical product for free movement within the EEA.
> 3. Remaining "permanently and continuously" at manufacturer's disposal.
> 4. Maintaining minimum qualifications through relevant scientific societies.

Results of inspections may be notified to the EMEA, other competent authorities, and other ethics committees.[70]

Where the IMP manufacturing site or sponsor's premises is established in a country outside the EEA, and that country has an agreement in place with the EU, an inspection of that site or premises may be carried out by qualified EU inspectors.[71]

10. Notification of Adverse Events and Suspected Unexpected Serious Adverse Reactions

The sponsor must notify the competent authorities of any serious adverse events (SAEs)[72] and suspected unexpected serious adverse reactions (SUSARs) (and in the case of SUSARs, also the ethics committee(s)) within prescribed time limits.[73] The sponsor must also provide an annual list of all SUSARs and a report on the safety of trial subjects to the relevant competent authorities and ethics committees.[74] Member States must add information on SUSARs to the central European pharmacovigilance database, EudraVigilance.[75] The database is only accessible to competent authorities, the EMEA, and the European Commission. A U.S. company conducting an international multi-centre trial should therefore be aware that SUSAR reporting requirements differ between the European Union and the United States (and indeed between the EU and other countries, such as Japan). Post-marketing pharmacovigilance obligations are discussed at section G.1 below.

11. Suspension of Trials

A competent authority may suspend or prohibit a clinical trial where it has objective grounds for considering that the original application is not being followed or for safety reasons.[76] Except in emergencies, sponsors and/or investigators are given one week in which to provide their opinion as to why the trial should not be stopped. Competent authorities may also require corrective action in the event that the sponsor or investigator or any other person involved in the conduct of the trial is not complying with the requirements of the Clinical Trials Directive. Where steps are taken, such as suspensions or the ordering of corrective action, those steps are communicated to other relevant competent authorities and ethics committees.

12. Effect of Noncompliance

Trials that are carried out without authorization or in breach of any authorization that has been granted will be the subject of enforcement through national courts/tribunals. By way of example, in the UK, the maximum penalty for noncompliance with the implementing Regulations is an unlimited fine and/or two years' imprisonment.[77]

13. Liability and Insurance

While the Clinical Trials Directive permits the sponsor to delegate trial-related tasks to third parties, the sponsor remains ultimately liable. The Clinical Trials Directive does not amend liabilities that already exist in law, so (for example) investigating institutions remain liable for clinical negligence and manufacturers of defective medicinal products remain liable under product liability law.

The Clinical Trials Directive requires insurance or some form of indemnity to cover the liability of the investigator and the sponsor,[78] but does not require no-fault compensation, nor does it contain any provisions that affect liabilities that exist in law. While the Directive does not, therefore, make insurance compulsory, many EEA countries do require insurance to be in place before a trial may start. Further, some countries do not specify a particular amount of cover to be in place, whereas other countries do. The risks associated with trials of, say, gene therapy products will clearly have a bearing on the availability, and cost, of insurance. The UK's Association of the British Pharmaceutical Industry has developed a form of indemnity to be given by sponsors in favor of trial subjects, and this is commonly used in UK trials. A U.S. sponsor offering an indemnity in such terms should first ensure that any insurance policy it has in place covers payments under that form of indemnity.

14. Clinical Trials and Data Protection (Privacy) Law

In Europe, the use of "personal data" (information relating to living individuals) is regulated by (among other legislation) the Data Protection Directive.[79] A key aspect of the Data Protection Directive is that personal data may not be processed by a company unless one or more preconditions have been met—for example, the individual has given his or her informed consent to the processing in question. Where the personal data contains health information, the preconditions are stricter. Those who process personal data are also generally required to notify their processing activities to the relevant national data protection supervisory authority or authorities. The obligations under data protection law exist in addition to general rules of confidentiality in a medical practitioner–patient relationship, and to ethical and legal requirements to obtain appropriate consent to participation in a clinical trial. The Data Protection Directive also prohibits the transfer of personal data from Europe to countries that are not deemed to have adequate data protection laws in place, unless one or more specified preconditions are met. The United States is not considered by Europe to have adequate data protection laws, and therefore, if a U.S. company is to transfer personal data from Europe to the United States, it must meet one or more of the preconditions. Consent[80] from the individual is one such precondition. Since the Clinical Trials Directive and ICH GCP guidelines require that informed consent to participation be obtained from trial patients, the trial consent form can be used to obtain informed consent for data transfer purposes. An alternative, but administratively more burdensome, approach is for the U.S. company to sign up to the so-called "Safe Harbor" scheme.[81] Note that anonymized data, such as purely statistical data, does not fall under European data protection legislation (but the act of anonymizing personal data is classified as processing of

> **Practice Points**
>
> Note that under the European Data Protection Directive, compliance with HIPAA does not of itself qualify as "adequate data protection" for the transfer of personal medical data from Europe to the United States.
>
> Companies seeking to collect personal data in the context of a European clinical trial and then transfer that personal data to the United States should:
>
> 1. Make sure that they have complied with the notification requirements of all relevant national data protection supervisory authorities.
> 2. Obtain the informed consent of patients, with the scope of the consent covering transfer of personal data to the United States.
> 3. Observe patient confidentiality rules and ethical/legal requirements for human subject research.

personal data). However, it may be difficult, if not impractical and contrary to the objectives of a trial, to anonymize all personal data collected in the context of a trial. It is also important to bear in mind that there are differences in the implementation of the Data Protection Directive between Member States and in procedures and standards adopted by national regulatory authorities. Other laws and professional standards as to confidentiality and use of patient data also differ between Member States. Therefore, companies located in more than one European Member State should obtain advice from local specialists in relation to all relevant states.

15. GCP and the GCP Directive

As noted above, under the Clinical Trials Directive, all clinical trials conducted within the EEA must be designed, conducted, and reported in accordance with GCP guidelines, and GCP inspections of investigational sites are required.[82] The European Commission has issued detailed GCP guidelines,[83] as has the Inspections Sector of the EMEA.

On April 8, 2005, the European Commission adopted a Directive with respect to GCP,[84] which Member States were required to implement into their national law by January 29, 2006.

The main features of the GCP Directive are:

a) codification of GCP principles;
b) rules for GCP inspectors and inspection procedures;
c) authorization requirements for manufacture and importation of IMPs; and
d) rules governing the trial master file.

E. Obtaining a Marketing Authorization in Europe[85]

1. Introduction

A medicinal product may only be placed on the market in the EEA if it has obtained a "marketing authorization."[86] If no marketing authorization has been granted anywhere in Europe for the medicinal product in question, there are two different routes to obtaining a marketing authorization throughout Europe:[87]

(i) the Centralized Procedure (which is conducted through the EMEA);

or

(ii) the Decentralized Procedure (which is conducted through a national competent authority and is then the subject of a multinational consensus and mutual recognition procedure).

The Centralized Procedure is mandatory for medicinal products developed by means of certain biotechnological processes,[88] namely:

a) immunological medicinal products, medicinal products derived from human blood and human plasma;[89]
b) medicinal products developed by means of one of the following biotechnology processes: recombinant-DNA technology, controlled expression of genes coding for biologically active proteins in prokaryotes and eukaryotes, including transformed mammalian cells, and hybridoma and monoclonal antibody methods;[90] and
c) advanced therapy medicinal products, which include gene therapy and somatic cell therapy medicinal products.[91]

> **Practice Points**
>
> A medicinal product may only be placed on the market in the EEA if it has obtained a "marketing authorization." The Centralized Procedure is the mandatory route for obtaining a marketing authorization in respect of biotechnology products, and is optional for certain other innovative products.

The Centralized Procedure is mandatory for certain other classes of medicinal products (the list was expanded as part of an extensive revision of European pharmaceutical legislation in 2004, the "Community Code Review"[92]), but optional for others (for example, applicants may request the EMEA to consider under the Centralized Procedure applications for products that have been developed by means of biotechnological processes other than those listed above and that are considered to constitute a significant innovation).

The Centralized Procedure provides a route for companies with biotechnology products to obtain a marketing authorization that is valid throughout the whole of the EEA, by means of a single procedure. This section of the chapter will focus on the Centralized Procedure.

2. What Information Must Be Contained in a Marketing Authorization Application?

In summary,[93] a full application[94] must include:

a) administrative information, such as a summary of product characteristics, information as to labeling, and the package leaflet and information about experts;
b) quality data (including a review of the information related to the chemical, pharmaceutical, and biological data);
c) non-clinical reports, including information as to pharmacology, pharmacokinetics, and toxicology; and
d) clinical reports derived from clinical studies.

Specific information must appear in the application in the cases of, among other classes of product, advanced therapy medicinal products (such as gene therapy medicinal products).

Where applicable, an applicant must provide a risk assessment overview evaluating possible risks to the environment due to the use and/or disposal of the medicinal product (for example, where the product contains or consists of GMOs).[95]

The European Commission has produced *Rules Governing Medicinal Products in the European Union*, which are set out in nine volumes and include a detailed *Notice to Applicants*, which provides information as to the form, presentation, and content of a marketing authorization application and includes Word format application forms.[96] The guidelines and notices set out in the *Rules* are not legally binding, but applicants must justify their processes where they deviate from those set out in the *Rules*. In addition, notes for guidance have been issued by the CHMP (sometimes in conjunction with the CVMP) of the EMEA to assist applicants in preparing marketing authorization applications. There are specific guidelines with respect to applications in respect of biotechnology products. Again, these guidelines are also not legally binding, but applicants must justify their processes where they deviate from those set out in the guidelines.

3. What Is the Format of a Marketing Authorization Application?

Regardless of whether the application for marketing authorization uses the Centralized Procedure or otherwise, the application must be in the five-module "EU-CTD" format.[97]

4. Summary of the Centralized Procedure

Prior to submitting a centralized application, an applicant liaises with the EMEA[98] as part of a "pre-submission phase." During that phase, the applicant may meet with the EMEA to discuss procedural, regulatory, and legal issues relating to the proposed submission. At least four to six months before submission of an application, applicants should notify the EMEA of their intention to submit an application, and provide certain information (including justification of the product's eligibility for evaluation under the Centralized Procedure). In addition, during this phase the CHMP appoints one of its members to act as a rapporteur (in effect, a go-between), and a second to act as a co-rapporteur.

Once the applicant has submitted a marketing authorization application to the EMEA, a scientific evaluation is carried out within the CHMP of the EMEA, by the national competent authorities. Together with scientific experts as appropriate, the rapporteur and co-rapporteur prepare an assessment report on which the CHMP makes its opinion. The opinion is sent to the European Commission. The European Commission then consults the Member States, drafts a Decision on a Community marketing authorization, and if the Decision is not challenged, grants a marketing authorization. The resulting authorization is valid throughout the EEA, and there are no national variations.

Legislation provides for a 210-day period for examining marketing authorization applications,[99] but an applicant may request an accelerated 150-day period if the medicinal product is "of major interest from the point of view of public health and in particular from the point of view of therapeutic innovation" and if "the request is duly substantiated."[100]

The holder of the marketing authorization (who need not be the manufacturer) must be established in the EEA.[101]

European and International Considerations

5. Duration of a Marketing Authorization

A marketing authorization has an initial term of five years.[102] After that period, the authorization may be renewed (for an indefinite period), following a risk/benefit assessment by the granting body (the EMEA in the case of centrally authorized products).[103] If a product is not actually placed on the market in the first three years following authorization, its marketing authorization becomes void.[104]

6. Responsibilities of the Holder of the Marketing Authorization

By law, the holder must fulfill certain obligations and assume certain responsibilities, including:

a) compliance with the content and terms of the authorization;
b) when the holder is not the manufacturer, entering into a written agreement with the manufacturer in order to guarantee that the manufacturing operations comply with the rules in force and the manufacturing conditions provided for in the dossier;
c) providing proof that the controls have been carried out on the finished product in accordance with the methods described in the documents that accompanied the application;
d) pharmacovigilance obligations (see section G.1 below);
e) responsibility for advertising of the medicinal product, and for ensuring compliance of advertising with the applicable provisions; and

> **Practice Points**
>
> The duties of a marketing authorization holder include:
> 1. Compliance with the content and terms of the authorization.
> 2. Putting in place a suitable written agreement with contract manufacturers.
> 3. Providing proof that the controls documented in the application have been carried out on the finished product.
> 4. Pharmacovigilance obligations.
> 5. Compliance with advertising regulation.
> 6. Document retention.

f) retaining and archiving all documentation on the medicinal product and, in particular, any documents related to clinical trials.

7. Can Patented Inventions Be Used for Uses Relating to Applying for a Marketing Authorization?

a. The Historical Position in Europe

National patent legislation in Europe provides for an exemption to patent infringement where an act is done for experimental purposes.[105] So far as trials of a patented product for the purposes of obtaining marketing authorization are concerned, however, there have been different interpretations of this exemption across Member States. In the UK, for example, the exemption has been construed rather narrowly. Acts may be within the exemption if they are carried out to discover something new about a patented product, but if they were done in order to provide information to satisfy a third party that something works *as has been claimed* (e.g., in order to obtain regulatory approval) then the exemption will not apply.[106] In Germany, it has been held that provided that trials are directed to yielding new knowledge about the subject matter of the invention, a collateral commercial purpose does not necessarily take the acts outside the exemption.[107]

Accordingly, without a specific exemption covering tests on patented products carried out in support of a marketing authorization application, such tests carried with them a significant risk of patent infringement. Companies have been discouraged from conducting such tests in the EEA. Rather than carrying out these tests after patent expiration, testing was carried out during the patent term, but outside the EEA, in countries where the product was not protected by patents or which had existing *Bolar* provisions.

b. The New Bolar Exemption

The Community Code Review has created an explicit *Bolar* exemption with a view to harmonizing the position in Europe with respect to the use, in the context of applications for marketing authorizations, of products that are the subject of patents or supplementary protection certificates:

Conducting the necessary studies and trials with a view to the application of paragraphs 1, 2, 3 and 4 [of this Article] and the consequential practical requirements shall not be regarded as contrary to patent rights or to supplementary protection certificates for medicinal products.[108]

Paragraph 1 referred to in the provision above sets out the data requirements for a "generic" marketing authorization application; this is examined in more detail below at section G.4.b. Paragraph 2 referred to in the provision above sets out the definitions of "reference medicinal product" and "generic medicinal product" as used in paragraph 1. Paragraph 3 covers the requirement for additional data to be submitted where, for example, the definition of "generic medicinal product" is not satisfied. Paragraph 4 covers the requirement for additional data in respect of applications for biological medicinal products similar to reference biological products but not meeting the definition of "generic medicinal product"; this is examined in more detail below at section G.4.c.

Accordingly, the new Community Code Review exempts testing in support of a generic application (for example, studies showing bioequivalence between generic and originator), testing in support of an application that does not satisfy the requirements of a generic application (for example, where the product is identical in all respects but its dose and additional safety and efficacy studies are required—commonly referred to as bridging data under previous law), and comparability studies in respect of biosimilar products. Consequential practical steps such as submitting samples with applications fall within the new exemption.

F. Clinical Trials and Marketing Authorizations: International Strategies and Issues

1. Product Development Strategies

Product development strategies must take into account international regulatory requirements and standards. While guidelines and scientific standards are being harmonized at an international level (see below), there are differences in processes, assessments, and interpretation between regions. Accordingly, companies must investigate the position in all applicable regions as it applies to their particular products, and take advice early on from local regulatory experts and supra-national or national agencies on a case-by-case basis, to understand the non-clinical and clinical data requirements in each territory in which their products are ultimately to be marketed.

If a U.S. biotech company already has non-clinical and/or clinical data from U.S. studies and is looking to make an application for a trial or a marketing authorization in Europe, the company should arrange to have its complete data package (including Chemistry, Manufacturing and Control (CMC) data) reviewed by European regulatory experts to identify any potential deficiencies or other adverse issues. It can be extremely difficult for a company to rebuild its regulatory dossier in the event that problems are identified at a late stage. A company may seek advice from the EMEA at any time and on any part of its dossier. Different levels of advice are available, depending on the company's requirements and on the stage of development of its product. Specific scientific advice may be obtained in cases where the company has a particular product under development. It is also possible for a company to have a more general discussion not confined to any particular product, in what is termed a "briefing meeting."[109]

> **Practice Points**
>
> Product development strategies must take into account international regulatory requirements and standards. Companies must investigate the position in all applicable regions as it applies to their particular products, and take advice early on from local regulatory experts and supra-national or national agencies on a case-by-case basis, to understand the non-clinical and clinical data requirements in each territory in which their products are ultimately to be marketed.

In late 2004 the EMEA and the FDA initiated a pilot program to provide parallel scientific advice. The aim of the program is to provide a mechanism for EMEA and FDA assessors and sponsors to exchange their views during the development phase of new medicinal products. Objectives of the program include the opportunity to optimize product development and avoid unnecessary testing replication or unnecessary diverse testing methodologies.[110] The pilot program was extended in March 2006.[111]

Many U.S. companies will look to a Contract Research Organization (CRO) to provide services at a local level. While the term "CRO" is used below in the singular, it should be borne in mind that in reality a U.S. company may not be able to identify one organization with all the necessary skills and expertise, and so may retain a number of service providers, or alternatively, the primary CRO may in turn subcontract out various specialist activities. The U.S. sponsor should look for a CRO with local expertise in all countries of interest, in terms of both regulatory knowledge and experience of conduct of trials in those countries. Where possible, the CRO should have experience of the therapeutic area under investigation. The U.S. sponsor may look to a European-based CRO to act as its "legal representative" under the Clinical Trials Directive. However, not all CROs are willing to take on this role, and alternative arrangements may have to be made (see section D.6 above).

2. Where to Conduct a Clinical Trial

Traditionally, most clinical trials have been carried out by U.S. and European companies in the United States and Western Europe.[112] However, it is becoming increasingly difficult to enroll sufficient numbers of patients for trials in those territories who are not already receiving treatment (i.e., patients who are "treatment naïve"), and there is increasing competition for both patients and investigators. At the same time, expertise in the conduct of clinical trials has increased significantly in other territories, such as Central and Eastern Europe, India, Latin America, and China, and there are other advantages to be had in conducting trials elsewhere, such as generally lower per-patient costs.

However, there may be problems and disadvantages, such as:

- marked differences in clinical practice for a given indication;
- underdeveloped legal and/or ethical framework;[113]
- lack of proper review of protocols by Institutional Review Boards;
- relatively poor documentation standards;
- lack of an appropriate structure with respect to adverse incident reporting;
- poor enforcement of local laws;
- material differences in genetics of the trial patient population; and
- material local environmental factors.

Individually or taken together, these problems can translate into refusal by regulatory authorities to accept the data generated. Acceptability of foreign clinical trials data is discussed further in the subsection below.

It should also be borne in mind that the location of clinical trials can influence whether a doctor will select the resulting approved product. Part of a development strategy may therefore include running clinical trials in a number of diverse regions, so as to provide an opportunity for doctors in those regions to become familiar with the product.

3. Use of U.S. Non-clinical and Clinical Trials Data to Support a Marketing Authorization Application

Whether a foreign competent authority accepts a given set of U.S. clinical trial and other data to support a marketing authorization application (or vice versa—the FDA accepts data generated outside the U.S.) should be checked on a case-by-case basis. Generally speaking, on the assumption that the relevant non-clinical and clinical standards have been complied with, U.S. data is acceptable to support a European marketing authorization application; there are no European legislative requirements to the effect that a marketing authorization application must be supported by data generated in Europe. However, particular circumstances can result in bars or impediments to the use of U.S. clinical trials data to support a European marketing authorization. For example:

a) problems are created where there are differences across regions in the way a particular medicine is used;
b) the comparator product used in U.S. pivotal studies may not be the standard of care (or is not authorized) in Europe; or
c) a product may be classified as a medicinal product in one region, having been classified as something else in another region (e.g., a cosmetic), leading to a lack of data of suitable quality to support a regulatory application.

In certain circumstances, it may be that the data are accepted, but only on the basis that local bridging studies are performed.[114]

European and International Considerations

4. International Coordination

a. Introduction: The ICH

Clearly, it is desirable, from an ethical point of view and a cost point of view, for any company carrying out non-clinical and clinical tests to minimize duplication of testing. It is also desirable for there to be uniformity between the administrative and regulatory processes of different regulatory authorities around the world. To those ends, there are various regional and global harmonization initiatives in place. The International Conference on Harmonization of Technical Requirements for Registration of Pharmaceuticals for Human Use (ICH) is a joint forum for the regulatory authorities of Europe, Japan, the United States, and experts from the pharmaceutical industry in the three regions to discuss scientific and technical aspects of product registration.[115] The aims of the harmonization are the more economical use of resources (including fewer animal experiments and human trials) and eliminating unnecessary delay in development and availability of new medicines, while maintaining quality, safety, and efficacy standards.

> **Practice Points**
>
> As part of an international product development strategy, timely advice should be obtained as to whether a foreign competent authority accepts U.S. clinical trial data to support a marketing authorization application, having regard to regional factors such as differences between regulatory regimes in the way the particular medicine is used, lack of a comparator, and/or difference in product classification between regions.

b. The Common Technical Document

In 2000, at ICH5 in San Diego, a Common Technical Document (CTD) was officially adopted by the regulatory authorities of the United States, European Union,[116] and Japan, with a view to providing a common format for the preparation of documentation to support a marketing authorization application made to national regulatory authorities.[117] The regulatory authorities of other countries, such as Australia,[118] have since adopted CTD. Regional differences (application requirements unique to certain regions) still remain and companies should, as part of their product development strategies, seek local advice from regulatory professionals as appropriate with respect to local content requirements and the level of detail generally sought by local competent authorities.

G. Post-marketing Issues in the EEA

1. Pharmacovigilance

a. Introduction

European legislation imposes an extensive set of pharmacovigilance obligations on marketing authorization holders (MAHs) and national competent authorities.[119] The Community Code Review (see above) has increased pharmacovigilance obligations further.

b. Roles and Responsibilities of an MAH

Roles and responsibilities of an MAH include:[120]

> **Practice Points**
>
> The post-marketing duties of a marketing authorization holder include:
> 1. Oversight of pharmacovigilance (through a qualified person on site).
> 2. Submission of a pharmacovigilance plan.
> 3. Safety and adverse event reporting.
> 4. Providing benefit/risk information to authorities.

(i) having permanently and continuously at its disposal, in the EEA, a qualified person responsible for pharmacovigilance, whose responsibilities include:

- establishing and maintaining a system for collection and collation of information about all serious adverse reactions (SARs) that are reported to the MAH;
- preparing for competent authorities certain prescribed safety reports, including a Periodic Safety Update Report (PSUR);[121]
- ensuring that any request from the competent authorities for the provision of additional information necessary for the evalua-

tion of the benefits and the risks afforded by a medicinal product is answered fully and promptly;
- the provision to the competent authorities of any other information relevant to the evaluation of the benefits and risks afforded by a medicinal product, including appropriate information on post-authorization safety studies; and

(ii) the submission of a pharmacovigilance plan as part of the marketing authorization application.

c. *Supervision and Enforcement*

Each Member State has established a pharmacovigilance system for the collection and evaluation of information relevant to the benefit-to-risk balance of medicinal products. The competent authority for centrally authorized products is the EMEA. The EMEA maintains a central database, known as "EudraVigilance," which contains adverse reaction reports received from national competent authorities and MAHs concerning medicines authorized in Europe. Competent authorities have the power to:

(i) inspect manufacturing/commercial establishments of manufacturers of medicinal products or active substances;
(ii) take samples with a view to carrying out independent tests;
(iii) examine documents relating to the object of the inspection (subject to some restrictions relating to the description of the manufacturing method); and
(iv) inspect premises, records, and documents of marketing authorization holder of certain firms employed by the manufacturing authorization holder.

Sanctions can include an inspection (followed by reinspection to ensure compliance achieved), a formal warning, fines,[122] product/batch recall, and the suspension, revocation, withdrawal or variation of the marketing authorization (which may be carried out with immediate effect if essential to patient safety). In the case of serious or persistent noncompliance, the MAH, its directors and managers, and/or the Qualified Person responsible for pharmacovigilance may be prosecuted.

The EMEA Pharmacovigilance Working Party provides a forum for Community-wide discussion and coordination of pharmacovigilance issues. Member States cooperate, via their national competent authorities, with the World Health Organization (WHO) Collaborating Centre for International Drug Monitoring.

2. Advertising, Promotion, and Labeling

At a European level, the advertising of medicinal products for human use is set out in Title VIII of Directive 2001/83/EC, as amended by Directive 2004/27/EC. Title VIII contains provisions with respect to matters such as advertising of medicinal products to the public, advertising to persons qualified to prescribe or supply medicinal products, visits by sales representatives to persons qualified to prescribe, the supply, of samples, the provision of inducements to prescribe or supply, and monitoring of advertising. Advertising of prescription-only medicines to the general public is prohibited, and advertising may not be misleading and should encourage the rational use of medicines. Advertising exclusively or mainly directed at children is expressly prohibited. Self-regulation is a key part of the regulatory framework for advertising and promotion, though the Directive requires Member States to have in place appropriate laws, should recourse to the courts or relevant administrative authority be necessary. In addition to this specific legislation, the advertising of medicines is also regulated under general advertising, broadcasting, and trading standards laws.

Title V of Directive 2001/83/EC (as amended by Directive 2004/27/EC) requires that all the information identifying the product (including product name, pharmaceutical form, contents, name and address of authorization holder, authorization number and batch number, composition, excipients, and method of administration), together with important warnings, be stated on the outer packaging. The labeling must be easily legible, clearly comprehensible and indelible, and in the language of the country in which the product is placed on the market. A package leaflet must be included inside the packet unless all the information to be given in the leaflet is already given on the outer packaging. The name of the medicinal product must also be expressed in Braille on the packaging and the package information leaflet must be available in formats appropriate for the blind and partially sighted.

3. Manufacture, Importation, Classification, and Inspections

a. *Manufacturing and Importing*

Title IV of Directive 2001/83/EC, as amended by Directive 2004/27/EC contains provisions governing the manufacture and importation of medicinal products. Manufacturers of medicinal products must be authorized by national competent authorities,[123] and their activities are subjected to inspection by those authorities.[124] Holders of manufacturing authorizations must (among other things) dispose of medicinal products in accordance with national law[125] and must have "permanently and continuously" at their disposal the services of at least one Qualified Person[126] (who must have certain minimum qualifications; see above at section D.8). All operations that are required to hold a manufacturing authorization must comply with the principles of GMP as set out in the GMP Directive[127] and with the detailed guidance set out in the Guide to Good Manufacturing Practice.[128] There are analogous authorization requirements in respect of importers of medicinal products into the EEA[129] and wholesale distributors.[130]

Imports of medicinal products into the EEA must have been made in accordance with standards at least equivalent to those required in the EEA.[131]

b. *Classification*

Whether a medicine is classified as prescription-only or over-the-counter is determined on a Member State-by-Member State basis, in accordance with principles set out in Title VI of Directive 2001/83/EC, as amended by Directive 2004/27/EC. The classification of a medicinal product affects the manner in which it may legally be advertised and sold, and may also affect its status under a national reimbursement scheme. Products may change classification; this is termed "switching."

c. *Inspections*

As noted above, national competent authorities regularly conduct inspections of manufacturers and other authorization holders within their jurisdiction, both in connection with national requirements and on behalf of the EMEA. The EMEA's Inspections Sector is responsible for coordinating any GMP, GCP or GLP inspections requested by the CHMP or CVMP. Inspections may be necessary to verify specific aspects of the clinical or laboratory testing or manufacture and control of medicinal products and/or to ensure compliance with GMP, GCP or GLP and quality assurance systems.[132]

The EEA has various mutual recognition agreements in place with third parties. Under the terms of those MRAs, medicinal products (including investigative medicinal products) may be imported from one party to the other, with national competent authorities accepting each other's inspection reports. The EMEA has issued guidance documents in relation to the interpretation and operation of those MRAs.[133]

4. Abridged Applications[134]

a. Introduction

Abridged application procedures are available in Europe, allowing manufacturers applying for marketing authorizations for "generic medicinal products" and similar biological medicinal products to rely on data submitted in support of an earlier application in respect of a reference product.

b. Abridged Applications for "Generic Medicinal Products"

A "generic medicinal product" is defined as a "medicinal product which has the same qualitative and quantitative composition in active substances and the same pharmaceutical form as the reference medicinal product, and whose bioequivalence with the reference medicinal product has been demonstrated by appropriate bioavailability studies."[135]

Different salts, esters, ethers, isomers, mixtures of isomers, complexes or derivatives of an active substance are considered to be the same active substance unless they differ significantly in safety and/or efficacy. In those cases, the applicant for a marketing authorization must supply additional information providing proof of the safety and/or efficacy of the various salts, esters or derivatives of an authorized active substance.[136]

Bioavailability studies are not required if the applicant "can demonstrate that the generic medicinal product meets the relevant criteria as defined in the appropriate detailed guidelines."[137]

c. Abridged Applications for Similar Biological Medicinal Products

The Community Code Review has created a specific regulatory pathway in respect of the approval of similar biological medicinal products (also known as "biosimilars" or "follow-on biologics"). (See Chapter 17 for a discussion of the comparable U.S. regulatory issues raised by follow-on biologics.)

Where a new biological medicinal product claimed to be "similar" to an original reference product that has been granted a marketing authorization does not meet the conditions in the definition of generic medicinal product (above) owing to, for example, differences in manufacturing processes, then a company wishing to obtain a marketing authorization in Europe in respect of it must provide "results of appropriate pre-clinical tests or clinical trials relating to these conditions."[138]

What is appropriate to evidence similarity (e.g., the type and amount of non-clinical and clinical data) will be determined on a case-by-case basis by the EMEA, which has issued draft and adopted guidance documents, and a set of "concept papers" on biosimilarity.[139]

The European Commission has stated that the EMEA is the only authority that may grant approvals in respect of biosimilars.[140]

5. Bibliographic or "Well-Established Use" Applications

An applicant does not have to provide results of pre-clinical tests or clinical trials if he can demonstrate that the active substances of the medicinal product have been in well-established medicinal use within Europe for at least 10 years, with recognized efficacy and an acceptable level of safety in terms of certain prescribed conditions. In those cases, test and trial results may be replaced by references to appropriate scientific literature.[141]

6. Regulatory Data and Marketing Exclusivity

Historically, the period of data exclusivity in European Member States for centrally approved products was 10 years after marketing authorization was granted. With respect to nationally approved products, the period was 10 years (in Belgium, France, Germany, Italy, Liechtenstein, Luxembourg, Netherlands, Sweden, and the UK) and six years (in Austria, Denmark,

Finland, Iceland, Norway, Portugal, Spain, Greece). The "accession countries" that joined the EU in 2004 opted for a six-year period (with Slovenia, Hungary, Lithuania, and Poland linking that to patent expiration).

The Community Code Review required European Member States to implement harmonizing legislation by October 30, 2005. The new law is as follows:

a) A generic application may be submitted if the reference product has been authorized for no less than eight years in a Member State.[142]
b) The generic may not be placed on the market until 10 years have elapsed from the initial marketing authorization of the reference product, i.e., a further two years of marketing exclusivity.
c) The period of exclusivity is extended by a further one year if, during the first eight years of the 10-year protection period, the marketing authorization holder obtains an authorization for a new therapeutic indication or indications that are considered to provide a "significant clinical benefit in comparison with existing therapies."[143]

This exclusivity period structure, which is subject to any remaining patent or supplementary certificate protection, has been termed the "8+2+1 solution." It applies to all products, whether approved through the Centralized or Decentralized Procedure. The new structure took effect in late 2005 and does not apply retrospectively. Therefore, the first applications for generic products under the "8+2+1" structure will not occur until late 2013.

Certain other exclusivity provisions have also been introduced, such as a one-year data exclusiv-

> **Practice Points**
>
> Under the "8+2+1 solution," products receiving marketing authorization after late 2005 will enjoy market exclusivity in any of the European Member States as follows:
>
> — No generic applications for not less than 8 years after marketing authorization, plus
> — No generic marketing for an additional 2 years, plus
> — No generic marketing authorizations for an additional 1 year if a qualifying new therapeutic indication is approved.

ity period for products switching from prescription-only to OTC status, on the basis of new pre-clinical or clinical data.[144]

7. Price Controls and Government Purchasing

Europe does not have a harmonized social security system, and there are different pricing and reimbursement schemes among the Member States. Prices for medicinal products (particularly prescription medicines) differ dramatically across Member States.[145] These price divergences drive parallel importation (see below).

8. Parallel Importation and Parallel Distribution

a. Parallel Importation

As noted above, national price divergences allow traders to buy medicinal products in one Member State where the price for those products is low (relative to the intended market) and sell them in another Member State where the price is high (relative to that in the original Member State).

The EC Treaty creates a system of free movement of goods within Europe. Among Member States, quantitative restrictions on exports and all measures having equivalent effect are banned. There are derogations from that principle, allowing prohibitions on imports in various circumstances—for example, the protection of health and life of humans or the protection of industrial and commercial property.

A national marketing authorization (as opposed to a marketing authorization obtained through the Centralized Procedure) permits marketing of a medicinal product only in one country. Accordingly, it can be seen that the national marketing authorization system could operate to prevent parallel importation. However, a series of cases heard before the European Court of Justice have established a set of conditions that, if satisfied, enable parallel importation to take place notwithstanding the national marketing authorization system, on the basis that the product being imported and the national reference product are identical or "essentially identical."[146]

Also of importance in the context of parallel imports is the issue of whether an owner of national intellectual property rights can use those rights to prevent parallel importation of products protected by his rights.

The basic rule is that once goods have been put on the market in the EEA by the intellectual property owner or with his consent (e.g., through a local licensee, agent or distributor), then the proprietor cannot use intellectual property infringement rights to prevent further commercial dealings in those goods (i.e., parallel importation). This is the "exhaustion of rights" rule developed by the Court of Justice of the European Communities (ECJ) under the competition and free movement of goods provisions of the EC Treaty (and now for the most part contained in various harmonized intellectual property laws, e.g., European Community (EC) trademarks law). The rule does not operate where goods are put on the market in the EEA by a third party independent of the intellectual property owner, nor where the proprietor is forced to market the goods through a compulsory licensing scheme. However, rights are exhausted irrespective of whether intellectual property protection was available in the Member State of first marketing.

The exhaustion of rights rule is Community-wide only.[147] Therefore, where the intellectual property owner or his licensee puts the goods on the market in a third country outside the EEA (e.g., the United States) the intellectual property rights are not exhausted in the EEA and the proprietor can stop the goods from being marketed in the Community by exercising his intellectual property infringement rights. Intellectual property rights are not exhausted when goods are merely passing through, or warehoused in, the Community in transit from one non-EEA country to another non-EEA country, nor are rights exhausted until the goods are actually sold to a consumer. Exhaustion of rights applies to each good separately.[148]

b. Trademark Issues: Repackaging and Relabeling

A special problem has arisen in EU law with the repackaging/relabeling of trademarked pharmaceuticals by parallel importers. The pharmaceuticals may be sold in different strengths/quantities in different Member States and will need to meet local labeling requirements. On the face of it, repackaging/relabeling amounts to infringement of trademark rights, but the parallel importer may have a defense provided he establishes that:

(i) the repackaging/relabeling is necessary in order to market the pharmaceuticals in the Member State of import;
(ii) the repackaging/relabeling cannot adversely affect the condition of the pharmaceuticals;

(iii) it is stated on the packaging by whom the repackaging/relabeling has been carried out;
(iv) the packaging must not be liable to damage the reputation of the trade mark and of its owner; thus, the packaging must not be defective, of poor quality, or untidy; and
(v) notice of the marketing of the repackaged/relabeled pharmaceutical has been given to the proprietor.[149]

Despite numerous references to, and rulings from, the ECJ during the last three decades, questions as to interpretation of European law with respect to repackaging and relabeling remain and continue to be referred to the ECJ. In April 2006, one of the eight Advocate-Generals of the ECJ, A.G. Sharpston of the UK, issued an opinion in which she concluded that (among other things) the five conditions above do not apply to overstickering of itself and, of the five conditions, the trademark owner bears the burden of proving serious risk of damage to itself or to the reputation of the trademarks (i.e., the fourth condition above), and the parallel importer bears the burden of proving the other conditions.[150] At the time of writing, the ECJ has not issued its decision, but typically ECJ decisions follow the opinions of the AGs.

c. Medicines Legislation

Following the Community Code Review, the manufacture of active substances expressly includes "the various processes of dividing up, packaging or presentation prior to [an active substance's] incorporation into a medicinal product, including repackaging or relabeling, such as are carried out by a distributor of starting materials."[151] Parallel importers must notify their intention to import to the marketing authorization holder and the competent authority in the Member State into which the product is to be imported.[152]

d. Parallel Distribution

A marketing authorization for a product obtained through the Centralized Procedure is valid throughout the EEA and as a consequence, that product may be put on the market in one Member State and marketed in any other part of the EEA by a "parallel distributor," independent of the marketing authorization holder. The only changes that parallel distributors may introduce to the packaging of a centrally authorized medicinal product are those that are strictly necessary to market the product in the Member State of destination (such as use of a different-language version(s) of labeling and package leaflet). Parallel distribution, therefore, is to be contrasted with parallel importation of medicinal products authorized nationally.

The parallel distributor must notify the marketing authorization holder and the EMEA, before distribution commences,[153] and is under a continuing duty to make sure that the product information remains in compliance with the EMEA.

9. Confidentiality and Freedom of Information

The Community Code Review included provision to increase transparency of the marketing authorization approval process (including refusals).[154] In addition to these transparency measures, certain jurisdictions in Europe (such as the UK and France) have implemented Freedom of Information legislation, which entitles individuals to request any information held by public/state bodies. In the UK, such bodies include the National Health Service and the national competent authority, the MHRA.

The UK's Freedom of Information Act 2000 contains absolute, unqualified exemptions to the right of access, for example, where disclosure would reveal "information provided in confidence." It also contains qualified exemptions under which information may be withheld only if the public interest in maintaining the exemption outweighs the public interest in disclosure. An example of a qualified exemption is where the "commercial interests" of any person would be, or are likely to be, prejudiced by disclosure.

The MHRA has published a Memorandum of Understanding, known as the "Traffic Light Document,"[155] setting out the likely decisions in the event that certain types of information are requested under the Freedom of Information Act 2000.

H. Other Areas of Regulation

1. Regulation of Human Embryonic Stem Cell Research

a. Introduction

The regulatory regimes in respect of human embryonic stem (ES) cell research differ widely in countries outside the United States. In Europe, some Member States are still grappling with the issues raised by ES cell research and reaching different conclusions from one another. The plurality of Europe's cultures and differing views on the moral status of the embryo have resulted in varying levels of regulation of human ES cell research and cloning between Member States.

b. The Council of Europe's Convention on Human Rights and Biomedicine[156]

The Council of Europe's Convention on Human Rights and Biomedicine was opened for signature and ratification in 1997. The Convention binds only those states that have ratified it.

The Convention leaves each Member State free to decide how to regulate ES research, subject to two conditions:[157]

(i) Where the law allows research on embryos *in vitro*, it shall ensure adequate protection for the embryo.
(ii) The creation of human embryos for research purposes is prohibited.

Neither the Convention nor the accompanying Explanatory Notes expand on what is meant by "adequate protection."

As of June 1, 2006, 19 states had ratified the Convention (some with formal reservations) and 14 states had signed it but not yet ratified it. Countries that have not signed and/or ratified the Convention include Finland, France, Germany, Ireland, Italy, Russia, Sweden, and the UK.[158]

There are currently three Additional Protocols to the Convention. The first prohibits human cloning,[159] the second contains provisions regarding the transplantation of organs and tissues of human origin for therapeutic purposes,[160] and the third sets out standards to be applied in biomedical research on human beings (including fetuses and embryos *in vivo*, but not embryos *in vitro*).¹⁶¹ The Additional Protocols are open to signature by signatories to the Convention.

As of June 1, 2006, 15 states had ratified the Additional Protocol on human cloning, including Croatia, Cyprus, Czech Republic, Greece, Hungary, Iceland, Portugal, Romania, and Spain.¹⁶²

While the Convention itself does not give individuals rights to bring proceedings before the European Court of Human Rights, matters that constitute a violation of the rights set out in the Convention may be considered in proceedings under the European Convention on Human Rights if they also constitute a violation of the rights set out in the latter.¹⁶³ The Additional Protocol on cloning stipulates that States that are bound by it must provide in their national legislation for penalties for offenses, such as prohibiting researchers and practitioners from practicing, revoking licenses, and the imposition of criminal penalties.

c. European Harmonizing Legislation—The Current Position

The European Commission has stated that it does not intend to legislate to harmonize regulation of human ES cell research across the EU, arguing that the diversity of views among Member States should be respected.¹⁶⁴ There have been differences between the Commission and the Parliament on this issue.

d. National Regulation within the EEA

Member States take differing positions on the regulation of human ES cell research. The UK regime is well established and relatively permissive.¹⁶⁵ Licenses may be (and have been) granted for a range of projects, including the creation of embryos for research purposes. Belgium and Sweden are also generally acknowledged to have comparatively liberal stem cell research regulations. Belgium, UK, and Sweden allow research using therapeutic cloning.

On the other hand, France and Germany¹⁶⁶ have adopted a more restrictive approach, and Italy a very restrictive approach.

e. Other Countries

By way of example, China, India,[167] Israel, and Singapore permit therapeutic cloning.[168] In Australia, the regulatory position has been in a state of uncertainty for some years, with debates at state and national levels.[169]

2. Human Tissue and Cells

a. Introduction

As with human ES cell research, the use of human tissue and cells in research and therapies raises complex legal and ethical questions. Europe has recently adopted a Directive on human tissues and cells, with a view to harmonizing standards in the EEA for aspects of human tissue donation, research, and use. At the time of writing, there is no European-wide regulation that specifically governs the authorization of tissue-engineering products for human application, and the regulatory framework for advanced therapies is incomplete. In particular, while products intended for gene and somatic cell therapy have been classified as medicinal products and are regulated as such in Europe, tissue-engineered products currently lie outside of any legislative framework.

However, the European Commission is working on a new regulatory framework to govern authorization, supervision, and post-authorization vigilance of advanced therapies (which include human tissue-engineering products, as well as gene and somatic cell therapies). This is discussed further at section 3 below.

The existing and proposed laws are important for any company using materials of human origin in its research, development and production, including (for example) a company establishing a "biobank."

b. The Human Tissues and Cells Directive

The Human Tissues and Cells Directive[170] entered into force on April 7, 2004, and Member States were required to implement it by no later than April 7, 2006.

This legislation is important for those involved in the transplantation of human tissues and cells, those involved in the movement of these materials within Europe, importation and exportation of these materials from

Europe, and patients for and donors of these materials. In the case of products made industrially from tissues and cells, the Directive applies only to donation, procurement, and testing—that is, the first steps of the manufacturing process. The other manufacturing steps are regulated by other European medicinal product legislation described previously in this chapter.

The Directive requires:

(i) the inspection and licensing of tissue establishments (which means a tissue bank or a unit of a hospital or another body where activities of processing, preservation, storage or distribution of human tissues are undertaken) by competent authorities in Member States;

(ii) tissue establishments to adopt appropriate control measures in order to ensure compliance with the requirements of the Directive. These control measures are evaluated by the competent authority in the course of the inspection regime. Tissue establishments are also required to maintain an up-to-date quality system with certain minimum documentary requirements, such as training manuals, donor records, and standard procedures, and to appoint a "responsible person." Records of the activities of tissue establishments and an annual report of those activities must be submitted to the competent authority;

(iii) that human tissues and cells intended, or used, for transplantation are traceable within and between Member States, including the implementation of donor identification systems and the requirement for tissue establishments to keep data necessary to ensure traceability;

(iv) Member States to ensure there is a system for reporting, investigating, registering, and transmitting information about serious adverse events and reactions that could influence the quality and safety of tissues and cells; and

(v) measures to be taken to regulate imports from and exports to non-EU countries of tissues and cells such that traceability is ensured and standards of quality and safety are met.

The Directive also empowers the Commission to establish and update technical requirements in relation to quality and safety of human tissues and cells. The first Technical Directive (in respect of the donation, procurement and testing of human tissues and cells) was adopted on February 8, 2006.[171] A second set of draft Technical Requirements (for the coding, processing, preservation, storage, and distribution of human tissues and cells) was issued on March 29, 2005, with responses requested by June 24, 2005.[172] A proposal for the second Technical Directive is anticipated in the second half of 2006.

3. Advanced Therapies

a. Europe

As noted above, at the time of writing, there is no European-wide regulation specifically governing the authorization of human tissue-engineering products. This leads to different national approaches as to their legal classification and authorization,[173] which in turn hinders the free movement of such products and patients' access to them and undermines industry development. However, with the aims of addressing these problems and providing legal certainty, in November 2005 the European Commission proposed a Regulation on advanced therapies.[174] The proposed Regulation governs human tissue-engineering products, gene therapies, and somatic cell therapies and includes:

- a compulsory centralized marketing authorization procedure;
- a new expert committee (Committee for Advanced Therapies) within the EMEA to assess advanced therapy products and follow scientific developments in the field;
- tailored technical requirements adapted to the particular scientific characteristics of these products;
- detailed guidance for the application of good manufacturing practice and good clinical practice to advanced therapies; and
- strengthened requirements for risk management and post-authorization traceability.

Decisions concerning the use or non-use of any specific type of human cells, however, would be left to the Member States.

b. International

The ICH has set up a Gene Therapy Discussion Group, the objectives of which are to:

(i) monitor emerging scientific issues;
(ii) proactively set out principles that may have a beneficial impact on harmonizing regulations of gene therapy products;
(iii) develop new ways of communication to ensure that the outcomes of ICH are well understood and widely disseminated; and
(iv) establish a publicly available ICH gene therapy Web page.[175]

4. Blood and Blood Components

European Directive 2002/98/EC[176] is a framework Directive setting out standards of quality and safety of human blood and blood components. It applies to the collection and testing of human blood and blood components, whatever their intended purpose.[177] Therefore, for example, the Directive covers blood and blood components that are used as starting materials for the manufacture of medicinal products. The Directive imposes obligations on Member States and "blood establishments"[178] in relation to quality and safety management, authorization and licensing requirements, and haemovigilance.

The Directive also contains provisions on the quality and safety of the blood and blood components themselves, on technical requirements, and on reporting and information.

The technical requirements for blood and blood components are set out in Directive 2004/33/EC.[179] From a biotechnological perspective, the storage, transport, and distribution conditions[180] and the quality and safety requirements for blood and blood components will be relevant to biotechnology medicinal products comprising blood/blood components. The requirements are set out in Annexes IV and V to the Directive, respectively. The Directive also sets out the detailed information that must be given to[181] and obtained from[182] donors, and criteria relating to the eligibility of donors.[183]

There is also a specific Directive concerning the traceability of blood and blood components[184] and a Directive setting out standards and specifications for quality systems for (among others) those who collect and test human blood or blood components, whatever their intended purpose.[185]

5. Medical Devices

In some cases, the distinction between a medicinal product and a medical device is blurred, such as in the case of devices that incorporate a medicine or stable derivates of human blood or human plasma as an integral part. Developers and manufacturers of such products need to understand which legislative regime they come under.[186]

Currently, three European Directives regulate the marketing and putting into service of medical devices:[187]

(i) Active Implantable Medical Devices;
(ii) Medical Devices Directive; and
(iii) In Vitro Diagnostic Directive.

These Directives define the essential requirements that devices must meet before being placed on the market, establish conformity assessment procedures, and set up vigilance and recall mechanisms. A manufacturer declares that the device meets the essential requirements by applying the "CE" mark to it in a specified manner. This "CE Marking" of conformity must be applied to medical devices (other than those that are custom-made or intended for clinical investigations) when they are placed on the market in Europe. Medical devices incorporating a biotechnology product may have to be the subject of both a marketing authorization and CE Marking.

The European Commission's Medical Devices Guidance document MEDDEV 2.1/3 Rev 2 sets out guidelines regarding the classification of products as medicinal products or medical devices.[188]

Recognizing the "blurring" mentioned above, the Medical Devices Directive is, at the time of writing, subject to a consultation exercise in which the drug/device issue is being considered.[189]

I. Regulation of GMOs

1. Regulation of GMOs: Legislation and Practice in the EEA

The use of GMOs is an area in which there has been much legislative activity in the past few years in the EEA and agricultural biotechnology is a particularly hot topic. GM crops represent the main form in which GMOs are released in the EEA, but the regulations governing the release and use of GM crops are applicable to any GMO.[190]

2. The EEA Legislative Framework with Respect to GMOs[191]

GMOs are subject to a number of different regulatory provisions in the EEA depending upon the uses they are put to. The legislation regulates all organisms, "with the exception of human beings, in which the genetic material has been altered in a way that does not occur naturally by mating and/or natural recombination."[192]

a. Experimental Release of GMOs into the Environment

Directive 2001/18/EC[193] (the "Deliberate Release Directive") governs the deliberate release of GMOs into the environment, and Part B is the key section applicable to experimental release of GMOs into the environment (e.g., for field testing). This Directive sets out the procedure to be followed by anyone wishing commercially to plant or otherwise release a GMO.

b. Placing on the Market of GMOs for Cultivation, Import, or Processing into Industrial Products

The Deliberate Release Directive also governs (mainly in Part C) the placing on the market of GMOs for cultivation, import or processing into industrial products, and again, sets out the procedure to be followed by anyone wishing commercially to plant or otherwise release a GMO. An applicant submits a notification to the competent national authority, which issues an assessment report. If favorable, the report is reviewed by other Member States. In the event of objections that are not resolved by dialogue between the relevant parties, the decision then moves to EU level, and the Commission asks the European Food Safety Authority (EFSA) to produce a report. Following consideration of the EFSA report, the Commission submits a draft decision on the authorization to the Regulatory Committee,[194] which votes on the decision. If a qualified majority is not reached then, the Commission submits the draft decision to the Council of Ministers for adoption or rejection, and again a qualified majority is required. The Commission can adopt the decision if the Council of Ministers does not arrive at a decision within three months. Therefore, it is possible that a GMO draft decision on approval that is rejected by a bare majority by both the Regulatory Committee and the Council of Ministers is adopted by the Commission.

c. Placing on the Market of GMOs for Food or Feed/Food or Feed Containing GMOs

Regulation (EC) 1829/2003[195] now governs applications to put products on the market in the EEA that either consist of GMOs or contain GMOs, or are produced from such organisms.[196] The authorization applies to use for both food and feed.[197]

This regulation is directed at producing a legislative regulatory framework for approving the use of GMO-derived food in the EEA while both protecting human health, environment, and consumer choice and preventing consumers being misled. It provides for a single authorization procedure whereby approval is obtained for the release of the GMO and its uses.[198] This would involve a single risk assessment, which would assess the risk of cultivation under criteria of the Deliberate Release Directive and risk of use in food/feed under Regulation (EC) 1829/2003. The result is dual authorization under both the Deliberate Release Directive and Regulation (EC) 1829/2003.

If a GMO is authorized, then approval lasts for 10 years provided the authorization holder demonstrates compliance with post-market monitoring requirements and is renewable for further 10-year periods.

d. Safeguard Clause

Approvals under the Deliberate Release Directive and Regulation 1829/2003 are not the last word in cultivating and marketing GMOs in the EEA. The provisions of the Deliberate Release Directive[199] permit Member States to invoke the so-called "safeguard clause."

The purpose of this clause is to permit Member States to require the withdrawal of a GMO or GMO-derived product from the market if they can demonstrate that it has justifiable reasons to consider the GMO in question to be a risk to human health and/or the environment.

e. Labeling and Traceability

Any GMO that has been authorized for release under either the Deliberate Release Directive or Regulation (EC) 1829/2003 is also subject to the provisions of Regulation (EC) 1830/2003[200] if it is to be marketed as food or feed. This regulation sets out the labeling and traceability regime that must be followed when food or feed consisting of, containing or produced from[201] GMOs is commercially released.

The adventitious presence of trace amounts of GMOs in food or feed does not make such food or feed subject to the requirements of Regulation (EC) 1829/2003 provided that the amount present does not exceed the thresholds set out in that regulation. However, individuals must be able to demonstrate to the competent authority that they are using appropriate steps to avoid the adventitious GMO presence even if sub-threshold levels are present. This has led to some confusion and certain environmental groups claiming that the setting of threshold levels is, in itself, inconsistent with the aims of the regulation, as it amounts to tacit authorization of an "acceptable" level of GMO contamination. The issue is, as yet, untested at law.

Regulation (EC) 1830/2003 is intended to facilitate the tracing of GMOs through the supply chain. The regulation requires businesses selling GMO-containing products to inform the purchaser of the origin of the product, giving them enough information to identify the particular GMO. As one of its main objectives, this regulation seeks to inform the public of the nature of the product, and an express goal is that GMO-derived food should not "mislead the public." Hence any food or feed containing, consisting of or produced from a GMO must be clearly labeled.

This regulation also provides wide-ranging powers for inspectors to visit and enter the premises of individuals and companies concerned in order to gather evidence of practices in confirmation of compliance with this regime.

f. Sanctions

EU legislation on GMOs often leaves the sanctions for breach to the discretion of the individual Member States but requires the penalties imposed to be "effective, proportionate and dissuasive."[202]

Few cases of GMO contamination have been discovered, but from those that have, it is clear that swift action is required to cooperate with the relevant authorities in order to resolve the situation.

g. Practical Implications for Industry

The GMO regulatory regime described above has wide-ranging implications for companies at all levels of the supply chain. It is possible that a number of these companies will not have taken a great deal of interest in GMO legislation in the past, and may not even have anything as fundamental as differential buying/storage/processing policies for GMO and conventional products and ingredients. In particular, industries that are directly affected by this legislation include:

- **Agriculture**—The regulation of the growing of GM crops is the most publicly visible aspect to the new GMO legislation. Companies selling bulk GM crop commodities need to obtain consent to import their produce into the EEA, whereas seed companies will need to obtain authorizations for cultivation of their products. In both cases the labeling and traceability regulations will apply to any products used to produce food or feed. Seed producers will also note the requirement to demonstrate that, even where the nature of the GMO contamination is such that it does not trigger compliance with the labeling and traceability regulations or require a release authorization, a company must be able to demonstrate that it is using "appropriate steps" to minimize the contamination.
- **Foodstuffs**—The retail food industry and its suppliers should have procedures in place to permit the tracing of GMO-derived ingredients through supply chains. Also, in the event that such ingredients are found to contain GMOs and are present in the end product, then, depending on the levels of GMO in the final product and whether or not the GMO is approved in the EEA, the company should review its labeling policies and/or switch ingredients.
- **Food processors**—Numerous products are used in the processing of food such as enzymes.[203] The production of these additives or processing aids often involves the use of GMOs because products such as enzymes can be produced using recombinant-DNA technology. The applicability of the deliberate release and labeling and traceability requirements to such products will depend in large part on the makeup of the final enzyme product. Producers should be aware of whether or not

the final preparation is a pure preparation of enzyme or whether the production process results in the "carry-over" of GMO DNA, GMO protein or even viable host organisms used to produce the enzyme. The presence of such contaminants may considerably influence the legal treatment of the final enzyme preparation.

Above all, each industry involved should be aware of the potential for a new wave of "dawn raids" by inspectors to investigate compliance with the new regime. In particular, companies should ensure that record keeping is of a standard that GMOs can be traced to customers and have been clearly followed throughout the supply chain. Also, companies' policies and procedures to avoid cross-contamination of conventional products with GMOs may be placed under scrutiny should any such adventitious GMO presence be discovered.

h. Developing and Marketing Authorizations for Medicinal Products Consisting of or Containing GMOs

The contained use (for example, in laboratory research) of genetically modified micro-organisms (GMmOs) is regulated by Directive 90/219/EC (the "Contained Use Directive").[204] The Contained Use Directive sets out (among other things) requirements for notification to competent authorities before GMmOs may be used for the first time.

As noted above in this chapter:

- There are specific legislative provisions governing clinical trials of products containing or consisting of GMOs, and GMO clinical trials must be conducted in accordance with clinical trial-specific legislation and guidance, but also in accordance with the Deliberate Use Directive and the Contained Use Directive.
- Marketing authorization applications for products containing or consisting of GMOs must contain particular information, including a risk assessment and evidence of compliance with the relevant provisions of the applicable GMO-related Directives. The EMEA has set out guidance for those developing medicinal products containing GMOs, advising potential applicants to discuss future applications with the EMEA between 6 months and a year in advance of

making a submission to the EMEA, and recommending that scientific advice from the EMEA[205] be obtained.

3. International GMO Regulation

Sitting alongside[206] the body of EU legislation described above is The Cartagena Protocol on Biosafety (the Protocol).[207] This Protocol was adopted in 2000 by members of the Convention on Biodiversity (a United Nations–backed organization) and came into force in September 2003, 90 days after the Republic of Palau became the 50th country to ratify it. The Protocol seeks to regulate the movement of GMOs across national boundaries, and central to it are the minimum standards of documentation that must accompany shipments containing GMOs and the level of information relating to the GMO that must be provided to the importing state in order for that state to be able to make an informed decision when agreeing to the importation.

Agricultural biotechnology is an important industry sector in India, and there is considerable state-supported crop biotechnology activity. India has implemented laws with respect to the use of GMOs and products derived from GMOs,[208] but concerns have been raised as to lack of effective enforcement of those laws.

Other nations, such as Australia and New Zealand, already have regimes in place to test and approve GMOs for release and/or use. The Australian government passed the Gene Technology Act in December 2000, which came into effect in June 2001 and, among other things, established the Office of the Gene Technology Regulator.[209] This Act makes a distinction between GMOs and products made with or using such GMOs. Such products are regulated by other regulatory agencies; for example, the use of GM products in food for human consumption is regulated by Food Standards Australia New Zealand,[210] and the use of GM products as human therapeutics is regulated by the Therapeutic Goods Administration.[211] New Zealand and Australia are both parties to the Convention on Biodiversity, but only New Zealand has ratified the Protocol as yet.[212]

For further information about GMOs (and other living modified organisms), including details of national laws and treaties, see the Biosafety Clearing House Web site at http://bch.biodiv.org/, maintained by the Secretariat of the Convention on Biological Diversity.

J. Intellectual Property

1. Introduction

The previous sections of this chapter have focused on the regulatory position in Europe and elsewhere with respect to medicinal products and genetically modified organisms. This section examines some key European intellectual property issues. It is not intended to be a general primer on intellectual property rights, but instead focuses on some key differences to the United States, key decisions in the field, and points to be aware of for U.S. companies. IP matters of importance for an expanding U.S. company include:

- What IP rights are available to protect inventions and works developed outside of the United States?
- What IP rights might someone else assert against the company?
- What differences are there in the procedures for, and approaches to, patenting in the biotechnology sector—what may or may not be patented?

2. Patents

a. Legislative Background

Of fundamental importance to any consideration of patent law in Europe is the 1973 European Patent Convention (EPC), which is principally concerned with the grant and validity of patents.[213] It provided for the establishment of the European Patent Office (EPO). Most of the signatories have brought their national law into line with the principles prescribed by the EPC. More recently, and specific to biotechnology, is Directive 98/44/EC of the European Parliament and of the Council of July 6, 1998 on the Legal Protection of Biotechnological Inventions (the Biotech Directive), which required Member States to bring their national laws into conformity with its provisions. Some of the provisions of the EPC and the Biotech Directive will be discussed below. The EPC is a Convention distinct from the EU Treaty (for example, Switzerland is an EPC signatory, but not an EU Member State), but the significance of that difference in this area may be limited.

b. Obtaining Patents in Europe

At present a separate patent is required for protection in each European state. Despite efforts to conclude legislation on the so-called Community patent in recent years, it is not yet possible to obtain a single (or "unitary") patent for the whole of Europe. Currently, therefore, patent protection covering European countries can be achieved by one of two procedures:

(i) filing separate applications in the national patent office of each Member State of interest. The patent office in each Member State examines the application to assess whether the requirements for patentability—novelty, inventiveness, industrial applicability—are met and that the subject matter does not fall within any excluded categories (as discussed below); or

(ii) filing a single application at the EPO. If successful, the European application will result in a bundle of national patents, one for each state designated in the application.[214]

The choice between separate national applications or a single application to the EPO is often made on the basis of cost, although procedural differences do exist. One important difference between a patent granted by the EPO (a European patent) and one by, say, the UK Patent Office is that the EPO provides an opportunity for a post-grant opposition procedure. If a European patent is successfully opposed, normally, all the national patents are maintained in an amended form or revoked together. By contrast, there is no post-grant opposition procedure for national patents granted by the UK Patent Office. Only the UK courts can revoke a national UK patent. To bring an opposition in the EPO, it must be initiated within nine months of grant.[215] EPO opposition proceedings have, however, been characterized by long time scales, often extending for several years, and this has been the subject of much criticism.

While the EPO examines and grants European patents and hears oppositions to European patents, infringement and validity actions are heard in the national court or courts of competent jurisdiction—not in the EPO.

c. Substantive Patentability Criteria; Differences to the U.S. Position

There are a number of aspects in which the substantive law governing availability of patents differs between Europe and the United States. Key differences include:

(i) The patent systems in Europe are so-called "first to file" systems. In other words, where two parties have independently made the same invention, the party first to file an application is the party entitled to the patent (leaving aside novelty requirements), even if the later filer could prove it made the invention first. While there are procedures to challenge title to a patent or an application to a patent, there is no procedure in Europe akin to the U.S. interference procedure.

(ii) The principles that govern what is and what is not prior art are also different. For the contents of an oral or written disclosure, or the details of a prior use, to be prior art, they have to have been "made available to the public" before the priority date.[216] There is no "grace period" in Europe. An oral or written disclosure, or a prior use, even a single day before the filing of the priority application, can be fatal to the chances of obtaining valid patent protection in Europe. It is thus essential to ensure that a patent application is filed before a journal article is published or a paper given at a conference. Ph.D. theses, which routinely appear on university library shelves, are another source of slip-ups

> **Practice Points**
>
> Key differences between U.S. and European patent protection:
> 1. Successful opposition of a patent filed with the EPO normally leads to amendment or revocation of all national patents.
> 2. "First to file," not "first to invent," determines patent rights.
> 3. No grace period for disclosure; any publication puts the intellectual property in the public domain.
> 4. Plant and animal varieties are not patentable.

in the European patenting process if the patent application is not filed in a timely manner. Under EPO case law, there is no quantitative requirement as to the numbers of persons to whom the disclosure is made for it to become "available to the public." It is sufficient if the disclosure is made to a single individual who is free to do with it as he or she wishes.[217] Therefore, if it is not possible for some reason to file a priority application before any disclosure to another party is made, it is essential to ensure that the disclosure is made under conditions of confidence. Preferably this should be under a signed non-disclosure agreement.

d. Excluded Subject Matter

Not all subject matter that is new and inventive at the priority date is patentable in Europe. Article 53(b) EPC contains certain specific exclusions. These include plant and animal varieties and "essentially biological processes for the production of plants or animals" (but see below).

A characteristic of European patent law for almost 30 years has been the exclusion from patentability of inventions the exploitation of which would be immoral, or in the wording of Article 53(a) EPC, would be "contrary to 'ordre public' or morality."[218]

e. Microbiological Processes and Products

The Article 53(b) EPC exclusion from patentability of "essentially biological processes for the production of plants or animals" expressly does not apply to "microbiological processes or the products thereof." Accordingly, the EPO is willing to grant patents for micro-organisms, plasmids, vectors, algae, and protozoa, as well as human, animal, and plant cells, assuming of course the subject matter meets the standard patentability criteria of novelty and inventive step.[219] By way of example, in decision T 0272/95, the EPO Technical Board of Appeal 3.3.4 upheld a patent granted to the Howard Florey Institute of Experimental Physiology and Medicine with a claim to a DNA fragment encoding human H2-preprorelaxin with a particular amino-acid sequence and another claim to a cell transformed by an appropriate DNA transfer vector.[220]

f. Human Material

The Biotech Directive contains specific detail regarding human material. The human body, at the various stages of its formation and development, and the simple discovery of one of its elements (including the sequence or partial sequence of a gene) cannot constitute patentable inventions.[221] On the other hand, an element isolated from the human body or otherwise produced by means of a technical process, including the sequence or partial sequence of a gene, may constitute a patentable invention, even if the structure of that element is identical to that of a natural element.[222] The industrial application of a sequence or partial sequence of a gene must, though, be disclosed in the patent application.[223]

Article 6 of the Biotech Directive states that the following inventions are unpatentable:

- processes for cloning human beings;
- processes for modifying the germ line genetic identity of human beings;
- use of human embryos for industrial or commercial purposes; and
- processes for modifying the genetic identity of animals that are likely to cause them suffering without any substantial medical benefit to man or animal, and animals resulting from such processes.

g. Morality: Stem Cells

The morality exclusion has played its part in the area of stem cells. In July 2002 the EPO Opposition Division rejected claims in a University of Edinburgh patent (EP 0695351) that were broad enough to cover human embryonic stem cells. Edinburgh appealed, and at the time of writing the matter is pending.

Moreover, in a statement in April 2003, the UK Patent Office stated that it would not grant patents for processes for obtaining stem cells from human embryos—that is, so-called "totipotent cells," which have the potential to develop into the entire human body (the human body at the various stages of its formation and development being excluded from the patentability under Article 5 of the Biotech Directive). The UK Patent Office would, however, in principle be prepared to grant patents for human embryonic pluripotent stem cells—those cells that arise from further division of totipotent cells and do not have the potential to develop into an entire human being.[224]

h. Morality: Transgenic Animals

The application of the morality exclusion in the case of transgenic animals has been considered at great length in the EPO in the course of the prosecution of, and opposition to, the Harvard/Oncomouse patent. The application was filed in 1985 and was eventually granted in 1991. Oppositions to the grant were filed by 16 parties. Some 13 years later, on July 6, 2004, an EPO Technical Board of Appeal upheld the patent in amended form.[225]

i. Transgenic Plants

Under Article 4(2) of the Biotech Directive, plants are patentable if "the technical feasibility of the invention is not confined to a particular plant or animal variety." Previously, in case T49/83 *CIBA-GEIGY/Propagating material*,[226] the EPO Technical Board of Appeal allowed claims to seeds treated with chemical agents to increase herbicide resistance. The invention was not considered to be contrary to the EPC plant varieties exclusion. This position was restated in 1999 by the EPO Enlarged Board of Appeal in decision G1/98 *Transgenic Plant/NOVARTIS II*, although in the interim (1995) the Enlarged Board had held, in decision G3/95, that a claim defining genetically modified plants as having a distinct, stable, herbicide-resistant genetic characteristic was not allowable, because the claimed genetic modification itself made the modified or transformed plant a "plant variety." For current practice of the EPO, reference should be made to EPO Guidelines for Examinations, Part C, Chapter IV, paragraph 3.4.1.

3. Trademarks

The law governing national trademarks in the EEA derives from the provisions of a European Directive,[227] so to a very large extent is consistent across the EEA.

While there are some differences in the way in which infringement is assessed, there are no differences between trademark law in the United States and the United Kingdom that are of particular significance to biotechnology companies. Like the United States, most European countries are signatories to the Madrid Protocol, and it is therefore possible to file an international trademark application in either the United States or a European Member State that covers both jurisdictions, as well as any others that are desired.

As well as filing national or international applications, it is possible in Europe to apply to the Office for Harmonization in the Internal Market[228] for a Community Trade Mark (CTM). This is a single, supra-national right that covers the entire European Community, with the same protection applying throughout. Unlike the European patent, the CTM is not a bundle of national rights and is enforced or, as the case may be, revoked in relation to the entire Community. The law that applies to CTMs is broadly similar to the law that applies under the Directive and national legislation. The European Community has recently become a member of the Madrid Protocol, so that it is now possible to extend an international registration to the whole of the EU as well as or instead of individual Member States.

4. Copyright and Database Right

The law of copyright in Europe is similar to that in the United States and protects the same categories of work, provided they qualify for protection.[229] Unlike in the United States, however, there is no means of registering copyright in Europe. This means it is potentially more difficult to establish ownership of copyright in Europe, though precautionary steps can be taken to identify significant copyright works, such as marking them with a copyright notice.

The European "database right" protects databases that are commercially valuable, by reason of the fact that there has been "substantial investment in the obtaining, verifying or presentation of the contents of the database." Therefore, even if a database does not qualify for copyright protection through not being "original," it may qualify for database right. The owner of the right can prevent someone else from "extracting" or "reutilizing" all or a substantial part of the database, and from repeatedly extracting or reutilizing small amounts. The database right is only available to companies established in the EEA or in a country or territory that has entered into an agreement with the EU mutually recognizing this form of database protection. To date, there is no reciprocal protection agreement with the United States.

5. Plant Breeders' Rights

Underpinning the international protection of plant varieties is a 1961 Convention established by the International Union for the Protection of New Varieties of Plants (UPOV).[230]

The plant variety right as provided for in the Convention provides a form of intellectual property protection that has been specifically adapted for the process of plant breeding and has been developed with the aim of encouraging breeders to develop new varieties of plants.

In Europe, applicants can apply to a central office, the Community Plant Variety Office (CPVO), for the "Community plant variety right" in respect of varieties that are distinct (from any other variety), uniform in characteristic, stable, and novel. The right can be considered as Europe's equivalent to the U.S. plant variety protection. The CPVO is a community organization that implements and applies the European system for protecting plant variety rights. Its site provides information on procedures for plant variety protection and issues such as the relationship between Community and national protection.[231]

6. The Interplay Between Intellectual Property Rights and European Community Law

There is an inherent conflict between the concept of a single market throughout the EEA and national intellectual property rights. This is a complex area, the detail of which is beyond the scope of this chapter, but key points to note with respect to the resolution of this conflict are:

- An intellectual property rights holder cannot rely on national law to resist the import and/or resale of a product put on the market anywhere in the EC by the owner or a connected undertaking with the owner's consent (unless the product has been tampered with). This is known as the doctrine of exhaustion of rights (see above, with respect to parallel importation).
- Many agreements with respect to intellectual property rights (such as technology transfer agreements and research and development agreements) are subject to EC competition law.
- Certain aspects of the protection afforded by intellectual property rights have been harmonized by Directives—for example, the duration of copyright.

7. Enforcement of Intellectual Property Rights

If a rights owner is seeking to enforce those rights against an actual or threatened infringer, the rights owner should seek timely legal advice from a local specialist on such matters as:

a) What remedies are available, such as temporary and final injunctions, search and seizure orders, damages, and accounts of profits?
b) What are the time scales for obtaining relief, and what are the associated costs?
c) Within Europe, where the infringement is taking place in more than one Member State, is there a tactical advantage in commencing proceedings in one country as opposed to another?
d) If applicable, are there remedies available through bodies other than the courts, such as Customs?
e) Does the local jurisdiction contain sanctions for making unjustifiable threats?

K. EC[232] Competition Law

1. Introduction

In the course of their business dealings with companies established in or doing business in Europe, companies must be aware of EC competition rules. Taking part in activities that prevent or distort trade between Member States, or that constitute an abuse of a dominant position, can result in severe sanctions.

The fundamental EC Treaty sets out a system of prohibitions of anticompetitive agreements and conduct. Unlike many competition regimes, the EC competition rules are also directed at ensuring the free movement of goods and services between EU Member States. As a result, many cases have involved restrictions on parallel imports between Member States—a concept that is alien to lawyers outside the EU.

2. EC Competition Procedures

The European Commission and national competition authorities each have wide-ranging powers to investigate and enforce the competition rules.

European and International Considerations

They can conduct on-site investigations or dawn raids and have the power to impose penalties of up to 10 percent of the worldwide group turnover.

3. Article 81

a. Introduction

Article 81(1) of the EC Treaty prohibits agreements and concerted practices between undertakings (organizations carrying on commercial activities), and decisions of trade associations that have the object or effect of preventing, restricting or distorting competition within the common market and that may affect trade between Member States.

A particular target of Article 81 is hardcore restrictions of competition involving price-fixing, market-sharing, limiting output, and bid-rigging. Businesses found to be engaging in any of these hardcore activities can expect to have severe financial penalties imposed on them.

As well as applying to agreements with an anticompetitive *intent*, Article 81 also applies to agreements with an anticompetitive *effect*. Consequently, even such apparently benign arrangements as joint research and development agreements between competitors, or distribution agreements, can be caught.

Where an agreement infringes Article 81(1), but its benefits outweigh its anticompetitive effects, it may be exempted under Article 81(3).

> **Practice Points**
>
> European competition (antitrust) law prohibits:
>
> - agreements and concerted practices between undertakings that have the object or effect of preventing, restricting or distorting competition within Europe and that may affect trade between Member States;
> - any abuse by one or more undertakings of a dominant position within Europe, insofar as it may affect trade between Member States.
>
> The European Commission and national competition authorities each have wide-ranging powers to investigate and enforce the competition rules. They can conduct on-site investigations or dawn raids and have the power to impose penalties of up to 10 percent of the worldwide group turnover.

Consequences of infringing Article 81(1) include being fined by the European Commission or national competition authorities, the offending provisions of the agreement (or even the whole agreement) being voided, and a damages claim by those who suffer loss as a result of the anticompetitive behavior. National courts can also grant injunctions to restrain anticompetitive behavior.

b. Block Exemptions

Exemption is possible by drafting the agreement to fall within the terms of one of a series of "block exemptions" covering certain common types of commercial agreement, such as exclusive distribution, R&D, and technology licensing agreements.[233] Provided that they do not contain serious restrictions of competition as mentioned above, agreements between non-competitors are exempted by these block exemptions if the market share of the supplier (or in certain circumstances, the buyer) is below a specified threshold. This new generation of block exemptions provide a safe harbor. An agreement does not necessarily fall within the prohibition imposed by Article 81 simply because it falls outside the scope of a block exemption.

4. Article 82

Article 82 of the EC Treaty prohibits any abuse by one or more undertakings of a dominant position within the common market or in a substantial part, insofar as it may affect trade between Member States. Article 82 applies only to businesses that are dominant in a market and only to the abuse of such power for anticompetitive ends.

The narrower the market, the greater the likelihood of an undertaking holding a position of market power.

Dominance is assessed on a case-by-case basis and depends on a number of factors, no one of which is conclusive, such as barriers to entry to the market (e.g., the cost of setting up manufacture, IP rights or product licenses) and constraints on market power (e.g., the strength of existing competitors and the extent of buyer power on the part of the undertaking's customers).

Dominant companies have a special responsibility to ensure that their behavior does not restrict competition. As a result, they may be precluded from engaging in certain types of behavior that is perfectly lawful for non-dominant companies. Examples include entering into certain types of exclusivity obligations and the prices, rebates, and discounts that dominant companies may offer.

Internet Links Referenced in This Chapter

This chapter includes many Internet links to legislative and regulatory sources and sources for further reading. In light of the rapid development of regulation and policy in the area of biotechnology, readers are advised when reading the main text to check the Internet links regularly for updates. Internet links referenced in the text and endnotes were accessed in or about June 2006.

Notes

1. The European Union (EU) Member States are Austria, Belgium, Czech Republic, Cyprus, Denmark, Estonia, Finland, France, Germany, Greece, Hungary, Ireland, Italy, Latvia, Lithuania, Luxembourg, Malta, Netherlands, Poland, Portugal, Slovakia, Slovenia, Spain, Sweden, and the UK. The Czech Republic, Cyprus, Estonia, Hungary, Latvia, Lithuania, Malta, Poland, Slovakia, and Slovenia joined the EU in 2004, and are sometimes referred to as the "accession states." The "European Economic Area," or "EEA," is made up of the countries of the EU together with Iceland, Liechtenstein, and Norway. Broadly speaking, EU laws on medicinal products extend by Treaty to the whole of the EEA.
2. *See* http://europa.eu.int/comm/dgs_en.htm.
3. *See* http://ec.europa.eu/enterprise/pharmaceuticals/index_en.htm.
4. *See* http://pharmacos.eudra.org/F2/advtherapies/index.htm.
5. *See* http://ec.europa.eu/enterprise/phabiocom/index_en.htm.
6. *See* http://pharmacos.eudra.org/F3/cosmetic/cosm_intro_NEW.htm.
7. *See* http://europa.eu.int/comm/enterprise/medical_devices/index_en.htm.
8. http://europa.eu.int/comm/food/food/biotechnology/index_en.htm.
9. http://europa.eu.int/comm/environment/biotechnology/index_en.htm.
10. http://ec.europa.eu/environment/chemicals/lab_animals/scientific_en.htm.
11. *See* http://ec.europa.eu/internal_market/indprop/invent/index_en.htm on "Biotechnological inventions."
12. http://europa.eu.int/comm/research/biosociety/index_en.htm, and see in particular the strategy paper "Life Sciences and Biotechnology—a Strategy for Europe," *available at* http://europa.eu.int/comm/research/biosociety/life_sciences/documents_en.htm.
13. *See* http://www.emea.eu.int for further information.
14. *See* http://www.emea.eu.int/Inspections/index.html for further information.

15. "Mandate, objectives and rules of procedure for the Working Party on Similar Biological Medicinal Products (BMWP)," March 18, 2005; *available at* http://www.emea.eu.int/pdfs/human/biosimilar/8065005en.pdf.

16. All of which are available from the EMEA Web site, http://www.emea.eu.int.

17. Copies of these guidance documents and concept papers are *available at* http://www.emea.eu.int/htms/human/itf/itfguide.htm.

18. This Web page also contains details of regulatory bodies of countries that have entered into Mutual Recognition Agreements with the EU in respect of various regulatory matters, and details of European and international health-care bodies. *See also*, as an alternative source of information on European competent authorities, the "Heads of Agencies" *at* http://heads.medagencies.org/.

19. This section, together with the sections on the regulation of product development, marketing authorizations, and post-marketing activities focus on human medicinal products. European regulation of veterinary medicinal products is governed, in many respects, by the same or a similar framework. Interested readers may refer to the volumes covering veterinary medicinal products in *The Rules Governing Medicinal Products in the European Union*—see section E.2 of this chapter.

20. Article 1(2) Directive 2001/83/EC, as amended by Directive 2004/27/EC of the European Parliament and of the Council of March 31, 2004 amending Directive 2001/83/EC on the Community Code relating to medicinal products for human use.

21. Article 2(2), *id*.

22. *See* note 1 for the definition of the EEA.

23. *See* http://www.europa.eu.int/comm/enterprise/chemicals/legislation/glp/index_en.htm for further information about GLP in the EEA.

24. *Available at* http://europa.eu.int/eur-lex/pri/en/oj/dat/2004/l_050/l_05020040220en00280043.pdf.

25. *Available at* http://europa.eu.int/eur-lex/pri/en/oj/dat/2004/l_050/l_05020040220en00440059.pdf.

26. *See* http://www.emea.eu.int/pdfs/human/ich/030295en.pdf.

27. Council Directive 86/609/EEC of November 24, 1986 on the approximation of laws, regulations, and administrative provisions of the Member States regarding the protection of animals used for experimental and other scientific purposes; *available at* http://europa.eu.int/comm/food/fs/aw/aw_legislation/scientific/86-609-eec_en.pdf.

28. Article 7, *id*.

29. Article 7(2), *id*.

30. Article 19, *id*.

31. Article 15, *id*.

32. The European Commission's Web site on laboratory animals, *available at* http://ec.europa.eu/environment/chemicals/lab_animals/home_en.htm, contains further information about the legislative framework, proposals for amendment, and statistics on animal use in the EU.

33. http://www.felasa.org/.

34. Documents and activities of the OECD in this area can be accessed from the OECD's GLP Web page *at* http://www.oecd.org/department/0,2688, en_2649_34381_1_1_1_1_1,00.html.

35. *See, e.g.,* http://www.nc3rs.org.uk/.

36. EC Directive 2001/20/EC on the approximation of laws, regulations, and administrative provisions of the Member States relating to the implementation of good clinical practice in the conduct of clinical trials on medicinal products for human use.

37. Commission Directive 2005/28/EC of April 8, 2005 laying down principles and detailed guidelines for good clinical practice as regards investigational medicinal products for human use, as well as the requirements for authorization of the manufacturing or importation of such products; copy *available at* http://pharmacos.eudra.org/F2/eudralex/vol-1/DIR_2005_28/DIR_2005_28_EN.pdf.

38. Commission Directive 2003/94/EC of October 8, 2003 laying down the principles and guidelines of good manufacturing practice in respect of medicinal products for human use and investigational medicinal products for human use; copy *available at* http://pharmacos.eudra.org/F2/eudralex/vol-1/DIR_2003_94/DIR_2003_94_EN.pdf.

39. Commission Directive 2005/28/EC of April 8, 2005 laying down principles and detailed guidelines for good clinical practice as regards investigational medicinal products for human use, as well as the requirements for authorization of the manufacturing or importation of such products. *Available at* http://pharmacos. eudra.org/F2/eudralex/vol-1/DIR_2005_28/DIR_2005_28_EN.pdf.

40. Guidelines are not legally binding, but applicants for authorization must justify their processes if they deviate.

41. http://pharmacos.eudra.org/F2/pharmacos/dir200120ec.htm.

42. *Available at* http://www.emea.europa.eu/index/indexh1.htm.

43. For example, while France passed national law to implement the Clinical Trials Directive in 2004, that law was not brought into force until April 2006.

44. So, for example, in the UK, the Clinical Trials Directive has been implemented into national law by the Medicines for Human Use (Clinical Trials) Regulations 2004, and someone carrying out trials in the UK will need to comply with that legislation, together with applicable guidelines adopted by the UK's competent authority, the Medicines and Healthcare Products Regulatory Agency: http://www.mhra.gov.uk.

45. The topic of testing of, and marketing, medicines for pediatric use is beyond the scope of this chapter, but it should be noted that there is considerable European legislative activity in this area. For further information, *see, e.g.*, the Proposal for a Regulation of the European Parliament and of the Council on Medicinal Products for Pediatric Use and Amending Regulation (EEC) No 1768/92, Directive 2001/83/EC and Regulation (EC) No 726/2004; European Commission COM(2005) 577 final, 10.11.2005, *available at* http://www.ec.europa.eu/enterprise/pharmaceuticals/paediatrics/docs/com_2005_0577_en.pdf.

46. *See* http://eudract.emea.eu.int.

47. Article 2(a) of the Clinical Trials Directive.

48. But Member States may have *other* laws in place applicable to such trials.

49. Article 9(3), *id.*

50. Article 10(a), *id.*

51. Article 16(4), *id.*

52. Article 17(1), *id.*

53. Article 17(2), *id.*

54. Article 3(2)(f), *id.*

55. *See, e.g.*, the guidance of the UK's Medicines and Healthcare Products Regulatory Agency, "How to submit a clinical trial authorisation (CTA)," *available at* http://www.mhra.gov.uk/home/idcplg?IdcService=SS_GET_PAGE&nodeId=723.

56. Article 7 of the Clinical Trials Directive.

57. In practice, some Ethics Committees in certain Member States are taking longer.

58. Article 9(4) of the Clinical Trials Directive.

59. While there is currently no mutual recognition procedure for clinical trial authorizations, this is an area under discussion within Europe, along with further harmonization measures.

60. Article 9(4) of the Clinical Trials Directive.

61. For an example from the UK, see the UK Gene Therapy Advisory Committee's guidance, *available at* http://www.advisorybodies.doh.gov.uk/genetics/gtac/applicform.htm.

62. Article 9(6) of the Clinical Trials Directive. Note that the Clinical Trials Directive is expressed to be without prejudice to the provisions of the Council Directives 90/219/EEC of April 23, 1990 on the contained use of genetically modified micro-organisms and 90/220/EEC of April 23, 1990 on the deliberate release into the environment of genetically modified organisms.

63. Article 9(6) of the Clinical Trials Directive.

64. "Detailed guidance for the request of an authorization of a clinical trial on a medicinal product for human use to the competent authorities, notification of substantial amendments and declaration of the end of the trial"; Revision 2 (Octo-

ber, 2005), *available at* http://eudract.emea.eu.int/docs/Detailed%20guidance%20CTA.pdf.

65. Article 13(1) of the Clinical Trials Directive.

66. Article 13(2), *id.*

67. *See* http://pharmacos.eudra.org/F2/mra/index.htm and http://www.emea.eu.int/Inspections/MRA.html for further information.

68. *See, e.g.,* the declaration form for use in the UK, "Qualified Person Declaration Concerning Investigational Medicinal Products Manufactured In Third Countries," *available at* http://www.mhra.gov.uk.

69. Article 15(1) of the Clinical Trials Directive.

70. Article 15(3), *id.*

71. Article 15(4), *id.*

72. A "serious adverse event or serious adverse reaction" is defined in Article 2 of the Clinical Trials Directive as "any untoward medical occurrence or effect that at any dose results in death, is life threatening, requires hospitalization, results in persistent or significant disability or incapacity, or is a congenital anomaly or birth defect.."

73. Article 17(1), *id.*

74. Article 17(2), *id.*

75. *See* http://www.eudravigilance.org/human/index.asp.

76. Article 12(1) of the Clinical Trials Directive.

77. Section 49 of The Medicines for Human Use (Clinical Trials) Regulations 2004.

78. Article 3(2)(f) of the Clinical Trials Directive.

79. Directive 95/46/EC; *see* http://europa.eu.int/comm/justice_home/fsj/privacy/index_en.htm. Note that the Data Protection Directive is not sector- or activity-specific, and as such its scope is much broader than that of HIPAA (see chapter 11).

80. "Consent" is defined by the Data Protection Directive as "any freely given, specific and informed indication of the data subject's wishes by which the subject signifies his agreement to personal data relating to him being processed."

81. Details of which can be found at http://www.export.gov/safeharbor/ (and in particular *see* http://www.export.gov/safeharbor/FAQ14PharmaFINAL.htm). There are other means of lawfully transferring personal data from the EEA to the U.S., but these are beyond the scope of this section.

82. Article 11(1)(f), *id.*

83. http://pharmacos.eudra.org/F2/pharmacos/docs/Doc2002/July/gcp_51_july.pdf.

84. Commission Directive 2005/28/EC of April 8, 2005, laying down principles and detailed guidelines for good clinical practice as regards investigational medicinal products for human use, as well as the requirements for authorization of the manufacturing or importation of such products. Copy *available at* http://pharmacos.eudra.org/F2/eudralex/vol-1/DIR_2005_28/DIR_2005_28_EN.pdf.

85. In this chapter, the European legislative regime with respect to marketing authorizations and post-marketing activities is discussed from the perspective of medicinal products for human (as opposed to veterinary) use.

86. Article 3(1), Regulation (EC) No. 726/2004 of the European Parliament and of the Council of March 31, 2004, laying down Community procedures for the authorization and supervision of medicinal products for human and veterinary use and establishing a European Medicines Agency.

87. Note that there is also a Mutual Recognition Procedure, allowing a marketing authorization already granted in one Member State (the "Reference Member State") to be recognized in some or all other Member States. For further information, *see* the European Commission's "Notice to Applicants Volume 2A - Procedures for marketing authorisation, Chapter 2, Mutual Recognition," dated November 2005, *copy available at* http://ec.europa.eu/enterprise/pharmaceuticals/eudralex/vol-2/a/vol2a_chap2_2005-11.pdf.

88. Paragraph 3.2.1.1(b), Annex I of Directive 2001/83/EC (as amended by Directive 2003/63/EC of June 25, 2003).

89. "Immunological medicinal products" are defined in Article 1(4) of Directive 2001/83/EC as amended, and "medicinal products derived from human blood or human plasma" are defined in Article 1(10) of the same.

90. Part A of the Annex to Council Regulation 726/2004.

91. Part IV, Annex I of Directive 2003/63/EC.

92. The Community Code Review package consists of: Regulation EC 726/2004; Directive 2004/27/EC on the Community Code relating to medicinal products for human use; Directive 2004/28/EC on the Community Code relating to medicinal products for veterinary use; and Directive 2004/24/EC on the Community Code relating to traditional herbal medicinal products. Copies of the relevant legislation can be found at the "Review of pharmaceutical legislation" area of the European Commission's Pharmaceuticals Web site, http://pharmacos.eudra.org/F2/review/index.htm.

93. For the legislative basis, see Article 8 and Annex I to Directive 2001/83/EC as amended by Directives 2003/63/EC and 2004/27. *See also* the European Commission Notice to Applicants (Volume 2 of the Rules Governing Medicinal Products in the European Union), *available at* http://pharmacos.eudra.org/F2/eudralex/vol-2/home.htm, and *see also* the specific and scientific EMEA Committee Guidelines, *available at* http://www.emea.eu.int.

94. Various abridged application procedures are available; these are discussed in section G.4 of this chapter.

95. For further information, see the EMEA Guidance "Medicinal Products containing or consisting of Genetically Modified Organisms," *available at* http://www.emea.eu.int/htms/human/presub/q20.htm.

96. *Available at* http://pharmacos.eudra.org/F2/eudralex/index.htm.

97. In accordance with the requirements of Annex I of Directive 2001/83/EC (as amended by Directives 2003/63/EC and 2004/27/EC).

98. http://www.emea.eu.int/htms/human/presub/PSG%20Compilation.pdf.
99. Article 6(3) Reg. 726/2004.
100. Article 14(9) Reg. 726/2004.
101. Article 2 Reg. 726/2004; *see also* the Guidance of the EMEA on "Establishment in the EEA," *available at* http://www.emea.eu.int/htms/human/presub/q16.htm.
102. Article 14(1) Reg. 726/2004; Article 24(1) of Directive 2001/83, as amended by Directive 2004/27.
103. Article 14(2) Reg. 726/2004; Article 24(2) of Directive 2001/83, as amended by Directive 2004/27.
104. Article 14(4) Reg. 726/2004; Article 24(4) of Directive 2001/83, as amended by Directive 2004/27. This provision is sometimes referred to as the "sunset clause."
105. *See, e.g.*, § 60(5)(b) Patents Act 1977 in the UK, corresponding to Article 27(b) of the European Patent Convention.
106. Monsanto v. Stauffer [1985], RPC 515.
107. *Klinische Versuche I (Interferon-gamma)* [1997] RPC 623) and *Klinische Versuche II (Erythropoietin)* [1998] RPC 423.
108. Article 10(6) of Directive 2001/83, as amended by Directive 2004/27.
109. *See, e.g.*, "Guideline on Pharmacogenetics Briefing Meetings" (Draft), March 17, 2005; EMEA/CHMP/20227/2004; *available at* http://www.emea.eu.int/pdfs/human/pharmacogenetics/2022704en.pdf.
110. For further information *see* "General Principles EMEA, FDA Parallel Scientific Advice Meetings Pilot Program," Sept. 17, 2004, *available at* http://www.fda.gov/oia/pilotprogram0904.html.
111. *See* "Cooperation on Medicines Regulation Intensified," Mar. 14, 2006, *available at* http://www.fda.gov/bbs/topics/news/2006/NEW01334.html.
112. Notwithstanding the size of the Japanese market for medicinal products, being second only to the United States.
113. Note that an applicant for a European marketing authorization must include in his application a statement to the effect that clinical trials conducted outside the EEA meet the ethical requirements of the Clinical Trials Directive.
114. *See, e.g.*, ICH Topic E5 Ethnic Factors in the Acceptability of Foreign Clinical Data, *available at* http://www.emea.eu.int/pdfs/human/ich/02899Sen.pdf.
115. http://www.ich.org.
116. *See* http://pharmacos.eudra.org/F2/pharmacos/docs.htm.
117. *See* the section "CTD" at http://www.ich.org.
118. http://www.tga.gov.au/docs/html/eugctd.htm.
119. For further information, *see* "EU Pharmacovigilance Rules for Human and Veterinary Medicinal Products," *available at* http://pharmacos.eudra.org/F2/eudralex/vol-9/home.htm.
120. Article 103 of Directive 2001/83, as amended by Directive 2004/27.
121. Article 4(6), *id.*

122. In which regard, see the consultation paper on a proposed regulation regarding penalties under Regulation 726/2004; *available at* http://pharmacos.eudra.org/F2/pharmacos/docs/Doc2005/02_05/Penalties%20-%20Public%20consultation%2002%202005.pdf.

123. Article 40(1) of Directive 2001/83, as amended by Directive 2004/27.

124. *See, e.g.,* Article 46(d) of Directive 2001/83, as amended by Directive 2004/27.

125. Article 46(b), *id.*

126. Article 48, *id.*

127. *See* note 39.

128. *See* http://pharmacos.eudra.org/F2/eudralex/vol-4/home.htm.

129. Article 40(3) of Directive 2001/83, as amended by Directive 2004/27.

130. Article 1(17) defines "wholesale distribution" as "All activities consisting of procuring, holding, supplying or exporting medicinal products, apart from supplying medicinal products to the public. Such activities are carried out with manufacturers or their depositories, importers, other wholesale distributors or with pharmacists and persons authorized or entitled to supply medicinal products to the public in the Member State concerned."

131. Article 4(2) of the GMP Directive.

132. For further information, see the Inspections section of the EMEA Web site, http://www.emea.eu.int/Inspections/index.html.

133. *See, e.g.,* "Mutual Recognition Agreements between the EU and the Parties Australia, Canada, New Zealand and Switzerland," *available at* http://www.emea.eu.int/Inspections/docs/0002203en.pdf, and "Questions and Answers on the EEA-Switzerland MRA," *available at* http://www.emea.eu.int/pdfs/technical/mra/ch/008402en.pdf.

134. This section sets out the position with respect to abridged applications following the 2004 Community Code review, rather than on the previous regime, which was based around a concept of "essential similarity."

135. Article 10(2)(b) of Directive 2001/83, as amended by Directive 2004/27.

136. *Id.*

137. *Id.*

138. Article 10(4) of Directive 2001/83, as amended by Directive 2004/27.

139. *See* the Biosimilar Medicinal Products Adopted Guidelines on the EMEA Web site at http://www.emea.eu.int/htms/human/biosimilar/biosimilarfin.htm, and the Biosimilar Medicinal Products Concept Papers *at* http://www.emea.eu.int/htms/human/biosimilar/biosimilarcon.htm

140. On April 12, 2006, the human growth hormone Omnitrope was the first biosimilar to be granted a marketing authorization by the EMEA and on April 24, 2006, Valtropin (another growth hormone) was the second.

141. Article 10a of Directive 2001/83, as amended by Directive 2004/27.
142. Article 10(1) of Directive 2001/83, as amended by Directive 2004/27.
143. *Id.*
144. Article 74a of Directive 2001/83, as amended by Directive 2004/27.
145. *See further* Commission Communication on the Single Market in Pharmaceuticals COM(98)588 Final, November 25, 1998, *available at* http://europa.eu.int/comm/enterprise/library/lib-regulation/doc/com-98-588_en.pdf.
146. Details are beyond the scope of this chapter, *but see, e.g., Smith & Nephew and Primecrown* (November 12, 1996; ECJ case C-201/94), *Rhône-Poulenc Rorer* (December 16, 1999; ECJ case C-94/98), and *Kohlpharma GmbH v. Bundesrepublik Deutschland* (April 1, 2004; ECJ case C-112/02).
147. The accession of countries into the EU raises difficult questions with respect to exhaustion of intellectual property rights that are beyond the scope of this chapter.
148. Thus the intellectual property rights in a line of Sebago shoes were not exhausted *in toto* by the sale of one consignment; *Sebago Inc and anor. v. G-B Unic SA* (July 1, 1999; ECJ Case C-173/98).
149. Bristol-Myers Squibb v. Paranova A/S (July 11, 1996; joined ECJ Cases C-427/93, 429/93 and 436/93); *also see* Boehringer Ingelheim KG and others v. Swingward Ltd. and another (April 23, 2002; ECJ Case C-143/00), *available at* http://curia.eu.int/en/content/juris/index_form.htm.
150. AG Opinion Boehringer Ingelheim KG and others v. Swingward Ltd. and another (April 6, 2006; ECJ Case C-348/04), *available at* http://curia.eu.int/en/content/juris/index_form.htm.
151. Article 46a of Directive 2001/83, as amended by Directive 2004/27.
152. Article 76(3) of Directive 2001/83, as amended by Directive 2004/27.
153. *See also* the *EMEA Post-Authorization Guidance on Parallel Distribution* dated July 19, 2006 (EMEA/Ho/2368/rev4), *available at* http://www.emea.eu.int/pdfs/human/parallel/236804en.pdf.
154. *See, e.g.,* Articles 11, 12, 13 and 14 of Regulation 726/2004, all of which contain provisions requiring the EMEA to make certain information publicly accessible.
155. Copy available from the Freedom of Information section of the MHRA's Web site, http://www.mhra.gov.uk/home/idcplg?IdcService=SS_GET_PAGE&nodeId=86.
156. *Convention for the Protection of Human Rights and Dignity of the Human Being with regard to the Application of Biology and Medicine*, opened for signature in Oviedo April 4, 1997, and coming into force on December 1, 1999; *available at* http://conventions.coe.int/treaty/en/treaties/html/164.htm.
157. Article 18 of the Convention.
158. *See* http://conventions.coe.int/Treaty/Commun/ChercheSig.asp?NT=164&CM=8&DF=6/8/2006&CL=ENG for details of signatories and ratifications.

159. *Additional Protocol to the Convention for the Protection of Human Rights and Dignity of the Human Being with regard to the Application of Biology and Medicine, on the Prohibition of Cloning Human Beings*, Paris, January 12, 1998, *available at* http://conventions.coe.int/treaty/en/treaties/html/168.htm.

160. *Additional Protocol to the Convention on Human Rights and Biomedicine, on Transplantation of Organs and Tissues of Human Origin*, Strasbourg, January 24, 2002, *available at* http://conventions.coe.int/treaty/en/treaties/html/186.htm.

161. *Additional Protocol to the Convention on Human Rights and Biomedicine, concerning Biomedical Research*, Strasbourg, Jan, 25, 2005, *available at* http://conventions.coe.int/treaty/en/treaties/html/195.htm.

162. *See* http://conventions.coe.int/Treaty/Commun/ChercheSig.asp?NT=168&CM=8&DF=6/8/2006&CL=ENG for details of signatories and ratifications.

163. Article 29 of the Convention and *see also* notes 164 and 165 of the accompanying Explanatory Report, *available at* http://conventions.coe.int/Treaty/EN/reports/html/164.htm.

164. For the position with respect to patenting, see section J.2.

165. Embryo research is governed by the 1990 Human Fertilization and Embryology Act, regulated by the Human Fertilization and Embryology Authority (HFEA). UK scientists have been allowed to conduct limited human cloning under license since February 2002. In 2001 the Human Reproduction Cloning Act banned reproductive cloning in the UK.

166. Germany has banned the creation of human embryos for research purposes. The importation and use of ES cell lines is regulated through the Stem Cell Act 2002, and certain further protection for embryos is set out in the Protection of Embryos Act 1990 (as amended). The Stem Cell Act sets out various tests concerning the necessity of ES cell research, and the standards to be adopted in any permitted research.

167. *See* the guidance on stem cell research, *available at* http://www.dbtindia.nic.in/policy/polimain.html.

168. European Commission press release, How does the European Commission deal with ethical issues within its Framework Programme for Research and Development? (May 17, 2005), *available at* http://europa.eu.int/rapid/pressReleasesAction. do?reference=MEMO/05/121&format=HTML&aged=&language=EN&gui Language=en.

169. *See, e.g.,* http://www.nhmrc.gov.au/embryos/index.htm.

170. *Available at* http://europa.eu.int/eur-lex/pri/en/oj/dat/2004/l_102/l_10220040407en00480058.pdf.

171. http://europa.eu.int/comm/health/ph_threats/human_substance/oc_tech_cell/oc_tech_cell_en.htm.

172. Commission Directive 2006/17/EC of February 8, 2006 implementing Directive 2004/23/EC of the European Parliament and of the Council as regards cer-

tain technical requirements for the donation, procurement and testing of human tissues and cells. *Copy available at* http://europa.eu.int/eur-lex/lex/LexUriServ/site/en/oj/2006/l_038/l_03820060209en00400052.pdf

173. Member States currently apply existing medicinal product and medical device legislation and approach advanced therapy products on a case-by-case basis.

174. "Proposal for a Regulation of the European Parliament and of the Council on advanced therapy medicinal products and amending Directive 2001/83/EC and Regulation (EC) No 726/2004" COM(2005) 567 Final; Nov. 16, 2005; *available at* http://pharmacos.eudra.org/F2/advtherapies/docs/COM_2005_567_EN.pdf. At the time of writing, the timetable for adoption (if at all) of the proposed regulation was anticipated to be between one and two years from fourth quarter of 2005. If adopted, the regulation will supplement existing European legislation on tissues and cells, medical devices, and medicinal products.

175. *See* the section "Gene Therapy Discussion Group" at http://www.ich.org.

176. Directive 2002/98/EC of the European Parliament and of the Council of January 27, 2003, setting standards of quality and safety for the collection, testing, processing, storage, and distribution of human blood and blood components and amending Directive 2001/83/EC; *available at* European Parliament and Council Directive 2004/23/EC of March 31, 2004, on setting standards of quality and safety for the donation, procurement, testing, processing, preservation, storage, and distribution of human tissues and cells; *available at* http://europa.eu.int/eur-lex/pri/en/oj/dat/2003/l_033/l_03320030208en00300040.pdf.

177. Article 2, Directive 2002/98/EC.

178. Article 3(e), Directive 2002/98/EC.

179. Commission Directive 2004/33/EC of March 22, 2004, implementing Directive 2002/98/EC of the European Parliament and of the Council as regards certain technical requirements for blood and blood components (http://europa.eu.int/eur-lex/pri/en/oj/dat/2004/l_091/l_09120040330en00250039.pdf).

180. Article 5, Directive 2004/33/EC.

181. Article 2 and Part A of Annex II, Directive 2004/33/EC.

182. Article 3 and Part B of Annex II, Directive 2004/33/EC.

183. Article 4 and Annex III, Directive 2004/33/EC.

184. Directive 2005/61/EC of Sept. 30, 2005 implementing Directive 2002/98/EC of the European Parliament and of the Council as regards traceability requirements and notification of serious adverse reactions and events; *available at* http://europa.eu.int/eur-lex/lex/LexUriServ/site/en/oj/2005/l_256/l_25620051001 en00320040.pdf.

185. Directive 2005/62/EC of Sept. 30, 2005 implementing Directive 2002/98/EC of the European Parliament and of the Council as regards Community standards and specifications relating to a quality system for blood establishments;

available at http://europa.eu.int/eur-lex/lex/LexUriServ/site/en/oj/2005/l_256/l_25620051001en00410048.pdf.

186. *See also* above at section B.

187. *See* the European Commission's medical devices Web site, http://europa.eu.int/comm/enterprise/medical_devices/index_en.htm for more information.

188. http://europa.eu.int/comm/enterprise/medical_devices/meddev/index.htm.

189. *See* http://europa.eu.int/comm/enterprise/medical_devices/consult.htm.

190. With the exception of crop co-existence measures that are specifically directed at permitting GM and organic agriculture to be practiced side by side.

191. For further information, *see* http://europa.eu.int/eur-lex/en/lif/reg/en_register_15102050.html. *See also* the European Commission press release of March 22, 2005, Questions and Answers on the Regulation of GMOs in the European Union, *available at* http://europa.eu.int/rapid/pressReleasesAction.do?reference=MEMO/05/104&format=HTML&aged=0&language=EN&guiLanguage=en.

192. Article 2, Directive 2001/18/EC.

193. In the UK this Directive is implemented primarily in Part IV of the Environmental Protection Act 1990 (as amended).

194. Composed of representatives of the Member States.

195. Enacted in England through the Genetically Modified Food (England) Regulations 2004.

196. N.B. does not apply to food produced "with" GMOs, such as milk from cattle fed GM feed.

197. The EU states that the regulation to obtain dual authority would avoid a Starlink-type situation occurring in the EU.

198. The EU refers to this as the "one door, one key principle."

199. Article 23 of Directive 2001/18/EC.

200. Enacted in England through the Genetically Modified Organisms (Traceability and Labeling) (England) Regulations 2004.

201. Food produced "with" GMOs, e.g., processing aids or animal feed, is not subject to the provisions of this regulation.

202. For example, in the UK it is a criminal offense to release unapproved GMOs into the environment and, depending on the offense committed, conviction on indictment could result in a prison term of up to five years: § 118(3)(b) Part IV of the Environmental Protection Act 1990 (as amended).

203. A draft regulation on enzymes has been prepared by the Commission.

204. Council Directive 90/219/EEC of April 23, 1990, on the contained use of genetically modified micro-organisms, as amended by Commission Directive 98/81/EC and Regulation (EC) No 1882/2003 of the European Parliament and of the Council of September 29, 2003.

205. A copy of the guidance is available from the EMEA Web site, http://www.emea.eu.int/htms/human/presub/q20.htm.
206. *See* http://europa.eu.int/comm/food/food/biotechnology/intlmatters/index_en.htm.
207. http://www.biodiv.org/doc/legal/cartagena-protocol-en.pdf.
208. For further information, see the Indian Department of Biotechnology's site at http://www.dbtindia.nic.in/thanks/biosafetymain.html.
209. *See* http://www.ogtr.gov.au/.
210. *See* http://www.foodstandards.gov.au/.
211. *See* http://www.ogtr.gov.au/about/index.htm.
212. For a list of countries that have ratified, accepted, acceded, or approved the Protocol, *see* http://www.biodiv.org/biosafety/signinglist.aspx?sts=rtf&ord=dt.
213. The EPC is accessible at http://www.european-patent-office.org/legal/epc/.
214. There is also a system, created under the Patent Cooperation Treaty (PCT), which simplifies international patent applications on almost a global scale (all countries of likely interest are now party to the PCT). It is administered by WIPO: *see* http://www.wipo.int/pct/en for further information.
215. Article 99 EPC.
216. Article 54 EPC.
217. *See, e.g.,* decision T482/89 *(TELEMACANIQUE/Power supply unit)* where the EPO Technical Board of Appeal held that a single sale is sufficient to render the article sold available to the public, provided the buyer was not bound by an obligation to maintain secrecy.
218. This is reflected in the optional provision of Article 27(2) of Agreement on Trade-Related Aspects of Intellectual Property (TRIPs).
219. Part C, Chapter IV, Paragraph 3.5, EPO Guidelines for Examination; http://www.european-patent-office.org/legal/gui_lines/.
220. *See* Decision at http://legal.european-patent-office.org/dg3/biblio/t950272eu2.htm.
221. Article 5(1) of the Biotech Directive.
222. Article 5(2), *id.*
223. Article 5(3), *id.*
224. *See* the UK Patent Office statement at http://www.patent.gov.uk/patent/p-decisionmaking/p-law/p-law-notice/p-law-notice-stemcells.htm.
225. *See* Decision at http://legal.european-patent-office.org/dg3/pdf/t030315ex1.pdf.
226. *See* Decision at http://legal.european-patent-office.org/dg3/biblio/t830049ep1.htm.
227. Council Directive 89/104/EEC of Dec. 21, 1988 on the approximation of laws of the member states relating to trademarks, *available at* http://oami.europa.eu/en/mark/aspects/direc/direc.htm

228. *See* www.oami.eu.int.

229. And UK copyright law does protect works authored by individuals domiciled in the United States.

230. *See* http://www.upov.int/index.html.

231. *See* http://www.cpvo.eu.int/default.php?lang=en.

232. The terms "EC" (European Community) and "EU" (European Union) are often used interchangeably. Strictly speaking, the competition rules should be referred to as EC competition rules rather than EU competition rules, since they are contained in the EC Treaty.

233. *See* Commission Regulation (EC) No. 772/2004 of April 27, 2004, on the application of Article 81(3) of the Treaty to categories of technology transfer agreements, *available at* http://europa.eu.int/eur-lex/pri/en/oj/dat/2004/l_123/l_12320040427en00110017.pdf, and its accompanying guidelines.

Chapter XIX

Biotechnology Patent Litigation for the Non-Patent Attorney

Julie Fleming Brown, Esq.
Orlando, Florida

The purpose of this chapter is to provide an overview of the substantive law, plus selected procedural and strategic concerns, that come into play in biotechnology patent litigation. However, details of all relevant aspects of patent litigation cannot be encapsulated in an overview chapter. The reader is urged to confer with competent counsel and/or to review any of the treatises devoted to patent litigation if faced with this expensive and difficult challenge.

Patent litigation has been growing precipitously over the last decade: patent cases filed in U.S. District Courts have increased by 78 percent as compared with an increase of only 12 percent in the total number of cases filed, according to statistics from the Administrative Office of the U.S. Courts. The rate of litigation is particularly high in biotechnology patents, with approximately 28 cases filed per 1,000 biotechnology patents as compared with 19 cases per thousand patents irrespective of technology.[1] As discussed in the remainder of this chapter, biotechnology patent litigation is expensive (in terms of both legal fees and the parties' costs in time that must be devoted to the litigation rather than to business priorities) and carries inherent uncertainty. The rewards of a successful suit may be high for a patentee: awards of lost profits, treble damages, and attorney's fees are not uncommon. But the potential upside carries with it the risk of having a patent declared invalid or unenforceable. Troublesome for both sides is the *Markman* process, the much-criticized process by which the court interprets patent terms as a matter of law, and the high reversal rate on patent cases, estimated to be between 34 and 47 percent.[2] In view of these issues, it is perhaps not surprising that a majority of biotechnology patent infringement cases settle before trial.

Although biotechnology cases have been on the rise over the last decade or so, they still constitute a relatively small percentage of decided cases. Accordingly, it is important to recognize (though perhaps unnecessary to explain at length) that the great majority of cases cited in the course of biotechnology patent litigation will fall outside the field. Even more critical is the awareness that the number of judges with any sort of training in biotechnology is minuscule. Judges often struggle with unfamiliar technology and find a way to fit it within the knowledge they already possess, but doing so with biotechnology is much more challenging. Parties to the litigation should consider very early in the case how to educate the judge about the technology. One approach that may be successful is requesting a court-appointed expert who would re-

> **Practice Points**
>
> How to present highly technical evidence in biotechnology patent cases:
>
> — Request a court-appointed expert
> — Submit videotape of explanation of relevant technology or process
> — Submit written explanation of technology or process with glossary
> — Consider organizing a site visit for the judge (and jury, if appropriate)
> — Work with a graphic artist to develop clear and simple demonstrative exhibits
>
> Note that, with the exception of demonstrative exhibits, each of these strategies may call for cooperation between the parties.

view the evidence with the judge and would be in a position to inform the judge on the technology itself. The parties would pay for such an expert, which increases the cost of the litigation, but the expense is well worthwhile if its effect is to provide the court with sufficient technical knowledge to make well-informed decisions throughout the litigation. In addition, demonstrative exhibits and lay comprehension of sophisticated technical testimony assume particular importance when a biotechnology case is tried to a jury. Where biotechnology patents are litigated, counsel must be prepared to educate as well as to advocate.

A. Judicial and Extrajudicial Proceedings

While many biotechnology patent disputes are resolved through litigation, litigation does carry significant downsides. Most notably, the expense of pursuing such a litigation action can be extremely burdensome. For example, a 2003 survey indicated that, generally speaking, the cost to bring a patent case through the discovery phase may be between $ 0.5 million if the amount in controversy is as little as $10 million, and $4 million if the amount in controversy is over $25 million.[3] An "average" patent case now costs about $2 million. Biotechnology patent cases may be even more expensive because fewer experts are available in this still-nascent field, though statistics to confirm that suspicion are not available. In legal fees alone, patent litigation is an expensive proposition—even without consideration of the possibility of treble damages.[4] The practitioner representing a biotechnology client should be aware that extrajudicial proceedings held in the Patent Office are available for the presentation of patent issues, though the scope of those proceedings is necessarily more limited than that of litigation. These proceedings, which are best characterized as patent-testing proceedings rather than measures to evaluate an infringement claim, bring prior art to the attention of the Patent Office in an effort either to invalidate or to strengthen the patent at issue, and the proceedings provoke a reexamination of the patent. While a full discussion of these proceedings is outside the scope of this chapter, the following sections provide a basic introduction. The two types of extrajudicial proceedings are reexamination and reissue.

1. Reexamination

An issued patent may be reexamined to evaluate the legal impact of prior art not considered by the examiner during the initial prosecution. In the litigation context, reexamination may be a useful tool for patentees facing an invalidity defense to an infringement accusation. "Any person at any time may file a request for reexamination by the Office of any claim of a patent on the basis of any prior art cited under the provisions of section 301 of this title."[5] Accordingly, a request for reexamination may be either *ex parte* or *inter partes*. In either case, it is important to note that once the reexamination begins, it is an unstoppable process and cannot be affected by settlement. Unlike patent litigation, in which the great majority of cases settle,[6] reexamination must continue to its conclusion.

a. Ex Parte Reexamination

An *Ex Parte* Reexamination (EPR) may be requested by a patentee or by a third party. A patentee may request reexamination to have the Patent Office review previously undisclosed prior art. As with all types of reexamination requests, the Patent Office will grant the request and perform the reexamination only if it determines that the newly submitted prior art creates a substantial new question as to the patentability of at least one claim in the patent at issue. Reexamination is not an automatic process—the Patent Office has discretion to determine whether to conduct a requested reexamination.

As described in 35 U.S.C. §§ 304-307, the process of reexamination is similar to that of the original patent prosecution, and the final conclusion may invalidate a claim or claims of the patent in issue in light of the new prior art, or the examiner may confirm that the invention (in whole or in part) is patentable over the prior art. Although an alleged infringer may cite the same prior art as a part of an invalidity defense in subsequent litigation, as a practical matter, the difficulty of persuading a factfinder that prior art invalidates a claim or claims increases when the claims have been not only confirmed but then reconfirmed by the Patent Office.[7] In short, a successful reexamination can considerably strengthen a patent against future challenges.

The patentee faces two primary dangers in the course of an EPR. First, if any claims of the patent are determined to be unpatentable, the patentee will be unable to bring an infringement suit on those claims. Second, the reexamination process can be lengthy—on the order of two years. This delay can create a laches problem for the patentee,[8] and although the patentee may bring suit while a reexamination is proceeding, the lawsuit may, in the court's discretion, be stayed until the reexamination concludes.[9] In the case of an EPR initiated by a third party, litigation is unlikely to be stayed unless the EPR is initiated early in the case.[10]

In contrast, a third-party requestor faces little risk in an EPR, and its identity need not be disclosed. Although a third-party EPR requestor has no right to respond to any arguments that may be raised in response to the newly submitted prior art and no right to participate in the appeal of a reexamination, serial EPRs are permitted and may fulfill the functions of response and/or appeal. A third-party requestor may file subsequent reexamination requests citing the same prior art, and if granted, those requests will merge with the previous request, thus permitting the requestor the opportunity to respond to the examiner's and the patentee's comments in the course of reexamination. One notable example of EPR is the reexamination of one of Pfizer's patents on Lipitor, initiated by the Public Patent Foundation (PUBPAT)[11] in 2004. In June 2005, the patent claims were rejected entirely under section 103(a), though Pfizer promised a response to the rejection.[12] As of the date of this writing, the reexamination is not yet final; nevertheless, it is safe to say that even if the subject patent emerges from reexamination with a scope similar to that previously granted, the exercise will have been expensive and inconvenient for Pfizer. However, if the patent survives reexamination, it will be stronger because of the process.

b. Inter Partes Reexamination

An *Inter Partes* Reexamination (IPR), available for any patent issued on an "original application" filed after November 29, 1999, allows a third party to request reexamination of a patent. As with EPR, an IPR request is not granted automatically but only upon the Patent Office's determination that the newly disclosed prior art creates a substantial new question of patentability. The request must identify the real party in interest[13] and provide the new prior art, which may consist only of patents and printed publications.[14] In addition, the requestor may submit written responses to the patent examiner's actions in the course of the reexamination. However, examiner interviews are unavailable. Unlike in the case of EPR, the principle of estoppel applies in IPR in several important ways. First, a third-party IPR requestor cannot institute serial IPRs against the same patent; if an IPR is unsuccessful, the requestor cannot have a second bite at the apple. Second, if a requestor is unsuccessful in IPR, that requestor and its successors, assigns, and licensees will be estopped from asserting in litigation the validity grounds that were *or could have been* asserted in the IPR. Finally, if an infringement defendant engaged in litigation claims that the patent is invalid and loses that challenge, that defendant may not subsequently initiate IPR.

The estoppel risks, the lack of examiner interviews, and the ability to present only limited prior art may limit the desirability of IPR, but a recent survey of those who have used IPR suggests that it generates a high-quality review of the prior art submitted and that it should be considered when a third party possesses very good prior art in the form of a patent or printed publication and lacks the substantial resources necessary for litigation.[15] One brewing question was raised by the Department of Health and Human Service's request for an IPR of Immunomedics, Inc.'s U.S. Patent No. 6,653,104 for an anti-cancer antibody:[16] whether the U.S. government should be permitted to use IPR—which was designed to reduce the amount of patent litigation—to request reexamination of a patent, or whether it should be limited to reexamination only through a Director-initiated reexam, discussed in the next section. Although this question is not at the heart of IPR, its resolution will prove notable, particularly since the request itself indicates a governmental interest in biotechnology patents.

c. *Director-Initiated Reexamination*

The Director of the Patent Office may also initiate a reexamination on a finding that a substantial new question of patentability exists based on patents or printed publications discovered by or revealed to the Director, even in the absence of an ex parte request for reexamination.[17] The mechanics of a

Director-initiated reexamination are identical to those of EPR and IPR except that no third party is involved. By Patent Office policy, few reexaminations are initiated by the Director.[18] As compared with EPR and IPR, Director-initiated reexaminations are more likely to result in cancellation of all reexamined claims and more likely than IPR, but approximately equally likely as EPR, to result in narrowing of the reexamined claims.[19]

2. Reissue

Reissue, discussed in Chapter II on patent prosecution, may be used as a tool for litigation because a patentee may file for reissue on the basis of prior art submitted to it by an alleged infringer.

B. General Overview of Patent Litigation Issues (Substantive)

A patent infringement suit must be filed in federal court and may be filed in any district court that has personal jurisdiction over the defendant and in which venue is proper. Several districts have acquired a reputation as being particularly patent-savvy and quick to resolve litigation, including the Eastern District of Virginia, the Western District of Wisconsin, and the Eastern District of Texas. These "rocket docket" courts have rules and procedures that speed cases from filing to trial in substantially less than the national average of about 22 months: the average in the Eastern District of Virginia and the Western District of Wisconsin is between eight and nine months, and the average in the Eastern District of Texas is about 17 months.[20] However, as courts become identified as "rocket docket" courts, the numbers of cases filed increases and the time to resolution decreases because of the higher caseload. For instance, the Eastern District of Texas is facing a 33 percent increase in the number of patent cases over the past year.[21] New "rocket dockets" tend to emerge as older ones lose speed, but it is not possible at this writing to predict where the new "rocket docket" courts will be. Although these courts are not known particularly for biotechnology skill, the speed with which a "rocket docket" advances litigation may well be sufficient reason to select one of those districts.

Patentees seeking quick resolution for infringement cases that involve infringing goods manufactured outside the United States and then imported may also consider filing suit at the U.S. International Trade Commission (ITC). Section 337 of the U.S. Tariff Act of 1930 (19 U.S.C. § 1337) prohibits unfair competition in import trade, and the ITC has become an excellent forum for resolution of patent infringement claims. Cases are initially assigned to an administrative law judge (ALJ), who generally hears the case within seven to nine months, and a full panel of the ITC commissioners reviews the ALJ's Initial Determination and issues a final decision, generally within 12 to 15 months of filing. Several downsides exist to the ITC's procedure: the ITC does not have jurisdiction over counterclaims, which must be removed to a district court with jurisdiction; it cannot grant damages to redress the infringement;[22] and an ITC decision has only persuasive effect in a subsequent (or parallel) federal case.[23] However, if the situation allows resort to the ITC and if the primary goal is to stop the infringement within the United States, resort to the ITC may have substantial advantages. For instance, the ITC found four patents owned by Genentech to have been infringed by recombinantly produced human growth hormone that Novo Nordisk was importing and selling in the United States.[24] Although district court litigation on the issue was subsequently settled, the ITC proceeding was a valuable first shot by Genentech to protect its patent rights in the United States.

Patent cases from every district are appealed to the Court of Appeals for the Federal Circuit, without regard to the "home" circuit. The Federal Circuit has exclusive jurisdiction over patent cases, as well as several other subjects.[25] Critics charge that the Federal Circuit, which was intended to provide predictable and consistent patent decisions (unlike the conflicting decisions issued by the various circuits before the Federal Circuit was founded in 1982), has instead generated a long string of opinions whose outcome depended on the panel hearing the case.[26] Nevertheless, the Federal Circuit has its admirers[27] and a strong body of case law.[28]

The parties for patent litigation include, of course, the patentee and the accused infringer. However, that simple statement requires some unpacking in view of the possibility that the patent will be licensed and perhaps sublicensed, leaving the question of whether the patentee, the (sub)licensee, or both may bring suit. The patentee and its successors in title have standing to file suit,[29] and a licensee with sufficient rights may have standing as a successor in interest. Generally speaking, the license agreement will control that decision, and a licensee who has the great bulk of rights associated with the patent will have the right to bring suit, while a licensee with fewer rights will not. Notably, however, the licensee's standing is a jurisdictional issue that is not subject to waiver, and bringing suit without standing may result in a dismissal with prejudice.[30]

1. Claim Interpretation

Claim interpretation is often a deciding phase of a patent case.[31] The determination of the precise meaning of each term and each claim is a matter of law, within the court's province.[32] Claim construction is reviewed de novo on appeal.[33] Claim terms are interpreted as they would have been by one of ordinary skill in the art at the time of the invention.[34] And because claim construction is solely a matter of law, previous interpretation may have preclusive effect on later litigation.[35] This concept may be somewhat frightening in light of the rampant uncertainty in claim interpretation. Judge Rader, of the Federal Circuit, observed in 1998 that nearly 40 percent of the claim construction decisions presented on appeal are reversed.[36] There is little evidence that the situation has improved in the ensuing years. Nevertheless, when claim terms are disputed, the court must interpret them. Construction may take place early in the litigation or not until during trial, and the court may hold a "Markman hearing" (discussed below) with or without fact and expert testimony, or it may render its decision based on written argument only. In short, no hard and fast rules exist, except those memorialized in the local patent rules that have been accepted in some districts.[37]

The uncertainty that claim construction generates has been criticized repeatedly and stridently, perhaps nowhere more so than in the Federal Circuit itself. In 2005, the Federal Circuit issued *Phillips v. AWH Corp.*, 415 F.3d 1303 (Fed. Cir. 2005) (en banc). The court had issued a previous order granting the en banc review and requesting amicus briefs on several questions concerning the appropriate use, if any, of dictionaries in the claim construction process. Chief Judge Mayer dissented from that decision, arguing that any attempt to refine the claim construction process while continuing to characterize it as a question of law would be futile. Judge Mayer dissented from the en banc decision as well, joined by Judge Newman, contending colorfully that repair of the claim construction process would be impossible without a complete overhaul: "The court's opinion today is akin to rearranging the deck chairs on the Titanic—the orchestra is playing as if nothing is amiss, but the ship is still heading for Davey Jones' locker."[38] Until Judge Mayer's view becomes the majority view (and there is little indication of such an occurrence), patentees must brace themselves for a daunting, expensive, and potentially deadly claim construction process by ensuring as cleanly prosecuted a patent as possible.

One maxim of claim interpretation is that if two or more interpretations are possible, the court should give preference to an interpretation that will preserve the claim's validity.[39] Claim terms are generally given their ordinary meanings, unless there is evidence in the patent that the inventor intended some other meaning.[40] Courts will generally focus their inquiry on evidence intrinsic to the patent, including the claims, the specification, and the prosecution history.[41] The Federal Circuit has directed focus on the intrinsic evidence,[42] although some judges of the Federal Circuit have recognized that extrinsic evidence, especially expert testimony, may be helpful.[43] Absent ambiguity in the intrinsic evidence, however, reliance on extrinsic evidence for claim construction is improper.[44]

Courts have in the past expressed confidence in "neutral" extrinsic evidence in the form of dictionaries and treatises.[45] However, the Federal Circuit recently expressed some doubt about the propriety of relying on such evidence, though a much-anticipated decision sidestepped the question.[46]

2. Definition of Infringement

Patent infringement occurs when one "without authority makes, uses, offers to sell, or sells any patented invention, within the United States or imports into the United States any patented invention during the term of the patent therefore."[47] A patentee who asserts infringement must prove infringement by a preponderance of the evidence. Patent infringement may be "literal," in which case every element of the asserted claim will be found to exist in the same form in the accused product, or infringement may exist under the doctrine of equivalents, in which case one or more claimed elements will be found in the accused product in a form that is substantially similar to the claimed element.

Determination of whether literal infringement exists requires a two-step process. First, if the meaning of any term used in the asserted claim(s) is disputed, the court must construe the meaning of the disputed terms as a matter of law in a Markman determination.[48] After the asserted claim has been construed, the accused product or activity is compared to the claim to determine as a matter of fact whether each element of the claim is present in the accused product. The patentee bears the burden of proving, by a preponderance of the evidence, the presence of each claimed element.[49] If all of the claimed elements are present in the accused product or process, patent infringement exists; conversely, if any claimed element is absent from the accused product or process, there is no literal infringement.[50]

Even if there is no literal infringement, however, infringement may still exist under the doctrine of equivalents. "[A] patentee may invoke this doctrine to proceed against the producer of a device 'if it performs substantially the same function in substantially the same way to obtain the same result.'"[51] This test of the doctrine of equivalents is often referred to as the "function-way-result" or "triple identity" test. Under *Warner-Jenkinson Co. v. Hilton Davis Chemical Co.*,[52] the Supreme Court established the "all elements rule," which requires application of the triple-identity test on an element-by-element basis rather than to the invention as a whole. The "all elements rule" is designed to reaffirm the fact that it is the patent claims that define the scope of the invention and that the public must be provided notice of the scope of the invention through the claims.[53] An example of infringement under the doctrine of equivalents lies in *Amgen, Inc. v. Hoechst Marion Roussel, Inc.*[54] In that case, the claimed protein sequence was depicted in a figure in the patent that included 166 amino acids, and the court concluded that the claimed sequence thus must include 166 amino acids. Since the allegedly infringing protein comprised only 165 amino acids, it did not literally infringe the patent. However, the court held that the 165-amino acid sequence was the equivalent of the claimed 166-amino acid sequence. Evaluating whether the patentee was estopped from laying claim to that equivalent (see discussion of prosecution history estoppel below), the court concluded that the amendment to reflect the 166-amino acid sequence was made only to claim the human form of the protein, thus to avoid a double-patenting rejection against a previous patent that claimed both human and non-human proteins, but not to claim any specific amino acid sequence. The court further concluded that the 165-amino acid sequence was not disclosed in the prior art and that the amendment was unnecessary to distinguish over the prior art, and the equivalent 165-amino acid sequence accordingly was held to infringe.

a. Types of infringement

- *Direct infringement*
  "Direct" patent infringement is the most common type of infringement, and it occurs when an alleged infringer commits the acts that constitute infringement, such as making, using, offering to sell, or selling a patented invention while the patent remains in force. Typical examples of infringement in the biotechnology industry involve the use of a drug or biologic material the composition or utility of which has been patented by another party or the use of drug discovery methods or "tools." See discussion below concerning the research exemption.
- *Induced infringement*
  Secondary infringement includes induced infringement and contributory infringement. The Patent Act provides that anyone who "actively induces infringement of a patent shall be liable as an infringer."[55] Active inducement of infringement occurs when a party, such as a product manufacturer or distributor, provides the necessary materials and information to allow another party, such as an end user, to infringe a patent. Unlike one accused of direct infringement, the inducing infringer must have actual knowledge of the patent at issue.[56] The patentee must prove direct infringement as a predicate for liability on the basis of active inducement to infringe.[57] In the biotech context, an example of induced infringement would be if a company produces a device for gene sequencing that does not itself infringe a patent, and further provides its customers instructions on how to use the device in an infringing manner with knowledge that such use will infringe a particular process patent.
- *Contributory infringement*
  The Patent Act defines contributory infringement as follows: "Whoever sells a component of a patented machine, manufacture, combination or composition, or a material or apparatus for use in practicing

a patented process, constituting a material part of the invention, knowing the same to be especially made or especially adapted for use in an infringement of such patent, and not a staple article or commodity of commerce suitable for substantial noninfringing use, shall be liable as a contributory infringer."[58] Designed to reach those who facilitate infringement by others without actually committing an infringing act, the doctrine of contributory infringement is limited to non-staple articles that lack substantial non-infringing uses. Accordingly, a common defense to a charge of contributory infringement includes the allegation that the accused product is a staple product or that it has a substantial non-infringing use.[59] Contributory infringement cannot exist in the absence of direct infringement.[60] Thus, a reagent manufacturer who sold the reagent along with instructions for its use in a patented process could be held liable for contributory infringement, assuming that the performance of the process infringed the asserted patent.

3. Proof of Infringement

a. Possible Defenses and Counterclaims

35 U.S.C. § 282 sets out a partial list of defenses that may be lodged in response to a patent infringement claim.

The following shall be defenses in any action involving the validity or infringement of a patent and shall be pleaded:

(1) Non-infringement, absence of liability for infringement or unenforceability;
(2) Invalidity of the patent or any claim in suit on any ground specified in part II of this title as a condition for patentability;
(3) Invalidity of the patent or any claim in suit for failure to comply with any requirement of sections 112 or 251 of this title;
(4) Any other fact or act made a defense by this title.

In addition to these defenses, other equitable defenses that are not special to patent cases are also permitted. Each of these categories of defenses will be discussed below.

b. Non-infringement

Non-infringement is, of course, the most immediate defense to a charge of infringement. A patentee must prove infringement by a preponderance of the evidence. The accused infringer may defend on the grounds that no infringement exists as alleged. To show that there is no literal infringement, a defendant need only demonstrate the absence of any claimed element.

To refute a claim of infringement under the doctrine of equivalents, however, an accused defender may rely on prosecution history estoppel or on prior art, either of which may limit the availability of the doctrine of equivalents. Prosecution history estoppel applies when an applicant made an amendment to a patent application in the course of prosecution to overcome an examiner's rejection of claims.[61] In 2002, the Supreme Court set the parameters of prosecution history estoppel by holding that prosecution history estoppel exists when an applicant amends an application to overcome rejections based on either prior art or section 112 (discussed below), although equivalents may remain despite an amendment to overcome prior art for "equivalents unforeseeable at the time of the amendment and beyond a fair interpretation of what was surrendered."[62] *Festo* also held that the patentee bears the burden of demonstrating that prosecution history estoppel does not apply. The bulk of the case law since *Festo* has further cut back on the availability of the doctrine of

> **Practice Points**
>
> Defenses to an allegation of patent infringement may include:
> — No literal infringement of any claimed elements
> — Prosecution history estoppel
> — Invalidity by anticipation or obviousness in view of prior art
> — Research exemption
> — Patent fails to satisfy an element of Section 112 (written description, enablement, best mode, or definiteness)
> — Patent unenforceable due to inequitable conduct of patentee
> — Patent misuse under antitrust laws
> — Standard defenses in equity such as laches or estoppel

equivalents, defining numerous situations that give rise to prosecution history estoppel.[63]

Similarly, the doctrine of equivalents may be restricted based on existing prior art because the doctrine may not be applied if its application would reach a prior art product.[64] The doctrine of equivalents is also barred when it would reach limitations that are disclosed but not claimed.[65] The availability of prosecution history estoppel to bar application of the doctrine of equivalents is illustrated in the context of the *Amgen, Inc. v. Hoescht Marion Roussel* case previously discussed in the context of the doctrine of equivalents.

A technical defense of non-infringement flows from the common-law research exemption, sometimes referred to as the "experimental use exception" or "experimental use privilege," which was first described in 1813 as a limited exemption for research using a patented invention "merely for philosophical experiments, or for the purpose of ascertaining the sufficiency of the [patented invention] to produce its described effects."[66] In *Madey v. Duke University*, the plaintiff, a physics professor, held patents on certain equipment used in the research laboratory where he served as director. Dr. Madey resigned following a dispute concerning management of the laboratory; Duke continued to use some of the equipment after Dr. Madey's departure; and Dr. Madey sued Duke for patent infringement. Reversing the district court's application of the research exemption, the Federal Circuit held that the experimental use exception is "very narrow and strictly limited," and that the exemption is inapplicable "so long as the act is in furtherance of the alleged infringer's legitimate business and is not solely for amusement, to satisfy idle curiosity, or for strictly philosophical inquiry."[67] Because the court defined Duke's business as "educating and enlightening students and faculty" and its secondary aim "to increase the status of the institution and lure lucrative research grants,"[68] the court held that its use of the patented equipment was in furtherance of its business objectives and was not subject to the experimental use exception. This broad scope of Duke's business objectives effectively ruled out any possibility of university research being included within the exemption, and the decision has been much criticized as exerting a "chilling impact" on university research.[69]

The research exemption was, in part, codified in 35 U.S.C. § 271 as a part of the Drug Price Competition and Patent Term Restoration Act of 1984 (Hatch-Waxman Act) and, in that form, is limited primarily to research on pharmaceuticals and medical devices that is performed to obtain marketing approval by the Food and Drug Administration.[70] The Federal Circuit followed the *Madey* decision and strictly construed the scope of § 271(e) in *Integra Lifesciences I, Ltd. v. Merck KgaA*.[71] The Supreme Court reversed that decision in 2005, holding that the section 271(e)(1) exemption flows to "all uses of patented compounds 'reasonably related' to the process of developing information for submission under *any* federal law regulating the manufacture, use, or distribution of drugs" without respect to the phase of research in which such information is developed or the submission in which such information could be included.[72] However, the Court explicitly left open the question of the applicability of section 271(e) to "research tools."[73]

The long-term effect of *Madey* and *Merck v. Integra* has yet to be determined. *Madey* appears to limit the research exemption quite dramatically, whereas the Supreme Court's *Merck* decision reopens the scope of the exemption as it exists under section 271(e). It appears likely, at this point, that basic research designed to identify a biotech product candidate would fall under *Madey* and could be infringing, whereas research designed to generate data for submission to the FDA for regulatory approval of the candidate would likely fall under *Merck* and be non-infringing. However, it will be important to follow subsequent cases, as the law is clearly in a state of flux.

c. Patent Invalidity (§§ 102, 103, 112)

An alleged infriger can, and very often will, assert that the patent at issue is invalid, but he or she must overcome a presumption of validity. "A patent shall be presumed valid. Each claim of a patent (whether in independent, dependent, or multiple dependent form) shall be presumed valid independently of the validity of other claims; dependent or multiple dependent claims shall be presumed valid even though dependent upon an invalid claim."[74] Accordingly, a patentee need not prove that its patent is valid. To overcome this presumption of validity, an accused infringer must show invalidity by clear and convincing evidence.[75] A patent may be held invalid for failure to comport with any of the requirements for patentability. Three grounds for invalidity will be discussed here: anticipation, obviousness, and the group of defenses classed as "Section 112" defenses.

i. Anticipation

35 U.S.C. § 102, discussed at length previously in Chapter II in the context of prosecution, sets forth each basis for a rejection of a patent application for lack of novelty. These bases for patent rejection also form the basis for the anticipation defense that alleges that an asserted patent is invalid because it is anticipated by prior art and thus lacks the novelty required. Anticipation under section 102 occurs only if every element of the asserted claim is found in a single prior art reference.[76] However, the doctrine of inherency prescribes that a reference may anticipate a claim even though it lacks an element of the claim if that element is inherent, or necessarily present, in the reference.[77] A recent decision has clarified that the doctrine of inherency may apply even if a personal of ordinary skill in the art would not have recognized the presence of the element before the critical date of the claim at issue.[78] The reference must be enabling and described in sufficient detail to be recognized by one of ordinary skill in the art at the time of the invention.[79]

The on-sale bar described in section 102(b), which provides that an invention is not patentable if it was sold more than one year prior to the date of the patent application, is worthy of special note. *Pfaff v. Wells Electronics, Inc.* held that the on-sale bar applies if the claimed invention was "the subject of a commercial offer for sale" and was "ready for patenting," whether by reduction to practice or by the existence of drawings or descriptions sufficiently specific to allow one of ordinary skill in the art to practice the invention.[80] Application of the on-sale bar is a question of law based upon underlying issues of fact.[81] An inventor may make experimental use of the invention and even may make experimental sales; assuming that these are bona fide experimental efforts, they will not operate under section 102(b) to invalidate a claim.[82] To determine whether the use is experimental, courts will consider factors such as "the length of the test period, whether the inventor received payment for the testing, any agreement by the user to maintain the use confidential, any records of testing, whether persons other than the inventor performed the testing, the number of tests, and the length of the test period in relation to tests of similar devices."[83] Notably, the Federal Circuit has held that clinical trials of a drug that are designed to test the drug's safety or efficacy, rather than "testing to perfect claimed features, or, in a few instances, testing to perfect features inherent to the claimed invention," fall outside the experimental use exception and thus start the clock under section 102(b).[84]

ii. Obviousness

If a single reference does not supply each element of an asserted claim but a combination of elements does so, the claim may be invalid as "obvious" under 35 U.S.C. § 103(a).[85] Obviousness must be determined on the invention as a whole, not on an element-by-element basis.[86] A question of law,[87] an obviousness analysis requires a determination of the scope and content of the prior art[88] and the claims at issue, a comparison between the prior art and the asserted claim(s), and consideration of the level of ordinary skill in the pertinent art.[89] The Supreme Court's seminal case on section 103, *Graham v. John Deere Co.*, set forth certain "secondary considerations" that are indicia of non-obviousness, including commercial success, long felt but unsolved needs, and failure of others.[90] The Federal Circuit has expanded the secondary factors to include the following:

- What the prior art patent as a whole discloses;
- What the prior art disclosed to workers in the art;
- Unexpected advances of the invention over the prior art;
- Failure of others to make the invention at issue to solve the problem, or long-felt need;
- Copying by others; and
- Commercial success, including extensive licensing of the patent at issue.[91]

Although the ultimate question of whether obviousness exists is a question of law, it rests on resolution of each of these underlying questions of fact.[92]

To use more than one reference for an obviousness analysis, a "motivation to combine" the references must exist.[93] The motivation to combine need not be express.[94] Instead, a suggestion to combine references may be found expressly in the prior art, in the knowledge and experience of one of ordinary skill in the art at the time of the invention at issue, or in the nature of the problem to be solved.[95] Thus, where a new drug combines two previously known drugs to achieve an enhanced efficacy that has not been disclosed in the prior art, the new drug would likely be held non-obvious. If, however, the prior art included a suggestion that the two older drugs might be combined, or even if the prior art included a reference suggesting that the two classes of drugs might be complementary, the new drug might instead be found to be obvious in view of the prior art.[96]

iii. Section 112 defenses

Section 112 defenses encompass several distinct, but somewhat related, requirements for patentability that, if absent, are grounds to invalidate a patent. These requirements are classed in shorthand as: (1) written description, (2) enablement, (3) best mode, and (4) definiteness.

The written description and enablement requirements spring from paragraph 1 of section 112, which provides as follows: "The specification shall contain a written description of the invention, and of the manner and process of making and using it, in such full, clear, concise, and exact terms as to enable any person skilled in the art to which it pertains, or with which it is most nearly connected, to make and use the same."

Although these two requirements are based in the same paragraph, they are nonetheless separate and distinct.[97] The written description requirement demands the patent application to convey to one of ordinary skill in the art that the inventor was in possession of the invention at the time of the application.[98] Accordingly, whether the specification and drawings of a patent in suit meets the written description requirement for a particular claim must be analyzed from the perspective of one of ordinary skill in the art, as applied at the time of the invention; expert testimony is often used to explore this issue.[99]

The written description requirement is particularly important in biotechnology cases. To meet the written description requirement demands, for example, that DNA claimed must be defined precisely.[100] "A definition by function, as we have previously indicated, does not suffice to define the genus because it is only an indication of what the gene does, rather than what it is. . . . It is only a definition of a useful result rather than a definition of what achieves that result. Many such genes may achieve that result. The description requirement of the patent statute requires a description of an invention, not an indication of a result that one might achieve if one made that invention."[101] The PTO has promulgated guidelines for satisfying the written description requirement for biotechnology applications; while the Federal Circuit has considered those guidelines, it does not hold them to be binding.[102]

    The Federal Circuit has, instead, set forth a somewhat conflicting and confusing line of cases on the written description requirement. The first of these, *Regents of the University of California v. Eli Lilly & Co.*, established a safeguard that prevents a patentee from disclosing one molecule with particular properties and acquiring rights to all other such molecules without identifying them.[103] Critics have charged that the *Lilly* case has established a higher written description requirement for biological inventions than for any other area of technology, a claim that was perhaps answered by the Federal Circuit's clarification in *Enzo Biochem, Inc. v. Gen-Probe, Inc.* that "Eli Lilly did not hold that all functional descriptions of genetic material necessarily fail as a matter of law to meet the written description requirement; rather, the requirement may be satisfied if in the knowledge of the art the disclosed function is sufficiently correlated to a particular, known structure."[104] The Federal Circuit's treatment of the written description requirement reached its most recent peak in *University of Rochester v. G.D. Searle & Co.*, which held the patent-in-suit invalid for its failure to disclose the identity of a compound that would perform the claimed activity of selectively inhibiting activity of the Cox-2 gene product in a human host when no knowledge existed in the art of a compound that would perform that function.[105] Accordingly, although the court appears not to require disclosure of a compound's identity if the art would know of it, the written description requirement remains a ripe ground for validity challenges by alleged infringers.

    Similarly, the test for a sufficiently enabling disclosure is whether the patent's disclosure would require one of ordinary skill in the art at the time of the invention to perform undue experimentation to practice the claimed invention.[106]

    The best-mode requirement also finds its basis in section 112, paragraph 1, which provides in pertinent part that "The specification . . . shall set forth the best mode contemplated by the inventor of carrying out his invention." Because a patent grants a time-limited monopoly in exchange for the full disclosure of an invention, the inventor is required to disclose the best mode, or most preferred embodiment, of the invention.

d. Patent Unenforceability

A patent may be held unenforceable on the basis of inequitable conduct, formerly known as "fraud on the Patent Office," in dealings with the Patent Office in the course of prosecution or after issue. An applicant has a duty of candor to the Office, which is formulated as a duty to disclose "all information known to the individual to be material to patentability."[107] If an applicant, the attorney or any other person who is actively involved in preparing or prosecuting the application makes affirmative representations or concealments material to patentability, intending to deceive the examiner, the patent may be held entirely unenforceable. A claim of inequitable conduct must be proven by clear and convincing evidence.[108] Once the duty of candor has been breached, the breach cannot be cured, and the entire patent is rendered unenforceable.[109]

35 C.F.R. § 1.56(b) defines information "material to patentability" as noncumulative information[110] that would establish a prima facie case of a claim's unpatentability or noncumulative information that is inconsistent with the applicant's position either opposing the Patent Office's assertion of unpatentability or supporting the applicant's assertion of patentability. Anticipatory prior art clearly qualified as material.[111] Information that is cumulative to or less pertinent than that actually considered by the examiner is not considered material.[112] It is, of course, in the great grey area between those two boundaries where cases are litigated. Intent to deceive is somewhat more readily recognized, however: "intent to deceive" has been interpreted to mean that "the inventor intended to deceive or mislead the examiner into granting the patent."[113] Because direct evidence of intent is generally not available, intent to deceive may be inferred from the facts and circumstances surrounding the applicant's acts.[114] All of the circumstantial evidence must be considered when deciding whether the applicant intended to deceive the examiner.[115]

When materiality and intent are shown, the determination of inequitable conduct is within the trial court's discretion.[116] When both materiality and intent to deceive have been demonstrated, the final decision as to whether the conduct was inequitable requires the court to weigh the evidence.[117] Upon substantial evidence of materiality, less evidence of intent to deceive is required, and vice versa.[118]

The remedy for a finding of inequitable conduct—unenforceability of the patent at issue and possibly of related patents as well, often along with an award of attorneys' fees—is devastating to the patentee. Consequently, inequitable conduct is sometimes raised almost out of habit, a practice that has been criticized by the courts.[119] Because of the high standard of proof, these defenses are rarely successful. If, however, an alleged infringer believes that an inequitable conduct claim is particularly strong, a Walker Process claim, in which antitrust liability may flow from the fraudulent procurement of a patent, should be considered.[120]

e. Antitrust

i. Patent Misuse

Patent misuse is an antitrust-based defense, in which the alleged infringer challenges the patentee's right to maintain a monopoly under the patent laws. Patent misuse results in the patent being held unenforceable as long as the misuse continues, but the misuse may be purged and enforceability restored.[121] The seminal Supreme Court case on patent misuse, *Dawson Chemical Co. v. Rohm and Haas Co.*,[122] surveyed the previous cases and held that section 271(c) and (d) (as since amended) establish the scope of patent misuse:

(c) Whoever sells a component of a patented machine, manufacture, combination or composition, or a material or apparatus for use in practicing a patented process, constituting a material part of the invention, knowing the same to be especially made or especially adapted for use in an infringement of such patent, and not a staple article or commodity of commerce suitable for substantial noninfringing use, shall be liable as a contributory infringer.

(d) No patent owner otherwise entitled to relief for infringement or contributory infringement of a patent shall be denied relief or deemed guilty of misuse or illegal extension of the patent right by reason of his having done one or more of the following:

(1) derived revenue from acts which if performed by another without his consent would constitute contributory infringement of the patent;
(2) licensed or authorized another to perform acts which if performed without his consent would constitute contributory infringement of the patent;
(3) sought to enforce his patent rights against infringement or contributory infringement;
(4) refused to license or use any rights to the patent; or
(5) conditioned the license of any rights to the patent or the sale of the patented product on the acquisition of a license to rights in another patent or purchase of a separate product, unless, in view of the circumstances, the patent owner has market power in the relevant market for the patent or patented product on which the license or sale is conditioned.

Patent misuse may arise from a tying arrangement in which patented products are sold only in combination with unpatented products.[123] As a general proposition, anytime a patented product is licensed or sold only in combination with another product, patent misuse may be at issue and should be thoroughly considered. Thus, if the patented product is a drug that may be delivered through a patch, and is sold only with that patch and in no other form, this may constitute a tying arrangement that could give rise to a patent misuse claim.

ii. Walker Process Counterclaim

When an inequitable conduct claim is presented, a Walker Process claim may also follow. "[T]he enforcement of a patent procured by fraud on the Patent Office may be violative of § 2 of the Sherman Act provided the other elements necessary to a § 2 case are present."[124] The basis of such a claim is the wrongful attempt to enforce a patent when the patentee engaged in inequitable conduct to obtain the patent. For example, if a patentee knowingly fails to cite material prior art in the course of prosecution, and if the patentee was aware of that fraudulent conduct in procuring the patent at the time it filed suit to enforce the patent, a Walker Process claim may be appropriate if the other elements of an antitrust case (such as relevant market, market power and antitrust injury) are present.[125]

iii. *Handgards* Counterclaim

Enforcement of a patent known to be invalid may also give rise to antitrust liability, under *Handgards, Inc. v. Ethicon, Inc.*[126] Unlike a Walker Process claim, *Handgards*-based antitrust claims are appropriate whenever a patentee sues on a patent with the knowledge that it is invalid; such liability does not require inequitable conduct. Thus, if a patentee sues on a patented protein sequence with knowledge—acquired after the patent had been granted—that the sequence had been disclosed in the prior art, a *Handgards* claim might be appropriate if the other indicia of antitrust liability are present.

f. *Other Defenses Not Special to Patent Cases*

No statute of limitation exists for a patent case, though 35 U.S.C. § 286 prohibits recovery of damages for infringements committed more than six years before the infringement claim was filed. The limitation cannot be tolled by other litigation or equitable defenses that can overcome a laches defense.[127]

The equitable defense of laches is available in patent infringement cases as in other cases and requires proof, by a preponderance of the evidence, of an unreasonable and unexcused delay in bringing the claim, which delay has cause material prejudice or injury to the opposing party.[128] Factors to be considered in evaluating a laches defense include "the length of delay, the seriousness of prejudice, the reasonableness of excuses, and the defendant's conduct or culpability. . . ."[129] A mere presentation of undue delay and prejudice is insufficient by itself to establish a laches defense, however; the court must, in its discretion, consider these other factors in deciding whether the laches defense should be denied.[130] A presumption of unreasonable delay may arise if the patentee delays filing suit for a six-year period, but the presumption is rebuttable.[131] If successful, the laches defense bars recovery for damages accrued before suit is filed but does not bar a claim in its entirety.[132]

Closely related to a standard laches defense is "prosecution laches," in which undue delay in the course of prosecution, coupled with material prejudice or injury to another party, operates to render the claims at issue unenforceable.[133]

Equitable estoppel is also available as a defense and, if successful, bars all relief on a claim.[134] To maintain an equitable estoppel defense, an alleged infringer must show misleading conduct by the patentee that led the alleged infringer to reasonably infer that the patentee did not intend to enforce its patent against the alleged infringer; reliance by the alleged infringer on the conduct; and material prejudice to the alleged infringer resulting from the reliance, if the patentee is permitted to proceed with the claim.[135] The court must consider evidence of other factors that may undermine the equitable estoppel defense, such as the alleged infringer's egregious conduct, such as intentional copying.[136] For example, a patentee may contact a competitor who manufactures a patented protein and assert that the protein falls within the scope of the patent. Following some discussion and clarification that the patentee believes the protein is infringing and the competitor maintains that there is no infringement, the patentee might inform the competitor that it is more interested in discussing licensing of some other, unrelated product or process. Time elapses and no more mention is made of the allegedly infringing protein. The competitor concludes that the patentee no longer intends to bring an infringement action and launches a new marketing campaign, touting the benefits of the protein at issue. If the patentee files suit at this point, the alleged infringer could assert an equitable estoppel defense given its reasonable and detrimental reliance on the patentee's course of conduct.

4. Damages Issues

"Upon finding for the claimant the court shall award the claimant damages adequate to compensate for the infringement, but in no event less than a reasonable royalty for the use made of the invention by the infringer, together with interest and costs as fixed by the court."[137] Thus, the baseline damages award is a "reasonable royalty," but upon appropriate proof, a patentee may recover its lost profits.

a. "No Less than a Reasonable Royalty"

Where proof of an analogous royalty rate is available, the reasonable royalty may be based on that information. In the absence of such proof, a variety of factors must be considered to determine the royalty rate that the parties would have agreed upon in a hypothetical, arm's-length licensing negotiation that would have occurred immediately before infringement began.[138] Both parties will, of course, present expert testimony as to when the infringing activity began. The prudent patentee would expect his expert to testify that the date on which the reasonable royalty rate is fixed is the date on which any infringing activity—even if, perhaps, not technically infringing because of the exceptions granted by section 271(e) and the common-law research exception—began. The alleged infringer may find an expert who would testify that it is at some earlier date, and the patentee's counsel would attack this on the ground that there is no rationale to select an independent date not tied to the facts to set the date of the hypothetical licensing negotiation. In the absence of some justification for picking another date, the court is likely to side with the patentee.

> **Practice Points**
>
> In providing relief for patent infringement, the court may provide:
>
> — Damages in an amount not less than a reasonable royalty OR lost profits
> — "Enhanced damages" (possibly including attorneys' fees) for willful infringement
> — Injunctive relief

Although several different methods of determining a reasonable royalty have been approved, the most common approach evaluates the Georgia Pacific factors:

- The royalties received by the patentee for the licensing of the patent in suit, proving or tending to prove an established royalty.
- The rates paid by the licensee for the use of other patents comparable to the patent in suit.
- The nature and scope of the license, as exclusive or non-exclusive; or as restricted or non-restricted in terms of territory or with respect to whom the manufactured product may be sold.

Biotechnology Patent Litigation for the Non-Patent Attorney

- The licensor's established policy and marketing program to maintain his patent monopoly by not licensing others to use the invention or by granting licenses under special conditions designed to preserve that monopoly.
- The commercial relationship between the licensor and licensee, such as whether they are competitors in the same territory in the same line of business or whether they are inventor and promoter.
- The effect of selling the patented specialty in promoting sales of other products of the licensee; the existing value of the invention to the licensor as a generator of sales of his non-patented items; and the extent of such derivative or convoyed sales.
- The duration of the patent and the term of the license.
- The established profitability of the product made under the patent, its commercial success, and its current popularity.
- The utility and advantages of the patent property over the old modes or devices, if any, that had been used for working out similar results.
- The nature of the patented invention; the character of the commercial embodiment of it as owned and produced by the licensor; and the benefits to those who have used the invention.
- The extent to which the infringer has made use of the invention and any evidence probative of the value of that use.
- The portion of the profit or of the selling price that may be customary in the particular business or in comparable businesses to allow for the use of the invention or analogous inventions.
- The portion of the realizable profit that should be credited to the invention as distinguished from non-patented elements, the manufacturing process, business risks, or significant features or improvements added by the infringer.
- The opinion testimony of qualified experts.
- The amount that a licensor (such as the patentee) and a licensee (such as the infringer) would have agreed upon (at the time the infringement began) if both had been reasonably and voluntarily trying to reach an agreement; that is, the amount which a prudent licensee—who desired, as a business proposition, to obtain a license to manufacture and sell a particular article embodying the patented

invention—would have been willing to pay as a royalty and yet be able to make a reasonable profit and which amount would have been acceptable by a prudent patentee who was willing to grant a license.[139]

A finding on reasonable royalty may be challenged only if it is so outrageously high or low that it is unsupportable.[140]

Russell L. Parr's *Royalty Rates for Pharmaceuticals & Biotechnology* (5th Edition) and *Patent Infringement Damages Statistics & Trends 1990—2004*, published by Navigant Consulting, Inc., provides useful information on royalty rates, but as is true of any form of patent damages, an expert witness will be necessary to present the case. Such information, while useful because it provides data as to royalty rates imposed for comparable technology, is somewhat less useful in the context of pharmaceuticals and biotechnology than in other areas because the rates that are reasonable depend so heavily on when the parties negotiate that rate. When a drug or biologic must be FDA-approved, for instance, a license might be negotiated in its early developmental stages when a high likelihood exists that the development will fail; in such a case, the royalty negotiated would be low in view of the high risk that the licensee would accept. Alternatively, the drug could be licensed on the eve of approval, at which point its likelihood of success would be fairly high and the royalty would be higher as a result. For the reasons previously discussed, however, these considerations are likely to impact the reasonable royalty rate only following determination of the point at which infringement began.

b. Lost Profits

Although a reasonable royalty is the floor below which a damages award may not fall, higher damages are available in the form of the patentee's lost profits. To recover lost profits, the patentee must establish causation, that "but for" the infringement, it would have made the infringer's sales, along with the quantum of profits lost.[141] The Federal Circuit has adopted the so-called *Panduit* factors as a non-exclusive method for determining an appropriate lost profits award: "to obtain as damages the profits on sales he would have made absent the infringement, i.e., the sales made by the infringer, a patent owner must prove: (1) demand for the patented product,

(2) absence of acceptable non-infringing substitutes, (3) his manufacturing and marketing capability to exploit the demand, and (4) the amount of the profit he would have made."[142]

Demand for the patented product is generally demonstrated by sales of the infringer and/or the patentee.[143] The absence of non-infringing substitutes requires proof that purchasers sought the patented product or process because of its features and a lack of then-available, competitive products with the same desired features.[144] The alleged substitute must be available on the market at the time of the infringement, although a known, viable, economically feasible substitute that was not actually available has also been considered as a non-infringing substitute for purposes of this analysis.[145] Alternatively, in lieu of proving the absence of acceptable, non-infringing substitutes, the patentee may offer proof of its market share in the relevant market and collect damages based upon its market share.[146] However, "[w]hen the patentee and the infringer are the only suppliers present in the market, it is reasonable to infer that the infringement probably caused the loss of profits."[147] The patentee must also submit proof that it had sufficient capacity at the time of the infringement to make the infringer's sales as well as its own.[148]

In addition to recovering its lost profits, a patentee may also be able to recover damages to account for price erosion if, but for the infringement, it would have been able to charge higher prices.[149] In general, the patentee at least potentially may recover damages on the basis of any foreseeable, economically provable injury.[150]

Similarly, under the entire market value rule, a patentee may recover profits lost on unpatented good or services that are normally sold with the patented product or as a result of a sale of the patented product.[151] However, the unpatented product must function with the patented product so as to form a single assembly, machine, or functional unit.[152]

c. Enhanced Damages

"[T]he court may increase the damages up to three times the amount found or assessed." 35 U.S.C. § 284. Enhanced damages are available if infringement is found to be willful or if the opposing party has exhibited bad faith.[153] The factors justifying enhanced damages must be proved by clear and convincing evidence.[154] Whether circumstances exist that would justify an award of enhanced damages is a question of fact[155] and the amount, if any, of an award of enhanced damages is a matter of the court's discretion.[156]

i. Willfulness

The determination of whether willful infringement exists is a question of fact,[157] reached based on the totality of the circumstances.[158] Factors to be considered in determining whether an infringer's conduct constitutes willful infringement include:

- Deliberate copying of patentee's invention;
- If the infringer was aware of the patent at issue, whether it considered the scope of the patent and formed a good-faith belief that the patent was invalid or not infringed;
- Defendant's behavior in the course of litigation;
- Defendant's size and financial condition;
- Closeness of the case;
- Duration of misconduct;
- Remedial action taken by defendant;
- Defendant's motivation for harm; and
- Whether defendant attempted to conceal misconduct.[159]

"[W]here . . . a potential infringer has actual notice of another's patent rights, he has an affirmative duty to exercise due care to determine whether or not he is infringing."[160] Until recently, this duty of due care de facto, even if not strictly speaking legally, included a duty to obtain an opinion from legal counsel.[161] In fact, the failure to present an opinion of counsel would permit the fact finder to make an adverse inference that no opinion had been obtained or that an opinion was obtained but that it did not exculpate the alleged infringer.[162] However, a recent en banc decision of the Federal Circuit has eliminated the adverse inference resulting from the failure to obtain an opinion of counsel.[163] *Knorr-Bremse* reaffirmed that an alleged infringer on notice of another's patent rights has a duty to investigate and determine whether he is infringing but concluded that inferring that a withheld opinion of counsel was adverse to the alleged infringer's position improperly invades the attorney-client relationship. Despite this conclusion, it is nevertheless prudent for one facing a potential patent infringement accusation to obtain an opinion of counsel, as there is no indication that the opinion will cease to be admissible evidence to rebut a charge of willfulness.

ii. Attorneys' Fees

In addition, in an "exceptional case" the court may award attorney fees to the prevailing party. 35 U.S.C. § 285. The award of fees is, however, within the court's discretion.[164] A finding of willful infringement often leads to an "exceptional case" finding; if not, the court is required to explain why the case does not qualify as exceptional.[165] Litigation misconduct and frivolous litigation may also support an "exceptional case" determination.[166]

d. Equitable Relief

Injunctions are frequently awarded in patent cases because the right to exclude others from making, using, selling, or offering for sale the patented article would be impotent if not specifically enforced following a finding of infringement. 35 U.S.C. § 283 provides that "[t]he several courts having jurisdiction of cases under this title may grant injunctions in accordance with the principles of equity to prevent the violation of any right secured by patent, on such terms as the court deems reasonable." Although the decision whether to grant injunctive relief is within the court's discretion, such relief is generally awarded.[167] Injunctive relief is, of course, awarded only during the lifespan of the patent at issue.[168]

C. Phases of a Patent Case (Procedural/Strategic)

Patent cases are subject to the *Federal Rules of Civil Procedure* and the *Federal Rules of Evidence*, as well as any local rules that may be in effect in the forum. Several courts have now adopted local patent rules. Reference to those rules is critical for conduct of a case pending in one of those courts, and may be helpful in fashioning a case management order for a case pending elsewhere.[169]

The case management order is often more structured in patent cases than in other kinds of civil litigation. Courts often require disclosures of the patentee's contentions on infringement, followed by the infringer's response and disclosure of contentions on invalidity and/or unenforceability, plus exchange of claims terms in dispute with an eye to sharpening the issues for a Markman hearing.

Biotech patent litigation resembles an odyssey, in which both the patentee and alleged infringer are subjected to multiple uncertainties and tests. Although the costs and risks are substantial, the rewards can be great for the patentee, both in immediate financial terms and through strengthening future negotiation position with a reputation for willingness to litigate. Nevertheless, the road is long and fraught with challenges, and experienced counsel is a necessary guide.

Notes

1. *See* Mark Schankerman, Enforcing Patent Rights and Competition, presented August 2003, and *available at* http://www.oecd.org/dataoecd/14/36/11741910.pdf. For additional background, *see* John R. Allison & Mark Lemley, *The Growing Complexity of the United States Patent System,* 82 B.U. L. REV. 77, 137 (2002).

2. Stephen P. Swinton & Adam A. Welland, Patent Injunction Reform and the Overlooked Problem of "False Positives," 70 BNA Patent, Trademark, and Copyright J. 1728, at n.4 (2005). The article is available on the Internet at http://www.lw.com/resource/publications/_pdf/pub1316_1.pdf.

3. 2003 AIPLA Economic Survey.

4. *See infra.*

5. 35 U.S.C. § 302.

6. *See* Jay P. Kesan & Gwendolyn G. Ball, "How Are Patent Cases Resolved? An Empirical Examination of the Adjudication and Settlement of Patent Disputes" (2005), U. Ill. Law & Economics Research Paper, http://ssrn.com/abstract=808347, which found that approximately 5% of patent cases go to trial and 8-9% are resolved on the merits through summary judgment.

7. Kaufman Co. v. Lantech, Inc., 807 F.2d 970, 973-74 (Fed. Cir. 1986).

8. See discussion of laches issues below.

9. Factors that the court should consider in determining whether to exercise its discretion to stay a case in view of a reexamination include the possible damage, hardship, and inequities to the parties, and whether the issues in question in the litigation might be simplified by the outcome of the reexamination. ASCII Corp. v. STD Entertainment USA, Inc., 844 F. Supp. 1378, 1380, 30 U.S.P.Q.2d (BNA) 1709 (N.D. Cal. 1994).

10. *See, e.g.,* Cognex Corp. v. National Instruments Corp., 2001 WL 34368283, No. Civ. A. 00-442-JJF (D. Del. June 29, 2001), in which the court denied a stay when the defendant/EPR requestor had been aware of the prior art for approximately six months before seeking reexamination.

11. PUBPAT is a nonprofit legal organization that "represents the public's interests against the harms caused by the patent system, particularly the harms caused by wrongly issued patents and unsound patent policy." *See* http://www.pubpat.org/About.htm for further information. The Web site also includes information about the reexamination request.

12. *See* Pfizer press release of June 22, 2005, *available at* http://www.pfizer.com/pfizer/are/news_releases/2005pr/mn_2005_0622.jsp.

13. 35 U.S.C. § 311. The purpose of requiring identification of the real party in interest is for determining the effect of the estoppel provided for litigation that follows an IPR.

14. See the later discussion on invalidity and Chapter II's discussion of section 102 for a full discussion of the varieties of prior art that may be submitted in the course of patent litigation.

15. *See* Joseph D. Cohen, *What's Really Happening in Inter Partes Reexamination*, 87 JPTOS 207 (2005). An updated version of this article is *available at* http://www.stoel.com/resources/articles/IP/InterPartes.pdf.

16. A copy of the Request for IPR is *available at* http://patentlaw.typepad.com/patent/95000062_20Original_20Request.pdf.

17. 37 C.F.R. § 1.520.

18. MANUAL OF PATENT EXAMINING PROCEDURE § 2239. Patent Office spokesperson Brigid Quinn has stated that only about 2% of reexaminations between 1981 and 2004 were director-initiated. *See* statistics cited in Michael D. Bednarek, Lawrence J. Gotts & Mark Koehn, *Katz Patent Reexaminations: A Change in Momentum Favoring RAKTL Targets*, *available at* http://library.findlaw.com/2004/Jun/9/133461.html.

19. *Id.*

20. Administrative Office of the United States Courts, 2003 Federal Court Management Statistics.

21. According to an *IP Law Bulletin* study reported at http://iplb.portfoliomedia.com/cgi-bin/absolutenm/anmviewer.asp?a=4329&z=31, the Eastern District of Texas has experienced a 33% increase in patent cases, as compared with a 5% increase in the Southern District of California and a 3% increase in the Northern District of Texas. Each of the other districts studied had a decrease in their patent dockets, notably including the Central District of California (-24%), the Southern District of New York (-23%), and the Districts of Delaware and New Jersey (-30% each).

22. The ITC may, however, issue orders to exclude infringing products from importation and may order removal or destruction of items that have already been imported. The U.S. Customs and Border Protection enforces the ITC's orders.

23. Bio-Technology Gen. Corp. v. Genentech, Inc., 80 F.3d 1553, 1558 (Fed. Cir. 1996); *cert. denied*, 117 S.Ct. 274 (1996).

24. The ITC's decision is *available at* http://info.usitc.gov/ouii/public/337inv.nsf/0/eb63108b844c92e8852566130071a31b?OpenDocument.

25. *See* 28 U.S.C. § 1295.

26. *See, e.g.,* Victoria Slind-Flor, *Federal Circuit Judged Flawed*, NAT'L L. J., Aug. 3, 1998.

27. *See, e.g.,* Charles Shifley, *Flawed or Flawless: Twenty Years of Federal Circuit Appeals*, 2 J. MARSHALL REV. INTELL. PROP. L. 178 (2003), *available at* http://www.jmls.edu/ripl/vol2/issue2/shifley.pdf.

28. An excellent resource on the jurisprudence of the Federal Circuit is ROBERT L. HARMON, PATENTS AND THE FEDERAL CIRCUIT (5th ed. 2003).

29. 35 U.S.C. §§ 100(d), 261, 281.

30. *See* Mentor H/S, Inc. v. Medical Device Alliance, Inc., 240 F.3d 1016 (Fed. Cir. 2001); Textile Productions, Inc. v. Mead Corp., 134 F.3d 1481, 1485 (Fed. Cir. 1998).

31. Claim interpretation is one of the most challenging steps in a patent litigation case. A detailed discussion of the many wrinkles and conflicting guidance in the case law is outside the scope of this chapter. Donald S. Chisum, *Chisum on Patents* (the gold standard of patent treatises) and Ronald B. Hildreth, *Patent Law: A Practitioner's Guide*, among others, provide an extensive exposition of the issues and considerations in *Markman* practice.

32. Markman v. Westview Instruments, Inc., 517 U.S. 370, 371 (1996).

33. Exxon Chemical Patents, Inc. v. Lubrizol Corp., 64 F.3d 1553, 1556 (Fed. Cir. 1995), *reh'g denied, en banc* suggestion declined, 77 F.3d 450 (Fed. Cir. 1996) ("on appeal we review the issue of claim interpretation independently without deference to the trial judge").

34. Hoganas AB v. Dresser Industries, Inc., 9 F.3d 948, 951 (Fed. Cir. 1993).

35. *Markman*, 517 U.S. 370 ("But whereas issue preclusion could not be asserted against new and independent infringement defendants even within a given jurisdiction, treating interpretive issues as purely legal will promote (though it will not guarantee) intra-jurisdictional certainty through the application of stare decisis on those questions not yet subject to interjurisdictional uniformity under the authority of the single appeals court."). In other words, once a claim term has been construed, its construction is accorded precedential weight where appropriate.

36. *Cybor Corp. v. FAS Tech., Inc.*, 138 F.3d 1448, 1476 (Fed. Cir. 1998).

37. See the following discussion of local patent rules.

38. *Phillips v. AWH Corp.*, 415 F.3d 1303, 1334-35 (Fed. Cir. 2005) (Mayer, J., dissenting).

39. *See, e.g., Eastman Kodak Co. v. Goodyear Tire & Rubber Co.*, 114 F.3d 1547, 1556 (Fed. Cir. 1997).

40. Johnson Worldwide Associates, Inc. v. Zebco Corp., 175 F.3d 985, 989 (Fed. Cir. 1999) (recognizing the "heavy" presumption that a term holds its ordi-

nary and accustomed meaning and stating, "[A] court must presume that the terms in the claim mean what they say, and, unless otherwise compelled, give full effect to the ordinary and accustomed meaning of claim terms."); Hoechst Celanese Corp. v. BP Chemicals Ltd., 78 F.3d 1575, 1578 (Fed. Cir. 1996) ("A technical term used in a patent document is interpreted as having the meaning that it would be given by persons experienced in the field of the invention, unless it is apparent from the patent and the prosecution history that the inventor used the term with a different meaning.").

41. C.R. Bard, Inc. v. Advanced Cardiovascular Systems, Inc., 911 F.2d 670, 673, 15 U.S.P.Q.2d (BNA) 1540 (Fed. Cir. 1990) ("Claim interpretation, which is a question of law, involves examination of the claim at issue, the specification, and the prosecution history.").

42. Vitronics Corp. v. Conceptronic, Inc., 90 F.3d 1576, 1582 (Fed. Cir. 1996).

43. *Cybor Corp.*, 138 F.3d at 1474, 1480.

44. *Vitronics*, 90 F.3d at 1583.

45. *Id.* at 1584 n.6 ("Although technical treatises and dictionaries fall within the category of extrinsic evidence, as they do not form a part of an integrated patent document, they are worthy of special note. Judges are free to consult such resources at any time in order to better understand the underlying technology and may also rely on dictionary definitions when construing claim terms, so long as the dictionary definition does not contradict any definition found in or ascertained by a reading of the patent documents.").

46. Phillips v. AWH Corp., 415 F.3d 1303 (Fed. Cir. 2005).

47. 28 U.S.C. § 271(a).

48. See previous discussion.

49. Graver Tank & Mfg. Co. v. Linde Air Prods. Co., 339 U.S. 605 (1950).

50. London v. Carson Pirie Scott & Co., 946 F.2d 1534, 1539 (Fed. Cir. 1991) ("There can be no infringement as a matter of law if a claim limitation is totally missing from the accused device.").

51. Graver Tank, 339 U.S. 605, 608 (1950), *quoting* Sanitary Refrigerator v. Winters, 280 U.S. 30 (1929).

52. 117 S. Ct. 1040 (1997).

53. Litigation application of the doctrine of equivalents is heavily dependent upon prosecution history estoppel issues, as discussed previously in the prosecution context (see Chapter Two) and below in this chapter.

54. 287 F. Supp. 2d 126 (D. Mass. 2003).

55. 35 U.S.C. § 271(b).

56. Water Tech. Corp. v. Calco Ltd., 850 F.2d 660 (Fed. Cir. 1988).

57. Micro Chem., Inc. v. Great Plains Chem. Co., 103 F.3d 1538 (Fed. Cir. 1997).

58. 35 U.S.C. § 271(c).

59. Mentor H/S, Inc. v. Medical Device Alliance, Inc., 244 F.3d 1365, 1379 (Fed. Cir. 2001).

60. Aro Mfg. Co. v. Convertible Top Replacement Co., 365 U.S. 336, 341 (1961) ("there can be no contributory infringement in the absence of a direct infringement"); Joy Technologies, Inc. v. Flakt, Inc., 6 F.3d 770, 774 (Fed. Cir. 1993) ("Liability for either active inducement of infringement or for contributory infringement is dependent upon the existence of direct infringement.").

61. Warner-Jenkinson Co. v. Hilton Davis Chem. Co., 117 S. Ct. 1040 (1997).

62. Festo Corp. v. Shoketsu Kinzoku Kogyo Kabushiki Co., 122 S. Ct. 1831, 62 U.S.P.Q.2d 1705 (2002).

63. *See, e.g.,* Honeywell Int'l Inc. v. Hamilton Sundstrand Corp., 370 F.3d 1131 (Fed. Cir. 2004) (en banc).

64. Tate Access Floors, Inc. v. Interface Architectural Res., Inc., 279 F.3d 1357, 61 U.S.P.Q.2d 1647 (Fed. Cir. 2002).

65. Johnson & Johnston Assocs. v. R.E. Serv. Co., 285 F.3d 1046, 62 U.S.P.Q.2d 1225 (Fed. Cir. 2002).

66. Whitemore v. Cutter, 29 F. Cas. 1120 (C.C. Mass. 1813) (Story, J.).

67. Madey v. Duke Univ., 307 F.3d 1351, 1362 (2002), *cert. denied*, 123 S. Ct. 2639 (2003).

68. *Id.*

69. *See, e.g.,* Brief for Assoc. of Am. Medical Colleges, et al., as Amici Curiae in Support of Petitioner at 14, Duke Univ. v. Madey, 123 S. Ct. 2639 (2003); Jennifer Miller, *Sealing the Coffin on Experimental Use*, 2003 DUKE L. & TECH. REV. 12 (2003).

70. *See* 35 U.S.C. § 271(e), which provides: "It shall not be an act of infringement to make, use, offer to sell, or sell within the United States or import into the United States a patented invention (other than a new animal drug or veterinary biological product . . . which is primarily manufactured using recombinant DNA, recombinant RNA, hybridoma technology, or other processes involving site-specific genetic manipulation techniques) solely for uses reasonably related to the development and submission of information under a Federal law which regulates the manufacture, use, or sale of drugs or veterinary biological products."

71. Integra Lifesciences I, Ltd. v. Merck KGaA, 331 F.3d 860, 872 (Fed. Cir. 2003).

72. Merck KGaA v. Integra Lifesciences I, Ltd., 125 S. Ct. 2372, 2383 (2005).

73. "Research tools" have been defined by the National Institutes of Health as "tools that scientists use in the laboratory, including cell lines, monoclonal antibodies, reagents, animal models, growth factors, combinatorial chemistry and DNA libraries, clones and cloning tools (such as PCR), methods, laboratory equipment and machines." Integra Lifesciences I, Ltd. v. Merck KGaA, 331 F.3d 860, 872 (Fed. Cir. 2003).

74. 35 U.S.C. § 282.

75. Bausch & Lomb, Inc. v. Barnes-Hind/Hydrocurve, Inc., 796 F.2d 443, 230 U.S.P.Q. 416 (Fed. Cir. 1986).

76. Glaxo Inc. v. Novopharm Ltd., 52 F.3d 1043, 1047, 34 U.S.P.Q.2d 1565 (Fed. Cir. 1995) ("A claim is anticipated and therefore invalid only when a single prior art reference discloses each and every limitation of the claim.").

77. Continental Can Co. v. Monsanto Co., 948 F.2d 1264, 1268 (Fed. Cir. 1991).

78. Schering Corp. v. Geneva Pharms. Inc., 339 F.3d 1373, 1377 (Fed. Cir. 2003).

79. ATD Corp. v. Lydall, Inc., 159 F.3d 534, 545, 48 U.S.P.Q.2d 1321 (Fed. Cir. 1998) ("An anticipating reference must describe the patented subject matter with sufficient clarity and detail to establish that the subject matter existed and that its existence was recognized by persons or ordinary skill in the field of the invention.").

80. Pfaff v. Wells Electronics, Inc., 525 U.S. 55, 67 (1998).

81. Micro Chemical, Inc. v. Great Plains Chemical Co., Inc., 103 F.3d 1538, 1544, 41 U.S.P.Q.2d 1238 (Fed. Cir. 1997).

82. *Pfaff*, 119 S. Ct. at 312.

83. Baxter Int'l, Inc. v. COBE Labs., Inc., 88 F.3d 1054, 1060, 39 U.S.P.Q.2d 1437 (Fed. Cir. 1996).

84. SmithKline Beecham Corp. v. Apotex Corp., 365 F.3d 1306, 1320 (Fed. Cir. 2004).

85. Section 103(a) provides: "A patent may not be obtained though the invention is not identically disclosed or described as set forth in section 102 of this title, if the differences between the subject matter sought to be patented and the prior art are such that the subject matter as a whole would have been obvious at the time the invention was made to a person having ordinary skill in the art to which said subject matter pertains. Patentability shall not be negatived by the manner in which the invention was made."

86. Kimberly-Clark Corp. v. Johnson & Johnson, 745 F.2d 1437, 1448, 223 U.S.P.Q. 603 (Fed. Cir. 1984) ("The proper approach to the obviousness issue must start with the claimed invention as a whole.").

87. Panduit Corp. v. Dennison Mfg. Co., 810 F.2d 1561, 1565-67, 1 U.S.P.Q.2d 1593 (Fed. Cir. 1987).

88. To qualify as prior art for purposes of a section 103 analysis, a reference must be of a type described in 35 U.S.C. § 102 (a), (b), (e), (f) or (g). Wang Labs., Inc. v. Toshiba Corp., 993 F.2d 858, 864, 26 U.S.P.Q.2d 1767 (Fed. Cir. 1993) ("Analogous art is that which is relevant to a consideration of obviousness under section 103. . . . Two criteria are relevant in determining whether prior art is analogous: (1) whether the art is from the same field of endeavor, regardless of

the problem addressed, and (2) if the art is not within the same field of endeavor, whether it is still reasonably pertinent to the particular problem to be solved.").

89. Graham v. John Deere Co., 383 U.S. 1, 17, 86 S. Ct. 684, 15 L. Ed. 2d 545 (1966).

90. *Id.* at 17.

91. Hughes Tool Co. v. Dresser Industries, Inc., 816 F.2d 1549, 1556, 2 U.S.P.Q.2d 1396 (Fed. Cir.), *cert. denied*, 481 U.S. 1052 (1987), 481 U.S. 1052 (1987) [("commercial success due to the invention; failure of others; long felt need; movement of the skilled in a different direction; skepticism of experts . . .; copying the invention in preference to the prior art . . . ; and other events proved to have actually happened in the real world (hence the description 'objective')")]; Panduit Corp. v. Dennison Mfg. Co., 810 F.2d 1561, 1566, 1 U.S.P.Q.2d 1593 (Fed. Cir. 1987).

92. Custom Accessories, Inc. v. Jeffrey-Allan Industries, Inc., 807 F.2d 955, 958, 1 U.S.P.Q.2d 1196 (Fed. Cir. 1986).

93. Heidelberger Druckmaschinen AG v. Hantscho Commercial Products, Inc., 21 F.3d 1068, 1072, 30 U.S.P.Q.2d 1377 (Fed. Cir. 1994) ("When the patented invention is made by combining known components to achieve a new system, the prior art must provide a suggestion or motivation to make such a combination."); Northern Telecom, Inc. v. Datapoint Corp., 908 F.2d 931, 934, 15 U.S.P.Q.2d 1321 (Fed. Cir. 1990), *cert. denied*, 498 U.S. 920 (1990) ("It is insufficient that the prior art disclosed the components of the patented device, either separately or used in other combinations; there must be some teaching, suggestion, or incentive to make the combination made by the inventor.").

94. Motorola, Inc. v. Interdigital Technology Corp., 121 F.3d 1461, 1472, 43 U.S.P.Q.2d 1481 (Fed. Cir. 1997) ("there is no requirement that the prior art contain an express suggestion to combine known elements to achieve the claimed invention. Rather, the suggestion to combine may come from the prior art, as filtered through the knowledge of one skilled in the art.").

95. *In re* Huston, 308 F.3d 1267, 1280, 64 U.S.P.Q.2d 1801 (Fed. Cir. 2002).

96. For a full discussion of a similar fact pattern, see Knoll Pharm. Co., Inc. v. Teva Pharms. USA, Inc., Case No. 03-1300 (Fed. Cir. May 19, 2004) (per curiam, Newman, Archer & Prost, JJ.), discussing the combination of an opioid and a non-steroidal anti-inflammatory drug. The opinion is *available at* http://caselaw.lp.findlaw.com/cgi-bin/getcase.pl?court=Fed&navby=case&no=031300.

97. Vas-Cath Inc. v. Mahurkar, 935 F.2d 1555, 1563-64, 19 U.S.P.Q.2d 1111 (Fed. Cir. 1991).

98. *Id.*

99. *Id.* at 1565-66.

100. Regents of the University of California v. Eli Lilly & Co., 119 F.3d 1559, 43 U.S.P.Q.2d 1398 (Fed. Cir. 1997) (held patent invalid for failure to provide adequate written description of claimed DNA when the protein encoded by the

DNA and method for generating the DNA were described, but the DNA itself was not described).

101. *Id.* at 1019.

102. *Id.* The Guidelines are *available at* http://www.uspto.gov/web/menu/written.pdf.

103. *See* 119 F.3d at 1019.

104. Moba, B.V. v. Diamond Automation, Inc., 325 F.3d 1306, 1320 (Fed. Cir. 2003), discussing the holding of Enzo Biochem, Inc. v. Gen-Probe, Inc., 296 F.3d 1316 (Fed. Cir. 2002).

105. Univ. of Rochester v. G.D. Searle & Co., 358 F.3d 916 (Fed. Cir. 2004).

106. Adang v. Fischoff, 286 F.3d 1346, 62 U.S.P.Q.2d 1504 (Fed. Cir. 2002).

107. 37 C.F.R. § 1.56.

108. Molins PLC v. Textron, Inc., 48 F.3d 1172, 1178 (Fed. Cir. 1995) ("One who alleges inequitable conduct arising from a failure to disclose prior art must offer clear and convincing proof of the materiality of the prior art, knowledge chargeable to the applicant of that prior art and of its materiality, and the applicant's failure to disclose the prior art, coupled with an intent to mislead the PTO.").

109. Kingsdown Medical Consultants, Ltd. v. Hollister Inc., 863 F.2d 867, 877 (Fed. Cir. 1988), *cert. denied*, 490 U.S. 1067 (1989) ("When a court has finally determined that inequitable conduct occurred in relation to one or more claims during prosecution of the patent application, the entire patent is rendered unenforceable.").

110. In this context, "noncumulative information" simply refers to information that goes beyond and does not duplicate references already disclosed to or located by the examiner.

111. Fox Industries, Inc. v. Structural Preservation Systems, Inc., 922 F.2d 801, 804 (Fed. Cir. 1990).

112. *Molins PLC*, 48 F.3d at 1179.

113. Therma-Tru Corp. v. Peachtree Doors Inc., 44 F.3d 988, 995 (Fed. Cir. 1995).

114. *Molins PLC*, 48 F.3d at 1180-81 ("Intent need not be proven by direct evidence; it is most often proven by a showing of acts, the natural consequences of which are presumably intended by the actor. . . . Generally, intent must be inferred from the facts and circumstances surrounding the applicant's conduct.").

115. Paragon Podiatry Lab., Inc. v. KLM Labs., Inc., 984 F.2d 1182, 1189 (Fed. Cir. 1993).

116. Heidelberger Druckmaschinen AG v. Hantscho Commercial Products, Inc., 21 F.3d 1068, 1073 (Fed. Cir. 1994) ("When these factual predicates [materiality and intent] are established, the determination of inequitable conduct is within the sound discretion of the trial court.").

117. *Molins PLC*, 48 F.3d at 1178 ("Once threshold findings of materiality and intent are established, the court must weigh them to determine whether the equities warrant a conclusion that inequitable conduct occurred. . . . In light of all the circumstances, an equitable judgment must be made concerning whether the applicant's conduct is so culpable that the patent should not be enforced.").

118. Critikon, Inc. v. Becton Dickinson Vascular Access, Inc., 120 F.3d 1253, 1256 (Fed. Cir. 1997) ("The more material the omission or the misrepresentation, the lower the level of intent required to establish inequitable conduct, and vice versa.").

119. *Kingsdown Medical Consultants*, 863 F.2d at 876, *quoting* Burlington Industries, Inc. v. Dayco Corp., 849 F.2d 1418, 1422 (Fed. Cir. 1988), *cert. denied*, 490 U.S. 1067 (1989) ("the habit of charging inequitable conduct in almost every major patent case has become an absolute plague").

120. See discussion of patent misuse below.

121. B. Braun Medical, Inc. v. Abbott Labs., 124 F.3d 1419, 1427 (Fed. Cir. 1997) ("When used successfully, this defense [of patent misuse] results in rendering the patent unenforceable until the misuse is purged. It does not, however, result in an award of damages to the accused infringer.").

122. 448 U.S. 176 (1980).

123. Morton Salt Co. v. G.S. Supplier Co., 314 U.S. 488 (1942).

124. Walker Process Equipment, Inc. v. Food Machinery & Chemical Corp., 382 U.S. 172, 172 (1965).

125. *See* Nobelpharma A.B. v. Implant Innovations Inc., 129 F.3d 1463 (Fed. Cir. 1997), *subseq. decision*, 1998 WL122399 (Fed. Cir. March 20, 1998), *pet. for reh'g denied* (April 29, 1998).

126. 601 F.2d 986 (9th Cir. 1979), *cert. denied*, 444 U.S. 1025 (1980).

127. A. Stucki Co. v. Buckeye Steel Castings Co., 963 F.2d 360, 363 (Fed. Cir. 1992).

128. Gasser Chair Co., Inc. v. Infanti Chair Mfg. Corp., 60 F.3d 770, 773 (Fed. Cir. 1995); A.C. Aukerman Co. v. R.L. Chaides Constr. Co., 960 F.2d 1020, 1045 (Fed. Cir. 1992).

129. *A.C. Aukerman*, 960 F.2d at 1034.

130. *Gasser Chair Co.*, 60 F.3d at 773.

131. Advanced Cardiovascular Systems, Inc. v. Scimed Life Systems, Inc., 988 F.2d 1157, 1163 (Fed. Cir. 1993) ("However, unlike a statutory period of limitation on suit, the presumption of laches is rebuttable. The presumption serves to place upon the patentee the burden of coming forward with evidence that the delay is reasonable or excusable.").

132. *Id.*

133. Symbol Technologies, Inc. v. Lemelson Medical, 277 F.3d 1361 (Fed. Cir.), *cert. denied*, 123 S. Ct. 113, *citing* Webster Elec. Co. v. Splitdorf Elec. Co., 264 U.S. 463.

134. ABB Robotics, Inc. v. GMFanuc Robotics Corp., 52 F.3d 1062, 1063 (Fed. Cir. 1995).

135. Hall v. Aqua Queen Mfg., Inc., 93 F.3d 1548, 1553 (Fed. Cir. 1996).

136. *A.C. Aukerman*, 960 F.2d at 1043-44.

137. 35 U.S.C. § 284.

138. Rite-Hite Corp. v. Kelley Co., 56 F.3d 1538, 1554 (Fed. Cir.), *cert. denied*, 516 U.S. 867 (1995).

139. Georgia-Pacific Corp. v. U.S. Plywood Corp., 318 F. Supp. 1116, 1120 (S.D. N.Y. 1970), *judgment modified on other grounds*, 446 F.2d 295 (2d Cir.), *cert. denied*, 404 U.S. 870 (1971).

140. Lindemann Maschinenfabrik GmbH v. American Hoist & Derrick Co., Harris Press & Shear Div., 895 F.2d 1403, 1406 (Fed. Cir. 1990) ("One challenging only the court's finding as to amount of damages awarded under the 'reasonable royalty' provision of § 284, therefore, must show that the award is, in view of all the evidence, either so outrageously high or so outrageously low as to be unsupportable as an estimation of a reasonable royalty.").

141. Rite-Hite Corp. v. Kelley Co., Inc., 56 F.3d 1538 (Fed. Cir. 1995) (en banc) ("To recover lost profits damages, the patentee must show a reasonable probability that, 'but for' the infringement, it would have made the sales that were made by the infringer.").

142. Panduit Corp. v. Stahlin Bros. Fibre Works, 575 F.2d 1152, 1156 (6th Cir. 1978).

143. *See, e.g.*, State Indus., Inc. v. Mor-Flo Indus., Inc., 883 F.2d 1573, 1578 (Fed. Cir. 1989).

144. Uniroyal, Inc. v. Rudkin-Wiley Corp., 939 F.2d 1540, 1545-46 (Fed. Cir. 1991).

145. Grain Processing Corp. v. Am. Maize-Prods. Co., 185 F.3d 1341, 1356 (Fed. Cir. 1999); *State Indus.*, 883 F.2d 1573, 1579 (Fed. Cir. 1989).

146. BIC Leisure Products, Inc. v. Windsurfing Int'l, Inc., 1 F.3d 1214, 1219 (Fed. Cir. 1993) ("This court has held that a patent owner may satisfy the second *Panduit* element by substituting proof of its market share for proof of the absence of acceptable substitutes.").

147. Kaufman Co., Inc. v. Lantech, Inc., 926 F.2d 1136, 1141, 1828 (Fed. Cir. 1991).

148. *See, e.g.*, Fonar Corp. v. Gen. Elec. Co., 107 F.3d 1543, 1553-54 (Fed. Cir.), *cert. denied*, 118 S. Ct. 266 (1997).

149. Minco, Inc. v. Combustion Eng'g, Inc., 95 F.3d 1109, 1119 (Fed. Cir. 1996).

150. *Rite-Hite Corp.*, 56 F.3d at 1546 ("We believe that under § 284 of the patent statute, the balance between full compensation, which is the meaning that the Supreme Court has attributed to the statute, and the reasonable limits of liability encompassed by general principles of law can best be viewed in terms

of reasonable, objective foreseeability. If a particular injury was or should have been reasonably foreseeable by an infringing competitor in the relevant market, broadly defined, that injury is generally compensable absent a persuasive reason to the contrary.").

151. Paper Converting Machine Co. v. Magna-Graphics Corp., 745 F.2d 11, 23 (Fed. Cir. 1984).

152. Tec Air, Inc. v. Denso Mfg. Michigan Inc., 192 F.3d 1353, 1362 (Fed. Cir. 1999).

153. Jurgens v. CBK, Ltd., 80 F.3d 1566, 1570, 38 U.S.P.Q.2d 1397 (Fed. Cir. 1996) ("Because increased damages are punitive, the requisite conduct for imposing them must include some degree of culpability.... An act of willful infringement satisfies this culpability requirement and is, without doubt, sufficient to meet the first requirement to increase a compensatory damages award.... Increased damages also may be awarded to a party because of the bad faith of the other side.").

154. State Industries, Inc. v. Mor-Flo Industries, Inc., 883 F.2d 1573, 12 U.S.P.Q.2d 1026 (Fed. Cir. 1989).

155. National Presto Industries, Inc. v. West Bend Co., 76 F.3d 1185, 1192-93, 37 U.S.P.Q.2d 1685 (Fed. Cir. 1996).

156. Odetics, Inc. v. Storage Technology Corp., 185 F.3d 1259, 1274, 51 U.S.P.Q.2d 1225 (Fed. Cir. 1999) ("The law is clear that while willful infringement may allow enhanced damages, such a finding does not compel the district court to grant them."); Modine Mfg. Co. v. Allen Group, Inc., 917 F.2d 538, 543, 16 U.S.P.Q.2d 1622 (Fed. Cir. 1990) ("The decision to increase damages is committed to the discretion of the trial judge and a district court's refusal to award increased damages will not be overturned absent a clear showing of abuse of discretion."), *cert. denied*, 500 U.S. 918 (1991).

157. L.A. Gear, Inc. v. Thom McAn Shoe Co., 988 F.2d 1117, 1126, 25 U.S.P.Q.2d 1913 (Fed. Cir. 1993) ("Willfulness of infringement is a question of fact, and the district court's finding thereon shall be sustained unless it is clearly in error.").

158. National Presto Industries, Inc. v. West Bend Co., 76 F.3d 1185, 1193, 37 U.S.P.Q.2d 1685 (Fed. Cir. 1996) ("All of the circumstances must be considered in determination of the issue of willful infringement.").

159. Read Corp. v. Portec, Inc., 970 F.2d 816, 826-27, 23 U.S.P.Q.2d 1426 (Fed. Cir. 1992). *See also* SRI Int'l, Inc. v. Advanced Tech. Labs. Inc., 127 F.3d 1462, 1465 (Fed. Cir. 1997); Rolls-Royce Ltd. v. GTE Valeron Corp., 800 F.2d 1101, 1110 (Fed. Cir. 1986); Bott v. Four Star Corp., 807 F.2d 1567, 1572 (Fed. Cir. 1986); Underwater Devices, Inc. v. Morrison-Knudsen Co., 717 F.2d 1380 (Fed. Cir. 1983).

160. *Underwater Devices*, 717 F.2d at 1389-90.

161. *Id.* at 1390.

162. Kloster Speedsteel AB v. Crucible Inc., 793 F.2d 1565, 1572-73 (Fed. Cir. 1986) ("a court must be free to infer that either no opinion was obtained or, if an opinion were obtained, it was contrary to the infringer's desire to initiate or continue its use of the patentee's invention").

163. Knorr-Bremse Systeme Fuer Nutzfahrzeuge GmbH v. Dana Corp., 383 F.3d 1337 (Fed. Cir. 2004) (*en banc*).

164. Amsted Industries Inc. v. Buckeye Steel Castings Co., 24 F.3d 178, 184 (Fed. Cir. 1994).

165. Modine Mfg. Co. v. Allen Group, Inc., 917 F.2d 538, 543 (Fed. Cir. 1990) ("When a trial judge denies attorney fees in spite of a finding of willful infringement, the court must explain why the case is not 'exceptional' within the meaning of the statute.").

166. Amsted Industries Inc. v. Buckeye Steel Castings Co., 23 F.3d 374, 376 (Fed. Cir. 1994) (litigation misconduct and frivolous suits may justify finding a case exceptional).

167. W.L. Gore & Assocs., Inc. v. Garlock, Inc., 842 F.2d 1275, 1281 (Fed. Cir. 1988) ("Although the district court's grant or denial of an injunction is discretionary depending on the facts of the case . . . injunctive relief against an adjudged infringer is usually granted.").

168. Kearns v. Chrysler Corp., 32 F.3d 1541, 1550 (Fed. Cir. 1994) ("When the rights secured by a patent are no longer protectable by virtue of expiration or unenforceability, entitlement to injunctive relief becomes moot because such relief is no longer available.").

169. The Northern District of California (http://www.cand.uscourts.gov/CAND/LocalRul.nsf/fec20e529a5572f0882569b6006607e0/4735a1c69bd18b418825695f00730cdd?OpenDocument), Northern District of Georgia (http://www.gand.uscourts.gov/documents/NDGARulesPatent.pdf), Western District of Pennsylvania (http://www.pawd.uscourts.gov/Documents/Forms/LocalPatentRules.pdf), and Eastern District of Texas (Appendix M at http://www.txed.uscourts.gov/) have adopted local patent rules.

Chapter XX

Litigation Issues

Robert F. Copple
Scottsdale, Arizona

Whether the new biotech enterprise succeeds or fails, litigation will likely occur. If the enterprise crashes, partners and investors will fight over the pieces. And shareholders may point at management's misdeeds as the cause of the demise. If, on the other hand, the enterprise is successful, markets a product, and makes a profit, it becomes a target for thieves, pretenders and, perhaps, some parties who have a legitimate complaint about the product or how the company is run. In addition, at many stages of the process the enterprise will file for various government approvals—patents, copyrights, FDA approval, SEC registration, etc.—and any rejection may force the enterprise to appeal that decision to a court.

Many business lawyers have nightmares about litigation. Despite their inherent toughness in negotiations, they tend to break out in a sweat at the first hint of a litigation dispute and hand the matter off to the nearest pit bull. Part of this litigation reluctance may have to do with the business lawyer's concern that he did something or missed something that gave rise to the dispute. The reality is that, given the vagaries of law, life, and chaos theory, no deal, no contract, no business relationship is litigation bulletproof. Both the biotech and the electronic tech booms have produced many examples of new enterprises with promising products that have been driven to the brink by a combination of SEC investigations, shareholder derivative suits, patent infringement claims, and products liability class actions. Therefore, biotech business lawyers can and should strive to become litigation issue spotters and risk managers during their representation of the new enterprise.

Litigation can be costly and even crippling. Particularly for the small or fledgling business, litigation costs can strain the resources of the new, already cash-strapped enterprise to the point of it being held hostage, no matter the likelihood of its liability. If nothing else, the management disruption caused by litigation alone can force key executives and inventors to lose their focus on the enterprise's primary goal of moving toward the market and profitability. Further, the investment community watches these public disputes closely. As a result, a large, ongoing litigation that creates the threat of substantial exposure to the enterprise, either in terms of dollar judgments or a finding of patent infringement, can have a real effect on investing confidence and on the enterprise's perceived value.

This chapter's purpose is not to turn business lawyers into litigators. There will be no pithy and erudite discussions of the rules of civil procedure or evidence. Instead, this chapter has two goals: (1) On a topical level, identify a number of issues particularly applicable to the biotech enterprise that may give rise to litigation; and (2) Discuss several techniques and processes that may help the business lawyer or general counsel and her client avoid or mitigate litigation and its effects.

A. Intellectual Property and Confidential Business Information

It almost goes without saying that invention and innovation are central to the biotech enterprise and its intellectual property are literally the family jewels. When one thinks about tech companies and intellectual property, patents are likely to be the first type of intellectual property that comes to mind. The subjects of patent prosecution and litigation have received expert treatment in Chapters II and XIX of this book.[1] In this chapter, biotech patent issues will only be addressed in the context of alternative dispute resolution. In addition to patents, however, there are other branches of intellectual property law, in particular trademark and trade secrets, that are crucial to protecting the biotech enterprise's brand and confidential business information.

Litigation Issues

1. Trademark Issues[2]

At some point in the biotech enterprise's development, the company or product brand may become almost as important as its patented inventions. Essentially, the brand is to the marketing side of the enterprise what the invention is to the research and development side. Trademark law is one of the tools available to protect the brand and, unlike patent law, is readily accessible to the business lawyer.

a. Registration and Protection

The purpose of allowing an exclusive right to use a trademark is to avoid consumer confusion between similar products. Trademark rights can be created at the federal level pursuant to the Lanham Act[3] by registration with United States Patent and Trademark Office (USPTO)[4] or by actual use. The advantage of USPTO registration is that it establishes certain presumptions regarding the trademark owner's right to use the trademark for a class of goods *nationwide*. The initial term of registration is 10 years, which may be extended indefinitely, assuming all of the statutory prerequisites are satisfied.[5] Registered trademarks should bear the symbol ® when used on or in conjunction with a product.

As defined by the Trademark Office, trademark protection can apply to "any word, name, symbol, or device, or any combination, used, or intended to be used, in commerce to identify and distinguish the goods of one manufacturer or seller from goods manufactured or sold by others, and to indicate the source of the goods. In short, a trademark is a brand name."[6] The key to protection is that the trademark distinguishes the particular product from other similar products. In determining whether a proposed trademark can be protected, the Trademark Office focuses on the distinctiveness of the mark. For example, the more fanciful or arbitrary the mark, the more likely it can be protected, as opposed to marks that are more suggestive or descriptive of a class of products. For example, "Biotech Chemical Solutions" would be harder to protect than "Novartis."

b. Litigation Claims—Infringement and Dilution

There are two general types of injury to trademark holders that can give rise to litigation. The first is infringement, which occurs when a second party uses a mark for a product that is the same as or similar to that of the trademark holder in a manner that is likely to confuse the consumer as to the source of the product. In determining the likelihood of confusion, federal courts look to the following factors: (1) the strength of the trademark; (2) the degree of similarity between the two marks; (3) the geographic and market proximity of the products; (4) the likelihood that the prior trademark owner may one day enter the market of the subsequent trademark holder; (5) actual consumer confusion; (6) the defendant's bad faith in adopting the mark; (7) the quality of the defendant's product; and (8) the sophistication of the consumers.[7]

Some of the best examples of trademark infringement involve the "knockoffs" of name-brand goods, such as watches (Rolex) and women's purses (Gucci), that are imported and sold in the United States under the trademark holder's mark. In these cases, it is clear that the seller of the knockoffs is seeking to confuse consumers, thus also establishing his bad faith, which can create a claim for treble damages. Even a slight variation of the name brand, such as "Rolec" or "Gucce" might be similarly actionable. If, however, the brand name Gucci was used for a line of farm tractors, as opposed to handbags, no infringement would have occurred, but there may be an action for the dilution of the trademark.

The second general category of trademark injury involves the dilution of the mark through blurring or tarnishment. At the outset, a claim for dilution requires that the trademark at issue be "famous."[8] Dilution does not involve the crucial infringement element of consumer confusion. Instead, the injury caused by dilution is the undermining or diminishment of the trademark's distinctiveness. Blurring occurs when a registered and longstanding trademark is used in conjunction with a dissimilar set of products, such as Gucci Tractors. Another example might be if a car manufacturer used the trademark "Viagra" for a new two-seat convertible sports car. Tarnishment occurs when the trademark is used by the second party in conjunction with low quality or unseemly products, such as the variation of the trademark "Toys R Us" used by an adult pornography Web site, "Adults R Us."[9] It is important to note that the U.S. Supreme Court has recently held that, to be successful, the plaintiff must demonstrate actual dilution of the trademark.[10] The primary defenses to infringement and dilution are "fair use"[11] and parody.[12]

This brief summary of trademark law leads to the following list of recommendations for business lawyers representing the new biotech enterprise:

(i) *Trademark Audit.* Prior to registration, counsel should conduct or arrange for a trademark audit. A proper audit involves both a review of existing trademarks registered with the USPTO and of other sources, such as through an Internet search, to determine if any of the proposed names are already registered or otherwise in use. The world of high tech is replete with stories of even large, sophisticated companies adopting a new product name or advertising slogan only later to be sued by a small business that had already adopted that name and demanded substantial settlement dollars for its use.

(ii) *Trademark Registration.* It is important for the new biotech enterprise to register both its company name and products' names as trademarks at the earliest opportunity in order both to have the benefit of using those names and to avoid infringement or dilution claims at a later time. It is not necessary for the named product actually to be for sale or in the stream of commerce at the time of the application for registration. What the applicant must assert is a bona fide intent to use the trademark in commerce.[13] Even so, the enterprise should look for every early opportunity to use the trademarks in interstate commerce, such as through letterhead and company promotions, in order to demonstrate its ownership of the mark. Registration will not be granted until the mark is "in use."

> **Practice Points**
> — Build a strong foundation with trademark audit and registration.
> — Register the range of domain names.
> — Respond quickly to infringement and dilution.

(iii) *Domain Name Registration.* Undoubtedly, the new enterprise will have its own Web site. Therefore, counsel should see to it that the new enterprise registers its domain names, as well as both the benign and malevolent variations of those domain names. By registering the primary domain name and similar variations, the enterprise can avoid future customer confusion, as well as the possible need to bring an expensive cybersquatting action[14] in the future or pay exorbitantly later for rights to the domain. By registering the less flattering variations, such as "enterprisesucks.com," the company can take a step toward closing the opportunity for Web sites attacking the company. In recent years, the cost of domain name registrations has dramatically decreased. As a result, for a few hundred dollars, the enterprise can register all of the obvious variations with one of the large registrars, such as godaddy.com and register.com.

(iv) *Response to Infringement or Dilution.* If counsel has followed the preceding steps, the enterprise will be in a good position to respond to any infringement or dilution of its marks. It is important to consider both federal and state remedies in contemplating an action, since state trademark and unfair competition laws cover a wider scope of activities and many times offer standards that are easier to meet than the federal counterparts. Remedies available under the relevant federal statutes, and often under state unfair competition laws, include injunction, deregistration, seizure and destruction of the offending products, disgorgement of profits and, in cases of bad faith, treble damages and attorneys' fees.[15] Of these remedies, injunction is usually the most important in stopping the infringement or dilution, generally by way of a temporary restraining order, preliminary injunction, and/or trial on the merits. The TRO and preliminary injunction tests in most federal and state jurisdictions require the plaintiff to prove that "irreparable harm" will take place if the offending action is not enjoined prior to a trial on the merits. Therefore, counsel should be mindful of the need to move quickly, first with a cease and desist letter, closely followed by a filed action. Delay in taking action will only cut against the enterprise's chances to prove irreparable harm and need for preliminary relief, thus forcing the enterprise to endure a long and expensive trial.

2. Trade Secrets

The trade secret branch of intellectual property law is somewhat amorphous in that it is potentially applicable to a wide range of information, some patentable and some not. Unlike patents, the term of the legal protection for a trade secret is indefinite. And, the protection is effective for as long as the secret is properly protected or not otherwise independently discovered. Again, this contrasts to patent law, which trades protection for full public disclosure of the invention. Protecting a trade secret, however, requires that the enterprise to whom the secret belongs take reasonable steps to protect the dissemination of the information. This problem of shepherding the secret becomes much more difficult in the volatile, fast-paced, and idea-driven tech sector where employees jump from one business to another, and companies compete nose to nose with their competitors to get the latest innovation to market. While it is certainly possible in this environment to develop an effective trade secret program, it requires that the enterprise institute the proper procedures and be prepared to move quickly when the secret is threatened.

a. Trade Secrets Defined

The best place to start a trade secret analysis is with the Uniform Trade Secrets Act (UTSA), which has been adopted by approximately 45 states. The UTSA defines a "trade secret" as:

> information, including a formula, pattern, compilation, program device, method, technique, or process, that: (i) derives independent economic value, actual or potential, from not being generally known to, and not being readily ascertainable by proper means by, other persons who can obtain economic value from its disclosure or use, and (ii) is the subject of efforts that are reasonable under the circumstances to maintain its secrecy.[16]

Therefore, trade secret protection potentially applies to a wide range of technical information, including inventions and/or methods that may be eligible for patent protection, and other information such as research and development background materials (engineer notebooks, plans for failed designs) that would not. In addition, trade secret status can attach to confidential business and financial information that would not be subject to other intellectual property protection. What is important is (i) that the information derives economic value from being secret and (ii) that it is not known or readily ascertainable by others. Accordingly, to qualify, the secret cannot be information available in the public domain or subject to easy discovery. And, if a competitor is able to reverse-engineer the information, the protection may not be available, at least as against that party.

b. Establishing the Foundation for Trade Secret Protection

It is not easy to define "reasonable efforts to secure the information," which will be dependent in part on the type of business involved. The goal is to develop and enforce a policy that demonstrates that the company has taken affirmative steps to protect its trade secrets. A confidentiality policy involving some or all of the following should be considered:

(i) *Notice, guidelines, and nondisclosure agreements.* Employees, vendors, contractors and other people given access to the information should be put on notice that the information is confidential, be provided with confidentiality guidelines, and individually sign separately enforceable nondisclosure agreements.

(ii) *Noncompete agreements.* Noncompete agreements, or covenants not to compete, for key employees represent a roundabout way of establishing trade secret protection by preventing those with key trade secret knowledge from going to work for a direct competitor. However, governing state law usually requires noncompete agreements to be limited as to scope, duration, and, sometimes, geography.

(iii) *Confidentiality labeling and training.* Documents, files, and other information repositories should be marked as confidential. Security protocols should be set up for computer systems, including login

> **Practice Points**
> — Treat the information as a trade secret.
> — Adopt internal guidelines and employer agreements.
> — Control access to the trade secret.

screens and passwords. Management should require training to be followed up with reminders of security protocols.

(iv) *Limit access.* Access to confidential information should be limited to those who need it in the course of their work. File cabinets and other repositories should be locked or housed in a secure area. Also, a sign-in system can be established for files.

(v) *Control or prevent copying.* Scientists and engineers have a tendency to create their own personal files of documents, both hard copy and electronic. To avoid this, the company should establish rules limiting copies, perhaps by creating a numbered set to be assigned. Computer copies can be prevented by setting up specific project files containing "read only" documents.

(vi) *General security measures.* Other general security measures can help bolster the case for trade secrets, including employee badges and sign-in systems for visitors.

(vii) *Departing Employees.* When an employee is terminated or gives notice of leaving the company, access to materials containing trade secrets should be curtailed. Departing employees should be asked during exit interviews about whether they have retained any confidential materials.

c. Misappropriation

Once the above foundation is set up, legal protection comes into play when the enterprise's trade secret has been wrongfully disclosed or misappropriated. The UTSA defines "misappropriation" as:

(i) acquisition of a trade secret of another by a person who knows or has reason to know that the trade secret was acquired by improper means; or

(ii) disclosure or use of a trade secret of another by a person who (A) used improper means to acquire knowledge of the trade secret, without express or implied consent of the owner; or (B) at the time of disclosure or use knew or had reason to know that his knowledge of the trade secret was (I) derived from or through a person who has utilized improper means to acquire it; (II) acquired under circumstances giving rise to a duty to maintain its secrecy or limit its use; or (III) derived from or through a person who owed a duty to the person seeking relief to maintain its secrecy or limit its use; or (C) before a material change of his position, knew or had reason to know that it was a trade secret and that knowledge of it had been acquired by accident or mistake.[17]

In any given trade secret misappropriation, wrongful acquisition, disclosure, and/or use by "improper means"[18] usually occur together as part of the same act. Examples include:

(i) Theft and/or copying of trade secret documents from secured or storage locations.
(ii) Acquiring trade secrets from existing employees who are bound by nondisclosure agreements or otherwise have notice of the confidential nature of the material.
(iii) Hiring employees from a competitor in order to acquire the trade secrets.
(iv) Industrial espionage, such as improper surveillance.
(v) Accidental disclosure when the recipient is aware of the confidential nature of the information and that it had been transmitted or disclosed by mistake.

When misappropriation is discovered or suspected, the enterprise and its attorneys must move quickly to prevent the detrimental use or further disclosure of the information. In addition, since the most immediate relief will be injunction, expedient action will be consistent with the argument that a pre-trial injunction is necessary to prevent irreparable harm, thus satisfying one of the standards for a temporary restraining order or preliminary injunction. The UTSA provides for other relief, including damages and attorneys' fees. In addition, counsel may want to consider other state law remedies, such as unfair competition statutes and contractual actions against employees or contractors.[19]

d. Inevitable Disclosure Doctrine

An offshoot of trade secret law, the inevitable disclosure doctrine, applies when an employee who has knowledge of a trade secret is hired by a competitor to perform the same or similar job. In such a situation, the concern is that the employee will not be able to separate his general technical skill, training, and experience from his knowledge of the trade secret and, eventually, will disclose the secret in the course of his work for the new employer.[20]

Interest in the doctrine has increased substantially with the mobility of employees within the tech sector. The problem is somewhat straightforward when the employee has entered into a noncompete agreement with the first employer, which can be enforced as a contractual right by injunction prohibiting the second employment.[21] It becomes much more difficult, however, when there is no contractual relationship between the employee and the first employer regarding trade secrets. In such cases, the courts have tended to reject the application of the doctrine as imposing an unbargained-for obligation on the employee and because it is inconsistent with a general policy favoring mobility of employees.[22] At this point in time, the best recommendation to the enterprise is to require all employees who may have access to trade secrets to enter into nondisclosure agreements at the beginning of their employment. Where allowed by law, noncompete agreements can provide for additional security, assuming such agreements are narrowly tailored in order to be enforceable.

B. Products Liability

Products liability, with its potential for mass tort exposure, nationwide class actions, and multimillion-dollar verdicts, is the greatest bane of the biotech industry. In fact, the plaintiff-side legal practice in biotech products liability has become a multibillion-dollar industry all by itself. It is not an exaggeration to conclude that no other legal practice area occupies so much Internet bandwidth and does so much television advertising seeking clients, has a more sophisticated network of attorneys and experts, and has such a well-developed information-sharing system. Lots of different types of lawyers try cases; however, when politicians complain about "the trial lawyers," they are really referring to the plaintiff-side personal injury lawyers, including products liability lawyers.

This subject, obviously, is much too large and dangerous to deal with adequately in this book. A products liability threat to the new biotech enterprise must be taken very seriously, including the retention of experienced defense counsel. However, there are a few basics that the business lawyer should be aware of in order to help manage his client's risks.

1. Defects and Causation

Products liability generally is a creature of state common law, although there are federal statutes relating to sufficient disclosure and other safety concerns. Products liability can reach any party in the chain, from manufacturer to final retail seller, but manufacturers, including the innovating company, are the primary targets. A products liability action may be based on negligence, breach of expressed warranty, or strict liability. Over time, the historic differences between these doctrines have tended to blur. As a result, the key questions in virtually any products liability analysis are: (1) whether the product is defective in that it is unreasonably dangerous for its intended use, and (2) whether the plaintiff's injuries were caused by the product. Defects generally fall into the categories of design defects, manufacturing defects, and marketing defects. The scope of potential damages includes compensatory damages and punitive damages.[23] The later is particularly troubling, as plaintiff's lawyers plead with juries to "send a message."

2. Establish a Record of Compliance and Responsibility

Despite the fact that products liability is the realm of the litigators, at least at the preventive level there is a role for the business attorney or general counsel in watching over his client to help avoid or mitigate potential products liability claims.

- At all points in the company's history, particularly during the testing and trial phase of the biotech product, make sure the company is carefully complying with all agency protocols, regulations, and information reporting and sharing requirements. Compliance and agency approval will not bar a subsequent products liability claim, but they can affect the weight of the claim and the scope of damages. On the other hand, evidence that the company took shortcuts, hid information, or lied to the agency will be the kiss of death in front of the jury.

Litigation Issues

- Carefully and conservatively construct all warranties, disclaimers, and public warnings in a manner to comply with law and agency regulations, and be truthful in their content.
- Assist your client in creating a document retention policy that complies with all agency requirements and centralizes document control.
- Encourage the company to hold training seminars for employees regarding proper business use of voicemail, instant messaging, and e-mail, and proper disposal of internally created documents. Sensitive issues, accusations, rash comments, and loose talk should not occur in these media.
- When the product has reached the marketplace, make sure your client keeps adequate records of consumer problems, complies with agency reporting regulations, and follows up on complaints as appropriate.
- Encourage your client to make use of the attorney-client communications privilege and the work-product doctrine. Proper use of these tools can go far to control dissemination of information and give a proper seriousness to discussion of potential liability. These devices cannot be used in a wholesale manner. Instead, they must be used judiciously and only when discussing matters relating to potential liability. This may include identifying a portion of a general business meeting or board meeting as privileged and ensure that no or few minutes or notes were taken and that participants do not leave the meeting with handouts. Take extra care when filing privileged documents. Remember that even classifying a discussion or a document as privileged does not mean that it is impervious to discovery. Also, these protections do not apply to facts and data. The attorney-client privilege can be pierced if it is shown that there is a likelihood that the issues discussed amounted to civil fraud or criminal activities.[24]

C. Business Liability

The previous sections of this chapter have set out specific areas of law that are important to the biotech enterprise, but that may not be part of the business lawyer's portfolio of experience and skill. Laws that give rise to business litigation are, however, the business lawyer's realm. This section is intended to provide a checklist of sorts briefly highlighting specific types of business litigation (not including the more mundane commercial litigation that all businesses must cope with) that are particularly pertinent to the new enterprise.

1. Corporate Disclosures and Insider Trading

Next to, or perhaps equal with, the products liability class action, the most devastating type of litigation the new enterprise can face is the securities class action. With corporate poster children such as Enron, Tyco, and Worldcom, securities law violations have taken on an entirely new seriousness. In addition, Sarbanes-Oxley and other congressional and SEC actions have raised the bar of what is required for minimal disclosure. Therefore, the business lawyer representing the new enterprise must be especially watchful, particularly as the new enterprise goes public.

a. *Misstatements and Omissions*

Perhaps the most common basis for a securities class action against a public company is Section 10(b) of the Securities Exchange Act of 1934 and the corresponding regulation, Rule 10b-5. A typical 10b-5 class action is based on claims by one or more purchasers of the stock, as representatives for all purchasers within the class, that the company intentionally or recklessly was responsible for a misstatement or omission of a material fact that impacted the price of the shares. Materiality, in this context, is a subjective question of fact relating to whether a reasonable purchaser would rely on the misstatement or omission in making a decision whether to purchase the stock. Rule 10b-5 cases tend to be based on a combination of official corporate documents, press releases, executive speeches, and reports to analysts, often followed by restatements of accounting reports that result in a price decrease for the stock. These cases sometimes are brought parallel to or including claims of insider trading on nonpublic information, as explained below.

When representing a new public company, the business lawyer can best serve his client by:

- Working with the enterprise to ensure that the prospectus, periodic filings, and other official corporate documents are well supported by fact and do not contain overenthusiastic projections about the company's financial or strategic prospects.
- Counseling company executives regarding the content of their speeches and other messages where they attempt to create interest in the company.
- Helping to establish internal controls with respect to public relations, investor relations, and accounting reports.
- Helping the company to plan ahead to adequately prepare future corporate disclosures.

b. Insider Trading

Another common source of securities litigation is insider trading under Section 16 of the Securities Exchange Act of 1934, and often in conjunction with Rule 10b-5. Insiders are those executives, directors, and others who have access to material information about the company that is not available to the public at large. Section 16 requires that insiders who possess 10% or more of the company's stock are required to report publicly any sale of stock. Even so, company executives and outsiders who possess insider information, usually about an upcoming event or announcement that will likely cause the stock to decline, are prohibited from trading on that information. In addition to class-action damages, penalties can include fines, disgorgement, and criminal sentences.

2. Corporate Governance

In response to corporate dishonesty and excesses, Congress passed the U.S. Public Company Accounting Reform and Investor Protection Act of 2002, also known as the Sarbanes-Oxley Act. Sarbanes-Oxley established new standards for corporate responsibility that sent a cold shiver through corporate America. This applies only to publicly reporting companies, in general, but it has set the standard for corporate practice, with its influence perhaps reaching also to larger, more broadly held "private" companies. As a result, business counsel for the biotech enterprise should educate herself on the act's requirements because the company will be looking to its counsel to help it chart a course of compliance.

Sarbanes-Oxley amends the Securities Act of 1934 to, among other things, require that:

- The CEO, CFO, and the company accounting firm certify the accuracy of financial statements in all periodic corporate reports, and it also establishes criminal penalties if those statements are inaccurate. In addition, all material information used in creating those reports and statements must be retained for five years and made available to the public in some instances upon request.
- Management establishes and takes responsibility for internal controls governing financial statements.
- The company reports material events.

3. False Claims and Whistleblowers

Congress passed the False Claims Act[25] in 1863 to prohibit fraudulent or dishonest business dealings with the U.S. government during the Civil War and to punish those who engaged in such activities. During modern history, the False Claims Act has been used to prosecute U.S. corporations for a variety of fraudulent dealings with the federal government. Under the authority of the act, private parties may sue individuals or corporations for such fraudulent behavior in what has become known as qui tam lawsuits. If successful, the court may order the defendant to pay treble damages based on the government's losses as a result of the fraudulent dealings, as well as additional fines. In addition, the act requires that the private parties who brought the suit be paid a "bounty" of up to 30 percent of the amount recovered by the government.

Recently, the False Claims Act has been asserted against a number of biotech companies, such as TAP Pharmaceuticals, Inc. in Boston, for Medicare/Medicaid drug fraud. The TAP case involved alleged illegal kickbacks to doctors who prescribed the companies' products and resulted in a settlement by TAP of $875 million.

The False Claims Act also provides protection for employees who bring, or participate in, qui tam lawsuits against their employers.[26] Sarbanes-Oxley has further strengthened the whistleblower protections. The treatment by the National Labor Relations Board and courts of these provisions are still in flux, but the statute imposes a high burden on a company that wants to terminate a whistleblower, even for unrelated causes. In addition, a number of states have their own versions of whistleblower laws.

4. Average Wholesale Price Drug Litigation

Another area of concern for biotech companies has to do with the class actions that have been filed against pharmaceutical companies Abbott Laboratories, Baxter, Glaxo, SmithKline, and Bristol. The plaintiffs claim that these companies established a cartel to inflate the average wholesale price for prescription drugs paid for by Medicaid and for which the companies are reimbursed. The case has been consolidated in Massachusetts federal court and is proceeding toward trial.

D. Document and Information Retention[27]

Document control, sharing, and preservation requirements of Sarbanes-Oxley, FDA regulations, and the Health Insurance Portability and Accountability Act of 1996 (HIPAA), as well as concerns about discovery in potential products liability lawsuits and securities actions, are very important issues for the new biotech enterprise. There are two problems, however, that further complicate any organized attempt at document retention. First, corporate document retention is not about saving every file, e-mail, or scrap of paper. Instead, effective retention requires a plan or strategy to determine what information to save and what to discard and the discipline to follow the plan. Second, for any new business that has been started in the last 10 years, it is likely that the vast majority of its records are stored in electronic, not hard copy, form. As discussed below, electronic recordkeeping presents it own document control problems.

American corporations are awash in electronic information. It is smeared across technology systems. Data resides in servers, laptop computers, handheld devices, old backup tapes, CD-ROM disks, thumb drives, and now, even cellular phones and pagers. Managing this morass of information is one of the most serious problems facing business today. Companies, large and small, often don't appreciate the ramifications until it is too late and they are already at risk of serious legal liability. At that point, trying to fix the problem can be dearly expensive and is often unsuccessful.

During the seemingly ancient days before computers and networks became the predominant business paradigm, most data was kept in the form of laboriously typed paper documents that were neatly filed and, at the end of their lifecycle, either thrown in the trash or sent to document storage facilities. Paper document preparation and storage were both burdensome and expensive. There was a natural limitation on the volume of documents produced and subsequently preserved. Computers and electronic data storage have changed all of that. Electronic document generation and storage is simple and cheap. The digital equivalent of a warehouse full of paper documents can now be stored in a small server no bigger then the average computer. As a result, rather than cull old files before storage, it is much quicker, easier, and cheaper just to save everything and buy extra storage disks. Effective data management requires thoughtful procedures governing what data to keep, what data to discard (we never say "destroy"), and how to control what's left.

1. Regulatory Record-Keeping Requirements

First, there is a growing collection of federal and state laws, as well as international rules, that require companies to preserve specific data for prescribed periods of time. In addition to Sarbanes-Oxley, HIPAA, the Internal Revenue Code, and the European Union Directives establish stringent policies governing the collection, storage, and use of personal information that will apply to any foray into international commerce. The FTC is following suit with its own studies and guidelines. Failure to abide by these regulations can subject companies to fines, penalties, and the forfeiture of the privilege of doing business in the respective jurisdictions. And the federal courts are now imposing strict penalties for spoliation of evidence.

2. Litigation Discovery Issues

If a business saves all of its electronic data, whether required to or not, litigation opening that data up to review can result in the company literally drowning in its digital waste. Electronic discovery can be debilitatingly expensive and may turn up difficult-to-explain documents or e-mails that the company had no obligation to save prior to the litigation. In addition, documents can be lost in all the volume, and heaven help you (because the court will not) if something is not disclosed in discovery that later turns up at trial. Once litigation is foreseeable, disposing of potentially relevant data can result in court-ordered sanctions or even a default judgment.

There are many examples where the failure to properly save or properly dispose of electronic data either saved the ship or sank it. Arthur Anderson and Enron went down, at least in part, because they illegally attempted to destroy documents after litigation was on the horizon. Likewise, we can't forget the litigation and the investment management firm stockbroker e-mails in which brokers trashed the very stocks they were trying to sell to the public.

3. Data Management Policy

With thought and planning, businesses can create electronic data life-cycle policies that will eliminate potential liability associated with either saving too much or too little of the company's data, or, more important, of losing control of what is there. An electronic data management policy can be built around several basic principles.

(i) *Identify the objectives of the enterprise.* First, it is critical that the company self-consciously devise "objectives" in maintaining its electronic records. This function has become more important, as it is easier to treat all records the same—just save everything, and let everything go unprotected on the "network." But depending on the business, different types of records have vastly different degrees of importance. Universities treat their academic records as sacrosanct, whereas payments for lawn care might be much lower on the scale. Companies hired to keep track of individuals crossing national borders might have strict record-keeping priorities and objectives for certain databases, but not others, such as their own committee meet-

> **Practice Points**
>
> A successful data management policy must be:
> — Simple
> — Focused
> — Enforced

ings. Health and insurance records are treated one way, and payment for staples and copy services another. Information categories are not the same. Importance and function vary by orders of magnitude in any enterprise. Accordingly, the first job is to prioritize. What is critical for the business? Devise information life-cycle management with such critical records in mind.

(ii) *Minimalism.* Next, data should be discarded unless there is a good business and/or legal reason to retain it. Implementation of this principle requires that a company, once again, take a hard look both at the types of data it collects and the regulatory constraints relating to that data. Data should also be preserved if it is potentially relevant to any ongoing or foreseeable litigation, now known as the *Zubulake* standard. The overall goal is to comply with law and to achieve business objectives, but not to save data that is not required by law or for business purposes. Given the fact the digital files can be copied *ad infinitum* onto different media, unless company controls access to data during the time it is stored by a business, it loses control over the ability to discard information. Maintaining such control is no easy task. Achieving it puts the company on the cutting edge of business process.

(iii) *Training and simplicity of procedure.* Of course, a data retention policy must be simple and easy to implement. As with all things corporate, there is a strong tendency for policy initiatives to become increasingly intricate to the point of dysfunction (only interpretable by those with graduate degrees in operations research). Once a policy becomes too complex, it is virtually guaranteed that employees will ignore it. For example, during the beginning of the Internet boom, the National Security Agency created complex internal rules for the transfer of sensitive data from one NSA employee to another. Rather than comply with the rules governing NSA's secured systems, employees discovered it was easier to simply send data to each other, around the NSA systems and through Internet as e-mail, thus defeating the policy. Therefore, any policy should strive for simplicity by establishing a limited number of broad subject matter categories and functions. While simplicity might result in some overinclusion of data retained, it nevertheless increases the odds that employees will actually comply with the policy.

(iv) *Adequacy of infrastructure.* There must be adequate hardware and software to accomplish the task, once objectives and policy are identified. It is, indeed, often astounding how "out of scale" a company's infrastructure is to accomplish appropriate data management. Here, as elsewhere, teamwork between higher management and IT workers is critical. Hardware is seldom the problem. The problem is the software and human systems infrastructure relating to information security, including access control, authenticity, retrievability, and auditability.

(v) *Information security.* Perhaps no practice can enhance data management better than appropriate "information security" procedures. Given that a theft incident may now trigger notice obligations, and perhaps liability, information security reigns supreme. It is fundamental to protecting the assets of the enterprise.

(vi) *Record authenticity.* Give thought to how one might prove the authenticity of one's own records if they are ever challenged in court, an administrative proceeding, or an audit. This implicates the need for proactive procedures. Authenticity, which has been stretched to the breaking point by the new information paradigm, should no longer be taken for granted.

(vii) *Retrievability.* One of the major problems with electronic record keeping is that when a request for information does come, for example, in discovery for litigation, it can be a six- to seven-figure chore just finding the data that formerly could be retrieved easily from a set of file cabinets. Accordingly, far more advance planning is now required to ensure that data can be retrieved. Businesses, therefore, must attack a mounting data retrieval issue. Just complying with one discovery request, when one has data stored hodgepodge on various media in various types of systems, could pay for an entirely new infrastructure. Don't be penny-wise and pound foolish.

(viii) *Distribution controls.* The interactive ease of networks, including the Internet, means that once access to specific data is acquired, the data can be transmitted to countless destinations around the globe in a matter of seconds. Once the digital genie is out of the electronic bottle, no amount of wishing can contain it. Every day there are new examples of this phenomenon. It can involve the public release of valuable intellectual property, such as the case of the Swedish man who released highly confidential DVD source code onto the Internet. At least when it comes to business data, unauthorized access can be reduced by employing network security controls. A different problem, however, arises in controlling the distribution of data by persons who have legitimate access to it. Whether the situation involves complex project files shared by a team of engineers or a simple e-mail communication, uncontrolled electronic replication can be a disaster. One answer is to employ one of the available software solutions that encrypt the data and allow the sender to specify the degree of republication rights granted to the recipient. Another important control is to ensure that when you notify any employee of impending termination, you have already restricted his or her access to critical information. Sophisticated companies are beginning to utilize these types of solutions as part of their overall data management strategy.

(ix) *Auditability.* With the new Sarbanes-Oxley accounting and auditing requirements, management of information will need to pass the various types of tests auditors will devise. Unless the data management system can pass an audit, a company is put in an unfortunate situation of potential violation. Any problem in internal controls potentially can result in a reserved accounting opinion, which can have a chilling effect on market trade of the company's stock. Accordingly, a sound data retention policy is at the same time a Sarbanes-Oxley compliance program. Along these lines, all companies should seriously consider using digital tools, such as digital signatures and network histories, to establish an auditable trail or chain of custody.

(x) *Consistency.* Data retention practices must be consistent. Inconsistent document retention actions will create a taint of intentional spoliation and wrongdoing. It's hard to explain why a company discarded data pursuant to your three-year-old policy for the first time just three days before being served with that antitrust complaint.

Therefore, the data retention policy must be implemented consistently. If there are dates or milestones for data review and disposal, they should be adhered to. Discipline is critical.

(xi) *Enforcement.* Enforcement must be simple and consistent. The policy should use both automated systems to dispose of unnecessary data and procedures to motivate employees to deal appropriately with the rest of the data that cannot be picked up through automated systems. So, for example, unnecessary e-mail accumulation can be limited either by strictly controlling the size of employee mailboxes, thus forcing employees to delete old e-mails in order to receive new ones, or by automated systems that automatically dispose of old e-mails after a set period of time (i.e., 30 days). Backup tapes also can present a glitch in a data retention policy. Backup tapes are intended primarily for one purpose: the emergency restoration of a computer system following a crash. Unfortunately, many businesses make the mistake of saving multiple sets of backup tapes as data archives. This action alone can create a nightmare of enormous litigation discovery costs if it is ever necessary to search those tapes. Therefore, a company should limit itself to no more than two sets of backup tapes, which are consistently recycled at particular intervals to capture the existing computer system. This procedure will make it unlikely that the backup tapes will ever be successfully demanded as a source of old and otherwise disposed-of data.

Information management is a dynamic concept that will need to change as data, software, and hardware co-evolve to create more complex computer ecosystems with greater capabilities. Therefore, establishing data life-cycle management policies is not a one-time process. The advent of electronic data storage and digital communications has provided business, consumers, and the public with untold benefits, including access to vast amounts of information and incredible speed in analysis and distribution. Implementing and maintaining a data life-cycle management system is a small but necessary price to pay for continuing to be a player in the marketplace.

E. Alternative Dispute Resolution

Alternative dispute resolution (ADR) is the single best litigation management tool available to businesses.[28] This tool can both reduce the costs and business disruption caused by prolonged litigation and result in many early settlements substantially lower than would have been predicted under a more typical single-track litigation scenario. Even so, many lawyers who are unfamiliar with these techniques reject ADR offhand as somehow a waste of time or a bad idea.

The reality is that most commercial litigation is simply a cost of doing business. Like any business cost, the goal is to reduce that cost to an optimum level that achieves the business strategy without negatively implicating the company's health. Recently, a number of previously "scorch the earth" corporations, such as Microsoft, have dramatically shifted their focus to ADR as a way to optimize litigation costs.

1. ADR Defined

Most typically, ADR involves enlisting a neutral third party to help resolve the dispute through a narrowly tailored private (arbitration) or through somewhat structured negotiations facilitated by an expert mediator (mediation).

a. Arbitration

ADR is really a group of techniques, all designed to assist warring parties in expediently and efficiently bringing disputes to an end. The leading ADR organizations, The CPR International Institute for Conflict Resolution (CPR) and the American Arbitration Association, host Web sites that contain a wealth of information regarding ADR technique, rules, and neutrals.[29] Arbitration can be described best as a private mini-trial before a trained neutral who acts as a judge, reviews evidence, hears testimony, and makes a decision concerning who, if anyone, is at fault and the dollars, if any, one party may owe to the other for the damages. The key to arbitration is that the parties, not the courts, determine the scope and focus of the arbitration and what is to be decided. By agreement between the parties, the process can be tailored to best fit their needs and goals. If the parties can agree to narrow the arbitration's scope, as well as to limit the amount of discovery that has to be done before presenting the case to the arbitrator, an arbitration can be substantially cheaper than a trial to the court by 25-50 percent. And arbitration can lead to a much quicker resolution of dispute, allowing the parties to put the matter behind them and focus on their core business objectives.

b. Mediation

Mediation is an entirely different process in which the parties retain a third-party neutral whose job is to look for ways to move the parties toward an amicable settlement. A successful mediator brings to the table a variety of psychological, business, and legal skills. The mediator's chief goal is to get the parties off their crystallized legal positions. In attempting to achieve settlement, the mediator will work to soften the individual parties' resolution by focusing on the weaknesses in their positions and the risks they may face by going to trial. Good mediators also employ creativity in looking for common interests between the parties that can displace the dispute, such as ongoing or future business relationships. Countless mediations have not only saved a strained business relationship between, say, a manufacturer and a supplier, but actually resulted in shared commitments to expand the volume of business conducted by the parties. However, mediation, including agreeing to the result, is voluntary, so it is possible to spend the time and incur the cost for the process with no final result.

2. ADR Myths and Misconceptions

Despite the fact that ADR has been used for years in a variety of contexts, there are a number of negative but unfounded perceptions about ADR that continue to persist.

a. A Sign of Weakness

One of the most common misconceptions is that the mere suggestion of ADR will be viewed as a sign of weakness and lack of resolve. On the contrary, sophisticated litigants are well aware of the costs, uncertainties, and risks of going to trial and generally see the advantage of entering into some form of ADR in order to achieve finality and stop the bleeding. It all comes down to understanding the parties' motivations. In most litigation between businesses, what the parties really want is to get the dispute finished (granted, on their own terms) and move on to pursuing their core business goals. In such disputes, ADR is a way to short-circuit the expensive and prolonged litigation process. Even in litigation brought by the individual person, the burdens of the case will eventually make ADR attractive. Whether the plaintiff has claimed a personal injury or the loss of an economic interest, the litigation-dollar burn rate will cause either the plaintiff (if paying attorneys' fees) or the attorney (if operating on a contingency) to desire a quicker, even if compromised, resolution. The strategy for the in-house attorney is to determine when it is most advantageous to suggest ADR.

b. Free Discovery

Another often-heard concern is that ADR will provide the opposing side with "free discovery." Since all forms of ADR require, to a greater or lesser extent, that the parties enter the process ready to persuade each other and the neutral of the strength of their individual cases, the parties must present, perhaps in an abbreviated form, their strongest arguments and evidence. However, under modern discovery rules, which require virtually complete disclosure of all evidence and legal arguments prior to trial, the days of litigation by ambush are over. Therefore, any minor loss of the element of surprise is largely outweighed by the potential for a cost-effective and early resolution. In fact, in most cases ADR will provide limited discovery opportunities and no information that would not otherwise be disclosed in traditional trial discovery.

3. An Integrated Strategy for ADR

Incorporating ADR as a systemic part of in-house representation can give the in-house lawyer much better control over her litigation portfolio and provide a definite strategic advantage.

a. Before the Dispute Arises

One of the first places to establish this advantage is in the corporation's transactional documents.[30] The inclusion of ADR clauses within those documents establishes a process should a dispute arise and avoids needing to persuade an opposing party to try the ADR route after tempers have already flared.

For example, the Army Corps of Engineers had great success in limiting litigation through a more complex variation of this strategy. The Corps used to assume that about 80 percent of its projects would result in some kind of post-construction litigation. In response to that enormous cost of doing business, the Corps came up with a partnering strategy that established milestones in its projects. The parties were required to identify and resolve through ADR any disputes that had arisen during each of the identified periods rather than fight it out at the end. As a result, the Corps estimates that its litigation has decreased to about 25 percent of its projects. This same process was used successfully in resolving construction disputes arising out of the "Big Dig" Boston underground transportation project.

> **Practice Points**
>
> Counsel should consider future use of ADR:
> — At the transaction stage
> — At the beginning of any dispute

For each type of transactional document, business counsel must understand fully the relationships that are being created and what is best for the company if a dispute arises. For example, in the case of a crucial supplier, the transactional obligations might require that disputes are submitted to ADR without disrupting the flow of necessary materials. Other types of transactions will require different formulations of the ADR requirement. Keep in mind which variation on this theme leaves your client with the most leverage. In customer agreements, the company might prefer to require a short mediation period before litigation so that if the problem is not resolved, the company can escalate its response quickly.

b. *In the Early Stages of the Dispute*

While there may be a perception that ADR usually comes into play after litigation is significantly developed and mature, the reality is that it may have its greatest potential impact during the infancy of the dispute. Once the litigation gauntlet has been thrown, there tends to be a psychological shift away from meaningful resolution and toward retribution and vindication. The Annenberg Institute has conducted extensive research into this phenomenon and has concluded that the longer a complaint or injury goes without resolution, the more crystallized the parties become in their litigation positions and the less likely they are to compromise and amicably resolve the dispute.[31] Therefore, counsel should evaluate each new dispute or potential dispute with an eye toward the possibility of getting the parties together for an early attempt at resolution before the relationships are irrevocably broken and the battle lines have been completely drawn.

c. Parallel Strategies

When litigation is unavoidable, ADR techniques give the litigation manager a powerful set of strategic tools to guide litigation to the optimal result. For each new matter, counsel should established parallel litigation/ADR strategies. The first strategy will usually involve a very aggressive litigation plan with every intention of driving the case through trial. The second strategy focuses on identifying the particular points in the case where the company's leverage might be greatest and present the optimal opportunity to move to ADR. This upfront planning can give counsel the ability to stay out ahead of opponents and to drive the litigation, even from a defendant's position.

d. Private Forums and Confidentiality

ADR also provides the company with a host of forums other than the traditional public courtroom. As a result, if a matter is particularly sensitive or involves confidential information, the parties may decide that it is best dealt with in a private proceeding. For example, ADR can be used to avoid taking the risk that a particular dispute, if handled through the public courts, might confuse or disrupt a related high-profile case, or create the potential for copycat cases. This element of confidentiality also can be of great advantage in an intellectual property dispute, whether it involves trade secrets or the legal validity of a patent that is crucial to a broader licensing program.

4. A Special Case for Patent Litigation[32]

The most difficult barrier to achieving resolution of a patent dispute in ADR is failing to understand the full financial complexity and competitive ramifications of a patent settlement or arbitration judgment. Most commercial litigation is resolved through the payment of a sum certain that is then incorporated into the balance sheets of the disputing companies and forgotten. It is more difficult, however, to quantify the value of a patent and its impact on future competition. That is, patent settlements and judgments often take the form of royalty fee per each use of the intellectual property. Past infringing use of intellectual property can be calculated with some degree of accuracy based on the number of units manufactured or sold. The uncertainty lies in attempting to estimate the number of times the intellectual property will be used in the future, that is, a thousand product units or a million product units. In addition, the risk for the settling party having to pay the royalty may be whether its future use of the intellectual property will be in a low-priced product or a small part of a high-priced product. A fee per use royalty may cause a future low-price product to be too expensive to manufacture and sell. For example, the same semiconductor chip set or computer interface might be used in a low-end computer peripheral or in a high-end computer system. Likewise, ADR settlements may prove to be inaccurate in cases of changing technology and markets, because what appeared to be very valuable turned out to have no future value to the business. For example, at one time hard-modem telephone intellectual property was extremely valuable. Now, however, with the advent of much more powerful computer microprocessors capable of performing "soft modem" tasks, hard-modem intellectual property may be of little or no value. In fact, since the parties can choose an expert or even a team of experts to handle the ADR, it is logical that the arbitrator or mediator is more likely to judge the respective positions and

> **Practice Points**
>
> Successful patent mediation requires:
> — Realistic estimate of value of the patent to the company
> — Early participation in the dispute process and agreement with valuation

values more accurately and arrive at a fair decision. Especially in biotechnology, it is difficult to explain complicated patent claims and genetic variations to a jury of people with little or no scientific background.

a. Participation by Senior Management

The financial complexities are not an insurmountable barrier to resolution of such disputes. What is important is that counsel and senior management understand these complexities and integrate the corporate strategy people into the early stages of a patent dispute and resolution. To put it another way, the purchase or sale of a patent license, even as a result of ADR, is not totally dissimilar from the sale or acquisition of another business. Therefore, it is only natural that the strategy experts should be engaged to help quantify and bless any such decision. With this kind of upfront preparation, ADR can be successful in dramatically reducing the transactional costs associated with patent dispute, as well as often leading to a more reasonable result between the parties. It is not unusual for patent mediations to result in settlement equal to 3 percent to 10 percent of the litigation demand. In this sense, patent litigation is like any other in that the damage claims become softer as they move toward the higher ranges. And, given the defendant's risk of losing patents, with the exception of the "lone inventors" who all believe they are the next Lemelson, most plaintiffs understand that one dollar today is better than the hope of two dollars tomorrow.

b. Advantages of ADR Confidentiality

It is important to remember that most patent cases do not stand alone. Instead, they are often part of ongoing licensing programs through which an inventor is systematically attempting to negotiate licenses with all of the manufacturers and users of the invention in a particular industry segment—for example, all semiconductor manufacturers who use the same piece of equipment or make the same type of microchip. Successful licensing programs are built upon a series of licensing negotiations enforced by the threat of litigation. However, patent litigation also creates risk to the plaintiff who, in order to bring a suit, must put its IP on the line. That is, litigation of patent disputes is not a zero-sum game that results in the plaintiff either getting a huge judgment or nothing. On the contrary, defendants will typically challenge the validity of the plaintiff's patents. If the patents are proven to be invalid to that defendant, they are invalid to the rest of the world, which means the end of the licensing program. Given these dangers, the plaintiff in a patent dispute often benefits from arguing for a risky patent in a private arbitration where the result will be confidential, will not have binding precedential effect, and, by agreement, the decision of the arbitrator will be limited to a simple statement of win or lose without substantive explanation.

c. ADR as an Alternative to Foreign Litigation

Finally, because of the global reach and applicability of intellectual property, there is a well-founded concern about whether governments and courts in some parts of the world have the ability or motivation to protect the intellectual property rights of non-citizen corporations. Even if there is a legal system to protect intellectual property rights, the prolonged time to trial and judgment in many countries may not address the infringement until well after the competitive damage is done or the infringer has become judgment-proof. In fact, such concerns about China and several other Asian nations in some cases are deterrents to foreign investment in those growth economies. Here again, the use of ADR might provide parties with more assurance of a fair evaluation and decision. One way to address these concerns proactively is by including mandatory ADR clauses in foundry agreements (where the inventor contracts with the manufacturer to produce the goods that will be branded and sold by the inventor). Therefore, if the foreign manufacturer uses the inventor's intellectual property for its own purposes, the infringement can be addressed in private arbitration rather than in the foreign courts. In addition, assuming the adequacy of personal jurisdiction over the manufacturer under the contract, this method creates an additional contract cause of action against the manufacturer in the United States, even though the actual infringement may fall outside of the jurisdiction of U.S. courts. Where there is no privity of contract between the inventor and the infringer, the trick is developing the

> **Practice Points**
>
> In international transactions, using ADR can avoid the delay and uncertainty of submitting a dispute to foreign courts.

leverage to motivate the infringer into arbitration. In either of the scenarios above, the ultimate issue will be ensuring that the arbitration judgment will be enforceable either in the foreign jurisdiction or in the United States. One word of warning, however: ADR results are not honored in every country, so it is critical to ensure that an ADR result, or even a clause in a contract requiring ADR, is likely to be enforced in the countries where the other party operates. With strategic planning, ADR presents the potential to sidestep the uncertainty of foreign courts and to enforce and protect intellectual property rights.

5. ADR Guidelines

Based on the above discussion, there are a few guidelines we can offer for using ADR effectively to reduce patent litigation costs and risks:

- At the inception of business relationships, try to lock ADR requirements into contracts with business partners who are in a position potentially to infringe your intellectual property.
- Every patent has two major components: liability and damages. Throughout the dispute process, give at least as much attention to the analysis of potential damages and business impact as you do to liability. The reality is that the liability issues are more subjective, and the technical part of the team can argue about them all day. Damages, however, are what really count and are much more suitable for early evaluation and handicapping. Understanding the damages exposure will better enable you to weigh the alternatives and the potential use of ADR.
- At first notice of the dispute, before litigation has commenced, take a hard look at exposure, impact, and costs, and consider the potential for an early mediation. The dispute research indicates that the longer a dispute goes on, the more the parties' positions crystallize, and the more the damage claims escalate. Too often, counsel and clients do not take these initial notices seriously and miss the opportunity to resolve a dispute for a small fraction of what the claim will grow into by trial.
- Once litigation commences, it is important to develop parallel strategies. That is, treat every litigation as if you fully intend to go through

trial. At the same time, it is important to step back and determine how you can direct and leverage the case into ADR.
- If the opposing side agrees to arbitration, take the time to create an agreement that limits the arbitration to the issues that actually need to be decided, limits discovery to what is necessary to try those issues, and carefully prescribes the arbitrator's authority and form of decision.
- If the parties agree to mediation, carefully select a negotiations team that has the expertise and authority necessary to resolve the case. Be ready to make a thoughtful and well-organized opening presentation with your best legal, technical, and business arguments. Although some neutrals will disagree about the value of opening presentations, the importance of such presentations is that often this is the first time the opposing party has heard the opposing position other than through the filter of its own counsel. Then, at the right time, be ready to put the technical liability arguments to the side in order to come to a business resolution. Focus on resolution, not on who's right.
- Just because litigation has commenced does not mean that the parties cannot move the case to arbitration. Once the litigation issues have taken form, the parties may begin to see the risks of trial (i.e., loss of patents versus high damages award) and the advantages of a more limited private forum. Knowing this, focus your litigation strategy on heightening your opponent's risk and leverage your opponent into arbitration.
- Finally, some parties, after spending millions of dollars on litigation costs, will then try to save a few bucks and choose their neutrals by price. This approach is foolish. The neutral fees will be insignificant compared to the litigation costs. Get the neutral who can best do the job.

Notes

1. For a less erudite discussion of patent litigation, *see* Robert F. Copple, *Behind the Magic Curtain*, CORPORATE COUNSEL 73 (May 2005).

2. For the most authoritative multivolume treatise on trademark law, *see* JEROME GILSON, TRADEMARK PROTECTION AND PRACTICE. There are also a host of

informative Web sites that provide the practitioner with an immediate source. *See, e.g.,* http://cyber.law.harvard.edu/metaschool/fisher/domain/tm.htm.

    3. 15 U.S.C. §§ 1051-1127.

    4. The USTPO Trademark Web site provides a wealth of information on trademark registration. *See* http://www.uspto.gov/main/trademarks.htm.

    5. *Id.* at §§ 1058-59.

    6. http://www.uspto.gov/web/offices/tac/tmfaq.htm#DefineTrademark.

    7. Polaroid Corp. v. Polared Electronics Corp., 287 F.2d 492, 495 (2d Cir. 1961).

    8. 15 U.S.C. § 1125(c)(1) sets out an eight-part test to determine whether a trademark is "famous."

    9. Toys R Us v. Akkaoui, 40 U.S.P.Q.2d 1836 (N.D. Cal. 1996).

    10. Moseley v. V. Secret Catalog, Inc., 537 U.S. 418 (2003).

    11. *See* Zatarain's, Inc. v. Oak Grove Smokehouse, Inc., 698 F.2d 786 (5th Cir. 1983).

    12. *See* L.L. Bean, Inc. v. Drake Publishers, Inc., 811 F.2d 26, 28 (1st Cir. 1987).

    13. 15 U.S.C. § 1051(1)(b)-(c).

    14. 15 U.S.C. § 11125(d)(1)(A).

    15. 15 U.S.C. §§ 1116-1125.

    16. Uniform Trade Secrets Act § 1(4).

    17. Uniform Trade Secrets Act § 1(2).

    18. Uniform Trade Secrets Act § 1(1) defines "improper means" as "theft, bribery, misrepresentation, breach or inducement of a breach of duty to maintain secrecy, or espionage through electronic or other means."

    19. Depending on the version of the UTSA adopted in the particular state, the act may or may not limit additional claims based on unfair competition statutes.

    20. PepsiCo Inc. v. Redmond, 54 F.3d 1262, 1269 (7th Cir. 1995) is considered the leading case on the inevitable disclosure doctrine.

    21. *See* Branson Ultrasonics v. Stratman, 921 F. Supp. 909 (D. Conn. 1996).

    22. *See* EarthWeb, Inc. v. Schlack, 71 F. Supp. 299, 310 (S.D.N.Y. 1999); Whyte v. Schlage Lock Co., 125 Cal. Rptr. 2d 272 (Ct. App. 2002).

    23. Sources of information on products liability law are far too numerous to begin to name. Even so, the products liability bible continues to be the American Law Institute's *Restatement of Law Third, Torts: Products*.

    24. For a very thorough resource on the attorney-client privilege and the work-product doctrine, *see* EDNA SELAN EPSTEIN, ATTORNEY-CLIENT PRIVILEGE AND THE WORK PRODUCT DOCTRINE (4th ed. 2001).

    25. 31 U.S.C. § 3729, *et seq.*

    26. *Id.* at § 3730(h).

27. Portions of this section were previously published in George L. Paul & Robert F. Copple, *Dealing With Data: No you can't call them documents anymore*, BUS. LAW TODAY 1 (March/April 2005). *See* Robert F. Copple, *Firms Must Pick Which Data to Save,* ARIZONA REPUBLIC (Sept. 12, 2004).

28. *See* Robert F. Copple & Susan Halverson, *Bulldozing Barriers to Patent Case ADR Use*, NATIONAL L.J. S1 (April 11, 2005); Robert F. Copple, *Long Before Those Tempers Flare*, LEGAL TIMES (Aug. 16, 2004); Robert F. Copple, *Alternatives to Litigation*, ARIZONA REPUBLIC (June 27, 2004).

29. *See* ADRCPR.com; Adr.com.

30. *See* Drafting Dispute Resolution Clauses: Better Solutions for Business (CPR).

31. *See* Proposal for the Reform of Libel Law: The Report of the Libel Reform Project of The Annenberg Washington Program (Rodney A. Smolla ed., 1988).

32. For a more extensive discussion of the use of mediation in patent disputes, *see* PATENT MEDIATION HANDBOOK: BETTER SOLUTIONS FOR BUSINESS (CPR Institute for Dispute Resolution 2004).

Chapter XXI

Biotechnology Resources

Jennifer Korpacz, JD, MSLS
Assistant Librarian, Research
Covington & Burling
Washington, D.C.

This chapter is intended as a tool for anyone starting research on a legal issue affecting biotechnology start-up companies or as a tool for someone building a library on biotechnology law.

Treatises

ALAN R. BROMBERG AND LARRY E. RIBSTEIN, BROMBERG AND RIBSTEIN ON PARTNERSHIP (Aspen Publishers, 1988 and updated twice annually, 2005).

BARRY R. FURROW, ET AL., HEALTH LAW, SECOND EDITION (Practitioner Treatise Series) (Thomson West, 2000).

DONALD S. CHISUM, CHISUM ON PATENTS (Matthew Bender, 1997, last updated with revisions 2005).

ELIZABETH S. MILLER AND ARTHUR J. JACOBSON, STATE LIMITED LIABILITY COMPANY AND PARTNERSHIP LAWS (Aspen Publishers, 2004, last updated with supplements 2005).

EMPLOYEE BENEFITS LAW, SECOND EDITION (Steven J. Sacher, et al. eds., American Bar Association, BNA Books, 2001).

FUNDAMENTALS OF LAW AND REGULATION (Robert P. Brady, et al. eds., Food and Drug Law Institute, 1999).

HAROLD EINHORN, PATENT LICENSING TRANSACTIONS (Matthew Bender, 1968, updated with revisions 2005).

INTELLECTUAL PROPERTY COUNSELING AND LITIGATION (Lester Horowitz and Ethan Horowitz eds., Matthew Bender, 1988, updated with revisions 2005).

J. WILLIAM CALLISON AND MAUREEN A. SULLIVAN, LIMITED LIABILITY COMPANIES: A STATE-BY-STATE GUIDE TO LAW AND PRACTICE (Thomson West, 2005 edition updated annually).

J. WILLIAM CALLISON AND MAUREEN A. SULLIVAN, PARTNERSHIP LAW AND PRACTICE: GENERAL AND LIMITED PARTNERSHIPS (Clark Boardman Callaghan, Thomson West, 1992, updated annually).

LARRY E. RIBSTEIN AND ROBERT R. KEATINGE, RIBSTEIN AND KEATINGE ON LIMITED LIABILITY COMPANIES (2d ed. 1995).

LARRY E. RIBSTEIN, BROMBERG AND RIBSTEIN ON LLPs, RUPA AND ULPA, 2001 (Aspen Publishers, 2005 edition updated with supplements).

LESTER HOROWITZ AND ETHAN HOROWITZ, PATENT LITIGATION: PROCEDURE & TACTICS (Matthew Bender, 1971, updated with supplements and revisions 2004).

MICHAEL J. HALLORAN, VENTURE CAPITAL & PUBLIC OFFERING NEGOTIATION (Thomson West, 1997, updated annually).

MICHAEL J. LENNON, TECHNOLOGY TRANSFER GUIDE (Aspen Publishers, 2000, supplemented annually).

MICHAEL J. MALINOWSKI, BIOTECHNOLOGY: LAW, BUSINESS, AND REGULATION (Aspen Publishers, 1999, updated with supplements 2003).

PHILIP W. GRUBB, PATENTS FOR CHEMICALS, PHARMACEUTICALS AND BIOTECHNOLOGY (Fundamentals of Global Law, Practice and Strategy) (Oxford University Press, 2005).

ROBERT L. HARMON, PATENTS AND THE FEDERAL CIRCUIT (5th ed., BNA Books 2003).

ROGER M. MILGRIM, MILGRIM ON LICENSING (Matthew Bender, 1991, updated with supplements and revisions).

RONALD B. HILDRETH, PATENT LAW: A PRACTITIONER'S GUIDE (Practising Law Institute, 1998).

THOMAS F. VILLENEUVE AND ROBERT V. GUNDERSON, JR., CORPORATE PARTNERING: STRUCTURING AND NEGOTIATING DOMESTIC AND STRATEGIC ALLIANCES (4th Edition, 1998, updated with supplements 2000).

National Academies Press

Animal Biotechnology: Science Based Concerns, National Research Council (National Academy Press, 2002).
http://www.nap.edu/books/0309084393/html/

Biosafety in the Laboratory: Prudent Practices for Handling and Disposal of Infectious Materials, National Research Council (National Academy Press, 1989).
http://www.nap.edu/books/0309039754/html/index.html

Guide for the Care and Use of Laboratory Animals, National Research Council (National Academy Press, 1996).
http://www.nap.edu/readingroom/books/labrats/

Prudent Practices in the Laboratory: Handling and Disposal of Chemicals, National Research Council (National Academy Press, 1995).
http://www.nap.edu/books/0309052297/html

Occupational Health and Safety in the Care and Use of Research Animals, National Academy Press (National Research Council, 1997).
http://www.nap.edu/books/0309052998/html/index.html

Current Awareness—Periodicals

BioCentury
http://www.biocentury.com/flash/flash.cfm

Biotechnology Law Report (Mary Ann Liebert, Inc. Publishers)
http://www.liebertpub.com/publication.aspx?pub_id=6

BioWorld Today (Thomson)
http://www.bioworld.com/

BNA Biotech Watch (BNA)
http://www.bna.com/products/ip/bwdm.htm

BNA Health Care Daily (BNA)
http://www.bna.com/products/health/hdln.htm

BNA Patent, Trademark & Copyright Daily (BNA)
http://www.bna.com/products/ip/ptdm.htm

BNA Pharmaeutical Law & Industry Report (BNA)
http://www.bna.com/products/health/plir.htm

Clinical Trials Advisor (FDAnews)
http://www.fdanews.com/cta/

FDA Week (Inside Washington Publishers)
http://www.iwpnews.com/050603_health_iwp.php

Genetic Engineering News
http://www.genengnews.com/

Health Information Privacy/Security Alert (Melamedia, LLC)
http://www.melamedia.com/

Inside CMS (Inside Washington Publishers)
http://www.iwpnews.com/050603_health_iwp.php

IN VIVO, The Business & Medicine Report (Windhover)
http://windhover.com/dotcom/publications/index.asp?page=invivo

Journal of Biolaw & Business
http://www.biolawbusiness.com/

Journal of International Biotechnology Law (Walter de Gruyter GmbH & Co. KG)
http://www.degruyter.de/rs/280_7046_ENU_h.htm

Journal of the Patent and Trademark Office Society (U.S. Patent and Trademark Office Society)
http://www.jptos.org/

Patent Strategy & Management (Law Journal Newsletters)
http://www.lawjournalnewsletters.com/pub/ljn_patent/

PCT Newsletter (Patent Cooperation Treaty Newsletter) (WIPO)
http://www.wipo.int/pct/en/newslett/index.jsp

Pharmaceutical Executive
http://www.pharmexec.com/pharmexec/

"The Pink Sheet" Prescription Pharmaceuticals and Biotechnology (FDC Reports)
http://www.thepinksheet.com/FDC/Weekly/pink/TOC.htm

"The Pink Sheet Daily" Prescription Pharmaceuticals and Biotechnology (FDC Reports)
http://www.thepinksheetdaily.com/FDC/Daily/PinkDaily/TOC.htm

Scrip World Pharmaceutical News (PJB Publications/ T&F Informa UK Ltd.)
http://www.pjbpubs.com/scrip/index.htm

Venture Capital Journal (Thomson/Venture Economics)
http://www.venturecapitaljournal.net/

Major Federal Acts

Age Discrimination in Employment Act of 1967, Pub. L. No. 90-202, 81 Stat. 602 (Dec. 15, 1967), as amended, codified at 29 U.S.C. §§ 621-634.

Americans with Disabilities Act of 1990, Pub. L. No. 101-336, 104 Stat. 327 (July 26, 1990), as amended, codified in numerous sections including 42 U.S.C. §§ 12,101 *et seq.*

Biotechnology Resources

Animal Drug Amendments of 1968, Pub. L. No. 90-399, 82 Stat. 342 (July 13, 1968), as amended, codified in numerous sections including 21 U.S.C. § 360b.

Animal Drug Availability Act of 1996, Pub. L. No. 104-250, 110 Stat. 3151 (Oct. 9, 1996), codified in numerous sections including 21 U.S.C. § 360b.

Animal Drug User Fee Act of 2003, Pub. L. No. 108-130, 117 Stat. 1361 (Nov. 18, 2003), codified at 21 U.S.C. § 301 note, and 18 U.S.C. §§ 379j-11, 379j-12.

The Animal Medicinal Drug Use Clarification Act of 1994, Pub. L. No. 103-396, 108 Stat. 4153 (Oct. 22, 1994), codified in numerous sections including 21 U.S.C. § 360b.

Animal Welfare Act (Laboratory Animal Act of 1966), Pub. L. No. 89-544, 80 Stat. 350 (Aug. 24, 1966), codified at 7 U.S.C. §§ 2131-2159.

Bayh-Dole Act (Bayh-Dole University and Small Business Patent Procedures Act), Pub. L. No. 96-517, 94 Stat. 3019 (Dec. 12, 1980), as amended, codified at 35 U.S.C. §§ 200-212.

Civil Rights Act of 1964 (Title VII), Pub. L. No. 88-352, 78 Stat. 241 (July 2, 1964), as amended, codified in numerous sections including 42 U.S.C. §§ 2000e *et seq.*

Clinical Laboratory Improvement Amendments of 1988, Pub. L. No. 100-578, 102 Stat. 2903 (Oct. 31, 1988), codified in numerous sections including 45 U.S.C. § 263a.

Cooperative Research and Technology Enhancement (CREATE) Act of 2004, Pub. L. No. 108-453, 118 Stat. 3596 (Dec. 10, 2004), codified at 35 U.S.C. §§ 1 note and 103.

Copyright Act, ch. 391, 61 Stat. 652 (July 30, 1947), as amended, codified in numerous sections including 17 U.S.C. §§ 1-215.

The Drug Amendments of 1962 (Kefauver-Harris Amendments), Pub. L. No. 87-781, 76 Stat. 780 (Oct. 10, 1962), codified in numerous sections including 21 U.S.C. §§ 348 and 360.

The Drug Price Competition and Patent Term Restoration Act of 1984 (Hatch-Waxman Act), Pub. L. No. 98-417, 98 Stat. 1585 (Sept. 24, 1984), codified in numerous sections including 21 U.S.C. § 355 and 35 U.S.C. § 156.

Employee Retirement Income Security Act of 1974 (ERISA), Pub. L. No. 93-406, 88 Stat. 829 (Sept. 2, 1974), as amended, codified in numerous sections including 29 U.S.C. §§ 1001 *et seq.*

Employee Polygraph Protection Act of 1988, Pub. L. No. 100-347, 102 Stat. 646 (June 27, 1988), as amended, codified at 29 U.S.C. § 2001 *et seq.*

Equal Pay Act of 1963, Pub. L. No. 88-38, 77 Stat. 56 (June 10, 1963), codified at 29 U.S.C. § 206.

Fair Credit Reporting Act, Pub. L. No. 90-321, Title VI (May 29, 1968), as added, Pub. L. No. 91-508, Title VI, 84 Stat. 1128 (Oct. 26, 1970), as amended, codified at 15 U.S.C. §§ 1681 *et seq.*

Fair Labor Standards Act of 1938, ch. 676, 52 Stat. 1060 (June 25, 1938), as amended, codified at 29 U.S.C. §§ 201 *et seq.*

Family and Medical Leave Act of 1993, Pub. L. No. 103-3, 107 Stat. 6 (Feb. 5, 1993), as amended, codified in numerous sections including 29 U.S.C. §§ 2601 *et seq.*

Federal Food, Drug, and Cosmetic Act of 1938, Pub. L. No. 75-717, ch. 675 (1938), 52 Stat. 1040 (June 25, 1938), as amended, codified in numerous sections including 21 U.S.C. §§ 301 *et seq.*

Federal Insecticide, Fungicide and Rodenticide Act (FIFRA), ch. 125, 61 Stat. 163 (June 25, 1947), codified in numerous sections including 7 U.S.C. §§ 136 *et seq.*

Food and Drug Administration Modernization Act of 1997, Pub. L. No.1-5-115, 111 Stat. 2296 (Nov. 21, 1997), codified in numerous sections including 21 U.S.C. § 301.

Food Additives Amendments (Delaney Amendment), Pub. L. No. 85-929, 72 Stat. 1784 (Sept. 6, 1958), as amended, codified in numerous sections including 21 U.S.C. § 321.

Generic Animal Drug and Patent Term Restoration Act, Pub. L. No. 100-670, 102 Stat. 3971 (Nov. 16, 1988), codified in numerous sections including 21 U.S.C. § 360b.

Health Insurance Portability and Accountability Act of 1996 ("HIPAA"), Pub. L. No. 104-191, 110 Stat. 1936 (August 21, 1996), as amended, codified in numerous sections including 42 U.S.C. §§ 1301 *et seq.*

Health Research Extension Act of 1985, Pub. L. No. 99-158, 99 Stat. 820 (Nov. 20, 1985), as amended, codified in numerous sections including 42 U.S.C. §§ 281 *et seq.*

The Homeland Security Act of 2002, Pub. L. No. 107-296, 116 Stat. 2135 (Nov. 25, 2002), as amended, codified in numerous sections including 6 U.S.C. §§ 101 *et seq.*

Immigration Reform and Control Act 1986, Pub. L. No. 99-603, 100 Stat. 3359 (Nov. 6, 1986), as amended, codified in numerous sections including 8 U.S.C. § 1324b.

Medicare Prescription Drug, Improvement and Modernization Act of 2003, Pub. L. No. 108-173, 117 Stat. 2066 (Dec. 8, 2003), in numerous sections including 42 U.S.C. § 1395w-141.

Minor Use and Minor Species Animal Health Act of 2004, Pub. L. No. 108-282, Title I, 118 Stat. 891 (Aug. 2, 2004), codified in numerous sections including 21 U.S.C. § 60b.

National Labor Relations Act, ch. 372, 49 Stat. 449 (July 5, 1935), as amended, codified at 29 U.S.C. §§ 151-169.

Occupational Safety and Health Act of 1970, Pub. L. No. 91-596, 84 Stat. 1590 (Dec. 29, 1970), as amended, codified in numerous sections including 29 U.S.C. §§ 651 *et seq.*

Orphan Drug Act, Pub. L. No. 97-414, 96 Stat. 2049 (Jan. 4, 1983), as amended, codified in numerous sections including 21 U.S.C. §§ 360aa-360dd.

Plant Protection Act, Pub. L. No. 106-224, Title IV, 114 Stat. 438 (June 20, 2000), as amended, codified in numerous sections including 7 U.S.C. §§ 7711-7718.

Prescription Drug User Fee of 1992 (PDUFA), Pub. L. No. 102-571, Title I, 106 Stat. 4491 (Oct. 29, 1992), codified in numerous sections including 21 U.S.C. §§ 379 and 343.

The Public Health Security and Bioterrorism Preparedness and Response Act of 2002, Pub. L. No. 107-188, 116 Stat. 594 (June 12, 2002), as amended, codified in numerous sections including 42 U.S.C. §§ 201 *et seq.*

Public Health Service Act, ch. 373, 58 Stat. 682 (July 1, 1944), as amended, codified in numerous sections including 42 U.S.C. §§ 201 *et seq.*

Resource Conservation and Recovery Act of 1976, Pub. L. No. 94-580, 90 Stat. 2795 (Oct. 21, 1976), codified at 42 U.S.C. §§ 6901 *et seq.*

Trademark Clarification Act of 1984, Pub. L. No. 98-620, Title I, 98 Stat. 3335 (Nov. 8, 1984), codified at numerous sections including 15 U.S.C. § 1064.

Uniformed Services Employment and Reemployment Rights Act of 1994, Pub. L. No. 103-353, 108 Stat. 3149 (Oct. 13, 1994), codified at numerous sections including 38 U.S.C. §§ v4301 *et seq.*

Virus-Serum-Toxin Act (VSTA), ch. 145, 37 Stat. 832 (Mar. 4, 1913), codified at 21 U.S.C. §§ 151-158.

Selected *Federal Register* Documents

Fraud, Untrue Statements of Material Facts, Bribery, and Illegal Gratuities, 56 Fed. Reg. 46,191 (November 10, 1991).

Human Cells, Tissues, and Cellular and Tissue-Based Products; Establishment Registration and Listing, 66 Fed. Reg. 5,547 (January 19, 2001).
http://www.fda.gov/OHRMS/DOCKETS/98fr/011901a.pdf

Eligibility Determination for Donors of Human Cells, Tissues, and Cellular and Tissue-Based Products Final Rule, 69 Fed. Reg. 29,786 (May 25, 2004).
http://www.fda.gov/OHRMS/DOCKETS/98fr/04-11245.pdf

Current Good Tissue Practice for Human Cell, Tissue, and Cellular and Tissue-Based Product Establishments; Inspection and Enforcement, 69 Fed. Reg. 68,612 (November 24, 2004).
http://www.fda.gov/OHRMS/DOCKETS/98fr/04-25798.pdf

Coordinated Framework for the Regulation of Biotechnology, 51 Fed. Reg. 23,302 (June 26, 1986).

Viruses, Serums, Toxins, and Analogous Products; Records and Reports, 70 Fed. Reg. 48,325 (2005) (to be codified at 9 C.F.R. Parts 101 and 116) (proposed August 17, 2005).
http://a257.g.akamaitech.net/7/257/2422/01jan20051800/
edocket.access.gpo.gov/2005/pdf/05-16266.pdf

Premarket Notice Concerning Bioengineered Foods, 66 Fed. Reg. 4,706 (2001) (to be codified at 21 C.F.R. Parts 192 and 592) (proposed January 18, 2001).
http://www.fda.gov/OHRMS/DOCKETS/98fr/011801a.pdf

Federal Agency Resources

Centers for Disease Control
http://www.cdc.gov/

Animal Policy Board
http://www.cdc.gov/od/ads/animal.htm

Biosafety in Microbiological and Biomedical Laboratories 12, CDC and NIH, DHHS. DHHS Publication No. (CDC) 93-8395. http://www.cdc.gov/od/ohs/biosfty/bmbl3toc.htm

Centers for Medicare & Medicaid Services (CMS)
http://www.cms.hhs.gov/default.asp

Agency for Healthcare Research and Quality
http://www.ahrq.gov/

Clinical Laboratory Fee Schedule
http://www.cms.hhs.gov/providers/pufdownload/clfdown.asp

Covered Entity Decision Tools
http://www.cms.hhs.gov/hipaa/hipaa2/support/tools/decisionsupport/default.asp

Department Appeals Board
http://www.hhs.gov/dab/

Form-1450 (Uniform Bill—UB-92)
http://www.cms.hhs.gov/providers/edi/edi5.asp#Form%20CMS-1450

Healthcare Common Procedure Coding System (HCPCS)
http://www.cms.hhs.gov/medicare/hcpcs/

ICD-9-CM—Diagnosis Codes—The International Classification of Diseases, 9th Revision, Clinical Modification
http://www.cms.hhs.gov/paymentsystems/icd9/

ICD-9-CM—Procedures Codes—The International Classification of Diseases, 9th Revision, Clinical Modification
http://www.cms.hhs.gov/paymentsystems/icd9/

Local Coverage Determinations
http://www.cms.hhs.gov/mcd/search.asp?

Manuals including the Medicare Claims Processing Manual
http://www.cms.hhs.gov/manuals/cmstoc.asp

Medicare Operations Division/The Medicare Appeals Council
http://www.hhs.gov/dab/MOD2005.html

National Coverage Determinations
http://www.cms.hhs.gov/coverage/default.asp

Place of Service Codes
http://www.cms.hhs.gov/states/poshome.asp

Department of Agriculture (USDA)
http://www.usda.gov/wps/portal/usdahome

Animal and Plant Health Inspection Service (APHIS)
http://www.aphis.usda.gov/

Animal Care Policy Manual
http://www.aphis.usda.gov/ac/polmanpdf.html

Animal Care Research Manual
http://www.aphis.usda.gov/ac/researchguide.html

Biotechnology Regulatory Services
http://www.aphis.usda.gov/brs/

Center for Veterinary Biologics
http://www.aphis.usda.gov/vs/cvb/

Institutional Animal Care and Use Committee (IACUC) Guidelines
http://www.aphis.usda.gov/ac/iacuc.pdf

Risk Analysis for Veterinary Biologics
http://www.aphis.usda.gov/vs/cvb/lpd/sifs.htm

Veterinary Services: Memorandum 800.50: Basic License Requirements and Guidelines for Submission of Materials in support of Licensure, May 28, 2002
http://www.aphis.usda.gov/vs/cvb/memos/2002/800_50.pdf

Department of Health and Human Services
http://www.dhhs.gov/

Common Rule for agency grantees, contractors and employees
http://www.hhs.gov/ohrp/policy/common.html

Office of Civil Rights—HIPAA
http://www.hhs.gov/ocr/hipaa

Office of Extramural Research Human Subjects
http://grants1.nih.gov/grants/policy/hs/index.htm

Office for Human Research Protections
http://www.hhs.gov/ohrp/

Office of the Inspector General (OIG), Compliance Program Guidance for Pharmaceutical Manufacturers (68 Fed. Reg. 23,731, 2003).
http://oig.hhs.gov/authorities/docs/03/050503FRCPGPharmac.pdf

Office of the Inspector General (OIG), Corporate Integrity Agreements (CIA)
http://oig.hhs.gov/fraud/cia/index.html

"The Nuremberg Code," *Trials of War Criminals before the Nuremberg Military Tribunals under Control Council Law No. 10,* Vol. 2, pp. 181-82 (Washington, D.C.: U.S. Government Printing Office, 1949).
http://www.hhs.gov/ohrp/references/nurcode.htm

"Review of Federal Policy for the Protection of Human Subjects," Presidential Memorandum (February 17, 1994).
http://www.hhs.gov/ohrp/humansubjects/guidance/hsdc94feb.htm

Department of Labor
http://www.dol.gov/

Fact Sheet #28—Family and Medical Leave Act (FMLA)
http://www.dol.gov/esa/regs/compliance/whd/whdfs28.htm

Foreign Labor Certification
http://www.plc.doleta.gov/

Office of Federal Contract Compliance Programs ("OFCCP")
http://www.dol.gov/esa/ofccp/

Department of State
http://www.state.gov/

Foreign Affairs Manual
http://foia.state.gov/regs/search.asp

Visa Bulletin
http://travel.state.gov/visa/frvi/bulletin/bulletin_1360.html

Environmental Protection Agency
http://www.epa.gov/

Biopesticides and Pollution Prevention Division (established within EPA's Office of Pollution Prevention (OPP))
http://www.epa.gov/pesticides/biopesticides/

Food and Drug Administration (FDA)
http://www.fda.gov/

Center for Biologics Evaluation and Research (CBER)
http://www.fda.gov/cber/index.html

CBER Commemorating 100 Years of Biologics Regulation
http://www.fda.gov/cber

CBER Frequently Asked Questions
http://www.fda.gov/cber/faq.htm

CBER Guidance, Guidelines, and Points to Consider Documents
http://www.fda.gov/cber/guidelines.htm

Guidance for Industry: Independent Consultants for Biotechnology Clinical Trial Protocols (August 2004)
http://www.fda.gov/cber/gdlns/bioclin.pdf

Manual of Standard Operating Procedures and Policies
http://www.fda.gov/cber/regsopp/regsopp.htm

Manual of Standard Operating Procedures and Policies, SOPP 8404, Version # 2, "Refusal to File Procedures for Biologic License Applications" (Oct. 2, 2002)
http://www.fda.gov/cber/regsopp/8404.htm

Manual of Standard Operating Procedures and Policies, SOPP 8405, "Complete Review and Issuance of Action Letters" (June 11, 1998)
http://www.fda.gov/cber/regsopp/8405.htm

Center for Drug Evaluation and Research (CDER)
http://www.fda.gov/cder/

Approved Drug Products with Therapeutic Equivalence Evaluations ("Orange Book")
http://www.fda.gov/cder/orange/default.htm

CDER Guidance Documents
http://www.fda.gov/cder/guidance/index.htm

Guidance for Industry: 180-Day Exclusivity When Multiple ANDAs Are Submitted on the Same Day (July 2003)
http://www.fda.gov/cder/guidance/5710fnl.pdf

Guidance for Industry: The Content and Format for Pediatric Use Supplements (Mar. 1996)
http://www.fda.gov/cder/guidance/clin1.pdf

Guideline for the Format and Content of the Microbiology Section of an Application (Feb. 1987)
http://www.fda.gov/cder/guidance/old031fn.pdf

Guidance for Industry: Fast Track Drug Development Programs—Designation, Development, and Application Review (July 2004)
http://www.fda.gov/cder/guidance/5645fnl.pdf

Guidance for Industry (Draft): Accelerated Approval Products—Submission of Promotional Materials (Mar. 1999)
http://www.fda.gov/cder/guidance/2197dft.pdf

Guidance for Industry: Consumer Directed Broadcast Advertisements (Aug. 1999)
http://www.fda.gov/cder/guidance/1804fnl.pdf

Guidance for Industry: Industry-Supported Scientific and Educational Activities (Nov. 1997)
http://www.fda.gov/cder/guidance/isse.pdf

Guidance for Industry (Draft): Applications Covered by Section 505(b)(2) (Oct. 1999)
http://www.fda.gov/cder/guidance/2853dft.pdf

Guidance for Industry: Content and Format of Investigational New Drug Applications (INDs) for Phase 1 Studies of Drugs, Including Well-Characterized, Therapeutic, Biotechnology-derived Products (Nov. 1995)
http://www.fda.gov/cder/guidance/clin2.pdf

Guidance for Industry: S6 Preclinical Safety Evaluation of Biotechnology-Derived Pharmaceuticals (July 1997)
http://www.fda.gov/cder/guidance/1859fnl.pdf

Guidance for Industry: General Considerations for the Clinical Evaluation of Drugs (1977)
http://www.fda.gov/cder/guidance/old034fn.pdf

Guidance for Industry: Disclosure of Information Provided to Advisory Committees in Connection with Open Advisory Committee Meetings Convened by the Center for Drug Evaluation and Research Beginning on January 1, 2000 (Nov. 1999)
http://www.fda.gov/cder/guidance/3431fnl.pdf

Guidance for Industry: Acceptance of Foreign Clinical Studies (Mar. 2001)
http://www.fda.gov/cder/guidance/fstud.pdf

Refusal to File Policy (July 12, 1993)
http://www.fda.gov/cder/guidance/rtf.pdf

"Managing the Risks from Medical Products Use: Creating a Risk Management Framework" (May 1999)
www.fda.gov/oc/cder/tfrm/riskmanagement.pdf

Manual of Policy and Procedures (MaPP)
http://www.fda.gov/cder/mapp.htm

Manual of Policy and Procedures, MaPP 4180.3, "Processing and Reviewing Voluntary Genomic Data Submissions (VGDSs)" (Mar. 2005)
http://www.fda.gov/cder/mapp/4180.3.pdf

Manual of Policy and Procedures (MaPP) 4512.1, "Formal Meetings Between CDER and CDER's External Constituents" (Mar. 1996)
http://www.fda.gov/cder/mapp/4512-1.pdf

Manual of Policy and Procedures (MaPP) 6010.5, "NDAs: Filing Review Issues" (May 2003)
http://www.fda.gov/cder/mapp/6010.5.pdf

Manual of Policy and Procedures, MaPP 6020.3, "Priority Review Policy" (Apr. 1996)
http://www.fda.gov/cder/mapp/6020-3.pdf

Manual of Policy and Procedures (MaPP) 6030.1, "IND Process and Review Procedures (Including Clinical Holds)" (May 1998)
http://www.fda.gov/cder/mapp/6030-1.pdf

Office of Orphan Products Development
http://www.fda.gov/orphan/index.htm

Office of Orphan Products Development Grant Program
http://www.fda.gov/orphan/grants/info.htm.

Center for Devices and Radiological Health (CDRH)
http://www.fda.gov/cdrh/

CDRH Guidance Documents
http://www.fda.gov/cdrh/guidance.html

CDRH Databases
http://www.fda.gov/cdrh/databases.html

Office of Regulatory Affairs
http://www.fda.gov/ora/default.htm

FDA Compliance Program Guidance Manual
http://www.fda.gov/ora/cpgm/default.htm

FDA Compliance Program Guidance Manual, Program # 7346.832, "PreApproval Inspections/Investigations" (Mar. 2005)
http://www.fda.gov/cder/gmp/PAI-7346832.pdf

FDA/ORA Bioresearch Monitoring Information
http://www.fda.gov/ora/compliance_ref/bimo/default.htm

Center for Food Safety and Applied Nutrition (CFSAN)
http://www.cfsan.fda.gov/list.html

CFSAN compilation of biotechnology documents
http://vm.cfsan.fda.gov/~lrd/biotechm.html

Guidance for Industry (Draft): Voluntary Labeling Indicating Whether a Food Have or Have Not Been Developed Using Biotechnology (Jan. 2001)
http://www.fda.gov/OHRMS/DOCKETS/98fr/001598gd.pdf

Statement of Policy: Foods Derived From New Plant Varieties, 57 Fed. Reg. 22,984 (May 29, 1992)
http://www.cfsan.fda.gov/~acrobat/fr920529.pdf

Center for Veterinary Medicine (CVM)
http://www.fda/cvm.gov

CVM Guidance Documents
http://www.fda.gov/cvm/Guidance/published.htm

Guidance for Industry, Animal Drug User Fees and Fee Waivers and Reductions, CVM Guidance # 170 (March 15, 2004)
http://www.fda.gov/cvm/Guidance/guide170.pdf

Guidance for Industry: Chemistry, Manufacturing and Controls Changes to an Approved NADA or ANADA, CVM Draft Guidance # 83 (June 1999)
http://www.fda.gov/cvm/Guidance/dguide83.PDF

Guidance for Industry: Drug Substance: Chemistry, Manufacturing, and Controls Information, CVM Draft Guidance # 169 (January 2004)
http://www.fda.gov/cvm/Guidance/3969DFT.pdf

Animal Drug Applications Expedited Review Guideline, CVM Program Policy and Procedures Guide # 1240.3135 (June 1990)
http://www.fda.gov/cvm/Guidance/3135.pdf

Guidance to Industry: Expedited Review for New Animal Drug Applications for Pathogen Reduction Claims, CVM Guidance # 121 (March 6, 2001)
http://www.fda.gov/cvm/Guidance/guide121.pdf

Guidance to Industry: Bioequivalence Guideline, CVM Guidance # 35 (October 9, 2002)
http://www.fda.gov/cvm/Guidance/bioequivalence_Oct02.pdf

Guidance to Industry: Target Animal Safety Guidelines for New Animal Drug, CVM Guidance # 33 (June 1989)
http://www.fda.gov/cvm/Guidance/Guideline33.htm

Guidance to Industry: General Principles for Evaluating the Safety of Compounds Used in Food-Producing Animals, CVM Guidance # 3 (June 2005)
http://www.fda.gov/cvm/Documents/GFI003.pdf

Guidance for Industry: Veterinary Feed Directive Regulation, CVM Guidance # 120 (March 1, 2001)
http://www.fda.gov/cvm/Guidance/guide120.pdf

Guidance for Industry: Dispute Resolution Procedures for Science-Based Decisions on Products Regulated by the Center for Veterinary Medicine (CVM), CVM Guidance # 79 (July, 2005).
http://www.fda.gov/cvm/Guidance/fguide79.pdf

Guidance to Industry: Target Animal Safety Guidelines for New Animal Drug, CVM Guidance # 33 (June 1989)
http://www.fda.gov/cvm/Guidance/Guideline33.htm

Guidance for Industry: Specifications: Test Procedures and Acceptance Criteria for New Biotechnological/Biological Veterinary Medicinal Products, VICH GL-40, CVM Draft Guidance # 177 (May 24, 2005)
http://www.fda.gov/cvm/Guidance/dguide177.pdf

The Minor Use and Minor Species Animal Health Act of 2004, Center for Veterinary Medicine compilation of guidance and related documents
http://www.fda.gov/cvm/minortoc.htm

Guidance for Industry: Drugs, Biologics, and Medical Devices Derived from Bioengineered Plants for Use in Humans and Animals, Draft Guidance (September 2002)
http://www.fda.gov/OHRMS/DOCKETS/98fr/02d-0324-gdl0001.pdf

Information for Consumers: How FDA Regulates Veterinary Devices, Center for Veterinary Medicine (May 2003)
http://www.fda.gov/cvm/regofdevices.htm

Animal Drug User Fee Act of 2003 (ADUFA), Center for Veterinary Medicine compilation of guidance and related documents
http://www.fda.gov/cvm/adufa.htm

CVM—Biotechnology in Animals and Feeds compilation of documents
http://www.fda.gov/cvm/bioengineered.html

CVM, Update on Livestock Cloning (July 13, 2001)
http://www.fda.gov/cvm/CVM_Updates/clones.htm

CVM, *Animal Cloning: A Risk Assessment*, Draft Executive Summary (October 21, 2003)
http://www.fda.gov/cvm/Documents/CLRAES.pdf

CVM Investigations with Bioengineered Animals: Letter to the University of Illinois (September 29, 2003)
http://www.fda.gov/cvm/FOI/UILetter.htm

CVM Investigations with Bioengineered Animals: Letter to Land Grant University Presidents (May 13, 2003)
http://www.fda.gov/cvm/FOI/LandGrantLtr.htm

FDA/CVM, *Information for Consumers: Questions and Answers and Answers About Transgenic Fish*
http://www.fda.gov/cvm/transgen.htm

FDA/CVM, *FDA Statement Regarding Glofish* (December 9, 2003)
http://www.fda.gov/bbs/topics/NEWS/2003/NEW00994.html

Animal Drugs and Genetically Engineered Animals—Center for Veterinary Medicine compilation of guidance and related documents
http://www.fda.gov/cvm/bio-drugs.html

Good Clinical Practice in FDA-Regulated Clinical Trials
http://www.fda.gov/oc/gcp/default.htm

FDA Regulations and the Common Rule Comparison
http://www.fda.gov/oc/gcp/comparison.html

Good Clinical Practices: FDA Regulations Relating to Good Clinical Practice and Clinical Trials
http://www.fda.gov/oc/gcp/regulations.html

Guidance for Institutional Review Boards and Clinical Investigators (1998 Update)
http://www.fda.gov/oc/ohrt/irbs/default.htm

Guidance for Industry-IRB Review of Stand-Alone HIPAA Authorizations Under FDA Regulations (Oct. 2003)
http://www.fda.gov/OHRMS/DOCKETS/98fr/03d-0204-gdl0001.pdf

FDA Forms
http://www.fda.gov/opacom/morechoices/fdaforms/fdaforms.html

Form FDA-356h, Application to Market a New Drug, Biologic, or an Antibiotic Drug for Human Use
http://www.fda.gov/opacom/morechoices/fdaforms/FDA-356h.pdf

FDA Form 1572, Statement of Investigator
http://www.fda.gov/opacom/morechoices/fdaforms/FDA-1572.pdf

Speeches and Articles

L. Crawford, *28th Annual National Food Policy Conference Speech*, September 19, 2005 (Washington, D.C.)
http://www.fda.gov/oc/speeches/2005/nfpc0919.html

L. Bren, "Cloning: Revolution or Evolution in Animal Production?," *FDA Veterinarian Newsletter*, Vol. XVIII, No. V (September/October 2003)
http://www.fda.gov/cvm/Sep-Oct03.htm

Michelle Meadows, *The FDA's Drug Review Process*, FDA CONSUMER MAGAZINE (July-Aug. 2002)
http://www.fda.gov/fdac.features/2002/402_drug.html

Miscellaneous

FDA Advisory Committees
http://www.fda.gov/oc/advisory/default.htm

FDA Dockets
http://www.fda.gov/ohrms/dockets/default.htm

FDA Final Decision of the Commissioner: Withdrawal of Approval of the New Animal Drug Application for Enrofloxacin in Poultry, Docket No. 2000N-1571 (July 27, 2005)
http://www.fda.gov/oc/antimicrobial/baytril.pdf

FDA Office of Combination Products
http://www.fda.gov/oc/combination/default.htm

Guidance for Industry (Draft): Exports and Imports Under the FDA Export Reform and Enhancement Act of 1996 (Feb. 1998)
http://www.fda.gov/oc/guidance/frexport.html

"The Prescription Drug Marketing Act—FDA's Report to Congress" (June 2001)
http://www.fda.gov/oc/pdma/report2001/

National Institutes of Health (NIH)

http://www.nih.gov/

Certificates of Confidentiality: Background Information
http://grants1.nih.gov/grants/policy/coc/background.htm

Certificates of Confidentiality: Frequently Asked Questions
http://grants1.nih.gov/grants/policy/coc/faqs.htm

Clinical Research and the HIPAA Privacy Rule
http://privacyruleandresearch.nih.gov/clin_research.asp

ClinicalTrials.gov
http://www.clinicaltrials.gov/

Declaration of Helsinki
http://ohsr.od.nih.gov/guidelines/helsinki.html

Grants Policy Statement (December 2003)
http://grants.nih.gov/grants/policy/nihgps_2003/index.htm

Guidelines for Research Involving Recombinant DNA Molecules, NIH, DHHS
http://www.4.od.nih.gov/oba/rac/guidelines/guidelines.html

HIPAA Authorization for Research
http://privacyruleandresearch.nih.gov/authorization.asp

Institution of Review Boards and HIPAA Privacy Rule
http://privacyruleandresearch.nih.gov/irb_default.asp

Institutional Animal Care and Use Committee Guidebook (2d Edition, OLAW and the Applied Research Ethics National Association, 2002)
http://www.grants.nih.gov/grants/olaw/Guidebook.pdf

Interagency Edison
https://s-edison.info.nih.gov/iEdison/

Memorandum of Understanding, APHIS, the Food and Drug Administration (FDA) and the NIH concerning laboratory animal welfare, Effective January 1, 2001
http://www.grants.nih.gov/grants/olaw/references/finalmou.htm

Office of Laboratory Animal Welfare
http://grants.nih.gov/grants/olaw/olaw.htm

Office of Technology Transfer
http://ott.od.nih.gov/

"Protecting Personal Health Information and Research: Understanding the HIPAA Privacy Rule"
http://privacyruleandresearch.nih.gov
http://privacyruleandresearch.nih.gov/pr_02.asp

Privacy Boards and the HIPAA Privacy Rule
http://privacyruleandresearch.nih.gov/privacy_boards_hipaa_privacy_rule.asp

Research Repositories, Databases, and the HIPAA Privacy Rule
http://privacyruleandresearch.nih.gov/research_repositories.asp

Workgroup Report
http://www.grants2.nih.gov/grants/policy/regulatoryburden/hazardouswastes.htm

Patent and Trademark Office (PTO)
http://www.uspto.gov/index.html

Manual of Patent Examining Procedure (MPEP) (8th edition, August 2001, Last Revision August 2005)
http://www.uspto.gov/web/offices/pac/mpep/

Patent Assignment Recordation Form—PTO-1595
http://www.uspto.gov/web/forms/pto1595.pdf

Synopsis of Application of Written Description Guidelines
http://www.uspto.gov/web/menu/written.pdf

U.S. Citizenship and Immigration Services (USCIS)
http://uscis.gov/graphics/

Forms
http://uscis.gov/graphics/formsfee/forms/index.htm

Other

Defense Contract Audit Agency—Defense Contract Audit Manual
http://www.dcaa.mil/cam.htm

Department of Defense—Small Business Innovation Research and Small Business Technology Transfer Programs Overviews
http://www.acq.osd.mil/sadbu/sbir/overview/index.htm

Equal Employment Opportunity Commission
http://www.eeoc.gov/

Federal Business Opportunities ("FedBizOpps")
http://www.fedbizopps.gov/

Federal Trade Commission
http://www.ftc.gov/

Occupational Safety and Health Administration (OSHA) (within the Department of Labor)
http://www.osha.gov/

Key Federal Cases

A. Stucki Co. v. Buckeye Steel Castings Co., 963 F.2d 360 (Fed. Cir. 1992).

ABB Robotics, Inc. v. GMFanuc Robotics Corp., 52 F.3d 1062 (Fed. Cir. 1995).

A.C. Aukerman Co. v. R.L. Chaides Constr. Co., 960 F.2d 1020 (Fed. Cir. 1992).

Advanced Cardiovascular Systems, Inc. v. Scimed Life Systems, Inc., 988 F.2d 1157 (Fed. Cir. 1993).

Adang v. Fischoff, 286 F.3d 1346, 62 U.S.P.Q.2d 1504 (Fed. Cir. 2002).

Amsted Industries Inc. v. Buckeye Steel Castings Co., 23 F.3d 374 (Fed. Cir. 1994).

Amsted Industries Inc. v. Buckeye Steel Castings Co., 24 F.3d 178 (Fed. Cir. 1994).

Aro Mfg. Co. v. Convertible Top Replacement Co., 365 U.S. 336 (1961).

ATD Corp. v. Lydall, Inc., 159 F.3d 534 (Fed. Cir. 1998).

ASCII Corp. v. STD Entertainment USA, Inc., 844 F. Supp. 1378 (N.D. Cal. 1994).

Bausch & Lomb, Inc. v. Barnes-Hind/Hydrocurve, Inc., 796 F.2d 443 (Fed. Cir. 1986).

Baxter Int'l, Inc. v. COBE Laboratories, Inc., 88 F.3d 1054 (Fed. Cir. 1996).

B. Braun Medical, Inc. v. Abbott Laboratories, 124 F.3d 1419 (Fed. Cir. 1997).

BIC Leisure Products, Inc. v. Windsurfing Int'l, Inc., 1 F.3d 1214 (Fed. Cir. 1993).

Bott v. Four Star Corp., 807 F.2d 1567 (Fed. Cir. 1986).

Burlington Industries, Inc. v. Dayco Corp., 849 F.2d 1418 (Fed. Cir. 1988), *cert. denied*, 490 U.S. 1067 (1989).

Burlington Industries v. Ellerth, 524 U.S. 742 (1998).

Cognex Corp. v. National Instruments Corp., 2001 WL 34368283, No. Civ. A. 00-442-JJF (D. Del. June 29, 2001).

Continental Can Co. v. Monsanto Co., 948 F.2d 1264 (Fed. Cir. 1991).

C.R. Bard, Inc. v. Advanced Cardiovascular Systems, Inc., 911 F.2d 670 (Fed. Cir. 1990).

Critikon, Inc. v. Becton Dickinson Vascular Access, Inc., 120 F.3d 1253 (Fed. Cir. 1997).

Custom Accessories, Inc. v. Jeffrey-Allan Industries, Inc., 807 F.2d 955 (Fed. Cir. 1986).

Cybor Corp. v. FAS Tech., Inc., 138 F.3d 1448 (Fed. Cir. 1998).

Eastman Kodak Co. v. Goodyear Tire & Rubber Co., 114 F.3d 1547 (Fed. Cir. 1997).

Eli Lilly & Co. v. Medtronic, Inc., 496 U.S. 661 (1990).

Enzo Biochem, Inc. v. Gen-Probe, Inc., 296 F.3d 1316 (Fed. Cir. 2002).

Exxon Chemical Patents, Inc. v. Lubrizol Corp., 64 F.3d 1553 (Fed. Cir. 1995), *reh'g denied, en banc suggestion declined*, 77 F.3d 450 (Fed. Cir. 1996).

Faragher v. City of Boca Raton, 524 U.S. 775 (1998).

Festo Corp. v. Shoketsu Kinzoku Kogyo Kabushiki Co., 122 S. Ct. 1831 (2002).

Fonar Corp. v. Gen. Elec. Co., 107 F.3d 1543 (Fed. Cir. 1997), *cert. denied*, 522 U.S. 908 (1997).

Fox Industries, Inc. v. Structural Preservation Systems, Inc., 922 F.2d 801 (Fed. Cir. 1990).

Franklin v. Parke-Davis, Division of Warner Lambert Co., 147 F. Supp. 2d 39 (D. Mass. 2001).

Gasser Chair Co., Inc. v. Infanti Chair Mfg. Corp., 60 F.3d 770 (Fed. Cir. 1995).

Georgia-Pacific Corp. v. U.S. Plywood Corp., 318 F. Supp. 1116 (S.D. N.Y. 1970), *judgment modified on other grounds*, 446 F.2d 295 (2d Cir.), *cert. denied*, 404 U.S. 870 (1971).

Glaxo Inc. v. Novopharm Ltd., 52 F.3d 1043 (Fed. Cir. 1995).

Graham v. John Deere Co., 383 U.S. 1, 17, 86 S. Ct. 684, 15 L. Ed. 2d 545 (1966).

Grain Processing Corp. v. Am. Maize-Prods. Co., 185 F.3d 1341 (Fed. Cir. 1999).

Grand Laboratories, Inc. v. Harris, 66 F.2d 1288 (8th Cir. 1981) (*en banc*).

Graver Tank & Mfg. Co. v. Linde Air Prods. Co., 339 U.S. 605 (1950).

Hall v. Aqua Queen Mfg., Inc., 93 F.3d 1548 (Fed. Cir. 1996).

Heidelberger Druckmaschinen AG v. Hantscho Commercial Products, Inc., 21 F.3d 1068, 30 U.S.P.Q.2d 1377 (Fed. Cir. 1994).

Hess & Clark, Inc. v. FDA, 497 F.2d 975 (D.C. Cir. 1974).

Hoganas AB v. Dresser Industries, Inc., 9 F.3d 948 (Fed. Cir. 1993).

Hoechst Celanese Corp. v. BP Chemicals Ltd., 78 F.3d 1575 (Fed. Cir. 1996).

Honeywell Int'l Inc. v. Hamilton Sunstrand Corp., 370 F.3d 1131 (*en banc*).

Hughes Tool Co. v. Dresser Industries, Inc., 816 F.2d 1549 (Fed. Cir.), *cert. denied*, 481 U.S. 1052 (1987).

Integra Lifesciences I, Ltd. v. Merck KGaA, 331 F.3d 860 (Fed. Cir. 2003).

In re Huston, 308 F.3d 1267, 1280, 64 U.S.P.Q.2d 1801 (Fed. Cir. 2002).

In re Pfizer, Inc., 81 F.T.C. 23 (1972).

Johnson & Johnson Assocs. v. R.E. Serv. Co., 285 F.3d 1046 (Fed. Cir. 2002).

Johnson Worldwide Associates, Inc. v. Zebco Corp., 175 F.3d 985 (Fed. Cir. 1999).

Joy Technologies, Inc. v. Flakt, Inc., 6 F.3d 770 (Fed. Cir. 1993).

Jurgens v. CBK, Ltd., 80 F.3d 1566 (Fed. Cir. 1996).

Kaufman Co., Inc. v. Lantech, Inc., 807 F.2d 970 (Fed. Cir. 1986).

Kaufman Co., Inc. v. Lantech, Inc., 926 F.2d 1136 (Fed. Cir. 1991).

Kearns v. Chrysler Corp., 32 F.3d 1541 (Fed. Cir. 1994).

Kimberly-Clark Corp. v. Johnson & Johnson, 745 F.2d 1437 (Fed. Cir. 1984).

Kingsdown Medical Consultants, Ltd. v. Hollister Inc., 863 F.2d 867 (Fed. Cir. 1988), *cert. denied*, 490 U.S. 1067 (1989).

Kloster Speedsteel AB v. Crucible Inc., 793 F.2d 1565 (Fed. Cir. 1986).

Knorr-Bremse Systeme Fuer Nutzfahrzeuge GmbH v. Dana Corp., 383 F.3d 1337 (Fed. Cir. 2004) (*en banc*).

Kordel v. United States, 335 U.S. 345 (1948).

L.A. Gear, Inc. v. Thom McAn Shoe Co., 988 F.2d 1117 (Fed. Cir. 1993).

Lindemann Maschinenfabrik GmbH v. American Hoist & Derrick Co., Harris Press & Shear Div., 895 F.2d 1403 (Fed. Cir. 1990).

London v. Carson Pirie Scott & Co., 946 F.2d 1534 (Fed. Cir. 1991).

Madey v. Duke Univ., 307 F.3d 1351 (Fed. Cir. 2002), *cert. denied*, 123 S. Ct. 2639 (2003).

Markman v. Westview Instruments, Inc., 517 U.S. 370 (1996).

Mentor H/S, Inc. v. Medical Device Alliance, Inc., 240 F.3d 1016 (Fed. Cir. 2001).

Mentor H/S, Inc. v. Medical Device Alliance, Inc., 244 F.3d 1365 (Fed. Cir. 2001).

Merck KGaA v. Integra Lifesciences I, Ltd., 545 U.S. at __, 125 S. Ct. 2372 (2005).

Micro Chem., Inc. v. Great Plains Chem. Co., 103 F.3d 1538 (Fed. Cir. 1997).

Minco, Inc. v. Combustion Engineering, Inc., 95 F.3d 1109 (Fed. Cir. 1996).

Moba, B.V. v. Diamond Automation, Inc., 325 F.3d 1306 (Fed. Cir. 2003).

Modine Mfg. Co. v. Allen Group, Inc., 917 F.2d 538 (Fed. Cir. 1990), *cert. denied*, 500 U.S. 918 (1991).

Molins PLC v. Textron, Inc., 48 F.3d 1172 (Fed. Cir. 1995).

Morton Salt Co. v. G.S. Supplier Co., 314 U.S. 488 (1942).

Motorola, Inc. v. Interdigital Technology Corp., 121 F.3d 1461 (Fed. Cir. 1997).

National Presto Industries, Inc. v. West Bend Co., 76 F.3d 1185 (Fed. Cir. 1996).

Northern Telecom, Inc. v. Datapoint Corp., 908 F.2d 931 (Fed. Cir. 1990), *cert. denied*, 498 U.S. 920 (1990).

Northwestern Memorial Hospital v. Ashcroft, 362 F.3d 923 (7th Cir. 2004).

Odetics, Inc. v. Storage Technology Corp., 185 F.3d 1259 (Fed. Cir. 1999).

Panduit Corp. v. Dennison Mfg. Co., 810 F.2d 1561 (Fed. Cir. 1987).

Panduit Corp. v. Stahlin Bros. Fibre Works, 575 F.2d 1152 (6th Cir. 1978).

Paper Converting Machine Co. v. Magna-Graphics Corp., 745 F.2d 11 (Fed. Cir. 1984).

Paragon Podiatry Laboratory, Inc. v. KLM Laboratories, Inc., 984 F.2d 1182 (Fed. Cir. 1993).

Perez v. Wyeth Laboratories, 734 A.2d 1245 (1999).

Pfaff v. Wells Electronics, Inc., 525 U.S. 55 (1998).

Phillips v. AWH Corp., 415 F.3d 1303 (Fed. Cir. 2005).

Read Corp. v. Portec, Inc., 970 F.2d 816 (Fed. Cir. 1992).

Regents of the University of California v. Eli Lilly & Co., 119 F.3d 1559 (Fed. Cir. 1997).

Rite-Hite Corp. v. Kelley Co., Inc., 56 F.3d 1538 (Fed. Cir. 1995) (en banc), *cert. denied*, 516 U.S. 867 (1995).

Roche Products, Inc. v Bolar Pharmaceuticals Co., 733 F.2d 858 (Fed. Cir. 1984).

Rhone-Poulenc Inc. v. FDA, 636 F.2d 750 (D.C. Cir. 1980).

Rolls-Royce Ltd. v. GTE Valeron Corp., 800 F.2d 1101 (Fed. Cir. 1986).

Sanitary Refrigerator v. Winters, 280 U.S. 30 (1929).

Schering Corp. v. Geneva Pharmaceuticals Inc., 339 F.3d 1373 (Fed. Cir. 2003).

SmithKline Beecham Corp. v. Apotex Corp., 365 F.3d 1306 (Fed. Cir. 2004).

SRI Int'l, Inc. v. Advanced Tech. Labs. Inc., 127 F.3d 1462 (Fed. Cir. 1997).

State Industries, Inc. v. Mor-Flo Industries, Inc., 883 F.2d 1573 (Fed. Cir. 1989).

Symbol Technologies, Inc. v. Lemelson Medical, 277 F.3d 1361 (Fed. Cir. 2002), *cert. denied*, 537 U.S. 825 (2002).

Tate Access Floors, Inc. v. Interface Architectural Res., Inc., 279 F.3d 1357 (Fed. Cir. 2002).

Tec Air, Inc. v. Denso Mfg. Michigan Inc., 192 F.3d 1353 (Fed. Cir. 1999).

Textile Productions, Inc. v. Mead Corp., 134 F.3d 1481 (Fed. Cir. 1998).

Therma-Tru Corp. v. Peachtree Doors Inc., 44 F.3d 988 (Fed. Cir. 1995).

Thompson v. Western States Medical Center, 535 U.S. 357 (2002).

Underwater Devices, Inc. v. Morrison-Knudsen Co., 717 F.2d 1380 (Fed. Cir. 1983).

Uniroyal, Inc. v. Rudkin-Wiley Corp., 939 F.2d 1540 (Fed. Cir. 1991).

Univ. of Rochester v. G.D. Searle & Co., 358 F.3d 916 (Fed. Cir. 2004).

U.S. ex rel. Pogue v. Diabetes Treatment Centers of America, No. 993298 (D.D.C., May 17, 2004).

U.S. ex rel. Stewart v. Louisiana Clinic, No. 99-1761 (E.D. La. June 4, 2003).

Vas-Cath Inc. v. Mahurkar, 935 F.2d 1555 (Fed. Cir. 1991).

Virginia State Board v. Virginia Citizens Council, 425 U.S. 748 (1976).

Vitronics Corp. v. Conceptronic, Inc., 90 F.3d 1576 (Fed. Cir. 1996).

Wang Laboratories, Inc. v. Toshiba Corp., 993 F.2d 858 (Fed. Cir. 1993).

Walker Process Equipment, Inc. v. Food Machinery & Chemical Corp., 382 U.S. 172 (1965).

Warner-Jenkinson Co. v. Hilton Davis Chem. Co., 117 S. Ct. 1040 (1997).

Washington Legal Foundation v. Friedman, 13 F. Supp. 2d 51 (D.D.C. 1998), amended by 36 F. Supp. 2d 16 (D.D.C. 1999), amended by, 36 F. Supp. 2d 418 (D.D.C. 1999), *mot. denied, summ. judgment granted*, 56 F. Supp. 2d 81 (D.D.C. 1999), *vacated in part sub nom. Washington Legal Foundation v. Henney*, 202 F.3d 331 (D.C. Cir. 2000), *mot. denied*, 128 F. Supp. 2d 11 (D.D.C. 2000).

Water Tech. Corp. v. Calco Ltd., 850 F.2d 660 (Fed. Cir. 1988).

Webster Elec. Co. v. Splitdorf Elec. Co., 264 U.S. 463 (1924).

Whittemore v. Cutter, 29 F. Cas. 1120 (no. 17, 600, c.c.d. Mass. 1813).

W.L. Gore & Associates, Inc. v. Garlock, Inc., 842 F.2d 1275 (Fed. Cir. 1988).

State Laws

Cornell Legal Information Institute: State Constitutions, Statutes and Related Legislative Information
http://www.law.cornell.edu/statutes.html#state

Health Privacy Project, *State Health Privacy Laws*, 2d edition (2002)
http://www.healthprivacy.org/info-url_nocat2304/info-url_nocat.htm

National Conference of State Legislatures
http://www.ncsl.org/

State Laws Concerning the Use of Animals in Research
http://www.nabr.org/Animallaw

Sandra P. Kaltman & John M. Isidor, *State Laws Affecting Institutional Review Boards*, 4 MED. RESEARCH LAW & POLICY 417 (2005).

Additional Resources

ABA Model Asset Purchase Agreement with Commentary (American Bar Association, June 2001)

ABA Model Stock Purchase Agreement with Commentary (American Bar Association, 1995)

Advanced Medical Technology Association Code of Ethics on Interactions with Health Care Professionals ("AdvaMed Code"), January 1, 2004
http://www.advamed.org/publicdocs/code_of_ethics.pdf

American Association of Laboratory Animal Science
http://www.aalas.org/index.aspx

American College of Laboratory Animal Medicine
http://www.aclam.org/

Animal Health Institute
http://www.ahi.org/

American Hospital Formulary Service Drug Information (AHFS-DI) (American Society of Health-System Pharmacists, 2005)
http://www.ashp.org/ahfs/

American Intellectual Property Law Association
http://www.aipla.org/

American Medical Association Ethical Guidelines on Gifts to Physicians from Industry ("AMA Guidelines") (June 1992)
http://www.ama-assn.org/ama/pub/category/5689.html
http://www.ama-assn.org/ama/pub/category/4001.html

American Medical Association's Council on Judicial and Ethical Affairs ("CEJA"), Clarification of Gifts to Physicians from Industry, CEJA Ethical Opinion 8.061—Clarifying Addendum
http://www.ama-assn.org/ama/pub/category/4263.html

American Medical Association's Council on Judicial and Ethical Affairs, "Guidelines on Gifts to Physicians from Industry: an Update," 56(1) *Food Drug Law J.* 27-40 (2001).

Association for Assessment and Accreditation of Laboratory Animal Care International
http://www.aaalac.org/

Association of American Medical Colleges
http://www.aamc.org/

Association of American Medical Colleges, "Guidelines for Academic Medical Centers on Security and Privacy." "Practical Strategies for Addressing the Health Insurance Portability and Accountability Act." (May 2001)
www.aamc.org/members/gir/gasp/start.htm.

Association of American Medical Colleges—HIPAA Resources
http://www.aamc.org/members/gir/gasp/hipaaresources.htm

Association of University Technology Managers (AUTM)
http://www.autm.net/aboutTT/aboutTT_faqs.cfm

Averill, *Lawyers Helping Lawyers: HIPAA Privacy Rules,* 51 L.A. BAR JNL. 280 (December 2003-January 2004).

Biotechnology Industry Organization
http://www.bio.org/

Biotechnology Industry Organization, "Biotechnology Industry Facts" excerpted from *BIO 2005-2006: Guide to Biotechnology* (2005)
http://www.bio.org/speeches/pubs/er/statistics.asp

Charles Shifley, *Flawed or Flawless: Twenty Years of Federal Circuit Appeals*, 2 J. MARSHALL REV. INTELL. PROP. L. 178 (2003)
http://www.jmls.edu/ripl/vol2/issue2/shifley.pdf.

Collaborations and Licensing in Global Pharmaceuticals and Biotech (Visiongain Management Reports, 2005)

Congressional Research Service, *The Virus-Serum-Toxin Act: A Brief History and* Analysis, Code RS22014 (January 3, 2005)
http://www.opencrs.com/document/RS22014/

Critical Factors for Alliance Formation: Insights from the Deloitte Research Biotech Alliance Survey, Deloitte Research, 2005.

Current Procedural Terminology (CPT)
http://www.ama-assn.org/ama/pub/category/3113.html

DRUGDEX® System (Thomson Micromedex, 2005)
http://www.micromedex.com/products/drugdex/

Duckett and Burns, *Responding to Subpoenas for Medical Records: In Compliance with HIPAA,* 39 Tenn. B.J. 18 (May 2003)

Growth Strategies for Large Biopharma Companies: Sustaining Future Growth Through Expanded Capabilities and Targeted Innovation (Deloitte Research, 2004)
http://www.deloitte.com/dtt/cda/doc/content/DTT_DR_Biopharma_Jan04.pdf

Dr. Jeremy Levin, Global Head of Strategic Alliances, Novartis Institutes for BioMedical Research, Speech given to the Massachusetts Biotechnology Council, October 2003.

Executive Office of the President, Council on Environmental Quality and Office of Science and Technology Policy, 2001, *Case Studies of Environmental Regulation of Biotechnology* (Washington, D.C., CEQ-OSTP 2001)
http://www.ostp.gov/html/012201.html

International Conference on Harmonisation of Technical Requirements for Registration of Pharmaceuticals for Human Use (ICH)
http://www.ich.org/cache/compo/276-254-1.html

International Trade Commission
http://www.usitc.gov/

IP Law Bulletin
http://www.iplawbulletin.com/Public/Default.aspx

Jennifer Miller, *Sealing the Coffin on Experimental Use*, 2003 DUKE LAW & TECH. REVIEW 12 (2003).

Joseph A. DiMasi, et al., *The Price of Innovation: New Estimates of Drug Development Costs*, 22 J. HEALTH ECONOMICS 151-85 (2003)
http://www.cptech.org/ip/health/econ/dimasi2003.pdf

Joseph D. Cohen, *What's Really Happening in Inter Partes Reexamination*, 87 *JPTOS* 207 (2005)
http://www.stoel.com/resources/articles/IP/InterPartes.pdf

Jay P. Kesan and Gwendolyn G. Ball, "How Are Patent Cases Resolved? An Empirical Examination of the Adjudication and Settlement of Patent Disputes," Univ. Ill. Law & Economics Research Paper (2005)
http://ssrn.com/abstract=808347

Kenneth S. Dueker, *Biobusiness on Campus; Commercialization of University-Developed Biomedical Technologies*, 52 FOOD DRUG L.J., 453 (1997).

Learning the Biopartnering Game: How to Achieve More from Your Alliance, IBM Business Consulting Services (2004)

Mandala Project, TED Case Studies Number 399, *Bovine Growth Hormone (rbST) and Dairy Trade*
http://www.american.edu/TED/bst.htm

The McKinsey Quarterly, 2004 Number 1 (McKinsey & Company)
http://www.mckinseyquarterly.com/

Michael D. Bednarek, et al., "Katz Patent Reexaminations: A Change in Momentum Favoring RAKTL Targets"
http://library.findlaw.com/2004/Jun/9/133461.html

OMB Circular A-110, "Uniform Administrative Requirements for Grants and Agreements With Institutions of Higher Education, Hospitals, and Other Non-Profit Organizations" (revised November 19, 1993, as further amended September 30, 1999)
http://www.whitehouse.gov/omb/circulars/a110/a110.html

Pew Initiative on Food and Biotechnology, *Biotech in the Barnyard: Implications of Genetically Engineered Animals*, Conference Proceedings, Dallas, Texas, September 24-25, 2002 (Washington, D.C.) (Pew, 2002)
http://www.pewagbiotech.org

Pew Initiative on Food and Biotechnology, *Bugs in the System: Issues in the Science and Regulation of Genetically Modified Insects* (Washington, D.C.) (Pew, 2004)
http://www.pewagbiotech.org

Pew Initiative on Food and Biotechnology, *Future Fish: Issues in Science and Regulation of TransgenicFish* (Washington, D.C.) (Pew, 2003)
http://www.pewagbiotec.org

Pharma Alliances: Bridging the Gap, The Kerdan Group, 2005.

Pharmaceutical Research and Manufacturers of America
http://www.phrma.org/

The Pharmaceutical Research and Manufacturers of America Code on Interactions with Healthcare Professionals ("PhRMA Code") (July 1, 2002)
http://www.phrma.org/publications/policy//2004-01-19.391.pdf

Policies and Procedures: Policy on the University's Relationship with a Faculty Start-up Company, Washington University in St. Louis (2001)
http://www.wustl.edu/policies/startup.html

The Public Patent Foundation
http://www.pubpat.org/

Report on Consensus Best Practices for Managing Hazardous Wastes in Academic Research Institutions, Howard Hughes Medical Institute (October 2001)
http://www.hhmi.org/research/labsafe/projects/report_congress.pdf

Robert L. Zeid, "Multi-Source Biotech-Derived Pharmaceuticals: Regulatory, Legal, and Scientific Issues in Development—Part 1" (2001)
http://www.drugdiscoveryonline.com/content/news/article.asp?DocID=%7B74DE2718-E0B5-11D4-A76E-00D0B7694F32%7D&Bucket=Guest+Columnists&VNETCOOKIE=NO

S. Nicholson, P. Danzon, and J. McCullough, "Biotech-Pharmaceutical Alliances as a Signal of Asset and Firm Quality," NBER Working Paper, No. 9007 (June 2002).

Dr. Sinead B. Clarke, et al., Learning the BioPartnering Game: How to Achieve More from Your Alliance, IBM Business Consulting Services (2004)
http://www-1.ibm.com/services/us/index.wss/ibvstudy/imc/a1005825

Stephen P. Swinton and Adam A. Welland, *Patent Injunction Reform and the Overlooked Problem of "False Positives,"* 70 BNA Patent, Trademark, and Copyright J. 1728 (2005)
http://www.lw.com/resource/publications/_pdf/pub1316_1.pdf

Tufts Center for the Study of Drug Development
http://csdd.tufts.edu/

USP DI, Drug Information for the Health Care Professional, Vol. 1 (Thomson Micromedex, 2005)
http://www.micromedex.com/products/uspdi/v1/

Victoria Slind-Flor, *Federal Circuit Judged Flawed*, Nat'l L. J. (Aug. 3, 1998).

What You Should Know About Intellectual Property, Research Collaborations, Materials Transfers, Consulting, and Confidential Disclosure Agreements, A Guide for Howard Hughes Medical Institute Investigators, Hughes Medical Institute Investigators (2005)
www.hhmi.org/pdf/investigator-guide.pdf.

Europe

Case Law

Case C-201/94, The Queen / The Medicines Control Agency, *ex parte* Smith & Nephew Pharmaceuticals and Primecrown / The Medicines Control Agency, 1996 E.C.R. I-5819
http://curia.eu.int/en/content/juris/index_form.htm

Case C-94/98, The Queen v. The Licensing Authority established by the Medicines Act 1968 (represented by the Medicines Control Agency), *ex parte* Rhône-Poulenc Rorer Ltd., May & Baker Ltd.,1999 E.C.R. I-8789
http://curia.eu.int/en/content/juris/index_form.htm

Case C-173/98, Sebago Inc. and Ancienne Maison Dubois et Fils SA. v. G-B Unic SA, 1999 E.C.R. I-4103
http://curia.eu.int/en/content/juris/index_form.htm

Case C-143/00, Boehringer Ingelheim KG and others v. Swingward Ltd. and another, 2002 E.C.R. I-3759
http://curia.eu.int/en/content/juris/index_form.htm

Case C-112/02, Kohlpharma GmbH v. Bundesrepublik Deutschland, 2004 O.J. (C 106) 8
http://curia.eu.int/en/content/juris/index_form.htm

Monsanto v. Stauffer [1985] R.P.C. 515.

Klinische Versuche I (Interferon-gamma) [1997] R.P.C. 623.

Klinische Versuche II (Erythropoetion) [1998] R.P.C. 423.

Directives

EudraLex, The Rules Governing Medicinal Products in the European Union
http://pharmacos.eudra.org/F2/eudralex/index.htm

Council Directive 86/609/EEC of 24 November 1986 on the approximation of laws, regulations and administrative provisions of the member states regarding the protection of animals used for experimental and other scientific purposes, 1986 *O.J. (L 358) 1*
http://europa.eu.int/comm/food/fs/aw/aw_legislation/scientific/86-609-eec_en.pdf

First Council Directive 89/104/EEC of 21 December 1988 to approximate the laws of the Member States relating to trade marks, 1989 O.J (L 040) 1
http://europa.eu.int/eur-lex/lex/LexUriServ/LexUriServ.do?uri=CELEX:31989L0104:EN:HTML

Council Directive 90/219/EEC of 23 April 1990 on the contained use of genetically modified micro-organisms, 1990 O.J. (L 117) 1
http://dg3.eudra.org/F2/eudralex/vol-1/pdfs-en/900219en.pdf

Council Directive 98/81/EC of 26 October 1998 amending Directive 90/219/EEC on the contained use of genetically modified micro-organisms, 1998 O.J. (L 330) 13
http://europa.eu.int/comm/environment/biotechnology/pdf/dir98_81.pdf

Directive 2001/18/EC of the European Parliament and of the Council of 12 March 2001on the deliberate release into the environment of genetically modified organisms and repealing Council Directive 90/220/EEC, 2001 O.J. (L 106) 1
http://europa.eu.int/eur-lex/pri/en/oj/dat/2001/l_106/l_10620010417en00010038.pdf

Directive 2001/20/EC of the European Parliament and of the Council of 4 April 2001 on the approximation of laws, regulations and administrative provisions of the member states relating to the implementation of good clinical practice in the conduct of clinical trials on medicinal products for human use, 2001 O.J. (L 121) 34

Directive 2001/20/EC, Implementing Texts
http://pharmacos.eudra.org/F2/pharmacos/dir200120ec.htm

Directive 2001/83/EC of the European Parliament and of the Council of 6 November 2001 on the Community Code relating to medicinal products for human use, 2001 O.J. (L 311) 67
http://pharmacos.eudra.org/F2/eudralex/vol-1/DIR_2001_83/DIR_2001_83_EN.pdf

Directive 2002/98/EC of the European Parliament and of the Council of 27 January 2003 setting standards of quality and safety for the collection, testing, processing, storage and distribution of human blood and blood components and amending Directive 2001/83/EC, 2003 O.J. (L 33) 30
http://pharmacos.eudra.org/F2/eudralex/vol-1/DIR_2002_98/DIR_2002_98_EN.pdf

Commission Directive 2003/94/EC of 8 October 2003 laying down the principles and guidelines of good manufacturing practice in respect of medicinal products for human use and investigational medicinal products for human use (Text with EEA relevance), 2003 O.J. (L 262) 22
http://pharmacos.eudra.org/F2/eudralex/vol-1/Dir_2003_94/Dir_2003_94_EN.pdf

Commission Directive 2003/63/EC of 25 June 2003 amending Directive 2001/83/EC of the European Parliament and of the Council on the Community code relating to medicinal products for human use (Text with EEA relevance), 2003 O.J. (L 159) 46
http://pharmacos.eudra.org/F2/eudralex/vol-1/DIR_2003_63/ DIR_2003_63_EN.pdf

Directive 2004/9/EC of the European Parliament and of the Council of 11 February 2004 on the inspection and verification of good laboratory practice (GLP) (Codified version) (Text with EEA relevance), 2004 O.J. (L 50) 28
http://europa.eu.int/eur-lex/pri/en/oj/dat/2004/l_050/ l_05020040220en00280043.pdf

Directive 2004/10/EC of the European Parliament and of the Council of 11 February 2004 on the harmonisation of laws, regulations and administrative provisions relating to the application of the principles of good laboratory practice and the verification of their applications for tests on chemical substances (codified version) (Text with EEA relevance), 2004 O.J. (L 50) 44
http://europa.eu.int/eur-lex/pri/en/oj/dat/2004/l_050/ l_05020040220en00440059.pdf

Directive 2004/23/EC of the European Parliament and of the Council of 31 March 2004 on setting standards of quality and safety for the donation, procurement, testing, processing, preservation, storage and distribution of human tissues and cells, 2004 O.J. (L 102) 48
http://europa.eu.int/eur-lex/pri/en/oj/dat/2004/l_102/ l_10220040407en00480058.pdf

Directive 2004/24/EC of the European Parliament and of the Council of 31 March 2004 amending, as regards traditional herbal medicinal products, Directive 2001/83/EC on the Community code relating to medicinal products for human use, 2004 O.J. (L 136) 85
http://pharmacos.eudra.org/F2/eudralex/vol-1/DIR_2004_24/ DIR_2004_24_EN.pdf

Directive 2004/27/EC of the European Parliament and of the Council of 31 March 2004 on the Community Code relating to medicinal products for human use, (Text with EEA relevance), 2004 O.J. (L 136) 34
http://pharmacos.eudra.org/F2/eudralex/vol-1/DIR_2004_27/ DIR_2004_27_EN.pdf

Directive 2004/28/EC of the European Parliament and of the Council of 31 March 2004 on the Community Code relating to veterinary medicinal products (Text with EEA relevance), 2004 O.J. (L 136) 58
http://pharmacos.eudra.org/F2/review/doc/final_publ/ Dir_2004_28_20040430_EN.pdf

Commission Directive 2004/33/EC of the European Parliament and of the Council of 22 March 2004 implementing Directive 2002/98/EC of the European Parliament and of the Council as regards certain technical requirements for blood and blood components (Text with EEA relevance), 2004 O.J. (L 91) 25
http://europa.eu.int/eur-lex/pri/en/oj/dat/2004/l_091/
l_09120040330en00250039.pdf

Commission Directive 2005/28/EC of 8 April 2005 laying down principles and detailed guidelines for good clinical practice as regards investigational medicinal products for human use, as well as the requirements for authorisation of the manufacturing or importation of such products (Text with EEA relevance), 2005 O.J. (L 91) 13
http://pharmacos.eudra.org/F2/eudralex/vol-1/DIR_2005_28/
DIR_2005_28_EN.pdf

Regulations

Regulation (EC) No. 1829/2003 of the European Parliament and of the Council of 22 September 2003 on genetically modified food and feed (Text with EEA relevance), 2003 O.J. (L 268) 1
http://europa.eu.int/eur-lex/pri/en/oj/dat/2003/l_268/
l_26820031018en00010023.pdf

Regulation (EC) No. 1882/2003 of the European Parliament and of the Council of 29 September 2003, adapting to Council Decision 1999/468/EC the provisions relating to committees which assist the Commission in the exercise of its implementing powers laid down in instruments subject to the procedure referred to in Article 251 of the EC Treaty, 2003 O.J. (L 284) 1.
http://europa.eu.int/eur-lex/pri/en/oj/dat/2003/l_284/
l_28420031031en00010053.pdf

Regulation (EC) No. 726/2004 of the European Parliament and of the Council of 31 March 2004 laying down Community procedures for the authorization and supervision of medicinal products for human and veterinary use and establishing a European Medicines Agency (Text with EEA relevance), 2004 O.J. (L 136) 1.
http://pharmacos.eudra.org/F2/eudralex/vol-1/REG_2004_726/
REG_2004_726_EN.pdf

Commission Regulation (EC) No. 772/2004 of 27 April 2004, on the application of Article 81(3) of the Treaty to categories of technology transfer agreements (Text with EEA relevance), 2004 O.J. (L 123) 11.

http://europa.eu.int/eur-lex/pri/en/oj/dat/2004/l_123/
l_12320040427en00110017.pdf

European Commission, DG Enterprise & Industry, Unit F2 'Pharmaceuticals', Human Tissue Engineering and Beyond: Proposal for a Community Regulatory Framework on Advanced Therapies, Proposal for a Regulation of the European Parliament and of the Council on Advanced Therapies and amending Regulation (EC) No. 726/2004 (20 May 2005).
http://pharmacos.eudra.org/F2/advtherapies/docs/DraftRegulation-Advanced%20Therapies-2005-May-04.pdf

Communication from the Commission to the Council, the European Parliament, the Economic and Social Committee and the Committee of the Regions, "Life Sciences and biotechnology—a Strategy for Europe," COM(2002) 27 final (Brussels, 23/1/2002).
http://europa.eu.int/eur-lex/en/com/cnc/2002/com2002_0027en01.pdf

Proposal for a Regulation of the European Parliament and of the Council on medicinal products for paediatric use and amending Regulation (EEC) No. 1768/92, Directive 2001/83/EC and Regulation (EC) No. 726/2004; European Commission COM(2004) 599 final (29/9/2004).
http://pharmacos.eudra.org/F2/Paediatrics/docs/_2004_09/EN.pdf

European Commission

European Commission—Directorates-General and Services
http://europa.eu.int/comm/dgs_en.htm

European Commission, Directorate-General Health and Consumer Protection (SANCO), Biotechnology
http://europa.eu.int/comm/food/food/biotechnology/index_en.htm

European Commission, Directorate-General Health and Consumer Protection, Biotechnology International Regulations
http://europa.eu.int/comm/food/food/biotechnology/intlmatters/index_en.htm

European Commission, Directorate-General Enterprise and Industry, Unit F2, Pharmaceuticals (Pharmacos Unit F2)
http://pharmacos.eudra.org/F2/home.html

European Commission, Directorate-General Enterprise and Industry, Unit F2, Pharmaceuticals (Pharmacos Unit F2), Advanced Therapies: Tissue Engineering, Cell Therapy and Gene Therapy
http://pharmacos.eudra.org/F2/advtherapies/index.htm

European Commission, Directorate-General Enterprise and Industry, Unit F2, Pharmaceuticals (Pharmacos Unit F2), Mutual Recognition Agreements (MRA)
http://pharmacos.eudra.org/F2/mra/index.htm

European Commission, Directorate-General Enterprise and Industry, *Detailed guidance for the request of an authorisation of a clinical trial on a medicinal product for human use to the competent authorities, notification of substantial amendments and declaration of the end of the trial*, Revision 1 (1 April 2004).
http://dg3.eudra.org/F2/pharmacos/docs/Doc2004/april/cp%20and%20guidance%20CA%20rev%2028%20Apr%2004%20Final%20.pdf

European Commission, Directorate-General Enterprise and Industry, Unit F3, Cosmetics and Medical Devices, Cosmetics
http://pharmacos.eudra.org/F3/cosmetic/cosm_intro_NEW.htm

European Commission, Directorate-General Enterprise and Industry, Unit F3, Cosmetics and Medical Devices, Medical Devices
http://europa.eu.int/comm/enterprise/medical_devices/index_en.htm

European Commission, Directorate-General Enterprise and Industry, Detailed Guidelines on the Principles of Good Clinical Practice in the Conduct in the EU of Clinical Trials on Medicinal Products for Human Use, Draft 5.1, ENTR/6416/01 (Brussels, July 2002).
http://pharmacos.eudra.org/F2/pharmacos/docs/Doc2002/July/gcp_51_july.pdf

European Commission, Directorate-General Enterprise and Industry, Good Laboratory Practice
http://www.europa.eu.int/comm/enterprise/chemicals/legislation/glp/index_en.htm

European Commission, Biotechnological Inventions
http://europa.eu.int/comm/internal_market/en/indprop/invent/index.htm

European Commission, Data Protection
http://europa.eu.int/comm/justice_home/fsj/privacy/index_en.htm

European Commission, Environment Policies: Biotechnology
http://europa.eu.int/comm/environment/biotechnology/index_en.htm

European Commission, Environment: Laboratory Animals
http://europa.eu.int/comm/environment/chemicals/lab_animals/index_en.htm

European Commission, Life Sciences & Biotechnology: A Strategic Vision
http://europa.eu.int/comm/biotechnology/intro_en.html

European Commission—Medical Devices

http://europa.eu.int/comm/enterprise/medical_devices/index_en.htm

European Commission, Guidelines relating to Medical Devices Directives
http://europa.eu.int/comm/enterprise/medical_devices/meddev/

European Commission, Research: Biosociety
http://europa.eu.int/comm/research/biosociety/index_en.htm

European Commission, Research: Biosociety, Documents on Life Sciences Issues for Health
http://europa.eu.int/comm/research/biosociety/life_sciences/documents_en.htm

European Commission Communication on the Single Market in Pharmaceuticals COM(98) 588 Final (Brussels, 25 November 1998).
http://europa.eu.int/comm/enterprise/library/lib-regulation/doc/com-98-588_en.pdf

European Commission Press Release, How Does the European Commission Deal with Ethical Issues Within Its Framework Programme for Research and Development? MEMO/05/121 (17 May 2005).
http://europa.eu.int/rapid/pressReleasesAction.do?reference=MEMO/05/121&format=HTML&aged=0&language=EN&guiLanguage=en

European Commission Press Release, "Questions and Answers on the Regulation of GMOs in the European Union," MEMO/05/104 (22 March 2005).
http://europa.eu.int/rapid/pressReleasesAction.do?reference=MEMO/05/104&format=HTML&aged=0&language=EN&guiLanguage=en

European Medicines Agency (EMEA)
http://www.emea.eu.int

European Medicines Agency, Human Medicines
http://www.emea.eu.int/index/indexh1.htm

European Medicines Agency, Inspections
http://www.emea.eu.int/Inspections/index.html

European Medicines Agency, Emerging Therapies and Technologies
http://www.emea.eu.int/htms/human/itf/itfguide.htm

European Medicines Agency, "Establishment in the EEA"
http://www.emea.eu.int/htms/human/presub/q16.htm

European Medicines Agency, "Mandate, objectives and rules of procedure for the Working Party on Similar Biological Medicinal Products (BMWP)," Doc. Ref. EMEA/CHMP/80650/2004 (London, 18 March 2005).
http://www.emea.eu.int/pdfs/human/biosimilar/8065005en.pdf

European Medicines Agency, Medicinal Products Containing or Consisting of Genetically Modified Organisms (GMOs)
http://www.emea.eu.int/htms/human/presub/q20.htm

European Medicines Agency, Mutual Recognition Agreements
http://www.emea.eu.int/Inspections/MRA.html

European Medicines Agency, Pharmacovigilance in the European Economic Area
http://www.eudravigilance.org/human/index.asp

European Medicines Agency, ICH Topic S6, Preclinical Safety Evaluation of Biotechnology-Derived Pharmaceuticals, Step 4, Consensus Guideline (16 July 1997).
http://www.emea.eu.int/pdfs/human/ich/030295en.pdf

European Medicines Agency, EMEA Pre-Submission Guidance for Users of the Centralised Procedure (London, February 2005).
http://www.emea.eu.int/htms/human/presub/PSG%20Compilation.pdf

European Medicines Agency, "General Principles EMEA, FDA Parallel Scientific Advice Meetings Pilot Program" (17 September 2004).
http://www.fda.gov/oia/pilotprogram0904.html

European Medicines Agency, ICH Topic E5, Ethnic Factors in the Acceptability of Foreign Clinical Data, Step 4, Consensus Guideline (5 February 1999).
http://www.emea.eu.int/pdfs/human/ich/02899Sen.pdf

European Medicines Agency, EMEA Post-Authorisation Guidance on Parallel Distribution, EMEA/Ho/2368/Rev 3 (London, 09 March 2005).
http://www.emea.eu.int/pdfs/human/parallel/236804en.pdf

European Medicines Agency, Committee for Proprietary Medicinal Products (CPMP), "Guideline on Comparability of Medicinal Products Containing Biotechnology-derived Proteins as Active Substance—Non-clinical and Clinical Issues," EMEA/CPMP/3097/02/Final (London, 17 December 2003).
http://www.emea.eu.int/pdfs/human/ewp/309702en.pdf

Council of Europe

Council of Europe, Treatise
http://conventions.coe.int/Treaty/EN/CadreListeTraites.htm

Additional Protocol to the Convention for the Protection of Human Rights and Dignity of the Human Being with regard to the Application of Biology and Medicine, on the Prohibition of Cloning Human Beings (Paris 12 January 1998).
http://conventions.coe.int/treaty/en/treaties/html/168.htm

Additional Protocol to the Convention on Human Rights and Biomedicine, on Transplantation of Organs and Tissues of Human Origin (Strasbourg 24 January 2002).
http://conventions.coe.int/treaty/en/treaties/html/186.htm

Additional Protocol to the Convention on Human Rights and Biomedicine, Concerning Biomedical Research (Strasbourg 25 January 2005).
http://conventions.coe.int/treaty/en/treaties/html/195.htm

Convention for the protection of Human Rights and dignity of the human being with regard to the application of Biology and Medicine, opened for signature in Oviedo 4 April 1997 and coming into force on 1 December 1999.
http://conventions.coe.int/treaty/en/treaties/html/164.htm

Convention for the protection of Human Rights and dignity of the human being with regard to the application of Biology and Medicine: Explanatory Report (April 1997).
http://conventions.coe.int/Treaty/EN/reports/html/164.htm

European Patent Office (EPO)

http://www.european-patent-office.org/index.en.php

European Patent Convention
http://www.european-patent-office.org/legal/epc/

European Patent Office, Decision of the EPO Boards of Appeal, *Telemechanique v. Siemens Nixdorf*, Case number T 0482/89—3.5.2 (11 December 1990).
http://legal.european-patent-office.org/dg3/biblio/t890482fx1.htm

European Patent Office, Decision of the EPO Boards of Appeal, *Howard Florey Institute of Experimental Physiology and Medicine*, Case number T 0272/95—3.3.4 (23 October 2002).
http://legal.european-patent-office.org/dg3/biblio/t950272eu2.htm

European Patent Office, Decision of the EPO Boards of Appeal, *The President and Fellows of Harvard College v. British Union for the Abolition of Vivisection, et al.*, Case number T 0315/03—3.3.8 (6 July 2004).
http://legal.european-patent-office.org/dg3/pdf/t030315ex1.pdf

European Patent Office, Decision of the EPO Boards of Appeal, *Ciba-Geigy*, Case number T 0049/83—3.3.1 (26 July 1983).
http://legal.european-patent-office.org/dg3/biblio/t830049ep1.htm

Guidelines for Examination in the European Patent Office
http://www.european-patent-office.org/legal/gui_lines/

Other

Community Plant Variety Office
http://www.cpvo.eu.int/default.php?lang=en

EudraCT European Community Clinical Trial System
http://eudract.emea.eu.int

European Economic Area (EEA) Legislative Framework: Chemicals, Industrial Risk and Biotechnology
http://europa.eu.int/eur-lex/en/lif/reg/en_register_15102050.html

Federation of European Laboratory Animal Science Associations
http://www.felasa.org/

Secretariat of the Convention on Biological Diversity, *Cartagena Protocol on Biosafety to the Convention on Biological Diversity: Text and Annexes* (Montreal, 2000)
http://www.biodiv.org/doc/legal/cartagena-protocol-en.pdf

Cartagena Protocol on Biosafety (Montreal, 29 January 2000)—Status of Ratification and Entry into Force
http://www.biodiv.org/biosafety/signinglist.aspx?sts=rtf&ord=dt

Heads of Agencies (Medicines)
http://heads.medagencies.org/

The International Conference on Harmonisation of Technical Requirements for Registration of Pharmaceuticals for Human Use (ICH)
http://www.ich.org

The International Union for the Protection of New Varieties of Plants
http://www.upov.int/index.html

The National Centre for the Replacement, Refinement and Reduction of Animals in Research
http://www.nc3rs.org.uk/

Office for Harmonization in the Internal Market—Trade Marks and Designs
http://oami.eu.int/en/default.htm

Organisation for Economic Co-operation and Development (OECD), Good Laboratory Practice
http://www.oecd.org/department/0,2688,en_2649_34381_1_1_1_1_1,00.html

World Intellectual Property Organization (WIPO)
http://www.wipo.int/portal/index.html.en

WIPO Patent Co-operation Treaty (PCT) Resources
http://www.wipo.int/pct/en/

Foreign Countries

Argentina

CONABIO, National Advisory Commission on Agricultural Biosafety
http://siiap.sagyp.mecon.ar/http-hsi/english/conabia/frameing.htm

Australia

Department of Health and Ageing, Office of the Gene Technology Regulator
http://www.ogtr.gov.au/

Department of Health and Ageing, Therapeutic Goods Administration
http://www.tga.gov.au/gene/index.htm

Food Standards Australia New Zealand
http://www.foodstandards.gov.au/

National Health and Medical Research Council
http://www.nhmrc.gov.au/index.htm

Brazil

National Technical Commission of Biosafety (CTNBio)
http://www.ctnbio.gov.br/

Canada

Canadian Food Inspection Agency (CFIA), Biotechnology
http://www.inspection.gc.ca/english/toc/bioteche.shtml

Environment Canada, New Substances (Biotechnology)
http://www.ec.gc.ca/substances/nsb/eng/index_e.htm

Health Canada, Food and Nutrition: Genetically Modified (GM) Foods & Other Novel
http://www.hc-sc.gc.ca/fn-an/gmf-agm/index_e.html

Health Canada, Science & Research: Biotechnology
http://www.hc-sc.gc.ca/sr-sr/biotech/index_e.html

Office of the Privacy Commissioner of Canada
http://www.privcom.gc.ca/index_e.asp

Speech by Jennifer Stoddart, Privacy Commissioner of Canada; "An overview of Canada's new private law—The *Personal Information Protection and Electronic Documents Act*" (Apr. 1, 2004)
http://www.privcom.gc.ca/speech/2004/vs/vs_sp-d_040331_e.asp

China

Ministry of Agriculture
http://www.agri.gov.cn/

India

Ministry of Science and Technology, Department of Biotechnology
http://www.dbtindia.nic.in/thanks/biosafetymain.html

United Kingdom

Medicines and Healthcare Products Regulatory Agency (MHRA)
http://www.mhra.gov.uk

UK Patent Office
http://www.patent.gov.uk/index.htm

UK Gene Therapy Advisory Committee (GTAC) http://www.advisorybodies.doh.gov.uk/genetics/gtac/index.htm

Index

A

Age Discrimination Act 329
Age Discrimination in Employment Act 273–74
Agency for Healthcare Research and Quality 581
Agreements
  business associate agreement disclosure 539–41
  confidentiality 122–25
  development and commercialization license 712–28
  employment contracts 288–99
  grants from federal agencies 326–52
  HIPAA authorizations 526–30
  license (patent and other) 171–79; 190–98; 710–12
  material transfer 124–26, 168–69
  non-compete 297
  research collaboration 126–28; 452–72
  SBIR and STTR grants 226–28; 344–46
  venture capital terms 230–35
Agricultural Bioterrorism Protection Act of 2002 646
Americans with Disabilities Act 270, 274–75
Animal and Plant Health Inspection Service 666
animal drugs 629–30
  administered in feed 635–36
  approval of new animal drugs. *See.*
  availability of 636–37
  Bureau of Veterinary Drugs 629
  different species, use in 636–37
  drugs for food animals. *See.*
  FFDCA, animal drug amendments to 629
  Minor Use and Minor Species Animal Health Act 637
  regulatory regime 630–33
Animal Health Protection Act 646
animal use in biomedical research and testing 408–24
  basic regulatory scheme 408–18
  Food and Drug Administration considerations 423–24
  Memorandum of Understanding Among Animal and Plant Health Inspection Service/U.S. Department of Agriculture 419
  National Institutes of Health considerations 420–23
    extramural research 421–22
    Guide for the Care and Use of Laboratory Animals 422
    Health Research Extension Act 420
    Institutional Animal Care and Use Committee Guidebook 422
  Principles for the Utilization and Care of Vertebrate Animals Used in Testing, Research and Training 418–19
  state law 424
    State Laws Concerning the Use of Animals in Research 424
animal use, regulation of biomedical products for 623–49
  animal health industry 625–27
    Association of American Feed Control Officials 627
    complexity 627
    development incentives 625
    gross revenues of 625
  animal health products 623–25
    Federal Food, Drug and Cosmetic Act 623

Federal Insecticide, Fungicide and Rodenticide Act 623
approval of new animal drugs 631–32
   compliance 632
   denial and withdrawal of approval 632
   enforcement 632
   expedited basis 631
   imminent hazard to human health 632
   inspection 632
   National Environmental Policy Act 631
   post-approval requirements 632
biotechnology products 639–41
biotechnology-derived products 628–29
   Animal and Plant Health Inspection Service 628
   Center for Veterinary Biologics 629
   Center for Veterinary Medicine 628
   Coordinated Framework for the Regulation of Biotechnology 628
Center for Veterinary Medicine 624, 633
   interacting with 637–41
drugs for food animals 633–35
   acceptable daily intake 635
   Center for Food Safety and Applied Nutrition 634
   Delaney Clause 634
   human food safety issues 633–35
   no observed effect level (NOEL) 634
   residues of animal drugs in edible tissue 634
   safe, Center for Veterinary Medicine definition of 633
   toxicology tests 634
government agencies relevant to animal health products 626
regulatory regime
   Center for Veterinary Medicine 630–33
   U.S. Department of Agriculture regulation of animal biological products, *See.*
Animal Welfare Act 329
Animal Welfare Act regulations 408–18
   Animal and Plant Health Inspection Service 412
   Animal Care Policy Manual 417
   civil penalties 410
   Federal Trade Secrets Act 416
   Freedom of Information Act 416
   Institutional Animal Care and Use Committee 410; 412–15
   implementation and enforcement of 417–20
   inspections 409
   intellectual property protection 411
   overview 408–11
   personnel qualifications 415
   procedures involving animals 413
   record keeping 415
   registration 412
   research facility 410
      defined 408
      requirements 409
   review of research activities 414
   U.S. Department of Agriculture 409
      authority, limits on 409
   veterinary care 415
anti-kickback statute 701–06
Association of American Feed Control Officials 627
Association of University Technology Managers 163

B

Bayh-Dole Act 163, 169, 174, 180–82
   applicability of 180–82
      license only" standard 181
      requirements of 180
      sublicensing 182
      title reversion right 181
      U.S. manufacturing preference 181
   requirements of 180

Index

Benefits Improvement and Protection Act
of 2000 572
biotech company life cycle 5–23
   challenges 10–23
      commercialization 11
      litigation 11–23
      regulatory oversight 11
   early development 8–9
      additional investment 8
      business growth 9
      complexity 9
      regulatory track 9
   later-stage development 10
   product approval 10
   start-up 6–8
      company formation 7
      intellectual property 6–7
      investment capital 7–23
biotech, defined 4–5
   three-branch approach 5
biotechnology, acquisition of 139–200
   biotechnology, transfer from academia. *See.*
   biotechnology, transfer from individuals. *See.*
   biotechnology, transfer from other nonprofit entity 184
   biotechnology transfer, forms of. *See.*
   technology, creation of. *See.*
biotechnology patent litigation for the non-patent attorney 813
   judicial and extrajudicial proceedings 815–19
      reexamination 816–19
      reissue 819
   patent case, phases of (procedural/strategic) 843–55
   patent litigation issues (substantive) 819–43
      claim interpretation 821–22
      damages 837–55
      infringement, defined 822–25
      infringement, proof of 825–37
      infringement, types of 824–25
biotechnology products in agricultural use, approval of 661–76

   Coordinated Federal Framework 662–64
   Food and Drug Administration, role of and states 668–71
      Federal Food, Drug and Cosmetic Act 668
      initial consultation 669
      labeling 669
      substances not "generally recognized as safe" 668
   other countries 671–76
      Argentina 672
      Brazil 672
      Canada 673
      China 674
      European Union 674
   state role in 670–71
   U.S. Department of Agriculture, role of 666–68
      and states 670–71
      Animal and Plant Health Inspection Service 666
      Environmental Assessment 667
      Environmental Impact Statement 667
      Plant Protection Act 666
   U.S. Environmental Protection Agency, role of 664–66
      and states 670
      Biopesticides and Pollution Prevention Division 664
      Federal Insecticide, Fungicide and Rodenticide Act 664
biotechnology products, legal requirements after approval 677–702. *See also* Food and Drug Administration.
   anti-kickback statute 701–06
      exceptions to 701
   False Claims Act 701
   Federal Trade Commission
      advertising regulation 678
   good manufacturing practice requirements 682–83
      strategies for compliance with 682
   import/export requirements 680–82

Certificate of a Pharmaceutical Product 681
Certificate to Foreign Government 681
export certificates 680
Office of Inspector General, Department of Health and Human Services 679
  anti-kickback statute 679
  Compliance Program Guidance for Pharmaceutical Manufacturers 679
  False Claims Act 679
sales and marketing regulations 686–700
  Prescription Drug Marketing Act 686
biotechnology, transfer from academia 162–84
  common restrictions 175–77
    audit 176
    cannot use university name 177
    government has a license 177
    indemnification 176
    license only, not an assignment 175
    license scope 176
    original licensee always liable 177
    restrictions on participation by the inventors 176
    sublicense approval 176
    sublicensee subject to license terms 176
    time limitations 176
  conflict between publication and protection of intellectual property 183–84
  "CREATE" Act of 2004 183
    prior art 183
  interests of other stakeholders 174–75
    Bayh-Dole Act 174
    Government Agencies 174
    National Institutes of Health 174
    nonprofits 175
    other underwriters 174
    special government considerations 174
  licensee considerations 171–72
    obtaining promise of cooperation from inventor 172
    policies and procedures 172
    public disclosure 173
    stakeholders 173
  principal investigator considerations 169–71
    Bayh-Dole Act 169
    conflict of commitment 170
    conflict of interest 169–70
    maintaining tax-free status of university 169
    special knowledge 171
  Trademark Clarification Act of 1984 180
  university considerations 162–68
    Association of University Technology Managers 163
    Bayh-Dole Act 163
    community considerations 167
    employee/researcher considerations 166
    main considerations 164
    society considerations 167
    University and Small Business Patent Procedure Act 162
  university license fees 177–79
    equity in the licensee 179
    equity protections 179
    lump-sum royalties 178
    milestone payments 178
    minimum annual payment 178
    participation in third-party payments 178
    periodic fees 178
    put of shares 179
    sales-based royalties 178
    standstill fee 177
    time for sale 179
    up-front fee 177
biotechnology, transfer from individuals 190–98
  common negotiation points 196–98
    confirmation of ownership 198

fees and royalties 196
indemnification 197
intellectual property matters 197
patent filing 199
price paid/consideration 196
records and reporting 197
warranty 197
terms 190
alternative dispute resolution 195
amendments 195
assignability 195
audit rights 194
boilerplate language 195
definitions 190
deliveries 193
follow-on and later-developed technology 192
indemnification 194
insurance 194
intellectual property protection 194
marketing responsibility 194
parties 190
payments 193
property licensed 190
recitals 190
reporting 194
representations and warranties of the inventor 194
retention of rights 193
right to sublicense 192
scope of assignment or license 191
term and renewal of license 192
termination 193
territory 191
biotechnology, transfer from other nonprofit entity 184–90
common misconceptions 187
Howard Hughes Medical Institute case study 188–89
assignment of rights 188
collaborations 189
equity ownership 189
sharing patent costs and royalties 189
start-up companies 189
time limitations 189

implications of nonprofit status 184–85
joint venturing 186
Small Business Innovation Research Program grants 186
Small Business Technology Transfer Program 187
priorities of nonprofit technology owner 185
unrelated business income tax 185
biotechnology transfer, forms of 155–61
acquisition of owner 155
and intellectual property 160
assignment 156
doctrine, effect on due diligence and intellectual property 160
employing the owner 155–56
fair use agreements 160
fair use and experimental use 158–60
experimental use doctrine in Europe and Japan 159
license 156–58
alternative to assignment 156–57
common form of transfer 156
license terms 157
public domain 161–62
sublicense 158
Board of Directors 70, 112–13
Board of Patent Appeals and Interferences 41
Byrd Anti-Lobbying Act 329

C

capital, pre-seed and seed 214–30
employee stock 218–21
commercial 221–43
corporate 220–21
incentive stock option 218
non-qualified stock options 218
plan basics 218
securities 219
tax 219
founders' stock 214–17
drag-along 217
lock-up 216
friends and family 223–24
corporate 224–25

        securities 223
    generating revenue to offset operating
        expense 225–26
        commercial 226
        intellectual property 225–43
        government funding 226–29
            advantages of 228
            disadvantages of 228
            Eligibility/51 Percent Rule 228
            Small Business Innovation Research grants 226
            Small Business Technology Transfer grants 227–28
        loans 224–25
        state resources 230
        stock to service or technology providers 221–23
            conflicts of interest 223
            securities 222
            tax 222
capital structure and stock grants 99–108
    common stock 105–08
    founders stock 100
    preferred stock 109–10
        key terms 110
    restricted stock 100
    securities law compliance 99
    stock options 100
capital, venture 230–36
    exit rights 233
        co-sale rights 235
        redemption rights 234
        registration rights 234
    financial rights 231–32
        accruing dividends 232
        liquidation preference 231
        participating preferred 231
        protection of ownership percentage 232
        valuation 231
    governance rights 233
        board representation 233–43
        class voting 233
        protective provisions 233
    Series B 235–36

Centers for Disease Control and Prevention 424, 581
Centers for Medicare and Medicaid Services 482, 565
Civil Rights Act of 1964 272, 329
clinical trials in the European Economic Area 743–812
    clinical trial authorization, applying for 747–812
    Clinical Trials Directive 743
        clinical trial, defined 745
        good clinical practice guidelines 753
        good clinical practice inspections 753
        insurance requirement 751
        provisions of 744–45
        sponsor, defined 746–47
    data protection law 751
    effect of noncompliance 751
    good clinical practice inspections 749
    good manufacturing practice inspections 749
    investigational medicinal product, defined 745
    investigational medicinal products 745–46
    liability and insurance 751
    manufacture, import of investigational medicinal products 748–49
        Qualified Person 749
    notification of adverse events 750
    regulatory framework 743–44
    serious adverse reactions 750
    suspected unexpected serious adverse reactions 750
    suspension of trials 750
company agreements, early stage 121–27
    confidentiality agreements 125–26
        disclosure of information 127
        exceptions to 126
        obligations with respect to the information received 126
        scope of 126
        term of 127
    material transfer agreements 128–37

Index

subject matter 128
research collaboration agreements 129–37
   ownership of intellectual property 127
   purpose of 130
review of intellectual property for non-intellectual property attorneys 121–22
   copyrights 124
   patents 121
   trademarks 122
   trade secrets 121
company formation 69–138
   board of directors, importance of 70–71
   capital structure and stock grants. *See.*
   company agreements, early stage. *See.*
   company models 73–79
      angel investor–funded 76
      charitable corporation or foundation 78
      corporate deal-funded 75–76
      debt-funded 79
      formed before in-licensing, R&D continues at university 74
      revenue-funded 75
      shoestring self-funded 77
      significant self-funded 77
      technology flip 75
      venture fund-launched 76
   company's attorneys, role of 73
   early participants, relationships with. *See.*
   entity selection, formation. *See.*
   fund raising 69–73
   incubators 118
   positioning for an exit 127–37
      generally accepted accounting principals 130
      public offerings 128
      sale of the company 128
      Sarbanes-Oxley Act 130
   simplicity 73
   timeliness 72
   university relationships 119–27
      arrangement guidelines 120
      policies for faculty members, staff, students 119
company formation 69-138 69
company formation
   company models
   "CREATE" Act of 2004 183

D

development and commercialization alliances 707–33
   anticipating changes of control 728–30
      licensee Issues 729–30
      licensor Issues 729
      tailoring a solution 730
   clinical stage licensing
      phase II 711
      phase III, clinical trials 711
   clinical-stage licensing 711
      phase 1 711
   Development and Commercialization License Agreement 712–28
      abandoned jurisdictions 723–24
      consideration for the license grant 716–23
      cooperation during regulatory approval process 725–26
      identifying subject technology 712–13
      intellectual property issues 723–25
      milestone payments 716–18
      nature and scope of license grant 712
      ongoing cooperation 724
      participation in the upside 726–31
      patent prosecution and maintenance 723
      prosecution of infringers 724
      punitive reduction in royalty rates 722–23
      retained rights of licensor 715–16
      rights granted 713–14
      royalty payments 718–21
         term of 721–22
      scope of rights 714
      trademarks, etc. 724

early-stage deals 709–10
   hits 710
   leads 710
   optimized leads 710
   target identification and validation 709
partners 707–08
   considerations in choosing 708
   reasons for choosing 707
pre-launch licensing 711–12
preclinical stage licensing
   ADME/Tox Studies 710–11
   investigational new drug application 711
preclinical-stage licensing 710–11
terminating agreement if alliance fails 730–32
   material breach by licensee 731
   material breach by licensor 732
   termination without cause 732

E

early participants, relationships with 111–14
  board of directors 112–13
   contacts of 113
   experience of 113
  employees 117
   confidentiality agreements 118
   flexibility, need for 117
   invention rights agreements 118
  founders 111–13
   role in company activities 112
  management 114–17
   chief executive officer 115–18
   chief financial officer 116
   chief scientific officer 116
   clinical 117
   regulatory 117
  scientific advisory board (SAB) 114–17
   compensation 114
Employee Polygraph Protection Act 288
Employee Retirement Income and Security Act 270–71, 285
employment contracts 288–99
  items to be covered 290–99
   boilerplate provisions 299
   compensation 291–99
   confidentiality 297
   disclosure of other pursuits 298
   duration 290
   duties and responsibilities 294
   fringe benefits 297
   noncompetition and nonsolicitation clauses 297
   position and title 291
   termination 295
   trade secret protection 297
  usefulness of 289–90
   confidentiality and intellectual property ownership 290
   defined compensation expectations 289–90
   defined performance expectations 289
   recruitment incentive 289
   security 289
employment issues 111–14, 265–316
  affirmative action obligations of government contracts 276
  Age Discrimination in Employment Act 273–74
   basic coverage 273
   Older Workers' Benefit Protection Act 273–74
  Americans with Disabilities Act 274–75
   basic coverage 274
   reasonable accommodation 274–75
  employee handbooks 299–303
   at-will statements 301
   description of benefits 303
   discipline policy 303–05
   disclaimers 301
   e-mail and computer usage policies 303
   Equal Employment Opportunity Commission policies 301–02
   Family and Medical Leave Act policies 302–03
   harassment policy 302
   items to be covered 301–04

Index 943

reasons for not using 300–01
reasons for using 299–317
employee or independent contractor 266–72
   Americans with Disabilities Act 270
   common-law control test 267
   economic reality test 270
   Employee Retirement Income and Security Act 270–71
   Internal Revenue Service control test 268
   Microsoft Corp. 271
   National Labor Relations Act 270
   potential liability 271–72
employer coverage under federal civil rights laws 272–75
employer coverage under state and local civil rights 275–76
employment at will 265
employment contracts. *See.*
equal opportunity obligations of government contra 276
Equal Pay Act 275
immigration options for biotech employees. *See.*
local laws and ordinances 275–77
Office of Federal Contract Compliance Programs 276
other federal employment laws 277–88
   Employee Polygraph Protection Act 288
   Employee Retirement Income and Security Act 285
   Fair Credit Reporting Act 287
   Fair Labor Standards Act. *See.*
   Family and Medical Leave Act 281
   Immigration Reform and Control Act 1986 286
   National Labor Relations Act. *See.*
   Occupational Safety and Health Act 285
   Uniformed Services Employment and Reemployment Rights Act 287
   Rehabilitation Act of 1973 276

state civil rights law 275
Title VII of the Civil Rights Act of 1964 272–73
   basic coverage 272–317
   U.S. Department of Labor 276
   sexual harassment 273
   Vietnam Veterans' Readjustment Assistance Act 276
entity selection, formation 81–137
   C-corporations 81–84
      centralized management 82
      classes of ownership 83
      incentive compensation 83
      limited liability 82–137
      owners 82
      taxation 83
      transferability of ownership 82
   choices 80
   exotic entity types 95
   limited liability companies 88–95
      organization of 91
      problems with 88
   name selection 97–99
      trademark law 97
   partnerships 80–81
   S-corporations 84–88
      conversions to C-corporations 87
      losses 87
      profits 87
      restrictions on 85
      termination of 87
   sole proprietorships 80–81
   state of organization 95–97
      Delaware 96
Equal Employment Opportunity Commission 301
Equal Pay Act 275
equity as primary consideration for license 179–80
European Commission 737–41; 796–812
   European Commission Competition Law 796–812
   European legislation 739–41
   European Medicines Agency 737–39
      activities of 738
   European Pharmacopoeia 739

national regulatory bodies 739
relevant directorates-general 737
European considerations 735
  advanced therapies 779
  blood and blood components 780
  clinical trials 759–64
    international coordination 763–64
    where to conduct 761–62
  good laboratory practice 741–43
    directives for 741
  human embryonic stem cell research 775–7
    Council of Europe's Convention on Human Rights and Biomedicine 775–76
    European harmonizing legislation 776
    National Regulation within the European Economic Area 776
  human tissue and cells 777–79
    Human Tissues and Cells Directive 777–79
  laboratory animal welfare 741–43
  marketing authorization in Europe. *See*.
  medical devices 781
  medicinal product, defined 740–41
  post-marketing issues in the European Economic Area, *See*.
  product development strategies 759–61
  standards for non-clinical tests 741–43
European Patent Office 56
exits 127–30
  exit rights 233–35

F

Fair Credit Reporting Act 287
Fair Labor Standards Act 277–80
  basic coverage 277
  basic requirements 277–81
  child labor 280
  minimum wage 277
  overtime pay 277
    white-collar exemptions 278–79
  record keeping 280
False Claims Act 586, 679, 701, 872
Family and Medical Leave Act 281, 302

federal contracts, research regulation through 332–37
  allowable and unallowable costs 340–42
    basic allowability requirements 340
    certification 341
    exceptions to applicability 340
    expressly unallowable cost 341
    government audits 342
    regulatory requirements 340
  Federal Acquisition Regulations 332
  Federal Procurement Requirements and Policy 332
  procurement integrity 337–44
    contractor bid or proposal information 338
    Freedom of Information Act 339
    Government Accountability Office 339
    restrictions on exchange of protected information 337–344
    source selection or procurement integrity-sensitive 337
    trade secrets 339
  product substitution 342–347
    defined 342
    quality assurance programs 342
    test requirements 343
  sale of commercial items and services 332–40
    evaluating vendor proposals 336
    evaluation procedures 334
    Federal Business Opportunities notices 334
    General Services Administration 337
    Obstruction of a Federal Audit statute 335
    procuring agency requirements 333
    representation and certification clauses 335
    U.S. Department of Health and Human Services 336
Federal False Claims Act. *See* False Claims Act

Index

Federal Food, Drug and Cosmetic Act 623, 629, 668, 677
Federal Food, Drug, and Cosmetics Act 479
Federal Insecticide, Fungicide and Rodenticide Act 623, 664
Federal Securities Act of 1933 209
Federal Trade Commission 678, 699–706
Federal Trade Secrets Act 416
financing a biotech company 69–70; 73–79; 203-43
  capital, pre-seed and seed. *See.*
  capital, venture. *See.*
  corporate investment 236–37
  drug development costs 204–06
  drug discovery process 207
  initial public offering 237–38
  IPO
    benefits of 237
    disadvantages of 238
  post-IPO financing 239–41
    convertible debt 240
    private investment in public equity 239–40
    project finance 241
  product development time lines 206–09
  securities law considerations 99–100; 209–13
    Federal Securities Act of 1933 209
    registration or exemption under the Securities Act 209
    Regulation D exempt transaction 210
    Rule 701—compensation plans 212
    Section 4(2) exempt transaction 210
    Securities and Exchange Commission 209
    state "blue sky" laws 213
Food and Drug Administration 43, 117, 358; 423–24; 479–93, 623, 668–70, 677–700
  approval, withdrawal of 700
  Center for Food Safety and Applied Nutrition 634
  Center for Veterinary Medicine 624
  Federal Food, Drug and Cosmetic Act 677
  guidance documents 678
  Office of Criminal Investigation 496
  regulation of advertising 687–91
  reporting requirements 683–86
Food and Drug Administration regulation of advertising 687–91
  advertising, examples 689
  broadcast advertisements: the major statement 692–93
  exchange of scientific information 695
  Federal Trade Commission 699–706
  First Amendment 696–99
  help-seeking advertisements 691
  label 687
  labeling 688
  notification 694
  off-label use, promotion of 694–95
  post-marketing notification 693
  print advertisements: the brief summary 692–700
  prior approval 693
  product claim advertisements 691
  product liability 699
  product-claim advertisements 691
  promotional materials 689
  reminder advertisements 691
Food and Drug Administration regulation of biomedical research 479–99
  clinical investigation, defined 481
  clinical research 481–83
  clinical trial 480
    record keeping 493–94
  clinical trial, anatomy of 490–99
    administrative actions 497
    audit 494–95
    bias, identification of 494
    Center for Biologics Evaluation and Research 495
    Center for Devices and Radiological Health 496
    Center for Drug Evaluation and Research 495

control of the trial 493–94
controlled clinical investigations. 491
informed consent form 491
inspections 495–97
inspections, preparing for 497–98
Office of Criminal Investigation 496
penalties 497
protocol, approval of 491
reporting 493–94
research stages 492
responding to allegations of misconduct 497–98
study advertisement 491
subject enrollment 491–92
submission 494–95
test article administration 491–92
contract research organization 484
contractual agreements 487
clinical trial agreement 487
principal investigator and study subject 489
sponsor and principal investigator 487
sponsor and the CRO 488
experiment, defined 481
Federal Food, Drug, and Cosmetics Act 479
goals of 483–90
Health Insurance Portability and Accountability Act 482
history, goals, purpose of 481
institutional review board 485
investigational device exemption 490–91
investigational new device application 483
investigational new drug application 483, 490
non-U.S. studies 499–501
clinical data 500
export of test article 500
EU clinical trial directive 500
principal investigator 486–90
Public Health Service Act 490

sponsor, defined 484
Food and Drug Administration reporting requirements 683–86
adverse experience reports 683
drug and biological products 683–84
medical devices 684
promotional materials 686
foreign patent portfolios 45–58
global patent strategies 45
options for filing in other jurisdictions 53–58
claim amendments 56
European Patent Office 56
international patent application 53
International Preliminary Examination Authority 54
International Preliminary Examination Report 55
International Search Authority 54
International Search Report 54
national filing 53
national phase 55–56
Patent Cooperation Treaty 54
Regional Patent Office filings 53
World Intellectual Property Organization 53
patent jurisdictions 46
patentability differences 49–51
novelty issues 51
prior art 51
prerequisites to filing 52
resident jurisdiction requirements 52
protection strategy 46–49
value of filing 48
where to file 46
which patent to file 47
founders 111–13
founders' stock 100-05; 214–17
Freedom of Information Act 61, 416
friends and family 223–24

G

General Services Administration 337
genetically modified organisms. regulation of, Europe 781–87

Index

Deliberate Release Directive 782–83
   labeling 783
      safeguard clause 783
      traceability 783
   experimental release into the environment 782
   legislation and practice 781–82
   marketing for cultivation, import, or industrial product processing 782
   marketing for food or feed 783
   medicinal products consisting of or containing genetically modified organisms 786–88
   practical implications industry 785–86
   sanctions 784
Government Accountability Office 339

H

Health Insurance Portability and Accountability Act 482, 509, 512–27
   authorization for disclosure 526–27
      Medical Records Release Form 526
   covered entities, defined 514
   exceptions to privacy regulations 543
   Federal Certificates of Confidentiality 545, 549–52
      explained 549–50
      National Institutes of Health statement on 550–61
   Federal Common Rule 545–51
   federal floor, establishment of 513
   individual rights
      access of to personal health information 521
      accounting of disclosures 524–26
      amendment or change of personal health information 523
      restriction of personal health information 521
      termination of agreement for restriction 521
   individually identifiable health information 513
      privacy and access requirements 514
      protected health information, defined 514
   mandated policies and procedures 516
   minimum standard 515
      exceptions to 515
   preemption issues 543–45
   privacy regulations 518–43
      individual rights 518–25
      notice of privacy practices 519–21
   privacy regulations for covered entities 512
   protection of individual health-care information 512
   research and business associate status 549
   research regulations 515
   research subject to 545–46
      permission to use or disclose research information 546–47
      Transactions Rule 545
      use or disclosure of information with authorization 547
      use or disclosure of information without authorization 546
   state laws 517
   U.S. Department of Health and Human Services 512
Howard Hughes Medical Institute 175, 188
human use, approval of products for 569–93
   biological products 605–07
      biological license application 606
      follow-ons biological product 607
      official lot release 606
      Public Health Service Act 606
   combination products 610–12
   content and format requirements 597–600
   drugs 591–605
      505(b)(2) applications 605
      Investigational New Drug Applications. See.
      preclinical 591–92
   future pathways to market 615
   generic drugs 603–05

abbreviated new drug applications 603
human cells, tissues, cellular and tissue-based products 607–08
medical devices 608–10
    510(k) notification process 609
    classifications 609
    investigational device exemption 610
    premarket application process 610
New Drug Applications. *See.*
special pathways to market 612–14
    fast-track programs 612–14
    orphan drug designation 614

I

immigration options for biotech employees 304–17
immigrant visas and permanent residence status 312–17
    employment-based preferences 312–14
    labor certification 314–15
    visa backlogs and priority dates 314
non-immigrant visas 305–11
    E-1 "Treaty Trader" visa 309
    E-2 "Treaty Investor" visas 309
    H-1B "Specialty Worker" visa 305
    L-1 "Intracompany Transfer" visa 308–09
    O-1 "Extraordinary Ability Alien" visa 310
    TN "NAFTA Professional" visa 307
obtaining a visa and U.S. entry 304–05
U.S. Citizenship & Immigration Services 304
U.S. Department of Homeland Security 304
Immigration Reform and Control Act 1986 286
incubators 114–15
intellectual property and confidential business information 117–22, 858–67
    trade secrets 118–19, 863–68
        defined 863–91
        establishing foundation for protection 864–65
        inevitable disclosure doctrine 866–70
        misappropriation 865–66
    trademarks 119–21, 859–67
        dilution 859–63
        domain name registration 861
        infringement 859–63
        infringement, response to 862
        registration and protection 859
        trademark audit 861
        trademark registration 861
intellectual property, Europe 788–94
    copyright 794
    database right 794
    enforcement of rights 796
    European community law, interplay with 795
    patents 788–93
        excluded subject matter 791
        human material 792
        microbiological processes and products 791
        obtaining 789
        stem cells, morality 792
        substantive patentability criteria; 790
        transgenic animals, morality 793
        transgenic plants 793
    plant breeders' rights 795
    trademarks 793–94
Intergovernmental Personnel Act 357
Internal Revenue Service 268
international considerations
    Gene Therapy Discussion Group 780
    genetically modified organism regulations 787–88
        Cartagena Protocol on Biosafety 787
International Preliminary Examination Authority 54
International Preliminary Examination Report 55
International Search Authority 54

International Search Report 54
inventor, defined 36
Investigational New Drug Applications 593–97
   clinical hold 593–94
      defined 594
   exemption from law 592
   Institutional Review Boards 593
      types of 595
   phases of clinical trials 595–97

L

litigation issues 835–67
litigation
   alternative dispute resolution 880–91
      arbitration 880–81
      defined 880–81
      guidelines 888–91
      integrated strategy for 882–84
      mediation 881
      myths and misconceptions 881–82
      patent litigation, special case for 885–88
   biotechnology patent litigation for the non-patent attorney. *See.*
   business liability 869–73
      average wholesale price drug litigation 873
      corporate disclosures 870–71
      corporate governance 871
      false claims 872
      False Claims Act 872
      insider trading 870–71
      misstatements and omissions 870
      Sarbanes-Oxley Act 871
      U.S. Public Company Accounting Reform and Investor Protection Act 871
      whistleblowers 872–73
   document and information retention 873–79
      data management policy 875–80
      discovery issues 874–75
      regulatory record-keeping requirements 874

intellectual property and confidential business information. *See.*
products liability 867–69
   defects and causation 868
   record of compliance and responsibility 868–70

M

marketing authorization in Europe 753–59
   Centralized Procedure 754
      summary of 756
   Decentralized Procedure 754
   duration of 757
   marketing application information requirements 755
   marketing authorization application, format of 756
   patented inventions 758
      Bolar exemption 758
      historical position in Europe 758
   responsibilities of authorization holder 757–58
   use of U.S. non-clinical and clinical trials data 762
material transfer agreements 168–69
medical reimbursement 563–89
   appeals 571–72
      Benefits Improvement and Protection Act of 2000 572
      fee-for-service appeals, comparison of 573
      steps for 571
   coding 569
      major coding systems 570
   compliance considerations 583–86
      discounts and related fraud and abuse considerations 586
      field locators 584
      Medicare Claims Processing Manual 583
      reimbursement support services 586
      requirements for proper billing 583–86
   coverage 564–68

coverage process 567–89
implications of coverage/non-
    coverage 567
Local Medical Review Policies
    568
medical necessity for patient 566
Medicare claims 567
Medicare Prescription Drug,
    Improvement and Modernization
    Act 565
National Coverage Determinations
    567
reasonable and necessary test 565–
    66
scope of benefits 564–65
specific exclusions from 565
drugs and biologicals 574–76
    Competitive Acquisition Program
        575
    Medicare, Part D 576
    Medicare, Part B 575
    pharmacy benefit managers 576
    prescription drug plans 576
durable medical equipment, prosthetics,
    orthotics, and supplies 578–79
in vitro diagnostics 579
investigational device
    exemptions 582
investigational products 581–83
    determination on costs of qualify-
        ing clinical trial 581–82
key terms and concepts 563–64
medical devices
    Food and Drug Administration
        approval of 576
medical devices 576–78
    Medicare Physicians' Fee Schedule
        577
new technologies 579–81
    ambulatory surgical centers,
        intraocular lenses 580
    inpatient prospective payment
        system 579–89
    outpatient prospective payment
        system 580
    private payer carve-outs 581

payers, identifying 574
    Medicaid 574
    Medicare 574
    private payers 574
payment law and policy 568
Medicare Prescription Drug, Improvement
    and Modernization Act 565
Microsoft Corp. 271
Minor Use and Minor Species Animal
    Health Act 637

N

National Aeronautics and Space Adminis-
    tration 330
National Cancer Institute 330
National Environmental Policy Act 631
National Institutes of Health 174, 325,
    329–30, 344–49, 358, 482, 581
    Grants Policy Manual 328
    Guidelines for Research Involving
        Recombinant DNA 329
National Labor Relations Act 270, 281–
    85
    applicability to non-union employers
        283–87
    coverage 281
    employee rights under 282
        Section 7 rights 282
    protected concerted activity 282
    union organizing 282–83
National Research Council 441
National Science Foundation 330
Neurontin case 679–80
    False Claims Act 680
    Pfizer 679
    Warner-Lambert Company 679
new drug applications 596–603
    advisory committees 602
    completion of review and decision 602
    content and format requirements 597–
        600
        refuse-to-file letter 598
    facility inspection 600
    labeling requirements 600
    labeling review 600–02
Nuclear Regulatory Commission 425

Index

O

Occupational Safety and Health Act 285
Office of Federal Contract Compliance Programs 276
Older Workers' Benefit Protection Act 273

P

patents 25–68. *See also* foreign patent portfolios; U.S. patent portfolios
   application formalities 35–38
      duty of candor and good faith 38
      Information Disclosure Statement 38
      inventive contribution 37
      inventor, defined 36
      Notice to File Missing Parts of Provisional Application 35–38
      Patent Cooperation Treaty 36
      priority claims 36
      provisional applications 35–38
      reduced fees 38
      small-entity status 38
   application preparation 34–35
      patentability search 34
   managing the company's patent estate 58–68
      blocking patents 66
      correspondence to products or business strategies 64–66
      current status report 58
      dominating patents 66
      Freedom of Information Act 61
      freedom to operate 66–68
      innovation management 59
      invalidity opinions 67
      loss prevention measures 60–62
      monitoring competitors 65
      monitoring newly issued patents 66
      nondisclosure agreements 62
      opinions of non-infringement 67
      patent asset evaluation 58
      patent estate audits 65
      rights of ownership 63–64
      third-party patent rights 59
      untimely disclosure 60
   patent prosecution 39–43
      Board of Patent Appeals and Interferences 41
      composition of matter claim 39
      divisional application 39
      examiner 39
      Examiner's Answer 42
      final rejections, appeal of 41–42
      first Office action 40
      method claim 39
      non-final Office action 40–41
      Notice of Allowance 40, 42–43
      Patent Term Adjustment 42
      prior art 40
      rejection of claim 40
      Request for Continued Examination 41
   post-issue patent considerations 43–46
      error corrections 44
      Food and Drug Administration 43
      inter partes reexamination 44
      Patent Term Adjustment 43–46
   publication of patent applications 38–39
      Patent Application Information Retrieval Web site 39
   requirements for patentability 31–34
      best mode 32, 33
      claim language 33
      determination of obviousness 32
      enablement requirement 32
      minimal beneficial use or utility 32
      prior art 31–32
      public disclosures 31
      scope of invention 32
      skilled artisan 32
      written description requirement 32
   types of 28–31
      continuing patent application practice 30–31
      provisional patent applications 29–31
Patent Cooperation Treaty 36, 54
Plant Protection Act 666

post-marketing Issues in the European
    Economic Area 764–74
  abridged applications 768–69
    generic medicinal products 768
    similar biological medicinal
      products 769–71
  advertising 766
  bibliographic applications 769
  classification 767
  confidentiality 774
  freedom of information 774
  government purchasing 771
  inspections 767–68
  labeling 766
  manufacturing and importing 767
  marketing exclusivity 770
    8+2+1 solution 770
  parallel distribution 773–75
  parallel importation 771–72
    medicines legislation 773
    relabeling 772–73
    repackaging 772
    trademark issues 772–73
  pharmacovigilance 764–66
    marketing authorization holders
      764–65
      roles and responsibilities of
        764–65
  price controls 771
  promotion 766
  regulatory data 770–71
preclinical research 407–42
  animal use in biomedical research and
    testing. See.
  categories of regulatory protections
    408
  Institutional Animal Care and Use
    Committee responsibility 434
  occupational safety and health considerations 438–42
    employee training 440
    hazardous chemicals standard 439
    measurements to monitor employee
      exposure 441
    medical attention 440
    National Research Council 441
    OSHA regulations 439–41
    resource tools 441
    resources 439
    standards 439
  precursor to therapeutic drug use 407
  protecting the environment and public
    health 425
    generator status 428
    hazardous waste, defined 426
    Nuclear Regulatory Commission
      425
    Resource Conservation and
      Recovery Act 425–32
    U.S. Department of Health and
      Human Services 425
    U.S. Department of Transportation
      425
    U.S. Environmental Protection
      Agency 425–32
    waste generators, standards for 430
  Public Health Security and Bioterrorism
    Preparedness and Response Act 434–
    38
  purpose of 407
  research facilities, applying environmental law to 433–34
    key issues 433
    Resource Conservation and
      Recovery Act 433
    U.S. Environmental Protection
      Agency 433
  research facility, defined 408
  select agents and toxins 434–38
    categories of 435
    defined 435
    regulation of 435
Prescription Drug Marketing Act 686
privacy issues 509–55
  academic medical centers and research
    551
  authorization for disclosure 526–27
    authorizations for marketing 529
    combined authorizations 528
    conditioning of authorizations 528
    core elements of 526
    defective authorization 528

Medical Records Release Form 526
  patient opportunity to agree or object 529
  psychotherapy notes 526
  revocation of authorizations 529
Canadian privacy legislation 551–61
  accuracy 554
  challenging compliance 555
  consent 553
  identifying purpose 553
  Individual Access 555
  limit use, disclosure, and retention 554
  limiting collection 554
  openness 554
  safeguards 554
Centers for Medicare and Medicaid Services 510
disclosure pursuant to business associate agreement 539–41
  satisfactory assurances 540
  written contracts, provisions of 540
disclosure pursuant to data use agreements 542–45
  limited data set 542
  provisions of agreement 542
disclosure pursuant to public policy exception 530–39
  as required by law 530
  cadaveric organ, eye or tissue donations 536
  decedents 536
  health oversight activities 534
  judicial and administrative proceedings 534
  law enforcement purposes 536
  research purposes 537
  specialized government functions 539
  threats to health or safety 539
  uses and disclosures for public health activities 531
  victims of abuse, neglect or domestic violence 532
  workers' compensation 539
Health Insurance Portability and Accountability Act 509
  covered entities, defined 509
  health-care operations 525
  defined 525
  national approach 512–44
    Health Insurance Portability and Accountability Act 512–18
  payment 525
  preemption issues 543–45
    exceptions to Health Insurance Portability and Accountability Act privacy regulations 543
  state approach to 545
  treatment 525
  U.S. Department of Health and Human Services 509
Public Health Security and Bioterrorism Preparedness and Response Act 434
Public Health Service Act 490, 606–07

R

Rehabilitation Act of 1973 276, 329
research and development collaborations 445–76
  alliances with third parties 475
    reliance on contractual protections 476
    right of first negotiation may have chilling effect 476
    right of first refusal may preclude other transactions 476
  post-closing pitfalls
    change in commitment to the project 472
    change in strategic fit 472
    communication issues 475
    control issues 475
    unrealistic expectations 475
  post-closing pitfalls that can derail collaboration 472–75
  research collaboration agreements. *See*.
  stakeholders in research collaboration 447

strategic partners, finding 446–49
　approaching big pharma 448
　importance of science 448
　third parties as valuable contacts 449
term sheets 449–52
　critical issues 450–51
　importance of 449–50
　issues to avoid 451–52
termination
　early 473–74
research collaboration agreements 452–72
　financial terms 462–66
　　approaches to structuring development rights 466
　　equity investments 463–65
　　milestone payments 465–69
　　research funding 463
　　signature payments 462–63
　governance of 452–54
　intellectual property 456–59
　　arising out of collaboration 458
　　background of larger funding partner 458
　　background of smaller partner 457
　　core of smaller partner 457
　　core the larger funding partner 457
　　developed during, but outside of, collaboration 458
　　that does not arise from existing property of either partner 459
　joint steering committee 452
　　composition of 452
　　decisionmaking by 453–55
　　duties of 453
　　meetings of 453
　license grants 459–62
　　cross-licenses 460
　　development and commercialization license 460
　　enabling license 461
　　freedom to operate 460
　　license as protection against infringement claims 461–62
　　research licenses 460

option to develop and commercialize 469–71
　notice of exercise 469
　right of first negotiation 470
　right of first refusal 469
option to develop and commercialize rights in unoptioned intellectual property 470
scope of collaboration 454–56
　field 455–78
　limitations based on patent family 456
　limitations based on project funding 456
　limitations based on timing 456
　limitations to 455
term 471
termination 471–72
　early 471–78
research, federal regulation of through funding 325–59
employment 353–61
　discussions with and hiring of U.S. government personnel 356
　Information Technology Exchange Program 357
　Intergovernmental Personnel Act 357
　U.S. Office of Government Ethics 357
ethics 353–61
　financial conflict of interest, grants 353
　misconduct in science and engineering, grants 354
　organizational conflicts of interest, contracts 354
　standards of conduct, grants 353
　U.S. Office of Government Ethics 357
federal contracts, research regulation through. See.
federal research grants 326–32
　Age Discrimination Act 329
　Animal Welfare Act 329
　Byrd Anti-Lobbying Act 329

Index 955

Civil Rights Act of 1964 329
Federal Acquisition Regulation 326
grantor agencies 330–32
National Aeronautics and Space Administration 330
National Cancer Institute 330
National Science Foundation 330
National Institutes of Health Grants Policy Manual 328
Rehabilitation Act 329
Small Business Innovation Research grants 330
Small Business Technology Transfer 330
subgrants 327–28
terms and conditions 328–30
Toxic Substances Control Act 330
U.S. Department of Defense 330
U.S. Health and Human Services Department 330
National Institutes of Health 325–30
Guidelines for Research Involving Recombinant DNA 329
outside activities 353–61
Food and Drug Administration regulations on 358
National Institutes of Health regulations on 358
Small Business Innovation Research. *See.*
Small Business Technology Transfer. *See.* 344
Resource Conservation and Recovery Act 425, 432–33
restricted stock 100–05

S

Sarbanes-Oxley Act 130, 871
scientific advisory board 114–17
Securities and Exchange Commission 209, 678
Small Business Innovation Research grants 344–53
amended applications 352
basic characteristics 346–47

criteria 351
defined 344
National Institutes of Health guidance 347–49
approach 348
environment 349
innovation 348
significance of 347–48
objectives of 345
participation requirements 345
phase I/phase II fast-track application review 352
phase II application review criteria 351
phase II—competing continuation application review 352
phases of 347
protection of human subjects 349–50
Data and Safety Monitoring Plan 350
Inclusion of Children Plan 350
Inclusion of Minorities Plan 350
Inclusion of Women Plan 350
National Institutes of Health policy 349
Scientific Review Groups 349
vertebrate animals 350–51
Small Business Technology Transfer grants 344–53
amended applications 352
basic characteristics 346–47
criteria 351
defined 345
National Institutes of Health guidance 347–49
approach 348
environment 349
innovation 348
significance of 347–61
participation requirements 346
phase I/phase II fast-track application review 352
phase II application review 351
phase II—competing continuation application review 352
phases of 347
protection of human subjects 349–50

Data and Safety Monitoring Plan 350
Inclusion of Children Plan 350
Inclusion of Minorities Plan 350
Inclusion of Women Plan 350
National Institutes of Health policy 349
Scientific Review Groups 349
vertebrate animals 350
Social Security Act 565
stock and stock options 100–07

T

technology, creation of 143–55
Canadian laws 146
effects of outside funding 152–55
manufacturing or sales restrictions 154
ownership 152–54
public domain 154
employee rights 145
European Union laws 147
joint venture ownership 148–49
necessary records 143
patent filing 149–52
continuing patent application 151
divisional patent application 151
foreign patent filing 152
patent claims and rights 150
patent requirements 149
provisional patent application 150
reasons for 149
stages of 150
types of patents 150
utility patent application 151
patent prosecution 151
post-issue considerations 151
protecting propriety of invention in early stages 140–43
company records 142–43
confidentiality agreements 140–41
determining who first invented product 141
state laws 145–46
trade secrets 147–48
applicability to biotechnology companies 148
defined 147
Uniform Trade Secrets Act 148
work made for hire 143–49
copyright law 143
employee v. contractor 144
shopright rule 143
Toxic Substances Control Act 330
Trademark Clarification Act of 1984 180

U

university relationships 115–17, 162–68
U.S. Citizenship & Immigration Services 304
U.S. Department of Agriculture 117, 409, 623, 666–68
U.S. Department of Agriculture regulation of animal biological products 641–48
Agricultural Bioterrorism Protection Act of 2002 646
Animal Health Protection Act 646–47
Animal and Plant Health Inspector Service regulatory requirements 642–46
adverse event reports 645
enforcement procedures 645
exemptions to 645–60
licensing 643–44
permits 644
record keeping 644
standard requirements 644
U.S. Veterinary Biologic Product License 643
U.S. Veterinary Biologics Establishment License 643
veterinary biologics, defined 642
special consideration for biotech biologics 647–60
summary information formats 647
Veterinary Biologics Product License 648
veterinary biologics 641–42
defined 642
Virus-Serum-Toxin Act 641

Index

U.S. Department of Defense 330, 581
U.S. Department of Health and Human Services 336, 425, 481, 509, 512, 632
  Office for Protection of Research Subjects 481
  Office of Inspector General 679
U.S. Department of Homeland Security 304
U.S. Department of Labor 276, 302
U.S. Department of Transportation 425
U.S. Department of Veterans Affairs 581
U.S. Department of Agriculture
  Animal and Plant Health Inspection Service 623
U.S. Environmental Protection Agency 425–33, 623, 664–66
  Biopesticides and Pollution Prevention Division 664
U.S. Food and Drug Administration. *See* Food and Drug Administration.
U.S. Health and Human Services Department 330
U.S. Office of Government Ethics 357
U.S. patent portfolios 26–45
  continuing patent application practice 30–31
  patent application formalities 35–38
  patent application, preparation of 34–35
  patent applications, publication of 38–39
  patent prosecution 39–43
    final rejections 41
    Notice of Allowance 42–57
  patent rights—claims 26–28
    patent monopoly 26
  post-issue patent considerations 43–46
  requirements for patentability 31
  types of patents 28–31
    provisional patent applications 29
U.S. Public Company Accounting Reform and Investor Protection Act 871
Uniform Trade Secrets Act 121, 148
Uniformed Services Employment and Reemployment Rights Act of 1994 287
University and Small Business Patent Procedure Act 162

V

Vietnam Veterans' Readjustment Assistance Act 276
Virus-Serum-Toxin Act 641–42

W

World Intellectual Property Organization 53